Contents

PREFACE   xv

Chapter One
ETHICAL THEORY AND BUSINESS PRACTICE   1

PART ONE: FUNDAMENTAL CONCEPTS AND PROBLEMS

Morality and Ethical Theory   1
Morality and Prudence   2
Morality and Law   4
The Rule of Conscience   6
Approaches to the Study of Morality   6
Justification in Ethics   8
Relativism and Objectivity of Belief   8
Moral Disagreements   12
The Problem of Egoism   14

PART TWO: NORMATIVE ETHICAL THEORY

The Role of Professional Standards   20
Utilitarian Theories   21
Kantian Ethics   28
Contemporary Challenges to the Dominant Theories   33
Common Morality Theories   34
Rights Theories   35
Virtue Ethics   38
Feminist Theories and the Ethics of Care   39
A Prologue to Theories of Justice   42

PART THREE: THE ANALYSIS OF CASES

    The Case Method in Law   43
    The Case Method in Business   44
    Using Ethical Theory for Case Analysis   45

Chapter Two
CORPORATE RESPONSIBILITY   49

INTRODUCTION

    Three Views on the Purpose of a Corporation   49
    Stakeholder Theory   54

THEORIES OF CORPORATE RESPONSIBILITY

    Milton Friedman, The Social Responsibility of Business Is
        to Increase Its Profits   55
    John G. Simon, Charles W. Powers, and *Jon P. Gunnemann,*
        The Responsibilities of Corporations and Their Owners   60
    Thomas M. Mulligan, The Moral Mission of Business   65

STAKEHOLDER ANALYSIS

    William M. Evan and *R. Edward Freeman,* A Stakeholder Theory
        of the Modern Corporation: Kantian Capitalism   75
    Kenneth E. Goodpaster, Business Ethics and Stakeholder Analysis   85

LEGAL PERSPECTIVES

    Michigan Supreme Court, *Dodge v. Ford Motor Company* (1919)   94
    Supreme Court of New Jersey, *A.P. Smith Manufacturing Co.*
        v Barlow (1953)   96

CASES

    Case 1: Shutdown at Eastland   98
    Case 2: The Sloane Products Case   99
    Case 3: Procter and Gamble and Toxic Shock Syndrome   100
    Case 4: H.B. Fuller in Honduras: Street Children
        and Substance Abuse   101

Suggested Supplementary Readings   102

Ethical Theory and Business

Ethical Theory and Business

Fourth Edition

Edited by

Tom L. Beauchamp

Department of Philosophy and Kennedy Institute of Ethics
Georgetown University

Norman E. Bowie

Elmer L. Andersen Chair in Corporate Responsibility
Department of Strategic Management and Organization
Curtis L. Carlson School of Management and Department of Philosophy
University of Minnesota

Prentice Hall, Englewood Cliffs, New Jersey 07632

Library of Congress Cataloging-in-Publication Data

Ethical theory and business / edited by Tom L. Beauchamp, Norman E. Bowie.—4th ed.

p. cm.

Includes bibliographical references.

ISBN 0–13–290347–4

1. Business ethics—United States. 2. Business ethics—United States—Case studies. 3. Industry—Social aspects—United States. 4. Industry—Social aspects—United States—Case studies. 5. Corporation law—United States—Cases. 6. Consumer protection— Law and legislation—United States—Cases. 7. n-us.

I. Beauchamp, Tom L.   II. Bowie, Norman E.,

HF5387.E82   1993

174′.4—dc20   92–19034
                                                 CIP

Editorial/production supervision
  and interior design: *Keith Faivre* and *Robert C. Walters*
Cover design: *Bruce Kenselaar*
Prepress buyer: *Herb Klein*
Manufacturing buyer: *Patrice Fraccio* and *Robert Anderson*
Acquisitions editor: *Ted Bolen*
Editorial Assistant: *Nicole Gray*

©1993, 1988, 1983, 1979 by Prentice-Hall, Inc.
A Simon & Schuster Company
Englewood Cliffs, New Jersey 07632

Printed in the United States of America

10 9 8 7 6 5 4 3 2 1

ISBN 0-13-290347-4

Prentice-Hall International (UK) Limited, *London*
Prentice-Hall of Australia Pty. Limited, *Sydney*
Prentice-Hall Canada Inc., *Toronto*
Prentice-Hall Hispanoamericana, S.A., *Mexico*
Prentice-Hall of India Private Limited, *New Delhi*
Prentice-Hall of Japan, Inc., *Tokyo*
Simon & Schuster Asia Pte. Ltd., *Singapore*
Editora Prentice-Hall do Brasil, Ltda., *Rio de Janeiro*

Chapter Three
THE REGULATION OF BUSINESS   104

INTRODUCTION

Self Regulation   104
Government Regulation   112

SELF-REGULATION

Kenneth J. Arrow, Business Codes and Economic Efficiency   118
Ian Maitland, The Limits of Business Self-Regulation   121
Richard T. DeGeorge, Ethical Responsibilities of Engineers in Large
        Organizations: The Pinto Case   130
Russell P. Boisjoly, Ellen Foster Curtis, and *Eugene Mellican,*
        Roger Boisjoly and the Challenger Disaster:
        The Ethical Dimensions   137

GOVERNMENT REGULATION

Steven Kelman, Regulation and Paternalism   151
Norman E. Bowie, Criteria for Government Regulations   158
Christopher D. Stone, Why The Law Can't Do It   162

LEGAL PERSPECTIVES

Licensee Responsibility to Review Records Before Their Broadcast   167
Supreme Court of the United States, *American Textile Manufacturers Institute,
        Inc. v. Raymond J. Donovan,* Secretary of Labor   169

CASES

Case 1: The Advertising Code Case   172
Case 2: Beech-Nut Corporation   173
Case 3: Regulating Insider Trading   174
Case 4: Flyover in Midland   177

Suggested Supplementary Readings   178

Chapter Four
ACCEPTABLE RISK   179

INTRODUCTION

Nature and Types of Risk   179
Product Safety and Risk to Consumers   181
Protecting Investors against Financial Risk   183
Worker Safety, Occupational Risk, and the Right to Know   185
Risk to Health and the Environment   187

CONSUMER RISK

Manuel G. Velasquez, The Ethics of Consumer Production   189
George G. Brenkert, Strict Products Liability
    and Compensatory Justice   198

OCCUPATIONAL RISK

Ruth R. Faden and *Tom L. Beauchamp,* The Right to Risk Information
    and the Right to Refuse Workplace Hazards   203

RISK TO THE ENVIRONMENT

Jang B. Singh and *V. C. Lakhan,* Business Ethics and the International Trade in
    Hazardous Wastes   210
W. Michael Hoffman, Business and Environmental Ethics   217

INVESTMENT RISK

Robert E. Frederick and *W. Michael Hoffman,* The Individual Investor
    in Securities Markets: An Ethical Analysis   223
Robert F. Bruner and *Lynn Sharp Paine,* Management Buyouts
    and Managerial Ethics   230

LEGAL PERSPECTIVES

Supreme Court of New Jersey, *Henningsen v. Bloomfield Motors, Inc. and Chrysler
    Corporation*   236
Supreme Court of the United States, *Automobile Workers v. Johnson Controls,
    Inc.*   241
Supreme Court of New Jersey, *State, Dept. of Environ. Protect. v. Ventron
    Corporation*   244

CASES

Case 1: Protecting Consumers Against Tobacco   247
Case 2: Do Apple Computer Shareholders Need Protection?   248
Case 3: Virazole and Investor Risk   249
Case 4: OSHA Noncompliance and Security   250

Suggested Supplementary Readings   251

Chapter Five
RIGHTS AND OBLIGATIONS OF EMPLOYERS AND EMPLOYEES   253

INTRODUCTION

Status and Scope of Employee Rights   253

Drug Testing and the Right to Privacy   255
Whistleblowing and the Duty of Loyalty   257
Trade Secrets and the Duty of Confidentiality   259

RIGHTS AND OBLIGATIONS IN HIRING AND FIRING

Patricia H. Werhane, Employment at Will and the Question
of Employee Rights   262
Jack M. Beermann and *Joseph William Singer,* Baseline Questions
in Legal Reasoning: The Example of Property in Jobs   270

DRUG TESTING

Mark A. Rothstein, Drug Testing in the Workplace: The Challenge to
Employment Relations and Employment Law   277
Joseph DesJardins and *Ronald Duska,* Drug Testing
in Employment   294

WHISTLEBLOWING

Sissela Bok, Whistleblowing and Professional Responsibility   305
Ronald Duska, Whistleblowing and Employee Loyalty   312
Susan Sauter, The Employee Health and Safety Whistleblower Protection Act
and the Conscientious Employee: The Potential for Federal Statutory
Enforcement of the Public Policy Exception to Employment at Will   317

TRADE SECRETS AND THE DUTY OF CONFIDENTIALITY

Michael S. Baram, Trade Secrets: What Price Loyalty   323
Robert E. Frederick and *Milton Snoeyenbos,* Trade Secrets, Patents,
and Morality   332

LEGAL PERSPECTIVES

Supreme Court of New Jersey, *Warthen v. Toms River Community Memorial
Hospital*   338
Supreme Court of New Jersey, *Potter v. Village Bank
of New Jersey*   342
Superior Court of Alaska, *Luedtke v. Nabors Alaska Drilling, Inc.*   346
Superior Court of California, *Futurecraft Corp. v. Clary Corp.*   355

CASES

Case 1: A Matter of Principle   359
Case 2: Probable Cause and Drug Testing   360
Case 3: Catching a Thief by Honesty Exams   360
Case 4: Old Secrets in a New Job   361

Suggested Supplementary Readings   362

Chapter Six
HIRING, FIRING, AND DISCRIMINATING   364

INTRODUCTION

The Basis of Preferential Policies   364
The Problem of Reverse Discrimination   367
Comparable Worth   369
The Problem of Sexual Harassment   371

AFFIRMATIVE ACTION AND REVERSE DISCRIMINATION

Thomas Nagel, A Defense of Affirmative Action   374
William Bradford Reynolds, Equal Opportunity, Not Equal Results   378
Tom L. Beauchamp, Goals and Quotas in Hiring and Promotion   382

PAY EQUITY AND COMPARABLE WORTH

Wil Waluchow, Pay Equity: Equal Value to Whom?   391
Helen Remick and *Ronnie J. Steinberg,* Comparable Worth
    and Wage Discrimination   397
Robert L. Simon, Comparable Pay for Comparable Work?   400

SEXUAL HARASSMENT

A. M. Koral, Dealing with Sexual Harassment in the Work Place   412
Larry May and *John C. Hughes,* Is Sexual Harassment Coercive?   415

LEGAL PERSPECTIVES

Supreme Court of the United States, *Local 28 of the Sheet Metal
    Workers' International Association v. Equal Employment Opportunity
    Commission*   420
Supreme Court of the United States, *City of Richmond
    v. J. A. Croson Company*   426
Supreme Court of the United States, *Meritor Savings Bank, FSB
    v. Vinson* Et al.   431

CASES

Case 1: "Harassment" at Brademore Electric   435
Case 2: Sing's Chinese Restaurant   437
Case 3: USAir's Hiring Channel   437
Case 4: Weber and the Kaiser Aluminum Steelworkers Plan   438
Case 5: Comparable Worth in the Female Section?   439

Suggested Supplementary Readings   440

Chapter Seven
GATHERING, CONCEALING, AND GILDING INFORMATION   442

INTRODUCTION

Free Choice or Unfair Influence?   443
Deception, Bluffing, and Strategic Disclosure   445
Disclosing and Concealing Information in Sales   447
Information Gathering   448

DISCLOSING AND BLUFFING

Albert Z. Carr, Is Business Bluffing Ethical?   449
Thomas L. Carson, Richard E. Wokutch, and *Kent F. Murrmann,* Bluffing in Labor
      Negotiations: Legal and Ethical Issues   455
Norman E. Bowie, Does It Pay to Bluff in Business?   460

SUPPRESSING FACTS IN SALES

David M. Holley, A Moral Evaluation of Sales Practices   462
James M. Ebejer and *Michael J. Morden,* Paternalism in the Marketplace: Should
    a Salesman Be His Buyer's Keeper?   472

TRUTH AND DECEPTION IN ADVERTISING

Tom L. Beauchamp, Manipulative Advertising   475
Richard L. Lippke, Advertising and the Social Conditions of Autonomy   484

COMPETITOR INTELLIGENCE GATHERING

Lynn Sharp Paine, Corporate Policy and the Ethics of Competitor Intelligence
    Gathering   489

LEGAL PERSPECTIVES

United States Court of Appeals, *Irving A. Backman
    v. Polaroid Corporation*   497
Supreme Court of the United States, *Federal Trade Commission
    v. Colgate-Palmolive Co. et al.*   500

CASES

Case 1: Food Labels and Artful Sales   504
Case 2: The Conventions of Lying on Wall Street   506
Case 3: Green Advertising   507
Case 4: Computer Math for Car Loans   508
Case 5: Marketing the Giant Quart   509

Suggested Supplementary Readings   510

Chapter Eight
ETHICAL ISSUES IN INTERNATIONAL BUSINESS   511

INTRODUCTION

Are There International Norms of Business Practice?   511
Exporting Hazardous Substances   514
The Regulation of International Business   516

INTERNATIONAL NORMS

Norman E. Bowie, The Moral Obligations
    of Multinational Corporations   519
Thomas Donaldson, Fundamental Rights and Multinational
    Duties   532

EXPORTING HAZARDOUS MATERIAL

Michael P. Walls, Chemical Exports and the Age of Consent: The High Cost of
    International Export Control Proposals   542
Lynn Sharp Paine, Regulating the International Trade in Hazardous Pesticides:
    Closing the Accountability Gap   547

THE FOREIGN CORRUPT PRACTICES ACT

Bartley A. Brennan, The Foreign Corrupt Practices Act Amendments
    of 1988: "Death" of a Law   557

TRANSNATIONAL CORPORATE CODES

William C. Frederick, The Moral Authority of Transnational
    Corporate Codes   564

LEGAL PERSPECTIVES

Supreme Court of Texas, *Dow Chemical Company and Shell Oil Company v.*
    Domingo Castro Alfaro et. al., No. C-7743   576
OECD, The Guidelines for Multinational Enterprises   582

CASES

Case 1: Foreign Assignment   587
Case 2: Transnational Oil Corporations in the Ecuadorian Amazon   588
Case 3: The Nestlé Corporation   590
Case 4: Foreign Payments   591
Case 5: Mitsubishi and Rockefeller Center   592

Suggested Supplementary Readings   593

Chapter Nine
SOCIAL AND ECONOMIC JUSTICE 595

INTRODUCTION

Theories of Distributive Justice   595
The Egalitarian Theory   597
Libertarian Theory   599
Communitarian Theory   600
Visions of Justice Beyond the Free Market   601
Conclusion   604

THEORIES OF SOCIAL JUSTICE

John Rawls, An Egalitarian Theory of Justice   604
Robert Nozick, The Entitlement Theory   612
Peter Singer, Rich and Poor   616
Michael Walzer, Spheres of Justice   622

INTERNATIONAL ECONOMIC JUSTICE

Thomas Donaldson, The Ethics of Conditionality
    in International Debt   630

JUSTICE UNDER CONDITIONS OF INDUSTRIAL MIGRATION

Judith Lichtenberg, On Alternatives to Industrial Flight:
    The Moral Issues   638

LEGAL PERSPECTIVES

Supreme Court of the United States, *William M. Ferguson, Attorney General for
    the State of Kansas* v. *Frank C. Skrupa . . . Credit Advisors*   645

CASES

Case 1: Baseball Economics   648
Case 2: Selling Cyclamates Abroad   649
Case 3: Cocaine at the Fortune-500 Level   650
Case 4: Covering the Costs of Health Care   651

Suggested Supplementary Readings   652

Preface

WHEN THE FIRST edition of *Ethical Theory and Business* went to press in 1977, business ethics had received little attention by philosophers, and was hidden under other labels in business schools. Much has changed since then. The American Assembly of Collegiate Schools of Business has insisted that ethics be a part of the business student's education, and an increasingly sophisticated literature has emerged.

The second and third editions published in 1983 and 1988 were radically restructured to keep up with the changing times, and the same forces of change have similarly convinced us to restructure the fourth edition. The chapter on ethical theory has been expanded, especially by incorporating an increased number of alternative perspectives on normative ethical theory, and there is an entirely new chapter on multinationals and international business. Thirty-three articles are new to this edition and include the topics of sexual harassment, investment risk, plant closings, international justice, suppressing facts in sales, corporate intelligence gathering, drug testing, and responsibility within organizations; and there is more material on case law than in the previous editions.

Many familiar landmarks remain, however, as we have retained twenty-six articles from the third edition and most of the topics, with the exception of "Conflicts of Interests and Roles." Employee rights, whistle-blowing, advertising ethics, affirmative action, and the obligations of business to protect the environment remain staple topics, as well as the chapters on social and economic justice, regulation, and corporate responsibility.

We have received many helpful suggestions from many people for improving this anthology, and although it is impossible to recognize everyone, we do extend special thanks to Denis Arnold, who assisted Norman Bowie with the bibliographic research, and to the six careful reviewers provided by

Prentice Hall. We also gratefully acknowledge earlier reviews by Robert Ashmore, J. David Newell, Michael A. Payne, Michael S. Pritchard, Michael Davis, Thomas M. Mulligan and Robert Ahuja. Our thanks also to John Cuddihy, Katy Cancro, Katie Marshall, Jennifer Givens, Ari Paparo, and Margaret Klumpp for their help with the research and redrafting. Through their effort we were able to push draft after draft of this new edition through our offices. They much improved the final product.

Tom L. Beauchamp
Norman E. Bowie

Ethical Theory
and Business Practice

CAN LARGE BUSINESS organizations be just? should the chief obligation of business be to look out for the bottom line? Is nonvoluntary employee drug testing immoral? How far should business go to protect and preserve the environment? These are some of the many questions that permeate discussions of the role of ethics in business.

The essays and cases in this book provide an opportunity to discuss these questions by reading and reflecting on influential arguments that have been made on these subjects. The goal of this first chapter is to provide a foundation in ethical theory sufficient for reading and critically evaluating the material in the ensuing chapters. The first part of this chapter introduces basic and recurring distinctions, definitions, and issues. The second part examines influential and relevant types of normative ethical theory. The third part discusses "the case method" as an exercise in moral reflection.

PART ONE: FUNDAMENTAL CONCEPTS AND PROBLEMS

Morality and Ethical Theory

The distinction between morality and ethical theory runs throughout this volume, but it is a tricky distinction. The term *morality* has a broad meaning that extends beyond the rules in professional codes of conduct adopted by corporations and professional associations. *Morality* suggests a social institution, composed of a set of standards pervasively acknowledged by the members of a culture. In this understanding, morality is concerned with practices defining right and wrong. These practices, together with other kinds of customs, rules, and mores, are transmitted within cultures and institutions from generation to generation.

Morality, then has an objective status as a body of guidelines for individual action. Similar to political constitutions and natural languages, morality exists prior to the acceptance (or rejection) of its standards by particular individuals. That is, individuals do not make their own rules; morality cannot be purely a personal policy or code.

The term *morality* fails to capture various aspects of moral reflection encountered in this volume. In contrast to *morality,* the terms *ethical theory* and *moral philosophy* suggest reflection on the nature and justification of right actions. These words refer to attempts to introduce clarity, substance, and precision of argument into the domain of morality. Many people go through life with an understanding of morality largely dictated by their culture. Other persons are not satisfied simply to conform to the morality of society. They want difficult questions answered: Is what our society forbids wrong? Are social values the best values? What is the purpose of morality? Does religion have anything to do with morality? Do the moral rules of society fit together in a unified whole? If there are conflicts and inconsistencies in our practices and beliefs, how should they be resolved? What should we do when facing a moral problem for which society has, as yet, provided no instruction?

Moral philosophers seek to answer such questions and to put moral beliefs and social practices of morality into a more unified and defensible package of guidelines and concepts. Sometimes this task involves challenging traditional moral beliefs by assessing the quality of moral arguments and suggesting modifications in existing beliefs. Morality, we might say, consists of what persons ought to do in order to conform to society's norms of behavior, whereas ethical theory consists of the philosophical reasons for or against the morality stipulated by society. Usually the latter effort centers on *justification:* Philosophers seek to justify a system of standards or some moral point of view on the basis of carefully analyzed and defended concepts and principles such as respect for autonomy, distributive justice, equal treatment, human rights, beneficence, and truthfulness.

Most moral principles are already embedded in public morality, but usually only in a vague and underanalyzed form. Justice is a good example. Recurrent topics in the pages of the *Wall Street Journal, Forbes, Business Week,* and other leading business journals justify the present system of corporate and individual taxation as well as the salaries paid to CEOs. However, an extended or detailed analysis of principles of justice is virtually never provided. Such matters are left at an intuitive or party-line level, where the correctness of a moral point of view is assumed, without argumentation. But the failure to provide anything more than superficial justification, in terms of intuitive principles learned from parents or peers, leaves us unable to defend our principles when challenged. In a society with many diverse views of morality, one can be fairly sure that one's principles will be challenged.

Before proceeding in our discussion of moral argument and ethical theory, we need to clarify some terms. *Ethics* is used as a general term referring to both moral beliefs and ethical theories. The terms *moral philosophy, ethical theory,* and *philosophical ethics,* by contrast, are reserved for philosophical theories, including philosophical reflection on social morality.

Morality and Prudence

Many students do not encounter moral philosophy as a topic of study until college or graduate school. Morality, however, is learned by virtually every young child as part of the acculturation process. The first step in this process is learning to distinguish moral rules from rules of prudence (self-interest). This task can be difficult, because the two kinds of rules are taught simultaneously, without being distinguished by their teachers. For example, people are constantly reminded in their early years to observe rules such as "Don't touch the hot stove," "Don't cross the street without looking both ways," "Brush your teeth after meals," and "Eat your vegetables." Most of these oughts and ought nots are instructions in self-interest; that is, they are instructions in prudence. At the same time, however, people are given oughts or ought nots of a moral kind. Parents, teachers, and peers teach that certain things ought not be done because they are "wrong" and certain things *ought* to be done because they are "right." "Don't pull your sister's hair." "Don't take money from your mother's pocketbook." "Share your toys." "Write a thank-you note to Grandma." These moral instructions seek to control actions that affect the interests of other people. As people mature, they learn what society expects of them in terms of taking into account the interests of other people.

One of the most common observations in business is that self-interest and good ethics can coincide, because it is often in one's interest to act morally. This fact makes evaluating another's conduct difficult. A simple example of both moral and prudential reasoning at work in business is found in an executive decision at Procter and Gamble to take off the market its Rely brand tampons, which had been causally linked to toxic shock syndrome.[1] Procter and Gamble had invested twenty years of research and approximately $75 million in the product's preparation. At first, when scientific research offered some evidence that the material in the tampons did not encourage bacterial growth, Edward G. Harness, then chairman of the board and chief executive officer, said he was "determined to fight for a brand, to keep an important brand from being hurt by insufficient data in the hands of a bureaucracy."[2] However, Procter and Gamble later stopped production of the Rely tampon, in part because of negative publicity and a report from the Center for Disease Control that statistically linked Rely to toxic shock syndrome, a report that Procter and Gamble's physicians, microbiologists, and epidemiologists were unable to refute.

"That was the turning point," Harness said. The company subsequently pledged its research expertise to the Center for Disease Control to investigate toxic shock syndrome and agreed to finance and direct a large educational program about the disease, as well as to issue a warning to women not to use Rely. Referring to the Rely case, Harness made the following public announcement:

> Company management must consistently demonstrate a superior talent for keeping profit and growth objectives as first priorities. However, it also must have enough breadth to recognize that enlightened self-interest requires the company to fill any reasonable expectation placed upon it by the community and the various concerned publics. Keeping priorities straight and maintaining the sense of civic responsibility will achieve important secondary objectives of the firm. Profitability and growth go hand in hand with fair treatment of employees, of direct customers, of consumers, and of the community.[3]

Here prudence and morality flow together, perhaps because an appeal to prudence persuades some in the audience while appeals to morality persuade others.

Such a mixture of moral language with the language of prudence is often harmless. Persons who are more concerned about the actions businesses take than about their motivations will be indifferent as to whether businesses use the language of prudence or the language of morality to justify what they do. The distinction is important to philosophers, however, because a business practice that might be prudential may nonetheless be morally wrong. History has shown how some actions that were long accepted or at least condoned in the business community have become condemned as immoral, for example, the discharge of pollution into the air and water, plant relocation purely for economic gain, and large political contributions to people of influence.

Because businesses exist within a larger social framework, businesspeople must reflect on the morality of their actions, not because it is prudent to do so but because it is right to do so. It is generally believed that acting morally is in the interest of business, and thus prudence seems to be a justifiable motive for acting ethically. However, as you read through this text, you will see that prudence often suggests a different business decision than does morality.

Morality and Law

Business ethics in the United States is currently involved in an entangled, complex, and mutually stimulating relationship with law as illustrated in the legal cases reprinted at the ends of the chapters. Morality and law share concerns over matters of basic social importance and often have in common certain principles, obligations, and criteria of evidence. Law is the public's agency for translating morality into explicit social guidelines and practices and for stipulating punishments for offenses. Chapter selections mention both case law (judge-made law expressed in court decisions) and statutory law (federal and state statutes and their accompanying administrative regulations). In these forms law has forced vital issues before the public. Case law, in particular, has established influential precedents that provide material for reflection on both legal and moral questions.

Some have said that corporate concern about business ethics can be reduced or eliminated by turning problems over to the legal department. The operative phrase here is: "Let the lawyers decide; if it's legal, it's moral." Although this tactic would simplify matters, moral evaluation needs to be distinguished from legal evaluation. Despite an intersection between morals and law, the law is not the repository of moral standards and values, even when the law is directly concerned with moral problems. A law-abiding person is not necessarily morally sensitive or virtuous, and the fact that something is legally acceptable does not imply that it is morally acceptable. For example, the doctrine of employment at will permits employers to fire employees for unjust reasons and is (within certain limits) legal, yet such firings are often morally unacceptable. Again, questions are raised in later chapters about the morality of business actions, such as plant relocation and mergers that cause unemployment, even though such actions are not illegal.

A typical example is the following: It was perfectly legal when Houston financier Charles E. Hurwitz doubled the rate of tree cutting in the nation's privately owned virgin redwood forest. He did so to reduce the debt he incurred when his company, the Maxxam Group, borrowed money to successfully complete a hostile takeover of Pacific Lumber Company, which owned the redwoods. Before the takeover, Pacific Lumber had followed a conservative cutting policy but nonetheless had consistently operated at a profit. Despite the clear legality of the new clear-cutting policy, it has been criticized as immoral.[4]

A related problem involves the belief that a person found guilty under law is therefore morally guilty. Such judgments are not necessarily correct but rather depend on the moral acceptability of the law on which the judgment has been reached. For example, before the Foreign Corrupt Practices Act was signed into law by President Jimmy Carter, slush funds, bribes, and the like had not been illegal for U.S. corporations dealing with foreign governments. Since the new and stringently restrictive legislation was enacted (perhaps as an overreaction to the Watergate scandals), an intense and still ongoing debate has surrounded the act's implications. It served to frustrate many businesses whose now illegal practices were deemed not only acceptable but necessary to the conduct of business in various foreign cultures. Many businesspeople believe that the act put U.S. business firms at a competitive disadvantage, because other industrialized countries have no such laws. Many today still believe there is nothing unethical or morally corrupt in these now illegal acts. The real problem, they contend, is a shortsightedness in the legislation.

Furthermore, the courts have often been accused, with some justification, of causing moral inequities through court judgments rendered against corporations. Here are some examples:[5] (1) Monsanto Chemical was successfully sued for $200 million, although the presiding judge asserted that there was no credible evidence linking Monsanto's Agent Orange to the severe harms that had been described in the case. (2) Chevron Oil was successfully sued for mislabeling its cans of paraquat, although the offending label conformed exactly to federal regulations, which permitted no other form of label to be used. (3) Although whooping cough vaccine indisputably reduces the risk of this disease for children who receive the vaccine, almost no manufacturer will produce it for fear of costly suits brought under product liability laws. In each of these instances it is easy to understand why critics have considered as morally unjustified various regulations, legislation, and decisions in case law. Taken together, these considerations lead to the following conclusion: If something is legal, it is not necessarily moral; if something is illegal, it is not necessarily immoral.

Although law and morality overlap heavily, they are distinct. Something else must be said against the view that if it is legal, it is moral. Often legal cases are themselves decided on moral grounds. The case of *Christopher Brothers v. DuPont* illustrates this point. In Beaumont, Texas, the DuPont Company was constructing a new plant for making methanol. An unknown third party, a DuPont competitor, hired defendants Rolfe and Gary Christopher to fly over the facility and take photographs. These photographs revealed DuPont's process for making methanol, a trade secret. The flyover was discovered and DuPont sued. In response, the Christophers argued that they had done nothing illegal. To an extent, the presiding judge agreed with the Christophers, who, he admitted, had neither trespassed nor breached a confidential relationship to obtain the information. Nonetheless, the judge found the Christophers' conduct ethically improper. As a colleague of ours once said, "If it stinks ethically, it will stink legally." Clearly judges often use morality to help decide a case in the absence of applicable law.

The Rule of Conscience

"I cannot in good conscience continue my . . . association with Mellon Bank Corporation," said J. David Barnes, a member of the bank's advisory board of directors, upon tendering his resignation.[6] Mellon Bank had offered to lend $150 million to T. Boone Pickens of Mesa Petroleum in his attempt to obtain control of Phillips Petroleum. In effect, Barnes resigned because he could not in good moral conscience condone the bank's money going to a person he regarded as a morally unscrupulous operator.

The slogan "Let your conscience be your guide" has long been, for many, what morality is all about. Yet, despite their admiration for persons of conscience, philosophers have typically judged appeals to conscience alone as insufficient and untrustworthy for ethical judgment. Consciences vary radically from person to person and time to time and are often altered by circumstance, religious belief, childhood, and training. For example, Stanley Kresge, the son of the founder of S. S. Kresge Company—now known as the K-Mart Corporation—is a teetotaler for religious reasons. When the company started selling beer and wine, Kresge sold all his stock. His conscience, he said, would not let him make a profit on alcohol. But the company dismissed his objection as "his own business" and said that it sees nothing wrong with earning profits on alcohol.[7]

The reliability of conscience, then, is not self-certifying. Moral justification must be based on a source external to conscience itself. This external source is often the common morality or ethical theory, as we shall see.

Approaches to the Study of Morality

Morality and ethical theory can be studied and developed by a variety of methods, but three general approaches have dominated the literature. Two of these approaches describe and analyze morality, presumably without taking moral positions. The other approach takes a moral position and appeals to morality or ethical theory to underwrite judgments. These three approaches can be outlined as follows:

Descriptive approaches
Conceptual approaches
Prescriptive (normative) approaches

These categories do not express rigid and always clearly distinguishable approaches. Nonetheless, when understood as broad, polar, and contrasting positions, they can serve as models of inquiry and as valuable distinctions.

Social scientists often refer to the *descriptive approach* as the scientific study of ethics. Factual description and explanation of moral behavior and beliefs, as performed by anthropologists, sociologists, and historians, are typical of this approach. Here moral attitudes, codes, and beliefs are described, to include corporate policies on sexual harassment, codes of ethics in trade associations, and so forth. Examples of this approach can be found in *Harvard Business Review* articles and *Forbes* magazine polls that report what business executives believe is morally acceptable and unacceptable.

The second approach involves the *conceptual study* of ethics. Here, the meanings of central terms in ethics such as *right, obligation, justice, good, virtue,* and *responsibility* are analyzed. Crucial terms in business ethics such as *trade secret* and *deception* can be given this same kind of careful conceptual attention. The proper analysis of the term *morality* (as defined at the beginning of this chapter) and the distinction between the moral and the nonmoral are typical examples of these conceptual problems.

The third approach, *prescriptive* or *normative ethics,* is a prescriptive study attempting to formulate and defend basic moral norms. Normative moral philosophy aims at determining what *ought* to be done, which needs to be distinguished from what *is,* in fact, practiced. Ideally, an ethical theory provides reasons for adopting a whole system of moral principles or virtues. *Utilitarianism* and *Kantianism* are widely discussed theories, but they are not the only such theories. Utilitarians argue that there is one and only one fundamental principle determining right action, which can be roughly stated as follows: "An action is morally right if and only if it produces at least as great a balance of value over disvalue as any available alternative action." Kantians, by contrast, have argued that one or more of these fundamental principles of ethics differ from the principle of utility, for instance, principles of obligation, such as "Never treat another person merely as a means to your own goals." Both forms of these theories, together with other dimensions of ethical theory, are examined in Part Two of this chapter.

Principles of normative ethics are commonly used to treat specific moral problems such as abortion, famine, conflict of interest, mistreatment of animals, and racial and sexual discrimination. This use of ethical theory is often referred to, somewhat misleadingly, as *applied ethics.* Philosophical treatment of medical ethics, engineering ethics, journalistic ethics, jurisprudence, and business ethics involves distinct areas that employ general ethical principles to attempt to resolve moral problems that commonly arise in the professions.

Substantially the same general ethical principles apply to the problems across professional fields and in areas beyond professional ethics as well. One might appeal to principles of justice, for example, to illuminate and resolve issues of taxation, health care distribution, environmental responsibility, criminal punishment, and reverse discrimination (see Chapters 6, 7, and 9). Similarly, principles of veracity (truthfulness) apply to debates about secrecy and deception in international politics, misleading advertisements in business ethics, balanced reporting in journalistic ethics, and disclosure of illness to a patient in medical ethics. Increased clarity about the general conditions under which truth must be told and when it may be withheld would presumably enhance understanding of moral requirements in each of these areas.

The exercise of sound judgment in business practice together with appeals to ethical theory are central in the essays and cases in this volume. Rarely is there a straightforward "application" of principles that mechanically resolves problems. Principles are more commonly *specified,* that is, made more concrete for the context, than applied. Much of the best work in contemporary business ethics involves arguments for how to specify principles to handle particular problems.

Justification in Ethics

Almost everyone interested in moral problems asks questions about whether certain views can be justified. What, then, counts as adequate justification? An easy answer to this question is that moral judgments are justified by giving reasons for them. However, not all reasons are good reasons, and not all good reasons are sufficient for justification. For example, a good reason for regulating various business practices, such as those of industries involved in the use of radioactive products, is that radioactivity presents a clear and present danger to others. Many believe that this reason is also sufficient to justify a broad set of regulatory practices, such as government protections against environmental contamination. But is it?

There is a good reason against government regulation: It involves a deprivation of liberty; it takes away the freedom to act in any way one wishes to act. To counter the contention that government regulation is not desirable because it involves a deprivation of liberty, additional reasons would have to be given to justify the deprivation of liberty, for example, the dire consequences to the public interest if government fails to intervene or the importance of protecting against inadvertent tragedies, such as the near disaster at the Three Mile Island nuclear generating station. A set of reasons is then offered to defend this perspective on the issues. In the example about radioactive materials, the set of *good* reasons for regulation might or might not count as *sufficient* justification for regulation, depending on the quality of the argument.

Every human belief is subject to challenge and, therefore, stands in need of justification by reasoned argument. But just as there are good and bad reasons, there are good and bad arguments. One must know whether the premises upon which these arguments rest are acceptable in order to know whether an argument proves or justifies anything. Are there such person-neutral premises?

Relativism and Objectivity of Belief

Some writers on ethics have contended that moral views simply express how one feels or how a culture accommodates the desires of its people. These sentiments are informal expressions of an important challenge to ethical theories: relativism. Individual relativists claim that what an individual person thinks is right or wrong *is* right or wrong for that person. Cultural relativists, on the other hand, believe that whatever a culture thinks is right or wrong *is* right or wrong in that culture. Thus, if the Irish tradition is to ban abortion, then abortion is morally wrong in Ireland. If the Swedish tradition allows abortion, then abortion is morally permissible in Sweden. Cultural relativism tells us that there is no way for us to show the true moral status of abortion, and hence the dispute between the Irish and Swedish cultures cannot be settled in principle.

For *individual* relativists it is impossible to settle moral disputes among individuals. For *cultural* relativists, it is impossible to settle moral disputes among cultures. Any justification of a universal moral principle that holds for all cultures could have no justification other than the fact that all cultures accept it. Each of these two types of relativism raises questions about the possibility of an objective morality.

Relativism has been defended because moral standards vary from place to place, with no absolute or universal moral standards applying to all persons at all times. Many relativists defend their theory by appealing to the existence of cultural or individual diversity of belief on matters of morality. Some of the most vivid and memorable facts supporting cultural diversity have been provided by anthropologists visiting "primitive" tribes in the South Sea Islands, Africa, and South America in the early twentieth century. Similar diversity today becomes apparent if U.S. culture is compared with that of other nations: Practices of business payoffs, employee treatment and loyalty, and corporate taxation are but three among thousands of possible practices whose acceptance varies from culture to culture.

Moral philosophers have tended to reject relativism, and we need to understand why. First, what does the argument from the fact of cultural diversity tell us? When early anthropologists probed beneath surface disagreements, they often discovered agreement on deeper levels. For example, one anthropologist discovered a tribe in which parents, after raising their children and still in a relatively healthy state, would climb a high tree. Their children would then shake the tree until the parents fell to the ground and died. This cultural practice seems vastly different from our own. The anthropologist discovered, however, that the tribe believed that people went into the afterlife in the same bodily state they left this life. Their children wanted them to enter the afterlife in a healthy state. The children in this tribe were no less concerned about their parents than are children in Western cultures. Although cultural disagreement exists concerning the afterlife, there is no ultimate moral disagreement over the moral principles determining how children should treat their parents.

Thus, despite differing practices and beliefs, people often do not disagree about ultimate moral standards. For example, personal payments for special services are common in some cultures and punishable as bribery in others; it is undeniable that these customs are different, but it does not follow that the underlying moral principles providing justification of the customs are different. The two cultures may agree about basic principles of morality, yet disagree how to live by these principles in particular situations.

This analysis implies that a fundamental conflict between cultural values could occur only if cultural disagreement about proper principles or rules exist at the deepest level of moral rules. It does not follow that the underlying moral standards differ even if beliefs, judgments, or actions do differ. People may differ because they have different factual beliefs rather than different normative standards. For example, individuals differ over appropriate actions to protect the environment, not because they have different sets of standards about environmental ethics, but because they hold different factual views about how certain discharges of chemicals and airborne particles will or will not harm the environment. Identical sets of normative standards might be invoked in their arguments about environmental protection, yet different policies and actions might be recommended.

One needs, then, to distinguish *relativism of judgments* from *relativism of standards*. This distinction rests on the fact that many different particular judgments call upon the same general standards for their justification. Moreover, relativism of judgment is so pervasive in human social life that it would be foolish to deny it: But when we differ about whether to buy one brand of telephone over another, it does not follow that we have different standards for telephones. Perhaps one person has had success with AT&T products in the past, whereas another person has not. Similarly in ethics, people may differ about whether one policy for keeping hospital information confidential is more acceptable than another, but it does not follow that they have different moral standards of confidentiality. They may hold the same moral standard on protecting confidentiality, but differ over how to implement that standard.

A relativism of standards, then, may not be a correct account even though relativism of judgment is correct. This possibility is worth serious consideration for two reasons. First, many prorelativism arguments are based on relativism of judgment, whose examples are then claimed to support a relativism of standards. If this were the only basis for a relativism of standards, it would be an empty theory. Second, many people react negatively to the idea that moral rules allow no flexibility for individual judgment. It seems to them that relativism is therefore preferable to an "iron-law" perspective. This view is shortsighted. Relativism of judgment does allow flexibility, but it, paradoxically, is consistent with a denial of the relativism of moral standards. People might agree that they should generally keep their promises, and yet they might disagree about the fulfillment of their promises in a particular circumstance (e.g., when the person to whom they made a promise turns out to be untrustworthy). A person who accepts nonrelative general standards can acknowledge that the rightness of a particular judgment or action depends on particular circumstances.

However, these observations do not decide whether a relativism of standards is true, and this shortcoming has been a major concern of moral relativism. If moral conflict did turn out to be fundamental, such conflict could not be removed even if there were perfect agreement about the facts, concepts, and background beliefs of a case.

Suppose, then, that disagreement exists at the deepest level of moral thinking; that is, suppose that two cultures disagree on basic or fundamental norms. It still does not follow from this relativity of standards that there is no ultimate norm or set of norms in which everyone *ought* to believe. Consider an analogy to religious disagreement: From the fact that people have incompatible religious or atheistic beliefs, it does not follow that there is no single correct set of religious or atheistic propositions. Nothing more than skepticism seems justified by the facts about religion that are adduced by anthropology; and nothing more than this skepticism would be justified if fundamental conflicts of belief were discovered in ethics.

Cultural Objectivity and Moral Stultification.   One can evaluate various (but not all) problems of relativism by focusing on (1) the objectivity of morals within cultures and (2) the stultifying consequences of a serious commitment to moral relativism. Because the first focus provides an argument against individual relativism and the second provides an argument against cultural relativism, each should be considered independently.

We noted previously that morality is concerned with practices of right and wrong transmitted within cultures from one generation to another. The terms of social life are set by these practices, whose rules are pervasively acknowledged and shared in that culture. Within the culture, then, is a significant measure of moral objectivity, because morality by its nature does not exist through a person's individual preferences. Individuals cannot create it by stipulation or correctly call a personal policy a morality. Such moral individualism is as dubious as anarchism in politics and law, and few readily accept a declaration that a person's political and legal beliefs are legitimately determined by that person alone. Nor can a corporation develop professional ethics alone. A hospital corporation like Humana cannot draw up a code brushing aside either the confidentiality of patient information or the requirement of obtaining adequate consents before surgery. Similarly, a brokerage house cannot simply define a conflict of interest according to its institutional preference. If these codes deviate significantly from standard or accepted rules, they must be rejected as subjective and mistaken.

Room for invention or alteration in morality is restricted by the broader understanding of morality in culture. Rules cannot be *moral* standards simply because an individual so labels them. Because individual relativism claims that they can be invented or labelled, this theory seems *factually* mistaken. This critique of individual relativism does not count against cultural relativism, however, because this criticism could be accepted by a cultural relativist.

Our discussion now can shift to the second argument, which is directed at cultural relativism and which projects the pragmatic consequences of accepting cultural relativism, especially if it would prevent serious reflection on, and resolution of, moral problems. In circumstances of disagreement, moral reflection would be in order whether or not cultural relativism is true. When two parties argue about some serious, divisive, and contested moral issue—for example, conflicts of interest in business—people tend to think that some fair and justified compromise may be reached. People seldom infer from the mere fact of a conflict between beliefs that there is no way to judge one view as correct or as better argued than the other. The more absurd the position advanced by one party, the more convinced others become that some views are mistaken or require supplementation. People seldom conclude that there is no correct ethical perspective or reasonable negotiation.

Moreover, a culture cannot develop just any set of moral principles. That a society exists at all indicates that the society has accepted certain moral principles to govern the behavior of its members. A society is possible only if the society has rules against lying to one another and against committing acts of random violence. We find as a matter of fact that certain moral rules are accepted by most, if not all, societies. Consider torture. How does a society respond when it is accused of torturing people? The accused society does not respond by saying that torturing people is acceptable in this society and hence is morally acceptable. Rather the accused society denies that torture occurs, tries to justify the torture, or charges the accuser with torture as well. Thus our hope for some agreement on fundamental moral principles may not be totally futile.

Nonetheless, moral disagreement among cultures and individuals is common. If one believes in reasoned debate and resolution of moral conflicts, one must accept the "rightness" of some moral perspective. What methods can be used to reduce moral disagreement? We examine ethical theories in Part Two of this chapter, but now, moral disagreements and their resolution need further discussion.

Moral Disagreements

In any pluralistic culture dilemmas involving conflicts of value exist. In this volume we examine a few of these dilemmas, such as withholding pertinent information in business deals, whistleblowing in industry, advertising on children's television, preferential hiring policies, and the like. Although some disagreements seem overwhelming, there are ways to resolve them or at least to reduce the level of disagreement. Let us examine several methods that have been employed in the past to deal constructively with moral disagreements, each of which deserves recognition as a method of easing disagreement and conflict.

Obtaining Objective Information. Many moral disagreements sometimes can be at least partially resolved by obtaining additional factual information on which moral controversies turn. We have already seen how useful such information can be in trying to ascertain whether cultural variations in belief are fundamental. Unfortunately, it has often been assumed that moral disputes are by definition produced solely by differences over moral principles or their application, and not by a lack of scientific or factual information. This assumption is misleading, inasmuch as moral disputes, that is, disputes over what morally ought or ought not to be done, often have nonmoral elements as their main ingredients. For example, debates over the allocation of tax dollars to prevent accidents or disease in the workplace often become bogged down in factual issues of whether particular measures such as masks or lower levels of toxic chemicals actually function best to prevent death and disease.

In a publicized controversy over the morality of "exaggerated claims" in advertising, the Federal Trade Commission (FTC) alleged that the Standard Oil Company of California (SOCAL) was guilty of intentionally misleading the public with its commercials for Chevron gasoline containing the additive F-310. Among the most damaging of the FTC's charges was the claim that SOCAL was falsely representing its F-310 additive as a unique product, thereby deceiving and misleading the public. Preliminary conferences and investigations, however, substantiated the validity of SOCAL's claims regarding its product's uniqueness, and the FTC thereupon withdrew its demonstrably unfounded charges. Although the dispute regarding other aspects of the F-310 advertising campaign continued, the appeal to the facts narrowed and focused the ground of disagreement and advanced the moral and legal controversy toward a resolution.

Controversial issues such as the use of Nutrasweet in diet sodas; toxic substances in the workplace; fluoridation of public waters; and the manufacture, dissemination, and advertisement of vaccines for medical use are laced with issues of both values and facts. The arguments used by disagreeing parties may turn on a dispute about liberty or justice, and therefore may be primarily moral; but they may also rest on factual disagreements over, for example, the efficacy of a product. Information may thus have only a limited bearing on the resolution of some controversies, yet it may have a direct and almost overpowering influence in others.

Definitional Clarity.   Sometimes controversies have been settled by reaching conceptual or definitional agreement over the language used by disputing parties. Controversies discussed in Chapter 6 over the morality of affirmative action, reverse discrimination, and comparable worth, for example, are often needlessly complicated because different senses of these expressions are employed, and yet disputing parties may have much invested in their particular definitions. If there is no common point of contention in such cases, parties will be addressing entirely separate issues through their conceptual assumptions. Often these parties will not have a bona fide moral disagreement.

Although conceptual agreement provides no guarantee that a dispute will be settled, it should at least facilitate direct discussion of the outstanding issues. For this reason, many essays in this volume dwell at some length on problems of conceptual clarity.

Example-Counterexample.   Resolution of moral controversies can also be aided by posing examples and opposed counterexamples, that is, by bringing forward cases or examples favorable to one point of view and counterexamples in opposition. For instance, in a famous case against AT&T a dispute over discriminatory hiring and promotion between the company and the Equal Employment Opportunities Commission (EEOC) was handled through the citation of statistics and examples that (allegedly) documented the claims made by each side. AT&T showed, for example, that 55 percent of the employees on its payroll were women and that 33 percent of all management positions were held by women. To sharpen its allegation of discriminatory practices in the face of this evidence, the EEOC countered by citing a government study demonstrating that 99 percent of all telephone operators were female, whereas only 1 percent of craft workers were female. Such a use of example and counterexample serves to weigh the strength of conflicting considerations.

Analysis of Arguments and Positions.   Finally, a serviceable method of philosophical inquiry is that of exposing the inadequacies in and unexpected consequences of arguments and positions. A moral argument that leads to conclusions that a proponent is not prepared to defend and did not previously anticipate will have to be changed, and the distance between those who disagree will perhaps be reduced by this process. Inconsistencies not only in reasoning but also in organizational schemes or pronouncements can be uncovered. However, in a context of controversy, sharp attacks or critiques are unlikely to eventuate in an agreement unless a climate of reason prevails. A fundamental axiom of successful negotiation is "reason and be open to reason." It holds for moral discussion as well as any other disagreement.

No contention is made here that moral disagreements can always be resolved or that every reasonable person must accept the same method for approaching such problems. Many moral disagreements may not be resolvable by any of the four methods we have discussed. A single ethical theory or method may never be developed to resolve all disagreements adequately, and the pluralism of cultural beliefs often presents a considerable barrier to the resolution of issues. Given the possibility of continual disagreement, the resolution of crosscultural conflicts such as those faced by multinational corporations may prove especially elusive. However, if something is to be done about these problems, a resolution seems more likely to occur if the methods outlined in this section are used.

The Problem of Egoism

Attitudes in business have often been deemed fundamentally egoistic. Executives and corporations are said to act from prudence—that is, each business is out to promote solely its interest. Some say the corporation has no other interest, because its goal is to be as successful in competition as possible.

The philosophical theory called *egoism* has familiar origins. Each of us has been confronted, for example, with occasions on which a choice must be made between spending money on ourselves or on some worthy charitable enterprise. When one elects to purchase new clothes for oneself rather than contribute to a university scholarship fund for poor students, self-interest is being given priority over the interests of others. Egoism generalizes beyond these occasions to all human choices. The egoist contends that all choices either involve or should involve self-promotion as their sole objective. Thus, a person's or corporation's only goal and perhaps only obligation is self-promotion. No sacrifices or obligations are owed to others.

Psychological Egoism.   There are two main varieties of egoism, psychological egoism and ethical egoism. Psychological egoism is the view that everyone is always motivated to act in his or her perceived self-interest. This factual theory regarding human motivation offers an explanation of human conduct, in contrast to a justification of human conduct. It claims that people always do what pleases them or what is in their interest. Popular ways of expressing this viewpoint include: "People are at heart selfish, even if they appear to be unselfish"; "People look out for Number One first"; "In the long run, everybody does what he or she wants to do"; and "No matter what a person says, he or she acts for the sake of personal satisfaction."

Psychological egoism presents a serious challenge to moral philosophy. If this theory is correct, there could be no purely altruistic moral motivation. Normative ethics (with the exception of ethical egoism) presupposes that people ought to behave in accordance with certain moral principles, whether or not such behavior promotes their own interests. If people *must act* in their own interest, to ask them to do otherwise would be absurd. Accordingly, if psychological egoism is true, the whole enterprise of normative ethics is futile.

Those who accept psychological egoism are convinced by their observation of themselves and others that people are entirely self-centered in their motivation. Conversely, those who reject the theory do so because they see many examples of altruistic behavior in the lives of friends, saints, heroes, and public servants, and because contemporary anthropology, psychology, and biology offer many compelling studies of sacrificial behavior. Even if it is conceded that people are basically selfish, critics of egoism say it seems undeniable that there are at least some outstanding examples of preeminently unselfish actions: when corporations cut profits in order to provide public services (see Chapter 2) and when employees "blow the whistle" on unsafe or otherwise improper business practices even though they could lose their jobs and suffer social ostracism (see Chapter 5).

The defender of psychological egoism is not impressed by the exemplary lives of saints and heroes or by social practices of sacrifice. The psychological egoist maintains that all persons who expend effort to help others, to promote fairness in competition, to promote the general welfare, or to risk their lives for the welfare of others are really acting to promote themselves: In loving others, they strengthen the love of others for themselves. By sacrificing for their children, parents receive satisfaction in their children's achievements. By following society's moral and legal codes, people avoid both the police and social ostracism.

Egoists maintain that no matter how self-sacrificing a person's behavior may at times seem, the desire behind the action is self-regarding. One is ultimately out for oneself, whether in the long or the short run, and whether one realizes it or not. Egoists view egoistic actions as perfectly compatible with behavior others categorize as altruistic. For example, many corporations have adopted "enlightened self-interest" policies through which they are responsive to community needs and promote worker satisfaction to promote their corporate image and ultimately their earnings. The clever person or corporation can appear to be unselfish, but the action's true character depends on the *motivation* behind the appearance. Apparently altruistic agents may simply believe that an unselfish appearance best promotes their long-range interests. From the egoist's point of view, the fact that some (pseudo?) sacrifices may be necessary in the short run do not count against egoism.

Consider a typical example. In mid-1985 Illinois Bell argued before the Illinois Commerce Commission that its competitors should be allowed full access to markets and that there should be no regulation to protect Illinois Bell from its competitors. Illinois Bell had long been protected by such regulation and under it had grown to be a successful, $2.7 billion company. Why, then, was it now arguing that a complete free market would be the fairest business arrangement? *Forbes* magazine asked, "Is this 'altruism' or is it 'enlightened self-interest'?" *Forbes* editors answered that, despite the appearance of altruism, what Illinois Bell wanted was "to get the state regulators off their backs" to be able to compete more successfully with fewer constraints and to avoid losing business to large companies that could set up their own telephone systems. Self-interest, not fairness, was, according to *Forbes,* the proper explanation of Illinois Bell's behavior.[8]

The psychological egoist maintains that all persons who expend effort to help others, to promote fairness in competition, to promote the general welfare, or even to risk their lives for the welfare of others are really acting to promote themselves. In loving others, for example, we strengthen their love for us. By sacrificing for our children, we take satisfaction in their achievements. By following society's moral codes, we avoid both the police and social ostracism. The psychological egoist concedes that people often do act contrary to their self-interest and that some people seem to act contrary to their self-interest most of the time. People simply make mistakes in assessing what is in their self-interest, and a few people stupidly overlook their best interest. Thus, the psychological egoist is not saying that people act in terms of their real self-interest. The egoist is only committed to the view that everyone always is motivated to act in accordance with perceived self-interest.

Is psychological egoism a correct theory? This question as a matter of psychological fact may not have an answer. However, because altruistic acts not in the interest of the individual performing them have occurred—for example, people giving up their own life to save another—some attempt to assess the adequacy of the egoist's arguments should be made. It is tempting for the psychological egoist to make the theory necessarily true because of the difficulties in proving it to be empirically true. When confronted with what looks like altruistic acts, egoists may appeal to unconscious motives of self-interest or claim that every act is based on some desire of the person performing the act and that acting on that desire is what is meant by *self-interest.*

The latter explanation seems to be a conceptual or verbal trick: The egoist has changed the meaning of *self-interest.* At first, *self-interest* meant acting exclusively on behalf of one's self-interest. Now the word has been redefined to mean acting on any interest one has. But the central questions remain unresolved: Are there different kinds of human motives? Do we sometimes have an interest in acting for ourselves and at other times on behalf of others, or do we simply act for ourselves? Philosophy and psychology have yet to establish that we never act contrary to perceived self-interest; for this reason psychological egoism remains a speculative hypothesis.

Ethical Egoism. Ethical egoism is a theory stating that the only valid standard of conduct is the obligation to promote one's well-being above everyone else's. Whereas psychological egoism is a descriptive, psychological theory about human motivation, ethical egoism is a normative theory about what people ought to do. According to psychological egoism, people always *do* act on the basis of perceived self-interest. According to ethical egoism, people always *ought* to act on the basis of perceived self-interest.

Ethical egoism is dramatically different from common morality. Consider maxims such as, "You're a sucker if you don't put yourself first and others second." This maxim is unacceptable by the norms of common morality, which requires that people return a lost wallet to a known owner and that they correct a bank loan officer's errors in their favor. Still, questions about why we should look out for the interests of others on such occasions have troubled many reflective persons. Some have concluded that acting against one's interest is contrary to reason. These thinkers regard conventional morality as tinged with irrational sentiment and indefensible constraints on the individual. These people are the supporters of ethical egoism. Their view does not entail that one ought never to take the interests of others into account, but rather that one should consider the interests of others only when it suits one's interest.

What would society be like if ethical egoism were the conventional, prevailing theory of proper conduct? Some philosophers and political theorists have argued that anarchism and chaos would result unless preventive measures were adopted. A classic statement of this position was made by the philosopher Thomas Hobbes. Imagine a world with limited resources, he says, where persons are approximately equal in their ability to harm one another and where everyone acts exclusively in his or her interest. Hobbes argued that in such a world everyone would be at everyone else's throat. Such a state of nature would be plagued by anxiety, violence, and constant danger. As Hobbes put it, life would be "solitary, poor, nasty, brutish, and short."[9] However, Hobbes also assumed that human beings are sufficiently rational to recognize their interests. To avoid the war of all against all, he urged his readers to form a powerful state to protect themselves.

Egoists accept Hobbes's view in the following form: Any clever person will realize that he or she has no moral obligations to others besides those he or she voluntarily assumes. One should accept moral rules and assume specific obligations only when doing so promotes one's self-interest. Even if one agrees to live under a set of laws of the state that are binding on everyone, one should obey rules and laws only to protect oneself and to bring about a situation of communal living that is personally advantageous. One should also back out of an obligation whenever it becomes clear that it is to one's long-range disadvantage to fulfill the obligation. When confronted by a social revolution, the questionable trustworthiness of a colleague, or an incompetent administration at one's place of employment, one is under no obligation to obey the law, fulfill one's contracts, or tell the truth. These obligations exist only because one assumes them, and one ought to assume them only as long as doing so promotes one's interest.

What can be said by way of criticism of this form of ethical egoism? One criticism is that the theory gives incompatible directives in circumstances of moral conflict: If everyone acted egoistically, it seems reasonably certain that protracted conflicts would occur, just as many international conflicts now arise among nations primarily pursuing their own interests. According to ethical egoism, both parties in a circumstance or conflict ought to pursue their best interests exclusively, and it is morally right for both to do so. For example, it is in the interest of a consumer activist to stop production and distribution of an automobile of hazardous design; and it is no less in the interest of the automobile manufacturer to prevent interruption of the production and distribution of the model. Egoism urges both parties to pursue their interests exclusively and holds both pursuits to be morally right.

The oddity of this situation can be highlighted by imagining that the consumer activist is an egoist. In order to be a consistent egoist, the activist must hold to a theory that the automobile manufacturer ought to pursue its interest, which would involve thwarting the activist's consumer objectives (all ought to pursue their interests and thwart others if necessary). In striving for theoretical consistency, the egoist supports a theory that works against his or her interest, and seems to fall into inconsistency. The egoist says that everyone ought to seek his or her maximal satisfaction, even if this pursuit would negatively affect the egoist's own pursuit of maximal satisfaction.

A plausible egoistic reply to this objection is that it springs from a misunderstanding of the rules and policies that an ethical egoist would promote. An arrangement whereby everyone acts on more or less fixed rules such as those found in conventional moral and legal systems would produce the most desirable state of affairs from a egoistic point of view. The reason is that such rules arbitrate conflicts and make social life more agreeable. These rules would include, for example, familiar moral and legal principles of justice that are intended to make everyone's situation more secure and stable.

Only an unduly narrow conception of self-interest, the egoist might argue, leads critics to conclude that the egoist would not willingly observe such rules of justice. If society can be structured to resolve personal conflicts through courts and other peaceful means, egoists will see it as in their interest to accept those binding social arrangements, just as they will see it as prudent to treat other individuals favorably in personal contacts. Notice that the egoist is not saying that his or her interests are served by promoting the good of others, but rather that personal interests are served by observing impartial rules irrespective of the outcome for others. Egoists do not care about the welfare of others except insofar as it affects their welfare, and this desire for personal well-being alone motivates acceptance of the conventional rules of morality.

Egoistic Business Practices and Utilitarian Results. A different view from that of Hobbes, and one that has been extremely influential in the philosophy of the business community, is found in Adam Smith's economic and moral writings. Smith believed that the public good evolves out of a suitably restrained clash of competing individual interests. As individuals pursue their self-interest, the interactive process is guided by an "invisible hand," ensuring that the public interest is achieved. Ironically, according to Smith, egoism in commercial transactions leads not to the war of all against all, but rather to a utilitarian outcome, that is, the largest number of benefits for the largest number of persons. The free market is, Smith thought, a better method of achieving the public good than the highly visible and authoritarian hand of Hobbes's all-powerful sovereign state.

Smith believed that government should be limited in order to protect individual freedom. At the same time, he recognized that concern with freedom and self-interest could get out of control. Hence he proposed that minimal state regulatory activity is needed to provide and enforce the rules of the competitive game. Smith's picture of a restrained egoistic world has captivated many in the business and economic community. They, like Smith, do not picture themselves as selfish and indifferent to the interests of others, and they recognize that a certain element of cooperation is essential if their interests are to flourish. At the same time, they recognize that when their interests conflict with the interests of others, they should pursue their interests within the established rules of the competitive game. Within the rules of business practice, they see ethics as the maxims of a suitably restrained egoist. It is egoistic because it is based on the active pursuit of personal interest. It is restrained because self-interest is kept within the bounds of the prevailing rules of business for the sake of the common good.

Many in the business community have actively supported the view that a restrained egoism leads to commendable utilitarian outcomes. This is one of the defenses of a free market economy: Competition advances the good of corporations, and competition among individual firms advances the good of society as a whole. Hence, a popular view of business ethics might be captured by the phrase "Ethical egoism leads to utilitarian outcomes." As Smith put it, corporations and individuals pursuing their individual interests also thereby promote the public good, so long as they abide by the rules that protect the public.

A controversial figure who defends his actions through this line of argument is America's highest-paid corporate executive, the previously mentioned T. Boone Pickens, chairman of Mesa Petroleum Company. Pickens is a corporate "raider": He works to spot undervalued corporations and then threatens to take them over. Using speculative stock purchases and hostile tender offers, raiders such as Pickens strike fear in the hearts of corporate managers, who sometimes modify their growth plans to defend the corporation from the takeover attempt. Pickens believes that he is simply drawing attention to undervalued companies whose true value comes to light through his activities. This benefits the stockholders (the only owners of public corporations in his view), whose stock suddenly increases in monetary value. Pickens's immediate ambition is self-interest—profit for himself and his company— but he claims that the public is a large benefactor of his efforts to improve his own financial position.

Many corporate managers vigorously disagree with Pickens, and many also disagree with the confident optimism underlying Adam Smith's more general perspective. Furthermore, they reject all forms of egoism. We can begin to understand their reservations by turning at this point to the study of ethical theory, and to utilitarian ethical theories in particular.

PART TWO: NORMATIVE ETHICAL THEORY

The central question discussed in Part Two is the following: What constitutes an acceptable ethical standard for business practice and by what authority is the standard acceptable? One time-honored answer is that the acceptability of a moral standard is determined by prevailing practices in business or authoritative, profession-generated documents such as codes. Many businesspersons find this viewpoint congenial and do not see any need for revisions in practices that they find comfortable and adequate.

Professional standards do play a role in business ethics, and we will discuss them in some detail. Ultimately, however, these standards need to be justified in terms of ethical theory, just as the moral norms of a culture need to be justified. For this reason, the later parts in this section are devoted to a discussion of utilitarianism and Kantianism, two widely discussed theories in modern history of Western philosophy.

The Role of Professional Standards

The professional practice standard holds that obligations and other standards of moral conduct are determined by the customary practices of a professional community. Proponents of this standard argue that a businessperson is charged with various responsibilities—for example, avoiding harm, honoring warranties, removing conflicts of interest, and obeying legal requirements—and that they must use proper professional criteria for determining appropriate actions. Professional custom establishes the standards of obligatory conduct such as "due care." Any person without expert knowledge is unqualified to determine what should be done, and for this reason the professional community is the appropriate source. This rule is applied to determine the obligation of due care in a person's performance when wrong conduct is suspected. For example, the standard is used by the courts to assess responsibility and liability for harm in negligence cases, usually because a client, patient, or customer seeks to punish the responsible party, be compensated, or both. Professional malpractice is an instance of negligence in which professional standards of care have not been followed, as when an accountant fails to follow accepted accounting practices.

One area of uncertainty in contemporary business involves a failure by professionals, such as accountants, to probe deeply enough in an investigative report, thereby harming those who do not receive the information that the professional had some responsibility to uncover. For example, since a scandal at Mckesson & Robbins in 1940, the Securities and Exchange Commission has held that an accountant performing a corporate audit has an obligation to uncover gross management overstatements. Although accountants have long resisted accusations of negligence for overlooking management fraud, some recent legal cases have suggested that the courts expect accountants to uncover fraud, no matter how subtle. Auditors failing to catch red flags of suspicious conduct are responsible for harms that result from their oversight according to this stringent SEC standard.

Despite its popularity in business, the professional practice standard has shortcomings. This particular standard of duty (and negligence) would surely be too high for some areas of practice. Even when the utmost care is exercised in some circumstances it is possible that some critical factor has been omitted or distorted because of lack of access to sources or documents. Whether a customary standard of disclosure exists within the relevant fields of business is questionable, and it is undecided how much consensus is required to establish such a standard, that is, how much consensus is needed for a norm to count as a standard prevalent in practice. A further objection is that negligent care might be perpetuated if professionals in the same field offer the same inferior set of precautions, warranties, technology, and auditing strategies, whether through ignorance, as a genuine conviction, or for reasons of professional solidarity. If the elements of negligent behavior are to serve as a workable model for business decisions, the established obligations cannot be set at such a low level that virtually any conduct is acceptable.

Another objection centers on a basic assumption of the professional practice standard: Relevant professionals have sufficient expertise to recognize the proper precautions, information, warranties, auditing strategies, and so forth. This assumption is empirical, yet there are no reliable data on these issues, and current research on the effects of professional standards is both sketchy and inconclusive. One might also doubt that professional standards should be set by professionals when they do possess the relevant expertise. It is the customers, employees, and consumers who desire more detailed disclosures or more extensive precautions as standards of due care than do professionals in practice. Usually, decisions about due care are not professional judgments, but ethical ones, and critics have a point in maintaining that they should not be made by the professional alone, or even primarily.

For example, during the 1970s and 1980s, drug use in the workplace became a serious national problem. What should a manager do to ensure a clean workplace unimpaired by drug use? The legally prudent action. These drug-use programs are becoming a commonly accepted business practice, but under what conditions are they morally acceptable? In answering that question, a number of perspectives are relevant. Some ethical theorists focus on the consequences of implementing a drug-testing program. According to these theorists, the moral manager must consider the drug-testing program and other viable alternatives for dealing with drug abuse by employees. The good and bad consequences of each policy must be determined in a way that enables the manager to compare the policies and choose the one that provides the greatest balance of good consequences over bad. This choice is made irrespective of whether or not it conforms to standards of professional practice. Many in the business community refer to this kind of reasoning as cost benefit analysis. Ethical theorists who reason in this way are called utilitarians.

Utilitarian Theories

Utilitarian theories hold that the moral worth of actions or practices is determined solely by their consequences. An action or practice is right if it leads to the best possible balance of good consequences over bad consequences for all the parties affected. In taking this perspective, utilitarians believe that the purpose or function of morality is to promote human welfare by minimizing harms and maximizing benefits.

The first developed utilitarian philosophical writings were those of David Hume (1711–1776), Jeremy Bentham (1748–1832), and John Stuart Mill (1806–1873). Mill's *Utilitarianism* (1863) is still today considered the major theoretical exposition. Mill discusses two foundations or sources of utilitarian thinking: a *normative* foundation in the principle of utility and a *psychological* foundation in human nature. He proposes the principle of utility—the "greatest happiness principle"—as the foundation of normative ethical theory: Actions are right, he says, in proportion to their tendency to promote happiness or absence of pain, and wrong insofar as they tend to produce pain or displeasure. Pleasure and freedom from pain, Mill argues, are alone desirable as ends. All desirable things (which are numerous) are desirable either for the pleasure inherent in them or as means to promote pleasure and prevent pain.

Mill's second foundation derives from his belief that most persons, and perhaps all, have a basic desire for unity and harmony with their fellow human beings. Just as people feel horror at crimes, he says, they have a basic moral sensitivity to the needs of others. He sees the purpose of morality as tapping natural human sympathies to benefit others, while controlling unsympathetic attitudes that cause harm to others. The principle of utility is conceived as the best means to these basic human goals.

Essential Features of Utilitarianism. Several essential features of utilitarianism may be extracted from the reasoning of Mill and other utilitarians. First, utilitarianism is committed to the maximization of the good and the minimization of harm and evil. It asserts that society ought always to produce the greatest possible balance of positive value or the minimum balance of disvalue for all persons affected. The means to maximization is efficiency, a goal that persons in business find congenial, because it is highly prized throughout the economic sector. Efficiency is a means to higher profits and lower prices, and the struggle to be maximally profitable seeks to obtain maximum production from limited economic resources. The utilitarian commitment to the principle of optimal productivity through efficiency is an essential part of the traditional business conception of society and a standard part of business practice. In this respect the enterprise of business harbors a fundamentally utilitarian conception of the good society.

The need both to minimize harm and to balance risks against benefits has been a perennial concern of the business community. For example, those in the petroleum industry know that oil and gas operations exist tenuously with wetlands areas, waterfowl, and fish. But if the demands of U.S. consumers are to be met, corporate and public policies must balance possible environmental harms against industrial productivity. Similarly, those in the nuclear power industry know that U.S. power plants are built with heavy containment structures to withstand internal failures; but they also recognize the possibility of a major disaster such as that at Chernobyl, then USSR, in 1986. Building safe structures is an attempt to balance public benefit, the predicted cost savings, the probability of failure, and the magnitude of harm in the event of failure. The utilitarian believes that such examples from public policy exhibit a general truth about the moral life.

However, utilitarianism involves more than valuing efficiency, reducing evil, and maximizing positive outcomes in the tradeoff situation. Hence a second essential feature must be considered—the utilitarian theory of *intrinsic value*. Efficiency itself is simply an instrumental good; that is, it is valuable strictly as a means to something else. In the corporation, efficiency is valuable as a means to growth and to profit maximization. Within the free enterprise system of competing firms, efficiency is valuable as a means toward maximizing the production of goods and services. Within utilitarian ethical theory, efficiency is the means for maximizing human good. But what is "good" according to the utilitarian?

We can begin to form an answer to this question by considering, as an illustration, the working of the New York stock market. Daily results on Wall Street are not intrinsically good. They are extrinsically good as a means to other ends, such as financial security and happiness. Utilitarians believe that people ought to seek certain experiences and conditions that are good in themselves without reference to further consequences, and that all values are ultimately to be gauged in terms of these intrinsic goods. Health, friendship, and freedom from pain would be included among such values. An intrinsic value, then, is a value in life that people wish to possess and enjoy just for its sake and not as a means to something else.

However, utilitarians disagree concerning what constitutes the complete range of things or states that are good. Bentham and Mill are hedonists. They believe that only pleasure or happiness (which we will consider synonymous for the purposes of this discussion) can be intrinsically good. Everything besides pleasure is instrumentally good to the end of pleasure. *Hedonistic utilitarians*, then, believe that any act or practice that maximizes pleasure (when compared with any alternative act or practice) is right. Later utilitarian philosophers, however, have argued that other values besides pleasure possess intrinsic worth, for example, friendship, knowledge, courage, health, and beauty. Utilitarians who believe in multiple intrinsic values are referred to as *pluralistic utilitarians*.

In recent philosophy, economics, and psychology, neither the approach of the hedonists nor that of the pluralists has prevailed. Both approaches have seemed relatively useless for purposes of objectively aggregating widely different interests. Another approach appeals to individual preferences. From this perspective, the concept of utility is understood, not in terms of states of affairs such as happiness, but rather in terms of the satisfaction of individual preferences, as determined by a person's behavior. In the language of business, utility is measured by a person's purchases or pursuits. To maximize a person's utility is to provide that which he or she has chosen or would choose from among the available alternatives. To maximize the utility of all persons affected by an action or policy is to maximize the utility of the aggregate group.

Although the preference-based utilitarian approach to value has been viewed by many as superior to its predecessors, it has not proved to be trouble-free as an ethical theory. A major theoretical problem arises when individuals have morally unacceptable preferences. For example, an airline pilot may prefer to have a few beers before going to work, or an employment officer may prefer to discriminate against women, yet such preferences are morally intolerable. Utilitarianism based purely on subjective preferences is satisfactory, then, only if a range of acceptable preferences can be formulated. This latter task has proved difficult in theory, and it may be inconsistent with a pure preference approach. Should products like cigarettes, fireworks, and semi-automatic rifles be legally prohibited because they cause such harm even though many people clearly would prefer to purchase them? How could a preference utilitarian answer that question?

One possible utilitarian response is to ask whether society is better off as a whole when these preferences are prohibited and when the choices of those desiring them are frustrated. If these products work against the larger objectives of utilitarianism (maximal public welfare) by creating unhappiness, the utilitarian could argue that preferences for these products should not be counted in the calculus of preferences. Preferences that serve to frustrate the preferences of others would then be ruled out by the goal of utilitarianism. As Mill argued, the cultivation of certain kinds of desires and the exclusion of antithetical desires are built into the ideal of utilitarianism.

A third essential feature of utilitarianism is its commitment to the measurement and comparison of goods. On the hedonistic view, people must be able to measure pleasurable and painful states and be able to compare one person's pleasures with another's to decide which is greater. Bentham, for example, worked out a measurement device that he called the *hedonic calculus*. He thought he could add the quantitative units of individual happiness, subtract the units of individual unhappiness, and thereby arrive at a total measure of happiness. By the use of this system we allegedly can determine the act or practice that will provide the greatest happiness to the greatest number of people.

Act and Rule Utilitarianism.
Utilitarian moral philosophers are conventionally divided into two types—act utilitarians and rule utilitarians. An *act utilitarian* argues that in all situations one ought to perform that act which leads to the greatest good for the greatest number. The act utilitarian regards rules such as "You ought to tell the truth in making contracts" as useful guidelines, but also as expendable. An act utilitarian would not hesitate to break any moral rule if breaking it would lead to the greatest number in a particular case. *Rule utilitarians,* however, reserve a more significant place for rules, which they do not regard as expendable on grounds that utility is maximized in the circumstances.

Consider the following case in which U.S. business practices and standards run up against the quite different practices of the Italian business community. The case involves the tax problems encountered by the Italian subsidiary of a major U.S. bank. It seems that in Italy the practices of corporate taxation typically involve elaborate negotiations among hired company representatives and the Italian tax service, and that the tax statement initially submitted by a corporation is regarded as a dramatically understated bid intended only as a starting point for the negotiating process. In the case in question, the U.S. manager of the Italian banking subsidiary decided, against the advice of locally experienced lawyers and tax consultants, to ignore the native Italian practices and file a conventional U.S.-style tax statement (that is, one in which the subsidiary's profits for the year were not dramatically understated). His reasons for this decision included his belief that the local customs violated the moral rule of truth telling.[10]

An act utilitarian might well take exception to this conclusion. Admittedly, to file an Italian-style tax statement would be to violate a moral rule of truth telling; but the act utilitarian would argue that such a rule is only a rule of thumb and can justifiably be violated to produce the greatest good. In the present case the greatest good would evidently be done by following the local consultants' advice and conforming to the Italian practices. Only by following those practices will the appropriate amount of tax be paid. This conclusion is strengthened by the ultimate outcome of the present case: The Italian authorities forced the bank to enter into the customary negotiations, a process in which the original, truthful tax statement was treated as an understated opening bid, and a dramatically excessive tax payment was consequently exacted.

In contrast to the position of act utilitarians, rule utilitarians hold that rules have a central position in morality that cannot be compromised by the demands of particular situations. Such compromise threatens the general effectiveness of the rules, the observance of which maximizes social utility. An example of rule utilitarian reasoning is found in a case involving John Zaccaro, the husband of 1984 vice-presidential candidate Geraldine A. Ferraro. In late 1982, Zaccaro was appointed the guardian of an elderly woman's estate. For his business purposes, Zaccaro borrowed $175,000 from the estate to be repaid at 12 percent interest. The propriety of Zaccaro's actions was questioned in court, where it was determined that he had not acted dishonestly or with malicious intent and may well have earned larger dividends for the woman than she would have reaped through more conservative investing. In effect, the court found that Zaccaro may have maximized the utility of everyone who was directly affected. Nonetheless, Zaccaro had placed himself in a position of conflict of interest, and the court found that "the rule is inflexible that a trustee shall not place himself in a position where his interest is or may be in conflict with his obligation." For this part, Zaccaro maintained that he acted in good faith and benefited the woman as best he could, but said, "I understand and accept the decision of the court that general principles of law must nevertheless be applied rigidly to guide the actions of other conservators."[11] In effect, both the judge and Zaccaro agreed that rule utilitarianism takes precedence over act utilitarianism. Even if Zaccaro had maximized everyone's ability in the circumstance, his act violated a basic, inflexible rule that had to take precedence.

For the rule utilitarian, then, actions are justified by appeal to abstract rules such as "Don't kill," "Don't bribe," and "Don't break promises." These rules, in turn, are justified by an appeal to the principle of utility. The rule utilitarian believes this position can escape the objections to act utilitarianism, because rules are not subject to change by the demands of individual circumstances. Utilitarian rules are in theory firm and protective of all classes of individuals, just as human rights are rigidly protective of all individuals regardless of social convenience and momentary need.

Act utilitarians, however, have a reply to these criticisms. They argue that there is a third option beyond ignoring rules and strictly obeying them: The rules should only be obeyed sometimes. An example of this act utilitarian form of reasoning is found in the defense offered by A. Carl Kotchian, former president of Lockheed Corporation, of $12 million in "grease payments" made to high Japanese officials to facilitate sales of Lockheed's TriStar plane. Kotchian recognized that "extortion," as he called it, was involved and that U.S. rules of business ethics forbid such payments. Kotchian advanced two arguments in defense of the payments: (1) "Such disbursements did not [at the time] violate American laws"; and (2) "the TriStar payments . . . would provide Lockheed workers with jobs and thus redounded to the benefit of their dependents, their communities, and stockholders of the corporation." Kotchian went on to argue that the financial consequences of "commercial success" and the public interest in both Japan and the United States were sufficient to override "a purely ethical and moral standpoint."[12] This is precisely the form of reasoning that rule utilitarians have generally rejected but act utilitarians have defended as at least meriting serious consideration. In the end, the act utilitarian view seems to invoke a prediction that society will be improved if people sometimes obey and sometimes disobey rules, because this kind of conduct will not fundamentally erode either moral rules or the general respect for morality.

Further, it is appropriate to ask whether rule utilitarians can escape the very criticisms they level at act utilitarians. There are often conflicts between moral rules. For example, rules of confidentiality conflict with rules protecting individual welfare. This issue surfaces in discussions of implementing genetic and drug-screening policies in the workplace. If the moral life were so ordered that one always knew which rules and rights should receive priority, there would be no serious problem for ethical theory. Yet such a ranking of rules seems impossible. Mill briefly considered this problem and held that the principle of utility should itself decide in any given circumstance which rule is to take priority. However, if this solution is accepted by rule utilitarians, their theory must, on some occasions, rely on the principle of utility to decide *directly* which actions are preferable to which alternatives in the absence of a governing rule. This view resembles those associated with act reasoning rather than with rule reasoning.

Criticisms of Utilitarianism. A major problem for utilitarianism is whether units of happiness or some other utilitarian value can be measured and compared in order to determine the best action among the alternatives. In deciding whether to open a pristine national wildlife preserve to oil exploration and drilling, for example, how does one compare the combined value of an increase in the oil supply, jobs, and consumer purchasing power, with the value of wildlife preservation and environmental protection? How does a corporate public affairs officer decide how to distribute the limited funds allocated for charitable contributions? If one attempted a corporate social audit (a picture of the company's sense of social responsibility), how could one measure and compare a corporation's ethical assets and liabilities?

Bentham's theory that pleasure alone is good and that it can be quantified has been a special object of criticism. Mill charged that, on Bentham's account, it would be better to be a satisfied pig than a dissatisfied Socrates. Human experience, Mill argued, is such that some pleasures are qualitatively better than others. To Mill, Socratic pleasures of the mind were qualitatively better than purely bodily pleasures. Confronted with the need to explain how "qualitative betterness" can be weighed and compared, he came up with no satisfactory answer. Moreover, it appears to many modern philosophers that Mill's strategy does not preserve hedonism. What special quality could a somewhat less pleasurable experience have that makes it qualitatively better? It cannot be the pleasure alone, so must not hedonism then be given up?

Utilitarians who are not hedonists have encountered other problems with measurement. Economists, for example, either appropriated the word *utility* to denote the experience of satisfaction of preference or they abandoned the word *utility* and talked about "preference ordering" instead. Many still doubt that construing utility in these ways resolves the measurability problem. Suppose Jim prefers to spend his $0.97 on milk, and Sally prefers to spend her $0.97 on bread. Then suppose that Sally and Jim have only $1.30 to distribute between them. What can utilitarianism advise when utility is limited to preference orderings? It seems that no advice is possible unless some inferences are made that enable us to go from known preferences to other considerations of welfare and happiness.

The utilitarian reply to these criticisms is that the alleged problem is either a pseudo-problem or else one that affects all ethical theories: People make crude, rough, and ready comparisons of values every day, including of pleasures and dislikes. For example, workers decide to go as a group to a bar rather than have an office party, because they think the bar function will satisfy more members of the group. Utilitarians readily acknowledge that accurate measurements of others' goods or preferences can seldom be provided because of limited knowledge and time. In everyday affairs such as purchasing supplies, administering business, or making legislative decisions, severely limited knowledge regarding the consequences of one's actions is often all that is available. Crucial, from the utilitarian perspective, is that one conscientiously attempts to determine the most desirable action and then with equal seriousness attempts to perform that action.

Utilitarianism has also been criticized on the grounds that it ignores nonutilitarian factors that are needed to make moral decisions. Much of the remainder of this chapter considers these alleged sins of omission. The most prominent omission cited is consideration of justice: The action that produces the greatest balance of value for the greatest number of people may bring about unjustified treatment of a minority. Suppose society decides that the public interest is served by denying health insurance of any sort to those testing positive for the AIDS virus. Moreover, in the interest of efficiency, suppose insurance companies are allowed to use as selective data lifestyle characteristics that are statistically associated with an enhanced risk of AIDS. Finally, suppose such policies would serve the larger public's financial interest. Utilitarianism seems to *require* that public law and insurance companies deny coverage to these AIDS victims. If so, would not this denial be unjust to those who have AIDS or are at high risk for contracting AIDS?

Many political philosophers and legal theorists have argued that documents such as the Bill of Rights in the United States Constitution contain rules that prohibit or constrain utilitarian calculations rather than serve as examples of utilitarian policy decision. The Bill of Rights, they say, was inserted into the Constitution because those rights protect individuals against slavery and other practices even if they are not rights that lead to the greatest good for the greatest number. Their justification thus seems nonutilitarian, because their purpose is to protect citizens from being sacrificed in the name of the public good.

In the last opinion he wrote for the U.S. Supreme Court (July 1986), former Chief Justice Warren Burger noted, "The fact that a given law or procedure is efficient, convenient and useful in facilitating functions of government, standing alone, will not save it if it is contrary to the Constitution. Convenience and efficiency are not the primary objectives, or the hallmarks, of democratic government."[13] Burger's criticism captures the essence of what many have argued against utilitarianism: It fails to account for basic principles in documents such as the Bill of Rights in the U.S. Constitution that morally and legally cannot be modified in the name of efficiency, productivity, and convenience.

Utilitarians insist against such criticisms that all entailed costs and benefits of an action or practice must be weighed, including, for example, the costs that would occur from modifying a constitution or statement of basic rights. In a decision that affects employee and consumer safety, say, the costs often include protests from labor and consumer groups, public criticism from the press, further alienation of employees from executives, the loss of customers to competitors, and the like. Second, rule utilitarians emphatically deny that narrow cost-benefit determinations are acceptable. They argue that general rules of justice (justified by broad considerations of utility) ought to constrain particular actions or uses of cost-benefit calculations in all cases. Rule utilitarians maintain that the criticisms of utilitarianism noted above are shortsighted because they focus on injustices that might be caused through a superficial or short-term application of the principle of utility. In a long-range view, utilitarians argue, promoting utility does not eventuate in overall unjust outcomes.

Kantian Ethics

Consider now a case involving the Plasma International Company.[14] After an earthquake in Nicaragua that produced a sudden need for fresh blood, Plasma International supplied the blood from underdeveloped West African countries, paying the donors as little as 15 cents per pint. Because of the shortage in Nicaragua, Plasma sold the blood at a premium price. The transaction ultimately yielded the firm nearly a quarter of a million dollars in profits. What is it about Plasma International's conduct that provokes moral outrage?

Immanuel Kant's (1724–1804) ethical theory may help define the basis of this outrage. He would argue that Plasma International treated human beings as though they were merely machines or capital. The company seemed to deny people the respect appropriate to their dignity as rational beings. Kant's respect-for-persons principle says that persons should be treated as ends and never only as means. Failure to respect persons is to treat them as means in accordance with one's *own* ends, and thus as if they were not independent agents. To exhibit a lack of respect for persons is either to reject a person's considered judgments, to ignore the person's concerns and needs, or to deny the person the liberty to act on those judgments. For example, manipulative advertising that attempts to make sales by interfering with the potential buyer's reflective choice violates the principle of respect for persons.

Respect for the human being is often said in Kantian theories to be demanded—not just as an option or at one's discretion—because human beings possess a moral dignity and therefore cannot be treated as if they had merely the conditional value possessed by machinery, industrial plants, robots, and capital. "Respect for persons" has sometimes been expressed in corporate contexts as "respect for the individual." An example is found in Hewlett-Packard, a U.S. firm that has been praised for its employee relationships. Because Hewlett-Packard does not fire employees (instead, it uses partial-hour layoffs and similar strategies) and attempts to make the corporate setting as pleasant as possible for workers, its employees tend to be tenaciously loyal and highly productive. Hewlett-Packard has thereby gained a reputation as a corporation that respects rather than exploits the individual.

Some have interpreted Kant to hold categorically that people can never treat another person as a means to their ends. This bald interpretation, however, misrepresents him. Kant did not prohibit the use of persons categorically and without qualification. He argued only that people must not treat another *exclusively* as a means to their ends. When employees are ordered to perform odious tasks, they are treated as a means to an employer's or supervisor's ends, but are not exclusively used for others' purposes, because they need not become mere servants or objects. Kant's principle demands only that such persons be treated with the respect and moral dignity to which every person is entitled, including those times when they are used primarily as means to the ends of others.

Kant's principle finds *motives* for actions morally important. It expects persons to make the right decisions *for the right reasons*. If persons are honest only because they believe that honesty pays, their "honesty" is cheapened. Indeed, it seems like no honesty at all, only an action that appears to be honest, for example, when corporate executives announce that the reason they made the morally correct decision was because it was good for their business. According to Kantian thinking, if a corporation does the right thing only when it is profitable or when it will enjoy good publicity, its decision is prudential, not moral.

Consider three examples of three people making personal sacrifices for a sick relative. Fred makes the sacrifices only because he fears the social criticism that would result if he failed to do so. He hates doing it and secretly resents being involved. Sam, by contrast, derives no personal satisfaction from taking care of his sick relative. He would rather be doing other things and makes the sacrifice purely from a sense of obligation. Bill, by contrast, is a kind-hearted person. He does not view his actions as a sacrifice at all. He is motivated by the satisfaction that comes from helping others. Assume in these three cases that the consequences of all the sacrificial actions are equally good and that the sick relative is adequately cared for as each agent intends. One can then ask which persons are behaving in a morally praiseworthy manner. Using utilitarian theory, such a question might be hard to answer, especially if act utilitarianism is the theory in question, because the good consequences in each case are identical. The Kantian believes, however, that motives count substantially in moral evaluation.

Nearly everyone would agree that Fred's motive is not a moral motive but a motive of prudence that springs from fear. This is not to say that Fred's action does not have good and intended consequences. Fred does not, however, deserve any moral credit for his act because it is not morally motivated. To recognize the prudential basis of the action does not detract from its good consequences. Given the purpose or function of the business enterprise, a motive of self-interest may be the most appropriate motive to ensure good consequences. The point, however, is that a business executive derives no special moral credit for acting in the corporate self-interest, even if society is benefited by and pleased by the action.

If Fred's motive is not moral, what about Bill's and Sam's? Here moral philosophers disagree. Kant maintained that moral action must be motivated by obligation alone. Sam, then, is the only individual whose actions may be appropriately described as moral in the Kantian view. Likewise, Bill deserves no more credit than Fred because Bill is motivated by sympathy and compassion, not by obligation alone. Bill is naturally kind-hearted or has been well socialized by his family, but this merits no moral praise. A Kantian believes that actions motivated by self-interest alone or compassion alone cannot be morally praiseworthy. To be deserving of moral praise one must act from obligation.

Kant insisted that all persons must act not only in accordance with obligation, but for the *sake* of obligation. That is, the person's motive for action must be a recognition of the duty to act. Kant tried to establish the ultimate basis for the validity of rules of obligation in pure reason, not in intuition, conscience, utility, or compassion. Morality provides a rational framework of principles and rules that constrain and guide all people, independent of their personal goals and preferences. He believed that all considerations of utility and self-interest are secondary, because the moral worth of an agent's action depends exclusively on the moral acceptability of the rule according to which the person is acting, or, as Kant preferred to say, moral acceptability depends on the rule that determines the agent's will.

An action has moral worth only if performed by an agent who possesses what Kant called a "good will." A person has a good will only if the sole motive for action is moral obligation, as determined by a universal rule. As we saw earlier, Kant developed this notion into a fundamental moral law—a categorical demand that persons be treated as ends in themselves and never solely as means to the ends of others. In other words, persons must be treated as having their autonomously established goals and must never be treated purely as the means to others' goals.

In another (separately developed) formulation, Kant advanced the following principle: "I ought never to act except in such a way that I can also will that my maxim should become a universal law." Kant called this principle the *categorical imperative*. It is categorical because it admits of no exceptions and is absolutely binding. It is imperative because it gives instruction about how one must act. He gave several controversial examples of imperative moral maxims: "Do not lie," "Help others in distress," "Do not commit suicide," and "Work to develop your abilities."

Kant's strategy was to show that the acceptance of certain practices causes the principles behind self-interested behavior to become self-defeating, as *universal* participation in that behavior undermines the practice itself. Some of the clearest cases involve persons who make a unique exception for themselves for purely selfish reasons. Consider the rule against breaking a promise. Suppose you consider breaking a promise that would be inconvenient to keep. According to Kant, you must first formulate your reason as a universal rule. The rule would say, "Everyone should break a promise whenever keeping it is inconvenient." Such a rule is contradictory, Kant said, because if one consistently recommended that all individuals should break their promises when it was inconvenient for them to do so, the practice of making promises would be senseless. Given the nature of a promise, a rule allowing people to break them when inconvenient makes the institution of promise making unintelligible. A rule that allows cheating on an exam negates the purpose of testing in the same way. For Kant, one doesn't keep promises because it pays or because one has a natural disposition to do so, but from respect for moral law that requires the obligation of promise keeping.

Kant's belief is that the conduct stipulated in these rules could not be made universal without some form of contradiction emerging. If a corporation kites checks to reap a profit in the way E. F. Hutton Brokerage did in a scandal of the early 1980s, it makes itself an exception to the system of monetary transfer, thereby cheating the system, which is established by certain rules. This conduct, if carried out consistently by other corporations, would violate the rules presupposed by the system, thereby rendering the system inconsistent. Kant's view is that actions involving invasion of privacy, theft, line cutting, cheating, kickbacks, and bribes are contradictory in that they are not consistent with the institutions or practices they presuppose.

Despite Kant's contributions to moral philosophy, his various accounts have been criticized as narrow and inadequate to handle various problems in the moral life. He has no place for moral emotions or sentiments such as sympathy and caring. Neither does Kant have much to say about character and virtue. John Stuart Mill even argued that Kant's theory does not successfully avoid an appeal to the utilitarian consequences of an action in determining its moral standing. On Mill's interpretation, the categorical imperative demands that an action should be morally prohibited if the consequences of adopting it would be disutilitarian. Kant fails in the extreme, Mill argued, to support moral rules by appealing to the idea of consistency.

Some also think that Kant emphasized universal obligations (obligations common to all people) at the expense of particular obligations (obligations that fall only on those in particular relationships or who occupy certain roles such as those of a business manager). Whereas the obligation to keep a promise is a universal obligation, the obligation to grade students fairly falls only on teachers. Many managerial obligations result from special roles played in business. For example, businesspersons tend to treat each customer according to the history of their relationship. If a person is a regular customer and the merchandise being sold is in short supply, the regular customer will be given preferential treatment because a relationship of commitment and trust has already been established. Japanese business has extended this notion to relations with suppliers and employees. At many firms, after a trial period, the regular employee has a job for life. Also the bidding system is used infrequently in Japan. Once a supplier has a history with a firm, the firm is loyal to its supplier and each trusts the other not to exploit the relationship.

However, considerations of particular obligations and special relationships may not be inconsistent with Kantianism because they may be formulated as universal. For example, the rule "Quality control inspectors have special obligations for customer safety" can be made into a "universal" law for all quality control inspectors. Although Kant wrote little about such particular duties, he would no doubt agree that a complete explanation of moral agency in terms of duty requires an account of *both* universal *and* particular duties.

A related aspect of Kant's ethical theory that has come under significant scrutiny by philosophers is his view that moral motivation involves *impartial* principles. Impartial motivation may be distinguished from the motivation one might have for treating someone in a certain way because one has a particular interest in the well-being of that person (a spouse or good friend, for example). A conventional interpretation of Kant's work suggests that if conflicts arise between one's obligation and other motivations—such as friendship, reciprocation, or love—the motive of obligation should always prevail. Against this moral view, some critics argue that one should show favoritism to one's loved ones, or at the least one should be entitled to do so. This criticism suggests that Kantianism (and utilitarianism as well) does not adequately account for those parts of the moral life involving intimate and special relationships.

The moral value of such a concern can be illustrated by an example. Imagine being sick in bed when a good friend comes to visit and cheer you up. It was inconvenient for her to make the trip and you thank her for coming. She tells you to think nothing of it. It is, she says, her obligation to visit all sick friends, and she acts only from obligation. She is completely sincere. How do you feel? Is there something missing from your friend's response? Critics of Kant argue that something is missing, namely, a concern for you as a particular individual, one with whom she has a special relationship. Acting from the motive of obligation in such situations seems to exclude a particular kind of moral value. Kantians fail to recognize this distinctive moral value, suggesting to many philosophers that there is something wrong with universal or impartialist ethical theories (including utilitarianism).

This notion of a special relationship with a unique history is often recognized in business. For example, the Unocal Corporation sharply criticized its principal bank, Security Pacific Corporation, for knowingly making loans of $185 million to a group that intended to use the money to buy shares in Unocal for a hostile takeover. Fred Hartley, chairman and president of Unocal, argued that the banks and investment bankers were "playing both sides of the game." Not only, he said, had

Security Pacific promised him that it would not finance such takeover attempts three months before doing so, but it had acted under conditions "in which the bank [has] continually received [for the last 40 years] confidential financial, geological, and engineering information from the company."[15] A forty-year history in which the bank has stockpiled confidential information cannot simply be cast aside for larger goals. Security Pacific had violated a special relationship it had with Unocal.

Nonetheless, impartiality is an irreplaceable moral concept, and ethical theory should recognize its centrality for many business relationships. For example, a major scandal occurred for some U.S. banks in 1991, because they were caught lending money to bank insiders.[16] The essence of federal rules is that banks can lend money to insiders if and only if insiders are treated exactly as outsiders are treated. Here the rule of impartiality is an essential moral constraint.

To conclude this section on Kantian ethics, almost no moral philosopher today finds Kant's system fully satisfactory. His contemporary defenders tended to say no more than that Kant provides the elements that are essential for a sound moral position. However, by using Kantian elements as a basis, some philosophers have attempted to construct a more encompassing theory. They use the Kantian notion of respect for persons as a ground for providing ethical theories of justice and rights. Considerable controversy persists as to whether Kantian theories are adequate to this task and whether they have been more successful than utilitarian theories.

Contemporary Challenges to the Dominant Theories

Thus far we have been examining utilitarian and Kantian theories, both of which meld a wide variety of moral considerations into a surprisingly systematized framework, centered around a single major principle. Much is attractive in these theories, and they have been the dominant models in ethical theory throughout much of the twentieth century. So dominant have the models been that they have sometimes been presented as the only types of ethical theory. From this perspective, one must choose between them, as if there were no available alternative. However, much recent philosophical writing has focused on defects in these theories and on ways in which the two theories actually affirm a similar conception of the moral life oriented around universal principles and rules.

These critics opt for some alternative to the utilitarian and Kantian models. They believe that the contrast between the two types of theory has been overestimated and that they do not merit the attention they have received and the lofty position they have occupied. Four popular replacements for, or perhaps supplements to, Kantian and utilitarian theories are (1) common morality theories (which are also obligation-based), (2) rights theories (based on human rights), (3) virtue theories (based on character traits), and (4) feminist theories and the ethics of care (which is disposition-based). These are the topics of the next four sections.

Each of these four types of theory has treated some problems well and has supplied insights not found in utilitarian and Kantian theories. The reader new to these outlooks may feel distressed by what sometimes seems an endless array of disagreements across the theories. But this reaction should be resisted. These theories are not in all respects competitive. In many ways they are complementary. The convergent insights in these theories are valuable, and we can complement our knowledge as we learn from each.

Common Morality Theories

One set of theories builds on the idea that there is a common morality that we all share by virtue of communal life. A straightforward example of this type of theory is found in Alan Donagan's *The Theory of Morality*. He locates the "philosophical core" of the common morality in the Hebrew-Christian tradition, whose morality he interprets in secular rather than religious terms. He identifies the fundamental principle of this tradition as "It is impermissible not to respect every human being, oneself or any other as a rational creature"[17] Donagan believes that all other moral rules in the common morality are derivative from this fundamental rule.

There are many versions of a common morality approach, but W. D. Ross's theory has had a particularly imposing influence. He argues that there are several basic rules of moral obligation and that they do not derive from either the principle of utility or Kant's categorical imperative. Some of Ross's basic rules are as follows: "Promises create obligations of fidelity"; "Wrongful actions create obligations of reparation"; "The generous gifts of friends create obligations of gratitude." Ross defends several additional obligations, such as obligations of self-improvement, nonmaleficence, beneficence, and justice.

Unlike Kant's system and the utilitarian system, Ross's list of obligations is not based on a single overarching principle. He defends it as a likeness of one's ordinary moral beliefs and judgments. He argues that to determine one's obligation, the greatest obligation in any given circumstance must be found based on the greatest balance of right over wrong in that particular context. To determine this balance, Ross introduces an influential distinction between *prima facie* obligations and *actual* obligations. *Prima facie* refers to an obligation that must be acted upon unless it conflicts on a particular occasion with an equal or stronger obligation. Such an obligation is right and binding, all other things being equal. A prima facie obligation becomes an obligation to be acted on in particular circumstances if it is not overridden or outweighed by some competing moral demand. One's actual obligation is determined by an examination of the respective weights of the competing prima facie obligations. Prima facie obligations are not absolute, but at the same time are binding in a way mere rules of thumb are not.

For example, Ross considers promise keeping a prima facie obligation. Does this mean that one must, under all circumstances, keep one's promise, as if promise keeping were a categorical imperative? No, there are situations in which breaking a promise is justified. To call promise breaking "prima facie wrong" means that promise breaking is wrong, unless some more weighty moral consideration in the circumstances is overriding. If the obligation to keep promises comes into conflict with the obligation to protect innocent persons, for example, then the actual obligation is to protect innocent persons (overriding the prima facie obligation of promise keeping).

The idea that moral principles are absolute has had a long, but troubled history. Both utilitarians and Kantians have defended their basic rule (the principle of utility and the categorical imperative) as absolute, but the claim that any rule or principle is absolute has been widely challenged. For Ross's reasons, among others, many moral philosophers have come to regard obligations and rights not as inflexible standards, but rather as strong prima facie moral demands that may be validly overridden in circumstances of competition with other moral claims. The idea of an exception-free hierarchy of rules and principles has virtually vanished, as has the claim that moral principles can be arranged in a hierarchical order that avoids conflict. This position also seems to entail that in cases of conflict there may not be a single right action, because two or more morally acceptable actions may be unavoidably in conflict and may prove to be of equal weight in the circumstances.

Rights Theories

Terms from moral discourse such as *value, goal,* and *obligation* have to this point dominated our discussion. Principles and rules in Kantian, utilitarian, and common morality theories have been understood as expressing obligations. Yet much that we encounter throughout this volume turns on rights, and public policy issues often concern rights or attempts to secure rights. Many current controversies in professional ethics and public policy involve the rights to property, work, privacy, and the like. In this section we see that rights have a distinctive character in ethical theory and yet are connected to the obligations we have previously examined.

In the twentieth century, public discussion about moral protections for persons vulnerable to abuse, enslavement, or neglect have typically been stated in terms of human rights. Many believe these rights transcend national boundaries and particular governments. Unlike legal rights, human rights are held independently of membership in a state or other social organization. Historically, human rights evolved from the notion of natural rights. As formulated by Locke and others in early modern philosophy, natural rights are claims the individual has against the state. If the state does not honor them, its legitimacy is in question. These rights were thought to consist primarily of rights to be free of interference, or liberty rights. Proclamations of rights to life, liberty, property, a speedy trial, and the pursuit of happiness subsequently formed the core of major Western political and legal documents. These rights came to be understood as powerful assertions demanding respect and status.

A number of influential philosophers have maintained that ethical theory or some part of it must be "rights-based."[18] They seek to ground ethical theory in an account of rights that is not reducible to a theory of obligations or virtues. Consider a theory we will encounter in Chapter 9 that insists liberty rights are basic. One representative of this theory, Robert Nozick, refers to his social philosophy (see

Chapter 9) as an "entitlement theory." The appropriateness of that description is apparent from the provocative line with which his book begins: "Individuals have rights, and there are things no person or group may do to them (without violating their rights)." Starting from this assumption, Nozick builds a political theory in which government action is justified only if it protects the fundamental rights of its citizens.

This political theory is also an ethical theory. Nozick takes the following rule to be basic: All persons have a right to be left free to do as they choose. The obligation not to interfere with a person follows from the right. That it *follows* is a clear indication of the priority of rights over obligations. That is, the obligation is derived from the right, not the other way around. A related rights-based conception uses *benefit* rights rather than *liberty* rights, as Alan Gewirth has proposed:

> Rights are to obligations as benefits are to burdens. For rights are justified claims to certain benefits, the support of certain interests of the subject or right-holder. Obligations, on the other hand, are justified burdens on the part of the respondent or obligation-bearer; they restrict his freedom by requiring that he conduct himself in ways that directly benefit not himself but rather the right-holder. But burdens are for the sake of benefits, and not vice versa. Hence obligations, which are burdens, are for the sake of rights, whose objects are benefits. . . .
> Respondents have correlative obligations *because* subjects have certain rights.[19]

These rights-based theories hold that rights form the justifying basis of obligations because they best express the purpose of morality, which is the securing of liberties or other benefits for a right-holder. Some might object that obligations are not necessarily burdens and that they may be welcomed as expressions of human rationality or as a basic form of human activity. But rights theorists insist that obligations are essentially what Mill and Kant said they were, namely, constraints on autonomy and, hence, burdens placed on autonomous action. Obligations restrict in a way rights do not, and the purpose of morality is to benefit, not burden.

Theories of moral rights have not traditionally been a major focus of business ethics, but this situation seems to be changing. For example, employees traditionally could be fired for what superiors considered disloyal conduct, and employees have had no internal right to "blow the whistle" on corporate misconduct. When members of minority groups complain about discriminatory hiring practices that violate their human dignity and self-respect, one plausible interpretation of these complaints is that those who register them believe that their moral rights are being infringed. Current theories of employee, consumer, and stockholder rights all provide frameworks for contemporary debates within business ethics.

The language of moral rights is greeted by some with skepticism because of the apparently absurd proliferation of rights and the conflict among diverse rights claims (especially in recent political debates). For example, it has been claimed by some parties that a pregnant woman has a right to abortion, whereas others claim that fetuses have a right to life that precludes the right to have an abortion. As we shall see throughout this volume, rights language has been extended to include such controversial rights as the right to financial privacy, rights of workers to information, the right to a pollution-free environment, the right to a job, and the right to health care.

Clashes between rights are often between what philosophers have distinguished as positive and negative rights. For instance, the right to well-being—that is, to receive goods and services when in need—is a positive right, whereas the right to liberty—the right not to be interfered with—is a negative right. The right to liberty is negative because no one has to act to honor it. Presumably all that must be done is leave people alone. The same is not true with respect to positive rights. To honor these rights, someone has to provide something. For example, if a starving person has a human right to well-being, someone has an obligation to provide that person with food.

The main difficulty is that positive rights place an obligation to provide something on others, who can respond that this requirement interferes with their property right to use their resources for their chosen ends. The distinction between positive and negative rights has often led those who would include a right to well-being on the list of human rights to argue that the obligation to provide for positive rights falls on the state. This distinction has intuitive appeal to many businesspersons, because they wish to limit the responsibilities of their firms, as well as the number of rights conflicts they must address.

This neat division of labor is suspicious, however. The government has already imposed some of the burden of positive rights on business. Employers contribute to retirement funds through contributions to social security, and firms are subject to the minimum wage laws. Moreover, many philosophers have doubts about the sharpness of the distinction between positive and negative rights. They argue that to protect a right to liberty, for example, society must do more than not interfere. Society needs to protect individuals with police forces and courts.

The existence of apparently intractable conflicts among rights is one of the more troublesome aspects of contemporary rights theory. But this conflict is not simply between negative and positive rights. An illustration of a conflict among negative rights is provided by a strike at the Adolph Coors Brewery in Golden, Colorado.[20] In April 1977, 1,400 workers at the brewery left their jobs in what was to become a prolonged and bitter walkout. At first, the action appeared to turn on technical questions involving seniority, the nature of the work week, and the like; but more general issues of employee rights and employer obligations gradually came to the fore as the dispute wore on. Citing such practices as the use of lie detector tests in screening job applicants and the tendency of company interviewers to ask non-job-related questions, union spokespersons claimed that Coors's management was not fulfilling its moral obligation to respect employee rights to privacy. Such negative rights, the striking workers might say, carve out a sphere or zone of protected activity with which the employer is morally obliged not to interfere. Nevertheless, Coors argued that it had the (negative) right to pursue its business in ways it believes are most conducive to profit.

Many writers in ethics now agree that a person can legitimately exercise a right to something only if sufficient justification exists—that is, when a right has an overriding status. Rights such as a right to equal economic opportunity, a right to do with one's property as one wishes, and a right to be saved from starvation may have to compete with other rights. Rights theorists have not provided a hierarchy for rights claims that has won even minimal acceptance, and this lack of an acceptable hierarchy may indicate that rights, like obligations, are prima facie claims, not absolute moral demands that cannot be overridden in particular circumstances by more stringent competing moral claims.

Virtue Ethics

In discussing utilitarian, Kantian, common morality, and rights-based theories, we have looked chiefly at obligations and rights. These theories do not typically emphasize the agents or actors who perform actions, have motives, and follow principles. Yet we commonly make judgments about good and evil persons, their traits of character, and their willingness to perform actions. In recent years, several philosophers have proposed that ethics should redirect its preoccupation with principles of obligation, directive rules, and judgments of right and wrong and look to decision making by persons of good character, that is, virtuous persons.

Virtue ethics, as it is called here, descends from the classical Hellenistic tradition represented by Plato and Aristotle. Here the cultivation of virtuous traits of character is viewed as morality's primary function. Aristotle held that virtue is neither a feeling nor an innate capacity, but rather a disposition bred from an innate capacity properly trained and exercised. People acquire virtues much as they do skills such as carpentry, playing an instrument, or cooking. They become just by performing just actions and become temperate by performing temperate actions. Virtuous character, says Aristotle, is neither natural nor unnatural; it is cultivated and made a part of the individual, much like a language or tradition.

But an ethics of virtue is more than habitual training. This approach relies even more than does Kant's theory on the importance of having a correct *motivational structure.* A just person, for example, not only has a disposition to act fairly, but has a morally appropriate desire to do so. The person characteristically has a moral concern and reservation about acting in a way that would be unfair. Having only the motive to act in accordance with a rule of obligation, as Kant demands, is not morally sufficient for virtue. Imagine a Kantian who always performs his or her obligation because it is an obligation, but intensely dislikes having to allow the interests of others to be of importance. Such a person, let us imagine, does not cherish, feel congenial toward, or think fondly of others, and respects them only because obligation requires it. This person can nonetheless, on a theory of moral obligation such as Kant's or Mill's, perform a morally right action, have an ingrained disposition to perform that action, and act with obligation as the foremost motive. But if the desire is not right, a necessary condition of virtue seems to be lacking, at least from the perspective of virtue ethics.

Consider an encounter with a tire salesperson. You tell him that safety is most important and that you want to be sure to get an all-weather tire. He listens carefully and then sells you exactly what you wanted, because he has been well trained by his manager to see his primary obligation as that of meeting the customer's needs. Acting this way is deeply ingrained in him. There is no more typical encounter in the business world than this one. But now let us go behind his behavior to his underlying motives and desires. This man detests his job and hates having to spend time with every customer who comes through the door. He cares not at all about being of service to people or creating a better environment in the office. All he wants to do is watch the television set in the waiting area and pick up his paycheck. Although this man meets his moral obligations, something in his character is deeply defective morally.

When people engage in business or take jobs simply for the profit or wages that will result, they may meet their obligations and yet not be engaged in a morally appropriate practice. But if they start a business because they believe in a quality product—a new, healthier yogurt, for example—and deeply desire to sell that product, their business is on the road to being a morally appropriate practice. The practice of business is morally better if it is sustained by truthfulness, justice, compassion, respectfulness, and patience. These traits seem to be morally deeper than actions based on obligation alone. Some interesting discussions in business ethics now center on the appropriate virtues of managers, employees, and other participants in business activity, as we will see many times in this book. These discussions have provided some much needed correctives to the approaches of Kant and the utilitarians.

There is a final reason why virtue ethics may be of constructive consequence for business ethics. A morally good person with right desires or motivations is more likely to understand what should be done, more likely to be motivated to perform required acts, and more likely to form and act on moral ideals than a morally bad person. A person who is ordinarily trusted is one who has an ingrained motivation and desire to perform right actions, and who characteristically cares about morally appropriate responses. A person who simply follows rules of obligation and who otherwise exhibits no special moral character, may not be trustworthy. Not the rule follower, then, but the person disposed *by character* to be generous, caring, compassionate, sympathetic, and fair is the one recommended, admired, praised, and held up as a moral model. Many experienced businesspersons say that such trust is the moral cement of the business world.

Feminist Theories and the Ethics of Care

Closely related to virtue ethics in several respects is a relatively new body of moral reflection that has come to be known as the "ethics of care." This theory develops some of the themes in virtue ethics about the centrality of character, but the ethics of care focuses on a set of character traits that people all deeply value in close personal relationships—sympathy, compassion, fidelity, love, friendship, and the like. Noticeably absent are universal moral rules and impartial utilitarian calculations such as those espoused by Kant and Mill.

Ethics of care has grown out of the eloquent work of a group of recent philosophers who are indebted to feminist theory. Feminist approaches to ethics may be characterized by at least two presuppositions. First, the subordination of women is wrong. Second, the experiences of women are worthy of respect and should be taken seriously. Although these may not seem to be extraordinary assumptions, feminist theorists argue that if they were acted upon, the theory and practice of business ethics would be radically transformed. Feminist scholars are committed to pointing out and excising male bias in the history of ethics, and to reformulating ethical theory in a manner that does not subordinate the interests of women. However, there is disagreement among feminists about how best to accomplish this task. The issues are complex, and feminists take different perspectives on matters such as equality, diversity, impartiality, community, autonomy, and the objectivity of moral knowledge. Nonetheless, several central components of feminist ethical thinking may be delineated.

Feminist philosophers point out that rationality in modern ethical theory, especially in Kantian and utilitarian theories, has most often been understood in terms of the formulation and impartial application of universally binding moral principles. Many of these scholars argue that universal principles are inadequate guides to action and that abstract formulations of hypothetical moral situations separate moral agents from the particularities of their individual lives and inappropriately separate moral problems from social and historical facts. Further, they have criticized the autonomous, unified, rational beings that typify both the Kantian and the utilitarian conception of the moral self. They argue that moral decisions often require a sensitivity to the situation, as well as an awareness of the beliefs, feelings, attitudes, and concerns of each of the individuals involved and of the relationships of those individuals to one another.

Feminist philosophers generally agree that Kantian and utilitarian impartiality fails to recognize the moral importance of valuing the well-being of another for her or his own sake. Further, they point out that impartiality has historically been associated with respect for the individual. They argue that impartiality undermines that very respect because it treats individuals impersonally, as anonymous and interchangeable moral agents without distinctive needs and abilities. In addition, impartial moral evaluations often pave over important differences in social, political, and economic power that are crucial to assessing the morally correct course of action in particular situations. Thus, they maintain that impartiality should be regarded as a vice and not a virtue in many situations. For example, a statistical evaluation indicating that 40 percent of a telecommunication company's work-force is comprised of women would suggest that the company is morally praiseworthy in this respect. However, a different assessment may be appropriate if 90 percent of the women are employed as telephone operators and clerical staff. Similarly, in evaluating a waste disposal company's competitive contract bid, feminist philosophers would urge management to look beyond the bottom line if, for example, 80% of the company's toxic waste disposal sites are located in poor, minority neighborhoods.

Kantian and utilitarian theories have also been widely criticized by contemporary feminist philosophers for advocating a conception of morality that leaves little room for virtues such as empathy, compassion, fidelity, love, and friendship. These philosophers argue that an understanding of the context of a situation is of particular importance when one takes into account the distinctive "voice" that many psychologists, philosophers, and management theorists have associated with women. This distinctive moral stance was first articulated by psychologist Carol Gilligan in her influential work *In a Different Voice*.[21] It is a voice of care and compassion, and although most feminist scholars do not associate this voice or perspective with women exclusively, they argue that it does represent an important contrast to the voice of rights and justice that is associated with men.

This distinct moral perspective is characterized by a concern with relationships, as opposed to individuals, by responsiveness to the particular needs of others, and by a commitment to their well-being. The ideas Gilligan advanced on the basis of her psychological studies have been developed by those who find the same "different voice" in contemporary philosophy. Kantian and utilitarian ethics are often criticized by these philosophers, as is the emphasis in modern moral philosophy on moral judgment as an instance of law or principle supported by universalistic ethical theories. Firmly rejected are contractarian models of ethics, with their emphasis on justice and rights, because they omit integral virtues and place a premium on *autonomous choice* among *free* and *equal* agents. Here the ethics of care offers a fundamental rethinking of the moral universe: The terms of social cooperation, especially in families and in communal decision making, are, as Annette Baier writes, *unchosen, intimate,* and among *unequals.* The contractarian model fails, Baier claims, to appreciate that parents and health professionals, for example, do not see their responsibilities to their children and patients in terms of contracts or universal rules, but rather in terms of care, needs, sustenance, and loving attachment. Only if every form of human relation were modeled on an exchange could these forms of caring be reduced to contract or moral law.[22]

Additional reasons exist for thinking that a morality centered on virtues of care and concern cannot be squeezed into a morality of rules. The frameworks are fundamentally dissimilar. Human warmth, friendliness, and trust in responding to others cannot be brought under rules of behavior. For example, a lawyer can follow all the rules of good legal practice in attending to the affairs of a bankrupt businessperson and still not display the sensitivity and warmth that this heartsick person needs; but such virtues of a good lawyer may be the most important part of the encounter.

Crucial to the ethics of care is a willingness to listen and to hear distinct and previously unacknowledged perspectives. For example, a manager considering the implementation of a mandatory drug testing program might come to an impasse because employers, employees, and customers have legitimate rights. Feminist philosophers and management theorists would urge the manager to help employees to feel concern for the customer while striving to make the workplace experience one where the worker is less alienated and hence less likely to take drugs. In order to do this, employees must feel that they can trust their mangers, and managers must be willing to listen and respond to their employees. The manager, in other words, must build solidarity among managers, employees, and customers.

This moral theory has the potential to transform business practice to exhibit more of the characteristics of a moral community. Traditional metaphors for business practice are competitive; they are war- and sports-oriented. Family metaphors seem out of place, as does the language of cooperation and compassion. Yet such language is undeniably central to morality, and if some contemporary management theorists are correct, such language is central to success in business as well. Cooperation among managers and employers is no less important for success than product quality. But this aspect of business has traditionally been ignored as "soft" and less important than a strong bottom line. Perhaps business at the end of this century and the beginning of the next will be more open to the contributions of the ethics of care, resulting in an improvement in both corporate morality and corporate productivity.

A Prologue to Theories of Justice

Many rules and principles form the terms of cooperation in society. Society is laced with implicit and explicit arrangements and agreements under which individuals are obligated to cooperate or abstain from interfering with others. Philosophers are much interested in the justice of these terms of cooperation. They pose questions such as: "What gives one person or group of people a right to expect cooperation from another person or group of people in some societal interchange (especially an economic one) if the former benefit and the latter do not?" "Is it just for some citizens to have more property than others? Is it fair for one person to gain an economic advantage over another, if both abide strictly by existing societal rules?"

In attempts to answer such questions, justice has been explicated in terms of the concepts of fairness and entitlement. A person has been treated justly when he or she has been given what is due or owed, what he or she deserves or can claim as a matter of entitlement. Some philosophers believe that diverse human judgments and beliefs about justice can be brought into systematic unity through a general theory of justice. Justice has been analyzed differently, however, in rival and often incompatible theories. These general theories of justice are treated exclusively in Chapter 9.

Here we need only note that in the literature on justice a key distinction between just *procedures* and just *results* exists. Ideally it is preferable to have both, but it is not always possible. For example, one might achieve a just result in redistributing wealth, but might use an unjust procedure, such as undeserved taxation of certain groups. By contrast, just procedures sometimes eventuate in unjust results, as when a fair trial finds the innocent guilty.

Many problems of justice that a cooperative society must handle involve the system or set of procedures that foster, but do not ensure, just outcomes. Once we agree on appropriate procedures, the outcome must be accepted as just, even if it produces inequalities that seem by other standards unjust. If procedural justice is the best that can be attained—as, for example, is claimed in the criminal justice system—society should accept the results of its system with a certain amount of humility and perhaps make allowances for inevitable inequalities and even inequities and misfortunes.

Some writers in business ethics are concerned with issues of procedural justice when they discuss just cause, ombudsmen, grievance procedures, peer review, arbitration procedures, and the like. If one considers again the question of drug-testing in the workplace, perhaps the manager's best solution is to bring the affected parties together to resolve the issues on their own, using clearly defined procedures. Procedural justice suggests decision making in which there is input from all the affected parties and a procedure for final resolution. Still, many problems about systems and principles of justice are beyond procedural justice. These problems are considered in Chapter 9.

Part Two has examined several central concepts and issues in ethical theory in order to explore options and distinctions promoting reflection on the cases and articles in subsequent chapters. Philosophy can help society find a reasoned and systematic approach to moral problems, but it does not supply mechanical solutions or definitive procedures for decision making. This lack of finality, however, is no cause for skepticism. Moral philosophy can produce well-constructed arguments and criticisms to help explore and advance the issues, but practical wisdom and sound judgment are philosophy's indispensable allies in decision-making contexts. In this respect, philosophy is neither inferior nor superior to other forms of reasoning such as those found in law, economics, and the behavioral sciences.

PART THREE: ANALYSIS OF CASES

Every subsequent chapter of this volume contains judicial opinions ("case law") and cases involving business activities. These materials do not derive from ethical theory, yet they merit moral analysis. The *case method*, as it is often called, has long been used in law and business for such purposes. However, only recently has philosophical ethics drawn attention to the importance of case studies and the case method, and their use is still controversial and unsettled.

Daniel Callahan and Sissela Bok have suggested that "case studies are employed most effectively when they can readily be used to draw out broader ethical principles and moral rules . . . [drawing] the attention of students to the common elements in a variety of cases, and to the implicit problems of ethical theory to which they may point."[23] Yet it is difficult to apply theory, draw out principles, or find common elements in these discussions. The history of case analysis in law and business involves much about discovering, modifying, and interpreting ethical principles, as we will now see.

The Case Method in Law

Case law establishes precedents of evidence and justification. The earliest developments in the law's use of the case method occurred around 1870, when Christopher Columbus Langdell revolutionized academic standards and teaching techniques by introducing this system at the Harvard Law School.[24] Langdell's textbooks were composed of cases selected and arranged to reveal the pervasive meaning of legal terms, as well as the rules and principles of law. He envisioned a dialectical or Socratic manner of argument to show students how concepts, rules, and principles are found in the legal reasoning of the judges who wrote the opinions. A teacher or legal scholar was to extract fundamental principles, much in the way a skillful biographer might extract the principles of a person's reasoning by studying his or her considered judgments.

However, Langdell's "principles" did not prove to be uniform across courts, contexts, or times, and incompatible and rival theories or approaches by judges tended to control in many precedent cases. Nevertheless, after Langdell's vision faded, the case method, with appropriate modifications, ultimately prevailed in U.S. law schools. It offers teachers and students a powerful tool for generalizing from cases. Spanning the tangled web of details in particular situations are overriding principles of legal reasoning. Legal theory and its fundamental doctrines can be both found in and applied to cases that came before courts. Moreover, training in the case method sharpens skills of legal reasoning. One can tear a case apart and then construct a better way of treating similar situations. In the thrust-and-parry classroom setting, teacher and student alike reach conclusions about a case's rights and wrongs.

The case method in law has come to be understood, then, as a way of learning to assemble facts and judge the weight of evidence—enabling the transfer of that weight to new cases. This task is accomplished by generalizing and mastering the principles that control the transfer, usually principles at work in the reasoning of judges.

The Case Method in Business

When the Harvard Business School was opened in 1908, its first dean, Edwin F. Gay, adopted the Law School curriculum as a prototype for courses on commercial law and eventually as a model throughout the business school. By 1919 the method had taken hold and eventually it came to dominate business schools that emphasize deliberation and decision making, weighing competing considerations, and reaching a decision in complex and difficult circumstances.[25] Judgment rather than doctrine, principle, or fact was taught. Cases involving puzzles and dilemmas that have no definitive solution by reference to principles or precedents were preferred for instructional purposes over those failing to present a difficult dilemma.

These cases are typically developed to recreate a managerial situation in which dilemmas are confronted. Cases are not primarily used to illustrate principles or rules, because the latter abstractions are invariably inadequate for final resolutions in real-world business situations. The objective is to develop a capacity to grasp problems and to find novel solutions that work in the context: *Knowing how* to think and act is more prized than *knowing that* something is the case.

This use of the case method in business schools springs from an ideal of education that puts the student in the decision-making role after an initial immersion into the facts of a complex situation. Theories and generalizations are downplayed, and the skills of thinking and acting in complex and uncertain environments are upgraded. The essence of the case method is to present a situation replete with the facts, opinions, and prejudices an executive might encounter (often an actual case) and to lead the student in making decisions in such an environment.

This method makes no assumption that there is a *right* answer to any problem, but only that there are more or less successful ways of handling problems. Understanding argument and analysis (roughly as outlined in Part One of this chapter) is more important than understanding substantive theories (as roughly outlined in Part Two). These forms of understanding need not be seen as antagonistic or competitive, but the case method in business schools has placed the premium on the problem-based form of analysis rather than on analysis by use of theory. It also avoids the authority-based method relied on in law schools, where judges and the body of law are overriding authorities. Similar to the Protestant rejection of authority in the Roman Catholic Church, business education has rejected any overriding authority in its use of cases.

Using Ethical Theory for Case Analysis

There are dangers in transferring the case method from either law or business to philosophical and business ethics. Not much is drearier than a tedious and unrewarding exposure to the moral opinions of those ignorant of the philosophical materials outlined in Parts One and Two. Accordingly, cases involving business ethics should be informed by theory. But theory also should not remain isolated from modification by case study. Several reasons support this judgment.

First, it seems mistaken to say that ethical theory is not extracted from the examination of cases but only applied to or specified in cases. Cases not only provide data for theory but are theory's testing ground as well. Revealing cases lead to modifications and refinements of theoretical commitments, especially by pointing to inadequacies in or limitations of theories. In thinking through the possible role of case analysis in ethics, one might consider John Rawls's celebrated account of "reflective equilibrium." In developing an ethical theory, he argues, it is appropriate to start with the broadest possible set of considered judgments about a subject and to erect a provisional set of principles that reflects them. Reflective equilibrium views investigation in ethics as a reflective testing of moral beliefs, moral principles, theoretical postulates, and other relevant moral beliefs to make them as coherent as possible. Starting with paradigms of what is morally proper or morally improper, one then searches for principles that are consistent with these paradigms as well as one another. Widely accepted principles of right action and considered judgments are taken, as Rawls puts it, "provisionally as fixed points," but also as "liable to revision."

Considered judgments is a technical term referring to "judgments in which our moral capacities are most likely to be displayed without distortion." Examples are judgments about the wrongness of racial discrimination, religious intolerance, and political conflict of interest. By contrast, judgments in which one's confidence level is low or in which one is influenced by the possibility of personal gain are strictly excluded from consideration. The goal is to match and prune considered judgments and principles in an attempt to make them coherent.[26]

Traditional ethical theory, from this perspective, has much to learn from practical decision-making contexts and vice versa. Ethical theory can profit from a close look at a wide variety of moral phenomena, and an understanding of right action could be constructed by generalizing from what is discovered. This effort should prevent theoreticians from streamlining and idealizing the complexity of the moral life. Major philosophical writings have been plagued by these problems and by a still more sobering difficulty: No theory is adequate to serve as the foundation for application to concrete moral problems. Accordingly, presumptions of a unilateral direction from ethical knowledge from theory to practice seem mistaken.

From this perspective, moral thinking is similar to other forms of theorizing: Hypotheses must be tested, buried, or modified through experimental thinking. Principles can be justified, modified, or refuted, and new insights gained, by examination of cases that function as experimental data. Similarly, one's principles allow one to interpret cases and arrive at moral judgments in a reflective manner. One promise of the case method is the opportunity it creates to increase the development and utility of ethical theories by more careful attention and testing of the scope, consistency, and adequacy of those theories.

A complaint heard frequently among university administrators and teachers is that their students learn technical skills but never develop moral reasoning that can be carried to real-life situations. Derek Bok complained in *Beyond the Ivory Tower* that students learn too much about increasing profits and too little about "applied ethics" that could teach them how to confront moral dilemmas. Steven Muller, former president of Johns Hopkins, complained that the modern university teaches marvelous lessons learned from the scientific method, but fails to teach that this method is neutral to morality, which is at least as important. The call is for a university environment in which informed decision-making skills involving moral judgment together with the technical skills and theoretical wisdom that dominate the curriculum. The case method has been cited as a promising entree, although not a complete solution, for teaching moral reflection in scientific and theoretical education.

We can now recall the previous discussions of relativism and moral disagreement. Often when discussing difficult cases many points of view will bounce around the classroom, and the controversies will seem intractable and not subject to a persuasive form of analysis transcending personal opinion. Far from an environment of learning, students may see their class as a bulletin board to which scores of opinions are tacked. It would be a mistake, however, to conclude that such discussion eventuates only in opinion. Many apparent dilemmas do turn out to be partially resolvable and often a consensus position emerges, even if no one entirely agrees on the best reasons for defending the position.

In the case analysis, dilemmas and disagreements should be avoided or minimized. A study of cases to determine how management might avoid problems can be profitable, as can reflection on procedures that deflect or defuse problems.

Cases need to be examined in terms of alternative strategies and actions. Invariably many alternatives could be proposed, but just as invariably they will not all be equally good. Even if intractable disagreement does occur, learning how to spot problems and resolve or deflect them may turn out to be as important as the substantive issues themselves.

One temptation should be avoided, however. Those who study the facts of cases invariably desire more facts. They see a solution as dependent on knowing more than is given about what transpired. If additional data can be discovered, they think, the problems can he handled and the dilemmas disentangled. A related temptation is to doctor the known facts, thereby presenting a hypothetical or new case, rather than an actual case. Both of these temptations should be avoided. Cases are interesting because only limited information is known. One is called upon to treat the problem under these real-life conditions of information scarcity. Professional business works under such conditions day in and day out, thus a case must be addressed as it is, and not as it might be in some possible world.

NOTES

1. Our discussion of this case is indebted to Richard Wokutch and also to Elizabeth Gatewood and Archie Carroll, "Anatomy of a Corporate Social Response: The Proctor and Gamble Rely Case," *Business Horizons,* September 1981.

2. Dean Rotbard and John A. Prestbo, "Killing a Product," *Wall Street Journal,* November 3, 1980.

3. Edward G. Harness, "Views on Corporate Responsibility," *Corporate Ethics Digest* 1 (September–October 1980).

4. Robert Lindsey, "Ancient Redwood Trees Fall to a Wall Street Takeover," *New York Times,* March 2, 1988, pp. A16–17.

5. Taken from Peter Huber, "The Press Gets Off Easy in Tort Law," *Wall Street Journal,* July 24, 1985, editorial page.

6. "Odds & Ends," *Wall Street Journal,* December 13, 1984, sec. 2, p. 1.

7. "Principle Sale," *Wall Street Journal,* May 22, 1985, p. 35.

8. "Bowing to the Inevitable," *Forbes,* August 12, 1985, p. 66.

9. Thomas Hobbes, *Leviathan,* Part I, Chap. 13, Par. 9.

10. Tom L. Beauchamp, ed., *Case Studies in Business, Society, and Ethics,* 3rd ed. (Englewood Cliffs, N.J.: Prentice Hall, 1993), Chap. 6.

11. As quoted in Charles R. Babcock, "Zaccaro Ousted as Guardian of Elderly Woman's Estate," *Washington Post,* August 31, 1984, sec. A, pp. 1, 8.

12. A. Carl Kotchian, *Saturday Review,* July 9, 1977.

13. See Al Kamen, "Budget Law Rejected by High Court," *Washington Post,* July 8, 1986, p. 1.

14. T. W. Zimmerer and P. L. Preston, "Plasma International," in R. D. Hay, and others, *Business and Society* (Cincinnati, Ohio: South-Western Publishing, 1976).

15. See Jennifer Hull, "Unocal Sues Bank," *Wall Street Journal,* March 13, 1985, p. 22; and Charles McCoy, "Mesa Petroleum Alleges Unocal Coerced Banks," *Wall Street Journal,* March 22, 1985, p. 6.

16. David S. Hilzenrath, "Taking Aim at Insider Bank Deals," *Washington Post,* September 30, 1991, Washington Business sec., p. 1.

17. See Alan Donagan, *The Theory of Morality* (Chicago: University of Chicago Press, 1977), p. 66.

18. Ronald Dworkin argues that *political* morality is rights-based in *Taking Rights Seriously* (London: Duckworth, 1977), p. 171. John Mackie has applied this thesis to *morality generally* in "Can There Be a Right-Based Moral Theory?" *Midwest Studies in Philosophy* 3 (1978): esp. p. 350.

19. Alan Gewirth, "Why Rights are Indispensable," *Mind* 95 (1986) p. 333.

20. This case is taken from Vincent Barry, *Moral Issues in Business* (Belmont: Calif.: Wadsworth, 1979), p. 149.

21. Carol Gilligan, *In a Different Voice* (Cambridge, Mass.: Harvard University Press, 1982).

22. Annette Baier, "Hume, The Women's Moral Theorist?" in *Women and Moral Theory,* edited by Eva Feder Kittay and Diana T. Meyers (Totowa, N.J.: Rowman and Littlefield, 1987), pp. 38ff; and Baier, *Postures of the Mind* (Minneapolis: University of Minnesota Press, 1985), pp. 210–219.

23. Daniel Callahan and Sissela Bok, *The Teaching of Ethics in Higher Education* (Hastings-on-Hudson, N.Y.: The Hastings Center, 1980), p. 69. See also Thomas Donaldson, ed., *Case Studies in Business Ethics* (Englewood Cliffs, N.J.: Prentice Hall, 1984), pp. 1–12.

24. Christopher Columbus Langdell's first casebook on *Contracts* is treated in Lawrence M. Friedman, *A History of American Law* (New York: Simon and Schuster, 1973), pp. 531f. The general account of the case method in this section is indebted to this source, and also to G. Edward White, *Tort Law in America: An Intellectual History* (New York: Oxford University Press, 1980).

25. See M. P. McNair, ed., *The Case Method at the Harvard Business School* (New York: McGraw-Hill, 1954).

26. John Rawls, *A Theory of Justice,* pp. 20ff, 46–48.

Chapter Two

Corporate Responsibility

T HIS CHAPTER FOCUSES on corporate social responsibility. The socially responsible corporation is the good corporation. Over two thousand years ago the Greeks thought they could answer questions about the goodness of things by knowing about the purpose of things. These Greek philosophers provided a functional analysis of good. For example, if one determines what a good racehorse is by knowing the purpose of racehorses (to win races) and the characteristics—for instance, speed, agility, and discipline—horses must have to win races, thus a good racehorse is speedy, agile, and disciplined. To adapt the Greeks' method of reasoning, one determines what a good (socially responsible) corporation is by investigating the purpose corporations should serve in society.

THREE VIEWS ON THE PURPOSE OF A CORPORATION

For many, the view that the purpose of the corporation is to make a profit for stockholders is beyond debate and is accepted as a matter of fact. But a statement about what the function of a corporation (or anything else) ought to be is not factual but normative. The statement "General Motors employs 100,000 people" makes a factual claim. The statement "General Motors ought to manage its resources in order to maximize profits for stockholders" is not a factual claim but a normative one. Many professors of business subjects treat the latter claim as a factual one but it is not.

Although capitalism, at the end of the twentieth century, is emerging as the preferred way to organize an economy, considerable disagreement exists concerning the fundamental purpose or goal of capitalist business organizations. The classical U.S. view that a corporation's primary and perhaps sole purpose is to maximize profits for stockholders is most often associated with the Nobel prize-winning economist Milton Friedman. This chapter presents arguments for and against the Friedmanite view that the purpose of a corporation is to maximize stockholder profits.

Friedman has two main arguments for his position. First, stockholders are the *owners* of the corporation and hence corporate profits *belong* to the stockholders. Managers are agents of the stockholders and have a moral obligation to manage the firm in the interest of the stockholders, that is, to maximize shareholder wealth. If the management of a firm donates some of the firm's income to charitable organizations, it is seen as an illegitimate use of stockholders' money. If individual stockholders wish to donate their dividends to charity, they are free to do so since the money is theirs. But managers have no right to donate corporate funds to charity. If society decides that private charity is insufficient to meet the needs of the poor, to maintain art museums, and to finance research for curing diseases, it is the responsibility of government to raise the necessary money through taxation. It should not come from managers purportedly acting on behalf of the corporation.

Second, stockholders are entitled to their profits as a result of a contract among the corporate stakeholders. A product or service is the result of the productive efforts of a number of parties—employees, managers, customers, suppliers, the local community, and the stockholders. Each of these stakeholder groups has a contractual relationship with the firm. In return for their services, the managers and employees are paid in the form of wages; the local community is paid in the form of taxes; and suppliers, under the constraints of supply and demand, negotiate the return for their products directly with the firm. Funds remaining after these payments have been made represent profit, and by agreement the profit belongs to the stockholders. The stockholders bear the risk when they supply the capital, and profit is the contractual return they receive for risk taking. Thus each party in the manufacture and sale of a product receives the remuneration it has freely agreed to.

Friedman believes that these voluntary contractual arrangements maximize economic freedom and that economic freedom is a necessary condition for political freedom. Political rights gain efficacy in a capitalist system. For example, private employers are forced by competitive pressures to be primarily concerned with a prospective employee's ability to produce rather than with that person's political views. Opposing voices are heard in books, in the press, or on television so long as there is a profit to be made. Finally, the existence of capitalist markets limits the number of politically-based decisions and thus increases freedom. Even political decisions reached democratically coerce the opposing minority. Once society votes on how much to spend for defense or for city streets, the minority must go along. In the market, each consumer can decide how much of a product or service he or she is willing to purchase. Thus Friedman entitled his book defending the classical view of the purpose of the firm *Capitalism and Freedom.*

The classical view that a corporation's primary responsibility is to maximize the stockholder profit is embodied in the legal opinion *Dodge v. Ford Motor Company* included in this chapter. The Court ruled that the benefits of higher salaries for Ford workers and the benefits of lower auto prices to consumers must not take priority over stockholder interests. According to *Dodge,* the interests of the stockholder are supreme.

It was not until 1953 in the case of *A. P. Smith Manufacturing Company v. Barlow et. al,* which permitted charitable contributions to Princeton University, that corporate officials had something approaching legal permission to undertake acts promoting the public good. In this appeal decision, which is reprinted in this chapter, Judge Jacobs recognized that corporations had public responsibilities as well as private ones.

What are these public responsibilities and how can they be justified? The justification for more public responsibilities has both a negative and a positive aspect. On the negative side, many have found Friedman's arguments for profit maximization to be inadequate. Limitations on the rights of ownership are already recognized as morally and legally legitimate. People cannot grow marijuana on their property, use their home for prostitution, or even keep dangerous animals as pets. Local ordinances place even more extreme restrictions on private property, and, of course, private property is taxed. Now most investment property is different from other kinds of personal property. Investment property is owned simply for its projected rate of return, and most stockholders are indifferent absentee owners who sell their stock whenever expedient. Consider the contrasting investment and care people take with personal property such as homes and cars. People seldom sell their homes just to make a quick financial killing. Since the owner of investment property has less incentive to take the same personal interest in managing, maintaining, and improving that property, there are even better arguments for regulating investment property for the public good.

As for the argument that profit-seeking firms maximize freedom, several things need pointing out. First, there are usually more people looking for work than there are jobs. Even a modest 5 percent unemployment rate means that one in twenty people is looking for work but cannot find it, and unemployment figures do not include those who have given up looking for work. Since the standard of living of most of the unemployed ranges from extremely modest to desperate, one is led to wonder how voluntary employment contracts really are. Second, many American firms operate under the employment-at-will doctrine where employees may be fired for many reasons unrelated to their contribution to the firm. In industries where the employment-at-will doctrine is practiced industrywide, employees with skills in those industries must accept employment at will if they want a job. Third, since the Bill of Rights does not apply in the corporate setting, many employees, in order to secure employment, are required to accept restrictions on their behavior on and off the job and are subject to honesty tests, drug tests, and other tests that many consider an invasion of privacy. (Employment at will and employee rights are considered at length in Chapter 5.) From this perspective, many employees hardly find the freedoms they want in the workplace.

Reasons independent of the criticisms of the Friedmanite view also indicate that corporations have purposes other than simply maximizing profits. In their essay contained here, John Simon, Charles Powers, and John Gunnemann maintain that all individuals and social institutions ought to adhere to certain moral standards which these authors refer to as the "moral minimum." If there is a genuine moral minimum to which all institutions, including businesses, must adhere, the pursuit of profit in violation of the moral minimum is morally irresponsible. In explaining the concept of the moral minimum, these authors draw on a distinction between negative injunctions and affirmative duties, a distinction that rests on the

further distinction between not causing harm and doing everything one can to promote the good. They argue that although society cannot legitimately impose affirmative duties on corporations to promote the general welfare, society can legitimately impose negative injunctions on corporations. That is, society can
legitimately insist that corporate activities not cause harm and that corporations
therefore must take active steps to prevent potentially harmful activities. Thus it is
morally acceptable for society to prevent companies from polluting our air but not
to impose on companies an obligation to donate to charity.

When the moral minimum is taken into account, the classical Friedmanite
view of the corporation has to be revised. On this amended view the purpose of the
corporation is to seek profits for stockholders while acting in conformity with the
moral minimum. That is, corporations may strive for profits so long as they commit
no harm.

Some argue that the obligation to avoid harm is too strong. The production
and distribution of products and services almost always involve risks and tradeoffs
among benefits and harms. For example, in the United States alone about 40,000
people die and over 200,000 are injured each year in automobile accidents. Such
death and injury are avoidable, but surely this does not suggest that automobile
companies should cease making automobiles.

This example points out the necessity of refining the avoidable harm criterion. It is a fundamental principle of ethics that "ought implies can". This expression means that one can be held accountable only for events that are within
one's power. Now since the overwhelming majority of automobile deaths and
injuries result from driver error and, to a lesser extent, from poor driving conditions due to inclement weather, the automobile manufacturer is not responsible
for those deaths and injuries. It is responsible only for harms resulting from defective parts and design.

However, the analysis above lets the automobile manufacturer off the hook
too easily. Simon, Powers, and Gunnemann understand that criteria for avoiding
harm include both not causing harm and preventing harm. Thus an automobile
manufacturer is obligated to decrease the incidence of death and injury due to
driver error and bad weather by building safer cars.

Is a company obligated to build a car as safe as it knows how? Surely there
must be some limitations on a corporation's obligation to prevent harm. Simon,
Powers, and Gunnemann suggest four conditions—need, proximity, capability,
and last resort—to assist corporations in determining their obligation to prevent
harm.

Would the capability condition help an automobile manufacturer with the
problem of auto safety? An auto executive might argue that the standards for safety
must leave the car's cost within the price range of the consumer ("ought implies
can" again). Comments about engineering and equipment capability are obvious
enough. But for a business, capability is also a function of profitability. For a company to build a maximally safe car at a cost that makes it impossible to sell at a profit
is beyond a company's capability. Whether tying capability to profitability is morally
acceptable should be considered by the reader.

In practice, many corporations believe that their moral obligations extend beyond the moral minimum of avoiding and preventing harm. In Minnesota many corporations, including some Fortune 500 companies like General Mills, H. B. Fuller, Honeywell, and 3M, annually donate 2 to 5 percent of their pretax profits to charity. So do the partners of the Minnesota offices of most of the major national accounting firms. These firms believe they have an affirmative obligation to contribute to the general good.

On what grounds do these obligations rest? Generally the argument for affirmative obligations to do good rests on considerations of competence, gratitude, and the responsibilities of citizenship. Because many corporations have both great power and considerable expertise in motivating people to meet goals productively, these corporations ought to use that power and expertise to benefit society. Great power is a gift, and it should be used to good ends. U.S. business has thrived in this representative democracy and as a result has tremendous resources at its disposal. These resources should be used wisely to assist in solving social ills.

Others argue that the social power and expertise of the corporation should be used to benefit the public because of the principle that one owes debts of gratitude to those who provide benefits, and corporations have benefited handsomely from society. The local community provides public education that trains workers; a legal system complete with police and courts to enforce corporate contracts; and a huge infrastructure of highways, sewage, garbage disposal, and public health facilities. Corporate taxes are not sufficient payment for the corporations' share of these resources. Therefore corporations have a duty out of gratitude to help solve social problems.

A related argument comes from the responsibilities of citizenship. Corporations are institutional members of society. If the individual members of society have an obligation to improve society—to leave the world better than they found it—corporations also have this responsibility. After all, corporations, unlike individuals, were created by society. Corporations are citizens and like all citizens have civic duties and responsibilities.

In this chapter, Thomas Mulligan's essay, "The Moral Mission of Business" represents the view that business firms have affirmative obligations to society. Mulligan rejects the view that consumer preferences should be taken as given and that business should simply give consumers what they want. Mulligan argues that business has the knowledge and competence to provide society with products and services that it really needs. One way of putting Mulligan's point is that business should lead consumers rather than simply follow them. Mulligan also reminds us that the employee—the maker or creator of the good or service—cannot be ignored. Workers will have a created sense of self-respect if they make worthy products and services. Businesses should develop a coherent plan for exercising social responsibility and then integrate this plan into its strategic vision. In Mulligan's view, contributing to the good of society is part of the mission of business.

But critical questions remain about affirmative obligations to do good. The obligations of the corporation to do good cannot be expanded without limit. All people have duties as citizens, but these duties are not open-ended. The injunction to take social responsibilities into account and to assist in solving social problems may make impossible demands on a corporation. At the practical level, the injunction ignores the impact that such activities have on profit. At the theoretical level, it turns every action into a moral action and hence makes the moral life too demanding. One consequence is this: If society asks too much of business, it might get nothing.

Moreover, who is going to define the social problems and determine which have priority? If business decides which social needs are good, some executives who are in their positions because their major forte is managing would be asked to decide what are and what are not worthy needs. Besides, as some defending Friedman's approach to corporate responsibility have argued, the business leader is not popularly elected and hence is accountable to no one. Government agents are elected to determine which social problems deserve attention and how they are to be resolved. In making these decisions, the officials are held accountable by the citizenry.

STAKEHOLDER THEORY

An alternative way to analyze the social responsibilities of business is to consider those affected by business decisions, referred to as *corporate stakeholders*. From the stakeholders' perspective, the classical view is problematic in that all emphasis is placed on one stakeholder—the stockholder. The interests of the other stakeholders are unfairly subordinated to the stockholders' interests. William Evan and R. Edward Freeman argue from a Kantian stakeholder approach that the classical view violates the Kantian categorical imperative that persons not be treated merely as a means for satisfying the interests of others. This Kantian line of analysis seems even more persuasive when we recall that stockholders are often absentee owners who can afford to lose some of their investment. Many employees, managers, and even local communities have much more than investment capital at stake. Their very livelihoods are at risk.

Although any person or group affected by corporate decisions is a stakeholder, most stakeholder analysis has focused on a special group of stakeholders: namely, members of groups whose existence was necessary for the firm's survival. Traditionally six stakeholder groups have been identified: stockholders, employees, customers, managers, suppliers, and the local community. Managers who manage from the stakeholder perspective see their task as harmonizing the legitimate interests of the primary corporate stakeholders. In describing stakeholder management, Evan and Freeman propose a set of principles and structural mechanisms that could make this kind of harmonizing possible.

Both in corporate and academic circles, stakeholder terminology has become very fashionable. However, many theoretical problems remain. Evan and Freeman seem to treat stakeholder interests as equal. However, as Kenneth E. Goodpaster points out in his article, managers have special obligations to the stockholders that they do not have to any other stakeholder group. Managers have fiduciary duties to stockholders but only nonfiduciary duties to other stakeholders. These fiduciary duties are established in law and are characterized as the duties that agents have to principals. In a principal-agent relationship, the agent is to act in the best interest of the principal.

That an agent is always to act in the interest of the principal, implies that whenever the interests of the stockholders conflict with the interests of another stakeholder group, the manager is obligated to honor the interests of the stockholders. If this view is justifiable, isn't Goodpaster really defending the classical Friedmanite position? Goodpaster thinks not, because even in a fiduciary relationship the principal cannot demand that the agent do something in his or her behalf that violates the basic moral principles of the community. But Friedman himself states something similar to this view when he concludes his article by saying, "There is one and only one social responsibility of business—to use it resources and engage in activities designed to increase its profits so long as it stays within the rules of the game, which is to say, engages in open and free competition without deception or fraud." If free competition without deception or fraud represents the community's view of business morality, little difference seems to exist between the views of Friedman and Goodpaster. On the other hand, if Goodpaster has a broader notion of the "basic moral principles of the community," he must say more about resolving conflicts concerning fiduciary duties to stockholders and nonfiduciary duties to other stakeholders.

Stakeholder theory is still in its early developmental stage. Much has been said of the obligations of managers to the other corporate stakeholders, but little has been said about the obligations of the other stakeholders, for instance, the community or employees, to the corporation. Do members of a community have an obligation to consider the moral reputation of a company when they make their purchasing decisions? Do employees have an obligation to stay with a company that has invested in their training even if they could get a slightly better salary by moving to another corporation?

Perhaps the most pressing problems for stakeholder theory is to specify in more detail the rights and responsibilities that each stakeholder group has and to suggest how the conflicting rights and responsibilities among the stakeholder groups can be resolved.

The Social Responsibility of Business Is to Increase Its Profits

Milton Friedman

When I hear businessmen speak eloquently about the "social responsibilities of business in a free-enterprise system," I am reminded of the wonderful line about the Frenchman who discovered at the age of 70 that he had been speaking prose all his life. The businessmen believe that they are defending free enterprise when they declaim that business is not concerned "merely" with profit but also with promoting desirable "social" ends; that business has a "social conscience" and takes seriously its responsibilities for providing employment, eliminating discrimination, avoiding pollution and whatever else may be the catchwords of the contemporary crop of reformers. In fact they are—or would be if they or anyone else took them seriously—preaching pure and unadulterated socialism. Businessmen who talk this way are unwitting puppets of the intellectual forces that have been undermining the basis of a free society these past decades.

The discussions of the "social responsibilities of business" are notable for their analytical looseness and lack of rigor. What does it mean to say that "business" has responsibilities? Only people can have responsibilities. A corporation is an artificial person and in this sense may have artificial responsibilities, but "business" as a whole cannot be said to have responsibilities, even in this vague sense. The first step toward clarity in examining the doctrine of the social responsibility of business is to ask precisely what it implies for whom.

Presumably, the individuals who are to be responsible are businessmen, which means individual proprietors or corporate executives. Most of the discussion of social responsibility is directed at corporations, so in what follows I shall mostly neglect the individual proprietors and speak of corporate executives.

In a free-enterprise, private-property system, a corporate executive is an employee of the owners of the business. He has direct responsibility to his employers. That responsibility is to conduct the business in accordance with their desires, which generally will be to make as much money as possible while conforming to the basic rules of the society, both those embodied in law and those embodied in ethical custom. Of course, in some cases his employers may have a different objective. A group of persons might establish a corpora-

tion for an eleemosynary purpose—for example, a hospital or a school. The manager of such a corporation will not have money profit as his objective but the rendering of certain services.

In either case, the key point is that, in his capacity as a corporate executive, the manager is the agent of the individuals who own the corporation or establish the eleemosynary institution, and his primary responsibility is to them.

Needless to say, this does not mean that it is easy to judge how well he is performing his task. But at least the criterion of performance is straightforward, and the persons among whom a voluntary contractual arrangement exists are clearly defined.

Of course, the corporate executive is also a person in his own right. As a person, he may have many other responsibilities that he recognizes or assumes voluntarily—to his family, his conscience, his feelings of charity, his church, his clubs, his city, his country. He may feel impelled by these responsibilities to devote part of his income to causes he regards as worthy, to refuse to work for particular corporations, even to leave his job, for example, to join his country's armed forces. If we wish, we may refer to some of these responsibilities as "social responsibilities." But in these respects he is acting as a principal, not an agent; he is spending his own money or time or energy, not the money of his employers or the time or energy he has contracted to devote to their purposes. If these are "social responsibilities," they are the social responsibilities of individuals, not of business.

What does it mean to say that the corporate executive has a "social responsibility" in his capacity as businessman? If this statement is not pure rhetoric, it must mean that he is to act in some way that is not in the interest of his employers. For example, that he is to refrain from increasing the price of the product in order to contribute to the social objective of preventing inflation, even though a price increase would be in the best interests of the corporation. Or that he is to make expenditures on reducing pollution beyond the amount that is in the best interests of the corporation or that is required by law in order to contribute to the social objective of improving the environment. Or that, at the expense of corporate profits, he is to hire "hardcore" unemployed instead of better qualified available workmen to contribute to the social objective of reducing poverty.

In each of these cases, the corporate executive would be spending someone else's money for a general social interest. Insofar as his actions in accord with his "social responsibility" reduce returns to stockholders, he is spending their money. Insofar as his actions raise the price to customers, he is spending the customers' money. Insofar as his actions lower the wages of some employees, he is spending their money.

The stockholders or the customers or the employees could separately spend their own money on the particular action if they wished to do so. The executive is exercising a distinct "social responsibility," rather than serving as an agent of the stockholders or the customers or the employees, only if he spends the money in a different way than they would have spent it.

But if he does this, he is in effect imposing taxes, on the one hand, and deciding how the tax proceeds shall be spent, on the other.

This process raises political questions on two levels: principle and consequences. On the level of political principle, the imposition of taxes and the expenditure of tax proceeds are governmental functions. We have established elaborate constitutional, parliamentary and judicial provisions to control these functions, to assure that taxes are imposed so far as possible in accordance with the preferences and desires of the public—after all, "taxation without representation" was one of the battle cries of the American Revolution. We have a system of checks and balances to separate the legislative function of imposing taxes and enacting expenditures from the executive function of collecting taxes and administering expenditure programs and from the judicial function of mediating disputes and interpreting the law.

Here the businessman—self-selected or appointed directly or indirectly by stockholders—is to be simultaneously legislator, executive and jurist. He is to decide whom to tax by how much and for what purpose, and he is to spend the proceeds—all this guided only by general exhortations from on high to restrain inflation, improve the environment, fight poverty and so on and on.

The whole justification for permitting the corporate executive to be selected by the stockholders is that the executive is an agent serving the interests of his principal. This justification disappears when the corporate executive imposes taxes and spends the proceeds for "social" purposes. He becomes in effect a public employee, a civil servant, even though he remains in name an employee of a private enterprise. On grounds of political principle, it is intolerable that such civil servants—insofar as their actions in the name of social responsibility are real and not just window-dressing—should be selected as they are now. If they are to be civil servants, then they must be elected through a political process. If they are to impose taxes and make expenditures to foster "social" objectives, then political machinery must be set up to make the assessment of taxes and to determine through a political process the objectives to be served.

This is the basic reason why the doctrine of "social responsibility" involves the acceptance of the socialist view that political mechanisms, not market mechanisms, are the appropriate way to determine the allocation of scarce resources to alternative uses.

On the grounds of consequences, can the corporate executive in fact discharge his alleged "social responsibilities?" On the other hand, suppose he could get away with spending the stockholders' or customers' or employees' money. How is he to know how to spend it? He is told that he must contribute to fighting inflation. How is he to know what action of his will contribute to that end? He is presumably an expert in running his company—in producing a product or selling it or financing it. But nothing about his selection makes him an expert on inflation. Will his holding down the price of his product reduce inflationary pressure? Or, by leaving more spending power in the hands of his customers, simply divert it elsewhere? Or, by forcing him to produce less because of the lower price, will it simply contribute to shortages? Even if he could answer these questions, how much cost is he justified in imposing on his stockholders, customers and employees for this social purpose? What is his appropriate share and what is the appropriate share of others?

And, whether he wants to or not, can he get away with spending his stockholders', customers' or employees' money? Will not the stockholders fire him? (Either the present ones or those who take over when his actions in the name of social responsibility have reduced the corporation's profits and the price of its stock.) His customers and his employees can desert him for other producers and employers less scrupulous in exercising their social responsibilities.

This facet of "social responsibility" doctrine is brought into sharp relief when the doctrine is used to justify wage restraint by trade unions. The conflict of interest is naked and clear when union officials are asked to subordinate the interest of their members to some more general purpose. If the union officials try to enforce wage restraint, the consequence is likely to be wildcat strikes, rank-and-file revolts and the emergence of strong competitors for their jobs. We thus have the ironic phenomenon that union leaders—at least in the U.S.—have objected to Government interference with the market far more consistently and courageously than have business leaders.

The difficulty of exercising "social responsibility" illustrates, of course, the great virtue of private competitive enterprise—it forces people to be responsible for their own actions and makes it difficult for them to "exploit" other people for either selfish or unselfish purposes. They can do good—but only at their own expense.

Many a reader who has followed the argument this far may be tempted to remonstrate that it is all well and good to speak of Government's having the responsibility to impose taxes and determine expenditures for such "social" purposes as controlling pollution or training the hard-core unemployed, but that the problems are too urgent to wait on the slow course of political processes, that the exercise of social responsibility by businessmen is a quicker and surer way to solve pressing current problems.

Aside from the question of fact—I share Adam Smith's skepticism about the benefits that can be expected from "those who affected to trade for the public good"—this argument must be rejected on grounds of principle. What it amounts to is an assertion that those who favor the taxes and expenditures in question have failed to persuade a majority of their fellow citizens to be of like mind and that they are seeking to attain by undemocratic procedures what they cannot attain by democratic procedures. In a free society, it is hard for "evil" people to do "evil," especially since one man's good is another's evil.

I have, for simplicity, concentrated on the special case of the corporate executive, except only for the brief digression on trade unions. But precisely the same argument applies to the newer phenomenon of calling upon stockholders to require corporations to exercise social responsibility (the recent G.M.

crusade for example). In most of these cases, what is in effect involved is some stockholders trying to get other stockholders (or customers or employees) to contribute against their will to "social" causes favored by the activists. Insofar as they succeed, they are again imposing taxes and spending the proceeds.

The situation of the individual proprietor is somewhat different. If he acts to reduce the returns of his enterprise in order to exercise his "social responsibility," he is spending his own money, not someone else's. If he wishes to spend his money on such purposes, that is his right, and I cannot see that there is any objection to his doing so. In the process, he, too, may impose costs on employees and customers. However, because he is far less likely than a large corporation or union to have monopolistic power, any such side effects will tend to be minor.

Of course, in practice the doctrine of social responsibility is frequently a cloak for actions that are justified on other grounds rather than a reason for those actions.

To illustrate, it may well be in the long-run interest of a corporation that is a major employer in a small community to devote resources to providing amenities to that community or to improving its government. That may make it easier to attract desirable employees, it may reduce the wage bill or lessen losses from pilferage and sabotage or have other worthwhile effects. Or it may be that, given the laws about the deductibility of corporate charitable contributions, the stockholders can contribute more to charities they favor by having the corporation make the gift than by doing it themselves, since they can in that way contribute an amount that would otherwise have been paid as corporate taxes.

In each of these—and many similar—cases, there is a strong temptation to rationalize these actions as an exercise of "social responsibility." In the present climate of opinion, with its wide-spread aversion to "capitalism," "profits," the "soulless corporation" and so on, this is one way for a corporation to generate goodwill as a by-product of expenditures that are entirely justified in its own self-interest.

It would be inconsistent of me to call on corporate executives to refrain from this hypocritical window-dressing because it harms the foundations of a free society. That would be to call on them to exercise a "social responsibility"! If our institutions, and the attitudes of the public make it in their self-interest to cloak their actions in this way, I cannot summon much indignation to denounce them. At the same time, I can express admiration for those individual proprietors or owners of closely held corporations or stockholders of more broadly held corporations who disdain such tactics as approaching fraud.

Whether blameworthy or not, the use of the cloak of social responsibility, and the nonsense spoken in its name by influential and prestigious businessmen, does clearly harm the foundations of a free society. I have been impressed time and again by the schizophrenic character of many businessmen. They are capable of being extremely far-sighted and clear-headed in matters that are internal to their businesses. They are incredibly short-sighted and muddle-headed in matters that are outside their businesses but affect the possible survival of business in general. This short-sightedness is strikingly exemplified in the calls from many businessmen for wage and price guidelines or controls or income policies. There is nothing that could do more in a brief period to destroy a market system and replace it by a centrally controlled system than effective governmental control of prices and wages.

The short-sightedness is also exemplified in speeches by businessmen on social responsibility. This may gain them kudos in the short run. But it helps to strengthen the already too prevalent view that the pursuit of profits is wicked and immoral and must be curbed and controlled by external forces. Once this view is adopted, the external forces that curb the market will not be the social consciences, however highly developed, of the pontificating executives; it will be the iron fist of Government bureaucrats. Here, as with price and wage controls, businessmen seem to me to reveal a suicidal impulse.

The political principle that underlies the market mechanism is unanimity. In an ideal free market resting on private property, no individual can coerce any other, all cooperation is voluntary, all parties to such cooperation benefit or they need not participate. There are no values, no "social" responsibilities in any sense other than the shared values and responsibilities of individuals. Society is a collection of individuals and of the various groups they voluntarily form.

The political principle that underlies the political mechanism is conformity. The individual must serve a more general social interest—whether that be determined by a church or a dictator or a majority. The individual may have a vote and say in what is to be done, but if he is overruled, he must conform. It is appropriate for some to require others to contribute to a general social purpose whether they wish to or not.

Unfortunately, unanimity is not always feasible. There are some respects in which conformity appears unavoidable, so I do not see how one can avoid the use of the political mechanism altogether.

But the doctrine of "social responsibility" taken seriously would extend the scope of the political mechanism to every human activity. It does not differ in philosophy from the most explicitly collectivist doctrine. It differs only by professing to believe that collectivist ends can be attained without collectivist means. That is why, in my book *Capitalism and Freedom,* I have called it a "fundamentally subversive doctrine" in a free society, and have said that in such a society, "there is one and only one social responsibility of business—to use its resources and engage in activities designed to increase its profits so long as it stays within the rules of the game, which is to say, engages in open and free competition without deception or fraud."

The Responsibilities of Corporations and Their Owners

John G. Simon, Charles W. Powers,
and Jon P. Gunnemann

... Our analysis of the controversies surrounding the notion of corporate responsibility—and the suggestion that the university as an investor should be concerned with corporate responsibility—proceeds in large part from our approach to certain issues in the area of social responsibility and public morals. In particular, we (1) make a distinction between negative injunctions and affirmative duties; (2) assert that all men have the "moral minimum" obligation not to impose social injury; (3) delineate those conditions under which one is held responsible for social injury, even where it is not clear that the injury was self-caused; and (4) take a position in the argument between those who strive for moral purity and those who strive for moral effectiveness.

NEGATIVE INJUNCTIONS AND AFFIRMATIVE DUTIES

A distinction which informs much of our discussion differentiates between injunctions against activities that injure others and duties which require the affirmative pursuit of some good. The failure to make this distinction in debate on public ethics often results in false dichotomies, a point illustrated by an article which appeared just over a decade ago in the *Harvard Business Review*. In that article, which provoked considerable debate in the business community, Theodore Levitt argued against corporate social responsibility both because it was dangerous for society and because it detracted from the primary goal of business, the making of profit. We deal with the merits of these arguments later; what is important for our immediate purpose, however, is Levitt's designation of those activities and concerns which constitute social responsibility. He notes that the corporation has become "more concerned about the needs of its employees, about schools, hospitals, welfare agencies and even aesthetics," and that it is "fashionable . . . for the corporation to show that it is a great innovator; more specifically, a great public benefactor; and, very particularly, that it exists 'to serve the public.'"[1] Having so delimited the notion of corporate responsibility, Levitt presents the reader with a choice between, on the one hand, getting involved in the management of society, "creating munificence for one and all," and, on the other hand, fulfilling the profit-making function. But such a choice excludes another meaning of corporate responsibility: the making of

profits in such a way as to minimize social injury. Levitt at no point considers the possibility that business activity may at times injure others and that it may be necessary to regulate the social consequences of one's business activities accordingly. . . .

Our public discourse abounds with similar failures to distinguish between positive and perhaps lofty ideals and minimal requirements of social organization. During the election campaigns of the 1950's and the civil rights movement of the early 1960's, the slogan, "You can't legislate morality," was a popular cry on many fronts. Obviously, we have not succeeded in devising laws that create within our citizens a predisposition to love and kindness; but we can devise laws which will minimize the injury that one citizen must suffer at the hands of another. Although the virtue of love may be the possession of a few, justice—in the minimal sense of not injuring others—can be required of all.

The distinction between negative injunctions and affirmative duties is old, having roots in common law and equity jurisprudence.[2] Here it is based on the premise that it is easier to specify and enjoin a civil wrong than to state what should be done. In the Ten Commandments, affirmative duties are spelled out only for one's relations with God and parents; for the more public relationships, we are given only the negative injunction: "Thou shalt not. . . . " Similarly, the Bill of Rights contains only negative injunctions.

AVOIDANCE AND CORRECTION OF SOCIAL INJURY AS A "MORAL MINIMUM"

We do not mean to distinguish between negative injunctions and affirmative duties solely in the interests of analytical precision. The negative injunction to avoid and correct social injury threads its way through all morality. We call it a "moral minimum," implying that however one may choose to limit the concept of social responsibility, one cannot exclude this negative injunction. Although reasons may exist why certain persons or institutions cannot or should not be required to pursue moral or social good in all situations, there are many fewer reasons why one should be excused from the injunction against injuring others. Any citizen, individual or institutional, may have competing obligations which could, under some circumstances, override this negative injunction. But these special circumstances do not wipe away the prima facie obligation to avoid harming others.

In emphasizing the central role of the negative injunction, we do not suggest that affirmative duties are never important. A society where citizens go well beyond the requirement to avoid damage to others will surely be a better community. But we do recognize that individuals exhibit varying degrees of commitment to promote affirmatively the public welfare, whereas we expect everyone equally to refrain from injuring others.

The view that all citizens are equally obligated to avoid or correct any social injury which is self-caused finds support in our legal as well as our moral tradition. H. L. A. Hart and A. M. Honoré have written:

> In the moral judgments of ordinary life, we have occasion to blame people because they have caused harm to others, and also, if less frequently, to insist that morally they are bound to compensate those to whom they have caused harm. These are the moral analogues of more precise legal conceptions: for, in all legal systems liability to be punished or to make compensation frequently depends on whether actions (or omissions) have caused harm. Moral blame is not of course confined to such cases of causing harm.[3]

We know of no societies, from the literature of anthropology or comparative ethics, whose moral codes do not contain some injunction against harming others. The specific notion of *harm* or *social injury* may vary, as well as the mode of correction and restitution, but the injunctions are present. . . .

We asserted earlier that it is easier to enjoin and correct a wrong than it is to prescribe affirmatively what is good for society and what ought to be done. Notions of the public good and the values that men actively seek to implement are subjects of intense disagreement. In this realm, pluralism is almost inevitable, and some would argue that it is healthy. Yet there can also be disagreement about what constitutes social injury or harm. What some people think are affirmative duties may be seen by others as correction of social injury. For example, the notion that business corporations should make special effort to train and employ members of minority groups could be understood by some to fulfill an affirmative duty on the part of corporations to meet society's problems; but it could be interpreted by others as the correction of a social injury caused by years of institutional racism. As a more extreme example, a Marxist would in all probability contend that *all* corporate activity is socially injurious and that therefore all social pursuits by corporations are corrective responses rather than affirmative actions.

Although the notion of *social injury* is imprecise and although many hard cases will be encountered in applying it, we think that it is a helpful designation and that cases can be decided on the basis of it. In the law, many notions (such as *negligence* in the law of torts or *consideration* in the law of contracts) are equally vague but have received content from repeated decision making over time. We would hope that under our proposed Guidelines similar "case law" would develop. Moreover, our Guidelines attempt to give some contents to the notion of *social injury* by referring to external norms: *social injury* is defined as "particularly including activities which violate, or frustrate the enforcement of, rules of domestic or international law intended to protect individuals against deprivation of health, safety or basic freedoms."

In sum, we would affirm the prima facie obligation of all citizens, both individual and institutional, to avoid and correct self-caused social injury. Much more in the way of affirmative acts may be expected of certain kinds of citizens, but none is exempt from this "moral minimum."

In some cases it may not be true—or at least it may not be clear—that one has caused or helped to cause social injury, and yet one may bear responsibility for correcting or averting the injury. We consider next the circumstances under which this responsibility may arise.

NEED, PROXIMITY, CAPABILITY, AND LAST RESORT (THE KEW GARDENS PRINCIPLE)

Several years ago the public was shocked by the news accounts of the stabbing and agonizingly slow death of Kitty Genovese in the Kew Gardens section of New York City while thirty-eight people watched or heard and did nothing.[4] What so deeply disturbed the public's moral sensibility was that in the face of a critical human need, people who were close to that need and had the power to do something about it failed to act.

The public's reaction suggests that, no matter how narrowly one may conceive of social responsibility, there are some situations in which a combination of circumstances thrusts upon us an obligation to respond. Life is fraught with emergency situations in which a failure to respond is a special form of violation of the negative injunction against causing social injury: a sin of omission becomes a sin of commission.

Legal responsibility for aiding someone in cases of grave distress or injury, even when caused by another, is recognized by many European civil codes and by the criminal laws of one of our states:

(A) A person who knows that another is exposed to grave physical harm shall, to the extent that the same can be rendered without danger or peril to himself or without interference with important duties owed to others, give reasonable assistance to the exposed person unless that assistance or care is being provided by others. . . .

(C) A person who wilfully violates subsection (A) of this section shall be fined not more than $100.00.[5]

This Vermont statute recognizes that it is not reasonable in all cases to require a person to give assistance to someone who is endangered. If such aid imperils himself, or interferes with duties owed to others, or if there are others providing the aid, the person is excepted from the obligation. These conditions of responsibility give some shape to difficult cases and are in striking parallel with the conditions which existed at Kew Gardens. The salient features of the Kitty Genovese case are (1) critical need; (2) the proximity of the thirty-eight spectators; (3) the capability of the spectators to act helpfully (at least to telephone the police); and (4) the absence of other (including official) help; i.e., the thirty-eight were the last resort. There would, we believe, be widespread agreement that a moral obligation to aid another arises when these four features are present. What we have called the "moral minimum" (the duty to avoid and correct self-caused social injury) is an obvious and easy example of fulfillment of these criteria—so obvious that there is little need to go through step-by-step analysis of these factors. Where the injury is not clearly self-caused, the application of these criteria aids in deciding responsibility. We have called this combination of features governing difficult cases the "Kew Gardens Principle." There follows a more detailed examination of each of the features:

Need. In cases where the other three criteria are constant, increased need increases responsibility. Just as there is no precise definition of social injury (one kind of need), there is no precise definition of need or way of measuring its extent.

Proximity. The thirty-eight witnesses of the Genovese slaying were geographically close to the deed. But proximity to a situation of need is not necessarily spatial. Proximity is largely a function of notice: we hold a person blameworthy if he knows of imperilment and does not do what he reasonably can do to remedy the situation. Thus, the thirty-eight at Kew Gardens were delinquent not because they were near but because nearness enabled them to know that someone was in need. A deaf person who could not hear the cries for help would not be considered blameworthy even if he were closer than those who could hear. So also, a man in Afghanistan is uniquely responsible for the serious illness of a man in Peoria, Illinois, if he has knowledge of the man's illness, if he can telephone a doctor about it, and if he alone has that notice. When we become aware of a wrongdoing or a social injury, we take on obligations that we did not have while ignorant.

Notice does not exhaust the meaning of proximity, however. It is reasonable to maintain that the sick man's neighbors in Peoria were to some extent blameworthy if they made no effort to inquire into the man's welfare. Ignorance cannot always be helped, but we do expect certain persons and perhaps institutions to look harder for information about critical need.[6] In this sense, proximity has to do with the network of social expectations that flow from notions of civic duty, duties to one's family, and so on. Thus, we expect a man to be more alert to the plight of his next-door neighbor than to the needs of a child in East Pakistan, just as we expect a man to be more alert to the situation of his own children than to the problems of the family down the block. The failure of the man to act

in conformance with this expectation does not give him actual notice of need, but it creates what the law would call *constructive notice.* Both factors—actual notice and constructive notice growing out of social expectation—enter into the determination of responsibility and blame.

Capability. Even if there is a need to which a person has proximity, that person is not usually held responsible unless there is something he can reasonably be expected to do to meet the need. To follow Immanuel Kant, *ought* assumes *can.* What one is reasonably capable of doing, of course, admits to some variety of interpretation. In the Kew Gardens incident, it might not have been reasonable to expect someone to place his body between the girl and the knife. It was surely reasonable to expect someone to call the police. So also it would not seem to be within the canons of reasonability for a university to sacrifice education for charity. . . . But if the university is able, by non-self-sacrificial means, to mitigate injury caused by a company of which it is an owner, it would not seem unreasonable to ask it to do so.

Last Resort. In the emergency situations we have been describing, one becomes more responsible the less likely it is that someone else will be able to aid. Physical proximity is a factor here, as is time. If the knife is drawn, one cannot wait for the policeman. It is important to note here that determination of last resort becomes more difficult the more complex the social situation or organization. The man on the road to Jericho, in spite of the presence of a few other travelers, probably had a fairly good notion that he was the only person who could help the man attacked by thieves. But on a street in New York City, there is always the hope that someone else will step forward to give aid. Surely this rationalization entered into the silence of each of the thirty-eight: there were, after all, thirty-seven others. Similarly, within large corporations it is difficult to know not only whether one alone has notice of a wrong-doing, but also whether there is anyone else who is able to respond. Because of this diffusion of responsibility in complex organizations and societies, the notion of last resort is less useful than the other Kew Gardens criteria in determining whether one ought to act in aid of someone in need or to avert or correct social injury. Failure to act because one hopes someone else will act—or because one is trying to find out who is the last resort—may frequently lead to a situation in which no one acts at all. This fact, we think, places more weight on the first three features of the Kew Gardens Principle in determining responsibility, and it creates a presumption in favor of taking action when those three conditions are present.

NOTES

1. Theodore Levitt, "The Dangers of Social Responsibility," *Harvard Business Review* (Sept.–Oct. 1958): 41–50.
2. We are grateful to President Edward Bloustein of Rutgers University for suggesting this terminology and for inviting our attention to its historical antecedents. Further analysis of the distinction between *negative injunctions* and *affirmative duties* is given in the following sections of this chapter.
3. H. L. A. Hart and A. M. Honoré, *Causation in the Law* (Oxford, 1959), p. 59.
4. See A. M. Rosenthal, *Thirty-Eight Witnesses* (New York, 1964).
5. "Duty to Aid the Endangered Act," *Vt. Stat. Ann.*, Ch. 12, §519 (Supp. 1968). See G. Hughes, "Criminal Omissions," 67 *Yale L. J.* 590 (1958).
6. See, for example, Albert Speer's reflection on his role during the Hitler regime: "For being in a position to know and nevertheless shunning knowledge creates direct responsibility for the consequences—from the very beginning." *Inside the Third Reich* (New York, 1970), p. 19.

The Moral Mission of Business

Thomas M. Mulligan

What purpose should business serve in society? Justice Louis Brandeis formulated his answer with characteristic clarity and resolve:

> In the field of modern business, so rich in opportunity for the exercise of man's finest and most varied mental faculties and moral qualities, mere money-making cannot be regarded as the legitimate end. Neither can mere growth in bulk or power be admitted as a worthy ambition. Nor can a man nobly mindful of his serious responsibilities to society view business as a game, since with the conduct of business human happiness or misery is inextricably interwoven.
>
> Real success in business is to be found in achievements comparable rather with those of the artist or the scientist, of the inventor or the statesman. And the joys sought in the profession of business must be like their joys and not the vulgar satisfaction which is experienced in the acquisition of money, in the exercise of power, or in the frivolous pleasure of mere winning. . . . As the profession of business develops, the great industrial and social problems . . . will one by one find solution.[1]

Copyright © 1992 by Thomas M. Mulligan. Used by permission of the author, who gratefully acknowledges the support of a grant by the Certified General Accountants Association of Ontario.

Brandeis saw business as a mighty instrument which we are morally obligated to use for the purpose of advancing civilization. I agree with him. In my view, we human beings have the autonomous power to add value to the world and to remove value from it. Our moral mission, individually and collectively, is to cultivate the wisdom and to do the work which, to the limit of our creativity and ability, will make this world better than we found it. By "better" I mean, for example, safer, healthier, more beautiful, more equitable, more loving, or more knowledgeable. There are many means by which we may try to fulfill this mission—such as by raising families; by pursuits in art, science, or government; and, hardly least, by means of transacting business.

My thesis is that the moral mission of business is to exercise all the imagination and initiative it can muster for the purpose of producing goods, services, and occasions for human achievement which make the world better. This mission is more important than any other function which business might perform. My position involves at least two claims: (1) that business people have enough moral insight to assess the goods and services they are capable of providing and to decide specifically which ones are morally worthy (i.e., which ones would contribute substantially to making the world better); and (2) that business people ought to work to create and market the specific goods and services which are morally worthy and to avoid those which are unworthy, even if such action is not legally required and even if such action does not consistently serve the firm's profitability.

OPPOSING VIEWS

These claims add up to a view distinctly at odds with the views of many academics and business practitioners, who believe it is wrong and even foolish to ask business to exercise imagination and initiative in order to make the world a better place. Instead, they think that laws, market prices, and public expectations are sufficient to determine both what resources business ought to consume and what outputs it ought to produce in the service of world betterment. They are mistaken:

Obeying the Law Is Not Enough

It is sometimes thought that transacting business is analogous to game playing. This is consistent with the practice, in both business research and education, of applying mathematical models borrowed from game theory to problems in business decision making. Supporters of this view sometimes observe that just as the fair, orderly conduct of games requires the players to follow rules, so too the conduct of business requires laws and regulations. Among their benefits, rules and laws maintain a level playing field where competitive advantages can be gained only as a result of honest effort or honest luck.

Nevertheless, in *Where the Law Ends* Christopher Stone argued that law fails to provide adequate control of business behavior.[2] He observed that, since laws are typically enacted in response to societal needs, there is often a delay between the time when social problems arise in the changing arena of business conduct and the time when answering directives are in the lawbooks. For example, in the late 1980s, after the apparently legal sale of poison gas factory equipment to Libya by European companies, critics were dismayed to find that American export controls would probably not bar U.S. companies from similar transactions. As a result, the process of changing U.S. law was begun.[3] Stone also pointed out that corporations routinely try to influence lawmakers by arousing public opinion, exemplified recently by the tobacco industry's promotional campaign on behalf of free speech, clearly intended to elicit support for the industry's desire to continue advertising tobacco products. Finally, Stone noted that in order to develop regulations for vast arrays of industries, governments frequently have little choice but to rely on business's own data and advice. The pitfalls of this reliance have been noted many times, including during the recent controversy surrounding the Food and Drug Administration's regulatory review of the bovine somatotropin growth hormone for dairy cows, in which a government veterinarian publicly criticized the FDA for working too closely with industry and relying too heavily on industry's allegedly biased test data.[4]

Stone's points are practical. They suggest that it is unwise to count on the law to define a worthy, impartial social mission for business. A more fundamental conceptual point also applies: The preeminent concern of law is to mitigate harm. Hence, the law characteristically does not tell us what to do; rather, it tells us what *not* to do. Law draws the line between acceptable and unacceptable conduct and specifies ever greater disincentives for crossing ever farther into the domain of the unacceptable. However, law typically does not tell business people who stay within the domain of legally acceptable conduct what acceptable actions to perform, nor does it provide guidelines or incentives for distinguishing between minimally acceptable and highly meritorious actions. Before the law, scoundrels, stinkers, and triflers who do nothing illegal are at one with the most industrious humanitarians. For these reasons, the law is not enough to stipulate, in any important affirmative respect, what the mission of business ought to be.

Heeding the Market Is Not Enough

Economists and other business thinkers sometimes see the market picking up where the law leaves off. While law concentrates on identifying the kinds of behavior which business should avoid, the market provides positive guidance concerning specifically what goods and services business should produce. Here is an outline of this concept of enterprise:

Reduced to its most fundamental elements, the economic world consists of two principal kinds of entities—firms and individual human beings (who are also called *householders*). In a free society, firms and householders interact by means of markets. There are two principal kinds of markets: (1) the market for the factors of production, in which firms buy such resources as labor, material, capital, and knowledge from householders, and (2) the market for products, in which householders buy goods and services from firms. The function of the firm is to receive as input the resources it buys in the factor market and efficiently transform them into the outputs it sells in the product market.

To perform this function successfully the firm can seek guidance from market prices. In both markets, householders are assumed to have preferences which affect their choices. It is further assumed that householders will demand the lowest prices for the factors of production they most prefer to part with and that householders will pay the highest prices for the products they most prefer to consume. Hence, prices communicate preferences. A successful firm is precisely one which takes the resources people most prefer to give up (and, therefore, will give up most cheaply) and transforms them into the goods and services people most prefer to consume (and for which they will, therefore, pay most dearly). Such a firm accomplishes two things at once: it maximizes its profit and it maximizes the satisfaction of human preferences. Profit therefore measures not just economic success, but also the firm's success in producing human satisfaction. This is the reasoning behind Adam Smith's famous observation that the firm which maximizes profit also creates social well-being, as surely as if it were guided by an invisible hand.

For the proponents of this concept of business, the ideal firm is in itself a purely preferenceless mechanism, efficiently responding to market prices in all of its decisions to buy and sell. It is a mathematical entity working on the mathematical problem of optimizing the diverse preferences of distinct sets of householders—workers in the labor market, vendors in the materials market, customers in the product market, and investors in the capital market. Because the whole responsibility of the firm is to respond faithfully to these human preferences, it would be irresponsible and undemocratic for the firm to develop its own independent preferences concerning the rightness or wrongness of using particular resources or of producing particular products. In the marketplace, the mission of business is to be a heeder, not a leader.

This vision of business has had far-reaching influence. It is widely accepted among business theorists. In politics, it has shaped the policies of a succession of U.S. administrations and internationally it has undoubtedly furthered the spread of free market practices along with the decline of communism.

An important implication of this view is that business should not directly consider moral issues when it makes decisions. The reason for this is that the moral preferences of workers, investors, vendors, and customers are already factored into market prices, along with all their other preferences. Milton Friedman, a persuasive champion of the free market, illustrates this point with the example of an industrial chemist who quits her job because she prefers not to provide labor to help manufacture napalm for incendiary weapons like those used in the Vietnam and Persian Gulf wars. "If many, many people feel that way," he says, "the cost of hiring people to make napalm will be high, napalm will be ex-

pensive, and less of it will be used. This is another way in which the free market does provide a much more sensitive and subtle voting mechanism than does the political system."[5] Hence, morality is already in the market—even the market for napalm—and business should not try to exercise any independent moral judgment.

I believe that this concept of the mission of business is mistaken in at least two respects.

First, the free market model takes human preferences as "givens" which markets express through prices and satisfy through exchange. However, this understanding of preferences strikes me as a serious oversimplification. I am not convinced that householders enter the marketplace with sure, ready-made preferences; human aims are not so clear and imagination is not so perfect. Customers, workers, vendors, and investors may not have settled, unequivocal notions of what constitutes good work, a good product, or the good life. For many people, the marketplace may function more as a testing ground, an experimental theatre, in which they seek completion of their incipient wants through work opportunities and product offerings which they envision only imperfectly, and which they look to business to define and create. In this vein, W. Edwards Deming, the quality control authority noted for his considerable influence on Japanese business philosophy, has expressed the sentiment that the consumer invents nothing. "New product and new types of service are generated," he states, "not by asking the consumer, but by knowledge, imagination, innovation, risk, trial and error on the part of the producer."[6]

In business, like art, there is no escaping the need to create things that are more detailed, more explicit, more real than anything the market can specify in advance. The resplendent images of heaven, hell, and things between which Michelangelo Buonarroti recorded on the Sistine ceiling did not and could not rise impeccably out of the collective preferences of his employers, assistants, admirers, and critics. It takes originative insight, initiative, and a difficult process of creatively grappling with the raw materials by the producer to introduce new goods, new services, and new experiences. So too home builders, computer makers, and restauranteurs are in the business not simply of heeding their respective markets, but of using their own imaginations to clarify, to concretize, and, inevitably, to affect the preferences operating in those markets.

I am proposing that there is a dialectic, a dynamic two-way relationship, between householder preferences and business offerings. Business develops offerings in response to householder preferences, but householders also develop preferences in response to business's offerings. Moral insight and moral initiative are needed on both sides of this mutually creative relationship, if the overall outcome is to be morally worthwhile. The producing firm is not simply a machine transforming incoming wants into outgoing products. It has original, discretionary power to define what will be offered in the marketplace and it is therefore obligated to think about what ought to be offered. To resume Milton Friedman's earlier example, it is not enough for a chemical company to maintain its own moral neutrality in deference to the supposed moral democracy of a profitable market in napalm, where the customer pays well and where only a non-critical number of workers, vendors, and investors refuses to participate. The doer of a deed has a responsibility to ask the self-referential moral question, "Is what I am doing honestly worth doing?" Maybe the decision makers at the napalm producing firm could, in the words of Control Data's Bill Norris, "check their gizzards" and in good faith answer "yes." Maybe not. But free market advocates are wrong to hold that the market system relieves that firm's leaders of the

responsibility to subject their offerings to moral scrutiny.

The second respect in which I believe the free market model is mistaken is in its acceptance of market prices as reliable measures not simply of economic value but also of moral value. Even if we were to grant that prices do sometimes adequately communicate well-defined householder preferences, prices still prove nothing concerning how morally worthy those preferences are. It is harsh reality that nasty preferences will engender nasty markets and that there is, therefore, no dependable connection between the economic value signified by market prices and the kind of value which makes the world a better place. Tobacco products, dial-a-porn services, handguns, and chemical warfare agents may be both profitable and legal market commodities, but they are at best of dubious social value and at worst genuinely decivilizing. Regrettably, the economic viability of nasty markets is only increased by technological advances, which typically allow production to be accomplished with less labor, material, or capital and thereby reduce the number of consenting human beings (workers, vendors, or investors) required to produce nasty products.

There is also a prospering marketplace, whose pageantry fills malls and radiates from TV screens, in which many offerings seem to be aimed only at indulging our unedifying but presumably harmless appetites for short-term comfort, peer attention, and mental reverie. This is the everyday realm of morally trivial products and services—of gossipy news, nutritionless food, escapist drama, and fashion accessories without end—which are easy to make and easy to sell in a society where consumption has itself become a recreational activity. In such a society what meaning or moral content can market preferences be trusted to have? Do the prices we find ourselves willing to pay for the latest vogues in jeans and jogging gear, high-tech sound systems, plastic turtle warriors, plush toys, prestigious cars, or closet loads of ties, belts, blouses, sweaters, and shoes provide an accurate measure of their contribution to the advance of civilization? I doubt that they do.

In the last analysis, it is a category error to reduce business morality to marketplace "voting." There is no guarantee that the morally optimal mix of goods and services will be found at the point where society's economic preferences converge, because there is no guarantee that those preferences aspired to world betterment in the first place. For business people committed to doing their moral best, market messages are not a useful substitute for their own moral insight and effort. They must look and decide for themselves where the best opportunities are for creating authentic civilization-building value.

Responding to Public Expectations Is Not Enough

Some thinkers have recognized that the market—at least the market as traditionally conceived—is not a satisfactory guide for business conduct and have proposed that business should also respond systematically to demands from its non-economic environment. There are two approaches to this: (1) the public policy approach, which holds that firms should take their social guidance from the expectations of society at large, and (2) stakeholder analysis, which urges each firm to be responsive in particular to those constituencies who are liable to be affected by the firm's actions (including, but not necessarily limited to, the firm's owners, employees, customers, suppliers, and the immediate community).

A classic advocacy of the public policy approach was provided by Lee Preston and James Post, who wrote that "guidelines for managerial performance are to be found not in the personal visions of the managers themselves . . . but rather in the larger society."[7] Stakeholder analysis is a more recent development and is sometimes championed by authorities on strategic management.

Most of us would likely have little respect for business leaders who failed to consider societal expectations or the concerns of their fellow stakeholders. However, these approaches tend to go beyond this, by supplanting the moral imagination and initiative of business people with an impersonal process of input, adaption, and response. Although their focus is not economic, these approaches are variants of heeding the market. "The organization should analyze and evaluate pressures and stimuli arising through public policy," acknowledged Preston and Post, "in precisely the same way that it analyzes and evaluates market experience."[8] Hence, proponents of both approaches typically apply empirical market survey techniques to the task of ascertaining society's or stakeholders' expectations and they often suggest organizational designs capable of adjusting efficiently to changing expectations.

If survey and response techniques are used simply to measure which way the social winds are blowing and to bend mechanically with those winds, then they are a miserable substitute for moral initiative. The winds of societal expectation, after all, blew strong and with a clear heading in Nazi Germany, but the firm which yielded unthinkingly to the Nazi concept of suitable business conduct did so at its moral peril. The moral mission of business is not fulfilled simply by doing what is required in order to survive in the social environment. A business must deserve to survive as a result of its honest choices and deliberate accomplishments.

The law, the market, and public expectations are inadequate substitutes for the moral imagination and initiative of business people because each of these proposed guides for business conduct still requires an appeal to a moral sense to fulfill it. Laws can be bad or good; markets can be bad or good; and public expectations can be bad or good. Ultimately, the only guide for righteous conduct is our irreducible moral sense and our power to act upon it with initiative. Advocates of obeying the law, heeding the market, and responding to public expectations have difficulty appreciating moral initiative, because they all conceive business as reactive, as a mechanism in a legal, economic, or social environment. Their thinking reflects the conceptual bias of the scientific world view, which dominates much of business theory and which models human behavior in terms of stimulus and response. Stimulation and response constitute an amoral process, and amorality is the common, troubling characteristic of all of the guidelines for business conduct which have been considered above and repudiated.

VALUE CREATION AND MORALITY

A few years ago, I saw a cartoon depicting a business school classroom. In it, the professor at the blackboard is drawing diagrams explaining the principles of production management; meanwhile a student in the back leans to another and says, "Things! I don't want to make *things*. I want to make *money*!"

This student, who may not be an entirely unfamiliar figure, would not have appreciated Justice Brandeis's earlier statement that "mere money making cannot be regarded as the legitimate end" of business. The student naively failed to grasp the essential dependence of making money on making things. In a world without productive achievement, money would have no meaning. Our productive achievements come first and matter most. Brandeis intimated this at the outset when he said that the achievements of business people ought to be comparable to those of artists, sci-

entists, inventors, or statesmen. An accomplished artist might create works of insight, beauty, or novel vision. A productive scientist might increase our understanding of how the world operates at the molecular or cosmic levels. A capable inventor might provide society with technical advances which promote healthier or more constructive living. A successful statesman might be a designer or implementer of a responsible, beneficial system of governance. Brandeis was saying that the success of business people should be measured, as it is for these other types of professional people, not by the quantity of their accumulated wealth, but by the quality of what they create and add to the world.

This concept of the moral mission of business has a number of features in its favor.

First, this concept places the focus of business morality at the center of business's native function, the production of goods and services. Much that has been written about business ethics depicts moral business conduct in terms of negative criteria or "extracurricular" contributions, such as avoiding criminal behavior or providing community service and charitable donations. There is no reason to dispute the merit of such conduct; however, those who emphasize it are overlooking the area where business has the greatest potential to produce positive moral achievements. Through the production of goods and services, business answers the call of the side of human nature named in the classical expression, *homo faber*—literally, man the maker. For many classical thinkers, our moral mission was to fulfill our human nature in the worthiest ways possible. By making worthy things, we makers make ourselves worthy people. Every day as they work, business people choose how well or how poorly they will fulfill the "maker" inherent in their natures, and, in so doing, they inevitably make an ongoing series of morally significant choices.

Second, this concept of the moral mission

of business facilitates the integration of moral conduct with effective strategic management. Just as goods and services should not be produced in *ad hoc* or haphazard ways by an organized, strategically managed firm, so too the moral contributions of that firm should not be devised *ad hoc* and delivered haphazardly. Critics of moral initiative by business sometimes assume that would-be morally engaged business people must be Lone Ranger types, who try singlehandedly and, of course, most unsuccessfully to implement *ad hoc* solutions to sweeping social problems like inflation, unemployment, poverty, illiteracy, pollution, or racism. Actually, there is no good reason why moral concerns need only be the pet agenda items of lone executives and "loose cannon" do-gooders. In its mission statement, standing policies, and long-range objectives, a strategically managed firm is expected to identify the kinds of goods and services it intends to offer and the market it intends to service. If the firm also intends those offerings to reflect moral imagination and initiative, then expression of this intent also belongs in the mission statement, policies, and objectives so that this intent can be built into the official agenda through all the subsequent stages of strategy development, revision, execution, and control. A company's moral initiatives in its choices concerning responsible resource consumption, philanthropic involvements and, above all, product characteristics can thus be conceived, articulated, budgeted, and implemented in the normal process of strategic management and can thereby represent the informed common will of the voluntary associates who comprise the business.

Third, this concept of the moral mission of business recognizes the moral relevance of a firm's product knowledge. The extensive knowledge a firm already has about its market offerings is precisely the knowledge which the firm requires and ought to use as a base for cultivating the moral insight needed if it is to

contribute in its own distinctive way to world betterment. No one is likely to know more than the producing firm about the potential benefits, hazards, and stakeholder concerns associated with its goods and services. When I was a child, one of the few pairs of shoes my father owned came unstitched. He took them to an elderly shoemaker in our neighborhood, who examined them and then tapped one of the shoes disapprovingly with his finger. "Bad work," he said. "But if they knew how to make them bad, they knew how to make them good." I think that the incident has stayed with me because I was struck by the moral indignation the old shoemaker felt toward the people who had made those shoes. In his view, those people had failed to live up to their business responsibilities; they had failed to use their knowledge to make their own small contribution to a better world.

Additionally, no one is better situated than the firm's decision makers to gather information and make a realistic assessment of the likely uses to which customers will put the firm's goods or services. Moral responsibility does not end at the shipping dock or retail counter, especially if it is possible to look beyond that point and anticipate with reasonable assurance that a product or service will be put to harmful use. The store clerk who sells a shotgun to a wild-eyed customer who is loudly voicing negative opinions about other people commits a morally significant error of judgment. A similar moral error is committed by weapons manufacturers when they arm fulminating dictators whose past behavior has shown a distinct propensity for waging war on their own subjects and immediate neighbors.

I am not claiming that business people can develop an infallible seer-like power to discern on every occasion which business choice is morally correct. However, I believe they are in a reasonable position to cultivate enough moral insight to assess their prospective product offerings and decide which of them would substantially add value to the world and which of them would subtract value from it.

PROFIT AND MORALITY

In free enterprise, a morally proactive firm needs and deserves to profit, because profitability empowers it to continue working at producing goods and services which make the world better. However, there is no denying that business people who choose their market interactions and product offerings based on a criterion of moral worthiness can run a greater risk of economic failure than business people who base their decisions directly on economic criteria. For one thing, morally committed business people may deliberately pass up some market opportunities. A publishing house, for example, may choose to avoid developing a line of third party reference manuals for popular software products, like those found in the computer sections of most bookstores, because it is not comfortable with the fact that the robust demand for these manuals is due largely to the proliferation of illegal copies of software. After all, if a friend gives someone a disk containing Word-Perfect, the recipient still needs a reference manual. Even though producing stand-alone reference manuals is perfectly legal, the publisher may decide it would be wrong to abet software piracy. That forsaken opportunity could translate into some forsaken profits.

Nevertheless, it would defy common sense to think that principled business people are obligated to operate with absolutely no regard for economic survival. Not even the most morally dedicated business people can feasibly fill their whole range of goods and services with morally exemplary offerings which generate no market interest, nor are they likely to make a lasting contribution to world betterment by selflessly "giving away the store" and running their companies into

ruin. Moral initiative by business requires a balance between moral and practical considerations. The firm's challenge is to develop offerings which it honestly considers to be morally worthy but which the market will also appreciate, or can be educated to appreciate, sufficiently to allow the firm to survive.

Business school educators usually have little to say about persuasive selling and persuasive advertising. Persuasion, after all, attempts to influence our preference functions, and it is not consistent with the mechanistic vision of firms outlined earlier to concede that they might have a rightful power to lead the market by actively working to create demand. However, for an innovative firm taking moral initiative, the selling function may properly involve morally educating the market by awakening an appreciation of the civilization-building value of the firm's goods or services, selling not simply the product, but trying to persuade market participants that the qualities of this product are the sort of qualities which right-minded people ought to prefer. This is a justifiable use of persuasion. A firm which commits to the extra effort and extra risks associated with trying to produce morally worthy products is a pioneer in the ongoing quest to better our world. Such a firm is entitled to attempt to increase the economic value of its goods and services, and hence the prospects for the firm's profitability, by advocating an enlightened change in the preference functions operating in the marketplace.

Hopefully, we are moving toward a world where, someday, market value will reliably express moral value. If we are to get there, moral education of the marketplace is needed, and, in a free society, this education is best administered in large part by business itself, which should take the initiative in showing the world that products and services which enhance civilization are preferable to those which are morally trivial or overtly harmful.

CONCLUSION

Justice Brandeis had high hopes for business's prospects for achieving its moral mission. "The great industrial and social problems," he predicted, "will one by one find solution." There are good reasons to share his optimism.

Even with its Malthusian population increases and periods of backsliding, the historical progress of civilization has on balance been for the better. The world is going, fitfully to be sure, through a long process of what social economist Kenneth Boulding calls "gentling," as a result of which "societies increasingly are held together not by threat but by exchange."[9] William Baumol has provided helpful measurements of the remarkable transformation of quality of life in the United States:

> From 1870 to 1979 U.S. output per work-hour increased by an astonishing 1100 percent. This was enough to permit the average number of hours worked per year to fall by some 40 percent while per capita output increased eightfold. To dramatize what such an explosion in living standards means we note that this implies . . . that our ancestors spent well over 90 percent of their incomes on food, clothing, and shelter, that vacations were virtually unknown, that the typical meal consisted of a "one-pot stew", shared by the entire family, and that home heating was so primitive that ink wells routinely froze in winter. Productivity has also exploded in agriculture. As late as the 17th century, when some 90 percent of the European work force was engaged in agriculture, outputs were still so small that regular famines, with widespread death by starvation, continued to be common. Today, the highly agricultural United States employs only 3 percent of its labor force in the production of farm outputs, usually providing a considerable overabundance.[10]

In this transformation, business, whose concern is economic exchange, has emerged as one of the world's principal civilizing influences. Business has been the implementer and often the author of the advances in labor utilization, shelter, and agriculture alluded to by Baumol, along with world-building improvements in the whole sustaining infrastructure for health and education. Business is now the repository and activator of much of our human creative energy and of our technical capacity for production. In our time, it is probably the greatest arena of human achievement.

The next step is for business leaders to recognize explicitly that world betterment is their true function and moral mission, and for them to pursue it with imagination and initiative. It is sometimes naively thought that business ethics is all about the choice between being a crook and not being a crook. Actually, crooks are not the most serious threat to the pursuit of business's moral mission. Rather, the major obstacle to be overcome is the widespread influence of the thinkers criticized earlier, who champion amoral and mistaken guidelines for business conduct. Their vision of business has lost sight of the moral mission of humankind and of the quest for its fulfillment inherent in business life.

NOTES

1. From an address at Brown University Commencement Day, 1912. Quoted in *The Social and Economic Views of Mr. Justice Brandeis,* ed. Alfred Lief (New York: Vanguard, 1930), pp. 387–388. It is noteworthy and regrettable that even as progressive a social thinker as Brandeis still, in 1912, referred to businesspeople only in male terms.

2. See Christopher Stone, *Where the Law Ends: The Social Control of Corporate Behavior* (Evanston, IL: Harper and Row, 1975), pp. 93–96. The points in this paragraph are summarized from Stone's highly regarded book; the examples are derived from more recent events.

3. See Michael R. Gordon with Stephen Engelberg, "Poison Gas Fears Lead U.S. to Plan

New Export Curbs," *New York Times*, 26 March 1989, p. 1.

4. See Julia Flynn Siler, "All Things Right and Dutiful: A Vet Who Blew the Whistle," *Business Week*, 2 September 1991, p. 75.

5. Milton Friedman, *There's No Such Thing as a Free Lunch* (LaSalle, IL: Open Court, 1975), p. 245. Also published as *An Economist's Protest,* 2nd ed. (Glen Ridge, NJ: Thomas Horton, 1975). The passage quoted was originally published in an interview of Friedman by John McClaughry in *Business and Society Review,* Spring 1972.

6. W. Edwards Deming, *Out of the Crisis* (Cambridge, MA: Massachusetts Institute of Technology, 1986), p. 182.

7. L. E. Preston and J. E. Post, *Private Management and Public Policy* (Englewood Cliffs, NJ: Prentice Hall, 1975), p. 102. In 1988 the abiding influence of this book was recognized when its authors were given the Howard Chase Book Award by the Social Issues in Management division of the Academy of Management.

8. Ibid., p. 143.

9. Robert Wright, *Three Scientists and Their Gods* (New York: Times Books, 1988), p. 267.

10. William J. Baumol, "Is There a U.S. Productivity Crisis?" *Science* 243 (1989): 611–612.

A Stakeholder Theory of the Modern Corporation: Kantian Capitalism

William M. Evan
and R. Edward Freeman

INTRODUCTION

Corporations have ceased to be merely legal devices through which the private business transactions of individuals may be carried on. Though still much used for this purpose, the corporate form has acquired a larger significance. The corporation has, in fact, become both a method of property tenure and a means of organizing economic life. Grown to tremendous proportions, there may be said to have evolved a "corporate system"—which has attracted to itself a combination of attributes and powers, and has attained a degree of prominence entitling it to be dealt with as a major social institution.[1]

Despite these prophetic words of Berle and Means (1932), scholars and managers alike continue to hold sacred the view that managers bear a special relationship to the stockholders in the firm. Since stockholders own shares in the firm, they have certain rights and privileges, which must be granted to them by management, as well as by others. . . . Sanctions, in the form of "the law of corporations," and other protective mechanisms in the form of social custom, accepted management practice, myth, and ritual, are thought to reinforce the assumption of the primacy of the stockholder.

The purpose of this paper is to pose several challenges to this assumption, from within the framework of managerial capitalism, and to suggest the bare bones of an alternative theory, *a stakeholder theory of the modern corporation.* We do not seek the demise of the modern corporation, either intellectually or in fact. Rather, we seek its transformation. In the words of Neurath, we shall attempt to "rebuild the ship, plank by plank, while it remains afloat."[2]

Our thesis is that we can revitalize the concept of managerial capitalism by replacing the notion that managers have a duty to stockholders with the concept that managers bear a fiduciary relationship to stakeholders. Stakeholders are those groups who have a stake in or claim on the firm. Specifically we include suppliers, customers, employees, stockholders, and the local community, as well as management in its role as agent for these groups. We argue that the legal, economic, political, and moral challenges to the currently received theory of the firm, as a nexus of contracts among the owners of the factors of production and customers, require us to revise this concept along essentially Kantian lines. That is, each of these stakeholder groups has a right not to be treated as a means to some end, and therefore must participate in determining the future direction of the firm in which they have a stake.[3] . . .

The crux of our argument is that we must reconceptualize the firm around the following question: For whose benefit and at whose expense should the firm be managed? We shall set forth such a reconceptualization in the form of a *stakeholder theory of the firm*. We shall then critically examine the stakeholder view and its implications for the future of the capitalist system.

THE ATTACK ON MANAGERIAL CAPITALISM

The Legal Argument

The basic idea of managerial capitalism is that in return for controlling the firm, management vigorously pursues the interests of stockholders. Central to the managerial view of the firm is the idea that management can pursue market transactions with suppliers and customers in an unconstrained manner.[4]

The law of corporations gives a less clearcut answer to the question: In whose interest and for whose benefit should the modern corporation be governed? While it says that the corporations should be run primarily in the interests of the stockholders in the firm, it says further that the corporation exists "in contemplation of the law" and has personality as a "legal person," limited liability for its actions, and immortality, since its existence transcends that of its members.[5] Therefore, directors and other officers of the firm have a fiduciary obligation to stockholders in the sense that the "affairs of the corporation" must be conducted in the interest of the stockholders. And stockholders can theoretically bring suit against those directors and managers for doing otherwise. But since the corporation is a legal person, existing in contemplation of the law, managers of the corporation are constrained by law.

Until recently, this was no constraint at all. In this century, however, . . . the law has evolved to effectively constrain the pursuit of stockholder interests at the expense of other claimants on the firm. It has, in effect, required that the claims of customers, suppliers, local communities, and employees be taken into consideration, though in general they are subordinated to the claims of stockholders. . . .

For instance, the doctrine of "privity of contract," as articulated in *Winterbottom v. Wright* in 1842, has been eroded by recent developments in products liability law. Indeed, *Greenman v. Yuba Power* gives the manufacturer strict liability for damage caused by its products, even though the seller has exercised all possible care in the preparation and sale of the product and the consumer has not bought the product from nor entered into any contractual arrangement with the manufacturer. Caveat emptor has been replaced, in large part, with caveat venditor.[6] The Consumer Product Safety Commission has the power to enact product recalls, and in 1980 one U.S. automobile company recalled more cars than it built. . . . Some industries are required to provide information to customers about a product's ingredients, whether or not the customers want and are willing to pay for this information.[7]

In short, the supplier-firm-customer chain is far from that visualized by managerial capitalism. In their roles as customers and suppliers, firms have benefitted from these constraints, but they have been harmed to the degree to which the constraints have meant loss of profit. . . .

The same argument is applicable to management's dealings with employees. The National Labor Relations Act gave employees the right to unionize and to bargain in good faith. It set up the National Labor Relations Board to enforce these rights with management. The Equal Pay Act of 1963 and Title VII of the Civil Rights Act of 1964 constrain management from discrimination in hiring practices; these have been followed with the Age Discrimination in Employment Act of 1967.[8] The emergence of a body of administrative case law arising from labor-management disputes and the historic settling of discrimination claims with large employers such as AT&T have caused the emergence of a body of practice in the corporation that is consistent with the legal guarantee of the rights of the employees. . . . The law has protected the due process rights of those employees who enter into collective bargaining agreements with management. As of the present, however, only 30 percent of the labor force are participating in such agreements; this has prompted one labor law scholar to propose a statutory law prohibiting dismissals of the 70 percent of the work force not protected.[9] . . .

The law has also protected the interests of local communities. The Clean Air Act and Clean Water Act have constrained management from "spoiling the commons." In an historic case, *Marsh v. Alabama,* the Supreme Court ruled that a company-owned town was subject to the provisions of the U.S. Constitution, thereby guaranteeing the rights of local citizens and negating the "property rights" of the firm. Some states and municipalities have gone further and passed laws preventing firms from moving plants or limiting when and how plants can be closed. In sum, there is much current legal activity in this area to constrain management's pursuit of stockholders' interests at the expense of the local communities in which the firm operates. . . .

We have argued that the result of such changes in the legal system can be viewed as giving some rights to those groups that have a claim on the firm, for example, customers, suppliers, employees, local communities, stockholders, and management. It raises the question, at the core of a theory of the firm: In whose interest and for whose benefit should the firm be managed? The answer proposed by managerial capitalism is clearly "the stockholders," but we have argued that the law has been progressively circumscribing this answer.

The Economic Argument

In its pure ideological form managerial capitalism seeks to maximize the interests of stockholders. In its perennial criticism of government regulation, management espouses the "invisible hand" doctrine. It contends that it creates the greatest good for the greatest number, and therefore government need not intervene. However, we know that externalities, moral hazards, and monopoly power exist in fact, whether or not they exist in theory. Further, some of the legal apparatus mentioned above has evolved to deal with just these issues.

The problem of the "tragedy of the commons" or the free-rider problem pervades the concept of public goods such as water and air. No one has an incentive to incur the cost of clean-up or the cost of nonpollution, since the marginal gain of one firm's action is small. Every firm reasons this way, and the result is pollution of water and air. Since the industrial revolution, firms have sought to internalize the benefits and externalize the costs of their actions. The cost must be borne by all, through taxation and regulation; hence we have the emergence of the environmental regulations of the 1970s.

Similarly, moral hazards arise when the purchaser of a good or service can pass along the cost of that good. There is no incentive to economize, on the part of either the producer or the consumer, and there is excessive use of the resources involved. The institutionalized practice of third-party payment in health care is a prime example.

Finally, we see the avoidance of competitive behavior on the part of firms, each seeking to monopolize a small portion of the market and not compete with one another. In a number of industries, oligopolies have emerged, and while there is questionable evidence that oligopolies are not the most efficient corporate form in some industries, suffice it to say that the potential for abuse of market power has again led to regulation of managerial activity. In the classic case, AT&T, arguably one of the great technological and managerial achievements of the century, was broken up into eight separate companies to prevent its abuse of monopoly power.

Externalities, moral hazards, and monopoly power have led to more external control on managerial capitalism. There are de facto constraints, due to these economic facts of life, on the ability of management to act in the interests of stockholders. . . .

A STAKEHOLDER THEORY OF THE FIRM

Foundations of a Theory

Two themes are present throughout our argument. The first is concerned with the rights and duties of the owners (and their agents) of private property, and the effects of this property on the rights of others. The second theme is concerned with the consequences of managerial capitalism and the effects of the modern corporation on the welfare of others. These themes represent two branches of modern moral theory, Kantianism and consequentialism, and they are pitted together as the main tension in most existing moral theories. Our purpose here is to argue that the stockholder theory of the firm seems to give precedence to one or the other interpretation, but that both are important in grounding a theory of the modern corporation. In other words, we need a theory that balances the rights of the claimants on the corporation with the consequences of the corporate form.

Those who question the legitimacy of the modern corporation altogether because of the evils of excessive corporate power usually believe that the corporation should have no right to decide how things are going to be for its constituents. While we believe that each person has the right to be treated not as a means to some corporate end but as an end in itself, we would not go so far as to say that the corporation has no rights whatsoever. Our more moderate stance is that if the modern corporation requires treating others as means to an end, then these others must agree on, and hence participate (or choose not to participate) in, the decisions to be used as such. Thus, property rights are legitimate but not absolute, particularly when they conflict with important rights of others. And any theory that is to be consistent with our considered judgment about rights must take such a balanced view. The right to property does not yield the right to treat others as means to an end, which is to say that property rights are not a license to ignore Kant's principle of respect for persons.

Those who question the legitimacy of the modern corporation altogether because of the resulting possibility of externalities or harm usually do not see that the corporation can be held accountable for its actions. We maintain that persons (even legal persons) are responsible for the consequences of their actions, regardless of how those actions are mediated, and must be able and willing to accept responsibility for them. Therefore, any theory that seeks to justify the corporate form must be based at least partially on the idea that the corporation and its managers as moral agents can be the cause of and can be held accountable for their actions.

In line with these two themes of rights and effects, . . . we suggest two principles that will serve as working rules, not absolutes, to guide us in addressing some of the foundational issues. We will not settle the thorny issues that these principles raise, but merely argue that any theory, including the stakeholder theory, must be consistent with these principles.

Principle of Corporate Rights (PCR). The corporation and its managers may not violate the legitimate rights of others to determine their own future.

Principle of Corporate Effects (PCE). The corporation and its managers are responsible for the effects of their actions on others.

The Stakeholder Concept

Corporations have stakeholders, that is, groups and individuals who benefit from or are harmed by, and whose rights are violated or respected by, corporate actions. The notion of stakeholder is built around the Principle of Corporate Rights (PCR) and the Principle of Corporate Effect (PCE). . . . The concept of stakeholders is a generalization of the notion of stockholders, who themselves have some special claim on the firm. Just as

stockholders have a right to demand certain actions by management, so do other stakeholders have a right to make claims. The exact nature of these claims is a difficult question that we shall address, but the logic is identical to that of the stockholder theory. Stakes require action of a certain sort, and conflicting stakes require methods of resolution. . . .

Freeman and Reed (1983)[10] distinguish two senses of *stakeholder*. The "narrow definition" includes those groups who are vital to the survival and success of the corporation. The "wide-definition" includes any group or individual who can affect or is affected by the corporation. While the wide definition is more in keeping with PCE and PCR, it raises too many difficult issues. We shall begin with a more modest aim: to articulate a stakeholder theory using the narrow definition.

Stakeholders in the Modern Corporation

Figure 1 depicts the stakeholders in a typical large corporation. The stakes of each are reciprocal, since each can affect the other in terms of harms and benefits as well as rights and duties. The stakes of each are not univocal and would vary by particular corporation. We merely set forth some general notions that seem to be common to many large firms.

Owners have financial stake in the corporation in the form of stocks, bonds, and so on, and they expect some kind of financial return from them. Either they have given money directly to the firm, or they have some historical claim made through a series of morally justified exchanges. The firm affects their livelihood or, if a substantial portion of their retirement income is in stocks or bonds, their ability to care for themselves when they can no longer work. Of course, the stakes of owners will differ by type of owner, preferences for money, moral preferences, and so on, as

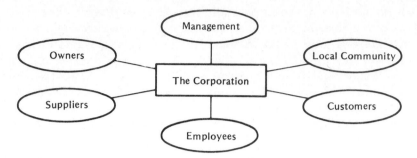

FIGURE 1.   A Stakeholder Model of the Corporation.

well as by type of firm. The owners of AT&T are quite different from the owners of Ford Motor Company, with stock of the former company being widely dispersed among 3 million stockholders and that of the latter being held by a small family group as well as by a large group of public stockholders.

Employees have their jobs and usually their livelihood at stake; they often have specialized skills for which there is usually no perfectly elastic market. In return for their labor, they expect security, wages, benefits, and meaningful work. In return for their loyalty, the corporation is expected to provide for them and carry them through difficult times. Employees are expected to follow the instructions of management most of the time, to speak favorably about the company, and to be responsible citizens in the local communities in which the company operates. Where they are used as means to an end, they must participate in decisions affecting such use. The evidence that such policies and values as described here lead to productive company-employee relationships is compelling. It is equally compelling to realize that the opportunities for "bad faith" on the part of both management and employees are enormous. "Mock participation" in quality circles, singing the company song, and wearing the company uniform solely to please management all lead to distrust and unproductive work.

Suppliers, interpreted in a stakeholder sense, are vital to the success of the firm, for raw materials will determine the final product's quality and price. In turn the firm is a customer of the supplier and is therefore vital to the success and survival of the supplier. When the firm treats the supplier as a valued member of the stakeholder network, rather than simply as a source of materials, the supplier will respond when the firm is in need. Chrysler traditionally had very close ties to its suppliers, even to the extent that led some to suspect the transfer of illegal payments. And when Chrysler was on the brink of disaster, the suppliers responded with price cuts, accepting late payments, financing, and so on. Supplier and company can rise and fall together. Of course, again, the particular supplier relationships will depend on a number of variables such as the number of suppliers and whether the supplies are finished goods or raw materials.

Customers exchange resources for the products of the firm and in return receive the benefits of the products. Customers provide the lifeblood of the firm in the form of revenue. Given the level of reinvestment of earnings in large corporations, customers indirectly pay for the development of new products and services. Peters and Waterman (1982)[11] have argued that being close to the customer leads to success with other stakeholders and that a distinguishing characteristic of some companies that have performed well is their emphasis on the customer. By paying attention to customers' needs, management automatically addresses the needs of suppliers and owners. Moreover, it seems that the ethic of customer service carries over to the community. Almost without fail the "excellent companies" in Peters and Waterman's study have good reputations in the community. We would argue that Peters and Waterman have found multiple applications of Kant's dictum, "Treat persons as ends unto themselves," and it should come as no surprise that persons respond to such respectful treatment, be they customers, suppliers, owners, employees, or members of the local community. The real surprise is the novelty of the application of Kant's rule in a theory of good management practice.

The local community grants the firm the right to build facilities and, in turn, it benefits from the tax base and economic and social contributions of the firm. In return for the provision of local services, the firm is expected to be a good citizen, as is any person, either "natural or artificial." The firm cannot expose the community to unreasonable hazards in the form of pollution, toxic waste, and so on. If for some reason the firm must leave a community, it is expected to work with local leaders to make the transition as smoothly as possible. Of course, the firm does not have perfect knowledge, but when it discovers some danger or runs afoul of new competition, it is expected to inform the local community and to work with the community to overcome any problem. When the firm mismanages its relationship with the local community, it is in the same position as a citizen who commits a crime. It has violated the implicit social contract with the community and should expect to be distrusted and ostracized. It should not be surprised when punitive measures are invoked.

We have not included "competitors" as stakeholders in the narrow sense, since strictly speaking they are not necessary for the survival and success of the firm; the stakeholder theory works equally well in monopoly contexts. However, competitors and government would be the first to be included in an extension of this basic theory. It is simply not true that the interests of competitors in an industry are always in conflict. There is no reason why trade associations and other multiorganizational groups cannot band together to solve common problems that have little to do with how to restrain trade. Implementation of stakeholder management principles, in the long run, mitigates the need for industrial policy and an increasing role for government intervention and regulation.

The Role of Management

Management plays a special role, for it too has a stake in the modern corporation. On the one hand, management's stake is like that of employees, with some kind of explicit or implicit employment contract. But, on the other hand, management has a duty of safeguarding the welfare of the abstract entity that is the corporation. In short, management, especially top management, must look after the health of the corporation, and this involves balancing the multiple claims of conflicting stakeholders. Owners want higher financial returns, while customers want more money spent on research and development. Employees want higher wages and better benefits, while the local community wants better parks and day-care facilities.

The task of management in today's corporation is akin to that of King Solomon. The stakeholder theory does not give primacy to one stakeholder group over another, though there will surely be times when one group will benefit at the expense of others. In general, however, management must keep the relationships among stakeholders in balance. When these relationships become imbalanced, the survival of the firm is in jeopardy.

When wages are too high and product quality is too low, customers leave, suppliers suffer, and owners sell their stocks and bonds, depressing the stock price and making it difficult to raise new capital at favorable rates. Note, however, that the reason for paying returns to owners is not that they "own" the firm, but that their support is necessary for the survival of the firm, and that they have a legitimate claim on the firm. Similar reasoning applies in turn to each stakeholder group.

A stakeholder theory of the firm must redefine the purpose of the firm. The stockholder theory claims that the purpose of the firm is to maximize the welfare of the stockholders, perhaps subject to some moral or social constraints, either because such maximization leads to the greatest good or because of property rights. The purpose of the firm is quite different in our view. If a stakeholder theory is to be consistent with the principles of corporate effects and rights, then its purpose must take into account Kant's dictum of respect for persons. The very purpose of the firm is, in our view, to serve as a vehicle for coordinating stakeholder interests. It is through the firm that each stakeholder group makes itself better off through voluntary exchanges. The corporation serves at the pleasure of its stakeholders, and none may be used as a means to the ends of another without full rights of participation in that decision. We can crystallize the particular applications of PCR and PCE to the stakeholder theory in two further principles. These stakeholder management principles will serve as a foundation for articulating the theory. They are guiding ideals for the immortal corporation as it endures through generations of particular mortal stakeholders.

Stakeholder Management Principles

P1: The corporation should be managed for the benefit of its stakeholders: its customers, suppliers, owners, employees, and local communities. The rights of these groups must be ensured, and, further, the groups must participate, in some sense, in decisions that substantially affect their welfare.

P2: Management bears a fiduciary relationship to stakeholders and to the corporation as an abstract entity. It must act in the interests of the stakeholders as their agent, and it must act in the interests of the corporation to ensure the survival of the firm, safeguarding the long-term stakes of each group.

P1, which we might call The Principle of Corporate Legitimacy, redefines the purpose of the firm to be in line with the principles of corporate effects and rights. It implies the legitimacy of stakeholder claims on the firm. Any social contract that justifies the existence of the corporate form includes the notion that stakeholders are a party to that contract. Further, stakeholders have some inalienable rights to participate in decisions that substantially affect their welfare or involve their being used as a means to another's ends. We bring to bear our arguments for the incoherence of the stockholder view as justification for P1. If in fact there is no good reason for the stockholder theory, and if in fact there are harms, benefits, and rights of stakeholders involved in running the modern corporation, then we know of no other starting point for a theory of the corporation than P1.

P2, which we might call The Stakeholder Fiduciary Principle, explicitly defines the duty of management to recognize these claims. It will not always be possible to meet all claims of all stakeholders all the time, since some of these claims will conflict. Here P2 recognizes the duty of management to act in the long-term best interests of the corporation, conceived as a forum of stakeholder interaction, when the interests of the group outweigh the interests of the individual parties to the collective contract. The duty described in P2 is a fiduciary duty, yet it does not suffer from the difficulties surrounding the fiduciary duty to stockholders, for the conflicts involved there are precisely those that P2 makes it mandatory for management to resolve. Of course, P2 gives no instructions for a magical resolution of the conflicts that arise from prima facie obligations to multiple parties. An analysis of such rules for decision making is a subject to be addressed on another occasion, but P2 does give these conflicts a legitimacy that they do not enjoy in the stockholder theory. It gives management a clear and distinct directive to pay attention to stakeholder claims.

P1 and P2 recognize the eventual need for changes in the law of corporations and other governance mechanisms if the stakeholder theory is to be put into practice. P1 and P2, if implemented as a major innovation in the structure of the corporation, will make manifest the eventual legal institutionalization of sanctions. . . .

Structural Mechanisms

We propose several structural mechanisms to make a stakeholder management conception practicable. We shall offer a sketch of these here and say little by way of argument for them.

1. *The Stakeholder Board of Directors.* We propose that every corporation of a certain size yet to be determined, but surely all those that are publicly traded or are of the size of those publicly traded, form a Board of Directors comprised of representatives of five stakeholder groups, including employees, customers, suppliers, stockholders, and members of the local community, as well as a representative of the corporation, whom we might call a "metaphysical director" since he

or she would be responsible for the metaphysical entity that is "the corporation." Whether or not each representative has an equal voting right is a matter that can be decided by experimentation; issues of governance lend themselves naturally to both laboratory and organizational experiments.

These directors will be vested with the duty of care to manage the affairs of the corporation in concert with the interests of its stakeholders. Such a Board would ensure that the rights of each group would have a forum, and by involving a director for the corporation, would ensure that the corporation itself would not be unduly harmed for the benefit of a particular group. In addition, by vesting each director with the duty of care for all stakeholders, we ensure that positive resolutions of conflicts would occur. . . . The task of the metaphysical director, to be elected unanimously by the stakeholder representatives, is especially important. The fact that the director has no direct constituency would appear to enhance management control. However, nothing could be further from the truth. To represent the abstract entity that is the corporation would be a most demanding job. Our metaphysical director would be responsible for convincing both stakeholders and management that a certain course of action was in the interests of the long-term health of the corporation, especially when that action implies the sacrifice of the interests of all. The metaphysical director would be a key link between the stakeholder representatives and management, and would spearhead the drive to protect the norms of the interests of all stakeholders. . . .

2. *Corporate Law.* The law of corporations needs to be redefined to recognize the legitimate purpose of the corporation as stated in P1. This has in fact developed in some areas of the law, such as products liability, where the claims of customers to safe products has emerged, and labor law, where the claims of

employees have been safeguarded. Indeed, in such pioneering cases as *Marsh v. Alabama* the courts have come close to a stakeholder perspective. We envision that a body of case law will emerge to give meaning to "the proper claims of stakeholders," and in effect that the "wisdom of Solomon" necessary to make the stakeholder theory work will emerge naturally through the joint action of the courts, stakeholders, and management.

While much of the above may seem utopian, there are some very practical transitional steps that could occur. Each large corporation could form a stakeholder advisory board, which would prepare a charter detailing how the organization is to treat the claims of each stakeholder. Initially this stakeholder advisory board would serve as an advisor to the current board of directors, and eventually it would replace that board. Simultaneously, a group of legal scholars and practitioners, such as the American Law Institute, could initiate discussion of the legal proposals and methods to change corporate charters, while business groups such as the Business Roundtable could examine the practical consequences of our proposals. Given the emergence of some consensus, we believe that a workable transition can be found. . . .

NOTES

1. Cf. A. Berle and G. Means, *The Modern Corporation and Private Property* (New York: Commerce Clearing House, 1932), 1. For a reassessment of Berle and Means' argument after 50 years, see *Journal of Law and Economics* 26 (June 1983), especially G. Stigler and C. Friedland, "The Literature of Economics: The Case of Berle and Means," 237–68; D. North, "Comment on Stigler and Friedland," 269–72; and G. Means, "Corporate Power in the Marketplace," 467–85.

2. The metaphor of rebuilding the ship while afloat is attributed to Neurath by W. Quine, *Word and Object* (Cambridge: Harvard University Press, 1960), and W. Quine and J. Ullian, *The Web of Belief* (New York: Random House, 1978). The point is that to keep the ship afloat during repairs we must replace a plank with one that will do a better job. Our argument is that Kantian capitalism can so replace the current version of managerial capitalism.

3. Kant's notion of respect for persons (i.e., that each person has a right not to be treated as a means to an end) can be be found in (1) Kant, *Critique of Practical Reason* (1838 edition). See J. Rawls, *A Theory of Justice* (Cambridge: Harvard University Press, 1971) for an eloquent modern interpretation.

4. For an introduction to the law of corporations see A. Conard, *Corporations in Perspective* (Mineola, NY: The Foundation Press, 1976), especially section 19; and R. Hamilton, *Corporations* (St. Paul: West Publishing, 1981), Chapter 8.

5. For a modern statement of managerial capitalism, see the literature in managerial economics, for example R. Coase, "The Nature of the Firm," *Economica* 4 (1937): 386–405; M. Jensen and W. Meckling, "Theory of the Firm: Managerial Behavior, Agency Costs and Ownership Structure," *Journal of Financial Economics* 3 (1976): 305–60; and O. Williamson, *The Economics of Discretionary Behavior* (London: Kershaw Publishing, 1965).

6. See R. Charan and E. Freeman, "Planning for the Business Environment of the 1980s," *The Journal of Business Strategy* 1 (1980): 9–19, especially p. 15 for a brief account of the major developments in products liability law.

7. See S. Breyer, *Regulation and Its Reform* (Cambridge: Harvard University Press, 1983), 133, for an analysis of food additives.

8. See I. Millstein and S. Katsh, *The Limits of Corporate Power* (New York: Macmillan, 1981), Chapter 4.

9. Cf. C. Summers, "Protecting All Employees Against Unjust Dismissal," *Harvard Business Review* 58 (1980): 136, for a careful statement of the argument.

10. See E. Freeman and D. Reed, "Stockholders and Stakeholders: A New Perspective on Corporate Governance," in C. Huizinga, ed., *Corporate Governance: A Definitive Exploration of the Issues* (Los Angeles: UCLA Extension Press, 1983).

11. See T. Peters and R. Waterman, *In Search of Excellence* (New York: Harper and Row, 1982).

Business Ethics
and Stakeholder Analysis

Kenneth E. Goodpaster

So we must think through what management should be accountable for; and how and through whom its accountability can be discharged. The stockholders' interest, both short- and long-term, is one of the areas. But it is only one.*

What is ethically responsible management? How can a corporation, given its economic mission, be managed with appropriate attention to ethical concerns? These are central questions in the field of business ethics. One approach to answering such questions that has become popular during the last two decades is loosely referred to as "stakeholder analysis." Ethically responsible management, it is often suggested, is management that includes careful attention not only to stockholders *but to stakeholders generally* in the decision-making process.

This suggestion about the ethical importance of stakeholder analysis contains an important kernel of truth, but it can also be misleading. Comparing the ethical relationship between managers and stockholders with their relationship to other stakeholders is, I will argue, almost as problematic as ignoring stakeholders (ethically) altogether—presenting us with something of a "stakeholder paradox."

DEFINITION

The term "stakeholder" appears to have been invented in the early '60s as a deliberate play on the word "stockholder" to signify that there are other parties having a "stake" in the

*Peter Drucker, 1988
Harvard Business Review

decision making of the modern, publicly held corporation in addition to those holding equity positions. Professor R. Edward Freeman, in his book *Strategic Management: A Stakeholder Approach* (Pitman, 1984), defines the term as follows:

> A stakeholder in an organization is (by definition) any group or individual who can affect or is affected by the achievement of the organization's objectives. (46)

Examples of stakeholder groups (beyond stockholders) are employees, suppliers, customers, creditors, competitors, governments, and communities. . . .

Another metaphor with which the term "stakeholder" is associated is that of a "player" in a game like poker. One with a "stake" in the game is one who plays and puts some economic value at risk.

Much of what makes responsible decision making difficult is understanding how there can be an ethical relationship between management and stakeholders that avoids being too weak (making stakeholders mere means to stockholders' ends) or too strong (making stakeholders quasistockholders in their own right). To give these issues life, a case example will help. So let us consider the case of General Motors and Poletown.

THE POLETOWN CASE

In 1980, GM was facing a net loss in income, the first since 1921, due to intense foreign competition. Management realized that major

From Kenneth E. Goodpaster, "Business Ethics and Stakeholder Analysis," *Business Ethics Quarterly* 1 (January 1991), pp. 53–73. Reprinted by permission.

capital expenditures would be required for the company to regain its competitive position and profitability. A $40 billion five-year capital spending program was announced that included new, state-of-the-art assembly techniques aimed at smaller, fuel-efficient automobiles demanded by the market. Two aging assembly plants in Detroit were among the ones to be replaced. Their closure would eliminate 500 jobs. Detroit in 1980 was a city with a black majority, an unemployment rate of 18% overall and 30% for blacks, a rising public debt and a chronic budget deficit, despite high tax rates.

The site requirements for a new assembly plant included 500 acres, access to long-haul railroad and freeways, and proximity to suppliers for "just-in-time" inventory management. It needed to be ready to produce 1983 model year cars beginning in September 1982. The only site in Detroit meeting GM's requirements was heavily settled, covering a section of the Detroit neighborhood of Poletown. Of the 3,500 residents, half were black. The whites were mostly of Polish descent, retired or nearing retirement. An alternative "green field" site was available in another midwestern state.

Using the power of eminent domain, the Poletown area could be acquired and cleared for a new plant within the company's timetable, and the city government was eager to cooperate. Because of job retention in Detroit, the leadership of the United Auto Workers was also in favor of the idea. The Poletown Neighborhood Council strongly opposed the plan, but was willing to work with the city and GM.

The new plant would employ 6,150 workers and would cost GM $500 million wherever it was built. Obtaining and preparing the Poletown site would cost an additional $200 million, whereas alternative sites in the midwest were available for $65 to $80 million.

The interested parties were many—stockholders, customers, employees, suppliers, the Detroit community, the midwestern alternative, the Poletown neighborhood. The decision was difficult. GM management needed to consider its competitive situation, the extra costs of remaining in Detroit, the consequences to the city of leaving for another part of the midwest, and the implications for the residents of choosing the Poletown site if the decision was made to stay. The decision about whom to talk to and *how* was as puzzling as the decision about *what* to do and *why*.

STAKEHOLDER ANALYSIS AND STAKEHOLDER SYNTHESIS

Ethical values enter management decision making, it is often suggested, through the gate of stakeholder analysis. But the suggestion that introducing "stakeholder analysis" into business decisions is the same as introducing ethics into those decisions is questionable. To make this plain, let me first distinguish between two importantly different ideas: stakeholder analysis and stakeholder synthesis. I will then examine alternative kinds of stakeholder synthesis with attention to ethical content.

The decision-making process of an individual or a company can be seen in terms of a sequence of six steps to be followed after an issue or problem presents itself for resolution. For ease of reference and recall, I will name the sequence PASCAL, after the six letters in the name of the French philosopher-mathematician Blaise Pascal (1623–1662), who once remarked in reference to ethical decision making that "the heart has reasons the reason knows not of."

1. PERCEPTION or fact gathering about the options available and their short- and long-term implications;
2. ANALYSIS of these implications with specific

attention to affected parties and to the decision-maker's goals, objectives, values, responsibilities, etc.;

3. SYNTHESIS of this structured information according to whatever fundamental priorities obtain in the mindset of the decision-maker;

4. CHOICE among the available options based on the synthesis;

5. ACTION or implementation of the chosen option through a series of specific requests to specific individuals or groups, resource allocation, incentives, controls, and feedback;

6. LEARNING from the outcome of the decision, resulting in either reinforcement or modification (for future decisions) of the way in which the above steps have been taken.

We might simplify this analysis, of course, to something like "input," "decision," and "output," but distinguishing interim steps can often be helpful. The main point is that the path from the presentation of a problem to its resolution must somehow involve gathering, processing, and acting on relevant information.

Now, by *stakeholder analysis* I simply mean a process that does not go beyond the first two steps mentioned above. That is, the affected parties caught up in each available option are identified and the positive and negative impacts on each stakeholder are determined. But questions having to do with processing this information into a decision and implementing it are *left unanswered*. These steps are not part of the *analysis* but of the *synthesis, choice,* and *action.*

Stakeholder analysis may give the initial appearance of a decision-making process, but in fact it is only a *segment* of a decision-making process. It represents the preparatory or opening phase that awaits the crucial application of the moral (or nonmoral) values of the decision-maker. So, to be informed that an individual or an institution regularly makes stakeholder analysis part of decision making or takes a "stakeholder approach" to management is to learn little or nothing about the

ethical character of that individual or institution. It is to learn only that stakeholders are regularly identified—*not why and for what purpose.* To be told that stakeholders are or must be "taken into account" is, so far, to be told very little. Stakeholder analysis is, as a practical matter, morally *neutral.* It is therefore a mistake to see it as a substitute for normative ethical thinking.

What I shall call "stakeholder synthesis" goes further into the sequence of decision-making steps mentioned above to include actual decision-making and implementation (S,C,A). The critical point is that stakeholder synthesis offers *a pattern or channel by which to move from stakeholder identification to a practical response or resolution.* Here we begin to join stakeholder analysis to questions of substance. But we must now ask: What kind of substance? And how does it relate to *ethics*? The stakeholder idea, remember, is typically offered as a way of integrating *ethical* values into management decision making. When and how does substance become *ethical* substance?

STRATEGIC STAKEHOLDER SYNTHESIS

We can imagine decision-makers doing "stakeholder analysis" for different underlying reasons, not always having to do with ethics. A management team, for example, might be careful to take positive and (especially) negative stakeholder effects into account for no other reason than that offended stakeholders might resist or retaliate (e.g., through political action or opposition to necessary regulatory clearances). It might not be *ethical* concern for the stakeholders that motivates and guides such analysis, so much as concern about potential impediments to the achievement of strategic objectives. Thus positive and negative effects on relatively powerless stakeholders may be ignored or discounted in the synthesis, choice, and action phases of the decision process.

In the Poletown case, General Motors might have done a stakeholder analysis using the following reasoning: our stockholders are the central stakeholders here, but other key stakeholders include our suppliers, old and new plant employees, the City of Detroit, and the residents of Poletown. These other stakeholders are not our direct concern as a corporation with an economic mission, but since they can influence our short- or long-term strategic interests, they must be taken into account. Public relation's costs and benefits, for example, or concerns about union contracts or litigation might well have influenced the choice between staying in Detroit and going elsewhere.

I refer to this kind of stakeholder synthesis as "strategic" since stakeholders outside the stockholder group are viewed instrumentally, as factors potentially affecting the overarching goal of optimizing stockholder interests. They are taken into account in the decision-making process, but as external environmental forces, as potential sources of either good will or retaliation. "We" are the economic principals and management; "they" are significant players whose attitudes and future actions might affect our short-term or long-term success. We must respect them in the way one "respects" the weather—as a set of forces to be reckoned with.

It should be emphasized that managers who adopt the strategic stakeholder approach are not necessarily *personally* indifferent to the plight of stakeholders who are "strategically unimportant." The point is that *in their role as managers*, with a fiduciary relationship that binds them as agents to principals, their basic outlook subordinates other stakeholder concerns to those of stockholders. . . . During the Poletown controversy, GM managers as individuals may have cared deeply about the potential lost jobs in Detroit, or about the potential dislocation of Poletown residents. But in their role as agents for the owners (stockholders)

they could only allow such considerations to "count" if they served GM's strategic interests (or perhaps as legal constraints on the decision).

The essence of a strategic view of stakeholders is not that stakeholders are ignored, but that all but a special group (stockholders) are considered on the basis of their actual or potential influence on management's central mission. The basic normative principle is fiduciary responsibility (organizational prudence), supplemented by legal compliance.

IS THE SUBSTANCE ETHICAL?

The question we must ask in thinking about a strategic approach to stakeholder synthesis is this: Is it really an adequate rendering of the *ethical* component in managerial judgment? Unlike mere stakeholder *analysis*, this kind of synthesis does go beyond simply *identifying* stakeholders. It integrates the stakeholder information by using a single interest group (stockholders) as its basic normative touchstone. If this were formulated as an explicit rule or principle, it would have two parts and would read something like this: (1) Maximize the benefits and minimize the costs to the stockholder group, short- and long-term, and (2) Pay close attention to the interests of other stakeholder groups that might potentially influence the achievement of (1). But while expanding the list of stakeholders may be a way of "enlightening" self-interest for the organization, is it really a way of introducing ethical values into business decision making?

There are really two possible replies here. The first is that as an account of how ethics enters the managerial mind-set, the strategic stakeholder approach fails not because it is *im*moral; but because it is *non*moral. By most accounts of the nature of ethics, a strategic stakeholder synthesis would not qualify as an ethical synthesis, even though it does represent a substantive view. The point is simply that while there is nothing necessarily *wrong* with strategic reasoning about the consequences of one's actions for others, the kind of concern exhibited should not be confused with what most people regard as *moral* concern. Moral concern would avoid injury or unfairness to those affected by one's actions because it is wrong, regardless of the retaliatory potential of the aggrieved parties.

The second reply does question the morality (*vs.* immorality) of strategic reasoning as the ultimate principle behind stakeholder analysis. It acknowledges that strategy, when placed in a highly effective legal and regulatory environment and given a time-horizon that is relatively longterm, may well avoid significant forms of anti-social behavior. But it asserts that as an operating principle for managers under time pressure in an imperfect legal and regulatory environment, strategic analysis is insufficient. In the Poletown case, certain stakeholders (e.g., the citizens of Detroit or the residents of Poletown) may have merited more *ethical* consideration than the strategic approach would have allowed. Some critics charged that GM only considered these stakeholders *to the extent that* serving their interests also served GM's interests, and that as a result, their interests were undermined.

Many, most notably Nobel Laureate Milton Friedman, believe that market and legal forces are adequate to translate or transmute ethical concerns into straightforward strategic concerns for management. He believes that in our economic and political system (democratic capitalism), direct concern for stakeholders (what Kant might have called "categorical" concern) is unnecessary, redundant, and inefficient, not to mention dishonest:

> In many cases, there is a strong temptation to rationalize actions as an exercise of "social responsibility." In the present climate of opinion, with its widespread aversion to "capitalism," "profits," the "soulless corporation" and so on, this is one way for a corporation to generate good will as a byproduct of expenditures that are entirely justified in its own self-interest. If our institutions, and the attitudes of the public make it in their self-interest to cloak their actions in this way, I cannot summon much indignation to denounce them. At the same time, I can express admiration for those individual proprietors or owners of closely held corporations or stockholders of more broadly held corporations who disdain such tactics as approaching fraud.

Critics respond, however, that absent a pre-established harmony or linkage between organizational success and ethical success, some stakeholders, some of the time, will be affected a lot but will be able to affect in only a minor way the interests of the corporation. They add that in an increasingly global business environment, even the protections of law are fragmented by multiple jurisdictions.

At issue then is (1) defining ethical behavior partly in terms of the (nonstrategic) decision-making values *behind* it, (2) recognizing that too much optimism about the correlation between strategic success and virtue runs the risk of tailoring the latter to suit the former.

Thus the move toward substance (from analysis to synthesis) in discussions of the stakeholder concept is not necessarily a move toward ethics. And it is natural to think that the reason for this has to do with the instrumental status accorded to stakeholder groups other than stockholders. If we were to treat all stakeholders by strict analogy with stockholders, would we have arrived at a more ethically satisfactory form of stakeholder synthesis? Let us now look at this alternative, what I shall call a "multi-fiduciary" approach.

MULTI-FIDUCIARY STAKEHOLDER SYNTHESIS

In contrast to a strategic view of stakeholders, one can imagine a management team processing stakeholder information by giving the same care to the interests of, say, employees, customers, and local communities as to the economic interests of stockholders. This kind of substantive commitment to stakeholders might involve trading off the economic advantages of one group against those of another, e.g., in a plant closing decision. I shall refer to this way of integrating stakeholder analysis with decision making as "multi-fiduciary" since all stakeholders are treated by management as having equally important interests, deserving joint "maximization" (or what Herbert Simon might call "satisficing").

Professor Freeman, quoted earlier, contemplates what I am calling the multi-fiduciary view at the end of his 1984 book under the heading *The Manager As Fiduciary to Stakeholders:*

> Perhaps the most important area of future research is the issue of whether or not a theory of management can be constructed that uses the stakeholder concept to enrich "managerial capitalism," that is, can the notion that managers bear a fiduciary relationship to stockholders or the owners of the firm, be replaced by a concept of management whereby the manager *must* act in the interests of the stakeholders in the organization? (249)

As we have seen, the strategic approach pays attention to stakeholders as factors that might affect economic interests and as market forces to which companies must pay attention for competitive reasons. They become actual or potential legal challenges to the company's exercise of economic rationality. The multi-fiduciary approach, on the other hand, views stakeholders apart from their instrumental, economic, or legal clout. On this view, the word "stakeholder" carries with it, by the deliberate modification of a single phoneme, a dramatic shift in managerial outlook.

In 1954, famed management theorist Adolf Berle conceded a long-standing debate with Harvard law professor E. Merrick Dodd that looks in retrospect very much like a debate between what we are calling strategic and multi-fiduciary interpretations of stakeholder synthesis. Berle wrote:

> Twenty years ago, [I held] that corporate powers were powers in trust for shareholders while Professor Dodd argued that these powers were held in trust for the entire community. The argument has been settled (at least for the time being) squarely in favor of Professor Dodd's contention.

The intuitive idea behind Dodd's view, and behind more recent formulations of it in terms of "multiple constituencies" and "stakeholders, not just stockholders" is that by expanding the list of those in whose trust corporate management must manage, we thereby introduce ethical responsibility into business decision making.

In the context of the Poletown case, a multi-fiduciary approach by GM management might have identified the same stakeholders. But it would have considered the interests of employees, the city of Detroit, and the Poletown residents *alongside* stockholder interests, not solely in terms of how they might *influence* stockholder interests. This may or may not have entailed a different outcome. But it probably would have meant a different approach to the decision-making process in relation to the residents of Poletown (talking with them, for example).

We must now ask, as we did of the strategic approach: How satisfactory is multi-fiduciary stakeholder synthesis as a way of giving ethical substance to management decision making? On the face of it, and in stark contrast to the strategic approach, it may seem that we have at last arrived at a truly moral view. But we should be cautious. For no sooner do we think we have found the proper interpretation of ethics in management than a major objection presents itself. And, yes, it appears to be a *moral* objection!

It can be argued that multi-fiduciary stakeholder analysis is simply incompatible with widely-held moral convictions about the special fiduciary obligations owed by management to stockholders. At the center of the objection is the belief that the obligations of agents to principals are stronger or different in kind from those of agents to third parties.

THE STAKEHOLDER PARADOX

Managers who would pursue a multi-fiduciary stakeholder orientation for their companies must face resistance from those who believe that a strategic orientation is the only *legitimate* one for business to adopt, given the economic mission and legal constitution of the modern corporation. This may be disorienting since the word "illegitimate" has clear negative ethical connotations, and yet the multi-fiduciary approach is often defended on ethical grounds. I will refer to this anomalous situation as the *Stakeholder Paradox:*

> It seems essential, yet in some ways illegitimate, to orient corporate decisions by ethical values that go beyond strategic stakeholder considerations to multi-fiduciary ones.

I call this a paradox because it says there is an ethical problem whichever approach management takes. Ethics seems both to forbid and to demand a strategic, profit-maximizing mind-set. The argument behind the paradox focuses on management's *fiduciary* duty to the stockholder, essentially the duty to keep a profit-maximizing promise, and a concern that the "impartiality" of the multi-fiduciary approach simply cuts management loose from certain well-defined bonds of stock-

holder accountability. On this view, impartiality is thought to be a *betrayal of trust.*

TOWARD A NEW STAKEHOLDER SYNTHESIS

We all remember the story of the well-intentioned Doctor Frankenstein. He sought to improve the human condition by designing a powerful, intelligent force for good in the community. Alas, when he flipped the switch, his creation turned out to be a monster rather than a marvel! Is the concept of the ethical corporation like a Frankenstein monster?

Taking business ethics seriously need not mean that management bears *additional* fiduciary relationships to third parties (non-stockholder constituencies) as multi-fiduciary stakeholder synthesis suggests. It may mean that there are morally significant *nonfiduciary* obligations to third parties surrounding any fiduciary relationship (See *Figure 1.*) Such moral obligations may be owed by private individuals as well as private-sector organizations to those whose freedom and well-being is affected by their economic behavior. It is these very obligations in fact (the duty not to harm or coerce and duties not to lie, cheat, or steal) that are cited in regulatory, legislative, and judicial arguments for constraining profit-driven business activities. These obligations are not "hypothetical" or contingent or indirect, as they would be on the strategic model, wherein they are only subject to the corporation's interests being met. They are "categorical" or direct. They are not rooted in the *fiduciary* relationship, but in other relationships at least as deep.

It must be admitted . . . that the jargon of "stakeholders" in discussions of business ethics can seem to threaten the notion of what corporate law refers to as the "undivided and unselfish loyalty" owed by managers and di-

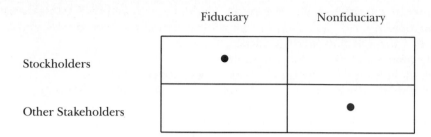

FIGURE 1.   Direct Managerial Obligations

rectors to stockholders. For this way of speaking can suggest a multiplication of management duties *of the same kind* as the duty to stockholders. What we must understand is that the responsibilities of management toward stockholders are of a piece with the obligations that *stockholders themselves* would be expected to honor in their own right. As an old Latin proverb has it, *nemo dat quod non habet,* which literally means "nobody gives what he doesn't have." Freely translating in this context we can say: No one can expect of an *agent* behavior that is ethically less responsible than what he would expect of himself. I cannot (ethically) *hire* to have done on my behalf something that I would not (ethically) *do* myself. We might refer to this as the "Nemo Dat Principle" (NDP) and consider it a formal requirement of consistency in business ethics (and professional ethics generally):

(NDP)   Investors cannot expect of managers (more generally, principals cannot expect of their agents) behavior that would be inconsistent with the reasonable ethical expectations of the community.

The NDP does not, of course, resolve in advance the many ethical challenges that managers must face. It only indicates that these challenges are of a piece with those that face us all. It offers a different kind of test (and so a different kind of stakeholder synthesis) that management (and institutional investors) might apply to policies and decisions.

The foundation of ethics in management—and the way out of the stakeholder paradox—lies in understanding that the conscience of the corporation is a logical and moral extension of the consciences of its principals. It is *not* an expansion of the *list* of principals, but a gloss on the principal-agent relationship itself. Whatever the structure of the principal-agent relationship, neither principal nor agent can ever claim that an agent has "moral immunity" from the basic obligations that would apply to any human being toward other members of the community.

Indeed, the introduction of moral reasoning (distinguished from multi-fiduciary stakeholder reasoning) into the framework of management thinking may *protect* rather than threaten private sector legitimacy. The conscientious corporation can maintain its private economic mission, but in the context of fundamental moral obligations owed by any member of society to others affected by that member's actions. Recognizing such obligations does *not* mean that an institution is a public institution. Private institutions, like private individuals, can be and are bound to respect moral obligations in the pursuit of private purposes.

Conceptually, then, we can make room for a moral posture toward stakeholders that is both *partial* (respecting the fiduciary relationship between managers and stockholders) and *impartial* (respecting the equally important nonfiduciary relationships between management and other stakeholders). . . .

Whether this conceptual room can be used *effectively* in the face of enormous pressures on contemporary managers and directors is another story, of course. For it is one thing to say that "giving standing to stakeholders" in managerial reasoning is conceptually coherent. It is something else to say that it is practically coherent.

Yet most of us, I submit, believe it. Most of us believe that management at General Motors *owed* it to the people of Detroit and to the people of Poletown to take their (nonfiduciary) interests very seriously, to seek creative solutions to the conflict, to do more than use or manipulate them in accordance with GM's needs only. We understand that managers and directors have a special obligation to provide a financial return to the stockholders, but we also understand that the word "special" in this context needs to be tempered by an appreciation of certain fundamental community norms that go beyond the demands of both laws and markets. There are certain class-action suits that stockholders ought not to win. For there is sometimes a moral defense.

CONCLUSION

The relationship between management and stockholders is ethically different in kind from the relationship between management and other parties (like employees, suppliers, customers, etc.), a fact that seems to go unnoticed by the multi-fiduciary approach. If it were not, the corporation would cease to be a private sector institution—and what is now called business ethics would become a more radical critique of our economic system than

is typically thought. On this point, Milton Friedman must be given a fair and serious hearing.

This does not mean, however, that "stakeholders" lack a morally significant relationship to management, as the strategic approach implies. It means only that the relationship in question is different from a fiduciary one. Management may never have promised customers, employees, suppliers, etc. a "return on investment," but management is nevertheless obliged to take seriously its extra-legal obligations not to injure, lie to or cheat these stakeholders *quite apart from* whether it is in the stockholders' interests.

As we think through the *proper* relationship of management to stakeholders, fundamental features of business life must undoubtedly be recognized: that corporations have a principally economic mission and competence; that fiduciary obligations to investors and general obligations to comply with the law cannot be set aside; and that abuses of economic power and disregard of corporate stewardship in the name of business ethics are possible.

But these things must be recognized as well: that corporations are not solely financial institutions; that fiduciary obligations go beyond short-term profit and are in any case subject to moral criteria in their execution; and that mere compliance with the law can be unduly limited and even unjust.

The *Stakeholder Paradox* can be avoided by a more thoughtful understanding of the nature of moral obligation and the limits it imposes on the principal-agent relationship. Once we understand that there is a practical "space" for identifying the ethical values shared by a corporation and its stockholders—a space that goes beyond strategic self-interest but stops short of impartiality—the hard work of filling that space can proceed.

Dodge v. Ford Motor Co.

Michigan Supreme Court

. . . When plaintiffs made their complaint and demand for further dividends, the Ford Motor Company had concluded its most prosperous year of business. The demand for its cars at the price of the preceding year continued. It could make and could market in the year beginning August 1, 1916, more than 500,000 cars. Sales of parts and repairs would necessarily increase. The cost of materials was likely to advance, and perhaps the price of labor; but it reasonably might have expected a profit for the year of upwards of $60,000,000. . . . Considering only these facts, a refusal to declare and pay further dividends appears to be not an exercise of discretion on the part of the directors, but an arbitrary refusal to do what the circumstances required to be done. These facts and others call upon the directors to justify their action, or failure or refusal to act. In justification, the defendants have offered testimony tending to prove and which does prove, the following facts: It had been the policy of the corporation for a considerable time to annually reduce the selling price of cars, while keeping up, or improving, their quality. As early as in June, 1915, a general plan for the expansion of the productive capacity of the concern by a practical duplication of its plant had been talked over by the executive officers and directors and agreed upon; not all of the details having been settled, and no formal action of directors having been taken. The erection of a smelter was considered, and engineering and other data in connection therewith secured. In consequence, it was determined not to reduce the selling price of cars for the year beginning August 1, 1915, but to maintain the price to accumulate a large surplus to pay for the proposed expansion of plant and equipment, and perhaps to build a plant for smelting ore. It is hoped, by Mr. Ford, that eventually 1,000,000 cars will be annually produced. The contemplated changes will permit the increased output.

The plan, as affecting the profits of the business for the year beginning August 1, 1916, and thereafter, calls for a reduction in the selling price of the cars. . . . In short, the plan does not call for and is not intended to produce immediately a more profitable business, but a less profitable one; not only less profitable than formerly, but less profitable than it is admitted it might be made. The apparent immediate effect will be to diminish the value of shares and the returns to shareholders.

It is the contention of plaintiffs that the apparent effect of the plan is intended to be the continued and continuing effect of it, and that it is deliberately proposed, not of record and not by official corporate declaration, but nevertheless proposed, to continue the corporation henceforth as a semi-eleemosynary institution and not as a business institution. In support of this contention, they point to the attitude and to the expressions of Mr. Henry Ford. . . .

"My ambition," said Mr. Ford, "is to employ still more men, to spread the benefits of this industrial system to the greatest possible number, to help them build up their lives and their homes. To do this we are putting the greatest share of our profits back in the business."

"With regard to dividends, the company paid sixty per cent, on its capitalization of two million dollars, or $1,200,000, leaving $58,000,000 to reinvest for the growth of the company. This is Mr. Ford's policy at present, and

204 Mich. 459, 170 N.W. 668, 3 A.L.R. 413. Majority opinion by Justice J. Ostrander.

it is understood that the other stockholders cheerfully accede to this plan."

He had made up his mind in the summer of 1916 that no dividends other than the regular dividends should be paid, "for the present."

> "Q. For how long? Had you fixed in your mind any time in the future, when you were going to pay—A. No."
> "Q. That was indefinite in the future? A. That was indefinite; yes, sir."

The record, and especially the testimony of Mr. Ford, convinces that he has to some extent the attitude towards shareholders of one who has dispensed and distributed to them large gains and that they should be content to take what he chooses to give. His testimony creates the impression, also, that he thinks the Ford Motor Company has made too much money, has had too large profits, and that, although large profits might be still earned, a sharing of them with the public, by reducing the price of the output of the company, ought to be undertaken. We have no doubt that certain sentiments, philanthropic and altruistic, creditable to Mr. Ford, had large influence in determining the policy to be pursued by the Ford Motor Company—the policy which has been herein referred to.

It is said by his counsel that—

> "Although a manufacturing corporation cannot engage in humanitarian works as its principal business, the fact that it is organized for profit does not prevent the existence of implied powers to carry on with humanitarian motives such charitable works as are incidental to the main business of the corporation." . . .

In discussing this proposition counsel have referred to decisions [citations omitted]. These cases, after all, like all others in which the subject is treated, turn finally upon the point, the question, whether it appears that the directors were not acting for the best interests of the corporation. We do not draw in question, nor do counsel for the plaintiffs do so, the validity of the general proposition stated by counsel nor the soundness of the opinions delivered in the cases cited. The case presented here is not like any of them. The difference between an incidental humanitarian expenditure of corporate funds for the benefit of the employees, like the building of a hospital for their use and the employment of agencies for the betterment of their condition, and a general purpose and plan to benefit mankind at the expense of others, is obvious. There should be no confusion (of which there is evidence) of the duties which Mr. Ford conceives that he and the stockholders owe to the general public and the duties which in law he and his codirectors owe to protesting, minority stockholders. A business corporation is organized and carried on primarily for the profit of the stockholders. The powers of the directors are to be employed for that end. The discretion of directors is to be exercised in the choice of means to attain that end, and does not extend to a change in the end itself, to the reduction of profits, or to the nondistribution of profits among stockholders in order to devote them to other purposes. . . . As we have pointed out, and the proposition does not require argument to sustain it, it is not within the lawful powers of a board of directors to shape and conduct the affairs of a corporation for the merely incidental benefit of shareholders and for the primary purpose of benefiting others, and no one will contend that, if the avowed purpose of the defendant directors was to sacrifice the interests of shareholders, it would not be the duty of the courts to interfere. . . . It is obvious that an annual dividend of 60 per cent, upon $2,000,000, or $1,200,000, is the equivalent of a very small dividend upon $100,000,000, or more.

The decree of the court below fixing and determining the specific amount to be distributed to stockholders is affirmed. . . .

A. P. Smith Manufacturing Co. v. Barlow

Supreme Court of New Jersey

The Chancery Division, in a well-reasoned opinion by Judge Stein, determined that a donation by the plaintiff The A. P. Smith Manufacturing Company to Princeton University was *intra vires*. Because of the public importance of the issues presented, the appeal duly taken to the Appellate Division has been certified directly to this court under Rule 1:5-1(a).

The company was incorporated in 1896 and is engaged in the manufacture and sale of valves, fire hydrants and special equipment, mainly for water and gas industries. Its plant is located in East Orange and Bloomfield and it has approximately 300 employees. Over the years the company has contributed regularly to the local community chest and on occasions to Upsala College in East Orange and Newark University, now part of Rutgers, the State University. On July 24, 1951 the board of directors adopted a resolution which set forth that it was in the corporation's best interests to join with others in the 1951 Annual Giving to Princeton University, and appropriated the sum of $1,500 to be transferred by the corporation's treasurer to the university as a contribution towards its maintenance. When this action was questioned by stockholders the corporation instituted a declaratory judgment action in the Chancery Division and trial was had in due course.

Mr. Hubert F. O'Brien, the president of the company, testified that he considered the contribution to be a sound investment, that the public expects corporations to aid philanthropic and benevolent institutions, that they obtain good will in the community by so doing, and that their charitable donations create favorable environment for their business operations. In addition, he expressed the thought that in contributing to liberal arts institutions, corporations were furthering their self-interest in assuring the free flow of properly trained personnel for administrative and other corporate employment. Mr. Frank W. Abrams, chairman of the board of the Standard Oil Company of New Jersey, testified that corporations are expected to acknowledge their public responsibilities in support of the essential elements of our free enterprise system. He indicated that it was not "good business" to disappoint "this reasonable and justified public expectation," nor was it good business for corporations "to take substantial benefits from their membership in the economic community while avoiding the normally accepted obligations of citizenship in the social community." Mr. Irving S. Olds, former chairman of the board of the United States Steel Corporation, pointed out that corporations have a self-interest in the maintenance of liberal education as the bulwark of good government. He stated that "Capitalism and free enterprise owe their survival in no small degree to the existence of our private, independent universities" and that if American business does not aid in their maintenance it is not "properly protecting the long-range interest of its stockholders, its employees and its customers." Similarly, Dr. Harold W. Dodds, President of Princeton University, suggested that if private institutions of higher learning were replaced by governmental institutions our society would be vastly different and private enterprise in other fields would fade out rather promptly.

98 A 2d 581 (1953). Opinion by Judge J. Jacobs.

Further on he stated that "democratic society will not long endure if it does not nourish within itself strong centers of non-governmental fountains of knowledge, opinions of all sorts not governmentally or politically originated. If the time comes when all these centers are absorbed into government, then freedom as we know it, I submit, is at an end." . . .

When the wealth of the nation was primarily in the hands of individuals they discharged their responsibilities as citizens by donating freely for charitable purposes. With the transfer of most of the wealth to corporate hands and the imposition of heavy burdens of individual taxation, they have been unable to keep pace with increased philanthropic needs. They have therefore, with justification, turned to corporations to assume the modern obligations of good citizenship in the same manner as humans do. Congress and state legislatures have enacted laws which encourage corporate contributions, and much has recently been written to indicate the crying need and adequate legal basis therefor[e]. . . .

During the first world war corporations loaned their personnel and contributed substantial corporate funds in order to insure survival; during the depression of the '30s they made contributions to alleviate the desperate hardships of the millions of unemployed; and during the second world war they again contributed to insure survival. They now recognize that we are faced with other, though nonetheless vicious, threats from abroad which must be withstood without impairing the vigor of our democratic institutions at home and that otherwise victory will be pyrrhic indeed. More and more they have come to recognize that their salvation rests upon sound economic and social environment which in turn rests in no insignificant part upon free and vigorous nongovernmental institutions of learning. It seems to us that just as the conditions prevailing when corporations were originally created required that

they serve public as well as private interests, modern conditions require that corporations acknowledge and discharge social as well as private responsibilities as members of the communities within which they operate. Within this broad concept there is no difficulty in sustaining, as incidental to their proper objects and in aid of the public welfare, the power of corporations to contribute corporate funds within reasonable limits in support of academic institutions. But even if we confine ourselves to the terms of the common-law rule in its application to current conditions, such expenditures may likewise readily be justified as being for the benefit of the corporation; indeed, if need be the matter may be viewed strictly in terms of actual survival of the corporation in a free enterprise system. The genius of our common law has been its capacity for growth and its adaptability to the needs of the times. Generally courts have accomplished the desired result indirectly through the molding of old forms. Occasionally they have done it directly through frank rejection of the old and recognition of the new. But whichever path the common law has taken it has not been found wanting as the proper tool for the advancement of the general good. . . .

In the light of all of the foregoing we have no hesitancy in sustaining the validity of the donation by the plaintiff. There is no suggestion that it was made indiscriminately or to a pet charity of the corporate directors in furtherance of personal rather than corporate ends. On the contrary, it was made to a preeminent institution of higher learning, was modest in amount and well within the limitations imposed by the statutory enactments, and was voluntarily made in the reasonable belief that it would aid the public welfare and advance the interests of the plaintiff as a private corporation and as part of the community in which it operates. We find that it was a lawful exercise of the corporation's implied and incidental powers under common-law principles and that it came within the express authority of the pertinent state legislation. As has been indicated, there is now widespread belief throughout the nation that free and vigorous non-governmental institutions of learning are vital to our democracy and the system of free enterprise and that withdrawal of corporate authority to make such contributions within reasonable limits would seriously threaten their continuance. Corporations have come to recognize this and with their enlightenment have sought in varying measures, as has the plaintiff by its contribution, to insure and strengthen the society which gives them existence and the means of aiding themselves and their fellow citizens. Clearly then, the appellants, as individual stockholders whose private interests rest entirely upon the well-being of the plaintiff corporation, ought not be permitted to close their eyes to present-day realities and thwart the long-visioned corporate action in recognizing and voluntarily discharging its high obligations as a constituent of our modern social structure.

The judgment entered in the Chancery Division is in all respects Affirmed.

CASE 1. *Shutdown at Eastland*

When Speedy Motors Company closed its assembly plant in Eastland, Michigan, lobbyists for organized labor cited the case as one more reason why the Federal government should pass a law regulating plant closings. With less than a month's notice, the company laid off nearly 2,000 workers and permanently shut down the facility, which had been in operation more than 20 years. The local union president called the action "a callous and heartless treatment of the workers and of the community."

Company executives defended the decision as inevitable in view of the harsh competitive realities of the automotive industry. "Purchases of the Speedy model produced at Eastland have fallen to almost nothing and there is nothing we can do about changes in consumer preferences," a company spokesman said.

Labor lobbyists insist that instances such as this show the need for a Federal law which would require companies to give as much as two years' notice before closing a major factory, unless they can demonstrate that an emergency exists. The proposed legislation would also require the employer to provide special benefits to workers and the community affected by the shutdown.

"Closing plants needlessly and without warning is an antisocial, criminal act," a union leader said. "Giant corporations don't give a thought to the hardships they are imposing on long-time employees and communities that depend on their jobs. The only thing they consider is their profit."

Opponents of the legislation maintain that the proposed law would strike at the heart of the free enterprise system. "Companies must be free to do business wherever they choose without being penalized," a corporate spokesman argued. "Plant closing legislation would constitute unjustified interference in private decision making. Laws which restrict the ability of management to operate a business in the most efficient manner are counterproductive and in direct conflict with the theory of free enterprise."

Adapted from a case by John P. Kavanagh, Emeritus Assistant Professor of Philosophy, Center for the Study of Values, University of Delaware. Reprinted by permission.

Questions

1. Does the closing of a plant when it ceases to be profitable violate the "moral minimum"?

2. Who are the affected stakeholders, and how should their interests be considered?

3. Who should take primary responsibility for those laid off or terminated due to a plant closing?

CASE 2. *The Sloane Products Case*

Sloane Products is a regional manufacturer of metal dispensers for paper products used in restaurants, hotels, and passenger terminals. The products bear the Sloane brand and are advertised in trade journals. Sloane sells its products through wholesalers. There is no information on the amount of output eventually sold in minority-operated establishments. Sloane assumes the amount is relatively small. The manufacturing plant, however, is in an older metropolitan area with a large black population, though the plant itself is far from the center of the black neighborhoods and the firm has only a few black employees.

In response to pleas from the metropolitan chapter of the National Alliance of Business, Sloane's board adopted the following policy on minority purchasing:

> Sloane managers are expected to make extra efforts to find minority suppliers and even to help minority enterprises adjust to Sloane's purchasing requirements. The board's instructions also made it clear that the effort was not expected to impose any serious disruption on Sloane's operations.

Right after the procurement directive was issued, Frank Gambetta, head of purchasing, had found a local firm, Diamond Carton Company, a black owned and managed producer of corrugated boxes for shipping merchandise. For quotation purposes, Gambetta's office had given Diamond information on quantity, quality, sizes, and delivery requirements.

Diamond had admitted being new to the business but assured the people at Sloane that Diamond could meet the product and delivery specifications.

Diamond had sent quotations to Gambetta's office. After some negotiation, Diamond was awarded a contract by Sloane, who then reduced quantities purchased from other sources.

However, Diamond did not provide samples for pre-production approval at the time specified in the original agreement. When samples eventually appeared, they proved to be below standard. Gambetta and production chief Sam Fritzel then spent time helping the managers at Diamond work out the defects, and eventually Diamond did produce samples that could be approved.

First production deliveries were satisfactory, but since then every delivery has been either late or substandard. This has been going on for four months.

Fritzel is ready to end the agreement on the grounds that the relationship with Diamond is disrupting Sloane's operations.

Questions

1. Has Sloane done enough for Diamond to justify ending the agreement at the present time?

Adapted from a case by Lawrence G. Lavengood, Professor of Business History, Graduate School of Management, Northwestern University. Reprinted by permission.

2. Is the fact that the relationship with Diamond is disrupting Sloane's operation good enough reason by itself for ending the agreement?

3. If Sloane does end the agrement with Diamond, does it have any obligation to find another minority supplier?

4. Given Sloane's geographical location, does it have any special moral responsibility to the black community at all?

CASE 3. *Procter and Gamble and Toxic Shock Syndrome*

In September 1980, Procter and Gamble reached a consent agreement with the Food and Drug Administration (FDA) to "demarket" its new super absorbent Rely tampon which had been twenty years in development. This agreement was reached one week after Procter and Gamble representatives were confronted by the FDA with results of a Center for Disease Control (CDC) study which found a strong correlation between the use of Rely tampons and Toxic Shock Syndrome (TSS). By then, TSS, a disease characterized by vomiting, high fever, diarrhea, and a rapid drop in blood pressure resulting in shock, had been blamed as the cause of death for 25 women in 1975. Subsequent deaths brought this number to about 100 by 1984.

Procter and Gamble was initially made aware of evidence linking tampon usage with TSS in June 1980 when it, along with other tampon manufacturers, received the results of a preliminary CDC study. Shortly thereafter, Procter and Gamble conducted its own studies of Rely, and found no significant link between TSS and this particular brand of tampons. Given a week to respond to the September CDC study, Procter and Gamble quickly assembled a previously selected independent panel of health and scientific experts to review the CDC findings. This panel reported that they did not find convincing evidence linking Rely in particular to TSS (as opposed to tampons in general). On the other hand, they reported that they could not refute the claims of the CDC study either.

As a result of this panel's findings, Procter and Gamble immediately discontinued sales of Rely. When its representatives next met with the representatives of the FDA, Procter and Gamble signed the consent agreement calling for the "withdrawal" of Rely from the market. Under this agreement Procter and Gamble attempted to buy back all of the product which was still in the hands of consumers or retailers through a concentrated campaign consisting of 340,000 letters and telegrams sent to retailers, and radio, television, and print advertisements directed at consumers.

According to the consent agreement, Procter and Gamble did not have to declare the product unsafe or defective and in fact they stated they had no evidence that it was. The motivation for reaching this agreement was at least partly the fear of being forced by the FDA into a "product recall" in which they would have to admit the product was unsafe—an admission that would certainly be used in product liability litigation. Procter and Gamble is also particularly sensitive to adverse publicity and this product withdrawal was viewed as a way to cut its losses on this dimension.

Toxic shock syndrome remains a mystery. New occurrences of the disease continue even after the withdrawal of Rely. Scientists believe

---

This case was prepared by Richard Wokutch, Associate Professor of Management, Virginia Polytechnic Institute and State University. Reprinted by permission.

it is caused by a virulent strain of bacteria, and evidence persists that contraction of the disease is linked to certain forms of tampon usage, but the precise connection is unclear. Both men and nonmenstruating women have contracted the disease.

For Procter and Gamble the withdrawal of Rely from the market was estimated to have cost $75 million after taxes (compared with total corporate profits of $640 million in the preceding year). Procter and Gamble was also left with no product in the $1 billion per year menstrual-products market, although they were considering new entries. The company's reputation, which suffered during the controversy, seems to have largely been redeemed. A public opinion survey conducted after the withdrawal found that the public gave Procter and Gamble high marks for its quick action.

A number of legal claims against Procter and Gamble are slowly making their way through the courts. Although accurate figures are hard to come by, several sources estimate that approximately 400 lawsuits were filed against Procter and Gamble for an estimated $4 billion. Other tampon manufacturers have also been sued.

The results of the lawsuits settled to date are even more difficult to assess since many were settled out of court. Most settlements, however, appear to have been for far less than the plaintiffs requested. Still, in the aggregate the financial burden to Procter and Gamble has been substantial.

In 1984 Procter and Gamble reentered the menstrual market with "Always," a line of absorbent sanitary napkins.

Questions

1. When confronted with the September CDC study, what were Procter and Gamble's response options?
2. Was the selected response strategy the most "socially responsible"? Was it the most profitable?
3. If Procter and Gamble had not been faced with the prospect of a government-mandated "product recall" do you think they would have responded any differently? What do you think they should have done in such a circumstance?
4. Discuss the factors you would consider in marketing a product where there is uncertainty about the risks involved.

CASE 4.   *H. B. Fuller in Honduras: Street Children and Substance Abuse*

Normally a marketing manager's dream is to have the name of a product it manufactures become the name for the generic product. Many companies beside Xerox make copiers but nearly everyone refers to all copy machines as *xerox machines*. At H. B. Fuller the marketing manager's dream had become a nightmare. Kativo Chemical Industries, a wholly owned foreign subsidiary of H. B. Fuller, sells a solvent-based adhesive (glue) in several countries in Latin America. The brand name of the glue is Resistol. In 1985 it came to H. B. Fuller's attention that large numbers of street children in the Central American country of Honduras were sniffing glue and that Resistol was among the glues

---

This case is based on a much longer case with the same name authored by Norman E. Bowie and Stefanie Lenway. The full "H. B. Fuller in Honduras: Street Children and Substance Abuse" was the Case award winner in the Columbia University Graduate School of Business Ethics in Business Program.

being abused. Indeed all these children who sniff glue are being referred to as *Resistoleros*.

That the name of a Fuller product should be identified with a social problem was a matter of great concern to the H. B. Fuller company. H. B. Fuller was widely known as a socially responsible corporation. Among its achievements were an enlightened employee relations policy that included giving each employee a day off on his or her birthday and, on the 10th anniversary of employment, bonus vacation time and a substantial check so that employees could travel and see the world. H. B. Fuller contributes 5 percent of its pretax profits to charity and continually wins awards for its responsibility to the environment. A portion of its corporate mission statement reads as follows:

> H. B. Fuller Company is committed to its responsibilities, in order of priority, to its customers, employees and shareholders. H. B. Fuller will conduct business legally and ethically, support the activities of its employees in their communities, and be a responsible corporate citizen.

The issue of the abuse of glue by Honduran street children received attention in the Honduran press as early as 1983. Initial responses to the problem were handled by officials at Kativo. These responses included requests to the press not to use "Resistolero" as a synonym for a street child glue sniffer and attempts to persuade the Honduran legislature not to require the addition of oil of mustard to its glue. Evidence indicated that oil of mustard was a carcinogen and hence was potentially dangerous to employees and consumers. Kativo officials believed that glue sniffing was a social problem and that Kativo was limited in what it could do about the problem. The solution was education.

From 1985 through 1989, officials at H. B. Fuller headquarters in St. Paul, Minnesota, were only dimly aware of the problem. While some of these officials assisted their Kativo subsidiary by providing information on the dangers of oil of mustard, the traditional policy of H. B. Fuller was to give great autonomy to foreign-owned subsidiaries. However, on June 7, 1989, Vice President for Corporate Relations Dick Johnson received a call from a stockholder whose daughter was in the Peace Corps in Honduras. The stockholder's question was how can a company like H. B. Fuller claim to have a social conscience and continue to sell Resistol which is "literally burning out the brains" of children in Latin America. Johnson knew that headquarters should become actively involved in addressing the problem. But given the nature of the problem and H. B. Fuller's policy of local responsibility, what should headquarters do?

Questions

1. To what extent can Honduran street children who obtain an H. B. Fuller product illegitimately be considered stakeholders? If they are stakeholders, how can their interests be represented?
2. What obligations does a company have to solve social problems?
3. Where does the responsibility for solving this problem rest—with the local subsidiary Kativo or with H. B. Fuller headquarters?
4. To what extent should officials at H. B. Fuller headquarters be concerned about potential criticisms that they are meddling in a problem where they don't understand the culture?

Suggested Supplementary Readings

BOWIE, NORMAN. "New Directions in Corporate Responsibility." *Business Horizons* 34 (July-August 1991):56–65.

EPSTEIN, EDWIN, M. "The Corporate Social Policy

Process, Beyond Business Ethics, Corporate Social Responsibility, and Corporate Social Responsiveness." *California Management Review* 29 (Spring 1987):99–114.

DONALDSON, THOMAS. *Corporations and Morality.* Englewood Cliffs, N.J.: Prentice Hall, 1982.

FREDERICK, WILLIAM C. "Toward CSR3: Why Ethical Analysis Is Indispensable and Unavoidable in Corporate Affairs." *California Management Review* 28 (Winter 1986):126–41.

FREEMAN, R. EDWARD. *Strategic Management: A Stakeholder Approach.* Boston: Pitman, 1984.

FREEMAN, R. EDWARD, AND DANIEL R. GILBERT, Jr. *Corporate Strategy and the Search for Ethics.* Englewood Cliffs, N.J.: Prentice Hall, 1988.

FRIEDMAN, MILTON. *Capitalism and Freedom.* Chicago University Press, 1962.

GOODPASTER, KENNETH E., AND JOHN B. MATTHEWS, Jr. "Can a Corporation Have a Conscience?" *Harvard Business Review* 60 (January-February 1982): 132–41.

LEVITT, THEODORE. "The Dangers of Social Responsibility." *Harvard Business Review* 36 (September-October 1958):41–50.

MINTZBERG, HENRY. "The Case for Corporate Social Responsibility." *Journal of Business Strategy* 4 (Fall 1983):3–15.

O'NEIL, ROBERT F. "Corporate Social Responsibility and Business Ethics: A European Perspective." *International Journal of Social Economics* 13:10 (1986):64–76.

O'TOOLE, JAMES. *Vanguard Management.* Garden City, N.Y.: Doubleday, 1985.

PETERS, THOMAS J., AND ROBERT H. WATERMAN, Jr. *In Search of Excellence.* New York: Warner Books, 1982.

RODEWALD, RICHARD A. "The Corporate Social Responsibility Debate: Unanswered Questions About the Consequences of Moral Reform." *American Business Law Journal* 25 (Fall 1987):443–466.

TULEJA, TAD. *Beyond the Bottom Line: How Business Leaders Are Turning Principles into Profits.* New York: Facts on File Publications, 1985.

WALTON, CLARENCE C. *The Moral Manager.* Cambridge, Mass.: Ballinger Publishing Company, 1988.

---*Chapter Three*---

The Regulation of Business

CHAPTER TWO ADDRESSED the general problem of corporate responsibility. This chapter explores the important subject of mechanisms for achieving corporate responsibility. We focus on how corporate performance is to be monitored, by whom may business be legitimately regulated, and how and by whom should the norms of corporate responsibility be enforced. In many respects irresponsible corporations are analogous to individuals who know what is right but who yield to temptation and do what they know is morally wrong. Such individuals are said to suffer from weakness of will. There are two fundamental strategies for overcoming weakness of will. One relies on voluntary internal mechanisms of self-control and the other on coercive or manipulative external constraints on behavior. In business, codes of ethics are an example of voluntary internal mechanisms of self-regulation, whereas government regulation is the most common external constraint. The strengths and weaknesses of self-regulation and government regulation are the central concerns of this chapter.

SELF-REGULATION

In the vast majority of cases business leaders prefer self-regulation to government regulation to overcome weakness of will. When pressed to argue for this preference, many business leaders invoke three arguments on behalf of the greater efficacy of self-regulation. First, businesspersons know their business and their roles and commitments better than any outsiders could. Hence, the duties of business seem best established by a knowledgeable community of practitioners. Second, businesspersons are best situated to bring pressures to bear on their members when they fail to perform their duties or when they abuse the public trust. A professional organization of businesspersons with the proper resources can run education programs about ethics, produce codes to conduct, monitor members' practices, and discipline and punish misconduct. Third, self-regulation is cheaper, more efficient, and more respectful of the autonomy of individual businesspersons and business firms than is government regulation. In other words, government regulation is expensive and coercive.

If this case for self-regulation is sound, it is reasonable to consider the methods and means by which self-regulation can be made to function in practice. Most businesspersons agree that society can expect a high level of ethical conduct on the part of businesspersons only if the practices and reward-and-punishment structures of business reinforce that behavior—inculcating appropriate senses of pride, shame, and responsibility. Many strategies exist for institutionalizing ethics, some of which require changes in the way corporations are managed.

On some occasions all that is needed to ensure moral behavior is a suitable procedure. Substantive requirements are not needed. For example, a number of advertising companies have a routine procedure of making surprise visits to television stations and checking their records as to whether they in fact broadcast commercials that they contracted to broadcast. Gary Pranzo, director of local broadcasting at Young & Rubicam, considers it "our fiduciary responsibility to our employees to do surprise audits."[1] These checks, then, serve a double moral purpose: They keep broadcasters honest, and they fulfill an advertising agency's fiduciary responsibility to its clients. This same monitoring practice was previously performed by the Federal Communications Commission, which stopped investigating stations' commercial logs as part of its massive effort at deregulation.

Other strategies for institutionalizing ethics require changes in the way information is processed. In ascertaining the cause of the 1979 crash of Air New Zealand TE-901 into Mt. Erebus, the Royal Commission investigating the crash identified the essential cause of the crash as the failure of the airline to inform Captain Collins of the change of the coordinates in the aircraft's internal computer system. Further investigation indicated that this communications failure was not simply the oversight of one individual. Rather, the communications gap resulted from general flaws in management procedure. To avoid another disaster, the management needed to improve the means of communication so that pilots were given complete information concerning the coordinates placed into the aircraft's computer. The lesson learned from these cases is that successful self-regulation in business requires persons who are responsible for ethical issues and sound management procedures for effecting ethical results. These procedures include adequate lines of communication, designations of responsibility, and clear opportunities for the ethical ramifications of corporate decisions to be discussed.

Codes of Ethics

Among the most common means to this end of self-regulation is the code of ethics directed at the amelioration of specific professional problems, as, for example, those used by physicians, nurses, bankers, advertising agents, chemical engineers, or lawyers. There are several advantages to such codes: First, they provide guidance in ethically ambiguous situations such as conflict-of-interest dangers. Suppose we adopt Michael Davis's definition of a conflict of interest: A situation when a person is in a relationship with another requiring him or her to exercise judgment in that other's service and when he or she also has an interest interfering with the proper exercise of judgment in that relationship.[2] Since these types of situations are a common occurrence in business, a code of ethics tells an individual what to do in many of the common types of conflict-of-interest situations.

With respect to insider information, IBM gives the following directives to its employees.[3]

> If IBM is about to announce a new product or make a purchasing decision and the news could affect the stock of a competitor or supplier, you must not trade in the stock of those companies.
>
> If IBM is about to make an announcement that could affect the price of its stock, you must not trade in IBM stock.
>
> If IBM is about to build a new facility, you must not invest in land or business near the new site.

And with respect to tips, gifts, and entertainment, IBM says,

> No IBM employee, or any member of his or her immediate family, can accept gratuities or gifts of money from a supplier, customer, or anyone in a business relationship. Nor can they accept a gift or consideration that could be perceived as having been offered because of the business relationship. "Perceived" simply means this: If you read about it in the local newspaper, would you wonder whether the gift just might have had something to do with a business relationship.
>
> No IBM employee can give money or a gift of significant value to a customer, supplier, or anyone if it could reasonably be viewed as being done to gain a business advantage.

The Wilmington *News Journal* treats favors and favoritism in its code of ethics in a similar fashion.[4]

> No employee shall accept gifts of money or items of value. Such things as pens and pocket diaries that appear to be worth no more than a few dollars may be accepted. . . .
>
> Free admissions to any event that is not free to the public are prohibited. If the public pays, the *News Journal* papers pay. . . .

A second advantage of a code of ethics is that it enables a company to do the morally responsible act that it wants to do but, because of competitive pressures, would otherwise be unable to do. In other words, sometimes the competitive nature of business makes it impossible for an individual corporation to do the morally appropriate act and survive. Suppose, for example, that textile company A is polluting a river and that expensive technology is now available to enable company A to reduce pollution. On the basis of the harm analysis provided by Simon, Powers, and Gunnemann (see Chapter Two), it seems that company A ought to install the pollution control device. However, suppose that company A can show that all other textile companies are similarly polluting rivers. If company A installs the pollution control devices and the other textile companies do not, company A's product will rise in price and hence will run the risk of becoming noncompetitive. Eventually company A may be forced out of business. The competitive situation thus makes it unfair and, from an economic perspective, impossible for company A to do the morally appropriate thing. Only a rule that requires all textile companies to install pollution control devices will be fair and effective. It is often maintained that in situations paralleling this textile pollution case, government regulation is the only viable answer.

Kenneth Arrow argues that the textile pollution case can potentially be adequately handled by an industry-wide code of ethics and that at least some evidence exists that industry-wide codes can work. Not all moral problems of personal conflict in society need to be resolved in courts by law or by regulatory agencies. Some are suitably handled by society's general moral codes or even by formal committee decisions. Indeed, if moral codes and practices were not widely efficacious, the courts and the regulatory systems would be overwhelmed.

The two major advantages of corporate codes of ethics are (1) they provide guidance in conflict-of-interest situations and (2) they provide socially responsible corporations the means to do the right thing. There are many other advantages as well. For example, a code can motivate through using peer pressure. A code holds up a generally recognized set of behavioral expectations that must be at least minimally considered in decision making. For example, one could not easily defend one's practices as an accountant if that person regularly violated the Standards of Ethical Conduct for Management Accountants.

Second, codes also provide more stable guides to right or wrong than do human personalities or continual ad hoc decisions. If one takes the notion of weakness of will seriously, it should be apparent that people are not completely objective. People tend to take the short-run point of view. The passions of a situation get in the way of a wise decision. These frailties of human nature require that decisions about ethics generally be a matter of law or rules.

Moreover, codes of ethics really do provide guidance, especially in ethically ambiguous situations. By tying a code of ethics to a job description, appropriate ethical conduct is clarified. Along these lines, empirical research supports the view that a clear set of rules does make a difference as to whether or not an employee will engage in an ethically dubious action. For example, W. Harvey Hagarty and Henry P. Sims, Jr., have done research with graduate students confronted with decision-making opportunities. Their results show that a clear company policy forbidding kickbacks lowers the tendency of the graduate students to permit kickbacks.[5]

In addition, codes of ethics not only guide the behavior of employees but they also control the autocratic power of employers. In theory at least, a business code of ethics can provide an independent ground of appeal when one is urged by an employer or supervisor to commit an unethical act. "I'm sorry, but company policy strictly forbids it" is a gracious and relatively safe way of ending a conversation about a "shady" deal.

Codes of business ethics also help specify the social responsibilities of business itself. One of the problems in business ethics is that no one seems to know what the rules are. As we have seen, most business leaders recognize that the social responsibilities of business must expand and that business executives should be held to higher ethical standards than in the past. However, a blanket ethical demand that business solves all social problems is arbitrary and unrealistic. Hence, business codes of ethics acceptable both to the business community and to the general public would help define what corporate social responsibility involves and bring some order out of the chaos.

Finally, the development of business codes of ethics is clearly in the interest of business itself. There is virtual unanimity in the business community that unethical business practices threaten to bring about increased government regulation of business. For reasons we discuss later, government regulation of business ethics is not viewed as the most desirable form of regulation. When compared with the specter of government regulation, many businesspeople agree that codes of ethics at least deserve a second look.

Codes of good business practice that have these advantages are not new. After all, one of the purposes of the Better Business Bureau is to protect both the consumer and the legitimate business operator from the fly-by-night operator. The Better Business Bureau ensures that business ethics not only is in the interest of the consumer but can also be in the vital interest of the business community. As noted, business activity depends on a high level of trust and confidence. If a firm or entire industry loses public confidence, it will have a difficult time selling its products.

In many cases, an industry-wide code of ethics provides the appropriate device for maintaining public trust. Such codes, when enforced properly, provide a means for ensuring that all who subscribe to the code will behave in the morally appropriate way. In that way the firms would remain competitive with one another and would reap the benefits of morality as well.

Despite the acknowledged advantages of codes of business ethics, such codes are often treated with great skepticism by many businesspeople and some consumers. What are their objections?

Initially, there is a very serious practical objection to industry-wide codes of ethics. Business leaders are reluctant to sit down together to write such codes for fear that they will be in violation of antitrust laws. However, antitrust laws allow discussion and development of industry-wide codes of ethics under government supervision. Since it seems highly likely that some way can and should be found to permit the development of industry-wide codes without violating antitrust laws, the objection is not too troubling.

A second criticism of professional codes of ethics is that they are too broad and amorphous. Consider four of the seventeen standards of the Public Relations Society of America (PRSA):

1. A member has a general duty of fair dealing toward his or her clients or employees, past and present, his or her fellow members, and the general public.
2. A member shall conduct his or her professional life in accord with the public welfare.
3. A member has the affirmative duty of adhering to generally accepted standards of accuracy, truth, and good taste.
4. A member shall not engage in any practice that tends to corrupt the integrity of channels of public communication.[6]

Because it uses terms such as *fair dealing, public welfare, generally accepted standards,* and *corrupt the integrity,* the PRSA code of standards is charged with being too broad and hazy.

However, language is always general and in need of interpretation. Moreover, whenever there is a definition, certain borderline cases generally exist. When is a person bald or middle aged? We used to think that 35 was middle aged. Now we are not so sure. These comments show that some of the criticisms of business codes are usually not criticisms of the codes but the language in the codes. This generality of the criticism provides the clue for mitigating the problem. After all, the institution known as the law is a well-entrenched social institution, and it is an institution that is grounded heavily in language. The same can be said of business practice. Contracts, collective-bargaining agreements, warranties, and the like are all linguistic devices that facilitate the practice of business. If language usage is as broad and amorphous as the critics contend, what accounts for the operational success of law and business?

Actually, language is not so broad and amorphous after all. The terms of a language have what H. L. A. Hart refers to as a "settled core of meaning."[7] Consider the rule that forbids vehicles from entering a public park. Clearly there are some borderline cases—roller skates, baby carriages, and so forth. But there are clear cases as well—automobiles, trucks, and so forth. If one accepts the notion of a "settled core of meaning," then most uses of words are clear enough. It is only at the borderline where controversies concerning application develop. The message for those constructing codes of business ethics seems quite clear. If the code is constructed with the settled core of meaning of the words in mind, ambiguity will be cut to a minimum. If the code of ethics is taken seriously, the choice of words will be taken seriously as well.

Still, ambiguities will remain. Codes will still need interpretation, and hence procedures must be adopted for interpreting what the code means and what it requires. However, interpretation is no more of a problem for a code of business ethics than it is for other uses of language. The law itself, even at the highest level represented by the Constitution, requires a Supreme Court to make a final decisive interpretation. Although frequently the law is the social institution most often appealed to when disagreements concerning the terms of a contract arise, other possibilities exist. The Better Business Bureau has an appeal procedure that can culminate in binding arbitration, a provision used frequently.

The third and perhaps most serious criticism of business codes of ethics is that they cannot be adequately enforced. A code of ethics without adequate enforcement is hardly a code at all. An effective code of ethics must be enforced and must have real penalties attached to it in order for it to bring about conformity. For example, in 1984 the National Association of Securities Dealers (NASD)—a national self-regulatory organization for 5,500 member firms—censured and disciplined for the fifth time the Springfield, Virginia, firm of Voss & Co. for violating the NASD's rules of fair practice. The findings indicated egregious abdications of responsibilities to customers and the pocketing of substantial monies. Fines totaling $4,000 and a five-day suspension of the firm's president were administered as penalties. The NASD noted that the company and its president "have demonstrated a chronic inability and unwillingness to comply with applicable requirements."[8] On the one hand, the NASD is to be commended for unusual vigilance. On the other hand, in light of the four previous violations and the substantial amount of money at stake, the punishment administered seems an unlikely deterrent.

For corporate codes of conduct and corporate social audits to be adequate, codes of conduct must be enforced and the message transmitted that ethics is taken seriously. Philip T. Drotning of Standard Oil of Indiana has put the point this way:

> Several generations of corporate history have demonstrated that any significant corporate activity must be locked into the mainstream of corporate operations or it doesn't get done. Social policies will remain placebos for the tortured executive conscience until they are implemented with the same iron fisted management tools that are routinely employed in other areas of activity to measure performance, secure accountability, and distribute penalties and rewards.

The most serious theoretical challenge to codes of ethics and indeed to most forms of self-regulation is presented by Ian Maitland. Maitland believes that most forms of self-regulation are unable to solve the assurance problem. From Maitland's perspective, Arrow's defense of an industry-wide code of ethics only solves half the problem. If a firm is not to be at a competitive disadvantage by doing the right thing, the firm must be assured that competing firms will also agree to do the right thing and will keep their agreements. An industry-wide code of ethics solves the first problem but not the second. The code provides the agreement but obviously no code can provide the assurance that parties to the agreement will in fact honor it. Although government regulation is one possible answer, Maitland suggests that associations (peak organizations) that are more complex than industry-wide associations should be a societal form of self-regulation.

Values and Responsibility: Individual versus Organizational

An especially difficult problem in regulation occurs when there is disagreement in an organization over whether an organization is behaving morally. The problem is especially acute when professionals within an organization believe that organizational decisions are compromising professional norms. This problem takes on added complexity if a corporate decision ends in disaster and society demands to know who should be held responsible. To what extent should the individuals who were opposed to the decision be held responsible? Many believe that determining the extent of responsibility of those who were opposed depends on how they behaved. Did they keep their opinions to themselves? Should they have gone to a higher authority, refused to sign off, or even resigned and blown the whistle? These issues are addressed in two articles that focus on two notoriously disastrous decisions by U.S. business firms—the decision by Ford regarding the placement of the gas tank in the Ford Pinto and the decision by Morton Thiokol to sign off on the launch of the space shuttle *Challenger*.

Richard T. De George defends the view that engineers are not morally responsible for general management decisions. Their responsibility is limited to bringing the relevant facts to the attention of management. In the Ford Pinto case, the engineers behaved responsibly because they informed management that a $6.65 modification would make the gas tank safer. Of course management received many other suggestions for improving the Pinto—some safety-related, some convenience-related. The task of management is to examine the total package of suggested improvements and their implication for the total cost of the car and finally to decide what improvements should be made and which should not be made so that the cost of the car can be competitive. That decision is a management decision and not an engineering decision. Thus even if the decision not to modify the gas tank in a Ford Pinto was an immoral one, the engineers who worked on the Ford Pinto are not morally responsible for that decision.

But do professionals have more responsibility than just informing management of the risks? In the case of the explosion of the *Challenger,* the senior scientist and other scientists had informed management over and over again of the dangers and probability of failure of the O-rings, especially during a launch in cold temperatures. Although Morton Thiokol appointed a Seal Erosion Task Team to investigate the problem, the team received little organizational support, much to the frustration of Roger Boisjoly and his colleagues. On January 27, 1986, Morton Thiokol's vice-president of engineering recommended against the next day's scheduled launch on the grounds that the predicted low temperature of 18 degrees could compromise the O-rings. NASA went directly to Joe Kilminster, vice-president of Space Booster Programs. At first Kilminster backed his engineers, but after continued pressure he held a caucus among five managers to make a "management decision." The managers overruled the engineers and approved the launch. Boisjoly noted his disapproval in his diary, but no public action was taken by any of the engineers. Should they have done more, and what responsibility, if any, do they bear for the *Challenger* disaster?

Russell J. Boisjoly, Ellen F. Curtis, and Eugene Mellican argue, in their essay included in this book, that there are two targets for assigning responsibility: individuals and organizations. Organizational responsibility is determined by examining organizational processes to see if the organization's rules for decision making were followed. If a decision has bad results, but the organization followed proper procedure, then no individuals within the organization are responsible for the unfortunate results. Although Russell Boisjoly, Curtis, and Mellican decry the notion of organizational responsibility, one must ask what the alternative should be. If the focus is one of individual responsibility, how should it be exercised? Should, contrary to De George, engineers be allowed to veto management decisions? One of the more difficult tasks that faces an organization is permitting a maximum degree of individual authority while avoiding anarchy and paralysis within the organization.

Government Regulation

History. As social and economic systems in European and North American nations have grown more complex, a correlative increase in the scope of government regulation of business (and of all economic activity) has occurred. Sometimes the government intervenes for the purpose of shoring up the economic system itself, whereas at other times intervention is undertaken to support certain socially approved goals. Whatever the exact purpose, government regulation of business is now an enormous undertaking. Because this phenomenon has emerged so rapidly and amid such constant controversy, an historical survey of the setting and reasons for modern regulation of U.S. business will be helpful.

In the nineteenth and early twentieth centuries, an individualist philosophy prevailed in both government and business, according to which the success of business was due largely to individual effort, which the government restricted only at society's economic peril. The proper role of government relative to industry was thus that of encouraging the growth of unregulated business. Action in light of this philosophy led to a situation in which the corporation was privileged. Tariffs intended to prevent foreign competition were erected, corporate taxes were kept at low levels, and the corporation enjoyed an advantaged status under law. Giant corporations quickly began to control the economy of the country. Before the turn of the twentieth century, the 200 largest corporations produced more of the GNP than the next 100,000 largest corporations combined. These monopolies stifled competition and inflated prices. Although their corporate profits rapidly increased, wages were decreasing and the cost of living was soaring. At the same time, these corporations engaged in a number of ethically unacceptable practices, such as lowering product quality without warning, watering down the value of stock, and so on.

In 1887, the Interstate Commerce Act was passed to protect farmers and small businesspersons from monopolistic practices, especially by the railroads. A federal regulatory agency, the Interstate Commerce Commission, was created to monitor the railroads, although it was given no real power to do so, and the act thus had little immediate effect. Only three years later, in 1890, the Sherman Antitrust Act was passed to protect small businesses from a wide variety of monopolistic practices. However, for many years thereafter, the courts continued to favor monopolistic interests, and not until Theodore Roosevelt's administration was a stricter interpretation placed on the Sherman Act. Finally, in 1914, both the Clayton Act and the Federal Trade Commission Act were established to control anticompetitive practices. The basic idea was to free the free enterprise system from monopoly and deceptive practices.

Shortly thereafter, a World War I boom restored confidence in business, and not until the Great Depression was there renewed pressure for further regulation. However, from 1930 until the 1980s, a broad range of federal legislation has been enacted to control those business activities believed to involve unfairness or inefficiencies analogous to those that earlier had resulted from unregulated industry. Thus, unfair advertising, deceptive trade, sluggish competition, powerful anticompetitive mergers, questionable investment practices, waste discharges, discrimination in hiring, and so on, all gradually came under federal regulation. Many state and local government controls were also enacted. Consequently, federal regulation has come to affect virtually every business in the country. There are now approximately 65 major federal agencies whose regulatory activities have a direct impact on business. As both regulation and deregulation have increased, so have the critical responses.

Presumably, everyone would like to see the federal regulatory process achieve vital social ends without obstructing the productive capacity of the marketplace. Sometimes this view is expressed in shorthand by saying that business should be regulated "in the public interest." Yet what is the public interest, and do regulatory agencies now function so that this interest is best served? Virtually no one is satisfied with the current state of regulatory practices in the United States or with much of the deregulation that has occurred. Critics across a wide spectrum of political opinion accuse federal agencies of either too much, too little, or inefficient regulation.

Advantages of Government Regulation

Competition is one of the rules of business practice, and the first instances of government regulation grew out of the unanimously recognized authority of government to interpret and enforce the rules of competition. In its initial phase, government regulation was designed to protect both business and the public from anticompetitive practices. This protection included the regulation of natural monopolies (for example, the utilities or telephone companies). In industries like these it was thought to make no sense to have competing companies. This anticompetitive regulatory task was later expanded to protect the public from unfair competitive practices as well. Government regulation expanded to focus on fraud, deception, and dishonesty. In this latter sphere, the public is perhaps most familiar with the government regulation of deceptive advertising by the Federal Trade Commission.

This type of government regulation—when conducted fairly and efficiently—both ought to be and in fact is supported by the business community. Such government regulation ought to be supported by the business community because it is regulation designed to support the rules of business activity itself. Practices that undermine competition, either through monopoly or deceit, cut away at a central tenet of business practice. From a market perspective, failure to support attempts to control and thwart anticompetitive practices would be self-defeating. The presence of regulatory activities increases investor, consumer, and competitor confidence in the integrity of the markets—and thus seems to work to everyone's advantage.

Theory, in this regard, is supported by practice. Complaints regarding deceptive advertising often are brought to the attention of government regulators by the competitors of the alleged offender. It was competing oil companies that successfully challenged Chevron's STP advertising claims. Similarly, it was competing drug companies that complained to the Federal Trade Commission about the claims of Sterling Drug on behalf of Bayer aspirin. Sterling used a report in the *New England Journal of Medicine,* which received partial financial support from the FTC itself, as "objective" proof for the superiority of Bayer aspirin. The competing companies alleged that the ads were misleading and deceptive. That dispute went all the way to the Supreme Court, which turned down the complaints of the competing drug companies (*F.T.C. v. Sterling Drug*). The Bayer aspirin dispute provides a perfect illustration of business reliance on government regulation and of its use of the judiciary to settle a dispute on a rule of business practice. Such government regulation is clearly in the interest of business.

In recent years a number of major corporations have expressed their fear that federal *deregulation* has produced unfairness in their industries; they want regulation back where controls have been lifted. For example, a number of grain and chemical shippers as well as public utilities want to reinstitute ICC controls of coal shipment rates on the same grounds we saw in the nineteenth century: Monopoly railroads are left free to "gouge" all shippers who must use a single railroad. Similarly, many insurance companies have asked that federal controls be applied to banks that are now competing in the insurance industry on grounds that banks are given an unfair advantage. One of the most interesting industries to watch is the airline industry, where major carriers have begun to collaborate in an effort to avoid crowded scheduling, thus assuming the old role of the now defunct Civil Aeronautics Board. Smaller airlines, which grew up under and generally favor deregulation, have begun to argue that there must be selective government regulation in order to maintain fair competition.

Sometimes unnoticed in the discussion of regulation is the massive *cooperative* interaction between government and industry that requires federal rule making. This cooperation is scarcely unique to the United States. In virtually every nation in the world, governments are intimately engaged in planning, financing, contracting, and otherwise subsidizing major sectors of the economy, often in collaboration with private industry. The rationale is to produce social efficiency, enhance international cooperation and competition, lower unemployment, reduce monopoly, stimulate ailing industries, and avoid wasteful duplicative activities such as research. Sometimes notorious business success stories are actually the result of cooperative planning between a government and private industry. The famous devastation of the U.S. steel industry by the Japanese, for example, came about through a plan of the Japanese government. During World War II the United States created a vast network of new and often efficient businesses because of national need—including steel and aluminum industries and pipeline companies—not to mention public utilities, which are actually privately owned by heavily regulated companies.

Government regulation can also serve another interest of business. In the absence of an effective code of ethics, industry-wide government regulation would enable the individual firm to undertake the action that is desirable from society's point of view without incurring a competitive disadvantage. For example, by setting universal air quality control standards, all firms polluting the air would be required to install scrubbers. In this way, government regulation enables some companies to do the good they believe should be done, but could not otherwise do because the competitive penalties would be too high. In such situations government regulation assists well-intentioned businesses to be the good citizens they want to be.

Yet another advantage of government regulation is that it controls indifferent or maleficent corporations and industries and forces them to adhere to the minimum requirements of morality. Much of the growth of government regulation can be attributed to the fact that society has broadened its notion of corporate social responsibility and therefore the need for governmental control. The public has demanded government regulation as a check on corporate misbehavior or inaction while simultaneously expanding the list of business activities that it finds ethically inappropriate or in need of investigation. Sometimes it is clear that self-regulatory action within an industry is out of the question as the method of regulation. For example, in recent years there have been a number of legislative battles over the regulation of video display terminals for computers, reservation systems, and the like. West Germany has an elaborate set of regulations concerning the manufacture and use of these devices, and legislation supported by various labor unions and women's groups has been introduced in twenty states in the United States to limit exposure to video displays in order to reduce eyestrain, fatigue, backaches, and headaches thought to be caused by daily use of these terminals in the automated office. None of these bills has passed (one passed the legislature in Oregon, but was vetoed by the governor) because the manufacturers of the equipment have been uniformly opposed to any form of regulation other than by local employers. For example, major manufacturers such as AT&T, Hewlett-Packard, IBM, and Tektronix all formed the Coalition for Office Technology to combat the regulatory efforts.[9]

In summary, the expansion of government regulation is the result of at least three factors. First, it results from the universally recognized authority of government to interpret and enforce the rules of business activity. Second, it results from requests from socially enlightened corporations that need government-imposed standards to enable them to take socially desirable actions without incurring serious competitive disadvantages. Third, it results from the demands of the general public that it be protected against a growing list of what are viewed as undesirable corporate practices.

Disadvantages of Government Regulation

Despite the advantages for business of some forms of government regulation, government regulation is often viewed on a scale from distrust to horror. There are several popular reasons why government regulation is opposed. These include:

1. Recognition that government regulation would diminish the power and the prestige of corporate officials
2. Fear that government officials would interfere with incentives and efficiency and hence reduce profit
3. Judgment that government officials do not understand business and hence that its regulations would be unreasonable and unworkable
4. Judgment that government officials are in no position to comment on the ethics of others

5. Judgment that the federal government is already too powerful in a pluralistic society so that it is inappropriate to increase the power of government in this way

6. Judgment that government regulation violates the legitimate freedom and moral rights of employers and stockholders

7. Judgment that inviting government to resolve problems of conflict is confrontational and socially divisive

One of the strongest and most influential opponents of government regulation has been Gary Becker, University Professor of Economics and Chairman of the Economics Department at the University of Chicago. He has presented a utilitarian case against regulation, largely focusing on the role of special-interest groups in a regulatory environment:

> Special-interest groups use political clout to obtain subsidies, favorable regulations, and other government help that enable them to resist making adjustments to adverse economic conditions. . . . Experience in the United States and other countries suggests that workers, management, and other interest groups will manipulate any industrial policy to promote their own interests rather than those of the whole country.[10]

Becker chalks up the failure of the U.S. steel industry less to Japanese ingenuity than to excessive demands in the United States by that industry for quotas and tariffs on imported steel, loan guarantees for steel companies, and government-directed programs to reinvest profits. These programs, he argues, raised prices and made U.S. steel noncompetitive. The major economic disasters in Israel, Russia, and Britain stem, in his judgment, from precisely such well-intentioned but ill-fated policies, which in the end do not even serve the special interests that lobby for them.

Although the seven items listed above and the statement by Becker present an accurate list of widespread objections to government regulation, some objections are either too sweeping—for example, point 4—or self-serving—for example, point 1. Philosophically, some general theoretical framework is needed to serve as the basis of criticism and to answer the question: Which regulations are reasonable and which ones are unreasonable? In 1964, Lon Fuller published his important book *The Morality of Law*, which provides eight criteria for evaluating good law and argues that extreme departures from those eight conditions threaten to undermine the legal system itself. In his article later in this chapter, Norman Bowie adapts Fuller's criteria for the special context of government regulation. Many government regulations fall short under the proposed criterion.

There are also general limitations inherent in the nature of law that limit its effectiveness as a means of regulation. If the only means of ensuring moral conduct were the law, serious social repercussions would result. At best society would be burdened with an expensive enforcement apparatus; at the extreme, society would become either totalitarian or collapse in anarchy. The Internal Revenue Service, for example, admits it would be powerless to prevent widespread cheating on income taxes, and if such cheating occurred the government could no longer use the income tax. In his article, Christopher Stone discusses some of the features of law that limit its effectiveness as a regulatory device.

Most businesspersons have already moved beyond the point of believing that the law is the definitive or sole word in setting standards of corporate ethics. The view "If it's legal, it's O.K." is not the prevailing notion in most corporations. Nonetheless, the first response of the public whenever it is unhappy is to argue for the passage of new laws. If Stone's analysis is correct, a constant attempt to regulate corporate conduct through law is doomed to failure. First, there is the time-lag problem. Laws are passed only after the damage has been done, and often the damage is severe. Some way of preventing the damage in the first place is needed, and we cannot reasonably look to the law for that degree or form of protection.

Stone also points out that government regulation works poorly when there is no consensus concerning what is right or wrong. In a democracy, the temptation is to identify the problem—for example, the degradation of the environment—and then to create a regulatory body with a broad mandate to "fix" the problem. However, the divisions that prevent Congress from drawing up specific regulations soon plague the regulatory agency itself.

Not all criticisms of government regulation are justified, however. A popular criticism of government regulation is that it is paternalistic because it forces people to do things for their own good on the grounds that it knows what is in their best interest better than they do. Some argue that laws requiring the use of seatbelts or requiring motorcyclists to wear helmets are passed on paternalistic grounds. Studies have shown over and over that the vast majority of drivers do not voluntarily wear seatbelts. Other research shows that many workers oppose various safety regulations—the wearing of helmets or safety goggles, for example. In his article, Steve Kelman agrees that paternalistic government regulation is either wrong or subject to criticism. However, he argues that the paternalistic charge is misplaced. His strategy is to show that in some cases the government really may know more than its constituents do, such as when people do not have the information to make individual decisions about the safety of a product. Moreover, as Kelman points out, even if individuals could get the information, obtaining it is often too costly. Sometimes the psychological cost of facing certain problems such as the prospect of illness and death are so high that people would rather have others think about them instead. What appears to be wrongful paternalism may turn out to be advantageous protection.

Government regulation, then, is neither a complete blessing nor a complete curse. Properly formulated, regulations applied in the appropriate situations can help assure proper corporate behavior. However, the complete job of business ethics cannot be done by regulatory action any more than by case law in the courts.

NOTES

1. As quoted in Ronald Alsop, "Efficacy of Global Ad Projects Is Questioned in Firm's Survey," *Wall Street Journal*, September 13, 1984, p. 31.

2. Michael Davis, "Conflicts of Interest," *Business and Professional Ethics Journal* 1 (Summer 1982): 21.

3. IBM Business Conduct Guidelines (internal document), 11–12.

4. "The News Journal's Code of Professionalism and Ethics," *Sunday News Journal,* August 29, 1982, p. H3.

5. W. Harvey Hegarty and Henry P. Sims, Jr., "Some Determinants of Unethical Decision Behavior: An Experiment," *Journal of Applied Psychology* 63(4) (August 1978): 451–457; and W. Harvey Hegarty and Henry P. Sims, Jr., "Organizational Philosophy, Policies and Objectives Related to Unethical Decision Behavior: A Laboratory Experiment," *Journal of Applied Psychology* 64(3) (June 1979): 331–338.

6. Ivan Hill, ed., *The Ethical Basis of Economic Freedom* (Chapel Hill, N.C.: American Viewpoint Inc., 1976), p. 292.

7. H. L. A. Hart, *The Concept of Law* (New York: Oxford University Press, 1961), pp. 124–141.

8. See Bruce Ingersoll, "SEC says NASD Was Too Lenient in Censure of Broker," *Wall Street Journal,* September 21, 1984, p. 36.

9. Henry Weinstein, "The VDT: Typhoid Mary or a Vision of the Future?" *International Herald Tribune,* August 21, 1985, p. 6.

10. Gary Becker, "The Best Industrial Policy Is None at All," *Business Week,* August 5, 1985, p. 14.

Business Codes and Economic Efficiency

Kenneth J. Arrow

This paper makes some observations on the widespread notion that the individual has some responsibility to others in the conduct of his economic affairs. It is held that there are a number of circumstances under which the economic agent should forgo profit or other benefits to himself in order to achieve some social goal, especially to avoid a disservice to other individuals. For the purpose of keeping the discussion within bounds, I shall confine my attention to the obligations that might be imposed on business firms. . . . Is it reasonable to expect that ethical codes will arise or be created? . . . This may seem to be a strange possibility for an economist to raise. But when there is a wide difference in knowledge between the two sides of the market, recognized ethical codes can be, as has already been suggested, a great contribution to economic efficiency. Actually we do have examples of this in our everyday lives, but in very limited areas. The case of medical ethics is the most striking. By its very nature there is a very large difference in knowledge between the buyer and the seller. One is, in fact, buying precisely the service of someone with much more knowledge than you have. To make this relationship a viable one, ethical codes have grown up over the centuries, both to avoid the possibility of exploitation by the physician and to assure the buyer of medical services that he is not being exploited. I am not suggesting that these are universally obeyed, but there is a strong presumption that the doctor

From Kenneth J. Arrow, "Social Responsibility and Economic Efficiency," *Public Policy* 21 (Summer 1973). Copyright © 1973 by the President and Fellows of Harvard College.

is going to perform to a large extent with your welfare in mind. Unnecessary medical expenses or other abuses are perceived as violations of ethics. There is a powerful ethical background against which we make this judgment. Behavior that we would regard as highly reprehensible in a physician is judged less harshly when found among businesspersons. The medical profession is typical of professions in general. All professions involve a situation in which knowledge is unequal on two sides of the market by the very definition of the profession, and therefore there have grown up ethical principles that afford some protection to the client. Notice there is a mutual benefit in this. The fact is that if you had sufficient distrust of a doctor's services, you wouldn't buy them. Therefore the physician wants an ethical code to act as assurance to the buyer, and he certainly wants his competitors to obey this same code, partly because any violation may put him at a disadvantage but more especially because the violation will reflect on him, since the buyer of the medical services may not be able to distinguish one doctor from another. A close look reveals that a great deal of economic life depends for its viability on a certain limited degree of ethical commitment. Purely selfish behavior of individuals is really incompatible with any kind of settled economic life. There is almost invariably some element of trust and confidence. Much business is done on the basis of verbal assurance. It would be too elaborate to try to get written commitments on every possible point. Every contract depends for its observance on a mass of unspecified conditions which suggest that the performance will be carried out in good faith without insistence on sticking literally to its wording. To put the matter in its simplest form, in almost every economic transaction, in any exchange of goods for money, somebody gives up his valuable asset before he gets the other's; either the goods are given before the money or the

money is given before the goods. Moreover there is a general confidence that there won't be any violation of the implicit agreement. Another example in daily life of this kind of ethics is the observance of queue discipline. People line up; there are people who try to break in ahead of you, but there is an ethic which holds that this is bad. It is clearly an ethic which is in everybody's interest to preserve; one waits at the end of the line this time, and one is protected against somebody's coming in ahead of him.

In the context of product safety, efficiency would be greatly enhanced by accepted ethical rules. Sometimes it may be enough to have an ethical compulsion to reveal all the information available and let the buyer choose. This is not necessarily always the best. It can be argued that under some circumstances setting minimum safety standards and simply not putting out products that do not meet them would be desirable and should be felt by the businessperson to be an obligation.

Now I've said that ethical codes are desirable. It doesn't follow from that that they will come about. An ethical code is useful only if it is widely accepted. Its implications for specific behavior must be moderately clear, and above all it must be clearly perceived that the acceptance of these ethical obligations by everybody does involve mutual gain. Ethical codes that lack the latter property are unlikely to be viable. How do such codes develop? They may develop as a consensus out of lengthy public discussion of obligations, discussion which will take place in legislatures, lecture halls, business journals, and other public forums. The codes are communicated by the very process of coming to an agreement. A more formal alternative would be to have some highly prestigious group discuss ethical codes for safety standards. In either case to become and to remain a part of the economic environment, the codes have to be accepted by the significant operating institutions and transmitted from one generation of executives to the next through standard operating procedures, through education in business schools, and through indoctrination of one kind or another. If we seriously expect such codes to develop and to be maintained, we might ask how the agreements develop and above all, how the codes remain stable. After all, an ethical code, however much it may be in the interest of all, is, as we remarked earlier, not in the interest of any one firm. The code may be of value to the running of the system as a whole, it may be of value to all firms if all firms maintain it, and yet it will be to the advantage of any one firm to cheat—in fact the more so, the more other firms are sticking to it. But there are some reasons for thinking that ethical codes can develop and be stable. These codes will not develop completely without institutional support. That is to say, there will be need for focal organizations, such as government agencies, trade associations, and consumer defense groups, or all combined to make the codes explicit, to iterate their doctrine and to make their presence felt. Given that help, I think the emergence of ethical codes on matters such as safety, at least, is possible. One positive factor here is something that is a negative factor in other contexts, namely that our economic organization is to such a large extent composed of large firms. The corporation is no longer a single individual; it is a social organization with internal social ties and internal pressures for acceptability and esteem. The individual members of the corporation are not only parts of the corporation but also members of a larger society whose esteem is desired. Power in a large corporation is necessarily diffused; not many individuals in such organizations feel so thoroughly identified with the corporation that other kinds of social pressures become irrelevant. Furthermore, in a large, complex firm where many people have to participate in any decision, there are likely to be some who are motivated to call attention to violations of the code. This kind of check has been conspicuous in government in recent years. The Pentagon Papers are an outstanding illustration of the fact that within the organization there are those who recognize moral guilt and take occasion to blow the whistle. I expect the same sort of behavior to occur in any large organization when there are well-defined ethical rules whose violation can be observed.

One can still ask if the codes are likely to be stable. Since it may well be possible and profitable for a minority to cheat, will it not be true that the whole system may break down? In fact, however, some of the pressures work in the other direction. It is clearly in the interest of those who are obeying the codes to enforce them, to call attention to violations, to use the ethical and social pressures of the society at large against their less scrupulous rivals. At the same time the value of maintaining the system may well be apparent to all, and no doubt ways will be found to use the assurance of quality generated by the system as a positive asset in attracting consumers and workers.

One must not expect miraculous transformations in human behavior. Ethical codes, if they are to be viable, should be limited in their scope. They are not a universal substitute for the weapons mentioned earlier, the institutions, taxes, regulations, and legal remedies. Further, we should expect the codes to apply in situations where the firm has superior knowledge of the situation. I would not want the firm to act in accordance with some ethical principles in regard to matters of which it has little knowledge. For example, with quality standards which consumers can observe, it may not be desirable that the firm decide for itself, at least on ethical grounds, because it is depriving the consumer of the freedom of choice between high-quality, high-cost and low-quality, low-cost products. It is in areas where someone is typically misinformed or imperfectly informed that ethical codes can contribute to economic efficiency.

The Limits of Business Self-Regulation

Ian Maitland

In a liberal democracy, there are limits to the extent to which socially responsible behavior can be ordered by law. Beyond a certain point, the costs of expanding the apparatus of state control become prohibitive—in terms of abridged liberties, bureaucratic hypertrophy, and sheer inefficiency. This fact probably accounts for the lasting appeal of the concept of self-regulation—the idea that we would be better off if we could rely on the promptings of a corporate "conscience" to regulate corporate behavior instead of the heavy hand of government regulation.

To its advocates, the virtues of self-regulation—or "corporate social responsibility"—seem self-evident. It promises simultaneously to allay business fears of further government encroachment and to restore the public's faith in business. What is more, it asks of business only that it behave in its own enlightened self-interest. While this entails a radical break with the way managers have conceived of their role in the past, it does not make any impossible or self-contradictory demands that an imaginative manager cannot adapt to. In any case, such things as the new awareness of the fragility of the physical environment, the quantum leap in the power of large corporations, and a New American Ideology, all demand no less.

The period from the mid-1950s to the mid-1970s saw a stream of proposals for the moral reconstruction of the corporation. The principal obstacle to self-regulation was diagnosed as managers' single-minded preoccupation with profits maximization. This, in turn, was attributed to intellectual short-comings—managers' insularity, their failure to keep up with changing values, their inability to see their role in a system-wide perspective, and their attachment to an outmoded ideology which defined the public interest as the unintended outcome of the pursuit of selfish interests. Also implicated were the organizational structure and culture of the modern corporation which supposedly embodied and perpetuated this orientation to profit. The advocates of self-regulation saw their task as being the proselytizing and scolding of managers into a broader definition of their role and the drawing up of blueprints for the socially responsible corporation.

This most recent wave of enthusiasm for self-regulation has largely receded, leaving behind it few enduring achievements. By and large, the exhortations appear to have fallen on deaf ears, or at best to have had only a marginal impact on corporate conduct. The primacy of profit maximization remains unchallenged and we continue to rely—and will do so for the foreseeable future—on legal compulsion administered by the state to regulate the undesirable consequences of economic activity.

If the marriage between the corporation and self-regulation was made in heaven, why

From Ian Maitland, "The Limits of Business Self-Regulation," *California Management Review* 27:3 (1985), © 1985 by the Regents of the University of California. By permission of the Regents.

has it not been consummated? The failure of self-regulation to live up to its promise is attributable to factors that have, for the most part, been overlooked by its advocates. In their attempts to make over managers' value systems and restructure the modern corporation, they have largely neglected the very real limits on managers' discretion that result from the operation of a market economy. As a consequence of these limits, managers are largely *unable* to consider their firms' impact on society or to subordinate profit-maximization to social objectives, no matter how well-intentioned they are.

A GAME THEORETIC ANALYSIS OF SELF-REGULATION

The crux of this argument is the recognition that an individual firm's interests as a competitor in the marketplace often diverge from its interests as a part of the wider society (or, for that matter, as a part of the business community). In this latter role, the firm is likely to welcome a cleaner environment, but as a competitor in the marketplace it has an interest in minimizing its own pollution abatement costs. It may philosophically favor a free market, but it will probably lobby in favor of protection for itself. This observation is a commonplace one, but its implications are rarely fully explored.

The firm's interests as part of a broader group typically take the form of collective or public goods. Using a rational choice model of behavior, Mancur Olson has demonstrated that it is not in the interest of a group member (let us say, the firm) to contribute to the costs of providing such goods.[1] Public goods (e.g., a cleaner environment or the free market) are goods that are available to all firms irrespective of whether or not they have contributed to their upkeep or refrained from abusing them. Since their availability is not contingent

on a firm having contributed, each firm has a rational incentive to free-ride, i.e., to leave the costs of providing them to other firms. However, if each firm succumbs to this temptation, as it must if it acts in its own rational self-interest, then the public good will not be provided at all. Thus, even when they are in agreement, "rational, self-interested individuals will not act to achieve their common or group interests."[2] In a rational world, Olson concludes, "it is certain that a collective good will *not* be provided unless there is coercion or some outside inducement."[3]

The typical objectives of business self-regulation and responsible corporate behavior—such as a cleaner environment—are public goods. Olson's theory therefore provides a basis for explaining why business self-regulation appears so hard to achieve.

Russell Hardin has pointed out that the logic underlying Olson's theory of collective action is identical to that of an n-person prisoner's dilemma (PD).[4] The strategy of not contributing toward the cost of a public good dominates the strategy of paying for it, in the sense that no matter what other firms do, any particular firm will be better off if it does not contribute.

. . . Ford Runge (following A.K. Sen) has argued that what appears to be a prisoner's dilemma proves, on closer inspection, to be an "assurance problem" (AP).[5] According to this theory, the group member (i.e., firm) does not withhold its contribution to a public good based on a rational calculation of the costs and benefits involved (as with the PD) but rather does so because it is unable to obtain the necessary assurance that other firms will contribute their fair share. In other words, the AP substitutes the more lenient assumption that firms prefer equal or fair shares for the PD's assumption that they invariably try to maximize their individual net gain. Under the AP, we can expect firms to regulate their own behavior in some larger interest so long as they are confident that other firms are doing the same.

But in a market economy, where decision making is highly dispersed, the prediction of other firms' behavior becomes problematic. As a consequence, no individual firm can be sure that it is not placing itself at a competitive disadvantage by unwittingly interpreting its own obligations more strictly than its competitors do theirs. In these circumstances, all firms are likely to undertake less self-regulation than they would in principle be willing (indeed, eager) to accept.

In spite of their differences, both the PD and the AP involve problems of collective action. In the case of the PD, the problem is that it is always in the rational interest of each firm to put its own individual interests ahead of its collective interests. In the case of the AP, the problem is that of coordinating firms' expectations regarding fair shares.

The sub-optimal supply of business self-regulation can be explained largely in terms of the barriers to collective action by firms. There are three levels of self-regulation: the firm level (corporate social responsibility); the industry level (industry self-regulation); and the level of the economy (business-wide self-regulation). It is only at the third level that the necessary collective action is likely to be of a socially benign variety.

THREE LEVELS OF SELF-REGULATION

Corporate Social Responsibility. Contemporary advocates of corporate social responsibility acknowledge the difficulties of implementing it, but they go on to proclaim its inevitability anyway. In their view, it has to work because nothing else will; at best, the law elicits grudging and literal compliance with certain minimal standards when what is needed is corporations' spontaneous and whole-hearted identification with the *goals* of

the law.[6] As Christopher Stone says, there are clear advantages to "encouraging people to act in socially responsible ways because they believe it the 'right thing' to do, rather than because (and thus, perhaps, only to the extent that) they are ordered to do so."[7]

Advocates of social responsibility have offered a number of prescriptions for curing firms' fixation on profit maximization. The weakness of these proposals lies in their assumption that social responsibility can be produced by manipulating the corporation. They overlook the extent to which the firm's behavior is a function of market imperatives rather than of managers' values or corporate structure. . . .

This point is . . . illustrated by cases where competitive pressures have prevented firms from acting responsibly even where it would be in their economic interest to do so. Robert Leone has described how aerosol spray manufacturers were reluctant to abandon the use of fluorocarbon propellants (which were suspected of depleting the ozone layer in the stratosphere) even though the alternative technology was cheaper. The problem was that "any individual company that voluntarily abandoned the use of such propellants ran the risk of a sizeable loss of market share as long as competitors still offered aerosol versions of their products [which the public values for their convenience]."[8] In situations of this kind it is not unusual for responsible firms, aware of their own helplessness, to solicit regulation in order to prevent themselves being taken advantage of by competitors who do not share their scruples about despoiling the environment or injuring the industry's reputation. Thus aerosol manufacturers did not oppose the ban on fluorocarbons in spite of the tenuous scientific evidence of their dangers. Similarly, following the Tylenol poisonings, the pharmaceutical industry sought and obtained from the FDA a uniform national rule on tamper-resistant packaging, because no individual firm had wanted to unilaterally incur the expense of such packaging.[9] The list of examples is endless.

In a market economy, firms are usually *unable* to act in their own collective interests because "responsible" conduct risks placing the firms that practice it at a competitive disadvantage unless other firms follow suit. Where there is no well-defined standard that enjoys general acceptance, it will take some sort of tacit or overt coordination by firms to supply one. Even if that coordination survives the attentions of the Antitrust Division and the FTC, compliance will still be problematic because of the free-rider problem. Arrow has pointed out that a "code [of behavior] may be of value to . . . all firms if all firms maintain it, and yet it will be to the advantage of any one firm to cheat—in fact the more so, the more other firms are sticking to it."[10] We are therefore faced with the paradox that the voluntary compliance of the majority of firms may depend on the coercive imposition of the code of behavior on the minority of free riders. Thus, although it is fashionable to view voluntarism and coercion as opposites—and to prefer the former for being more humane and, ultimately, effective—they are more properly seen as interdependent.[11]

Industry Self-Regulation. If responsible corporate conduct must ultimately be backed by coercion, there remains the question of who is to administer the coercion. Is self-regulation by a trade association or other industry body a practical alternative to government regulation? The classic solution to the public goods dilemma is "mutual coercion, mutually agreed upon."[12] The possibility of "permitting businesses to coerce themselves" has been raised by Thomas Schelling who adds that such an approach "could appeal to firms which are prepared to incur costs but only on condition that their competitors do also."[13]

The record of industry self-regulation in the United States suggests that it does indeed commonly arise in response to the public goods problem. David A. Garvin explains the development of self-regulation in the advertising industry in this way.[14] Michael Porter has noted that self-regulation may be of particular importance to an emerging industry which is trying to secure consumer acceptance of its products. At this stage of its life cycle, an industry's reputation could be irretrievably injured by the actions of a single producer.[15] Thus the intense self-regulation in the microwave industry is understandable in terms of the industry's need to "overcome the inherent suspicion with which many people view 'new' technology like microwave ovens."[16] Nevertheless, industry self-regulation remains the exception in the United States. This is so because it is a two-edged sword: the powers to prevent trade abuses are the same powers that would be needed to restrain trade.

Because of the potential anti-competitive implications of industry self-regulation, its scope has been strictly limited. Anti-trust laws have significantly circumscribed the powers of trade associations. Legal decisions have proscribed industry-wide attempts to eliminate inferior products or impose ethical codes of conduct. Major oil firms were frustrated by the anti-trust statutes when they tried to establish an information system to rate the quality of oil tankers in an attempt to reduce the incidence of oil spills from substandard vessels.[17] Airlines have had to petition the Civil Aeronautics Board for antitrust immunity so that they could discuss ways of coordinating their schedules in order to reduce peak-hour overcrowding at major airports.[18]

In short, industry or trade associations appear to hold out little promise of being transformed into vehicles for industry self-regulation. The fear is too entrenched that industry self-regulation, however plausible its initial rationale, will eventually degenerate into industry protectionism.

Business Self-Regulation. If self-regulation at the level of the individual firm is of limited usefulness because of the free-rider problem, and if industry self-regulation is ruled out by anti-trust considerations, we are left with self-regulation on a business-wide basis, presumably administered by a confederation or peak organization. An "encompassing" business organization of this sort would be less vulnerable to the anti-trust objections that can be levelled at industry associations. This is so because the diversity of its membership would inhibit such an organization from aligning itself with the sectional interests of particular firms or industries. Because it would embrace, for example, both producers and consumers of steel, it would be unable to support policies specifically favoring the steel industry (such as a cartel or tariffs) without antagonizing other parts of its membership that would be injured by such policies. A business peak organization would thus be constrained to adopt a pro-competitive posture.[19]

How might a peak organization contribute to resolving the assurance problem and the prisoner's dilemma? In the case of the AP, we saw that the principal impediment to cooperation is the difficulty of predicting others' behavior—without which coordination is impossible. By defining a code of responsible corporate conduct—and/or making authoritative rulings in particular cases—a peak organization might substantially remove this difficulty. In particular, if it is equipped to *monitor* compliance with the code, it could provide cooperating firms with the necessary assurance that they were not shouldering an unfair burden.

The point here is not that a peak organization would necessarily be more competent to make ethical judgments or that its code would

be ethically superior; it is that the code would be a *common* one that would enable firms to coordinate their behavior. As we have seen, where there is a multiplicity of standards, there is effectively no standard at all, because no firm can be confident that its competitors are playing by the same rules.

A common external code would also help defuse two contentious issues in top management's relations with the firm's stockholders. First managers would be at least partly relieved of the task of making subjective (and often thankless) judgments about the firm's obligations to various stakeholders—a task for which they are generally not equipped by training, by aptitude, or by inclination. Second, such a code would permit them to heed society's demands that the firm behave responsibly while at the same time protecting them from the charge that their generosity at the stockholders' expense was jeopardizing the firm's competitive position.[20]

So far we have assumed that each firm *wants* to cooperate (i.e., to contribute to the realization of the public good, in this case by acting responsibly) provided other firms do the same. As long as there is some means of coordinating their behavior, then firms can be counted on to cooperate. What happens if we allow for the likelihood that, while most firms may be disposed to comply with the code, some number of opportunistic firms will choose to defect?

A code of conduct—even if only morally binding—can be expected to exert a powerful constraining influence on the behavior of would-be defectors. Such a code would embody "good practice" and so would serve as a standard against which corporate behavior could be judged in individual cases. Consequently, firms which violated the code would be isolated and the spotlight of public indignation would be turned on them. In the cases where moral suasion failed, the code would still offer certain advantages (at least from business's standpoint). First, an adverse ruling by the peak organization would serve to distance the business community as a whole from the actions of a deviant firm and so would counter the impression that business was winking at corporate abuses.[21] Second, the standards defined by the peak organization might become the basis for subsequent legislation or regulatory rulemaking. By setting the agenda in this fashion, the peak organization might forestall more extreme or onerous proposals.

However, the defection of even a handful of firms (if it involved repeated or gross violation of the code) would undermine the social contract on which the consent of the majority was based. Their continued compliance would likely be conditional on the code being effectively policed. Therefore, it seems inconceivable that business self-regulation could be based on moral suasion alone. . . .

Thus, if we modify the AP to reflect the real-world probability that some number of opportunistic firms will disregard the code, the case for investing the peak organization with some powers of compulsion becomes unanswerable. The case is stronger still if we accept the axiom of the PD that firms will invariably defect when it is in their narrow self-interest to do so. Some form of sovereign to enforce the terms of the social contract then becomes indispensable. . . .

THE CONSEQUENCES OF PEAK ORGANIZATION

Peak (or "encompassing") organizations are not merely larger special interest organizations. By virtue of the breadth and heterogeneity of their membership, they are transformed into a qualitatively different phenomenon. Indeed, peak organizations are likely to exert pressure on the behavior of their members in the direction of the public interest.

In the interests of its own stability, any organization must resist efforts by parts of its membership to obtain private benefits at the expense of other parts. It follows that the more inclusive or encompassing the organization, the larger the fraction of society it represents, and so the higher the probability that it will oppose self-serving behavior (by sections of its membership) that inflicts external costs on the rest of society. . . .

The officers of business peak organizations in Germany, Japan, and Sweden have a quasi-public conception of their role that is far removed from the American interest group model. According to Andrew Shonfield, Germany's two business *Spitzenverbände* "have typically seen themselves as performing an important public role, as guardians of the long-term interests of the nation's industries."[22] The same finding is reported by an American scholar who evidently has difficulty in taking at face value the claims made by leaders of the BDI (Confederation of German Industry): "To avoid giving an impression that it is an interest group with base, selfish and narrow aims, the BDI constantly identifies its own goals with those of the entire nation."[23] Finally, David Bresnick recently studied the role of the national confederation of employers and trade unions of six countries in the formation and implementation of youth employment policies. In Germany, these policies were largely made and administered by the confederations themselves. In Bresnick's words, "The system in Germany has evolved with minimal government regulation and maximum protection of the interests of the young, while promoting the interests of the corporations, trade unions and the society in general. It has reduced the government role to one of occasional intervenor. It has taken the government out of the business of tax collector and achieved a degree of social compliance that is extraordinary."[24]

A similar account is given by Ezra Vogel of

the role of the Japanese business peak organization, *Keidanren*.[25] Keidanren concentrates on issues of interest to the business community as a whole and "cannot be partial to any single group or any industrial sector." Vogel reports that Japanese business leaders are surprised at "the extent to which American businessmen thought only of their own company and were unprepared to consider business problems from a broader perspective." In Japan, this "higher level of aggregation of interests within the business community tends to ensure that the highest level politicians also think in comparably broad terms."[26] . . .

While the data on . . . German and Japanese peak organizations are too unsystematic to constitute a strict test concerning the consequences of peak organizations, they do shed a revealing light on the role such an organization might play in the U.S. In particular, in administering a system of self-regulation, a peak organization would be in a position to take into account a broader range of interests than is catered for by our present structures of interest representation. Also, a peak organization might promote more harmonious business-government relations without entailing the cooptation or capture of either one by the other.

PROSPECTS

What are the prospects of [a] system of business self-regulation administered by a peak organization taking root in the U.S.? What incentives would an American peak organization be able to rely on to secure firms' compliance with its standards and rulings? We have seen that, by itself, recognition of the mutuality of gains to be had from a peak organization cannot guarantee such compliance. In order to overcome the free-rider problem, the would-be peak organization must be able to offer firms private benefits or "selective in-

centives" that are unavailable outside the organization but that are sufficiently attractive to induce firms to comply.[27]

Students of organizations have identified an array of incentives—both positive and negative—that have been used to attract and hold members. These include: selective access to information (e.g., about government actions, technical developments, and commercial practices) under the organization's control; regulation of jurisdictional disputes between members; predatory price-cutting; boycotts; withdrawal of credit; public disparagement; fines; social status; and conviviality. . . . Finally, purposive incentives—"intangible rewards that derive from the sense of satisfaction of having contributed to the attainment of a worthwhile cause"—have provided at least a transient basis for organization. . . .

The difficulties encountered by trade associations that try to influence their members' behavior are compounded in the case of a would-be peak organization. A peak organization has access to fewer selective benefits with which to maintain members' allegiance, and its goals are even further removed from the immediate concerns of most firms. Moreover, these goals tend to be public goods (e.g., maintaining the private enterprise system or avoiding higher taxes). Wilson notes that "no single businessman has an incentive to contribute to the attainment of what all would receive if the organized political efforts are successful." In these circumstances, "the creation and maintenance of an association such as the [U.S.] Chamber, which seeks to represent all business in general and no business in particular has been a considerable achievement."[28]

The Chamber, of course, seeks only to speak for business's collective interests. It is not difficult to imagine how much more precarious its existence would be if it also tried to set and enforce standards of conduct. It follows that if trade associations have generally been ineffective except when their powers have been underwritten by the government, a peak organization is *a fortiori* likely to be dependent on government support. And, in fact, in Western Europe, it appears that "many of the peak associations . . . reached their hegemonic status with major contributions from the more or less official recognition of key government agencies."[29]

What form would such public support have to take in the U.S.? It might involve waiving anti-trust laws in the case of the peak organization, e.g., by permitting it to punish free-riding behavior by imposing fines or administering boycotts. Government might grant it certain prerogatives—e.g., privileged access to key policy deliberations or agency rulemaking, which it might in turn use to obtain leverage over recalcitrant firms. The government might require—as in Japan[30]—that every firm be a registered member of the peak organization. All these actions would serve to strengthen the peak organization vis-á-vis its members.

However, the chances are slight that actions of this kind could be taken in the U.S. In the first place, as Salisbury says, "American political culture is so rooted in individualist assumptions that [interest] groups have no integral place."[31] In contrast with Europe, associations have not been officially incorporated into the process of policy formation; bureaucrats in the U.S. deal directly with constituent units (individual firms, hospitals, universities, etc.) not with associations.[32] Given the dubious legitimacy of interest organizations in general, it seems improbable that semi-official status or privileged access would be granted to a peak organization.

A second obstacle is the structure of American government. The fragmentation of power in the American system—federalism, separation of powers, legislators nominated and elected from single-member districts—has created multiple points of access for inter-

ests that want to influence the policy process. Wilson has persuasively argued that a country's interest group structure is largely a reflection of its political structure. Thus a centralized, executive-led government is likely to generate strong national interest associations and, conversely, "the greater decentralization and dispersion of political authority in the United States helps explain the greater variety of politically active American voluntary associations."[33] In the American context, then, it is virtually inconceivable that a peak organization could secure a monopolistic or privileged role in public policymaking in even a few key areas; but without superior access of this sort it is deprived of one of the few resources available to influence its members' behavior. . . .

CONCLUSION

. . . This article has examined the ways it might be possible for firms to coordinate their behavior (both in their own larger interests and the public interest) while at the same time minimizing the risk that this coordination would be exploited for anti-social purposes. Such a benign outcome could be obtained by permitting collective action to be administered by a business-wide peak organization. At this level of coordination, a competitive market economy could coexist with effective self-regulation. However, the United States—given its distinctive political institutions—is not likely to provide a congenial soil for such an organization to take root.

NOTES

1. Mancur Olson, *The Logic of Collective Action* (Cambridge, MA: Harvard University Press, 1965).
2. Ibid., p. 2.

3. Ibid., p. 44.

4. Russell Hardin, "Collective Action as an Agreeable n-Prisoner's Dilemma," *Behavioral Science*, vol. 16 (1971), pp. 472–79.

5. C. Ford Runge, "Institutions and the Free Rider: The Assurance Problem in Collective Action," *Journal of Politics*, vol. 46 (1984), pp. 154–81.

6. Cf. Henry Mintzberg, "The Case for Corporate Social Responsibility," *Journal of Business Strategy*, vol. 14 (1983), pp. 3–15.

7. Christopher Stone, *Where the Law Ends* (New York, NY: Harper Torchbooks, 1975), p. 112.

8. Robert A. Leone, "Competition and the Regulatory Boom," in Dorothy Tella, ed., *Government Regulation of Business: Its Growth, Impact, and Future* (Washington, D.C.: Chamber of Commerce of the United States, 1979), p. 34.

9. Susan Bartlett Foote, "Corporate Responsibility in a Changing Legal Environment," *California Management Review*, vol. 26 (1984), pp. 217–28.

10. Kenneth J. Arrow, "Social Responsibility and Economic Efficiency," *Public Policy*, vol. 21 (1973), p. 315.

11. See Thomas Schelling on "the false dichotomy of voluntarism and coercion," in "Command and Control," in James W. McKie, ed., *Social Responsibility and the Business Predicament* (Washington, D.C.: Brookings, 1974), p. 103.

12. The phrase is from Garrett Hardin's "The Tragedy of the Commons," *Science*, vol. 162 (1968), p. 1247.

13. Schelling, op. cit., p. 103.

14. David Garvin, "Can Industry Self-Regulation Work?" *California Management Review*, vol. 25 (1983), p. 42.

15. Michael Porter, *Competitive Strategy* (New York, NY: Free Press, 1980), p. 230.

16. Thomas P. Grumbly, "Self-Regulation: Private Vice and Public Virtue Revisited," in Eugene Bardach and Robert Kagan, eds., *Social Regulation: Strategies for Reform* (San Francisco, CA: Institute for Contemporary Studies, 1982), p. 97.

17. Garvin, op. cit., pp. 155, 156.

18. Christopher Conte, "Transport Agency's Dole Vows to Restrict Traffic at 6 Busy Airports if Carriers Don't," *Wall Street Journal*, August 16, 1984, p. 10.

19. Mancur Olson, *The Rise and Decline of Nations* (New Haven, CT: Yale University Press, 1982), pp. 47–48.

20. These objections lie at the heart of the complaint that the doctrine of corporate social responsibility provides no operational guidelines to assist managers in making responsible choices. The most sophisticated (but, I think, ultimately unsuccessful) attempt to supply an objective, external standard (located in what they call the public policy process) is Lee Preston and James Post, *Private Management and Public Policy* (Englewood Cliffs, NJ: Prentice-Hall, 1975).

21. See on this point the remarks of Walter A. Haas, Jr., of Levi Strauss quoted in Leonard Silk and David Vogel, *Ethics and Profits* (New York, NY: Simon & Schuster, 1976), pp. 25–27.

22. Andrew Shonfield, *Modern Capitalism* (New York and London: Oxford University Press, 1965), p. 245.

23. Gerard Baunthal, *The Federation of German Industries in Politics* (Ithaca, NY: Cornell University Press, 1965), pp. 56–57.

24. David Bresnick, "The Youth Employment Policy Dance: Interest Groups in the Formulation and Implementation of Public Policy," paper presented at the American Political Science Association meetings in Denver, September 2–5, 1982, p. 33.

25. Ezra Vogel, *Japan as Number 1* (New York, NY: Harper Colophon, 1979), chapter 5.

26. Ibid.

27. This is, of course, the essence of the argument in Olson's *Logic*, op. cit. This section draws heavily on James Q. Wilson, *Political Organizations*, op. cit.; Robert H. Salisbury, "Why No Corporatism in America?," in Philippe Schmitter and Gerhard Lehmbruch, *Trends Toward Corporatist Intermediation* (Beverly Hills: Sage, 1979); and Philippe Schmitter and Donald Brand, "Organizing Capitalists in the United States: The Advantages and Disadvantages of Exceptionalism," presented at a workshop at the International Institute of Management, Berlin, November 14–16, 1979.

28. James Q. Wilson, *Political Organizations* (New York, NY: Basic Books, 1973), pp. 153, 161.

29. Salisbury, op. cit., p. 215. See also Wilson, op. cit., p. 82.

30. Vogel, *Japan as Number 1*, op. cit., p. 112.

31. Salisbury, op. cit. p. 222.

32. Schmitter and Brand, op. cit., p. 71.

33. Wilson, op. cit., p. 83; see generally chapter 5.

Ethical Responsibilities of Engineers in Large Organizations: The Pinto Case

Richard T. De George

The myth that ethics has no place in engineering has been attacked, and at least in some corners of the engineering profession has been put to rest.[1] Another myth, however, is emerging to take its place—the myth of the engineer as moral hero. A litany of engineering saints is slowly taking form. The saints of the field are whistle blowers, especially those who have sacrificed all for their moral convictions. The zeal of some preachers, however, has gone too far, piling moral responsibility upon moral responsibility on the shoulders of the engineer. This emphasis, I believe, is misplaced. Though engineers are members of a profession that holds public safety paramount,[2] we cannot reasonably expect engineers to be willing to sacrifice their jobs each day for principle and to have a whistle ever by their sides ready to blow if their firm strays from what they perceive to be the morally right course of action. If this is too much to ask, however, what then is the actual ethical responsibility of engineers in a large organization?

I shall approach this question through a discussion of what has become known as the Pinto case, i.e., the trial that took place in Winamac, Indiana, and that was decided by a jury on March 16, 1980.

In August 1978 near Goshen, Indiana, three girls died of burns in a 1973 Pinto that was rammed in traffic by a van. The rear-end collapsed "like an accordian,"[3] and the gas tank erupted in flames. It was not the first such accident with the Pinto. The Pinto was introduced in 1971 and its gas tank housing was not changed until the 1977 model. Between 1971 and 1978 about fifty suits were brought against Ford in connection with rear-end accidents in the Pinto.

What made the Winamac case different from the fifty others was the fact that the State prosecutor charged Ford with three (originally four, but one was dropped) counts of reckless homicide, a *criminal* offense, under a 1977 Indiana law that made it possible to bring such criminal charges against a corporation. The penalty, if found guilty, was a maximum fine of $10,000 for each count, for a total of $30,000. The case was closely watched, since it was the first time in recent history that a corporation was charged with this criminal offense. Ford spent almost a million dollars in its defense.

With the advantage of hindsight I believe the case raised the right issue at the wrong time.

The prosecution had to show that Ford was reckless in placing the gas tank where and how it did. In order to show this the prosecu-

---

From Richard T. De George, "Ethical Responsibilities of Engineers in Large Organizations: The Pinto Case," *Business and Professional Ethics Journal* 1 (Fall 1981).

tion had to prove that Ford consciously disregarded harm it might cause and the disregard, according to the statutory definition of "reckless," had to involve "substantial deviation from acceptable standards of conduct."[4]

The prosecution produced seven witnesses who testified that the Pinto was moving at speeds judged to be between 15 and 35 mph when it was hit. Harly Copp, once a high-ranking Ford engineer, claimed that the Pinto did not have a balanced design and that for cost reasons the gas tank could withstand only a 20 mph impact without leaking and exploding. The prosecutor, Michael Cosentino, tried to introduce evidence that Ford knew the defects of the gas tank, that its executives knew that a $6.65 part would have made the car considerably safer, and that they decided against the change in order to increase their profits.

Federal safety standards for gas tanks were not introduced until 1977. Once introduced, the National Highway Traffic Safety Administration (NHTSA) claimed a safety defect existed in the gas tanks of Pintos produced from 1971 to 1976. It ordered that Ford recall 1.9 million Pintos. Ford contested the order. Then, without ever admitting that the fuel tank was unsafe, it "voluntarily" ordered a recall. It claimed the recall was not for safety but for "reputational" reasons.[5] Agreeing to a recall in June, its first proposed modifications failed the safety standard tests, and it added a second protective shield to meet safety standards. It did not send out recall notices until August 22. The accident in question took place on August 10. The prosecutor claimed that Ford knew its fuel tank was dangerous as early as 1971 and that it did not make any changes until the 1977 model. It also knew in June of 1978 that its fuel tank did not meet federal safety standards; yet it did nothing to warn owners of this fact. Hence, the prosecution contended, Ford was guilty of reckless homicide.

The defense was led by James F. Neal who had achieved national prominence in the Watergate hearings. He produced testimony from two witnesses who were crucial to the case. They were hospital attendants who had spoken with the driver of the Pinto at the hospital before she died. They claimed she had stated that she had just had her car filled with gas. She had been in a hurry and had left the gas station without replacing the cap on her gas tank. It fell off the top of her car as she drove down the highway. She noticed this and stopped to turn around to pick it up. While stopped, her car was hit by the van. The testimony indicated that the car was stopped. If the car was hit by a van going 50 mph, then the rupture of the gas tank was to be expected. If the cap was off the fuel tank, leakage would be more than otherwise. No small vehicle was made to withstand such impact. Hence, Ford claimed, there was no recklessness involved. Neal went on to produce films of tests that indicated that the amount of damage the Pinto suffered meant that the impact must have been caused by the van's going at least 50 mph. He further argued that the Pinto gas tank was at least as safe as the gas tanks on the 1973 American Motors Gremlin, the Chevrolet Vega, the Dodge Colt, and the Toyota Corolla, all of which suffered comparable damage when hit from the rear at 50 mph. Since no federal safety standards were in effect in 1973, Ford was not reckless if its safety standards were comparable to those of similar cars made by competitors; that standard represented the state of the art at that time, and it would be inappropriate to apply 1977 standards to a 1973 car.[6]

The jury deliberated for four days and finally came up with a verdict of not guilty. When the verdict was announced at a meeting of the Ford Board of Directors then taking place, the members broke out in a cheer.[7]

These are the facts of the case. I do not wish to second-guess the jury. Based on my reading of the case, I think they arrived at a proper decision, given the evidence. Nor do I wish to comment adversely on the judge's ruling that prevented the prosecution from introducing about 40% of his case because the evidence referred to 1971 and 1972 models of the Pinto and not the 1973 model.[8]

The issue of Ford's being guilty of acting recklessly can, I think, be made plausible, as I shall indicate shortly. But the successful strategy argued by the defense in this case hinged on the Pinto in question being hit by a van at 50 mph. At that speed, the defense successfully argued, the gas tank of any subcompact would rupture. Hence that accident did not show that the Pinto was less safe than other subcompacts or that Ford acted recklessly. To show that would require an accident that took place at no more than 20 mph.

The contents of the Ford documents that Prosecutor Cosentino was not allowed to present in court were published in the *Chicago Tribune* on October 13, 1979. If they are accurate, they tend to show grounds for the charge of recklessness.

Ford had produced a safe gas tank mounted over the rear axle in its 1969 Capri in Europe. It tested that tank in the Capri. In its over-the-axle position, it withstood impacts of up to 30 mph. Mounted behind the axle, it was punctured by projecting bolts when hit from the rear at 20 mph. A $6.65 part would help make the tank safer. In its 1971 Pinto, Ford chose to place the gas tank behind the rear axle without the extra part. A Ford memo indicates that in this position the Pinto has more trunk space, and that production costs would be less than in the over-the-axle position. These considerations won out.[9]

The Pinto was first tested it seems in 1971, after the 1971 model was produced, for rear-end crash tolerance. It was found that the tank ruptured when hit from the rear at 20 mph. This should have been no surprise, since the Capri tank in that position had rup-

tured at 20 mph. A memo recommends that rather than making any changes Ford should wait until 1976 when the government was expected to introduce fuel tank standards. By delaying making any change, Ford could save $20.9 million, since the change would average about $10 per car.[10]

In the Winamac case Ford claimed correctly that there were no federal safety standards in 1973. But it defended itself against recklessness by claiming its car was comparable to other subcompacts at that time. All the defense showed, however, was that all the subcompacts were unsafe when hit at 50 mph. Since the other subcompacts were not forced to recall their cars in 1973, there is *prima facie* evidence that Ford's Pinto gas tank mounting was substandard. The Ford documents tend to show Ford knew the danger it was inflicting on Ford owners; yet it did nothing, for profit reasons. How short-sighted those reasons were is demonstrated by the fact that the Pinto thus far in litigation and recalls alone has cost Ford $50 million. Some forty suits are still to be settled. And these figures do not take into account the loss of sales due to bad publicity.

Given these facts, what are we to say about the Ford engineers? Where were they when all this was going on, and what is their responsibility for the Pinto? The answer, I suggest, is that they were where they were supposed to be, doing what they were supposed to be doing. They were performing tests, designing the Pinto, making reports. But do they have no moral responsibility for the products they design? What after all is the moral responsibility of engineers in a large corporation? By way of reply, let me emphasize that no engineer can morally do what is immoral. If commanded to do what he should not morally do, he must resist and refuse. But in the Ford Pinto situation no engineer was told to produce a gas tank that would explode and kill people. The engineers were not instructed to make an unsafe car. They were morally responsible for knowing the state of the art, including that connected with placing and mounting gas tanks. We can assume that the Ford engineers were cognizant of the state of the art in producing the model they did. When tests were made in 1970 and 1971, and a memo was written stating that a $6.65 modification could make the gas tank safer,[11] that was an engineering assessment. Whichever engineer proposed the modification and initiated the memo acted ethically in doing so. The next step, the administrative decision not to make the modification was, with hindsight, a poor one in almost every way. It ended up costing Ford a great deal more not to put in the part than it would have cost to put it in. Ford still claims today that its gas tank was as safe as the accepted standards of the industry at that time.[12] It must say so, otherwise the suits pending against it will skyrocket. That it was not as safe seems borne out by the fact that only the Pinto of all the subcompacts failed to pass the 30 mph rear impact NHTSA test.

But the question of wrongdoing or of malicious intent or of recklessness is not so easily solved. Suppose the ordinary person were told when buying a Pinto that if he paid an extra $6.65 he could increase the safety of the vehicle so that it could withstand a 30 mph rear-end impact rather than a 20 mph impact, and that the odds of suffering a rear-end impact of between 20 and 30 mph was 1 in 250,000. Would we call him or her reckless if he or she declined to pay the extra $6.65? I am not sure how to answer that question. Was it reckless of Ford to wish to save the $6.65 per car and increase the risk for the consumer? Here I am inclined to be clearer in my own mind. If I choose to take a risk to save $6.65, it is my risk and my $6.65. But if Ford saves the $6.65 and I take the risk, then I clearly lose. Does Ford have the right to do that without informing me, if the going stan-

dard of safety of subcompacts is safety in a rear-end collision up to 30 mph? I think not. I admit, however, that the case is not clear-cut, even if we add that during 1976 and 1977 Pintos suffered 13 firey fatal rear-end collisions, more than double that of other U.S. comparable cars. The VW Rabbit and Toyota Corolla suffered none.[13]

Yet, if we are to morally fault anyone for the decision not to add the part, we would censure not the Ford engineers but the Ford executives, because it was not an engineering but an executive decision.

My reason for taking this view is that an engineer cannot be expected and cannot have the responsibility to second-guess managerial decisions. He is responsible for bringing the facts to the attention of those who need them to make decisions. But the input of engineers is only one of many factors that go to make up managerial decisions. During the trial, the defense called as a witness Francis Olsen, the assistant chief engineer in charge of design at Ford, who testified that he bought a 1973 Pinto for his eighteen-year-old daughter, kept it a year, and then traded it in for a 1974 Pinto which he kept two years.[14] His testimony and his actions were presented as an indication that the Ford engineers had confidence in the Pinto's safety. At least this one had enough confidence in it to give it to his daughter. Some engineers at Ford may have felt that the car could have been safer. But this is true of almost every automobile. Engineers in large firms have an ethical responsibility to do their jobs as best they can, to report their observations about safety and improvement of safety to management. But they do not have the obligation to insist that their perceptions or their standards be accepted. They are not paid to do that, they are not expected to do that, and they have no moral or ethical obligation to do that.

In addition to doing their jobs, engineers can plausibly be said to have an obligation of loyalty to their employers, and firms have a right to a certain amount of confidentiality concerning their internal operations. At the same time engineers are required by their professional ethical codes to hold the safety of the public paramount. Where these obligations conflict, the need for and justification of whistle blowing arises. If we admit the obligations on both sides, I would suggest as a rule of thumb that engineers and other workers in a large corporation are morally *permitted* to go public with information about the safety of a product if the following conditions are met:

1. if the harm that will be done by the product to the public is serious and considerable;
2. if they make their concerns known to their superiors; and
3. if, getting no satisfaction from their immediate superiors, they exhaust the channels available within the corporation, including going to the board of directors.

If they still get no action, I believe they are morally *permitted* to make public their views; but they are not morally *obliged* to do so. Harly Copp, a former Ford executive and engineer, in fact did criticize the Pinto from the start and testified for the prosecution against Ford at the Winamac trial.[15] He left the company and voiced his criticism. The criticism was taken up by Ralph Nader and others. In the long run it led to the Winamac trial and probably helped in a number of other suits filed against Ford. Though I admire Mr. Copp for his actions, assuming they were done from moral motives, I do not think such action was morally required, nor do I think the other engineers at Ford were morally deficient in not doing likewise.

For an engineer to have a moral *obligation* to bring his case for safety to the public, I think two other conditions have to be fulfilled, in addition to the three mentioned above.[16]

4. He must have documented evidence that would convince a reasonable, impartial observer that his view of the situation is correct and the company policy wrong.

Such evidence is obviously very difficult to obtain and produce. Such evidence, however, takes an engineer's concern out of the realm of the subjective and precludes that concern from being simply one person's opinion based on a limited point of view. Unless such evidence is available, there is little likelihood that the concerned engineer's view will win the day simply by public exposure. If the testimony of Francis Olsen is accurate, then even among the engineers at Ford there was disagreement about the safety of the Pinto.

5. There must be strong evidence that making the information public will in fact prevent the threatened serious harm.

This means both that before going public the engineer should know what source (government, newspaper, columnist, TV reporter) will make use of his evidence and how it will be handled. He should also have good reason to believe that it will result in the kind of change or result that he believes is morally appropriate. None of this was the case in the Pinto situation. After such public discussion, five model years, and failure to pass national safety standards tests, Ford plausibly defends its original claim that the gas tank was acceptably safe. If there is little likelihood of his success, there is no moral obligation for the engineer to go public. For the harm he or she personally incurs is not offset by the good such action achieves.[17]

My first substantive conclusion is that Ford engineers had no moral *obligation* to do more than they did in this case.

My second claim is that though engineers in large organizations should have a say in setting safety standards and producing cost-benefit analyses, they need not have the last word. My reasons are two. First, while the degree of risk, e.g., in a car, is an engineering problem, the acceptability of risk is not. Second, an engineering cost-benefit analysis does not include all the factors appropriate in making a policy decision, either on the corporate or the social level. Safety is one factor in an engineering design. Yet clearly it is only one factor. A Mercedes-Benz 280 is presumably safer than a Ford Pinto. But the difference in price is considerable. To make a Pinto as safe as a Mercedes it would probably have to cost a comparable amount. In making cars as in making many other objects some balance has to be reached between safety and cost. The final decision on where to draw the balance is not only an engineering decision. It is also a managerial decision, and probably even more appropriately a social decision. . . .

Engineers in large corporations have an important role to play. That role, however, is not usually to set policy or to decide on the acceptability of risk. Their knowledge and expertise are important both to the companies for which they work and to the public. But they are not morally responsible for policies and decisions beyond their competence and control. Does this view, however, let engineers off the moral hook too easily?

To return briefly to the Pinto story once more, Ford wanted a subcompact to fend off the competition of Japanese imports. The order came down to produce a car of 2,000 pounds or less that would cost $2000 or less in time for the 1971 model. This allowed only 25 months instead of the usual 43 months for design and production of a new car.[18] The engineers were squeezed from the start. Perhaps this is why they did not test the gas tank for rear-end collision impact until the car was produced.

Should the engineers have refused the order to produce the car in 25 months? Should they have resigned, or leaked the story to the newspapers? Should they have re-fused to speed up their usual routine? Should they have complained to their professional society that they were being asked to do the impossible—if it were to be done right? I am not in a position to say what they should have done. But with the advantage of hindsight, I suggest we should ask not only what they should have done. We should especially ask what changes can be made to prevent engineers from being squeezed in this way in the future.

Engineering ethics should not take as its goal the producing of moral heroes. Rather it should consider what forces operate to encourage engineers to act as they feel they should not; what structural or other features of a large corporation squeeze them until their consciences hurt? Those features should then be examined, evaluated, and changes proposed and made. Lobbying by engineering organizations would be appropriate, and legislation should be passed if necessary. In general I tend to favor voluntary means where possible. But where that is utopian, then legislation is a necessary alternative. . . .

The means by which engineers with ethical concerns can get a fair hearing without endangering their jobs or blowing the whistle must be made part of a corporation's organizational structure. An outside board member with primary responsibility for investigating and responding to such ethical concerns might be legally required. . . . Another way of achieving a similar end is by providing an inspector general for all corporations with an annual net income of over $1 billion. An independent committee of an engineering association might be formed to investigate charges made by engineers concerning the safety of a product on which they are working;[19] a company that did not allow an appropriate investigation of employee charges would become subject to cover-up proceedings. Those in the engineering industry can suggest and work to implement other ideas. I have elsewhere outlined a set of ten such changes for the ethical corporation.[20] . . .

Many of the issues of engineering ethics within a corporate setting concern the ethics of organizational structure, questions of public policy, and so questions that frequently are amenable to solutions only on a scale larger than the individual—on the scale of organization and law. The ethical responsibilities of the engineer in a large organization have as much to do with the organization as with the engineer. They can be most fruitfully approached by considering from a moral point of view not only the individual engineer but the framework within which he or she works. We not only need moral people. Even more importantly we need moral structures and organizations. Only by paying more attention to these can we adequately resolve the questions of the ethical responsibility of engineers in large organizations.

NOTES

1. The body of literature on engineering ethics is now substantive and impressive. See, *A Selected Annotated Bibliography of Professional Ethics and Social Responsibility in Engineering*, compiled by Robert F. Ladenson, James Choromokos, Ernest d'Anjou, Martin Pimsler, and Howard Rosen (Chicago: Center for the Study of Ethics in the Professions, Illinois Institute of Technology, 1980). A useful two-volume collection of readings and cases is also available: Robert J. Baum and Albert Flores, *Ethical Problems in Engineering*, 2nd edition (Troy, N.Y.: Rensselaer Polytechnic Institute, Center for the Study of the Human Dimensions of Science and Technology, 1980). See also Robert J. Baum's *Ethics and Engineering Curricula* (Hastings-on-Hudson, N.Y.: Hastings Center, 1980).

2. See, for example, the first canon of the 1974 Engineers Council for Professional Development Code, the first canon of the National Council of Engineering Examiners Code, and the draft (by A. Oldenquist and E. Slowter) of a "Code of Ethics for the Engineering Profes-

sion" (all reprinted in Baum and Flores, *Ethical Problems in Engineering*.

3. Details of the incident presented in this paper are based on testimony at the trial. Accounts of the trial as well as background reports were carried by both the *New York Times* and the *Chicago Tribune*.

4. *New York Times*, February 17, 1980, IV, p. 9.

5. *New York Times*, February 21, 1980, p. A6; *Fortune*, September 11, 1978, p. 42.

6. *New York Times*, March 14, 1980, p. 1.

7. *Time*, March 24, 1980, p. 24.

8. *New York Times*, January 16, 1980, p. 16; February 7, 1980, p. 16.

9. *Chicago Tribune*, October 13, 1979, p. 1. and Section 2, p. 12.

10. *Chicago Tribune*, October 13, 1979, p. 1; *New York Times*, October 14, 1979, p. 26.

11. *New York Times*, February 4, 1980, p. 12.

12. *New York Times*, June 10, 1978, p. 1; *Chicago Tribune*, October 13, 1979, p. 1, and Section 2, p. 12. The continuous claim has been that the Pinto poses "no serious hazards."

13. *New York Times*, October 26, 1978, p. 103.

14. *New York Times*, February 20, 1980, p. A16.

15. *New York Times*, February 4, 1980, p. 12.

16. The position I present here is developed more fully in my book *Business Ethics* (New York: Macmillan, 1981). It differs somewhat from the dominant view expressed in the existing literature in that I consider whistle blowing an extreme measure that is morally obligatory only if the stringent conditions set forth are satisfied. Cf. Kenneth D. Walters, "Your Employees' Right to Blow the Whistle," *Harvard Business Review*, July–August, 1975.

17. On the dangers incurred by whistle blowers, see Gene James, "Whistle Blowing: Its Nature and Justification," *Philosophy in Context*, 10 (1980), pp. 99–117, which examines the legal context of whistle blowing; Peter Raven-Hansen, "Dos and Don'ts for Whistleblowers: Planning for Trouble," *Technology Review*, May 1980, pp. 34–44, which suggests how to blow the whistle; Helen Dudar, "The Price of Blowing the Whistle," *The New York Times Magazine*, 30 October, 1977, which examines the results for whistleblowers; David W. Ewing, "Canning Directions," *Harpers*, August 1979, pp. 17–22, which indicates "how the government rids itself of troublemakers" and how legislation

protecting whistleblowers can be cir-
cumvented; and Report by the U.S. General
Accounting Office, "The Office of the Special
Counsel Can Improve Its Management of
Whistleblower Cases," December 30, 1980
(FPCD-81-10).

18. *Chicago Tribune,* October 13, 1979, Section 2,
    p. 12.

19. A number of engineers have been arguing for
    a more active role by engineering societies in
    backing up individual engineers in their at-
    tempts to act responsibly. See, Edwin Layton,
    Revolt of the Engineers (Cleveland: Case West-
    ern Reserve, 1971); Stephen H. Unger, "Engi-

neering Societies and the Responsible Engineer," *Annals of the New York Academy of Sciences,* 196 (1973), pp. 433–37 (reprinted in
Baum and Flores, *Ethical Problems in Engineering,* pp. 56–59; and Robert Perrucci and Joel
Gerstl, *Profession Without Community: Engineers
in American Society* (New York: Random
House, 1969).

20. Richard T. De George, "Responding to the
    Mandate for Social Responsibility," *Guidelines
    for Business When Societal Demands Conflict*
    (Washington, D.C.: Council for Better Busi-
    ness Bureaus, 1978), pp. 60–80.

Roger Boisjoly and the *Challenger* Disaster: The Ethical Dimensions

Russell P. Boisjoly
Ellen Foster Curtis
Eugene Mellican

INTRODUCTION

On January 28, 1986, the space shuttle *Challenger* exploded 73 seconds into its flight, killing the seven astronauts aboard. As the nation mourned the tragic loss of the crew
members, the Rogers Commission was
formed to investigate the causes of the disaster. The Commission concluded that the explosion occurred due to seal failure in one of
the solid rocket booster joints. Testimony
given by Roger Boisjoly, Senior Scientist and
acknowledged rocket seal expert, indicated
that top management at NASA and Morton
Thiokol had been aware of problems with the
O-ring seals, but agreed to launch against the
recommendation of Boisjoly and other engineers. Boisjoly had alerted management to

problems with the O-rings as early as January
1985, yet several shuttle launches prior to the
Challenger had been approved without correcting the hazards. This suggests that the
management practice of NASA and Morton
Thiokol had created an environment which
altered the framework for decision making,
leading to a breakdown in communication
between technical experts and their supervisors, and top level management, and to
the acceptance of risks that both organizations had historically viewed as unacceptable. With human lives and the national interest at stake, serious ethical concerns are
embedded in this dramatic change in management practice.

In fact, one of the most important aspects
of the *Challenger* disaster—both in terms of

the causal sequence that led to it and the lessons to be learned from it—is its ethical dimension. Ethical issues are woven throughout the tangled web of decisions, events, practices, and organizational structures that resulted in the loss of the *Challenger* and its seven astronauts. Therefore, an ethical analysis of this tragedy is essential for a full understanding of the event itself and for the implications it has for any endeavor where public policy, corporate practice, and individual decisions intersect.

The significance of an ethical analysis of the *Challenger* disaster is indicated by the fact that it immediately presents one of the most urgent, but difficult, issues in the examination of corporate and individual behavior today, i.e., whether existing ethical theories adequately address the problems posed by new technologies, new forms of organization, and evolving social systems. At the heart of this issue is the concept of responsibility. No ethical concept has been more affected by the impact of these changing realities. Modern technology has so transformed the context and scale of human action that not only do the traditional parameters of responsibility seem inadequate to contain the full range of human acts and their consequences, but even more fundamentally, it is no longer the individual that is the primary locus of power and responsibility, but public and private institutions. Thus, it would seem, it is no longer the character and virtues of individuals that determine the standards of moral conduct, it is the policies and structures of the institutional settings within which they live and work.

Many moral conflicts facing individuals within institutional settings do arise from matters pertaining to organizational structures or questions of public policy. As such, they are resolvable only at a level above the responsibilities of the individual. Therefore, some writers argue that the ethical responsibilities of the engineer or manager in a large corporation have as much to do with the organization as with the individual. Instead of expecting individual engineers or managers to be moral heroes, emphasis should be on the creation of organizational structures conducive to ethical behavior among all agents under their aegis. It would be futile to attempt to establish a sense of ethical responsibility in engineers and management personnel and ignore the fact that such persons work within a sociotechnical environment which increasingly undermines the notion of individual, responsible moral agency (Boling and Dempsey, 1981; De George, 1981).

Yet, others argue that precisely because of these organizational realities individual accountability must be re-emphasized to counteract the diffusion of responsibility within large organizations and to prevent its evasion under the rubric of collective responsibility. Undoubtedly institutions do take on a kind of collective life of their own, but they do not exist, or act, independently of the individuals that constitute them, whatever the theoretical and practical complexities of delineating the precise relationships involved. Far from diminishing individuals' obligations, the reality of organizational life increases them because the consequences of decisions and acts are extended and amplified through the reach and power of that reality. Since there are pervasive and inexorable connections between ethical standards and behavior of individuals within an organization and its structure and operation, "the sensitizing of professionals to ethical considerations should be increased so that institutional structures will reflect enhanced ethical sensitivities as trained professionals move up the organizational ladder to positions of leadership" (Mankin, 1981, p. 17).

By reason of the courageous activities and testimony of individuals like Roger Boisjoly, the *Challenger* disaster provides a fascinating illustration of the dynamic tension between organizational and individual responsibility. By focusing on this central issue, this article seeks to accomplish two objectives: first, to demonstrate the extent to which the *Challenger* disaster not only gives concrete expression to the ethical ambiguity that permeates the relationship between organizational and individual responsibility, but also, in fact, is a result of it; second, to reclaim the meaning and importance of individual responsibility within the diluting context of large organizations.

In meeting these objectives, the article is divided into two parts: a case study of Roger Boisjoly's efforts to galvanize management support for effectively correcting the high risk O-ring problems, his attempt to prevent the launch, the scenario which resulted in the launch decision, and Boisjoly's quest to set the record straight despite enormous personal and professional consequences; and an ethical analysis of these events.

PREVIEW FOR DISASTER

On January 24, 1985, Roger Boisjoly, Senior Scientist at Morton Thiokol, watched the launch of Flight 51-C of the space shuttle program. He was at Cape Canaveral to inspect the solid rocket boosters from Flight 51-C following their recovery in the Atlantic Ocean and to conduct a training session at Kennedy Space Center (KSC) on the proper methods of inspecting the booster joints. While watching the launch, he noted that the temperature that day was much cooler than recorded at other launches, but was still much warmer than the 18 degree temperature encountered three days earlier when he arrived in Orlando. The unseasonably cold weather of the past several days had produced the worst citrus crop failures in Florida history.

When he inspected the solid rocket boost-

ers several days later, Boisjoly discovered evidence that the primary O-ring seals on two field joints had been compromised by hot combustion gases (i.e., hot gas blow-by had occurred) which had also eroded part of the primary O-ring. This was the first time that a primary seal on a field joint had been penetrated. When he discovered the large amount of blackened grease between the primary and secondary seals, his concern heightened. The blackened grease was discovered over 80 degree and 110 degree arcs, respectively, on two of the seals, with the larger arc indicating greater hot gas blow-by. Post-flight calculations indicated that the ambient temperature of the field joints at launch time was 53 degrees. This evidence, coupled with his recollection of the low temperature the day of the launch and the citrus crop damage caused by the cold spell, led to his conclusion that the severe hot gas blow-by may have been caused by, and related to, low temperature. After reporting these findings to his superiors. Boisjoly presented them to engineers and management at NASA's Marshall Space Flight Center (MSFC). As a result of his presentation at MSFC, Roger Boisjoly was asked to participate in the Flight Readiness Review (FRR) on February 12, 1985 for Flight 51-E which was scheduled for launch in April, 1985. This FRR represents the first association of low temperature with blow-by on a field joint, a condition that was considered an "acceptable risk" by Larry Mulloy, NASA's Manager for the Booster Project, and other NASA officials.

Roger Boisjoly had twenty-five years of experience as an engineer in the aerospace industry. Among his many notable assignments were the performance of stress and deflection analysis on the flight control equipment of the Advanced Minuteman Missile at Autonetics, and serving as a lead engineer on the lunar module of Apollo at Hamilton Standard. He moved to Utah in 1980 to take a position in the Applied Mechanics Department as a Staff Engineer at the Wasatch Division of Morton Thiokol. He was considered the leading expert in the United States on O-rings and rocket joint seals and received plaudits for his work on the joint seal problems from Joe C. Kilminster, Vice President of Space Booster Programs, Morton Thiokol (Kilminster, July, 1985). His commitment to the company and the community was further demonstrated by his service as Mayor of Willard, Utah from 1982 to 1983.

The tough questioning he received at the February 12th FRR convinced Boisjoly of the need for further evidence linking low temperature and hot gas blow-by. He worked closely with Arnie Thompson, Supervisor of Rocket Motor Cases, who conducted subscale laboratory tests in March, 1985, to further test the effects of temperature on O-ring resiliency. The bench tests that were performed provided powerful evidence to support Boisjoly's and Thompson's theory: Low temperatures greatly and adversely affected the ability of O-rings to create a seal on solid rocket booster joints. If the temperature was too low (and they did not know what the threshold temperature would be), it was possible that neither the primary or secondary O-rings would seal!

One month later the post-flight inspection of Flight 51-B revealed that the primary seal of a booster nozzle joint did not make contact during its two minute flight. If this damage had occurred in a field joint, the secondary O-ring may have failed to seal, causing the loss of the flight. As a result, Boisjoly and his colleagues became increasingly concerned about shuttle safety. This evidence from the inspection of Flight 51-B was presented at the FRR for Flight 51-F on July 1, 1985; the key engineers and managers at NASA and Morton Thiokol were now aware of the critical O-ring problems and the influence of low temperature on the performance of the joint seals.

During July, 1985, Boisjoly and his associates voiced their desire to devote more effort and resources to solving the problems of O-ring erosion. In his activity reports dated July 22 and 29, 1985, Boisjoly expressed considerable frustration with the lack of progress in this area, despite the fact that a Seal Erosion Task Force had been informally appointed on July 19th. Finally, Boisjoly wrote the following memo, labelled "Company Private," to R. K. (Bob) Lund, Vice President of Engineering for Morton Thiokol, to express the extreme urgency of his concerns. Here are some excerpts from that memo:

> This letter is written to insure that management is fully aware of the seriousness of the current O-ring erosion problem. . . . The mistakenly accepted position on the joint problem was to fly without fear of failure . . . is now drastically changed as a result of the SRM 16A nozzle joint erosion which eroded a secondary O-ring with the primary O-ring never sealing. If the same scenario should occur in a field joint (and it could), then it is a jump ball as to the success or failure of the joint. . . . The result would be a catastrophe of the highest order—loss of human life. . . .
>
> It is my honest and real fear that if we do not take immediate action to dedicate a team to solve the problem, with the field joint having the number one priority, then we stand in jeopardy of losing a flight along with all the launch pad facilities (Boisjoly, July, 1985a).

On August 20, 1985, R. K. Lund formally announced the formation of the Seal Erosion Task Team. The team consisted of only five full-time engineers from the 2500 employed by Morton Thiokol on the Space Shuttle Program. The events of the next five months would demonstrate that management had not provided the resources necessary to carry out the enormous task of solving the seal erosion problem.

On October 3, 1985, the Seal Erosion Task Force met with Joe Kilminster to discuss the problems they were having in gaining organizational support necessary to solve the O-ring problems. Boisjoly later stated that Kilminster summarized the meeting as a "good bullshit session." Once again frustrated by bureaucratic inertia, Boisjoly wrote in his activity report dated October 4th:

> ... NASA is sending an engineering representative to stay with us starting Oct. 14th. We feel that this is a direct result of their feeling that we (MTI) are not responding quickly enough to the seal problem ... upper management apparently feels that the SRM program is ours for sure and the customer be damned (Boisjoly, October, 1985b).

Boisjoly was not alone in his expression of frustration. Bob Ebeling, Department Manager, Solid Rocket Motor Igniter and Final Assembly, and a member of the Seal Erosion Task Force, wrote in a memo to Allan McDonald, Manager of the Solid Rocket Motor Project, "HELP! The seal task force is constantly being delayed by every possible means. . . . We wish we could get action by verbal request, but such is not the case. This is a red flag" (McConnell, 1987).

At the Society of Automotive Engineers (SAE) conference on October 7, 1985, Boisjoly presented a six-page overview of the joints and the seal configuration to approximately 130 technical experts in hope of soliciting suggestions for remedying the O-ring problems. Although MSFC had requested the presentation, NASA gave strict instructions not to express the critical urgency of fixing the joints, but merely to ask for suggestions for improvement. Although no help was forthcoming, the conference was a milestone in that it was the first time that NASA allowed information on the O-ring difficulties to be expressed in a public forum. That NASA also recognized that the O-ring problems were not receiving appropriate attention and manpower considerations from Morton Thiokol management is further evidenced by Boisjoly's October 24

log entry, " . . . Jerry Peoples (NASA) has informed his people that our group needs more authority and people to do the job. Jim Smith (NASA) will corner Al McDonald today to attempt to implement this direction."

The October 30 launch of Flight 61-A of the *Challenger* provided the most convincing, and yet to some the most contestable, evidence to date that low temperature was directly related to hot gas blow-by. The left booster experienced hot gas blow-by in the center and aft field joints without any seal erosion. The ambient temperature of the field joints was estimated to be 75 degrees at launch time based on post-flight calculations. Inspection of the booster joints revealed that the blow-by was less severe than that found on Flight 51-C because the seal grease was a grayish black color, rather than the jet black hue of Flight 51-C. The evidence was now consistent with the bench tests for joint resiliency conducted in March. That is, at 75 degrees the O-ring lost contact with its sealing surface for 2.4 seconds, whereas at 50 degrees the O-ring lost contact for 10 minutes. The actual flight data revealed greater hot gas blow-by for the O-rings on Flight 51-C which had an ambient temperature of 53 degrees than for Flight 61-A which had an ambient temperature of 75 degrees. Those who rejected this line of reasoning concluded that temperature must be irrelevant since hot gas blow-by had occurred even at room temperature (75 degrees). This difference in interpretation would receive further attention on January 27, 1986.

During the next two and one-half months, little progress was made in obtaining a solution to the O-ring problems. Roger Boisjoly made the following entry into his log on January 13, 1986, "O-ring resiliency tests that were requested on September 24, 1985 are now scheduled for January 15, 1986."

THE DAY BEFORE THE DISASTER

At 10 a.m. on January 27, 1986. Arnie Thompson received a phone call from Boyd Brinton, Thiokol's Manager of Project Engineering at MSFC, relaying the concerns of NASA's Larry Wear, also at MSFC, about the 18 degree temperature forecast for the launch of flight 51-L, the *Challenger,* scheduled for the next day. This phone call precipitated a series of meetings within Morton Thiokol, at the Marshall Space Flight Center; and at the Kennedy Space Center that culminated in a three-way telecon involving three teams of engineers and managers, that began at 8:15 p.m. E.S.T.

Joe Kilminster, Vice President, Space Booster Programs, of Morton Thiokol began the telecon by turning the presentation of the engineering charts over to Roger Boisjoly and Arnie Thompson. They presented thirteen charts which resulted in a recommendation against the launch of the *Challenger.* Boisjoly demonstrated their concerns with the performance of the O-rings in the field joints during the initial phases of *Challenger's* flight with charts showing the effects of primary O-ring erosion, and its timing, on the ability to maintain a reliable secondary seal. The tremendous pressure and release of power from the rocket boosters create rotation in the joint such that the metal moves away from the O-rings so that they cannot maintain contact with the metal surfaces. If, at the same time, erosion occurs in the primary O-ring for any reason, then there is a reduced probability of maintaining a secondary seal. It is highly probable that as the ambient temperature drops, the primary O-ring will not seat then there will be hot gas blow-by and erosion of the primary O-ring; and that a catastrophe will occur when the secondary O-ring fails to seal.

Bob Lund presented the final chart that included the Morton Thiokol recommendations that the ambient temperature including wind must be such that the seal temperature would be greater than 53 degrees to proceed with the launch. Since the overnight low was predicted to be 18 degrees, Bob Lund recommended against launch on January 28, 1986, or until the seal temperature exceeded 53 degrees.

NASA's Larry Mulloy bypassed Bob Lund and directly asked Joe Kilminster for his reaction. Kilminster stated that he supported the position of his engineers and he would not recommend launch below 53 degrees.

George Hardy, Deputy Director of Science and Engineering at MSFC, said he was "appalled at that recommendation," according to Allan McDonald's testimony before the Rogers Commission. Nevertheless, Hardy would not recommend to launch if the contractor was against it. After Hardy's reaction, Stanley Reinartz, Manager of Shuttle Project Office at MSFC, objected by pointing out that the solid rocket motors were qualified to operate between 40 and 90 degrees Fahrenheit.

Larry Mulloy, citing the data from Flight 61-A which indicated to him that temperature was not a factor, strenuously objected to Morton Thiokol's recommendation. He suggested that Thiokol was attempting to establish new Launch Commit Criteria at 53 degrees and that they couldn't do that the night before a launch. In exasperation Mulloy asked, "My God, Thiokol, when do you want me to launch? Next April?" (McConnell, 1987). Although other NASA officials also objected to the association of temperature with O-ring erosion and hot gas blow-by, Roger Boisjoly was able to hold his ground and demonstrate with the use of his charts and pictures that there was indeed a relationship: The lower the temperature the higher the probability of erosion and blow-by and the greater the likelihood of an accident. Finally, Joe Kilminster asked for a five-minute caucus off-net.

According to Boisjoly's testimony before the Rogers Commission, Jerry Mason, Senior Vice President of Wasatch Operations, began the caucus by saying that "a management decision was necessary." Sensing that an attempt would be made to overturn the no-launch decision, Boisjoly and Thompson attempted to re-review the material previously presented to NASA for the executives in the room. Thompson took a pad of paper and tried to sketch out the problem with the joint, while Boisjoly laid out the photos of the compromised joints from Flights 51-C and 61-A. When they became convinced that no one was listening, they ceased their efforts. As Boisjoly would later testify, "There was not one positive pro-launch statement ever made by anybody" (Report of the Presidential Commission, 1986, IV, p. 792, hereafter abbreviated as R.C.).

According to Boisjoly, after he and Thompson made their last attempts to stop the launch, Jerry Mason asked rhetorically, "Am I the only one who wants to fly?" Mason turned to Bob Lund and asked him to "take off his engineering hat and put on his management hat." The four managers held a brief discussion and voted unanimously to recommend *Challenger's* launch.

Exhibit I shows the revised recommendations that were presented that evening by Joe Kilminster after the caucus to support management's decision to launch. Only one of the rationales presented that evening supported the launch (demonstrated erosion sealing threshold is three times greater than 0.038″ erosion experienced on SRM-15). Even so, the issue at hand was sealability at low temperature, not erosion. While one other rationale could be considered a neutral statement of engineering fact (O-ring pressure leak check places secondary seal in outboard position which minimizes sealing time), the other seven rationales are negative, anti-launch, statements. After hearing Kilminster's presentation, which was accepted without a single probing question, George Hardy asked him to sign the chart and telefax it to Kennedy Space Center and Marshall Space Flight Center. At 11 p.m. E.S.T. the teleconference ended.

Aside from the four senior Morton Thiokol executives present at the teleconference, all

EXHIBIT 1   MTI Assessment Of Temperature Concern on SRM-25 (51L) Launch

- CALCULATIONS SHOW THAT SRM-25 O-RINGS WILL BE 20° COLDER THAN SRM-15 O-RINGS
- TEMPERATURE DATA NOT CONCLUSIVE ON PREDICTING PRIMARY O-RING BLOW-BY
- ENGINEERING ASSESSMENT IS THAT:
  - COLDER O-RINGS WILL HAVE INCREASED EFFECTIVE DUROMETER ("HARDER")
- "HARDER" O-RINGS WILL TAKE LONGER TO "SEAT"
  - MORE GAS MAY PASS PRIMARY O-RING BEFORE THE PRIMARY SEAL SEATS (RELATIVE TO SRM-15)
  - DEMONSTRATED SEALING THRESHOLD IS 3 TIMES GREATER THAN 0.038″ EROSION EXPERIENCED ON SRM-15
  - IF THE PRIMARY SEAL DOES NOT SEAT, THE SECONDARY SEAL WILL SEAT
  - PRESSURE WILL GET TO SECONDARY SEAL BEFORE THE METAL PARTS ROTATE
  - O-RING PRESSURE LEAK CHECK PLACES SECONDARY SEAL IN OUTBOARD POSITION WHICH MINIMIZES SEALING TIME
- MTI RECOMMENDS STS-51L LAUNCH PROCEED ON 28 JANUARY 1986
  - SRM-25 WILL NOT BE SIGNIFICANTLY DIFFERENT FROM SRM-15

Joe C. Kilminster, Vice President Space Booster Programs.

others were excluded from the final decision. The process represented a radical shift from previous NASA policy. Until that moment, the burden of proof had always been on the engineers to prove byond a doubt that it was safe to launch. NASA, with their objections to the original Thiokol recommendation against the launch, and Mason, with his request for a "management decision," shifted the burden of proof in the opposite direction. Morton Thiokol was expected to prove that launching *Challenger* would not be safe (R.C., IV, p. 793).

The change in the decision so deeply upset Boisjoly that he returned to his office and made the following journal entry:

> I sincerely hope this launch does not result in a catastrophe. I personally do not agree with some of the statements made by Joe Kilminster's written summary stating that SRM-25 is okay to fly (Boisjoly, 1987).

THE DISASTER AND ITS AFTERMATH

On January 28, 1986, a reluctant Roger Boisjoly watched the launch of the *Challenger*. As the vehicle cleared the tower, Bob Ebeling whispered, "We've just dodged a bullet." (The engineers who opposed the launch assumed that O-ring failure would result in an explosion almost immediately after engine ignition.) To continue in Boisjoly's words, "At approximately T+60 seconds Bob told me he had just completed a prayer of thanks to the Lord for a successful launch. Just thirteen seconds later we both saw the horror of the destruction as the vehicle exploded" (Boisjoly, 1987).

Morton Thiokol formed a failure investigation team on January 31, 1986, to study the *Challenger* explosion. Roger Boisjoly and Arnie Thompson were part of the team that was sent to MSFC in Huntsville, Alabama. Boisjoly's first inkling of a division between himself and management came on February 13 when he was informed at the last minute that he was to testify before the Rogers Commission the next day. He had very little time to prepare for his testimony. Five days later, two Commission members held a closed session with Kilminster, Boisjoly, and Thompson. During the interview Boisjoly gave his memos and activity reports to the Commissioners. After that meeting, Kilminster chastised Thompson and Boisjoly for correcting his interpretation of the technical data. Their response was that they would continue to correct his version if it was technically incorrect.

Boisjoly's February 25th testimony before the Commission, rebutting the general manager's statement that the initial decision against the launch was not unanimous, drove a wedge further between him and Morton Thiokol management. Boisjoly was flown to MSFC before he could hear the NASA testimony about the pre-flight telecon. The next day, he was removed from the failure investigation team and returned to Utah.

Beginning in April, Boisjoly began to believe that for the previous month he had been used solely for public relations purposes. Although given the title of Seal Coordinator for the redesign effort, he was isolated from NASA and the seal redesign effort. His design information had been changed without his knowledge and presented without his feedback. On May 1, 1986, in a briefing preceding closed sessions before the Rogers Commission, Ed Garrison, President of Aerospace Operations for Morton Thiokol, chastised Boisjoly for "airing the company's dirty laundry" with the memos he had given the Commission. The next day, Boisjoly testified about the change in his job assignment. Commission Chairman Rogers criticized Thiokol management, " . . . if it appears that you're punishing the two people or at least two of the people who are right about the decision and objected to thc launch which ultimately resulted in criticism of Thiokol and then they're demoted or feel that they are being retaliated against, that is a very serious matter. It would seem to me, just speaking for myself, they should be promoted, not demoted or pushed aside" (R.C., V, p. 1586).

Boisjoly now sensed a major rift developing within the corporation. Some co-workers perceived that his testimony was damaging the company image. In an effort to clear the air, he and McDonald requested a private meeting with the company's three top executives, which was held on May 16, 1986. According to Boisjoly, management was unreceptive throughout the meeting. The CEO told McDonald and Boisjoly that the company "was doing just fine until Al and I testified about our job reassignments" (Boisjoly, 1987). McDonald and Boisjoly were nominally restored to their former assignments, but Boisjoly's position became untenable as time passed. On July 21, 1986, Roger Boisjoly requested an extended sick leave from Morton Thiokol.

ETHICAL ANALYSIS

It is clear from this case study that Roger Boisjoly's experiences before and after the *Challenger* disaster raise numerous ethical questions that are integral to any explanation of the disaster and applicable to other management situations, especially those involving highly complex technologies. The difficulties and uncertainties involved in the management of these technologies exacerbate the kind of bureaucratic syndromes that generate ethical conflicts in the first place. In fact, Boisjoly's experiences could well serve as a paradigmatic case study for such ethical problems, ranging from accountability to corporate loyalty and whistle blowing. Underlying all these issues, however, is the problematic relationship between individual and organi-

zational responsibility. Boisjoly's experiences graphically portray the tensions inherent in this relationship in a manner that discloses its importance in the causal sequence leading to the *Challenger* disaster. The following analysis explicates this and the implications it has for other organizational settings.

By focusing on the problematic relationship between individual and organizational responsibility, this analysis reveals that the organizational structure governing the space shuttle program became the locus of responsibility in such a way that not only did it undermine the responsibilities of individual decision makers within the process, but it also became a means of avoiding real, effective responsibility throughout the entire management system. The first clue to this was clearly articulated as early as 1973 by the board of inquiry that was formed to investigate the accident which occurred during the launch of *Skylab 1:*

> The management system developed by NASA for manned space flight places large emphasis on rigor, detail, and thoroughness. In hand with this emphasis comes formalism, extensive documentation, and visibility in detail to senior management. While nearly perfect, such a system can submerge the concerned individual and depress the role of the intuitive engineer or analyst. It may not allow full play for the intuitive judgment or past experience of the individual. An emphasis on management systems can, in itself, serve to separate the people engaged in the program from the real world of hardware (Quoted in Christiansen, 1987, p. 23).

To examine this prescient statement in ethical terms is to see at another level the serious consequences inherent in the situation it describes. For example, it points to a dual meaning of responsibility. One meaning emphasizes carrying out an authoritatively prescribed review process, while the second stresses the cognitive independence and input of every individual down the entire chain of authority. The first sense of responsibility shifts the ethical center of gravity precipitously away from individual moral agency onto the review process in such a way that what was originally set up to guarantee flight readiness with the professional and personal integrity of the responsible individuals, instead becomes a means of evading personal responsibility for decisions made in the review process.

A crucial, and telling, example of this involves the important question asked by the Rogers Commission as to why the concerns raised by the Morton Thiokol engineers about the effects of cold weather on the O-rings during the teleconference the night before the launch were not passed up from Level III to Levels II or I in the preflight review process. The NASA launch procedure clearly demands that decisions and objections methodically follow a prescribed path up all levels. Yet, Lawrence Mulloy, operating at Level III as the Solid Rocket Booster Project Manager at MSFC, did not transmit the Morton Thiokol concerns upward (through his immediate superior, Stanley Reinartz) to Level II. When asked by Chairman Rogers to explain why, Mr. Mulloy testified:

> At that time, and I still consider today, that was a Level III issue, Level III being a SRB element or an external tank element or Space Shuttle main engine element or an Orbiter. There was no violation of Launch Commit Criteria. There was no waiver required in my judgment at that time and still today (R.C., I, p. 98).

In examining this response in terms of shifting responsibility onto the review process itself, there are two things that are particularly striking in Mr. Mulloy's statement. The first is his emphasis that this was a "Level III issue." In a formal sense, Mr. Mulloy is correct. However, those on Level III also had the authority—and, one would think, especially in this instance given the heated discussion

on the effects of cold on the O-rings, the motivation—to pass objections and concerns on to Levels II and I. But here the second important point in Mr. Mulloy's testimony comes into play when he states, "there was no violation of Launch Commit Criteria." In other words, since there was no Launch Commit Criteria for joint temperature, concerns about joint temperature did not officially fall under the purview of the review process. Therefore, the ultimate justification for Mr. Mulloy's position rests on the formal process itself. He was just following the rules by staying within the already established scope of the review process.

This underscores the moral imperative executives must exercise by creating and maintaining organizational systems that do not separate the authority of decision makers from the responsibility they bear for decisions, or insulate them from the consequences of their actions or omissions.

Certainly, there can be no more vivid example than the shuttle program to verify that, in fact, "an emphasis on management systems can, in itself, serve to separate the people engaged in the program from the real world of hardware." Time and time again the lack of communication that lay at the heart of the Rogers Commission finding that "there was a serious flaw in the decision making process leading up to the launch of flight 51-L" (R.C., I, p. 104) was explained by the NASA officials or managers at Morton Thiokol with such statements as, "that is not my reporting channel," or "he is not in the launch decision chain," or "I didn't meet with Mr. Boisjoly, I met with Don Ketner, who is the task team leader" (R.C., IV, p. 821, testimony of Mr. Lund). Even those managers who had direct responsibility for line engineers and workmen depended on formalized memo writing procedures for communication to the point that some "never talked to them directly" (Feynman, 1988, p. 33).

Within the atmosphere of such an ambiguity of responsibility, when a life threatening conflict arose within the management system and individuals (such as Roger Boisjoly and his engineering associates at Morton Thiokol) tried to reassert the full weight of their individual judgments and attendant responsibilities, the very purpose of the flight readiness review process, i.e., to arrive at the "technical" truth of the situation, which includes the recognition of the uncertainties involved as much as the findings, became subverted into an adversary confrontation in which "adversary" truth, with its suppression of uncertainties, became operative (Wilmotte, 1970).

What is particularly significant in this radical transformation of the review process, in which the Morton Thiokol engineers were forced into "the position of having to prove that it was unsafe instead of the other way around" (R.C., IV, p. 822; see also p. 793), is that what made the suppression of technical uncertainties possible is precisely that mode of thinking which, in being challenged by independent professional judgments, gave rise to the adversarial setting in the first place: groupthink. No more accurate description for what transpired the night before the launch of the *Challenger* can be given than the definition of groupthink as:

> . . . a mode of thinking that people engage in when they are deeply involved in a cohesive in-group, when the members' strivings for unanimity override their motivation to realistically appraise alternative courses of action. . . . Groupthink refers to the deterioration of mental efficiency, reality testing, and moral judgment that results from in-group pressures (Janis, 1972, p. 9).

From this perspective, the full import of Mr. Mason's telling Mr. Lund to "take off his engineering hat and put on his management hat" is revealed. He did not want another technical, reality-based judgment of an independent professional engineer. As he had already implied when he opened the caucus by stating "a management decision was necessary," he wanted a group decision, specifically one that would, in the words of the Rogers Commission, "accommodate a major customer" (R.C., I. p. 104). With a group decision the objections of the engineers could be mitigated, the risks shared, fears allayed, and the attendant responsibility diffused.

This analysis is not meant to imply that groupthink was a pervasive or continuous mode of thinking at either NASA or Morton Thiokol. What is suggested is a causal relationship between this instance of groupthink and the ambiguity of responsibility found within the space shuttle program. Whenever a management system, such as NASA's generates "a mindset of 'collective responsibility' " by leading "individuals to defer to the anonymity of the process and not focus closely enough on their individual responsibilities in the decision chain," (N.R.C. Report, 1988, p. 68) and there is a confluence of the kind of pressures that came to bear on the decision making process the night before the launch, the conditions are in place for groupthink to prevail.

A disturbing feature of so many of the analyses and commentaries on the *Challenger* disaster is the reinforcement, and implicit acceptance, of this shift away from individual moral agency with an almost exclusive focus on the flaws in the management system, organizational structures and/or decision making process. Beginning with the findings of the Rogers Commission investigation, one could practically conclude that no one had any responsibility whatsoever for the disaster. The Commission concluded that "there was a serious flaw in the decision making process leading up to the launch of flight 51-L. A well structured and managed system emphasizing safety would have flagged the rising doubts about the Solid Rocket Booster joint seal." Then the Commission report immediately states, "Had these matters been clearly stated and emphasized in the flight readiness process in terms reflecting the views of most of the Thiokol engineers and at least some of the Marshall engineers, it seems likely that the launch of 51-L might not have occurred when it did" (R.C., I, p. 104). But the gathering and passing on of such information was the responsibility of specifically designated individuals, known by name and position in the highly structured review process. Throughout this process there had been required "a series of formal, legally binding certifications, the equivalent of airworthiness inspections in the aviation industry. In effect the myriad contractor and NASA personnel involved were guaranteeing *Challenger's* flight readiness with their professional and personal integrity" (McConnell, 1987, p. 17).

When the Commission states in its next finding that "waiving of launch constraints appears to have been at the expense of flight safety," the immediate and obvious question would seem to be: Who approved the waivers and assumed this enormous risk? And why? This is a serious matter! A launch constraint is only issued because there is a safety problem serious enough to justify a decision not to launch. However, the Commission again deflects the problem onto the system by stating, "There was no system which made it imperative that launch constraints and waivers of launch constraints be considered by all levels of management" (R.C., 1986, I, p. 104).

There are two puzzling aspects to this Commission finding. First, the formal system already contained the requirement that project offices inform at least Level II of launch constraints. The Commission addressed the explicit violation of this requirement in the case of a July 1985 launch constraint that had been imposed on the Solid Rocket Booster because of O-ring erosion on the nozzle:

NASA Levels I and II apparently did not realize Marshall had assigned a launch constraint within the Problem Assessment System. This communication failure was contrary to the requirement, contained in the NASA Problem Reporting and Corrective Action Requirements System, that launch constraints were to be taken to Level II (R.C., 1986, I, pp. 138-139; see also p. 159).

Second, the Commission clearly established that the individual at Marshall who both imposed and waived the launch constraint was Lawrence Mulloy, SRB Project Manager. Then why blame the management system, especially in such a crucial area as that of launch constraints, when procedures of that system were not followed? Is that approach going to increase the accountability of individuals within the system for future flights?

Even such an independent minded and probing Commission member as Richard Feynman, in an interview a year after the disaster, agreed with the avoidance of determining individual accountability for specific actions and decisions. He is quoted as saying, "I don't think it's correct to try to find out which particular guy happened to do what particular thing. It's the question of how the atmosphere could get to such a circumstance that such things were possible without anybody catching on." Yet, at the same time Feynman admitted that he was not confident that any restructuring of the management system will ensure that the kinds of problems that resulted in the *Challenger* disaster—"danger signs not seen and warnings not heeded"— do not recur. He said, "I'm really not sure that any kind of simple mechanism can cure stupidity and dullness. You can make up all the rules about how things should be, and they'll go wrong if the spirit is different, if the attitudes are different over time and as personnel change" (Chandler, 1987, p. 50).

The approach of the Rogers Commission

and that of most of the analyses of the *Challenger* disaster is consistent with the growing tendency to deny any specific responsibility to individual persons within corporate or other institutional settings when things go wrong. Although there are obviously many social changes in modern life that justify the shift in focus from individuals to organizational structures as bearers of responsibility, this shift is reinforced and exaggerated by the way people think about and accept those changes. One of the most pernicious problems of modern times is the almost universally held belief that the individual is powerless, especially within the context of large organizations where one may perceive oneself, and be viewed, as a very small, and replaceable, cog. It is in the very nature of this situation that responsibility may seem to become so diffused that no one person IS responsible. As the National Research Council committee, in following up on the Rogers Commission, concluded about the space shuttle program:

> Given the pervasive reliance on teams and boards to consider the key questions affecting safety, 'group democracy' can easily prevail . . . in the end all decisions become collective ones . . . (N.R.C. Report, pp. 68 and 70).

The problem with this emphasis on management systems and collective responsibility is that it fosters a vicious circle that further and further erodes and obscures individual responsibility. This leads to a paradoxical—and untenable—situation (such as in the space shuttle program) in which decisions are made and actions are performed by individuals or groups of individuals but not attributed to them. It thus reinforces the tendency to avoid accountability for what anyone does by attributing the consequences to the organization or decision making process. Again, shared, rather than individual, risktaking and responsibility became operative. The end result can be a cancerous attitude that so permeates an organization or management system that it metastasizes into decisions and acts of life-threatening irresponsibility.

In sharp contrast to this prevalent emphasis on organizational structures, one of the most fascinating aspects of the extensive and exhaustive investigations into the *Challenger* disaster is that they provide a rare opportunity to re-affirm the sense and importance of individual responsibility. With the inside look into the space shuttle program these investigations detail, one can identify many instances where personal responsibility, carefully interpreted, can properly be imputed to NASA officials and to its contractors. By so doing, one can preserve, if only in a fragmentary way, the essentials of the traditional concept of individual responsibility within the diluting context of organizational life. This effort is intended to make explicit the kind of causal links that are operative between the actions of individuals and the structures of organizations.

The criteria commonly employed for holding individuals responsible for an outcome are two: (1) their acts or omissions are in some way a cause of it; and (2) these acts or omissions are not done in ignorance or under coercion (Thompson, 1987, p. 47). Although there are difficult theoretical and practical questions associated with both criteria, especially within organizational settings, nevertheless, even a general application of them to the sequence of events leading up to the *Challenger* disaster reveals those places where the principle of individual responsibility must be factored in if our understanding of it is to be complete, its lessons learned, and its repetition avoided.

The Rogers Commission has been criticized—and rightly so—for looking at the disaster "from the bottom up but not from the top down," with the result that it gives a clearer picture of what transpired at the lower levels of the *Challenger's* flight review process than at its upper levels (Cook, 1986). Nevertheless, in doing so, the Commission report provides powerful testimony that however elaborately structured and far reaching an undertaking such as the space shuttle program may be, individuals at the bottom of the organizational structure can still play a crucial, if not deciding, role in the outcome. For in the final analysis, whatever the defects in the *Challenger's* launch decision chain were that kept the upper levels from being duly informed about the objections of the engineers at Morton Thiokol, the fact remains that the strenuous objections of these engineers so forced the decision process at their level that the four middle managers at Morton Thiokol had the full responsibility for the launch in their hands. This is made clear in the startling testimony of Mr. Mason, when Chairman Rogers asked him: "Did you realize, and particularly in view of Mr. Hardy's (Deputy Director of Science and Engineering at MSFC) point that they wouldn't launch unless you agreed, did you fully realize that in effect, you were making a decision to launch, you and your colleagues?" Mr. Mason replied, "Yes, sir" (R.C., 1986, IV, p. 770).

If these four men had just said no, the launch of the *Challenger* would not have taken place the next day. . . .

Although fragmentary and tentative in its formulation, this set of considerations points toward the conclusion that however complex and sophisticated an organization may be, and no matter how large and remote the institutional network needed to manage it may be, an active and creative tension of responsibility must be maintained at every level of the operation. Given the size and complexity of such endeavors, the only way to ensure that tension of attentive and effective responsibility is to give the primacy of responsibility to that ultimate principle of all moral conduct: the human individual—even if this does necessitate, in too many instances under present circumstances, that individuals such as Roger Boisjoly, when they attempt to exercise their responsibility, must step forward as moral heroes. In so doing, these individuals do not just bear witness to the desperate need for a system of full accountability in the face of the immense power and reach of modern technology and institutions. They also give expression to the very essence of what constitutes the moral life. As Roger Boisjoly has stated in reflecting on his own experience, "I have been asked by some if I would testify again if I knew in advance of the potential consequences to me and my career. My answer is always an immediate 'yes'. I couldn't live with any self-respect if I tailored my actions based upon the personal consequences . . ." (Boisjoly, 1987).

REFERENCES

Boisjoly, Roger M.: 1985a, Applied Mechanics Memorandum to Robert K. Lund, Vice President, Engineering, Wasatch Division, Morton Thiokol, Inc., July 31.

Boisjoly, Roger M.: 1985b, Activity Report, SRM Seal Erosion Task Team Status, October 4.

Boisjoly, Roger M.: 1987, Ethical Decisions: Morton Thiokol and the Shuttle Disaster. Speech given at Massachusetts Institute of Technology, January 7.

Boling, T. Edwin and Dempsey, John: 1981, "Ethical dilemmas in government: Designing an organizational response," *Public Personnel Management Journal* 10, 11–18.

Chandler, David: 1987. "Astronauts gain clout in 'revitalized' NASA," *Boston Globe* 1 (January 26):50.

Christiansen, Donald: 1987, "A system gone awry," *IEEE Spectrum* 24(3):23.

Cook, Richard C.: 1986, "The Rogers commission failed," *The Washington Monthly* 18 (9), 13–21.

De George, Richard T.: 1981, "Ethical responsibilities of engineers in large organizations: The Pinto Case," *Business and Professional Ethics Journal* 1, 1–14.

Feynman, Richard P.: 1988, "An outsider's view of the Challenger inquiry" *Physics Today* 41 (2):26–37.

Janis, Irving L.: 1972, *Victims of Groupthink,* Boston, MA: Houghton Mifflin Company.

Kilminster, J. C.: 1985, Memorandum (E000-FY86-003) to Robert Lund, Vice President, Engineering, Wasatch Division, Morton Thiokol, Inc., July 5.

McConnell, Malcolm: 1987, *Challenger, A Major Malfunction: A True Story of Politics, Greed, and the Wrong Stuff,* Garden City, N.J.: Doubleday and Company, Inc.

Mankin, Hart T.: 1981, "Commentary on 'Ethical responsibilities of engineers in large organizations: The Pinto Case,'" *Business and Professional Ethics Journal* 1, 15–17.

National Research Council: 1988, *Post-Challenger Evaluation of Space Shuttle Risk Assessment and Management,* Washington, D.C.: National Academy Press.

Report of the Presidential Commission on the Space Shuttle Challenger Accident: 1986, Washington, D.C.: U.S. Government Printing Office.

Thompson, Dennis F.: 1987, *Political Ethics and Public Office,* Cambridge, MA: Harvard University Press.

Wilmotte, Raymond M.: 1970, "Engineering truth in competitive environments," *IEEE Spectrum* 7 (5):45–49.

Regulation and Paternalism

Steven Kelman

Opposition to paternalism plays an important role in the current national debate over the appropriate scope for government regulation, especially consumer protection regulation on behalf of safety and health. It is frequently summoned in condemning calls to ban saccharin or laetrile. It is pronounced likewise against proposals to require people to wear seatbelts or motorcycle helmets. And it appears in criticisms of safety standards for lawnmowers or autos, since such standards, although they neither ban nor mandate use of the product in question, do require that consumers pay for certain safety features if they wish to buy the product. The antipaternalistic contention is simple. If people know the risks of, say, saccharin and choose to run these risks for themselves in order to obtain the benefits they believe they will gain, who are we to interfere with that choice?

I believe that it is correct to oppose paternalism, but incorrect to tar most government consumer protection health and safety regulations with a paternalistic brush. . . .

There are, in other words, good nonpaternalistic arguments for such regulation, although these arguments are often mistaken for paternalistic ones. In the final section, I will discuss explicitly the question of whether there are ever any occasions when regulation might be justified on avowedly paternalistic grounds. . . .

DECISION-MAKING COSTS AND VOLUNTARY RENUNCIATION OF CHOICE AUTHORITY

In this section, I argue that when there are costs associated with deciding what choice to make, it is rational in some situations for an individual to renounce his authority to make the choice for himself, and to hand over such authority to a third party who will make the choice in the individual's interest. Such third-party choices are not paternalistic, because they are not made against the person's wishes. They introduce a new category, separate both from choices one makes oneself and from choices made paternalistically. Much government safety regulation of consumer products, I believe, falls into this category.

The probability that one would want to renounce the authority to choose increases (1) the more that the decision-making costs for the person exceed those for the third party, and (2) the closer the choice the third party makes is to the choice the person would have made. . . .

The costs of decision making include information-gathering costs, information-processing costs, and possibly psychological costs of choice. Information gathering costs are the costs of determining the existence of all the relevant features across which the different types of a product can vary and the different values these variables take across the different types of product. Information-processing costs are the costs of calculating the implication of the different values for a judgment of the benefits of the product, given one's preferences. Psychological costs are the frustration that may be felt from information overload or the trauma that may be experienced from having to make difficult choices.

An immense disservice to intelligent discussion of the safety regulation of consumer products occurs because of the tendency to base such discussions on a small number of dramatic instances—saccharin, seatbelts, laetrile. A statement such as, "People know that it's more risky to drive without seatbelts than with them, and if they choose to take that risk to avoid the discomfort of wearing the belts, that should be up to them," may be made with a straight face. People know the feature they are making a choice about (that is, they know what seatbelts are). They know what values the variable can take (the seatbelts may be

worn or not worn). They know the implications of these different values for their judgments about the choice (wearing seatbelts decreases risk but may increase discomfort).

The problem is that such individual dramatic examples are unrepresentative of the universe of choices that consumers would have to make for themselves in a world where they had to make all decisions about the safety features of products they buy themselves. Statements about consumers knowing the risks of failing to use seatbelts or consuming saccharin and choosing to bear them are plausible. Statements such as the following are far less so: "People know that if the distance between the slats on the infant crib is $2\frac{3}{8}$th inches there is little risk that an infant will strangle himself falling through the slats, while if the distance is $3\frac{1}{4}$th inches the risk is much greater, and if they choose to take this risk to get a crib that is less expensive, that should be up to them." The reader may ask himself if he would feel confident identifying which one of the four following substances that may be present in food is far more risky than the other three: calcium hexametaphosphate, methyl paraben, sodium benzoate, and trichloroethylene. Or he may ask himself how confident he would feel making decisions about what safety features to buy in order to guard against power lawnmower accidents or to protect against a radio exploding or electrocuting him. If he does know, how confident does he feel that he understands the risks associated with various levels of the substance? Is five parts per million of benzene hexachloride a lot or a little? If the bacteria count in frozen egg is one million per gram, should we be alarmed?

What these examples suggest—they could be multiplied manyfold—is that consumers do not ordinarily have anything approaching perfect information for judging the safety of most consumer products themselves, the misleading examples from widely publicized regulatory controversies over issues such as seatbelts and saccharin to the contrary notwithstanding. Compared with their knowledge of product features such as appearance, convenience, or taste, knowledge of safety features is typically very small.

One conclusion sometimes drawn is that lack of knowledge demonstrates lack of concern. If people do not know about safety features, it is sometimes argued, that means they do not care about them. This conclusion does not follow from the premise. When information-gathering costs something, the amount of information gathered depends not only on the perceived benefits of the information but also on how costly it would be to gather. I may "care" about two product features equally, but if information on one is cheap to obtain and information on the other is expensive, I will gather more information on the first feature than on the second. Information on product features such as appearance or convenience is often relatively easy to get. Information on a product's appearance is garnered by simple observation. For a product that does not cost very much and that is frequently repurchased, experience is a cheap way to gain information about the product's convenience or taste. I may buy a certain brand of orange soda or paper tissue and try it. Then I will know whether I like it.

By contrast, gathering information on safety features is often very costly. Frequently, arcane or technical facts must be understood, and the recourse to experience is not available in the same way as with many other product features. Using a risky product does not always lead to an accident. Drinking a brand of orange soda will always lead to information on its taste, but not on its additives. To go through the pain of an injury or illness is a very high cost to pay for gathering information about a product's safety. . . .

The first criterion for a situation in which it would be rational for an individual to hand over decision-making authority to a third party is when the third party can gather the information more cheaply than the individual can. This criterion often applies in the case of safety features. The per consumer cost of gathering safety information is likely to be much less for an expert third party gathering it for a large group of consumers than for an individual. An expert has an easier time finding out about and evaluating different technical safety features. Since only one gathering process need occur, its cost can be divided among the large group for whom it is undertaken, rather than having to be separately borne by each individual consumer assembling similar information for himself.

The second cost associated with the act of choosing is the cost in information-processing. This involves taking information about a product feature and evaluating its significance in light of one's preferences. Memory and other cognitive limitations make it costly or simply impossible to process large amounts of information about a product, even if the information is available. Information processing costs clearly vary across people and situations, but the more information that must be processed, the higher the processing costs. Furthermore, there is evidence that at some point "information overload" occurs, where the brain has too much information to process. Under the circumstances, one's skill at evaluating information can decrease so much that the choice reflects one's preferences worse than a choice made where less information was available, but could be processed better. . . . Overload may appear not only when we must process a lot of information for a single choice, but also when we must process little information for many choices.

Choice may carry with it psychological costs as well. To be sure, there are many instances, as noted earlier, where people relish the opportunity to choose. In other instances, people might not relish the process, but believe that a choice made by a third party is likely to be so inferior to the choice they make themselves that they are willing to pay possible psychological costs. But this is not always the case. Life would be unbearable if we constantly had to make all decisions for ourselves. Information overload may produce not only evaluations poorer in quality but also feelings of frustration growing out of the realization that our brains are not processing information as well as they usually do. Furthermore, people can find some kinds of decisions very unpleasant to make. These might include choices that are complicated, ones that involve thinking about distasteful things, or ones where all the alternatives are disagreeable. Everyday experience is filled with instances where people try to avoid making unpleasant decisions—if this were not the case, Harry Truman would never have placed the sign "The buck stops here" in his office. Linus, the Peanuts comic strip character, expressed the trauma that can accompany difficult choices when he said, "No problem is so big or so complicated that it can't be run away from." . . .

As with costs of information-gathering, the costs of information-processing and the psychological costs of choice are likely frequently to be lower for an expert third party, as far as safety is concerned, than for the individual. Decisions about safety, because they involve so much technical information, are likely to be those where information overload makes processing costly. They are also likely to be decisions that many people find unpleasant to make. They require that one contemplate the prospect of illness, disfigurement, or even death. They also necessitate thought about tradeoffs between saving money and taking risks—thoughts that most people also find unpleasant, as can be seen by looking at how politicians, agency officials, and even business spokesmen themselves squirm when such

topics are raised. In fact, I believe this uneasiness is one of the main reasons why safety decisions are handed over to government. . . .

Objections to the Information Argument for Intervention

Different objections might be made to the argument developed so far. One that is frequently heard runs something like this: If the consumer has difficulty making choices about safety features because he lacks information, then let the government see that the requisite information is provided, rather than mandating safety features or banning products. To do more, the argument goes, would be to throw out the baby of individual choice with the bathwater of imperfect information. . . .

Another objection is sometimes raised: Voluntary renunciation of consumer choice to *some* third party need not justify *government* standards or product bans. Consumers might hire a personal agent to make the choice for them. Or the government might be limited to certify that a product meets whatever safety standards the agency determines to be appropriate. All these methods, it is argued, allow voluntary renunciation of the authority to choose without mandatory government regulation.

I will first consider arguments claiming that the government's role should be limited to information provision—or even that such an information provision role is unjustified. For the government to mandate provision of information or to provide it itself does indeed lower information-gathering costs. To require its dissemination in nontechnical form lowers these costs further. And to make the information conveniently available (as part of labeling) lowers it still further. These steps sometimes do lower decision-making costs enough to make it worthwhile for consumers to retain their authority to choose. An example would be in the area of product quality, where the psychological costs of choice are low and preferences differ widely across consumers. In these cases, government should stick to such tasks. But in other situations, all these steps still would not lower decision-making costs enough to make it rational for a consumer to retain his authority to choose. Under such a regime, consumers still might be confronted frequently with columns of fine print presenting large numbers of product features and risk information about each. The information-processing costs of evaluating this information in the light of one's preferences remain unaffected by the cheaper information-gathering. Any psychological decision-making costs are unaffected as well. . . .

Let us turn now to objections that the third party need not be the government. Consumers might choose to let decisions be made for them by friends they trust or by expert agents they hire to make the decisions in their interests. Mandatory government regulation, the argument continues, is a poor vehicle for making decisions that a consumer chooses to renounce, because it binds not only those who choose *not* to make the choice themselves, but also those who *would* have wanted to do so.

Certainly there are instances where choice by agents that a consumer seeks out might be preferable to decisions by government. Consumers use doctors as agents, for instance, and to some limited extent retail stores act as agents as well. One advantage such choices have is that the agent can be apprised of the client's individual preferences. By contrast, a government agency must make a single choice, despite the existence of diverse preferences among citizens. But in other instances, looking for, paying, and monitoring a privately hired agent would be more expensive than having the government undertake the same tasks. This greater expense might outweigh the advantages of a choice personally tailored to the client's preferences. Fur-

thermore, the private provision of the information-gathering aspect of the agent's job creates the same public goods problems as any private provision of information. And for a person to seek an agent in any individual instance, he must have enough knowledge of the existence of dimensions along which he wishes to judge the product in question to know that he needs an agent in the first place.

Another way for a person to renounce his authority to choose without requiring mandatory government regulation is for the government to certify the safety of products and for the consumer, who wished to renounce his authority, to choose simply to buy the certified product. In certifying a product, the government would decide on appropriate safety features. The only difference would be that it would not be mandatory that all products comply with the features. Only those that did comply, however, would be certified. If a consumer decides to buy a certified product, he in effect has let the government make his decision for him. But those who wish to decide for themselves would have the choice of buying a product without the certified safety feature package.

Choosing to buy certified products might be an appropriate form for voluntary renunciation of the authority to choose. But it might not be a consumer's preferred alternative either. Most important as a reason for preferring mandatory regulation to certification is the fear that despite one's general resolution to buy only certified products, one might be tempted in individual cases to depart from one's resolution and buy noncertified ones. . . .

Even if we end up not giving in to temptation, we might wish to be spared temptation so as to avoid the anxiety costs of realizing that one might, at any time, give in. Thus, a person might well prefer mandatory regulation to certification out of fear that in many specific instances, with one lawnmower in front of him that is certified and another that is not, he might "take a chance" and get the cheaper, noncertified one, although as a general matter of considered reflection he would wish to buy only certified products. People frequently choose to have an alternative withheld from them at later times just to avoid temptation. . . .

It may be accepted that there are people who would rather have government set mandatory safety standards than hire private agents or have the government certify product safety. Yet it still might be protested that others who would prefer to make the decisions themselves (or to hire their own agents or choose with the help of government certification) should not be forced to pay for safety features they do not want.

Under the circumstances, one group or the other will end up being hurt. Either those opposed to mandatory safety standards are harmed by being forced to buy products with mandated features, or those favoring mandatory standards are hurt by having to do without the mandatory standards they seek. Whether the social decision finally made responds to the wishes of the first group or the second has, then, external effects on the group whose wishes are denied. . . . Those seeking mandatory regulation are demanding something that will help themselves and hurt those who would prefer to choose for themselves. The latter group, then, may be seen as passive victims of the acts of those demanding regulation. The *prima facie* duty to do justice suggests sympathy with passive victims against active encroachers. Nevertheless, considerations of the size of the groups seeking and wishing to avoid regulation, as well as of the nature of the interference contemplated, are relevant to such judgments. In regard to the size of the groups in the case of government safety regulation, there exist unambiguous survey data. In a 1974 poll, respondents were asked whether the government should "make sure that each packaged, canned, or frozen food is safe to eat." An overwhelming 97% agreed, a degree of unanimity hard to replicate for any government policy. In a 1976 poll, respondents were asked a similar question about government product safety standards and 85% agreed.[1] As for the extent of interference, it is not generally great. Those opposed to regulation are interfered with to the extent of having to pay some extra money for safety features they would have preferred to avoid. Their homes are not broken into. They are not restrained by physical force from moving around where they wish. Their fortunes are not decimated. My own conclusion is that it would be wrong to prevent the vast majority of Americans who prefer to turn the general run of decisions about product safety over to the government from doing so.

The figures on the percentages of those who wish to turn safety decisions over to the government also shed light on the earlier brief examination of whether decisions made by government safety regulators were likely to be sufficiently similar to those that consumers would make themselves, if fully informed, to make it rational for consumers voluntarily to hand such choices over to regulators. If government agencies did make decisions frequently that wildly departed from those that consumers would make themselves, one would expect the survey results to have been dramatically different. Instead, they show a broad vote of confidence for the efforts of government agencies regulating product safety. . . .

EXTERNAL EFFECTS AND THE OVERRULING OF A PERSON'S OWN CHOICE

John Stuart Mill affirmed in *On Liberty* that the restriction against interference with a person's authority to choose applied to acts that affected only the individual himself and not to those acts affecting others. Ever since Mill, however, this distinction has come under withering attack. Government intervention in people's choice may occur not out of a desire to overrule paternalistically an individual's choices insofar as they regard only himself, but out of a desire to protect others against the negative consequences of those choices. Thus, banning saccharin or requiring people to wear seatbelts might be justified on nonpaternalistic grounds even if people did not want to hand these decisions to the government, because of the effects bladder cancer or auto accidents have, not on the individual himself, but on others. The distinction between intervention on paternalistic grounds and intervention on the grounds that others must be protected against the negative consequences of a person's behavior is often lost in the general public debate on regulation, where opposition to both kinds of intervention tends to get lumped together as complaints against "government interference." Thus, the resentment of businessmen against OSHA or EPA regulations should not be confused with resentment against a bureaucrat who believes he knows what is good for a person better than the person does himself.

The discussions of external effects, such as pollution, in introductory economics textbooks tend to obscure the issue, because they imply that most actions lack external effects. That "no man is an island" dashes any attempt to make such neat categorizations. . . .

If a person becomes sick or is injured or if he dies because he purchased an unsafe product, clearly his action in buying the product had external effects on friends and loved ones. If a person is insured, other policyholders ultimately foot the bills. If a person is not insured and suffers great financial hardship, other members of society still end up paying. When the victim appears before us after a sad fate has befallen him, the rest of us pay cash to help the uninsured victim out—or pay in the form of the guilty feelings occasioned by turning our backs on the victim, even if we attempt the justification that the victim made his bed and now should have to lie in it. The fact that we end up either saving people from the really bad consequences of their choices or feeling guilty if we do not is an argument, based on external effects and not on paternalism, for intervening in the original choices. Consequently, we require people to provide for their old age through Social Security, give the poor inkind rather than cash transfers, or mandate safety regulations.

None of this means that our every move should be subject to government restrictions. Almost everyone who has thought seriously about the implications of the ubiquity of external effects has come to the conclusion that society must establish which acts individuals have a right to do or refrain from doing, despite the harm the act may inflict on others, and which are too harmful to permit to go unhindered or be left undone, despite the fact that the individual would prefer to behave otherwise. . . .

To decide in a given case whether an individual should have the right to make decisions about what risks to take, despite the harm that the bad consequences of such decisions can cause others, raises difficult questions to which answers cannot be cranked out deductively. It will not do to argue, as is sometimes done, that external effects arguments must never be used to justify restricting risks because it would be possible to use such arguments to eradicate all exercises of liberty. For the fact is that *everyone*, even libertarians, recognizes that at some point the external effects of an individual's acts become great enough to justify taking away the individual's right to act. Thus, all agree that murder or assault are not rightful displays of liberty. We cannot escape a controversial balancing process in which the extent of the external effects that the person's actions produce, the importance of the act for the individual, and possible deontological considerations regarding *prima facie* duties, are weighed against one another. . . .

The purpose of this article has not been to defend or criticize any specific examples of government safety regulation. Rather, I have attempted to defend the justifiability, in principle, of such regulation against the specific accusation that it inevitably involves paternalism and hence should be condemned. I have agreed with the general condemnation of pa-

ternalism, while suggesting nonpaternalistic justifications for such intervention and arguing that there are certain cases where cautious paternalistic intervention might be justified. . . .

NOTE

1. These figures are from Food and Drug Administration (1976). *Consumer Nutrition Knowledge Survey, Report I*, Washington, DC: FDA, p. 39.

Criteria for Government Regulations

Norman E. Bowie

In a penetrating analysis of law (*The Morality of Law*), Lon Fuller identified eight conditions that any legal system must fulfill if it is to be considered a good legal system.[1] These eight conditions include (1) laws must be general (laws are not made to apply to one individual), (2) laws must be publicized, (3) laws cannot be made retroactively, (4) laws must be understandable, (5) the set of laws should not contain rules that are contradictory, (6) laws must be within the power of citizens to obey them, (7) laws must maintain a certain stability through time, and (8) laws as announced must be in agreement with their actual administration.

Fuller's eight conditions for a good legal system have such a ring of self-evidence about them that explanatory comments can be kept to a minimum. However, in the course of sup-

plying some explanatory comment, the extent to which government regulation violates these eight conditions for good law will become obvious. The condition of generality is clearly related to the analyses of justice and the universalizability required by Kant's categorical imperative. Rules are not directed toward a single person but rather are to apply to a class of persons. Relevantly similar persons are to be treated similarly. What is a reason in one case must be a reason in all similar cases.

Despite this requirement of generality, much regulatory law proceeds in an opposite direction. Fuller says,

> In recent history perhaps the most notable failure to achieve general rules has been that of certain of our regulatory agencies, particularly

Adapted from Norman E. Bowie, *Business Ethics*, pp. 118–124, © 1982. Reprinted by permission of Prentice Hall, Englewood Cliffs, N.J.

those charged with allocative functions. . . . [T]hey were embarked on their careers in the belief that by proceeding at first case by case they would gradually gain an insight which would enable them to develop general standards of decision. In some cases this hope has been almost completely disappointed; this is notably so in the case of the Civil Aeronautics Board and the Federal Communications Commission.[2]

If general rules are essential to good regulatory law as has been argued, then the case-by-case method is inadequate. If the government takes a position regarding water pollution from one of Bethlehem Steel's plants, the president of Bethlehem Steel should be able to conclude that the government will take a similar position on similar conditions at all Bethlehem's plants. Moreover, the president of Bethlehem Steel should be able to conclude that the same position will be taken when the same situation exists at other competing steel plants. If Fuller's description is right, the state of regulatory law is such that the president of Bethlehem Steel could *not* conclude that a similar position would be taken and hence much regulatory law is seriously deficient.

The second condition is that the laws be publicized. This condition goes hand in hand with the conditions of generality and stability. One cannot obey the law if one does not know what the law is. Regulatory law does conform—on the whole—to this condition. The regulations do appear in federal documents such as the *Federal Register*. However, any academic researcher who has worked with government documents knows that finding a rule or regulation is often no easy task. Large corporations have legal teams to assist them in knowing what the law is. However, as government regulations grow, the small business houses suffer a distinct handicap in their capability to know the law. To the extent the regulations change rapidly over time, the publicity requirement becomes harder and harder to meet.

Third, laws should not be made retroactively, and generally they are not. The reason for this requirement is clear. Laws are designed to guide behavior. A retroactive law violates the fundamental purpose of laws since it obviously cannot guide conduct. It punishes behavior that was legal at the time it was done. Business leaders complain that government regulators at least approach violating this condition when they threaten firms with penalties for environmental damage when there is no way for the firm to have known that some of its activities were causing environmental damage. A company should not be penalized for damage it caused to the earth's ozone layer when it produced fluorocarbons in the 1960s.

The fourth requirement of clarity is, to many business executives, the condition that government regulations most often violate. Loaded with jargon and bad grammar, these regulations often present a nightmare for highly trained corporate legal staffs and an impossible situation for small companies. An example to illustrate the point:

212.75 Crude Oil Produced and Sold from Unitized Properties.
(b) Definitions. For purposes of this section— "Current unit cumulative deficiency" means (1) for months prior to June 1, 1979, the total number of barrels by which production and sale of crude oil from the unitized property was less than the unit base production control level subsequent to the first month (following the establishment of a unit base production control level for that unitized property) in which any crude oil produced and sold from that unit was eligible to be classified as actual new crude oil (without regard to whether the amount of actual new crude oil was exceeded by the amount of imputed new crude oil), minus the total number of barrels of domestic crude oil produced and sold in each prior month from that unitized property (following the establishment of a unit base production control level for that unit-

ized property) which was in excess of the unit base production control level for that month, but which was not eligible to be classified as actual new crude oil because of this requirement to reduce the amount of actual new crude oil in each month by the amount of the current unit cumulative deficiency.[3]

Fifth, a system of laws that contains laws contradicting one another is inadequate because a situation covered by the contradictory laws requires the impossible. Fuller focuses on the federal Food, Drug, and Cosmetic Act.

Section 704 of that act defines the conditions under which an inspector may enter a factory; one of these conditions is that he first obtain the permission of the owner. Section 331 makes it a crime for the owner of the factory to refuse "to permit entry or inspection as authorized by section 704." The Act seems, then, to say that the inspector has a right to enter the factory but that the owner has a right to keep him out by refusing permission.[4]

Actually, the instances of contradiction cited by businesspersons are not so obvious as those in the case given. Most contradictions in laws governing business practice result from two sources: (1) from contradictory rules issued by independent agencies responsible for the same area and (2) from contradictory rules issued by independent agencies on separate matters but when applied in a specific case lead to contradiction.

To illustrate just how complex the issue of the contradictory nature of law can become, consider, for example, the Sears suit against a number of federal agencies or officers, including the attorney general, the secretary of Labor, the chairman of the Equal Opportunity Commission (EOC), and seven other cabinet officers and federal agencies. The issue of contention is antidiscrimination statutes. Employers like Sears are not to discriminate on the basis of race, sex, age, or physical and mental handicaps. Yet the employer is required to give preference to veterans. But

since veterans are overwhelmingly male, the required preference for veterans is in contradiction with the requirement that no preference be given to sex. Preferences for veterans ipso facto give preference to males. It is reported that

The Company [Sears] asked the court to grant an injunction requiring the defendants "to coordinate the employment of anti-discrimination statutes" and to issue uniform guidelines that would tell employers "how to resolve existing conflicts between affirmative-action requirements based on race and sex and those based on veterans' status, age, and physical or mental handicaps."[5]

Without judging either Sears' motives for the suit or its behavior with respect to nondiscrimination, the Sears request for consistency is warranted in point of logic and good regulation.

Sixth, laws requiring the impossible violate the fundamental purpose of law—the guidance of human conduct. This point seems so obvious that it hardly needs comment. Yet a tradition is growing in legal circles that clearly violates this principle. Strict liability holds a person or corporation liable for an act even when they are not responsible for it. Fuller points out the absurdity of allowing strict liability to expand so that it covers all activities.

If strict liability were to attend, not certain specified forms of activity, but all activities, the conception of a causal connection between the act and the resulting injury would be lost. A poet writes a sad poem. A rejected lover reads it and is so depressed that he commits suicide. Who "caused" the loss of his life? Was it the poet, or the lady who jilted the deceased, or perhaps the teacher who aroused his interest in poetry? A man in a drunken rage shoots his wife. Who among those concerned with this event share the responsibility for its occurrence—the killer himself, the man who lent the gun to him, the liquor dealer who provided the gin, or was it perhaps the friend who dissuaded him from securing a divorce that would have ended an unhappy alliance?[6]

Hence, to conform to this requirement of good law, the government regulations of business must rest on an adequate theory that delineates a class of undesirable acts that can result from business activity and then assesses the extent to which business must be shown to be responsible for their acts before being held liable. It may well be, for example, that some activities (blasting) are so dangerous that strict liability should be invoked to discourage the activity in question. However, in many cases strict liability is not the appropriate legal category and business people are quite right in being concerned about its ever-growing application.

Another condition that seems constantly violated in the government regulation of business is Fuller's seventh requirement of constancy through time. Government regulations are in a constant state of flux. One person replaces another in the White House and the rules of the game change. Let there be a change in the leadership of a major congressional committee and the rules change again.

During the early years of the environmental crisis, companies were forced or encouraged to abandon coal because it tended to be a highly polluting fuel. Now that the energy crisis is here, companies are being encouraged or forced to return to coal to save precious oil. The expenses involved in these transitions are staggering. Something must be done to control the anarchic flux so characteristic of the government regulation of business.

Finally, there should be agreement between the law and the way it is administered. It is one thing to discover what the law is. It is quite another to have the law enforced as written. Business people argue that the federal and state regulatory bureaucracies are filled with petty individuals whose only means of gaining self-respect is by blocking the legitimate plans or aims of business. The time and effort involved in fighting these people discourages the growth of small business and encourages large businesses to provide either a

psychic or monetary bribe to clear the roadblocks. There has been much talk about protecting employee rights within the firm. Devices must also be found to protect the legitimate interests of individual businesses from the government bureaucracy.

To balance this criticism, the reader should know that Fuller's eight conditions for good law represent an ideal for a legal system. The reader should also realize that Fuller's ideal works best for statutes; it works somewhat less well for administrative decisions. No legal system can conform completely to Fuller's ideals. Take the condition that the law must be stable through time. Change, including change in the conditions that produced the law in the first place, requires change in the law as well. Before OPEC and the oil crisis, cleaning up the atmosphere required regulations that discouraged the burning of coal. The oil embargo changed all that. Strategic considerations required encouragement for the use of coal. This shift in policy was expensive, but, given the changes in the world situation, the shift was necessary.

Fuller would agree here. Indeed, that is why he refers to his eight conditions as constituting a morality of the ideal rather than a morality of duty. However, Fuller is right in indicating that departures from these eight conditions do have costs, including the cost of undermining the law itself.

Others might argue that regulatory law is something of a misnomer. Regulatory "law" has less in common with law than it does with judicial decisions or executive decisions. What constitutes the disanalogy, Fuller's critics believe, is that judicial decisions or executive decisions are geared to specific situations and hence have less of the characteristics of generality than do statutes. Fuller might concede much of this point yet insist, correctly I believe, that his eight conditions still serve as an ideal for judicial and executive decisions as well. After all, Supreme Court *decisions* are viewed by everyone as establishing precedents. Perhaps the rule for the pricing of gas at the pumps need not be clear to everyone, but it should at least be clear to the oil companies, shouldn't it?

With these cautions in mind, Fuller's eight conditions for good law are fundamentally sound. Even when Fuller's eight conditions are recognized as an ideal, the fact that so much government regulatory policy stands in violation of them points out a serious inadequacy in the use of government regulation for achieving ethical corporate behavior. After all, government through its judicial system and through some regulation is, as we have seen, a requirement for a stable business environment. Both the law and business are rule-governed activities. When the rules that apply to business or that sustain and protect business violate the conditions for good law, business is harmed. Laws that are not stable do adversely affect incentives and efficiency.

Laws that are not clear or that require the impossible, or that apply retroactively, or that are contradictory are unreasonable and unworkable. Both the business community and the public at large have every right to insist that the laws regulating business should confirm to the criteria for good law.

NOTES

1. Lon Fuller, *The Morality of Law*, rev. ed. (New Haven, Conn.: Yale University Press, 1964), p. 39.
2. Ibid., p. 46.
3. *Federal Register*, vol. 44, no. 69, April 9, 1979.
4. Fuller, *The Morality of Law*, p. 67.
5. "Sears Turns the Tables," *Newsweek*, February 5, 1979, pp. 86–87.
6. Fuller, *The Morality of Law*, p. 76.

Why the Law Can't Do It

Christopher D. Stone

Wherever the market is inadequate as a control, one can, of course, act to shore it up by law. . . . If the majority of the people believe the market and present laws inadequate to keep corporations within socially desirable bounds, the society can, through its democratic processes, make tougher laws. . . . But I am . . . suggesting that even if the corporation followed the law anyway, it would not be enough. The first set of reasons involves what I shall call the "time-lag problem"; the second concerns limitations connected with the making of law; the third concerns limitations connected with the mechanisms for implementing the law.

THE TIME-LAG PROBLEM

Even if we put aside the defects in the impact of the sanctions, there still remains the problem that the law is primarily a reactive institution. Lawmakers have to appreciate and respond to problems that corporate engineers, chemists, and financiers were anticipating (or could have anticipated) long before—that the drugs their corporations are about to produce can alter consciousness or damage the gene pool of the human race, that they are on the verge of multinational expansion that will endow them with the power to trigger worldwide financial crises in generally unforeseen ways, and so on. Even if laws could be passed to deal effectively with these dangers, until they are passed a great deal of damage—some perhaps irreversible—can be done. Thus, there is something grotesque—and socially dangerous—in encouraging corporate managers to believe that, until the law tells them otherwise, they have no responsibilities beyond the law and their impulses (whether their impulses spring from the id or from the balance sheet). We do not encourage human beings to suppose so. And the dangers to society seem all the more acute where corporations are concerned.

LIMITATIONS CONNECTED WITH THE MAKING OF LAW

To claim society's desires will be realized so long as the corporations "follow the edict of the populus" fails to take into account *the role of corporations in making the very law that we trust to bind them.* This is, incidentally, not an especially modern development or one peculiar to laws regulating corporations. The whole history of commercial law is one in which, by and large, the "legislation" has been little more than an acknowledgment of rules established by the commercial sector, unless there are the strongest and most evident reasons to the contrary. Thus, in many areas such as food, drug, and cosmetic regulation, and, more recently, with respect to the promulgation of safety rules by the Department of Transportation, the government effectively adopts the standards worked out with the industry. Such processes do not always bespeak, as is sometimes intimated, sinister sales of power. The real roots are more cumbersome, more bureaucratic, more "necessary," and therefore more difficult to remedy: The regulating body is considerably outstaffed and relatively uninformed; it knows

that it has to "live with" the industry it is regulating; it does not want to set standards that it always will be having to fight to enforce. . . .

Even the specialized regulatory agencies, much less the Congress, cannot in their rulemaking capacities keep technically abreast of the industry. Are employees who work around asbestos being subjected to high risks of cancer? What psychological and physical dangers lurk in various forms of manufacturing processes? What are the dangers to field workers, consumers, and the environment of various forms of pesticides? Congress and the various regulatory bodies can barely begin to answer these questions. The companies most closely associated with the problems may not know the answers either; but they certainly have the more ready access to the most probative information. It is their doctors who treat the employees' injuries; it is their chemists who live with and test the new compounds; it is their health records that gather absentee data. Granted, there are practical problems of getting corporations to gather and come forward with the relevant data, . . . But at this juncture my point is only this: Here, too, it is a lame argument that working within traditional legal strategies, we can keep corporations in line.

In many cases lawmaking is an unsatisfactory way to deal with social problems not because of a lack of "facts" in the senses referred to above, but because we, as a society, *lack consensus as to the values we want to advance.* For example, people do not want corporations to deplete natural resources "too fast," but desiring the luxuries that the resources can yield, differ on what "too fast" means. Then, too, we who live in the present do not know how to take into account the values that future generations might attach to the resources. Problems of this sort exist everywhere we look. Consider a drug that can benefit 99 percent of people who suffer from some disease, but could seriously injure 1 percent: Should it be banned from the market? People value inexpensive power. They also value a clean environment. These factors point toward construction of nuclear generating stations. But such stations put a risk on life. The problem ushered in is not merely a "factual" one in the narrow sense—for example, what is the probability over any time horizon of an accident that will cause such and such a magnitude of disaster. It is more complex still. For even if we could agree upon these "facts," how can we agree upon and factor into our decision the various values involved—the value of human life, the value of a relatively clean environment, those "fragile" values so easily lost in the shuffle of a technological society with its computers geared for the consumption of hard, quantifiable facts?

A closely related difficulty involves our increasing *lack of confidence as to causes and effects.* Let me explain this by a contrast. Suppose A shoots B, intending to kill him, and B dies. We place A on trial for murder. Why A? No one who has reflected upon the matter would be so naive as to suppose that A was the "sole cause" of B's death either in any valid scientific sense or from a broader social perspective. As the defense attorney might remind us, "A was a product of a broken family, an intolerable social environment," and so on. What is more, by focusing on A as the legally responsible entity, we are overlooking the effect that a judgment of guilt will have on those other than A. His family will also be hurt by meting out "justice" to A. If he was a productive worker, the whole society will suffer to some degree. Thus, when we select A as the focus of legal responsibility, we are making simplifying judgments both on the causality side—supposing him to be the sole cause—and on the effect side—overlooking the effects on others. . . .

There are today, however, a whole host of major social problems that remain so for the reason that we cannot accept the simplified judgments as to causality and effect that traditional legal solutions demand. Take, as example of a major contemporary social dilemma, the problem of "inner-city blight." What entities can we single out for responsibility, either pragmatically or morally? The slum dwellers? Slum landlords? City employers who take their operations to other states? How complex, uncertain, and even counterintuitive are the implications of any particular remedy that we may try. Worse, our uncertainties seem only to increase the more we develop methods and machinery to take into account the variety of factors we are increasingly capable of seeing are involved. A sort of legislative paralysis results—or worse, a legislative panic.

Even in those instances when the relevant facts can be established, and the relevant values are matters of consent, we may be able to agree upon what to do only in the most general way, inadequately for translation into viable legal rules. As the earth gets more and more crowded, and life more complex, increasingly such problems arise. For example, while we all agree that bad odors ought to be held to a tolerable level in residential or mixed residential areas, it is not easy to translate this decision into enforceable legal machinery. How does one spell out a rule so that those bound by it know how to orient their behavior. . . .

The vagueness problem has even more serious ramifications than appear on first glance. For one thing, the administration of justice in this country depends upon most litigation being settled out of court, and the more vague a statute, the more in doubt an outcome, and thus the more likely we are to find our court dockets crowded with cases that neither side is prepared to concede. A related point is that when standards are vague, the persons against whom they are turned are apt to feel personally and arbitrarily selected out for persecution, victims of men, rather than of the laws. When people—or corporations—feel themselves to have had no fair warning, increased friction between industry and government is likely to result, a development that has numerous regrettable ramifications. (The vagueness of the antitrust laws, real and imagined, is a common point of complaint among businesspersons and serves as a justification for the short shrift they would like to give laws and "government interference" generally.) What is more, if the language really is vague, the law is that much less likely to be an effective force in the face of competing, more definite constraints on the organization, such as the "need" to return profits, increase price-earnings ratios, and the like.

One can, of course, try to obviate the vagueness by seeking more and more precision in the law's language. But in doing so we risk making matters considerably worse. There is the possibility that once we have unleashed the regulators to make finer and finer regulations, the regulations become an end in themselves, a cumbersome, frustrating, and pointless web for those they entangle. Second, what all too often happens when legislatures try to turn vague value sentiments into tangible, measurable legal terms is that the rules they come up with have lost touch with the values they were originally designed to advance. There is a fascinating example of this in the area of water pollution. In their study of the attempt to reduce pollution in the Delaware River area, Bruce Ackerman and James Sawyer have shown that the regulators have emphasized dissolved oxygen content (D.O.) as a critical standard—the amount of D.O. in the water being taken as an inverse measure of how badly the water is polluted. What Ackerman and Sawyer show, however, is that if one looks at the values that lie behind efforts to minimize water pollution —boating and swimming, potable water, support of fish life—actually over a broad range of D.O. content, D.O. is an inadequate measure of whether or not any of those values are being advanced. Thus, while D.O. has the attractiveness

of being traditionally recognized among sanitary engineers (it is "hard" and computerizable), gearing laws to it makes limited sense, at best. . . .

LIMITATIONS CONNECTED WITH IMPLEMENTING THE LAW

When we do push ahead even in the face of our doubts as to values, our uncertainty as to facts, and the myriad difficulties of fashioning our wants into legal language, further problems lie ahead. Each of them raises its own doubts as to the virtue of a society in which the outer bounds of a corporation's responsibility are established by the limits we can set down through law.

The fact is that a combination of factors, including the increased expectations of today's citizens and the increasingly technical nature of the society, have left our traditional legal mechanisms unsatisfactory to cope with the problems that currently concern people. Consider for example, the law of torts, the ordinary rule for recovering damages against someone who has injured you. A model tort case is one in which Smith, who is walking across the street, is accidentally but negligently driven into by Jones. Smith falls, suffering internal injuries, and sues for damages. Now, I call this "a model" case because certain of its features make it so well suited to traditional legal recovery. Note that (a) Smith knows *the fact* that he has been injured; (b) Smith knows *who* has caused the injury; (c) one can assess, fairly well, the *nature and extent* of his injuries; and (d) the *technical inquiry* involved in analyzing causality is not too extensive—that is, simple laws of physics are involved, not beyond commonsense experience.

But contrast that model case—a case in which the tort laws may be fairly adequate to make restitution—with the sort of case that is increasingly of concern in the society today.

The food we will eat tonight (grown, handled, packaged, distributed by various corporations) may contain chemicals that are killing us, or at least reducing our life expectancy considerably. But (a) we cannot know with certainty the fact that we are being injured by any particular product; (b) it is difficult determining who might be injuring us—that is, even if we know that our bodies are suffering from a buildup of mercury, we are faced with an awesome task of pinning responsibility on any particular source of mercury; (c) we would have a difficult time proving the extent of our injuries (the more so proving the extent attributable to any particular source); and (d) the nature of the evidence that would have to be evaluated by the court is far more complex and technical than that in the "model" case above—perhaps too technical realistically to trust to courts or even agencies to handle. Thus, it seems inevitable that a certain percentage of harmful, even seriously harmful activity is not going to be contained by trusting to traditional legal mechanisms.

Then, too, at some point the costs of enforcing the law are going to transcend the benefits, and the law may not, on balance, be worth the effort. We can, for example, prohibit employers from discriminating on the basis of sex, and if we are using the law merely as a means of declaring social policy, it may make good sense to do so. But if we were to undertake serious systematic enforcement, the policing and prosecution costs (absent a strong sense by the employer that the law is right) would be questionably high. Some of the costs of falling back on law are obvious: administering court systems and staffing administrative agencies. . . . But there are other sorts of less direct "costs" hidden in such a system. There are various sorts of costs that arise from the attendant government-industry friction. A network of rules and regulations, backed by threats of litigation, breeds distrust, destruction of documents, and an attitude that "I won't do anything more than I am absolutely required to do."

The counterproductiveness of law can be extreme. I have already referred to the manner in which threatening directors and officers with legal liability impedes an ideal flow of information within the corporation, keeping potentially "tainting" knowledge away from those with most authority to step in and remedy the wrongdoing. But the law's bad effects on information are more pervasive still. To develop a system of total health care delivery demands not only a proper flow of information *within* pharmaceutical houses, but between the pharmaceutical houses and hospitals, doctors' offices, and coroners' laboratories. Information that doctors and hospital administrators should be regularly developing is, however, a potential source of medical malpractice liability. Because of the law, it may be best not to gather it and keep it on hand. . . .

Let me close by observing that in these and many criticisms of the federal agencies, I often find myself in strong agreement with the so-called anti's. But, in my mind, they fail to draw from their skepticism the correct implication for the corporate social-responsibility debate. If the agencies—or the other public control mechanisms—*were* effective, then it would be proper to brush aside the calls for corporate social responsibility by calling on the law to keep corporations in line. But the weaknesses of the agencies are simply a further argument that trust in our traditional legal machinery as a means of keeping corporations in bounds is misplaced—and that therefore something more is needed.

Licensee Responsibility to Review Records Before Their Broadcast

A number of complaints received by the Commission concerning the lyrics of records played on broadcasting stations relate to a subject of current and pressing concern: the use of language tending to promote or glorify the use of illegal drugs as marijuana, LSD, "speed," etc. This Notice points up the licensee's long-established responsibilities in this area.

Whether a particular record depicts the dangers of drug abuse, or, to the contrary, promotes such illegal drug usage is a question for the judgment of the licensee. The thrust of this Notice is simply that the licensee must make that judgment and cannot properly follow a policy of playing such records without someone in a responsible position (i.e., a management level executive at the station) knowing the content of the lyrics. Such a pattern of operation is clearly a violation of the basic principle of the licensee's responsibility for, and duty to exercise adequate control over, the broadcast material presented over his station. It raises serious questions as to whether continued operation of the station is in the public interest, just as in the case of a failure to exercise adequate control over foreign-language programs.

In short, we expect broadcast licensees to ascertain, before broadcast, the words or lyrics of recorded musical or spoken selections played on their stations. Just as in the case of the foreign-language broadcasts, this may also entail reasonable efforts to ascertain the meaning of words or phrases used in the lyrics. While this duty may be delegated by licensees to responsible employees, the licensee remains fully responsible for its fulfillment.

Thus, here as in so many other areas, it is a question of responsible, good faith action by the public trustee to whom the frequency has been licensed. No more, but certainly no less, is called for.

Action by the Commission February 24, 1971. Commissioners Burch (Chairman), Wells and Robert E. Lee with Commissioner Lee issuing a statement, Commissioners H. Rex Lee and Houser concurring and issuing statements, Commissioner Johnson dissenting and issuing a statement, and Commissioner Bartley abstaining from voting.

STATEMENT OF COMMISSIONER ROBERT E. LEE

I sincerely hope that the action of the Commission today in releasing a "Public Notice" with respect to *Licensee Responsibility to Review Records Before Their Broadcast* will discourage, if not eliminate the playing of records which tend to promote and/or glorify the use of illegal drugs.

We are all aware of the deep concern in our local communities with respect to the use of illegal drugs particularly among the younger segment of our population. Public officials, at all levels of government, as well as all interested citizens are attempting to cope with this problem.

It is in this context that I expect the Broadcast Industry to meet its responsibilities of reviewing records before they are played. Obviously, if such records promote the use of illegal drugs, the licensee will exercise appropriate judgment in determining whether the broadcasting of such records is in the public interest.

Public Notice of March 5, 1971, 28 F.C.C. 2d 409. Commission decision with statements by Robert E. Lee and H. Rex Lee, Federal Communications Commission.

CONCURRING STATEMENT
OF COMMISSIONER H. REX LEE

While the title of the notice seemingly applies to the licensee's responsibility to review all records before they are broadcast, the notice itself is directed solely at records which allegedly use "language tending to promote or glorify the use of illegal drugs. . . . "

Although I am concurring, I would have preferred it if the Commission had not decided to restrict today's notice to so-called "drug lyrics." The Commission may appear to many young people as not being so concerned with other pressing broadcasting problem areas. And to many of these young people (and not just to that segment who use illegal drugs) the Commission may appear as "an ominous government agency" merely out to clamp down on *their* music.

A preferable approach would have been to repeat, with an additional reference to drug abuse of all kinds, our 1960 *Program Policy Statement* wherein we stated:

> Broadcast licensees must assure responsibility for all material which is broadcast through their facilities. *This includes all programs and advertising material which they present to the public. . . .* This duty is personal to the licensee and may not be delegated. He is obligated to bring his positive responsibility affirmatively to bear upon all who have a hand in providing broadcast material for transmission through his facilities so as to assure the discharge of his duty to provide acceptable program schedule consonant with operating in the public interest in his community.[1] [Emphasis added.]

Because of the Commission's expressed concern with the drug problem, I would hope that we could initiate action with other appropriate Federal agencies to require a reassessment by pharmaceutical manufacturers, advertisers, and the media, looking toward the reform of advertising practices in the nonprescription drug industry. *Advertising Age* expressed its concern with the increased use of drugs—both the legal and illegal types—when it stated in an editorial:

> With an estimated $289,000,000 being spent annually on TV advertising of medicines, this serious question is being raised: Is the flood of advertising for such medicines so pervasive that it is convincing viewers that there is a medical panacea for any and all of their problems, medical and otherwise? Are we being so consistently bombarded with pills for this and pills for that and pills for the other thing that we have developed a sort of Pavlovian reaction which makes us reach for a pill everytime we are faced with an anxious moment, be it of physical or psychic origin?[2]

Drug abuse *is* a serious problem in the United States. It is found in every sector of the population, not merely among the young who listen to hard rock music.

I believe the broadcasting industry has made a good start in helping to discourage illegal drug abuse. Many local radio and television stations and the four networks have broadcast documentaries and specials, carried spot announcements, helped to raise funds for local drug abuse clinics and information centers, and have helped to establish "tie-lines" and "switchboards" where all people can call for free medical and psychological help and guidance. These activities represent "communicating" in the best sense of the word.

My concurrence in this notice, therefore, should not be regarded as a reflection on the good start that I think that most broadcasters have made in dealing with this problem. They must continue with even more determination and support from everyone.

NOTES

1. *Report and Statement of Policy re: Commission En Banc Programming Inquiry*, FCC 60-970, 20 R.R. 1901, 1912–1913 (July 27, 1960).
2. *Advertising Age* (May 11, 1970), p. 24.

American Textile Manufacturers Institute, Inc., v. Raymond J. Donovan, Secretary of Labor

Supreme Court of the United States

. . . Congress enacted the Occupational Safety and Health Act of 1970 (the Act) "to assure so far as possible every working man and woman in the Nation safe and healthful working conditions. . . ." The Act authorizes the Secretary of Labor to establish, after notice and opportunity to comment, mandatory nationwide standards governing health and safety in the workplace. In 1978, the Secretary, acting through the Occupational Safety and Health Administration (OSHA), promulgated a standard limiting occupational exposure to cotton dust, an airborne particle byproduct of the preparation and manufacture of cotton products, exposure to which induces a "constellation of respiratory effects" known as "byssinosis." This disease was one of the expressly recognized health hazards that led to passage of the Occupational Safety and Health Act of 1970.

Petitioners in these consolidated cases, representing the interests of the cotton industry challenged the validity of the "Cotton Dust Standard" in the Court of Appeals for the District of Columbia Circuit pursuant to § 6 (f) of the Act, 29 U. S. C. § 655 (f). They contend in this Court, as they did below, that the Act requires OSHA to demonstrate that its Standard reflects a reasonable relationship between the costs and benefits associated with the Standard. Respondents, the Secretary of Labor and two labor organizations, counter that Congress balanced the costs and benefits in the Act itself, and that the Act should there-

fore be construed not to require OSHA to do so. They interpret the Act as mandating that OSHA enact the most protective standard possible to eliminate a significant risk of material health impairment, subject to the constraints of economic and technological feasibility. The Court of Appeals held that the Act did not require OSHA to compare costs and benefits. . . .

I

. . . In enacting the Cotton Dust Standard, OSHA interpreted the Act to require adoption of the most stringent standards to protect against material health impairment, bounded only by technological and economic feasibility. OSHA therefore rejected the industry's alternative proposal for a PEL of 500 $\mu g/m^2$ in yarn manufacturing, a proposal which would produce a 25% prevalence of at least Grade $\frac{1}{2}$ byssinosis. The agency expressly found the Standard to be both technologically and economically feasible based on the evidence in the record as a whole. Although recognizing that permitted levels of exposure to cotton dust would still cause some byssinosis, OSHA nevertheless rejected the union proposal for a 100 $\mu g/m^2$ PEL because it was not within the "technological capabilities of the industry." Similarly, OSHA set PELS for some segments of the cotton industry at 500 $\mu g/m^2$ in part because of limitations of tech-

---

452 U.S. 490 (1981). Majority opinion by Justice William J. Brennan.

nological feasibility. Finally, the Secretary found that "engineering dust controls in weaving may not be feasible even with massive expenditures by the industry," and for that and other reasons adopted a less stringent PEL of 750 μg/m² for weaving and slashing.

The Court of Appeals upheld the Standard in all major respects. The court rejected the industry's claim that OSHA failed to consider its proposed alternative or give sufficient reasons for failing to adopt it. The court also held that the Standard was "reasonably necessary and appropriate" within the meaning of § 3(8) of the Act, 29 U.S.C. § 652(8), because of the risk of material health impairment caused by exposure to cotton dust. Rejecting the industry position that OSHA must demonstrate that the benefits of the Standard are proportionate to its costs, the court instead agreed with OSHA's interpretation that the Standard must protect employees against material health impairment subject only to the limits of technological and economic feasibility. The court held that "Congress itself struck the balance between costs and benefits in the mandate to the agency" under § 6 (b) (5) of the Act, 29 U. S. C. § 655 (b) (5), and that OSHA is powerless to circumvent that judgment by adopting less than the most protective feasible standard. Finally, the court held that the agency's determination of technological and economic feasibility was supported by substantial evidence in the record as a whole.

We affirm in part, and vacate in part.

II

The principal question presented in this case is whether the Occupational Safety and Health Act requires the Secretary, in promul-gating a standard pursuant to § 6 (b) (5) of the Act, 29 U. S. C. § 655 (b) (5), to determine that the costs of the standard bear a reasonable relationship to its benefits. Relying on § § 6 (b) (5), and 3(8) of the Act, 29 U. S. C. § § 655 (b) (5), 652(8), petitioners urge not only that OSHA must show that a standard addresses a significant risk of material health impairment, but also that OSHA must demonstrate that the reduction in risk of material health impairment is significant in light of the costs of attaining that reduction. Respondents on the other hand contend that the Act requires OSHA to promulgate standards that eliminate or reduce such risks "to the extent such protection is technologically and economically feasible." To resolve this debate, we must turn to the language, structure, and legislative history of the Occupational Safety and Health Act. . . .

The legislative history of the Act, while concededly not crystal clear, provides general support for respondents' interpretation of the Act. The congressional reports and debates certainly confirm that Congress meant "feasible" and nothing else in using that term. Congress was concerned that the Act might be thought to require achievement of absolute safety, an impossible standard, and therefore insisted that health and safety goals be capable of economic and technological accomplishment. Perhaps most telling is the absence of any indication whatsoever that Congress intended OSHA to conduct its own cost-benefit analysis before promulgating a toxic material or harmful physical agent standard. The legislative history demonstrates conclusively that Congress was fully aware that the Act would impose real and substantial costs of compliance on industry, and believed that such costs were part of the cost of doing business. . . .

Not only does the legislative history confirm that Congress meant "feasible" rather than "cost-benefit" when it used the former term, but it also shows that Congress understood that the Act would create substantial costs for employers, yet intended to impose such costs when necessary to create a safe and healthful working environment. Congress viewed the costs of health and safety as a cost of doing business. Senator Yarborough, a cosponsor of the Williams bill, stated: "We know the costs would be put into consumer goods but that is the price we should pay for the 80 million workers in America." He asked:

> One may well ask too expensive for whom? Is it too expensive for the company who for lack of proper safety equipment loses the services of its skilled employees? Is it too expensive for the employee who loses his hand or leg or eyesight? Is it too expensive for the widow trying to raise her children on meager allowance under workmen's compensation and social security? And what about the man—a good hardworking man—tied to a wheel chair or hospital bed for the rest of his life? That is what we are dealing with when we talk about industrial safety. . . . We are talking about people's lives, not the indifference of some cost accountants.

Senator Eagleton commented that "[t]he costs that will be incurred by employers in meeting the standards of health and safety to be established under this bill are, in my view, *reasonable and necessary costs of doing business.*"

Other Members of Congress voiced similar views. Nowhere is there any indication that Congress contemplated a different balancing by OSHA of the benefits of worker health and safety against the costs of achieving them. Indeed Congress thought that the *financial costs* of health and safety problems in the workplace were as large or larger than the *financial costs* of eliminating these problems. In its statement of findings and declaration of pur-

pose encompassed in the Act itself, Congress announced that "personal injuries and illnesses arising out of work situations impose a substantial burden upon, and are a hindrance to, interstate commerce in terms of lost production, wage loss, medical expenses, and disability compensation payment." The Senate was well aware of the magnitude of these costs:

> [T]he economic impact of industrial deaths and disability is staggering. Over $1.5 billion is wasted in lost wages, and the annual loss to the Gross National Product is estimated to be over $8 billion. Vast resources that could be available for productive use are siphoned off to pay workmen's compensation benefits and medical expenses. . . .

V

When Congress passed the Occupational Safety and Health Act in 1970, it chose to place pre-eminent value on assuring employees a safe and healthful working environment, limited only by the feasibility of achieving such an environment. We must measure the validity of the Secretary's actions against the requirements of that Act. For "[t]he judicial function does not extend to substantive revision of regulatory policy. That function lies elsewhere—in Congressional and Executive oversight or amendatory legislation."

Accordingly, the judgment of the Court of Appeals is affirmed in all respects except to the extent of its approval of the Secretary's application of the wage guarantee provision of the Cotton Dust Standard at 29 CFR § 1910.1043 (f) (2) (v). To that extent, the judgment of the Court of Appeals is vacated and the case remanded with directions to remand to the Secretary for further proceedings consistent with this opinion. . . .

CASE 1.   *The Advertising Code Case*

The Advertising Code of American Business was part of a program of industry self-regulation announced 28, September, 1971. This program arose in response to mounting public criticism of the advertising industry, to more aggressive action by federal regulatory agencies, and to fear of even greater government control in the future.

In announcing the new program of self-regulation, enforcement was emphasized. Complaints are received or initiated by the National Advertising Division (NAD) of the Council of Better Business Bureaus. During the first year, 337 complaints were placed on the table. Of these 337, investigations were completed on 184. Seventy-two of those complaints were upheld. In every case, the advertiser either agreed to withdraw the objectionable ad or to modify it. Six of the cases which were dismissed were appealed to a higher body, the National Advertising Review Board. Of the six cases, the NARB accepted the decision of the NAD in four cases, but agreed with two complaints. In these two cases, the challenged ads were withdrawn. All complaints were settled within several months. Supporters of the NAD applaud their time record for handling complaints as compared with frequent delays of several years in federal suits.*

The Advertising Code of American Business reads as follows:

1. *Truth*. Advertising shall tell the truth, and shall reveal significant facts, the concealment of which would mislead the public.
2. *Responsibility*. Advertising agencies and advertisers shall be willing to provide substantiation of claims made.
3. *Taste and Decency*. Advertising shall be free of statements, illustrations or implications which are offensive to good taste or public decency.
4. *Bait Advertising*. Advertising shall offer only merchandise or services which are readily available for purchase at the advertised price.
5. *Guarantees and Warranties*. Advertising of guarantees and warranties shall be explicit. Advertising of any guarantee or warranty shall clearly and conspicuously disclose its nature and extent, the manner in which the guarantor or warrantor will perform, and the identity of the guarantor or warrantor.
6. *Price Claims*. Advertising shall avoid price or savings claims which are false or misleading, or which do not offer provable bargains or savings.
7. *Unprovable Claims*. Advertising shall avoid the use of exaggerated or unprovable claims.
8. *Testimonials*. Advertising containing testimonials shall be limited to those of competent witnesses who are reflecting a real and honest choice.

Questions

1. How should rule 7 which forbids exaggerated claims be interpreted?
2. Is the set of rules comprehensive enough to forbid deceptive advertising?
3. Evaluate the described enforcement mechanism. Suggest improvements if you think any are needed.
4. Is the rule on "taste and decency" too broad and amorphous?

---

*These figures may be found in Howard H. Bell's "Self-Regulation by the Advertising Industry," in *The Unstable Ground: Corporate Social Policy in a Dynamic Society*, ed. S. Prakash Sethi (Los Angeles: Melville Publishing Company, 1974).

Adapted from "Advertising Code of American Business," 1971. Reprinted by permission of the American Advertising Federation and the author, Norman E. Bowie.

CASE 2. *Beech-Nut Corporation*

Beech-Nut Corporation was the second-largest baby food company in the United States. It was founded in 1891 and was incorporated in the state of Pennsylvania. The company primarily produced and distributed baby food and dietetic specialty products. Over the years, Beech-Nut had built a reputation on purity, high-quality products, and natural ingredients. Because of competition and other difficulties, however, Beech-Nut was eventually forced to reduce its product line to a single product, which was baby food. This product line, unfortunately, had almost never turned a profit.[1] Its market share in 1977 was only 15 percent compared with a 70 percent market share attained by the Gerber company, its major competitor. By 1978, Beech-Nut, burdened with losses, owed millions of dollars to suppliers and was under great financial pressure.[2]

To cope with the threat of insolvency, Beech-Nut executives switched to a supplier that offered apple juice concentrate at a price 20 percent below market. At that time, rumors of apple juice adulteration had already spread in the industry, and therefore the purchase of concentrate at 20 percent below market raised suspicions among the employees in Beech-Nut's Research and Development Department.[3] In 1977, tests by a company-hired laboratory suggested that the cheap apple concentrate that Beech-Nut bought from Universal Juice Company might be adulterated. The company, however, continued to claim that its products contained no artificial ingredients.

In 1981, Jerome J. LiCari, director of research and development at Beech-Nut, mounted a major drive to improve adulteration testing. He found that the apple juice concentrate Beech-Nut was buying to use in its juice and other products was a blend of beet sugar, cane syrup, and other synthetic ingredients. With this fresh evidence, LiCari informed Niels Hoyvald and John Lavery, then president and vice-president of Beech-Nut, respectively, that the concentrate was bogus, and he suggested getting another concentrate supplier. He believed that continuing to deal with Universal could jeopardize the productline restructuring that Beech-Nut was planning, which would emphasize nutritional values and the absence of artificial ingredients in its products.[4] Despite LiCari's efforts, Hoyvald and Lavery took no action, and the company continued to produce and distribute adulterated apple juice under the label "100% fruit juice."

In 1982, federal and state agencies started investigations and established that Universal's concentrate was bogus. Beech-Nut immediately canceled its apple concentrate contracts, but it continued to distribute millions of bottles of "fake" apple juice at deep discounts in the U.S. market as well as other parts of the world. Despite warnings from the Food and Drug Administration and the New York State Agriculture Department, Beech-Nut did not issue a national apple juice recall until late October of the year and continued to unload its $3.5 million of inventory of adulterated apple juice. This behavior gave the prosecutors reason to believe that the company's main concern was making money even if it meant selling a phony product.[5]

This case was prepared by Rogene Buchholz of Loyola University, New Orleans, and reprinted from *Business Environment and Public Policy,* Prentice Hall, 1992.

NOTES

1. Chris Welles, "What Led Beech-Nut Down the Road to Disgrace.[2] *Business Week,* February 22, 1988, p. 125.
2. Ibid.
3. Ibid.
4. Ibid., p. 125.
5. Leonard Burder, "Two Former Executives of Beech-Nut Guilty in Phony Juice Case," *Wall Street Journal,* February 18, 1988, p. D-3.

Questions

1. After reporting his findings to Hoyvald and Lavery, did LiCari have any additional moral responsibility to expose the distribution of the adulterated apple juice?
2. In what ways is LiCari's position as director of research and development at Beech-Nut similar to Boisjoly's at Morton Thiokol? To the engineers in charge of the Ford Pinto?
3. Who is responsible for distribution of the adulterated apple juice in 1977? In 1981?
4. Evaluate the options available to LiCari after he reported his findings to Beech-Nut's senior management.

CASE 3. *Regulating Insider Trading*

Trading stocks on "insider information" has long been banned in the United States, and the Securities and Exchange Commission (SEC) has vigorously pursued rules against such trading since the Securities Exchange Act of 1934. Under the terms of this law, an insider is forbidden by law to use information obtained on the inside to buy or sell securities or to pass the information on to others so that they might benefit. In the important precedent case of *SEC v. Texas Gulf Sulphur,* a court held that "Anyone in possession of material inside information must either disclose it to the investing public, or, if he is disabled from disclosing it in order to protect a corporate confidence, or he chooses not to do so, must abstain from trading in or recommending the securities concerned while such inside information remains undisclosed."

However, "insider-trading" has proved difficult to define. An inside trader is someone who has material nonpublic information obtained by virtue of a relationship with the corporation and who trades in the stock of the corporation. Some believe that the information a trader has must be relevant to the price of the stock and should not include any inside-derived information that might have a bearing on one's purchase of the stock. For example, one might have confidential information that could not be disclosed and yet would not likely affect the stock's price even if it were known. The SEC has said that one must not *misappropriate* the nonpublic infor-

---

This case was prepared by Tom L. Beauchamp and Norman Bowie based on Jonathan R. Macey, "SEC Vigilant on Insider Trading—But Is It Within Law?" *Wall Street Journal,* May 28, 1986, p. 34; "Insider Trading Case Reinforces Belief That Small Investor Is at a Disadvantage," *Wall Street Journal,* May 20, 1986, p. 2; "The War on Insider Trading," *Business Week* (May 26, 1986): 38; Daniel Seligman, "An Economic Defense of Insider Trading," *Fortune* (September 5, 1983): 47–48; "Greed on Wall Street," *Newsweek* (May 26, 1986): 44–46; "The Levine Case: New Names," *Newsweek* (July 14, 1986): 55; Larry Elkin, "Lawyers File Appeals for 3 in Winans Case," *Washington Post,* November 27, 1985, p. D2; "Ex-Reporter Says He Believed Leaks on His Journal Articles Weren't Illegal," *Wall Street Journal,* March 19, 1985, p. 12; "Those Hobnailed Boots; The SEC Has Put the Workings of the Market in Jeopardy," *Barron's* (June 2, 1986): 11; "Winans Says He Knew Leaks Would Bring Dismissal," *Wall Street Journal,* March 21, 1985, p. 10; Editorial, *Business Week* (April 29, 1985): 79, 128.

mation, but a definition of "misappropriate" has proved difficult and tortuous.

In late 1985 and mid-1986 the financial world was stunned by two prominent insider trading "scandals" in a row. The first case involved a reporter, R. Foster Winans of the *Wall Street Journal.* He had taken advantage of his position as a reporter for personal financial gain (not very effectively) and had also helped his friends and associates gain financially (very effectively). Winans was one of the reporters who wrote the column "Heard on the Street," which frequently influences stock prices. A Winans-recommended stock jumped, on average, 6.5 percent on a day it was touted in his column. Winans and his friends enjoyed a trading advantage over members of the general public, who did not have access to the same information as did a surrogate for the public who was presumed to hold it in trust for the public until it was published. The *Journal* has a policy requiring that such information be held in trust and not acted upon in order to avoid conflict of interest—particularly in the tempting case of the "Heard on the Street" column—because of the opportunity to cause sharp movements in the price of a stock.

In spring 1986 a more consequential case erupted. Dennis Levine, a Managing Director who specialized in mergers and acquisitions at Drexel Burnham Lambert, was arrested for allegedly trading the securities of 54 companies (including major companies such as Nabisco and McGraw-Edison) on insider information in order to earn over $12.6 million. Levine was one of Wall Street's most successful figures and had taken home $3 million in salary and bonuses during the previous year. He had also just pulled off a major deal in his advising of Pantry Pride Inc. in its takeover of Revlon Inc.

Levine's walk on the wrong side of the Street evidently began on a trip to the Bahamas in 1980, where he deposited $170,000 at secret branches of a Swiss bank. He used code names and ultimately set up two dummy Panamanian corporations, which traded through the Bahamian bank. On or about March 22, 1984, Levine bought 75,000 shares of Jewell Companies, Inc. He sold them on June 5, 1984. In 1985, he bought 145,000 shares of American Natural Resources Co. on February 14, and sold them March 4. A continuous pattern of such trading developed, netting Levine the $12.6 million in a short period of time. On the basis of a tip, the SEC launched its investigation and built its case on the pattern of suspicious well-timed stock trading.

The Levine case reinforced a view that is strongly held at the SEC: Insider trading is rampant on Wall Street. Repeatedly, the stock of a takeover target will jump in price immediately before a takeover offer is announced to the public. For example, just before Levine's arrest, General Electric acquired RCA. Immediately prior to the announcement the stock had jumped a dramatic 16 points. The SEC immediately began a massive investigation. It became clear then that the SEC is dedicated to major policing efforts in the attempt to contain insider trading. Since Levine's arrest, several other prominent Wall Street figures have been arrested.

The view that insider trading is rampant is widely held beyond the SEC as well. In reporting on the Winans case, *Business Week* pointed out in a cover story: "Executives do it. Bankers do it. Accountants, secretaries, and messengers do it. And so do printers, cabdrivers, waiters, housewives, hairdressers—and mistresses. Some do it on their own. Others work in rings with connections as far away as Switzerland and Hong Kong. But they all work the shadowy side of Wall Street by trading on inside information to make money in the stock market. Insider trading is running rampant, despite a major law enforcement crackdown and toughened penalties." *Business Week* maintained in an editorial in the same issue that "Insider trading violates a felt ethical sense," but was unable to offer a single reason for the conclusion that it is ethically improper.

The purpose of laws against insider trading—as the SEC interprets them—is essentially a moral one: to preserve fairness in the market place. If some investors have inside information not publicly available, they are thought to be unfairly advantaged. The underlying principles are that all investors should have equal access to information in a free market, that securities markets must operate on faith and trust, and that insider trading undermines public confidence in the marketplace. The United States Supreme Court has taken a slightly different view of the moral purpose from the SEC's. The Court has held that an insider trader must be one who has a fiduciary duty to retain confidential information; inside trading is therefore like stealing from an employer.

However, there is considerable moral ambiguity surrounding insider trading in general, and not every authority considers it unfair. Several scholars have argued that permitting insider trades would make the securities markets more efficient. The activities of the traders would be spotted and the market would respond more quickly to essential information. Ben R. Murphy, a partner in a merchant banking firm in Dallas, argues as follows: "My theory is that if we didn't have [insider trading laws] the market would eventually discount all the leaks and rumors and become more efficient. People would have to take a risk on believing the rumors or not." It is noteworthy that over $50 billion of securities trade daily on American exchanges, and no one is prepared to argue that even as much as 1 percent involves insider trading or any form of illegal transactions.

Jonathan Macey, Professor of Law at Emory University, has argued that a person who locates undervalued shares in a company

through inside information can provide a valuable service to the market by the discovery, whether insider trading occurs or not. But in order to encourage such discovery, the person or institution must be allowed to profit. This is basically what stock analysts do; they all try to get information not yet public before their rivals do in order to reward clients who pay them for their activities. The amateur investing public has no chance against such professional knowledge and can only hope that the market price already reflects insider information. Macey concludes that "A complete ban on trading by those with confidential information about a company would be disastrous to the efficiency of the capital markets. If such a rule were enforced, nobody would have an incentive to engage in a search for undervalued firms, stock prices would not accurately reflect company values, and, perhaps worst of all, investment capital would not flow to its most highly valued users. Thus, we would all be better off if the SEC would deescalate its war on insider trading."

The status of the law against insider trading is uncertain and very difficult to enforce. The leading investment journal, *Barron's,* has maintained that the SEC is "riding roughshod over due process of law," drying up the free flow of information, and harming the interests of those it is sworn to protect. *Barron's* adamantly insisted that Winans had done no legal wrong and that the SEC had twisted the idea of "misappropriation" of information to the breaking point in getting a conviction of Winans. Winans' only wrong, said *Barron's,* was the moral wrong of violating the *Wall Street Journal's* rules of ethics.

Questions

1. Does the fact that prohibitions against insider trading are difficult to enforce make any difference in determining whether

they are immoral or should be made illegal?

2. Should the law have anything to say about insider trading? Should morality?

3. Would self-regulation be a better way to control insider trading than government regulation?

4. If permitting insider trading would indeed make markets more efficient, does that fact establish that such trading practices should be permitted?

CASE 4. *Flyover in Midland*

On February 7, 1978, an aerial photography team commissioned by the EPA flew over and took detailed aerial photographs of the Midland, Michigan, plant of The Dow Chemical Company. The company had no knowledge that the flight was taking place.

Prior to February 1978 the EPA had been conducting an investigation to determine whether to approve a consent order, issued by the State of Michigan, under the Clean Air Act. The order had to do with emissions from Dow power plants at its Midland location. The EPA later admitted that they had had "the full cooperation of Dow, and Dow withheld nothing" that their inspectors had asked to see during their preliminary investigation in September 1977. In addition, one month later when the EPA requested schematic drawings of the power plants, Dow voluntarily provided them.

In December 1977 the EPA again requested access to the Midland plants, this time indicating that they intended to take pictures. In order to protect its trade secrets, it is Dow's policy not to allow cameras into its plants. After being informed of this policy, the chemical engineer employed at the EPA's Region V office apparently made comments that were interpreted by one of his subordinates to be an authorization for the flyover. Dow found out about the flyover a month after it occurred and promptly filed suit against the EPA in Federal Court.

Such flyovers are not unusual, however. The agency's Environmental Photographic Interpretation Center has a staff of 50 pilots, photographers, and map readers. The EPA maps hazardous waste dumps and takes high resolution pictures from small aircraft.

On April 19, 1982, the Eastern District of Michigan U.S. District Court ruled that the overflight violated the law. The EPA appealed and in 1984 won a victory in the U.S. Court of Appeals. The Court specifically rejected the company's argument that the EPA action amounted to a search that violated the company's constitutional right to privacy. As of this writing the case is on appeal to the U.S. Supreme Court.

Questions

1. Should the EPA be required to inform a corporation when a flyover is to be made? After a flyover has been made?

2. What obligations, if any, does the EPA have to protect a company's trade secrets?

3. Should the Freedom of Information Act apply to material gathered by the EPA on flyovers?

4. If a decision were to be made solely on moral grounds, how should a company's right to protect trade secrets be balanced against society's right to enforce environmental regulations?

This case was prepared by Norman E. Bowie based on articles by Edward M. Nussbaum and Garry L. Hamlin in *Chemical Engineering Progress* (April 1981) and from "The EPA's Eye in the Sky Has Companies Seeing Red," *Business Week* (October 28, 1985): 90.

Suggested Supplementary Readings

ACQUAAH, KWAMENA. *International Regulation of Transnational Corporations*. New York: Praeger, 1986.

ARTHUR, E., EUGENE. "The Ethics of Corporate Governance." *Journal of Business Ethics* 6 (January 1987): 59–70.

BARAM, MICHAEL S. *Alternatives to Regulation*. Lexington: Mass.: Lexington Books, 1981.

BOWIE, NORMAN E. "Fair Markets." *Journal of Business Ethics* 7 (January-February 1988): 89–98.

BROOKS, LEONARD J. "Ethical Codes of Conduct: Deficient in Guidance for Canadian Accounting Profession." *Journal of Business Ethics* 8 (May 1989): 325–335.

———. "Corporate Codes of Conduct." *Journal of Business Ethics* 8 (February-March 1989): 117–129.

CORLETT, J. ANGELO. "Corporate Responsibility and Punishment." *Public Affairs Quarterly* 2 (January 1988): 1–16.

DEGEORGE, RICHARD T. "GM and Corporate Responsibility." *Journal of Business Ethics* 5 (June 1986): 177–179.

GARRETT, JAN EDWARD. "Unredistributable Corporate Moral Responsibility." *Journal of Business Ethics* 8 (July 1989): 535–545.

GETZ, KATHLEEN A., "International Codes of Conduct: An Analysis of Ethical Reasoning" *Journal of Business Ethics* 9 (July 1990): 567–77.

HILL, IVAN. *The Ethical Basis of Economic Freedom*. Chapel Hill, N.C.: American Viewpoint Inc., 1976.

HOFFMAN, W. MICHAEL, JENNIFER MILLS MOORE, and DAVID FEDO, eds. *Corporate Governance and Institutionalizing Ethics*. Lexington, Mass.: Lexington Books, 1984.

MATHEWS, M. C.: "Codes of Ethics: Organizational Behaviour and Misbehaviour." *Research in Corporate Social Performance* 9 (1987): 107–130.

MEINERS, ROGER E., and BRUCE YANDLE, eds. *Regulation and the Reagan Era*. New York: Holmes and Meier, 1989.

MITNICK, BARRY M. *The Political Economy of Regulation*. New York: Columbia University Press, 1980.

NIELSEN, RICHARD P. "What Can Managers Do About Unethical Management?" *Journal of Business Ethics* 6 (May 1987): 309–320.

SCHULTZE, CHARLES L. *The Public Use of the Private Interest*. Washington, D.C.: The Brookings Institution, 1977.

STONE, CHRISTOPHER D. *Where the Law Ends: The Social Control of Corporate Behavior*. New York: Harper and Row, 1975.

WEIDENBAUM, MURRAY L. *The Future of Business Regulation*. New York: AMACON, 1979.

WERHANE, PATRICIA H. "Engineers and Management: The Challenge of the *Challenger* Incident." *Journal of Business Ethics* 10 (August 1991): 605–616.

Chapter Four

Acceptable Risk

GOVERNMENT IS CONSTITUTED to protect citizens from risk to the environment, risk from external invasion, risk to health, risk from crime, risk from fire, risk of highway accidents, and similar risks. A natural extension of this idea is that the social contract obligates government to protect citizens against risks to health, bodily safety, financial security, and the environment. However, society has not yet decided on the extent to which government should restrain free-market business for health, safety, financial security, and environmental interests. It is now widely agreed that the primary responsibilities for risk reduction and disclosure of risk rest on corporations, but the government continues to play a controversial role in enforcing corporate responsibilities.

Corporate activities present several types of risk of harm. In this chapter, we concentrate on judgments of acceptable risk for consumers, workers, investors, and the environment. We focus more on the responsibilities of business and methods for reducing risk, and less on the nature and types of harm caused. These risk-reduction methods include disclosure of information about risks as well as risk-reduction techniques.

NATURE AND TYPES OF RISK

Courts have long held that businesses "must pay the freight" when their activities present risk and then cause harm.[1] However, articulating this rule is difficult without shared definitions of *harm* and *risk*.

The Nature of Harm

Competing conceptions of harm exist, but Joel Feinberg has supplied a useful working definition:

> [Interests] can be blocked or defeated by events in impersonal nature or by plain bad luck. But they can only be "invaded" by human beings, . . . singly, or in groups and organizations. . . . One person harms another in the present sense, then, by invading,

and thereby thwarting or setting back, his interest. The test . . . of whether such
an invasion has in fact set back an interest is whether that interest is in a worse
condition than it would otherwise have been in had the invasion not occurred at
all. . . . Not all invasions of interest are wrongs, since some actions invade
another's interests excusably or justifiably, or invade interests that the other has no
right to have respected.[2]

Causing a setback to interests in health, financial goals, or the environment
can constitute a harm without necessarily being an unjustifiable harm. Almost everyone would agree that harming another person's interests is blameworthy if the
harm results in little compensating benefit and the damage could easily be avoided.
But we rarely, if ever, experience such a clear and uncomplicated scenario. Benefits
that offset risk usually exist, and the risk of harm is often expensive to eliminate or
control. Some heated debates over products that appeared to be harmful—for example, presweetened children's cereals—have shown that they also create substantial benefits. In the workplace it has become increasingly difficult simply to banish
dangerous chemicals that provide major social benefits. In each case their risks
must be weighed against their benefits.

Kinds of Risk

Different kinds of risk raise distinct issues. For example, risks of psychological
harm, physical harm, legal harm, and economic harm require different analyses
and different remedies. Some representative risks pertinent to the material in this
chapter are the following:

> *Risks to Consumers (and their Families)*
> Prepared foods (increased fat and sugar)
> Drugs (side effects such as G. I. bleeding)
> Cigarettes (lung cancer)
> *Risks to Workers (and their Families)*
> Benzene (leukemia)
> Asbestos (asbestosis)
> Lead (destruction of reproductive capacities)
> *Risks to the Public and the Environment*
> Coal-dust emissions (respiratory complications)
> Carbon and other fuel emissions (respiratory complications)
> Toxic chemicals (genetic defects)
> *Risks to Investors*
> Savings accounts (decline in the rate of return)
> Stocks (decline of principal)
> Real estate (loss of liquidity)

Problems of Risk Assessment

Society has not yet adequately grasped the risks inherent in thousands of toxic
chemicals, foods, drugs, sources of energy, machines, and environmental emissions. Some have serious, irreversible consequences; others do not. Moreover,

the *probability* of exposure to a risk may be known with some precision, whereas virtually nothing may be known about the harm's *magnitude;* or the magnitude may be precisely expressible, whereas the probability remains too indefinite to be calculated accurately. "Wild guess" sometimes best describes the accuracy with which physical and chemical risks may be determined, for example, for a worker who constantly changes locations, who works with multiple toxic substances, and whose physical condition can be attributed in part to factors independent of the workplace such as smoking.

PRODUCT SAFETY AND RISK TO CONSUMERS

It is safe to say that we all consume products that carry minor, significant, and unknown risks. No household is complete without several dozen potentially hazardous products, including ovens, electrical lines, furniture cleaners, spray paints, insecticides, medicines, and video display terminals. Millions of people in North America are the victims of household and office accidents involving these products every year, and more of our young people die from failures and accidents involving products than from disease. Thousands of law suits are filed by businesses against other businesses each year because of product failure, hazard, and harm, and there are related problems about deceptive marketing practices and inadequate warranties.

Some responsibility for the occurrence of these harms rests primarily on the consumer, who may carelessly use products or fail to read clearly written instructions. But some risks can be described as inherent in the product: A cautious and reasonable judgment of acceptable risk has been made that the product cannot be made less risky without unduly increasing cost or limiting use. Still other problems of risk derive from use of cheap materials, careless design, poor construction, or new discovery about risk in an already marketed product.

Disclosure of Risk Information

A consumer presumably controls what to purchase, because the seller must satisfy consumers or fail to sell the product and be driven from the market. However, this principle works only if the consumer understands relevant information about risk and performance. But serious questions exist about whether the information supplied to the consumer is adequate for making an informed and free choice. For example, are we told how a kerosene heater should be cleaned and stored and how often new filters should be installed? Are the side effects of a drug disclosed when a prescription is filled? Sellers may list only a minimal set of facts about known hazards, especially regarding technologically advanced products, because a seller attempts to sell in the most cost-effective manner. Disclosure of risk information costs money and adversely affects sales. Thus, the seller has an economic incentive to keep disclosure to a selective minimum.

These topics of disclosure and understanding have been under intense discussion in recent years. By the late 1970s a major right-to-know movement had taken hold in consumer affairs and in the U.S. workplace. Numerous laws were passed, notably the Consumer Product Safety Act of 1972, to protect consumers by setting safety standards, examining consumer product marketing, providing more adequate risk information, and upgrading the quality of warranty statements.

Product Safety and Quality Control

Quality control is a strategy in addition to disclosure of risk information. Corporations such as Johns Manville (asbestos) and A. H. Robins (the Dalkon Shield) have faced massive product liability judgments in recent years. Although higher standards of quality control would also protect manufacturers, both theoretical and practical problems exist in establishing and enforcing such standards. Methods of consumer protection incur significant costs that increase product cost and frequently force companies to abandon the market. For example, some lawn mower prices almost doubled after the introduction of new safety requirements was initiated; and several companies floundered in the process. Liberty issues are also at stake. For example, the freedom to put a new "junk food" on the market might be jeopardized (in theory, the freedom to produce junk foods would be eliminated), and the freedom to buy cheap, substandard products would be lost (because they could not be marketed).

These quality control controversies raise questions about liability and manufacturer warranties, discussed in this chapter in *Henningsen v. Bloomfield Motors and Chrysler Corporation.* In this case, the court held Chrysler as well as the dealer liable for an injury caused by a defective steering gear, without finding any evidence of negligence. The court argued that an implied warranty of suitability for use is owed the purchaser and contended that a major assumption behind free-market "contracting"—bargaining among equals—can be questioned when products prove to be defective. The *Henningsen* case cast doubt on the efficacy of disclaimers by manufacturers, and it quickly came to be applied to many products, including glass doors, guns, and stoves.

Manuel G. Velasquez considers in his essay how to differentiate between the obligations of consumers to themselves and the obligations of manufacturers to consumers. He distinguishes three theories of business obligations, showing that each strikes a different balance between consumer and manufacturer obligations. The first theory rests on an account of the social contract between consumers and business (under which Velasquez situates *Henningsen* as a classic example), and the second provides a theory of due care. The third theory presents an account of strict liability, a topic to which we now turn.

Liability for Harm

Two tests affecting liability are that professionals should conform to the minimally acceptable professional standards and that they should perform any actions that a reasonably prudent person would perform in the circumstances. Sometimes when the utmost care has been exercised, an accident or lack of information or documents might still cause harm. But if due care has been exercised to make a product safe (and affected parties have been apprised of known risks), a business would seem not to be at fault for any harm caused, even if the business helped bring about the harm.

This rule suggests that a manufacturer can be held liable for unsafe or inefficacious products or unsafe workplaces only if the manufacturer knew or *should have known* about the risks involved. Although attractive, it does not require much ingenuity to realize how difficult it is to determine what an employer or manufacturer "should have known." A product or technique can be so thoroughly researched and delayed that it will ensure a manufacturer's loss rather than profit. Is one to hold businesses to this kind of economic risk? If so, how could one determine that enough research and development had been carried out? Can the problem be handled through adequate insurance? Or is a modified conception of liability needed?

It has recently been suggested that manufacturers should be held liable not only to a standard of prudent behavior but to a stronger standard: liability for injuries caused to parties by defects in the manufacturing process, even if the manufacturer exercised due diligence and still could not have reasonably foreseen the problem. This principle is referred to as *strict product liability*, that is, liability without fault. Here questions of good faith, negligence, and absence of knowledge are not pertinent to a determination of liability. The advocates of this no-fault principle use primarily utilitarian arguments. They maintain that manufacturers are in the best position to pay and recover the costs of injury because they can pass the costs on through the product's price and, moreover, will have the added benefit of increasing manufacturer's objectivity, diligence, and prudence before marketing a product. This argument envisions a shift from the traditional doctrine of "let the buyer beware" (*caveat emptor*) to "let the seller beware."

This utilitarian justification is controversial and is assessed in this chapter by George G. Brenkert, who thinks it more important to ask whether strict liability conforms to principles of justice, in particular, whether it is just to ask manufacturers to bear the cost of injury merely because they are in the best position to do so. Brenkert maintains that in a free market society it is just to use strict liability because it is essential to maintain a consumer's equal opportunity to function. Using premises of compensatory justice and equal opportunity rather than utility, Brenkert argues that it is fair to place the burden of strict liability on manufacturers.

PROTECTING INVESTORS AGAINST FINANCIAL RISK

Many issues about risk of economic harm to consumers apply equally well to investors. At issue is a complex set of relationships that contains problems of conflict of interest as well as problems of deception and manipulation through improper disclosures. Brokerage houses, money managers, and investment counselors demand as much freedom as possible to deal with their clients. In these markets time spent making disclosures to customers is uncompensated and restricted by business requirements. Brokers with a large client base often do not adequately grasp the risk attached to the financial instruments they sell. Monitoring systems are usually loose, and direct supervisors do not closely track how investments are sold or which, if any, disclosures are made to clients. For example, Paine Webber, Inc. was fined $900,000 by the New York Stock Exchange in early 1992 for ignoring these problems and allowing its brokers to make hundreds of overly risky recommendations to customers.

Small investors who use brokerage houses and banks usually do not have the same access to relevant information available to professional investors. Amateur investors stand little chance against such professional knowledge and can only hope that their brokers possess good information or that the market price already reflects the relevant information. Even if brokers possess sufficient information, the house policy may be more aggressive and may introduce more risk than the average customer appreciates. For example, the firm may be primarily interested in limited partnerships in real estate, fully margined common stock, futures and commodities, and oil and gas drilling partnerships, rather than the more mundane unit investment trusts, certificates of deposit, and municipal bonds that a particular customer needs.

A broker has little incentive to match client needs with investments aside from the desire to maintain the business relationship. Although brokerage firms often advertise a full range of products and free financial planning by experts, brokers dislike financial planning per se, because it requires a large amount of time and carries no commission. They also dislike pedestrian forms of investing such as certificates of deposit and no-load mutual funds. Riskier investments generally carry higher commissions, and brokerage houses typically give brokers complete discretion to recommend a range of investments to their clients. At the same time, brokers are skillfully taught to be salespersons, to avoid lengthy phone calls, and to flatter clients who pride themselves on making their own decisions. In some firms brokers are taught to make recommendations to clients based primarily on the commission. Consequently, brokers are motivated to sell risky and complicated forms of investment to unsuspecting clients.

An inherent conflict of interest troubles many industry critics: The broker has a fiduciary responsibility to make recommendations based on the client's financial best interest. But the broker is also a salesperson who makes a living by selling securities and who is obligated to maximize profits for the brokerage house. The more trades made, the better for the broker, but this rule seldom works to the client's advantage. Commissions are an ever-present temptation influencing a recommendation, and the structure of incentives drives up the risk for the client.

The law requires securities firms to disclose commissions to clients. However, statistics on the full range of fees involved in many instruments are rarely mentioned to clients. When available, the figures are usually buried beneath a pile of information in a thick prospectus that clients do not read prior to a purchase. Most clients do not obtain the prospectus until after the purchase, which often places no dollar figure on the commission. Brokers are not required to disclose commissions in advance of a sale to clients, and they are not required to disclose that they are given additional, expensive free vacations for selling large numbers of certain mutual funds. Moreover, clients virtually never ask the commission amount or the range of fees. The reason is not lack of interest, but rather the sense that it will harm their relationship with the broker.

The U.S. Securities and Exchange Commission (SEC) was created by the Securities Exchange Act of 1933 to regulate a wide variety of manipulative stock practices. Although sensitive to issues such as insider trading, the SEC does not set ceilings on commissions and does not require brokers to receive written consent from clients prior to purchase. The SEC occasionally determines that a brokerage house's markup is so high that the commission amounts to fraud, but these cases are rare.

In recent years ethical brokerage houses have increasingly realized that tighter SEC control and a more developed sense of moral responsibility may serve their best interest. Ethical lapses are so common to the financial markets that the whole industry has been tarred with the brush of greed. Many reformers who lack an adequate understanding of the industry have introduced new legislation to more tightly control the industry. Significant reforms are beginning to emerge, but their outline is not yet clear.

One proposal for protecting investors seriously considered in this chapter's essay by Robert E. Frederick and W. Michael Hoffman is that the at-risk investor be denied access to securities markets to safeguard them from financial harm. They argue that restricting access to markets is justified only in cases in which rights not to be harmed by exposure to excessive risk are being protected.

In a second article, Robert F. Bruner and Lynn Sharp Paine argue that the managers' fiduciary obligations to shareholders are jeopardized in a circumstance of management buyouts. These managers have an obligation to maximize the shareholders' interest by keeping the price high, but they have a strong incentive to negotiate a low price on their own behalf, thereby minimizing shareholders' interests. Buyouts place investors at risk of managers taking advantage of shareholders through their superior knowledge and control over information and by their intentionally understating the stock's value. The authors note that the management buyout functions to undermine shareholder trust in corporate leadership, and yet buyouts often present shareholders with a rich opportunity to protect their investments and sell at the highest possible price. Bruner and Paine argue for standards whereby a buyout offer should at least equal the value shareholders could achieve on their own. Such standards, they maintain, protect the at-risk investor and satisfy management's fiduciary obligations to shareholders.

WORKER SAFETY, OCCUPATIONAL RISK, AND THE RIGHT TO KNOW

Critics of business and government have long contended that uninformed workers are routinely, and often knowingly, exposed to dangerous conditions. For example, employers did not tell asbestos workers for many years of the known dangers of contracting asbestosis. Although little is currently known about the knowledge and comprehension of workers, evidence from at least some industries shows that ignorance is a causal factor in occupational illness or injury. In a detailed study at the Hurley Reduction Works, a smelter owned by Kennecott Copper, investigators concluded that "the smelter's work force has little or no understanding of occupational health hazards, their evaluation, or prevention," especially regarding airborne arsenic, sulfur dioxide, and copper dust, all of which appear in high to very high levels.[3] The simple solution is to ban hazardous productions from use, but to do so would be to shut down a large segment of industrial manufacturing. Hundreds of products still use asbestos because no functional substitute is available.

The implications of worker ignorance are chillingly present in the following worker's testimony before an OSHA hearing on the toxic agent DBCP:

> We had no warning that DBCP exposure might cause sterility, testicular atrophy, and perhaps cancer. If we had known that these fumes could possibly cause the damage that we have found out it probably does cause, we would have worn equipment to protect ourselves. As it was, we didn't have enough knowledge to give us the proper respect for DBCP.[4]

The regulation of workplace risks has consistently sought to determine an objective level of acceptable risk and then to ban or limit exposure above that level. However, the goal of safety is not the primary justification for disclosures of risk. Individuals need the information upon which the objective standard is based to determine whether the risk it declares acceptable is *to them*. Here a subjective standard of acceptable risk seems more appropriate than an objective standard established by "experts." Choosing to risk testicular atrophy seems rightly a worker's personal choice, one not fully decidable by health and safety standards established for groups of workers. Even given objective standards, substantial ambiguity prevails when the risks are uncertain by expert assessment and the dose levels raising concern for health and safety cannot be further clarified.

Problems also surface about both the strategy of information disclosure and the strategy of protective schemes if either is used in isolation. Often no meaningful figures define the relationship between acceptable risk and the ease with which the risk can be eliminated or controlled. There also may be no consensus on which levels of probability of serious harm, such as death, constitute risks sufficiently high that steps ought to be taken to reduce or eliminate the risk or to provide information to those affected.

Both the employer's responsibility to inform employees and the employee's right to refuse hazardous job assignments are the concern of the essay by Ruth Faden and Tom L. Beauchamp. They support a standard of information disclosure and consider three possible standards for determining the justifiability of a refusal to work or a safety walkout. Also included in the legal perspectives section of this chapter is the case of *Automobile Workers v. Johnson Controls, Inc.*, which determined that employers cannot legally adopt "fetal protection policies" that exclude women of childbearing age from a hazardous workplace, because such policies involve illegal sex discrimination. However, the Supreme Court decision was, in some respects, narrow; it left U.S. corporations in uncertainty over an acceptable policy for protecting fetuses from reproductive hazards.

RISK TO HEALTH AND THE ENVIRONMENT

Controversy over protecting the environment and preventing the depletion of natural resources has mushroomed in the last three decades, a period that has caught business, government, and the general public unprepared to handle environmental problems. In the 1960s and 1970s the government instituted regulatory programs, and ever since the public has become increasingly concerned about the environmental impact of chemical dumping, supersonic transport, burning coal, nuclear power, the Alaska pipeline, and the like. In this debate, environmental deterioration is often linked to corporate actions, and thus corporate responsibility has become a major issue.

Environmental issues have traditionally been envisaged in free-market terms: Natural resources are available to entrepreneurs who are free to purchase and use them. Markets transfer resources, and rules of private property and free choice allow use of the environment to maximize profits. Conflicts were traditionally handled by relatively simple procedures that balanced conflicting interests. Those who polluted, for example, could be prosecuted and fined. People assumed that the environment, once properly tended to, was sufficiently resilient to return to its former state.

Recently this optimistic outlook has been vigorously challenged. First, it became apparent that a market conception of resource use did not fit the environment, because air, water, and much of the land environment is owned in common, and their value is not determined by prices in the market. Also, new technology and increased production seem now to have damaged the environment to a point at which unrectifiable and uncontrollable global imbalances may emerge. Yet, corporations still "externalize" rather than internalize costs by passing on the costs of pollution to the public. Attempts to bring market "externalities" such as pollution into standard pricing mechanisms—by, say, taxing effluents—have proved inadequate to handle environmental problems.

Virtually all nations over the last thirty years have increased government planning and legal adjudication of problems, especially for the setting of standards for the emission of industrial pollutants into air and water. The trend is also toward an authoritative regulatory scheme of allocational priorities to resolve the problem of accumulative harms—that is, those harms, like automobile emissions, caused not by isolated individuals but by cooperative large groups.

Some writers depict the environment as analogous to a common range land where competing cattle ranchers graze so many cattle in search of profits (as it is economically rational for each cattle rancher to do) that eventually the common land is overgrazed and can no longer support animal life. As businesspersons pursue their economic interests, collectively they work toward the ruin of all. This analysis has been disputed by those who see environmental problems as involving tradeoffs that need not do irreversible damage to "the commons." However, society acknowledges that some tradeoffs will require additional tradeoffs that may only mortgage the future. For example, air-pollution scrubbers used in industry to remove sulfur dioxide from flue gas produce three to six tons of sludge for every ton of sulfur dioxide they remove. The sludge is then buried in landfills, creating a risk of water pollution. Efforts to clean the air risk polluting the water.

Classic conflicts between public and private interests have emerged in these environmental debates. For example, attempts have been made to show that fluorocarbons in aerosol spray cans sufficiently damage the earth's ozone shield that serious repercussions may accompany continued use—for example, melting of polar ice caps, flooding of cities along the world's coasts, and radioactive contamination. Critics have charged that the food industry rapes the land by its failure to balance high-level methods of food production with the land's lower-level production capacity. Environmentalists have accused the timber industry of deforestation without replenishment. Responsibility for various forms of pollution has been given to the bottle and can industries, plastics industries, smelters, chemical industries, and the oil industry. In recent years industrial disposal of hazardous wastes that include mercury, benzene, and dioxin have been faulted for the contamination of groundwater, landfills, and even waste recovery plants.

Those who promote a new environmental ethic argue that Western culture has a special problem because of entrenched attitudes about the use of nature for human enjoyment and betterment. In this conception, humans live less as part of the ecosystem than as external dwellers. Others argue, however, that people should view the environment in a different way only to the extent that doing so would improve the quality of life and continued existence. They maintain that environmental concerns are valid only if they improve the human situation and not because animals, plants, or ecosystems have rights. This approach emphasizes the freedom of businesses to use the environment unless their activities harm other individuals in society.

Many now believe that only severe curbs on industry and severe judicial penalties will protect the environment, whereas others believe that environmental impact statements and other now standard practices are sufficient. The core of the environmental problem is how to balance the liberty rights of those who want to use the environment in typical free-market style against the rights to safe workplaces and products and our right to a contamination-free environment.

Prevalent has been a tendency to look to legal and regulatory approaches to resolve these vital social problems. However, it has become progressively clear that the combined effects of statutory law, case law, and regulatory guidelines will not suffice. Problems regarding the quality of the environment and the adequacy of health and safety protections will require corporate initiatives and a keener sense of responsibility on everyone's part.

Three readings in this chapter are concerned with these problems of environmental risk and protection. The Supreme Court of New Jersey held, in the case of *State Dept. of Environmental Protection v. Ventron Corporation,* that corporations which create problems of mercury pollution for state waterways are liable for all resultant damages of their actions under common-law principles. The court found that toxic wastes are "abnormally dangerous" discharges that assess *strict liability* for harm, including liability for all clean-up costs. The court's conclusion that "even if they did not intend to pollute or adhered to the standards of the time, all [corporate] parties remain liable" is of far-reaching significance.

The article by Jang B. Singh and V. C. Lakhan shows the extent of the annual production of hazardous wastes and how it has increased since the 1940s. They are particularly concerned with a diverse set of moral problems in the thriving international trade in hazardous substances. Finally, W. Michael Hoffman explores the relationship between business activities and the current interest in a broad environmental ethics. He argues that corporations have moral obligations to protect the environment that exceed the standards of environmental law and that corporations should be eager to cooperate with the government in protecting and cleaning up the environment. However, he denies that the slogans "good ethics is good business" or "protect the environment in order to protect human health" should be used as the moral basis of corporate environmental programs. He argues for a deeper moral perspective that focuses on the value of the environment itself.

NOTES

1. *Buckley v. New York Post,* 373 F.2d 175 (1967), at 182.
2. Joel Feinberg, *Harm to Others* (New York: Oxford University Press, 1984), 34–35.
3. Manuel Gomez, and others, "Kennecott/Hurley," in *At Work in Copper: Occupational Health and Safety in Copper Smelting* Vol. 3 (New York: Inform, 1979), 132.
4. Occupational Safety and Health Administration, "Access to Employee Exposure and Medical Records-Final Rules," *Federal Register,* May 23, 1980, p. 35222.

The Ethics of Consumer Production

Manuel G. Velasquez

Where . . . does the consumer's duties to protect his or her own interests end, and where does the manufacturer's duty to protect consumers' interests begin? Three different theories on the ethical duties of manufacturers have been developed, each one of which strikes a different balance between the consumer's duty to himself or herself and the manufacturer's duty to the consumer: the contract view, the "due care" view, and the social costs view. The contract view would place the greater responsibility on the consumer, while the "due care" and social costs views

place the larger measure of responsibility on the manufacturer. We will examine each of these views.

THE CONTRACT VIEW OF BUSINESS' DUTIES TO CONSUMERS

According to the contract view of the business firm's duties to its customers, the relationship between a business firm and its customers is essentially a contractual relationship, and the firm's moral duties to the customer are those

From Manuel G. Velasquez, *Business Ethics: Concepts and Cases,* 3rd ed. (Englewood Cliffs, NJ: Prentice Hall, 1992), pp. 277–92. © 1992 Prentice Hall, Inc. Reprinted by permission.

created by this contractual relationship.[1] When a consumer buys a product, this view holds, the consumer voluntarily enters into a "sales contract" with the business firm. The firm freely and knowingly agrees to give the consumer a product with certain characteristics and the consumer in turn freely and knowingly agrees to pay a certain sum of money to the firm for the product. In virtue of having voluntarily entered this agreement, the firm then has a duty to provide a product with those characteristics, and the consumer has a correlative right to get a product with those characteristics. . . .

Traditional moralists have argued that the act of entering into a contract is subject to several secondary moral constraints:

1. Both of the parties to the contract must have full knowledge of the nature of the agreement they are entering.
2. Neither party to a contract must intentionally misrepresent the facts of the contractual situation to the other party.
3. Neither party to a contract must be forced to enter the contract under duress or undue influence.

These secondary constraints can be justified by the same sorts of arguments that Kant and Rawls use to justify the basic duty to perform one's contracts. Kant, for example, easily shows that misrepresentation in the making of a contract cannot be universalized, and Rawls argues that if misrepresentation were not prohibited, fear of deception would make members of a society feel less free to enter contracts. But these secondary constraints can also be justified on the grounds that a contract cannot exist unless these constraints are fulfilled. For a contract is essentially a *free agreement* stuck between two parties. Since an agreement cannot exist unless both parties know what they are agreeing to, contracts require full knowledge and the absence of misrepresentation. And since freedom implies the absence of coercion, contracts must be made without duress or undue influence.

The contractual theory of business's duties to consumers, then, claims that a business has four main moral duties: The basic duty of (1) complying with the terms of the sales contract, and the secondary duties of (2) disclosing the nature of the product, (3) avoiding misrepresentation, and (4) avoiding the use of duress and undue influence. By acting in accordance with these duties, a business respects the right of consumers to be treated as free and equal persons, that is, in accordance with their right to be treated only as they have freely consented to be treated.

The Duty to Comply

The most basic moral duty that a business firm owes its customers, according to the contract view, is the duty to provide consumers with a product that lives up to those claims that the firm expressly made about the product, which led the customer to enter the contract freely, and which formed the customer's understanding concerning what he or she was agreeing to buy. In the early 1970s, for example, Winthrop Laboratories marketed a painkiller that the firm advertised as "nonaddictive." Subsequently, a patient using the painkiller became addicted to it and shortly died from an overdose. A court in 1974 found Winthrop Laboratories liable for the patient's death because, although it had expressly stated that the drug was nonaddictive, Winthrop Laboratories had failed to live up to its duty to comply with this express contractual claim.[2]

As the above example suggests, our legal system has incorporated the moral view that firms have a duty to live up to the express claims they make about their products. The Uniform Commercial Code, for example, states in Section 2-314:

Any affirmation of fact or promise made by the seller to the buyer that related to the goods and becomes part of the basis of the bargain creates an express warranty that the goods shall conform to the affirmation or promise.

In addition to the duties that result from the *express* claim a seller makes about the product, the contract view also holds that the seller has a duty to carry through on any *implied* claims he or she knowingly makes about the product. The seller, for example, has the moral duty to provide a product that can be used safely for the ordinary and special purposes for which the customer, relying on the seller's judgment, has been led to believe it can be used. . . .

The express or implied claims that a seller might make about the qualities possessed by the product range over a variety of areas and are affected by a number of factors. Frederick Sturdivant classifies these areas in terms of four variables: "The definition of product quality used here is: the degree to which product performance meets predetermined expectation with respect to (1) reliability, (2) service life, (3) maintainability, and (4) safety."[3]

Reliability. Claims of reliability refer to the probability that a product will function as the consumer is led to expect that it will function. If a product incorporates a number of interdependent components, then the probability that it will function properly is equal to the result of multiplying together each component's probability of proper functioning.[4] As the number of components in a product multiplies, therefore, the manufacturer has a corresponding duty to ensure that each component functions in such a manner that the total product is as reliable as he or she implicitly or expressly claims it will be. This is especially the case when malfunction poses health or safety hazards. The U.S. Consumer Product Safety Commission lists hundreds of examples of hazards from product malfunctions in its yearly report.[5]

Service Life. Claims concerning the life of a product refer to the period of time during which the product will function as effectively as the consumer is led to expect it to function. Generally, the consumer implicitly understands that service life will depend on the amount of wear and tear to which one subjects the product. In addition, consumers also base some of their expectations of service life on the explicit guarantees the manufacturer attaches to the product.

A more subtle factor that influences service life is the factor of obsolescence.[6] Technological advances may render some products obsolete when a new product appears that carries out the same functions more efficiently. Or purely stylistic changes may make last year's product appear dated and less desirable. The contract view implies that a seller who knows that a certain product will become obsolete has a duty to correct any mistaken beliefs he or she knows buyers will form concerning the service life they may expect from the product.

Maintainability. Claims of maintainability are claims concerning the ease with which the product can be repaired and kept in operating condition. Claims of maintainability are often made in the form of an express warranty. Whirlpool Corporation, for example, appended this express warranty on one of its products:

> During your first year of ownership, all parts of the appliance (except the light bulbs) that we find are defective in materials or workmanship will be repaired or replaced by Whirlpool free of charge, and we will pay all labor charges. During the second year, we will continue to assume the same responsibility as stated above except you pay any labor charges.[7]

But sellers often also imply that a product may be easily repaired even after the expiration date of an express warranty. In fact, however, product repairs may be costly, or even impossible, due to the unavailability of parts.

Product Safety. Implied and express claims of product safety refer to the degree of risk associated with using a product. Since the use of virtually any product involves some degree of risk, questions of safety are essentially questions of *acceptable known levels* of risk. That is, a product is safe if its attendant risks are known and judged to be "acceptable" or "reasonable" by the *buyer* in view of the benefits the buyer expects to derive from using the product. This implies that the seller complies with his or her part of a free agreement if the seller provides a product that involves only those risks he or she says it involves, and the buyer purchases it with that understanding. The National Commission on Product Safety, for example, characterized "reasonable risk" in these terms:

> Risks of bodily harm to users are not unreasonable when consumers understand that risks exist, can appraise their probability and severity, know how to cope with them, and voluntarily accept them to get benefits they could not obtain in less risky ways. When there is a risk of this character, consumers have reasonable opportunity to protect themselves; and public authorities should hesitate to substitute their value judgments about the desirability of the risk for those of the consumers who choose to incur it. But preventable risk is not reasonable (a) when consumers do not know that it exists; or (b) when, though aware of it, consumers are unable to estimate its frequency and severity; or (c) when consumers do not know how to cope with it, and hence are likely to incur harm unnecessarily; or (d) when risk is unnecessary in that it could be reduced or eliminated at a cost in money or in the performance of the product that consumers would willingly incur if they knew the facts and were given the choice.[8]

Thus the seller of a product (according to the contractual theory) has a moral duty to provide a product whose use involves *no greater risks* than those the seller *expressly* communicates to the buyer or those the seller *implicitly* communicates by the implicit claims made when marketing the product for a use whose normal risk level is well known. . . .

The Duty of Disclosure

An agreement cannot bind unless both parties to the agreement know what they are doing and freely choose to do it. This implies that the seller who intends to enter a contract with a customer has a duty to disclose exactly what the customer is buying and what the terms of the sale are. At a minimum, this means the seller has a duty to inform the buyer of any facts about the product that would affect the customer's decision to purchase the product. For example, if the product the consumer is buying possesses a defect that poses a risk to the user's health or safety, the consumer should be so informed. Some have argued that sellers should also disclose a product's components or ingredients, its performance characteristics, costs of operation, product ratings, and any other applicable standards.[9]

Behind the claim that entry into a sales contract requires full disclosure is the idea that an agreement is free only to the extent that one knows what alternatives are available: Freedom depends on knowledge. The more the buyer knows about the various products available on the market and the more comparisons the buyer is able to make among them, the more one can say that the buyer's agreement is voluntary. . . .[10]

Since entry into a contract requires *freely* given consent, the seller has a duty to refrain from exploiting emotional states that may induce the buyer to act irrationally against his or her own best interests. For similar reasons, the seller also has the duty not to take advantage of gullibility, immaturity, ignorance, or any other factors that reduce or eliminate the buyer's ability to make free rational choices.

Problems with the Contractual Theory

The main objections to the contract theory focus on the unreality of the assumptions on which the theory is based. First, critics argue, the theory unrealistically assumes that manufacturers make direct agreements with consumers. Nothing could be farther from the truth. Normally, a series of wholesalers and retailers stand between the manufacturer and the ultimate consumer. The manufacturer sells the product to the wholesaler, who sells it to the retailer, who finally sells it to the consumer. The manufacturer never enters into any direct contract with the consumer. How then can one say that manufacturers have contractual duties to the consumer?

Advocates of the contract view of manufacturers' duties have tried to respond to this criticism by arguing that manufacturers enter into "indirect" agreements with consumers. Manufacturers promote their products through their own advertising campaigns. These advertisements supply the promises that lead people to purchase products from retailers who merely function as "conduits" for the manufacturer's product. Consequently, through these advertisements, the manufacturer forges an indirect contractual relationship not only with the immediate retailers who purchase the manufacturer's product but also with the ultimate consumers of the product. The most famous application of this doctrine of broadened indirect contractual relationships is to be found in a 1960 court opinion, *Henningsen v. Bloomfield Motors*.[11] . . .

A second objection to the contract theory focuses on the fact that a contract is a two-edged sword. If a consumer can freely agree to buy a product *with* certain qualities, the consumer can also freely agree to buy a product *without* those qualities. That is, freedom of contract allows a manufacturer to be released from his or her contractual obligations by explicitly *disclaiming* that the product is reliable, serviceable, safe, etc. Many manufacturers fix such disclaimers on their products. . . . The contract view, then, implies that if the consumer has ample opportunity to examine the product and the disclaimers and voluntarily consents to buy it anyway, he or she assumes the responsibility for the defects disclaimed by the manufacturer, as well as for any defects the customer may carelessly have overlooked. Disclaimers can effectively nullify all contractual duties of the manufacturer.

A third objection to the contract theory criticizes the assumption that buyer and seller meet each other as equals in the sales agreement. The contractual theory assumes that buyers and sellers are equally skilled at evaluating the quality of a product and that buyers are able to adequately protect their interests against the seller. . . . In practice, this laissez-faire ideology gave birth to the doctrine of "caveat emptor": let the buyer take care of himself.

In fact, sellers and buyers do not exhibit the equality these doctrines assume. A consumer who must purchase hundreds of different kinds of commodities cannot hope to be as knowledgeable as a manufacturer who specializes in producing a single product. Consumers have neither the expertise nor the time to acquire and process the information on which they must base their purchase decisions. Consumers, as a consequence, must usually rely on the judgment of the seller in making their purchase decisions, and are particularly vulnerable to being harmed by the seller. Equality, far from being the rule, as the contract theory assumes, is usually the exception.

THE DUE CARE THEORY

The "due care" theory of the manufacturer's duties to consumers is based on the idea that consumers and sellers do not meet as equals and that the consumer's interests are particularly vulnerable to being harmed by the manufacturer who has a knowledge and an expertise that the consumer does not have. Because manufacturers are in a more advantaged position, they have a duty to take a special "care" to ensure that consumers' interests are not harmed by the products that they offer them. The doctrine of "caveat emptor" is here replaced with a weak version of the doctrine of "caveat vendor": let the seller take care. . . .

The "due care" view holds, then, that because consumers must depend upon the greater expertise of the manufacturer, the manufacturers not only has a duty to deliver a product that lives up to the express and implied claims about it, but in addition the manufacturer has a duty to exercise due care to prevent others from being injured by the product, *even if the manufacturer explicitly disclaims such responsibility and the buyer agrees to the disclaimer*. The manufacturer violates this duty and is "negligent" when there is a failure to exercise the care that a reasonable person could have foreseen would be necessary to prevent others from being harmed by use of the product. Due care must enter into the design of the product, into the choice of reliable materials for constructing the product, into the manufacturing processes involved in putting the product together, into the quality control used to test and monitor production, and into the warnings, labels, and instructions attached to the product. In each of these areas, according to the due care view, the manufacturer, in virtue of a greater expertise and knowledge, has a positive duty to take whatever steps are necessary to ensure that when the product leaves the plant it is as safe as possible, and the customer has a right to such assurance. Failure to take such steps is a breach of the moral duty to exercise due care and a violation of the injured person's right to expect such care, a right that rests on the consumer's need to rely on the manufacturer's expertise. . . .

The Duty to Exercise Due Care

According to the due care theory, manufacturers exercise sufficient care when they take adequate steps to prevent whatever injurious effects they can foresee that the use of their product may have on consumers after having conducted inquiries into the way the product will be used and after having attempted to anticipate any possible misuses of the product. A manufacturer, then, is *not* morally negligent when others are harmed by a product and the harm was not one that the manufacturer could possibly have foreseen or prevented. Nor is a manufacturer morally negligent after having taken all reasonable steps to protect the consumer and to ensure that the consumer is informed of any irremovable risks that might still attend the use of the product. A car manufacturer, for example, cannot be said to be negligent from a moral point of view when people carelessly misuse the cars the manufacturer produces. A car manufacturer would be morally negligent only if the manufacturer had allowed unreasonable dangers to remain in the design of the car that consumers cannot be expected to know about or that they cannot guard against by taking their own precautionary measures.

What specific responsibilities does the duty to exercise due care impose on the producer? In general, the producer's responsibilities would extend to three areas:

Design. The manufacturer should ascertain whether the design of an article conceals any dangers, whether it incorporates all feasible safety devices, and whether it uses materials that are adequate for the purposes the product is intended to serve. The manufacturer is responsible for being thoroughly acquainted with the design of the item, and to conduct research and tests extensive enough to uncover any risks that may be involved in employing the article under various conditions of use. . . .

Production. The production manager should control the manufacturing processes to eliminate any defective items, to identify any weaknesses that become apparent during production, and to ensure that short-cuts, substitution of weaker materials, or other economizing measures are not taken during manufacture that would compromise the safety of the final product. To ensure this, there should be adequate quality controls over materials that are to be used in the manufacture of the product and over the various stages of manufacture.

Information. The manufacturer should fix labels, notices, or instructions on the production that will warn the user of all dangers involved in using or misusing the item and that will enable the user to adequately guard himself or herself against harm or injury. These instructions should be clear and simple, and warnings of any hazards involved in using or misusing the product should also be clear, simple, and prominent. . . .

Problems with "Due Care"

The basic difficulty raised by the "due care" theory is that there is no clear method for determining when one has exercised enough "due care." That is, there is no hard and fast rule for determining how far a firm must go to ensure the safety of its product. Some authors have proposed the general utilitarian rule that the greater the probability of harm and the larger the population that might be harmed, the more the firm is obligated to do. But this fails to resolve some important issues. Every product involves at least some small

risk of injury. If the manufacturer should try to eliminate even low-level risks, this would require that the manufacturer invest so much in each product that the product would be priced out of the reach of most consumers. Moreover, even *attempting* to balance higher risks against added costs involves measurement problems: How does one quantify risks to health and life?

A second difficulty raised by the "due care" theory is that it assumes that the manufacturer can discover the risks that attend the use of a product before the consumer buys and uses it. In fact, in a technologically innovative society new products whose defects cannot emerge until years or decades have passed will continually be introduced into the market. Only years after thousands of people were using and being exposed to asbestos, for example, did a correlation emerge between the incidence of cancer and exposure to asbestos. Although manufacturers may have greater expertise than consumers, their expertise does not make them omniscient. Who, then, is to bear the costs of injuries sustained from products whose defects neither the manufacturer nor the consumer could have uncovered beforehand?

Thirdly, the due care view appears to some to be paternalistic. For it assumes that the *manufacturer* should be the one who makes the important decisions for the consumer, at least with respect to the levels of risks that are proper for consumers to bear. But one may wonder whether such decisions should not be left up to the free choice of consumers who can decide for themselves whether or not they want to pay for additional risk reduction.

THE SOCIAL COSTS VIEW OF THE MANUFACTURER'S DUTIES

A third theory on the duties of the manufacturer would extend the manufacturer's duties beyond those imposed by contractual relationships and beyond those imposed by the duty to exercise due care in preventing injury or harm. This third theory holds that a manufacturer should pay the costs of *any* injuries sustained through any defects in the product, *even when the manufacturer exercised all due care in the design and manufacture of the product and has taken all reasonable precautions to warn users of every foreseen danger.* According to this third theory a manufacturer has a duty to assume the risks of even those injuries that arise out of defects in the product that no one could reasonably have foreseen or eliminated. The theory is a very strong version of the doctrine of "caveat vendor": let the seller take care.

This third theory, which has formed the basis of the legal doctrine of "strict liability," is founded on utilitarian arguments. The utilitarian arguments for this third theory hold that the "external" costs of injuries resulting from unavoidable defects in the design of an artifact constitute part of the costs society must pay for producing and using an artifact. By having the manufacturer bear the external costs that result from these injuries as well as the ordinary internal costs of design and manufacture, all costs will be internalized and added on as part of the price of the product. Internalizing all costs in this way, according to proponents of this theory, will lead to a more efficient use of society's resources. First, since the price will reflect *all* the costs of producing and using the artifact, market forces will ensure that the product is not overproduced, and that resources are not wasted on it. (Whereas if some costs were not included in the price, then manufacturers would tend to produce more than is needed.) Second, since manufacturers have to pay the costs of injuries, they will be motivated to exercise greater care and to thereby reduce the number of accidents. Manufacturers will therefore strive to cut down the social costs of injuries, and this

means a more efficient care for our human resources. In order to produce the maximum benefits possible from our limited resources, therefore, the social costs of injuries from defective products should be internalized by passing them on to the manufacturer, even when the manufacturer has done all that could be done to eliminate such defects. And third, internalizing the costs of injury in this way enables the manufacturer to distribute losses among all the users of a product instead of allowing losses to fall on individuals who may not be able to sustain the loss by themselves.

Underlying this third theory on the duties of the manufacturer are the standard utilitarian assumptions about the values of efficiency. The theory assumes that an efficient use of resources is so important for society that social costs should be allocated in whatever way will lead to a more efficient use and care of our resources. On this basis, the theory argues that a manufacturer should bear the social costs for injuries caused by defects in a product, even when no negligence was involved and no contractual relationship existed between the manufacturer and the user.

Problems with the Social Costs View

The major criticism of the social costs view of the manufacturer's duties is that it is unfair.[12] It is unfair, the critics charge, because it violates the basic canons of compensatory justice. Compensatory justice implies that a person should be forced to compensate an injured party only if the person could foresee and could have prevented the injury. By forcing manufacturers to pay for injuries that they could neither foresee nor prevent, the social costs theory (and the legal theory of 'strict liability' that flows from it) treats manufacturers unfairly. Moreover, insofar as the social costs theory encourages passing the costs of injuries on to all consumers (in the form of higher prices), consumers are also being treated unfairly.

A second criticism of the social costs theory attacks the assumption that passing the costs of all injuries on to manufacturers will reduce the number of accidents.[13] On the contrary, critics claim, by relieving consumers of the responsibility of paying for their own injuries, the social costs theory will encourage carelessness in consumers. And an increase in consumer carelessness will lead to an increase in consumer injuries.

A third argument against the social costs theory focuses on the financial burdens the theory imposes on manufacturers and insurance carriers. Critics claim that a growing number of consumers successfully sue manufacturers for compensation for any injuries sustained while using a product, even when the manufacturer took all due care to ensure that the product was safe.[14] Not only have the number of "strict liability" suits increased, critics claim, but the amounts awarded to injured consumers have also escalated. Moreover, they continue, the rising costs of the many liability suits that the theory of "strict liability" has created have precipitated a crisis in the insurance industry because insurance companies end up paying the liability suits brought against manufacturers. . . .

The arguments for and against the social costs theory deserve much more discussion than we can give them here. The theory is essentially an attempt to come to grips with the problem of allocating the costs of injuries between two morally innocent parties: The manufacturer who could not foresee or prevent a product-related injury, and the consumer who could not guard himself or herself against the injury because the hazard was unknown. This allocation problem will arise in any society that, like ours, has come to rely upon a technology whose effects do not become evident until years after the technol-ogy is introduced. Unfortunately, it is also a problem that may have no "fair" solution.

NOTES

1. See Thomas Garrett and Richard J. Klonoski, *Business Ethics,* 2nd ed. (Englewood Cliffs, NJ: Prentice Hall, 1986), p. 88.

2. *Crocker v. Winthrop Laboratories, Division of Sterling Drug, Inc.,* 514 Southwestern 2d 429 (1974).

3. Frederick D. Sturdivant, *Business and Society,* 3rd ed. (Homewood, IL: Richard D. Irwin, Inc., 1985), p. 392.

4. Ibid., p. 393.

5. U.S. Consumer Products Safety Commission, *1979 Annual Report* (Washington, DC: U.S. Government Printing Office, 1979), pp. 81–101.

6. A somewhat dated but still incisive discussion of this issue is found in Vance Packard, *The Wastemakers* (New York: David McKay Co., Inc., 1960).

7. Quoted in address by S. E. Upton (vice-president of Whirlpool Corporation) to the American Marketing Association in Cleveland, OH: 11 December 1969.

8. National Commission on Product Safety, *Final Report,* quoted in William W. Lowrance, *Of Acceptable Risk* (Los Altos, CA: William Kaufmann, Inc., 1976), p. 80.

9. See Louis Stern, "Consumer Protection via Increased Information," *Journal of Marketing,* 31, no. 2 (April 1967).

10. Lawrence E. Hicks, *Coping with Packaging Laws* (New York: AMACOM, 1972). p. 17.

11. *Henningsen v. Bloomfield Motors, Inc.,* 32 New Jersey 358, 161 Atlantic 2d 69 (1960). [See this text, pp. 236–40.]

12. George P. Fletcher, "Fairness and Utility in Tort Theory," *Harvard Law Review,* 85, no. 3 (January 1972): 537–73.

13. Posner, *Economic Analysis of Law,* 2nd ed. (Boston: Little, Brown and Co., 1977), pp. 139–42.

14. See "Unsafe Products: The Great Debate Over Blame and Punishment," *Business Week,* 30 April 1984; Stuart Taylor, "Product Liability: the New Morass," *New York Times,* 10 March 1985; "The Product Liability Debate," *Newsweek,* 10 September 1984.

Strict Products Liability and Compensatory Justice

George G. Brenkert

I

Strict products liability is the doctrine that the seller of a product has legal responsibilities to compensate the user of that product for injuries suffered because of a defective aspect of the product, even when the seller has not been negligent in permitting that defect to occur.[1] Thus, even though a manufacturer, for example, has reasonably applied the existing techniques of manufacture and has anticipated and cared for nonintended uses of the product, he may still be held liable for injuries a product user suffers if it can be shown that the product was defective when it left the manufacturer's hands.

To say that there is a crisis today concerning this doctrine would be to utter a commonplace which few in the business community would deny. The development of the doctrine of strict products liability, according to most business people, threatens many businesses financially. Furthermore, strict products liability is said to be a morally questionable doctrine, since the manufacturer or seller has not been negligent in permitting the injury-causing defect to occur. On the other hand, victims of defective products complain that they deserve full compensation for injuries sustained in using a defective product whether or not the seller is at fault. Medical expenses and time lost from one's job are costs no individual should have to bear by himself. It is only fair that the seller share such burdens.

In general, discussions of this crisis focus on the limits to which a business ought to be

held responsible. Much less frequently, discussions of strict products liability consider the underlying question of whether the doctrine of strict products liability is rationally justifiable. But unless this question is answered it would seem premature to seek to determine the limits to which businesses ought to be held liable in such cases. In the following paper I discuss this underlying philosophical question and argue that there is a rational justification for strict products liability which links it to the very nature of the free enterprise system.

II

. . . To begin with, it is crucial to remember that what we have to consider is the relationship between an entity doing business and an individual. The strict liability attributed to business would not be attributed to an individual who happened to sell some product he had made to his neighbor or a stranger. If Peter sold an article he had made to Paul and Paul hurt himself because the article had a defect which occurred through no negligence of Peter's, we would not normally hold Peter morally responsible to pay for Paul's injuries. . . .

It is different for businesses. They have been held to be legally and morally obliged to pay the victim for his injuries. Why? What is the difference? The difference is that when Paul is hurt by a defective product from corporation X, he is hurt by something produced in a socioeconomic system purportedly embodying free enterprise. In other words, among other things:

Used by permission of the author.

1. Each business and/or corporation produces articles or services it sells for profit.
2. Each member of this system competes with other members of the system in trying to do as well as it can for itself not simply in each exchange, but through each exchange for its other values and desires.
3. Competition is to be "open and free, without deception or fraud."
4. Exchanges are voluntary and undertaken when each party believes it can benefit thereby. One party provides the means for another party's ends if the other party will provide the first party the means to its ends.
5. The acquisition and disposition of ownership rights—that is, of private property—is permitted in such exchanges.
6. No market or series of markets constitutes the whole of a society.
7. Law, morality, and government play a role in setting acceptable limits to the nature and kinds of exchange in which people may engage.

What is it about such a system which would justify claims of strict products liability against businesses? . . . In the free enterprise system, each person and/or business is obligated to follow the rules and understandings which define this socioeconomic system. Following the rules is expected to channel competition among individuals and businesses to socially positive results. In providing the means to fulfill the ends of others, one's own ends also get fulfilled.

Though this does not happen in every case, it is supposed to happen most of the time. Those who fail in their competition with others may be the object of charity, but not of other duties. Those who succeed, qua members of this socioeconomic system, do not have moral duties to aid those who fail. Analogously, the team which loses the game may receive our sympathy but the winning team is not obligated to help it to win the next game or even to play it better. Those who violate the rules, however, may be punished or pe-

nalized, whether or not the violation was intentional and whether or not it redounded to the benefit of the violator. Thus, a team may be assessed a penalty for something that a team member did unintentionally to a member of the other team but which injured the other team's chances of competition in the game by violating the rules.

This point may be emphasized by another instance involving a game that brings us closer to strict products liability. Imagine that you are playing table tennis with another person in his newly constructed table tennis room. You are both avid table tennis players and the game means a lot to both of you. Suppose that after play has begun, you are suddenly and quite obviously blinded by the light over the table—the light shade has a hole in it which, when it turned in your direction, sent a shaft of light unexpectedly into your eyes. You lose a crucial point as a result. Surely it would be unfair of your opponent to seek to maintain his point because he was faultless—after all, he had not intended to blind you when he installed that light shade. You would correctly object that he had gained the point unfairly, that you should not have to give up the point lost, and that the light shade should be modified so that the game can continue on a fair basis. It is only fair that the point be played over.

Businesses and their customers in a free enterprise system are also engaged in competition with each other. The competition here, however, is multifaceted as each tries to gain the best agreement he can from the other with regard to the buying and selling of raw materials, products, services, and labor. Such agreements must be voluntary. The competition which leads to them cannot involve coercion. In addition, such competition must be fair and ultimately result in the benefit of the entire society through the operation of the proverbial invisible hand.

Crucial to the notion of fairness of competition are not simply the demands that the competition be open, free, and honest, but also that each person in a society be given an equal opportunity to participate in the system in order to fulfill his or her own particular ends. . . .

. . . Equality of opportunity requires that one not be prevented by arbitrary obstacles from participating (by engaging in a productive role of some kind or other) in the system of free enterprise, competition, and so on in order to fulfill one's own ends ("reap the benefits"). Accordingly, monopolies are restricted, discriminatory hiring policies have been condemned, and price collusion is forbidden.

However, each person participates in the system of free enterprise *both* as a worker/producer *and* as a consumer. The two roles interact; if the person could not consume he would not be able to work, and if there were no consumers there would be no work to be done. Even if a particular individual is only (what is ordinarily considered) a consumer, he or she plays a theoretically significant role in the competitive free enterprise system. The fairness of the system depends upon what access he or she has to information about goods and services on the market, the lack of coercion imposed on that person to buy goods, and the lack of arbitrary restrictions imposed by the market and/or government on his or her behavior.

In short, equality of opportunity is a doctrine with two sides which applies both to producers and to consumers. If, then, a person as a consumer or a producer is injured by a defective product—which is one way his activities might arbitrarily be restricted by the action of (one of the members of) the market system—surely his free and voluntary participation in the system of free enterprise will be seriously affected. Specifically, his equal opportunity to participate in the system in order to fulfill his own ends will be diminished.

Here is where strict products liability enters the picture. In cases of strict liability the manufacturer does not intend for a certain aspect of his product to injure someone. Nevertheless, the person is injured. As a result, he is at a disadvantage both as a consumer and as a producer. He cannot continue to play either role as he might wish. Therefore, he is denied that equality of opportunity which is basic to the economic system in question just as surely as he would be if he were excluded from employment by various unintended consequences of the economic system which nevertheless had racially or sexually prejudicial implications. Accordingly, it is fair for the manufacturer to compensate the person for his losses before proceeding with business as usual. That is, the user of a manufacturer's product may justifiably demand compensation from the manufacturer when its product can be shown to be defective and has injured him and harmed his chances of participation in the system of free enterprise.

Hence, strict liability finds a basis in the notion of equality of opportunity which plays a central role in the notion of a free enterprise system. That is why a business which does *not* have to pay for the injuries an individual suffers in the use of a defective article made by that business is felt to be unfair to its customers. Its situation is analogous to that of a player's unintentional violation of a game rule which is intended to foster equality of competitive opportunity.

A soccer player, for example, may unintentionally trip an opposing player. He did not mean to do it; perhaps he himself had stumbled. Still, he has to be penalized. If the referee looked the other way, the tripped player would rightfully object that he had been treated unfairly. Similarly, the manufacturer of a product may be held strictly liable for a product of his which injures a person who uses that product. Even if he is faultless, a consequence of his activities is to render the user of his product less capable of equal participation in the socioeconomic system. The manufacturer should be penalized by way of compensating the victim. Thus, the basis upon which manufacturers are held strictly liable is compensatory justice.

In a society which refuses to resort to paternalism or to central direction of the economy and which turns, instead, to competition in order to allocate scarce positions and resources, compensatory justice requires that the competition be fair and losers be protected.[2] Specifically, no one who loses should be left so destitute that he cannot reenter the competition. Furthermore, those who suffer injuries traceable to defective merchandise or services which restrict their participation in the competitive system should also be compensated.

Compensatory justice does not presuppose negligence or evil intentions on the part of those to whom the injuries might ultimately be traced. It is not perplexed or incapacitated by the relative innocence of all parties involved. Rather, it is concerned with correcting the disadvantaged situation an individual experiences due to accidents or failures which occur in the normal working of that competitive system. It is on this basis that other compensatory programs which alleviate the disabilities of various minority groups are founded. Strict products liability is also founded on compensatory justice.

An implication of the preceding argument is that business is not morally obliged to pay, as such, for the physical injury a person suffers. Rather, it must pay for the loss of equal competitive opportunity—even though it usually is the case that it is because of a (physical) injury that there is a loss of equal opportunity. Actual legal cases in which the injury which prevents a person from going about his or her daily activities is emotional or mental, as well as physical, supports this thesis. If a person were neither mentally nor physically harmed, but still rendered less capable of participating competitively because of a defective

aspect of a product, there would still be grounds for holding the company liable.

For example, suppose I purchased and used a cosmetic product guaranteed to last a month. When used by most people it is odorless. On me, however, it has a terrible smell. I can stand the smell, but my co-workers and most other people find it intolerable. My employer sends me home from work until it wears off. The product has not harmed me physically or mentally. Still, on the above argument, I would have reason to hold the manufacturer liable. Any cosmetic product with this result is defective. As a consequence my opportunity to participate in the socioeconomic system is curbed. I should be compensated.

III

There is another way of arriving at the same conclusion about the basis of strict products liability. To speak of business or the free enterprise system, it was noted above, is to speak of the voluntary exchanges between producer and customer which take place when each party believes he has an opportunity to benefit. Surely customers and producers may miscalculate their benefits; something they voluntarily agreed to buy or sell may turn out not to be to their benefit. The successful person does not have any moral responsibilities to the unsuccessful person—at least as a member of this economic system. If, however, fraud is the reason one person does not benefit, the system is, in principle, undermined. If such fraud were universalized, the system would collapse. Accordingly, the person committing the fraud does have a responsibility to make reparations to the one mistreated.

Consider once again the instance of a person who is harmed by a product he bought or used, a product that can reasonably be said to be defective. Has the nature of the free enterprise system also been undermined or corrupted in this instance? Producer and consumer have exchanged the product but it has not been to their mutual benefit; the manufacturer may have benefited, but the customer has suffered because of the defect. Furthermore, if such exchanges were universalized, the system would also be undone.

Suppose that whenever people bought products from manufacturers the products turned out to be defective and the customers were always injured, even though the manufacturers could not be held negligent. Though one party to such exchanges might benefit, the other party always suffered. If the rationale for this economic system—the reason it was adopted and is defended—were that in the end both parties share the equal opportunity to gain, surely it would collapse with the above consequences. Consequently, as with fraud, an economic system of free enterprise requires that injuries which result from defective products be compensated. The question is: Who is to pay for the compensation?

There are three possibilities. The injured party could pay for his own injuries. However, this is implausible since what is called for is compensation and not merely payment for injuries. If the injured party had simply injured himself, if he had been negligent or careless, then it is plausible that he should pay for his own injuries. No compensation is at stake here. But in the present case the injury stems from the actions of a particular manufacturer who, albeit unwittingly, placed the defective product on the market and stands to gain through its sale.

The rationale of the free enterprise system would be undermined, we have seen, if such actions were universalized, for then the product user's equal opportunity to benefit from the system would be denied. Accordingly, since the rationale and motivation for an individual to be part of this socioeconomic system is his opportunity to gain from participation in it, justice requires that the injured product user receive compensation for his injuries. Since the individual can hardly compensate himself, he must receive compensation from some other source.

Second, some third party—such as government—could compensate the injured person. This is not wholly implausible if one is prepared to modify the structure of the free enterprise system. And, indeed, in the long run this may be the most plausible course of action. However, if one accepts the structure of the free enterprise system, this alternative must be rejected because it permits the interference of government into individual affairs.

Third, we are left with the manufacturer. Suppose a manufacturer's product, even though the manufacturer wasn't negligent, always turned out to be defective and injured those using his products. We might sympathize with his plight, but he would either have to stop manufacturing altogether (no one would buy such products) or else compensate the victims for their losses. (Some people might buy and use his products under these conditions.) If he forced people to buy and use his products he would corrupt the free enterprise system. If he did not compensate the injured users, they would not buy and he would not be able to sell his products. Hence, he could partake of the free enterprise system—that is, sell his products—only if he compensated his user/victims. Accordingly, the sale of this hypothetical line of defective products would be voluntarily accepted as just or fair only if compensation were paid the user/victims of such products by the manufacturer.

The same conclusion follows even if we consider a single defective product. The manufacturer put the defective product on the market. Because of his actions others who seek the opportunity to participate on an equal basis in this system in order to benefit therefrom are unable to do so. Thus, a result of his actions, even though unintended, is to undermine the system's character and integrity. Accordingly, when a person is injured in his attempt to participate in this system, he is owed compensation by the manufacturer. The seller of the defective article must not jeopardize the equal opportunity of the product user to benefit from the system. The seller need not guarantee that the buyer/user will benefit from the purchase of the product; after all, the buyer may miscalculate or be careless in the use of a nondefective product. But if he is not careless or has not miscalculated, his opportunity to benefit from the system is illegitimately harmed if he is injured in its use because of the product's defectiveness. He deserves compensation.

It follows from the arguments in this and the preceding section that strict products liability is not only compatible with the system of free enterprise but that if it were not attributed to the manufacturer the system itself would be morally defective. And the justification for requiring manufacturers to pay compensation when people are injured by defective products is that the demands of compensatory justice are met.[3]

NOTES

1. This characterization of strict products liability is adapted from Alvin S. Weinstein et al., *Products Liability and the Reasonably Safe Product* (New York: John Wiley & Sons, 1978), ch. 1. I understand the seller to include the manufacturer, the retailer, distributors, and wholesalers. For the sake of convenience, I will generally refer simply to the manufacturer.

2. I have drawn heavily, in this paragraph, on the fine article by Bernard Boxhill, "The Morality of Reparation," reprinted in *Reverse Discrimination*, ed. Barry R. Gross (Buffalo, New York: Prometheus Books, 1977), pp. 270–278.

3. I would like to thank the following for providing helpful comments on earlier versions of this paper: Betsy Postow, Jerry Phillips, Bruce Fisher, John Hardwig, and Sheldon Cohen.

The Right to Risk Information and the Right to Refuse Workplace Hazards

Ruth R. Faden and Tom L. Beauchamp

In recent years, the right of employees to be informed about health hazards in the workplace has become a major issue in occupational health policy. We focus on several philosophical and policy-oriented problems concerning the right to know and correlative obligations to disclose relevant information. Related rights are also addressed, including the right to refuse hazardous work and the right of workers to contribute to workplace safety standards.

I

A government and industry consensus has gradually evolved that workers have a right to know about occupational risks, and correlatively that there is a moral and a legal obligation to disclose relevant information to workers. The National Institute for Occupational Safety and Health (NIOSH) and other U.S. federal agencies informed the U.S. Senate as early as July, 1977, that "workers have the right to know whether or not they are exposed to hazardous chemical and physical agents regulated by the Federal Government."[1] The Occupational Safety and Health Administration (OSHA) implemented regulations in 1980 guaranteeing workers access to medical and exposure records,[2] and then developed regulations in 1983, 1986, and 1988 regarding the right to know about hazardous chemicals and requiring right-to-know training programs in many industries.[3] Numerous states and municipalities have passed additional legislation.[4] Many corporations—including Monsanto, DuPont, and Hercules—have initiated model right-to-know programs.

Although the view that workers have some form of right to risk information is now well established under law, no consensus exists about the nature and extent of an employer's moral obligation to disclose such information, and the legal obligation remains unsettled. Considerable ambiguity also attends the nature and scope of the right—i.e., which protections and actions the right entails, and to whom these rights apply. For example, corporations and workers usually do not distinguish between the obligation to disclose currently available information, to seek information through literature searches, to generate information through new research, and to communicate hazards through educational or other training programs. The relevant literature also does not discuss whether corporations owe workers information that exceeds federal and state requirements.

II

A diverse set of recent U.S. laws and federal regulations reflect the belief that citizens in general, and workers in particular, have a right to learn about significant risks. These include The Freedom of Information Act, The Federal Insecticide, Fungicide, and Ro-denticide Amendments and Regulations, The Motor Vehicle and School Bus Safety Amendments, The Truth-in-Lending Act, The Pension Reform Act, The Real Estate Settlement Procedures Act, The Federal Food, Drug, and Cosmetic Act, The Consumer Product Safety Act, and The Toxic Substances Control Act. Taken together, this legislation communicates the implicit message that manufacturers and other businesses have a moral (and often a legal) obligation to disclose information needed by individuals to decide about their participation, employment, or enrollment.

Recent developments in the right to know in the workplace have consistently held to this general trend towards disclosure and have included an expanded notion of corporate responsibility to provide adequate information to workers. These developments could revolutionize corporate workplace practices. Until the 1983 OSHA Hazard Communication Standard (HCS) went into effect in 1986 for the manufacturing sector and in 1988 for the non-manufacturing sector,[5] workers did not routinely receive extensive information from many employers. Today, by contrast, some corporations have established model programs. For example, the Monsanto Company has a right-to-know program in which it distributes information on hazardous chemicals to its employees, and both notifies and monitors past and current employees exposed to carcinogenic and toxic chemicals. Hercules Inc. has videotape training sessions that incorporate frank discussions of workers' anxieties. The tapes depict workplace dangers and on-the-job accidents. Those employees who have seen the Hercules film are then taught how to read safety data and how to protect themselves.[6]

Job-training programs, safety data sheets, proper labels, and a written program are all now HCS-mandated. According to the present standards, all employers must "establish hazard-communication programs to transmit information on the hazards of chemicals to their employees." The training of new employees must occur before they are exposed to hazardous substances, and each time a new hazard is introduced. Each employee must sign a written acknowledgment of training, and OSHA inspectors may interview employees to check on the effectiveness of the training sessions.[7]

The sobering statistics on worker exposure and injury and on dangerous chemicals in the workplace make such corporate programs essential. The annual Registry of Toxic Effects of Chemical Substances lists over 25,000 hazardous chemicals, at least 8,000 of which are present in the workplace. As OSHA mentioned in the preamble to its Hazard Communication Standard, an estimated 25 million largely uninformed workers in North America (one in four workers) are exposed to toxic substances regulated by the federal government. Approximately 6,000 U.S. workers die from workplace injuries each year, and perhaps as many as 100,000 deaths annually are caused to some degree by workplace exposure and consequent disease. One percent of the labor force is exposed to known carcinogens, and over 44,000 U.S. workers are exposed full-time to OSHA-regulated carcinogens.[8]

Despite OSHA's HCS regulations, compliance problems persist. By March 1989, OSHA had recorded over 49,000 HCS violations in the workplace. The agency described the noncompliance rate as "incredible."[9] Part of the problem stems from ignorance both about the dangers and current OSHA requirements.

III

The most developed models of general disclosure obligations and the right to know are presently found in the extensive literature on informed consent, which also deals with in-

formed refusal. This literature developed largely from contexts of fiduciary relationships between physicians and patients, where there are broadly recognized moral and legal obligations to disclose known risks (and benefits) associated with a proposed treatment or research maneuver. No parallel obligation has traditionally been recognized in nonfiduciary relationships, such as that between management and workers. Workmen's compensation laws originally designed for problems of accident in instances of immediately assessable damage largely handled risks in this environment. Obligations to warn or to disclose remained undeveloped, because they are irrelevant under the "no-fault" conception operative in workmen's compensation.

However, needs for information in clinical medicine and in the workplace have gradually become associated with occupational disease—in particular, knowledge about the serious long-term risks of injury, disease, and death from exposure to toxic substances. In comparison to traditional accident and safety issues, these risks to health in the workplace carry increased need for information on the basis of which a person may wish to take various actions, including choosing to forego employment completely, to refuse certain work environments within a place of employment, to request improved protective devices, or to request lowered levels of exposure.

Employee-employer relationships—unlike physician-patient relationships—are often confrontational, with few common goals, and therefore present to workers a constant danger through undisclosed risk. This danger and the relative powerlessness of employees in the employer-employee relationship may not be sufficient to justify employer disclosure obligations in all industries, but placing relevant information in the workers' hands is morally appropriate in all hazardous conditions. By what criteria, then, shall such disclosure obligations be determined?

One plausible argument is the following: Because large employers, unions, and government agencies must deal with multiple employees and complicated causal conditions, no standard should be more demanding than the so-called objective reasonable person standard. This standard is what a fair and informed member of the relevant community believes is needed. Under this standard, no employer, union, or other party should be held responsible for disclosing information beyond that needed to make an informed choice about the adequacy of safety precautions, industrial hygiene, long-term hazards, and the like, as determined by what the reasonable person in the community would judge to be the worker's need for information material to a decision about employment or working conditions.

However, this standard of disclosure is not adequate for all individual disclosures. In the case of serious hazards—such as those involved in short-term, but concentrated doses of radiation—a *subjective* standard tied to individual persons may be more appropriate. In cases where disclosures to individual workers may be expected to have significant subjective impact that varies with each individual, the reasonable person standard should perhaps be supplemented by a standard that addresses each worker's personal informational needs. A viable alternative might also include, as a component of all general disclosures under the reasonable person standard, the statement, "If you are concerned about the possible effect of hazards on your individual health, and you seek clarification or personal information, make an appointment to consult a company physician." Perhaps the best solution to the problem of a general standard is a compromise between a reasonable-person and a subjective standard: Whatever a reasonable person would judge material to the decision-making process should be disclosed, and in addition any remaining information that is material to an individual worker should be provided through a process of asking whether he or she has any additional or special concerns.

Any such standard should avoid a narrow focus on the employer's obligation to disclose information and should seek to ensure the quality of a worker's understanding and consent. From this perspective, the problems center on communication rather than the abstract issues about proper legal standards of disclosure. The key to effective communication is to invite participation by workers in a dialogue. Asking questions, eliciting concerns, and establishing a climate that encourages questions may be more meaningful than the full corpus of disclosed information. Different levels of education, linguistic ability, and sophistication about the issues needs to be accommodated.

We need also to consider which groups of workers will be included. Former workers, for example, often have as much of a pressing need for the information as do presently employed workers. The federal government has the names of approximately 250,000 former workers whose risk of cancer, heart disease, and lung disease has been increased by exposure to asbestos, polyvinyl chloride, benzene, arsenic, betanaphthyalamine, and dozens of other chemicals. Employers have the names of several million such workers. The U.S. Congress has passed a bill to notify those workers at greatest risk, so that checkups and diagnosis of disease can be made before a disease's advanced stage.[10] But at this writing, neither industry nor the government has developed a systematic program. They claim that the expense of notification would be prohibitive, that many workers would be unduly alarmed, and that existing screening and surveillance programs should prove adequate in monitoring and treating disease. Critics rightly charge, however, that existing programs are inadequate and that workers have a right to know in order to investigate potential problems at their initiative.[11]

IV

Despite the apparent consensus on the desirability of having some form of right to know in the workplace, hurdles exist that will make it difficult to implement this right. Complicated questions arise about the kinds of information to be disclosed, by whom, to whom, and under what conditions. Trade secrets have also been a long-standing thorn in the side of progress,[12] because companies resist disclosing information about an ingredient or process claimed as a trade secret. Also, economic or other constraints sometimes inhibit workers from exercising their full range of workplace options. For example, in industries in which ten people apply for every available position, bargaining for increased protection is an unlikely event. However, we must set these problems aside in order to consider perhaps the most perplexing difficulty about the right to know in the workplace: the right to refuse hazardous work assignments and to have effective mechanisms for workers to reduce the risks they face.

In a limited range of cases, informed workers can reject employment because they regard accompanying health and safety conditions as unacceptable. This decision is more likely to occur in a job market in which workers have alternative employment opportunities or in which a worker has been offered a new assignment with the option of remaining in his or her current position. More commonly, however, workers are not in a position to act on information about health hazards by seeking alternative employment elsewhere. For the information to be useful, workers must be able to effect reforms.

The U.S. Occupational Safety and Health Act of 1970 (OSH Act)[13] confers a series of

rights on employees that appear to give increased significance to the corporate obligation to disclose hazards in the workplace. Specifically, the OSH Act grants workers the right to request an OSHA inspection if they believe an OSHA standard has been violated or an imminent hazard exists. Under the Act, employees also have the right to "walk-around," i.e., to participate in OSHA inspections of the worksite and to consult freely with the inspection officer. Most importantly, the OSH Act expressly protects employees who request an inspection or otherwise exercise their rights under the OSH Act from discharge or any discriminatory treatment in retaliation for legitimate safety and health complaints.[14]

While these worker rights under the OSH Act are essential, they are not sufficiently strong to assure that all workers have effective mechanisms for initiating inspections of suspected health hazards. The OSH Act does not cover small businesses (those employing fewer than ten workers) or federal, state, and municipal employees. Questions remain about OSHA's ability to enforce these provisions of the OSH Act. But if workers are to effectively use disclosed information on health hazards, they must have access to a workable and efficient regulatory system.

Workers must also have an adequately protected right to refuse unsafe work and the right to refuse an employer's request that they sign OSHA-mandated forms acknowledging that they have been trained about hazardous chemicals. One cannot easily determine the current extent to which these rights are legally protected.[15] Although the OSH Act does not grant a general right to refuse unsafe work, provisions to this effect exist in some state occupational safety laws. In addition, former Secretary of Labor Ray Marshall issued a regulation that interprets the OSH Act as including a limited right to refuse unsafe work, a right upheld by the U.S. Supreme

Court in 1980.[16] The Labor-Management Relations Act (LMRA) also provides a limited right of refusal, which is also included implicitly in the National Labor Relation Act (NLRA).[17]

These statutory protections have not established uniform conditions granting to workers a right to refuse. For example, OSHA regulations allow workers to walk off the job if there is a "real danger of death or serious injury," while the LMRA permits refusals only under "abnormally dangerous conditions."[18] Under the LMRA, the nature of the occupation determines the extent of danger justifying refusal, while under OSHA the character of the threat, or so-called imminent danger, determines worker action. By contrast, under the NLRA a walk-out by two or more workers may be justified for even minimal safety problems, so long as the action can be construed as a "concerted activity" for mutual aid and protection and a no-strike clause does not exist in any collective bargaining agreements. While the NLRA appears to provide the broadest protection to workers, employees refusing to work under the NLRA can lose the right to be reinstated in their positions if permanent replacements can be hired.

The relative merits of the different statutes are further confused by questions of overlapping authority, called "preemption." It is not always clear (1) whether a worker is eligible to claim protection under a given law, (2) which law affords a worker maximum protections or remedies in a particular circumstance, and (3) whether or under what conditions a worker can seek relief under another law or through the courts, once a claim under a given law has been rejected or invalidated.

The current legal situation concerning the right to refuse hazardous work also fails to resolve other questions. Consider, for example, whether a meaningful right to refuse hazardous work entails an obligation to continue to pay nonworking employees, or to award the employees back-pay if the issue is resolved in their favor. On the one hand, workers without union strike benefits or other income protections would be unable to exercise their right to refuse unsafe work due to economic pressures. On the other hand, to permit such workers to draw a paycheck is to legitimize strike with pay, a practice traditionally considered unacceptable by management and by Congress. The situation does not resolve whether the right to refuse unsafe work should be restricted to cases of obvious, imminent, and serious risks to health or life (the current OSHA and LMRA position) or should be expanded to include lesser risks and uncertain risks—for example, exposure to suspected toxic or carcinogenic substances that although not immediate threats, may prove more dangerous over time. In order for "the right to know" to lead to meaningful worker action, workers must be able to remove themselves from exposure to suspected hazards, as well as obvious or known hazards.

The question of the proper standard for determining whether a safety walkout is justified is connected to this issue. At least three different standards have been applied in the past: a good-faith subjective standard, which requires only that the worker honestly believe that a health hazard exists; a reasonable person standard, which requires that the belief be reasonable under the circumstances as well as sincerely held; and an objective standard, which requires evidence—commonly established by expert witnesses—that the threat exists. Although the possibility of worker abuse of the right to refuse has been a major factor in a current trend to reject the good faith standard, recent commentary has argued that this trend raises serious equity issues in the proper balancing of this concern with the needs of workers confronted with basic self-preservation issues.[19]

No less important is whether the right to refuse hazardous work should be protected only until a formal review of the situation is initiated (at which time the worker must return to the job) or whether the walk-out should be permitted until the alleged hazard is at least temporarily removed. So long as the hazards covered under a right to refuse are restricted to risks that are obvious in the environment and that are easily established as health hazards, this issue is relatively easy to resolve. However, if the nature of the risk is less apparent, any meaningful right to refuse must call attention to an alleged hazard and compel regulatory action. If this chain of events is set in motion, then requirements that workers continue to be exposed while OSHA or the NLRB conduct investigations may prove unacceptable to workers, especially if they consider the magnitude of potential harm to be significant. However, compelling employers to remove suspected hazards during the evaluation period may also result in intolerable economic burdens. We need, then, to delineate the conditions under which workers may be compelled to return to work during an alleged hazard investigation and the conditions that can compel employers to remove alleged hazards.

V

Legal rights will prove useless if workers remain ignorant of their options. Despite recent requirements that employers initiate training programs, it remains doubtful that many workers, particularly nonunion workers and those in small businesses, are aware that they have a legally protected right to refuse hazardous work, let alone that at least three statutory provisions protect that right. Even if workers were to learn of such a right, they could probably not weave their way through the maze of legal options unaided. OSHA officials have acknowledged that both employers and workers are puzzled about proper strategies of education and compliance.[20] But

if the workplace is to have a meaningful right to know, workers must have an adequate program to educate them not only about hazards but also about their rights and how to exercise them.

Many corporations hopefully will follow the model guidelines and programs established by Monsanto and Hercules on the right to know and will confirm and explain the right to (at least temporarily) refuse work under unduly hazardous conditions. Such programs of information and training in hazards are as important for managers as for workers. In several recent court cases corporate executives have been tried—and in some cases convicted—for murder and manslaughter, because they negligently caused worker deaths by failing to warn of hazards. In Los Angeles and Chicago occupational deaths are investigated as possible homicides.[21] An improved system of corporate disclosures of risk and the rights of workers will therefore benefit everyone.

NOTES

1. NIOSH, et al., "The Right to Know: Practical Problems and Policy Issues Arising from Exposures to Hazardous Chemical and Physical Agents in the Workplace" (Washington, D.C.: July 1977), pp. 1 and 5.

2. Occupational Safety and Health Administration, "Access to Employee Exposure and Medical Records—Final Rules," *Federal Register*, May 23, 1980, pp. 35212–77.

3. OSHA, Regulations 29 CFR 1910.1200 et seq; printed in 48 FR 53, 278 (1983) and (1986). See also *United Steelworkers v. Auchter*, No 83-3554 et al.; 763 F.2d 728 (3rd Cir., 1985).

4. See Deborah Shalowitz, "OSHA to Ease State Right-to-Know Burdens," *Business Insurance* 22 (Jan. 11, 1988), p. 17. OSHA wrote these workplace requirements to override conflicting state right-to-know laws, unless the states can show a compelling need for additional legislation.

5. 29 CFR 1910.1200; 48 FR 53, 280 (1983); and see Linda D. McGill, "OSHA's Hazard Communication Standards: Guidelines for Com-

pliance," *Employment Relations Today* 16 (Autumn 1989): 181–87.

6. Laurie Hays, "New Rules on Workplace Hazards Prompt Intensified on the Job Training Programs," *Wall Street Journal,* July 8, 1986, p. 31; Cathy Trost, "Plans to Alert Workers," *Wall Street Journal,* March 28, 1986, p. 15.

7. "Hazard Communication," *Federal Register,* August 24, 1987; and see William J. Rothwell, "Complying with OSHA," *Training & Development Journal* 43 (May 1989): 53–54; McGill, "OSHA's Hazard Communication Standards," p. 184.

8. See 48 CFR 53, 282 (1983); Office of Technology Assessment, *Preventing Illness and Injury in the Workplace* (Washington, D.C.: U.S. Government Printing Office, 1985).

9. Current Reports, *O.S.H. Reporter* (March 15, 1989), p. 1747, as quoted in McGill, "OSHA's Hazard Communication Standard," p. 181.

10. High Risk Occupational Disease Notification and Prevention Act, HR 1309.

11. See Cathy Trost, "Plans to Alert Workers to Health Risks Stir Fears of Lawsuits and High Costs," *Wall Street Journal,* March 28, 1986, p. 15; Peter Perl, "Workers Unwarned," *Washington Post,* January 14, 1985, pp. A1, A6.

12. Under current standards, an employer is not required to disclose the name or any information about a hazardous chemical that would require disclosure of a bona fide trade secret; but in a medical emergency the company must disclose this information to physicians or nurses as long as confidentiality is assured.

13. 29 U.S.C. §651–658 (1970).

14. OSH Act 29 U.S.C. 661(c). If the health or safety complaint is not determined to be legitimate, there are no worker protections.

15. The right to refuse an employer's request to sign a training acknowledgment form is upheld in *Beam Distilling Co. v. Distillery and Allied Workers' International,* 90 Lab. Arb. 740 (1988).

16. *Whirlpool v. Marshall* 445 US 1 (1980).

17. See the detailed exposition in Susan Preston, "A Right Under OSHA to Refuse Unsafe Work or a Hobson's Choice of Safety or Job?" *University of Baltimore Law Review* 8 (Spring 1979), pp. 519–550.

18. 29 U.S.C. §143 (1976), and 29 CFR §1977.12 (1979).

19. James C. Robinson, "Labor Union Involvement in Occupational Safety and Health, 1957–1987," *Journal of Health Politics, Policy, and Law* 13 (Fall 1988), p. 463; Nancy K. Frank, "A Question of Equity: Workers' Right to Refuse Under OSHA Compared to the Criminal Necessity Defense," *Labor Law Journal* 31 (October 1980), pp. 617–626.

20. McGill, "OSHA's Hazard Communication Standard," p. 181.

21. See *Illinois v. Chicago Magnet Wire Corporation,* No. 86–114, *Amicus Curiae* for The American Federation of Labor and Congress of Industrial Organizations; R. Henry Moore, "OSHA: What's Ahead for the 1990s," *Personnel* 67 (June 1990), p. 69; and Jonathan Tasini, "The Clamor to Make Punishment Fit the Corporate Crime," *Business Week,* February 10, 1986, p. 73.

Business Ethics and the International Trade in Hazardous Wastes

Jang B. Singh
and V. C. Lakhan

The export of hazardous wastes by the more developed countries to the lesser developed nations is escalating beyond control. The ethical implications and environmental consequences of this trade in hazardous wastes highlight the need for international controls

Journal of Business Ethics 8 (1989):889–99. © 1989 Kluwer Academic Publishers. Reprinted by permission of Kluwer Academic Publishers.

and regulations in the conduct of business by corporations in the more developed countries. In the late 1970s, the Love Canal environmental tragedy awakened the world to the effects of ill conceived and irresponsible disposal of hazardous by-products of industries. Today, the media focuses its attention on the alleged illegal dumping of hazardous wastes in the lesser developed countries (see Barthos, 1988, and Harden, 1988). The most recent dramatic case so far is that of Koko, Nigeria where more than eight thousand drums of hazardous wastes were dumped, some of which contained polychlorinated biphenyl (PCB), a highly carcinogenic compound and one of the world's most toxic wastes (Tifft, 1988). . . .

THE INTERNATIONAL TRADE IN HAZARDOUS WASTES AND ATTENDANT PROBLEMS

Miller (1988) defined hazardous waste as any material that may pose a substantial threat or potential hazard to human health or the environment when managed improperly. These wastes may be in solid, liquid or gaseous form and include a variety of toxic, ignitable, corrosive, or dangerously reactive substances. Examples include acids, cyanides, pesticides, solvents, compounds of lead, mercury, arsenic, cadmium, and zinc, PCB's and dioxins, fly ash from power plants, infectious waste from hospitals, and research laboratories, obsolete explosives, herbicides, nerve gas, radioactive materials, sewage sludge, and other materials which contain toxic and carcinogenic organic compounds.

Since World War II, the amount of toxic byproducts created by the manufacturers of pharmaceuticals, petroleum, nuclear devices, pesticides, chemicals, and other allied products has increased almost exponentially. From an annual production of less than 10 million metric tonnes in the 1940's, the world now produces more than 320 million metric tonnes of extremely hazardous wastes per year. The United States is by far the biggest producer, with "over 275 million metric tonnes of hazardous waste produced each year" (Goldfarb, 1987). The total is well over one tonne per person. But the United States is not alone. European countries also produce millions of tonnes of hazardous wastes each year (Chiras, 1988). Recent figures reported by Tifft (1988) indicate that the twelve countries of the European Community produce about 35 million tonnes of hazardous wastes annually. . . .

The United States and certain European countries are now turning to areas in Africa, Latin America, and the Caribbean to dump their wastes. Historically, the trade in wastes has been conducted among the industrialized nations. A major route involving industrialized nations is that between Canada and the United States. The movement of wastes from the United States into Canada is governed by the Canada-U.S.A. Agreement on the Transboundary Movement of Hazardous Waste which came into effect on November 8, 1986 (Environment Canada). In 1988, the United States exported 145,000 tonnes. Of this amount, only one third was recyclable, leaving approximately 96,667 tonnes of hazardous organic and inorganic wastes such as petroleum by-products, pesticides, heavy metals, and organic solvents and residues for disposal in the Canadian environment. Of interest is the fact that Canada restricts the import of nuclear waste, but not toxic, flammable, corrosive, reactive, and medical wastes from the United States.

Most of the United States hazardous wastes are shipped from the New England states, New York and Michigan and enter Ontario and Quebec which in 1988 received approximately 81,899 and 62,200 tonnes respectively. The neutralization and disposal of the imported hazardous wastes are done by several Canadian companies, with the two largest being Tricil and Stablex Canada Inc. Tricil with several locations in Ontario, imports wastes from more than 85 known American companies which it incinerates and treats in lagoons and landfill sites. Stablex Canada imports a wide variety of hazardous wastes from more than 300 U.S. companies. It uses various disposal methods, including landfills and cement kilns which burn not only the components needed for cement but also hazardous waste products. With the established Canada-U.S. Agreement on the Transboundary Movement of Hazardous Waste companies like Tricil and Stablex may increase their importation of hazardous wastes generated in the United States. As it stands, the United States Environmental Protection Agency estimates that over 75% of the wastes exported from the U.S. is disposed of in Canada (Vallette, 1989). This estimate will likely have to be raised in the near future. Canada-United States trade in hazardous wastes is not a one-way route. It is believed that all of the hazardous wastes imported by the United States (estimated at 65,000 tonnes in 1988) is generated in Canada (Ibid).

An especially controversial trend in the international trade in hazardous wastes is the development of routes between industrialized and "lesser developed countries." For example, according to the United States Environmental Protection Agency there have been more proposals to ship hazardous wastes from the United States to Africa during 1988, than in the previous four years (Klatte et al., 1988).

African nations have recently joined together to try to completely ban the dumping of toxic wastes on their continent. They have referred to the practice as "toxic terrorism" performed by Western "merchants of death." Some African government officials are so disturbed by the newly exposed practices that they have threatened to execute guilty individuals by firing squad. Recently, Lagos offi-

cials seized an Italian and a Danish ship along with fifteen people who were associated with transporting toxic wastes in the swampy Niger River delta into Nigeria. This occurred shortly after the discovery of 3,800 tonnes of hazardous toxic wastes, which had originated in Italy. Local residents immediately became ill from inhaling the fumes from the leaking drums and containers which were filled with the highly carcinogenic compound PCB, and also radioactive material.

Companies in the United States have been responsible for sending large quantities of hazardous wastes to Mexico. Although Mexico only accepts hazardous wastes for recycling, which is referred to as "sham re-cycling," there are numerous reports of illegal dumping incidents. . . .

Given the fact that hazardous wastes are:

1. Toxic
2. Highly reactive when exposed to air, water, or other substances that they can cause explosions and generate toxic fumes
3. Ignitable that they can undergo spontaneous combustion at relatively low temperatures
4. Highly corrosive that they can eat away materials and living tissues
5. Infectious
6. Radioactive

Miller (1988) has, therefore, emphasized correctly that the proper transportation, disposal, deactivation, or storage of hazardous wastes is a grave environmental problem which is second only to nuclear war.

The practice of transporting and dumping hazardous wastes in lesser developed nations, where knowledge of environmental issues is limited is causing, and will pose, major problems to both human health and the environment. Several comprehensive studies have outlined the detrimental impacts which hazardous waste can have on humans and natural ecosystems. Epstein et al., (1982) have provided a thorough and dramatic coverage of the impacts of hazardous wastes, while Regenstein (1982), in his book *America the Poisoned*, gives a good overview of the implications of hazardous wastes. Essentially, hazardous wastes not only contaminate ground water, destroy habitats, cause human disease, contaminate the soil; but also enter the food chain at all levels, and eventually damage genetic material of all living things. . . .

The hazardous wastes can also directly threaten human health through seeping into the ground and causing the direct pollution of aquifers, which supply "pure" drinking water. Today, in the United States, a long list of health related problems are caused by hazardous chemicals from "leaking underground storage tanks" (LUST). Investigations now show that human exposure to hazardous wastes from dumpsites, water bodies, and processing and storage areas can cause the disposed synthetic compounds to interact with particular enzymes or other chemicals in the body, and result in altered functions. Altered functions have been shown to include mutagenic (mutation-causing), carcinogenic (cancer-causing), and teratogenic (birth-defect causing) effects. In addition, they may cause serious liver and kidney dysfunction, sterility and numerous lesser physiological and neurological problems (see Nebel, 1987). . . .

THE ETHICAL IMPLICATIONS

The international trade in hazardous wastes raises a number of ethical issues. The rest of this paper examines some of these.

The Right to a Livable Environment

The desire for a clean, safe and ecologically balanced environment is an often expressed sentiment. This is especially so in industrial-ized countries where an awareness of environmental issues is relatively high—a fact that is gaining recognition in political campaigns. However, expression of the desire for a clean, safe environment is not the same as stating that a clean, safe environment is the right of every human being. But the right of an individual to a livable environment is easily established at the theoretical level. Blackstone (1983) examines the right to a livable environment from two angles—as a human right and as a legal right. The right to a clean, safe environment is seen as a human right since the absence of such a condition would prevent one from fulfilling one's human capacities.

> Each person has this right qua being human and because a livable environment is essential for one to fulfill his human capacities. And given the danger to our environment today and hence the danger to the very possibility of human existence, access to a livable environment must be conceived as a right which imposes upon everyone a correlative moral obligation to respect. (Blackstone, 1983, p. 413)

Guerrette (1986) illustrates this argument by reference to the Constitution of the United States. He proposes that people cannot live in a chemically toxic area, they cannot experience freedom in an industrially polluted environment and they cannot be happy worrying about the quality of air they breathe or the carcinogenic effects of the water they drink (Guerrette, 1986, p. 409). Some even argue (e.g., Feinberg, 1983) that the right to a livable environment extends to future generations and that it is the duty of the present generation to pass on a clean, safe environment to them.

Establishing the right to a livable environment as a human right is not the same as establishing it as a legal right. This requires the passing of appropriate legislation and the provision of a legal framework that may be used to seek a remedy if necessary. Such provisions are more prevalent in the industrialized countries and this is one of the push factors in the export of hazardous wastes to the lesser developed countries. This points to the need for a provision in international law of the right to a decent environment which with accompanying policies to save and preserve our environmental resources would be an even more effective tool than such a framework at the national level (Blackstone, 1983, p. 414). As ecologists suggest, serious harm done to one element in an ecosystem will invariably lead to the damage or even destruction of other elements in that and other ecosystems (Law Reform Commission of Canada, 1987, p. 262) and ecosystems transcend national boundaries. . . .

A more direct harmful effect of the international trade in hazardous wastes is the damage to the health of workers involved in the transportation and disposal of these toxic substances. For example, prolonged exposure to wastes originating in Italy and transported by a ship called Zanoobia is suspected of causing the death of a crew person and the hospitalization of nine others (Klatte et al., 1983, p. 12). Whereas worker rights in workplace health and safety are gaining wider recognition in many industrialized nations this is not so in the "less developed" countries which are increasingly becoming the recipients of hazardous wastes. Widespread violation of workers' rights to a clean, safe work environment should therefore be expected to be a feature of the international trade in hazardous wastes.

Racist Implications

The recent trend of sending more shipments of hazardous wastes to Third World countries has led to charges of racism. *West Africa*, a weekly magazine, referred to the dumping of

toxic wastes as the latest in a series of historical traumas for Africa. . . . Charges of racism in the disposal of wastes have been made before at the national level in the United States. A study of waste disposal sites found that race was the most significant among variables tested in association with the location of commercial hazardous wastes facilities. The findings of this national study which were found to be statistically significant at the 0.0001 level showed that communities with the greatest number of commercial hazardous wastes facilities had the highest concentration of racial minorities (Lee, 1987, pp. 45–46). The study found that although socio-economic status appeared to play a role in the location of commercial hazardous wastes facilities, race was a more significant factor.

In the United States, one of the arguments often advanced for locating commercial waste facilities in lower income areas is that these facilities create jobs. This is also one of the arguments being advanced for sending wastes to poor lesser developed countries. . . . Nearly all the countries receiving hazardous wastes have predominantly coloured populations. This is the reason why charges of racism are being made against exporters of wastes. However, it must be noted that even though the trend of sending wastes to other countries . . . has recently gained strength, the bulk of the international trade in hazardous wastes is still within industrialized Europe and North America which have predominantly noncoloured populations.

For example, the United States Environmental Protection Agency estimates that as much as 75% of the wastes exported from the United States is disposed of in Canada (Klatte et al., 1988, p. 9). Another striking example is that a dump outside Schonberg, East Germany, is the home of well over 500,000 tonnes of waste a year from Western Europe (Rubbish Between Germans, March 1, 1986, p. 46). Thus, while charges of racism in the export of hazardous wastes are being made by some Third World leaders, figures on the international trade in such substances do not substantiate these claims.

Corporate Responsibility

The international trade in hazardous wastes basically involves three types of corporations—the generators of wastes, the exporters of wastes and the importers of wastes. These entities, if they are to act in a responsible manner, should be accountable to the public for their behaviour.

> Having a corporate conscience means that a company takes responsibility for its actions, just as any conscientious individual would be expected to do. In corporate terms, this means that a company is accountable to the public for its behaviour not only in the complex organizational environment but in the natural physical environment as well. A company is thus responsible for its product and for its effects on the public. (Guerrette, 1986, p. 410)

Using Guerrette's definition of corporate responsibility, it seems clear that a corporation involved in the international trade in hazardous wastes is not likely to be a responsible firm. The importer of hazardous wastes is clearly engaged in activities that will damage the environment while the exporter being aware that this is a possibility, nevertheless, sends these wastes to the importer. However, it is the generator of hazardous wastes that is the most culpable in this matter. If the wastes are not produced then obviously their disposal would not be necessary. Therefore, in view of the fact that virtually no safe method of disposing hazardous wastes exists, a case of corporate irresponsibility could easily be formulated against any corporation involved in the international trade in these substances.

Government Responsibility

Why do countries export wastes? A major reason is that many of them are finding it difficult to build disposal facilities in their own countries because of the NIMBY syndrome mentioned earlier. Other reasons are that better technologies may be available in another country, facilities of a neighboring country may be closer to a generator of waste than a site on national territory and economies of scale may also be a factor. However, to these reasons must be added the fact that corporations may be motivated to dispose of waste in another country where less stringent regulations apply (Transfrontier Movements, March 1984, p. 40). It is the responsibility of governments to establish regulations governing the disposal of wastes. In some countries these regulations are stringent while in others they are lax or non-existent. Moreover, some countries have regulations governing disposal of wastes within national boundaries as well as regulations relating to the export of hazardous wastes. For example, companies in the United States that intend to export hazardous wastes are requested to submit notices to the Environmental Protection Agency (EPA) and to demonstrate that they have the permission of the receiving country (Porterfield and Weir, 1987, p. 341). However, the effectiveness of these controls is in question. The General Accounting Office has found that "the E.P.A. does not know whether it is controlling 90 percent of the existing waste or 10 percent. Likewise it does not know if it is controlling the wastes that are most hazardous" (Ibid.). Moreover, there is evidence indicating that other U.S. government agencies are encouraging the export of hazardous wastes. The Navy, the Army, the Defense Department, the Agriculture Department and the Treasury Department are some government agencies that have provided hazardous wastes to known exporters.

Also, major U.S. cities, sometimes with the approval of the State Department, have been suppliers to the international trade in hazardous wastes (Porterfield and Weir, 1987, p. 342).

While more stringent regulations, higher disposal costs, and heightened environmental awareness are pushing many companies in industrial countries to export hazardous wastes, it must be, nevertheless, realized that the governments of lesser developed countries are allowing such imports into their countries because of the need for foreign exchange. These governments are willing to damage the environment in return for hard currency or the creation of jobs. One must assume that on the basis of cost-benefit analysis these governments foresee more benefits than harm resulting from the importation of hazardous wastes. However, these benefits go mainly to a few waste brokers while the health of large numbers of people is put at risk. In some cases decisions to import wastes are made by governments which hold power by force and fraud. For example, Haiti which has imported wastes is ruled by a military dictatorship and Guyana which is actively considering the importation of industrial oil wastes and paint sludge is ruled by a minority party which has rigged all elections held in that country since 1964. The ethical dilemma posed by this situation is that of whether or not an unrepresentative government of a country could be trusted to make decisions affecting the life and health of its citizens. In fact, a larger question is whether or not any government has the right to permit business activity that poses a high risk to human life and health.

Generally, governments of waste generating countries, in reaction to political pressure, have imposed stringent regulations on domestic disposal and some restrictions on the export of hazardous wastes; However, as the examples above illustrate, the latter restrictions are not strictly enforced, hence, indicating a duplicitous stance on the part of the generating countries. The governments of importing countries, in allowing into their countries, wastes that will disrupt ecosystems and damage human health, deny their citizens the right to a livable environment.

CONCLUSION

Hazardous wastes are, in the main, by-products of industrial processes that have contributed significantly to the economic development of many countries. Economic development, in turn, has led to lifestyles which also generate hazardous wastes. To export these wastes to countries which do not benefit from waste generating industrial processes or whose citizens do not have lifestyles that generate such wastes is unethical. It is especially unjust to send hazardous wastes to lesser developed countries which lack the technology to minimize the deleterious effects of these substances. Nevertheless, these countries are increasingly becoming recipients of such cargoes. The need for stringent international regulation to govern the trade in hazardous wastes is now stronger than ever before. However, this alone will not significantly curb the international trade in hazardous wastes. International regulation must be coupled with a revolutionary reorganization of waste-generating processes and change in consumption patterns. Until this is achieved the international trade in hazardous wastes will continue and with it a plethora of unethical activities.

BIBLIOGRAPHY

Barthos, G.: 1988, "Third World Outraged at Receiving Toxic Trash," *Toronto Star*, June 26, pp. 1, 4.
Blackstone, W. T.: 1983, "Ethics and Ecology," in Beauchamp, T. L. and Bowie, N. E. (Eds), *Ethi-*

cal *Theory and Business* 2nd. edition (Prentice Hall, Englewood Cliffs, New Jersey), pp. 411–424.

Brooke, J.: 1988, "Africa Fights Tide of Western Wastes," *Globe and Mail,* July 18, p. A10.

Chiras, D. D.: 1988, *Environmental Science* (Benjamin Commings Publishing Co. Inc., Denver).

Environment Canada: 1986, *Canada-U.S.A. Agreement on the Transboundary Movement of Hazardous Waste* (Environment Canada, Ottawa).

Epstein, S. S., Brown, L. O., and Pope, C.: 1982, *Hazardous Waste in America* (Sierra Club Books, San Francisco).

Feinberg, J.: 1983, "The Rights of Animals and Unborn Generation," in Beauchamp, T. L., and Bowie, N. E., (Eds), *Ethical Theory and Business,* 2nd. edition. (Prentice Hall, Englewood Cliffs, New Jersey) pp. 428–436.

Goldfarb, T. D.: 1987, *Taking Sides: Clashing Views on Controversial Environmental Issues.* (Dushkin Publishing Co., Inc., CT).

Guerrette, R. H.: 1986, "Environmental Integrity and Corporate Responsibility," *Journal of Business Ethics* Vol. 5. pp. 409–415.

Harden, B.: 1988, "Africa Refuses to Become Waste Dump for the West," *Windsor Star,* July 9, p. A–6.

Klatte, E., Palacio, F., Rapaport, D., and Vallette, J.: 1988. *International Trade in Toxic Wastes: Policy and Data Analysis* (Greenpeace International, Washington, D.C.).

Law Reform Commission of Canada: 1987, "Crimes Against the Environment" in Poff, D. and Waluchow, W., *Business Ethics in Canada* (Prentice Hall, Canada Inc., Scarborough), pp. 261–264.

Lee, C.: Summer 1987, "The Racist Disposal of Toxic Wastes," *Business and Society Review,* Vol. 62, pp. 43–46.

Miller, T.: 1988, *Living in the Environment* (Wadsworth Publishing Co., California).

Montreal Gazette: April 27, 1987, "Mexico Sends Back U.S. Barge Filled With Tonnes of Garbage," p. F9.

Morrison, A.: 1988, "Dead Flowers to U.S. Firms that Plan to Send Waste to Guyana," *Catholic Standard,* Sunday, May 8.

Nobel, B. J.: 1987, *Environmental Science* (Prentice Hall, New Jersey).

OECD Observer: March 1984, "Transfrontier Movements of Hazardous Wastes: Getting to Grips with the Problem," pp. 39–41.

Porterfield, A. and Weir, D.: 1987, "The Export of U.S. Toxic Wastes," *The Nation,* Vol. 245, Iss. 10 (Oct. 3), pp. 341–344.

Regenstein, L.: 1982, *America the Poisoned* (Acropolis Books, Washington, D.C.).

The Economist: March 1, 1986, "Rubbish Between Germans," p. 46.

Tifft, S.: 1988, "Who Gets the Garbage," *Time* July 4, pp. 42–43.

Vallette, J.: 1989, *The International Trade in Wastes: A Greenpeace Inventory,* 4th edition. (Greenpeace International, Luxembourg).

Business and Environmental Ethics

W. Michael Hoffman

. . . Concern over the environment is not new. Warnings came out of the 1960s in the form of burning rivers, dying lakes, and oil-fouled oceans. Radioactivity was found in our food, DDT in mother's milk, lead and mercury in our water. Every breath of air in the North American hemisphere was reported as contaminated. Some said these were truly warnings from Planet Earth of eco-catastrophe, unless we could find limits to our growth and changes in our lifestyle.

Over the past few years Planet Earth began to speak to us even more loudly than before, and we began to listen more than before. The message was ominous, somewhat akin to God warning Noah. It spoke through droughts, heat

From W. Michael Hoffman, "Business and Environmental Ethics," *Business Ethics Quarterly* 1 (1991):169–84. Reprinted by permission.

waves, and forest fires, raising fears of global warming due to the buildup of carbon dioxide and other gases in the atmosphere. It warned us by raw sewage and medical wastes washing up on our beaches, and by devastating oil spills—one despoiling Prince William Sound and its wildlife to such an extent that it made us weep. It spoke to us through increased skin cancers and discoveries of holes in the ozone layer caused by our use of chlorofluorocarbons. It drove its message home through the rapid and dangerous cutting and burning of our primitive forests at the rate of one football field a second, leaving us even more vulnerable to greenhouse gases like carbon dioxide and eliminating scores of irreplaceable species daily. It rained down on us in the form of acid, defoliating our forests and poisoning our lakes and streams. Its warnings were found on barges roaming the seas for places to dump tons of toxic incinerator ash. And its message exploded in our faces at Chernobyl and Bhopal, reminding us of past warnings at Three Mile Island and Love Canal. . . .

I

In a 1989 keynote address before the "Business, Ethics and the Environment" conference at the Center for Business Ethics, Norman Bowie offered some answers to the first two questions.

> Business does not have an obligation to protect the environment over and above what is required by law; however, it does have a moral obligation to avoid intervening in the political arena in order to defeat or weaken environmental legislation.[1]

I disagree with Bowie on both counts.

Bowie's first point is very Friedmanesque.[2] The social responsibility of business is to produce goods and services and to make profit

for its shareholders, while playing within the rules of the market game. These rules, including those to protect the environment, are set by the government and the courts. To do more than is required by these rules is, according to this position, unfair to business. In order to perform its proper function, every business must respond to the market and operate in the same arena as its competitors. As Bowie puts this:

> An injunction to assist in solving societal problems [including depletion of natural resources and pollution] makes impossible demands on a corporation because, at the practical level, it ignores the impact that such activities have on profit.[3]

If, as Bowie claims, consumers are not willing to respond to the cost and use of environmentally friendly products and actions, then it is not the responsibility of business to respond or correct such market failure.

Bowie's second point is a radical departure from this classical position in contending that business should not lobby against the government's process to set environmental regulations. To quote Bowie:

> Far too many corporations try to have their cake and eat it too. They argue that it is the job of government to correct for market failure and then they use their influence and money to defeat or water down regulations designed to conserve and protect the environment.[4]

Bowie only recommends this abstinence of corporate lobbying in the case of environmental regulations. He is particularly concerned that politicians, ever mindful of their reelection status, are already reluctant to pass environmental legislation which has huge immediate costs and in most cases very long-term benefits. This makes the obligations of business to refrain from opposing such legislation a justified special case.

I can understand why Bowie argues these points. He seems to be responding to two extreme approaches, both of which are inappropriate. Let me illustrate these extremes by the following two stories.

At the Center's First National Conference on Business Ethics, Harvard Business School Professor George Cabot Lodge told of a friend who owned a paper company on the banks of a New England stream. On the first Earth Day in 1970, his friend was converted to the cause of environmental protection. He became determined to stop his company's pollution of the stream, and marched off to put his new-found religion into action. Later, Lodge learned his friend went broke, so he went to investigate. Radiating a kind of ethical purity, the friend told Lodge that he spent millions to stop the pollution and thus could no longer compete with other firms that did not follow his example. So the company went under, 500 people lost their jobs, and the stream remained polluted.

When Lodge asked why his friend hadn't sought help from the state or federal government for stricter standards for everyone, the man replied that was not the American way, that government should not interfere with business activity, and that private enterprise could do the job alone. In fact, he felt it was the social responsibility of business to solve environmental problems, so he was proud that he had set an example for others to follow.

The second story portrays another extreme. A few years ago "Sixty Minutes" interviewed a manager of a chemical company that was discharging effluent into a river in upstate New York. At the time, the dumping was legal, though a bill to prevent it was pending in Congress. The manager remarked that he hoped the bill would pass, and that he certainly would support it as a responsible citizen. However, he also said he approved of his company's efforts to defeat the bill and of the firm's policy of dumping wastes in the meantime. After all, isn't the proper role of business to make as much profit as possible within the bounds of law? Making the laws—setting the rules of the game—is the role of government, not business. While wearing his business hat the manager had a job to do, even if it meant doing something that he strongly opposed as a private citizen.

Both stories reveal incorrect answers to the questions posed earlier, the proof of which is found in the fact that neither the New England stream nor the New York river was made any cleaner. Bowie's points are intended to block these two extremes. But to avoid these extremes, as Bowie does, misses the real managerial and ethical failure of the stories. Although the paper company owner and the chemical company manager had radically different views of the ethical responsibilities of business, both saw business and government performing separate roles, and neither felt that business ought to cooperate with government to solve environmental problems.[5]

If the business ethics movement has led us anywhere in the past fifteen years, it is to the position that business has an ethical responsibility to become a more active partner in dealing with social concerns. Business must creatively find ways to become a part of solutions, rather than being a part of problems. Corporations can and must develop a conscience, as Ken Goodpaster and others have argued—and this includes an environmental conscience.[6] Corporations should not isolate themselves from participation in solving our environmental problems, leaving it up to others to find the answers and to tell them what not to do.

Corporations have special knowledge, expertise, and resources which are invaluable in dealing with the environmental crisis. Society needs the ethical vision and cooperation of all its players to solve its most urgent problems, especially one that involves the very survival of the planet itself. Business must work with government to find appropriate solutions. It should lobby for good environmental legislation and lobby against bad legislation, rather than isolating itself from the legislative process as Bowie suggests. It should not be ethically quixotic and try to go it alone, as our paper company owner tried to do, nor should it be ethically inauthentic and fight against what it believes to be environmentally sound policy, as our chemical company manager tried to do. Instead business must develop and demonstrate moral leadership.

There are examples of corporations demonstrating such leadership, even when this has been a risk to their self-interest. In the area of environmental moral leadership one might cite DuPont's discontinuing its Freon products, a $750-million-a-year business, because of their possible negative effects on the ozone layer, and Proctor and Gamble's manufacture of concentrated fabric softener and detergents which require less packaging. But some might argue, as Bowie does, that the real burden for environmental change lies with consumers, not with corporations. If we as consumers are willing to accept the harm done to the environment by favoring environmentally unfriendly products, corporations have no moral obligation to change so long as they obey environmental law. This is even more the case, so the argument goes, if corporations must take risks or sacrifice profits to do so. . . .

Even Bowie admits that perhaps business has a responsibility to educate the public and promote environmentally responsible behavior. But I am suggesting that corporate moral leadership goes far beyond public educational campaigns. It requires moral vision, commitment, and courage, and involves risk and sacrifice. I think business is capable of such a challenge. Some are even engaging in such a challenge. Certainly the business ethics

movement should do nothing short of encouraging such leadership. I feel morality demands such leadership.

II

If business has an ethical responsibility to the environment which goes beyond obeying environmental law, what criterion should be used to guide and justify such action? Many corporations are making environmentally friendly decisions where they see there are profits to be made by doing so. They are wrapping themselves in green where they see a green bottom line as a consequence. . . .

The frequent strategy of the new environmentalists is to get business to help solve environmental problems by finding profitable or virtually costless ways for them to participate. They feel that compromise, not confrontation, is the only way to save the earth. By using the tools of the free enterprise system, they are in search of win-win solutions, believing that such solutions are necessary to take us beyond what we have so far been able to achieve.

I am not opposed to these efforts; in most cases I think they should be encouraged. There is certainly nothing wrong with making money while protecting the environment, just as there is nothing wrong with feeling good about doing one's duty. But if business is adopting or being encouraged to adopt the view that good environmentalism is good business, then I think this poses a danger for the environmental ethics movement—a danger which has an analogy in the business ethics movement.

As we all know, the position that good ethics is good business is being used more and more by corporate executives to justify the building of ethics into their companies and by business ethics consultants to gain new clients. . . .

Is the rationale that good ethics is good business a proper one for business ethics? I think not. One thing that the study of ethics has taught us over the past 2,500 years is that being ethical may on occasion require that we place the interests of others ahead of or at least on par with our own interests. And this implies that the ethical thing to do, the morally right thing to do, may not be in our own self-interest. What happens when the right thing is not the best thing for the business?

Although in most cases good ethics may be good business, it should not be advanced as the only or even the main reason for doing business ethically. When the crunch comes, when ethics conflicts with the firm's interests, any ethics program that has not already faced up to this possibility is doomed to fail because it will undercut the rationale of the program itself. We should promote business ethics, not because good ethics is good business, but because we are morally required to adopt the moral point of view in all our dealings—and business is no exception. In business, as in all other human endeavors, we must be prepared to pay the costs of ethical behavior.

There is a similar danger in the environmental movement with corporations choosing or being wooed to be environmentally friendly on the grounds that it will be in their self-interest. There is the risk of participating in the movement for the wrong reasons. But what does it matter if business cooperates for reasons other than the right reasons, as long as it cooperates? It matters if business believes or is led to believe that it only has a duty to be environmentally conscientious in those cases where such actions either require no sacrifice or actually make a profit. And I am afraid this is exactly what is happening. . . .

I am not saying we should abandon attempts to entice corporations into being ethical, both environmentally and in other ways, by pointing out and providing opportunities where good ethics is good business. And there are many places where such attempts fit well in both the business and environmental ethics movements. But we must be careful not to cast this as the proper guideline for business's ethical responsibility. Because when it is discovered that many ethical actions are not necessarily good for business, at least in the short-run, then the rationale based on self-interest will come up morally short, and both ethical movements will be seen as deceptive and shallow.

III

What is the proper rationale for responsible business action toward the environment? A minimalist principle is to refrain from causing or prevent the causing of unwarranted harm, because failure to do so would violate certain moral rights not to be harmed. There is, of course, much debate over what harms are indeed unwarranted due to conflict of rights and questions about whether some harms are offset by certain benefits. . . .

Some naturalistic environmentalists only include other sentient animals in the framework of being deserving of moral consideration; others include all things which are alive or which are an integral part of an ecosystem. This latter view is sometimes called a biocentric environmental ethic as opposed to the homocentric view which sees all moral claims in terms of human beings and their interests. Some characterize these two views as deep *versus* shallow ecology.

The literature on these two positions is vast and the debate is ongoing. The conflict between them goes to the heart of environmental ethics and is crucial to our making of environmental policy and to our perception of moral duties to the environment, including business'. I strongly favor the biocentric view. And although this is not the place to try to adequately argue for it, let me unfurl its banner for just a moment.

A version of R. Routley's "last man" example[7] might go something like this: Suppose you were the last surviving human being and were soon to die from nuclear poisoning, as all other human and sentient animals have died before you. Suppose also that it is within your power to destroy all remaining life, or to make it simpler, the last tree which could continue to flourish and propagate if left alone. Furthermore you will not suffer if you do not destroy it. Would you do anything wrong by cutting it down? The deeper ecological view would say yes because you would be destroying something that has value in and of itself, thus making the world a poorer place.

It might be argued that the only reason we may find the tree valuable is because human beings generally find trees of value either practically or aesthetically, rather than the atoms or molecules they might turn into if changed from their present form. The issue is whether the tree has value only in its relation to human beings or whether it has a value deserving of moral consideration inherent in itself in its present form. The biocentric position holds that when we find something wrong with destroying the tree, as we should, we do so because we are responding to an intrinsic value in the natural object, not to a value we give to it. This is a view which argues against a humanistic environmental ethic and which urges us to channel our moral obligations accordingly.

Why should one believe that nonhuman living things or natural objects forming integral parts of ecosystems have intrinsic value? . . .

I suspect Arne Naess gives as good an answer as can be given. Faced with the ever returning question of "Why?," we have to stop somewhere. Here is a place where we well might stop. We shall admit that the value in itself is something shown in intuition. We attribute intrinsic value to ourselves and our nearest, and the validity of further identification can be contested, and *is* contested by many. The negation may, however, also be attacked through a series of "whys?" Ultimately, we are in the same human predicament of having to start somewhere, at least for the moment. We must stop somewhere and treat where we then stand as a foundation.[8]

In the final analysis, environmental biocentrism is adopted or not depending on whether it is seen to provide a deeper, richer, and more ethically compelling view of the nature of things.

If this deeper ecological position is correct, then it ought to be reflected in the environmental movement. Unfortunately, for the most part, I do not think this is being done, and there is a price to be paid for not doing so. . . .

Furthermore, there are many cases where what is in human interest is not in the interest of other natural things. Examples range from killing leopards for stylish coats to destroying a forest to build a golf course. I am not convinced that homocentric arguments, even those based on long-term human interests, have much force in protecting the interests of such natural things. Attempts to make these interests coincide might be made, but the point is that from a homocentric point of view the leopard and the forest have no morally relevant interests to consider. It is simply fortuitous if nonhuman natural interests coincide with human interests, and are thereby valued and protected. Let us take an example from the work of Christopher Stone. Suppose a stream has been polluted by a business. From a homocentric point of view, which serves as the basis for our legal system, we can only correct the problem through finding some harm done to human beings who use the stream. Reparation for such harm might involve cessation of the pollution and restoration of the stream, but it is also possible that the business might settle with the people by paying them for their damages and continue to pollute the stream. Homocentrism provides no way for the stream to be made whole again unless it is in the interests of human beings to do so. In short it is possible for human beings to sell out the stream[9]. . . .

At the heart of the business ethics movement is its reaction to the mistaken belief that business only has responsibilities to a narrow set of its stakeholders, namely its stockholders. Crucial to the environmental ethics movement is its reaction to the mistaken belief that only human beings and human interests are deserving of our moral consideration. I suspect that the beginnings of both movements can be traced to these respective moral insights.

NOTES

1. Norman Bowie, "Morality, Money, and Motor Cars," *Business, Ethics, and the Environment: The Public Policy Debate,* ed., W. Michael Hoffman, Robert Frederick, and Edward S. Petry, Jr. (New York: Quorum Books, 1990), p. 89.
2. See Milton Friedman, "The Social Responsibility of Business Is to Increase Its Profits," *The New York Times Magazine* (September 13, 1970).
3. Bowie, p. 91.
4. Bowie, p. 94.
5. Robert Frederick, Assistant Director of the Center for Business Ethics, and I have developed and written these points together. Frederick has also provided me with invaluable assistance on other points in this paper.
6. Kenneth E. Goodpaster, "Can a Corporation have an Environmental Conscience?" *The Corporation, Ethics, and the Environment,* ed., W. Michael Hoffman, Robert Frederick, and Edward S. Petry, Jr. (New York: Quorum Books, 1990).
7. Richard Routley, and Val Routley, "Human Chauvinism and Environmental Ethics," *Environmental Philosophy,* Monograph Series, No. 2, ed., Don Mannison, Michael McRobbie, and Richard Routley (Australian National University, 1980), pp. 121ff.
8. Arne Naess, "Identification as a Source of Deep Ecological Attitudes," *Deep Ecology,* ed., Michael Tobias (San Marcos, CA: Avant Books, 1988), p. 266.
9. Christopher D. Stone, "Should Trees Have Standing?—Toward Legal Rights for Natural Objects," in *People, Penguins, and Plastic Trees,* pp. 86–87.

The Individual Investor in Securities Markets: An Ethical Analysis

Robert E. Frederick and W. Michael Hoffman

Securities markets are full of pitfalls for individual investors. Examples of fraud and regulatory violations in the markets are common. For instance, a recent *Business Week* cover story reports that investors are being duped out of hundreds of millions a year in penny stock scams in spite of SEC regulations.[1] A report in the *Wall Street Journal* on the Chicago futures trading fraud highlights the "danger of being ripped off in futures markets" by unscrupulous floor brokers filling customers' "market orders"—a type of order that "individual investors should avoid using."[2]

Journal of Business Ethics 9 (1990):579–89. © 1990 Kluwer Academic Publishers. Reprinted by permission of Kluwer Academic Publishers.

But securities markets present risks to individual investors that go beyond clear violations of regulations and fraud. The above *Wall Street Journal* story, for example, also issued a more general warning to investors,

> Futures are fast moving, risky investment vehicles that are unsuitable for anyone who can't afford to lose and who doesn't have time to pay close attention to trading positions.[3]

Furthermore, it is not only the high risk futures and commodities markets that are perilous for investors. For example, the North American Securities Administration reports that "the securities industry isn't responding well to the problems of small investors in the wake of the stock market crash," problems such as poor execution of trades and being misled by brokers.[4] Even the bond markets, which in the past at least gave the outside appearance of stability, are in increasing turmoil. For instance, the SEC is now investigating the possibility that securities firms dumped billions of dollars of risky municipal bonds on individual investors because they were unable to sell them to institutions.[5] And MetLife is suing RJR-Nabisco on the grounds that individual investors were unjustifiably harmed when the A rated corporate bonds they purchased lost millions in value due to the junk bond financing of the RJR-Nabisco leveraged buyout.[6]

In light of these and many other examples that could be given, suppose the SEC announced that individual investors, for their own protection, no longer have access to securities markets. They are no longer permitted to buy stocks, bonds, or commodities or futures options. If this were to happen there surely would be a public outcry of protest, even moral outrage. The reasons for such outrage probably would revolve around the belief that some fundamental right had been violated, perhaps the presumed right that markets should be free and open so that everyone has an opportunity to better his or her position and enjoy the goods and services of society.

A quick look, however, reveals that not all markets have unrestricted access. Nor is there a generally accepted belief that any rights are being unjustifiably violated in such cases. In consumer markets, for example, individuals under a certain age are prohibited from voting, buying alcoholic beverages, and seeing certain movies. Regardless of age, not just anyone can buy a fully automatic rifle or order a few dozen hand grenades. In fact, not just anyone can drive a car; one must pass a test and be licensed to do that. Furthermore, even after being allowed to drive, this privilege can be revoked if it is abused. And, of course, none of our citizens is legally permitted to participate in certain drug markets, such as cocaine.

But it will be argued that there is good reason for these and other such restrictions. We are attempting to prevent people, the argument goes, from harming themselves or causing harm to others. This is what makes it morally permissible, or even obligatory, to restrict access to certain kinds of consumer products. The ethical principle here is that, when possible, persons ought to be protected from undue harm. Hence, the restrictions in question are justified.

Yet might not this be exactly the rationale behind a possible SEC ban against individual investors entering securities markets? Just as unrestricted access to some drugs is thought to present unacceptable risks to consumers, trading in today's securities markets may present unacceptable risks to many investors, resulting in great financial rather than physical harm. And since we feel justified in prohibiting consumers from buying what we take to be highly dangerous drugs or other consumer products, shouldn't we, by analogy, be justified in prohibiting certain investors from buying highly risky financial instruments? . . .

EXACTLY WHAT KIND OF INVESTOR ARE WE TALKING ABOUT?

The type of investor we will be concerned with, and the type we take to be the most likely candidate for the SEC prohibition mentioned earlier, is one that (a) is at relatively *high risk*, where risk is a function of the probability of a certain market event occurring and the degree of harm the investor would suffer were the event to occur, and (b) an investor who is relatively *unsophisticated* about the functioning of the market and hence unappreciative of the degree of risk they face. For example, suppose Jones invests his life savings in high yield bonds issued to finance an LBO, and suppose a few months later the company that issued the bonds suddenly announces that it is going into Chapter 11 bankruptcy. The value of the bonds drops precipitously and for all practical purposes in a matter of hours Jones' savings are wiped out. If Jones did not realize that the high return he was initially receiving was a reflection of the risky nature of the bonds, then he would fall within the category of investors with which we are concerned even assuming he had several million dollars invested. . . .

DO AT RISK INVESTORS HAVE A RIGHT TO PARTICIPATE IN SECURITIES MARKETS?

Obviously at risk investors are legally permitted to invest in securities markets, but do they have a right to do so? And if they do, what kind of right is it? These questions are important since how they are answered will determine in large part what kind of justification will be required to restrict or suspend investments by at risk investors, or whether a justification is possible at all.

Since the word "right" is used in many different senses, we will give rough definitions of the sense in which we will use "right" and associated terms. A "claim right," as we will understand it, is a right established within a system of rules. To have such a right is to have a valid or justified claim for action or forbearance against some person or institution. The notion of a "liberty" is weaker than that of a right. To have a liberty is not to have a duty or obligation to act toward a person or institution in a certain way. Rights imply liberties, but one may have a liberty without an associated right. A still weaker notion is that of a "privilege." To have a privilege is to have revocable permission to act in a certain way.[7]

Claim rights, liberties, and privileges can be either legal or moral depending on whether the rules in question are established by legislative action or follow from a system of morality. It is important to see that legal rights and moral rights need not be the same. A moral right may not be recognized by law, and one may have a legal right to engage in an immoral action.

If at risk investors have claim rights to invest in the market, then the government has a corresponding duty not to interfere with their activity. On the other hand, if they have a liberty to invest, they have no duty not to invest. If they have a privilege, then they are permitted to invest but such permission can be withdrawn. Now, if at risk investors have a claim right to invest, as opposed to a weaker liberty or an even weaker privilege to invest, then the justification required for infringing on that right will be very different from that required if they have a liberty or privilege. Hence it is important to decide, as best we can, exactly which they have.

We believe a strong case can be made that at risk investors have a moral claim right to invest in the market, and that this right follows from the classic "right to freedom" that is so much a part of the American tradition. . . .

It follows from the right to freedom that it

is morally permissible for persons to choose to invest in any way they deem appropriate within the bounds of law and a proper regard for the wrongful effects their actions may have on the lives of others.

If this is correct, then any interference with this right, whether by some individual or government agency, is prima facie unjustified. There are, however, several objections that could be raised. One of them is that persons simply have no such moral right because they have no rights at all other than those granted by law. Thus, no moral right is violated if the legal right to invest is altered or eliminated. Another is that although persons have moral rights, they do not have the right to freedom that we have attributed to them. . . .

There is one other objection to the right of freedom that we proposed. It is that even if all competent persons have an equal right to freedom, it still does not follow that they have the right to make any choice within the sphere of choices that do not wrongfully harm others. It does not follow, for example, that they have the right to make choices that seriously harm themselves. Intervention in such cases may be justified to prevent harm.

But is it? In order to decide, we must consider the possible justifications for interfering with the choices of others.

WHAT SORT OF JUSTIFICATION MIGHT BE OFFERED FOR RESTRICTING THE INVESTMENTS OF AT RISK INVESTORS?

One kind of justification that might be proposed is paternalistic. By paternalism we roughly mean interfering with a person's actions or preferences by restricting their freedom of action or the range of choices normally available to them for the reason that such a restriction promotes or preserves their good, welfare, happiness, or interests. A pa-

ternalistic justification for restricting at risk investors would be that exposure to risk for many investors is too great to permit them to continue without some sort of protection that reduces the risk to an acceptable degree. For certain investors an acceptable degree may be no risk at all. For others some risk may be permissible. In either case, the argument goes, as long as the intent of intervention is to protect or promote the good of at risk investors, and as long as it does not wrong other persons, then intervention is at least permissible and may be obligatory. It is only in this way that harm to many investors can be prevented.

The standard objection to paternalistic justifications is something like this: If people choose to run the risk to gain what they believe will be the rewards, who are we to interfere? From where do we derive a special dispensation to overrule their choices and interfere with their lives?

Although there is a kernel of truth in this objection, it is much too facile. Some paternalistic acts are clearly justified. Paternalistic reasoning is commonly used to justify restricting the choices of children and people judged incompetent or otherwise unable rationally to consider the consequences of their acts. Moreover, paternalistic justifications are not obviously unreasonable even in cases where the competence of the person is not in question. It is at least initially credible that some consumer products, such as prescription drugs, are not in unrestricted circulation precisely because of paternalistic reasons.

Let us confine our discussion to those persons ordinarily taken to be competent and rational. We still do not believe that paternalism *per se* justifies restricting at risk investors that fall within this category. One reason is that it may be impossible to find out just what the good or welfare of an individual investor is. Not only is there the thorny problem of trying to reach a common and precise understanding of the vague idea of the "good" of a person, there are immense practical difficulties in discovering whether a certain individual's good is served by restricting his or her access to the market. There may be situations where an individual's good is not served, and intervention in those cases would be a wrongful violation of his or her rights.

But suppose regulators do know the good of some individuals. Would paternalism then justify intervening to preserve or promote their good? We believe not in cases where regulators and the person in question have differing conceptions of that person's good. Even if regulators happen to know a person's "true" good better than he or she does themselves, imposing on that person a conception of his or her good they do not accept is not justified. Regulators may attempt to persuade at risk investors to take a different course or provide them with information that they need to make an informed decision, but it is not permissible to deny them the right to direct their lives. . . .

Although paternalism as characterized thus far does not justify interference with the choices of at risk investors, there are circumstances in which intervention is justified. This can best be explained by using an example not related to investing. Suppose Jones mistakenly believes the food he is about to eat is wholesome but we have good reason to think it is contaminated with botulism. As he raises the fork to his mouth we only have time to strike it away. At first he is angry, but after we explain the reason for our action he is grateful. The act of striking the fork away is an example of paternalistic intervention since it is done for Jones' good but against his wishes. It seems obvious, however, that we acted properly. Intervention in this case is justified since if Jones were fully aware of the circumstances he would act differently or would agree to have us intervene on his behalf. He would consent to our action. Hence, intervention here respects his right to freedom since it is

compatible with his goals and does not force upon him some version of his good he would not accept.

Note that it is not merely our superior knowledge of the situation that justifies interference, but also our judgment that Jones would agree that our actions preserve or promote his good. The case would be different were Jones attempting suicide instead of trying to have a decent meal. Paternalistic intervention may not be justified when a person voluntarily undertakes an action harmful to him- or herself, provided that person has a reasonably complete understanding of his or her circumstances and the consequences of the action. But it is at least prima facie justified, we suggest, when an action is based on incomplete information and thus is, in one sense, less than fully voluntary.

Now suppose there are compelling grounds to believe that some otherwise competent investors are unappreciative of the high degree of risk they face, and that if they were presented with information about those risks they would act either to reduce or eliminate them, or would consent to having restrictions placed on the kinds of investments they could make. Since they would consent to intervention or act differently were they fully aware of the circumstances, intervention on their behalf is justified just as it was justified for Jones. Their rights are not violated since nothing is imposed on them that they would not consent to were they fully aware of the dangers they faced.

A major difference between the Jones case and at risk investors is that we dealt with Jones as an individual, but a regulatory or legislative body would have to deal with at risk investors as a group. There simply is no way to reach them all individually. Furthermore, although such bodies may be able to make reasonable assumptions about the kinds of risks acceptable to most at risk investors, and about the kinds of restrictions to which most of them would agree, it seems inevitable that there will be some investors that would not consent to restrictions because, for example, they have an unusual conception of their good or welfare, or because they find the restrictions highly offensive. For these people restrictions on investing will impose a foreign conception of their good on them and thus is not compatible with their right to direct their lives. . . .

If the *reason* given for intervening is promoting the good of at risk investors as a group, then, as we have tried to argue, it is not justified. Suppose, however, the reason is not only that the good of some investors is promoted, but that there is a duty to intervene to protect certain *rights,* in particular, the right of investors not to be harmed. The argument would go something like this: There is good reason to believe that some at risk investors would consent to having restrictions placed on them to protect their financial position and prevent them from suffering financial harm. Since it is a basic function of government to protect its citizens from harm, there is a duty to protect these investors. Hence, placing restrictions on their investment activities is justified even though such restrictions may violate the right of other investors to direct their lives as they see fit.

If this argument is plausible, then there is a conflict of rights between two groups of at risk investors. This is a genuine moral dilemma that can only be resolved by deciding whose rights are to prevail. We believe it should be the right not to be harmed. An analogy with prescription drugs may be helpful here. One reason there are restrictions on access to drugs is to prevent harm to persons who do not know how to use them correctly. These restrictions are justified, in our view, even supposing there are some individuals willing to take the risk. The right to freedom of this latter group should be and should remain a serious consideration in devising restrictions on

drugs, but it does not override the right of others not to be exposed to excessive risk and possible serious harm.

The same holds true of at risk investors. The right of some of them not to be exposed to excessive risk and possible serious financial harm overrides the right of others to invest without restrictions. We emphasize, however, that the right to freedom cannot be lightly dismissed, and must be given due consideration when formulating policies and regulations governing the markets. . . .

IF SOME INVESTORS ARE RESTRICTED, HOW SHOULD IT BE DONE?

Since we are not experts in the regulation of securities markets, the best we can do here is make a few suggestions that seem to us worthy of additional investigation. It is a basic premise, essential for any just system of regulation and law, that relevantly different classes of persons be treated in relevantly different ways. Hence, it clearly would be unjust to restrict the activities of all investors to protect some of them. It also follows from this basic premise that distinctions must be drawn within the class of at risk investors. It may turn out in the end that there is no workable method of protecting some at risk investors while preserving the rights of all of them, but it would be a mistake to begin with this assumption.

In light of this it might be suggested that the only plausible course of action is to make sure that at risk investors have all the information they need to make investment decisions. This has at least three advantages. The first is that providing information does not seriously infringe any rights. And establishing stringent policies to ensure that the information is received also may be reasonable. For example, suppose that to demonstrate a minimum level of competence persons must pass an examination before investing, just as they have to pass a driving exam before driving. Different kinds of exams could be given for different kinds of investments. Would such a procedure violate any rights? It certainly would be costly and inconvenient, but we doubt that it is an inordinate restriction on the right to freedom.

A second advantage is that providing information is already one function of the Securities and Exchange Commission. According to the Commission's pamphlet "Consumers' Financial Guide" the three main responsibilities of the Commission are:

1. To require that companies that offer their securities for sale in "interstate commerce" register with the Commission and make available to investors complete and accurate information.
2. To protect investors against misrepresentation and fraud in the issuance and sale of securities.
3. To oversee the securities markets to ensure they operate in a fair and orderly manner.

Although the pamphlet goes on to advise investors that "whatever the choice of investment, make sure that you have complete and accurate information before investing to ensure that you use your funds wisely," it also emphasizes that the SEC does not see itself as the guarantor of investments:

> Registration . . . does not insure investors against loss of their investments, but serves rather to provide information upon which investors may base an informed and realistic evaluation of the worth of a security.

Thus providing information to at risk investors is consistent with the mission of the SEC and would not require massive restructuring of the Commission.

The third advantage is that providing information would be the most direct way to discover whether investors would consent to restrictions. Earlier we argued that restrictions on some at risk investors are justified because they would consent to intervention if they were fully aware of the risk they faced. But instead of imposing regulations based on what investors *would* do were they to have all the relevant information, it is preferable to give them the information whenever possible and see what they *actually* do. This would avoid the danger of imposing on them a conception of their good that they do not accept.

We agree that providing information to at risk investors is a good idea, and propose that methods be initiated that ensure that investors receive the information, rather than just having it available for those that seek it out. However, this may not be enough to eliminate unacceptable risks for at risk investors. Consider the prescription drug market again, and assume that the FDA made strenuous efforts to provide consumers with complete information about drugs. Supposing for a moment that it is legally permissible for consumers to buy drugs, as it is in some countries, this might be enough to eliminate unacceptable risk of harm from drugs for the few that had the time, energy, and expertise to use the information. But for most people it would be an overwhelming blizzard of paper that would be of no real use. As Steven Kelman has argued, the cost of organizing and understanding the information may be so high that the most sensible course of action for most people would be to assign their right to select drugs to some individual or institution with special expertise, provided the choice was made with their best interests in mind.[8] Merely providing information about drugs does not protect persons from harm unless the information is understood. When it appears unlikely that a large class of people will devote the time needed to understand it, then it is appropriate, we believe, to place legal restrictions on their choices. This protects them from harm, but is not an intolerable limitation of freedom.

The same reasoning applies in the securities markets. So much information is available and it is so complex that for many investors beyond a certain point it would be too costly to make the investment in time required to assimilate it all. Having "complete and accurate information," as the SEC suggests, is not enough. Leaving aside the issue of how one determines whether it is complete and accurate (note that not even the SEC does that), there remains the problem of understanding it well enough to make a wise investment decision. Perhaps it could be done, but would it be done by most at risk investors? We are inclined to think not. So we suggest that, just as with prescription drugs, at risk investors be required by law to engage the services of an expert. This would go a long way toward eliminating unacceptable risks for them, and given the significant possibility of harm many investors face, we do not feel it would be an excessive restriction on their freedom. Exceptions would have to be made for those investors willing to become expert in the markets (since they would no longer meet the definition of an at risk investor), and some system of qualifications would need to be established to identify investment counselors capable of advising the other investors. . . .

NOTES

1. "The Penny Stock Scandal," *Business Week*, 23 Jan. 1989, pp. 74–82.
2. "Investors Can Take a Bite Out of Fraud," *Wall Street Journal*, 24 Jan. 1989, p. C1.
3. *Wall Street Journal* 24 Jan. 1989, p. C1.
4. "Many Crash Complaints Unresolved," *Wall Street Journal* 10 Oct. 1988, p. C1. For additional information on problems faced by individual investors, see John L. Casey, *Ethics in the Financial Marketplace*, (Scudder, Stevens & Clark, New York, 1988).
5. "SEC Studies Municipals in Trusts," *Wall Street Journal*, 11 Oct. 1988, p. C1.
6. "Bondholders Are Mad as Hell—And No Wonder," *Business Week*, 5 Dec. 1988, p. 28.
7. Joel Feinberg, *Social Philosophy* (Prentice Hall, Englewood Cliffs, NJ, 1973), pp. 55–56. These definitions are based on the ones given by Feinberg.
8. Steven Kelman, "Regulation and Paternalism," in *Ethical Theory and Business* eds. T. L. Beauchamp and N. E. Bowie (Prentice Hall, Englewood Cliffs, NJ, 1988), p. 153.

Management Buyouts and Managerial Ethics

Robert F. Bruner
and Lynn Sharp Paine

Because of their unusual terms, size, and number, management buyouts (MBOs) have emerged as one of the more arresting features in the corporate landscape. W. T. Grimm and Company estimated that in 1979 the value of firms going private was $636 million.[1] By 1986, Mergers and Acquisitions estimated the value of firms going private to be

$40.9 billion.[2] As the volume of management buyouts rises, so does the volume of criticism. There are several avenues of attack. For instance, many critics doubt the social value of these transactions. They argue that MBOs threaten the financial stability of the American economy and are only financial rearrangements having no effect on the utilization of real assets.[3]

The attack most interesting from the standpoints of directors, senior managers, and shareholders rests on the claim that buyouts are unethical because of management's conflict of interest. In a buyout, managers' personal interests are pitted against their fiduciary duties to shareholders. Critics ask whether stockholders are getting the managerial loyalty to which they are entitled.[4] . . .

THE PROBLEM WITH BUYOUTS

In recent years, management buyouts have offered shareholders attractive returns. The cash flow gains from increased leverage and depreciation have permitted buyers to pay a premium over market price and at the same time to earn supernormal rates of return. On average, it appears that sellers receive almost a 30 percent premium for their equity claim. On the buyers' side, detailed case analyses suggest substantial internal rates of return on investment ranging from 25 to 50 percent. Superficially at least, it appears that both sides of the transaction win. Why, then, has management's role in buyouts been so heavily criticized?

The criticism is about fairness for the public shareholders. Management's position on both sides of the bargaining table may make buyout prices suspect even when shareholders are bought out at premiums. Critics find it difficult to see how management members of the buyout team can serve effectively as fiduciaries of selling shareholders and at the same time negotiate on their own behalf as buyers. As fiduciary, management's objective should be to obtain the highest price possible. As members of the buyout team, however, it would be natural for management to try to push the price as low as possible. A low price makes the purchase more attractive and enhances the potential future gains from going public again.

The risk is that management may take advantage of shareholders; but even if the buyout team offers shareholders a fair deal—one that satisfies its fiduciary obligations—the deal may not be perceived as fair by those who are aware of management's conflict of interest. The bevy of shareholder derivative lawsuits that have followed recent buyouts, even those at premium prices, and the criticisms produced by academics and policy makers indicate that shareholders lack confidence in the fairness of the prices they are offered.

Management's conflicting objectives are one source of concern about buyouts, but other issues are also involved. Management's superior knowledge exacerbates the problem of conflicting objectives. As insiders, managers have privileged access to information, sometimes secret, about the firm's prospects, and they have a unique feel for the company's value which comes from experience in handling its day-to-day affairs. Their knowledge of the firm and their special appreciation for its value give managers a decided advantage vis-à-vis shareholders and potential competitors when proposing a buyout price. A price which appears fair in light of publicly available information may be unfair when undisclosed plans, discoveries, and inventions are taken into account.

Management also has the ability to affect the company's stock price by controlling the flow of information, by its choice of accounting procedures, and by timing its strategic decisions. Opportunities to manipulate share price in conjunction with a buyout bid are significant. Quite apart from any deliberate efforts to manipulate stock prices, however, management has a unique ability to choose the most opportune time to propose a buyout.

Presumably, management proposes or participates in a buyout only if it is advantageous to management to do so. If management believes the share price is significantly below what could be obtained by releveraging or liquidating the company, it makes sense for management to buy the company and take steps to redeploy its assets. Under these circumstances shareholders may justifiably wonder whether management is taking for itself some opportunity that properly belongs to the corporation. Traditionally, under the corporate opportunity doctrine, the law has prohibited officers, directors, and senior managers from taking personal advantage of opportunities that come to them in their official capacities and are of potential benefit to the corporation.[5] If corporate leaders exploit corporate opportunities for themselves, the law permits shareholders to impose a trust on the profits earned. Couldn't management relever or liquidate directly to benefit shareholders rather than first taking the company private? On the face of it, the MBO appears to be a mechanism for transferring value from shareholders to management.

MANAGEMENT'S FIDUCIARY OBLIGATIONS

The concerns about conflicting interests, insider advantages, and misappropriation of corporate opportunities reflect management's special obligations to the corporation and its shareholders. In contrast to the arm's-length relationship that normally obtains between buyers and sellers in the marketplace, managers have a fiduciary responsibility toward the corporation and shareholders for whom they work.

According to the orthodox theory of the corporation, shareholders own—or at least invest in—the firm, while management runs it. In order for this arrangement to work, shareholders must be able to trust the management will devote adequate attention to corporate business and run the business competently in a way that promotes the shareholders' interests. This trust is in part promoted through the board of directors, whose job it is to monitor management's performance on behalf of shareholders. But it depends more fundamentally on the continuing good faith performance by men and women in management positions.

The classic legal statement of the responsibility of corporate fiduciaries is found in the well-known case of *Guth v. Luft* decided by the Supreme Court of Delaware in 1939:

> A public policy, existing through the years, and derived from a profound knowledge of human characteristics and motives . . . demands of a corporate officer or director . . . the most scrupulous observance of his duty, not only affirmatively to protect the interests of the corporation committed to his charge, but also to refrain from doing anything that would work injury to the corporation, or to deprive it of profit or advantage which his skill and ability might properly bring to it, or to enable it to make in the reasonable and lawful exercise of its powers.[6]

The central element of this ideal is that management be dedicated to advancing the interests of the corporation, but most especially that management should not advance its own interests at the expense of the corporation.

The separation of ownership and control which underlies the modern public corporation is possible only if shareholders trust corporate leadership. In the absence of trust, monitoring management's performance becomes very costly. Without some fundamental assurance that their interests will be protected, equity investors would have little incentive to put their capital in the hands of professional managers. The benefits of corporate enterprise that flow to consumers, employees, suppliers, communities, and the general public—as well as to shareholders—are in jeopardy if management loses sight of its fiduciary obligations.

AN ETHICAL PERSPECTIVE ON MANAGEMENT BUYOUTS

Management buyouts threaten to undermine shareholder trust in corporate leadership if they are seen as or used as techniques for shrewd managers to benefit at shareholders' expense. Management's personal interest in buyouts, coupled with the absence of any generally accepted standard of fairness for evaluating buyout bids, make them especially potent threats to investor confidence. If there were no potential benefits for shareholders in these arrangements, there would be every reason to prohibit them. But, as noted earlier, buyouts sometimes offer shareholders the best alternative for protecting their investment or realizing its value. For example, management may be able, because of its position and superior knowledge, to see potential where outsiders do not, and thus be willing to take a seemingly moribund company private and rejuvenate it.[7] Management may, because of its position, be able to take a company private to ward off a hostile takeover bid offering a lower price.[8] Even in the absence of threatening conditions, a buyout may offer shareholders the best opportunity to realize the value of their investment because of the tax advantages and leveraging opportunities available as a result of going private. Any discussion of buyouts must recognize that sometimes they may be in shareholders' best interests.

From the perspective of managerial ethics, the practical challenge, then, is both to specify the conditions under which going private is consistent with management's fiduciary obligations and to motivate managers to propose only buyouts which satisfy those conditions.

MANAGEMENT'S CONFLICT OF INTEREST

Some observers consider buyouts inherently inconsistent with management's fiduciary obligations because of management's conflicting personal interests. These observers and many others apparently take the position that it is unethical to place oneself in a position in which personal interest may conflict with obligation. The appeal of such a position is obvious. In conflict of interest situations, there is always the possibility that personal interest will overwhelm obligation, that an abuse of trust will occur. However, the principle may be criticized on two grounds.

First, it is based on a misconception of conflicts of interest, one which sees potential conflict as characteristic of discrete, identifiable situations—which can be easily marked off from the normal state of affairs.

In fact, whenever a person is charged to act for the benefit of another—as corporate fiduciary, as parent, as employee—a conflict between personal interest and obligation to promote the interests of the other can erupt. The conflict may arise in connection with almost any type of decision or activity. An employee's decision not to search more widely for a competitive supplier, for example, may involve such a conflict. Potential conflict is not limited to exchanges between the agent and principal. Recognition that the potential for conflict exists continuously in every agency relationship renders the principle requiring avoidance of potential conflict totally unworkable. It is impossible to eliminate all potential conflicts without eliminating the relationships that give rise to them, and that would be too great a price to pay. Practical judgment is required to identify situations in which the potential gain to the agent or loss to the principle is great enough to warrant steps to monitor or restrain the agent's behavior.

The principle requiring avoidance of all potential conflict situations may also be criticized because it sometimes penalizes the very party it is meant to protect. If, for example, corporate directors were flatly prohibited from doing business with the corporations they serve, some opportunities advantageous to the corporation would have to be foregone. Courts and state legislatures have long recognized the possibility that a flat prohibition on dealing between a corporation and its directors can in some circumstances work to the detriment of the corporation.

Conflicts of interest are problematic not because they are themselves unethical, but because they may lead to conduct that is unethical. It may be difficult to do what obligation requires when important personal interests seem to point in a different direction. More commonly, personal interest may threaten the objectivity or integrity of professional judgment. When personal interests loom large, the decision maker may have difficulty determining where his firm's interests lie. There is a very natural tendency to want to see the interests of the firm and self-interest as aligned, even if, from a more objective perspective, they are not.

While there is little reason to recommend avoiding all situations in which personal interest may conflict with fiduciary obligation, there is good reason for looking more closely at situations in which a conflict creates a risk of significant losses to the principal or benefits to the agent. A buyout is just such a situation. . . .

FAIR PRICE

Who is entitled to the gains from management buyouts? Selling shareholders may believe that the gains from the buyout should be theirs. The value created derives from unused debt capacity and a depreciable asset base. Shareholders own both of these before the transaction. Buyers, no doubt, believe that their ability to leverage the company beyond the level normally available to a public corporation entitles them to the gains. In a normal arm's-length transaction, buyers and sellers negotiate from these different perceptions to reach a mutually acceptable price. Should the situation be any different in a management buyout? Should the normal arm's-length standard for fair price apply in the buyout context? Sometimes it is assumed that if buyouts give shareholders a premium over market price, then there should be no complaints. Shareholders should gladly accept the premium and be grateful to management for having taken the initiative to unlock some added value. This position, however, fails to take into account management's fiduciary obligation and the foundation upon which it rests.

A buyout proposal is, in effect, a proposal to convert a fiduciary relationship into an arm's-length relationship. Whether the buyout group should be held to a fiduciary standard under these circumstances is central to the analysis of fair price. Our discussion of disclosure and review was based on the view that management's fiduciary obligations continue even after a buyout is proposed. Permitting management unilaterally to divest itself of its responsibilities to the firm by making a buyout proposal and then permitting the buyout group to negotiate on the basis of information and resources management acquired in its capacity as fiduciary would seriously undermine shareholder confidence. From the time a buyout is proposed until it is consummated or the proposal dropped, management should be held to a fiduciary standard. Unlike the approach which says that anything over market price is fair, our approach to fair price takes management's fiduciary responsibility into account.

As stated earlier, at the heart of management's fiduciary responsibility is the obligation to promote the corporation's interests. But most especially, management must not benefit at the expense of shareholders. Sometimes it is easy to see when corporate fiduciaries are benefiting at the expense of shareholders. When they misappropriate corporate assets for themselves, for example, the harm to shareholders and the corresponding benefit to the fiduciaries is simply measured by the value of the assets taken. Determining the harm to shareholders in a buyout case is more difficult. While shareholders may benefit to the extent that the price exceeds market value, they may be harmed to the extent that the price is less than it ought to be by some other standard. For example, a buyout bid might be higher than market price, but still not as high as the price the shares would bring if management took certain initiatives such as relevering the company to improve share price.

Moreover, when a fiduciary steals from the corporation, there is no uncertainty about entitlements: the assets belong to the corporation and no reasonable person can claim to have any entitlement to them by virtue of his status in the corporation. However, where the question is the appropriate division of newly created wealth, particularly wealth created through the combined efforts of many people, entitlements are ambiguous. In order to determine whether one party is benefiting at the expense of another, there must be some benchmark or standard for the appropriate division of the gains. In the buyout situation, if shareholders get too little, then the buyout group benefits at their expense. Part of the

problem of identifying buyouts which satisfy managements' fiduciary obligations is to specify a standard for determining whether the price is appropriate or fair.

Perhaps the most obvious standard is the firm's stock price before the buyout. Under the theory of capital market efficiency, the firm's value in the open market is fair in the sense that it reflects all public information about the company. One defect of this standard for evaluating buyout bids is that it is vulnerable to the asymmetry of information between insiders (i.e., managers) and outsiders (i.e., public shareholders). Asymmetries can arise because of differences in technical expertise between managers and the public, the possibly high cost of information gathering, and the size and complexity of the firm. A second defect of this standard is that it fails to distinguish between management's existing policies and those that might prevail if the firm were restructured or the management incentive scheme changed. To the extent that stock price before a buyout reflects managers' failure to utilize all their skills and abilities to maximize shareholder wealth, using it as a standard of fair price endorses managerial inefficiency.

A second standard is the price the firm would fetch if sold in an open auction. This standard explicitly controls for the fact that the buyout bid is not derived from arm's-length bidding. Certainly any bid lower than what an open market auction would bring is too low and may indicate that management is seeking to take advantage of shareholders. But the open market rule has the limitation that competing arm's-length bids are rarely available unless solicited, and even then may not be forthcoming. Nevertheless, this is an important standard because competing open market bidders have been known to intervene in instances of apparently low management bids.[9] Some commentators advocate a rule of open bidding once a management buyout is proposed. Such a rule has much to be said for it, but in the absence of actual interested bidders, it fails to give much guidance for assessing buyout bids.

A third and more useful standard of comparison is the value shareholders could obtain if they synthesized the buyout on their own: borrowed heavily, repurchased a large percentage of shares, and increased the shareholdings of managers (by sale or outright gift). Even the value created by depreciation tax shields can be synthesized by selling plant and equipment and then leasing them back. This standard is not only more useful, since it does not depend on the presence of competing bidders, but it is also more consistent with management's duty of loyalty to shareholders. Management's fiduciary duty requires that it put forth its best efforts on shareholders' behalf. . . .

NOTES

1. News release, Doremus & Company, Chicago, January 12, 1984, p. 2.

2. "1987 Profile," *Mergers & Acquisitions* (May/June 1986): 71.

3. Louis Lowenstein, "No More Cozy Management Buyouts," *Harvard Business Review* (January/February 1986): 147–156.

4. Benjamin J. Stein, "Going Private Is Unethical," *Fortune,* November 11, 1985, p. 169.

5. For instance, *Durfee v. Durfee & Canning, Inc.,* 323 Mass. 187 (1948). See generally, Victor Brudney and Robert Charles Clark, "A New Look at Corporate Opportunities," *Harvard Law Review,* 94 (1981): 997–1062.

6. *Guth v. Loft,* 5A.2d 503, 510 (Del. Supr. 1939).

7. For instance, employees at Weirton Steel saved it from imminent closing, then took a 19 percent pay cut, and raised $300 million to buy the assets in 1983. Since then, Weirton has embarked on a significant modernization program.

8. For instance, in April 1987, Dart Group, Inc., made an unsolicited takeover bid for Supermarkets General Corporation for $1.75 billion. Two weeks later, management offered to take the company private for $1.8 billion.

9. For example, competitive bidders intervened in response to J. B. Fuqua's 1981 attempt to buy out Fuqua Industries and in response to Chairman David Mahoney's 1983 proposal to take Norton Simon, Inc., private.

Henningsen v. Bloomfield Motors, Inc. and Chrysler Corporation

Supreme Court of New Jersey

Claus H. Henningsen purchased a Plymouth automobile, manufactured by defendant Chrysler Corporation, from defendant Bloomfield Motors, Inc. His wife, plaintiff Helen Henningsen, was injured while driving it and instituted suit against both defendants to recover damages on account of her injuries.

Her husband joined in the action seeking compensation for his consequential losses. The complaint was predicated upon breach of express and implied warranties and upon negligence. At the trial the negligence counts were dismissed by the court and the case was submitted to the jury for determination solely

Atlantic Reporter 161 A2d 69, pp. 73–75, 78–81, 83–87, 93–96, 102. This opinion was written by Justice John J. Francis.

on the issues of implied warranty of merchantability.* Verdicts were returned against both defendants and in favor of the plaintiffs. Defendants appealed and plaintiffs cross-appealed from the dismissal of their negligence claim. . . .

. . . The particular car selected was described as a 1955 Plymouth, Plaza "6," Club Sedan. The type used in the printed parts of the [purchase order] form became smaller in size, different in style, and less readable toward the bottom where the line for the purchaser's signature was placed. The smallest type on the page appears in the two paragraphs, one of two and one-quarter lines and the second of one and one-half lines, on which great stress is laid by the defense in the case. These two paragraphs are the least legible and the most difficult to read in the instrument, but they are most important in the evaluation of the rights of the contesting parties. They do not attract attention and there is nothing about the format which would draw the reader's eye to them. In fact, a studied and concentrated effort would have to be made to read them. De-emphasis seems the motive rather than emphasis. . . . The two paragraphs are:

"The front and back of this Order comprise the entire agreement affecting this purchase and no other agreement or understanding of any nature concerning same has been made or entered into, or will be recognized. I hereby certify that no credit has been extended to me for the purchase of this motor vehicle except as appears in writing on the face of this agreement.

"I have read the matter printed on the back hereof and agree to it as a part of this order the same as if it were printed above my signature. . . . "

The testimony of Claus Henningsen justifies the conclusion that he did not read the two fine print paragraphs referring to the back of the purchase contract. And it is uncontradicted that no one made any reference to them, or called them to his attention. With respect to the matter appearing on the back, it is likewise uncontradicted that he did not read it and that no one called it to his attention.

. . . The warranty, which is the focal point of the case, is set forth [on the reverse side of the page]. It is as follows:

"7. It is expressly agreed that there are no warranties, express or implied, *made* by either the dealer or the manufacturer on the motor vehicle, chassis, or parts furnished hereunder except as follows.

"The manufacturer warrants each new motor vehicle (including original equipment placed thereon by the manufacturer except tires), chassis or parts manufactured by it to be free from defects in material or workmanship under normal use and service. Its obligation under this warranty being limited to making good at its factory any part or parts thereof which shall, within ninety (90) days after delivery of such vehicle *to the original purchaser* or before such vehicle has been driven 4,000 miles, whichever event shall first occur, be returned to it with transportation charges prepaid and which its examination shall disclose to its satisfaction to have been thus defective: *This warranty being expressly in lieu of all other warranties expressed or implied, and all other obligations or liabilities on its part,* and it neither assumes nor authorizes any other person to assume for it any other liability in connection with the sale of its vehicles. . . . ' " [Emphasis added] . . .

The new Plymouth was turned over to the Henningsens on May 9, 1955. No proof was adduced by the dealer to show precisely what

---

*["Merchantability": The articles shall be of the kind described and be fit for the purpose for which they were sold. Fitness is impliedly warranted if an item is merchantable, Ed.]

was done in the way of mechanical or road testing beyond testimony that the manufacturer's instructions were probably followed. Mr. Henningsen drove it from the dealer's place of business in Bloomfield to their home in Keansburg. On the trip nothing unusual appeared in the way in which it operated. Thereafter, it was used for short trips on paved streets about the town. It had no servicing and no mishaps of any kind before the event of May 19. That day, Mrs. Henningsen drove to Asbury Park [New Jersey]. On the way down and in returning the car performed in normal fashion until the accident occurred. She was proceeding north on Route 36 in Highlands, New Jersey, at 20–22 miles per hour. The highway was paved and smooth, and contained two lanes for northbound travel. She was riding in the right-hand lane. Suddenly she heard a loud noise "from the bottom, by the hood." It "felt as if something cracked." The steering wheel spun in her hands; the car veered sharply to the right and crashed into a highway sign and a brick wall. No other vehicle was in any way involved. A bus operator driving in the left-hand lane testified that he observed plaintiff's car approaching in normal fashion in the opposite direction; "all of a sudden [it] veered at 90 degrees . . . and right into this wall." As a result of the impact, the front of the car was so badly damaged that it was impossible to determine if any of the parts of the steering wheel mechanism or workmanship or assembly were defective or improper prior to the accident. The condition was such that the collision insurance carrier, after inspection, declared the vehicle a total loss. It had 468 miles on the speedometer at the time. . . .

The terms of the warranty are a sad commentary upon the automobile manufacturers' marketing practices. Warranties developed in the law in the interest of and to protect the ordinary consumer who cannot be expected to have the knowledge or capacity or even the opportunity to make adequate inspection of mechanical instrumentalities, like automobiles, and to decide for himself whether they are reasonably fit for the designed purpose. . . . But the ingenuity of the Automobile Manufacturers Association, by means of its standardized form, has metamorphosed the warranty into a device to limit the maker's liability. To call it an "equivocal" agreement, as the Minnesota Supreme Court did, is the least that can be said in criticism of it.

The manufacturer agrees to replace defective parts for 90 days after the sale or until the car has been driven 4,000 miles, whichever is first to occur, *if the part is sent to the factory, transportation charges prepaid, and if examination discloses to its satisfaction that the part is defective.* . . .

Chrysler points out that an implied warranty of merchantability is an incident of a contract of sale. It concedes, of course, the making of the original sale to Bloomfield Motors, Inc., but maintains that this transaction marked the terminal point of its contractual connection with the car. Then Chrysler urges that since it was not a party to the sale by the dealer to Henningsen, there is no privity of contract* between it and the plaintiffs, and the absence of this privity eliminates any such implied warranty.

There is no doubt that under early common-law concepts of contractual liability only those persons who were parties to the bargain could sue for a breach of it. In more recent times a noticeable disposition has appeared in a number of jurisdictions to break through the narrow barrier of privity when dealing with sales of goods in order to give realistic recognition to a universally accepted fact. The fact is that the dealer and the ordinary

---

*["Privity of contract": A contractual relation existing between parties that is sufficiently close to confer a legal claim or right. Ed.]

buyer do not, and are not expected to, buy goods, whether they be foodstuffs or automobiles, exclusively for their own consumption or use. Makers and manufacturers know this and advertise and market their products on that assumption; witness the "family" car, the baby foods, etc. The limitations of privity in contracts for the sale of goods developed their place in the law when marketing conditions were simple, when maker and buyer frequently met face to face on an equal bargaining plane and when many of the products were relatively uncomplicated and conducive to inspection by a buyer competent to evaluate their quality. With the advent of mass marketing, the manufacturer became remote from the purchaser, sales were accomplished through intermediaries, and the demand for the product was created by advertising media. In such an economy it became obvious that the consumer was the person being cultivated. Manifestly, the connotation of "consumer" was broader than that of "buyer." He signified such a person who, in the reasonable contemplation of the parties to the sale, might be expected to use the product. Thus, where the commodities sold are such that if defectively manufactured they will be dangerous to life or limb, then society's interests can only be protected by eliminating the requirement of privity between the maker and his dealers and the reasonably expected ultimate consumer. In that way the burden of losses consequent upon use of defective articles is born by those who are in a position to either control the danger or make an equitable distribution of the losses when they do occur. . . .

Under modern conditions the ordinary layman, on responding to the importuning of colorful advertising, has neither the opportunity nor the capacity to inspect or to determine the fitness of an automobile for use; he must rely on the manufacturer who has control of its construction, and to some degree on the dealer who, to the limited extent called for by the manufacturer's instructions, inspects and services it before delivery. In such a marketing milieu his remedies and those of persons who properly claim through him should not depend "upon the intricacies of the law of sales. The obligation of the manufacturer should not be based alone on privity of contract. It should rest, as was once said, upon 'the demands of social justice.'" . . .

In a society such as ours, where the automobile is a common and necessary adjunct of daily life, and where its use is so fraught with danger to the driver, passengers, and the public, the manufacturer is under a special obligation in connection with the construction, promotion, and sale of his cars. Consequently, the courts must examine purchase agreements closely to see if consumer and public interests are treated fairly. . . .

What influence should these circumstances have on the restrictive effect of Chrysler's express warranty in the framework of the purchase contract? As we have said, warranties originated in the law to safeguard the buyer and not to limit the liability of the seller or manufacturer. It seems obvious in this instance that the motive was to avoid the warranty obligations which are normally incidental to such sales. The language gave little and withdrew much. In return for the delusive remedy of replacement of defective parts at the factory, the buyer is said to have accepted the exclusion of the maker's liability for personal injuries arising from the breach of the warranty, and to have agreed to the elimination of any other express or implied warranty. An instinctively felt sense of justice cries out against such a sharp bargain. But does the doctrine that a person is bound by his signed agreement, in the absence of fraud, stand in the way of any relief? . . .

The warranty before us is a standardized

form designed for mass use. It is imposed upon the automobile consumer. He takes it or leaves it, and he must take it to buy an automobile. No bargaining is engaged in with respect to it. In fact, the dealer through whom it comes to the buyer is without authority to alter it; his function is ministerial—simply to deliver it. The form warranty is not only standard with Chrysler but, as mentioned above, it is the uniform warranty of the Automobile Manufacturers Association. . . . Of these companies, the "Big Three" (General Motors, Ford, and Chrysler) represented 93.5% of the passenger-car production for 1958 and the independents 6.5%.[1] And for the same year the "Big Three" had 86.72% of the total passenger vehicle registrations. . . .

In the context of this warranty, only the abandonment of all sense of justice would permit us to hold that, as a matter of law, the phrase "its obligation under this warranty being limited to making good at its factory any part or parts thereof" signifies to an ordinary reasonable person that he is relinquishing any personal injury claim that might flow from the use of a defective automobile. Such claims are nowhere mentioned. . . .

In the matter of warranties on the sale of their products, the Automobile Manufacturers Association has enabled them to present a united front. From the standpoint of the purchaser, there can be no arms length negotiating on the subject. Because his capacity for bargaining is so grossly unequal, the inexorable conclusion which follows is that he is not permitted to bargain at all. He must take or leave the automobile on the warranty terms dictated by the maker. He cannot turn to a competitor for better security.

Public policy is a term not easily defined. Its significance varies as the habits and needs of a people may vary. It is not static and the field of application is an ever increasing one. A contract, or a particular provision therein, valid in one era may be wholly opposed to the public policy of another. Courts keep in mind the principle that the best interests of society demand that persons should not be unnecessarily restricted in their freedom to contract. But they do not hesitate to declare void as against public policy contractual provisions which clearly tend to the injury of the public in some way. . . .

In the framework of this case, illuminated as it is by the facts and the many decisions noted, we are of the opinion that Chrysler's attempted disclaimer of an implied warranty of the merchantability and of the obligations arising therefrom is so inimical to the public good as to compel an adjudication of its invalidity. . . .

The principles that have been expounded as to the obligation of the manufacturer apply with equal force to the separate express warranty of the dealer. This is so, irrespective of the absence of the relationship of principle and agent between these defendants, because the manufacturer and the Association establish the warranty policy for the industry. The bargaining position of the dealer is inextricably bound by practice to that of the maker and the purchaser must take or leave the automobile, accompanied and encumbered as it is by the uniform warranty. . . .

Under all of the circumstances outlined above, the judgments in favor of the plaintiffs and against the defendants are affirmed.

NOTES

1. Standard and Poor (Industrial Surveys, Autos, Basic Analysis, June 25, 1959), p. 4109.

Automobile Workers v. Johnson Controls, Inc.

Supreme Court of the United States

In this case we are concerned with an employer's gender-based fetal-protection policy. May an employer exclude a fertile female employee from certain jobs because of its concern for the health of the fetus the woman might conceive?

I

Respondent Johnson Controls, Inc., manufactures batteries. In the manufacturing process, the element lead is a primary ingredient. Occupational exposure to lead entails health risks, including the risk of harm to any fetus carried by a female employee.

Before the Civil Rights Act of 1964, 78 Stat. 241, became law, Johnson Controls did not employ any woman in a battery-manufacturing job. In June 1977, however, it announced its first official policy concerning its employment of women in lead-exposure work. . . .

Johnson Controls "stopped short of excluding women capable of bearing children from lead exposure," *id.*, at 138, but emphasized that a woman who expected to have a child should not choose a job in which she would have such exposure. The company also required a woman who wished to be considered for employment to sign a statement that she had been advised of the risk of having a child while she was exposed to lead. . . .

Five years later, in 1982, Johnson Controls shifted from a policy of warning to a policy of exclusion. Between 1979 and 1983, eight employees became pregnant while maintaining blood lead levels in excess of 30 micrograms per deciliter. Tr. of Oral Arg. 25, 34. This appeared to be the critical level noted by the Occupational Health and Safety Administration (OSHA) for a worker who was planning to have a family. See 29 CFR § 1910.1025 (1989). The company responded by announcing a broad exclusion of women from jobs that exposed them to lead:

> " . . . [I]t is [Johnson Controls'] policy that women who are pregnant or who are capable of bearing children will not be placed into jobs involving lead exposure or which could expose them to lead through the exercise of job bidding, bumping, transfer or promotion rights." App. 85–86.

The policy defined "women . . . capable of bearing children" as "[a]ll women except those whose inability to bear children is medically documented." *Id.*, at 81. It further stated that an unacceptable work station was one where, "over the past year," an employee had recorded a blood lead level of more than 30 micrograms per deciliter or the work site had yielded an air sample containing a lead level in excess of 30 micrograms per cubic meter. *Ibid.*

II

In April 1984, petitioners filed in the United States District Court for the Eastern District of Wisconsin a class action challenging John-

89 U.S. 1215 (1991). Opinion delivered by Justice Blackmun.

son Controls' fetal-protection policy as sex discrimination that violated Title VII of the Civil Rights Act of 1964, as amended, 42 U. S. C. §2000e *et seq.* Among the individual plaintiffs were petitioners Mary Craig, who had chosen to be sterilized in order to avoid losing her job. . . .

III

The bias in Johnson Controls' policy is obvious. Fertile men, but not fertile women, are given a choice as to whether they wish to risk their reproductive health for a particular job. Section 703(a) of the Civil Rights Act of 1964, 78 Stat. 255, as amended, 42 U. S. C. §2000e-2(a), prohibits sex-based classifications in terms and conditions of employment, in hiring and discharging decisions, and in other employment decisions that adversely affect an employee's status. Respondent's fetal-protection policy explicitly discriminates against women on the basis of their sex. The policy excludes women with childbearing capacity from lead-exposed jobs and so creates a facial classification based on gender. Respondent assumes as much in its brief before this Court. Brief for Respondent 17, n. 24.

Nevertheless, the Court of Appeals assumed, as did the two appellate courts who already had confronted the issue, that sex-specific fetal-protection policies do not involve facial discrimination. . . . The court assumed that because the asserted reason for the sex-based exclusion (protecting women's unconceived offspring) was ostensibly benign, the policy was not sex-based discrimination. That assumption, however, was incorrect.

First, Johnson Controls' policy classifies on the basis of gender and childbearing capacity, rather than fertility alone. Respondent does not seek to protect the unconceived children of all its employees. Despite evidence in the

record about the debilitating effect of lead exposure on the male reproductive system, Johnson Controls is concerned only with the harms that may befall the unborn offspring of its female employees. . . . Johnson Controls' policy is facially discriminatory because it requires only a female employee to produce proof that she is not capable of reproducing.

Our conclusion is bolstered by the Pregnancy Discrimination Act of 1978 (PDA), 92 Stat. 2076, 42 U. S. C. §2000e(k), in which Congress explicitly provided that, for purposes of Title VII, discrimination "on the basis of sex" includes discrimination "because of or on the basis of pregnancy, childbirth, or related medical conditions." "The Pregnancy Discrimination Act has now made clear that, for all Title VII purposes, discrimination based on a woman's pregnancy is, on its face, discrimination because of her sex." *Newport News Shipbuilding & Dry Dock Co. v. EEOC,* 462 U. S. 669, 684 (1983). In its use of the words "capable of bearing children" in the 1982 policy statement as the criterion for exclusion, Johnson Controls explicitly classifies on the basis of potential for pregnancy. Under the PDA, such a classification must be regarded, for Title VII purposes, in the same light as explicit sex discrimination. Respondent has chosen to treat all its female employees as potentially pregnant; that choice evinces discrimination on the basis of sex. . . .

The beneficence of an employer's purpose does not undermine the conclusion that an explicit gender-based policy is sex discrimination under § 703(a) and thus may be defended only as a BFOQ [bona fide occupational qualification].

The enforcement policy of the Equal Employment Opportunity Commission accords with this conclusion. On January 24, 1990, the EEOC issued a Policy Guidance in the light of the Seventh Circuit's decision in the present case. . . .

In sum, Johnson Controls' policy "does not pass the simple test of whether the evidence shows 'treatment of a person in a manner which but for that person's sex would be different.'" . . .

IV

Under § 703(e)(1) of Title VII, an employer may discriminate on the basis of "religion, sex, or national origin in those certain instances where religion, sex, or national origin is a bona fide occupational qualification reasonably necessary to the normal operation of that particular business or enterprise." 42 U. S. C. §2000e-2(e)(1). We therefore turn to the question whether Johnson Controls' fetal-protection policy is one of those "certain instances" that come within the BFOQ exception. . . .

The PDA's amendment to Title VII contains a BFOQ standard of its own: unless pregnant employees differ from others "in their ability or inability to work," they must be "treated the same" as other employees "for all employment-related purposes." 42 U. S. C. §2000e(k). This language clearly sets forth Congress' remedy for discrimination on the basis of pregnancy and potential pregnancy. Women who are either pregnant or potentially pregnant must be treated like others "similar in their ability . . . to work." *Ibid.* In other words, women as capable of doing their jobs as their male counterparts may not be forced to choose between having a child and having a job. . . .

V

We have no difficulty concluding that Johnson Controls cannot establish a BFOQ. Fertile women, as far as appears in the record,

participate in the manufacture of batteries as efficiently as anyone else. Johnson Controls' professed moral and ethical concerns about the welfare of the next generation do not suffice to establish a BFOQ of female sterility. Decisions about the welfare of future children must be left to the parents who conceive, bear, support, and raise them rather than to the employers who hire those parents. Congress has mandated this choice through Title VII, as amended by the Pregnancy Discrimination Act. Johnson Controls has attempted to exclude women because of their reproductive capacity. Title VII and the PDA simply do not allow a woman's dismissal because of her failure to submit to sterilization.

Nor can concerns about the welfare of the next generation be considered a part of the "essence" of Johnson Controls' business. . . .

Johnson Controls argues that it must exclude all fertile women because it is impossible to tell which women will become pregnant while working with lead. This argument is somewhat academic in light of our conclusion that the company may not exclude fertile women at all; it perhaps is worth noting, however, that Johnson Controls has shown no "factual basis for believing that all or substantially all women would be unable to perform safely and efficiently the duties of the job involved." *Weeks v. Southern Bell Tel. & Tel. Co.*, 408 F. 2d 228, 235 (CA5 1969), quoted with approval in *Dothard*, 433 U. S., at 333. Even on this sparse record, it is apparent that Johnson Controls is concerned about only a small minority of women. Of the eight pregnancies reported among the female employees, it has not been shown that any of the babies have birth defects or other abnormalities. The record does not reveal the birth rate for Johnson Controls' female workers but national statistics show that approximately nine percent of all fertile women become pregnant each year. The birthrate drops to two percent for blue collar workers over age 30. See Becker, 53 U. Chi. L. Rev., at 1233. Johnson Controls' fear of prenatal injury, no matter how sincere, does not begin to show that substantially all of its fertile women employees are incapable of doing their jobs. . . .

It is no more appropriate for the courts than it is for individual employers to decide whether a woman's reproductive role is more important to herself and her family than her economic role. Congress has left this choice to the woman as hers to make.

The judgment of the Court of Appeals is reversed and the case is remanded for further proceedings consistent with this opinion.

State, Dept. of Environ. Protect. v. Ventron Corp.

Supreme Court of New Jersey

This appeal concerns the responsibility of various corporations for the cost of the cleanup and removal of mercury pollution seeping from a forty-acre tract of land into Berry's Creek, a tidal estuary of the Hackensack River that flows through the Meadowlands. The plaintiff is the State of New Jersey, Department of Environmental Protection (DEP); the primary defendants are Velsicol Chemical Corporation (Velsicol), its former subsidiary, Wood Ridge Chemical Corporation (Wood Ridge), and Ventron Corporation (Ventron), into which Wood Ridge was merged. . . .

Beneath its surface, the tract is saturated by an estimated 268 tons of toxic waste, primarily mercury. For a stretch of several thousand feet, the concentration of mercury in Berry's Creek is the highest found in fresh water sediments in the world. The waters of the creek are contaminated by the compound methyl mercury, which continues to be released as the mercury interacts with other elements. Due to depleted oxygen levels, fish no longer inhabit Berry's Creek, but are present only when swept in by the tide and, thus, irreversibly toxified.

The contamination at Berry's Creek results from mercury processing operations carried on at the site for almost fifty years. In March, 1976, DEP filed a complaint against Ventron, Wood Ridge, Velsicol, Berk, and the Wolfs, charging them with violating the "New Jersey Water Quality Improvement Act of 1971," *N.J.S.A.* 58:10–23.1 to –23.10, and *N.J.S.A.* 23:5–28, and further, with creating or maintaining a nuisance. . . .

After a fifty-five-day trial, the trial court determined that Berk and Wood Ridge were jointly liable for the cleanup and removal of the mercury; [and] that Velsicol and Ventron were severally liable for half of the costs; . . .

The Appellate Division substantially affirmed the judgment, but modified it in several respects, including the imposition of joint and several liability on Ventron and Velsicol for all costs incurred in the cleanup and removal of the mercury pollution in Berry's Creek. . . . We modify and affirm the judgment of the Appellate Division.

94 N.J. 473 (1983). Opinion delivered by Justice J. Pollock.

I

From 1929 to 1960, first as lessee and then as owner of the entire forty-acre tract, Berk operated a mercury processing plant, dumping untreated waste material and allowing mercury-laden effluent to drain on the tract. Berk continued uninterrupted operations until 1960, at which time it sold its assets to Wood Ridge and ceased its corporate existence.

In 1960, Velsicol formed Wood Ridge as a wholly-owned subsidiary for the sole purpose of purchasing Berk's assets and operating the mercury processing plant. . . . Wood Ridge continued to operate the processing plant on the 7.1-acre tract from 1960 to 1968, when Velsicol sold Wood Ridge to Ventron. . . .

In 1968, Velsicol sold 100% of the Wood Ridge stock to Ventron, which began to consider a course of treatment for plant wastes. Until this time, the waste had been allowed to course over the land through open drainage ditches. In March 1968, Ventron engaged the firm of Metcalf & Eddy to study the effects of mercury on the land, and three months later, Ventron constructed a weir to aid in monitoring the effluent. . . .

In 1970, the contamination at Berry's Creek came to the attention of the United States Environmental Protection Agency (EPA), which conducted a test of Wood Ridge's waste water. The tests indicated that the effluent carried two to four pounds of mercury into Berry's Creek each day. . . .

On February 5, 1974, Wood Ridge granted to Robert Wolf, a commercial real estate developer, an option to purchase the 7.1-acre tract on which the plant was located, and on May 20, 1974, Ventron conveyed the tract to the Wolfs. The Wolfs planned to demolish the plant and construct a warehousing facility. In the course of the demolition, mercury-contaminated water was used to wet down the structures and allowed to run into the creek. The problem came to the attention of DEP,

which ordered a halt to the demolition, pending adequate removal or containment of the contamination. DEP proposed a containment plan, but the Wolfs implemented another plan and proceeded with their project. DEP then instituted this action. . . .

The trial court concluded that the entire tract and Berry's Creek are polluted and that additional mercury from the tract has reached, and may continue to reach, the creek via ground and surface waters. Every operator of the mercury processing plant contributed to the pollution; while the plant was in operation, the discharge of effluent resulted in a dangerous and hazardous mercurial content in Berry's Creek. The trial court found that from 1960–74 the dangers of mercury were becoming better known and that Berk, Wood Ridge, Velsicol, and Ventron knew of those dangers. . . .

II

The lower courts imposed strict liability on Wood Ridge under common-law principles for causing a public nuisance and for "unleashing a dangerous substance during non-natural use of the land." . . .

Twenty-one years ago, without referring to either *Marshall v. Welwood* or *Rylands v. Fletcher*, this Court adopted the proposition that "an ultrahazardous activity which introduces an unusual danger into the community . . . should pay its own way in the event it actually causes damage to others." *Berg v. Reaction Motors Div., Thiokol Chem. Corp.*, 37 N.J. 396, 410 (1962). . . .

We believe it is time to recognize expressly that the law of liability has evolved so that a landowner is strictly liable to others for harm caused by toxic wastes that are stored on his property and flow onto the property of others. Therefore, we . . . adopt the principle of liability originally declared in *Rylands v.*

Fletcher. The net result is that those who use, or permit others to use, land for the conduct of abnormally dangerous activities are strictly liable for resultant damages. . . .

Under the *Restatement [(Second) of Torts]* analysis, whether an activity is abnormally dangerous is to be determined on a case-by-case basis, taking all relevant circumstances into consideration. As set forth in the *Restatement:*

> In determining whether an activity is abnormally dangerous, the following factors are to be considered:
> a. existence of a high degree of risk of some harm to the person, land or chattels of others;
> b. likelihood that the harm that results from it will be great;
> c. inability to eliminate the risk by the exercise of reasonable care;
> d. extent to which the activity is not a matter of common usage;
> e. inappropriateness of the activity to the place where it is carried on; and
> f. extent to which its value to the community is outweighed by its dangerous attributes.
> [*Restatement (Second) of Torts* § 520 (1977)].

Pollution from toxic wastes that seeps onto the land of others and into streams necessarily harms the environment. . . . The lower courts found that each of those hazards was present as a result of the contamination of the entire tract. . . . With respect to the ability to eliminate the risks involved in disposing of hazardous wastes by the exercise of reasonable care, no safe way exists to dispose of mercury by simply dumping it onto land or into water. . . .

Even if they did not intend to pollute or adhered to the standards of the time, all of these parties remain liable. Those who poison the land must pay for its cure.

We approve the trial court's finding that Berk, Wood Ridge, Velsicol, and Ventron are liable under common-law principles for the abatement of the resulting nuisance and damage. . . .

III

We agree with the trial court's finding that both Berk and Wood Ridge violated the statute by intentionally permitting mercury-laden effluent to escape onto the land surrounding Berry's Creek. . . .

In an appropriate exercise of its original jurisdiction under *R.* 2:10–5, the Appellate Division found that the record overwhelmingly supported the conclusion that the mercury pollution in Berry's Creek and the surrounding area presented a substantial and imminent threat to the environment, thus satisfying the requirement for a retroactive application of the act. Our independent analysis leads us to the same conclusion. Thus, we find Berk, Wood Ridge, and Velsicol liable under the Spill Act. Ventron is liable because it expressly assumed the liabilities of Wood Ridge in their merger. . . .

As amended, the Spill Act provides: "Any person who has discharged a hazardous substance *or is in any way responsible* for any hazardous substance . . . shall be strictly liable, jointly and severally, without regard to fault, for all clean up and removal costs." *N.J.S.A.* 58:10–23.11g(c) (emphasis added). . . .

From 1967 to 1974, and thereafter, Velsicol could have controlled the dumping of mercury onto its own thirty-three-acre tract. By permitting Wood Ridge, even after it became a Ventron subsidiary in 1968, to use that tract as a mercury dump, Velsicol made possible the seepage of hazardous wastes into Berry's Creek. Furthermore, from 1960 to 1968, Velsicol was the sole shareholder of Wood Ridge and all members of the Wood Ridge Board of Directors were Velsicol employees. Velsicol personnel, officers, and directors were involved in the day-to-day operation of Wood Ridge. In addition to constant involvement in Wood Ridge's activities, Velsicol permitted the dumping of waste material on the thirty-three-acre tract. When viewed together, those facts compel a finding that Velsicol was "responsible" within the meaning of the Spill Act for the pollution that occurred from 1960 to 1968. . . .

Through the merger of Wood Ridge into Ventron, the latter corporation assumed all of Wood Ridge's liabilities, including those arising out of the pollution of Berry's Creek. See *N.J.S.A.* 14A:10–6(c). Ventron, however, did not assume Velsicol's liability.

Pursuant to the mandate of the Spill Act, see *N.J.S.A.* 58:10–23.11g(c), Berk, Wood Ridge, Velsicol, and Ventron are jointly and severally liable without regard to fault. Only Ventron and Velsicol remain in existence, and we affirm that portion of the Appellate Division judgment that holds them jointly and severally liable for the cleanup and removal of mercury from the Berry's Creek area.

IV

. . . As modified, the judgment of the Appellate Division is affirmed.

CASE 1. *Protecting Consumers Against Tobacco*

The dangers of smoking cigarettes are now generally conceded by almost everyone except tobacco companies. Far less decided is how to protect the consumer and the potential consumer of cigarettes. A major source of marketing—perhaps the major source—is newspaper advertising. Newspapers are also a major source, and probably the major source, of information transmitted to the public about the dangers of smoking cigarettes. Newspapers thus have an interest in revenue from cigarette advertising and an interest in informing the public about the dangers of what they advertise. No one needs to be reminded that most newspapers are businesses interested in making a profit but also interested in customer satisfaction.

The American Newspaper Publishers Association and the Magazine Publishers Association have appealed to First Amendment protections of the right to advertise and to present the facts as newspapers see fit in order to justify their view that this matter should be left up to each individual newspaper.

The New Republic commissioned reporter David Owen to write an article on cancer and the cigarette lobby. He wrote a piece so blunt in stating the issues and laying blame that *The New Republic*'s editors killed it. According to *USA Today*, "In the candid (and no doubt regretted) words of Leon Wieseltier, the editor who assigned it, the threat of 'massive losses of advertising revenue' did it in." The editors of *The New Republic* had been willing to report on the dangers of smoking and on the pressures brought by lobbyists, but were not willing to support the forcefulness with which Owen stated his case. Owen later published his piece in the *Washington Monthly*, where he wrote that "The transcendent achievement of the cigarette lobby has been to establish the

This case was prepared by Tom L. Beauchamp. The case is based on the following sources: Charles Trueheart, "The Tobacco Industry's Advertising Smoke Screen," *USA Today,* March 15, 1985, p. 3D; Kenneth E. Warner, "Cigarette Advertising and Media Coverage of Smoking and Health," *New England Journal of Medicine,* Vol. 312, No. 6, February 7, 1985, pp. 384–388; Sam Zagoria, "Smoking and the Media's Responsibility," *Washington Post,* December 18, 1985, p. A26; Elizabeth Whelan, "Second Thoughts on a Cigarette-Ad Ban," *Wall Street Journal,* December 28, 1985, p. 28; Sam Zagoria, "Consumer Watchdogs," *Washington Post,* April 24, 1985, p. A24; Robert J. Samuelson, "Pacifying Media Hype," *Washington Post,* October 9, 1985, pp. F1, F12.

cancer issue as a 'controversy' or a 'debate' rather than as the clear-cut scientific case that it is." Owen portrayed an industry that intentionally uses newspapers and magazines to enhance its appeal by depicting the young smoker as healthy and sexy.

According to research by Kenneth E. Warner, rejection of Owens' article is one of many cases in which American news media refused to report on smoking hazards for fear of loss of advertising revenue. This general problem prompted *Washington Post* ombudsman Sam Zagoria to chide newspapers for a failure to see the issues as moral rather than legal:

> Couldn't the newspapers of the country agree—voluntarily and collectively—to refuse cigarette advertising? Couldn't they do what is right rather than only what is not prohibited by law? Most papers take great pride in the service they render to their communities, not only in providing information but also in philanthropic activities that provide scholarships and underwrite athletic tournaments. Is not helping some youngster avert the tortures of life-shortening lung cancer even a greater gift? . . . Is there any media group for social responsibility?

Only 6 out of 1,700 daily American newspapers, Zagoria noted (using statistics taken from the *New York State Journal of Medicine*),

attempt wholeheartedly to report on the dangers of smoking.

During National Consumer Week in 1985, Zagoria wrote another column in which he took the position that the press has a "watchdog" role to play not only in government, but in consumer safety as well. Few journalists disagree with Zagoria's judgment that this role is legitimate or that a newspaper can validly choose to emphasize reporting on the risks of smoking without introducing a bias. However, Zagoria's contentions that the press has an *obligation* to promote the interests of consumers has met a hostile reaction in newspaper front offices.

Questions

1. Has Zagoria confused the industry's responsibility and the government's responsibility to protect the public with that of the media's responsibilities, as many managers at newspapers believe?
2. Does anyone's obligation to protect consumers stretch as far as Zagoria suggests?
3. Are stiff warnings on packages of cigarettes adequate to protect consumers? potential consumers?

CASE 2.   *Do Apple Computer Shareholders Need Protection?*

In 1982 the Apple Computer Inc. announced its new disk drive "Twiggy." The drive was introduced to the market in the spring of 1983, but was discontinued the following September. The price of Apple's stock dropped 25% ($8 a share) the day after the drive was scrapped. Apple stockholders brought suit against the company and some of its officers, charging them with making materially mis-

leading statements about the product in 1982 news releases. The case worked its way to the courts in May 1991.

The disk drive had a failure rate as high as 40% when it was released on the market. As a result, Apple had to recall the product. Since Apple technicians and executives knew there were problems with the disk, stockholders argued that the company's officer's should be

This case was prepared by Tom L. Beauchamp.

held morally and legally responsible not only for the quality of the product but for the decline in the stock price. The stockholders argued that they were due compensation for the money they lost.

Stockholders noted that more is at stake than a conflict of interest between management's responsibility to the stockholders and their profit objective. Stockholders rely on having materially correct information about developments they cannot confirm or disconfirm first hand. Because they were given incomplete information about the market risks of the product, stockholders believe management failed to make honest disclosures and thereby failed in its fiduciary obligations.

Questions

1. Should management put profitability above responsibilities to disclose full information to shareholders?
2. Do managers have a responsibility to pay the stockholders all or some of the money they lost?
3. Were the officers deliberately misleading investors in failing to make a full disclosure?
4. Does management's duty to the stockholders require reports of the risks of a new technology, even when so doing might jeopardize future sales of the product?

CASE 3.   *Virazole and Investor Risk*

On October 7, 1991, the U.S. Securities and Exchange Commission (SEC) filed suit against two pharmaceutical firms in a District of Columbia federal District Court, charging that the companies had falsely and misleadingly represented to investors a product's promise for combating the AIDS virus. The suit grew out of a four-year SEC investigation of ICN Pharmaceuticals and its Costa Mesa, California-based subsidiary, Viratek, Inc. The U.S. Food and Drug Administration (FDA) had approved the companies to market the drug ribavirin under the trade name Virazole, for hospital use in treating respiratory syncitial virus. In a January 1987 press conference, the companies announced that ribavirin had, in addition, proved effective in delaying the onset of AIDS symptoms in HIV-infected patients. Shortly after this announcement Viratek stock climbed from $14 a share to $70

a share. On the date the SEC filed suit, the stock declined to $5.12 a share.

The company provided a summary of its scientific findings, but AIDS advocacy groups maintained that ICN and Viratek had supplied few hard facts and test results to substantiate the conclusions announced. The SEC lawsuit alleged that corporate officials in 1987 deliberately made untrue claims regarding virazole's effectiveness. According to SEC officials, in the placebo-controlled clinical trials, the patients who received placebos had exhibited severely weakened immune systems before the trial and so were certain to fare worse than the patients receiving the drug being tested. The placebo patients also showed an unusually rapid progression toward acute AIDS symptoms. Consequently, the ribavirin patients appeared to benefit from treatment only because their AIDS

This case was prepared by John Cuddihy, based in part on a report by Tracy Thompson in *The Washington Post*, "Drug Maker Settles SEC Suit over Notification of Investors," October 8, 1991, D3.

symptoms developed more slowly in comparison with their placebo counterparts. In April 1987, the FDA declined to approve ribavirin for AIDS treatment, based on its analysis of the clinical trials. When ICN and Viratek subsequently neglected to inform investors of the results of clinical trials, the SEC launched its investigation.

After the SEC filed its lawsuit, ICN and Viratek officials signed a consent order that did not address corporate culpability, but did stipulate that the corporations involved would take precautions not to make potentially "misleading statements to investors" in the future. At the same time, company spokespersons denied any wrongdoing in the ribavirin controversy. They held that the consent order was signed only because it was the fastest way to resolve the affair. According to Viratek's CEO, "We have always operated our business with integrity, and as good citizens we will continue to do so." The company

claimed that it had a different view of the scientific evidence than did the SEC and that it had no moral or legal obligation to make disclosures to investors of the sort proposed by the SEC. Investors did not file suit in the case.

Questions

1. What should Viratek have told stockholders and potential stockholders? Should any information disclosure include a full, conservatively stated estimate of the scientific evidence?
2. Did Viratek officials manipulate potential investors into buying the stock through an incomplete disclosure?
3. Assuming trade secrets are involved, is the scientific evidence proprietary to the company and also confidential? If so, could hard facts and test results be disclosed without damage to the company?

CASE 4.   *OSHA Noncompliance and Security*

TMW Corporation produces three-quarters of the world's micro-synchronizers, an integral part of apartment vacuum systems. This corporation has plants mostly in the Midwest, although a few are scattered on both the East and West Coasts. The plants in the Midwest employ Electronic Worker's Union members under a contract that became effective last August and is in force for three years. This union is strong and the employees will do anything to preserve and maintain the strong union benefits that have been won.

Last year an OSHA official visited the St. Louis plant and discovered several discrepancies with the standards established by the OSH Act, including the absence of safety gog-

gles on employees who weld tiny wires together, and also an automatic shut-off switch on the wire-splicing machine. OSHA issued warnings to TMW of the noncompliances and informed company officials that it would impose drastic fines if they did not correct them.

The company immediately proceeded to correct the problems. They had to shut parts of the Midwest plants down on a rotating basis to alter the wire-splicing machines. These measures upset the union members, because the employer laid off older employees, not the new trainees on the machines. They threatened a walkout.

The safety goggles presented the company with another OSHA compliance hur-

---

This case was prepared by Professor Kenneth A. Kovach. Printed with permission.

dle. When told of the need to wear their goggles, the welders refused, saying they could not see as well. The welders said they would take responsibility for not wearing the goggles. The unions backed the welders in their refusal.

Questions

1. Was the TMW Corporation wrong in laying off the senior employees?
2. Should the company force the welders to comply with the safety goggle requirements? Since the welders refused to comply and assumed responsibility, is the company released of all responsibility in the event of an accident?
3. Should OSHA intervene and fine those responsible for any violations of OSHA standards? Is this case too minor for such intervention?

Suggested Supplementary Readings

Consumer Protection

CAVANILLAS MUGICA, SANTIAGO. "Protection of the Weak Consumer Under Product Liability Rules." *Journal of Consumer Policy* 13 (1990).

LUTHANS, FRED, and others. *Social Issues in Business.* New York: Macmillan, 1984. Part III.

OWEN, DAVID G. "Rethinking the Policies of Strict Products Liability." *Vanderbilt Law Review* 33 (1980).

PROSSER, WILLIAM L. "The Assault Upon the Citadel (Strict Liability to the Consumer)." *Yale Law Journal* 69 (1960).

SCHWARTZ, ALAN. "Views of Addiction and the Duty to Warn." *Virginia Law Review* 75 (April 1989).

VISCUSI, W. KIP, "Toward a Proper Role for Hazard Warnings in Products Liability Cases." *Journal of Products Liability* 13 (1991).

Worker Protection

BEAUCHAMP, TOM L. *Case Studies in Business, Society, and Ethics.* 3rd ed. Englewood Cliffs, N.J.: Prentice Hall, 1993. Chaps. 1, 5.

BRUENING, JOHN. "Risk Communication." *Occupational Hazards* 52 (October 1990).

EZORSKY, GERTRUDE, ed. *Moral Rights in the Workplace.* Albany: State University of New York Press, 1987.

GIBSON, MARY. *Workers Rights.* Totowa, N.J.: Rowman and Littlefield, 1983.

GOLDSMITH, WILLIS. "The Expanding Scope of Employers' Duties Under the Hazard Communication Standard and State and Local Right-to-Know Laws." *Employee Relations Law Journal* 12 (Spring 1987).

HUNT, VILMA R. "Perspective on Ethical Issues in Occupational Health." In *Biomedical Ethics Reviews 1984,* edited by R. Almeder and J. Humber. Clifton, N.J.: Humana Press, 1984.

MURRAY, THOMAS, and RONALD BAYER. "Ethical Issues in Occupational Health." In *Biomedical Ethics Reviews 1984,* edited by R. Almeder and J. Humber. Clifton, N.J.: Humana Press, 1984.

SASS, ROBERT. "The Worker's Right to Know, Participate, and Refuse Hazardous Work: A Manifesto Right." *Journal of Business Ethics* 5 (April 1986).

WALTERS, VIVIENNE, and MARGARET DENTON. "Workers' Knowledge of Their Legal Rights and Resistance to Hazardous Work." *Industrial Relations* 45 (Summer 1990).

Environmental Protection

ATTFIELD, ROBIN. *The Ethics of Environmental Concern.* New York: Columbia University Press, 1983.

BLACKSTONE, WILLIAM T., ed. *Philosophy and Environmental Crisis.* Athens: University of Georgia Press, 1974.

BRIDGMAN, HOWARD. *Global Air Pollution: Problems for the 1990s.* New York: Columbia University Press, 1992.

ENGEL, J. RONALD, and JOAN GIBB ENGEL, eds. *Ethics of Environment and Development.* Tucson: University of Arizona Press, 1991.

Environmental Ethics. "An Interdisciplinary Journal

Dedicated to the Philosophical Aspects of Environmental Problems." 1979 to present.

GIBSON, MARY. *To Breathe Freely: Risk, Consent, and Air.* Totowa, N.J.: Rowman and Littlefield, 1985.

GOODIN, ROBERT E. "Property Rights and Preservationist Duties." *Inquiry* 33 (1991).

HARRIS, CHRISTOPHER, and others. "Criminal Liability of Federal Hazardous Waste Law: The 'Knowledge' of Corporations and their Executives." *Wake Forest Law Review* 23 (1988).

HOFFMAN, W. MICHAEL, and others, eds. *Business, Ethics, and the Environment: The Public Policy Debate.* New York: Quorum Books, 1990.

————, eds. *The Corporation, Ethics, and the Environment.* New York: Quorum Books, 1990.

LEOPOLD, ALDO. "The Land Ethic." In *A Sand County Almanac.* New York: Oxford University Press, 1966.

MILLER, ALAN S. *Gaia Connections: An Introduction to Ecology, Ecoethics, and Economics.* Totowa, N.J.: Rowman and Littlefield, 1991.

NAESS, ARNE. *Ecology, Community, and Lifestyle,* trans. by D. Rothenberg. New York: Cambridge University Press, 1990.

REGAN, TOM, ed. *Earthbound: New Introductory Essays in Environmental Ethics.* New York: Random House, 1984.

ROLSTON, HOLMES, III. *Philosophy Gone Wild: Environmental Ethics.* Buffalo, N.Y.: Prometheus Books, 1991.

SAGOFF, MARK. *The Economy of the Earth.* New York: Cambridge University Press, 1990.

SCHERER, DONALD, and THOMAS ATTIG, eds. *Ethics and the Environment.* Englewood Cliffs, N.J.: Prentice Hall, 1983.

SKORPEN, ERLING. "Images of the Environment in Corporate America." *Journal of Business Ethics* 10 (1991).

Investor Protection

ALMEDER, ROBERT F., and MILTON SNOEYENBOS. "Churning: Ethical and Legal Issues." *Business and Professional Ethics Journal* 6 (Spring 1987).

BROWN, DONNA. "Environmental Investing: Let the Buyer Beware." *Management Review* 79 (June 1990).

DAMM, RICHARD E. "A Question of Bias." *Best's Review* 86 (December 1985).

HEACOCK, MARIAN, and others. "Churning: An Ethical Issue in Finance." *Business and Professional Ethics Journal* 6 (Spring 1987).

HINNANT, WALTER R. "Fiduciary Duties of Directors: How Far Do They Go?" *Wake Forest Law Review* 23 (1988).

HOFFMAN, W. MICHAEL, and RALPH J., McQUADE. "A Matter of Ethics." *Financial Strategies and Concepts* 4 (1986).

MOORE, JENNIFER. "What Is Really Unethical About Insider Trading?" *Journal of Business Ethics* 9 (March 1990).

"Note: Recent Trends in the Organization and Regulation of Securities Markets." *Financial Market Trends* 46 (May 1990).

SCHADLER, F. P., and J. E. KARNS. "The Unethical Exploitation of Shareholders in Management Buyout Transactions." *Journal of Business Ethics* 9 (July 1990).

WILLIAMS, OLIVER, and others. *Ethics and the Investment Industry.* Savage, Md.: Rowman and Littlefield, 1989.

Chapter Five

Rights and Obligations of Employers and Employees

TRADITIONALLY, BUSINESS FIRMS are organized hierarchically, with production line employees at the bottom and the CEO at the top. Also the interests of the stockholders are given priority over the interests of the other stakeholders. However, much recent literature presents a challenge to these arrangements, especially to underlying classical economic assumptions whereby labor is treated as analogous to land, capital, and machinery, that is, as replaceable and as a means to profit. Employees primarily want to be treated as persons who are genuine partners in the business enterprise. They want decent salaries and job security, as well as appreciation from supervisors, a sense of accomplishment, and fair opportunities to display their talents. Many employees are also interested in participating in planning the future directions of the company, defining the public responsibilities of the corporation, evaluating the role and quality of management, and—most especially—helping to set the tasks assigned to their jobs.[1] These new developments in labor relations are all to the good, but they must be understood in light of a very different tradition whereby an employee is clearly subordinate to the employer, is legally obligated to obey the employer's orders, and has few rights except the right to quit.

STATUS AND SCOPE OF EMPLOYEE RIGHTS

In the traditional view, the freedom of the employee to quit, the freedom of the employer to fire, and the right of the employer to order the employee to do his or her bidding define the essence of the employment contract. The legal principle behind the traditional view is called the *employment-at-will principle*. This principle says that in the absence of a specific contract or law, an employer may hire, fire, demote, or promote an employee whenever the employer wishes. Moreover, the employer may act with justification, with inadequate justification, or with no justification at all. In the selection that opens this chapter, Patricia Werhane considers the arguments for and against the employment-at-will doctrine.

Over the years this master-servant relationship, which is at the core of the employment-at-will doctrine, has been legally constrained. Once unions were given legal protection, collective bargaining produced contracts that constrained the right of employers to fire at will. Employees who were protected by union contracts usually could be fired only for cause and then only after a lengthy grievance process. During the height of the union movement, the chief protection against an unjust firing was the union-negotiated contract. However during the 1980s and early 1990s the percentage of the U.S. workforce belonging to unions fell into the teens, and as a result the protection offered by the union-negotiated contract covers millions fewer workers.

Some might argue that the decline in the number of U.S. workers who belong to unions has not significantly increased the number of employees who are at risk of an unjust dismissal. These people argue that a large number of enlightened companies have adopted policies that provide the same type of protection against unjust dismissal as was previously found in union-negotiated contracts. Moreover, where such policies exist they have the force of law. For example, on May 9, 1985, the New Jersey Supreme Court held that Hoffman-LaRoche Inc. was bound by job security assurances that were implied in an employee manual. The manual seemed to pledge that employees could be fired only for just cause and then only if certain procedures were followed. Hoffman-LaRoche argued that although the company manual gave company policy, adherence to it was voluntary and not legally enforceable. The court, however, said employers cannot have it both ways without acting unfairly and so illegally. Hoffman-LaRoche had to reinstate an employee who had been fired on grounds that his supervisor had lost confidence in his work.

In response to this and similar rulings, a number of corporations have taken steps to make it more difficult for employees to use company manuals and policy statements to protect their jobs. Some are simply eliminating the manuals and dismantling their grievance procedure apparatus. Sears Roebuck and other employers have their employees sign a form declaring that they can be fired "with or without just cause." Finally several companies have developed internal procedures that examine every dismissal case as though it were a specific contract with a just-cause-for-firing provision in it.[2]

Others point out that during the 1980s and early 1990s, certain grounds for firing employees have been made illegal by federal or state law. Antidiscrimination statutes protect workers from being fired because of their race or sex, because they are handicapped, or because of age. Federal law also protects workers from being fired because they resist sexual advances from their bosses or refuse to date them. The protection given employees from this and other forms of sexual harassment is discussed in Chapter 6.

Although such laws are needed to curb past abuses, they are not always clear nor always effective. For example, are people who test positive for the virus that causes AIDS handicapped under the law? In the recession of 1991 many highly qualified white collar middle management employees who were over 40 and laid off found it virtually impossible to find similar employment elsewhere. Rightly or wrongly, many of these people thought their age was a factor in their inability to obtain similar employment.

Yet another important development is the evolution of a common law protection to one's job if an employee disobeys an employer on the grounds that the employer ordered him or her to do something illegal or immoral. The notion that employees should not lose their jobs because they refuse to behave illegally or immorally might seem obvious, but as the two recent New Jersey cases included in this chapter show, the situation is more complex than it might appear. On some issues there is near unanimity that a course of action is right or wrong. But on other matters there is considerable difference of opinion. As we saw in the discussions of the Ford Pinto and the *Challenger* in Chapter 2, conflicts concerning what is morally appropriate often occur between managers and engineers. As a practical matter, a large corporation cannot allow employees to refuse to abide by a corporate decision whenever it conflicts with a personal moral position. On the other hand, the public must support employees who refuse to obey an order or accept a decision that threatens the public with serious harm. *Potter v. Village Bank of New Jersey* and *Warthen v. Toms River Community Memorial Hospital* illustrate how the courts try to balance the public interest and legitimate business concerns on this issue.

Even more important, these laws do not provide sufficient protection for what many employees consider their most important workplace right—the right to a job. From the perspective of most employees, the most important contribution of capitalism is providing work. Job security is often ranked higher than increased pay in terms of what employees most want from employers. The desire for job security is captured in employee demands that workers have a right to a job and that this right deserves protection. The claim that a person has a right to a job has two components. First, workers believe they have a right to a job in the first place. Second, as employees continue to work at a job, they believe they have a right to retain that job. Provision of the right to a job in the first place is usually considered to be the responsibility of government and is not discussed here. However, the notion that employees gain rights to a job that they have been holding is a new idea and is the subject of the article by Jack M. Beermann and Joseph William Singer. Beermann and Singer attempt to show that the traditional understanding of property rights in employment relationships is biased in favor of the employers. They propose two alternative ways to view the employer-employee relationship that would give workers a property right in their job. Beermann and Singer argue that workers gain property rights to their jobs from their reasonable reliance on a relationship with the employer who as owner has made access to the property available in the past and from the fact that jobs themselves should be recognized as legally protected property interests.

DRUG TESTING AND THE RIGHT TO PRIVACY

Although a right to one's job may be the workplace right that employees most value and want honored, they believe they have other rights that should be honored as well. Many people believe that the rights guaranteed by the Bill of Rights in the Constitution are rights that each U.S. citizen has in all aspects of his or her life. But this is not the case. Americans are protected against government infringements of the Bill of Rights but they are not protected against corporate infringement of these rights. The Bill of Rights does not apply within the corporation. Thus there is no right to free speech within the corporation. Many believe that such a gap in the protection of the Constitution for individual citizens seems unjustified. They argue that since business activity takes place within U.S. society, business activity should be conducted consistent with the Bill of Rights. Others argue, however, that applying the Bill of Rights in the corporate setting would create great inefficiencies because discipline would break down. Besides there are many companies in the United States for which a person can work, but there is only one U.S. government. Thus it is more important to have a Bill of Rights to protect individuals from government than to have a Bill of Rights to protect individuals from their boss.

Debates regarding the extent and scope of employee rights are commonplace in U.S. business. Theft by employees and customers is a huge problem accounting for billions of dollars in losses every year. Until recently a common technique for deterring theft was to subject employees to polygraph (lie detector) tests. However, doubts about their accuracy and arguments that the tests invaded the privacy of employees led to a legal prohibition on their use, enacted initially by some states and then by the federal government. Now employers are turning to honesty tests that are based on statistical correlations between the answers to certain questions on the honesty test and the likelihood that an employee will commit theft.[3] The same issues of accuracy and invasion of privacy that confronted use of polygraphs confront the use of honesty tests. However, the American Psychological Association has certified the validity of some tests, and the tests have escaped serious legal challenge up to the present time.[4]

Another serious problem facing corporate America is the rising cost of health insurance. In order to reduce their insurance premiums, many corporations are taking a great interest in the personal habits of their employees. Some will not hire people who smoke.[5] Others will insist that employees lose weight, exercise, and abstain from risky activities off the job.[6] These attempts to regulate individual employee behavior off the job are extremely controversial and perhaps the most controversial is the attempt by corporations to prevent employees from using drugs. Many corporations now give drug tests to prospective employees.[7] If they fail, they are not hired. An increasing number of companies are giving drug tests to persons they already employ. If any of these employees fail, companies take different actions. Some fire the employee outright; some retest the employee after a period of supposed abstinence and fire the employee if he or she tests positive again; still others insist that employees enroll in a drug treatment program. However, there is a common thread to all these approaches: The use of drugs even off the job will not be tolerated.

Rules that prohibit an employee from smoking either tobacco or marijuana violate both an employee's right to liberty and an employee's right to privacy. Employers argue that such violations are necessary with respect to tobacco in order to keep the cost of health insurance under control and are necessary with respect to marijuana and other drugs to protect customers, other employees, and the public at large. Are these arguments decisive?

In most matters the authority of the boss ends at the company gate. What employees do on their own time is the employees' business. However, some conduct off the job may affect the employees' performance on the job or interfere with the employer's right to make a living by damaging the perception of the company and driving away customers. Even recreational use of relatively harmless drugs like marijuana are alleged to have these effects. In his article, Mark A. Rothstein documents the economic harm to employers caused by drugs, how drug testing works, what it measures, and how accurate it is. He then assesses the legal arguments against drug testing and concludes that drug testing is legal so long as it is reasonable. Rothstein ends by describing the elements of a legal, ethical, and effective drug-testing program.

Despite the fact that the vast majority of companies do some drug testing and the fact that well-constructed drug-testing programs are legal, a few companies still do not test for drugs. One of the most remarkable is the Drexelbrook Engineering Company, a 300 employee company in Horsham, Pennsylvania, that designs and manufactures electronic systems that measure and control levels of hazardous chemicals. Drexelbrook's vice-president and general counsel, Lewis Maltby, admits that one of its employees on drugs could cause a disaster as tragic as the one that occurred in Bhopal, India, but despite the huge potential legal liability, they still won't test their employees for drugs. According to Maltby, the fundamental flaw with drug testing is that it tests the wrong thing. "A realistic program to detect workers whose condition puts the company or other people at risk would test for the condition that actually creates the danger. . . . A serious program would recognize that the real problem is worker's impairment and test for that."[8] A philosophical defense of Maltby's position is provided by the article by Joseph DesJardins and Ronald Duska.

Although the notion of testing for job impairment rather than drug use is appealing from the ethical point of view, there are certainly some occupations—teaching and law, for example—in which tests for impairment would be difficult to devise. In other situations testing for job impairment might be inordinately expensive. How much would it cost a school district to test its school bus drivers every school day? Thus the outlook for employee rights is mixed. Current trends indicate that a larger number of employee rights will be recognized and that some that are currently recognized will be expanded. On the other hand, the pressure on corporations to control cost will continue and, as a result, so will the pressures to avoid expenditures for honoring rights.

WHISTLEBLOWING AND THE DUTY OF LOYALTY

To suggest that the moral problems in employee-employer relationships are all about employee rights would, of course, be one-sided. No less important are employee obligations. Employees have moral obligations to respect the property of the corporation, to abide by employment contracts, and to operate within the bounds of the company's procedural rules. Indeed it is legally established that an employer has a right to loyalty. This right is captured in the so-called law of agency.

For example, Section 387 of the Restatement of Agency (1958) expresses the general principle that "an agent is subject to his principle to act solely for the benefit of the principle in all matters connected with his agency."[9] Specifically, the "agent is also under a duty not to act or speak disloyally," and the agent is to keep confidential any information acquired by him as an employee that might damage the agent or his business.[10]

Even if an employer is legally entitled to loyalty, is he or she morally entitled to loyalty? Ronald Duska has argued that loyalty can apply only in a relationship that transcends self-interest and must be based on a stable relationship of trust and confidence. The relationship of an employee to the corporation is not that kind of relationship, in his view, because it is a relationship of mutual self-interest. In this form of relationship, the employee does not have an obligation of loyalty to the employer.

If a corporation takes the position advocated by Milton Friedman in Chapter 2, then Duska's argument seems persuasive and indeed Friedman himself would probably accept it. As you recall, in Friedman's view the only concern of the firm is to manage its assets in order to obtain profits for the stockholders and the only concern of the workers is to get the best working conditions they can. Loyalty simply isn't in the picture. But if a broader stakeholder theory like William M. Evan and R. Edward Freeman's is adopted, the corporation does have genuine obligations to employees. In a stakeholder-managed firm, the relationship between the employer and the employee is more likely to be characterized as a relationship of trust and confidence that transcends self-interest. If Duska accepted this characterization of the stakeholder account, these firms would be morally entitled to loyalty.

However, the duty of loyalty is not absolute. That an employee should be loyal is a *prima facie* duty. The object of the employee's duty must be deserving if the duty is genuine and overriding rather than *prima facie*. The virtue of loyalty does not require that the employee accept blindly the boss or corporate cause to which he or she is loyal. Nor does it require that when loyalty to the employer conflicts with other duties—such as protecting the public from harm—the duty to the employer is always overriding. Indeed, when a corporation is engaged in activity that is seriously wrong, employees may have a higher obligation to be disloyal to their employer and blow the whistle.

In her article, Sissela Bok attempts to define whistleblowing and to indicate the conditions under which it is justified. Since from the business organization's standpoint, whistleblowing is an accusation against the hierarchy and hence disloyal, Bok argues that the evil being exposed should be immediate and specific and should be done from a moral motive. Whistleblowing should benefit the public; should be done only after internal channels within the business firm have been exhausted; should treat the one accused fairly; and usually should be done openly, rather than anonymously.

Well-publicized cases of whistleblowing bring public acclaim to the whistleblower but little else. The whistleblower finds it nearly impossible to get an equivalent job in the same industry and difficult enough to get another job at all. Many corporate executives share the sentiments of the former president of General Motors James M. Roche.

Some of the enemies of business now encourage an employee to be disloyal to the enterprise. They want to create suspicion and disharmony, and pry into the propri- etary interests of the business. However this is labelled—industrial espionage, whistleblowing, or professional responsibility—it is another tactic for spreading dis- unity and creating conflict.[11]

Although Roche illegitimately confuses industrial espionage and whistleblowing, the attitude expressed by his remarks explains why it is so difficult for the whistleblower to find another job. In her article Susan Sauter argues for the need for a federal law to protect whom she calls the health and safety whistleblower. After documenting the in- adequacy of current protection in state law and common law, she describes what a fed- eral statute would look like and how it could be implemented.

TRADE SECRETS AND THE DUTY OF CONFIDENTIALITY

We have already seen that among the specific legal requirements of an employee duty of loyalty is the duty to keep confidential information that might cause finan- cial damage to one's employer if it were made public. One of the best examples of such information is a trade secret. The legal definition of a trade secret is provided in Section 757 of the *Restatement of Torts*. A *trade secret* is a pattern, device, formula, or compilation of information used in business and designed to give the employer an opportunity to obtain an advantage over his or her competitors who neither know nor use the information. A trade secret is a type of intellectual property. Moreover, to qualify as a trade secret the information must be the particular secret of an owner and not general secrets maintained in a trade. In addition, a trivial advance or difference in a known formula, process, or device is not a trade secret. Needless to say, many bitter court fights turn on whether an advance or difference really is trivial.

A trade secret is different from a patent. A *patent* is issued for an invention by the federal government and gives the patent holder the right to use or license oth- ers to use the invention for seventeen years. At the end of the seventeen-year period the patent expires and the invention enters the public domain. An unpatented in- vention is almost always treated as a trade secret by a company, but trade secrets can include industrial processes, lists of customers, market data, and research pro- posals. In their article, Robert E. Frederick and Milton Snoeyenbos discuss the ad- vantages and disadvantages of obtaining a patent as opposed to keeping something a trade secret.

The mere intent of an employer to treat something as confidential is not suf- ficient to make it a trade secret. There is no trade secrecy if a process can be ascer- tained either by the application of general skill and knowledge to a sold product, for example, by analyzing a product to discover its chemical formula, or by what is called *reverse engineering,* that is, by an engineering examination that starts with a known product and works backward to discover the process through which the product was produced. For example, a computer engineer might be able to dis- cover how a computer head is made by examining the layers and types of film de- posited on the head of a computer.[12]

Furthermore, it is not necessarily an employee's disclosure that can cause loss of secrecy. The company's own carelessness can be the cause of the problem, and courts therefore expect companies to take reasonable precautions to protect themselves, even against discovery by corporate spies. When the Kellogg Company stopped its famous plant tours in April 1986, the primary reason was a fear that the tours created a legitimate opportunity for industrial spies to take the tours and steal state-of-the-art manufacturing secrets.[13]

Issues about whether a change in a process is trivial or nontrivial or whether a company has taken adequate precautions to protect a trade secret, although important, pale beside the issue of what rights the corporation has to protect its trade secrets from being given to competitors by former employees. Under the law, an employee leaving a job cannot utilize or disclose a trade secret. For example, the formula for Coca-Cola is the property of the Coca-Cola Company. If an employee gave the formula to Pepsi, a trade secret would have been disclosed. Although the Coca-Cola example is clear, most claims of former employee disclosure of trade secrets are more complicated. If not framed carefully, what might be called the "Coca-Cola Model" of trade secret disclosure may prove more misleading than illuminating.

The "Coca-Cola Model" assumes there are no issues surrounding the company's claim to ownership of the formula, device, or process that a former employee is accused of disclosing. But often the former employee helped create or advance the formula, device, or process through his or her own ingenuity or skill. Indeed the former employee might have played an essential role in the development of what the company claims to be its trade secret. The greater part an employee played in creating or otherwise improving the confidential information or property, the more the employee seems to have a right to use it, and the less an employer seems to have a right to claim sole possession. Thus when an employee leaves to take a position at another firm, serious conflicts can arise over proprietary information.

The chief bone of contention is what belongs to the employer and what belongs to the employee. For tangible items such as the formula for Coca-Cola, the issue can be settled rather easily. The item belongs to the company and cannot be disclosed. Indeed most companies require that employees sign statements giving the company ownership of anything they invent. However, much proprietary information is not as tangible as a formula but is general knowledge about processes, management methods, and research directions that has become part of the employee's knowledge and thinking. Since it is this general knowledge that makes the employee valuable to another firm, to always decide in favor of protecting the employer's trade secret would in effect prevent the employee from taking a job elsewhere. Such a system would have the effect of reducing many employees to the status of indentured servants. Thus, as seen in *Futurecraft Corp. v. Clary Corp.* at the end of this chapter, the court must balance an employer's right to protect its trade secrets with the employee's right to leave a firm for a better opportunity elsewhere. Indeed, many courts have dropped the assumption that the transfer of intellectual property is simple theft and have adopted a "balancing model" of trade secret protection according to which the employee's mobility and opportunity should be weighed against the employer's rights in determining the scope of protection afforded to confidential information. Such courts have attempted to weigh a public policy favoring the protection of trade secrets against a competing public policy favoring the interest of an employee to use skills and knowledge acquired in a field in order to earn a livelihood.[14]

The operating principle of the balancing model is that the employer's interest in maintaining the secret must outweigh both the interest of the employee in using the knowledge to earn a living and the interest of the public in having the knowledge transmitted. On this principle, if the employee would be absolutely foreclosed from competition, whereas the employer in losing the trade secret would be only minimally damaged, the court would deny trade secret protection. The rationale for this approach is the goal of not placing employees in a situation of servitude while not precluding incentives for the firm to innovate.

Note too that the balancing principle would also permit the employer's interest in maintaining the secret to be outweighed by a public interest in having the knowledge disclosed. This aspect of the "balancing model" has nothing to do with employees' rights but has to do instead with the debate in the technology and innovation literature over whether the strict protection of trade secrets stifles or promotes technological discovery and U.S. competitiveness. Those who maintain that "strict trade secret protection stifles innovation" argue that if the flow of scientific information were sped up, firms would be forced to be more innovative and U.S. industry would be more competitive against European and Japanese multinationals. Those who believe that "strict trade secret protection promotes innovation" argue that innovation requires large capital outlays and that companies won't make that investment unless the courts will protect their trade secrets.

The model of balancing the competing interests of employees and employers is a utilitarian and pragmatic model that has emerged through a U.S. court system charged with weighing such competing interests. This model may not be better than the older model fashioned on the goal of protecting the employer's property. However, one thing is clear from the recent analysis of trade secrets: The issues about trade and proprietary information are more complex and more extensive in business than has been appreciated in the past.

As the courts have moved toward the "balancing model," some corporations have decided to manage the protection of their trade secrets internally rather than relying on the courts to do it for them. In his article, Michael S. Baram attempts to sketch a management policy that protects a corporation's intellectual property while remaining sensitive to the bona fide rights of employees.

In conclusion, many types of obligations to past employers might be violated when an employee takes a new position, including those established by contractual obligations, keeping promises, truthfulness, confidentiality, and loyalty. Any assessment of what a former employee owes to the employing company would involve a careful scrutiny of each of these obligations. Moreover, any discussion of employee rights must include employee obligations as well. Thus if the courts begin to recognize a property right to a job, it may become appropriate for the courts to balance that employee right with stricter rules for protecting an employer's trade secrets and enforcing the corresponding employee's duty to keep such information confidential.

NOTES

1. Brian Dumaine, "Who Needs a Boss?" *Fortune*, May 7, 1990, pp. 52–60.

2. See "Fear of Firing," *Forbes* December 2, 1985, p. 90; and John Hoerr, and others, "Beyond Unions: A Revolution in Employee Rights in the Making," *Business Week*, July 8, 1985, p. 72.

3. Peggy Schmidt, "Lie-Detector Tests in a New Guise," *New York Times*, October 1, 1989, pp. 29, 31.

4. Gilbert Fuchsberg, "Prominent Psychologists Group Gives Qualified Support to Integrity Tests," *Wall Street Journal*, March 2, 1991.

5. "If You Light Up on Sunday, Don't Come in on Monday," *Business Week*, August 26, 1991, pp. 68–72.

6. "Privacy," *Business Week*, March 28, 1988, pp. 61–68.

7. See, for example, Ron Winslow, "Study May Spur Job-Applicant Drug Screening," *Wall Street Journal*, November 28, 1990, p. B1.

8. Lewis Maltby, "Why Drug Testing Is a Bad Idea," *Inc.*, June 1987, p. 153.

9. Quoted from Phillip I. Blumberg, "Corporate Responsibility and the Employee's Duty of Loyalty and Obedience," in *Ethical Theory and Business,* edited by Thomas Beauchamp and Norman E. Bowie (Englewood Cliffs, N.J.: Prentice Hall, 1979), 307.

10. Ibid., pp. 308, 307.

11. James M. Roche, "The Competitive System, to Work, to Preserve, and to Protect," *Vital Speeches of the Day* (May 1971), p. 445.

12. See *Videotronics, Inc. v. Bend Electronics,* 564 F. Supp. 1471 at 1475 (Nev. 1983); *Sarkes Tarzian, Inc. v. Audio Devices Inc.,* 166 F. Supp. at 265; *Aetna Building Maintenance Co. v. West,* 39 Cal. 2d 198, 206 (1952); *Hollingsworth Solderless Terminal Co. v. Turley,* 622 F. 2d 1324 at 1334; *Kewanee Oil Co. v. Bicron Corp.,* 416 U.S. at 476.

13. Damon Darlin, "Kellogg Is Snapping Its 80 Year Tradition of Cereal Tours," *Wall Street Journal*, April 10, 1986, p. 1.

14. See, for example, *Cambridge Filter v. Intern Filter Company, Inc.* 548 F. Supp. 1301 at 1307 (1982).

Employment at Will and the Question of Employee Rights

Patricia H. Werhane

EMPLOYMENT AT WILL

The principle of employment at will, hereafter abbreviated EAW, is a common-law doctrine stating that in the absence of law or contract employers have the right to hire, promote, demote, and fire whomever and whenever they please. The principle was stated explicitly in 1887 in a document by H. G. Wood entitled, *Master and Servant.* Wood said, "A general or indefinite hiring is prima facie a hiring at will."[1] The term "master-ser-

From Patricia H. Werhane, *Persons, Rights, and Corporations* (Englewood Cliffs, NJ: Prentice Hall, 1985). Reprinted by permission.

vant," a medieval expression referring to employer-employee relationships, persists in some areas of the law even today.[2] In this country EAW has been interpreted as the rule that employers whose employees are not specifically covered by statute or contract "may dismiss their employees at will . . . for good cause, for no cause, *or even for causes morally wrong*, without being thereby guilty of legal wrong."[3]

EAW has been upheld in the courts of this country as recently as 1982 when the Supreme Court of Hawaii refused to question this principle. In that case EAW was invoked to justify the dismissal of a hotel employee allegedly fired so that she would be unavailable to testify to federal investigators who wanted to find out about the Hawaiian hotel practice of exchanging room price information. Even though the court recognized the abusiveness of the employer demand, the court ruled that the hotel had the right to discharge her "at will."[4] The firing of Daisy Alomar, the social worker, and George Geary whose casing proved faulty were also upheld by the courts on the basis of Employment at Will. It should be noted that other recent court decisions have ruled in favor of the employee. For example, Ms. Nees, the woman who was fired for fulfilling jury duty was reinstated after taking the case to court, as were Mr. Sventko and Ms. Kelsay, the persons who filed worker's compensation claims. Some courts have even overreacted against the principle of EAW. However, in none of these instances has the employee been reinstated on the basis that EAW is a questionable doctrine. Rather it was decided that public policy was violated in each rescinded case.

Defending the Principle of EAW

While the Principle of EAW may appear to be unjust in some cases where it is invoked, it has been strongly defended not only in the courts but in philosophical theory as well. The principle is often justified for one or more of the following reasons:

1. The right to private ownership guarantees that employers may employ whomever and whenever they wish.
2. Employee rights that go beyond EAW often conflict with employer freedoms.
3. EAW defends employee and employer rights equally, in particular the right to freedom of contract.
4. In freely taking a job, an employee voluntarily commits herself to role responsibilities and company loyalty, both of which are undermined by the intrusion of certain employee rights.
5. Extending rights in the workplace often interferes with the efficiency and productivity of the business organization and thus in the long run reduces the benefits of free enterprise.
6. Employee rights require institution by public policy, such as legislation and/or regulation. This spells the end of voluntarism in the marketplace, which is essential to capitalism.

Let us examine each of these arguments in more detail. The principle of EAW is sometimes maintained purely on the basis of rights to private ownership. It is contended that the right to freedom and to private ownership are valid entitlements, and that they include the right freely to use and improve what one owns, including all aspects of one's business, so long as one does not violate the basic moral rights of others. Whether one defines "basic moral rights" as merely negative rights or as more positive entitlements remains an issue in spelling out the limits of property rights. Traditionally, at least from a libertarian perspective, basic moral rights have by and large been conceived as negative rights. According to this view, because employers have these property rights, an employer has the right to dispose of an employee's work freely because that work changes the employer's production. In dismissing or demoting employees, the employer is not denying rights to *persons*.

Rather, the employer is simply excluding that person's *labor* from the organization. Instituting employee rights restricts the employer's legitimate freedom to do what she wishes with her production, thus violating her property rights.

Second, provisions that extend employee rights beyond EAW conflict with or override employer rights. In particular, extending employee entitlements by instituting due process procedures when firing or demoting, allowing freedom of expression when this might conflict with employer interests (as in cases of whistle blowing), or expanding employee privacy rights when information valuable to the business is at stake, conflict with an employer's right to do as she pleases. The employee in these circumstances enjoys *greater* freedom than the employer because the employee can act as he pleases while the employer is restricted by the institutional strictures of employee rights.

This reasoning leads to the third defense of EAW. Contrary to what is sometimes contended, EAW defends employee and employer rights equally. An employer's right to hire and fire "at will" is balanced by a worker's right to accept or reject employment. The institution of any employee right that restricts "at will" hiring and firing would be unfair unless this restriction were balanced by a similar restriction controlling employee job choice in the workplace. Such programs would do irreparable damage by preventing both employees and employers from continuing in voluntary employment arrangements. These arrangements are guaranteed by the right to "freedom of contract," which, one will recall, is the right of persons or organizations to enter into any voluntary agreement with which all parties of the agreement are in accord. Employee rights restrict freedom of contract and thus are clearly coercive, because they force persons and organizations to accept behavioral restraints that place unnecessary constraints on voluntary employment agreements.

Fourth, an employee freely commits himself to certain loyalties and responsibilities when taking a job. This voluntary commitment is threatened by the expansion of employee rights. Extending rights in the workplace implicitly implies that in fact an employee need not be loyal to his employer, a phenomenon which, if true, would mean the end of employee responsibility and accountability as it is commonly expected in employee-employer relationships. More will be said about loyalty and role responsibilities in the next chapter.

EAW is most often defended on practical grounds. From a utilitarian perspective hiring and firing "at will" is deemed necessary in productive organizations to ensure maximum efficiency and productivity, the goals of such organizations. To disrupt this would defeat the primary purposes of free enterprise organizations in a capitalist economy. In the absence of EAW unproductive employees, workers who were no longer needed, and even troublemakers would be able to stay in the employ of a business. Even if a business *could* rid itself of undesirable employees, the lengthy procedure of due process required by an extension of employee rights would be costly, it would be distracting to other employees, thus slowing production, and would be harmful to the morale of other employees. Permissive whistle blowing is especially bothersome, because it calls the employer's integrity into question and may harm innocent workers allegedly involved in the activity in question.

The strongest reason for not instituting a full set of employee rights in the workplace, at least in the private sector of the economy, has to do with the nature of business in a free society. Businesses are privately owned voluntary organizations of all sizes from small entrepreneurships to large corporations. As such, they are not subject to the restrictions governing public and political institutions. Political procedures such as due process, needed to safeguard the public against the arbitrary exercise of power, do not apply to voluntary private organizations. Extending these to the workplace would require public policies interfering both with the right of persons and organizations not to be forced into activities not of their choosing and with their correlative freedom of contract. Thus the institution of a full set of employee rights would spell the end of free enterprise as it should be, because guaranteeing rights in the workplace would require restrictive legislation and regulation. Corporations would lose their freedom. Voluntary market arrangements, so vital to free enterprise and guaranteed by freedom of contract would be sacrificed for the alleged public interest of employee claims. Therefore, according to defenders of EAW, this principle is crucial to preserve employer and employee freedoms, to insure the continued economic success of free enterprise, which benefits employees as well as employers, and to safeguard the voluntarism that is essential to democratic capitalism.

EMPLOYEE RIGHTS AND A REFUTATION OF EAW

The foregoing defenses of the practice of EAW make a number of questionable judgments. First, a defense of EAW on the basis of property rights appears to ignore the fact that employees are persons and thus require, *morally* require, different treatment than robots or property. The argument that EAW is a free, efficient practice of voluntary organizations is also based on the questionable assumptions: (a) that employers in these organizations do not exercise arbitrary power in their positions, and (b) that "at will" employment practices are fair and noncoercive. So EAW may eschew the exercise of freedom in favor of the employer. There is also a

failure to recognize that the absence of rights in the workplace puts employees at an unfair disadvantage vis-à-vis other employees, a disadvantage that creates harmful inequalities and thus injustices in the workplace. Let us examine these criticisms.

Property Rights

EAW has been defended on the grounds that every person has the right to own and accumulate property and the freedom to dispose of what they own as they see fit. To say that employers have the right to dispose of what they own "at will" is a legitimate claim that follows from the right to private ownership. But two preconditions for this right are important. First, ownership rights are equal rights. Employers do not, for example, have the right to dispose of their properties if or when this activity violates the equally important rights of employees.

Second, . . . property rights are neither basic rights nor absolute rights. In a free society if ownership is defined as ownership of material possessions, then property rights can hardly be rights on the same par with, or overriding, say, the right to free expression in the form of legitimate whistle blowing. This is because free expression, the prima facie right to speak out within the constraints of decency, national security, and the avoidance of slander, is part of the basic right to freedom, even when freedom is defined merely as the negative right to be left alone. Not being able to express oneself and to tell the truth would interfere with one's right to be left alone. In a democratic society property rights are based on the right to freedom, in this case the freedom to acquire unowned or available property when such acquisitions do not harm others. This right too, is grounded on the moral right to the freedom to do as one pleases so long as one does not harm the freedom of others. But because of this, rights to ownership cannot override rights to freedom, because the latter are preconditions for the legitimacy of the former.

Some contemporary theorists will complain that this argument criticizing EAW is based on a seventeenth-century Lockean notion of property and property ownership. The relation of an employer to property today is much different from that of earlier times. Today employers are, by and large, corporations. The corporation is owned by stockholders who have little or no say in the management and hence in the employment practices of the corporation, and is run by managers who hire and fire but who do not own the business and are themselves employees. A defense of employee rights cannot be sustained by criticizing abuses of property rights, but must be argued for on other grounds.

This criticism correctly points out the enormous changes that have occurred in employer-property relationships. But the evolution of property from single ownership to the corporate arrangement is not fully reflected in the employment policies embedded in EAW. This is because those in a position to hire—foremen, managers and executives—are given the so-called privileges of ownership to treat the noncontractual employees under their jurisdiction "at will" when firing, promoting, or demoting them. The question is, *do* these "at will" employment practices violate the rights of employees? That this is the case will be shown in considering the weakest point in the defense of EAW: the contention that labor is a form of property.

Persons, Labor, Property, and Firing Without Cause

The relationship between a person or an institution and the property he, she or it owns is different from the relationship between a person and his or her work. A person (or an insti-

tution) is distinct from his or her material possessions, but it cannot be said that a person is entirely separate from his or her labor. Disposing of the labor of the employee is not the same as disposing of a product of labor or of other property. It is the confusion of these that may be the basis for the allegation that arbitrarily firing employees does not violate their rights. Let us see why this is so. . . .

The term "labor" is sometimes used collectively to refer to the work force as a whole. Labor also refers to the activity of working. Other times it refers to the productivity or "fruits" of that activity. The latter, the productivity of working, is what is traded for remuneration in employee-employer work agreements. Productivity, labor in the third sense, might be thought of as a form of property or at least as something convertible into property. For example, suppose an advertising agency hires an expert known for her creativity in developing new commercials. This person trades her ideas, the product of her work (thinking), for pay. The ideas are not literally property, but they are tradeable items because, when laid out on paper or on television, they become a form of property and are separable from their creator. But the activity of working (thinking in this case) cannot be sold or transferred. Caution is necessary, however, in thinking of productivity as identical to material property, for there is an obvious difference between productivity and material property. Productivity requires the past or present activity of working, and thus the presence of the person performing this activity.

Person, property, labor, and productivity are all different in this important sense. A person can be distinguished from his or her possessions, a distinction that allows for the creation of legally fictional persons such as corporations or trusts that can "own" property. But persons cannot be distinguished from their working, and this activity is necessary for creating productivity, a tradeable product of one's working. Incidentally, this is why slavery violates more rights than the nationalization of private property without compensation. Slavery does not merely deny an employee pay in trade for productivity; it also treats persons as property.

Returning to the principle of EAW, EAW allows the employer to fire or demote employees without giving any reasons at all. In allowing such actions this doctrine confuses the activity of working with its productivity. In dismissing an employee, a well-intentioned employer aims to rid the corporation of the productivity of that employee. The problem in normal employment situations is that an employer must also eliminate the employee's opportunity to work at the place of employment, that is, the activity that generated the productivity, and thus must fire persons. So ordinarily when an employer treats the productivity of working arbitrarily she treats persons arbitrarily as well.

When an employer fires persons without cause or without giving reason, the employer is presuming that he or she has the right to decide what should be done to his or her business even when exercising that right violates the rights of other persons. This presumption is in itself highly questionable. Treating employees "at will" is analogous to considering an employee as a piece of property at the disposal of the employer, because arbitrary firing treats rational persons as things. When I "fire" a robot, I do not have to give reasons, because a robot is not a rational being. It has no use for reasons. On the other hand, if I fire a person arbitrarily I make the assumption that she does not need reasons either. And this logic is faulty, for if I have hired rational adults, then in firing them I should treat them as such. This does not preclude firing. It merely asks employers to give reasons for their actions, for reasons are appropriate when one is dealing with persons. Later we shall argue that employers should have *good*

reasons for dismissing employees. Here the criticism is of EAW's position that employers do not have to give *any* reasons whatsoever. This does not mean that the employer does not have reasons. He may even have good ones, but unless he feels morally obliged to state them, he is not treating his employee as a rational adult.

Freedom of Contract and the Equal Exercise of Freedom

Let us examine EAW from another perspective which involves the notion of freedom. Voluntary private organizations argue that they should be as free as possible from coercive and restrictive procedures. The requirement of due process before firing might be termed such a procedure because it restricts the decisions and action of voluntary organizations by (a) requiring impartial mechanisms for evaluating employee treatment, and (b) restraining certain actions of employers vis-à-vis employees, thereby (c) interfering with their freedom of contract. However one needs to evaluate the role of the employer and the coercive nature of "at will" employment in voluntary organizations more carefully before accepting that conclusion.

Despite the fact that private employers are independent businesses and employment arrangements are voluntarily entered into by employees, employers are in a position of power relative to employees. This in itself is not a good reason to restrict employer activities. Rather, the possible abuses of this power are what is at issue. By means of his or her position, the employer can arbitrarily hire or fire an employee. Of course the employee can arbitrarily quit too, but an "at will" employee is seldom in a position within the law to inflict harm on an employer by resigning. Legally sanctioned "at will" treatment by employers of employees can, on the other hand, harm employees.

The following analogy illustrates this point. When a business goes bankrupt it is commonly supposed, whether or not there is good reason, that the business deserved this bankruptcy because of mismanagement or some other failing. Persons connected with bankruptcy often have difficulties afterwards borrowing money or getting new jobs because it is suspected that they are bad managers. It is assumed, rightly or wrongly, that the owner or manager in question *deserved* this loss.

Similarly, when one is demoted or fired the reduction or loss of the job is only part of what the employee suffers. It is commonly taken for granted that he or she deserved the demotion or firing, whether or not this is the case. Without a hearing or an objective appraisal of this treatment, an employee cannot appeal if he or she is mistreated, nor has the employee any way to demonstrate to others that he or she was fired arbitrarily or without good reason. Fired or demoted employees, therefore, have more difficulty getting new jobs than those who are not fired, even when the dismissal was unwarranted. The absence of due process procedures in the workplace, in particular those that would afford objective hearings about employee treatment, places an employee at an unfair disadvantage relative to other workers, for those who do not deserve to be fired are treated the same as those who do. That is, it is assumed in both cases that the firing was warranted.

EAW could be defended as the best available policy for protecting the rights of employers and employees. However, this is not the case. The Principle of EAW is to the advantage of the owner or employer and to the unfair disadvantage of the employee, because the employee's so-called "right" to change jobs is restricted by whether or not the employee was fired or demoted, while the employer's right to fire or demote is not constrained. Thus, because of EAW, employers can exercise their freedom with less restraint

than employees, at least in regard to hiring/accepting employment or firing/quitting.

Worse, "at will" practices violate the very right upon which EAW is based. Part of the appeal of EAW is that it protects an employer's and an employee's freedom of contract. It is the contention that instituting employee rights is coercive because this violates freedom of contract by forcing employers and employees involuntarily to change their employment practices. But "at will" employment practices are or can be, coercive. This is because when employees are fired without reason they are placed in a disadvantageous and personally harmful position not of their choosing and perhaps not justified by their behavior. They are forced to find new employment with the stigma of having been fired when their dismissal may have been unjustified. Of course not all fired employees are in the same position. Some deserve to be fired for a variety of reasons. But when an employer need not give reasons for dismissals, there is no way to distinguish those who deserve to be fired from those who do not. The latter, then, may be said to have been coerced, because they are undeservedly out of a job and have no means of redress. According to the principle of freedom of contract, employment agreements are voluntary arrangements agreed upon by both parties. But it is hard to imagine that rational people would agree in advance to being fired arbitrarily in an employment contract. It is, then, difficult to defend "at will" employment practices on the basis of freedom of contract since these practices themselves are, or can be, coercive to at least one party of the "agreement."

If "at will" employment can be coercive, why do persons agree to such employment by accepting jobs? Sometimes a person must take a job for economic reasons, because jobs are scarce, or because his or her talents are limited. In these cases the prospective employee often thinks he is not in a position to bargain for his rights at the time of employment. Sometimes employees are simply not fully informed about their rights as "at will" employees. Often employment is accepted because a potential employee enters into the employment agreement in good faith, assuming good faith and fair treatment in return on the part of the employer. None of these reasons can justify subsequent arbitrary treatment of employees by employers.

These reasons point to the fact that freedom of contract, like other freedoms, is a prima facie right. It cannot be used as an excuse to limit other freedoms without contradicting its own premises. This much is clear from earlier arguments. Moreover, it is also clear that freedom of contract cannot be appealed to as a reason for restricting other employee rights unless the employee was fully informed about such restrictions at the time of employment. This sort of information is often missing in employment agreements. In any case, freedom of contract cannot be used to override another basic moral right even if this should be agreed upon in a voluntary employee-employer contract.

Utilitarian Arguments

"At will" treatment of employees is also advocated as a means of maximizing efficiency. Unproductive or disruptive employees harm business and hamper productivity. A company must have the liberty to hire whomever and whenever they wish. But what is to prevent an employer from hiring a mentally retarded son-in-law or firing a good employee on personal grounds, actions which are themselves damaging to efficiency? Unless they have to give reasons for hiring or firing, there is no assurance that some employers will not misuse their "at will" privilege to the detriment of the business.

Many utilitarians would not accept the foregoing defense of EAW as a good utilitar-ian argument. They would say that one cannot justify harming someone, in particular restraining their freedom, for the sake of some collective or corporate benefit. Some of these philosophers would make the more restricted argument that one can restrain a person's freedom only if that action would alleviate very great collective or corporate harms, or more narrowly, only if that action reduced a greater collective loss of freedom than the freedom to be given up. Economic harms which affect a large majority override individual claims to rights, then, only in serious instances when these harms endanger societal freedoms. One may use this argument, however, to criticize EAW as well. One could say that abolishing EAW in the workplace would alleviate harms—harms to employees disadvantaged by the absence of rights. While EAW does positive harm to employees, specifically to their freedoms, instituting employee rights would not harm an employer's freedom. Because of the serious nature of this harm to employees, the benefits of employee moral rights outweigh any alleged loss of productivity or efficiency that might result from abolishing EAW. Thus the institution of moral rights in the workplace may be defended from a utilitarian perspective.

Voluntarism versus Public Policy

Finally, critics of employee rights argue that the extension of rights in the workplace requires enforcement through public policy. But this is not necessarily the case. Voluntary institution of employee moral rights in the workplace is feasible and would preclude regulation since it would make public policies unnecessary. Voluntary employee rights programs would, moreover, be consistent with the ideals of democratic capitalism, which defends the cooperative and free institution of equal rights for all persons in all settings. Employers are rightfully wary of employee rights, because they compare our voluntary system to that of Northern Europe where, by law, employees virtually cannot be fired. But this is because European law focuses on *employee* claims while neglecting equal *employer* rights. A voluntary program that institutes *equal* employer and employee rights, one set of rights complementing and balancing the other, would avoid this difficulty. . . .

The principle of EAW, then, can neither be defended as a principle that preserves equal moral rights nor on utilitarian grounds. It advocates treating persons as forms of property, it eschews equal freedoms, and is to the unfair disadvantage of the employee.

NOTES

1. H. G. Wood, *A Treatise on the Law of Master and Servant* (Albany, N.Y.: John D. Parsons, Jr., 1877), p. 134.
2. For example, until the end of 1980 the *Index of Legal Periodicals* indexed employee-employer relationships under this rubric.
3. Lawrence E. Blades, "Employment at Will versus Individual Freedom: On Limiting the Abusive Exercise of Employer Power," *Columbia Law Review*, 67 (1967), p. 1405, quoted from *Payne v. Western*, 81 Tenn. 507 (1884), and *Hutton v. Watters*, 132 Tenn. 527, S.W. 134 (1915).
4. *Parnar v. Americana Hotels, Inc.* Hawaii, 652 P. 2d 625 (1982).

Baseline Questions in Legal Reasoning: The Example of Property in Jobs

Jack M. Beermann and Joseph William Singer

PROPERTY RIGHTS AND CONTROL OF THE WORKPLACE

Employers as Owners and Workers as Non-Owners

The employment-at-will doctrine rests on a particular construction of property rights as well as contract rights. It protects employers' property rights against claims by workers that they have a right of access to employers' property.[1] The social vision underlying this scheme identifies employers as owners of property and employees as non-owners. The

employer, as owner, has the power to determine the terms on which others are granted access to the employer's property. Like any landowner, the employer has the power to grant non-owners a license to enter her property. Moreover, licenses are presumed to be revocable at will. If a non-owner wants continued access to property owned by another, she must purchase that right by negotiating a contract that provides for continued access, buying an easement or leasing the property. The presumption is that the owner retains the right to exclude non-owners from her property unless she explicitly gives up that right.

From Jack M. Beermann and Joseph William Singer, "Baseline Questions in Legal Reasoning: The Example of Property in Jobs," *Georgia Law Review*, V. 23:911, pp. 946–956. Reprinted by permission.

When courts define employers' property rights in the workplace as the baseline, workers' arguments in favor of job security are doomed before they can be made. This is because constructions of social relationships that define one party as an owner and the other party as a non-owner inevitably bias the analysis in favor of the owner. They do so by creating a presumption that owners retain whatever rights to control contested resources that they do not give away.

What alternative constructions of property rights in employment relationships would shift the baseline and constitute a social vision favoring worker interests? We propose two alternative ways to conceptualize the employer-employee relationship. First, we argue that workers gain property rights in the workplace from their reasonable reliance on a relationship with the owner that made access to the property available in the past. Our discussion here uses some examples from the common law to illustrate that non-owners are sometimes conceptualized as owners and granted protection against unjustified loss of access to property on which they have relied in the past. Second, we argue that jobs themselves should be recognized as legally protected property interests.

The Reliance Interest in the Workplace

A more communitarian social vision of property rights would start from the assumption that property rights are almost always shared, rather than unitary, and that they ordinarily are created in the context of relationships. This is true in the most important areas of social life, including the family, the workplace, and housing. It is especially true in the context of labor relations. Instead of identifying one party as the owner and the other as the non-owner, we should focus on the social relationships the workplace comprises and define

the just contours of those relationships. In this view, property rights do not represent zones of autonomy for actors who control sets of social resources. Instead, they arise out of relationships of mutual dependence. Under this understanding of market relationships, property rights are normally distributed between the parties to those relationships. This means that, for some purposes, it is useful to describe the "non-owner" as possessing property rights in the relationship. We should understand the employment relationship as a device for allocating control over resources between the parties. In this view, property rights in employment relations are shared and distributed among the parties to the relationship. The allocation of property rights between employers and employees is based on a variety of factors, including their contributions to the joint enterprise, their needs and the needs of others, and notions of what kinds of labor relations are just. With a relational conception of property rights as a baseline, workers may have legitimate claims to protection from unjustified discharge.

In a variety of instances, the common law has redefined nonowners as owners. For example, mortgage law developed to protect the interests of landowners who conveyed their property to others in return for a loan. The borrower/owner conveyed title to the property to the lender, which the lender agreed to return if the borrower paid the debt by a certain day. . . . This arrangement vested all current property interests in the lender, with the borrower retaining only a future interest. Originally, the lender exercised the right of the owner to possess the property as a way to earn rents and collect profits. Later, the lender allowed the mortgagor to possess the property, although the lender retained the right to take possession at any time. If the borrower did not repay the loan on the appointed day, his future interest would be forfeited. This was an absolute rule and would apply even if the mortgagor could not find the mortgagee to pay him. If the borrower did not repay the debt, the lender would retain fee simple ownership of the entire property, even if its value far exceeded the amount of the unpaid debt.

The equity courts intervened to regulate these transactions. They allowed the borrower to recover title to the property even if he had not complied with the terms of the right of entry. By the seventeenth century, mortgagors had the right to recover both title and possession after full title had shifted to the mortgagee by tendering the amount of the unpaid debt. The mortgagee was allowed to cut off this right by foreclosure procedures. The equity courts decided that the lender's only legitimate interest in the land was as security for the debt. They therefore ignored the terms of the contractual arrangements which vested title to the property in the lender and gave the borrower the right to get the land back for the amount of the debt. The courts called the borrower's right to buy back the land before foreclosure the "equity of redemption." This equity of redemption was a new, judicially-created property right.

It is important to recognize how extraordinary this intervention in the market was. We have become so accustomed to treating mortgages in this way that we fail to appreciate the historical basis of the equity of redemption. At the time the equity courts heard the case, they had before them an owner, the lender who held title to the land, and a non-owner, the borrower and *prior owner*, who now had no legal rights *of any kind* in the land. The courts ignored entirely the parties' contractual arrangement and the current owner's legal title. They seized from the lender/owner all rights in the land other than the right to force a sale of the property to assure repayment of the loan. The courts then vested in the nonowner title to the property (if the borrower could

repay the loan) which the court had appropriated from the owner/lender. If the borrower could not repay the loan, the court forced the owner to sell the property and seized the proceeds of sale above the amount of the unpaid loan from the title holder and gave it to the borrower. Thus the courts redefined the borrower/non-owner's interest as a property interest, which they called the "equity of redemption."

This arrangement recognizes property interests in the party to a relationship who, by the terms of the contractual arrangement, has no legally enforceable property interests. It divides property interests between the parties, calling the mortgagor the "equitable owner" and the mortgagee the "legal owner." It strips the mortgagee of absolute control over the property and limits the mortgagee's rights to those of a secured lender. Of the bundle of numerous rights that ordinarily accompany fee simple ownership of property, the mortgagee was allowed to retain only one—the right to sell the property to recover the unpaid loan. At the same time, the courts identified the borrower as an owner whose rights are defined in relation to those of the lender. The process of redefining property rights in this situation was so successful that the legal method of accomplishing the transaction changed to fit the new allocation of rights so that instead of absolute title, the homeowner now grants the lender an interest denominated a "mortgage." The lender who holds title is not thought of as an owner at all, but merely a secured lender.

The equity of redemption protects the interests of homeowners in relying on continued access to their homes. And far from usurping the role of the legislature in creating new property rights, the courts' creation of this property right has been ratified by legislation implementing and regulating the foreclosure procedure in a manner protecting the homeowner's right to redeem the property before the foreclosure sale. This legislation regulates the contractual arrangement between the borrower and lender by making the right of redemption before foreclosure nondisclaimable. Calling this right a property right invests the borrower with the honorific title of mortgagor or "homeowner." This language of property rights expresses the moral claim of the mortgagor to exert control over property purportedly transferred to another.

Similarly, adverse possession law defines the adverse possessor, the non-owner, as the owner of property. The rules in force shift ownership from the title holder to the adverse possessor if the possession has been sufficiently open, longstanding and without the owner's permission. As with mortgage law, the rules in force transfer property from the true owner to a non-owner who has relied in the past on a relationship with the owner that made access to the property possible. As with the equity of redemption, the adverse possessor is implicitly vested with the moral or economic claim of the owner. The owner has effectively abandoned the property by not exercising her right to bring a trespass claim and the adverse possessor has acquired property interests because of longstanding use. The adverse possessor has acted in a way that would create property rights in unowned property. Despite the true owner's legal title, we shift our sympathies to the adverse possessor and conceptualize the adverse possessor as the "owner."

The rules in force treat the adverse possessor, who is in fact a *trespasser*, as the owner, because we assume the adverse possessor would experience a significant loss if the property were taken away—perhaps even a blow to her personhood. In contrast, the true owner would experience renewed possession as a windfall gain—a benefit less substantial than the harm to the adverse possessor. The courts create property rights in the non-owner because judges believe that society benefits by

forcing a transfer. This benefit is based on the belief that the adverse possessor will use the property more productively and that the adverse possessor will be harmed more than the true owner if the property is taken away. The harm to the adverse possessor is thought to be greater than the harm to the true owner because the adverse possessor, not the true owner, develops personhood interests in long use of the property.

Land reform is a legislative realignment of property rights to protect individuals who need continued access to land for an affordable price. Our example is the Hawaii land reform program at issue in the Supreme Court case, *Hawaii Housing Authority v. Midkiff.*[2] In Hawaii, many homeowners leased the land on which their homes sat from a few rich and powerful landholders. Under the scheme that the Supreme Court upheld in the case, the legislature granted to the leaseholders the right to purchase the land from the owners, against the wishes of the owners. The Hawaii legislature thought that the needs of the tenants (the possessors) were more important than the property rights of the landowners. The legislature effectively treated the lessees as the owners of the property and the lessors as mere investors. As with adverse possessors and mortgagors, the tenants here were invested with the moral claims of the owner to possession of the property, while the landlord was relegated to mere compensation.

These examples all illustrate legal rules that allocate property rights between the parties to an ongoing relationship. We learn from these examples that the rules in force sometimes implement a social vision of property rights that focuses on the needs of both parties to the relationship that may go beyond and even contradict the terms of their agreement. The rules may protect the needs of the less powerful party to a relationship by guaranteeing access to property on which that person has relied in the past. This communitarian social vision of property rights is embodied in property doctrines that realign property interests in the face of contracts that apparently grant rights to stronger parties. In these cases, the law grants a weaker, more vulnerable party ownership of property that has been contractually allocated to the stronger party.

A communitarian social vision might explain these examples in two ways. First, they may rest on the notion that property rights between the parties to an ongoing relationship are open to realignment in the social interest. Adverse possession may protect the interests of one who has made productive use of property. Homeowners are granted the equity of redemption both to encourage home ownership and to prevent the social dislocation that may occur from loss of home or family wealth. The Hawaii land reform program was intended to correct a market failure by creating a competitive market for fee simple ownership of land.

Second, property rights are subject to realignment when the interests of the parties are such that a non-owner needs the property more than the recognized owner and the relationship is such that we consider it fair to place this obligation on the owner. The homeowner, the long-term tenant, and the adverse possessor depend on access to land, and have relied on a relationship with the owner that made such access possible. They depend on continued use of the property and need it more than the true owner. Their interest is likely to be personal. In contrast, the title holder's interest in these cases is likely to be merely financial, and therefore fungible. In allocating control over property between the parties, the law grants a certain amount of protection to both parties. In so doing, it recognizes that the more vulnerable party may have personal interests in continued access to the property, while the true owners' interests are merely financial.

These same arguments apply to workers' interests in their jobs. These personhood and productivity arguments apply to employees as well as adverse possessors, mortgagors and long-term tenants. Employees can claim that after long tenure in a job, the employee should be granted rights to continue working. Job security induces the employee to care about the success of the common enterprise. Job security may increase productivity by promoting trust among market participants and increasing the sense of participating in a common enterprise. A long-term employee suffers more from the harm of losing a job than the owner gains from the right to fire. After a long term of employment, the worker needs continued access to employment more than the owner needs the right to exclude. Employees, because of their relative inability to diversify, might be more dependent on continued access than the employer is on the ability to exclude through firing. These needs may exist regardless of the contract between the parties, and perhaps, should overcome the contract—especially if the contract is itself the product of disparities in power.

Employment-at-will is justified by a construction of property rights that emphasizes the employer's property interests and ignores the property interests of the employee. The difference between judicial treatment of employment-at-will, on the one hand, and judicial treatment of mortgages and adverse possession, on the other hand, revolves around the concept of ownership. In the employment case, the employee is conceptualized as a non-owner while the manager is, or represents, the owner. The loss of managerial control is valued more highly than the loss of a job *partly* because the job is not conceptualized as a property interest, while control of the workplace (and of one's land) *is* conceptualized as an aspect of ownership of the workplace. The choice of a baseline may therefore significantly affect our assessment of the appropriate contours of the relationship between the parties.

Jobs as Property

An alternative conceptualization of a communitarian property regime might recognize property rights in the activities themselves. Under this conception, workers would not only be "part-owners" of the workplace, but would have a separate property interest in their jobs. This reconceptualization of jobs as property would be consistent with Charles Reich's landmark article, *The New Property*.[3] In that article, Reich argued that government benefits in modern society serve many of the same functions as traditional property and should therefore be recognized as property which cannot arbitrarily be taken away. It is now well settled that government jobs may be protected under the fourteenth amendment as property interests that cannot be taken without due process.[4] The same reasoning should apply to jobs in the private sector—a worker's job is likely to be her most valuable asset and the worker may depend on it for her continued ability to remain a functioning member of society.[5]

Congress recently passed a plant closing notification bill which requires reasonable notice as a prerequisite to layoffs of large groups of employees.[6] This requirement treats jobs like tenancies, which cannot be ended without notice. A notification requirement effectively treats jobs as property interests that are defeasible only on certain conditions.

Property rights in jobs could exist in a variety of forms. The narrowest definition would prohibit employers from firing employees for reasons of malice or in bad faith. A broader definition, advocated here, would adopt the just cause termination principle. Employees have the right to keep their jobs unless the employer can demonstrate just cause to fire

them. Other conceptions of workers' property rights are also conceivable under which the right to fire would be as limited as the right to remove an owner from real property. This definition could grant employees an almost absolute right to continued employment. Under this construction, the employer could only sever the employment relation by buying the job back from the employee. The employer would have to pay the employee enough to induce the employee to give up the right to continued employment. The employee may forfeit the job for extreme misconduct, as for instance, real and personal property owners may forfeit property if the property is used for, or acquired with the proceeds of, distribution of illegal drugs. And perhaps abandonment or inattention could lead to forfeiture as in adverse possession.

A conception of property in jobs could grant employees the right to manage the business. This conception would treat employers like mortgagees or bondholders, whose interests are generally limited to recovering a reasonable return on their investment. Employees could then exercise other property rights, including the right to manage the business. Under this redefinition of property rights, investors, like creditors or shareholders, would be granted rights sufficient to protect their legitimate interests in their investments. Indeed, our entire conception of property rights in the workplace may need radical restructuring to bring democratic values into the workplace. The separation of ideals of democracy from the marketplace in general is difficult to justify.

Jobs should be conceptualized as property rights to invest employees with the moral authority of owners whose right of access to their livelihood may not be destroyed without justification. The threat of firing, and the general lack of job security, places control over important aspects of the employee's life in the employer's hands. Hierarchical social structures, such as the employer-employee relationship, deny to the parties at the lower end of the hierarchy important aspects of their personhood. Indeed, the employees' ability to try to change the workplace for the better may be hampered by the potential for management reaction against an employee who "rocks the boat" even if the employee has useful ideas.

Conceptualizing jobs as property shifts the baseline for discussing what constitutes justice in employment relations. If we applied the empirical and moral claims underlying mortgages, adverse possession, and land reform to the employment relation, our assessment of the relative costs and benefits would shift. Employees, like adverse possessors, invest their personhood in their jobs. Loss of a job is a serious blow, not only because it entails loss of possibly the largest portion of one's wealth—a steady income—but also because it entails loss of part of one's identity. Firing thus should be viewed as a significant harm. In contrast, a just cause rule would still allow employers to fire workers for cause, interfering in the employers' control of the workplace only by making their firing decisions subject to worker challenge. Viewed in this light, a just cause rule protects both the employers' and the employees' property interests while the at-will rule ignores the employees' property interests entirely. Defining the workers' interests as property interests changes the baseline by investing those interests with the moral authority of ownership. It therefore shifts the burden of proof by forcing the proponent of employment-at-will to justify a rule that allows an employer to strip an employee of property rights arbitrarily and without just cause. Stated in this way, the argument for employment-at-will appears to be weak indeed.

NOTES

1. Compare Charles Reich, "The New Property," 73 *Yale L.J.* 733 (1964) (government benefits should be considered and protected as property to prevent government control over the integrity of the individual). The courts' reluctance to move beyond traditional property rights has been noted by Cass Sunstein in his recent article, "Constitutionalism After the New Deal," 101 *Harv. L. Rev.* 421 (1987). For an excellent analysis of employers' property rights claims underlying labor law, see J. Atleson, *Values and Assumptions in American Labor Law* (Amherst: University of Massachusetts Press, 1983).

2. 467 U.S. 229 (1984). Professor Williamson Chang has argued that the Hawaii land reform program actually represented a redistribution from a relatively disempowered group —native Hawaiians—to a politically powerful group. Conversations with Williamson Chang, Professor of Law, University of Hawaii School of Law (1989).

3. See Reich, Note 1. See also Clyde W. Summers, "Labor Law as the Century Turns: A Changing of the Guard," 67 *Neb. L. Rev.* 7, 15–16 (1988) (describing nascent conceptions of property rights in jobs).

4. See *Board of Regents of State Colleges v. Roth*, 408 U.S. 564, 576–77 (1972) (holding that fourteenth amendment requires a hearing prior to nonrenewal of nontenured state teacher's contract if teacher can show that he was deprived of "property" interest in continued employment). But see *Bishop v. Wood*, 426 U.S. 341 (1976) (holding that existence of a property interest in continued employment depends on state law, rather than mutual understandings growing out of the employment relationship).

5. In the public sector, the Supreme Court has recognized the new property, but only to the extent that the government benefit in question is an entitlement that is protected by law from termination or alteration. Need is not a factor in determining whether a property interest exists. This approach can be criticized for failing to recognize how important need is to Reich's analysis. See Beermann, *Government Official Torts and the Takings Clause: Federalism and State Sovereign Immunity*, 68 B.U.L. Rev 277, 301–02, 303 & n.110, 304–05 (1988).

6. Worker Adjustment and Retraining Notification Act, 29 U.S.C.A. §§ 2101–2109 (West 1988), stating that an employer shall not order a plant closing or mass layoff until the end of a 60-day-period after the employer serves written notice thereof to affected employees.

Drug Testing in the Workplace: The Challenge to Employment Relations and Employment Law

Mark A. Rothstein

THE PROBLEM OF DRUG ABUSE

Drug abuse is one of America's most pervasive, serious, tragic, and seemingly intractable social problems. According to the National Institute on Drug Abuse (NIDA), over seventy million Americans have experimented with illegal drugs and twenty-three million Americans are currently using some type of illegal substance.[1] Over twenty-two million Americans have experimented with cocaine and ten million are cocaine-dependent. In the last ten years there has been a 200% increase in cocaine-related deaths and a 500% increase in admissions to drug abuse treatment programs.[2]

The abuse of legal drugs, especially alcohol, also is a source for great concern. Over 100 million Americans use alcohol and there may be as many as eighteen million adult alcoholics in the United States. Alcohol is involved in nearly half of all automobile accidents and homicides, one-fourth of all suicides, and four-fifths of all family court cases. . . .[3]

With regard to illicit drug use, more educated and affluent people had a significant decline in drug use, while less educated and poor people had little or no decline in drug use. With the exception of heroin and crack (a smokable form of cocaine) used by the poor, the use of illegal drugs, although still high, seems to have peaked. . . .

Drug abuse exacts a heavy toll from society: from the health care system, from the criminal justice system, and from drug abusers and their families. Drug abuse is also very costly to employers. According to one estimate, ninety percent of drug and alcohol abusers work and a significant number of employees use drugs on the job.

Different occupations often tend to have a particular type of drug problem. For instance, marijuana use on the job is most prevalent in the entertainment/recreation industry (17%), construction industry (13%), personal services (11%), and manufacturing of durable goods (10%).[4] On the other hand, alcohol abuse is most prevalent among "blue collar" workers.[5] Undoubtedly, age, education, income, and other characteristics of the work force are responsible for these trends.

Regardless of the drug involved, it is clear that employee drug abuse is very costly to employers. The costs of employee drug abuse borne by employers can be divided into six categories: (1) lost productivity; (2) accidents and injuries; (3) insurance; (4) theft and other crimes; (5) employee relations; and (6) legal liability.

From Mark A. Rothstein, "Drug Testing in the Workplace: The Challenge to Employment Relations and Employment Law," *Chicago-Kent Law Review* 63:3 (1987). Reprinted by permission of ITT Chicago-Kent College of Law.

Lost Productivity

Several studies have attempted to measure whether the use of drugs by employees adversely affects their performance on the job. Using verbal, written, physiological, and physical testing, the studies concluded that drug abusers were functioning at only 50% to 67% capacity.[6] Specifically, drug abusers demonstrated poor work quality, failure to follow up or complete assignments, inadequate preparation, impaired memory, lethargy, reduced coordination, carelessness, mistakes, and slowdowns.[7]

A second measure of lost productivity attributed to drug abuse is absenteeism. Drug-abusing employees have a higher rate of absenteeism, with estimates ranging from 2.5 to 16 times higher than employees who do not use drugs.[8] Thus, employers are faced with increased costs for additional sick leave and medical insurance.

Finally, drug abusers have a higher turnover rate.[9] According to one study, illicit drug users (particularly marijuana users who also use alcohol or other drugs) had average termination dates ten months earlier for males and sixteen months earlier for females.[10]

Estimates of the total financial impact of lost productivity from drugs borne by American business vary widely. The most frequently cited estimates are those of the Research Triangle Institute, which estimates that lost productivity totals $99 billion annually, with two-thirds attributable to alcohol.[11]

Accidents and Injuries

In 1984 American business lost an estimated $81 billion due to accidents, and many people believe that drug abuse is responsible for a significant share of the losses.[12] In the last ten years there have been a number of highly publicized accidents where employee drug abuse was a factor, including thirty-seven deaths in the railroad industry. Overall, it has been reported that drug users have three to four times as many accidents as nonusers.[13]

There has been little scientific study, however, of the relationship between drugs and accidents. In a study by the National Institute for Occupational Safety and Health (NIOSH), out of 2,979 workplace injuries in the chemical industry in 1984 and 1985, drugs were a primary factor in only two injuries and a partial factor in only six more.[14] Similarly, a study by the Mine Safety and Health Administration (MSHA), found only ten accidents in four years involved drugs.[15]

Despite any doubts raised by these contradictory studies, there is a perception that many workplace accidents are caused by drugs, and there is certainly the potential for drug-related accidents. Thus, many policies appear to be based on the assumption of a causal relationship between drugs and accidents.

Insurance

Drug and alcohol abuse may increase insurance costs by as much as $50 billion annually.[16] Employers that provide employees with insurance coverage as a part of the employee benefits package pay a substantial part of these increased costs. For example, employees with drug problems are more likely to use medical insurance and file workers' compensation claims.

Theft and Other Crimes

A common concern about the employment of people who use drugs is that to support their drug habit they are likely to steal from their employer, embezzle money, sell company products or trade secrets without authorization, steal from coworkers or customers, and sell drugs on company premises. Although these concerns have not been proven empirically, there is anecdotal evidence, and many employer policies appear to be based on the assumption that these concerns are valid.

Employee Relations

Another cost associated with drug abuse that is difficult to quantify is the negative impact of drugs on employee relations. Lost productivity, safety risks, and "work shifting" (nonusers being forced to do more than their share of work) can lower employee morale. Employees who use drugs also may try to sell drugs to coworkers or to spread the use of drugs to coworkers. Consequently, management must resolve intraemployee frictions and disputes. Meanwhile, management energies also must be committed to drug detection, crime prevention, drug education, quality control, accident prevention, and rehabilitation—all without invading employee privacy or undermining labor-management relations.

Legal Liability

Employer policies dealing with drugs in the workplace also must consider the issue of legal liability. Every injured person, damaged piece of property, defective product, breached contact, or other wrongful act attributable to employee drug usage has the potential for substantial employer liability. On the other hand, overzealous efforts to combat drug abuse in the workplace also have the potential for liability. Thus, employers must navigate a careful course between insouciance and overreaction to the threat of drugs in the workplace.

DRUG TESTING—HOW IT WORKS AND WHAT IT MEASURES

Drug Testing Technology

In the last decade, technological advances in drug testing and the commercial exploitation of these advances have made workplace drug testing commonplace. Despite the frequency of drug testing, however, there remains widespread misunderstanding about how the tests work, what they measure, and how their accuracy is determined.

Drug tests analyze a body specimen for the presence of drugs or their by-products, metabolites. The most commonly used specimen for workplace testing is urine, although blood, breath, saliva, hair, and other specimens have been used in settings other than the workplace. Blood testing by employers is mostly limited to retrospective testing after the occurrence of an accident.

Scientifically valid drug testing is a two-step process. In the initial step, a "screening" test eliminates from further testing those specimens with negative results, indicating either the absence of targeted substances or the presence of levels below a designated threshold or "cut-off" point. A result which reveals substance levels at or above the cut-off is considered positive. All positive specimens are then retested using a "confirmatory" test. According to the Toxicology Section of the American Academy of Forensic Sciences, the confirmatory test must be "based upon different chemical or physical principles than the initial analysis method(s)."[17] Confirmatory testing is essential to establish both the identity and quantity of the substances in the specimen.

There are three main types of initial screening tests: color or spot tests, thin layer chromatography and immunoassays. The most widely used are the immunoassays, which are of three types, enzyme, radio, and fluorescence. All of these latter tests are based on immunological principles. A known quantity of the tested-for drug is bound to an enzyme or radioactive iodine and is added to the urine. If the urine contains the drug, the added, "labeled" drug competes with the drug in the specimen and cannot bind to the antibodies. As a result, the enzyme or radioactive iodine remains active. By measuring enzyme activity or radioactivity, the presence and amount of the drug can be determined.

The most commonly used immunoassay is the enzyme multiplied immunoassay technique or EMIT. An advantage of EMIT is that it tests for a broad spectrum of drugs and their metabolites, including opiates, barbiturates, amphetamines, cocaine and its metabolite, benzodiazepines, methaqualone, methadone, phencyclidine, and cannabinoids. It is also fast and cheap. A single test may cost about five dollars. In addition, portable kits starting at $300 are sold for on-site use by individuals with minimal training.

The radioimmunoassay (RIA) can measure only one drug at a time, but has broad-spectrum detection capabilities similar to EMIT. RIA is more expensive than EMIT, however, and requires a more highly trained technician. The fluorescence polarization immunoassay (FPIA) is a relatively new technique and, as yet, not widely used.

The most widely used confirmatory test is gas chromatography/mass spectrometry (GC/MS). In GC the sample is pretreated to extract drugs from the urine. The drugs are converted to a gaseous form and transported through a long glass column of helium gas. By application of varying temperatures to the column the compounds are separated according to their unique properties, such as molecular weight and rate of reaction. These particular properties are used to identify the compound. Although GC can be used alone, the superior method combines it with a mass spectrometer (MS), which breaks down the compound molecules into electrically charged ion fragments. Each drug or metabolite produces a unique fragment pattern, which can be detected by comparison with known fragment patterns. GC/MS requires expensive equipment and highly trained technicians to prepare the sample and interpret test results. The process is also time-consuming because

only one sample and one drug per sample may be tested at a time. High performance liquid chromatography (HPLC) is also used as a confirmatory test, but GC/MS has become the standard confirmatory test.

The pricing structures for drug tests vary widely. Some laboratories charge customers a flat fee per specimen tested; others divide the fee so that those samples requiring a confirmatory test incur an additional charge. Other factors affecting price are the type of analysis used, the number of specimens tested, and the types of drugs tested for. In general, laboratory charges for single-procedure methods range from $5 to $20; GC/MS confirmation costs from $30 to $100.[18]

What the Tests Measure

It is essential to understand that a positive result on a drug test does not indicate impairment of the subject. Drug metabolites detected in urine are the inert, inactive byproducts of drugs and cannot be used to determine impairment. Although a blood test can reveal the presence of drugs in the blood in their active state, with the exception of ethanol, there is no known correlation between the detection of metabolites in urine and blood concentrations. Moreover, there is no agreement among experts on what level of drug indicates impairment.

Many variables influence how a drug will affect an individual user, including the type of drug, dose, time lapse from administration, duration of effect and use, the interactions with other drugs. The individual's age, weight, sex, general health state, emotional state, and drug tolerance also are important factors. Consequently, the wide individual variations make generalizing extremely speculative. According to one expert:

Table 1 Approximate Duration of Detectability of Selected Drugs in Urine[20]

Drugs	Approximate Duration of Detectability
Amphetamines	2 days
Barbiturates	1–7 days
Benzodiazepines	3 days
Cocaine metabolites	2–3 days
Methadone	3 days
Codeine	2 days
PCP	8 days
Cannabinoids	
Single use	3 days
Moderate smoker (4 times/week)	5 days
Heavy smoker (daily)	10 days
Chronic heavy smoker	21 days

Testing does only one thing. It detects what is being tested. It does not tell us anything about the recency of use. It does not tell us anything about how the person was exposed to the drug. It doesn't even tell us whether it affected performance.[19]

A final factor that complicates interpretation of a positive result is the often-considerable duration of detectability of drugs in urine. As indicated in the following table, drug metabolites can be detected in urine from one day to several weeks following exposure. The usual *effects* of most drugs persist for only a few hours after use. Therefore, drugs are detectable long after their effects have subsided and any correlations between a positive test and impairment are impossible.

How Accurate Are the Tests?

Before discussing the accuracy of drug tests, it is important to review how accuracy in medical tests is measured. The key concepts are "sensitivity" and "specificity." The sensitivity of a test is a measure of its ability to identify persons with the tested-for condition. It is the percentage of persons with the condition who register a positive test result:

$$\frac{\text{True positive test results}}{\substack{\text{Persons with condition} \\ \text{(True positives + False negatives)}}} \times 100 \text{ percent}$$

Therefore, if 100 persons have a condition and the test is able to identify 90 of them, the test would be 90% sensitive.

The specificity of a test is a measure of its ability to identify persons who do not have a condition. It is the percentage of persons free of the condition who register a negative test result:

$$\frac{\text{True negative test results}}{\substack{\text{Persons free of conditions} \\ \text{(True negatives + False positives)}}} \times 100 \text{ percent}$$

Therefore, if 100 persons are free of a condition and the test is able to identify 90 of them, the test would be 90% specific.

The "positive predictive value" of a test refers to the value of a positive test result in identifying the presence of a condition. It is the percentage of persons whose test results are positive who actually have the condition:

$$\frac{\text{Persons with condition (True positives)}}{\text{Positive test results (True positives + False positives)}} \times 100 \text{ percent}$$

According to independent studies,[21] the EMIT test has a sensitivity of about 99% and a specificity of about 90%.[22] The positive predictive value of the test, however, varies greatly depending on the prevalence of drug usage in the tested population. The following tables illustrate how important prevalence is to the predictive value of a test.

Table 2 assumes a 50% prevalence—perhaps individuals in a drug treatment program or, in a workplace setting, individuals selected for testing based upon reasonable suspicion. The test correctly identifies 4950 of the 5000 true positives, with 50 false negatives. It correctly identifies 4500 of the 5000 true negatives, with 500 false positives. Therefore, of the 5450 positives, 4950 are true positives. The positive predictive value of the test is 4950/5450 or 90.8%.

Table 3 assumes a 5% prevalence—a reasonable estimate of the prevalence of recent drug users among job applicants. The test correctly identifies 495 of the 500 true positives, with 5 false negatives. It correctly identifies 8550 of the 9500 true negatives, with 950 false positives. Therefore, of the 1445 positives, 495 are true positives. The positive predictive value of the test is 495/1445 or 34.3%.

Table 3 demonstrates why it is essential to use confirmatory tests. Two out of three positives identified by the test will be false positives. Unfortunately, pre-employment drug tests, where the prevalence and predictive values are low, are also the tests least likely to be confirmed due to cost considerations.

Because drug tests detect metabolites of drugs rather than the drugs themselves, commonly used screening tests (and to a lesser extent confirmatory tests as well) sometimes incorrectly identify as metabolites of illicit drugs the metabolites of other substances or normal human enzymes such as lysozyme and malate dehydrogenase. Table 4 indicates some of the substances for which this effect, cross-reactivity, has been documented.

The problem of cross-reactivity is one important reason why it is important to use pretest questionnaires inquiring about medications and other cross-reactants and to give individuals an opportunity to explain a positive result. A related concern is that a drug test will be positive because of "passive inhalation." There is disputed evidence about whether a marijuana test using a cutoff of 20 nanograms per milliliter of urine will test positive if the subject was exposed to the marijuana smoke of other peo-

Table 2   Predictive Value of EMIT Test with 99% Sensitivity, 90% Specificity, 50% Prevalence, and 10,000 Subjects

Subjects	True Positives	False Negatives
5000+	4950	50
	False Positives	True Negatives
5000−	500	4500

Table 3 Predictive Value of EMIT Test with 99% Sensitivity, 90% Specificity, 5% Prevalence, and 10,000 Subjects

Subjects	True Positives	False Negatives
500+	495	5
	False Positives	True Negatives
9500–	950	8550

Table 4 Some Commonly Available Substances That Cross-React with Widely Tested-For Drugs

Type of Drug	Cross-Reactants
Amphetamines	1. over-the-counter cold medications (decongestants)
	2. over-the-counter and prescription dietary aids
	3. asthma medications
	4. anti-inflammatory agents
Barbiturates	1. anti-inflammatory agents
	2. phenobarbital (used to treat epilepsy)
Cocaine	1. herbal teas (made from coca leaves)
Marijuana (cannabinoids)	1. nonsteroidal anti-inflammatory agents
	2. Ibuprofen (Advil, Motrin, Nuprin)
Morphine, opiates	1. codeine
	2. prescription analgesics and antitussives
	3. poppy seeds
	4. over-the-counter cough remedies
Phencyclidine (PCP)	1. prescription cough medicines
	2. Valium

ple. Using a higher cutoff, however, such as 100 nanograms per milliliter of urine, will eliminate this problem.

The accuracy of drug tests also may be affected by several other factors. Alteration of the specimen, such as by substitution or dilution, improper calibration of equipment or cleaning of equipment (the so-called carry-over effect), mislabeling, contamination, or technician error all may undermine test accuracy. Indeed, even the best methodologies will yield valid results only to the extent that the testing laboratory adheres to rigid standards of quality control. Laboratory proficiency criteria, however, have been extremely inadequate. . . .

PRIVATE EMPLOYERS AS DRUG TESTERS

Although drug testing began in the private sector, it was not until public employers began testing that private sector drug testing became so widespread. For the most part, it is the large companies that have embraced drug testing. Among *Fortune* 500 corporations, only ten percent performed urinalysis in 1982; by 1985 the figure had reached twenty-five percent;[23] and by 1987 nearly fifty percent of the largest corporations performed drug testing.[24]

As the size of the company declines, so too

does the prevalence of drug testing. In a 1987 survey of companies with more than 500 employees, seventeen percent of the companies tested current workers for drugs and twenty-three percent tested applicants.[25] Smaller companies reported less testing. Transportation and manufacturing companies were most likely to test, electronics/communications and insurance/finance companies were least likely to test. The specifics of drug testing also vary by size of the company, geography, industry, and other factors. Larger companies are more likely to use confirmatory testing and refer those testing positive to an employee assistance program; smaller companies are more likely to use only screening tests and to respond to a positive test with summary dismissal.

According to one study, almost all of the companies (94.5%) that perform urinalysis test job applicants and nearly three-fourths of the companies (73%) test current employees on a "for cause" basis.[26] Only fourteen percent conducted random tests and those companies tended to be smaller, with a significant number of them testing people in jobs of a "sensitive or high risk nature."[27] The most widely cited reason for testing (37%) was health and safety.[28] Other reasons for testing were the identification of a workplace substance abuse problem (21%), the awareness of drugs as a national problem (11%), and the high-risk nature of the job (9%).[29]

It is also valuable to consider why the companies without drug testing programs have declined to engage in testing. According to the American Management Association, the most common reasons for not performing drug testing are as follows: moral issues or privacy (68%); inaccuracy of tests (63%); negative impact on morale (53%); tests show use, not abuse (43%); employee opposition (16%); and union opposition (7%).[30] Interestingly, fear of litigation was not mentioned, but it

certainly may be an increasingly significant consideration.

LEGAL ISSUES

A number of constitutional arguments have been raised to challenge the legality of employee drug testing. Because of the governmental action requirement, federal constitutional protections are limited to public employees and private employees where drug testing is mandated by federal, state, or local governments.

The most frequently raised argument is that drug testing constitutes an unreasonable search and seizure in violation of the fourth amendment. In *Schmerber v. California,* the Supreme Court held that taking a blood sample from a criminal defendant to determine whether he was intoxicated was a search within the meaning of the fourth amendment. Lower court decisions after *Schmerber* have recognized that requiring a urine sample is far less intrusive than extracting blood, but have nonetheless concluded that a mandatory urine screen also is a search for purposes of the fourth amendment. The limited nature of the intrusion, however, may be important in determining the validity of the search.

The fourth amendment does not bar all searches, only unreasonable ones. Therefore, it must be determined whether the drug test is unreasonable. This in turn often depends on the nature of the search: who is searched, when the search is made, how it is made, and what is done with the results. Courts balance the degree of intrusion of the search on the person's fourth amendment right of privacy against the need for the search to promote some legitimate governmental interest.

One essential factor is whether the individual has a reasonable expectation of privacy relative to the circumstances of the search. Government employees have a reasonable expectation of privacy at work and "do not surrender their fourth amendment rights merely because they go to work for the government."[31] Yet, government employers maintain rights in conducting warrantless searches "for the proprietary purpose of preventing future damage to the agency's ability to discharge effectively its statutory responsibilities."[32]

Three distinct privacy interests have been identified in urinalysis. First is the expectation of privacy as to the urine itself. According to one court, "[a]n individual cannot retain a privacy interest in a waste product that, once released, is flushed down the drain."[33] Another court, however, has observed that "[t]he urine excreted for a drug test . . . is not expected to be a waste product, flushed down a toilet. Indeed, precautions are taken in the test procedure to prevent the sample from being thus disposed of."[34] Second is the expectation of privacy in the information contained in the urine. "Obviously, one does not expect that he will be made to discharge urine so that it can be analyzed in order to discover the personal physiological secrets it may hold. Thus, as with blood, there is an expectation of privacy concerning the 'information' body fluids may hold."[35] Third is the expectation of privacy in the process of urination. "[T]he act of urination is a private one and, if interfered with, protected by the Fourth Amendment."[36] Therefore, policies requiring direct observation of an individual urinating would be more difficult to sustain.

An interesting issue is whether the fourth amendment protects an individual's refusal to submit to a mandatory urinalysis. In *Everett v. Napper*, the Atlanta Bureau of Fire Services was conducting an investigation into drug trafficking by fire fighters and one of the subjects of the investigation listed the plaintiff as one of the fire fighters who had purchased drugs from him. The plaintiff denied the allegation and refused to submit to a urinalysis. After his discharge for refusal to cooperate

with the investigation, he sued claiming, among other things, a violation of his fourth amendment rights. The Eleventh Circuit, in upholding the discharge, held that "since Everett did not submit to the urinalysis, there was no 'search' and therefore no possible fourth amendment violation."[37]

The court's reasoning in *Everett* is disturbing. Although the court could have sustained the discharge on the ground that the intended search was reasonable, it is questionable whether the court could flatly state that because he refused to take the drug test there was no search and therefore no fourth amendment violation. It is unlikely that the court would want to embrace the notion that one must acquiesce in an illegal search in order to have standing to challenge the search when negative consequences already have attached to the refusal. At the least, it would seem to violate substantive due process to discharge a public employee for refusal to consent to an unlawful act.

Other courts to consider this issue, unlike the *Everett* court, have not focused on whether the refusal negated the search, but whether it was lawful for the government to require consent to the search. For example, in *McDonell v. Hunter*, the Eighth Circuit stated: "If a search is unreasonable, a government employer cannot require that its employees consent to that search as a condition of employment."[38]

A related but distinct constitutional protection has been established to protect the "right of privacy." Although this right is not explicit in the Constitution, the Supreme Court has found that it includes the individual's interest in avoiding disclosure of personal matters and independence in making certain kinds of important decisions, such as marriage, procreation, and family relationships. This privacy interest, however, is not absolute and must be balanced against legitimate governmental interests in disclosure.

In the context of drug testing, the courts

have been reluctant to apply privacy principles distinct from those recognized under the fourth amendment.

> The "privacy" rights of the public employees have been vindicated under the Fourth Amendment by this court's determination that [the transit agency's] random program is unreasonable. To find that the testing procedure implicates a further, separate protection would require an expansive reading of the Fourteenth Amendment that this court is unwilling to undertake.[39]

Another constitutional argument often raised in drug testing cases is procedural due process. The argument has been used to challenge both test procedures and employee termination procedures. As to the former, it has been held that termination of employment on the basis of an unconfirmed EMIT test violated due process and that it violated due process when voluntarily-submitted urine samples were destroyed before they could be sent out for independent testing. Even the addition of confirmatory testing may not satisfy due process concerns about the proper handling of the specimen and cleaning and calibration of test equipment. As to the latter, employee termination procedures, the termination of an individual's employment must be preceded by notice and opportunity for a hearing appropriate to the nature of the case, although a full, predischarge hearing is not required. . . .

Although the specific legal criteria vary with the source of the legal protection, essentially the courts seek to determine whether a challenged drug testing program is reasonable under the circumstances. One way of looking at the issue is to see whether reasonable grounds exist to suspect that the testing will turn up evidence of work-related drug use and whether the measures adopted are not excessively intrusive. Another way is to focus upon the following four factors: who is tested, when is the testing performed, how is the test-

ing performed, and what is done with test results.

Who Is Tested?

The starting point for determining whether any particular drug testing is reasonable is to look at the individual being tested. In other words, the job description and responsibilities of the person tested are very important. The courts have been more willing to sanction the use of drug testing where employees and co-workers may be endangered by drug impairment. Drug testing in other job classifications is less likely to be upheld.

When Is the Testing Performed?

Drug testing may be conducted at a variety of stages during the employment relationship, including pre-employment, periodic, upon return to work following a leave of absence, after an accident, based on suspicion of drug use, and randomly. The timing or circumstances of the test often affect the legality of the test.

Pre-employment testing is the most prevalent form of drug testing. It is also the most likely to be upheld. Applicants do not have any vested rights in their jobs and if they are denied a job because of a drug test they have only lost an expectancy as opposed to current employees whose loss probably would be considered more tangible.

Periodic testing, especially when used as part of an overall medical evaluation of fitness, also is likely to be upheld. For other types of testing, without a particularized or individualized need for testing, the courts are more inclined to find that testing is unnecessary and therefore unreasonable. Random testing, particularly unsystematic random testing, where the individuals to be tested are selected subjectively, has been looked upon with distrust by the courts who are fearful of abuses in selection. Similarly, surprise, mass testing has been held to be unlawful.

With specific evidence of the need to test, the courts are more inclined to uphold the testing. Drug testing of certain employees who were identified in reports as drug users has been upheld. Post-accident testing also has been upheld. In *Division 241, Amalgamated Transit Union v. Suscy,* the Seventh Circuit upheld the Chicago Transit Authority's rule mandating drug testing for bus drivers involved in a serious accident or suspected of being intoxicated.

The courts have not required "probable cause" before upholding an individual drug test. "Reasonable suspicion," a lesser standard, has been widely adopted. "The 'reasonable suspicion' test requires that to justify this intrusion, officials must point to specific, objective facts and rational inferences that they are entitled to draw from these facts in the light of their experience."[40]

Reasonable suspicion goes to individual drug testing. An unresolved issue is whether evidence of widespread drug abuse in the community or a problem within a group of workers is needed to justify wider testing. In *Lovvorn v. City of Chattanooga,* the drug testing of fire fighters was struck down because of a lack of reasonable suspicion of the need to test:

> The City has not pointed to any objective facts concerning deficient job performance or physical or mental deficiencies on the part of its fire fighters, either in general or with respect to specific personnel, which might lead to a reasonable suspicion upon which tests could be based.[41]

How Is the Testing Performed?

The testing procedures used may affect the legality of the testing. In *Jones v. McKenzie,* the court held that the use of an unconfirmed EMIT test, which violated a specific regulation mandating confirmation, was arbitrary and capricious. Confirmatory testing, such as the use of gas chromatography/mass spectrometry to confirm an initial immunoassay, will increase the accuracy of the test and the likelihood of legality. In *National Treasury Employees Union v. Von Raab,* the Fifth Circuit upheld drug testing by the Customs Service in large part because of specific measures to ensure the reliability of test results. These measures included confirmatory testing, chain-of-custody procedures, allowing the employee to choose a laboratory for re-testing, and a quality assurance program.[42]

Safeguarding the chain-of-custody of the specimen is necessary to eliminate the possibility of confusion, mishandling, or sabotage. In addition, it may be necessary to retain the sample to allow for independent confirmation of the results. In *Banks v. FAA,* the discharges of air traffic controllers were set aside because the urine samples had been destroyed before they could be re-tested by an independent laboratory.

A final issue relates to sample collection. The courts have recognized a substantial privacy interest in urination.

> There are few activities in our society more personal or private than the passing of urine. Most people describe it by euphemisms if they talk about it at all. It is a function traditionally performed without public observation; indeed, its performance in public is generally prohibited by law as well as social custom.[43]

Consequently, direct observation of urination is unlikely to be upheld. In *Caruso v. Ward,* police officers were required to urinate in the presence of a superior officer of the same sex to ensure the regularity of the sample. The court found this process especially troublesome. "[T]he subject officer would be required to perform before another person what is an otherwise very private bodily function which necessarily includes exposing one's private parts, an experience which even if courteously supervised can be humiliating and degrading. . . . "[44]

What Is Done with Test Results

Workplace drug-testing programs are more likely to be upheld if individuals who test positively are rehabilitated rather than discharged. This often relates closely with the duty to make reasonable accommodation to handicapped workers. For example, in *Hazlett v. Martin Chevrolet, Inc.,* an employer was found to have violated Ohio's handicap discrimination law by discharging an employee suffering from drug and alcohol addiction and refusing to grant a one month disability or sick leave so that the employee could obtain treatment. Employees with other illnesses previously had been given leaves.

THE ELEMENTS OF A LEGAL, ETHICAL, AND EFFECTIVE DRUG TESTING PROGRAM

If there is one general criticism that can be leveled at managers in the public and private sectors regarding drug testing, it is that they have too eagerly embraced drug testing as *the* solution to the problem of workplace drug abuse. Before drug testing is implemented there must be a detailed and thoughtful consideration of whether there is a workplace drug abuse problem, whether drug testing is essential to combat the problem, whether the benefits of drug testing outweigh the costs to employers and employees, and whether drug testing can be undertaken in a way that will ensure accuracy, fairness, and privacy.

While some people have recommended unrestricted drug testing or no drug testing at all, there is a growing consensus—from the AFL-CIO to the AMA—that limited drug testing is permissible. For example, the AMA's Council on Scientific Affairs recommended:

That the AMA take the position that urine drug and alcohol testing of employees should be limited to: (a) preemployment examinations of those persons whose jobs affect the health and safety of others, (b) situations in which there is reasonable suspicion that an employee's job performance is impaired by drug and alcohol use, and (c) monitoring as part of a comprehensive program of treatment and rehabilitation of alcohol and drug abuse or dependence.[45]

Placing careful controls on drug testing is an attempt to accommodate the legitimate concerns about test accuracy and privacy with legitimate concerns about public health and safety. It is even more difficult to move beyond generalities to concrete guidelines on workplace drug testing. A legal, ethical, and effective drug testing program should satisfy each of the following requirements.

1. *Reasonable suspicion exists to believe that there is at least some class-wide problem of drug abuse among the relevant group of employees.*

Drug testing is an extreme measure and it should not be undertaken lightly. The only compelling reason to test is to protect employee and public safety. Although drug testing should not be started only *after* a tragic accident, there are sound reasons why it should not be initiated unless there is at least some evidence of a drug abuse problem in the locality, in a particular profession or job classification, or at a particular employer. One way of determining whether there is a drug abuse problem at a particular workplace is for all employees to take a drug test anonymously. The results will indicate whether there is a problem and, if so, its nature and scope. This information also is valuable in designing education and rehabilitation programs.

2. *There are no feasible alternatives to detecting impairment, including supervision and simulation.*

The primary concern underlying drug testing is that drug-impaired employees will be impaired on the job. Drug testing, however, does not measure impairment. It measures prior exposure, which is used as a surrogate for impairment based on one of the two following theories. First, employees who use drugs off the job are more likely to use drugs on the job or to report to work under the influence of drugs. Second, prior drug use may impede performance even though no impairment is noticeable. If impairment or the effects of impairment are detectable, then there is no need for drug testing. One way to detect impairment is through regular, close supervision. Another way is for the employee to demonstrate fitness via simulation.

3. *The drug testing program is limited to workers who, if working while impaired, would pose a substantial danger to themselves, other persons, or property.*

Among the numerous asserted justifications for employee drug testing are the following: (1) drug use is illegal and therefore employers have a responsibility to discover employees who may be breaking the law; (2) drug abusing employees often need substantial sums of money to buy drugs and these employees are likely to steal from their employer or to accept bribes on the job; (3) employees using drugs are likely to have a reduction in their productivity; (4) maintaining a drug-free workplace is essential to an employer's public image; and (5) drug testing is essential to protect safety and health.

First, as to illegality, it is clear that employers are not concerned about illegality per se. If they were concerned simply about lawbreaking, measures other than drug testing are likely to be much more effective in detecting wrongdoing. For example, an employee (and management) federal income tax return screening every April 15th would undoubtedly be quite revealing. Of course, it is the province of the Internal Revenue Service and not the employer to detect tax irregularities. Similarly, it is the responsibility of law enforcement agencies and not employers to prevent illegal drug use.

Second, as to theft and bribery, the sudden need for more money to support a drug habit is only one reason why an employee might become dishonest. To be thorough, employers would need to know if an employee were gambling, suffering losses in the stock market, or even having an extra-marital affair. Pre-employment background and reference checks and post-hiring supervision and auditing are much more effective in preventing theft and bribery than urinalysis.

Third, productivity is a legitimate concern of an employer. Productivity, however, is directly measurable and is done so on a continual basis by employers. A decline in productivity is an end point and it is irrelevant whether the decline is caused by boredom, personal problems, or drug abuse. Lack of productivity is a better measure of lack of productivity than urinalysis.

Fourth, from a legal and policy standpoint, public image is a deeply troubling rationale for employment policies. Historically, many forms of employment discrimination have been defended on grounds such as "customer preference." The law has correctly rejected such asserted defenses. Public image is not only so vague as to justify nearly any action, but in the case of drug testing, it is a two-edged sword. Drug abuse in the United States is a pervasive, intractable social problem and the fact that an employer has, among its employees, one or more individuals with a substance abuse problem is unlikely to generate public disdain. The way in which the employer deals with the problem, however, may directly affect a public image. Indiscriminate and heedless drug testing without regard for employee rights can influence the way in which the employer is regarded by current employees, potential employees, customers, and shareholders.

Fifth, safety is the only justifiable reason for employee drug testing. It is true that current drug tests do not measure impairment and only measure prior exposure. Nevertheless, there is ample evidence that individuals who use drugs often take them at work or report to work impaired. For employees in safety-sensitive positions, prudence demands that public safety considerations outweigh even the legitimate concerns of employees. For employees not in safety-sensitive positions, such as retail or clerical workers, there is no justification for drug testing. Reasonable supervision will ensure that satisfactory performance is not impeded for any reason, including drugs.

If safety is the only compelling reason for drug testing, the nature of this exception needs to be further defined. The danger posed by an impaired worker must be *substantial*. This is based on the severity of the consequences, the likelihood of danger, and the immediacy of the harm. To justify drug testing, the risk of harm from an impaired worker also must be otherwise unpreventable (as by supervision, quality control, and work review) and the consequences irreparable. Nuclear power, chemical plant, and transportation workers are the best examples. Even as to these employees, however, the other elements still need to be satisfied.

4. *Testing not based on individualized, reasonable suspicion is limited to pre-employment and periodic testing.*

Pre-employment and periodic testing (especially as part of a pre-employment or annual medical examination) are the least objectionable forms of testing. They permit the discovery of individuals who have a substance abuse problem within the context of a medical examination. There is no stigma attached to supplying a urine sample in this context. The medical setting also helps to encourage truthful disclosure by a substance-abusing employee, protects confidentiality, and facilitates treatment.

The other acceptable time for testing is when there is reasonable suspicion of impairment. This is a closer case. If an employee in a safety-sensitive job is observed to be drowsy, dizzy, disoriented, or otherwise is suspected of

being impaired, regardless of the results of a drug test, the employee should not be permitted to continue work and should be referred to a physician. Thus, the need for a drug test under these circumstances may be questioned because the behavior establishing reasonable cause also demands action immediately and cannot await the results of a drug test. The other issue raised by reasonable cause testing is that clear guidelines must be established for determining reasonable cause. Without such guidelines there is a danger of arbitrariness in selecting the employee for testing.

Despite the drawbacks of reasonable cause testing, employers should be provided with some basis for a periodic or unprogrammed testing. Recreational as well as compulsive drug users may be able to forego the use of drugs for a short period of time each year to test negatively. In those job categories where drug testing is acceptable, it ought to be effective. Reasonable cause testing, including post-accident testing, should be permissible.

Some people have suggested (and some statutes have used the approach) that the *only* permissible drug testing is for reasonable cause. For employees working alone (such as truck drivers), it is hard to imagine that there ever would be reasonable cause until after a tragic accident occurred. Thus, reasonable cause testing should not be the only basis for drug testing.

Random testing and surprise, round-up testing are unacceptable. As noted earlier, these tests have been struck down in several public sector cases on constitutional grounds.

5. *State of the art screening and confirmatory test procedures are performed by trained professionals, off-site, under laboratory conditions.*

Employers that use "do-it-yourself" drug testing kits and unconfirmed screening tests are engaged in a false economy. Unless the best technology is used, drug test results are unreliable and likely to be challenged in court. Even the best analytical techniques are only as good as the people performing the tests. Careful laboratory selection and ongoing quality review are essential.

6. *Specimen collection is not observed.*

With the growth of employee drug testing there have been numerous reports of employees attempting to substitute "clean urine" or otherwise tampering with specimens. Some employers, in response, have taken to observing employees in the act of urination. For many employees, this aspect of drug testing is the most objectionable, degrading, and insensitive element. It is highly unlikely that the benefits of observation (preventing tampering by a few individuals whose drug problems were not otherwise detectable) outweigh the human relations, employment relations, and public relations costs of observation.

7. *Testing is performed for the presence of prescription drugs and alcohol as well as illicit drugs.*

If the underlying purpose of drug testing is safety, there is no reason why drug testing should be limited to illicit drugs. In terms of the number of people who abuse them and the fatalities, injuries, and property damage caused by their effects in the workplace, alcohol and prescription drugs (often in combination) pose a much greater threat than illicit drugs.

8. *There is valid employee consent before the testing and an opportunity to explain a positive test result.*

An argument could be made that consent to drug testing is never voluntary (or valid) when employees are likely to be discharged or applicants not hired if they refuse. Nevertheless, if drug testing is essential to protect public safety in the face of a drug abuse problem by certain employees, and if the other criteria for testing are met, an employer ought to be able to make consent to drug testing a condition of employment. Employers, however, should not perform drug testing surreptitiously, such as by simply testing all urine samples obtained as part of a pre-employment or periodic medical examination.

A related issue is whether applicants and employees should be given advance notice that a pre-employment or periodic drug test will be performed. Some federal and state laws specifically mandate advance notice, but there is generally no such legal requirement. The obvious drawback to notice is that it permits individuals to abstain before being tested and then to resume drug use after the test. This drawback, however, may be outweighed by the following considerations. First, providing employees with notice improves employee acceptability of the program. It indicates that the purpose of the testing is to promote public safety and not to "catch" employees. Second, as to applicants, company resources will be saved because habitual drug users will not proceed further with their application. Third, individuals genuinely interested in obtaining or retaining employment may cease using drugs before the test, and surveillance, supervision, and re-testing may ensure that they do not resume drug use.

Finally, individuals should be given an opportunity to explain a positive test result. As noted earlier, even state of the art confirmatory testing may produce false positive results due to laboratory error or cross-reactivity with some medicines and foods.

9. *Test results are kept confidential.*

Drug test results should be regarded in the same way as other medical records. Specifically, the data should be stored in the medical department (assuming there is one) and access should be limited to medical personnel. Supervisory and managerial employees should only be notified of the consequences of the results (e.g., employee A is medically unfit for work), but not the specific results. Other information essential to personnel actions should be provided only on a "need-to-know" basis. When an initial drug screen is positive and a confirmatory test is scheduled, no results should be released until after the confirmatory test. The failure to maintain confidentiality may lead to liability based on invasion of privacy, defamation, intentional infliction of emotional distress, or other torts.

10. *The test procedures or resulting personnel actions do not violate applicable legal rights of applicants and employees.*

As discussed previously, a wide range of constitutional, statutory, and common law doctrines may be implicated by drug testing. Both the testing itself and any personnel actions based on the testing must be in accordance with these legal requirements.

11. *Drug testing is only part of an overall drug abuse program, including education and rehabilitation.*

Drug testing should be only one part, and indeed should be the least important part, of a comprehensive drug abuse program. The other two components of the program should be drug awareness and employee assistance.

Drug awareness programs are educational activities aimed at supervisors and employees. Supervisors need to be trained to recognize some of the "suspect changes in employee job performance and behavior that may portend a drug abuse problem."[46] They also need to be trained in how to respond to employees suspected of having a drug abuse problem.

Employees also should be involved in a separate drug education program. Although there are several different models of programs, all programs teach employees to recognize the signs of drug abuse in themselves, family, friends, and co-workers. All programs also discuss the dangers of drug abuse and describe company and community services available for dealing with drug abuse.

The other essential part of a drug abuse program is an employee assistance program (EAP). There are 8,000[47] to 10,000[48] EAPs today, giving about twenty percent of the work force access to such a program.[49] Most of the EAPs are in large companies. Some of the programs are run in-house, others are run on a contract basis. Both types of EAPs work the same way. An employee may volun-

tarily enter the program or may be referred by a supervisor. The employee contacts the EAP and works out an individual treatment program. Participation in an EAP is kept confidential. In some instances, employer discipline is waived on the condition that the employee complete the EAP.

CONCLUSION

Drug abuse in America and drug abuse in American workplaces are complicated problems. Drug abuse will not be eliminated or even brought under control simply through law enforcement, military action, public relations campaigns, rehabilitation, legalization of certain drugs, or prohibiting any current drug user from obtaining private or public employment. Similarly, a facile solution to the problem of workplace drug abuse will not be found in a specimen jar or a million specimen jars.

At best, drug testing is a sometimes-necessary evil that is part of a comprehensive program to insure the public health and safety. At worst, it is an unholy alliance of politics, profiteering, unrestrained technology, and heedless personnel policies.

The efficacy and desirability of drug testing in the workplace will continue to be weighed by judges, legislators, and policy makers in the public and private sectors. In making these decisions, it is essential to consider the limits of technology, the inability of drug testing to resolve the underlying problem of drug abuse, and the human and organizational costs of implementing drug testing programs. Drug testing must be considered in the light of established employment law principles, such as equal opportunity, job-related decisionmaking, and reasonable accommodation. Drug testing also must be viewed in the larger context of a society that is built on values of autonomy, privacy, and dignity.

NOTES

1. Press Office, National Institute on Drug Abuse, "Highlights of the 1985 National Household Survey on Drug Abuse," *NIDA Capsules* (Nov. 1986 rev.) [hereinafter NIDA Highlights].

2. Smith, Deborah W., and Andrew S. Silberman, "Treatment Resources for Chemical Dependency," 1 *Seminars in Occup. Med.* 265 (1986) (citing the National Institute on Alcohol Abuse and Alcoholism (NIAAA), "Fifth Special Report to Congress on Alcohol and Health" (1984)).

3. Ross, Robert N., and Diana Chapman Walsh, "Treatment for Chemical Dependency and Mental Illness: The Payer's Perspective," 1 *Seminars in Occup. Med.* 277 (1986).

4. Walsh, J. Michael, and Steven W. Gust, "Drug Abuse in the Workplace: Issues, Policy Decisions, and Corporate Response," 1 *Seminars in Occup. Med.* (1986) (citing C.R. Shuster, Testimony Before the House Select Committee on Narcotics Abuse and Control (May 7 1986)), 237–38.

5. Ross and Walsh, Note 3, at 285.

6. Dogoloff, Lee I., "Drug Abuse in the Workplace," 1 *Occup. Med.: State of the Art Rev's* 643 (1986) (67%); Imwinkelried, Edward J., "Some Preliminary Thoughts on the Wisdom of Governmental Prohibition or Regulation of Employee Urinalysis Testing," 11 *Nova L. Rev.* 563, 565 (1987) (65%); *Alcohol, Drug Factor in Accidents Discussed, Disputed at Montreal Session,* 17 O.S.H. Rep. (BNA) 93 (1987) (50–65%) [hereinafter Montreal Session].

7. P. Bensinger, *Drugs in the Workplace: Employers' Rights and Responsibilities* 1 (1984), at 1.

8. Dogoloff, Note 6, at 645 (2.5 times); Imwinkelreid, Note 6, at 565 (16 times).

9. Walsh & Gust, Note 4, at 237.

10. *Id.* (citing study by Kandel, D., and Yamaguchi, K.).

11. BNA Special Report, "Alcohol & Drugs in the Workplace: Costs, Controls, and Controversies," 7(1986), at 7.

12. *Id.* at 7 (quoting P. Bensinger).

13. P. Bensinger, Note 7, at 1 (3.5 times); "BNA Special Report," Note 11, at 8 (3 to 4 times) (quoting P. Bensinger); Dogoloff, Note 6, at 645 (3.6 times); "Montreal Session," Note 6, at 93 (4 times) (quoting an industrial hygienist for the Department of Agriculture).

14. "Montreal Session," Note 6, at 93–94.

15. *Id.* See also *Few Sound Studies Link Drug, Alcohol Abuse with Workplace Accident Rates, Physician Says,* 17 O.S.H. Rep. (BNA) 825 (1987) (quoting Dr. Bob Brewer of the Rush Occupational Health Network).

16. "Study: $50 Billion Wasted Annually from Abuse of Drugs and Alcohol," 1 *Employee Rel. Weekly* (BNA) 1554 (1986) (citing a study by the Comprehensive Care Corp.).

17. Dubowski, Kurt M., "Drug-Use Testing: Scientific Perspectives," 11 *Nova L. Review* (1987), at 437.

18. Hoyt, David W., Robert E. Finnigan, Thomas Nee, Theodore F. Shults, and Thorne J. Butler, "Drug Testing in the Workplace—Are Methods Legally Defensible?," 258 *J.A.M.A.* 504, 508 (1987). See also Hudner, Edward J., "Urine Testing for Drugs," 11 Nova L. Rev. 553, 555 (1987); McBay, Arthur J., "Efficient Drug Testing: Addressing the Basic Issues," 11 Nova L. Rev. 647, 648 (1987); Morikawa, Dennis J., Peter J. Hurtgen, Terence G. Connor and Joseph J. Costello, "Implementation of Drug and Alcohol Testing in the Unionized Workplace," 11 *Nova L. Rev.* 653, 656 (1987); Schroeder, Patricia, and Andrea L. Nelson, "Drug Testing in the Federal Government," 11 *Nova L. Rev.* 685, 688–89 (1987).

19. Professor Ronald K. Seigel of UCLA Medical School, forensic psychopharmacologist, quoted in Denenberg, Tia Schneider, and Richard V. Denenberg, "Drug Testing from the Arbiter's Perspective," 11 *Nova L. Rev.* (1987), at 399.

20. Council on Scientific Affairs, American Medical Association, "Scientific Issues in Drug Testing," 257 *J.A.M.A.* (1987), at 3112.

21. Fenton, John, Michael Schaffer, Nancy W. Chen, and E. W. Bermes, Jr., "A Comparison of Enzyme Immunoassay and Gas Chromatography/Mass Spectrometry in Forensic Toxicology," 25 *J. Forensic Sci.* 314 (1980).

22. False positive rates vary based on the substance tested for and the test procedure used. The EMIT test false positive rates are: cocaine—10%; opiates—5.6%; barbiturates—5.1%; amphetamines—12.5%; and marijuana—19%. *Id.* The average is about 10%, for a specificity of 90%.

23. Chapman, "The Ruckus Over Medical Testing," *Fortune,* Aug. 19, 1985, at 57, 58.

24. Boyer, "ABC to Conduct Drug-Use Tests on Applicants for Full-Time Jobs," *N.Y. Times,*

July 10, 1987, at Y 44; "Labor Letter: Drug Tests Spread," *Wall St. J.*, April 7, 1987, at 1.

25. "Drug Testing Popular," *Occup. Health & Safety*, Aug. 1987, at 12 (based on survey by Business and Legal Reports).

26. "Survey Shows Little Use of Random Test Programs," 1 *Nat'l Rep. on Substance Abuse* (BNA), Sept. 16, 1987, at 2 (citing study at Executive Knowledgeworks).

27. *Id.*

28. *Id.*

29. *Id.*

30. Teleconference on Drug Testing, *U.S.A. Today*, Feb. 5, 1987, at 1.

31. *Allen v. City of Marietta*, 601 F. Supp. 482, 491 (N.D. Ga. 1985).

32. *Id.*

33. *Turner v. Fraternal Order of Police*, 500 A.2d 1005, 1011 (D.C. 1985).

34. *National Treasury Employees Union v. Von Raab*, 816 F. 2d 170, 175 (5th Cir. 1987).

35. *Caruso v. Ward*, 133 Misc. 2d 544, 547, 506 N.Y.S.2d 789, 792 (Sup. Ct. 1986).

36. *Turner*, 500 A.2d at 1011.

37. 825 F.2d 341 (11th Cir. 1987), at 345.

38. 809 F.2d 1302 (8th Cir. 1987), at 1310. *Accord*

National Fed'n of Fed. Employees, 818 F.2d at 943.

39. *Amalgamated Transit Union, Local 1277, AFL-CIO v. Sunline Transit Agency*, 663 F. Supp. 1560, 1572 (C.D. Cal. 1987). See also *Shoemaker v. Handel*, 795 F.2d 1136 (3d Cir. 1986).

40. *City of Palm Bay*, 475 So. 2d at 1326.

41. 647 F. Supp. 875 (E.D. Tenn. 1986), at 882.

42. 816 F.2d 170 (5th Cir. 1987), at 181–82.

43. *National Treasury Employees Union*, 816 F.2d at 175.

44. 133 Misc. 2d 544, 506 N.Y.S. 2d 789 (Sup. Ct. 1986), at 548, 506 N.Y.S.2d at 793.

45. Council on Scientific Affairs, American Medical Association, "Issues in Employee Drug Testing," 258 *J.A.M.A.* 2089 (1987), at 2095. In the interest of disclosure, it should be noted that the author was the legal consultant to the American Medical Association in the drafting of this recommendation.

46. Jack E. Nelson, "Drug Abusers on the Job," 23 *J. Occup. Med.* 403 (1981).

47. Masi, Dale A., "Employee Assistance Programs," 1 *Occup. Med.: State of the Art Rev's* 653 (1986).

48. Bureau of National Affairs, "Alcohol and Drugs in the Workplace" 15 (1986) at 39.

49. *Id.* at 40.

Drug Testing in Employment

*Joseph DesJardins
and Ronald Duska*

According to one survey, nearly one-half of all *Fortune* 500 companies were planning to administer drug tests to employees and prospective employees by the end of 1987.[1] Counter to what seems to be the current trend in favor of drug testing, we will argue that it is rarely legitimate to override an employee's or applicant's right to privacy by using such tests or procedures.

OPENING STIPULATIONS

We take privacy to be an "employee right" by which we mean a presumptive moral entitlement to receive certain goods or be protected from certain harms in the workplace.[2] Such a right creates a *prima facie* obligation on the part of the employer to provide the relevant goods or, as in this case, refrain from the rele-

From Joseph DesJardins and Ronald Duska, "Drug Testing in Employment," *Business & Professional Ethics Journal* 6 (1987). Reprinted by permission of the authors.

vant harmful treatment. These rights prevent employees from being placed in the fundamentally coercive position where they must choose between their job and other basic human goods.

Further, we view the employer-employee relationship as essentially contractual. The employer-employee relationship is an economic one and, unlike relationships such as those between a government and its citizens or a parent and a child, exists primarily as a means for satisfying the economic interests of the contracting parties. The obligations that each party incurs are only those that it voluntarily takes on. Given such a contractual relationship, certain areas of the employee's life remain their own private concern and no employer has a right to invade them. On these presumptions we maintain that certain information about an employee is rightfully private, i.e., the employee has a right to privacy.

THE RIGHT TO PRIVACY

According to George Brenkert, a right to privacy involves a three-place relation between a person A, some information X, and another person B. The right to privacy is violated only when B deliberately comes to possess information X about A, and no relationship between A and B exists which would justify B's coming to know X about A.[3] Thus, for example, the relationship one has with a mortgage company would justify that company's coming to know about one's salary, but the relationship one has with a neighbor does not justify the neighbor's coming to know that information. Hence, an employee's right to privacy is violated whenever personal information is requested, collected and/or used by an employer in a way or for any purpose that is *irrelevant to* or *in violation of* the contractual relationship that exists between *employer and employee*.

Since drug testing is a means for obtaining information, the information sought must be relevant to the contract in order for the drug testing not to violate privacy. Hence, we must first decide if knowledge of drug use obtained by drug testing is job-relevant. In cases where the knowledge of drug use is *not* relevant, there appears to be no justification for subjecting employees to drug tests. In cases where information of drug use is job-relevant, we need to consider if, when, and under what conditions using a means such as drug testing to obtain that knowledge is justified.

IS KNOWLEDGE OF DRUG USE JOB RELEVANT INFORMATION?

There seem to be two arguments used to establish that knowledge of drug use is job relevant information. The first argument claims that drug use adversely affects job performance thereby leading to lower productivity, higher costs, and consequently lower profits. Drug testing is seen as a way of avoiding these adverse effects. According to some estimates $25 billion ($25,000,000,000) are lost each year in the United States because of drug use.[4] This occurs because of loss in productivity, increase in costs due to theft, increased rates in health and liability insurance, and such. Since employers are contracting with an employee for the performance of specific tasks, employers seem to have a legitimate claim upon whatever personal information is relevant to an employee's ability to do the job.

The second argument claims that drug use has been and can be responsible for considerable harm to the employee him or herself, fellow employees, the employer, and/or third parties, including consumers. In this case drug testing is defended because it is seen as a way of preventing possible harm. Further, since employers can be held liable for harms done both to third parties, e.g., customers, and to the employee or his or her fellow employees, knowledge of employee drug use will allow employers to gain information that can protect themselves from risks such as liability. But how good are these arguments? We turn to examine the arguments more closely.

THE FIRST ARGUMENT: JOB PERFORMANCE AND KNOWLEDGE OF DRUG USE

The first argument holds that drug use leads to lower productivity and consequently implies that a knowledge of drug use obtained through drug testing will allow an employer to increase productivity. It is generally assumed that people using certain drugs have their performances affected by such use. Since enhancing productivity is something any employer desires, any use of drugs that reduces productivity affects the employer in an undesirable way, and that use is, then, job-relevant. If such production losses can be eliminated by knowledge of the drug use, then knowledge of that drug use is job-relevant information. On the surface this argument seems reasonable. Obviously some drug use in lowering the level of performance can decrease productivity. Since the employer is entitled to a certain level of performance and drug use adversely affects performance, knowledge of that use seems job-relevant.

But this formulation of the argument leaves an important question unanswered. To what level of performance are employers entitled? Optimal performance, or some lower level? If some lower level, what? Employers have a valid claim upon some *certain level* of performance, such that a failure to perform up to this level would give the employer a justification for disciplining, firing or at least finding fault with the employee. But that does not necessarily mean that the employer has a right to a maximum or optimal level of performance, a level above and beyond a certain level of acceptability. It might be nice if the employee gives an employer a maximum effort or optimal performance, but that is above and beyond the call of the employee's duty and the employer can hardly claim a right at all times to the highest level of performance of which an employee is capable.

That there are limits on required levels of performance and productivity becomes clear if we recognize that job performance is person related. It is person-related because one person's best efforts at a particular task might produce results well below the norm, while another person's minimal efforts might produce results abnormally high when compared to the norm. For example a professional baseball player's performance on a ball field will be much higher than the average person's since the average person is unskilled at baseball. We have all encountered people who work hard with little or no results, as well as people who work little with phenomenal results. Drug use by very talented people might diminish their performance or productivity, but that performance would still be better than the performance of the average person or someone totally lacking in the skills required. That being said, the important question now is whether the employer is entitled to an employee's maximum effort and best results, or merely to an effort sufficient to perform the task expected.

If the relevant consideration is whether the employee is producing as expected (according to the normal demands of the position and contract) not whether he or she is producing as much as possible, then knowledge of drug use is irrelevant or unnecessary. Let's see why.

If the person is producing what is expected, knowledge of drug use on the grounds of production is irrelevant since, *ex hypothesi* the production is satisfactory. If, on the other hand, the performance suffers, then, to the extent that it slips below the level justifiably expected, the employer has *prima facie* grounds for warning, disciplining or releasing the employee. But the justification for this is the person's unsatisfactory performance, not the person's use of drugs. Accordingly, drug use information is either unnecessary or irrelevant and consequently there are not sufficient grounds to override the right of privacy. Thus, unless we can argue that an employer is entitled to optimal performance, the argument fails.

This counter-argument should make it clear that the information which is job-relevant, and consequently which is not rightfully private, is information about an employee's level of performance and not information about the underlying causes of that level. The fallacy of the argument which promotes drug testing in the name of increased productivity is the assumption that each employee is obliged to perform at an optimal, or at least quite high, level. But this is required under few, if any, contracts. What is required contractually is meeting the normally expected levels of production or performing the tasks in the job-description adequately (not optimally). If one can do that under the influence of drugs, then on the grounds of job-performance at least, drug use is rightfully private. If one cannot perform the task adequately, then the employee is not fulfilling the contract, and knowledge of the cause of the failure to perform is irrelevant on the contractual model.

Of course, if the employer suspects drug use or abuse as the cause of the unsatisfactory performance, then she might choose to help the person with counseling or rehabilitation. However, this does not seem to be something morally required of the employer. Rather, in the case of unsatisfactory performance, the employer has a *prima facie* justification for dismissing or disciplining the employee.

Before turning to the second argument which attempts to justify drug testing, we should mention a factor about drug use that is usually ignored in talk of productivity. The entire productivity argument is irrelevant for those cases in which employees use performance enhancing drugs. Amphetamines and steroids, for example, can actually enhance some performances. This points to the need for care when tying drug testing to job-performance. In the case of some drugs used by athletes, for example, drug testing is done because the drug-influenced performance is too good and therefore unfair, not because it leads to inadequate job-performance. In such a case, where the testing is done to ensure fair competition, the testing may be justified. But drug testing in sports is an entirely different matter than drug testing in business.

To summarize our argument so far. Drug use may affect performances, but as long as the performance is at an acceptable level, the knowledge of drug use is irrelevant. If the performance is unacceptable, then that is sufficient cause for action to be taken. In this case an employee's failure to fulfill his or her end of a contract makes knowledge of the drug use unnecessary.

THE SECOND ARGUMENT: HARM AND THE KNOWLEDGE OF DRUG USE TO PREVENT HARM

Even though the performance argument is inadequate, there is an argument that seems somewhat stronger. This is an argument based on the potential for drug use to cause harm. . . . One could argue that drug testing might be justified if such testing led to knowledge that would enable an employer to prevent harm. Drug use certainly can lead to harming others. Consequently, if knowledge of such drug use can prevent harm, then, knowing whether or not one's employee uses drugs might be a legitimate concern of an employer in certain circumstances. This second argument claims that knowledge of the employee's drug use is job-relevant because employees who are under the influence of drugs can pose a threat to the health and safety of themselves and others, and an employer who knows of that drug use and the harm it can cause has a responsibility to prevent it. Employers have both a general duty to prevent harm and the specific responsibility for harms done by their employees. Such responsibilities are sufficient reason for an employer to claim that information about an employee's drug use is relevant if that knowledge can prevent harm by giving the employer grounds for dismissing the employee or not allowing him/her to perform potentially harmful tasks. Employers might even claim a right to reduce unreasonable risks, in this case the risks involving legal and economic liability for harms caused by employees under the influence of drugs, as further justification for knowing about employee drug use.

This second argument differs from the first in which only a lowered job performance was relevant information. In this case, even to allow the performance is problematic, for the performance itself, more than being inadequate, can hurt people. We cannot be as sanguine about the prevention of harm as we can about inadequate production. Where drug use can cause serious harms, knowledge of that use becomes relevant if the knowledge of such use can lead to the prevention of harm and drug testing becomes justified as a means for obtaining that knowledge.

As we noted, we will begin initially by accepting this argument . . . where restrictions on liberty are allowed in order to prevent harm to others. . . . In such a case an employer's obligation to prevent harm may over-ride the obligation to respect an employee's privacy.

But let us examine this more closely. Upon examination, certain problems arise, so that even if there is a possibility of justifying drug testing to prevent harm, some caveats have to be observed and some limits set out.

JOBS WITH POTENTIAL TO CAUSE HARM

To say that employers can use drug-testing where that can prevent harm is not to say that every employer has the right to know about the drug use of every employee. Not every job poses a serious enough threat to justify an employer coming to know this information.

In deciding which jobs pose serious enough threats certain guidelines should be followed. First the potential for harm should be *clear* and *present*. Perhaps all jobs in some extended way pose potential threats to human well-being. We suppose an accountant's error could pose a threat of harm to someone somewhere. But some jobs like those of airline pilots, school bus drivers, public transit drivers and surgeons, are jobs in which unsatisfactory performance poses a clear and present danger to others. It would be much harder to make an argument that job performances by auditors, secretaries, executive vice-presidents for public relations, college teachers, professional athletes, and the like, could cause harm if those performances were carried on under the influence of drugs. They would cause harm only in exceptional cases.

NOT EVERY PERSON IS TO BE TESTED

But, even if we can make a case that a particular job involves a clear and present danger for causing harm if performed under the influence of drugs, it is not appropriate to treat everyone holding such a job the same. Not every job-holder is equally threatening.

There is less reason to investigate an airline pilot for drug use if that pilot has a twenty-year record of exceptional service than there is to investigate a pilot whose behavior has become erratic and unreliable recently, or than one who reports to work smelling of alcohol and slurring his words. Presuming that every airline pilot is equally threatening is to deny individuals the respect that they deserve as autonomous, rational agents. It is to ignore previous history and significant differences. It is also probably inefficient and leads to the lowering of morale. It is the likelihood of causing harm, and not the fact of being an airline pilot *per se,* that is relevant in deciding which employees in critical jobs to test.

So, even if knowledge of drug use is justifiable to prevent harm, we must be careful to limit this justification to a range of jobs and people where the potential for harm is clear and present. The jobs must be jobs that clearly can cause harm, and the specific employee should not be someone who is reliable with a history of such reliability. Finally, the drugs being tested should be those drugs, the use of which in those jobs is really potentially harmful.

LIMITATIONS ON DRUG TESTING POLICIES

Even when we identify those jobs and individuals where knowledge of drug use would be job relevant information, we still need to examine whether some procedural limitations should not be placed upon the employer's testing for drugs. We have said that in cases where a real threat of harm exists and where evidence exists suggesting that a particular employee poses such a threat, an employer could be justified in knowing about drug use in order to prevent the potential harm. But we need to recognize that as long as the employer has the discretion for deciding when

the potential for harm is clear and present, and for deciding which employees pose the threat of harm, the possibility of abuse is great. Thus, some policy limiting the employer's power is called for.

Just as criminal law places numerous restrictions protecting individual dignity and liberty on the state's pursuit of its goals, so we should expect that some restrictions be placed on an employer in order to protect innocent employees from harm (including loss of job and damage to one's personal and professional reputation). Thus, some system of checks upon an employer's discretion in these matters seems advisable. Workers covered by collective bargaining agreements or individual contracts might be protected by clauses in those agreements that specify which jobs pose a real threat of harm (e.g., pilots but not cabin attendants) and what constitutes a just cause for investigating drug use. Local, state, and federal legislatures might do the same for workers not covered by employment contracts. What needs to be set up is a just employment relationship—one in which an employee's expectations and responsibilities are specified in advance and in which an employer's discretionary authority to discipline or dismiss an employee is limited.

Beyond that, any policy should accord with the nature of the employment relationship. Since that relationship is a contractual one, it should meet the condition of a morally valid contract, which is informed consent. Thus, in general, we would argue that only methods that have received the informed consent of employees can be used in acquiring information about drug use.[5]

A drug-testing policy that requires all employees to submit to a drug test or to jeopardize their job would seem coercive and therefore unacceptable. Being placed in such a fundamentally coercive position of having to choose between one's job and one's privacy does not provide the conditions for a truly free consent. Policies that are unilaterally established by employers would likewise be unacceptable. Working with employees to develop company policy seems the only way to insure that the policy will be fair to both parties. Prior notice of testing would also be required in order to give employees the option of freely refraining from drug use. It is morally preferable to prevent drug use than to punish users after the fact, since this approach treats employees as capable of making rational and informed decisions.

Further procedural limitations seem advisable as well. Employees should be notified of the results of the test, they should be entitled to appeal the results (perhaps through further tests by an independent laboratory) and the information obtained through tests ought to be kept confidential. In summary, limitations upon employer discretion for administering drug tests can be derived from the nature of the employment contract and from the recognition that drug testing is justified by the desire to prevent harm, not the desire to punish wrong doing.

EFFECTIVENESS OF DRUG TESTING

Having declared that the employer might have a right to test for drug use in order to prevent harm, we still need to examine the second argument a little more closely. One must keep in mind that the justification of drug testing is the justification of a means to an end, the end of preventing harm, and that the means are a means which intrude into one's privacy. In this case, before one allows drug testing as a means, one should be clear that there are not more effective means available.

If the employer has a legitimate right, perhaps duty, to ascertain knowledge of drug use to prevent harm, it is important to examine exactly how effectively, and in what situations, the *knowledge* of the drug use will prevent the harm. So far we have just assumed that the *knowledge* will prevent the harm. But how?

Let us take an example to pinpoint the difficulty. Suppose a transit driver, shortly before work, took some cocaine which, in giving him a feeling of invulnerability, leads him to take undue risks in his driving. How exactly is drug-testing going to contribute to the knowledge which will prevent the potential accident?

It is important to keep in mind that; (1) if the knowledge doesn't help prevent the harm, the testing is not justified on prevention grounds; (2) if the testing doesn't provide the relevant knowledge it is not justified either; and finally, (3) even if it was justified, it would be undesirable if a more effective means for preventing harm were discovered.

Upon examination, the links between drug testing, knowledge of drug use, and prevention of harm are not as clear as they are presumed to be. As we investigate, it begins to seem that the knowledge of the drug use even though relevant in some instances is not the most effective means to prevent harm.

Let us turn to this last consideration first. Is drug testing the most effective means for preventing harm caused by drug use?

Consider. If someone exhibits obviously drugged or drunken behavior, then this behavior itself is grounds for preventing the person from continuing in the job. Administering urine or blood tests, sending the specimens out for testing and waiting for a response, will not prevent harm in this instance. Such drug testing because of the time lapse involved, is equally superfluous in those cases where an employee is in fact under the influence of drugs, but exhibits no or only subtley impaired behavior.

Thus, even if one grants that drug testing somehow prevents harm an argument can be made that there might be much more effective methods of preventing potential harm such as administering dexterity tests of the type employed by police in possible drunk-driving cases, or requiring suspect pilots to pass flight simulator tests.[6] Eye-hand coordination, balance, reflexes, and reasoning ability can all be tested with less intrusive, more easily administered, reliable technologies which give instant results. Certainly if an employer has just cause for believing that a specific employee presently poses a real threat of causing harm, such methods are just more effective in all ways than are urinalysis and blood testing.

Even were it possible to refine drug tests so that accurate results were immediately available, that knowledge would only be job relevant if the drug use was clearly the cause of impaired job performance that could harm people. Hence, testing behavior still seems more direct and effective in preventing harm than testing for the presence of drugs *per se.*

In some cases, drug use might be connected with potential harms not by being causally connected to motor-function impairment, but by causing personality disorders (e.g., paranoia, delusions, etc.) that affect judgmental ability. Even though in such cases a *prima facie* justification for urinalysis or blood testing might exist, the same problems of effectiveness persist. How is the knowledge of the drug use attained by urinalysis and/or blood testing supposed to prevent the harm? Only if there is a causal link between the use and the potentially harmful behavior, would such knowledge be relevant. Even if we get the results of the test immediately, there is the necessity to have an established causal link between specific drug use and anticipated harmful personality disorders in specific people.

But it cannot be the task of an employer to determine that a specific drug is causally related to harm-causing personality disorders. Not every controlled substance is equally likely to cause personality changes in every person in every case. The establishment of the causal link between the use of certain drugs and harm-causing personality disorders is not the province of the employer, but the province of experts studying the effects of drugs. The burden of proof is on the employer to establish that the substance being investigated has been independently connected with the relevant psychological impairment and then, predict on that basis that the specific employee's psychological judgment has been or will soon be impaired in such a way as to cause harm.

But even when this link is established, it would seem that less intrusive means could be used to detect the potential problems, rather than relying upon the assumption of a causal link. Psychological tests of judgment, perception and memory, for example, would be a less intrusive and more direct means for acquiring the relevant information which is, after all, the likelihood of causing harm and not the presence of drugs *per se.* In short, drug testing even in these cases doesn't seem to be very effective in preventing harm on the spot.

Still, this does not mean it is not effective at all. Where it is most effective in preventing harm is in its getting people to stop using drugs or in identifying serious drug addiction. Or to put it another way, urinalysis and blood tests for drug use are more effective in preventing potential harm when they serve as a deterrent to drug use *before* it occurs, since it is very difficult to prevent harm by diagnosing drug use *after* it has occurred but before the potentially harmful behavior takes place.

Drug testing can be an effective deterrent when there is regular or random testing of all employees. This will prevent harm by inhibiting (because of the fear of detection) drug use by those who are occasional users and those who do not wish to be detected.

It will probably not inhibit or stop the use by the chronic addicted user, but it will allow an employer to discover the chronic user or addict, assuming that the tests are accurately administered and reliably evaluated. If the chronic user's addiction would probably lead to harmful behavior of others, the harm is prevented by taking that user off the job. Thus regular or random testing will prevent harms done by deterring the occasional user and by detecting the chronic user.

There are six possibilities for such testing:

1. Regularly scheduled testing of all employees
2. Regularly scheduled testing of randomly selected employees
3. Randomly scheduled testing of all employees
4. Randomly scheduled testing of randomly selected employees
5. Regularly scheduled testing of employees selected for probable cause,
6. Randomly scheduled testing of employees selected for probable cause

Only the last two seem morally acceptable as well as effective.

Obviously, randomly scheduled testing will be more effective than regularly scheduled testing in detecting the occasional user, because the occasional users can control their use to pass the tests, unless of course tests were given so often (a practice economically unfeasible) that they needed to stop altogether. Regular scheduling probably will detect the habitual or addicted user. Randomly selecting people to test is probably cheaper, as is random scheduling, but it is not nearly as effective as testing all. Besides, the random might miss some of the addicted altogether, and will not deter the risk takers as much as the risk aversive persons. It is, ironically, the former who are probably potentially more harmful.

But these are merely considerations of efficiency. We have said that testing without probable cause is unacceptable. Any type of regular testing of all employees is unaccept-

able. We have argued that testing employees without first establishing probable cause is an unjustifiable violation of employee privacy. Given this, and given the expense of general and regular testing of all employees (especially if this is done by responsible laboratories), it is more likely that random testing will be employed as the means of deterrence. But surely testing of randomly selected innocent employees is as intrusive to those tested as is regular testing. The argument that there will be fewer tests is correct on quantitative grounds, but qualitatively the intrusion and unacceptability are the same. The claim that employers should be allowed to sacrifice the well-being of (some few) innocent employees to deter (some equally few) potentially harmful employees seems, on the face of it, unfair. Just as we do not allow the state randomly to tap the telephones of just any citizen in order to prevent crime, so we ought not allow employers to drug test all employees randomly to prevent harm. To do so is again to treat innocent employees solely as a means to the end of preventing potential harm.

This leaves only the use of regular or random drug-testing as a deterrent in those cases where probable cause exists for believing that a particular employee poses a threat of harm. It would seem that in this case, the drug testing is acceptable. In such cases only the question of effectiveness remains: Are the standard techniques of urinalysis and blood-testing more effective means for preventing harms than alternatives such as dexterity tests? It seems they are effective in different ways. The dexterity tests show immediately if someone is incapable of performing a task, or will perform one in such a way as to cause harm to others. The urinalysis and blood-testing will prevent harm indirectly by getting the occasional user to curtail their use, and by detecting the habitual or addictive user, which will allow the employer to either give treatment to the addictive personality or remove them from the job. Thus we can conclude that drug testing is effective in a limited way, but aside from inhibiting occasional users because of fear of detection, and discovering habitual users, it seems problematic that it does much to prevent harm that couldn't be achieved by other means.

Consider one final issue in the case of the occasional user. They are the drug users who do weigh the risks and benefits and who are physically and psychologically free to decide. The question in their case is not simply "will the likelihood of getting caught by urinalysis or blood-testing deter this individual from using drugs?" Given the benefits of psychological tests and dexterity tests described above, the question is "will the rational user be more deterred by urinalysis or blood testing than by random psychological or dexterity tests?" And, if this is so, is this increase in the effectiveness of a deterrent sufficient to offset the increased expense and time required by drug tests? We see no reason to believe that behavioral or judgment tests are not, or cannot be made to be, as effective in determining what an employer needs to know (i.e., that a particular employee may presently be a potential cause of harm). If the behavioral, dexterity and judgment tests can be as effective in determining a potential for harm, we see no reason to believe that they cannot be as effective a deterrent as drug tests. Finally, even if a case can be made for an increase in deterrent effect of drug testing, we are skeptical that this increased effectiveness will outweigh the increased inefficiencies.

In summary, we have seen that deterrence is effective at times and under certain conditions allows the sacrificing of the privacy rights of innocent employees to the future and speculative good of preventing harms to others. However, there are many ways to deter drug use when that deterrence is legitimate and desirable to prevent harm. But random testing, which seems the only practicable means which has an impact in preventing harm is the one which most offends workers rights to privacy and which is most intrusive of the rights of the innocent. Even when effective, drug testing as a deterrent must be checked by the rights of employees. . . .

DRUG TESTING FOR PROSPECTIVE EMPLOYEES

Let's turn finally to drug testing during a pre-employment interview. Assuming the job description and responsibilities have been made clear, we can say that an employer is entitled to expect from a prospective employee whatever performance is agreed to in the employment contract. Of course, this will always involve risks, since the employer must make a judgment about future performances. To lower this risk, employers have a legitimate claim to some information about the employee. Previous work experience, training, education, and the like are obvious candidates since they indicate the person's ability to do the job. Except in rare circumstances drug use itself is irrelevant for determining an employee's ability to perform. (Besides, most people who are interviewing know enough to get their systems clean if the prospective employee is going to test them.)

We suggest that an employer can claim to have an interest in knowing (a) whether or not the prospective employee *can* do the job and (b) whether there is reason to believe that once hired the employee *will* do the job. The first can be determined in fairly straightforward ways: past work experience, training, education, etc. Presumably past drug use is thought more relevant to the second question. But there are straightforward and less intrusive means than drug testing for resolving this issue. Asking the employee "Is there anything that might prevent you from doing this job?" comes first to mind. Hiring the employee on a probationary period is another way. But to inquire about drug use here is to claim a right to know too much. It is to claim a right to know not only information about what an employee *can* do, but also a right to inquire into whatever background information *might* be (but not necessarily *is*) causally related to what an employee *will* do. But the range of factors that could be relevant here, from medical history to psychological dispositions to family plans, is surely too open-ended for an employee to claim as a *right* to know.

It might be responded that what an employee is entitled to expect is not a certain level of output, but a certain level of effort. The claim here would be that while drug use is only contingently related to what an employee *can* do, it is directly related to an employee's *motivation* to do the job. Drug use then is *de facto* relevant to the personal information that an employee is *entitled* to know.

But this involves an assumption mentioned above. The discussion so far has assumed that drugs will adversely affect job performance. However, some drugs are performance *enhancing* whether they are concerned with actual *output* or *effort*. The widespread use of steroids, pain-killers, and dexadrine among professional athletes are perhaps only the most publicized instances of performance enhancing drugs. (A teacher's use of caffeine before an early-morning class is perhaps a more common example.) More to the point, knowledge of drug use tells little about motivation. There are too many other variables to be considered. Some users are motivated and some are not. Thus the motivational argument is faulty.

We can conclude, then, that whether the relevant consideration for prospective employees is output or effort, knowledge of drug use will be largely irrelevant for predicting. Employers ought to be positivistic in their approach. They should restrict their informa-

tion gathering to measurable behavior and valid predictions, (What has the prospect done? What can the prospect do? What has the prospect promised to do?) and not speculate about the underlying *causes* of this behavior. With a probationary work period always an option, there are sufficient non-intrusive means for limiting risks available to employers without having to rely on investigations into drug use.

In summary, we believe that drug use is information that is rightfully private and that only in exceptional cases can an employer claim a right to know about such use. Typically, these are cases in which knowledge of drug use could be used to prevent harm. However, even in those cases we believe that there are less intrusive and more effective means available than drug testing for gaining the information that would be necessary to prevent the harm. Thus, we conclude that drug testing of employees is rarely justified, and mostly inefficacious.

NOTES

1. *The New Republic,* March 31, 1986.
2. "A Defense of Employee Rights," Joseph Des-Jardins and John McCall, *Journal of Business Ethics* 4, (1985). We should emphasize that our concern is with the *moral* rights of privacy for employees and not with any specific or prospective *legal* rights. Readers interested in pursuing the legal aspects of employee drug testing should consult: "Workplace Privacy Issues and Employee Screening Policies" by Richard Lehe and David Middlebrooks in *Employee Relations Law Journal* (Vol. 11, no. 3) pp. 407–21; and "Screening Workers for Drugs: A Legal and Ethical Framework" by Mark Rothstein, in *Employee Relations Law Journal* (vol. 11, no. 3) pp. 422–36.
3. "Privacy, Polygraphs, and Work," George Brenkert, *Business and Professional Ethics Journal* Vol. 1, no. 1 (Fall 1981). For a more general discussion of privacy in the workplace see "Privacy in Employment" by Joseph Des-

Jardins, in *Moral Rights in the Workplace* edited by Gertrude Ezorsky, (SUNY Press, 1987). A good resource for philosophical work on privacy can be found in "Recent Work on the Concept of Privacy" by W. A. Parent, in *American Philosophical Quarterly* (Vol. 20, Oct. 1983) pp. 341–56.

4. *U.S. News and World Report,* Aug. 1983; *Newsweek,* May 1983.

5. The philosophical literature on informed consent is often concerned with "informed consent" in a medical context. For an interesting discussion of informed consent in the workplace, see Mary Gibson, *Worker's Rights* (Rowman and Allanheld, 1983), especially pp. 13–14 and 74–75.

6. For a reiteration of this point and a concise argument against drug testing, see Lewis L. Maltby, "Why Drug Testing Is a Bad Idea," *Inc.* June 1987, pp. 152–53. "But the fundamental flaw with drug testing is that it tests for the wrong thing. A realistic program to detect workers whose condition puts the company or other people at risk would test for the condition that actually creates the danger. The reason drunk or stoned airline pilots and truck drivers are dangerous is their reflexes, coordination, and timing are deficient. This impairment could come from many situations—drugs, alcohol, emotional problems—the list is almost endless. A serious program would recognize that the real problem is workers' impairment, and test for that. Pilots can be tested in flight simulators. People in other jobs can be tested by a trained technician in about 20 minutes—at the job site," p. 152.

Whistleblowing and Professional Responsibility

Sissela Bok

"Whistleblowing" is a new label generated by our increased awareness of the ethical conflicts encountered at work. Whistleblowers sound an alarm from within the very organization in which they work, aiming to spotlight neglect or abuses that threaten the public interest.

The stakes in whistleblowing are high. Take the nurse who alleges that physicians enrich themselves in her hospital through unnecessary surgery; the engineer who discloses safety defects in the braking systems of a fleet of new rapid-transit vehicles; the Defense Department official who alerts Congress to military graft and overspending: all know that they pose a threat to those whom they denounce and that their own careers may be at risk.

MORAL CONFLICTS

Moral conflicts on several levels confront anyone who is wondering whether to speak out about abuses or risks or serious neglect. In the first place, he must try to decide whether, other things being equal, speaking out is in fact in the public interest. This choice is often made more complicated by factual uncertainties: Who is responsible for the abuse or neglect? How great is the threat? And how likely is it that speaking out will precipitate changes for the better?

In the second place, a would-be whistleblower must weigh his responsibility to serve the public interest against the responsibility he owes to his colleagues and the institution

From Sissela Bok, "Whistleblowing and Professional Responsibility," *New York University Education Quarterly,* 11 (Summer 1980): 2–7. Reprinted with permission.

in which he works. While the professional ethic requires collegial loyalty, the codes of ethics often stress responsibility to the public over and above duties to colleagues and clients. Thus the United States Code of Ethics for Government Servants asks them to "expose corruption wherever uncovered" and to "put loyalty to the highest moral principles and to country above loyalty to persons, party, or government."[1] Similarly, the largest professional engineering association requires members to speak out against abuses threatening the safety, health, and welfare of the public.[2]

A third conflict for would-be whistleblowers is personal in nature and cuts across the first two: even in cases where they have concluded that the facts warrant speaking out, and that their duty to do so overrides loyalties to colleagues and institutions, they often have reason to fear the results of carrying out such a duty. However strong this duty may seem in theory, they know that, in practice, retaliation is likely. As a result, their careers and their ability to support themselves and their families may be unjustly impaired.[3] A government handbook issued during the Nixon era recommends reassigning "undesirables" to places so remote that they would prefer to resign. Whistleblowers may also be downgraded or given work without responsibility or work for which they are not qualified; or else they may be given many more tasks than they can possibly perform. Another risk is that an outspoken civil servant may be ordered to undergo a psychiatric fitness-for-duty examination,[4] declared unfit for service, and "separated" as well as discredited from the point of view of any allegations he may be making. Outright firing, finally, is the most direct institutional response to whistleblowers.

Add to the conflicts confronting individual whistleblowers the claim to self-policing that many professions make, and professional responsibility is at issue in still another way. For an appeal to the public goes against everything that "self-policing" stands for. The question for the different professions, then, is how to resolve, insofar as it is possible, the conflict between professional loyalty and professional responsibility toward the outside world. The same conflicts arise to some extent in all groups, but professional groups often have special cohesion and claim special dignity and privileges.

The plight of whistleblowers has come to be documented by the press and described in a number of books. Evidence of the hardships imposed on those who chose to act in the public interest has combined with a heightened awareness of professional malfeasance and corruption to produce a shift toward greater public support of whistleblowers. Public service law firms and consumer groups have taken up their cause; institutional reforms and legislation have been proposed to combat illegitimate reprisals.[5]

Given the indispensable services performed by so many whistleblowers, strong public support is often merited. But the new climate of acceptance makes it easy to overlook the dangers of whistleblowing: of uses in error or in malice; of work and reputations unjustly lost for those falsely accused; of privacy invaded and trust undermined. There comes a level of internal prying and mutual suspicion at which no institution can function. And it is a fact that the disappointed, the incompetent, the malicious, and the paranoid all too often leap to accusations in public. Worst of all, ideological persecution throughout the world traditionally relies on insiders willing to inform on their colleagues or even on their family members, often through staged public denunciations or press campaigns.

No society can count itself immune from such dangers. But neither can it risk silencing those with a legitimate reason to blow the whistle. How then can we distinguish between different instances of whistleblowing? A society that fails to protect the right to speak out even on the part of those whose warnings turn out to be spurious obviously opens the door to political repression. But from the moral point of view there are important differences between the aims, messages, and methods of dissenters from within.

NATURE OF WHISTLEBLOWING

Three elements, each jarring, and triply jarring when conjoined, lend acts of whistleblowing special urgency and bitterness: dissent, breach of loyalty, and accusation.

Like all dissent, whistleblowing makes public a disagreement with an authority or a majority view. But whereas dissent can concern all forms of disagreement with, for instance, religious dogma or government policy or court decisions, whistleblowing has the narrower aim of shedding light on negligence or abuse, or alerting to a risk, and of assigning responsibility for this risk.

Would-be whistleblowers confront the conflict inherent in all dissent: between conforming and sticking their necks out. The more repressive the authority they challenge, the greater the personal risk they take in speaking out. At exceptional times, as in times of war, even ordinarily tolerant authorities may come to regard dissent as unacceptable and even disloyal.[6]

Furthermore, the whistleblower hopes to stop the game; but since he is neither referee nor coach, and since he blows the whistle on his own team, his act is seen as a violation of loyalty. In holding his position, he has assumed certain obligations to his colleagues and clients. He may even have subscribed to a loyalty oath or a promise of confidentiality. Loyalty to colleagues and to clients comes to be pitted against loyalty to the public interest, to those who may be injured unless the revelation is made.

Not only is loyalty violated in whistleblowing, hierarchy as well is often opposed, since the whistleblower is not only a colleague but a subordinate. Though aware of the risks inherent in such disobedience, he often hopes to keep his job.[7] At times, however, he plans his alarm to coincide with leaving the institution. If he is highly placed, or joined by others, resigning in protest may effectively direct public attention to the wrongdoing at issue.[8] Still another alternative, often chosen by those who wish to be safe from retaliation, is to leave the institution quietly, to secure another post, and then to blow the whistle. In this way, it is possible to speak with the authority and knowledge of an insider without having the vulnerability of that position.

It is the element of accusation, of calling a "foul," that arouses the strongest reactions on the part of the hierarchy. The accusation may be of neglect, of willfully concealed dangers, or of outright abuse on the part of colleagues or superiors. It singles out specific persons or groups as responsible for threats to the public interest. If no one could be held responsible—as in the case of an impending avalanche—the warning would not constitute whistleblowing.

The accusation of the whistleblower, moreover, concerns a present or an imminent threat. Past errors or misdeeds occasion such an alarm only if they still affect current practices. And risks far in the future lack the immediacy needed to make the alarm a compelling one, as well as the close connection to particular individuals that would justify actual accusations. Thus an alarm can be sounded about safety defects in a rapid-transit system that threaten or will shortly threaten passengers, but the revelation of safety defects in a system no longer in use, while of historical interest, would not constitute whistleblowing. Nor would the revelation of potential problems in a system not yet fully designed and far from implemented.[9]

Not only immediacy, but also specificity, is needed for there to be an alarm capable of pinpointing responsibility. A concrete risk must be at issue rather than a vague foreboding or a somber prediction. The act of whistleblowing differs in this respect from the lamentation or the dire prophecy. An immediate and specific threat would normally be acted upon by those at risk. The whistleblower assumes that his message will alert listeners to something they do not know, or whose significance they have not grasped because it has been kept secret.

The desire for openness inheres in the temptation to reveal any secret, sometimes joined to an urge for self-aggrandizement and publicity and the hope for revenge for past slights or injustices. There can be pleasure, too—righteous or malicious—in laying bare the secrets of co-workers and in setting the record straight at last. Colleagues of the whistleblower often suspect his motives: they may regard him as a crank, as publicity-hungry, wrong about the facts, eager for scandal and discord, and driven to indiscretion by his personal biases and shortcomings.

For whistleblowing to be effective, it must arouse its audience. Inarticulate whistleblowers are likely to fail from the outset. When they are greeted by apathy, their message dissipates. When they are greeted by disbelief, they elicit no response at all. And when the audience is not free to receive or to act on the information—when censorship or fear of retribution stifles response—then the message rebounds to injure the whistleblower. Whistleblowing also requires the possibility of concerted public response: the idea of whistleblowing in an anarchy is therefore merely quixotic.

Such characteristics of whistleblowing and strategic considerations for achieving an impact are common to the noblest warnings, the most vicious personal attacks, and the delusions of the paranoid. How can one distinguish the many acts of sounding an alarm that are genuinely in the public interest from all the petty, biased, or lurid revelations that pervade our querulous and gossip-ridden society? Can we draw distinctions between different whistleblowers, different messages, different methods?

We clearly can, in a number of cases. Whistleblowing may be starkly inappropriate when in malice or error, or when it lays bare legitimately private matters having to do, for instance, with political belief or sexual life. It can, just as clearly, be the only way to shed light on an ongoing unjust practice such as drugging political prisoners or subjecting them to electroshock treatment. It can be the last resort for alerting the public to an impending disaster. Taking such clearcut cases as benchmarks, and reflecting on what it is about them that weighs so heavily for or against speaking out, we can work our way toward the admittedly more complex cases in which whistleblowing is not so clearly the right or wrong choice, or where different points of view exist regarding its legitimacy—cases where there are moral reasons both for concealment and for disclosure and where judgments conflict. Consider the following cases:[10]

A. As a construction inspector for a federal agency, John Samuels (not his real name) had personal knowledge of shoddy and deficient construction practices by private contractors. He knew his superiors received free vacations and entertainment, had their homes remodeled and found jobs for their relatives—all courtesy of a private contractor. These superiors later approved a multimillion no-bid contract with the same "generous" firm.

Samuels also had evidence that other firms were hiring nonunion laborers at a low wage while receiving substantially higher payments from the government for labor costs. A former superior, unaware of an office dictaphone, had incautiously instructed Samuels on how to accept bribes for overlooking sub-par performance.

As he prepared to volunteer this information to various members of Congress, he became tense and uneasy. His family was scared and the fears were valid. It might cost Samuels thousands of dollars to protect his job. Those who had freely provided Samuels with information would probably recant or withdraw their friendship. A number of people might object to his using a dictaphone to gather information. His agency would start covering up and vent its collective wrath upon him. As for reporters and writers, they would gather for a few days, then move on to the next story. He would be left without a job, with fewer friends, with massive battles looming, and without the financial means of fighting them. Samuels decided to remain silent.

B. Engineers of Company "A" prepared plans and specifications for machinery to be used in a manufacturing process and Company "A" turned them over to Company "B" for production. The engineers of Company "B," in reviewing the plans and specifications, came to the conclusion that they included certain miscalculations and technical deficiencies of a nature that the final product might be unsuitable for the purposes of the ultimate users, and that the equipment, if built according to the original plans and specifications, might endanger the lives of persons in proximity to it. The engineers of Company "B" called the matter to the attention of appropriate officials of their employer who, in turn, advised Company "A." Company "A" replied that its engineers felt that the design and specifications for the equipment were adequate and safe and that Company "B" should proceed to build the equipment as designed and specified. The officials of Company "B" instructed its engineers to proceed with the work.

C. A recently hired assistant director of admissions in a state university begins to wonder whether transcripts of some applicants accurately reflect their accomplishments. He knows that it matters to many in the university community, including alumni, that the football team continue its winning tradition. He has heard rumors that surrogates may be available to take tests for a fee, signing the names of designated applicants for admission, and that some of the transcripts may have been altered. But he has no hard facts. When he brings the question up with the director of admissions, he is told that the rumors are unfounded and asked not to inquire further into the matter.

INDIVIDUAL MORAL CHOICE

What questions might those who consider sounding an alarm in public ask themselves? How might they articulate the problem they see and weigh its injustice before deciding whether or not to reveal it? How can they best try to make sure their choice is the right one? In thinking about these questions it helps to keep in mind the three elements mentioned earlier: dissent, breach of loyalty, and accusation. They impose certain requirements—of accuracy and judgment in dissent; of exploring alternative ways to cope with improprieties that minimize the breach of loyalty; and of fairness in accusation. For each, careful articulation and testing of arguments are needed to limit error and bias.

Dissent by whistleblowers, first of all, is expressly claimed to be intended to benefit the public. It carries with it, as a result, an obligation to consider the nature of this benefit and to consider also the possible harm that may come from speaking out: harm to persons or institutions and, ultimately, to the public interest itself. Whistleblowers must, therefore, begin by making every effort to consider the effects of speaking out versus those of remaining silent. They must assure themselves of the accuracy of their reports, checking and rechecking the facts before speaking out; specify the degree to which there is genuine impropriety; consider how imminent is the threat they see, how serious, and how closely linked to those accused of neglect and abuse.

If the facts warrant whistleblowing, how can the second element—breach of loyalty—be minimized? The most important question here is whether the existing avenues for change within the organization have been explored. It is a waste of time for the public as well as harmful to the institution to sound the loudest alarm first. Whistleblowing has to remain a last alternative because of its destructive side effects: it must be chosen only when other alternatives have been considered and rejected. They may be rejected if they simply do not apply to the problem at hand, or when there is not time to go through routine channels or when the institution is so corrupt or coercive that steps will be taken to silence the whistleblower should he try the regular channels first.

What weight should an oath or a promise of silence have in the conflict of loyalties? One sworn to silence is doubtless under a stronger obligation because of the oath he has taken. He has bound himself, assumed specific obligations beyond those assumed in merely taking a new position. But even such promises can be overridden when the public interest at issue is strong enough. They can be overridden if they were obtained under duress or through deceit. They can be overridden, too, if they promise something that is in itself wrong or unlawful. The fact that one has promised silence is no excuse for complicity in covering up a crime or a violation of the public's trust.

The third element in whistleblowing—accusation—raises equally serious ethical concerns. They are concerns of fairness to the persons accused of impropriety. Is the message one to which the public is entitled in the first place? Or does it infringe on personal and private matters that one has no right to invade? Here, the very notion of what is in the public's best "interest" is at issue: "accusations" regarding an official's unusual sexual or religious experiences may well appeal to the public's interest without being information relevant to "the public interest."

Great conflicts arise here. We have witnessed excessive claims to executive privilege and to secrecy by government officials during the Watergate scandal in order to cover up for abuses the public had every right to discover. Conversely, those hoping to profit from prying into private matters have become adept at invoking "the public's right to know." Some

even regard such private matters as threats to the public: they voice their own religious and political prejudices in the language of accusation. Such a danger is never stronger than when the accusation is delivered surreptitiously. The anonymous accusations made during the McCarthy period regarding political beliefs and associations often injured persons who did not even know their accusers or the exact nature of the accusations.

From the public's point of view, accusations that are openly made by identifiable individuals are more likely to be taken seriously. And in fairness to those criticized, openly accepted responsibility for blowing the whistle should be preferred to the denunciation or the leaked rumor. What is openly stated can more easily be checked, its source's motives challenged, and the underlying information examined. Those under attack may otherwise be hard put to defend themselves against nameless adversaries. Often they do not even know that they are threatened until it is too late to respond. The anonymous denunciation, moreover, common to so many regimes, places the burden of investigation on government agencies that may thereby gain the power of a secret police.

From the point of view of the whistleblower, on the other hand, the anonymous message is safer in situations where retaliation is likely. But it is also often less likely to be taken seriously. Unless the message is accompanied by indications of how the evidence can be checked, its anonymity, however safe for the source, speaks against it.

During the process of weighing the legitimacy of speaking out, the method used, and the degree of fairness needed, whistleblowers must try to compensate for the strong possibility of bias on their part. They should be scrupulously aware of any motive that might skew their message: a desire for self-defense in a difficult bureaucratic situation, perhaps, or the urge to seek revenge, or inflated expectations regarding the effect their message will have on the situation. (Needless to say, bias affects the silent as well as the outspoken. The motive for holding back important information about abuses and injustice ought to give similar cause for soulsearching.)

Likewise, the possibility of personal gain from sounding the alarm ought to give pause. Once again there is then greater risk of a biased message. Even if the whistleblower regards himself as incorruptible, his profiting from revelations of neglect or abuse will lead others to question his motives and to put less credence in his charges. If, for example, a government employee stands to make large profits from a book exposing the iniquities in his agency, there is danger that he will, perhaps even unconsciously, slant his report in order to cause more of a sensation.

A special problem arises when there is a high risk that the civil servant who speaks out will have to go through costly litigation. Might he not justifiably try to make enough money on his public revelations—say, through books or public speaking—to offset his losses? In so doing he will not strictly speaking have *profited* from his revelations: he merely avoids being financially crushed by their sequels. He will nevertheless still be suspected at the time of revelation, and his message will therefore seem more questionable.

Reducing bias and error in moral choice often requires consultation, even open debate:[11] methods that force articulation of the moral arguments at stake and challenge privately held assumptions. But acts of whistleblowing present special problems when it comes to open consultation. On the one hand, once the whistleblower sounds his alarm publicly, his arguments will be subjected to open scrutiny; he will have to articulate his reasons for speaking out and substantiate his charges. On the other hand, it will then be too late to retract the alarm or to

combat its harmful effects, should his choice to speak out have been ill-advised.

For this reason, the whistleblower owes it to all involved to make sure of two things: that he has sought as much and as objective advice regarding his choice as he can *before* going public; and that he is aware of the arguments for and against the practice of whistleblowing in general, so that he can see his own choice against as richly detailed and coherently structured a background as possible. Satisfying these two requirements once again has special problems because of the very nature of whistleblowing: the more corrupt the circumstances, the more dangerous it may be to seek consultation before speaking out. And yet, since the whistleblower himself may have a biased view of the state of affairs, he may choose not to consult others when in fact it would be not only safe but advantageous to do so; he may see corruption and conspiracy where none exists.

NOTES

1. Code of Ethics for Government Service passed by the U.S. House of Representatives in the 85th Congress (1958) and applying to all government employees and office holders.

2. Code of Ethics of the Institute of Electrical and Electronics Engineers, Article IV.

3. For case histories and descriptions of what befalls whistleblowers, see Rosemary Chalk and Frank von Hippel, "Due Process for Dissenting Whistle-Blowers," *Technology Review* 81 (June–July 1979): 48–55; Alan S. Westin and Stephen Salisbury, eds., *Individual Rights in the Corporation* (New York: Pantheon, 1980); Helen Dudar, "The Price of Blowing the Whistle," *New York Times Magazine,* 30 October 1979, pp. 41–54; John Edsall, *Scientific Freedom and Responsibility* (Washington, D.C.: American Association for the Advancement of Science, 1975), p. 5; David Ewing, *Freedom Inside the Organization* (New York: Dutton, 1977); Ralph Nader, Peter Petkas, and Kate Blackwell, *Whistle*

Blowing (New York: Grossman, 1972); Charles Peter and Taylor Branch, *Blowing the Whistle* (New York: Praeger, 1972).

4. Congressional hearings uncovered a growing resort to mandatory psychiatric examinations.

5. For an account of strategies and proposals to support government whistleblowers, see Government Accountability Project, *A Whistleblower's Guide to the Federal Bureaucracy* (Washington, D.C.: Institute for Policy Studies, 1977).

6. See, e.g., Samuel Eliot Morison, Frederick Merk, and Frank Friedel, *Dissent in Three American Wars* (Cambridge: Harvard University Press, 1970).

7. In the scheme worked out by Albert Hirschman in *Exit, Voice and Loyalty* (Cambridge: Harvard University Press, 1970), whistleblowing represents "voice" accompanied by a preference not to "exit," though forced "exit" is clearly a possibility and "voice" after or during "exit" may be chosen for strategic reasons.

8. Edward Weisband and Thomas N. Franck, *Resignation in Protest* (New York: Grossman, 1975).

9. Future developments can, however, be the cause for whistleblowing if they are seen as resulting from steps being taken or about to be taken that render them inevitable.

10. Case A is adapted from Louis Clark, "The Sound of Professional Suicide," *Barrister*, Summer 1978, p. 10; Case B is Case 5 in Robert J. Baum and Albert Flores, eds., *Ethical Problems of Engineering* (Troy, N.Y.: Rensselaer Polytechnic Institute, 1978), p. 186.

11. I discuss these questions of consultation and publicity with respect to moral choice in chapter 7 of Sissela Bok, *Lying* (New York: Pantheon, 1978); and in *Secrets* (New York: Pantheon Books, 1982), Ch. IX and XV.

Whistleblowing and Employee Loyalty

Ronald Duska

. . . There are proponents on both sides of the issue—those who praise whistleblowers as civic heroes and those who condemn them as "finks." Maxwell Glen and Cody Shearer, who wrote about the whistleblowers at Three Mile Island say, "Without the *courageous* breed of assorted company insiders known as whistleblowers—workers who often risk their livelihoods to disclose information about construction and design flaws—the Nuclear Regulatory Commission itself would be nearly as idle as Three Mile Island. . . .That whistleblowers deserve both gratitude and protection is beyond disagreement."[1]

Still, while Glen and Shearer praise whistleblowers, others vociferously condemn them. For example, in a now infamous quote, James Roche, the former president of General Motors said:

Some critics are now busy eroding another support of free enterprise—the loyalty of a management team, with its unifying values and cooperative work. Some of the enemies of business now encourage an employee to be *disloyal* to the enterprise. They want to create suspicion and disharmony, and pry into the proprietary interests of the business. However this is labeled—industrial espionage, whistle blowing, or professional responsibility—it is another tactic for spreading disunity and creating conflict.[2]

From Roche's point of view, not only is whistleblowing not "courageous" and not deserving of "gratitude and protection" as Glen and Shearer would have it, it is corrosive and impermissible.

Discussions of whistleblowing generally revolve around three topics: (1) attempts to define whistleblowing more precisely, (2) de-

Reprinted by permission of the author.

bates about whether and when whistleblowing is permissible, and (3) debates about whether and when one has an obligation to blow the whistle.

In this paper I want to focus on the second problem, because I find it somewhat disconcerting that there is a problem at all. When I first looked into the ethics of whistleblowing it seemed to me that whistleblowing was a good thing, and yet I found in the literature claim after claim that it was in need of defense, that there was something wrong with it, namely that it was an act of disloyalty.

If whistleblowing is a disloyal act, it deserves disapproval, and ultimately any action of whistleblowing needs justification. This disturbs me. It is as if the act of a good Samaritan is being condemned as an act of interference, as if the prevention of a suicide needs to be justified.

In his book *Business Ethics*, Norman Bowie claims that "whistleblowing . . . violate(s) a *prima facie* duty of loyalty to one's employer." According to Bowie, there is a duty of loyalty that prohibits one from reporting his employer or company. Bowie, of course, recognizes that this is only a *prima facie* duty, that is, one that can be overridden by a higher duty to the public good. Nevertheless, the axiom that whistleblowing is disloyal is Bowie's starting point.[3]

Bowie is not alone. Sissela Bok sees "whistleblowing" as an instance of disloyalty:

> The whistleblower hopes to stop the game; but since he is neither referee nor coach, and since he blows the whistle on his own team, his act is seen as a *violation of loyalty*. In holding his position, he has assumed certain obligations to his colleagues and clients. He may even have subscribed to a loyalty oath or a promise of confidentiality. . . . Loyalty to colleagues and to clients comes to be pitted against loyalty to the public interest, to those who may be injured unless the revelation is made.[4]

Bowie and Bok end up defending whistleblowing in certain contexts, so I don't necessarily disagree with their conclusions. However, I fail to see how one has an obligation of loyalty to one's company, so I disagree with their perception of the problem and their starting point. I want to argue that one does not have an obligation of loyalty to a company, even a *prima facie* one, because companies are not the kind of things that are properly objects of loyalty. To make them objects of loyalty gives them a moral status they do not deserve and in raising their status, one lowers the status of the individuals who work for the companies. Thus, the difference in perception is important because those who think employers have an obligation of loyalty to a company fail to take into account a relevant moral difference between persons and corporations.

But why aren't companies the kind of things that can be objects of loyalty? To answer that we have to ask what are proper objects of loyalty. John Ladd states the problem this way, "Granted that loyalty is the wholehearted devotion to an object of some kind, what kind of thing is the object? Is it an abstract entity, such as an idea or a collective being? Or is it a person or group of persons?"[5] Philosophers fall into three camps on the question. On one side are the idealists who hold that loyalty is devotion to something more than persons, to some cause or abstract entity. On the other side are what Ladd calls "social atomists," and these include empiricists and utilitarians, who think that at most one can only be loyal to individuals and that loyalty can ultimately be explained away as some other obligation that holds between two people. Finally, there is a moderate position that holds that although idealists go too far in postulating some superpersonal entity as an object of loyalty, loyalty is still an important and real relation that holds between people, one that cannot be dismissed by reducing it to some other relation.

There does seem to be a view of loyalty that is not extreme. According to Ladd, " 'loyalty' is taken to refer to a relationship between persons—for instance, between a lord and his vassal, between a parent and his children, or between friends. Thus the object of loyalty is ordinarily taken to be a person or a group of persons."[6]

But this raises a problem that Ladd glosses over. There is a difference between a person or a group of persons, and aside from instances of loyalty that relate two people such as lord/vassal, parent/child, or friend/friend, there are instances of loyalty relating a person to a group, such as a person to his family, a person to this team, and a person to his country. Families, countries, and teams are presumably groups of persons. They are certainly ordinarily construed as objects of loyalty.

But to what am I loyal in such a group? In being loyal to the group am I being loyal to the whole group or to its members? It is easy to see the object of loyalty in the case of an individual person. It is simply the individual. But to whom am I loyal in a group? To whom am I loyal in a family? Am I loyal to each and every individual or to something larger, and if to something larger, what is it? We are tempted to think of a group as an entity of its own, an individual in its own right, having an identity of its own.

To avoid the problem of individuals existing for the sake of the group, the atomists insist that a group is nothing more than the individuals who comprise it, nothing other than a mental fiction by which we refer to a group of individuals. It is certainly not a reality or entity over and above the sum of its parts, and consequently is not a proper object of loyalty. Under such a position, of course, no loyalty would be owed to a company because a company is a mere mental fiction, since it is a

group. One would have obligations to the individual members of the company, but one could never be justified in overriding those obligations for the sake of the "group" taken collectively. A company has no moral status except in terms of the individual members who comprise it. It is not a proper object of loyalty. But the atomists go too far. Some groups, such as a family, do have a reality of their own, whereas groups of people walking down the street do not. From Ladd's point of view the social atomist is wrong because he fails to recognize the kinds of groups that are held together by "the ties that bind." The atomist tries to reduce these groups to simple sets of individuals bound together by some externally imposed criteria. This seems wrong.

There do seem to be groups in which the relationships and interactions create a new force or entity. A group takes on an identity and a reality of its own that is determined by its purpose, and this purpose defines the various relationships and roles set up within the group. There is a division of labor into roles necessary for the fulfillment of the purposes of the group. The membership, then, is not of individuals who are the same but of individuals who have specific relationships to one another determined by the aim of the group. Thus we get specific relationships like parent/child, coach/player, and so on, that don't occur in other groups. It seems then that an atomist account of loyalty that restricts loyalty merely to individuals and does not include loyalty to groups might be inadequate.

But once I have admitted that we can have loyalty to a group, do I not open myself up to criticism from the proponent of loyalty to the company? Might not the proponent of loyalty to business say: "Very well. I agree with you. The atomists are short-sighted. Groups have some sort of reality and they can be proper objects of loyalty. But companies are groups. Therefore companies are proper objects of loyalty."

The point seems well taken, except for the fact that the kinds of relationships that loyalty requires are just the kind that one does not find in business. As Ladd says, "The ties that bind the persons together provide the basis of loyalty." But all sorts of ties bind people together. I am a member of a group of fans if I go to a ball game. I am a member of a group if I merely walk down the street. What binds people together in a business is not sufficient to require loyalty.

A business or corporation does two things in the free enterprise system: It produces a good or service and it makes a profit. The making of a profit, however, is the primary function of a business as a business, for if the production of the good or service is not profitable, the business would be out of business. Thus nonprofitable goods or services are a means to an end. People bound together in a business are bound together not for mutual fulfillment and support, but to divide labor or make a profit. Thus, while we can jokingly refer to a family as a place where "they have to take you in no matter what," we cannot refer to a company in that way. If a worker does not produce in a company of if cheaper laborers are available, the company—in order to fulfill its purpose—should get rid of the worker. A company feels no obligation of loyalty. The saying "You can't buy loyalty" is true. Loyalty depends on ties that demand self-sacrifice with no expectation of reward. Business functions on the basis of enlightened self-interest. I am devoted to a company not because it is like a parent to me; it is not. Attempts of some companies to create "one big happy family" ought to be looked on with suspicion. I am not devoted to it at all, nor should I be. I work for it because it pays me. I am not in a family to get paid, I am in a company to get paid.

The cold hard truth is that the goal of profit is what gives birth to a company and forms that particular group. Money is what ties the group together. But in such a commercialized venture, with such a goal, there is no loyalty, or at least none need be expected. An employer will release an employee and an employee will walk away from an employer when it is profitable for either one to do so.

Not only is loyalty to a corporation not required, it more than likely is misguided. There is nothing as pathetic as the story of the loyal employee who, having given above and beyond the call of duty, is let go in the restructuring of the company. He feels betrayed because he mistakenly viewed the company as an object of his loyalty. Getting rid of such foolish romanticism and coming to grips with this hard but accurate assessment should ultimately benefit everyone.

To think we owe a company or corporation loyalty requires us to think of that company as a person or as a group with a goal of human fulfillment. If we think of it in this way we can be loyal. But this is the wrong way to think. A company is not a person. A company is an instrument, and an instrument with a specific purpose, the making of profit. To treat an instrument as an end in itself, like a person, may not be as bad as treating an end as an instrument, but it does give the instrument a moral status it does not deserve; and by elevating the instrument we lower the end. All things, instruments and ends, become alike.

Remember that Roche refers to the "management team" and Bok sees the name "whistleblowing" coming from the instance of a referee blowing a whistle in the presence of a foul. What is perceived as bad about whistleblowing in business from this perspective is that one blows the whistle on one's own team, thereby violating team loyalty. If the company can get its employees to view it as a team they belong to, it is easier to demand loyalty. Then the rules governing teamwork and team loyalty will apply. One reason the appeal to a team and team loyalty works so well in business is that businesses are in competition with one another. Effective motivation turns business practices into a game and instills teamwork.

But businesses differ from teams in very important respects, which makes the analogy between business and a team dangerous. Loyalty to a team is loyalty within the context of sport or a competition. Teamwork and team loyalty require that in the circumscribed activity of the game I cooperate with my fellow players, so that pulling all together, we may win. The object of (most) sports is victory. But winning in sports is a social convention, divorced from the usual goings on of society. Such a winning is most times a harmless, morally neutral diversion.

But the fact that this victory in sports, within the rules enforced by a referee (whistleblower), is a socially developed convention taking place within a larger social context makes it quite different from competition in business, which, rather than being defined by a context, permeates the whole of society in its influence. Competition leads not only to victory but to losers. One can lose at sport with precious few consequences. The consequences of losing at business are much larger. Further, the losers in business can be those who are not in the game voluntarily (we are all forced to participate) but who are still affected by business decisions. People cannot choose to participate in business. It permeates everyone's lives.

The team model, then, fits very well with the model of the free market system, because there competition is said to be the name of the game. Rival companies compete and their object is to win. To call a foul on one's own

teammate is to jeopardize one's chances of winning and is viewed as disloyalty.

But isn't it time to stop viewing corporate machinations as games? These games are not controlled and are not ended after a specific time. The activities of business affect the lives of everyone, not just the game players. The analogy of the corporation to a team and the consequent appeal to team loyalty, although understandable, is seriously misleading, at least in the moral sphere where competition is not the prevailing virtue.

If my analysis is correct, the issue of the permissibility of whistleblowing is not a real issue since there is no obligation of loyalty to a company. Whistleblowing is not only permissible but expected when a company is harming society. The issue is not one of disloyalty to the company, but of whether the whistleblower has an obligation to society if blowing the whistle will bring him retaliation.

NOTES

1. Maxwell Glen and Cody Shearer, "Going After the Whistle-blowers," *Philadelphia Inquirer,* Tuesday, August 2, 1983, Op-ed page, p. 11A.

2. James M. Roche, "The Competitive System, to Work, to Preserve, and to Protect," *Vital Speeches of the Day* (May 1971): 445.

3. Norman Bowie, *Business Ethics* (Englewood Cliffs, N.J.: Prentice Hall, 1982), pp. 140–143.

4. Sissela Bok, "Whistleblowing and Professional Responsibilities," *New York University Education Quarterly* 2 (1980): 3, and here p. 294.

5. John Ladd, "Loyalty," *The Encyclopedia of Philosophy* 5: 97.

6. Ibid.

The Employee Health and Safety Whistleblower Protection Act and the Conscientious Employee: The Potential for Federal Statutory Enforcement of the Public Policy Exception to Employment at Will

Susan Sauter

THE PURPOSE OF THE EMPLOYEE HEALTH AND SAFETY WHISTLEBLOWER PROTECTION ACT

On February 23, 1989, Senators Metzenbaum and Grassley introduced Senate Bill 436, the Employee Health and Safety Whistleblower Protection Act [the "Bill"]. The Bill . . . would protect private sector employees who disclose violations of federal health and safety laws from retaliatory disciplinary measures taken by their employers. The Bill is purportedly designed merely "to strengthen and improve" existing federal whistleblower protection. . . .

Findings and Purposes of the Bill

. . . The "Purposes" section of the Bill stated the five objectives that constituted the drafters' plan for implementing remedies for the three problems identified in the "Findings." These objectives will be evaluated in conjunction with the Findings section.

In the "Findings" section, the Bill stated that Congress determined that:

1. Employees who report unlawful or hazardous activities are performing an important public service by helping to ensure the health and safety of workers and the general public;

2. Employees should be able to report unlawful or hazardous activities without fear of reprisal; and

3. Employees who make such reports are not adequately protected against reprisal by the current Federal laws designed to protect private sector whistleblowers.

Employees Should Be Free from Retaliation for Reporting Their Employers' Wrongdoing. As stated in the "Purposes" section, the objectives of the Bill include extending protection from retaliation to all private sector employees who disclose their employers' violations of health and safety laws and who currently cannot bring an action under an existing statute. The Bill would remedy this gap in the law by granting those employees a federal cause of action against their employers. By affirming the right of an employee to be free from retaliatory actions of his employer, the sponsors of the Bill created a federal statutory exception to employment at will, the principal doctrine currently governing the employment relationship between nonunion, private sector employees and their employers. . . .

Employees are Inadequately Protected by Existing Whistleblower Protection. The summary of the Whistleblower Act included in the

Hearings before the Senate Subcommittee on Labor stated that the current system of federal whistleblower protection left "enormous gaps" in coverage. . . .

Currently, the federal statutes providing for whistleblower protection vary in their treatment of investigative agencies, adjudicatory agencies, statutes of limitation, judicial review, the good faith standard, protected activity, exhaustion of employer remedies, and relief available. The agency responsible for violations of the substantive statute is almost never the same as the agency responsible for investigation of the whistleblower's claim, and the adjudicatory agency is never the same for each investigative agency. For example, a person bringing a claim under the Asbestos Hazard Emergency Response Act, whose program agency is the Environmental Protection Agency, has his claim investigated by the Department of Labor and adjudicated in the district courts. However, an employee bringing a claim under the Clean Air Act, whose program agency is also the Environmental Protection Agency, has his claim investigated by the Wage and Hour Division and adjudicated by the Office of Administrative Law Judges [hereinafter ALJ]. Furthermore, the former employee would have 90 days to pursue his claim while the latter would have only 30 days. Moreover, the former employee is also denied the judicial review provided the latter employee. Similar discrepancies among the other statutes result in inconsistent resolution of whistleblowers' claims. . . .

Analysis of Findings and Purposes Sections of the Proposed Bill

The policies expressed in the "Findings" section of the Bill and reaffirmed in objectives stated in the "Purposes" section reflect controversial value judgments and indicate that Congress is accomplishing far more than the purported strengthening and improving of existing federal law. The implications of the federal law on state statutory and common law are far reaching in that the proposed Bill would create a federal uniform exception to the employment-at-will doctrine, the doctrine that continues to govern the employment relationship in the private sector despite the limited exceptions recognized by state courts and legislatures. The differences between the existing federal laws in investigation, adjudication, judicial review and enforcement as well as the lack of coverage for employees whose jobs substantially affect the public health and safety provide the bases for the argument that federal law inadequately protects whistleblowers.

Despite the apparent dual purpose of the Bill, its primary effect would be to establish broad protection of employees from termination. . . . The testimony at the Hearings consisted in large part of a "parade of horrors"— testimony from employees in the airline, energy, and meat packing industries that emphasized not only the atrocious working conditions and health and safety violations of the employers, but the callous and willful termination of publicly minded employees who attempted to expose the violations. . . .

The emphasis on employee protection is consistent with the public policy exception, which, sounding in tort, emphasizes the injury to the employee. Creating an independent cause of action for such claims, as some states have done, does not alter the nature of the claim: it remains an exception to the employment-at-will doctrine as is any other wrongful termination action. The whistleblower exception has also been called the *right* of the employee to dissent from the illegal actions of his employer without retaliation, emphasizing the protection of the employee and not the public good. Under such a definition, public policy demands merely that an employer not fire an employee who is attempting to protect the public interest, whether or not the employee in fact does so.

PROTECTION AFFORDED BY THE BILL

Defining Employees and Whistleblowing Activities Protected Under the Proposed Bill

Persons Protected Under the Bill. Using Congress's broad commerce power, the drafters of the Bill provided that every private sector employer whose business affects commerce would be subject to the provisions of the Act, expressly including agents of employees, states and political subdivisions of the states, and interstate governmental agencies, while expressly excluding the United States and the United States Postal Service. . . . Considering the narrow scope of the existing federal laws, the reach of the proposed statute is extensive. The reach of the existing federal statutes is limited to employees of employers who are subject to the conduct-regulating aspects of the particular law. The proposed law would extend whistleblowing protection to any employee who reports a violation or perceived violation of *any* federal law that has the purpose or effect of protecting the health or safety of the public. . . .

What the Employer May Not Do: Retaliatory Acts. The Bill prohibits employers from discharging or discriminating against an employee who discloses his employer's violation of a health and safety law. The Bill does not state explicitly what retaliatory acts of the employer would constitute discrimination. Senator Metzenbaum, however, upon introducing the Bill into the Senate, indicated that the Bill was designed to prevent demotion, harassment, or intimidation. At the Hearings before the Subcommittee on Labor and Human Re-

sources, testimony of whistleblowers showed that transfers, reductions in responsibilities, threats of reprisal, refusal of privileges, and even interference with an employee's mail and telephone calls can result from an employee's whistleblowing activities. The language of the Bill and the interpretation provided by Senator Metzenbaum seem broad enough to encompass all the activities described in the testimonials.

What the Employee Is Protected in Doing: Whistleblowing Acts. Determining which acts of an employee are protected involves first identifying the precise violations of law that will give rise to the privilege of protected whistleblowing and then identifying the employee's actions taken consequent to the violations that would fall under the purview of the statute. Section 3(6) of the Bill defines the types of laws whose violations may give rise to the rights specified under the act, while § 4(a)(1)–(3) sets out the conduct of an employee that would be protected.

The Employee Health and Safety Whistleblower Protection Act contemplates protecting only those employees who blow the whistle on their employers' violations of certain federal and state statutes. The drafters of the Bill set out the parameters of permissible whistleblowing by limiting protection to those employees who disclose their employers' violations of "Federal health or safety law[s]," a limitation that embraces the belief that the Bill will help protect the public interest in health and safety. Further, the Bill protects employees who disclose what they *believe* constitutes a violation of a health or safety law whether or not the conduct is in fact unlawful. . . .

An employer could not discriminate against an employee for (1) disclosing or evincing an intent to disclose that the employer has violated a health or safety law; (2) intending to or actually instigating or aiding or participating in a proceeding related to an employer's activity, policy or practice that violates health or safety laws, enactment or implementation of a federal health or safety law, or implementation of the Act itself; or (3) refusing to participate in an activity that constitutes an actual violation of a federal health and safety law or that the employee reasonably believes would cause serious injury to the employee or others. For the third category of behavior to be protected, the employee must show that he first sought a remedy of the problem and could not obtain one, or show that seeking a remedy was futile under the circumstances. The Bill excepts from coverage any employee who acted without direction from his employer and intentionally caused a violation of law.

The proposed statute would cover the issues that case law designates as traditional whistleblower complaints, wherein an employee alleges that he has been fired in retaliation for reporting the employer's wrongful acts, as well as the "good faith refusal to work," wherein the employee claims he was discharged because he refused to violate the law or refused to participate in an activity that he reasonably believed would either violate a law or cause serious harm to himself or others. These two categories of whistleblowing will be considered separately. . . .

Under the traditional whistleblower section of the Bill, the statute states that an employee would have a right to "disclose" the employer's violation, but it does not state to whom the employee is required to disclose. The legislative history of the Bill does not specify whether internal disclosures to a supervisor in the company or external disclosures to some appropriate agency or other entity or both would be protected. However, the testimony of the whistleblowers at the Congressional Hearing showed that employees are equally subject to harassment when they report to their employers as when they report to outside agencies. Their statements

and the responses of Senator Metzenbaum demonstrate that the Bill is intended to provide protection for the types of whistleblowers whose cases were presented at the Hearing, suggesting that the drafters of the Bill would support protection for internal as well as external whistleblowing. Clearly the proponents of the Bill see it as a mechanism for enforcing the underlying laws. Requiring external whistleblowing would increase the chances of outside enforcement of the laws and thus serve that objective of the Bill. However, the Bill also contains a provision for reporting the employer's violations to the appropriate agency at the time the wrongful discharge claim is brought. Thus, the whistleblower protection could be extended to internal and external whistleblowers and still advance the enforcement aspect of the Bill.

Persons commenting on the Bill during the Hearings have addressed the subject and offered different alternatives for Congress to consider. Members of the law firm Bishop, Cook, Purcell & Reynolds, who, at Senator Metzenbaum's request, submitted comments on the Bill to the Subcommittee, advocated including language that would require an employee to report violations of federal law "to a competent federal agency." The firm contended that extending protection to those employees who report health and safety violations to their employers would abuse the rights created by the Bill by calling into question even the most legitimate of disciplinary measures if there had been a recent internal communication concerning health and safety. . . .

Requiring internal reporting, however, might ultimately weaken protection of the employee. Professors Devine and Aplin identified employer strategies that fall short of termination or demotion but that effectively silence employee whistleblowers who pursue internal channels. Inhibiting the free flow of information by isolating the employee physically from relevant material is only one of several methods for "neutralizing" the employee-dissenter and his disclosures. Other strategies include transferring the employee to a "bureaucratic Siberia," where he would suffer reduced responsibility; putting the employee in charge of correcting the problem, making it impossible for him to do so, and then firing him for incompetence; responding with outrageous charges against the whistleblower's character; eliminating or redefining the dissenter's job so that he no longer has an opportunity for investigating the allegedly unlawful condition; undercutting the employee's support base, which can involve revocation of research privileges or elimination or reduction of staff; preventing a written record of the company's activities by limiting employee input to oral statements, by issuing gag orders, or through simple peer pressure.

These covert responses to internal whistleblowing illustrate the risks an employee faces when pursuing whatever employer-controlled channels might be available. The possibility that such subtle retaliation might result weakens the viability of employer initiated grievance procedures designed to intercept employee disclosures and allow the employer the first opportunity to react to the dissent. The methods of retaliation identified by Professors Devine & Aplin, furthermore, might not be actionable even if the proposed Bill protected internal as well as external whistleblowing. Thus, encouraging internal whistleblowing might impose an unintended penalty on the conscientious employee. . . .

The argument in favor of encouraging internal whistleblowing is predicated on a theory of employer autonomy and is supported by the business community. Proponents of internal whistleblowing believe that employers who are alerted to health and safety violations should be permitted to try to amend the problem themselves first, before external entities invade the purview of the employer.

This position also implies that whistleblower laws must strike a balance in the employment relationship as well as a balance between the employee's loyalty to his employer and his duty to protect his community. While employers should not be able to retaliate against an employee for refusing to remain silent about a work condition that poses health or safety threats to the employee or to the public at large, employers should retain some control over the company's operational compliance and the law. As a matter of policy, an employer ought to be given a chance to comply with the law before the decision is taken out of its hands.

Whether the drafters of the Bill intended to protect internal or external whistleblowing or both, the Bill will have to be amended to include a specification of the exact disclosure protected. To advance the primary purposes of the Bill, the amendment should protect both internal and external whistleblowing. If an employee is fired for internal whistleblowing, his loyalty would be punished twice: by his employer for the discharge and then by the Bill by refusing him a cause of action for retaliatory termination. Protecting only internal disclosures might have the effect of frustrating investigation into validity of the claim that a health or safety violation has been committed because the employee would be required to exhaust his internal remedies first even in futile situations. Proving health or safety violations, moreover, is a pre-requisite for recovery for wrongful discharge; thus, mandatory internal whistleblowing might impede the objectives of the Bill: to protect employees from wrongful discharge and to identify and prevent violations of the substantive laws. Protecting both internal reporting when possible and external reporting when necessary would advance both of the objectives of the Bill. Internal whistleblowing may facilitate the correction of the health or safety law's violation; if the employee is fired for the disclosure and the situation remains uncorrected, the employee can bring a claim under the federal act and, according to the scheme of the act, the violation would be reported to the federal agency responsible for enforcement of the law and the violation will be remedied by the outside agency. When internal disclosure is futile, the employee can feel safe in going to an external agency, knowing that if his employer retaliates, he has a cause of action under the Bill.

While refusals to work are not generally included in the traditional definition of whistleblowing, a good faith refusal to work has been included in several state whistleblower statutes and has been included in the public policy exception as recognized by some state courts. The proposed statute would protect the employee against retaliation for refusal to work in two distinct situations. First, the employee could not be retaliated against for refusing to participate in an activity that he believes constitutes a violation of health or safety laws. Second, the employee may refuse to participate in any activity or practice when the employee has a reasonable fear that his participation would result in serious harm to him or to the public at large. Two conditions are placed on the second situation: the employee's apprehension of harm must be such that a reasonable person facing the same circumstances would conclude that there is a legitimate danger of "an accident, injury or serious impairment of health or safety," and the employee must show that before refusing to work, he sought to have the dangerous situation remedied and was unsuccessful.

Like the traditional whistleblower provisions, the refusal to work provision would require an employee to point to the precise law that the employer violated in order to invoke the privilege. As the Bill is written, the employee would have to identify the particular law violated only when his refusal is not based on a reasonable belief that he or the public is in imminent danger of serious injury. The employee's reasonable belief would protect him only when the employer's practice was so egregious as to warrant a belief that serious harm would result from the employee's participation.

Common law protection of whistleblowers in the public policy exception context demonstrates that good faith refusals to work are the basis for a substantial number of retaliatory discharge claims. The cases indicate that courts are most sympathetic to claims of wrongful termination when the employee himself has risked incurring penalties for the wrongful act. Courts and commentators state that employees should not be put in the position of committing an illegal act or losing their jobs. Loyalty to the company breaks down when the company's practices require an employee to honor his duty to the company at the expense of his moral duty to the public.

While critics of the Bill do not dispute the propriety of permitting employees to refuse to commit violations of law, they charge that the standard for determining when an employee is privileged in refusing to work is so nebulous that neither employer nor employee will know when a refusal is protected and when it is not. The business constituency argues in favor of a stricter standard so that employees would not be protected for insubordination when they simply disagree with an employer's methods or policies and do not actually fear violating the law or causing serious injury to themselves or the public.

Analysis of the Bill's Provisions Defining Employees and Whistleblowing Activities

The proposed statute would afford broad protection to all private sector employees who suffer retaliation for their whistleblowing activities. The Bill would protect disclosures of the employer's violations of federal health and safety laws as well as good faith refusals to work. Considerable disagreement exists as to the activities of an employee that should be protected under the guise of whistleblowing safeguards. Employers and the business community as a whole, as well as some scholars, advocate narrowly defining the scope of whistleblower protection to maintain employer autonomy and to prevent employees from abusing the protection. Employees, who are arguably in the best position to discover and identify violations of health and safety laws, want to be free from retaliation for their efforts to eliminate the dangers those violations pose to them, their fellow employees, and the public. The drafters of the Bill apparently agree. . . .

CONCLUSION

The Employee Health and Safety Whistleblower Act seeks to protect private sector employees from retaliation by their employers for disclosing the employer's violations of federal and some state laws. The Bill was proposed in response to a perceived gap in existing coverage in federal law that enabled employers to terminate employees who reported practices of their employers that posed substantial dangers to the public at large and to the employee. The findings of the Bill showed that the drafters believed that such employees were entitled to the protection of law regardless of whether the existing employment relationship was at will. . . .

The Employee Health and Safety Whistleblower Protection Act could be one of the most important pieces of legislation for the protection of private sector employees. The common law public policy exception to employment at will has gone far in abrogating the employment-at-will doctrine that continues to plague modern employment relationships. Several states have already passed statutory whistleblower protection statutes, sounding the death knell for the at-will relationship and bringing private sector employment relations into the twentieth century. However, some states cling anachronistically to the idea that the will of the parties should govern the employment relationship, while others so severely limit the definition of public policy that they offer no real protection at all. A national declaration of public policy, as embodied by the Bill, is a necessary and long overdue modification to the contemporary employment relationship.

Trade Secrets: What Price Loyalty?

Michael S. Baram

In 1963, the Court of Appeals of Ohio heard an appeal of a lower court decision from The B.F. Goodrich Company. The lower court had denied Goodrich's request for an injunction, or court order, to restrain a former employee, Donald Wohlgemuth, from disclosing its trade secrets and from working in the space suit field for any other company.

This case, as it was presented in the Court of Appeals, is a fascinating display of management issues, legal concepts, and ethical dilemmas of concern to research and development organizations and their scientist and engineer employees. The case also represents an employer-employee crisis of increasing incidence in the young and vigorous R&D sector of U.S. industry. Tales of departing employees and threatened losses of trade secrets or proprietary information are now common.

Such crises are not surprising when one considers the causes of mobility. The highly educated employees of R&D organizations place primary emphasis on their own development, interests, and satisfaction. Graduates of major scientific and technological institutions readily admit that they accept their first jobs primarily for money and for the early and brief experience they feel is a prerequisite for seeking more satisfying futures with smaller companies which are often their own. Employee mobility and high personnel turnover rates are also due to the placement of new large federal contracts and the termination of others. One need only look to the Sunday newspaper employment advertisements for evidence as to the manner in which such programs are used to attract highly educated R&D personnel.

This phenomenon of the mobile employee seeking fulfillment reflects a sudden change in societal and personal values. It also threatens industrial reliance on trade secrets for the protection of certain forms of intellectual property. There are no union solutions, and the legal framework in which it occurs is an ancient structure representing values of an earlier America. The formulation of management responses—with cognizance of legal, practical, and ethical considerations—is admittedly a difficult task, but one which must be undertaken.

In this article I shall examine the basic question of industrial loyalty regarding trade secrets, using the Goodrich-Wohlgemuth case as the focal point of the challenge to the preservation of certain forms of intellectual property posed by the mobile employee, and then offer some suggestions for the development of sound management policies.

THE APPEALS CASE

Donald Wohlgemuth joined The B.F. Goodrich Company as a chemical engineer in 1954, following his graduation from the University of Michigan, and by 1962 he had become manager of the space suit division. As the repository of Goodrich know-how and secret data in space suit technology, he was indeed a key man in a rapidly developing technology of interest to several government agencies. Nevertheless, he was dissatisfied with his salary ($10,644) and the denial of his requests for certain additional facilities for his department.

A Goodrich rival, International Latex, had recently been awarded the major space suit subcontract for the Apollo program. Following up a contact from an employment agency hired by Latex, Wohlgemuth negotiated a position with Latex, at a substantial salary increase. In his new assignment he would be manager of engineering for industrial products, which included space suits. He then notified Goodrich of his resignation, and was met with a reaction he apparently did not expect. Goodrich management raised the moral and ethical aspects of his decision, since the company executives felt his resignation would result in the transfer of Goodrich trade secrets to Latex.

After several heated exchanges, Wohlgemuth stated that "loyalty and ethics have their price and International Latex has paid this price. . . . " Even though Goodrich threatened legal action, Wohlgemuth left Goodrich for Latex. Goodrich thereupon requested a restraining order in the Ohio courts.

At the appeals court level, the Goodrich brief sought an injunction that would prevent Wohlgemuth from working in the space suit field for *any* other company, prevent his disclosure of *any* information on space suit technology to *anyone*, prevent his consulting or conferring with *anyone* on Goodrich trade secrets, and finally, prevent *any* future contact he might seek with Goodrich employees.

These four broad measures were rejected by the Ohio Court of Appeals. All were too wide in scope, and all would have protected much more than Goodrich's legitimate concern of safeguarding its trade secrets. In addition, the measures were speculative, since no clear danger seemed imminent. In sum, they represented a form of "overkill" that would have placed undue restraints on Wohlgemuth.

The court did provide an injunction restraining Wohlgemuth from disclosure of Goodrich trade secrets. In passing, the court noted that in the absence of any Goodrich employment contract restraining his employment with a competitor, Wohlgemuth could commence work with Latex. With ample legal precedent, the court therefore came down on both sides of the fence. Following the decision, Wohlgemuth commenced his career with Latex and is now manager of the company's Research and Engineering Department.

COMMON-LAW CONCEPTS

The two basic issues in crises such as the Goodrich-Wohlgemuth case appear irreconcilable: (1) the right of the corporation to its intellectual property—its proprietary data or trade secrets; and (2) the right of the individual to seek gainful employment and utilize his abilities—to be free from a master servant relationship.

There are no federal and but a few state statutes dealing with employment restraints and trade secrets. The U.S. courts, when faced with such issues, have sought to apply the various common-law doctrines of trade secrets and unfair competition at hand to attain an equitable solution. Many of these common-law doctrines were born in pre-industrial England and later adopted by English and U.S. courts to meet employment crises of this nature through ensuing centuries of changing industrial and social patterns. In fact, some of the early cases of blacksmiths and barbers seeking to restrain departing apprentices are still cited today.

To the courts, the common legal solution, as in *Goodrich v. Wohlgemuth,* is pleasing because it theoretically preserves the rights of both parties. However, it is sadly lacking in practicality, since neither secrets nor individual liberty are truly preserved.

The trade secrets which companies seek to protect have usually become an integral portion of the departing employee's total capabilities. He cannot divest himself of his intellectual capacity, which is a compound of information acquired from his employer, his co-workers, and his own self-generated experiential information. Nevertheless, all such information, if kept secret by the company from its competition, may legitimately be claimed as corporate property. This is because the employer-employee relationship embodied in the normal employment contract or other terms of employment provides for corporate ownership of all employee-generated data, including inventions. As a result, a departing employee's intellectual capacity may be, in large measure, corporate property.

Once the new position with a competitor has been taken, the trade secrets embodied in the departing employee may manifest themselves quite clearly and consciously. This is what court injunctions seek to prohibit. But, far more likely, the trade secrets will manifest themselves subconsciously and in various forms—for example, as in the daily decisions by the employee at his new post, or in the many small contributions he makes to a large team effort—often in the form of an intuitive sense of what or what not to do, as he seeks to utilize his overall intellectual capacity. Theoretically, a legal injunction also serves to prohibit such "leakage." However, the former employer faces the practical problem of securing evidence of such leakage, for little will be apparent from the public activities and goods of the new employer. And if the new employer's public activities or goods appear suspicious, there is also the further problem of distinguishing one's trade secrets from what may be legitimately asserted as the self-generated technological skills or state of the art of the new employer and competitor which were utilized.

This is a major stumbling block in the attempt to protect one's trade secrets, since the possessor has no recourse against others who independently generate the same information. It is therefore unlikely that an injunction against disclosure of trade secrets to future employers prevents any "unintentional" transfer (or even intentional transfer) of information, except for the passage of documents and other physical embodiments of the secrets. In fact, only a lobotomy, as yet not requested nor likely to be sanctioned by the courts, would afford security against the transfer of most trade secrets.

Conversely, the departing employee bears the terrible burden of sensitivity. At his new post, subconscious disclosure and mental and physical utilization of what he feels to be no more than his own intellectual capacity may result in heated exchanges between companies, adverse publicity, and litigation. He is marked, insecure, and unlikely to contribute effectively in his new position. In fact, new co-workers may consider him to be a man with a price, and thus without integrity. Frequently,

caution on the part of his new employer will result in transfer to a nonsensitive post where he is unlikely to contribute his full skills, unless he has overall capability and adaptability.

The fact that neither secrets nor individual liberty will be truly preserved rarely influences the course of litigation. Similarly, these practical considerations are usually negligible factors in the out-of-court settlements which frequently terminate such litigation, because the settlements primarily reflect the relative bargaining strengths of disputing parties.

Finally, there is the full cost of litigation to be considered. In addition to the obvious court costs and attorney's fees, there is the potentially great cost to the company's image. Although the drama enacted in court reflects legitimate corporate concerns, the public may easily fail to see more than an unequal struggle between the powerful corporate machine and a lonely individual harassed beyond his employment tenure. Prospective employees, particularly new and recent graduates whose early positions are stepping stones, may be reluctant to accept employment with what appears to be a vindictive and authoritarian organization.

Practical and Legal Aspects

Trade secrets are, of course, a common form of intellectual property. Secrecy is the most natural and the earliest known method of protecting the fruits of one's intellectual labors. Rulers of antiquity frequently had architects and engineers murdered, after completion of their works, to maintain secrecy and security. The medieval guilds and later the craftsmen of pre-industrial Europe and America imposed severe restraints on apprentices and their future activities.

Recognition and acceptance of the practice of protecting intellectual property by secrecy is found throughout Anglo-American common or judge-made law, but statutory protection has not been legislated. Perhaps the failure to do so is because of the recognition by the elected officials of industrial societies that secrecy is not in the public interest and that the widest dissemination of new works and advances in technology and culture is necessary for optimal public welfare. . . .

To summarize this common law briefly, virtually all information—ranging from full descriptions of inventions to plant layouts, shop knowhow, methods of quality control, customer and source lists, and marketing data—is eligible for protection as trade secrets. No standards of invention or originality are required. If such information is not known to the public or to the trade (or it is known but its utility is not recognized), and if such information is of value to its possessor, it is eligible for protection by the courts.

Further, and of greatest importance in terms of favorably impressing the courts, there must be evidence that the possessor recognized the value of his information and treated it accordingly. In the context of confidential relationships, "treatment" normally means that the possessor provided for limited or no disclosure of trade secrets. This means many things: for example, total prohibition of disclosure except to key company people on a need-to-know basis; provision of the information to licensees, joint ventures, or employees having contractual restraints against their unauthorized disclosure or use; division of employee responsibilities so that no employee is aware of more than a small segment of a particular process; and use in labs of unmarked chemicals and materials.

There must also be evidence that particular efforts were expended for the purpose of preserving secrecy for the specific data claimed as trade secrets. General company policies indiscriminately applied to data and employees or licensees will not suffice in the legal sense to convince the courts of the presence of trade secrets.

When the possessor and his information do fulfill such criteria, court recognition and the award of compensation to damaged parties, or injunctive restraints to protect parties in danger of imminent or further damage, will follow. If there is evidence of (a) breach of confidential relationships (contracts or licenses) which were established to preserve the secrecy of company information, (b) unauthorized copying and sale of secrets, or (c) conspiracy to damage the possessor, the courts will act with greater certitude. But in many cases, such as in the Goodrich-Wohlgemuth litigation, no such evidence is present.

Finally, the courts will not move to protect trade secrets when an action is brought by one party against another who independently generated similar information, or who "reverse-engineered" the publicly sold products of the party petitioning the court, unless there is some contractual, fiduciary, or other relationship based on trust connecting the parties in court.

Other Considerations

In addition to the foregoing practical and legal aspects, basic questions of industrial ethics and the equitable allocation of rights and risks should be examined to provide management with intelligent and humane responses to employer-employee crises that involved intellectual property. The patent and copyright systems for the stimulation and protection of such property are premised on dissemination of information and subsequent public welfare. These systems reflect public concern with the proper use of intellectual property, which the common law of trade secrets lacks.

Will the courts continue to utilize common-law concepts for the protection of trade secrets, when such concepts are based solely on the rights of the possessors of secret information, and when the application of such concepts has a detrimental effect on both the rights of employees and the public welfare? Since current court practice places the burden of industrial loyalty solely on the employee, the skilled individual has to pay the price. In other words, the law restricts the fullest utilization of his abilities. And the detrimental effect on public welfare can be inferred from recent federal studies of technology transfer, which indicate that employee mobility and the promotion of entrepreneurial activities are primary factors in the transfer of technology and the growth of new industries.

The continuation of trade secret concepts for the preservation of property rights in secret information at the expense of certain basic individual freedoms is unlikely. The law eventually reflects changing societal values, and the mobile R&D employee who seeks career fulfillment through a succession of jobs, frequently in sensitive trade secret areas, is now a reality—one not likely to disappear. Thus it is probable that the courts will eventually adopt the position that those who rely on trade secrets assume the realities or risks in the present context of public concern with technological progress and its relationship to the public good, and with the rights of the individual. Resulting unintentional leakage of secret information through the memory of a departing employee is now generally accepted as a reasonable price to pay for the preservation of these societal values. However, the courts will never condone the theft or other physical appropriation of secret information, nor are the courts likely to condone fraud, conspiracy, and other inequitable practices resulting in some form of unfair competition.

The failings of the statutory systems serve, not as justification for the inequitable applica-

tion of medieval trade secret concepts, but as the basis for legislative reform. Injunctive restraints against the unintentional leakage of secrets and the harassment of departing employees through litigation should not be part of our legal system. This is especially true when there is a growing body of evidence that management can respond, and has intelligently done so, to such crises without detriment to the individual employee, the public good, or the company itself.

MANAGEMENT RESPONSE

How then shall managers of research and development organizations respond to the reality of the mobile employee and his potential for damage to corporate trade secrets?

Contractual Restraints

Initial response is invariably consideration of the use of relevant contractual prohibitions on employees with such potential. For a minority of companies, this means the institution of employment contracts or other agreements concerning terms of employment. For most, a review of existing company contracts, which at a minimum provide for employee disclosure of inventions and company ownership of subsequent patents, will be called for to determine the need for relevant restraints.

Contractual prohibitions vary somewhat, but they are clearly of two general types: (1) restraints against unauthorized disclosure and use of company trade secrets or proprietary information by employees during their employment tenure or at any time thereafter; (2) restraints against certain future activities of employees following their employment tenure.

A restraint against unauthorized disclosure or use is normally upheld in the courts, provided it is limited to a legitimate company concern—trade secrets. But it is usually ineffective, due to the unintentional leakage and subconscious utilization of trade secrets, and the difficulties of "policing" and proving violation, as discussed earlier. In fact, several authorities feel that this type of restraint is ineffective unless coupled with a valid restraint against future employment with competitors. . . .

Courts have been naturally reluctant to extend protection to trade secrets when the freedom of an individual to use his overall capability is at stake. In addition, the former employer faces the practical difficulty of convincing almost any court that a prohibition of future employment is necessary, since the court will look for clear and convincing evidence that the ex-employee has, or inevitably will, exercise more than the ordinary skill a man of his competence possesses. A few states—such as California by statute and others by consistent court action—now prohibit future employment restraints.

It therefore appears that a contractual prohibition of future employment in a broad area, which prevents an ex-employee from using his overall capability, is invalid in most states. . . .

Internal Policies

Another response of R&D management to the mobile employee and his potential for damage to corporate trade secrets is the formulation of internal company policies for the handling of intellectual property of trade secret potential. Such policies may call for the prior review of publications and addresses of key employees, prohibition of consulting and other "moonlighting," dissemination of trade secrets on a strict "need to know" basis to designated employees, and prohibitions on the copying of trade secret data. More "physical" policies may restrict research and other operational areas to access for designated or "badge" employees only and divide up operations to prevent the accumulation of extensive knowledge by any individual—including safety and other general plant personnel. Several companies I know of distribute unmarked materials—particularly chemicals—to employees.

Although internal policies do not necessarily prevent future employment with competitors, they can serve to prevent undue disclosures and lessen the criticality of the departure of key personnel. All must be exercised with a sophisticated regard for employee motivation, however, because the cumulative effect may result in a police state atmosphere that inhibits creativity and repels prospective employees.

Several farsighted R&D organizations are currently experimenting with plans which essentially delegate the responsibility for nondisclosure and nonuse of their trade secrets to the key employees themselves. These plans include pension and consulting programs operative for a specified post-employment period. In one company, for example, the pension plan provides that the corporate monies which are contributed to the employee pension fund in direct ratio to the employee's own contributions will remain in his pension package following his term of employment, provided he does not work for a competing firm for a specified number of years. In another company, the consulting plan provides that certain departing employees are eligible to receive an annual consulting fee for a given number of years following employment if they do not work for a competitor. The consulting fee is a preestablished percentage of the employee's annual salary at the time of his departure.

Obviously, such corporate plans are subject to employee abuse, but if limited to truly key employees, they may succeed without abuse in most cases. They not only have the merit of providing the employee with a choice, an equitable feature likely to incur employee loyalty, but they also have no apparent legal defects.

Another valid internal practice is the debriefing of departing employees. The debriefing session, carried out in a low-key atmosphere, affords management an excellent opportunity to retrieve company materials and information in physical form, to impart to the employee a sense of responsibility regarding trade secrets and sensitive areas, and to discuss mutual anxieties in full.

External Procedures

Several management responses relating to external company policies are worth noting, as they also serve to protect trade secrets in cases involving employee departures. Among several industries, such as in the chemical field, it is common to find gentlemen's agreements which provide mutuality in the nonhiring of competitor's key employees, following notice. Employees who have encountered this practice have not found the experience a pleasant one. This same practice is also found in other areas, such as the industrial machinery industry, that are in need of innovation; and it appears that the presence of such agreements helps to depict these industries in an unappealing fashion to the types of employees they need.

Another external response for management consideration is company reliance on trademarks. Given a good mark and subsequent public identification of the product with the mark, a company may be able to maintain markets despite the fact that its intellectual property is no longer a trade secret. Competitors may be hesitant about utilizing the former trade secrets of any company whose products are strongly identified with trademarks and with the company itself.

Some trade secrets are patentable, and management faced with the potential loss of such secrets should consider filing for patent protection. The application is treated confidentially by the U.S. Patent Office and some foreign patent offices up to the time of award. Moreover, if the application is rejected, the secrecy of the information is not legally diminished. In any case, the subject matter of the application remains secret throughout the two-to-three year period of time normally involved in U.S. Patent Office review.

CONCLUSION

A major concern of our society is progress through the promotion and utilization of new technology. To sustain and enhance this form of progress, it is necessary to optimize the flow of information and innovation all the way from conception to public use. This effort is now a tripartite affair involving federal agencies, industry, and universities. A unique feature of this tripartite relationship is the mobility of R&D managers, scientists, and engineers who follow contract funding and projects in accordance with their special competence. Neither the federal agencies nor the universities rely on trade secret concepts for the protection of their intellectual property. However, industry still does, despite the fact that trade secret concepts bear the potential ancillary effect of interfering with employee mobility.

It is becoming increasingly clear that new societal values associated with the tripartite approach to new technology are now evolving, and that the common law dispensed by the courts has begun to reflect these values. A victim of sorts is trade secret law, which has not only never been clearly defined, but which has indeed been sustained by court concepts of unfair competition, equity, and confidence derived from other fields of law. The day when courts restrict employee mobility to preserve industrial trade secrets appears to have passed, except—as we noted earlier—in cases involving highly charged factors such as conspiracy, fraud, or theft.

In short, it is now unwise for management to rely on trade secret law and derivative employee contractual restraints to preserve trade secrets. Companies must now carefully weigh the nature and value of their intellectual property, present and potential employees, competition, and applicable laws in order to formulate sound management policies.

PROGRAMMED APPROACH

Regarding the challenge to the preservation of trade secrets posed by the mobile employee, sophisticated management will place its primary reliance on the inculcation of company loyalty in key employees, and on the continual satisfaction of such key employees. For example, management might consider adopting the following five-step basis for developing an overall approach to the challenge:

1. Devise a program for recognition of employee achievement in the trade secret area. At present, this form of recognition is even more neglected than is adequate recognition of employee inventions.

2. Make an appraisal of trade secret activities. This should result in a limitation of (a) personnel with access to trade secrets, (b) the extent of trade secrets available to such personnel, and (c) information which truly deserves the label of trade secret.

3. Review in-house procedures and the use of physical safeguards, such as restrictions on access to certain specified areas and on employee writings for outside publication. Restrictions may tend to stifle creativity by in-

hibiting communication and interaction conducive to innovation. Striking the balance between too few and too many safeguards is a delicate process and depends on employee awareness of what is being sought and how it will benefit them.

4. Appraise the legal systems available for the protection of intellectual property. Utility and design patents may be advisable in some cases. The copyright system now offers some protection to certain types of industrial designs and computer software. Trademarks may be adroitly used to maintain markets.

5. Recognize that all efforts may fail to persuade a key employee from leaving. To cope with this contingency, the "gentle persuasion" of a pension or consulting plan in the post-employment period has proved effective and legally sound. A thorough debriefing is a further safeguard. Other cases wherein employee mobility is accompanied by fraud, unfair competition, or theft will be adequately dealt with by the courts.

The problem of the departing employee and the threatened loss of trade secrets is not solved by exhortations that scientists and engineers need courses in professional ethics. Management itself should display the standards of conduct expected of its employees and of other companies.

Finally, let me stress again that success probably lies in the inculcation of company loyalty in key employees, not in the enforcement of company desires or in misplaced reliance on the law to subsidize cursory management. Better employee relations—in fact, a total sensitivity to the needs and aspirations of highly educated employees—requires constant management concern. In the long run, total sensitivity will prove less costly and more effective than litigation and the use of questionable contractual restraints.

Trade Secrets, Patents, and Morality

Robert E. Frederick
and Milton Snoeyenbos

Suppose that company M develops a super-computer that gives it a competitive advantage, but decides that, rather than marketing it, it will use the computer to provide services to users. In doing so, it keeps its technical information secret. If another company, N, were to steal the computer, N would be subject to moral blame as well as legal penalty. But suppose that, without M's consent, N obtained M's technical information, which thereby enabled N to copy M's computer. Should N then be subject to moral blame and legal penalty?

At first glance it seems that N should be held morally and legally accountable; but N has a line of defense which supports its position. Information, or knowledge, unlike a physical asset, can be possessed by more than one individual or firm at any one time. Thus, in obtaining M's information N did not diminish M's information; since M possesses exactly the same information it had before, N cannot be said to have stolen it. Furthermore, everyone regards the dissemination of knowledge as a good thing; it has obvious social utility. M's competitive advantage, moreover, was not a good thing, since it could have enabled M to drive other firms out of the computer service business; M might have established a monopoly. Thus, M has no right to keep the information to itself, and, in the interests of social utility, N had a right to obtain M's information. Hence, N should be praised rather than blamed for its act.

This defense of N raises the general question of whether a firm's use of trade secrets or

patents to protect information is justifiable. If it is not, then N may at least be morally justified in using clandestine means to obtain M's information. If there is a justification for allowing trade secrets and patents, then, not only is N's act unjustifiable, but we also have a basis for saying that the release of certain information in certain contexts to N by an employee of M is unjustifiable. In this paper we argue that there are both consequentialist and nonconsequentialist reasons for allowing firms to protect *their* proprietary information via patents and trade secrets. On the other hand, an individual has a right to liberty and a right to use *his* knowledge and skills to better himself. These rights place certain constraints on what can qualify as a trade secret or patentable item of information. We begin with a discussion of present patent and trade secret law.

Patents differ significantly from trade secrets. A patent provides a legal safeguard of certain information itself, but the information must be novel. Some internal information generated by a firm may not meet the U.S. Patent Office's standards of inventiveness. Then, too, even if an item is patentable, there may be disadvantages to the firm in seeking and securing a patent on it and/or advantages to the firm in just trying to keep the information secret. There are legal costs in securing a patent, and patents have to be secured in every country in which one wishes to protect the information. In the U.S. a patent expires in 17 years, and, since it is not renewable, the information then becomes public domain. Furthermore, since a patent is a public document, it both reveals research directions and encourages competitors to invent related products that are just dissimilar enough to avoid a patent infringement suit. So there are ample reasons for a firm to keep information secret and not attempt to secure a patent. If a firm can keep the information secret, it may have a longterm advantage over competitors. The disadvantage is that, unlike a patented device or information, the law provides no protection for a trade secret itself. A competitor can analyze an unpatented product in any way, and, if it discovers the trade secret, it is free to use that information or product. For example, if a firm analyzes Coca-Cola and uncovers the secret formula, it can market a product chemically identical to it, although, of course, it cannot use the name "Coca-Cola," since that is protected by trademark law.

It is, however, unlawful to employ "improper means" to secure another's trade secret. Legal protection of trade secrets is based on the agent's duty of confidentiality. Section 395 of the *Restatement of Agency* imposes a duty on the agent "not to use or communicate information confidentially given to him by the principal or acquired by him during the course of or on account of his agency . . . to the injury of the principal, on his own account or on behalf of another . . . unless the information is a matter of general knowledge." This duty extends beyond the length of the work contract; if the employee moves to a new job with another firm, his obligation to not disclose his previous principal's trade secrets is still in effect.

Since patents are granted by the U.S. Patent Office in accordance with the U.S. Patent Code, patent law cases are federal cases, whereas trade secrets cases are handled by state courts in accordance with state laws. Although there is no definition of "trade secret" adopted by every state, most follow the definition in Section 757 of the *Restatement of Torts*,

according to which a trade secret consists of a pattern, device, formula or compilation of information used in business and designed to give the employer an opportunity to obtain an advantage over his competitors who neither know nor use the information. On this definition virtually anything an employer prefers to keep confidential could count as a trade secret.

In practice, however, the *Restatement* specifies several factors it suggests that courts should consider in deciding whether information is legally protectable: (1) the extent to which the information is known outside the business, (2) the extent to which it is known to employees in the firm, (3) the extent to which the firm used measures to guard secrecy of the information, (4) the value of the information to the firm and to its competitors, (5) the amount of money the firm spent to develop the information, and (6) how easily the information may be developed or properly duplicated.

According to (1), (2), (4), (5), and (6), not all internally generated information will count legally as a trade secret. And, via (3), the firm must take measures to guard its secrets: " . . . a person entitled to a trade secret . . . must not fail to take all proper and reasonable steps to keep it secret. He cannot lie back and do nothing to preserve its essential secret quality, particularly when the subject matter of the process becomes known to a number of individuals involved in its use or is observed in the course of manufacturing in the plain view of others" (*Gallowhur Chemical Corp. v. Schwerdle*, 37 N. J. Super. 385, 397, 117 A2d 416, 423; *J. T. Healy & Son, Inc., v. James Murphy & Son, Inc.*, 1970 Mass. Adv. Sheets 1051, 260 NE2d 723 (Ill. App. 1959)). In addition to attempting to keep its information secret, the firm must inform its employees as to what data are regarded as secret: there "must be a strong showing that the knowledge was gained in confidence," (*Wheelabrator Corp. v. Fogle*, 317 F. Supp. 633

(D. C. La. 1970)), and employees must be warned that certain information is regarded as a trade secret (*Gallo v. Norris Dispensers, Inc.,* 315 F. Supp. 38 (D. C. Mo. 1970)). Most firms have their employees sign a document that (a) specifies what its trade secrets or types of trade secrets are, and (b) informs them that improper use of the trade secrets violates confidentiality and subjects them to litigation.

If a firm has information that really is a legitimate trade secret, if it informs its employees that this information is regarded as secret, and informs them that improper use violates confidentiality, then it may be able to establish its case in court, in which case it is entitled to injunctive relief and damages. But the courts also typically examine how the defendant in a trade secret case obtained the information. For example, if an employee transfers from company M to company N, taking M's documents with him to N, then there is clear evidence of a breach of confidentiality (or "bad faith") if the evidence can be produced by M. But trade secret law is equity law, a basic principle of which is that bad faith cannot be presumed. In equity law the maxim "Every dog has one free bite" obtains, i.e., a dog cannot be presumed to be vicious until he bites someone. Thus, if the employee took no producible hard evidence in the form of objects or documents, but instead took what was "in his head" or what he could memorize, then M may have to wait for its former employee to overtly act. By then it may be very difficult to produce convincing evidence that would establish a breach of confidentiality.

In considering possible justifications of patents and trade secrets, we have to take into consideration the public good or social utility, the firm's rights and interests, and the individual's rights and interests. Our aim should be to maximize utility while safeguarding legitimate rights.

As Michael Baram has noted, "A major concern of our society is progress through the promotion and utilization of new technology. To sustain and enhance this form of progress, it is necessary to optimize the flow of information and innovation all the way from conception to public use."[1] Given the assumption that technological progress is conducive to social utility, and that the dissemination of technological information is a major means to progress, the key issue is how to maximize information generation and dissemination.

One answer is to require public disclosure of all important generated information, and allow unrestricted use of that information. In some cases this is appropriate, e.g., government sponsored research conducted by a private firm is disclosed and can be used by other firms. Within a capitalistic context, however, it is doubtful that a general disclosure requirement would maximize social utility. The innovative firm would develop information leading to a new product only to see that product manufactured and marketed by another firm at a lower price because the latter firm did not incur research costs. The proposal probably would also result in less competition; only firms with strong financial and marketing structures would survive. Small, innovative firms would not have the protection of their technological advantages necessary to establish a competitive position against industry giants. If both research effort and competition were diminished by this proposal, then the "progress" Baram mentions would not be maximized—at least not in the area of marketable products.

In a market economy, then, there are reasons grounded in social utility for allowing firms to have some proprietary information. The laws based on such a justification should, in part, be structured with an eye to overall utility, and in fact they are so structured. Patents, for example, expire in 17 years. While the patent is in force it allows the firm to recoup research expenses and generate a profit by charging monopolistic prices. Patent protection also encourages the generation of new knowledge. The firm holding the patent, and realizing profits because of it, is encouraged to channel some of those profits to research, since its patent is of limited duration. Given that its patent will expire, the firm needs to generate new, patentable information to maximize profits. Competitors are encouraged to develop competing products that are based on new, patentable information.

Patent protection should not, however, extend indefinitely; it would not only extend indefinitely the higher costs that consumers admittedly bear while a patent is in force, but in certain cases, it could also stifle innovation. A firm holding a basic patent might either "sit on" it or strengthen its monopoly position. A company like Xerox, for example, with the basic xerography patent, might use its profits to fund research until it had built up an impenetrable patent network, but then cut reproductive graphics research drastically and rest relatively secure in the knowledge that its competitors were frozen out of the market. Patents allow monopoly profits for a limited period of time, but patent law should not be structured to forever legitimatize a monopoly.

Richard De George has recently offered another argument to the conclusion that the right to proprietary information is a limited right:

> Knowledge is not an object which one can keep locked up as long as one likes. . . . Whatever knowledge a company produces is always an increment to the knowledge developed by society or by previous people in society and passed from one generation to another. Any new invention is made by people who learned a great deal from the general store of knowledge before they could bring what they knew to bear on a particular problem. Though we can attribute them to particular efforts of individuals or teams, therefore, inventions and discoveries also are the result of those people who developed them and passed on their knowledge to others. In this way every advance in knowledge is social and belongs ultimately to society, even though for practical purposes we can assign it temporarily to a given individual or firm.[2]

Allowing the firm to use proprietary information has utility, but the right to such information is limited. In point of fact, although we have stressed the utility of allowing use of proprietary information, U.S. patent and copyright laws were enacted during the industrial revolution to reduce secrecy. Patent laws allow limited monopolies in return for public disclosure of the information on which the patent is based. Thus, patent laws provide information to competitors and encourage them to develop their own patentable information that not only generates new products, but also adds to the store of available knowledge.

If allowing limited use of proprietary information has utility, it is still an open question as to the proper limits of such use. Does the present 17-year patent limit maximize utility? This is an empirical question that we will not attempt to answer. Although most experts and industry representatives believe the present limit is about right, U.S. drug firms have recently argued that research and development time and Federal Drug Administration (FDA) testing and licensing requirements are so extensive that social disutility results, as well as disutility for innovative firms.

Although patents expire and the information protected can then be used by anyone, trade secrets can extend indefinitely according to present law. In 1623, the Zildjian family in Turkey developed a metallurgical process for making excellent cymbals. Now centered in Massachusetts, the family has maintained their secret to the present day, and they still produce excellent cymbals.

Preservation of such secrets may well have utility for firms holding the secrets, but does it have social utility? Not necessarily, as the following case illustrates. Suppose that Jones, a shadetree mechanic, develops a number of small unpatentable improvements in the internal combustion engine's basic design. The result is an engine that is cheap, reliable, and gets 120 miles per gallon. With no resources to mass produce and market his engine, Jones decides to sell to the highest bidder. XYZ oil company, with immense oil reserves, buys the information. To protect its oil interests, it keeps the information secret. Now suppose it is in fact against XYZ's interests to divulge the information. Then, to calculate overall utility we have to weigh the social disutility of keeping the information secret against the social utility of keeping the existing oil industry intact. Although utility calculations are difficult, it seems clear that disutility would arise from allowing the information to be kept secret.

If the preservation of *some* secrets has social disutility, it also seems clear that requiring immediate disclosure of *all* trade secrets in a capitalistic context would have disutility as well. The arguments here parallel those we developed in discussing patents. Again, specification of the appropriate duration of a trade secret is a utility calculation. The calculation will, however, have to take into consideration the fact that the law provides no protection for the secret itself. The firm with a significant investment in a trade secret always runs the risk that a competitor may legitimately uncover and use the secret.

Allowing patents and trade secrets has obvious utility for the firm that possesses them, but the firm also has a *right* to at least the limited protection of its information. It has a *legal* right to expect that its employees will live up to their work contracts, and employees have a correlative duty to abide by their contracts. The work contract is entered into voluntarily by employer and employee; if a prospective employee does not like the terms of a (legitimate) trade secret provision of a contract, he does not have to take the job. The normal employment contract specifies that the firm owns all employee-generated information. Even if the employee transfers from firm M to firm N, M still owns the information produced when he was employed there, and the employee is obligated not to reveal that information.

The moral basis of contract enforceability, including contractual provisions for the protection of proprietary information, is twofold. First, as argued, allowing trade secrets has social utility in addition to utility for the firm. The institution of contract compliance is necessary for the systematic and orderly functioning of business, and a sound business environment is essential to general social utility. However, if only a few people broke their contracts, business would continue to survive. This leads to the second moral basis for adhering to the provisions of one's contract.

If an individual breaks his contract, then he must either regard himself as an exception to the rule banning contract-breaking, or he must believe, in Kant's terms, that a maxim concerning contract-breaking is universalizable. But if we agree that in moral matters everyone ought to adopt the moral point of view, and that point of view requires that one not make himself an exception to the rule, it follows that the person in question is not justified in breaking the rule. On the other hand, if he claims that breaking the contract is in accordance with a maxim, then we can properly demand to have the maxim specified. Clearly the maxim cannot be something like: "I will keep my promises, except on those occasions where it is not to my advantage to keep the promises." For if everyone followed this maxim, there would be no institution of promising or promise-keeping. Since the maxim is not universalizable, it cannot legitimately be appealed to as a sanction for action. Of course, other maxims are available, and the contract-breaker may claim that his act is in accordance with one of these maxims. But note that this reply at least tacitly commits the person to the moral point of view; he is agreeing that everyone ought to act only on universalizable maxims. The only dispute, then, is whether his maxim is in fact universalizable. If we can show him that it is not, he is bound to admit that he is not morally justified in breaking the contract. As a standard, then, contracts should be kept, and where an individual breaks, or contemplates breaking, a contract, the burden is on him to produce a universalizable maxim for his action.

Our analysis does not, however, imply that a person is morally obligated to abide by all contracts; some contracts, or provisions of certain contracts, may be morally and/or legally unacceptable. A person does have a right to liberty and a right to use his knowledge and skills to earn a living. Thus, firm M cannot legitimately specify that *all* knowledge an employee gains while at M is proprietary. This would prohibit the person from obtaining employment at another firm; in effect the work contract would amount to a master-slave relationship. As the *Restatement of Torts* appropriately specifies, only certain information qualifies as a legitimate trade secret. Furthermore, the employee brings to his job certain knowledge and skills that typically are matters of public domain, and, on the job, the good employee develops his capacities. As the court noted in *Donahue v. Permacil Tape Corporation:* an ex-employee's general knowledge and capabilities "belong to him as an individual for the transaction of any business in which he may engage, just the same as any part of the skill, knowledge, information or education which was received by him before entering the employment. . . . On terminating his employment, he has a right to take them with him."[3]

Given that an individual's rights to liberty and to use his knowledge and skills to better himself are primary rights, and hence cannot be overridden by utility considerations, the burden clearly is on the firm to: (1) specify to employees what it regards as its trade secrets, and (2) make sure the secrets are legitimate trade secrets. In addition, a company can employ certain pragmatic tactics to protect its trade secrets. It can fragment research activities so that only a few employees know all the secrets. It can restrict access to research data and operational areas. It can develop pension and consulting policies for ex-employees that motivate them not to join competitors for a period of time. More importantly, it can develop a corporate atmosphere that motivates the individual to remain with the firm.

We began by sketching an argument that company N was justified in obtaining information about company M's computer without M's consent. Our conclusion is that N's argument is specious. Utility considerations justify allowing M to keep its information secret for a period of time, and any employee of M who divulges M's secret information to N is morally blameworthy because he violates his contractual obligations to M.

NOTES

1. Michael S. Baram, "Trade Secrets: What Price Loyalty?" *Harvard Business Review*, vol 46, No. 6 (Nov.–Dec., 1968), pp. 66–74 [reprinted here, pp. 323–331].
2. Richard T. DeGeorge, *Business Ethics* (New York: Macmillan, 1982), p. 207.
3. Cited in Baram, p. 71.

Warthen v. Toms River Community Memorial Hospital

Superior Court of New Jersey

Plaintiff Corrine Warthen appeals from a summary judgment of the Law Division dismissing her action against defendant Toms River Community Memorial Hospital (Hospital). Plaintiff sought to recover damages for her allegedly wrongful discharge in violation of public policy following her refusal to dialyze a terminally ill double amputee patient because of her "moral, medical and philosophical objections" to performing the procedure.

The facts giving rise to this appeal are not in dispute and may be summarized as follows. The Hospital, where plaintiff had been employed for eleven years as a registered nurse, terminated plaintiff from its employment on August 6, 1982. For the three years just prior to her discharge, plaintiff had worked in the Hospital's kidney dialysis unit. It is undisputed that plaintiff was an at-will employee.

Plaintiff alleges that during the summer of 1982 her supervisor periodically assigned her to dialyze a double amputee patient who suffered from a number of maladies. On two occasions plaintiff claims that she had to cease treatment because the patient suffered cardiac arrest and severe internal hemorrhaging during the dialysis procedure. During the first week of 1982 plaintiff again was scheduled to dialyze this patient. She approached her head nurse and informed her that "she had moral, medical, and philosophical objections" to performing this procedure on the patient because the patient was terminally ill and, she contended, the procedure was causing the patient additional complications. At

that time the head nurse granted plaintiff's request for reassignment.

On August 6, 1982, the head nurse again assigned plaintiff to dialyze the same patient. Plaintiff once again objected, apparently stating that she thought she had reached agreement with the head nurse not to be assigned to this particular patient. She also requested the opportunity to meet with the treating physician, Dr. DiBello. Dr. DiBello informed plaintiff that the patient's family wished him kept alive through dialysis and that he would not survive without it. However, plaintiff continued to refuse to dialyze the patient, and the head nurse informed her that if she did not agree to perform the treatment, the Hospital would dismiss her. Plaintiff refused to change her mind, and the Hospital terminated her.

Plaintiff subsequently instituted this action alleging that she was wrongfully discharged by the Hospital without justification and in violation of public policy. The Hospital denied liability to plaintiff and alleged, by way of a separate defense, that plaintiff's termination was appropriate because she had the status of an at-will employee. Following completion of pretrial discovery, the Hospital moved for summary judgment, which the trial court denied because it perceived "that there [was] . . . a question of fact as to whether or not there is a public policy as articulated in the nurses' code of ethics that would permit somebody in the nursing profession to refuse to participate in a course of treatment which is against her principles in good faith." However, upon re-

488 A.2d 299 (1985). Opinion by Judge Michels.

consideration, the trial court granted the motion, concluding that "the nurses' code of ethics is a personal moral judgment and permits the nurse to have a personal moral judgment, but it does not rise to a public policy in the face of the general public policies that patients must be cared for in hospitals and patients must be treated basically by doctors and doctors' orders must be carried out." This appeal followed.

Plaintiff contends that the trial court erred in granting summary judgment because her refusal to dialyze the terminally-ill patient was justified as a matter of law by her adherence to the *Code for Nurses*, a code of ethics promulgated by the American Nurses Association, and that determining whether adherence to the *Code* "constitutes a public policy question" is a question of fact which should be resolved by a jury, not by the trial court. We disagree. . . .

Plaintiff relies on the "public policy" exception to the "at-will employment" doctrine to justify her claim that defendant wrongfully discharged her. As has often been stated at common law, "in the absence of an employment contract, employers or employees have been free to terminate the employment relationship with or without cause." . . . Recently, in *Pierce v. Ortho Pharmaceutical Corp., supra*, the Supreme Court recognized a developing exception to the traditional "at-will employment" doctrine, holding that "an employee has a cause of action for wrongful discharge when the discharge is contrary to a clear mandate of public policy." . . .

As a preliminary matter plaintiff contends that identifying the "clear mandate of public policy" constitutes a genuine issue of material fact for the jury rather than, as occurred in the instant case, a threshold question for the trial judge. To support her contention plaintiff cites *Kalman v. Grand Union Co.*, . . . in which we said:

It is the employee's burden to identify "a specific expression" or "a clear mandate" of public

policy which might bar his discharge. [Citation omitted]. What constitutes a qualifying mandate is a fact question. . . .

However, quoting the following explanatory language from *Ortho Pharmaceutical,* we went on to emphasize that "the judiciary must define the cause of action in case-by-case determinations." . . .

In *Ortho Pharmaceutical* plaintiff, a physician and research scientist, was dismissed because of her opposition to continued laboratory research, development and testing of the drug loperamide, which Ortho intended to market for the treatment of diarrhea. The plaintiff was opposed to the drug because it contained saccharin and because she believed that by continuing work on loperamide she would violate her interpretation of the Hippocratic oath. The Court held, *as a matter of law*, that where plaintiff merely contended saccharin was controversial, not dangerous, and the FDA had not yet approved human testing of loperamide, the Hippocractic oath did not contain a clear mandate of public policy preventing the physician from continuing research. Then, not finding any issue of material fact, the Supreme Court remanded the case to the trial court for the entry of summary judgment.

Thus, identifying the mandate of public policy is a question of law, analogous to interpreting a statute or defining a duty in a negligence case. . . . As the Chancery Court said in *Schaffer v. Federal Trust Co.*, . . .

"Public policy has been defined as that principle of law which holds that no person can lawfully do that which has a tendency to be injurious to the public, or against the public good." . . . The term admits of no exact definition. . . . The source of public policy is the statutes enacted by the legislature and in the decisions of the courts; there we find what acts are considered harmful to the public and therefore unlawful.

Public policy is not concerned with minutiae, but with principles. Seldom does a single clause of a statute establish public policy; policy is discovered from study of the whole statute, or even a group of statutes *in pari materia*. . . .

Based on the foregoing, we hold that where a discharged at-will employee asserts wrongful discharge on public policy grounds, the trial court must, as a matter of law, determine whether public policy justified the alleged conduct. Then, assuming the pleadings raise a genuine issue of material fact, it is for the jury to determine the truth of the employee's allegations. Here, therefore, the issue of whether the *Code for Nurses* represented a clear expression of public policy did not present a genuine issue of material fact precluding the entry of summary judgment.

Plaintiff next contends that, as a matter of law, the *Code for Nurses* constitutes an authoritative statement of public policy which justified her conduct and that the trial court therefore improperly granted defendant's motion for summary judgment. In *Ortho Pharmaceutical* the Supreme Court discussed the role of professional codes of ethics as sources of public policy in "at-will employment" cases:

> In certain instances, a professional code of ethics may contain an expression of public policy. However, not all such sources express a clear mandate of public policy. For example, a code of ethics designed to serve only the interests of a profession or an administrative regulation concerned with technical matters probably would not be sufficient. Absent legislation, the judiciary must define the cause of action in case-by-case determinations. An employer's right to discharge an employee at will carries a correlative duty not to discharge an employee who declines to perform an act that would require a violation of a clear mandate of public policy. However, unless an employee at will identifies a specific expression of public policy, he may be discharged with or without cause. . . .

The Court carefully warned against confusing reliance on professional ethics with reliance on personal morals:

> Employees who are professionals owe a special duty to abide not only by federal and state law, but also by the recognized codes of ethics of their professions. That duty may oblige them to decline to perform acts required by their employers. However, an employee should not have the right to prevent his or her employer from pursuing its business because the employee perceives that a particular business decision violates the employee's personal morals, as distinguished from the recognized code of ethics of the employee's profession. . . .

The burden is on the professional to identify "a specific expression" or "a clear mandate" of public policy which might bar his or her dismissal. . . .

Here, plaintiff cites the *Code for Nurses* to justify her refusal to dialyze the terminally ill patient. She refers specifically to the following provisions and interpretive statement:

THE NURSE PROVIDES SERVICES WITH RESPECT FOR HUMAN DIGNITY AND THE UNIQUENESS OF THE CLIENT UNRESTRICTED BY CONSIDERATIONS OF SOCIAL OR ECONOMIC STATUS, PERSONAL ATTRIBUTES, OR THE NATURE OF HEALTH PROBLEMS.

1.4 THE NATURE OF HEALTH PROBLEMS

The nurse's concern for human dignity and the provision of quality nursing care is not limited by personal attitudes or beliefs. If personally opposed to the delivery of care in a particular case because of the nature of the health problem or the procedures to be used, the nurse is justified in refusing to participate. Such refusal should be made known in advance and in time for other appropriate arrangements to be made for the client's nursing care. If the nurse must knowingly enter such a case under emergency circumstances or enters unknowingly, the obligation to provide the best possible care is observed. The nurse withdraws from this type of situation only when assured that alternative sources of nursing care are available to the client. If a client requests information or counsel in an area that is legally sanctioned but contrary to the nurse's personal beliefs, the nurse may refuse to provide these services but must advise the client of sources where such service is available. [American Nurses Association, *Code for Nurses with Interpretive Statements*. . . .

Plaintiff contends that these provisions constitute a clear mandate of public policy justifying her conduct. . . .

It is our view that as applied to the circumstances of this case the passage cited by plaintiff defines a standard of conduct beneficial only to the individual nurse and not to the public at large. The overall purpose of the language cited by plaintiff is to preserve human dignity; however, it should not be at the expense of the patient's life or contrary to the family's wishes. The record before us shows that the family had requested that dialysis be continued on the patient, and there is nothing to suggest that the patient had, or would have, indicated otherwise. . . .

Recently, in *In re Conroy, supra,* our Supreme Court confirmed this State's basic interest in the preservation of life, . . . and our recognition, embraced in the right to self-determination, that all patients have a fundamental right to expect that medical treatment will not be terminated against their will. . . . This basic policy mandate clearly outweighs any policy favoring the right of a nurse to refuse to participate in treatments which he or she personally believes threatens human dignity. Indeed, the following passage from the *Code for Nurses* echoes the policy cited by *Conroy* and severely constrains the ethical right of nurses to refuse participation in medical procedures:

1.4 THE NATURE OF HEALTH PROBLEMS
The nurse's respect for the worth and dignity of the individual human being applies irrespective of the nature of the health problem. It is reflected in the care given the person who is disabled as well as the normal; the patient with the long-term illness as well as the one with the acute illness, or the recovering patient as well as the one who is terminally ill or dying. It extends to all who require the services of the nurse for the promotion of health, the prevention of ill-

ness, the restoration of health, and the alleviation of suffering. [American Nurses Association, *Code for Nurses with Interpretive Statements*. . . .

The position asserted by plaintiff serves only the individual and the nurses' profession while leaving the public to wonder when and whether they will receive nursing care. . . . Moreover, as the Hospital argues, "[i]t would be a virtual impossibility to administer a hospital if each nurse or member of the administration staff refused to carry out his or her duties based upon a personal private belief concerning the right to live. . . . "

Concededly, plaintiff had to make a difficult decision. Viewing the facts in a light most beneficial to plaintiff, she had dialyzed the particular patient on several occasions in the past, and on two of those occasions plaintiff says the patient had suffered cardiac arrest and severe internal hemorrhaging during the dialysis procedure. The first time plaintiff objected to performing the procedure her head nurse agreed to reassign her, and at that time plaintiff apparently believed she had an agreement with the head nurse not to be assigned to this particular patient. She also believed she had fulfilled her ethical obligation by making her refusal to participate in the procedure "known in advance and in time for other appropriate arrangements to be made for the client's nursing care."

Nonetheless, we conclude as a matter of law that even under the circumstances of this case the ethical considerations cited by plaintiff do not rise to the level of a public policy mandate permitting a registered nursing professional to refuse to provide medical treatment to a terminally ill patient, even where that nursing professional gives his or her superiors advance warning. Beyond this, even if we were to make the dubious assumption that the *Code for Nurses* represents a clear expression of public policy, we have no hesitancy in concluding on this record that plaintiff was motivated by her own personal morals, precluding application of the "public policy" exception to the "at-will employment" doctrine. Plaintiff alleged that each time she refused to dialyze the patient she told the head nurse that she had "moral, medical and philosophical objections" to performing the procedure. She makes no assertion that she ever referred to her obligations and entitlements pursuant to her code of ethics. In addition, the very

basis for plaintiff's reliance on the *Code for Nurses* is that she was personally opposed to the dialysis procedure. By refusing to perform the procedure she may have eased her own conscience, but she neither benefited the society-at-large, the patient, nor the patient's family.

Accordingly, the judgment under review is affirmed.

Potter v. Village Bank of New Jersey

Superior Court of New Jersey

The crucial question raised in this appeal is whether a bank president and chief executive officer who blows the whistle on suspected laundering of Panamanian drug money is protected from retaliatory discharge by the public policy of this State. We answer in the affirmative. We also hold that the retaliatory discharge in this case constituted an intentional tort which exposed defendants to compensatory and punitive damages. We affirm the judgment.

A

Plaintiff Dale G. Potter became the president and chief executive officer of the Village Bank of New Jersey (Village Bank) on November 15, 1982. His employment was terminated in May or June 1984. On June 13, 1984 plaintiff filed a complaint in the Chancery Division against Village Bank alleging that his job had been wrongfully terminated. Plaintiff sought reinstatement to his position as chief executive officer and president of the bank. . . .

After the matter was transferred to the Law

Division, plaintiff filed an amended complaint. . . . In the four-count amended complaint plaintiff sought compensatory and punitive damages based on (1) fraudulent inducement, (2) breach of contract, (3) tortious interference with the employment relationship and (4) wrongful termination.

The case was tried to a jury over a four-day period. . . . At the end of plaintiff's case, the trial judge granted defendants' motion for involuntary dismissal of plaintiff's claims of fraudulent inducement, breach of contract and wrongful interference with the employment relationship. The only remaining claim was for wrongful discharge. . . .

The claim of wrongful discharge was submitted to the jury as to the remaining defendants, Village Bank and Em Kay. The jury answered the following special interrogatories:

Q1. Did the Defendants wrongfully discharge the plaintiff?
A. Yes.
Q2. Was the plaintiff damaged by such wrongful discharge?
A. Yes.
Q3. What amount of compensatory damages,

543 A.2d 80 (1985). Opinion by Judge J. H. Coleman.

if any, should the plaintiff be awarded for such wrongful discharge?
A. $50,000.
Q4. What amount of punitive damages, if any, should the plaintiff be awarded for such wrongful discharge?
A. $100,000.

After the trial judge denied defendants' motion for judgment notwithstanding the verdict, final judgment was entered in the sum of $162,575.40, which consisted of $100,000 in punitive damages, $50,000 in compensatory damages plus $12,575.40 in prejudgment interest on the compensatory damages.

Village Bank and Em Kay Holding Corporation have appealed from the entire judgment. Plaintiff has cross-appealed from the involuntary dismissals at the end of plaintiff's evidence.

The pivotal issue presented to the jury was whether plaintiff resigned or was discharged in violation of a clear mandate of public policy. Based on the evidence presented, the jury concluded he was fired contrary to a clear mandate of public policy. The following evidence supports that finding. Em Kay Holding Corporation (Em Kay) owns 93% of the stock of Village Bank. The remaining 7% is distributed among other shareholders. Em Kay is owned by the Em Kay Group which has its headquarters in Panama City, Panama. Em Kay Group is owned by Mory Kraselnick and Moises Kroitoro.

Bart and Kraselnick negotiated with plaintiff for employment at Village Bank. In September 1982 when the president of Village Bank suffered a heart attack, plaintiff was offered and accepted a position with the bank as a "holding company consultant." Plaintiff became president and chief executive officer of Village Bank two months later. Between then and January 1983, Kraselnick frequently telephoned plaintiff to request that Village Bank make large loans to companies that did business with Kraselnick and companies owned by Kraselnick. With few exceptions, plaintiff refused these requests.

After a January 21, 1983 meeting Kraselnick told plaintiff: "[I]f I ever ask you to do anything wrong, I'll stand up in front of you." At the time, plaintiff did not understand the meaning of the statement. Over the next couple of months, however, many cash deposits of between $8,000 and $9,300 were made into the accounts of Kraselnick, Bart, Noel Kinkella (office manager of Em Kay Equities whose president was Bart) and several of the companies in the Em Kay Group.

On March 24, 1983 plaintiff learned that Village Bank was advertising his job in the *Wall Street Journal*. When plaintiff confronted Kraselnick about this, he was told "You're not as outspoken and enthusiastic as I want you to be when you meet me." After plaintiff defended his position, the two temporarily reconciled.

On March 31, 1983 Kinkella went to Village Bank with a shopping bag filled with money. She made seven $9,000 deposits to accounts held by Kraselnick, Bart, Kinkella and four Em Kay related companies. Plaintiff became suspicious that drug money was being laundered so he called the New Jersey Commissioner of Banking and reported the transactions and requested advice. Before plaintiff could meet with the Commissioner, Kinkella deposited another package of about $50,000 in cash. When plaintiff asked Bart about the money, Bart told him that it was for lease payments between two related aeronautical companies in the Em Kay Group. Plaintiff became more suspicious that the large cash deposits were related to laundering of Panamanian drug money. When the Commissioner eventually met with plaintiff, he told plaintiff to maintain anonymity and that a full investigation would be undertaken. The jury was not informed about the details of plaintiff's suspicions.

Audits of the bank were conducted starting around the end of April or the beginning of May 1983. On June 28, 1983 plaintiff advised Village Bank's board of directors of the examination, but not of his meeting with the Commissioner. In July 1983 plaintiff filed currency transaction reports with the Department of the Treasury reporting the cash deposits.

In September 1983 Village Bank's board of directors raised plaintiff's salary from $65,000 to $75,000. Kraselnick also offered plaintiff a $10,000 bonus in cash so he "wouldn't pay income taxes" on it. When plaintiff refused to accept the bonus in cash, the bonus was not paid. In December 1983 the United States Attorney's Office for New Jersey issued subpoenas to the bank for the production of documents "on a list of accounts" related to the Em Kay Group. Plaintiff was also interviewed by representatives from that office.

On January 6, 1984 plaintiff executed his first written employment contract with Village Bank. The term was for one year beginning November 15, 1983. The contract provided for a base salary of $75,000, with a bonus at the discretion of the board of directors.

At some time between July and December 1983, plaintiff told Steven S. Radin, secretary to the Village Bank board of directors, that he "had gone to the Commissioner and reported the [cash] transactions." In January 1984 Radin informed Bart and Kraselnick of what plaintiff had told him. This angered Kraselnick. At the next scheduled board meeting, the directors were informed.

Immediately after the board meeting, Kraselnick asked plaintiff why he went to the Commissioner of Banking. When plaintiff responded "I thought that it was drug money," Kraselnick stated "you're probably right." From that point on, plaintiff contended that he was isolated from running the bank effectively since his subordinates in the bank were ordered not to talk to him. Further, there

were several instances where Kraselnick questioned plaintiff's judgment and accused him of doing things incorrectly.

Plaintiff testified that Radin and at least two of Village Bank's directors advised him that he was about to be fired before plaintiff wrote a letter on May 22, 1984. The letter was written to Kraselnick which stated in pertinent part:

> I wanted to be able to communicate directly with you and since my requests for a face to face meeting with you have been rejected, I am using this as my only recourse. At this point in time, I am considering myself "de facto" fired since Allan Bart has told several directors and John Bjerke, among others, that "Potter's gone" and in turn at least one director has communicated the same to several customers who have even discussed it with people in the Bank including myself. Needless to say, the lack of discretion in discussing this situation in this way can only serve to hurt the Bank and the people in it. However, it has been done and the effect of it, in my opinion, has been that I consider myself at this point in time essentially to be terminated only without the pre-requisite action of the Board of Directors.

Shortly after the letter was written, plaintiff told members attending a board meeting that the letter was not intended as a letter of resignation. He reiterated this point in a May 31, 1984 letter to Radin.

By letter dated June 1, 1984, Radin notified plaintiff that

> . . . it was the consensus of the Board that the Bank pay you full salary until the termination (November 15, 1984) of your present contract. During that period of time you would have the use of a car, office and secretarial assistance. Also you would receive all ordinary employee benefits. In consideration of these severance terms the Board requested a general release from you for the Bank, its directors and officers. The Board gave you until June 1, 1984 to accept to reject this offer. From May 24, 1984 until June 1, 1984 you were placed on leave of absence with pay.

Plaintiff rejected the proposal made by the board. When plaintiff attempted to attend a June 11 board meeting with his attorney, the board asked him to leave the bank. . . .

B

Subsequent to the trial in this matter Kraselnick, Bart, Bjerke and Village Bank were indicted by a federal grand jury for the District of New Jersey for allegedly conspiring to defraud the United States and making fraudulent statements in violation of 31 *U.S.C.* § 5311 *et seq.*, 31 *C.F.R.* § 103.22 *et seq.*, and 18 *U.S.C.* §§ 371, 1001 and 1002. The alleged criminal violations are based on their failure to report large cash transactions at Village Bank during the time Potter was president and chief executive officer.

31 *U.S.C.* § 5313(a) provides, in pertinent part:

> (a) When a domestic financial institution is involved in a transaction for the . . . receipt . . . of United States coins or currency (or other monetary instruments the Secretary of the Treasury prescribes), in an amount, denomination, or amount and denomination, or under circumstances the Secretary prescribes by regulation, the institution and any other participant in the transaction the Secretary may prescribe shall file a report on the transaction at the time and in the way the Secretary prescribes. A participant acting for another person shall make the report as the agent or bailee of the person and identify the person for whom the transaction is being made.

Pursuant to this authority, the Secretary of the Treasury promulgated regulations which mandate the reporting of transactions in currency of more than $10,000.

Because the deposits in this case were slightly less than $10,000, plaintiff was not required by the strict wording of the statute and regulations to report the cash transactions.

However, there is existing authority holding that a bank officer may not structure a single transaction in currency as multiple transactions to avoid the reporting requirements. A financial institution must aggregate all transactions by one customer in one day.

. . . Potter did much more than "protest [] [the] directors' improprieties" relating to a regulatory scheme. He blew the whistle on suspected criminal conduct involving one or more directors. Hence, Potter's termination relates to the public policy designed to encourage citizens to report suspected criminal violations to the proper authorities in order to ensure proper enforcement of both state and federal penal laws. . . . Nowhere in our society is the need for protection greater than in protecting well motivated citizens who blow the whistle on suspected white collar and street level criminal activities. If "no person can lawfully do that which has a tendency to be injurious to the public or against the public good" because of public policy, *Allen v. Commercial Casualty Insurance Co.*, . . . surely whistle blowers of suspected criminal violations must be protected from retaliatory discharge. It stands to reason that few people would cooperate with law enforcement officials if the price they must pay is retaliatory discharge from employment. Clearly, that would have a chilling effect on criminal investigations and law enforcement in general.

Additionally, after the plaintiff's employment was terminated, the Legislature enacted the Conscientious Employee Protection Act, . . . effective September 5, 1986. Under the act, an employee who has been terminated because of reporting suspected criminal violations, has the right to file a retaliatory tort claim in addition to other remedies. We read this legislative enactment as a codification of public policy established through judicial decisions. . . .

We hold that the public policy of the State of New Jersey should protect at will employees—including bank presidents—who in good faith blow the whistle on one or more bank directors suspected of laundering money from illegal activities. . . .

C

We hold that an at will employee who has sustained a retaliatory discharge in violation of a clear mandate of public policy is entitled to recover economic and noneconomic losses. Such an employee may recover (1) the amount he or she would have earned from the time of wrongful discharge for a reasonable time until he or she finds new employ-ment, including bonuses and vacation pay, less any unemployment compensation received in the interim, . . . (2) expenses associated with finding new employment and mental anguish or emotional distress damages proximately related to the retaliatory discharge, . . . and (3) the replacement value of fringe benefits such as an automobile and insurance for a reasonable time until new employment is obtained. . . .

The jury awarded $50,000 in compensatory damages. In addition, the jury awarded $100,000 in punitive damages. We are completely satisfied that both the compensatory and punitive damages awarded are supported by sufficient credible evidence and were consonant with the law. . . .

Luedtke v. Nabors Alaska Drilling, Inc.

Superior Court of Alaska

This case addresses one aspect of drug testing by employers. A private employer, Nabors Alaska Drilling, Inc. (Nabors), established a drug testing program for its employees. Two Nabors employees, Clarence Luedtke and Paul Luedtke, both of whom worked on drilling rigs on the North Slope, refused to submit to urinalysis screening for drug use as required by Nabors. As a result they were fired by Nabors. The Luedtkes challenge their discharge on the following grounds:

1. Nabors' drug testing program violates the Luedtkes' right to privacy guaranteed by article I, section 22 of the Alaska Constitution;

2. Nabors' demands violate the covenant of good faith and fair dealing implicit in all employment contracts;

3. Nabors' urinalysis requirement violates the public interest in personal privacy, giving the Luedtkes a cause of action for wrongful discharge; and

4. Nabors' actions give rise to a cause of action under the common law tort of invasion of privacy.

Nabors argues that the Luedtkes were "at will" employees whose employment relationship could be terminated at any time for any reason. Alternatively, even if termination had to be based on "just cause," such cause existed because the Luedtkes violated estab-

---

768 P. 2d 1123 (1989). Opinion by Judge Compton.

lished company policy relating to employee safety by refusing to take the scheduled tests.

This case raises issues of first impression in Alaska law including: whether the constitutional right of privacy applies to private parties; some parameters of the tort of wrongful discharge; and the extent to which certain employee drug testing by private employers can be controlled by courts.

FACTUAL AND PROCEDURAL BACKGROUND

The Luedtkes' cases proceeded separately to judgment. Because they raised common legal issues, on Nabors' motion they were consolidated on appeal.

Paul's Case

Factual Background. Paul began working for Nabors, which operates drilling rigs on Alaska's North Slope, in February 1978. He began as a temporary employee, replacing a permanent employee on vacation for two weeks. During his two weeks of temporary work, a permanent position opened up on the rig on which he was working and he was hired to fill it. Paul began as a "floorman" and was eventually promoted to "driller." A driller oversees the work of an entire drilling crew.

Paul started work with Nabors as a union member, initially being hired from the union hall. During his tenure, however, Nabors "broke" the union. Paul continued to work without a union contract. Paul had no written contract with Nabors at the time of his discharge.

During his employment with Nabors, Paul was accused twice of violating the company's drug and alcohol policies. Once he was suspended for 90 days for taking alcohol to the

North Slope. The other incident involved a search of the rig on which Paul worked. Aided by dogs trained to sniff out marijuana, the searchers found traces of marijuana on Paul's suitcase. Paul was allowed to continue working on the rig only after assuring his supervisors he did not use marijuana.

In October 1982, Paul scheduled a two-week vacation. Because his normal work schedule was two weeks of work on the North Slope followed by a week off, a two-week vacation amounted to 28 consecutive days away from work. Just prior to his vacation, Paul was instructed to arrange for a physical examination in Anchorage. He arranged for it to take place on October 19, during his vacation. It was at this examination that Nabors first tested Paul's urine for signs of drug use. The purpose of the physical, as understood by Paul, was to enable him to work on off-shore rigs should Nabors receive such contracts. Although Paul was told it would be a comprehensive physical he had no idea that a urinalysis screening test for drug use would be performed. He did voluntarily give a urine sample but assumed it would be tested only for "blood sugar, any kind of kidney failure [and] problems with bleeding." Nabors' policy of testing for drug use was not announced until November 1, 1982, almost two weeks after Paul's examination.

In early November 1982, Paul contacted Nabors regarding his flight to the North Slope to return to work. He was told at that time to report to the Nabors office in Anchorage. On November 5, Paul reported to the office where a Nabors representative informed him that he was suspended for "the use of alcohol or other illicit substances." No other information was forthcoming from Nabors until November 16 when Paul received a letter informing him that his urine had tested positive for cannabinoids. The letter informed him that he would be required to pass two subsequent urinalysis tests, one on November 30 and the other on December 30, before he would be allowed to return to work. In response Paul hand delivered a letter drafted by his attorney to the Manager of Employee Relations for Nabors, explaining why he felt the testing and suspension were unfair. Paul did not take the urinalysis test on November 30 as requested by Nabors. On December 14, Nabors sent Paul a letter informing him he was discharged for refusing to take the November 30 test.

Procedural Background. Following his discharge, Paul applied for unemployment compensation benefits with the Alaska State Department of Labor (DOL). DOL initially denied Paul benefits for the period of December 12, 1982 through January 22, 1983 on the ground that his refusal to take the urinalysis test was misconduct under AS 23.30.379(a). Paul appealed that decision and on January 27, 1983, the DOL hearing officer concluded that the drug re-test requirement was unreasonable. On that basis, the hearing officer held that Paul's dismissal was not for misconduct. Nabors appealed to the Commissioner of Labor, who sustained the decision of the appeals tribunal.

Paul initiated this civil action in November 1983. He asserted claims for wrongful dismissal, breach of contract, invasion of privacy, and defamation. Nabors moved for and was granted summary judgment on the invasion of privacy claim, on both the constitutional and common law tort theories. Prior to trial Paul voluntarily dismissed his defamation claim. The trial court, in a non-jury trial, held for Nabors on Paul's wrongful dismissal and breach of contract claims.

Paul appeals the trial court's rulings with regard to his wrongful dismissal, breach of contract, and invasion of privacy claims.

Clarence's Case

Factual Background. Clarence has had seasonal employment with Nabors, working on drilling rigs, since the winter of 1977–78. Prior to beginning his first period of employment, he completed an employment application which provided for a probationary period.

In November 1982 Clarence became subject to the Nabors drug use and testing policy. In mid-November a list of persons scheduled for drug screening was posted at Clarence's rig. His name was on the list. The people listed were required to complete the test during their next "R & R" period. During that next "R & R" period Clarence decided he would not submit to the testing and informed Nabors of his decision.

Nabors offered to allow Clarence time to "clean up" but Clarence refused, insisting that he thought he could pass the test, but was refusing as "a matter of principle." At that point Nabors fired Clarence. The drug test that would have been performed on Clarence was the same as that performed on Paul.

Procedural Background. Following his discharge Clarence also sought unemployment compensation benefits with the DOL. Nabors objected because it believed his refusal to submit to the drug test was misconduct under AS 23.20.379(a). After a factual hearing and two appeals, the Commissioner of Labor found that "Nabors has not shown that there is any connection between off-the-job drug use and on-the-job performance." Thus, there was no showing that Nabors' test policy was related to job misconduct. Furthermore, the Commissioner adopted factual findings that 1) no evidence had been submitted by Nabors linking off-duty drug use with on-the-job accidents, and 2) Nabors was not alleging any drug use by Clarence.

Clarence filed his complaint in this case in November 1984. He alleged invasion of privacy, both at common law and under the Alaska Constitution, wrongful termination, breach of contract, and violation of the implied covenant of good faith and fair dealing. The trial court granted summary judgment in favor of Nabors on all of Clarence's claims. No opinion, findings of fact or conclusions of law were entered.

Clarence appeals the award of summary judgment on all counts.

DISCUSSION

The Right to Privacy

The right to privacy is a recent creation of American law. The inception of this right is generally credited to a law review article published in 1890 by Louis Brandeis and his law partner, Samuel Warren. Brandeis & Warren, *The Right to Privacy*, 4 Harv.L.Rev. 193 (1890). Brandeis and Warren observed that in a modern world with increasing population density and advancing technology, the number and types of matters theretofore easily concealed from public purview were rapidly decreasing. They wrote:

> Recent inventions and business methods call attention to the next step which must be taken for the protection of the person, and for securing to the individual what Judge Cooley calls the right "to be let alone." Instantaneous photographs and newspaper enterprise have invaded the sacred precincts of private and domestic life; and numerous mechanical devices threaten to make good the prediction that "what is whispered in the closet shall be proclaimed from the housetops."

Id. at 195 (footnotes omitted). Discussing the few precedential cases in tort law in which courts had afforded remedies for the publication of private letters or unauthorized photographs, Brandeis and Warren drew a common thread they called "privacy." They defined this right as the principle of "inviolate personality." *Id.* at 205.

While the legal grounds of this right were somewhat tenuous in the 1890's, American jurists found the logic of Brandeis and Warren's arguments compelling. The reporters of the first Restatement of Torts included a tort entitled "Interference with Privacy." By 1960, Professor Prosser could write that "the right of privacy, in one form or another, is declared to exist by the overwhelming majority of the American courts." . . . He cited cases in which private parties had been held liable in tort for eavesdropping on private conversations by means of wiretapping and microphones, or for peering into the windows of homes. In addition, while Brandeis and Warren were mainly concerned with the publication of private facts, Professor Prosser identified four different manifestations of the right to privacy: intrusion upon the plaintiff's seclusion; public disclosure of embarrassing private facts; publicity which places the plaintiff in a false light; and appropriation, for the defendant's pecuniary advantage of the plaintiff's name or likeness. Professor Prosser's categories form the framework of the expanded tort of invasion of privacy found in the Restatement (Second) of Torts.

Eventually the right to privacy attained sufficient recognition to be incorporated in several state constitutions. Alaska (adopted 1972); Cal. (adopted 1972); Haw. (adopted 1978); Mont. (adopted 1972).

Interpreting the Constitution of the United States, the United States Supreme Court in 1965 held that a Connecticut statute banning the use of birth control devices by married couples was "repulsive to the notions of privacy surrounding the marriage relationship." . . . The Supreme Court wrote that "specific guarantees in the Bill of Rights have penumbras, formed by emanations from those guarantees that help give them life and substance. Various guarantees create zones of privacy." . . . Justice Goldberg's concurrence suggested that the right of marital privacy was fundamental to the concept of liberty. . . . Since *Griswold* the Supreme Court has found the federal constitutional right of privacy to apply to a number of other situations. . . .

In this case the plaintiffs seek to fit their cases within at least one of four legal frameworks in which the right to privacy has found expression: constitutional law, contract law, tort law, and the emerging mixture of theories known as the public policy exception to the at-will doctrine of employment law.

The Right to Privacy Under the Alaska Constitution.

The Alaska Constitution was amended in 1972 to add the following section:

> *Right of Privacy.* The right of the people to privacy is recognized and shall not be infringed. The legislature shall implement this section.

We observe initially that this provision, powerful as a constitutional statement of citizens' rights, contains no guidelines for its application. Nor does it appear that the legislature has exercised its power to apply the provision; the parties did not bring to our attention any statutes which "implement this section."

The Luedtkes argue that this court has never clearly answered the question of whether article I, section 22 applies only to state action or whether it also governs private action. The Luedtkes urge this court to hold that section 22 governs private action. This question was broached in *Allred v. State. In Allred* this court was faced with the question of whether a psychotherapist-patient privilege exists in Alaska. We found the privilege in the

common law rather than under the constitutional right to privacy:

> Since it is apparent that [the psychotherapist] was not a police agent, we do not perceive any state action that would trigger the constitutional privacy guarantees. . . .

Our dictum in *Allred* comports with traditional constitutional analysis holding that the constitution serves as a check on the power of government: "That all lawful power derives from the people and must be held in check to preserve their freedom is the oldest and most central tenet of American constitutionalism." L. Tribe, *American Constitutional Law.* In the same vein, we have written in regard to Alaska's constitutional right to privacy: "[T]he primary purpose of these constitutional provisions is the protection of 'personal privacy and dignity against unwarranted intrusions by the State.'" . . .

[1] The parties in the case at bar have failed to produce evidence that Alaska's constitutional right to privacy was intended to operate as a bar to private action, here Nabors' drug testing program. Absent a history demonstrating that the amendment was intended to proscribe private action, or a proscription of private action in the language of the amendment itself, we decline to extend the constitutional right to privacy to the actions of private parties.

Wrongful Termination

[2] In *Mitford v. de LaSala,* this court held that at-will employment contracts in Alaska contain an implied covenant of good faith and fair dealing. In *Knight v. American Guard & Alert, Inc.* (Alaska 1986), we acknowledged that violation of a public policy could constitute a breach of that implied covenant. We wrote:

The [plaintiff's] claim, concerning alleged termination in violation of public policy, is in accord with a theory of recovery accepted in many states. We have never rejected the public policy theory. Indeed, it seems that the public policy approach is largely encompassed within the implied covenant of good faith and fair dealing which we accepted in *Mitford*.

We conclude that there is a public policy supporting the protection of employee privacy. Violation of that policy by an employer may rise to the level of a breach of the implied covenant of good faith and fair dealing. However, the competing public concern for employee safety present in the case at bar leads us to hold that Nabors' actions did not breach the implied covenant.

The Luedtkes Were At-Will Employees. [3, 4] First, we address the Luedtkes' arguments that they were not at-will employees, but rather that they could be fired only for good cause. The key difference between these two types of employment is whether the employment contract is for a determinable length of time. Employees hired on an at-will basis can be fired for any reason that does not violate the implied covenant of good faith and fair dealing. However, employees hired for a specific term may not be discharged before the expiration of the term except for good cause. Neither of the Luedtkes had any formal agreements for a specified term, so any such term, if it existed, must be implied.

In *Eales v. Tanana Valley Medical-Surgical Group, Inc.*, 663 P.2d 958 (Alaska 1983), we held that where an employer promised employment that would last until the employee's retirement age, and that age was readily determinable, a contract for a definite duration would be implied. We also held that no additional consideration need be given the employee to create a contract for a definite term.

The Luedtkes' cases are distinguishable from that of the plaintiff in *Eales*. The Luedtkes received benefits, such as medical insurance and participation in a pension or profit sharing plan, which continued as long as they were employed. However, Nabors never gave an indication of a definite duration for their employment, nor a definite endpoint to their employment. Instead, Nabors merely provided benefits consistent with modern employer/employee relations.

There Is a Public Policy Supporting Employee Privacy. The next question we address is whether a public policy exists protecting an employee's right to withhold certain "private" information from his employer. We believe such a policy does exist, and is evidenced in the common law, statutes and constitution of this state. . . .

Alaska law clearly evidences strong support for the public interest in employee privacy. First, state statutes support the policy that there are private sectors of employee's lives not subject to direct scrutiny by their employers. For example, employers may not require employees to take polygraph tests as a condition of employment. AS 23.10.037. In addition, AS 18.80.200(a) provides:

> It is determined and declared as a matter of legislative finding that discrimination against an inhabitant of the state because of race, religion, color, national origin, age, sex, marital status, changes in marital status, pregnancy, or parenthood is a matter of public concern and that this discrimination not only threatens the rights and privileges of the inhabitants of the state but also menaces the institutions of the state and threatens peace, order, health, safety and general welfare of the state and its inhabitants.

This policy is implemented by AS 18.80.220, which makes it unlawful for employers to inquire into such topics in connection with prospective employment. This statute demonstrates that in Alaska certain subjects are placed outside the consideration of employers in their relations with employees. The protections of AS 18.80.220 are extensive. This statute has been construed to be broader than federal anti-discrimination law. . . . We believe it evidences the legislature's intent to liberally protect employee rights.

Second, as previously noted, Alaska's constitution contains a right to privacy clause. While we have held, *supra,* that this clause does not proscribe the private action at issue, it can be viewed by this court as evidence of a public policy supporting privacy. . . .

Third, there exists a common law right to privacy. The Restatement (Second) of Torts § 652B provides:

Intrusion upon Seclusion One who intentionally intrudes, physically or otherwise, upon the solitude or seclusion of another or his private affairs or concerns, is subject to liability to the other for invasion of his privacy, if the intrusion would be highly offensive to a reasonable person.

While we have not expressly considered the application of this tort in Alaska, we have recognized its existence.

Thus, the citizens' right to be protected against unwarranted intrusions into their private lives has been recognized in the law of Alaska. The constitution protects against governmental intrusion, statutes protect against employer intrusion, and the common law protects against intrusions by other private persons. As a result, there is sufficient evidence to support the conclusion that there exists a public policy protecting spheres of employee conduct into which employers may not intrude. The question then becomes whether employer monitoring of employee drug use outside the work place is such a prohibited intrusion.

The Public Policy Supporting Employee Privacy Must Be Balanced Against the Public Policy Supporting Health and Safety. Since the recent advent of inexpensive urine tests

for illicit drugs, most litigation regarding the use of these tests in the employment context has concerned government employees. The testing has been challenged under the proscriptions of federal fourth amendment search and seizure law. This body of law regulates only governmental activity, and as a result is of limited value to the case at bar, which involves private activity. However, the reasoning of the federal courts regarding the intrusiveness of urine testing can illuminate this court's consideration of the extent to which personal privacy is violated by these tests.

In *Capua v. City of Plainfield,* 643 F. Supp. city firefighters sued to enjoin random urinalysis tests conducted by the fire department. The court wrote:

Urine testing involves one of the most private of functions, a function traditionally performed in private, and indeed, usually prohibited in public. The proposed test, in order to ensure its reliability, requires the presence of another when the specimen is created and frequently reveals information about one's health unrelated to the use of drugs. If the tests are positive, it may affect one's employment status and even result in criminal prosecution.

We would be appalled at the spectre of the police spying on employees during their free time and then reporting their activities to their employers. Drug testing is a form of surveillance, albeit a technological one. Nonetheless, it reports on a person's off-duty activities just as surely as someone had been present and watching. It is George Orwell's "Big Brother" Society come to life.

While there is a certain amount of hyperbole in this statement, it does portray the *potential* invasion that the technology of urinalysis makes possible. It is against this potential that the law must guard. Not all courts view urine testing with such skepticism, believing the intrusion justified in contemporary society.

Judge Patrick Higginbotham assumed a more cynical stance in *National Treasury Employees Union v. Von Raab,* observing that there is little difference between the intrusiveness of urine testing and the intrusiveness of other affronts to privacy regularly accepted by individuals today. He wrote:

The precise privacy interest asserted is elusive, and the plaintiffs are, at best, inexact as to just what that privacy interest is. Finding an objectively reasonable expectation of privacy in urine, a waste product, contains inherent contradictions. The district court found such a right of privacy, but, in fairness, plaintiffs do not rest there. Rather, it appears from the plaintiffs' brief that it is the manner of taking the samples that is said to invade privacy, because outer garments in which a false sample might be hidden must be removed and a person of the same sex remains outside a stall while the applicant urinates. Yet, apart from the partial disrobing (apparently not independently challenged) persons using public toilet facilities experience a similar lack of privacy. The right must then be a perceived indignity in the whole process, a perceived affront to personal identity by the presence in the same room of another while engaging in a private body function.

It is suggested that the testing program rests on a generalized lack of trust and not on a developed suspicion of an individual applicant. Necessarily there is a plain implication that an applicant is part of a group that, given the demands of the job, cannot be trusted to be truthful about drug use. The difficulty is that just such distrust, or equally accurate, care, is behind every background check and every security check; indeed the information gained in tests of urine is not different from that disclosed in medical records, for which consent to examine is a routine part of applications for many sensitive government posts. In short, given the practice of testing and background checks required for so many government jobs, whether any expectations of privacy by these job applicants were objectively reasonable is dubious at best. Certainly, to ride with the cops one ought to expect inquiry, and by the surest means, into whether he is a robber.

. . . As Judge Higginbotham observes, society often tolerates intrusions into an individual's privacy under circumstances similar to those present in urinalysis. We find this persuasive. It appears, then, that it is the reason the urinalyais is conducted, and not the conduct of the test, that deserves analysis.

This court discussed, on the one hand, the reasons society protects privacy, and, on the other hand, the reasons society rightfully intrudes on personal privacy in *Ravin v. State, Ravin* addressed the issue of whether the state could prohibit the use of marijuana in the home. We held that it could not. We observed that "the right to privacy amendment to the Alaska Constitution cannot be read so as to make the possession or ingestion of marijuana itself a fundamental right." Rather, we "recognized the distinctive nature of the home as a place where the individual's privacy receives special protection." However, we recognized also that this "fundamental right" was limited to activity which remained in the home. We acknowledged that when an individual leaves his home and interacts with others, competing rights of others collectively and as individuals may take precedence:

Privacy in the home is a fundamental right, under both the federal and Alaska constitutions. We do not mean by this that a person may do anything at anytime as long as the activity takes place within a person's home. There are two important limitations on this facet of the right to privacy. First, we agree with the Supreme Court of the United States, which has strictly limited the *Stanley* guarantee to possession for purely private, noncommercial use in the home. And secondly, we think this right must yield when it interferes in a serious manner with the health, safety, rights and privileges of others or with the public welfare. No one has an absolute right to do things in the privacy of his own home which will affect himself or others adversely. Indeed, one aspect of a private matter is that it is private, that is, that it does not adversely affect persons beyond the actor, and hence is none of their business. When a matter does affect the public, directly or indirectly, it loses its wholly private character, and can be made to yield when an appropriate public need is demonstrated.

The *Ravin* analysis is analogous to the analysis that should be followed in cases construing the public policy exception to the at-will employment doctrine. That is, there is a sphere of activity in every person's life that is closed to scrutiny by others. The boundaries of that sphere are determined by balancing a person's right to privacy against other public policies, such as "the health, safety, rights and privileges of others." . . .

The Luedtkes claim that whether or not they use marijuana is information within that protected sphere into which their employer, Nabors, may not intrude. We disagree. As we have previously observed, marijuana can impair a person's ability to function normally:

> The short-term physiological effects are relatively undisputed. An immediate slight increase in the pulse, decrease in salivation, and a slight reddening of the eyes are usually noted. There is also impairment of psychomotor control. . . .

We also observe that work on an oil rig can be very dangerous. We have determined numerous cases involving serious injury or death resulting from accidents on oil drilling rigs. In addition, in Paul's case the trial court expressly considered the dangers of work on oil rigs. It found:

> 13. It is extremely important that the driller be drug free in the performance of his tasks in order to insure the immediate safety of the other personnel on the particular drill rig.
> 14. It is extremely important that the driller be drug free in the performance of his tasks in order to insure the safety and protection of the oil field itself and the oil resource contained within it.

[5] Where the public policy supporting the Luedtkes privacy in off-duty activities conflicts with the public policy supporting the protection of the health and safety of other workers, and even the Luedtkes themselves, the health and safety concerns are paramount. As a result, Nabors is justified in determining whether the Luedtkes are possibly impaired on the job by drug usage off the job.

We observe, however, that the employer's prerogative does have limitations.

First, the drug test must be conducted at a time reasonably contemporaneous with the employee's work time. The employer's interest is in monitoring drug use that may directly affect employee performance. The employer's interest is not in the broader police function of discovering and controlling the use of illicit drugs in general society. In the context of this case, Nabors could have tested the Luedtkes immediately prior to their departure for the North Slope, or immediately upon their return from the North Slope when the test could be reasonably certain of detecting drugs consumed there. Further, given Nabors' need to control the oil rig community, Nabors could have tested the Luedtkes at any time they were on the North Slope.

Second, an employee must receive notice of the adoption of a drug testing program. By requiring a test, an employer introduces an additional term of employment. An employee should have notice of the additional term so that he may contest it, refuse to accept it and quit, seek to negotiate its conditions, or prepare for the test so that he will not fail it and thereby suffer sanctions.

[6, 7] These considerations do not apply with regard to the tests both Paul and Clarence refused to take. Paul was given notice of the future tests. He did not take the November 30 test. As a result, Nabors was justified in discharging Paul. Clarence had notice and the opportunity to schedule his test at a reasonable time. However, he refused to take any test. As a result, Nabors was justified in discharging Clarence. Neither discharge violated the implied covenant of good faith and fair dealing. . . .

Common Law Right to Privacy Claims

We recognize that "[t]he [common law] right to be free from harassment and constant intrusion into one's daily affairs is enjoyed by all persons." *Siggelkow v. State*, ... As previously discussed, that law is delineated in the Restatement (Second) of Torts § 652B, entitled Intrusion upon Seclusion. That section provides: "One who intentionally intrudes . . . upon the solitude or seclusion of another or his private affairs or concerns, is subject to liability . . . if the intrusion would be highly offensive to a reasonable person."

[8, 9] It is true, as the Luedtkes contend, that publication of the facts obtained is not necessary. Instead, the liability is for the offensive intrusion. . . . However, courts have construed "offensive intrusion" to require either an unreasonable manner of intrusion, or intrusion for an unwarranted purpose. . . . Paul has failed to show either that the manner or reason for testing his urine was unreasonable. During his physical, he voluntarily gave a urine sample for the purpose of testing.

Therefore, he cannot complain that urine testing is "highly offensive." . . . Paul can only complain about the purpose of the urine test, that is, to detect drug usage. However, we have held, *supra*, that Nabors was entitled to test its employees for drug usage. As a result, the intrusion was not unwarranted. Paul complains additionally that he was not aware his urine would be tested for drug usage. In this regard we observe that Paul was not aware of any of the tests being performed on his urine sample. Nor did he know the ramifications of those tests. But he did know that whatever the results were they would be reported to Nabors. Therefore, his complaint about a particular test is without merit. We conclude that for these reasons Paul could not maintain an action for invasion of privacy with regard to the urinalysis conducted October 19.

As to the urinalyses Paul and Clarence refused to take, we hold that no cause of action for invasion of privacy arises where the intrusion is prevented from taking place. . . .

Futurecraft Corp. v. Clary Corp.

Superior Court of California

This is an unfair competition action brought by Futurecraft Corporation (hereinafter referred to as Futurecraft) for an injunction, damages and an accounting against a former employee, Roderick Koutnik (hereinafter referred to as Koutnik) and Koutnik's new employer, Clary Corporation (hereinafter referred to as Clary), for the wrongful use and disclosure of certain valve designs claimed to be confidential to and the trade secrets of

Futurecraft. Futurecraft appeals from a judgment in favor of both defendants entered by the court below after a trial limited by that court to the following issue: "What, if any, trade secret, embraced within the issues as established by the pleadings, stipulations and pretrial order, *became entrusted to the defendant Roderick Koutnik while he was an employee of the plaintiff*?" (Emphasis added.) . . .

The basis of plaintiff's claim for relief is, as

set forth in the opening brief, "(1) that the various *design features* are protectible trade secrets, as such, and (2) that, at any rate, Koutnik had expressly agreed that he would not utilize these designs (and particularly the paragraph V design) in competition with Futurecraft." (Emphasis added.)

Futurecraft and Clary are, and since at least 1953 or early 1954 have been, competitors in the design, manufacture and sale of valves and valve components for guided missiles and rockets for the defense program of the United States. Koutnik was employed by Futurecraft during three separate periods (part-time from 1949 to 1951, and full-time from July 1, 1951, to April 25, 1952, and from January 31, 1953, to March 17, 1956) for the purpose of inventing, designing and developing such valves and valve components.

Koutnik had been employed by the California Institute of Technology at its Jet Propulsion Laboratory from September 15, 1947, to May 11, 1951, and from April 28, 1952, to January 25, 1953.

The trial court stated in his memorandum of decision (footnote 1, par. IX) that when Koutnik entered the employ of Futurecraft, "he carried with him a good deal of knowledge concerning the art, science and mechanics of valve design and manufacture, and a good deal of skill in the application of that knowledge . . . [and that] [m]uch, probably most, of that knowledge had been acquired at the Jet Propulsion Laboratory of the California Institute of Technology. . . ."

The particular valve designs forming the subject matter of this action . . . consist of two types of valve mechanisms. . . . The information alleged by Futurecraft to be confidential to it consists of a number of specific design features of the respective valves. . . .

It is appropriately stated in appellant's opening brief:

" . . . this Court will be presented with two basically divergent approaches, or view-

points, on this definitional problem. The defendants successfully urged the trial court to adopt a rigidly narrow and absolutist view, based upon a concept that a trade secret must be 'an item of private property' and that one can have no 'property rights' in an idea if someone else—anyone else—knows about it.

"In contrast to defendants' property rights concept, plaintiff urged below and urges here a more realistic, equitable and common sense approach (which is widely accepted and applied in other jurisdictions), based upon the Restatement view that a trade secret may consist of anything which is ' . . . used in one's business, and which gives him an opportunity to obtain an advantage over *competitors who do not know or use it. . . .* ' (Emphasis added.) Rest., Torts, § 757, Comment b."

[1a] Before turning to the "definitional problem" of what constitutes a trade secret, it is well to mention a basic underlying problem, namely, the legal basis upon which plaintiff predicates its right to relief. This problem stems from the fact that ownership of a trade secret does not give the owner a monopoly in its use, but merely a proprietary right which equity protects against usurpation by unfair means. . . .

" ' . . . The employer thus has the burden of showing two things: (1) a legally protectable trade secret; and (2) *a legal basis,* either a covenant or a confidential relationship, *upon which to predicate relief,*'" (Emphasis added.)

The case of *Wexler v. Greenberg, supra,* 160 A.2d 430, deals primarily with the "legal basis . . . upon which to predicate relief" problem. In many respects the *Wexler* case aptly illustrates the situation presented in the case at bar.

In *Wexler,* defendant Greenberg was a qualified chemist in the sanitation and maintenance field. In March of 1949 he was employed by plaintiff as its chief chemist and continued there for approximately eight years. In the performance of his duties he spent approximately half of his working time in plaintiff's laboratory where he would analyze and duplicate competitor's products and then use the resulting information to develop various new formulas. In August 1957 defendant Greenberg left plaintiff and went to work for defendant corporation. Plaintiff sought to enjoin the defendants from disclosing and using certain formulas and processes pertaining to the manufacture of certain sanitation and maintenance chemicals which plaintiff claimed to be its trade secrets. The Chancellor found that the formulas constituted trade secrets and that their appropriation was in violation of the duty that Greenberg owed to plaintiff by virtue of his employment and the trust reposed in him.

The Supreme Court of Pennsylvania assumed that certain of the formulas were trade secrets of the plaintiff but reversed and stated in pertinent part as follows:

"[2] We are initially concerned with the fact that the final formulations claimed to be trade secrets were not *disclosed to* Greenberg by the appellees during his service or because of his position. [Italics shown.] Rather, the fact is that these formulas had been developed by Greenberg himself, while in the pursuit of his duties as Buckingham's [i.e., plaintiff] chief chemist, or under Greenberg's direct supervision. We are thus faced with the problem of determining the extent to which a former employer, *without the aid of any express covenant* [italics shown], can restrict his ex-employee, a highly skilled chemist, in the uses to which this employee can put his knowledge of formulas and methods he himself developed during the course of his former employment because this employer claims these same formulas, as against the rest of the world, as his trade secrets. *This problem becomes particularly significant when one recognizes that Greenberg's situation is not uncommon. In this era of electronic, chemical, missile and atomic development, many skilled technicians and expert employ-*

ees are currently in the process of developing potential trade secrets. Competition for personnel of this caliber is exceptionally keen, and the interchange of employment is commonplace. One has but to reach for his daily newspaper to appreciate the current market for such skilled employees. *We must therefore be particularly mindful of any effect our decision in this case might have in disrupting this pattern of employee mobility, both in view of possible restraints upon an individual in the pursuit of his livelihood and the harm to the public in general in forestalling to any extent widespread technological advances."* (P. 433.) (Emphasis added.) . . .

"The usual situation involving misappropriation of trade secrets in violation of a confidential relationship is one in which an employer *discloses to his employee* a pre-existing trade secret (one already developed or formulated) so that the employee may duly perform his work. . . . In such a case the trust and confidence upon which legal relief is predicated stems from the instance of the employer's *turning over to the employee* the pre-existing trade secret. [Italics shown.] It is then that a pledge of secrecy is impliedly extracted from the employee, a pledge which he carries with him even beyond the ties of his employment relationship. Since it is conceptually impossible, however, to elicit an implied pledge of secrecy from the sole act of an employee turning over to his employer a trade secret which he, the employee, has developed, as occurred in the present case, the appellees must show a different manner in which the present circumstances support the permanent cloak of confidence cast upon Greenberg by the Chancellor. The only avenue open to the appellees is to show that the nature of the employment relationship itself gave rise to a duty of nondisclosure.

"The burden the appellees must thus meet brings to the fore a problem of accommodating competing policies in our law: the right of a businessman to be protected against unfair competition stemming from the usurpation of his trade secrets and the right of an individual to the unhampered pursuit of the occupations and livelihoods for which he is best suited. There are cogent socio-economic arguments in favor of either position. Society as a whole greatly benefits from technological improvements. Without some means of post-employment protection to assure that valuable developments or improvements are exclusively those of the employer, the businessman could not afford to subsidize research or improve current methods. In addition, it must be recognized that modern economic growth and development has pushed the business venture beyond the size of the one-man firm, forcing the businessman to a much greater degree to entrust confidential business information relating to technological development to appropriate employees. While recognizing the utility in the dispersion of responsibilities in larger firms, the optimum amount of "entrusting" will not occur unless the risk of loss to the businessman through a breach of trust can be held to a minimum.

"On the other hand, any form of post-employment restraint reduces the economic mobility of employees and limits their personal freedom to pursue a preferred course of livelihood. The employee's bargaining position is weakened because he is potentially shackled by the acquisition of alleged trade secrets; and thus, paradoxically, he is restrained, because of his increased expertise, from advancing further in the industry in which he is most productive. Moreover, as previously mentioned, society suffers because competition is diminished by slackening the dissemination of ideas, processes and methods." (Pp. 434–435.) . . .

The court concluded that Greenberg was privileged to disclose and use the formulas which he had developed—they being a part of the technical knowledge and skill that he had acquired by virtue of his employment (p. 437). Therefore, even though the formulas were plaintiff's trade secrets, Greenberg was privileged to use them.

It is apparent that the trial judge in the case at bar did give careful consideration to the "legal basis . . . upon which to predicate relief" problem even though he ultimately held that there was no trade secret. This is evident from the trial court's framing of the issue to be: "What, if any, trade secret . . . became entrusted to the defendant Roderick Koutnik while he was an employee of the plaintiff" and by what was stated in paragraph IX of the notice of decision. . . .

Appellant asserts in its reply brief that the fact that Koutnik utilized knowledge and skill which he obtained at Jet Porpulsion Laboratory in developing the Paragraph V valve design is immaterial. While it might well be immaterial on the "definitional problem" of what constitutes a trade secret, it is material on the "legal basis . . . upon which to predicate relief" phase of the problem. In other words, as illustrated by the *Wexler* case, *supra,* plaintiff may well have a trade secret yet defendant Koutnik be privileged to use it by virtue of there being no covenant or breach of confidence. . . .

. . . The court cannot compel a man who changes employers to wipe clean the slate of his memory. . . . To grant plaintiff the relief prayed for would in effect restrain Koutnik from the pursuit of his profession. He would be deprived of the use of knowledge and skill which he gained which did not originate with plaintiff. . . .

Mr. Julian O. von Kalinowski in an excellent article entitled "Key Employees and Trade Secrets" in 47 *Virginia Law Review* 583 states in the conclusion of the article at page 599:

"Protection should be afforded when, and only when, the information in question has value in the sense that it affords the plaintiff [i.e., ex-employer] a competitive advantage over competitors who do not know of it [i.e., the trade secret], *and where the granting of such protection will not unduly hamstring the ex-employee in the practice of his occupation or profession.* This simple balancing process will invariably protect all of the pertinent interests—those of the former employer, of the former employee, and of the public." (Emphasis added.) . . .

The appellant's remaining contentions either have already been dealt with or are without merit.

For the reasons stated the judgment is affirmed.

CASE 1. *A Matter of Principle*

Nancy Smith was hired May 1, 1988, as the associate director of Medical Research at a major pharmaceutical company. The terms of Ms. Smith's employment were not fixed by contract, and as a result she is considered to be an "at-will" employee. Two years later Ms. Smith was promoted to Director of Medical Research Therapeutics, a section that studied nonreproductive drugs.

One of the company's research projects involved the development of loperamide—a liquid treatment for acute and chronic diarrhea to be used by infants, children, and older persons who were unable to take solid medication. The formula contained saccharin in an amount that was 44 times higher than that the Food and Drug Administration permitted in 12 ounces of an artificially sweetened soft drink. There are, however, no promulgated standards for the use of saccharin in drugs.

The research project team responsible for the development of loperamide unanimously agreed that because of the high saccharin content, the existing formula loperamide was unsuitable for distribution in the United States (apparently the formula was already being distributed in Europe). The team estimated that the development of an alternative formula would take at least three months.

The pharmaceutical's management pressured the team to proceed with the existing formula, and the research project team finally agreed. Nancy Smith maintained her opposition to the high saccharin formula and indicated that the Hippocratic Oath prevented her from giving the formula to old people and children. Nancy Smith was the only medical person on the team, and the grounds for her decision was that saccharin was a possible carcinogen. Therefore Nancy Smith was unable to participate in the clinical testing.

Upon learning that she was unwilling to participate in the clinical testing, the management removed her from the project and gave her a demotion. Her demotion was posted, and she was told that management considered her unpromotable. She was charged specifically with being irresponsible, lacking in good judgment, unproductive, and uncooperative with marketing. Nancy Smith had never been criticized by supervisors before. Nancy Smith resigned because she believed she was being punished for refusing to pursue a task she thought unethical.

Questions:

1. Was Nancy Smith terminated, or did she resign voluntarily?

This case was prepared by Norman E. Bowie on the basis of the appeal decision in *Pierce v. Ortho Pharmaceutical Corporation,* Superior Court of New Jersey, 1979.

2. Should the parmaceutical's management have the right to terminate Nancy Smith if she refused to participate in the clinical testing?

3. Under the circumstances of her "resigna-tion," should she have the right to sue for reinstatement to her position as Director of Medical Research Therapeutics?

4. If you were the judge in such a court case, how would you rule and on what grounds?

CASE 2. *Probable Cause and Drug Testing*

Global Concern, Inc., is a small import-export company located in Seattle. Beth Sandino is the second shift shipping and receiving supervisor for Global Concern. Over a period of several weeks Beth has noticed a change in the behavior of Steve Osterhaut, one of the second shift inventory clerks. Steve's job is to record all incoming and outgoing shipments in the company's somewhat antiquated computer database. Steve is normally stoical and introverted. Recently, however, he has been more talkative and given to outbreaks of laughter. He has also been more productive and has approached Beth on several occasions with ideas for updating the inventory management system.

Beth has noticed that this change in Steve's behavior is most apparent after Steve has had lunch with Jim Morrison, the new second shift forklift operator. Jim's performance has been consistently satisfactory since the day he began work for Global Concern. As far as Beth can tell, his personal behavior has also been consistent since he began work. One day after lunch Beth noticed an empty package of cigarette papers in Steve's wastebasket. She suspects that Steve and Jim have been smoking marijuana during their lunch break.

Questions

1. Do you think Beth would be justified in having Steve tested for drug use? Would she be justified in having Jim tested for drug use? Explain.

2. Would DesJardins and Duska support the decision to test Steve? To test Jim? Explain.

3. Assume that Beth decided to bring the matter of testing Steve and Jim to senior management. If the senior management of Global Concern were to request legal advice from Mark Rothstein, how would he advise them on this matter? Would you agree with Rothstein's advice?

4. In justifying a decision to test or not to test, do you think it would make a difference if Global Concern specialized in the import and export of industrial explosives? Would it make a difference to DesJardins and Duska? to Rothstein? Explain.

CASE 3. *Catching a Thief by Honesty Exams*

Employee theft is a serious problem. The American Management Association estimates that as many as 20 percent of the firms that go out of business do so because of employee theft. Since the polygraph or lie detector has been restricted in at least twenty states, a number of firms have turned to honesty tests. As described in the *Wall Street Journal*, the tests are given in the employer's office, take about an hour, and are relatively cheap, at $6

This case was prepared by D. G. Arnold. Reprinted by permission.
Case prepared by Norman Bowie. Reprinted by permission.

to $14 a test. Among the questions on the test are the following: What's your favorite alcoholic drink? Which drugs have your tried? Did you ever make a false insurance claim? Do you blush often? Have you ever gotten really angry at someone for being unfair to you?[1] Let us assume that the questions are statistically correlated with employee theft, that the tests are administered by the test manufacturer, and that persons failing the test are given an opportunity to establish their innocence on other grounds.

Many employees answer the questions openly, and many provide damaging information. As one corporate spokesperson said, "You become amazed at how many people believe it is acceptable conduct to steal just a little bit, maybe 50 cents, maybe a dollar a day."

Nonetheless, the tests have come under severe criticism from some unions, some lawyers, and the American Civil Liberties Union. They criticize many of the questions as non-job-related and as violations of rights of privacy. Others find the use of the tests intimidating.

Questions

1. Does the honesty test violate an employee's right to privacy? Could a test be devised that didn't?
2. Is the use of honesty tests to curtail theft morally justifiable? Explain.
3. Would your answer to question 2 be any different if the management of the firm used one-way mirrors or "plants" instead of honesty tests to deter employee theft?
4. How would you deter employee theft, and what arguments would you give for the moral acceptability of your plan?

CASE 4. *Old Secrets in a New Job*

William Stapleton, a chemical engineer with considerable experience in offset printing processes, had been hired recently as an engineering supervisor in Western Chemical's Printing Products Division. Until then he had been employed as a research chemist by a competing firm and during the past two years had personally developed a new formula and manufacturing process for press blankets. The new blanket was now on the market and was gaining an increasing share of the market from Stapleton's former employer.

In the offset process, the rubber blanket cylinder on the press receives the image from the inked printing plate and transfers this image to the paper. The blanket is thus an important determinant of printing quality.

Stapleton's formula and manufacturing process resulted in a blanket which not only produced superior quality but also gave longer wear, reducing the cost of materials and the cost of press down-time for blanket changes.

Western executives who had interviewed Stapleton had made no mention to him of the new offset blanket. They had indicated it was his managerial potential which interested them since the company was expanding and would soon need many more managers with scientific experience than were presently available. Stapleton had been anxious to move out of the laboratory and into management work for some time, but his former employer had not afforded him the opportunity.

The responsibilities of supervision and ad-

Case prepared by William McInnes, S.J., Fairfield University. Reprinted by permission.
[1]*Wall Street Journal,* August 3, 1981

ministration had brought Stapleton to grips with new kinds of problems, as he had hoped would be the case. One problem, however, currently sitting on his desk in the form of a memo from George Curtis, the Division's director of Engineering, was giving him particular concern. It read as follows:

> Please see me this afternoon for the purpose of discussing formulas and manufacturing processes for offset press blankets.

This was the first reference anyone had made to the use of specific past technical information in his new job. Stapleton realized he would have to decide immediately to what extent he would reveal data concerning the secret processes being used by his former employer.

Questions

1. Is the new formula and manufacturing process for press blankets the kind of trade secret that should be protected?
2. Suppose an employee knew quite a lot about the manufacturing process, but did not know the new formula. If the employee gave Western Chemical his knowledge of the manufacturing process, would that violate a legitimate trade secret?
3. Would Stapleton violate a trade secret if his new employer were in a noncompetitive industry?
4. Is Stapleton morally obligated to refuse the information to Western Chemical, even if his refusal would cost him his job?

Suggested Supplementary Readings

Employee Rights and Responsibilities

BRENKERT, GEORGE. "Privacy, Polygraphs, and Work." *Business and Professional Ethics Journal* 1 (Fall 1981): 19–34.

DEGEORGE, RICHARD. "The Right to Work: Law and Ideology." *Valparaiso University Law Review,* 19 (Fall 1984): 15–35.

DESJARDINS, JOSEPH R., AND JOHN J. MCCALL. "A Defense of Employee Rights." *Journal of Business Ethics* 4 (October 1985): 367–376.

EWING, DAVID W. *Freedom Inside the Organization: Bringing Civil Liberties to the Workplace.* New York: E. P. Dutton, 1977.

EXTEJT, MARIAN M., and WILLIAM N. BOCKANIC. "Issues Surrounding the Theories of Negligent Hiring and Failure to Fire." *Business and Professional Ethics Journal* 8 (Winter 1989): 21–34.

EZORSKY, GERTRUDE, ed. *Moral Rights in the Workplace.* Albany, N.Y.: State University of New York Press, 1987.

HANSON, KAREN. "The Demands of Loyalty." *Idealistic Studies* 16 (April 1986): 195–204.

KUPFER, JOSEPH. "Privacy, Autonomy, and Self-Concept." *American Philosophical Quarterly* 24 (January 1987): 81–89.

LEE, BARBARA A. "Something Akin to a Property Right: Protections for Job Security." *Business and Professional Ethics Journal* 8 (Fall 1989): 63–81.

LIPPKE, RICHARD L. "Work, Privacy, and Autonomy." *Public Affairs Quarterly* 3 (April 1989): 41–53.

MAITLAND, IAN, "Rights in the Workplace: A Nozickian Argument." *Journal of Business Ethics* 8 (December 1989): 951–954.

MOORE, JENNIFER. "Drug Testing and Corporate Responsibility: The 'Ought Implies Can' Argument." *Journal of Business Ethics* 8 (April 1989): 279–287.

NIXON, JUDY L., AND JUDY F. WEST. "The Ethics of Smoking Policies." *Journal of Business Ethics* 8 (December 1989): 409–414.

RUST, MARK. "Drug Testing." *ABA Journal* 1 (November 1986): 51–54.

STIEBER, JACK, AND MICHAEL MURRAY. "Protection Against Unjust Discharge: The Need for a Federal Statute." *Journal of Law Review* 16 (Winter 1983): 319–341.

WESTIN, ALAN F., AND STEVEN SALISBURY. *Individual Rights in the Corporation: A Reader on Employee Rights.* New York: Pantheon, 1980.

WINSTON, MORTON E. "Aids, Confidentiality, and the Right to Know." *Public Affairs Quarterly* 2 (April 1988): 91–104.

Whistleblowing and the Duty of Loyalty

DANDEKAR, NATALIE. "Contrasting Consequences: Bringing Charges of Sexual Harassment Compared with Other Cases of Whistleblowing." *Journal of Business Ethics* 9 (February 1990): 151–158.

ELLISTON, FREDERICK. "Anonymity and Whistleblowing." *Journal of Business Ethics* 1 (August 1982): 167–177.

———. "Anonymous Whistleblowing: A Conceptual and Ethical Analysis." *Business and Professional Ethics Journal* 1 (Winter 1982): 39–58.

ELLISTON, FREDERICK, AND OTHERS. *Whistleblowing and Whistleblowing Research.* 2 Vols. New York: Praeger, 1985.

FISHER, BRUCE D. "The Whistleblower Protection Act of 1989: A False Hope for Whistleblowers." *Rutgers Law Review* 43 (Spring 1991): 355–416.

GLAZER, M. P., AND P. M. GLAZER. *The Whistle Blowers: Exposing Corruption in Government and Industry.* New York: Basic Books, 1989.

GREENBERGER, DAVID, MARCIA MICELI, AND DEBRA COHEN. "Oppositionists and Group Norms: The Reciprocal Influence of Whistleblowers and Co-workers." *Journal of Business Ethics* 6 (October 1987): 527–542.

HIRSCHMAN, ALBERT. *Exit, Voice and Loyalty.* Cambridge, Mass.: Harvard University Press, 1970.

KEELEY, MICHAEL, and JILL W. GRAHAM. "Exit, Voice and Ethics." *Journal of Business Ethics* 10 (May 1991): 349–355.

NADER, RALPH, PETER J. PETKAS, AND KATE BLACKWELL, eds. *Whistle Blowing: The Report of the Conference on Professional Responsibility.* New York: Grossman, 1972.

NEAR, JANEY P., and MARCIA P. MICELI. "Whistle-Blowers in Organizations: Dissidents or Reformers?" *Research in Organizational Behavior* 9 (1987): 321–368.

PETTIT, PHILIP. "The Paradox of Loyalty." *American Philosophical Quarterly* 25 (April 1988): 163–171.

Trade Secrets and the Duty of Confidentiality

AMERICAN LAW INSTITUTE. *Restatement of Torts* (1939), No. 757.

BOK, SISSELA. "Trade and Corporate Secrecy." In *Secrets: On the Ethics of Concealment and Revelation.* New York: Pantheon Books, 1982.

CAVA ANITA. "Trade Secrets and Covenants Not to Compete: Beware of Winning the Battle and Losing the War." *Journal of Small Business Management* 28 (October 1990): 99–103.

DOERFER, GORDON L. "The Limits of Trade Secret Law Imposed by Federal Patent and Antitrust Supremacy." *Harvard Law Review* 80 (May 1967): 1432–1462.

FRIEDMAN, DAVID D., WILLIAM H. LANDES, AND RICHARD A. POSNER. "Some Economics of Trade Secrets Law." *Journal of Economic Perspectives* 5 (Winter 1991): 61–72.

MILGRAM, ROGER M. *Protecting and Profiting from Trade Secrets.* New York: Practicing Law Institute, 1979.

———. *Trade Secrets.* New York: Matthem Bender, 1978.

NOVOTNY, ERIC J. "Who Owns Your Ideas?" *Module Series in Applied Ethics.* Dubuque, Iowa: Kendall/Hunt, 1985.

Olney, Claude W. "The Secret World of the Industrial Spy." *Business and Society Review* 64 (Winter 1988): 28–32.

STEVENSON, RUSSELL B. "Corporations and Information: Secrecy, Access and Disclosure," Baltimore: Johns Hopkins University Press, 1980.

WEXLER, MARK N. "Conjectures on the Dynamics of Secrecy and the Secrecy Business." *Journal of Business Ethics* 6 (August 1987): 469–480.

Chapter Six

Hiring, Firing, and Discriminating

FOR DECADES BLACKS, women, and many minorities were barred from some of the most desirable institutions in the United States. Even when declared unconstitutional, the discrimination often persisted. The history of discrimination in North America suggests that justice demands effective policies favoring groups previously and presently discriminated against. Recently, however, policies that establish goals, timetables, and quotas intended to ensure more equitable opportunities have provoked controversy. Contemporary controversy has centered on whether *affirmative action* programs, *reverse discrimination,* and criteria of *comparable worth* are appropriate forms of remedy.

The term *affirmative action* refers to positive steps taken to hire persons from groups previously and presently discriminated against. The term is used broadly to refer to everything from open advertisement of positions to employment quotas. For over two decades U.S. federal laws have required corporations to advertise jobs fairly and to promote the hiring of members of groups formerly discriminated against. As a result, corporate planning has often used employment goals or targeted employment outcomes to eliminate the vestiges of discrimination.

There is a crucial symbolic difference between a *goal* and a *quota,* although both can be expressed in percentages. Goals are mandated or negotiated targets and timetables, whereas quotas symbolize for many, policies that can easily result in reverse discrimination, primarily against white males. The term *preferential hiring* refers to hiring that gives preference in recruitment and ranking to groups previously and presently discriminated against. This preference can be in the form of goals or quotas or in the act of choosing minorities over other candidates having equal credentials.

THE BASIS OF PREFERENTIAL POLICIES

Not all employment discrimination is unjustified. It depends on whether the criteria used to discriminate are relevant. For example, federal regulations prohibit pilots and co-pilots from staying in their jobs beyond age sixty, on grounds that age is relevant to their performance and others' safety. A pilot may, however, be retained as a flight engineer beyond age sixty. Because there is a justified reason for what appears to be age discrimination, the use of age to demote pilots is not a form of age bias or unjustified discrimination by an employer. Despite this federal law, TransWorld Airlines, American Airlines, Western Airlines, and United Airlines were successfully sued for age bias because they not only demoted pilots at age sixty but forced them to retire.[1] The rationale for having different rules for pilots and flight engineers rests on the premise that age is relevant to a pilot's performance but irrelevant to a flight engineer's performance. In several of the controversies discussed in this chapter, it is alleged that race, sex, age, and religion are irrelevant properties that someone has unjustifiably claimed to be relevant to hiring or promoting.

Affirmative action programs have affected U.S. businesses in profound ways. Consider, for example, the impact on the Monsanto Chemical Company. In 1971 Monsanto found itself with few black or female employees. In that same year the Department of Labor announced that affirmative action would be enforced. In complying, Monsanto tripled the number of minority employees in the next fourteen years, aggressively promoted women and blacks into middle management positions, and eliminated racial hiring patterns in technical and craft positions. Monsanto achieved these goals without diluting the quality of its employees. Today the firm has no intention of abandoning its affirmative action programs. The focus of the programs has, however, shifted from hiring minority employees to the promotion of minorities within the company.[2]

Preferential policies are often said to have their foundations in the principle of compensatory justice, which requires that if an injustice has been committed, just compensation or reparation is owed the injured person(s). If an individual has been injured by past discrimination, he or she should be recompensed for the past injustice. However, a significant controversy has arisen over whether past discrimination against groups such as women and minorities justifies compensations for group members. Many now hold that only identifiable discrimination against individuals calls for compensation.

Ronald Reagan was the first U.S. President to oppose preferential hiring. Reagan and his successor, George Bush, campaigned against quotas and then sought to roll them back. The Department of Justice was the administration's vanguard, but others were intimately involved. In 1985 Chairman of the U.S. Civil Rights Commission Clarence Pendleton reported to the President his conviction that the Commission had succeeded in making racial and group quotas a "dead issue." He maintained that public controversy over preferential treatment had been replaced with a vision of a color-blind society that is an "opportunity society" rather than a "preference society."[3]

Although this conclusion is questionable, given current civil rights law and business practice, it does illustrate a split between two primary, competing positions in U.S. society: (1) that the only means to the end of a color-blind, sex-blind society is preferential treatment and (2) that a color-blind, sex-blind society can be achieved by guaranteeing equal opportunities to all citizens. According to the second position, employers must never use criteria favoring color, sex, or any such irrelevant consideration when hiring or promoting personnel. The goal is to eradicate discrimination, not to perpetuate it through reverse discrimination. These two competing positions agree that compensation is justified for particular victims of discrimination, but they disagree about whether compensation is owed to individuals as members of groups.

Reagan, Bush, and Pendleton vigorously promoted their vision of equal opportunity. Assistant Attorney General for Civil Rights in the Department of Justice, William Bradford Reynolds (an author in this chapter), was chief federal officer in charge of enforcing this viewpoint during the Reagan years. Reynolds pursued a number of lawsuits that sought to overturn municipal preferential programs containing hiring goals—even if the programs were voluntary or had been enacted by negotiation. He contended that such programs discriminate against white males by setting hiring goals. However, Reynolds sued city governments if they established barriers that made it difficult to hire blacks as city employees. For example, he sued seven nearly all-white Chicago suburbs on grounds that their residency requirements for jobs were a de facto way of keeping blacks out of municipal positions.

Reynolds promoted the view that he and the Reagan administration stood, in the tradition of Martin Luther King, Jr., and other civil rights leaders, for equal opportunity in a color-blind society. Reynolds's opponents, he still believes, have distorted the idea of *equal opportunity* into that of *equal results,* meaning numerical outcomes (quotas) that discriminate against whites. Similarly, he argues that the right to individual opportunity has been distorted into the idea of group entitlements. He has vigorously opposed the principle that federal contractors should hire qualified women and minorities in proportion to their availability in the labor pool and has opposed the use of quotas to achieve racial and sexual hiring goals.

The articles in this chapter by Reynolds and by philosopher Thomas Nagel address the ethical issues that have emerged from congressional, executive, and judicial conclusions about the moral and legal responsibilities of businesses to eradicate discrimination. A major moral issue is whether preferential policies requiring that preference be given to minority candidates over otherwise better qualified white males (i.e., if the circumstances had been anonymous) is a justified instance of compensatory justice or unjust discrimination. The dispute centers on whether such practices of preferential treatment are either (1) just, (2) unjust, or (3) not just but still permissible.

1. Those who claim that such compensatory measures are just, or are required by justice, argue that past discrimination persists in the present. Blacks who were victims of past discrimination are still handicapped or discriminated against, whereas the families of past slave owners are still being unduly enriched by inheritance laws. Those who have inherited wealth accumulated by iniquitous practices have no more right to their wealth than the sons of slaves, who have some claim to it as a matter of compensation. In the case of women, the argument is that our culture is structured to equip them with a lack of self-confidence, that it prejudicially excludes them from much of the work force, and that it treats them as a low-paid auxiliary labor unit. Consequently, only highly independent women can be expected to compete with males on initially fair terms. A slightly stronger argument

is that compensation is fair because it is owed to those who have suffered unjust treatment. For example, if veterans are owed preferential treatment because of their service and sacrifice to country, blacks and women are owed preferential treatment because of their economic sacrifices, systematic incapacitation, and consequent family and group losses.

2. Those who claim that group compensatory measures are unjust argue that no criteria exist for measuring just compensation, that discrimination is presently minor and controllable, and that those harmed by past discrimination are no longer alive to be compensated. Instead of providing compensation, they argue, strict equality and merit should be enforced while attacking the roots of discrimination. Also, some now successful but once underprivileged minority groups argue that their long struggle for equality is being jeopardized by programs of "favoritism" to blacks and women. Some of these arguments are developed in Reynolds's article.

3. The third view is that some compensatory measures are not just because they violate principles of justice, but are still justifiable by moral principles other than justice. A proponent of this view, Thomas Nagel, argues that "there is an element of individual unfairness" in strong affirmative action plans, but these plans are justified as a means to the end of eradicating an intolerable social situation. Tom L. Beauchamp argues that even some measure of reverse discrimination can be justified as a means to the end of a nondiscriminatory society.

THE PROBLEM OF REVERSE DISCRIMINATION

The U.S. Supreme Court has held that federal law permits private employers to set up plans that favor groups traditionally discriminated against. The moral justification, if any, for such plans and the acceptability of any reverse discrimination created by the plans, however, remain controversial.

Among writers who support policies of reverse discrimination, a mainline approach has been to argue that under certain conditions compensation owed for past wrongs justifies present policies that produce reverse discrimination. Beauchamp argues, however, that reverse discrimination is permissible to eliminate or alleviate *present* discriminatory practices against classes, not to compensate classes for *past* wrongs. He introduces factual evidence for his claim that discrimination is pervasive. This evidence supports the claim that reverse discrimination is sometimes justified. Because discrimination now prevails, Beauchamp contends that policies that may eventuate in reverse discrimination are essential to eliminate the ongoing discrimination.

Opponents of this position argue that reverse discrimination violates fundamental, overriding principles of justice and cannot be justified. Policies that discriminate in reverse violate principles of equal opportunity and fair treatment. Additional arguments against reverse discrimination include the following: (1) Some persons who are not responsible for the past discrimination (for example, qualified young white males) pay the price; preferential treatment is discriminatory because innocent persons are penalized solely on the basis of their race rather than for having harmed another individual. (2) Male members of minority groups such as Poles, Irish, Italians—who were previously discriminated against—bear a heavy and unfair burden of compensating women and other minority groups. (3) Many individual members of any class selected for preferential treatment never have been unjustly treated and therefore do not deserve preferential policies. (4) Compensation can be provided to individuals who were previously treated unfairly without resorting to reverse discrimination.

As the court cases in this chapter indicate, the problems associated with preferential and discriminatory hiring are surprisingly complicated. *Memphis Fire Department et al. v. Carl W. Stotts* (otherwise known as *Firefighters v. Stotts*) has received national attention and occupies a prominent role in Reynolds's essay, which was written shortly after the court announced its opinion. Reynolds, then Assistant Attorney General, interpreted the case as the dismantling of affirmative action, specifically all affirmative action plans that contain specific numerical goals. He further interpreted *Stotts* as asserting that preferential remedies apply only to actual victims of a jurisdiction's discriminatory hiring patterns. However, this interpretation has been disputed. The primary issue in *Firefighters* was layoffs. The court held that seniority rather than race can legitimately be the criterion for who will be laid off. Whether the court meant the opinion to extend beyond layoffs to hiring and promotion is not discussed specifically, and no criterion is set forth for valid affirmative action plans.

In three cases between July 1986 and March 1987 the Supreme Court supported the permissibility of specific numerical goals in affirmative action plans that are intended to combat a manifest imbalance in traditionally segregated job categories (even if the particular workers drawn from minorities were not victims of past discrimination). In *Local 28 v. Equal Employment Opportunity Commission,* otherwise known as *Sheet Metal Workers,* a specific minority hiring goal of 29.23 percent had been established. The Court held that quotas involved in the 29 percent goal are justified when dealing with persistent or egregious discrimination. The Supreme Court held that the history of Local 28 was one of complete "foot-dragging resistance" to the idea of hiring for their apprenticeship training programs from minority groups. The Court argued that

> even where the employer or union formally ceases to engage in discrimination, informal mechanisms may obstruct equal employment opportunities. An employer's reputation for discrimination may discourage minorities from seeking available employment. In these circumstances, affirmative race-conscious relief may be the only means available to assure equality of employment opportunities and to eliminate those discriminatory practices and devices which have fostered racially stratified job environments to the disadvantage of minority citizens.

However, in a 1989 opinion also included in this chapter, the Supreme Court held in *City of Richmond v. J. A. Croson* that Richmond, Virginia, officials could not require contractors to set aside 30 percent of their budget for subcontractors who owned "minority business enterprises." The Court held that this plan did not exhibit sufficient government interest to justify the plan and that the plan was not written to remedy the effects of prior discrimination. The Court found that this kind of fixed percentage based on race, in the absence of evidence of identified past discrimination, denied citizens an equal opportunity to compete for the subcontracts.

COMPARABLE WORTH

The slogan "equal pay for equal worth" has been at the center of discussions about workplace discrimination, and the gap between men's and women's pay has been the focus. *Comparable worth* refers to comparable pay for work of comparable value. The comparable *worth* of work is the criterion for whether the work is *equal.* That is, comparable worth is used to refer to a set of several diverse principles that assert that persons should be paid on an identical scale for jobs requiring the same competence, education, effort, stress, and responsibility. Robert Simon, another author in this chapter, discusses these principles, each of which is an attempt to grasp the idea of "comparable pay for comparable worth." Each principle suggests the need to adjust corporate pay scales so that persons in different jobs can be paid similarly if the demands of job are relevantly similar.

The term *comparable worth* continues to be unpopular in the corporate environment, because adjusting pay scales to eliminate discrimination undercuts setting pay scales according to free market values. In the corporate world, rating scales and employment practices modeled on the idea of comparable pay are typically referred to as schemes of "pay equity" or "internal equity," rather than comparable worth.

Federal law in the United States holds that workers in the same job cannot be paid differently merely because of race or sex. The Equal Pay Act of 1963 specifies that employers must pay employees the same wages for equal work in jobs requiring equal skill, effort, and responsibility. However, a pay differential may be permissible if based on merit, seniority, or the quality or quantity of production. Few would dispute these premises, but the principle of comparable worth extends beyond the notions of "same job" and "equal work" to "jobs of the same value." For example, San Francisco's Amfac Corp. hired a consultant to ensure that their "french-fry cooker in Portland is paid the same as [their] sugar-cane worker in Hawaii,[4] under the assumption that their jobs are of the same value to the corporation.

Comparable worth is based on the idea that traditionally male positions such as miner and truck driver can be rated comparably to traditionally female positions such as secretary and nurse. Any unjustified differential in pay can be reduced. The goal is to pay women, especially, according to their responsibilities, experience, contributions, and training. Jobs that are equal in value with respect to these characteristics are to be considered identical in value, despite the fact that women in these positions have typically been paid less than men. Comparable-worth advocates believe that a system that values women's work less is discriminatory.

In the mid-1980s, the U.S. Civil Rights Commission adopted a report that urged federal agencies to reject the principle of comparable worth. The Commission's chairman once called the principle of comparable worth "the looniest idea since 'Looney Tunes' came on the screen." The Commission held that employers should be held accountable for individual discriminatory acts and policies but be required to combat social attitudes or to alter industry-preferred forms of evaluating the worth of jobs. Two months later the Equal Employment Opportunity Commission unanimously adopted the principle that federal law does not require comparable worth and that factual differences in pay scales are no grounds for asserting discrimination. Shortly thereafter, Reynolds and the Justice Department filed its first "friend-of-the-court" brief in a comparable-worth case and sided with the state of Illinois in a case in which nurses were seeking higher pay on comparable-worth grounds. In this context, Reynolds argued that the comparable-worth theory made "a mockery of the ideal of pay equity" and would necessarily depend on "subjective evaluations" by those who made judgments of comparability.[5]

Part of this dispute is conceptual. As Robert Simon notes, there are different meanings attached to "comparable worth" and to principles that would implement it. The Reagan administration defined *comparable worth* as requiring that all jobs of the same value to society be paid equally. Their understanding would require a wholesale restructuring of wage scales and would be extremely difficult to implement. However, many who favor comparable worth and believe it can be implemented use a different definition based on the idea of pay equity as specified in the Equal Pay Act of 1963: All differentials in wages must be justified by nondiscriminatory and relevant considerations such as seniority, merit pay, skills, and stress.

Corporate America has usually been negative about comparable worth in its public statements, as have the *Wall Street Journal*'s editors, the U.S. Chamber of Commerce, and the National Association of Manufacturers, among others. This skepticism may, in part, stem from the conceptual confusion over the definition of *comparable worth*. Opponents of comparable worth argue that it cannot be implemented because it is beyond the capacity of experts to determine objective values for different jobs. They claim that its enforcement would require massive federal intervention, even if it could be implemented. In addition, comparable worth invites exorbitant contract disputes and unending litigation, disturbs the flexibility and diversity in hiring and promotion that is essential to a free market, and neglects the facts that women have less work experience, less seniority, and a lower rate of unionization. Several of the criticisms of comparable worth are analyzed and criticized in the essay by Helen Remick and Ronnie J. Steinberg.

Proponents of comparable worth, such as Remick and Steinberg, believe the principle itself is an essential tool needed to eliminate the systematic undervaluation of the women's contributions. Proponents additionally argue that policies of comparable worth are essential to fairness. Policies can be implemented and structured along the lines of models already being used in traditional job-analysis and job-evaluation processes. Proponents point out that corporations have tried to implement "equal value to the company" by using ratings, pay scales, job-evaluation systems, and so forth. Management has furthered this attempt by using market-wage survey techniques. From this perspective, comparable worth expresses the need for a unified system of job evaluation that measures the relative value of all positions in the corporation. Comparable worth introduces a broader element of fairness into employment practices and reduces or possibly eliminates institutionalized systems of injustice. Proponents often admit that unfairness cannot be completely eliminated, but they point out that unfairnesses can be carefully monitored.

The idea of "equal value to the company" is one of the main topics addressed in this chapter by Wil Waluchow, who considers different criteria that might be employed in explicating notions such as equal value, comparable worth, and comparable pay. Waluchow addresses the question, "How does one determine the worth or value of someone's work so as to compare it with the work of others" and argues for an appropriate standard that would redress situations of pay inequity.

Implementation of comparable-worth criteria has been particularly controversial. Presumably implementation can proceed by (1) negotiation at the bargaining table, (2) internal development at corporations, or (3) external imposition by governments. All three means are currently under discussion and experiment. The first approach to comparable worth has been heavily promoted by the American Federation of State, County, and Municipal Employees (AFSCME), which won impressive precedential comparable-worth pay adjustments in Chicago, Los Angeles, Iowa, Minnesota, Wisconsin, New York, and Connecticut. These changes were achieved by labor negotiation, not court battles.

Some corporations have begun to develop programs of comparable worth. For example, major corporations such as AT&T, BankAmerica, Chase Manhattan, IBM, Motorola, and Tektronix have introduced systems of job comparisons that will allow the cross-job evaluations essential for comparable worth. In these systems, factors that express a job's "worth"—years of education, degree of responsibility, necessary skill, amount of noise in the work environment, and physical labor—are rated on a point scale. Jobs with equal points are to be compensated equally. For example, AT&T worked with its unions to devise a plan in which fourteen measurements were adopted to evaluate by point ratings such factors as keyboard skills, job stress, and abilities to communicate.[6]

A similar set of potentially revolutionary changes that would be externally imposed on corporations are under scrutiny in several state legislatures, but these developments have slowed in recent years. Minnesota was the first to adopt such a plan for state employees and has subsequently been an active state. The U.S. federal government has been largely uninterested. Meanwhile, other countries have been more aggressive. Canada enacted a comparable-worth law that covers all workers under federal jurisdiction, and in Great Britain a similar law was imposed on an unwilling Prime Minister.

THE PROBLEM OF SEXUAL HARASSMENT

One of the oldest forms of discrimination in the workplace and one of the newest in business ethics and U.S. courts is sexual harassment. Statistics on its prevalence are somewhat unreliable, but studies and surveys strongly suggest that between 15 and 65 percent of working women encounter some form of sexual harassment. Studies also reveal that there was a constant increase of sexual harassment cases during the five-year period from 1986 to 1991. The landmark U.S. Supreme Court case of *Meritor Savings Bank v. Vinson* (reprinted in this chapter) was decided in 1986. This case made it clear that a wide range of activities in the workplace constitute sexual harassment under Title VII of the Civil Rights Act of 1964. The case has significantly impacted discussions of workplace discrimination and the development of corporate policies to police it.

The most widespread form of sexual harassment now seems to be offensive sexual innuendo and suggestion that generate embarrassment and anger, rather than coercive threats demanding sexual favors or physical abuse. Some studies suggest that sexual harassment has recently become less overt, but not less commonplace. Forms of sexual harassment that condition a job or promotion on sexual favors have declined. But an increase has occurred in unwanted sexual advances such as straightforward propositions, offensive posters, degrading comments, kisses, improper joking and teasing, and the like.

Men and women often have different views of what constitutes an unwelcome sexual advance, comment, or environment. But in *Meritor,* the Supreme Court extended protections against sexual harassment beyond circumstances of asking for sexual favors to any form of offensive remark and sexual conduct that creates a hostile working environment.

Establishing a precise definition of *sexual harassment* has proved difficult. The centerpiece of any definition is persistent behavior involving unwelcome sexual remarks, advances, or requests that negatively affects working conditions. The conduct need not make a sexual favor a condition of employment or promotion, and it need not be imposed on persons who are in no position to resist the conduct. Even someone in a strong position to resist the approach can be sexually harassed. Derogatory gestures, offensive touching, and leering can affect workers' performance or sense that the workplace is inhospitable, irrespective of their ability to resist. The conduct need not be "sexual" in a narrow sense. The conduct can be gender-specific, involving demeaning remarks about, for example, how women underperform in their job assignments.

Before *Meritor,* sexual harassment was often thought to involve attempted coercion: a threat the person approached could not reasonably resist. In the typical case, a person's job or promotion was conditioned on performing a sexual favor. However, after *Meritor,* it has been widely agreed that many forms of sexual harassment do not involve an irresistible threat and are not coercive. In this chapter, Larry May and John C. Hughes argue that sexual harassment is inherently coercive. Their reason is not that they want to exclude noncoercive sexual innuendo from counting as sexual harassment. Rather, they believe that the different types of sexual harassment are all coercive and that society has lost sight of their coercive character. They note especially the close connection between sexual harassment and supervisors who hold the power to fire or promote those they approach. These approaches worsen the situation of the person approached, thereby constituting a harm and making the workplace hostile.

Although the notion of causing or allowing a "hostile working environment" has been at the forefront of recent attempts to define *sexual harassment*, it has proved difficult to define both terms so that they are not overly broad. What makes for a hostile or intimidating workplace? Do teasing and denigrating remarks count? What is it to denigrate? Which forms of conduct overstep the bounds of being friendly and humorous? Employees in some corporations have complained that corporate policies are written so that asking someone out for a drink after work or sexual humor can easily be construed as unwelcome conduct that creates a hostile working environment.

Standards of offensive or unwelcome sexual behavior have been as difficult to formulate as definitions. The "reasonable person" standard of what counts as offensive or unwelcome has been replaced in some courts with a "reasonable woman" standard that tries to determine whether a male's comments or advances directed toward a woman would be considered offensive by taking the reasonable woman's point of view rather than the reasonable person's point of view. This shift from a gender-neutral standard should make it easier for women to file lawsuits successfully, because men might not find offensive what a woman would. However, if one takes the view, as many now do, that harassment is in large measure a matter of how the individual feels when approached by another person, then the standard of the reasonable woman will be too weak. The standard would have to be whether *this person* finds conduct offensive, not whether the reasonable woman so finds it. Although the law is not likely to move in the direction of a subjective standard, ethics literature is increasingly moving in this direction.

Efforts to remove sexual harassment from the corporate workplace appear to have increased since the 1986 *Meritor* decision, although there is controversy about how seriously to take the increased interest. Many major corporations now have some form of training and grievance policies. Corporations with sexual harassment policies for all management levels report that unwelcome comments and touching have declined significantly after initiating the policies. One reason for increased corporate interest is that corporations have been held legally liable in a few cases for the behavior of supervisors, even when other supervisors were unaware of the behavior. Although these lawsuits and corporate policies have made corporations more sensitive to the issues, little evidence exists that top executives have given urgent priority to the improvement and enforcement of sexual harassment policies. The article by A. M. Koral in this chapter cites several reasons why top executives should take these issues more seriously than they have to date.

NOTES

1. Stephen Wermiel, "High Court Rules TWA Discriminated Against Pilots on the Basis of Their Age," *Wall Street Journal,* January 9, 1985, p. 5; Al Kamen, "Court Backs TWA Workers in Age-Discrimination Case," *Washington Post,* January 9, 1985, p. A2.
2. Aric Press, and others, "The New Rights War," *Newsweek,* December 30, 1985, pp. 66–69.

3. Juan Williams, "Quotas Are a 'Dead Issue,' Rights Panel Chairman Says," *Washington Post,* January 30, 1985, p. A2.
4. "Labor Letter," *Wall Street Journal,* April 16, 1985, p. 1, col. 5.
5. Brief filed with the 7th U.S. Circuit Court of Appeals in Chicago. See Los Angeles Times Service, "U.S. Court Brief Assails 'Comparable Worth' Pay," *International Herald Tribune,* August 19, 1985, p. 3.
6. Cathy Trost, "Pay Equity, Born in Public Sector, Emerges as an Issue in Private Firms," *Wall Street Journal,* July 8, 1985, p. 15.

A Defense of Affirmative Action

Thomas Nagel

The term "affirmative action" has changed in meaning since it was first introduced. Originally it referred only to special efforts to ensure equal opportunity for members of groups that had been subject to discrimination. These efforts included public advertisement of positions to be filled, active recruitment of qualified applicants from the formerly excluded groups, and special training programs to help them meet the standards for admission or appointment. There was also close attention to procedures of appointment, and sometimes to the results, with a view to detecting continued discrimination, conscious or unconscious.

More recently the term has come to refer also to some degree of definite preference for members of these groups in determining access to positions from which they were formerly excluded. Such preference might be allowed to influence decisions only between candidates who are otherwise equally qualified, but usually it involves the selection of women or minority members over other candidates who are better qualified for the position.

Let me call the first sort of policy "weak affirmative action" and the second "strong affirmative action." It is important to distinguish them, because the distinction is sometimes blurred in practice. It is strong affirmative action—the policy of preference—that arouses controversy. Most people would agree that weak or precautionary affirmative action is a good thing, and worth its cost in time and energy. But this does not imply that strong affirmative action is also justified.

I shall claim that in the present state of things it is justified, most clearly with respect to blacks. But I also believe that a defender of the practice must acknowledge that there are serious arguments against it, and that it is defensible only because the arguments for it have great weight. Moral opinion in this country is sharply divided over the issue because significant values are involved on both sides. My own view is that while strong affirmative action is intrinsically undesirable, it is a legitimate and perhaps indispensable method of pursuing a goal so important to the national welfare that it can be justified as a temporary, though not short-term, policy for both public and private institutions. In this respect it is like other policies that impose burdens on some for the public good.

Testimony before the Subcommittee on the Constitution of the Senate Judiciary Committee, June 18, 1981. Reprinted by permission of Professor Nagel.

THREE OBJECTIONS

I shall begin with the argument against. There are three objections to strong affirmative action: that it is inefficient; that it is unfair; and that it damages self-esteem.

The degree of inefficiency depends on how strong a role racial or sexual preference plays in the process of selection. Among candidates meeting the basic qualifications for a position, those better qualified will on the average perform better, whether they are doctors, policemen, teachers, or electricians. There may be some cases, as in preferential college admissions, where the immediate usefulness of making educational resources available to an individual is thought to be greater because of the use to which the education will be put or because of the internal effects on the institution itself. But by and large, policies of strong affirmative action must reckon with the costs of some lowering in performance level: the stronger the preference, the larger the cost to be justified. Since both the costs and the value of the results will vary from case to case, this suggests that no one policy of affirmative action is likely to be correct in all cases, and that the cost in performance level should be taken into account in the design of a legitimate policy.

The charge of unfairness arouses the deepest disagreements. To be passed over because of membership in a group one was born into, where this has nothing to do with one's individual qualifications for a position, can arouse strong feelings of resentment. It is a departure from the ideal—one of the values finally recognized in our society—that people should be judged so far as possible on the basis of individual characteristics rather than involuntary group membership.

This does not mean that strong affirmative action is morally repugnant in the manner of racial or sexual discrimination. It is nothing like those practices, for though like them it employs race and sex as criteria of selection, it does so for entirely different reasons. Racial and sexual discrimination are based on contempt or even loathing for the excluded group, a feeling that certain contacts with them are degrading to members of the dominant group, that they are fit only for subordinate positions or menial work. Strong affirmative action involves none of this: it is simply a means of increasing the social and economic strength of formerly victimized groups, and does not stigmatize others.

There is an element of individual unfairness here, but it is more like the unfairness of conscription in wartime, or of property condemnation under the right of eminent domain. Those who benefit or lose out because of their race or sex cannot be said to deserve their good or bad fortune.

It might be said on the other side that the beneficiaries of affirmative action deserve it as compensation for past discrimination, and that compensation is rightly exacted from the group that has benefited from discrimination in the past. But this is a bad argument, because as the practice usually works, no effort is made to give preference to those who have suffered most from discrimination, or to prefer them especially to those who have benefited most from it, or been guilty of it. Only candidates who in other qualifications fall on one or other side of the margin of decision will directly benefit or lose from the policy, and these are not necessarily, or even probably, the ones who especially deserve it. Women or blacks who don't have the qualifications even to be considered are likely to have been handicapped more by the effects of discrimination than those who receive preference. And the marginal white male candidate who is turned down can evoke our sympathy if he asks, "Why me?" (A policy of explicitly *compensatory* preference, which took into account each individual's background of poverty and discrimination, would escape some of these objections, and it has its defenders, but it is not the policy I want to defend. Whatever its merits, it will not serve the same purpose as direct affirmative action.)

The third objection concerns self-esteem, and is particularly serious. While strong affirmative action is in effect, and generally known to be so, no one in an affirmative action category who gets a desirable job or is admitted to a selective university can be sure that he or she has not benefited from the policy. Even those who would have made it anyway fall under suspicion, from themselves and from others: it comes to be widely felt that success does not mean the same thing for women and minorities. This painful damage to esteem cannot be avoided. It should make any defender of strong affirmative action want the practice to end as soon as it has achieved its basic purpose.

JUSTIFYING AFFIRMATIVE ACTION

I have examined these three objections and tried to assess their weight, in order to decide how strong a countervailing reason is needed to justify such a policy. In my view, taken together they imply that strong affirmative action involving significant preference should be undertaken only if it will substantially further a social goal of the first importance. While this condition is not met by all programs of affirmative action now in effect, it is met by those which address the most deep-seated, stubborn, and radically unhealthy divisions in the society, divisions whose removal is a condition of basic justice and social cohesion.

The situation of black people in our country is unique in this respect. For almost a century after the abolition of slavery we had a rigid racial caste system of the ugliest kind, and it only began to break up twenty-five years ago. In the South it was enforced by law, and in the North, in a somewhat less severe form, by social convention. Whites were thought to be defiled by social or residential proximity to blacks, intermarriage was taboo, blacks were denied the same level of public goods—education and legal protection—as whites, were restricted to the most menial occupations, and were barred from any positions of authority over whites. The visceral feeling of black inferiority and untouchability that this system expressed were deeply ingrained in the members of both races, and they continue, not surprisingly, to have their effect. Blacks still form, to a considerable extent, a hereditary social and economic community characterized by widespread poverty, unemployment, and social alienation.

When this society finally got around to moving against the caste system, it might have done no more than to enforce straight equality of opportunity, perhaps with the help of weak affirmative action, and then wait a few hundred years while things gradually got better. Fortunately it decided instead to accelerate the process by both public and private institutional action, because there was wide recognition of the intractable character of the problem posed by this insular minority and its place in the nation's history and collective consciousness. This has not been going on very long, but the results are already impressive, especially in speeding the advancement of blacks into the middle class. Affirmative action has not done much to improve the position of poor and unskilled blacks. That is the most serious part of the problem, and it requires a more direct economic attack. But increased access to higher education and upper-level jobs is an essential part of what must be achieved to break the structure of drastic separation that was left largely undisturbed by the legal abolition of the caste system.

Changes of this kind require a generation or two. My guess is that strong affirmative action for blacks will continue to be justified into the early decades of the next century, but that by then it will have accomplished what it can and will no longer be worth the costs. One point deserves special emphasis. The goal to be pursued is the reduction of a great social injustice, not proportional representation of the races in all institutions and professions. Proportional racial representation is of no value in itself. It is not a legitimate social goal, and it should certainly not be the aim of strong affirmative action, whose drawbacks make it worth adopting only against a serious and intractable social evil.

This implies that the justification for strong affirmative action is much weaker in the case of other racial and ethnic groups, and in the case of women. At least, the practice will be justified in a narrower range of circumstances and for a shorter span of time than it is for blacks. No other group has been treated quite like this, and no other group is in a comparable status. Hispanic-Americans occupy an intermediate position, but it seems to me frankly absurd to include persons of oriental descent as beneficiaries of affirmative action, strong or weak. They are not a severely deprived and excluded minority, and their eligibility serves only to swell the numbers that can be included on affirmative action reports. It also suggests that there is a drift in the policy toward adopting the goal of racial proportional representation for its own sake. This is a foolish mistake, and should be resisted. The only legitimate goal of the policy is to reduce egregious racial stratification.

With respect to women, I believe that except over the short term, and in professions or institutions from which their absence is particularly marked, strong affirmative action is not warranted and weak affirmative action is enough. This is based simply on the expectation that the social and economic situation of women will improve quite rapidly under conditions of full equality of opportunity. Re-

cent progress provides some evidence for this. Women do not form a separate hereditary community, characteristically poor and uneducated, and their position is not likely to be self-perpetuating in the same way as that of an outcast race. The process requires less artificial acceleration, and any need for strong affirmative action for women can be expected to end sooner than it ends for blacks.

I said at the outset that there was a tendency to blur the distinction between weak and strong affirmative action. This occurs especially in the use of numerical quotas, a topic on which I want to comment briefly.

A quota may be a method of either weak or strong affirmative action, depending on the circumstances. It amounts to weak affirmative action—a safeguard against discrimination—if, and only if, there is independent evidence that average qualifications for the positions being filled are no lower in the group to which a minimum quota is being assigned than in the applicant group as a whole. This can be presumed true of unskilled jobs that most people can do, but it becomes less likely, and harder to establish, the greater the skill and education required for the position. At these levels, a quota proportional to population, or even to representation of the group in the applicant pool, is almost certain to amount to strong affirmative action. Moreover it is strong affirmative action of a particularly crude and indiscriminate kind, because it permits no variation in the degree of preference on the basis of costs in efficiency, depending on the qualification gap. For this reason I should defend quotas only where they serve the purpose of weak affirmative action. On the whole, strong affirmative action is better implemented by including group preference as one factor in appointment or admission decisions, and letting the results depend on its interaction with other factors.

I have tried to show that the arguments

against strong affirmative action are clearly outweighed at present by the need for exceptional measures to remove the stubborn residues of racial caste. But advocates of the policy should acknowledge the reasons against it, which will ensure its termination when it is no longer necessary. Affirmative action is not an end in itself, but a means of dealing with a social situation that should be intolerable to us all.

Equal Opportunity, Not Equal Results

William Bradford Reynolds

No one disputes that "affirmative action" is a subject of vital significance for our society. The character of our country is determined in large measure by the manner in which we treat our individual citizens—whether we treat them fairly or unfairly, whether we ensure equal opportunity to all individuals or guarantee equal results to selected groups. As the Assistant Attorney General, I am faced daily with what seem to have emerged on the civil rights horizon as the two predominant competing values that drive the debate on this issue—that is, the value of equal opportunity and the value of equal results—and I have devoted a great deal of time and attention to the very different meanings they lend to the phrase "affirmative action."

Typically—to the understandable confusion of almost everyone—"affirmative action" is the term used to refer to both of these contrasting values. There is, however, a world of difference between "affirmative action" as a measure for ensuring equality of opportunity and "affirmative action" as a tool for achieving equality of results.

In the former instance, affirmative steps are taken so that all individuals (whatever their race, color, sex, or national origin) will be given the chance to compete with all others on equal terms; each is to be given his or her place at the starting line without advantage or disadvantage. In the latter, by contrast, the promise of affirmative action is that those who participate will arrive at the finish in prearranged places—places allocated by race or sex.

I have expressed on a number of occasions my conviction that the promise of equal results is a false one. We can never assure equal results in a world in which individuals differ greatly in motivation and ability; nor, in my view, is such a promise either morally or constitutionally acceptable. This was, in fact, well understood at the time that the concept of "affirmative action" was first introduced as a remedial technique in the civil rights arena. In its original formulation, that concept embraced only non-preferential affirmative efforts, in the nature of training programs and enhanced recruitment activities, aimed at opening wide the doors of opportunity to all Americans who cared to enter. Thus, President Kennedy's Executive Order 10925, one of the earliest to speak to the subject, stated that federal contractors should "take affirmative action to ensure that the applicants are employed, and that employees are treated during employment, without regard to their race, creed, color, or national origin."

This principle was understood by all at that

From William Bradford Reynolds, "Equal Opportunity, Not Equal Rights," in Robert K. Fullinwider and Claudia Mills, eds., *The Moral Foundations of Civil Rights* (Totowa, N.J.: Rowman and Littlefield, 1986). Reprinted with permission.

time to mean simply that individuals previously neglected in the search for talent must be allowed to apply and be considered along with all others for available jobs or contracting opportunities, but that the hiring and selection decisions would be made from the pool of applicants without regard to race, creed, color, or national origin—and later sex. No one was to be afforded a preference, or special treatment, because of group membership; rather, all were to be treated equally as individuals based on personal ability and worth.

This administration's commitment is, of course, to this "original and undefiled meaning"—as Morris Abram, Vice Chairman of the Civil Rights Commission, calls it—of "affirmative action." Where unlawful discrimination exists, we see that it is brought to an abrupt and uncompromising halt; where that discrimination has harmed any individual, we ensure that every victim of the wrongdoing receives "make-whole" relief; and affirmative steps are required in the nature of training programs and enhanced recruitment efforts to force open the doors of opportunity that have too long remained closed to far too many.

The criticism, of course, is that we do not go far enough. The remedial use of goals-and-timetables, quotas, or other such numerical devices—designed to achieve a particular balance as to race or sex in the work force—has been accepted by the lower federal courts as an available instrument of relief, and therefore, it is argued, such an approach should not be abandoned. There are several responses to this sort of argumentation.

The first is a strictly legal one and rests on the Supreme Court's recent decision in *Firefighters Local Union v. Stotts*, No. 82–206 (decided June 12, 1984). The Supreme Court in *Stotts* did not merely hold that federal courts are prohibited from ordering racially preferential layoffs to maintain a certain racial per-

centage, or that courts cannot disrupt bona fide seniority systems. To be sure, it did so rule; but the Court said much more, and in unmistakably forceful terms. As Justice Stevens remarked during his recent commencement address at Northwestern University, the decision represents "a far-reaching pronouncement concerning the limits on a court's power to prescribe affirmative action as a remedy for proven violations of Title VII of the Civil Rights Act." For the *Stotts* majority grounded the decision, at bottom, on the holding that federal courts are without *any* authority under Section 706(g)—the remedial provision of Title VII—to order a remedy, either by consent decree or after full litigation, that goes beyond enjoining the unlawful conduct and awarding "make-whole" relief for actual victims of the discrimination. Thus, quotas or other preferential techniques that, by design, benefit nonvictims because of race or sex cannot be part of Title VII relief ordered in a court case, whether the context is hiring, promotion, or layoffs.

A brief review of the opinion's language is particularly useful to understanding the sweep of the decision. At issue in *Stotts* was a district court injunction ordering that certain white firefighters with greater seniority be laid off before blacks with less seniority in order to preserve a certain percentage of black representation in the fire department's work force. The Supreme Court held that this order was improper because "there was no finding that any of the blacks protected from layoff had been a victim of discrimination."[1] Relying explicitly on Section 706(g) of Title VII, the court held that Congress intended to "provide make-whole relief only to those who have been actual victims of illegal discrimination."[2] . . .

After *Stotts*, it is, I think, abundantly clear that Section 706(g) of Title VII does not tolerate remedial action by courts that would grant to nonvictims of discrimination—at the expense of wholly innocent employees or potential employees—an employment preference based solely on the fact that they are members of a particular race or gender. Quotas, or any other numerical device based on color or sex, are by definition victim-blind: they embrace without distinction and accord preferential treatment to persons having no claim to "make-whole" relief. Accordingly, whether such formulas are employed for hiring, promotion, layoffs, or otherwise, they must fail under any reading of the statute's remedial provision.

There are equally strong policy reasons for coming to this conclusion. The remedial use of preferences has been justified by the courts primarily on the theory that they are necessary to cure "the effects of past discrimination" and thus, in the words of one Supreme Court Justice, to "get beyond" racism."[3] This reasoning is twice flawed.

First, it is premised on the proposition that any racial imbalance in the employer's work force is explainable only as a lingering effect on past racial discrimination. The analysis is no different where gender-based discrimination is involved. Yet, in either instance, equating "underrepresentation" of certain groups with discrimination against those groups ignores the fact that occupation selection in a free society is determined by a host of factors, principally individual interest, industry, and ability. It simply is not the case that applicants for any given job come proportionally qualified by race, gender, and ethnic origin in accordance with U.S. population statistics. Nor do the career interests of individuals break down proportionally among racial or gender groups. Accordingly, a selection process free of discrimination is no more likely to produce "proportional representation" along race or sex lines than it is to ensure proportionality among persons grouped according to hair color, shoe size, or any other irrelevant personal characteristic. No human endeavor,

since the beginning of time, has attracted persons sharing a common physical characteristic in numbers proportional to the representation of such persons in the community. "Affirmative action" assumptions that one might expect otherwise in the absence of race or gender discrimination are ill-conceived.

Second, and more important, there is nothing *remedial*—let alone *equitable*—about a court order that *requires* the hiring, promotion, or retention of a person who has not suffered discrimination solely because that person is a member of the same racial or gender group as other persons who were victimized by the discriminatory employment practices. The rights protected under Title VII belong to individuals, not to groups. The Supreme Court made clear some years ago that [t]he basic policy of [Title VII] requires that [courts] focus on fairness to individuals rather than fairness to classes."[4] The same message was again delivered in *Stotts*. As indicated, remedying a violation of Title VII requires that the individual victimized by the unlawful discrimination be restored to his or her "rightful place." It almost goes without saying, however, that a person who is *not* victimized by the employer's discriminatory practices has no claim to a "rightful place" in the employer's work force. And, according preferential treatment to *nonvictims* in no way remedies the injury suffered by persons who have in fact been discriminated against in violation of Title VII.

Moreover, racial quotas and other forms of preferential treatment unjustifiably infringe on the legitimate employment interests and expectations of third parties, such as incumbent employees, who are free of any involvement in the employer's wrongdoing. To be sure, awarding retroactive seniority and other forms of "rightful place" relief to individual victims of discrimination also unavoidably infringes upon the employment interests and expectations of innocent third parties. Indeed, this fact has compelled some, including Chief Justice Burger, to charge that granting rightful place relief to victims of racial discrimination is on the order of "robbing Peter to pay Paul."[5]

The legitimate "rightful place" claims of identifiable victims of discrimination, however, warrant imposition of a remedy that calls for a sharing of the burden by those innocent incumbent employees whose "places" in the work force are the product of, or at least enhanced by, the employer's unlawful discrimination. Restoring the victim of discrimination to the position he or she would have occupied but for the discrimination merely requires incumbent employees to surrender some of the largesse discriminatorily conferred upon them. In other words, there is justice in requiring Peter, as a kind of third-party beneficiary of the employer's discriminatory conduct, to share in the burden of making good on the debt to Paul created by that conduct. But, an incumbent employee should not be called upon as well to sacrifice or otherwise compromise legitimate employment interests in order to accommodate persons *never wronged* by the employer's unlawful conduct. An order directing Peter to pay Paul in the absence of any proof of a debt owing to Paul is without remedial justification and cannot be squared with basic notions of fairness.

Proponents of the so-called remedial use of class-based preferences often counter this point with a two-fold response. First, they note that the effort to identify and make whole all victims of the employer's discriminatory practices will never be 100 percent successful. While no one can dispute the validity of this unfortunate point, race- and gender-conscious preferences simply do not answer this problem. The injury suffered by a discriminatee who cannot be located is in no way ameliorated—much less remedied—by conferring preferential treatment on other, randomly selected members of his or her race

or sex. A person suffering from appendicitis is not relieved of the pain by an appendectomy performed on the patient in the next room.

Second, proponents of judicially imposed numerical preferences also argue that they are necessary to ensure that the employer does not return to his or her discriminatory ways. The fallacy in this reasoning is self-evident. Far from *preventing* future discrimination, imposition of such remedial devices *guarantees* future discrimination. Only the color or gender of the ox being gored is changed.

It is against this backdrop that the Court's decision in *Stotts* assumes so much significance in the "affirmative action" debate. The inescapable consequence of *Stotts* is to move government at the federal, state, and local levels noticeably closer to the overriding objective of providing all citizens with a truly equal opportunity to compete on merit for the benefits that our society has to offer—an opportunity that allows an individual to go as far as the person's energy, ability, enthusiasm, imagination, and efforts will allow and not be hemmed in by the artificial allotment given to his or her group in the form of a numerical preference. The promise is that we might now be able to bring an end to that stifling process by which government and society view its citizens as possessors of racial or gender characteristics, not as the unique individuals they are; where advancements are viewed not as hard-won achievements, but as conferred "benefits."

The use of race or sex in an effort to restructure society along lines that better represent someone's preconceived notions of how our limited educational and economic resources should be allocated among the many groups in our pluralistic society necessarily forecloses opportunities to those having the misfortune—solely by reason of gender or skin color—to be members of a group whose allotment has already been filled. Those so denied, such as the more senior white Memphis firefighters laid off to achieve a more perfect racial balance in the fire department, are discriminated against every bit as much as the black Memphis firefighters originally excluded from employment. In our zeal to eradicate discrimination from society, we must be ever vigilant not to allow considerations of race or sex to intrude upon the decisional process of government. That was precisely the directive handed down by Congress in the Civil Rights Act of 1964, and, as *Stotts* made clear, the command has full application to the courts. Plainly, "affirmative action" remedies must be guided by no different principle. For the simple fact remains that wherever it occurs, and however explained, "no discrimination based on race [or sex] is benign . . . no action disadvantaging a person because of color [or gender] is affirmative."[6]

NOTES

1. Slip opinion at p. 16.
2. Slip opinion at p. 17.
3. *University of California Regents v. Bakke,* 438 U.S. 265, 407 (Justice Blackmun, concurring).
4. *Los Angeles Department of Water & Power v. Manhart,* 435 U.S. 702, 708 (1978).
5. *Franks v. Bowman Transportation Co.,* 424 U.S. 747, 781 (1976) (Justice Burger, dissenting).
6. *United Steelworkers of America, AFL-CIO v. Weber,* 443 U.S. 193, 254 (1979) (Justice Rehnquist, dissenting).

Goals and Quotas in Hiring and Promotion

Tom L. Beauchamp

Since the 1960s, government and corporate policies that set goals for hiring women and minorities have been sharply criticized. Their opponents maintain that many policies establish indefensible quotas and discriminate in reverse against sometimes more qualified white males. In 1991 President George Bush referred to the word *quota* as the "dreaded q-word." Bush finally agreed to new civil rights legislation in October 1991, after years of resisting changes. Quotas, he said, had "finally" been eliminated from congressional consideration. Such opposition is understandable. No worker wants to lose a job to a less qualified person, and no employer wants to be restricted in its hiring and promotion by a quota policy.

Although I agree that some policies that set target goals and adopt quotas sometimes violate rules of fair and equal treatment, I believe such policies can be justified. My objective in this paper is to defend policies that set goals and quotas, despite their unpopularity. I argue that goals and quotas, rightly conceived, are congenial to management—not hostile as they are often depicted. Both the long-range interest of corporations and the public interest should be well served by carefully selected preferential policies.

TWO POLAR POSITIONS

In 1965 President Lyndon Johnson issued an executive order that announced a toughened federal initiative requiring goals and timetables for equal employment opportunity.[1] This initiative was the prevailing regulatory approach for many years. But recently two competing schools of thought on the justifiability of preferential programs have come into sharp conflict, one mirroring the views of Bush, and the other mirroring those of Johnson.

The first school, like Bush, stands in opposition to quotas, accepting the view that all persons are entitled to an equal opportunity and to constitutional guarantees of equal protection in a color-blind, nonsexist society. Civil rights laws, in this approach, should offer protection only to individuals who have been demonstrably victimized by specific acts of discrimination. Hiring goals, timetables, and quotas do not isolate specific acts and work to create new victims of discrimination.

The second school, like Johnson, supports strong affirmative action policies. The justification of affirmative action programs is viewed as the correction of discriminatory employment practices. This second school views the first school as construing "equal opportunity" and "civil rights" so narrowly that those affected by discrimination do not receive any practical aid in overcoming the side effects of prejudice. This second school believes that mandated hiring ensures fairness and erodes discrimination, whereas the identification of individual victims of discrimination would be, as the editors of the *New York Times* once put it, the "project of a century and [would] leave most victims of discrimination with only empty legal rights."[2]

These two schools may not be as far apart morally as they first appear. If legal enforcement could efficiently and comprehensively identify discriminatory treatment and could protect its victims, both schools would agree that the legal-enforcement strategy is preferable. But there are at least two reasons why this solution will not be accepted by the second school. First, there is the unresolved issue of whether those in contemporary society who have been advantaged by *past* discrimination (for example, wealthy owners of family businesses) deserve their advantages. Second, there is the issue of whether *present*, ongoing discrimination can be successfully, comprehensively, and fairly combatted by identifying and prosecuting violators without resorting to quotas. This second issue is the more pivotal.

A "quota," in the sense in which I use the term, does not mean that fixed numbers of employees should be hired regardless of an individual's qualification for a position. Quotas are target employment percentages. In some cases a less qualified person may be hired or promoted; but it has never been a part of affirmative action to hire below the threshold of "basically qualified."[3] Quotas, then, are numerically expressible goals that one is morally obligated to pursue with good faith and due diligence. If it is impossible to hire the basically qualified persons called for by the goals in a given time frame, the schedule can be relaxed, as long as the target goals, the due diligence, and the good faith continue. The word *quota* (as defined below) does not mean "fixed number" in any stronger sense.

DATA ON DISCRIMINATION

Discrimination affecting hiring and promotion is not present everywhere in our society, but it is pervasive. An impressive body of statistics constituting prima facie evidence of discrimination has been assembled in recent years. It indicates that (1) women with identical credentials are promoted at approximately one-half the rate of their male counterparts; (2) 69% or more of the white-collar positions in the United States are held by women, but only approximately 10% of the management positions are held by women; (3) 8.7% of all professionals in the private business sector are of Asian origin, but they constitute only 1.3% of the management positions; (4) in the total U.S. population, 3 out of 7 employees hold white-collar positions, whereas the ratio is only 1 of 7 for blacks; (5) blacks occupy over 50% of the nation's jobs as garbage collectors and maids, but only 4% of the nation's management positions.[4]

Such statistics are not decisive indicators of discrimination, but additional facts support the conclusion that racist and sexist biases powerfully influence the marketplace. Consider prevailing biases in real estate rentals and sales. Studies have shown that there is an 85% probability that blacks will encounter discrimination in rental housing and a 50% probability that blacks will suffer discrimination in purchasing a house; that blacks suffer more discrimination than other economically comparable minority groups; and that there may be as many as two million instances of discrimination in the U.S. housing market each year in the United States. One recent study indicates that approximately 80% of American residential neighborhoods in the largest 29 metropolitan areas remained entirely segregated from 1960 to 1980. Not socioeconomic status, but race, is the clear difference in real estate sales and loans.[5]

If we shift from housing to jobs, a similar pattern is found, especially for black males, for whom employment has become steadily more difficult in almost every sector from the mid-1970s through the early 1990s.[6] In 1985 the Grier Partnership and the Urban league produced independent studies that reveal striking disparities in the employment levels of college-trained blacks and whites in Washington, D.C., one of the best markets for blacks. Both studies found that college-

trained blacks have much more difficulty than their white counterparts in securing employment. Both cite discrimination as the major underlying factor.[7]

A 1991 study by the Urban Institute is a still more powerful illustration of the problem. This study examined employment practices in Washington, D.C., and Chicago. Equally qualified, identically dressed white and black applicants for jobs were used to test for bias in the job market, as presented by newspaper-advertised positions. Whites and blacks were matched identically for speech patterns, age, work experience, personal characteristics, and physical build. Investigators found repeated discrimination against black male applicants. The higher the position, the higher they found the level of discrimination to be. The white men received job offers three times more often than the equally qualified blacks who interviewed for the same position. The authors of the study concluded both that discrimination against black men is "widespread and entrenched" and that fears of reverse discrimination by white males are unfounded because the effects of discrimination more than offset any effects of reverse discrimination.[8]

These statistics help us frame the significance of racial and sexual discrimination in the United States. Although much is now known about patterns of discrimination, much remains to be discovered, in part because it is hidden and difficult to uncover.

PROBLEMS OF PROOF AND INTENTION

Although we typically conceive racism and sexism as an intentional form of favoritism or exclusion, major problems confronting American business and government arise from unintended institutional practices. Employees are frequently hired through a network that, without design, excludes women or minority groups. For example, hiring may occur through personal connections or by word of mouth, and layoffs may be ruled by a seniority system. The actual hiring policies themselves may be racially and sexually neutral. Nonetheless, they can have an adverse effect on the ability of minorities in securing positions. There may be no intention to discriminate against anyone, but the system still works to this end. In some cases, past discrimination that led to unfair hiring practices and an imbalanced work force are perpetuated even when there is no desire to perpetuate them.

Including unconscious forms of screening is essential to an adequate and comprehensive picture of discrimination. In 1985 the U.S. Supreme Court unanimously held that states may be held guilty of discriminating against persons with disabilities when there is no "invidious animus, but rather [a discriminatory effect] of thoughtlessness and indifference—of benign neglect." The Court appropriately held that discrimination would be difficult if not impossible to prohibit if *intentional* discrimination alone qualified as discrimination.[9]

In addition to the unconscious consequences of hiring patterns, the effects of irrelevant criteria for jobs should be considered, especially when an employer falsely believes the criteria to be relevant. In a seminal 1971 discrimination case, *Griggs v. Duke Power Company*[10], the U.S. Supreme Court argued that in a social climate with a history of racism, discrimination, and underfunded schools, any hiring qualification that has a negative effect on the ability of blacks to obtain employment must be demonstrated to be a "business necessity."[11] In *Griggs,* workers at the Duke Power Company were required to have credentials that were not essential for performance of the job. The court held that to combat discrimination corporations must test for fairness in every phase of their operation: hiring systems, job classifications, seniority systems, recruitment policies, etc. all must be revised as necessary to combat unconscious as well as overt discrimination. This decision became the backbone of affirmative action and established the much disputed antidiscrimination rule that a company should hire approximately the same percentage of minority workers as there are minorities in the "relevant work force."

This decision was vigorously attacked by the former chairman of the Equal Employment Opportunity Commission and now Supreme Court Justice Clarence Thomas. He maintained that this rule has been interpreted in some quarters of American society as meaning that blacks and women must be hired by companies *in proportion* to their numbers in the relevant work force and that any company failing to do so is discriminating. Thomas held that this rule surpasses what is reasonable because there may be justifiable reasons why a group is proportionally underrepresented.[12] I believe this attack misrepresents Supreme Court rulings and the reasons for those rulings.

Griggs presents the Court's recognition that institutional hiring criteria and practices can work to discriminate when conscious discrimination is not present. More than twenty years after *Griggs,* the discrimination is still not recognized as such by many who discriminate. As a result, discrimination remains a major social problem. Because much of our social world is built on a foundation of discrimination, it is difficult for many to see how employment practices function to exclude women and minorities from positions and promotions in the workplace. This, in my judgment, is the main reason quotas are an indispensable government and management tool: They are sometimes the only way to break down old patterns of discrimination and thereby change the configuration of the workplace.

Courts in the United States have on a few occasions resorted to quotas for this reason: An employer had an intractable history and a bullheaded resistance to change that necessitated strong measures. The Supreme Court, however, has never directly supported quotas using the term *quota*. Rather, it has upheld affirmative action programs that contain numerically expressed hiring formulas that are intended to reverse the patterns of both intentional and unintentional discrimination.[13] At the same time, the Supreme Court has suggested that other programs that use such formulas have gone too far.[14] Whether the formulas are excessive depends on the facts in an individual case. From this perspective, there is no inconsistency between *Fullilove v. Klutznick* (1980), which allowed percentage set-asides for minority contractors, and *City of Richmond v. J. A. Croson* (1989), which disallowed such set-asides.

I believe the Supreme Court has consistently maintained this view since *Griggs* and that it is the right moral perspective as well as the proper framework for American law. Numerical goals or quotas should be implemented only when it is necessary to overcome the discriminatory impact of insensitive institutional policies and irrelevant criteria used for employment. Proposed formulas can be excessive here just as they can elsewhere.

Although I have suggested that one can distinguish between conscious discriminatory practices and unconscious practices that have discriminatory impact, the distinction should not be pushed too far. The two often work together. For example, the practices and framework of policies in a corporation may be nondiscriminatory, but those implementing the practices and policies may have discriminatory attitudes. Fair rules can easily be exploited or evaded by both personnel officers and unions, who often operate using criteria for hiring and promotion such as "self-confidence," "fitting in," "collegiality," and "per-

sonal appearance," among other superficial characteristics.[15]

Issues about the breadth and depth of discrimination may divide us as a society more than any other issue about affirmative action. If one believes there is but a narrow slice of surface discrimination, one is likely to agree with what I have called the first school. But if one believes discrimination is deeply, almost invisibly entrenched in our society, one is apt to agree with the second school. I have been arguing for the perspective taken by the second school, but this perspective needs to be specified to prevent it from assuming the same bullheaded insensitivity that it pretends to locate elsewhere. Discriminatory attitudes and practices are likely to be deep-seated in some institutions, while shallow or absent in others. Society is not monolithic in the depth and breadth of discrimination. This means that in some cases affirmative action programs are not needed, in other cases only modest good faith programs are in order, and in still others enforced quotas are necessary to break down discriminatory patterns.

Because we disagree about the depth, breadth, and embeddedness of discrimination, we disagree further over the social policies that will rid us of the problem. Those like William Bradford Reynolds and George Bush who believe discrimination is relatively shallow and detectable look for formulas and remedies that center on *equal opportunity*. Those like Thomas Nagel and Lyndon Johnson who believe discrimination is deep, camouflaged, and embedded in society look for formulas that center on *measurable outcomes*.[16]

PROBLEMS OF ENFORCEMENT

One revealing example of resistance to efforts to erase discrimination is the Supreme Court's decision in *Local 28 v. Equal Employment Opportunity Commission*, commonly known as *Sheet*

Metal Workers.[17] In a 1975 trial, the U.S. District Court found a record "replete with instances of bad faith" and, in turn, ordered the establishment of a "remedial racial goal of 29% nonwhite membership (based on the percentage of nonwhites in the local labor pool). An appellate court then found that the union had "consistently and egregiously violated" the law of the land (Title VII, in particular). By 1981, after 22 years of struggle, virtually nothing had been done to modify the discriminatory hiring practices. In 1982 and 1983 court fines and civil contempt proceedings were issued to the union, with little effect.

The Supreme Court held, in reviewing this case, that one need not produce "identified victims" of discrimination and that goals such as the 29% quota are justified in cases in which "an employer or a labor union has been engaged in persistent or egregious discrimination, or where necessary to dissipate the lingering effects of pervasive discrimination." The quoted rule, which the Court has cited many times in other cases,[18] is particularly instructive: Goals and quotas are needed in cases in which there are ongoing, stubborn effects of pervasive preference for particular groups or discriminatory attitudes that control hiring. Otherwise, goals and quotas are dispensable.

As the Supreme Court notes in *Sheet Metal Workers,* present laws in the United States were enacted by Congress to prevent "pervasive and systematic discrimination in employment." Innumerable cases since the Philadelphia Plan in 1969 have shown that only numerical remedies will facilitate recruitment and combat racism and sexism in a tenacious, intractable environment of discrimination. The Supreme Court has not said, nor have I, that there cannot be a case of reverse discrimination in which a white male has unjustifiably been excluded from consideration and has a right to compensation. Unwarranted reverse discrimination is no better than any other form of unwarranted discrimination. But the following should also be considered: Reverse discrimination should be distinguished from what merely *appears* to be reverse discrimination. Sometimes persons will be hired or admitted who appear to be displacing better applicants, but the appearance is the result of another person's discriminatory perceptions of the person's qualifications. On other occasions, there will be genuine reverse discrimination, and on many occasions it will be impossible to determine whether this consequence occurs. The investigators reached this same conclusion in the aforementioned 1991 study by the Urban Institute of employment practices in Washington, D.C., and Chicago: Discrimination against black men is sufficiently entrenched that the effects of discrimination more than offset any effects of reverse discrimination.

WHY CORPORATIONS SHOULD WELCOME GOALS AND QUOTAS

Little has been said to this point about corporate policy, which will be well served by acceptance of goals and targets to eradicate discrimination throughout the 1990s. I shall discuss only so-called voluntary programs that use target goals and quotas. Although they stand in sharp contrast to legally enforced goals and quotas, the U.S. Department of Justice has sought in recent years to ban voluntary corporate programs, on grounds that these policies result in reverse discrimination. There are at least three reasons why it is in the interest of responsible businesses to use aggressive plans that incorporate goals and quotas: (1) an improved workforce, (2) stability of good working conditions and maintenance of a bias-free corporate environment, and (3) congeniality to managerial planning.

1. First, corporations that discriminate will

fail to look at the full range of qualified persons in the market and, as a result, will employ a higher percentage of second-best employees than the market presents. The U.S. work force is projected to be 80% women, minorities, and immigrants by the year 2000, and corporations are already reporting both that they are finding fewer qualified workers for available positions and that they have profited from vigorous internally-generated rules of nonracial, nonsexist hiring.[19] Hal Johnson, a senior vice-president at Travelers Cos., appropriately stated the benefits in adopting goals and quotas: "In [the 1990s] more of the work force is going to be minorities—Hispanics, blacks—and women. The companies that started building bridges back in the 1970s will be all right. Those that didn't won't."[20]

Goals and quotas that are properly conceived should yield superior, not inferior employees. It is a myth that tampering with the free market produces inferior hiring. No one would argue, for example, that baseball has poorer talent for dropping its free-market color barrier. To find the best baseball talent, bridges had to be built that extended, for example, into the population of Puerto Rico. Businesses will be analogously improved if they extend their boundaries and provide proper training and diversity programs. Bill McEwen of the Monsanto Corporation and spokesperson for the National Association of Manufacturers (NAM) notes that this extension has long been happening at NAM companies:

> We have been utilizing affirmative action plans for over 20 years. We were brought into it kicking and screaming. But over the past 20 years we've learned that there's a reservoir of talent out there, of minorities and women that we hadn't been using before. We found that [affirmative action] works.[21]

Maintaining a high quality work force is consistent with the management style already implemented in many companies. For example, James R. Houghton, Chairman of Corning Glass, has established voluntary quotas to increase the quality of employees, not merely the number of women and black employees. Corning established the following increased-percentage targets for the total employment population to be met between 1988 and 1991: women professionals to increase from 17.4% to 23.2%, black professionals to increase from 5.1% to 7.4%, the number of black senior managers to increase from 1 to 5, and the number of women senior managers to increase from 4 to 10. Corning management interpreted the targets as follows: "Those numbers were not commandments set in stone. We won't hire people just to meet a number. It will be tough to meet some of [our targets]." Corning found that it could successfully recruit in accordance with these targets, but found severe difficulty in maintaining the desired numbers in the workforce because of a continuing attrition problem. The company continues to take the view that in an age in which the percentage of white males in the employment pool is constantly declining, a "total quality company" must vigorously recruit women and minorities using target goals.[22]

A diverse work force can, additionally, create a more positive employment environment and better serve its customers. According to Jack MacAllister, CEO of U S West, "If a company is going to serve a diverse society, then its employees at every level—including its top decision makers—must reflect that society." An internal U S West study recently found that white males were ten times more likely to be promoted than minority women (black, Hispanic, and Asian). As a result, the company designed a plan to promote its female employees and to prepare employees for more demanding positions. U S West adopted the view that a diverse group of employees is better suited to develop new and creative ideas than a homogeneous group approaching problems from a similar perspective and that racial and sexual patterns of discrimination in hiring have to be combatted by target-driven hiring programs. They therefore explicitly targeted Women of Color for training and promotion.[23]

Many corporations have found that vigorous affirmative action has economic benefits, not merely social benefits. Diversity in the workforce produces diversity of ideas, different perspectives on strategic planning, and improved, more open personnel policies. As a result, as the director of personnel at Dow Chemical puts it, "If anything there is [in the corporate world] a new push on affirmative action plans because of the increasing number of women and minorities entering the work force."[24]

2. Second, pulling the foundations from beneath affirmative-action hiring would open old wounds at municipalities and corporations that have been developing target goals and quotas through either a consent-decree process with courts or direct negotiations with representatives of minority groups and unions. These programs have, in some cases, been agonizingly difficult to develop and would disintegrate if goals and timetables were ruled impermissible. The P.Q. Corporation, for example, reports that it has invested years of training in breaking down managerial biases and stereotypes while getting managers to hire in accordance with affirmative action guidelines. The corporation is concerned that without the pressure of affirmative action programs, managers will fail to recognize their own biases and use of stereotypes. Removal of voluntary programs might additionally stigmatize a business by signalling to minorities that a return to older patterns of discrimination is permissible. Such stigmatization is a serious blow in today's competitive market.[25]

3. Third, affirmative action programs in-

volving quotas have been successful for the corporations that have adopted them, and there is no need to try to fix what is not broken. As the editors of *Business Week* maintained, "Over the years business and regulators have worked out rules and procedures for affirmative action, including numerical yardsticks for sizing up progress, that both sides understand. It has worked and should be left alone."[26] It has worked because of the above mentioned improved workforce and because of a businesslike approach typical of managerial planning: Managers set goals and timetables for almost everything—from profits to salary bonuses. From a manager's point of view, setting goals and timetables is a basic way of measuring progress.

A survey of 200 major American corporations found that the same approach has often been taken to the management of affirmative action: Over 75% of these corporations already use "voluntary internal numerical objectives to assess [equal employment opportunity] performance." Another survey of 300 top corporate executives reported that 72% believe that minority hiring improves rather than hampers productivity, while 64% said there is a need for the government to help bring women and minorities into the mainstream of the workforce. Many corporations have used their records in promotion and recruitment to present a positive image of corporate life in public reports and recruiting brochures. Such reports and brochures have been published, for example, by Schering-Plough, Philip Morris, Exxon, AT&T, IBM, Westinghouse, and Chemical Bank.[27]

Affirmative action has also worked to increase productivity and improved consumer relationships. Corporations in consumer goods and services industries report increased respect and increased sales after achieving noticeable affirmative action results. They report that they are able to target some customers they otherwise could not reach, enjoy increased competitiveness, and better understand consumer complaints as a result of a more diverse workforce. Corporations with aggressive affirmative action programs have also been shown to outperform their competitors.[28]

CONCLUSION

If the social circumstances of discrimination were to be substantially altered, my conclusions in this paper would be modified. I agree with critics that the introduction of preferential treatment on a large scale runs the risk of producing economic advantages to individuals who do not deserve them, protracted court battles, congressional lobbying by power groups, a lowering of admission and work standards, reduced social and economic efficiency, increased racial and minority hostility, and the continued suspicion that well-placed minorities received their positions purely on the basis of quotas. These reasons constitute a strong case against affirmative action policies that use numerical goals and quotas. However, this powerful case is not sufficient to overcome the still stronger counterarguments.

NOTES

1. Executive Order 11,246. C.F.R. 339 (1964–65). This order required all federal contractors to construct affirmative action policies.
2. "Their Right to Remedy, Affirmed," *New York Times,* July 3, 1986, p. A30.
3. This standard has been recognized at least since *EEOC v. AT&T,* No. 73–149 (E.D. Pa. 1973).
4. See National Center for Education Statistics, *Faculty in Higher Education Institutions, 1988, Contractor Survey Report,* compiled Susan H. Russell, et al. (Washington: U.S. Dept. of Education, March 1990), pp. 5–13; Herman Schwartz, "Affirmative Action," *Minority Re-*

port, ed. L. W. Dunbar (New York: Pantheon Books, 1984), pp. 61–62; Betty M. Vetter, ed., *Professional Women and Minorities: A Manpower Data Resource Service,* 8th ed. (Washington: Commission on Science and Technology, 1989); Irene Pave, "A Woman's Place Is at GE, Federal Express, P&G . . . ." *Business Week,* June 23, 1986, pp. 75–76; Winifred Yu, "Asian Americans Charge Prejudice Slows Climb to Management Rank," *Wall Street Journal,* September 11, 1985, p. 35.

5. See *A Common Destiny: Blacks and American Society,* Gerald D. Jaynes and Robin M. Williams, Jr., eds., Committee on the Status of Black Americans, Commission on Behavioral and Social Sciences and Education, National Research Council (Washington: NAS Press, 1989), pp. 12–13, 138–48; "Business Bulletin," *Wall Street Journal,* February 28, 1985, p. 1; Constance L. Hays, "Study Says Prejudice in Suburbs Is Aimed Mostly at Blacks," *New York Times,* November 23, 1988, p. A16.
6. Paul Burstein, *Discrimination, Jobs, and Politics* (Chicago: University of Chicago Press, 1985); Bureau of Labor Statistics, *Employment and Earnings* (Washington, D.C.: U.S. Dept. of Labor, Jan. 1989); Jaynes and Williams, eds., *A Common Destiny,* op. cit., pp. 16–18, 84–88.
7. As reported by Rudolf A. Pyatt, Jr., "Significant Job Studies," *Washington Post,* April 30, 1985, pp. D1–D2.
8. Margery Austin Turner, Michael Fix, and Raymond Struyk, *Opportunities Denied, Opportunities Diminished: Racial Discrimination in Hiring* (Washington, D.C.: Urban Institute Report 91–9, 1991).
9. *Alexander v. Choate,* 469 U.S. 287, at 295.
10. 401 U.S. 424 (1971).
11. The court relaxed this standard in *Wards Cove Packing Co. v. Atonio,* 109 S.Ct. 2115 (1989). However, much of the argument in *Wards Cove* was nullified by civil rights legislation passed in October 1991, which required a return to the "business necessity" rule in *Griggs.*
12. Juan Williams, "EEOC Chief Cites Abuse of Racial Bias Criteria," *Washington Post,* December 4, 1984, p. A13.
13. *Fullilove v. Klutznick,* 448 U.S. 448 (1980); *United Steelworkers v. Weber,* 443 U.S. 193 (1979); *United States v. Paradise,* 480 U.S. 149 (1987); *Johnson v. Transportation Agency,* 480 U.S. 616 (1987)

14. *Firefighters v. Stotts*, 467 U.S. 561 (1984); *City of Richmond v. J. A. Croson*, 109 S.Ct. 706 (1989); *Wygant v. Jackson Bd. of Education*, 476 U.S. 267 (1986); *Wards Cove Packing v. Atonio*, 490 U.S. 642.

15. See the argument to this effect in Gertrude Ezorsky, *Racism & Justice: The Case for Affirmative Action* (Ithaca, N.Y.: Cornell University Press, 1991), Chap. 1.

16. For a balanced article on this topic, see Robert K. Fullinwider, "Affirmative Action and Fairness," *Report from the Institute for Philosophy & Public Policy* 11 (University of Maryland, Winter 1991): 10–13.

17. *Local 28 of the Sheet Metal Workers' International Association v. Equal Employment Opportunity Commission*, 106 S.Ct. 3019. All quotations below are from this case.

18. A strong reaffirmation is found in *United States v. Paradise*, 480 U.S. 149. This 1986 case concluded that "even under a strict scrutiny analysis, the one-black-for-one white promotion requirement is permissible . . . [and] justified by a compelling governmental interest in eradicating the Department's pervasive, systematic, and obstinate discriminatory exclusion of blacks. . . . The one-for-one requirement is necessary to eliminate the effects of the Department's long-term, open, and pervasive discrimination" (150). The court rejects arguments directed against quotas and reverse discrimination (156, 163).

19. See L. Joseph Semien, "Opening the Utility Door for Women and Minorities," *Public Utilities Fortnightly*, July 5, 1990, pp. 29–31; Pave, "A Woman's Place," p. 76.

20. As quoted in Walter Kiechel, "Living with

Human Resources," *Fortune*, August 18, 1986, p. 100.

21. As quoted in Peter Perl, "Rulings Provide Hiring Direction: Employers Welcome Move," *Washington Post*, July 3, 1986, pp. A1, A11.

22. Tim Loughran, "Corning Tries to Break the Glass Ceiling," *Business & Society Review* 76 (Winter 1991), pp. 52–55. For its efforts, Corning (along with Avon Products, DuPont, and Gannett News) was given an award by *Catalyst*, a foundation that honors companies that initiate aggressive and successful recruitment programs for women.

23. Richard Remington, "Go West, Young Woman!" in *Telephony* 215 (Nov. 1988), pp. 30–32; Diane Feldman, "Women of Color Build a Rainbow of Opportunity, *Management Review* 78 (Aug. 1989), pp. 18–21.

24. Loughran, op. cit., p. 54.

25. See Jeanne C. Poole and E. Theodore Kautz, "An EEO/AA Program That Exceeds Quotas—It Targets Biases," *Personnel Journal* 66 (Jan. 1987), pp. 103–105. Mary Thornton, "Justice Dept. Stance on Hiring Goals Resisted," *Washington Post*, May 25, 1985, p. A2; Linda Williams, "Minorities Find Pacts with Corporations Are Hard to Come By and Enforce," *Wall Street Journal*, August 23, 1985, p. 13.

26. Editorial, "Don't Scuttle Affirmative Action," *Business Week*, April 5, 1985, p. 174.

27. "Rethinking *Weber:* The Business Response to Affirmative Action," *Harvard Law Review* 102 (Jan. 1989), p. 661, note 18; Robertson, "Why Bosses Like to Be Told," p. 2.

28. See "Rethinking *Weber,*" esp. pp. 668–70.

Pay Equity: Equal Value to Whom?

Wil Waluchow

A fundamental principle of justice upon which many of our moral and legal practices are founded is that equals should be treated equally: that in the absence of relevant differences between them, people should be treated the same. This principle, associated with the Greek philosopher Aristotle, accounts for many of our beliefs about fairness

Journal of Business Ethics 7 (1988): 185–189. © 1988 *by D. Reidel Publishing Company.* Reprinted by permission.

and underlies the common law doctrines of legal precedent. It is also a principle which lies at the heart of the pay equity controversy. Work of equal value performed by men and women in the workplace (traditionally conceived) does not always appear to be rewarded with equal or even comparable pay. There is a wage gap (some estimate it as high as 36%) which seems undeniably due, in part, to the persistent, wholly unwarranted undervaluation of work performed by women. An irrelevant difference, sex, has been and is functioning as though it were relevant. The result is injustice; equals are not being treated equally.

The major difficulties in overcoming these injustices through social or legal means seem to fall largely into four categories. First, there has been much controversy over the nature or cause of the wage gap and therefore over how best and whether to tackle it. We cannot, the critics rightly point out, simply infer from the fact that there is a gap between the wages of men and women that sexual discrimination is the cause or even a significant part of the cause of its existence.[1] Some argue that only a very small percentage of the gap is attributable to this factor. Alternative explanations range from the premise that women, as the marriage partners largely responsible, traditionally, for maintaining homes and rearing children have in comparison with men been able to invest less "human capital" in the marketplace, thus accounting for their lower wages;[2] to the premise that the relatively sudden influx of women onto the job market in post-war years resulted in a fierce competition for the relatively few, lower paying jobs more established participants—i.e. the men— were inclined to avoid.[3] But however much of the wage gap we can attribute to such additional factors, it is clear that there is a considerable remainder which can be explained only by the fact of discrimination.[4]

A second set of objections is based on the high, and in the view of some unfair, costs to business and government (and ultimately the taxpayer) of increased wages for women in the private and public sectors respectively. To this there is a simple reply. If business, government, and the male work force are, and have been for some time, profiting from the suppressed wages of women, then we have a clear case of unjust enrichment; and it is anything but unfair to demand the return of unjustly appropriated goods.

A third set of objections follows from the second. Increased wages for women will result, it has been argued, in a decreased demand for labour, especially in those sectors of the job market in which women happen to be concentrated. Thus we encounter a dilemma: our well-intentioned efforts will bring about more harm than good for those very people we are trying to help. To this there are at least three replies. First, the objection seems analogous to ones often formulated by people who were opposed to the abolition of slavery. To be sure, many Blacks did suffer in the short run; but there is no denying the long term gains. Secondly, when personal welfare competes with justice even the victim will often choose the latter. Witness the reluctance of many strikers to relinquish their cause even in the face of grave financial burdens. A third reply is that it is far from clear that the harmful consequences will be all that severe. The experience of Australia, which took major steps toward pay equity in the 1970s offers some grounds for hope. As Paul Weiler notes: "Although we cannot hold out comparable worth as an unqualified boon for women . . . the fact is that when one sums up both . . . wage and employment effects, there was a sharp net improvement in the condition of Australian women on the whole."[5] So there is hope that the choice isn't quite as bleak as all that.

A fourth set of objections to movements toward pay equity involves a question which Aristotle's principle leaves entirely unanswered. We are instructed to treat equals equally. But precisely how do we determine who is equal and who is therefore entitled to equal or comparable pay? What criteria should we use in determining relevant and irrelevant differences? The conceptual and practical difficulties encountered in answering these questions have led many to condemn pay equity out of hand. According to Clarence Pendleton, chairman of the United States Civil Rights Commission, equal or comparable worth is the "looniest idea since 'Looney Tunes' came on the screen."[6] Were we unable to unearth conceptually sound and workable criteria, Pendleton would have a strong case. Unless we have appropriate criteria and are confident that they can be applied in a consistent, principled manner, we run the risk of perpetuating, even increasing, the injustice we set out to eradicate. If we have the wrong criteria, then equals may be treated even more unequally.

On what basis, then, should we determine whose work is equal in value to whose? I'm afraid I have no easy solution—mainly worries and difficulties, in particular worries about a phrase which has figured in several landmark American legal cases and which one sometimes encounters in Canadian media reports: "work of equal value *to the employer*."[7] My concern is that continued use of this phrase may lead to the continued undervaluation of certain forms of work. It may result in the very same injustices we are trying to eliminate. In what follows I shall try to make clear the sources of my concern.

In beginning, we must first distinguish two very different principles as they apply to women and pay equity. The first, the "Equal Work Principle" (EWP) states that women should receive equal pay for equal—i.e. identical—work. The second, the "Equal [or Comparable] Value Principle" (EVP) says that women should receive equal pay, not only for identical work, but for different work of equal

value. The EWP applies, of course, in cases where men and women perform precisely the same tasks, more or less equally well. Some men might perform the relevant tasks better than some women; but the reverse applies as well. Here we encounter no significant difficulties. We have a clear-cut criterion. The work performed is equal; so the value of the work must be equal; and so it follows from the EWP that women who do this work are, all else being equal, entitled to the same pay as men. How valuable the work in question really is and how much each should therefore receive are difficult questions, of course. But they are also ones which are beyond the scope of the EWP. It is purely comparative and specifies one limited circumstance in which men and women should receive equal pay. It says nothing about the absolute value of those equal forms of work or about how much they merit in the way of financial reward.

It's a well-documented fact that the EWP is a relatively powerless tool in addressing the wage gap. For a number of reasons, women and men as a whole have tended to land in different jobs and different industries, though we can hope that pay equity will go some way towards eliminating this feature of our society in the future. In such cases, we lack the clear-cut criterion provided by the EWP and must instead invoke the EVP with all its attendant difficulties. How do we compare very different jobs? Is it really like comparing apples and oranges, as the critics are so fond of saying? If not, how can we determine whether and how the differences between two different types of work are relevant for purposes of value and pay? One thing seems clear. We cannot, as we could with the EWP, answer these questions without asking *how much* a particular task is worth as compared with another. We cannot help asking whether, in terms of the relevant criteria, the value of a particular level or brand of secretarial work is greater than, equal to, or less than, the value of warehouse work or the work of electricians and carpenters. And so we inevitably encounter serious conceptual difficulties. these difficulties result largely from the fact that many different conceptions and associated criteria seem to be suggested by the amorphous phrase "equal value." At least that's what I'd now like to argue.

Consider for a moment the range of possible answers to the following question:

How does one determine the worth or value of someone's work so as to compare it with the work of others?

Here is a partial list of possible answers suggesting different criteria not all of which yield the same evaluations in all cases.

A. By whatever the *existing market*—i.e. an employer—will pay for it;
B. By whatever a *fair market* would pay for it;
C. By what she *deserves* for doing it;
D. By how much her work *contributes to the success of the firm;*
E. By how much her work *contributes to the community or society;*
F. By whatever is *the going rate in "the industry"* for people who do the same work;
G. By whatever value her work is assigned by her employer's *declared or explicit wage policy;*
H. By whatever value her work is assigned by her employer's *implicit wage policy.*

Answers A and B are favorites of those enamoured of neo-classical economic theory. Answer C appeals to desert, D and E to one's contribution to an enterprise broadly construed. Answers F–H, like the EWP, are purely comparative. They require the consistent enforcement of existing standards or policies.

Much needs to be said about these eight competing, and possibly overlapping, criteria. Each has its merits; though each has its obvious problems as well. A is neat and tidy, but of no use in dealing with pay inequities.

The existing market is unfair to women and largely responsible for the present wage gap. B allows us to purge the market of at least some of its undesirable forces, but it is anything but neat and tidy. The criterion suggested involves counterfactual speculation about what a fair market—i.e. one which, among other things, did not pander to prejudice against women—*would* pay for one's work *if* a whole set of non-existent conditions obtained. Such counterfactual speculation should be avoided if at all possible. Answer C seems *prima facie* appealing and acceptable, but it begs all sorts of questions, desert being an eminently contestable notion. D and E are very popular and often used to justify, for instance, very high wages for corporate executives and doctors. F and H pose problems of their own. To the extent that they appeal to existing standards which themselves may be based on prejudice, they will of course be of no help. F also ignores such things as regional differences, the different histories of collective bargaining within particular firms, and possibly even the different levels of productivity among different companies within the same industry.[8] G is often invoked by defenders of pay equity. Firms, at least sizeable ones, often have sophisticated internal procedures for ranking labour and management positions. These involve criteria which, if consistently applied without latent prejudice against women and so-called women's work, could sometimes eliminate inequities. But there are at least two problems with this solution. First, as noted earlier, to the extent that the internal standards are themselves biased, the result of their unbiased enforcement will still be unjust. A second problem is that many firms, in particular many smaller ones, simply lack explicit standards and procedures. This is one reason in favour of criterion H, a version of which has been developed by Treiman, Hartman and Roos.[9] On this model, one sets out to discover the implicit values underlying an employer's wage structure for its various non-female (i.e. predominantly male or mixed) positions, on the assumption that the values the employer actually places on various job factors will not be skewed by sexual prejudice in such instances. Once found, these values can then be used to compare what the employer actually pays for these same factors when they are found in the predominantly female jobs. One could, in this way, discover how an employer objectively valued, say, educational credentials versus the assumption of risk of injury. The unbiased values might be revealed by what he pays for such jobs as electrician as opposed to predominantly male administrative or professional jobs like engineer.[10] Whatever values we discovered we would then have a basis for comparing how much the employer pays for these same factors when they figure in the predominantly female positions such as secretary or plant nurse. If we found a difference, we would have a clear case for equalization.

This seems to be a promising proposal which deserves serious consideration, especially given the general reluctance of governments to allow anything more than comparisons of how men and women fare on existing pay structures within one and the same firm of "establishment." But its limitations are obvious and must be acknowledged. First, it applies only to large firms with a wide variety of different jobs upon the basis of which the appropriate comparisons can be made. Second, it fails to provide a solution for companies where the employees are almost exclusively women. Here something more than this entirely internal, comparative test is required. And third, the values discovered in the nonfemale jobs might still be skewed by other non-sexual forms of bias.

One could go on discussing the eight criteria in some detail. But instead I should now like to turn to my main worry, which can now be expressed in terms of the desert and con-

tribution criteria (C–E). Once we distinguish these different criteria, it is clear that the phrase "work of equal value" is radically ambiguous. The contribution criteria suggests that a work's value is instrumental in nature; it depends on, or exists in relation to, its *functional role* in bringing about desired states of affairs. These states of affairs can include such things as satisfactory production levels, profits, or as in the case of public nurses and doctors, a healthy population. On such a model, it is principally one's *work* which is of value, a value which can properly be expressed as its value to the employer or to society. The more a person's work contributes to securing the relevant desired states of affairs, the more valuable it is. We might call this *functional value*, and (somewhat tentatively) add that, all else being equal, work of higher skill and responsibility (two of the four factors normally mentioned in discussions of pay equity; effort and working conditions being the others) will be functionally more valuable. The contribution criteria, then, provide the best explanation of their relevance.

The desert criterion, however, operates very differently. Here, we might say, the value lies not so much in *the work* and its functional role in achieving desired states of affairs. Rather the value—more precisely, the *merit*—lies in *the worker herself*. The work of an employee who toils under conditions of physical or mental danger or miscomfort, or who puts in a much greater effort in preparing for a job or in carrying it out, is not *necessarily* of greater value to her employer. Her work may actually be of little functional value as compared with, say, the relatively cushy work of the corporate executive. The latter may score high in terms of responsibility and skill, i.e. in terms of the contribution criteria, but not necessarily the desert criterion. As for the former, her *work* might score very low on the contribution criterion, but *she herself* will rate very high on the desert criterion. And the reason is clear. All else being equal, one who makes a greater effort or endures undesirable conditions to achieve desirable ends, merits greater reward, regardless of the functional value of her work, of how much it *contributes* to securing those ends. This again, is because desert, unlike functional value, attaches principally to the worker not her work.

In so far as the desert and contribution criteria apply to different things—the worker vs. her work—they involve very different conceptions of value and often yield crucially different results. These important differences are masked by the phrase "work of equal value." We should always ask: "Equal with respect to what or to whom?" How we rank different jobs will depend crucially on how we answer this question.

I am now in a position to formulate my worry about the phrase "equal value to the employer." These words strongly suggest *functional value* (and the contribution criterion) at the expense of *worker's* value (and the desert criterion). It follows that use of this phrase in formulating, describing or even conceiving pay equity policy can easily lead to the undervaluation of important factors such as effort and working conditions. The result can only be injustice: workers will still be treated unequally. One final point: to the extent that many women are at present clustered in so-called "ghetto jobs", a number of which could well score very low on the contribution criteria but comparatively high on the desert criterion, this result should be of particular concern to proponents of pay equity for women. We have here a case where our choice of words might make a considerable difference both in conception and ultimately practice.[11]

NOTES

1. C.f. R. Abella, *Equality in Employment: A Royal Commission Report*, Government of Canada, 1984.

2. See G. Becker, "Human Capital, Effort, and the Sexual Division of Labor", *J. Lab. Econ.* **2,** 33 (1985).

3. This argument is outlined in "Comparable Worth: Theory, Policy and Equity Issue", Christian Dick, M. A. Thesis, McMaster University, 1986, pp. 48–58.

4. See Paul Weiler, "The Wages of Sex: The Uses and Limits of Comparable Worth", *Harvard Law Review* **99:** 1728 (1986) at 1790–91. See also, Corcoran & Duncan, "Work History, Labor Force Attachment, and Earnings Differences Between the Races and Sexes", *J. Human Resources* 3 (1979); England, "The Failure of Human Capital Theory to Explain Occupational Sex Segregation", *J. Hum. Resources* **17,** 358 (1982); Roos, "Sex Stratification in the Workplace: Male Female Differences in Economic Returns to Occupation", *Soc. Sci. Research* **10** (1981); Treiman, Hartman, and Roos, "Assessing Pay Discrimination Using National Data", in *Comparable Worth and Wage Discrimination: Technical Possibilities and Political Realities*, H. Remick, ed. (1984); and *Women, Work, and Wages: Equal Pay for Jobs of Equal Value*, Treiman & Hartman, ed. (Washington, D.C.: National Academy Press, 1981).

5. Weiler, p. 1777. Weiler's conclusions are based on Gregory & Duncan, "Segmented Labor Market Theories and the Australian Experience of Equal Pay for Women", *J. Post-Keynesian Econ.* **3,** 403 (1981); and Gregory, McMahon, and Whittingham, "Women in the Australian Labor Force: Trends, Causes, and Consequences", *J. Lab. Econ.* **3.** S293 (1985).

6. *New York Times*, Sept. 5, 1985, A25. Cited in Weiler, p. 1729.

7. See, for example, *AFSCME v. Washington*, 770 F.2d 1401 (9th Cir. 1985) where the court claimed that "the value of a particular job *to an employer* is but one factor influencing the rate of compensation for that job" (emphasis added). . . .

8. This may pose a problem for the EWP too, if the equal work in question is not restricted to one and the same "establishment", to use the phrase adopted in the *Canadian Human Rights Act*.

9. See Treiman, Hartman, and Roos; and Treiman and Hartman, *supra* Note 4. The model is outlined and defended by Weiler in *supra* Note 2.

10. The example is borrowed from Weiler, *Supra* Note 4.

11. An earlier version of this paper was read at a conference entitled 'Women and Economic Equity: The Canadian Context' which was held on January 23–5 at Mount St. Vincent University, Halifax. I wish to acknowledge the assistance of several of the participants, in particular Deborah Poff and Alex Michalos.

Comparable Worth and Wage Discrimination

Helen Remick
and Ronnie J. Steinberg

Comparable worth contradicts fundamental economic assumptions, stretches legal interpretations, challenges stereotypes of women workers, and causes scrutiny of accepted management tools. It questions some of our deepest beliefs about the nature and value of work. . . .

Cultural beliefs underlying the differentiation of men's and women's work are so strong (though obviously changeable) that widespread debate on a comparable worth policy would have been unthinkable twenty—perhaps even ten—years ago. The concept of comparable worth was introduced as "equal pay for work of equal value" at the close of the Second World War. . . .

The diversity that exists in the approaches to salary setting allows one to assess whether any one method or approach shows less bias than others. To date, studies using a number of different methods show surprisingly similar results: all demonstrate the systematic undervaluation of work done by women. We need not have a single means of setting salaries as long as the many ways are free of systematic bias against women. As the goal of comparable worth has evolved from a political demand into a policy with serious economic consequences for employers, opponents have developed a number of arguments against it. . . .

APPLES AND ORANGES

A *Fortune* magazine article described comparable worth as "a fallacious notion that apples are equal to oranges and that prices for both should be the same." (Smith, 1978:58). The apples-and-oranges comparison refers to the supposed impossibility of finding a method to describe, evaluate, and establish equivalencies among dissimilar jobs. However, both suggestions—that no method for comparing dissimilar jobs can be found and that apples could not be equal to oranges—are themselves fallacious.

Of course, any particular apple may not be equal to any particular orange, nor are all apples identical. Yet there are general characteristics of fruit, such as the number of calories, the vitamin and mineral content, and so on, that make it possible to compare specific apples with specific oranges. Along some of these dimensions of comparison, the apples and oranges compared may, in fact, be equivalent, and therefore be of equal value.

Likewise, certain dissimilar jobs may comprise functional tasks and characteristics that, from the employer's point of view, are equivalent in value. Job evaluation systems describe and analyze jobs in terms of an array of underlying features such as prerequisites, tasks, and responsibilities. While far from perfect, these systems have been and continue to be used to classify dissimilar jobs,especially in large firms and at the management level. It is surprising, then, that the same employer groups that have supported job evaluation systems when they have been used to create and justify an existing organization hierarchy and wage structure contend that such systems cannot be used to compare male-dominated and female-dominated jobs within that wage structure.

THE FREE MARKET

Critics also contend that comparable worth will destroy the free market as the basic mechanism for setting wages. This argument assumes, first, that wages are largely set through the impersonal forces of supply and demand and, second, that this is the best possible way to set wages. Government intervention will sabotage the invisible hand. This criticism of comparable worth policy is troublesome on three counts: it misrepresents the intent of comparable worth policy; it inflates out of all proportion the deleterious consequences to the market of establishing government-backed labor standards to protect employees against wage discrimination; and it assumes that the market now functions impersonally and fairly.

The goal of comparable worth policy is to pay a fair market wage to jobs historically done by women. This means that the wage rate should be based on the productivity-based job content characteristics of the jobs and not on the sex of the typical job incumbent. In other words, . . . comparable worth advocates seek to disentangle and remove discrimination from the market. The laissez-faire doctrine underlying the free market ideology assumes that employers and employees bargain as equals. Comparable worth policy can contribute toward a more smoothly running marketplace. Ironically, by giving less powerful women the power resource of a legally backed right to be paid at a nondiscriminatory wage rate, comparable worth policy removes a market imperfection. . . .

"Society" has always established limits on the actions that can be taken in the marketplace when such actions have gone beyond what is considered fair and appropriate. State child labor laws are one example, and we also have the Fair Labor Standards Act, the Occupational Health and Safety Act, and Title VII of the Civil Rights Act of 1964.

We interfere with the free market all the time in at least two other ways. First, government intervenes in the free market to protect employers. For example, the federal government provided funds to Chrysler, Amtrak, and Lockheed when it was seemingly necessary to keep these major companies from bankruptcy. Second, employers themselves repeatedly interfere with the free market. Price fixing, wage setting,and control of a particular product market are not necessarily the activities of personally evil individual employers; rather, they are often rational economic responses designed to minimize risk, reduce costs, and increase profits, thus allowing firms to remain in business.

An interesting example of employer collusion in wage setting is drawn from the comparable worth case *Lemons v. City of Denver* (22 FEP Cases 959). In the city of Denver, nurses were paid less than gardeners or tree trimmers. The nurses presented evidence that administrators of all the local hospitals met annually to set the salary levels that would be paid to nurses in the Denver metropolitan area. The judge failed to comment on the wage-and price-fixing activities of the hospital administrators when, as Mary Heen notes in Chapter 12, he ruled against the nurses. Under these circumstances, it would be virtually impossible for an individual nurse to bargain a "free market" wage.

THE COST

Critics of comparable worth policy also argue that the financial costs of adjusting female wages up to male standards would be prohibitive: employer advocacy groups have presented estimates that range from $2 billion to $150 billion. . . . But the assumption underlying these estimates is that *all* wage discrimination in *all* work organizations is going to be rectified all at once and tomorrow. This assumption has no basis in history; nor does it reflect the approach thus far taken *within* work organizations to correct for systematic undervaluation or for other forms of discrimination.

Most legal reforms that impact upon the labor market have been implemented in stages: either the scope of coverage is initially restricted and gradually expanded to cover a larger proportion of employees over time. . . .

The cost of implementing comparable worth policy will probably be spread out at the very least over the next two decades. While no doubt costly, the length of this implementation process should reduce the impact of its cost for any year or even any decade. The goal of the proponents of comparable worth is to balance fairness with fiscal responsibility. . . .

There has been a tendency in several recent lawsuits to focus on eliminating discrimination at the entry level as the key to closing the wage gap; both *IUE v. Westinghouse* (23 FEP Cases 588) and *Taylor v. Charley Brothers Co.* (25 FEP Cases 602) make this point. In some employment situations, overt discrimination by the employer does occur at entry; at both Charley Brothers and Westinghouse, the jobs in question required no previous training, and the employer chose employment assignments. In many, perhaps most, employment situations, however, previous education, training, and experience are required by the employer, and potential employees indicate their preferences by applying for the specific jobs for which they have already acquired the necessary skills. Given the skill requirements of many jobs, successful implementation of the integration strategy would require extensive retraining programs similar to those funded under the Comprehensive Employment and Training Act, or more recently, the Job Partnership Training Act. . . . Without subsidized retraining programs, women must either retrain at their own expense (if they have the resources to do so) or compete with men for less skilled, higher-paid jobs in order to improve their economic well-being. While these strategies have some potential for solving the earnings problems of a few individuals, they are simply inadequate as an approach to a systemic problem. . . .

PART-TIME WORK

Many women, especially those with young children, prefer part-time to full-time employment. Shorter work hours are their only way of dealing with the many demands in their lives. For mothers of school-aged children, work during school hours may be best; work hours for mothers of younger children are often chosen to fall outside the work hours of the husband, so that he can take care of the children while she works, and vice versa.

The increase in the number of working women has caused a shift in the peak working hours of many service industries. Grocery stores, for example, are quiet on weekdays from nine to four, when the few shoppers are primarily women with small children and people of retirement age. The stores are crowded in the early evening and on weekends. Retail stores follow much the same pattern of use. This concentration of hours of heavy use has caused many employers to create part-time, peak-hour jobs and to cut back in the number of full-time positions. The fact that women are more willing to accept part-time work than men are is causing a rapid feminization of these kinds of jobs.

Women's tendency to choose part-time work as a solution to role demands presents interesting compensation issues. Traditionally, part-time workers receive poorer benefit packages and lower hourly wages than full-time workers, even within the same firm. . . . Economists tend to explain the lower compensation in terms of lower return to the employer for training and lower commitment by the employee. But are part-time workers really less productive and therefore worth less? Or is this a *post hoc* rationalization justifying a lower wage for female workers? Particularly for tedious jobs, our experience has shown two half-time workers to be more productive than one full-time employee.

Because most part-time workers are women, we must use care in sorting out how much of the lower pay is due to the sex of the workers and how much to their relative productivity. Part-time workers often have attributed to them the same kind of stereotypes attributed to women in general: they lack job commitment, they have no need for good wages or benefit packages, they offer no payoff for on-the-job training, and so on. . . .

Moreover, as more firms adopt comparable worth, the resultant salary adjustments will permeate the wage structure of local labor markets. Through the process of pressure, innovation, imitation, and adjustment, the wages paid for work done primarily by women will catch up with the reality that women represent a large, permanent, and highly productive set of employees. These concrete actions will, no doubt, eventually transform a highly charged and controversial political demand into a routine and institutionalized feature of equal employment policy.

Comparable Pay for Comparable Work?

Robert L. Simon

"Equal pay for equal work" is one of the most defensible and most widely accepted principles to have been implemented in this country in the name of equal opportunity. However, implementation of the principle of equal pay for equal work has not significantly closed the gap between the pay men receive and the pay women receive in the marketplace. Thus, in 1955, women's earnings were about 60 percent of the earnings of men, and today women continue to make only about 60 cents for every dollar men make in the workplace.[1]

One fact that helps explain a significant

Reprinted by permission of the author, who gratefully acknowledges the National Endowment for the Humanities for a summer stipend that supported the work on this paper.

portion of this gap between men's and women's earnings is the concentration of women in low-paying job categories. Roughly four-fifths of all women work in 25 of the 420 job categories listed by the Department of Labor.[2] Clearly, implementation of the principle of equal pay for equal work will not close the gap between the earnings of males and earnings of females as long as, on the average, men and women are not doing the *same* work.

Accordingly, the support of many advocates of pay equity has shifted from the principle of equal pay for equal work to a new principle: the principle of *comparable pay for work of comparable worth* (PCW). Proponents of PCW argue that if the jobs in which women are concentrated are equal in worth to traditionally male jobs but pay less, then unequal pay across these jobs categories is inequitable and unjust.

Such an approach is not entirely new. For example, systems of job evaluation have been employed by the federal government and by many private employees to assess comparative pay of different job categories.[3] On a more intuitive level, who has not wondered whether some highly paid job category is really more important than a lower paid one? Is the work done by police officers of less worth than that performed by better paid corporate vice presidents in charge of advertising? Isn't the work of teachers equal in value to that of many lawyers, professional athletes, or entertainers?

Advocates of comparable worth want to generate a social policy from the sentiments that lie behind such questions. However, implementation of some version of PCW should take place only after extensive debate and consideration. If the difficulties PCW generates are not understood and faced, this principle is all too likely to become a purely political weapon that, while capable of generating intense feelings of discontent, is unlikely to

result in more equity in the workplace. In the following pages we will explain and examine some of these difficulties in an effort to evaluate comparable worth as a social policy.

THE MEANING OF COMPARABLE WORTH

As we will see, many questions can be raised about the justice and fairness of various versions of PCW. However, before turning to such fundamental *moral* concerns, we must be clear about the notion of comparable worth itself. In particular, what does it *mean* to say that two jobs are of comparable worth? How are we to tell when two jobs are comparable? These questions, sometimes blurred together under the heading "the measurement problem," are of fundamental importance. Principles such as PCW can guide conduct only if they are clear enough so that those to whom they apply can understand what is being required of them.

As suggested above, the measurement problem really has two distinct parts. The first is to explain what is meant by "comparable worth." The second is to formulate a criterion for measuring comparable worth, as so defined. Without solutions to these problems, enforcement of PCW would be arbitrary and inequitable. Jobs judged comparable by one conception of comparable worth would not be so judged by another. Even if there were agreement on a conception of comparable worth, different criteria of measurement would yield different rankings of job categories. But justice and equity cannot vary arbitrarily; they require consistent application of defensible principles so that similar cases are treated alike.

We can begin with the question of meaning. What does it mean to say that two jobs are of comparable worth? Unfortunately, comparable worth can be understood in a variety of ways, many of which are irrelevant to understanding what advocates have in mind. For example, if we take the worth of a job to refer to its *intrinsic moral worth,* jobs would be comparable only when their intrinsic moral worth was equivalent. To the extent that this notion is intelligible at all (for it is far from clear that jobs even have intrinsic moral worth, let alone different degrees of it), it might rest on intuitions that some jobs—for example modeling for pornographic pictures—seem less worthy than others—for example that of a dedicated physician.

However, this clearly is not what advocates of comparable worth have in mind, and for good reason. It is difficult to see how an overall ranking of the intrinsic moral worth of different jobs is to be derived, or what would make it defensible. Moreover, it is doubtful if any one such ranking, even if it could be shown to be defensible, should be implemented in a pluralistic society in which the intuitions of many individuals and groups are likely to differ significantly.

If advocates of comparable worth do not mean to refer to the moral value of jobs, what do they mean? Perhaps the best clue is the reliance by advocates on job evaluation studies as measuring devices. These studies assess such factors as the degree of responsibility a job requires, the quality of working conditions, the training needed to do the work, the degree of skill required, and so forth. This list suggests that advocates of comparable worth conceive of the worth of a job as its "level of demand," where the demand a job makes on a worker is a function of the application of a variety of demand-making criteria. Different jobs are comparable when they make equivalent demands on the worker, as measured by a variety of demand-making factors. "Level of demand" here is being used as a technical term to refer to the aggregate of factors held to be criteria of what the job requires. So, in this view, secretaries are underpaid relative to

truck drivers if and only if truck drivers make more than secretaries but their jobs are no more demanding.

The problem with this view is that there does not appear to be any one favored set of demand-making criteria specifying the "level of demand" of particular jobs. On the contrary, job evaluations themselves rest on controversial value judgments. For example, should enhanced responsibility be viewed as a burden that makes a job more difficult or as an asset that makes a job more stimulating? Is outdoor work more demanding than indoor work since workers may have to be on the job in inclement weather, or is it less demanding since workers get fresh air and are not chained to a desk? Even if we could arrive at uncontroversial answers to questions regarding criteria for the level of demand, how would we *weigh* such criteria in case of conflict? If librarians require more training than city bus drivers, but the bus drivers work under greater stress, which job is of greater worth? Clearly, each of these questions calls for complex evaluations which raise normative issues rather than ones that can be settled by straightforward observation of the "facts."

Conceptions of comparable worth can vary, then, according to the criteria for the level of demand that are employed and the weight assigned to each. Therefore, we should think of comparable worth not as one principle but as a related family of principles that differ from one another, often in significant respects. Thus, in any debate about comparable worth, it is important to make sure that all parties involved are considering the same conception.

Perhaps more importantly, if there is no way of showing that one conception of comparable worth is more defensible than others, application of any one conception rather than another seems arbitrary. Even if there is a defensible conception, if we can't tell what it is, implementation of comparable worth will be open to charges of inequity and unfairness. Jobs will be rated as comparable or non-comparable without a justified basis for doing so.

So far we have been talking only about the meaning of comparable worth. However, even if we could agree on the nature and weight of the criteria of comparable worth, application of such criteria also involves normative issues. For example, even if we agree that, all else being equal, greater responsibility entails a greater level of demand, how are we to measure responsibility? Is responsibility related to the number of people one supervises, the level of decision making one holds within a firm, the costs of misjudgment, or what? Thus, an airline mechanic may supervise few people but has a great deal of responsibility for people's lives. Is the mechanic's responsibility greater than that of top executives in the airline's office? How are we to tell?

The problems of meaning and measurement often are claimed to undermine completely the case for comparable worth. How can comparable worth be an instrument for securing social justice if there are no defensible criteria of comparability, no defensible assignments of weight to conflicting criteria, and no clear way to measure application of the criteria in controversial cases?

At this point advocates of comparable worth may agree that comparison of jobs does rest on arguable value judgments. It does not follow, they will point out, that such judgments must be entirely arbitrary or indefensible. For one thing, even though many judgments about comparability will be controversial, many more may not. For example, most of us would agree that normally a person who has the responsibility for evaluating the work of many employees has more responsibility than an employee who performs routine clerical tasks. Moreover, even if it is arguable in theory that a routine job should receive greater compensation than one that

involves stimulating responsibilities, which presumably are their own reward, that is not the way the market traditionally has worked. Males with responsible jobs generally have received greater compensation than those performing routine tasks. Accordingly, proponents of comparable worth can argue that there are widely shared intuitions and inherited practices that can form a core of standards for evaluating conceptions of comparable worth. Although the core will have to be expanded in controversial ways to deal with difficult cases, advocates claim that it is equally controversial to rely on the market alone.

In other words, advocates of comparable worth can argue that starting with relatively uncontested judgments and practices, society, through debate, can work toward a *reflective equilibrium* on job comparability.[4] Such a reflective equilibrium will have been reached when the jobs we intuitively feel are comparable are shown to be so by principles we are willing to accept and which yield no conflicting or counterintuitive decisions in other cases. The process of reaching such a reflective equilibrium involves the mutual adjustment and readjustment of judgments and principles until they fit together in harmony. While a reflective equilibrium is reached, if at all, only after an extended process of consideration and debate, the process itself is likely to move us closer to consensus. In any case, advocates would argue that the results are likely to be less unjust and unfair than the way the market currently treats women.

Such an approach does at least show that problems of meaning and measurement are not necessarily unresolvable. Since the process of achieving reflective equilibrium takes considerable time, it will be unclear at any given point in the process whether particular job comparisons are warranted. This would count substantially against attempts to impose standards of comparable worth in one giant leap; for example, through congressional action or Supreme Court decision. Without actually going through the process, we would have no reason to place confidence in the defensibility of the imposed standards.

Moreover, even if this problem could be avoided, perhaps by having individual firms autonomously adopt their own standards of comparable worth, greater problems remain. For one thing, there is no guarantee that a social consensus about comparability will emerge. Individuals may arrive at their own personal reflective equilibriums, but why should those individual systematizations be in agreement with one another? Perhaps even more importantly, even if such a social agreement were to emerge from individual reflection, what moral weight would it have? Why should it be equated with the dictates of equity and justice rather than being regarded as a socially determined political consensus reflecting persuasion and political tradeoffs? How are we to distinguish a mere consensus from rational convergence on a common and defensible point of view?[5]

While such objections surely have force, they may not be decisive. After all, while there is no guarantee that a defensible equilibrium will be reached, there is no guarantee in other areas of social policy either. To the extent that the process of open discussion and democratic decision making is itself justifiable, it is as defensible in the area of comparable worth as in other areas of policy making. At the very least, by encouraging free discussion and criticism of prevailing views, biases are likely to be detected and criteria of comparability are likely to be gradually improved by exposure to the light of rational examination.

Our discussion suggests, then, that although questions of meaning are fundamental, they may not be so severe as to entirely undermine the case for comparable worth. Of course, if there is no clear account of how comparable worth is to be understood, it is

likely to become a political football employed simply to advance the interests of groups that would benefit by its implementation. That may or may not be good policy, but it should not be confused with social justice. Nevertheless, it is at least arguable that defensible standards of comparability, initially based on considered judgments and existing practice, will emerge from the democratic decision-making process. Surely the burden of proof may still be on advocates to show that a given conception of comparable worth is defensible. Nevertheless, there may exist a procedure that would enable them to meet the task. Although healthy scepticism about that procedure may be warranted, it has not been established by the arguments we have considered that comparable worth is a necessarily unintelligible notion to be thrown out on grounds of incomprehensibility alone.

COMPARABLE WORTH AND SOCIAL JUSTICE

As we have seen, women tend to work in only a few of the occupations listed by the Labor Department, and there tend to be very few males in these occupations. For example, 97 percent of registered nurses are female, 99 percent of secretaries are female, and 84 percent of elementary school teachers are female. Moreover, as the number of males in a job category increases, so does the pay.[6] For example, household workers, 95 percent of which are female, make about half the average salary of janitors, 85 percent of which are males. Secretaries make only about three-fourths the average salary of truck drivers, virtually all of whom are male.[7] As stated earlier, overall women's earnings tend to be about 60 percent of the earnings of men in the marketplace.

This suggests a rationale for comparable worth. Most advocates of some version of PCW do not view it as a principle of ideal social justice, which any society must implement if it is to be fully just. . . . However, they argue that when differences in wages reflect sex discrimination, then the market has not operated properly, and corrective application of PCW is called for. . . . The point of instituting comparable worth is to correct for a breakdown in the market involving discrimination against women. Hence, comparable worth need not be instituted across the board, but only in those areas where women have been victimized by unfair treatment.

What is the evidence that women have been discriminated against? The wage gap itself often is cited as evidence of overt discrimination against women by employers. But while it cannot be doubted that such overt discrimination exists, there is considerable disagreement over whether it explains a significant proportion of the wage gap. Broad generalizations of the form, "Women make only X percent of what men make," tend not to be helpful, since it is the significance of such statistical claims that is at issue.

Many labor economists cite such premarket factors as the greater tendency of women to interrupt their careers, sex differences in educational background, and the greater willingness of women to sacrifice career goals for family responsibilities as explanations for a significant part of the wage gap.[8] Thus, according to one recent study of a corporation, even when offered promotions and responsibilities commensurate with those of men, women tend to turn them down more often.[9] Many labor economists argue further that when women make the same market choices as men, they are similarly rewarded, as comparisons of the earnings of never-married working men and women suggest.[10] One typical statement by a labor economist asserts that "perhaps half of the overall 40 percent differential between the earnings of men and women is due to premarket factors."[11]

Statistics by themselves will not show whether the wage gap, as well as the disproportionate representation of women in certain job categories, results from discrimination, the choices women make, or some complex interaction between the two. According to the theory of rational choice, women make rational decisions, based on their own values, to subordinate career to family responsibilities to a greater extent than men. According to critics of such a view, women make such decisions only because their expected return on the market is much less than men because of discrimination, and hence they have less incentive to pursue careers.[12]

We cannot decide between these two views here, but several points can be made. First, even if overt discrimination does play some role in contributing to the wage gap, it is far from clear that comparable worth is an appropriate or necessary response. Existing equal opportunity legislation prohibits the kind of on-the-job discrimination by employers that is at issue. Second, even if on the job discrimination were eliminated, the wage gap would persist so long as women remain concentrated in lower-paying job categories. Such concentration does not seem to be caused primarily by employer discrimination, since it occurs when women first enter the job market and overt discrimination would take place after women were actually on the job.

However, advocates of comparable worth might plausibly distinguish overt on-the-job discrimination from the more systematic and covert discrimination that limits women's choices in the market. For example, until very recently, not only were many jobs held largely by males (such as that of bartender) deemed unsuitable for females, but such prejudices were upheld by the courts.[13] Since women saw that their opportunities in the job market were limited, it became rational for them to devote more time to family than to their careers. Women, in other words, are caught in a vicious circle. "Women stay home because of low wages; women earn low wages because they stay at home."[14] It is widespread social and economic barriers, ranging from guidance counselors who steer women into "acceptable" career paths to socially enforced stereotypes about unsuitable jobs for women, that keep women concentrated in low-paying job categories.

Such theories of covert discrimination seem more relevant to the case for comparable worth than appeals to overt discrimination by employers, since they call into question the legitimacy of the initial situation within which women first make economic choices. However, such approaches are not free from difficulty. For one thing, they run the risk of degenerating into the kind of feminist theories about socialization and conditioning that deny that women function as autonomous agents in the first place. It seems far too self-serving to dismiss the traditional preferences of many women as simply the products of conditioning while always assuming that preferences more to one's liking are the truly autonomous ones. Such a claim might sometimes be true, but is makes it all too easy, as one writer sympathetic to feminism points out, "to slide into the convenient idea that *whenever* women make choices which feminists think they ought not to make, they must be conditioned, so giving feminists an excuse to discount those opinions. . . . The attempt to free women turns into a different way of coercing them."[15] Indeed, the picture of women as brainwashed puppets is unacceptable—and in fact is contradicted by the recent behavior of women in the work force who have integrated many predominantly male job categories.

However, advocates of the theory of covert discrimination need not dismiss the claim that women make autonomous choices. Indeed, the fact that women are moving into predominantly male job categories suggests

that when given the same opportunities and the same expected return, many women will make market choices that are similar to those of men. In this view, the concentration of women in low-paying job categories does reflect women's choices, but their choices frequently don't reflect the values women would express in a fair and equal context for decision making. Rather, they are rational responses to the illegitimately confining set of incentives that women face.

This argument is not implausible, especially when it is shown to be compatible with some aspects of rational choice theory. However, its connection with comparable worth is not clear. Advocates assume that if covert discrimination is a principal factor underlying the wage gap, comparable worth is justified. But is that assumption correct?

For one thing, comparable worth does not seem to be a form of compensation for individual victims of discrimination. Comparable worth affects everyone in a benefited job category, whether or not they have individually suffered from discrimination. Indeed, not only does comparable worth ignore the important principle that compensation should be proportional to injury; it virtually stands it on its head. Older women, who have fewer years left to work but who presumably are most likely to have been victims of discrimination, will receive the fewest benefits. Younger women, particularly those just entering the job market, who are least likely to have been victims of discrimination, will work the greatest number of years under comparable worth and hence will receive the greatest benefits.

Advocates of comparable worth rightly will reply that their goal is not to compensate individuals for discrimination. But what then is the connection between comparable worth and alleged discrimination in the market? Perhaps it is that since the market wage scale is heavily influenced by sex discrimination, comparable worth provides an untainted and therefore fairer standard of compensation. It is not that market wages, set by supply and demand, are *inherently* unfair. Rather, it is that since women in our society have not been in a fair market, comparable worth should replace the wage standards set by a tainted pseudomarket procedure.

Before adopting such a procedure, however, we should be sure that adoption of some form of comparable worth does promote overall fairness. If the adoption of comparable worth would itself generate serious problems of justice and fairness, we would need to consider whether overall gains, in terms of social justice, outweigh losses before recommending adoption.

Consider, first, the problems that would arise if a single standard of comparable worth were promulgated through legislation or as the result of a major court decision. How would such a single standard be arrived at? On what basis would it be selected? What would justify the standard employed? If, as suggested earlier, judgments of comparability are all too likely to rest upon highly controversial and contestable value judgments, why should the new pay scale be any more equitable than the old one? If the standard cannot be justified, those who are disadvantaged by it will have no reason to accept the resulting wage scale as fair. Thus, even without considering the kinds of complications to be discussed below, it is doubtful whether clear gains in equity would be achieved by implementation of a single standard of comparable worth, at least so long as judgments of comparability lack a substantial basis.

Perhaps this difficulty can be avoided by implementing comparable worth on a piece-meal basis, in a long-term effort to reach a reflective equilibrium on comparability. In this view, individual firms, or perhaps individual localities, adopt their own internal comparable worth plans, and these need not be identical.

But this piece-meal approach also raises problems of justice and fairness. One such problem is that workers doing the same job in different firms might have their jobs evaluated totally differently. In Firm X security guards and secretaries might be regarded as comparable while in Firm Y they might not be regarded as comparable. Suppose that as a result of comparability rankings, secretaries in X were paid more than secretaries in Y, even though all the secretaries do the same work. Of course, secretaries in different firms are presently paid differently, just as assistant professors at Harvard may receive higher compensation than assistant professors at a less highly rated institution; but this would not be a result of a purely internal job evaluation scheme that might later be found to be in sharp conflict with our considered judgments.

Perhaps some initial arbitrariness must be expected as the price to be paid as we move toward a less arbitrary reflective equilibrium. After all, as advocates of comparable worth would claim, the market itself reflects inequity in the treatment of women. The temporary unfairness generated by piece-meal approaches to comparable worth may be less than the unfairness that would persist if the status quo were simply allowed to stand.

Even though such a rejoinder has force, other serious problems of equity remain. Some of these are not problems of pure theory, but may become particularly acute when some form of comparable worth is applied in the real world. For example, the piece-meal approach to comparable worth generates economic incentives for firms to select those evaluators whose conceptions of comparable worth create the least economic disadvantage. Each employer reasons that if other employers adopt comparable worth plans without regard to market advantage, she can do better by adopting a less disadvantageous plan. Indeed, even employers with some genuine commitment to comparable worth may have to act in such fashion as a defensive measure against other firms that use comparable worth to secure market gains. In either case, it is rational for the employer to select the conception of comparable worth that departs least from the wage structure the market would have dictated. We are left with the inequitable result that employers most seriously committed to comparable worth are most open to exploitation by less-committed competitors. Indeed, without a defensible standard of comparable worth, how are employers who take unfair advantage of the system even to be identified?

The evaluation of equity becomes even more complicated when other costs of comparable worth are considered. It is extremely likely, for instance, that implementation of some form of comparable worth will lead to an overall rise in wages. Thus, if the work of a firm's clerical staff is found to be comparable to that of higher-paid truckers, it is unlikely that pay cuts can be forced on the truckers. Instead, the salaries of the clerical workers will be raised to a comparable level. This means that the firm's overall costs of production will rise. These costs are generally passed on to consumers, but firms in weak positions may be unable to do this and in some cases may even be forced out of business.

Suppose that costs are passed on to consumers in the form of higher prices. It is by no means clear that such costs will be passed on equitably. If the firm produces necessities, the poor will pay a disproportionate share of the cost, since they spend a higher percentage of their income on necessities than do the more affluent. When the employer in question is the federal, state, or local government, services may be cut in an effort to avoid tax hikes that pay increases would otherwise require. Again these cuts in services may disproportionately affect the relatively poor and powerless.

Perhaps most importantly, many economists argue that comparable worth may not help (and may even harm) the very group it is designed to benefit.[16] If comparable worth raises the employer's costs of doing business, it creates an incentive to reduce the number of employees whose salaries are above the market price. In other words, if comparable worth makes the cost of employing people in certain job categories excessive, employers will have an incentive to reduce the number of people holding such jobs. Since the jobs in question are those held predominantly by women, comparable worth may ultimately create fewer employment opportunities for women than would otherwise have existed.[17]

Of course, it is possible that such dire empirical consequences will not come about, or that negative consequences will be outweighed by gains. The issues here are in part empirical as well as conceptual and moral. The moral point, however, is that harmful or inequitable consequences must be given adequate weight in the evaluation of comparable worth and must not be ignored because of perhaps justified indignation about the economic situation of women in the market.

Finally, when considering questions of equity and fairness, we need to consider how much *weight* comparable worth should be given when it is in conflict with other values, such as efficiency. Suppose, for example, that a state's job evaluation plan finds that electrical engineers and city planners do comparable work but that the state is faced with a shortage of electrical engineers and a surplus of city planners. One way of luring talented engineers to the area, or of inducing students to study electrical engineering, is to raise the wages of the electrical engineers. But if in order to do so the state must also raise the wages of all workers in comparable jobs, not only may the costs be prohibitive but the incentive effects of higher wages would be lost. In spite of social needs, individuals would find it just as desirable to become city planners as electrical engineers. Comparable worth, then, is inefficient in so far as it limits our ability to use higher compensation to attract people to positions where they are needed.

Of course, some losses in efficiency may be warranted by gains in the overall justice of the system. Indeed, it is plausible to think that small gains in justice and fairness outweigh larger losses in overall efficiency, since it is normally wrong to make some people better off by treating others unjustly. On the other hand, losses in efficiency may become so great as to outweigh minor gains in justice or equity, or may themselves constitute an injustice if sufficiently great and distributed in unfair or questionable ways. Clearly, enormous losses in efficiency normally are not justified by small gains in the overall justice or fairness of a system. We have already seen that the costs of comparable worth may be borne disproportionately by the relatively poor and powerless or perhaps even by some of those women the policy was designed to help. But even if these costs are ignored, the inefficiencies generated by departure from the pricing system have to be balanced against whatever gains comparable worth may promote. Thus, before implementing any particular conception of comparable worth, we must decide *the degree to which implementation will be restricted in case of conflict with other values.* In other words, if comparable worth is not to be an absolute to be applied regardless of other costs, what tradeoffs should we be prepared to make?

It will be well to remember here that the line between such values as efficiency, on one hand, and equity and justice, on the other, is not always a sharp one. If the costs of inefficiency are borne disproportionately by the least advantaged and the least powerful, questions of equity and social justice are raised. Our discussion suggests that this may actually be the case with comparable worth. At the very least, we need good reason to think the costs will be fairly distributed before we hop aboard the comparable worth bandwagon.

Finally, before concluding our discussion of equity and fairness, we need to consider in what sense comparable worth might be a "remedy" for the concentration of women in low-paying job categories. It is unlikely that it will eliminate such concentration; in fact, it may perpetuate it. Since institution of comparable worth would remove much of the economic incentive for women to follow the same career paths as men, by compensating "women's" work comparably to "men's" work, it could be argued that women would have less reason to leave traditional female career paths than under the present system.[18] As a matter of empirical fact, in recent years, there has been significant movement of women into some previously male-dominated jobs. In 1960, for example, only 9 percent of insurance adjusters were female, while in 1981, 58 percent were female. Similarly, recent figures reveal that 47 percent of bartenders now are women—a significant change from times when the courts refused even to allow women to be bartenders on the paternalistic grounds that women were too pure to be sullied by such work.[19] Gains in female representation also have been made in law, medicine, and business, although many other job categories tend to remain almost exclusively male. Would comparable worth remove financial incentives for even more sexual integration in the workplace?

We need to be careful of trying to have it both ways on this point. It is surely possible that higher pay for traditionally female jobs will draw more male candidates, contributing to sexual integration through the back door. In turn, increased competition may require more and more women to try for employment in traditionally male job categories. The empirical issues here are difficult, and no prediction is likely to be uncontroversial. But it is at least possible that comparable worth will result in a reduction of jobs in traditionally female employment categories, the consequent forcing out of women who are unprepared for or who prefer not to engage in traditionally male work, and only minimal male interest in traditionally female jobs. While this is undoubtedly a "worst possible case" scenario, is it any less probable than more favorable alternatives? On the other hand, if we don't promulgate a version of comparable worth, will more women in the work force be worse off than if we did? What kind of evidence do we need before we decide? Morally, what is the fairest way of distributing benefits and burdens? What should public policy be under conditions of uncertainty and even radical disagreement on such fundamental points?

CONCLUSIONS

What does our discussion suggest about the overall case for comparable worth? For one thing, it suggests that simplistic approaches and political analysis by slogan are to be rejected. Clarence Pendleton, Chair of the U.S. Civil Rights Commission in 1985, who referred to comparable worth as "looney tunes," surely is mistaken. On the other hand, unquestioning adherence to comparable worth simply because the intent of the policy is to benefit women, or because of support by some feminists, may also be unwarranted.

Just because the situation is complex, it does not follow that nothing sensible can be said about it. One thing rational analysis can do, even when no entirely satisfactory alternative is available, is to set out the costs of holding different positions. This not only puts each of us in a better position to see what objections need to be answered and to see which policy best coheres with our other moral judgments, it may also promote reasonable choice under conditions of uncertainty.

In particular, proponents of comparable worth face serious difficulties. For one thing, it is at best unclear whether jobs can be compared in the way required. Imposition of a single nationwide standard of comparability

seems unjustified, given the difficulties of justification that we have explored. Alternatively, even if we might eventually achieve a societal reflective equilibrium on comparability through the piece-meal approach, we do not have one now. Hence, promulgation of some form of comparable worth will not necessarily promote more equity in the workplace, particularly at the start. Moreover, it also is unclear whether comparable worth will help women as a class, or whether it will only help some women perhaps at significant expense to others. Finally, comparable worth may assign costs to those least able to bear them and may encourage gerrymandering of individual comparable worth plans to secure market advantages.

Proponents of comparable worth may acknowledge these difficulties, but they reply that the overall costs, including any possible inequities, are less serious than those generated by present reliance on the market. Be that as it may, such a reply seems insufficient to justify adoption of comparable worth, at least at the present time. For one thing, as we have seen, the degree to which the wage gap is explained by discrimination, even of the covert variety, is controversial. But even leaving that point aside, is it sensible to adopt a new broad-scale social formula for setting wages without any guarantee, or even reasonable assurances, that gains in equity and social justice will result? Without such reasonable assurances, comparable worth looks more and more like a social policy that will benefit some groups at the expense of others rather than a requirement of social justice.

In short, we started out with the claim that comparable worth is needed to remedy the unjust treatment of women in the workplace. Our discussion suggests, however, that the burden of proof remains on advocates of comparable worth. That is, while the evidence we have considered warrants neither total rejection nor total acceptance of comparable worth, it does support a healthy skepticism. Unless there is good reason to believe that comparisons of jobs will be supportable, that the costs of implementation will be distributed fairly, and that some mechanism will be instituted to balance comparable worth against other values in case of conflict, adoption of comparable worth seems premature at best. Perhaps these problems can be resolved, but adoption of this policy in advance of a resolution would be unwarranted.

This does not mean that the plight of women in the job market should be ignored. Greater enforcement of equal opportunity legislation surely is needed. Where possible, work options such as "flex-time" and the institution of regulated day-care centers can help all workers, male or female, to reconcile responsibilities to both family and career. Greater sensitivity among educators and guidance personnel can contribute to even greater sexual integration in the work force. Finally, the economic contribution that women make to their families can receive greater recognition and protection by law.

Accordingly, before we implement some version of comparable worth, we need to resolve the problems it presents. In view of the real difficulties facing it, we should not just assume that it is a clear requirement of justice and fairness in the workplace. Rather, we need to consider whether comparable worth really is a defensible remedy for social injustice rather than a device that will simply replace old problems with new ones while moving us no closer to the goals of fairness and justice that we all should seek.

NOTES

1. Ronald G. Ehrenberg and Robert S. Smith, *Modern Labor Economics* (Glenview, Ill.: Scott, Foresman and Company, 1982), 396. If a different base year is selected, different results

are obtained. Thus, if 1964 is taken as the base, one finds a slight decrease in the gap by 1979. Clearly, great care must be taken in the use of statistics in this area.

2. "Paying Women What They're Worth," *Report from the Center for Philosophy & Public Policy* 3 (1983): 1–2.

3. For discussion, see Sharon P. Smith, *Equal Pay in the Public Sector: Fact or Fantasy* (Princeton, N.J.: Princeton University Press, 1977).

4. The idea of reflective equilibrium is developed and applied to the justification of a theory of justice by John Rawls, in his *A Theory of Justice* (Cambridge: Harvard University Press, 1971), especially pp. 46–48, 577–579.

5. R. M. Hare argues that appeal to reflective equilibrium amounts to little more than appeal to accepted beliefs in his "Rawls' Theory of Justice," *The Philosophical Quarterly*, 23 (1973): 144–155, 241–251.

6. Bureau of Labor Statistics, 1981, reprinted in "Paying Women What They're Worth."

7. Bureau of Labor Statistics, 1982, reprinted in "Paying Women What They're Worth."

8. For discussion, see Michael Evan Gold, *A Dialogue on Comparable Worth* (Ithaca: Cornell University Press, 1983), and Ehrenberg and Smith, *Modern Labor Economics*, 395–397.

9. See Carl Hoffmann and John Shelton Reed, "Sex Discrimination?—the XYZ Affair," *The Public Interest* 62 (1980): 21–39.

10. U.S. Bureau of Labor Statistics, *Handbook of Labor Statistics*, Table 60. However, other figures show that some significant inequality of results persists even when never married men and women are compared; see Ehrenberg and Smith, *Modern Labor Economics*, pp. 397–398.

11. Ehrenberg and Smith, *Modern Labor Economics*, p. 39.

12. For discussion, see Gold, *A Dialogue on Comparable Worth*, pp. 14–16.

13. See, for example, *Goesaert v. Cleary*, 335 U.S. 464 (1948), upholding a Michigan law which provided that no woman (unless she was the wife or daughter of the male owner) could obtain a bartender's license.

14. Gold, *A Dialogue on Comparable Worth*, p. 14.

15. Janet Radcliffe Richards, *The Sceptical Feminist* (Boston: Routledge and Kegan Paul, 1980).

16. For discussion, see George Hildebrand, "The Market System," in *Comparative Worth*, ed. Rob-

ert Libernash (Washington, D.C.: Equal Treatment Advisory Council, 1980), especially p. 106.

17. This point is debated throughout Gold, *A Dialogue on Comparable Worth.*

18. Conversely, higher salaries for traditionally fe-

male jobs may attract males to compete for such positions. However, this incentive effect may be less than expected if there is a stigma attached to men doing "women's work."

19. "More Women Work at Traditional Male Jobs," *New York Times*, No. 15, 1982, p. C26.

Dealing with Sexual Harassment in the Work Place

A.M. Koral

In the past two years, employers have been faced with a continuing flood of sexual harassment cases—but with a new twist. Increasingly, employees' charges of sexual harassment have been based not on "quid pro quo" requests for sexual favors but on allegations that the employer has created—or permitted—a sexually hostile work environment.

The influx of cases in this emotionally charged area follows the Supreme Court's 1986 decision in *Meritor v. Vinson* [this text, pp. 431–35]. . . .

Cases of environmental sexual harassment have generally arisen in three contexts: (1) supervisors' misconduct, (2) co-workers' sexually harassing activities, and (3) nonemployees' (customers or the public) behavior. . . .

SUPERVISORS' MISCONDUCT

The EEOC guidelines [as discussed in *Meritor*] make employers absolutely liable for sexual harassment perpetrated by supervisors. The employer is liable even if it was not informed about the offensive conduct and even

if it has a clear policy prohibiting and providing a means of reporting sexual harassment.

In *Meritor*, however, the Court specifically rejected the EEOC view that employers are automatically liable for sexual harassment perpetrated by supervisors. But the Supreme court also rejected the opposing view that an employer cannot be held liable unless it received actual notice of the supervisor's misconduct, even if the employer has a general policy against sexual harassment and a reporting procedure that was ignored by the plaintiff. Rather, the Court adopted the view that common-law "agency" principles should be applied in formulating rules of employer liability for supervisor misconduct.

It is impossible to run a sophisticated business without delegating authority to supervisors who will be considered the employer's "agents" under the law. It is, however, quite possible to teach supervisors that certain kinds of conduct will not be tolerated. Several recent cases illustrate instances of improper supervisory behavior and what could have been done to avoid it.

In *Huddleston v. Roger Dean Chevrolet, Inc.*, 845 F.2d 900 (11th Cir. 1988), a female former sales representative in a car dealership brought an action against the dealership and her former supervisor, claiming that she was subjected to sexual harassment in violation of Title VII. According to the court's findings, Huddleston was subjected to repeated and unwelcome sexual harassment by both her co-workers and her supervisor. She was frequently berated by her supervisor in the presence of other salesmen and, on one occasion, was grabbed by the arm and forcibly moved across the sales floor. The supervisor was also present at several sales meetings when sexually derogatory comments were made about Huddleston. The court held that because the supervisor had "actual and apparent authority to alter [the plaintiff's] employment status—including authority to fire her," the plaintiff did not have to prove that the employer knew or should have known of the conduct in question.

What is noteworthy in *Huddleston* is that the conduct complained of was not really sexual at all. Rather, the claim was really very close to a traditional disparate-treatment claim, in that Huddleston alleged little more than that she was treated abusively because she was a woman. The environment created by the supervisor and co-workers was truly hostile, offensive, and intimidating, not because of sexual jokes and innuendos, but because of hostility to Huddleston's gender. Ideally, top management of the enterprise should have anticipated that a hostile situation might arise when a woman began working in a job traditionally occupied by men. The company could then have prepared for the situation by training its supervisors and co-workers and by providing them with an explicit statement of the firm's policy against harassment.

In a similar case, *Hicks v. The Gates Rubber Company*, 44 Empl. Prac. Dec. (CCH) ¶ 37,542 (1987), the Tenth Circuit held that physically aggressive conduct by a male supervisor toward a female employee, even though not overtly sexual, can be considered to establish a hostile environment. The court stated that any pervasive pattern of harassment of an employee that would not occur *but for* the sex of the employee may constitute a hostile work environment. . . .

Clearly, employers that delegate authority to hire and fire to supervisors and managers must see that the authority is not abused. Supervisors must be made to understand that the *threat* to abuse their authority may create liability equal to the liability that actual quid pro quo demands and retaliatory actions could create.

Another feature of the *Sparks* and *Huddleston* cases that should be of interest both to supervisors and employers is that the plaintiffs sued not only their respective employers but also the supervisors *individually*. This phenomenon is not uncommon, and supervisors should understand that they are risking not only their employers' money when they participate in or condone environmental sexual harassment. . . .

Supervisors should be made to understand that company policies against sexual harassment are as serious as other policies and that failure to adhere to these policies will lead to discipline up to and including termination. Employers must be careful how they handle this kind of discipline, however. In several cases, an employer's publicizing the fact that a supervisor was fired for perpetrating sexual harassment has provoked a lawsuit from the ex-supervisor alleging defamation or breach of privacy. . . .

Above all, the employer must see to it that no retaliatory actions by supervisors or co-workers are tolerated. Retaliation against a person for asserting his or her Title VII rights is as serious as any other violation of Title VII, even if the employee is incorrect and there was no underlying harassment.

If the accused harasser does not possess the authority to alter the employment status of another employee, that person is not an "agent" of the employer, and the employer is not liable for that person's action unless it has received notice of them and failed to take prompt reasonable measures to stop the harassing activities. Such notice, however, does not have to be a formal complaint by the victim of the harassment. The fact that a supervisor or other management employee knows or should now of the harassment is sufficient to constitute notice.

HARASSMENT NOT OVERTLY SEXUAL

As with supervisory misconduct, co-workers' harassment can create a hostile environment even though the conduct is not explicitly sexual. In *Hall v. Gus Construction Company, Inc.*, 842 F.2d 1010 (8th Cir. March 25, 1988), three female road construction workers claimed that male members of their construction crew inflicted persistent verbal and physical abuse upon them, creating a hostile work environment that caused their constructive discharge (i.e., they resigned). All three plaintiffs had complained to their supervisor, but the conduct continued, often in the supervisor's presence.

The employer and supervisor argued that several of the allegedly offensive incidents should not have been considered by the court because they were not sexual in nature. The court rejected the defendant's claim, noting that, although much of the name-calling and practical joking inflicted upon the plaintiffs was devoid of sexual overtones, "the predicate acts underlying a sexual harassment claim need not be clearly sexual in nature in order to make out a claim of hostile work environment." The court emphasized that "intimidation and hostility toward women because they are women can obvi-

ously result from conduct other than explicit sexual advances."

In addition to the fact that conduct having no sexual content whatever may create "hostile work environment," it appears that virtually anything having an offensive sexual content can lead to liability. In *Bennett v. Corroon & Black Corp.*, 46 Fair Empl. Prac. Cas. (BNA) 1329 (5th Cir. 1988), for example, an employee discovered that obscene cartoons bearing her name and portraying a variety of exotic sexual acts had been placed in the public men's room in the office building in which she worked. After the cartoons had been up for a week, the company's chief executive saw them, but did nothing to remove them until learning of the plaintiff's strong emotional reaction. Bennett subsequently resigned, and the employer continued to pay her full salary and psychiatric bills until she obtained employment elsewhere.

The employer argued that the alleged harassment was not "based on" the plaintiff's sex, to which the court of appeals responded that "any reasonable person would have to regard [the] cartoons as highly offensive to a woman who seeks to deal with her fellow employees and clients with professional dignity and without the barrier of sexual differentiation and abuse.". . .

CONCLUSION

It is never possible in a culture as traditionally individualistic and independent as ours to control the behavior of all supervisors and employees at all times. However, it is both possible and desirable to define conduct that is unacceptable and to facilitate reporting and correction of unacceptable conduct. . . .

Is Sexual Harassment Coercive?

Larry May
and John C. Hughes

If sexual harassment is to be treated as something more than a purely personal dispute, how do we distinguish the social problem from benevolent forms of social interaction between members of a work hierarchy? We will argue here that sexual harassment of women workers is a public issue because it is inherently coercive, regardless of whether it takes the form of a threat for noncompliance, or of a reward for compliance. We will further argue that the harm of harassment is felt beyond the individuals immediately involved because it contributes to a pervasive pattern of discrimination and exploitation based on sex.

The term *sexual harassment* refers to the intimidation of persons in subordinate positions by those holding power and authority over them in order to exact sexual favors that would ordinarily not have been granted. Sexual harassment of male subordinates by female superiors is conceivable, and probably occurs, albeit infrequently. Positions of authority are more likely to be occupied by males, while women are predominantly relegated to positions of subservience and dependency. Furthermore, strong cultural patterns induce female sexual passivity and acquiescence to male initiative. These factors combine to produce a dominant pattern of male harassment of females. However, it might bear reflecting that the poisoning of the work environment that may result from sexual intimidation may affect members of both sexes, so that sexual harassment should be viewed as more than merely a women's issue.

Truly systematic empirical studies of the incidence of sexual harassment are yet to be done. Most of the studies by social scientists to date suffer from severe methodological flaws. Nevertheless, they reveal a pattern of sexual harassment of working women that is too strong to ignore. Perhaps the most telling study is that conducted by Peggy Crull.[1] Working with a self-selected sample, Crull sought to discern the nature, extent, and effects of sexual harassment on women, as well as the predominant relationship between harasser and victim. Her data show the victims of harassment to be likely to occupy low-status and low-paying positions of economic vulnerability. Fifty-three percent of the victims on her survey were clerical workers (including secretaries, typists, and general office help), with another 15 percent occupying service positions (waitresses, hospital aids, and the like). The most frequent pattern involved verbal harassment, but over half of Crull's respondents also reported incidents of physical harassment that persisted over time despite their protestations, with 39 percent reporting fondling. Twelve percent claimed to have been physically restrained during incidents of sexual harassment.

What is perhaps most significant in Crull's finding is that 79 percent of the men involved held power to fire or promote the victim, while only 16 percent threatened an explicit employment sanction. Seventy-nine percent of the victims complained about the incident to the harasser or to someone in authority (often though not always the same person), but in only 9 percent of the cases did the be-

---

From *Moral Rights in the Workplace*, G. Ezorsky, ed. (Albany, NY: State University of New York Press). Reprinted by permission.

havior stop. Forty-nine percent of the women who complained felt their claims were not taken seriously, while 26 percent experienced retaliation for their complaints. Crull also discovered that whether the victim complained or not, her experience of harassment placed her job in jeopardy. A full 24 percent of Crull's respondents were soon fired, while another 42 percent were pressured into resigning by the intolerable working conditions that resulted from the behavior of their supervisors. If this figure is not striking enough, 83 percent claimed the harassment interfered in some way with their job performance. Indeed, 96 percent reported symptoms of emotional stress, with 63 percent reporting symptoms of physical stress. Twelve percent sought some form of therapeutic help in dealing with these symptoms. Faced with such results, it seems fair to say that sexual harassment is a problem that must be taken seriously.

I

Like most interpersonal transactions, sexual advances may take many forms. There is of course the sincere proposal, motivated by genuine feeling for another, made in a context of mutual respect for the other's autonomy and dignity. Such offers are possible between members of a work hierarchy, but are of no concern here. Rather, we are interested in advances that take the following forms: (1) Sexual threat: "If you don't provide a sexual benefit, I will punish you by withholding a promotion or a raise that would otherwise be due, or ultimately fire you." (2) Sexual offer: "If you provide a sexual benefit, I will reward you with a promotion or a raise that would otherwise not be due." There are also sexual harassment situations that are merely annoying, but without demonstrable sanction or reward. It is worth noting at the outset that all three forms of sexual harassment have been

proscribed under recently promulgated Equal Employment Opportunity Commission guidelines implementing Title VII.[2]

Sexual harassment in the form of threats is coercive behavior that forces the employee to accept a course of conduct she wouldn't otherwise accept. What is wrong with this? Why can't she simply resist the threats and remain as before? Viewed in the abstract, one can seemingly resist threats, for unlike physical restraint, threatening does not completely deny individual choice over her alternatives. A person who is physically restrained is literally no longer in control of her own life. The victim is no longer reaching decisions of her own and autonomously carrying them out. Threats do not have this dramatic effect on a person's autonomy. Rather, the effect of the threat is that the recipient of a threat is much less inclined to act as she would have absent the threat—generally out of fear. Fear is the calculation of expected harm and the decision to avoid it. Reasonably prudent individuals will not, without a sufficiently expected possibility of gain, risk harm. The first thing wrong with sexual threats then is that, for the reasonable person, it now takes a very good reason to resist the threat, whereas no such strength of reasoning was required before to resist a sexual advance.

Sexual threats are coercive because they worsen the objective situation the employee finds herself in. To examine this claim, consider her situation before and after the threat has been made (preproposition stage and postproposition stage).[3] In the preproposition stage, a secretary, for example, is judged by standards of efficiency to determine whether she should be allowed to retain her job. She would naturally view her employer has having power over her, but only in the rather limited domain concerning the job-related functions she performs. Her personal life would be her own. She could choose her own social relationships, without fear that these decisions might adversely affect her job. In the postproposition stage, she can no longer remain employed under the same conditions while not choosing to have relations with her employer. Further, the efficient performance of job-related functions is no longer sufficient for the retention of her job. She can no longer look to her supervisor as one who exercises power merely over the performance of her office duties. He now wields power over a part of her personal life. This may help to explain Crull's finding that many women leave their jobs after such a proposition has been tendered. They cannot simply go on as before, for their new situation is correctly perceived as worse than the old situation.

It is the worsening of the woman's situation after the threat has been made that contributes to the likelihood of her acquiescence to the threat. The perception of job insecurity created by the threat can only be alleviated by her acceptance of the sexual proposition. But what of the woman who prefers to have a sexual relationship with her employer than not to do so? Has this woman also been made objectively worse off than she was before the threat occurred? We contend that she has, for before the threat was made she could pursue her preference without feeling forced to do so. If the liaison developed and then turned sour, she could quit the relationship and not so clearly risk a worsening of her employment situation. Now, however, her continued job success might be held ransom to the continued sexual demands of her employer. This also may adversely affect other women in the business organization. What the employer has done is to establish a precedent for employment decisions based upon the stereotype that values women for their sexuality rather than for their job skills. This has a discriminatory impact on women individually and as a group. Focusing on this effect will shed some light on the harm of both sexual threats and sexual offers.

II

Consider the following case.[4] Barnes was hired as an administrative assistant by the director of a federal agency. In a preemployment interview, the director, a male, promised to promote Barnes, a female, within ninety days. Shortly after beginning her job, (1) the director repeatedly asked her for a date after work hours, even though she consistently refused; (2) made repeated remarks to her that were sexual in nature; and (3) repeatedly told her that if she did not cooperate with him by engaging in sexual relations, her employment status would be affected. After consistently rebuffing him, she finally told him she wished for their relationship to remain a strictly professional one. Thereafter the director, sometimes in concert with others, began a campaign to belittle and demean her within the office. Subsequently she was stripped of most of her job duties, culminating in the eventual abolition of her job. Barnes filed suit, claiming that these actions would not have occurred but for the fact that she was a woman.

Under Title VII, it is now widely accepted that the kind of sexual threat illustrated by this case is an instance of sex discrimination in employment. Such threats treat women differently than men in employment contexts even though gender is not a relevantly applicable category for making employment-related decisions. The underlying principle here is that like persons should be treated alike. Unless there are relevant differences among persons, it is harmful to disadvantage one particular class of persons. In the normal course of events, male employees are not threatened sexually by employers or supervisors. The threats disadvantage a woman in that an additional requirement is placed in her path for successful job retention, one not placed in the path of male employees. When persons who are otherwise similarly situated are distinguished on the basis of their sex, and rewards or burdens are apportioned according to these gender-based classifications, illegal sex discrimination has occurred. Applying this theory of discrimination to Barnes' complaint, the federal appellate court ruled:

> So it was, by her version, that retention of her job was conditioned upon submission to sexual relations—an exaction which the supervisor would not have made of any male. It is much too late in the day to contend that Title VII does not outlaw terms of employment for women which differ appreciably from those set for men and which are not genuinely and reasonably related to the performance on the job. . . . Put another way, she became the target of her superior's sexual desires because she was a woman and was asked to bow to demands as the price for holding her job.[5]

There is a second way in which this behavior might be viewed as discriminatory. Sexual threats also contribute to a pervasive pattern of disadvantaged treatment of women as a group. Under this approach, the harm is not viewed as resulting from the arbitrary and unfair use of gender as a criterion for employment decisions. Rather, emphasis is on the effect the classification has of continuing the subordination of women as a group. The harm results regardless of whether the specific incident could be given an employment rationale or not. Sexual harassment perpetuates sex discrimination, and illustrates the harm that occurs for members of a group that have historically been disadvantaged. This theory was applied to sexual harassment in another federal lawsuit, *Tomkins v. Public Service Gas and Electric Co.*[6] The plaintiff's lawyers argued that employer tolerance of sexual harassment and its pattern of reprisals had a disparate impact upon women as an already disadvantaged group and was inherently degrading to all women.

Sexual threats are harmful to the individual woman because she is coerced and treated unfairly by her employer, disadvantaging her for no good reason. Beyond this, such practices further contribute to a pervasive pattern of disadvantaged status for her and all women in society. The sexual stereotyping makes it less likely, and sometimes impossible, that women will be treated on the basis of job efficiency, intelligence, or administrative skill. These women must now compete on a very different level, and in the case where sexual threats are common or at least accepted, this level is clearly inferior to that occupied by men. The few male employees who are harassed in the workplace suffer the first harm but not the second. We shall next show that there are also two harms of sexual offers in employment, only one of which can also be said to befall men.

III

The harm of sexual offers is much more difficult to identify and analyze. Indeed, some may even see sexual offers as contributing to a differentiation based on sex that advantages rather than disadvantages women, individually and as a group. After all, males cannot normally gain promotions by engaging in sexual relations with their employers. We shall argue, on the contrary, that a sexual offer disadvantages the woman employee by changing the work environment so that she is viewed by others, and may come to view herself, less in terms of her work productivity and more in terms of her sexual allure. This change, like the threat, makes it unlikely that she can return to the preproposition stage even though she might prefer to do so. Furthermore, to offset her diminished status and to protect against later retaliation, a prudent woman would feel that she must accept the offer. Here, sexual offers resemble the coercive threat. The specific harm to women becomes clearer when one looks at the group impact of sexual offers in employment. Women are already more economically vulnerable and socially passive than men. When sexual offers are tendered, exploitation of a woman employee is accomplished by taking advantage of a preexisting vulnerability males generally do not share.

Seduction accomplished through sexual offers and coercive threats blend together most clearly in the mixed case of the sexual offer of a promotion with the lurking threat of retaliation if the offer is turned down. Both combine together to compel the woman to engage in sexual relations with her employer. Gifts are so rare in economic matters that it is best to be suspicious of all offers and to look for their hidden costs. As Crull's study showed, only 16 percent of those harassed were explicitly threatened. Yet 24 percent were fired, and another 42 percent reported that they were forced to resign. This evidence leads us to surmise that sexual offers often contain veiled threats and are for that reason coercive.

Why are the clearly mixed cases, where there is both an offer and a (sometimes only implied) threat, coercive rather than noncoercive? To return to our initial discussion, why is it that one is made worse off by the existence of these proposals? In one sense they enable women to do things they couldn't otherwise do, namely, get a promotion that they did not deserve, thus seeming to be noncoercive. On the other hand, if the woman prefers not having sexual relations with her employer (while retaining her job) to having sexual relations with him (with ensuing promotion), then it is predominantly a threat and more clearly coercive. The best reason for not preferring the postproposition stage is that she is then made worse off if she rejects the proposition, and if she accepts, she nonetheless risks future harm or retaliation. This latter condition is also true for more straightforward offers, as we shall now show.

A number of contemporary philosophers have argued that offers place people in truly advantageous positions, for they can always be turned down with the ensuing return to the preoffer stage.[7] In the case of sexual offers, however, the mere proposal of a promotion in exchange for sexual relations changes the work environment. Once sexual relations are seriously proposed as a sufficient condition for employment success, the woman realizes that this male employer sees her (and will probably continue to see her) as a sex object as well as an employee. A prudent women will henceforth worry that she is not being regarded as an employee who simply happens to be a woman, but rather as a woman made more vulnerable by the fact that she happens to be an employee. If she accepts the offer, she lends credence to the stereotype, and because of this, it is more likely that she may experience future offers or even threats. She would thus worry about her ability to achieve on the basis of her work-related merits. If she rejects the offer, she would still worry about her employer's attitude toward her status as a worker. Furthermore, because of the volatility of sexual feelings, these offers cannot be turned down without the risk of offending or alienating one's employer, something any employee would wish to avoid. She may reasonably conclude from these two considerations that neither postoffer alternative is desirable. This is one of the hidden costs of sexual offers in the workplace.

It may be claimed that such environmental changes are no different for men who can also be the objects of sexual offers in the workplace. One needs to show that the changed environment is worse for those who are women. Sexual employment offers take advantage of unequal power relations that exist between employer and employee so as to force a particular outcome further benefitting those who are already in advantageous positions. But beyond this, sexual offers are doubly exploitative for female employees, because women already enter the employment arena from a position of vulnerability. As we have indicated, this is true because of the history of their economic powerlessness and because of their culturally ingrained passivity and acquiescence in the face of male initiatives. . . .

By blocking a return to the more preferable preoffer alternative, the male employer has acted similarly to the employer who uses sexual threats. The woman is forced to choose between two undesirable alternatives because she cannot have what she would have chosen before the proposal was made. Stressing these hidden costs, which are much greater for women than for men, exposes the coercive element inherent in sexual offers as well as in sexual threats. We are thus led to conclude that both of these employment practices are harmful to women and recently were properly proscribed by the U.S. Equal Employment Opportunity Commission.

NOTES

1. Peggy Crull, "The Impact of Sexual Harassment on the Job: a Profile of the Experiences of 92 Women," *Sexuality in Organizations*, ed. D. A. Neugarten and J. M. Shafritz (Oak Park, Ill.: Moore Publishing Co., 1980), 67–72.

2. 45 Fed. Reg. 74, 677 (1980); 29 C.F.R. 1604.11 (a)

3. We proceed from the general analysis developed by Robert Nozick, "Coercion," *Philosophy, Science and Method*, ed. Morgenbesser, Suppes, and White (New York: St. Martin's Press, 1969).

4. Summary of the facts for *Barnes v. Costel*, 561 F.2d 984 (D.C. Cir. 1977).

5. 561 F.2d 989, 990, 992 n. 68 (D.C. Cir. 1977).

6. 568 F.2d 1044 (3rd Cir. 1977).

7. See Michael Bayles, "Coercive Offers and Public Benefits," *The Personalist*, Vol. 55 (1974); Donald Vandeveer, "Coercion, Seduction and Rights," *The Personalist* Vol. 58 (1977); and Nozick, "Coercion," among others.

Local 28 of the Sheet Metal Workers' International Association v. Equal Employment Opportunity Commission

Supreme Court of the United States

In 1975, petitioners were found guilty of engaging in a pattern and practice of discrimination against black and Hispanic individuals (nonwhites) in violation of Title VII of the Civil Rights Act of 1964, 42 U.S.C. § 2000e *et seq.*, and ordered to end their discriminatory practices, and to admit a certain percentage of nonwhites to union membership by July

106 S.Ct. 3019 (1986).

1981. In 1982 and again in 1983, petitioners were found guilty of civil contempt for disobeying the District Court's earlier orders. They now challenge the District Court's contempt finding, and also the remedies the court ordered both for the Title VII violation and for contempt. Principally, the issue presented is whether the remedial provision of Title VII, see 42 U.S.C. § 2000e–5(g), empowers a district court to order race-conscious relief that may benefit individuals who are not identified victims of unlawful discrimination.

Petitioner Local 28 of the Sheet Metal Workers' International Association (Local 28) represents sheet metal workers employed by contractors in the New York City metropolitan area. Petitioner Local 28 Joint Apprenticeship Committee (JAC) is a management-labor committee which operates a 4-year apprenticeship training program designed to teach sheet metal skills. . . .

Petitioners, joined by the EEOC, argue that the membership goal, the [Employment, Training, Education and Recruitment Fund ("the Fund")] order, and other orders which require petitioners to grant membership preferences to nonwhites are expressly prohibited by § 706(g), 42 U.S.C. § 2000e–5(g), which defines the remedies available under Title VII. Petitioners and the EEOC maintain that § 706(g) authorizes a district court to award preferential relief only to the actual victims of unlawful discrimination. They maintain that the membership goal and the Fund violate this provision, since they require petitioners to admit to membership, and otherwise to extend benefits to, black and Hispanic individuals who are not the identified victims of unlawful discrimination. We reject this argument, and hold that § 706(g) does not prohibit a court from ordering, in appropriate circumstances, affirmative race-conscious relief as a remedy for past discrimination. Specifically, we hold that such relief may be appropriate where an employer or a labor union

has engaged in persistent or egregious discrimination, or where necessary to dissipate the lingering effects of pervasive discrimination.

Section 706(g) states: "If the court finds that the respondent has intentionally engaged in or is intentionally engaging in an unlawful employment practice . . . , the court may enjoin the respondent from engaging in such unlawful employment practice, and order such affirmative action as may be appropriate, which may include, but is not limited to, reinstatement or hiring of employees, with or without back pay . . . , or any other equitable relief as the court deems appropriate. . . . No order of the court shall require the admission or reinstatement of an individual as a member of a union, or the hiring, reinstatement, or promotion of an individual as an employee, or the payment to him of any back pay, if such individual was refused admission, suspended, or expelled, or was refused employment or advancement or was suspended or discharged for any reason other than discrimination on account of race, color, religion, sex, or national origin in violation of . . . this title." 78 Stat. 261, as amended and as set forth in 42 U.S.C. § 2000e–5(g).

The language of § 706(g) plainly expresses Congress' intent to vest district courts with broad discretion to award "appropriate" equitable relief to remedy unlawful discrimination. . . . Nevertheless, petitioners and the EEOC argue that the last sentence of § 706(g) prohibits a court from ordering an employer or labor union to take affirmative steps to eliminate discrimination which might incidentally benefit individuals who are not the actual victims of discrimination. This reading twists the plain language of the statute.

The last sentence of § 706(g) prohibits a court from ordering a union to admit an individual who was "refused admission . . . for any reason other than discrimination." It does not, as petitioners and the EEOC suggest, say that a court may order relief only for the actual victims of past discrimination. The sentence on its face addresses only the situation where a plaintiff demonstrates that a union (or an employer) has engaged in unlawful discrimination, but the union can show that a particular individual would have been refused admission even in the absence of discrimination, for example, because that individual was unqualified. In these circumstances, § 706(g) confirms that a court could not order the union to admit the unqualified individual. . . . In this case, neither the membership goal nor the Fund order required petitioners to admit to membership individuals who had been refused admission for reasons unrelated to discrimination. Thus, we do not read § 706(g) to prohibit a court from ordering the kind of affirmative relief the District Court awarded in this case.

The availability of race-conscious affirmative relief under § 706(g) as a remedy for a violation of Title VII also furthers the broad purposes underlying the statute. Congress enacted Title VII based on its determination that racial minorities were subject to pervasive and systematic discrimination in employment. . . . Title VII was designed "to achieve equality of employment opportunities and remove barriers that have operated in the past to favor an identifiable group of white employees over other employees. . . . In order to foster equal employment opportunities, Congress gave the lower courts broad power under § 706(g) to fashion "the most complete relief possible" to remedy past discrimination. . . .

In most cases, the court need only order the employer or union to cease engaging in discriminatory practices, and award make-whole relief to the individuals victimized by those practices. In some instances, however, it may be necessary to require the employer or union to take affirmative steps to end discrimination effectively to enforce Title VII. Where an employer or union has engaged in particu-

larly longstanding or egregious discrimination, an injunction simply reiterating Title VII's prohibition against discrimination will often prove useless and will only result in endless enforcement litigation. In such cases, requiring recalcitrant employers or unions to hire and to admit qualified minorities roughly in proportion to the number of qualified minorities in the work force may be the only effective way to ensure the full enjoyment of the rights protected by Title VII. . . .

Affirmative race-conscious relief may be the only means available "to assure equality of employment opportunities and to eliminate those discriminatory practices and devices which have fostered racially stratified job environments to the disadvantage of minority citizens.". . . .

Finally, a district court may find it necessary to order interim hiring or promotional goals pending the development of nondiscriminatory hiring or promotion procedures. In these cases, the use of numerical goals provides a compromise between two unacceptable alternatives: an outright ban on hiring or promotions, or continued use of a discriminatory selection procedure. . . .

Many opponents of Title VII argued that an employer could be found guilty of discrimination under the statute simply because of a racial imbalance in his work force, and would be compelled to implement racial "quotas" to avoid being charged with liability. *Weber*, 443 U.S., at 205, 99 S.Ct., at 2728. At the same time, supporters of the bill insisted that employers would not violate Title VII simply because of racial imbalance, and emphasized that neither the Commission nor the courts could compel employers to adopt quotas solely to facilitate racial balancing. *Id.*, at 207, n. 7, 99 S.Ct., at 2729, n. 7. The debate concerning what Title VII did and did not require culminated in the adoption of § 703(j), which stated expressly that the statute did not require an employer or labor union to adopt quotas or preferences simply because of a racial imbalance. However, while Congress strongly opposed the use of quotas or preferences merely to maintain racial balance, it gave no intimation as to whether such measures should be acceptable as *remedies* for Title VII violations. . . .

The purpose of affirmative action is not to make identified victims whole, but rather to dismantle prior patterns of employment discrimination and to prevent discrimination in the future. Such relief is provided to the class as a whole rather than to individual members; no individual is entitled to relief, and beneficiaries need not show that they were themselves victims of discrimination. In this case, neither the membership goal nor the Fund order required petitioners to indenture or train particular individuals, and neither required them to admit to membership individuals who were refused admission for reasons unrelated to discrimination. . . .

The court should exercise its discretion with an eye towards Congress' concern that race-conscious affirmative measures not be invoked simply to create a racially balanced work force. In the majority of Title VII cases, the court will not have to impose affirmative action as a remedy for past discrimination, but need only order the employer or union to cease engaging in discriminatory practices and award make-whole relief to the individuals victimized by those practices. However, in some cases, affirmative action may be necessary in order effectively to enforce Title VII. As we noted before, a court may have to resort to race-conscious affirmative action when confronted with an employer or labor union that has engaged in persistent or egregious discrimination. Or such relief may be necessary to dissipate the lingering effects of pervasive discrimination. Whether there might be other circumstances that justify the use of court-ordered affirmative action is a matter that we need not decide here. We note only that a court should consider whether affirmative action is necessary to remedy past dis-

crimination in a particular case before imposing such measures, and that the court should also take care to tailor its orders to fit the nature of the violation it seeks to correct. In this case, several factors lead us to conclude that the relief ordered by the District Court was proper.

First, both the District Court and the Court of Appeals agreed that the membership goal and Fund order were necessary to remedy petitioners' pervasive and egregious discrimination. The District Court set the original 29% membership goal upon observing that "[t]he record in both state and federal courts against [petitioners] is replete with instances of their bad faith attempts to prevent or delay affirmative action." 401 F.Supp., at 488. The court extended the goal after finding petitioners in contempt for refusing to end their discriminatory practices and failing to comply with various provisions of RAAPO. In affirming the revised membership goal, the Court of Appeals observed that "[t]his court has twice recognized Local 28's long continued and egregious racial discrimination . . . and Local 28 has presented no facts to indicate that our earlier observations are no longer apposite." 753 F.2d, at 1186. In light of petitioners' long history of "foot-dragging resistance" to court orders, simply enjoining them from once again engaging in discriminatory practices would clearly have been futile. Rather, the District Court properly determined that affirmative race-conscious measures were necessary to put an end to petitioners' discriminatory ways.

Both the membership goal and Fund order were similarly necessary to combat the lingering effects of past discrimination. In light of the district Court's determination that the union's reputation for discrimination operated to discourage nonwhites from even applying for membership, it is unlikely that an injunction would have been sufficient to extend to nonwhites equal opportunities for employment. Rather, because access to admission, membership, training, and employment in the industry had traditionally been obtained through informal contacts with union members, it was necessary for a substantial number of nonwhite workers to become members of the union in order for the effects of discrimination to cease. The Fund, in particular, was designed to insure that nonwhites would receive the kind of assistance that white apprentices and applicants had traditionally received through informal sources. On the facts of this case, the District Court properly determined that affirmative, race-conscious measures were necessary to assure the equal employment opportunities guaranteed by Title VII.

Second, the District Court's flexible application of the membership goal gives strong indication that it is not being used simply to achieve and maintain racial balance, but rather as a benchmark against which the court could gauge petitioners' efforts to remedy past discrimination. The court has twice adjusted the deadline for achieving the goal, and has continually approved of changes in the size of the apprenticeship classes to account for the fact that economic conditions prevented petitioners from meeting their membership targets; there is every reason to believe that both the court and the administrator will continue to accommodate *legitimate* explanations for petitioners' failure to comply with the court's orders. Moreover, the District Court expressly disavowed any reliance on petitioners' failure to meet the goal as a basis for the contempt finding, but instead viewed this failure as symptomatic of petitioners' refusal to comply with various subsidiary provisions of RAAPO. In sum, the District Court has implemented the membership goal as a means by which it can measure petitioners' compliance with its orders, rather than as a strict racial quota.

Third, both the membership goal and the Fund order are temporary measures. Under

AAAPO "[p]referential selection of [union members] will end as soon as the percentage of [minority union members] approximates the percentage of [minorities] in the local labor force." *Weber,* 443 U.S., at 208–209, 99 S.Ct., at 2730; see *United States v. City of Alexandria,* 614 F.2d, at 1366. Similarly, the Fund is scheduled to terminate when petitioners achieve the membership goal, and the court determines that it is no longer needed to remedy past discrimination. The District Court's orders thus operate "as a temporary tool for remedying past discrimination without attempting to 'maintain' a previously achieved balance." *Weber,* 443 U.S., at 216, 99 S.Ct., at 2734 (Blackmun, J., concurring).

Finally, we think it significant that neither the membership goal nor the Fund order "unnecessarily trammel[s] the interests of white employees." *Id.* 443 U.S., at 208, 99 S.Ct., at 2730; *Teamsters,* 431 U.S., at 352–353, 97 S.Ct., at 1863–1864. Petitioners concede that the District Court's orders did not require any member of the union to be laid off, and did not discriminate against *existing* union members. See *Weber, supra,* 443 U.S., at 208, 99 S.Ct., at 2729–2730; see also 30 St. Louis U.L.J., at 264. While whites seeking admission into the union may be denied benefits extended to their nonwhite counterparts, the court's orders do not stand as an absolute bar to such individuals; indeed, a majority of new union members have been white. See *City of Alexandria, supra,* at 1366. Many provisions of the court's orders are race-neutral (for example, the requirement that the [Joint Apprenticeship Committee (JAC)] assign one apprentice for every four journeyman workers), and petitioners remain free to adopt the provisions of AAAPO and the Fund order for the benefit of white members and applicants.

Petitioners also allege that the membership goal and Fund order contravene the equal protection component of the Due Process Clause of the Fifth Amendment because they deny benefits to white individuals based on race. We have consistently recognized that government bodies constitutionally may adopt racial classifications as a remedy for past discrimination. . . . We conclude that the relief ordered in this case passes even the most rigorous test—it is narrowly tailored to further the Government's compelling interest in remedying past discrimination.

In this case, there is no problem . . . with a proper showing of prior discrimination that would justify the use of remedial racial classifications. Both the District Court and Court of Appeals have repeatedly found petitioners guilty of egregious violations of Title VII, and have determined that affirmative measures were necessary to remedy their racially discriminatory practices. More importantly, the District Court's orders were properly tailored to accomplish this objective. First, the District Court considered the efficacy of alternative remedies, and concluded that, in light of petitioners' long record of resistance to official efforts to end their discriminatory practices, stronger measures were necessary. . . . Again, petitioners concede that the District Court's orders did not disadvantage *existing* union members. While white applicants for union membership may be denied certain benefits available to their nonwhite counterparts, the court's orders do not stand as an absolute bar to the admission of such individuals; again, a majority of those entering the union after entry of the court's orders have been white. We therefore conclude that the District Court's orders do not violate the equal protection safeguards of the Constitution.

Finally, Local 28 challenges the District Court's appointment of an administrator with broad powers to supervise its compliance with the court's orders as an unjustifiable interference with its statutory right to self-governance. See 29 USC § 401(a). Preliminarily, we note that while AAAPO gives the administrator broad powers to oversee petitioners' membership practices, Local 28 retains complete control over its other affairs. Even with respect to membership, the administrator's job is to insure that petitioners comply with the court's orders and admit sufficient numbers of nonwhites; the administrator does not select the particular individuals that will be admitted, that task is left to union officials. In any event, in light of the difficulties inherent in monitoring compliance with the court's orders, and especially petitioners' established record of resistance to prior state and federal court orders designed to end their discriminatory membership practices, appointment of an administrator was well within the District Court's discretion. . . .

To summarize our holding today, six members of the Court agree that a district court may, in appropriate circumstances, order preferential relief benefitting individuals who are not the actual victims of discrimination as a remedy for violations of Title VII, . . . that the District Court did not use incorrect statistical evidence in establishing petitioners' nonwhite membership goal, that the contempt fines and Fund order were proper remedies for civil contempt, and that the District Court properly appointed an administrator to supervise petitioners' compliance with the court's orders. Five members of the Court agree that in this case, the District Court did not err in evaluating petitioners' utilization of the apprenticeship program, and that the membership goal and the Fund order are not violative of either Title VII or the Constitution. The judgment of the Court of Appeals is hereby *Affirmed*. . . .

City of Richmond v. J.A. Croson Company

Supreme Court of the United States

In this case, we confront once again the tension between the Fourteenth Amendment's guarantee of equal treatment to all citizens, and the use of race-based measures to ameliorate the effects of past discrimination on the opportunities enjoyed by members of minority groups in our society. . . .

I

On April 11, 1983, the Richmond City Council adopted the Minority Business Utilization Plan (the Plan). The Plan required prime contractors to whom the city awarded construction contracts to subcontract at least 30% of the dollar amount of the contract to one or more Minority Business Enterprises (MBEs). Ordinance No. 83–69–59, codified in Richmond, Va., City Code, § 12–156(a) (1985). The 30% set-aside did not apply to city contracts awarded to minority-owned prime contractors. *Ibid.*

The Plan defined an MBE as "[a] business at least fifty-one (51) percent of which is owned and controlled . . . by minority group members." § 12–23, p. 941. "Minority group members" were defined as "[c]itizens of the United States who are Blacks, Spanish-speaking, Orientals, Indians, Eskimos, or Aleuts." *Ibid.* There was no geographic limit to the Plan; an otherwise qualified MBE from anywhere in the United States could avail itself of the 30% set-aside. The Plan declared that it was "remedial" in nature, and enacted "for

the purpose of promoting wider participation by minority business enterprises in the construction of public projects." § 12–158(a). The Plan expired on June 30, 1988, and was in effect for approximately five years. *Ibid.*

The Plan authorized the Director of the Department of General Services to promulgate rules which "shall allow waivers in those individual situations where a contractor can prove to the satisfaction of the director that the requirements herein cannot be achieved." § 12–157. To this end, the Director promulgated Contract Clauses, Minority Business Utilization Plan (Contract Clauses). Section D of these rules provided: "No partial or complete waiver of the foregoing [30% set-aside] requirement shall be granted by the city other than in exceptional circumstances. To justify a waiver, it must be shown that every feasible attempt has been made to comply, and it must be demonstrated that sufficient, relevant, qualified Minority Business Enterprises . . . are unavailable or unwilling to participate in the contract to enable meeting the 30% MBE goal.". . .

The Plan was adopted by the Richmond City Council after a public hearing. App. 9–50. Seven members of the public spoke to the merits of the ordinance: five were in opposition, two in favor. Proponents of the set-aside provision relied on a study which indicated that, while the general population of Richmond was 50% black, only .67% of the city's prime construction contracts had been awarded to minority businesses in the 5-year period from 1978 to 1983. . . .

There was no direct evidence of race discrimination on the part of the city in letting contracts or any evidence that the city's prime contractors had discriminated against minority-owned subcontractors. . . .

. . . On September 6, 1983, the city of Richmond issued an invitation to bid on a project for the provision and installation of certain plumbing fixtures at the city jail. On September 30, 1983, Eugene Bonn, the regional manager of J.A. Croson Company (Croson), a mechanical plumbing and heating contractor, received the bid forms. The project involved the installations of stainless steel urinals and water closets in the city jail. Products of either of two manufacturers were specified, Acorn Engineering Company (Acorn) or Bradley Manufacturing Company (Bradley). Bonn determined that to meet the 30% set-aside requirement, a minority contractor would have to supply the fixtures. The provision of the fixtures amounted to 75% of the total contract price. . . .

Bonn subsequently began a search for potential MBE suppliers. The only potential MBE fixture supplier was Melvin Brown, president of Continental Metal Hose, hereafter referred to as "Continental." However, because of Continental's inability to obtain credit approval, Continental was unable to submit a bid by the due date of October 13, 1983. Shortly thereafter and as a direct result, Croson submitted a request for a waiver of the 30% set-aside. Croson's waiver request indicated that Continental was "unqualified" and that the other MBEs contacted had been unresponsive or unable to quote. Upon learning of Croson's waiver request, Brown contacted an agent of Acorn, the other fixture manufacturer specified by the city. Based upon his discussions with Acorn, Brown subsequently submitted a bid on the fixtures to Croson. Continental's bid was $6,183.29 higher than the price Croson had included for the fixtures in its bid to the city. This constituted a 7% increase over the market price for the fixtures. With added bonding and insurance, using Continental would have raised the cost of the project by $7,663.16. On the same day that Brown contacted Acorn, he also called city procurement officials and told them that Continental, an MBE, could supply the fixtures specified in the city jail contract. On November 2, 1983, the city denied Croson's waiver request, indicating that Croson had 10 days to submit an MBE Utilization Commitment Form, and warned that failure to do so could result in its bid being considered unresponsive.

Croson wrote the city on November 8, 1983. In the letter, Bonn indicated that Continental was not an authorized supplier for either Acorn or Bradley fixtures. He also noted that Acorn's quotation to Brown was subject to credit approval and in any case was substantially higher than any other quotation Croson had received. Finally, Bonn noted that Continental's bid had been submitted some 21 days after the prime bids were due. In a second letter, Croson laid out the additional costs that using Continental to supply the fixtures would entail, and asked that it be allowed to raise the overall contract price accordingly. The city denied both Croson's request for a waiver and its suggestion that the contract price be raised. The city informed Croson that it had decided to rebid the project. On December 9, 1983, counsel for Croson wrote the city asking for a review of the waiver denial. The city's attorney responded that the city had elected to rebid the project, and that there is no appeal of such a decision. Shortly thereafter Croson brought this action under 42 U.S.C. § 1983 in the Federal District Court for the Eastern District of Virginia, arguing that the Richmond ordinance was unconstitutional on its face and as applied in this case.

The District Court upheld the Plan in all respects . . . [and held that] the 30% figure was "reasonable in light of the undisputed fact that minorities constitute 50% of the population of Richmond." *Ibid.*

Croson sought certiorari from this Court. We granted the writ, vacated the opinion of the Court of Appeals, and remanded the case for further consideration in light of our intervening decision in *Wygant v. Jackson Board of Education,* 476 U.S. 267, 106 S.Ct. 1842, 90 L.Ed.2d 260 (1986). . . .

On remand, a divided panel of the Court of Appeals struck down the Richmond set-aside program as violating both prongs of strict scrutiny under the Equal Protection Clause of the Fourteenth Amendment. *J.A. Croson Co. v. Richmond,* 822 F.2d 1355 (CA4 1987) (*Croson II*). . . .

In this case, the debate at the city council meeting "revealed no record of prior discrimination by the city in awarding public contracts. . . . " *Croson II, supra,* at 1358. Moreover, the statistics comparing the minority population of Richmond to the percentage of *prime* contracts awarded to minority firms had little or no probative value in establishing prior discrimination in the relevant market, and actually suggested "more of a political than a remedial basis for the racial preference." 822 F.2d, at 1359. The court concluded that, "[i]f this plan is supported by a compelling governmental interest, so is every other plan that has been enacted in the past or that will be enacted in the future." *Id.,* at 1360.

The Court of Appeals went on to hold that even if the city had demonstrated a compelling interest in the use of a race-based quota, the 30% set-aside was not narrowly tailored to accomplish a remedial purpose. The court found that the 30% figure was "chosen arbitrarily" and was not tied to the number of minority subcontractors in Richmond or to any other relevant number. *Ibid.* The dissenting judge argued that the majority had "misconstrue[d] and misapplie[d]" our decision in

Wygant. 822 F.2d, at 1362. We noted probable jurisdiction of the city's appeal, . . . and we now affirm the judgment.

II

. . . Congress, unlike any State or political subdivision, has a specific constitutional mandate to enforce the dictates of the Fourteenth Amendment. The power to "enforce" may at times also include the power to define situations which *Congress* determines threaten principles of equality and to adopt prophylactic rules to deal with those situations. . . .

That Congress may identify and redress the effects of society-wide discrimination does not mean that, *a fortiori,* the States and their political subdivisions are free to decide that such remedies are appropriate. Section 1 of the Fourteenth Amendment is an explicit *constraint* on state power, and the States must undertake any remedial efforts in accordance with that provision. To hold otherwise would be to cede control over the content of the Equal Protection Clause to the 50 state legislatures and their myriad political subdivisions. The mere recitation of a benign or compensatory purpose for the use of a racial classification would essentially entitle the States to exercise the full power of Congress under § 5 of the Fourteenth Amendment and insulate any racial classification from judicial scrutiny under § 1. We believe that such a result would be contrary to the intentions of the Framers of the Fourteenth Amendment, who desired to place clear limits on the States' use of race as a criterion for legislative action, and to have the federal courts enforce those limitations. . . .

It would seem equally clear, however, that a state or local subdivision (if delegated the authority from the State) has the authority to eradicate the effects of private discrimination within its own legislative jurisdiction. This authority must, of course, be exercised within the constraints of § 1 of the Fourteenth Amendment. . . . As a matter of state law, the city of Richmond has legislative authority over its procurement policies, and can use its spending powers to remedy private discrimination, if it identifies that discrimination with the particularity required by the Fourteenth Amendment. . . .

Thus, if the city could show that it had essentially become a "passive participant" in a system of racial exclusion practiced by elements of the local construction industry, we think it clear that the city could take affirmative steps to dismantle such a system. It is beyond dispute that any public entity, state or federal, has a compelling interest in assuring that public dollars, drawn from the tax contributions of all citizens, do not serve to finance the evil of private prejudice. . . .

III.A

The Equal Protection Clause of the Fourteenth Amendment provides that "[N]o State shall . . . deny to *any person* within its jurisdiction the equal protection of the laws" (emphasis added). As this Court has noted in the past, the "rights created by the first section of the Fourteenth Amendment are, by its terms, guaranteed to the individual. The rights established are personal rights." *Shelley v. Kraemer,* 334 U.S. 1, 22, 68 S.Ct. 836, 846, 92 L.Ed. 1161 (1948). The Richmond Plan denies certain citizens the opportunity to compete for a fixed percentage of public contracts based solely upon their race. To whatever racial group these citizens belong, their "personal rights" to be treated with equal dignity and respect are implicated by a rigid rule erecting race as the sole criterion in an aspect of public decision making. . . .

Classifications based on race carry a danger of stigmatic harm. Unless they are strictly

reserved for remedial settings, they may in fact promote notions of racial inferiority and lead to a politics of racial hostility. . . .

III.B

The District Court found the city council's "findings sufficient to ensure that, in adopting the Plan, it was remedying the present effects of past discrimination in the *construction industry*." Supp.App. 163 (emphasis added). Like the "role model" theory employed in *Wygant,* a generalized assertion that there has been past discrimination in an entire industry provides no guidance for a legislative body to determine the precise scope of the injury it seeks to remedy. It "has no logical stopping point." *Wygant, supra,* at 275, 106 S.Ct., at 1847 (plurality opinion). "Relief" for such an ill-defined wrong could extend until the percentage of public contracts awarded to MBEs in Richmond mirrored the percentage of minorities in the population as a whole.

Appellant argues that it is attempting to remedy various forms of past discrimination that are alleged to be responsible for the small number of minority businesses in the local contracting industry. Among these the city cites the exclusion of blacks from skilled construction trade unions and training programs. This past discrimination has prevented them "from following the traditional path from laborer to entrepreneur." Brief for Appellant 23-24. The city also lists a host of nonracial factors which would seem to face a member of any racial group attempting to establish a new business enterprise, such as deficiencies in working capital, inability to meet bonding requirements, unfamiliarity with bidding procedures, and disability caused by an inadequate track record. *Id.,* at 25–26, and n. 41.

While there is no doubt that the sorry history of both private and public discrimination in this country has contributed to a lack of opportunities for black entrepreneurs, this observation, standing alone, cannot justify a rigid racial quota in the awarding of public contracts in Richmond, Virginia. Like the claim that discrimination in primary and secondary schooling justifies a rigid racial preference in medical school admissions, an amorphous claim that there has been past discrimination in a particular industry cannot justify the use of an unyielding racial quota.

It is sheer speculation how many minority firms there would be in Richmond absent past societal discrimination, just as it was sheer speculation how many minority medical students would have been admitted to the medical school at Davis absent past discrimination in educational opportunities. Defining these sorts of injuries as "identified discrimination" would give local governments license to create a patchwork of racial preferences based on statistical generalizations about any particular field of endeavor.

These defects are readily apparent in this case. The 30% quota cannot in any realistic sense be tied to any injury suffered by anyone. . . .

There is nothing approaching a prima facie case of a constitutional or statutory violation by *anyone* in the Richmond construction industry. . . .

The District Court accorded great weight to the fact that the city council designated the Plan as "remedial." But the mere recitation of a "benign" or legitimate purpose for a racial classification, is entitled to little or no weight. . . . Racial classifications are suspect, and that means that simple legislative assurances of good intention cannot suffice. . . .

In this case, the city does not even know how many MBEs in the relevant market are qualified to undertake prime or subcontracting work in public construction projects. . . . Nor does the city know what percentage of total city construction dollars minority firms now receive as subcontractors on prime contracts let by the city.

To a large extent, the set-aside of sub-contracting dollars seems to rest on the unsupported assumption that white prime contractors simply will not hire minority firms. . . . Without any information on minority participation in subcontracting, it is quite simply impossible to evaluate overall minority representation in the city's construction expenditures.

The city and the District Court also relied on evidence that MBE membership in local contractors' associations was extremely low. Again, standing alone this evidence is not probative of any discrimination in the local construction industry. There are numerous explanations for this dearth of minority participation, including past societal discrimination in education and economic opportunities as well as both black and white career and entrepreneurial choices. Blacks may be disproportionately attracted to industries other than construction. . . . The mere fact that black membership in these trade organizations is low, standing alone, cannot establish a prima facie case of discrimination. . . .

While the States and their subdivisions may take remedial action when they possess evidence that their own spending practices are exacerbating a pattern of prior discrimination, they must identify that discrimination, public or private, with some specificity before they may use race-conscious relief. . . .

In sum, none of the evidence presented by the city points to any identified discrimination in the Richmond construction industry. We, therefore, hold that the city has failed to demonstrate a compelling interest in apportioning public contracting opportunities on the basis of race. To accept Richmond's claim that past societal discrimination alone can serve as the basis for rigid racial preferences would be to open the door to competing claims for "remedial relief" for every disadvantaged group. The dream of a Nation of equal citizens in a society where race is irrelevant to personal opportunity and achievement would be lost in a mosaic of shifting preferences based on inherently unmeasurable claims of past wrongs. . . .

IV

Since the city must already consider bids and waivers on a case-by-case basis, it is difficult to see the need for a rigid numerical quota. . . .

Given the existence of an individualized procedure, the city's only interest in maintaining a quota system rather than investigating the need for remedial action in particular cases would seem to be simple administrative convenience. But the interest in avoiding the bureaucratic effort necessary to tailor remedial relief to those who truly have suffered the effects of prior discrimination cannot justify a rigid line drawn on the basis of a suspect classification. . . . Under Richmond's scheme, a successful black, Hispanic, or Oriental entrepreneur from anywhere in the country enjoys an absolute preference over other citizens based solely on their race. We think it obvious that such a program is not narrowly tailored to remedy the effects of prior discrimination.

V

. . . Because the city of Richmond has failed to identify the need for remedial action in the awarding of its public construction contracts, its treatment of its citizens on a racial basis violates the dictates of the Equal Protection Clause. Accordingly, the judgment of the Court of Appeals for the Fourth Circuit is Affirmed.

Meritor Savings Bank, FSB v. Vinson Et al.

Supreme Court of the United States

This case presents important questions concerning claims of workplace "sexual harassment" brought under Title VII of the Civil Rights Act of 1964, 78 Stat. 253, as amended, 42 U. S. C. § 2000e *et seq.*

I

In 1974, respondent Mechelle Vinson . . . started as a teller-trainee, and thereafter was promoted to teller, head teller, and assistant branch manager. She worked at the same branch for four years, and it is undisputed that her advancement there was based on merit alone. In September 1978, respondent notified her supervisor, Sidney Taylor that she was taking sick leave for an indefinite period. On November 1, 1978, the bank discharged her for excessive use of that leave.

Respondent brought this action against Taylor and the bank, claiming that during her four years at the bank she had "constantly been subjected to sexual harassment" by Taylor in violation of Title VII. She sought injunctive relief, compensatory and punitive damages against Taylor and the bank, and attorney's fees.

At the 11-day bench trial, the parties presented conflicting testimony about Taylor's behavior during respondent's employment.† Respondent testified that during her probationary period as a teller-trainee, Taylor treated her in a fatherly way and made no sexual advances. Shortly thereafter, however, he invited her out to dinner and, during the course of the meal, suggested that they go to a motel to have sexual relations. At first she refused, but out of what she described as fear of losing her job she eventually agreed. According to respondent, Taylor thereafter made repeated demands upon her for sexual favors, usually at the branch, both during and after business hours; she estimated that over the next several years she had intercourse with him some 40 or 50 times. In addition, respondent testified that Taylor fondled her in front of other employees, followed her into the women's restroom when she went there alone, exposed himself to her, and even forcibly raped her on several occasions. These activities ceased after 1977, respondent stated, when she started going with a steady boyfriend.

Respondent also testified that Taylor touched and fondled other women employees of the bank, and she attempted to call witnesses to support this charge. But while some supporting testimony apparently was admitted without objection, the District Court did not allow her "to present wholesale evidence of a pattern and practice relating to sexual advances to other female employees in her case in chief, but advised her that she might well be able to present such evidence in rebuttal to the defendants' cases." *Vinson v. Taylor*, 22 EPD ¶30,708, p. 14,693, n. 1, 23 FEP Cases 37, 38–39, n. 1 (DC 1980). Respondent did not offer such evidence in rebuttal. Finally, respondent testified that be-

cause she was afraid of Taylor she never reported his harassment to any of his supervisors and never attempted to use the bank's complaint procedure.

Taylor denied respondent's allegations of sexual activity, testifying that he never fondled her, never made suggestive remarks to her, never engaged in sexual intercourse with her, and never asked her to do so. He contended instead that respondent made her accusations in response to a business-related dispute. The bank also denied respondent's allegations and asserted that any sexual harassment by Taylor was unknown to the bank and engaged in without its consent or approval.

The District Court denied relief and . . . ultimately found that respondent "was not the victim of sexual harassment and was not the victim of sexual discrimination" while employed at the bank.

Although it concluded that respondent had not proved a violation of Title VII, the District Court nevertheless went on to address the bank's liability. After noting the bank's express policy against discrimination, and finding that neither respondent nor any other employee had ever lodged a complaint about sexual harassment by Taylor, the court ultimately concluded that "the bank was without notice and cannot be held liable for the alleged actions of Taylor."

The Court of Appeals for the District of Columbia Circuit reversed. . . . The court stated that a violation of Title VII may be predicated on either of two types of sexual harassment: harassment that involves the conditioning of concrete employment benefits on sexual favors, and harassment that, while not affecting economic benefits, creates a hostile or offensive working environment. . . . Believing that "Vinson's grievance was clearly of the [hostile environment] type," and that the District Court had not considered whether a violation of this type had occurred, the court concluded that a remand was necessary.

---

†Like the Court of Appeals, this Court was not provided a complete transcript of the trial. We therefore rely largely on the District Court's opinion for the summary of the relevant testimony.

The court further concluded that the District Court's findings that any sexual relationship between respondent and Taylor "was a voluntary one" did not obviate the need for a remand. . . .

As to the bank's liability, the Court of Appeals held that an employer is absolutely liable for sexual harassment practiced by supervisory personnel, whether or not the employer knew or should have known about the misconduct. The court relied chiefly on Title VII's definition of "employer" to include "any agent of such a person," 42 U. S. C. §2000e(b), as well as on the EEOC Guidelines. The court held that a supervisor is an "agent" of his employer for Title VII purposes, even if he lacks authority to hire, fire, or promote, since "the mere existence—or even the appearance—of a significant degree of influence in vital job decisions gives any supervisor the opportunity to impose on employees.". . . .

In accordance with the foregoing, the Court of Appeals reversed the judgment of the District Court and remanded the case for further proceedings. . . .

II

Title VII of the Civil Rights Act of 1964 makes it "an unlawful employment practice for an employer . . . to discriminate against any individual with respect to his compensation, terms, conditions, or privileges for employment, because of such individual's race, color, religion, sex, or national origin.". . . .

Respondent argues, and the Court of Appeals held, that unwelcome sexual advances that create an offensive or hostile working environment violate Title VII. Without question, when a supervisor sexually harasses a subordinate because of the subordinate's sex, that supervisor "discriminate[s]" on the basis of sex. . . .

First, the language of Title VII is not limited to "economic" or "tangible" discrimination. The phrase "terms, conditions, or privileges of employment" evinces a congressional intent " 'to strike at the entire spectrum of disparate treatment of men and women' " in employment. . . .

Second, in 1980 the EEOC issued Guidelines specifying that "sexual harassment," as there defined, is a form of sex discrimination prohibited by Title VII. . . .

In defining "sexual harassment," the Guidelines first describe the kinds of workplace conduct that may be actionable under Title VII. These include "[u]nwelcome sexual advances, requests for sexual favors, and other verbal or physical conduct of a sexual nature." 29 CFR § 1604.11(a) (1985). Relevant to the charges at issue in this case, the Guidelines provide that such sexual misconduct constitutes prohibited "sexual harassment," whether or not it is directly linked to the grant or denial of an economic *quid pro quo*, where "such conduct has the purpose or effect of unreasonably interfering with an individual's work performance or creating an intimidating, hostile, or offensive working environment.". . . .

In concluding that so-called "hostile environment" (*i. e.*, non *quid pro quo*) harassment violates Title VII, the EEOC drew upon a substantial body of judicial decisions and EEOC precedent holding that Title VII affords employees the right to work in an environment free from discriminatory intimidation, ridicule, and insult. . . .

Since the Guidelines were issued, courts have uniformly held, and we agree, that a plaintiff may establish a violation of Title VII by proving that discrimination based on sex has created a hostile or abusive work environment. . . .

For sexual harassment to be actionable, it must be sufficiently severe or pervasive "to alter the conditions of [the victim's] employment and create an abusive working environment." *Ibid.* Respondent's allegations in this case—which include not only pervasive harassment but also criminal conduct of the most serious nature—are plainly sufficient to state a claim for "hostile environment" sexual harassment. . . .

The fact that sex-related conduct was "voluntary," in the sense that the complainant was not forced to participate against her will, is not a defense to a sexual harassment suit brought under Title VII. The gravamen of any sexual harassment claim is that the alleged sexual advances were "unwelcome." 29 CFR § 1604.11(a) (1985). While the question whether particular conduct was indeed unwelcome presents difficult problems of proof and turns largely on credibility determinations committed to the trier of fact, the District Court in this case erroneously focused on the "voluntariness" of respondent's participation in the claimed sexual episodes. The correct inquiry is whether respondent by her conduct indicated that the alleged sexual advances were unwelcome, not whether her actual participation in sexual intercourse was voluntary. . . .

III

Although the District Court concluded that respondent had not proved a violation of Title VII, it nevertheless went on to consider the question of the bank's liability. Finding that "the bank was without notice" of Taylor's alleged conduct, and that notice to Taylor was not the equivalent of notice to the bank, the court concluded that the bank therefore could not be held liable for Taylor's alleged actions. The Court of Appeals took the opposite view, holding that an employer is strictly liable for a hostile environment created by a supervisor's sexual advances, even though the employer neither knew nor reasonably

could have known of the alleged misconduct. The court held that a supervisor, whether or not he possesses the authority to hire, fire, or promote, is necessarily an "agent" of his employer for all Title VII purposes, since "even the appearance" of such authority may enable him to impose himself on his subordinates. . . .

The EEOC, in its brief as *amicus curiae*, contends that courts formulating employer liability rules should draw from traditional agency principles. Examination of those principles has led the EEOC to the view that where a supervisor exercises the authority actually delegated to him by his employer, by making or threatening to make decisions affecting the employment status of his subordinates, such actions are properly imputed to the employer whose delegation of authority empowered the supervisor to undertake them. . . . Thus, the courts have consistently held employers liable for the discriminatory discharges of employees by supervisory personnel, whether or not the employer knew, should have known, or approved of the supervisor's actions. . . .

The EEOC suggests that when a sexual harassment claim rests exclusively on a "hostile environment" theory, however, the usual basis for a finding of agency will often disappear. In that case, the EEOC believes, agency principles lead to

"a rule that asks whether a victim of sexual harassment had reasonably available an avenue of complaint regarding such harassment, and, if available and utilized, whether that procedure was reasonably responsive to the employee's complaint. If the employer has an expressed policy against sexual harassment and has implemented a procedure specifically designed to resolve sexual harassment claims, and if the victim does not take advantage of that procedure, the employer should be shielded from liability absent actual knowledge of the sexually hostile environment (obtained, *e. g.*, by the filing of a charge with the EEOC or a comparable state agency). In all other cases, the employer will be liable if it has actual knowledge of the harassment or if, considering all the facts of the case, the victim in question had no reasonably available avenue for making his or her complaint known to appropriate management officials." Brief for United States and EEOC as *Amici Curiae* 26.

As respondent points out, this suggested rule is in some tension with the EEOC Guidelines, which hold an employer liable for the acts of its agents without regard to notice. 29 CFR § 1604.11(c) (1985). The Guidelines do require, however, an "examin[ation of] the circumstances of the particular employment relationship and the job [f]unctions performed by the individual in determining whether an individual acts in either a supervisory or agency capacity."

We hold that the Court of Appeals erred in concluding that employers are always automatically liable for sexual harassment by their supervisors. For the same reason, absence of notice to an employer does not necessarily insulate that employer from liability. *Ibid.*

Finally, we reject petitioner's view that the mere existence of a grievance procedure and a policy against discrimination, coupled with respondent's failure to invoke that procedure, must insulate petitioner from liability. While those facts are plainly relevant, the situation before us demonstrates why they are not necessarily dispositive. Petitioner's general nondiscrimination policy did not address sexual harassment in particular, and thus did not alert employees to their employer's interest in

correcting that form of discrimination. App. 25. Moreover, the bank's grievance procedure apparently required an employee to complain first to her supervisor, in this case Taylor. Since Taylor was the alleged perpetrator, it is not altogether surprising that respondent failed to invoke the procedure and report her grievance to him. Petitioner's contention that respondent's failure should insulate it from liability might be substantially stronger if its procedures were better calculated to encourage victims of harassment to come forward.

IV

In sum, we hold that a claim of "hostile environment" sex discrimination is actionable under Title VII, that the District Court's findings were insufficient to dispose of respondent's hostile environment claim, and that the District Court did not err in admitting testimony about respondent's sexually provocative speech and dress. As to employer liability, we conclude that the Court of Appeals was wrong to entirely disregard agency principles and impose absolute liability on employers for the acts of their supervisors, regardless of the circumstances of a particular case.

Accordingly, the judgment of the Court of Appeals reversing the judgment of the District Court is affirmed, and the case is remanded for further proceedings consistent with this opinion.

CASE 1.   *"Harassment" at Brademore Electric*

Maura Donovan is a recent graduate of UCLA who now works as a low-level administrative assistant for Keith Sturdivant at the Brademore Electric Corporation, a large Los

Angeles electrical contractor. Keith interviewed and hired Maura to work directly under him.

Maura had been employed at Brademore

only three weeks when Keith approached her to go out on the weekend. Maura was taken somewhat by surprise and declined, thinking it best not to mix business and pleasure. But two days later Keith persisted, saying that Maura owed him something in return for his "getting" her the job. Maura was offended by this comment, knowing that she was well qualified for the position, but Keith seemed lonely, almost desperate, and she agreed to go with him to the Annual Renaissance Fair on Saturday afternoon. As it turned out, she did not have an enjoyable time. She liked the fair, but found Keith a bit crude and at times almost uncivil in the way he treated employees at the Fair. She hoped he would not ask her out again.

But Monday morning he came back with the idea that they go on an overnight sailboat trip with some of his friends the next weekend. Maura politely declined. But Keith persisted, insisting that she owed her job to him. Maura found herself dreading the times she saw Keith coming down the corridor. What had been a very nice work environment for her had turned into a place of frequent dread. She spent a lot of time working to avoid Keith.

For four straight weeks, Keith came up with a different idea for how they might spend the weekend—always involving an overnight trip. Maura always declined. After the second week, she lied and told him that she was dating a number of other men. She said she was quite interested in two of these men and that she did not see any future with Keith. Keith's reaction was to become even more insistent that they had a future together and to continue to ask her out.

Keith had become quite infatuated with Maura. He watched her every movement, whenever he had the opportunity. Sometimes he openly stared at her as she walked from one office to another. He began to have sex-ual fantasies about her, which he disclosed to two male supervisors. However, he never mentioned to Maura that he had in mind any form of sexual relationship.

Keith's direct supervisor, Vice President B. K. Singh, became aware of Keith's interest in Maura from two sources. First, he was told about the sexual fantasies by one of Keith's two male friends to whom Keith made the disclosures. Second, Maura had that same day come to his office to complain about what she considered sexual harassment. Mr. Singh became concerned about a possible contaminated work environment, but he did not think that he or Maura could make any form of harassment charge stick. The company had no corporate policy on harassment. Mr. Singh considered the situation to be just another case of one employee asking another out and being overly persistent. Mr. Singh decided not to do anything right away, not even to discuss the problem with Keith. He was worried that if he did take up the matter with Keith at such an early stage, he would himself be creating a hostile work environment. He believed Keith's advances would have to worsen before he should intervene or take the problem to the President.

Questions

1. Is Keith's conduct a case of sexual harassment? Is it a clear case, a borderline case, or no case at all?
2. Is it justifiable for Mr. Singh to adopt a position of nonintervention? Should he speak with Keith? What would you do if you were in his position?
3. Does the fact that Maura agreed to go out with Keith once mean that she has encouraged him to make further requests? If so, was she sufficiently discouraging at a later point?

CASE 2. *Sing's Chinese Restaurant**

The Bali Hai Corporation started as a small Chinese restaurant in Boston, Massachusetts, in 1959. The restaurant was an exact replica of a Chinese pagoda. Over the years, the restaurant, owned and managed by Arnold Sing, became known for its food and atmosphere. Customers were made to feel as if they were actually in China. In the last few years, Sing decided to incorporate and open other similar restaurants throughout the country. Sing, who had come to the United States from China in the early 1940s, was very strict in keeping up his reputation of good food and atmosphere. He had a policy of hiring only waiters of Oriental descent. He felt this added to his customers' dining pleasure and made for a more authentic environment. For kitchen positions, though, Sing hired any qualified applicants.

About a year ago in Sing's Bali Hai of Washington, D.C., there was a shortage of waiters. An advertisement was placed in the newspaper for waiters, and the manager of the store was instructed by Sing to hire only Orientals. The manager was also reminded of Bali Hai's commitment to a reputation of good food and atmosphere. Two young men, one black and one white, both with considerable restaurant experience, applied for the waiter's jobs. The manager explained the policy of hiring only Orientals to the young men, and he also told them he could get them work in his kitchen. The two men declined the positions and instead went directly to the area Equal Employment Office and filed a complaint. Sing's defense was that the policy was only to preserve the atmosphere of the restaurant. He said the Oriental waiters were needed to make it more authentic. Sing added that he hired blacks, whites, and other races for his kitchen help.

Questions

1. Is Sing's defense a good one under the law? Why or why not?
2. Is Sing's defense a good one under the standards of morality? Why or why not?
3. Is this a case of "preferential hiring"? "Of reverse discrimination"?

CASE 3. *USAir's Hiring Channel*†

In June 1991 USAir agreed to abandon an informal hiring practice it had long used: USAir employees and influential friends of the company would no longer be invited to recommend pilots who were their acquaintances or relatives directly to the two vice-presidents of Flying, thereby skirting the usual company screens for minimum qualifications. Under this former policy, a vice president could pursue or otherwise act on these recommendations as he or she saw fit. All other pilot applicants were first screened in the front office. Only white pilots had ever been hired through the alternative hiring channel.

Two black pilots who became employed by USAir—one through a standard system of application and the other through a corporate merger—complained that they would have

---

*Copyright Kenneth A. Kovach and reprinted with permission of the author.
†This case was prepared by Tom L. Beauchamp on the basis of *Garland v. USAir, Inc.*, 767 F. Supp. 715 (April 25, 1991), and 56 Fair Empl. Prac. Cas. (BNA) 377 (June 10, 1991).

been hired earlier if USAir's backdoor policy had not been in place. They claimed the policy was a preferential hiring system for friends and relatives of employees and that it discriminated against blacks. These two pilots claimed rights to back pay and seniority. They sued for both.

A federal judge held that they were entitled to immediate back pay and seniority, dating to the time they likely would have been hired but were not because of the preferential policy. The court found that several white pilots who had been hired instead of the two black pilots did not meet minimum objective criteria used in standard front-office screens. Conversely, many black applicants who did meet these criteria had never been hired. The court also found that the alternative hiring channel lacked access to black applicants, and, therefore, was a segregated system that advantaged whites and intentionally discriminated against blacks on the basis of race. In

the final settlement, USAir agreed both to discontinue all existing special channels of recommendation and hiring *and* to establish a new special channel for recruiting black employees for the next thirty months.

Questions

1. Does the new "special channel for recruiting black employees" unjustifiably discriminate against new white applicants? Is this special channel an instance of affirmative action?

2. Was USAir guilty of intentional discrimination? Did the corporate policy create a segregated system?

3. Is it justifiable for businesses to use any form of hiring that bypasses screens in employment offices? For example, in small family businesses, can family members legitimately bypass normal screens?

CASE 4.   *Weber and the Kaiser Aluminum Steelworkers Plan*

In 1974 the United Steelworkers of America and Kaiser Aluminum & Chemical Corp. established an employment agreement that addressed an overwhelming racial imbalance in employment in Kaiser plants. Of primary concern was the lack of skilled black craftsworkers. This concern arose because of an ongoing exclusion of black craftsworkers. In an attempt to remove the disparity and create a fair employment policy, an affirmative action plan ("the plan") was agreed to, whereby

> black craft-hiring goals were set for each Kaiser plant equal to the percentage of blacks in the respective local labor forces . . . [and] to enable plants to meet these goals, on-the-job training programs were established to teach unskilled workers—black and white—the skills necessary to become craftsworkers (443 U.S. 198 [1979]).

Under the guidelines of the plan, 50 percent of those selected for the newly instituted training program were to be black employees *until* the goals of the plan were accomplished, after which the 50 percent provision would be discontinued.

Such a plan was instituted at the Gramercy, Louisiana, plant from which the major problems had arisen and where blacks constituted less than 2 percent of the skilled craftsworkers, although they were approximately 39 percent of the Gramercy labor force. Subsequently, thirteen trainees, of which seven were black, were selected in accordance with the guidelines of the plan. The black trainees had less seniority than many white production workers who were denied training status. Brian Weber, one such production worker, argued that he and others had been unduly

---

This case was abstracted from Supreme Court materials by Katie Marshall and Tom L. Beauchamp.

discriminated against. He thought the plan was a violation of Title VII of the Civil Rights Act of 1964. A District Court and a Court of Appeals held that Title VII had been violated. The U.S. Supreme Court then addressed the issue of whether employers were forbidden from enacting such affirmative action plans to alleviate racial imbalances.

The Supreme Court held that forbidding such affirmative action plans under Title VII would be in direct contradiction to its purpose, because the statutory words call upon "employers and unions to self-examine and to self-evaluate their employment practices and to endeavor to eliminate, so far as possible, the vast vestiges of an unfortunate and ignominious page in this country's history" (433 U.S. 204 [1978]). The Supreme Court concluded that the Kaiser plan purposes "mirror[ed] those of the statute," because both

the plan and the statute "were designed to break down old patterns of racial segregation [and] both were structured to open employment opportunities for Negroes in occupations which have been traditionally closed to them." The Supreme Court reversed the opinions of the lower courts (433 U.S. 208 [1978]).

Questions

1. Are the percentage figures in this case "quotas"? Are they justified under the circumstances?
2. Does Kaiser have a fair employment policy? If not, how should it be revised?
3. Is there reverse discrimination against Weber? If so, is it justified?

CASE 5.   *Comparable Worth in the Female Section*

During the early 1970s, the County of Washington, Oregon, established salary scales for its guards in the county jail. Female guards in the female section were paid one-third to one-eighth less than male guards of the comparable rank and experience in the male section.

The female guards complained that they were paid unequal wages for work substantially equal to that performed by male guards and that the underlying reason was sex discrimination. The pay scale for males had been determined by the county's survey of outside markets for guards, but the pay scale for females was not similarly set. The survey indicated that the average outside pay standard is that female correctional officials are paid about 95 percent as much as male correctional officials. Nonetheless, the County of Washington decided to pay women only 70 percent of the salary paid to men. The county

thus had scaled down the female guards' work below the outside market level. However, the county had not had difficulty hiring women in the local region at its pay scales.

The county said there were two major differences in the jobs for men and women: The male guards supervised more than ten times as many prisoners per guard as did the female guards, and the females, unlike the males, were required to spend part of their time on clerical jobs (considered less valuable by the county). The county therefore held that the females' jobs were not substantially equal to those of the male guards and merited less than equal pay. The county objected to the idea that any outside authority such as the courts could evaluate its pay scales without placing virtually every employer at risk of scrutiny by the courts for not paying comparable wages.

This case was prepared by Tom L. Beauchamp.

Questions

1. Is this a "comparable worth" case, or a case involving sex discrimination or a simple case of fair salaries? Is it all of these?
2. Are there relevant differences between the male jobs and the female jobs that would justify a lower scale for women?

Suggested Supplementary Readings

ARVEY, RICHARD D. "Sex Bias in Job Evaluation Procedures." *Personnel Psychology* 39 (1986).

BOXILL, BERNARD. *Blacks and Social Justice*. Totowa, N.J.: Rowman and Littlefield, 1992.

BROWNE, M. NEIL, AND ANDREA M. GIAMPETRO. "The Socially Responsible Firm and Comparable Worth." *American Business Law Journal* 25 (Fall 1987).

BURSTEIN, PAUL. *Discrimination, Jobs, and Politics*. Chicago: University of Chicago Press, 1985.

COHEN, MARSHALL, THOMAS NAGEL, AND THOMAS SCANLON, eds. *Equality and Preferential Treatment*. Princeton, N.J.: Princeton University Press, 1977.

DANDEKER, NATALIE. "Contrasting Consequences: Bringing Charges of Sexual Harassment Compared with Other Cases of Whistleblowing." *Journal of Business Ethics* 9 (1990).

EXTEJT, MARIAN M., AND M. BOCKANIC. "Issues Surrounding the Theories of Negligent Hiring and Failure to Fire." *Business and Professional Ethics Journal* 8, No. 4 (1989).

EZORSKY, GERTRUDE. *Racism and Justice*. Ithaca, N.Y.: Cornell University Press, 1991.

FISCHEL, DANIEL, AND EDWARD LAZEAR. "Comparable Worth and Discrimination in Labor Markets." *University of Chicago Law Review* 53 (Summer 1986).

FULLINWIDER, ROBERT. *The Reverse Discrimination Controversy*. Totowa, N.J.: Rowman and Allanheld, 1980.

GRIDER, DOUG, AND MIKE SHURDEN. "The Gathering Storm of Comparable Worth." *Business Horizons* 30 (1987).

GUNDERSON, MORLEY. "Male-Female Wage Differentials and Policy Responses." *Journal of Economic Literature* 27 (March 1989).

HOFFMANN, CARL C. AND KATHLEEN HOFFMANN. "Does Comparable Worth Obscure the Real Issues?" *Personnel Journal* 66 (January 1987).

LEAP, TERRY L., AND LARRY R. SMELTZER. "Racial Remarks in the Workplace: Humor or Harassment?" *Harvard Business Review* 62 (1984).

LYNCH, F. R. *Invisible Victims: White Males and the Crisis of Affirmative Action*. Westport, Conn.: Greenwood Press, 1989.

MICELI, MARCIA P., and others. "Employers' Pay Practices and Potential Responses to 'Comparable Worth' Litigation." *Journal of Business Ethics* 7 (May 1988).

NEWTON, LISA. "Bakke and Davis: Justice, American Style." *National Forum: The Phi Kappa Phi Journal* 58 (Winter 1978).

OLNEY, PETER B., JR. "Meeting the Challenge of Comparable Worth." *Compensation and Benefits Review* 19 (March-April 1987).

ORAZEM, PETER F., AND J. PETER MATTILA. "The Implementation Process of Comparable Worth." *Journal of Political Economy* 98 (February 1990).

PHILIPS, MICHAEL. "Preferential Hiring and the Question of Competence." *Journal of Business Ethics* 10 (1991).

POSNER, RICHARD. "The Bakke Case and the Future of 'Affirmative Action.'" *California Law Review* 67 (January 1979).

————. "An Economic Analysis of Sex Discrimination Laws." *University of Chicago Law Review* 56 (Fall 1989).

RAISIAN, JOHN, and others. "Pay Equity and Comparable Worth." *Contemporary Policy Issues* 4 (1986).

REMICK, HELEN. *Comparable Worth and Wage Discrimination*. Philadelphia: Temple University Press, 1984.

SCHEIBAL, WILLIAM. "*AFSCME v. Washington:* The Continued Viability of Title VII Comparable Worth Actions." *Public Personnel Management* 17 (Fall 1988).

SCHRAGE, LAURIE. "Some Implications of Comparable Worth." *Social Theory and Practice* 13 (1987).

SHANEY, MARY JO. "Perceptions of Harm: The Consent Defense in Sexual Harassment Cases." *Iowa Law Review* 71 (1986).

SINGER, M. S. AND A. E. SINGER. "Justice in Preferential Hiring." *Journal of Business Ethics* 10 (1991).

SULLIVAN, FREDERICK. "Sexual Harassment: The Supreme Court's Ruling." *Personnel* 63 (1986).

THOMAS, LAURENCE. "On Sexual Offers and Threats." In *Moral Rights in the Workplace*, edited by Gertrude Ezorsky. Albany, N.Y.: State University of New York Press, 1987.

Thought and Action 5 (Spring 1989). Special issue on sexual harassment.

U.S. Supreme Court. *Burwell v. Eastern Air Lines, Inc.* 450 U.S. 965 (1981).

————. *Firefighters v. Stotts*, 467 U.S. 561 (1984).

————. *Johnson v. Transportation Agency*, 480 U.S. 616 (1987).

————. *McDonnell Douglas Corp. v. Green*, 411 U.S. 792 (1973).

————. *Price Waterhouse v. Hopkins*, 490 U.S. ____, 104 L.Ed. 268 (1989).

————. *United Steelworkers v. Weber*, 443 U.S. 193 (1979).

————. *United States v. Paradise*, 480 U.S. 149 (1987).

————. *Watson v. Forth Worth Bank & Trust*, 487 U.S. 977 (1988).

————. *Wygant v. Jackson Bd. of Education*, 476 U.S. 267 (1986).

WASSERSTROM, RICHARD. "Racism, Sexism and Preferential Treatment: An Approach to the Topics." *UCLA Law Review* 24 (1977).

YORK, KENNETH M. "Defining Sexual Harassment in Workplaces: A Policy-Capturing Approach." *Academy of Management Journal* 32 (1989).

Chapter Seven

Gathering, Concealing, and Gilding Information

ADVERTISING IS A noticeable way businesses present information to the public, but it is neither the only form of communication nor the most important use of information in business. Sales information, government reports, annual reports containing financial audits, public relations presentations, warranties, trade secrets, and public education and public health campaigns are other vital means by which corporations manage and communicate information.

A wide array of moral problems stalk these activities. Some problems are commonplace—for example, withholding vital information, distorting truth, and bluffing. Other problems of information control are more subtle. These include using information to manipulate customers, using annual reports as public relations devices, giving calculated "news releases" to the press, avoiding disclosures to workers that directly affect their health and welfare, and industrial spying.

Rights of autonomy and free choice are at the center of these discussions. In some forms, withholding information and manipulating advertising messages threaten to undermine the consumer's free choice. Deceptive and misleading statements limit freedom by restricting the range of choice and causing a person to do what he or she otherwise might not do.

Aside from these *autonomy*-based problems, there are *harm*-based problems that may have little to do with issues of free choice. For example, when the Nestle Corporation was pressured to suspend infant formula advertising and aggressive marketing products in developing countries, the controversy focused less on the freedom-based issue of poor dissemination of information than on the felt need to educate a population about breastfeeding and about the risks and benefits of the use of infant formula. Harm-based issues are mentioned in this chapter, but restrictions of free choice by manipulative influence is a focal point.

FREE CHOICE OR UNFAIR INFLUENCE?

A classic defense of American business practice is that business provides the public with what it wants. In the free enterprise system the consumer is king, and the market responds to consumer demands. This response to consumer demand is said to represent the chief strength of a market economy over a collectivist system: Freedom of consumer choice is unaffected by government and corporate controls.

But consider the following controversy about freedom of choice. The Federal Trade Commission (FTC) in late 1984 and early 1985 "reconsidered" its rule prohibiting supermarket advertising of items not in stock. The rule had been enacted in 1971 to combat frustration among shoppers who found empty shelves in place of advertised goods and often wound up substituting more expensive items. FTC officials suggested that the rule may have been unduly burdensome for the supermarket industry and that "market forces" would eliminate or curtail those who dishonestly advertise. Consumer groups argued that relaxing the rule would permit more expensive stores to lure shoppers by advertising low prices, leading many shoppers to spend more overall than they would have spent in a low-budget store. Mark Silbergeld of the Consumers Union argued that the Commission was acting in ignorance of the *real purpose* of supermarket advertising, which is to present a "come-on to get people into their stores."[1]

On the one hand, if advertisements do succeed in manipulating persons to buy products through false or empty advertising, these purchase decisions may not be as free as consumers think or as supermarket companies suggest. On the other hand, shoppers can refuse to buy substitutes for the missing goods or can return later for the unavailable items. Does such advertising, then, represent a deprivation of free choice, or is it rather an example of how free choice determines market forces? Can it function as both for certain populations of persons?

Control over a person is exerted through some form of influence, but not all influences serve to control. Influences are of many types. Some are desired and accepted by those who are influenced, whereas others are unwelcome. Many influences can easily be resisted by most persons; others can prove irresistible. In many cases human reactions to influences such as corporate-sponsored information and advertising presentations cannot be determined nor can they be easily studied. Frank Dandrea, vice-president of marketing for Schiefflin & Co., the importer of Hennessy's Cognac, reports that in their advertisements "The idea is to show a little skin, a little sex appeal, a little tension."[2] This effect is accomplished by showing a scantily clad woman holding a brandy snifter and staring provocatively in response to a man's interested glance. Hennessy uses sex and humor. Other companies use rebates and coupons. These are attempts to influence, and little question remains that they are at least partially successful. But the influence of these strategies and the moral acceptability of these influences are not well understood.

However, there is a continuum of controlling influence in our daily lives, running from coercion, at the controlling end of the continuum, to persuasion and education, both noncontrolling influences. Coercion requires an intentional and successful influence through an irresistible threat of harm. Coercion negates freedom because it entirely controls action. Persuasion, by contrast, involves a successful appeal to reason in order to convince a person to freely accept what is advocated by the persuader. Like informing, persuading is entirely compatible with free choice.

Manipulation covers the great gray area of influence. It is a catch-all category that suggests getting people to do what is advocated without resort to coercion and without appeal to reasoned argument. In the case of *informational* manipulation, on which parts of this chapter concentrate, information is managed so that the manipulee will do what the manipulator intends. Whether such uses of information necessarily compromise or restrict free choice is an unresolved issue. One plausible view is that some manipulations—for instance the use of rewards such as free trips or lottery coupons in direct mail advertising—are compatible with free choice, whereas others—such as deceptive offers or tantalizing ads aimed at young children—are not compatible with free choice. Beer and wine advertising aimed at teenagers and young adults has been under particularly harsh criticism in recent years, on grounds that sex, youth, fun, and beauty are directly linked to dangerous products, with noticeable success.

Many problems with advertising fall somewhere between acceptable and unacceptable manipulation. Consider two examples: Anheuser-Busch ran a television commercial for its Budweiser Beer showing some working men heading for a brew at day's end. The commercial begins with a shot of the Statue of Liberty in the background, includes close-up shots of a construction crew working to restore the Statue, and ends with the words, "This Bud's for you, you know America takes pride in what you do." This may seem innocent, but the Liberty-Ellis Island Foundation accused Anheuser-Busch of a "blatant attempt to dupe [i.e., manipulate] consumers" by implying that Budweiser was among the sponsors helping to repair the Statue. Moreover, Anheuser-Busch had refused such a sponsorship when invited by the Foundation and its rival, Stroh Brewing Company, had subsequently accepted an exclusive brewery sponsorship.[3]

A second case comes from Kellogg's advertising for its All-Bran product. The company ran a campaign linking its product to the prevention of cancer, apparently causing an immediate increase in sales of 41 percent for All-Bran. Many food manufacturers advertise the low-salt, low-fat, low-calorie, or high-fiber content of their products, but Kellogg went further, citing a specific product as a way to combat a specific disease. It is illegal to make claims about the health benefits of a specific food product without FDA approval, and Kellogg did not have this approval. Yet officials at both the National Cancer Institute and FDA found the ads perplexing. On the one hand, officials at these agencies agree that a high-fiber, low-fat diet containing some of the ingredients in All-Bran does help prevent cancer. On the other hand, no direct association exists between eating a given product and preventing cancer, and certainly no single food product can function like a drug as a preventative or remedy for such a disease.

The Kellogg ad strongly suggested that eating All-Bran was all one needs to do to prevent cancer. Such a claim is potentially misleading in several respects. The ad does not suggest how much fiber people should eat, nor does it note that people can consume too much fiber while neglecting other essential minerals. Furthermore, no direct scientific evidence links consuming this product and preventing cancer, and this product could not be expected to affect all types of cancer. Does Kellogg promise a reward that is manipulative, or is the ad, as Kellogg claims, basically a truthful, health-promotion campaign? Does it contain elements of both?

These examples help illustrate the broad categories on the continuum of controlling influences that are under examination in this chapter. Other forms of influence such as *indoctrination* and *seduction* might be mentioned, but in the end, especially for advertising, the difference between manipulation and persuasion will prove to be the key variation.

DECEPTION, BLUFFING, AND STRATEGIC DISCLOSURE

Manipulation can take many forms: offering rewards, threatening punishments, instilling fear, and so forth. The principal form discussed in this chapter is the manipulation of information. Here the manipulator modifies a person's sense of options by affecting the person's understanding of the situation. Deception, bluffing, and the like are used by the manipulator to change not the person's *actual* options but only the person's *perception* of the options. The more a person is deprived of a relevant understanding in the circumstances, the greater the effect on the person's free choice.

One does not need extensive experience in business to know that many deceptive practices, like bluffing and slick sales techniques, are both widely practiced and widely accepted. It is common knowledge that automobile dealers do not expect people to pay the sticker price for automobiles. A certain amount of quoting of competitors, bargaining, moving "extras" under the basic price, and going to managers for approval is part of the game. A similar situation prevails in real estate transactions, where the asking price for a house is seldom the anticipated selling price, and at bargaining sessions where labor leaders overstate wage demands and management understates the wage increases it is willing to grant.

The intent is to manipulate, however gently. In his article, "Is Business Bluffing Ethical?" Albert Z. Carr recognizes that such practices are characteristic of business and maintains that they are analogous to the game of poker. Just as conscious misstatement, concealment of pertinent facts, exaggeration, and bluffing are morally acceptable in poker, they are also acceptable in business. What makes such practices acceptable, Carr says, is that all parties understand the rules of the game. In advertising, for example, exaggeration and bluffing are understood to be part of the selling game. Only an extraordinarily naive person would believe advertisements without casting a skeptical eye on the images and words coming from a television set.

But there are moral limits to the game, even if the rules of the game are grasped by all. Suppose that Pamela is willing to sell her home for $60,000 if that is the best price she can get. She puts the home on the market for $70,000. A potential buyer's initial offer is $60,000. She turns it down and tells him that $65,000 is her rock-bottom price. He purchases the home for $65,000. Many people would characterize her behavior as shrewd bluffing rather than an immoral lie. Many people would think more of her, rather than less. However, suppose she manufactured the claim that another party was writing up a contract to buy the house for $65,000 and that she would sell it to him for the same $65,000 price because both she and he were Baptists. In this case many people would maintain that she had told at least one lie, probably two. But are the lies unjustified or merely part of the game? Would it make any moral difference if she were to have her brother pretend to make her an offer and draw up a fake contract so that the prospective buyer would be pressured to buy?

The sophistication of the audience, standard practice, and the intention of the informer all need to be considered to decide whether gilded information is unacceptably presented. Manipulation and deception can result as much from what is not said as from what is said. For example, true information can be presented out of context and hence can be misleading. The reasoning of Chief Justice Earl Warren in *FTC v. Colgate-Palmolive Co.* demonstrates how the omission of facts can be misleading at times, whereas the omission of others is not misleading. At issue is a television commercial depicting someone shaving sandpaper that had been generously lathered with Rapid Shave. The FTC found that Rapid Shave could soften and shave sandpaper, but the sandpaper needed to soak in Rapid Shave for approximately eighty minutes before it could be shaved. On this basis, the FTC declared the ad a deceptive trade practice because the television viewer was not informed about the eighty-minute period in which the sandpaper had to soak. This omission constituted a misrepresentation of the product's moisturizing power.

Colgate-Palmolive disagreed. It compared its "experiment" to the use of mashed potatoes substituted for ice cream in television ice cream ads. Just as the television lights made the use of ice cream impossible—a fact ice cream ads do not disclose—so the eighty-minute duration made showing an actual experiment with Rapid Shave impossible. The court rejected the analogy, on grounds that the mashed potatoes prop was not used for proof of the quality of the product, whereas the Rapid Shave commercial was attempting to provide such proof. The decision could be generalized as follows: Whether undisclosed information is an example of deception and manipulation depends on whether the information relates to claims about the quality of the product.

Another problem about disclosure of information appears in *Backman v. Polaroid Corporation.* In this case investors alleged that Polaroid had obtained negative information about its product Polavision but had failed to disclose to investors known unfavorable facts about the product. In effect, the claim is that Polaroid manipulated investors into purchasing the stock at a higher value than its worth. A similar charge led to accusations against Salomon Inc. in late 1991 for both moral and legal failures to properly disclose to shareholders a stock option plan and cash bonus plan that benefited top corporate executives. Investors charged that such compensation diluted the value of the stock. Salomon responded that it had "followed the rules" of disclosure in its mailings to stockholders.[4]

Despite such examples, Carr's view is that it is morally permissible to try to deceive others in these ways as long as everyone knows that such actions are accepted in the business world. Carr would presumably say that neither Polaroid nor Salomon did anything wrong so long as it is accepted that unfavorable facts about a product or compensation scheme do not have to be disclosed. In two articles following Carr's, one by Thomas L. Carson, Richard E. Wokutch, and Kent F. Murrmann and the other by Norman E. Bowie, Carr's public openness criterion is rejected. Bowie argues that bluffing, "white lies," and lack of disclosure interfere with markets, create instability, hurt productivity and hence competition, and threaten the business community itself in the long run. Carson, Wokutch, and Murrmann argue that many (but not all) forms of bluffing typically constitute lying that is prima facie wrong. They claim that bluffing is legitimate only if both sides understand the rules and both parties can bluff each other. By contrast to Carr, they argue that bluffing tends to be immoral when the attempt to lie or bluff is unilateral rather than bilateral. They insist not only that the rules of the game be understood, but that the game be played on a level playing surface.

DISCLOSING AND CONCEALING INFORMATION IN SALES

All of these issues about disclosure, deception, and manipulation are as prominent in sales as in advertising. As the marketplace for products has grown more complex and sophisticated, buyers have become more dependent upon salespersons to know their products and to tell the truth about them. The implicit assumption in some sales contexts is that bargaining and deception about a selling price are parts of the game, just as they are in real estate and labor negotiations. But this "flea market" and "horse-trader" model of sales is unsuited to many contemporary markets. The salesperson is expected to have superior knowledge and is treated as an expert on the product, or at least as one who obtains needed information about a product. In this climate, it seems unethical for salespersons to take advantage of a buyer's implicit trust by using deceptive or manipulative techniques. But if it is unethical to disclose too little, does it follow that the ethical salesperson has an obligation to disclose everything that might be of interest to the customer? For example, does the salesperson have to disclose that his or her company charges more than a competitor? What principles rightly govern the transfer of information during sales?

James M. Ebejer and Michael J. Morden point out in their article in this chapter that some salespersons view their relationship to the customer under the model of *caveat emptor* (let the buyer beware), whereas on the other extreme some salespersons see their role as that of paternalistic protector of the customer's interests. These authors argue for a professional sales ethic that they describe as "limited paternalism." According to this standard, a salesperson should be his or her "buyers' keeper" by identifying the needs of customers and disclosing information essential to meeting those needs. The salesperson is obligated to use this approach even if customers do not understand what their best interests are. These authors believe this approach maximizes mutual exchange and mutual advantage, evidently a utilitarian criterion for proper sales disclosures.

In a second article on sales practices, David M. Holley maintains that a commitment to the free-market system requires a business commitment to certain kinds of information disclosure. As he sees it, the primary obligation of salespersons is to avoid undermining the conditions of acceptable exchange. This criterion appears to be more permissive than limited paternalism: One is required to act paternalistically on behalf of a customer only if such conduct is necessary to avoid undermining the conditions of fair bargaining and freely chosen exchange. Nonetheless, by comparison to contemporary practice, Holley's argument is likely to require more, rather than less, education of the customer.

INFORMATION GATHERING

Proprietary information was introduced in Chapter 5 as an issue of intellectual property rights and trade secrets. A related issue is treated in the present chapter: how corporations should gather information about competitors and their products. It is commercial stealing to use proprietary information without permission, and using espionage, bribery, and trespass to obtain information is clearly unethical. However, many gray areas remain between theft and legitimate collection of information about competitors.

Some form of intelligence gathering about competitors is practiced by almost all corporations the size of those in the *Fortune* 500, and is generally considered by managers to be essential to compete adequately. Some methods of obtaining information are ethically and legally dubious, and litigation over property rights and criminal charges of pirated materials has increased in recent years. Management surveys suggest that a wide range of questionable activities in the pursuit of intelligence gathering now exists. Attempts to obtain research data and newly developed technologies through employee piracy, industrial espionage, and sensitive listening devices that monitor conversations at a distance are typical problems. Deceit, bribery, raiding of employees, invading confidential data banks, and covert surveillance have all been used by U.S. corporations. These activities are rarely discussed in corporations as ethically questionable activities and are almost never included in corporate codes of conduct. However, some significant changes have recently taken place in defense-related industries as a result of some 1990–1991 accusations and resignations involving secret procurement of Pentagon Documents by Navy contractors such as Bath Iron Works, Martin Marietta, United Technologies, and Unisys.

In her article in this chapter, Lynn Sharp Paine identifies ways in which intelligence gathering takes place, especially in the use of misrepresentation, improper influence, and various strategies that undermine relationships of trust and confidence. Many of the techniques she discusses involve manipulation not of customers or competitors but of employees, potential employees, or trusted associates of competitors. She then points to relevant principles that would help us draw the line between legitimate and illegitimate methods of acquiring information. She also points to the costs that corporations and the public will incur if they fail to pay closer attention to these problems than they have in the past.

Paine's arguments are not intended to suggest that intelligence gathering per se is unwelcome or immoral. Market success may require some forms of intelligence gathering about development efforts, plans for expansion, reasons for price reductions, sales strategy, customer base, pricing, and the like. Some consulting firms and societies specialize in acquiring and then rapidly disseminating information about a wide range of products in some part of the industry. Successful competition has proved difficult in some parts of business unless a data base is maintained on competitors' products and plans.

Sometimes when information transfers occur that a company might hope to have kept secret, the transfer is not necessarily an invalid discovery or disclosure of information. The company's carelessness in using the information can be the source of the problem, and it is expected that the company will take reasonable precautions to protect itself against discovery by industrial spies. When the Kellogg Company stopped its famous plant tours in 1986, the primary reason was a fear that the tours created a legitimate opportunity for industrial sleuths to discover state-of-the-art manufacturing secrets.[5]

Accordingly, discussion of intelligence gathering suggests a need to distinguish between legitimate methods of acquiring information and illegitimate methods. The line is often difficult to draw, and some borderline cases are inevitable. Only slight shades of difference sometimes exists between what one is inclined to think appropriate and what one judges inappropriate. But it is essential to try to draw that line not only to meet one's moral responsibility, but also to stop the tide of litigation.

1. Sari Horwitz, "FTC Considers Letting Food Stores Advertise Out-of-Stock Items," *Washington Post*, December 27, 1984, p. E1.
2. As quoted in Amy Dunkin, and others, "Liquor Makers Try the Hard Sell in a Softening Market," *Business Week*, May 13, 1985, p. 56.
3. "Anheuser-Busch Sued on Ad Showing Statue of Liberty," *Wall Street Journal*, November 28, 1984, p. 43.
4. Robert J. McCartney, "Investors Hit Salomon on Bonuses," *Washington Post*, October 23, 1991, pp. C1, C5.
5. Damon Darlin, "Kellogg Is Snapping Its 80-Year Tradition of Cereal Tours," *Wall Street Journal*, April 10, 1986, p.1

Is Business Bluffing Ethical?

Albert Z. Carr

A respected businessman with whom I discussed the theme of this article remarked with some heat, "You mean to say you're going to encourage men to bluff? Why, bluffing is nothing more than a form of lying! You're advising them to lie!"

From Albert Z. Carr, "Is Business Bluffing Ethical?" *Harvard Business Review* (January/February 1968). Reprinted by permission of the *Harvard Business Review*. Copyright © 1968 by the President and Fellows of Harvard College; all rights reserved.

I agreed that the basis of private morality is a respect for truth and that the closer a businessman comes to the truth, the more he deserves respect. At the same time, I suggested that most bluffing in business might be regarded simply as game strategy—much like bluffing in poker, which does not reflect on the morality of the bluffer.

I quoted Henry Taylor, the British statesman who pointed out that "falsehood ceases to be falsehood when it is understood on all sides that the truth is not expected to be spoken"—an exact description of bluffing in poker, diplomacy, and business. I cited the analogy of the criminal court, where the criminal is not expected to tell the truth when he pleads "not guilty." Everyone from the judge down takes it for granted that the job of the defendant's attorney is to get his client off, not to reveal the truth; and this is considered ethical practice. I mentioned Representative Omar Burleson, the Democrat from Texas, who was quoted as saying, in regard to the ethics of Congress, "Ethics is a barrel of worms"[1]—a pungent summing up of the problem of deciding who is ethical in politics.

I reminded my friend that millions of businessmen feel constrained every day to say *yes* to their bosses when they secretly believe *no* and that this is generally accepted as permissible strategy when the alternative might be the loss of a job. The essential point, I said, is that the ethics of business are game ethics, different from the ethics of religion.

He remained unconvinced. Referring to the company of which he is president, he declared: "Maybe that's good enough for some businessmen, but I can tell you that we pride ourselves on our ethics. In 30 years not one customer has ever questioned my word or asked to check our figures. We're loyal to our customers and fair to our suppliers. I regard my handshake on a deal as a contract. I've never entered into price-fixing schemes with my competitors. I've never allowed my sales-

men to spread injurious rumors about other companies. Our union contract is the best in our industry. And, if I do say so myself, our ethical standards are of the highest!"

He really was saying, without realizing it, that he was living up to the ethical standards of the business game—which are a far cry from those of private life. Like a gentlemanly poker player, he did not play in cahoots with others at the table, try to smear their reputations, or hold back chips he owed them.

But this same fine man, at that very time, was allowing one of his products to be advertised in a way that made it sound a great deal better than it actually was. Another item in his product line was notorious among dealers for its "built-in obsolescence." He was holding back from the market a much-improved product because he did not want to interfere with sales of the inferior item it would have replaced. He had joined with certain of his competitors in hiring a lobbyist to push a state legislature, by methods that he preferred not to know too much about, into amending a bill then being enacted.

In his view these things had nothing to do with ethics; they were merely normal business practice. He himself undoubtedly avoided outright falsehoods—never lied in so many words. But the entire organization that he ruled was deeply involved in numerous strategies of deception.

PRESSURE TO DECEIVE

Most executives from time to time are almost compelled, in the interests of their companies or themselves, to practice some form of deception when negotiating with customers, dealers, labor unions, government officials, or even other departments of their companies. By conscious misstatements, concealment of pertinent facts, or exaggeration—in short, by bluffing—they seek to persuade others to agree with them. I think it is fair to say that if the individual executive refuses to bluff from time to time—if he feels obligated to tell the truth, the whole truth, and nothing but the truth—he is ignoring opportunities permitted under the rules and is at a heavy disadvantage in his business dealings.

But here and there a businessman is unable to reconcile himself to the bluff in which he plays a part. His conscience, perhaps spurred by religious idealism, troubles him. He feels guilty; he may develop an ulcer or a nervous tic. Before any executive can make profitable use of the strategy of the bluff, he needs to make sure that in bluffing he will not lose self-respect or become emotionally disturbed. If he is to reconcile personal integrity and high standards of honesty with the practical requirements of business, he must feel that his bluffs are ethically justified. The justification rests on the fact that business, as practiced by individuals as well as by corporations, has the impersonal character of a game—a game that demands both special strategy and an understanding of its special ethics.

The game is played at all levels of corporate life, from the highest to the lowest. At the very instant that a man decides to enter business, he may be forced into a game situation, as is shown by the recent experience of a Cornell honor graduate who applied for a job with a large company.

This applicant was given a psychological test which included the statement, "Of the following magazines, check any that you have read either regularly or from time to time, and double-check those which interest you most. *Reader's Digest, Time, Fortune, Saturday Evening Post, The New Republic, Life, Look, Ramparts, Newsweek, Business Week, U.S. News & World Report, The Nation, Playboy, Esquire, Harper's, Sports Illustrated.*"

His tastes in reading were broad, and at one time or another he had read almost all of these magazines. He was a subscriber to The New Republic, an enthusiast for Ramparts, and an avid student of the pictures in Playboy. He was not sure whether his interest in Playboy would be held against him, but he had a shrewd suspicion that if he confessed to an interest in Ramparts and The New Republic, he would be thought a liberal, a radical, or at least an intellectual, and his chances of getting the job, which he needed, would greatly diminish. He therefore checked five of the more conservative magazines. Apparently it was a sound decision, for he got the job.

He had made a game player's decision, consistent with business ethics.

A similar case is that of a magazine space salesman who, owing to a merger, suddenly found himself out of a job:

This man was 58, and, in spite of a good record, his chance of getting a job elsewhere in a business where youth is favored in hiring practice was not good. He was a vigorous, healthy man, and only a considerable amount of gray in his hair suggested his age. Before beginning his job search he touched up his hair with a black dye to confine the gray to his temples. He knew that the truth about his age might well come out in time, but he calculated that he could deal with that situation when it arose. He and his wife decided that he could easily pass for 45, and he so stated his age on his résumé.

This was a lie: yet within the accepted rules of the business game, no moral culpability attaches to it.

THE POKER ANALOGY

We can learn a good deal about the nature of business by comparing it with poker. While both have a large element of chance, in the long run the winner is the man who plays with steady skill. In both games ultimate victory requires intimate knowledge of the rules, insight into the psychology of the other players, a bold front, a considerable amount of self-discipline, and the ability to respond swiftly and effectively to opportunities provided by chance.

No one expects poker to be played on the ethical principles preached in churches. In poker it is right and proper to bluff a friend out of the rewards of being dealt a good hand. A player feels no more than a slight twinge of sympathy, if that, when—with nothing better than a single ace in his hand—he strips a heavy loser, who holds a pair, of the rest of his chips. It was up to the other fellow to protect himself. In the words of an excellent poker player, former President Harry Truman, "If you can't stand the heat, stay out of the kitchen." If one shows mercy to a loser in poker, it is a personal gesture, divorced from the rules of the game.

Poker has its special ethics, and here I am not referring to rules against cheating. The man who keeps an ace up his sleeve or who marks the cards is more than unethical; he is a crook, and can be punished as such—kicked out of the game or, in the Old West, shot.

In contrast to the cheat, the unethical poker player is one who, while abiding by the letter of the rules, finds ways to put the other players at an unfair disadvantage. Perhaps he unnerves them with loud talk. Or he tries to get them drunk. Or he plays in cahoots with someone else at the table. Ethical poker players frown on such tactics.

Poker's own brand of ethics is different from the ethical ideals of civilized human relationships. The game calls for distrust of the other fellow. It ignores the claim of friendship. Cunning deception and concealment of one's strength and intentions, not kindness and openheartedness, are vital in poker. No one thinks any the worse of poker on that account. And no one should think any the worse of the game of business because its standards of right and wrong differ from the prevailing traditions of morality in our society. . . .

'WE DON'T MAKE THE LAWS'

Wherever we turn in business, we can perceive the sharp distinction between its ethical standards and those of the churches. Newspapers abound with sensational stories growing out of this distinction:

> We read one day that Senator Philip A. Hart of Michigan has attacked food processors for deceptive packaging of numerous products.[2]
>
> The next day there is a Congressional to-do over Ralph Nader's book, *Unsafe At Any Speed*, which demonstrates that automobile companies for years have neglected the safety of car-owning families.[3]
>
> Then another Senator, Lee Metcalf of Montana, and journalist Vic Reinemer show in their book, *Overcharge*, the methods by which utility companies elude regulating government bodies to extract unduly large payments from users of electricity.[4]

These are merely dramatic instances of a prevailing condition; there is hardly a major industry at which a similar attack could not be aimed. Critics of business regard such behavior as unethical, but the companies concerned know that they are merely playing the business game.

Among the most respected of our business institutions are the insurance companies. A group of insurance executives meeting recently in New England was startled when their guest speaker, social critic Daniel Patrick Moynihan, roundly berated them for "unethical" practices. They had been guilty, Moynihan alleged, of using outdated actuarial tables to obtain unfairly high premiums. They habitually delayed the hearings of lawsuits against them in order to tire out the plaintiffs and win cheap settlements. In their employment policies they use ingenious devices to discriminate against certain minority groups.[5]

It was difficult for the audience to deny the validity of these charges. But these men were business game players. Their reaction to Moynihan's attack was much the same as that of the automobile manufacturers to Nader, of the utilities to Senator Metcalf, and of the food processors to Senator Hart. If the laws governing their businesses change, or if public opinion becomes clamorous, they will make the necessary adjustments. But morally they have in their view done nothing wrong. As long as they comply with the letter of the law, they are within their rights to operate their businesses as they see fit.

The small business is in the same position as the great corporation in this respect. For example:

> In 1967 a key manufacturer was accused of providing master keys for automobiles to mail-order customers, although it was obvious that some of the purchasers might be automobile thieves. His defense was plain and straightforward. If there was nothing in the law to prevent him from selling his keys to anyone who ordered them, it was not up to him to inquire as to his customers' motives. Why was it any worse, he insisted, for him to sell car keys by mail, than for mail-order houses to sell guns that might be used for murder? Until the law was changed, the key manufacturer could regard himself as being just as ethical as any other businessman by the rules of the business game.[6]

Violations of the ethical ideals of society are common in business, but they are not necessarily violations of business principles. Each year the Federal Trade Commission orders hundreds of companies, many of them of the first magnitude, to "cease and desist" from practices which, judged by ordinary standards, are of questionable morality but which are stoutly defended by the companies concerned.

In one case, a firm manufacturing a well-known mouthwash was accused of using a cheap form of alcohol possibly deleterious to health. The company's chief executive, after testifying in Washington, made this comment privately:

> "We broke no law. We're in a highly competitive industry. If we're going to stay in business, we have to look for profit wherever the law permits. We don't make the laws. We obey them. Then why do we have to put up with this 'holier than thou' talk about ethics? It's sheer hypocrisy. We're not in business to promote ethics. Look at the cigarette companies, for God's sake! If the ethics aren't embodied in the laws by the men who made them, you can't expect businessmen to fill the lack. Why, a sudden submission to Christian ethics by businessmen would bring about the greatest economic upheaval in history!"

It may be noted that the government failed to prove its case against him.

CAST ILLUSIONS ASIDE

Talk about ethics by businessmen is often a thin decorative coating over the hard realities of the game. . . .

The illusion that business can afford to be guided by ethics as conceived in private life is often fostered by speeches and articles containing such phrases as, "It pays to be ethical," or, "Sound ethics is good business." Actually, this is not an ethical position at all; it is a self-serving calculation in disguise. The speaker is really saying that in the long run a company can make more money if it does not antagonize competitors, suppliers, employees, and customers by squeezing them too hard. He is saying that oversharp policies reduce ultimate gains. That is true, but it has nothing to do with ethics. The underlying attitude is much like that in the familiar story of the shopkeeper who finds an extra $20 bill in the cash register, debates with himself the ethical problem—should he tell his partner? —and finally decides to share the money because the gesture will give him an edge over the s.o.b. the next time they quarrel.

I think it is fair to sum up the prevailing attitude of businessmen on ethics as follows:

We live in what is probably the most competitive of the world's civilized societies. Our customs encourage a high degree of aggression in the individual's striving for success. Business is our main area of competition, and it has been ritualized into a game of strategy. The basic rules of the game have been set by the government, which attempts to detect and punish business frauds. But as long as a company does not transgress the rules of the game set by law, it has the legal right to shape its strategy without reference to anything but its profits. If it takes a long-term view of its profits, it will preserve amicable relations, so far as possible, with those with whom it deals. A wise businessman will not seek advantage to the point where he generates dangerous hostility among employees, competitors, customers, government, or the public at large. But decisions in this area are, in the final test, decisions of strategy, not of ethics.

. . . If a man plans to make a seat in the business game, he owes it to himself to master the principles by which the game is played, including its special ethical outlook. He can then hardly fail to recognize that an occasional bluff may well be justified in terms of the game's ethics and warranted in terms of economic necessity. Once he clears his mind on this point, he is in a good position to match his strategy against that of the other players. He can then determine objectively whether a bluff in a given situation has a good chance of succeeding and can decide when and how to bluff, without a feeling of ethical transgression.

To be a winner, a man must play to win. This does not mean that he must be ruthless, cruel, harsh, or treacherous. On the contrary, the better his reputation for integrity, honesty, and decency, the better his chances of victory will be in the long run. But from time to time every businessman, like every poker player, is offered a choice between certain loss or bluffing within the legal rules of the game. If he is not resigned to losing, if he wants to rise in his company and industry, then in such a crisis he will bluff—and bluff hard. . . .

In the last third of the twentieth century even children are aware that if a man has become prosperous in business, he has sometimes departed from the strict truth in order to overcome obstacles or has practiced the more subtle deceptions of the half-truth or the misleading omission. Whatever the form of the bluff, it is an integral part of the game, and the executive who does not master its techniques is not likely to accumulate much money or power.

NOTES

1. *The New York Times,* March 9, 1967.
2. *The New York Times,* November 21, 1966.
3. New York, Grossman Publishers, Inc., 1965.
4. New York, David McKay Company, Inc., 1967.
5. *The New York Times,* January 17, 1967.
6. Cited by Ralph Nader in "Business Crime," *The New Republic,* July 1, 1967, p. 7.

Bluffing in Labor Negotiations:
Legal and Ethical Issues

Thomas L. Carson,
Richard E. Wokutch,
and Kent F. Murrmann

More than a decade ago a *Harvard Business Review* article entitled 'Is Business Bluffing Ethical' (Carr, 1968) created a storm of controversy when the author defended bluffing and other questionable business practices on the grounds that they are just part of the game of business. The controversy over the ethics of bluffing and alleged deception in business negotiations erupted again recently with the publication of the Wall Street Journal article, 'To Some at Harvard, Telling Lies Becomes a Matter of Course' (Bulkeley, 1979). This detailed a negotiations course taught at Harvard Business School in which students were allowed to bluff and deceive each other in various simulated negotiation situations. Student's grades were partially determined by the settlements they negotiated with each other, and hence some alleged that this course encouraged and taught students to bluff, lie to, and deceive negotiating partners. These controversies raised issues concerning the morality, necessity, and even the legality of bluffing in business negotiations which were never adequately resolved. It is the aim of this paper to shed some light on these issues. . . .

BLUFFING AND BARGAINING SUCCESS

Bluffing is an act in which one attempts to misrepresent one's intentions or overstate the strength of one's position in the bargaining process. This is possible because neither party knows for sure the other party's true intentions or 'sticking point'. Bluffing often involves making deceptive statements. For instance, the union bargaining representative may boldly state, "There is no way that our people will accept such a small wage increase", when he/she knows full well that they would gladly accept management's offer rather than go out on strike. However, bluffing can be entirely nonverbal. Nodding confidently as one raises the bet while holding a poor hand in a game of poker is a paradigm case of bluffing. Getting up from the bargaining table in a huff and going out the door is another example of nonverbal bluffing. Through these and similar types of statements and behavior either party can convey to the other an exaggerated portrayal of its ability to impose or endure costs, and thereby can increase its actual ability to gain concessions in the bargaining process.

In addition, aggressive bluffing can be used to test the other party's resolve or otherwise prod the other party to concede certain points. This use of bluffing on different bargaining issues over a period of time, say spanning several bargaining sessions, can significantly increase one's understanding of the other party's true strength, and thus can enhance one's ability to accurately estimate the other party's sticking points on various issues.

There can be no doubt that bluffing is an

Journal of Business Ethics 1 (1982):13–22. Copyright © 1982 *by D. Reidel Publishing Co., Dordrecht, Holland and Boston,* *U.S.A.* Reprinted by permission.

important bargaining tool. It can be employed to create impressions of enhanced strength as well as to probe the other party to find out the level of its critical sticking points. Through these methods either party can attempt to gain a more favorable settlement than the other party would otherwise be willing to allow. And, labor and management alike are more apt to fully abide by those terms of employment that they know were established through a free and vigorous use of their best bargaining skills.

THE ALLEGED NECESSITY OF BLUFFING

While bluffing can obviously be advantageous in labor negotiations, one might ask whether it is 'economically necessary'. This does not appear to be the case. Where one of the parties has an extremely strong negotiating position (e.g. an employer in a one company town with a high unemployment rate, a slavemaster, or a surgeon who is the only one capable of performing a new surgical procedure necessary to save one's life) wages and working conditions can simply be dictated by the stronger party.

What about the claim that bluffing is a necessary part of the negotiation of any *voluntary* labor agreement between parties of relatively equal power? This also seems false. Suppose that two very scrupulous parties are attempting to reach a wage settlement and neither wants to engage in bluffing. Assuming that they trust each other and honestly reveal their 'sticking points', they could agree to some formula such as splitting the difference between the sticking points. This is of course unlikely to occur in real life, but only because few individuals are honest or trusting enough for our assumption to hold. . . .

THE HONEST CLAIMS DOCTRINE

Of particular interest with respect to the legal status of bluffing is the 'honest claims' doctrine, established by the U.S. Supreme Court in its Truitt Mfg. Co. decision (*NLRB v. Truitt Mfg. Co.*, 1956). This states that "good faith necessarily requires that claims made by either party should be honest claims". The central issue in the Truitt Case was whether the employer would be required to substantiate its claim that it could not afford to pay a certain wage increase. In addition to enunciating its 'honest claims' doctrine, the court declared that if an "inability to pay argument is important enough to present in the give and take of bargaining it is important enough to require some sort of proof of its accuracy" (*NLRB v. Truitt Mfg. Co.*, 1956, p. 152). This 'honest claims' policy has been consistently upheld and applied in numerous court decisions to this day. Thus, it is clear that the law requires honesty in collective bargaining. However, the 'honest claims' requirement applies only to those types of claims that pertain directly to issues subject to bargaining and the employer's ability to provide certain conditions of employment. Thus, the 'honest claims' policy requires a union to refrain from presenting false information to management concerning the level of wages and fringe benefits provided by employers under other union contracts. Likewise, the employer must refrain from falsely claiming an inability to provide a certain benefit.

BLUFFING AND THE HONEST CLAIMS DOCTRINE

How does the 'honest claims' doctrine apply to the practice of bluffing? It is clear that bluffing that involves the presentation of false information about issues subject to bargaining (i.e., wages, hours, and condition of employment) is a violation. However bluffing about objective issues not subject to negotiation such as one's ability to withstand a strike (e.g. the size of the union strike fund, or the union membership's vote on the question of whether or not to go out on strike) is allowable. Also, bluffing that is limited to representations of one's bargaining intentions or one's willingness to impose or endure costs in order to win a more favorable contract does not constitute a violation. Of course, this type of bluffing is more effective and more prevalent because it can not be as easily discredited through reference to objective information as can false statements about working conditions. In sum, though the Truitt decision requires honesty with regard to the making of claims concerning bargaining topics, it does not proscribe the more effective and important forms of bluffing commonly used in bargaining today.

BLUFFING AND THE CONCEPT OF LYING

Suppose (example 1) that I am a management negotiator trying to reach a strike settlement with union negotiators. I need to settle the strike soon and have been instructed to settle for as much as a 12% increase in wages and benefits if that is the best agreement I can obtain. I say that the company's final offer is a 10% increase. Am I lying? Consider also whether any of the following examples constitute lying:

2. Management negotiators misstating the profitability of a subsidiary to convince the union negotiating with it that the subsidiary would go out of business if management acceded to union wage demands.
3. Union officials misreporting the size of the union strike fund to portray a greater ability to strike than is actually the case.
4. Management negotiators saying, "We can't af-

ford this agreement", when it would not put the firm out of business but only reduce profits from somewhat above to somewhat below the industry average.
5. Union negotiators saying, "The union membership is adamant on this issue", when they know that while one half of the membership is adamant, the other half couldn't care less.
6. Union negotiators saying, "If you include this provision, we'll get membership approval of the contract", when they know they'll have an uphill battle for approval even with the provision.

Defining Lying

What is lying? A lie must be a false statement[1], but not all false statements are lies. If I am a salesman and say that my product is the best on the market and *sincerely believe this to be the case,* my statement is not a lie, even if it is untrue. A false statement is not a lie unless it is somehow deliberate or intentional. . . . The following definition is more plausible than . . . [competitors]:

> A lie is a deliberate false statement which is either intended to deceive others or foreseen to be likely to deceive others. . . .

Suppose that a management negotiator asks a union negotiator the size of the union strike fund. The union negotiator responds by saying it is three times its actual amount. [Some definitions imply] that this statement is not a lie since the management negotiator didn't have a right to know the information in question and the union didn't explicitly promise to tell the truth about this. But surely this is a lie. The fact that management has no right to know the truth is just cause for withholding the information, but responding falsely is a lie nonetheless.

There is, to the best of our knowledge, no plausible definition of lying which allows us to say that typical instances of bluffing in labor and other sorts of business negotiations do not involve lying. We should stress that it is only bluffing which involves making false statements which constitutes lying. One is not lying if one bluffs another by making the true statement "We want a 30% pay increase". Similarly, it is not a lie if one bluffs without making any statements as in a game of poker or overpricing (on a price tag) a product where bargaining is expected (e.g. a used car lot or antique store).

The Concept of Deception

At this point it would be useful to consider the relationship between lying and the broader concept of deception. Deception may be defined as intentionally causing another person to have false beliefs. (It is not clear whether preventing someone from having true beliefs should count as deception). As we have seen, lying always involves the intent to deceive others, or the expectation that they will be deceived as a result of what one says, or both. But one can lie without actually deceiving anyone. . . .

It seems that one can often avoid lying in the course of a business negotiation simply by phrasing one's statements very carefully. In negotiations instead of lying and saying that 10% is the highest wage increase we will give, I could avoid lying by making the following true, but equally deceptive statement: "Our position is that 10% is our final offer" (without saying that this position is subject to change). It is questionable whether this is any less morally objectionable than lying. . . .

MORAL ISSUES IN LYING

Common sense holds that lying is a matter of moral significance and that lying is *prima facie* wrong, or wrong everything else being equal.

This can also be put by saying that there is a presumption against lying, and that lying requires some special justification in order to be considered permissible. Common sense also holds that lying is not always wrong, it can sometimes be justified (Ross, 1930). Almost no one would agree with Kant's (1797) later view in 'On the Supposed Right to Tell Lies from Benevolent Motives', that it is wrong to lie even if doing so is necessary to protect the lives of innocent people. According to this view it would be wrong to lie to a potential murderer concerning the whereabouts of an intended victim. Common sense also seems to hold that there is a presumption against simple deception.

Assuming the correctness of this view about the morality of lying and deception, and assuming that we are correct in saying that bluffing involves lying, it follows that bluffing and other deceptive business practices require some sort of special justification in order to be considered permissible.

We will now attempt to determine whether there is any special justification for the kind of lying and deception which typically occurs in labor and other sorts of business negotiations. Bluffing and other sorts of deceptive strategies are standard practice in these negotiations and they are generally thought to be acceptable. Does the fact that these things are standard practice or 'part of the game' show that they are justified? We think not. The mere fact that something is standard practice, legal, or generally accepted is not enough to justify it. Standard practice and popular opinion can be in error. Such things as slavery were once standard practice, legal and generally accepted. But they are and *were* morally wrong. Bluffing constitutes an attempt to deceive others about the nature of one's intentions in a bargaining situation. The *prima facie* wrongness of bluffing is considerably *diminished* on account of the fact that the lying and deception involved typically concern matters about which the other parties have no particular right to know. The others have no particular right to know one's bargaining position—one's intentions. However, there is still some presumption against lying or deceiving other people, even when they have no right to the information in question. A stranger has no right to know how old I am. I have no obligation to provide him/her with this information. Other things being equal, however, it would still be wrong for me to lie to this stranger about my age.

In our view the main justification for bluffing consists in the fact that the moral presumption against lying to or deceiving someone holds only when the person or persons with whom you are dealing is/are not attempting to lie to or deceive you. Given this, there is no presumption against bluffing or deceiving someone who is attempting to bluff or deceive you on that occasion. The prevalence of bluffing in negotiations means that one is safe in presuming that one is justified in bluffing in the absence of any special reasons for thinking that one's negotiating partners are not bluffing (e.g., when one is dealing with an unusually naive or scrupulous person).

CONCLUSIONS

Granted that bluffing and deception can be permissible given the exigencies and harsh realities of economic bargaining in our society, isn't it an indictment of our entire economic system that such activities are necessary in so many typical circumstances? Even those who defend the practice of bluffing (Carr, 1968) concede that a great deal of lying and deception occurs in connection with the economic activities of our society. Much of this (particularly in the area of bargaining or negotiating) is openly condoned or encouraged by both business and labor. While lying and deception are not generally condoned in other contexts, they often occur as the result of pressures generated by the highly competitive nature of our society. For example, few would condone the behavior of a salesperson who deliberately misrepresents the cost and effectiveness of a product. However, a salesperson under pressure to sell an inferior product may feel that he/she must either deceive prospective customers or else find a new job. . . .

It can be argued that [certain] objections to competitive economic systems such as our own rest on a mistaken view about the nature of moral goodness and the moral virtues. One's moral goodness and honesty are not a direct function of how frequently one tells lies. Thor Hyerdahl did not tell any lies during the many months in which he was alone on the KonTikki. But we would not conclude from this that he was an exceptionally honest man during that period of time. Similarly, the fact that a businessperson who has a monopoly on a vital good or service does not misrepresent the price or quality of his/her goods or services does not necessarily mean that he/she is honest. There is simply no occasion or temptation to be dishonest. The extent to which a person possesses the different moral virtues is a function of how that person is *disposed* to act in various actual and possible situations. My courage or cowardice is a function of my ability to master fear in dangerous situations. . . . This is not to deny that the economic institutions of our society can in some cases alter a person's basic behavioral dispositions and thereby also his/her character for the worse. For example, the activities of a negotiator may cause him/her to be less truthful and trusting in his/her personal relationships. Our claim is only that most of the 'undesirable moral effects' attributed to our economic institutions involve actualizing pre-existing dispositions, rather than causing any fundamental changes in character.

NOTES

1. Arnold Isenberg however disputes this in "Conditions for Lying," in *Ethical Theory and Business,* Tom Beauchamp and Norman Bowie (eds.) (Prentice Hall, Englewood Cliffs, N.J., 1979), pp. 466–468.

BIBLIOGRAPHY

Bulkeley, W. M.: 1979, "To Some at Harvard, Telling Lies Becomes a Matter of Course," *Wall Street Journal,* January 15, pp. 1, 37.

Carr, A. Z.: 1968, "Is Business Bluffing Ethical?," *Harvard Business Review* **46,** 143–153.

Isenberg, A.: 1965, "Conditions for Lying," in T. Beauchamp and N. Bowie (eds.), *Ethical Theory and Business* (Prentice Hall, Englewood Cliffs, N.J., 1979), pp. 466–468.

Kant, I.: 1775–1780, *Lectures on Ethics* (Louis Infield, Trans., Harper and Row, New York, 1963).

Kant, I.: 1797, "On a Supposed Right to Tell Lies from Benevolent Motives," in B. Brody (ed.), *Moral Rules and Particular Circumstances* (Prentice Hall, Englewood Cliffs, N.J., 1970), pp. 31–36.

National Labor Relations Act, as amended, 29 USC 151 *et seq.* (1970).

NLRB v. *Truitt Mfg. Co.,* 351US149, 38LRRM2042 (1956).

Ross, D.: 1930, *The Right and the Good* (Oxford University Press, Oxford).

Does It Pay to Bluff in Business?

Norman E. Bowie

Albert Carr has argued in an influential article[1] that the ethics of business is best understood on the model of the ethics of poker.

Wouldn't it be in the best interest of business to adopt the poker model of business ethics? I think not. Let us consider labor relations, where Carr's poker model is implicitly if not explicitly adopted. In collective bargaining the relationship between the employer and the employee is adversarial. Collective bargaining is competitive through and through. The task of the union is to secure as much in pay and benefits as possible. The task of the employer's negotiators is to keep the pay and benefits as low as possible.

In the resulting give-and-take, bluffing and deception are the rule. Management expects the union to demand a percentage pay increase it knows it won't get. The union expects the company to say that such a pay increase will force it to shut down the plant and move to another state. Such demands are never taken at face value although they are taken more seriously on the ninetieth day of negotiations than they are on the first day.

Recently the conventional view of collective bargaining practice has been under attack. One of the most prominent criticisms of current practice is its economic inefficiency. The adversarial relationship at the bargaining table carries over to the workplace. As a result of the hostility between employee and employer, productivity suffers and many American products are at a competitive disadvantage with respect to foreign products. Japanese labor-management relations are not so adversarial and this fact accounts for part of their success. This particular criticism of collective bargaining has received much attention in the press and in popular business magazines. The most recent manifestation of the recognition of the force of this criticism is the host of decisions General Motors has made to ensure that labor relations are different at its new assembly plant for the Saturn.

Second, the practice of bluffing and deception tends to undermine trust. As some American firms lost ground to foreign competition, the management of many of the firms asked for pay reductions, commonly called "give backs." Other managers in firms not threatened by foreign competition cited the "dangers" of foreign competition to request pay cuts for their employees—even though they were not needed. Use of this tactic will only cause future problems when and if the competitive threat really develops. This utilitarian point was not lost on participants in a labor-management relations seminar I attended.

Participant I: In the past, there was a relationship of mutual distrust.

Participant II: These are the dangers in crying "wolf." When the company is really in trouble, no one will believe them.

Participant III: To make labor/management participation teams work, you need to generate mutual trust. It only takes one bad deal to undermine trust.

These individuals are indicating that the practices of bluffing and deception have bad consequences in employer/employee relationships. These unfortunate consequences have been well documented by philosophers—most recently by Sissela Bok. Bok's critique of "white lies" and the use of placebos applies equally well to deception in the collective bargaining process.

Triviality surely does set limits to when moral inquiry is reasonable. But when we look more closely at practices such as placebo-giving, it becomes clear that all lies defended as "white" cannot be so easily dismissed. In the first place, the harmlessness of lies is notoriously disputable. What the liar perceives as harmless or even beneficial may not be so in the eyes of the deceived. Second, the failure to look at an entire practice rather than at their own isolated case often blinds liars to cumulative harm and expanding deceptive activities. Those who begin with white lies can come to resort to more frequent and more serious ones. Where some tell a few white lies, others may tell more. Because lines are so hard to draw, the indiscriminate use of such lies can lead to other deceptive practices. The aggregate harm from a large number of marginally harmful instances may, therefore, be highly undesirable in the end—for liars, those deceived, and honesty and trust more generally.[2]

However, there is more at stake here than the bad consequences of lying. Bluffing, exaggeration, and the nondisclosure of information also undermine a spirit of cooperation that is essential to business success. The poker model, with its permitted bluffing and the like, is a competitive model. What the model overlooks is the fact that the production of a good or service in any given plant or office is a cooperative enterprise. Chrysler competes with General Motors and Toyota but the production of Chrysler K cars in that assembly plant in Newark, Delaware, is a cooperative enterprise. Lack of cooperation results in poor quality vehicles.

Hence the competitive model of collective bargaining sets wages and working conditions for what at the local level is a cooperative enterprise. Labor-management negotiators forget the obvious truth that the production of goods and services cannot succeed on a purely competitive basis. There have to be some elements of cooperation somewhere in the system. Why shouldn't the collective bargaining process use cooperative rather than competitive techniques? When bargaining is conducted industrywide, as it is with automobiles, the competitive mode seems natural. Auto production is a competitive industry. But just because Chrysler is competitive with General Motors, why must Chrysler management be in a competitive relationship with its own employees? Indeed, couldn't it be argued that the fact that Chrysler's management does see itself in competition with its unionized employees undercuts its competitive position vis-à-vis other automobile producers. To use the language of competition, if Chrysler is at war with itself, how can it win the war against others?

As long as collective bargaining is essentially adversarial and characterized by bluffing and exaggeration on both sides, the cooperative aspect of business will be underemphasized. The costs of ignoring the cooperative aspect are great—both for society and for business itself.

Hence this distrust that so concerned the participants in the seminar is only in part a function of the deceit and bluffing that go on in collective bargaining. It is in large part a function of using the wrong model. We shouldn't look at collective bargaining as a game of poker.

With this discussion of collective bargaining as instance, let us evaluate Carr's proposal on utilitarian grounds. Should the stockholders applaud a chief executive officer whose operating procedure is analogous to the operating procedure of a poker player? In Carr's view, "A good part of the time the businessman is trying to do unto others as he hopes others will not do unto him." But surely such a practice is very risky. The danger of discovery is great, and our experience of the past several years indicates that many corporations that have played the game of business like the game of poker have suffered badly. Moreover, if business practice consisted essentially of these conscious misstatements, exaggerations, and the concealment of pertinent facts, it seems clear that business practice would be inherently unstable. Contemporary business practice presupposes such stability, and business can only be stable if the chief executive officer has a set of moral standards higher than those that govern the game of poker. The growth of the large firm, the complexity of business decisions, the need for planning and stability, and the undesirable effects of puffery, exaggeration, and deception all count against Carr's view that the ethics of business should be the ethics of a poker game.

NOTES

1. Albert Z. Carr, "Is Business Bluffing Ethical?" *Harvard Business Review,* 46 (January-February 1968): 143–153.
2. Sissela Bok, *Lying: Moral Choice in Public and Private Life* (New York: Pantheon Books, 1978), pp. 19,31.

A Moral Evaluation of Sales Practices

David M. Holley

A relatively neglected area in recent literature on business ethics is the ethics of sales practices. Discussions of the moral dimensions of marketing have tended to concentrate almost exclusively on obligations of advertisers or on the moral acceptability of the advertising system. By contrast, little attention has been given to the activities of individual salespersons.[1]

This neglect is surprising on several

counts. First, efforts to sell a product occupy a good deal of the time of many people in business. Developing an advertising campaign may be a more glamorous kind of activity, but it is sales on the individual level that provides the revenue, and for most businesses the number of persons devoted to selling will far exceed the number devoted to advertising. Second, the activity of selling something is of intrinsic philosophical significance. It furnishes a paradigm case of persuasive communication, raising such issues as deception, individual autonomy, and the social value of a marketing-oriented system for distributing goods and services. While the practice of advertising raises these same issues, the potential for manipulation of vulnerable consumers comes into much sharper focus at the level of individual sales.

In this paper I will attempt to develop a framework for evaluating the morality of various sales practices. Although I recognize that much of the salesforce in companies is occupied exclusively or primarily with sales to other businesses, my discussion will focus on sales to the individual consumer. Most of what I say should apply to any type of sales activity, but the moral issues arise most clearly in cases in which a consumer may or may not be very sophisticated in evaluating and responding to a sales presentation.

My approach will be to consider first the context of sales activities, a market system of production and distribution. Since such a system is generally justified on teleological grounds, I describe several conditions for its successful achievement of key goals. Immoral sales practices are analyzed as attempts to undermine these conditions.

I

The primary justification for a market system is that it provides an efficient procedure for meeting people's needs and desires for goods and services.[2] This appeal to economic benefits can be elaborated in great detail, but at root it involves the claim that people will efficiently serve each other's needs if they are allowed to engage in voluntary exchanges.

A crucial feature of this argument is the condition that the exchange be voluntary. Assuming that individuals know best how to benefit themselves and that they will act to achieve such benefits, voluntary exchange can be expected to serve both parties. On the other hand, if the exchanges are not made voluntarily, we have no basis for expecting mutually beneficial results. To the extent that mutual benefit does not occur, the system will lack efficiency as a means for the satisfaction of needs and desires. Hence, this justification presupposes that conditions necessary for the occurrence of voluntary exchange are ordinarily met.

What are these conditions? For simplicity's sake, let us deal only with the kind of exchange involving a payment of money for some product or service. We can call the person providing the product the *seller* and the person making the monetary payment the *buyer*. I suggest that voluntary exchange occurs only if the following conditions are met:

1. Both buyer and seller understand what they are giving up and what they are receiving in return.
2. Neither buyer nor seller is compelled to enter into the exchange as a result of coercion, severely restricted alternatives, or other constraints on the ability to choose.
3. Both buyer and seller are able at the time of the exchange to make rational judgments about its costs and benefits.

I will refer to these three conditions as the knowledge, noncompulsion, and rationality conditions, respectively.[3] If the parties are uninformed, it is possible that an exchange might accidentally turn out to benefit them. But given the lack of information, they would not be in a position to make a rational judgment about their benefit, and we cannot reasonably expect beneficial results as a matter of course in such circumstances. Similarly, if the exchange is made under compulsion, then the judgment of personal benefit is not the basis of the exchange. It is possible for someone to be forced or manipulated into an arrangement that is in fact beneficial. But there is little reason to think that typical or likely.[4]

It should be clear that all three conditions are subject to degrees of fulfillment. For example, the parties may understand certain things about the exchange but not others. Let us posit a theoretical situation in which both parties are fully informed, fully rational, and enter into the exchange entirely of their own volition. I will call this an *ideal exchange*. In actual practice there is virtually always some divergence from the ideal. Knowledge can be more or less adequate. Individuals can be subject to various irrational influences. There can be borderline cases of external constraints. Nevertheless, we can often judge when a particular exchange was adequately informed, rational, and free from compulsion. Even when conditions are not ideal, we may still have an *acceptable exchange*.

With these concepts in mind, let us consider the obligations of sales personnel. I suggest that the primary duty of salespeople to customers is to avoid undermining the conditions of acceptable exchange. It is possible by act or omission to create a situation in which the customer is not sufficiently knowledgeable about what the exchange involves. It is also possible to influence the customer in ways that short-circuit the rational decision-making process. To behave in such ways is to undermine the conditions that are presupposed in teleological justifications of the market system. Of course, an isolated act is not sufficient to destroy the benefits of the system. But the moral acceptability of the system may become questionable if the conditions of acceptable exchange are widely abused. The individual who attempts to gain personally by undermining these conditions does that which, if commonly practiced, would produce a very different system from the one that supposedly provides moral legitimacy to that individual's activities.

II

If a mutually beneficial exchange is to be expected, the parties involved must be adequately informed about what they are giving up and what they are receiving. In most cases this should create no great problem for the seller[5], but what about the buyer? How is she to obtain the information needed? One answer is that the buyer is responsible for doing whatever investigation is necessary to acquire the information. The medieval principle of *caveat emptor* encouraged buyers to take responsibility for examining a purchase thoroughly to determine whether it had any hidden flaws. If the buyer failed to find defects, that meant that due caution had not been exercised.

If it were always relatively easy to discover defects by examination, then this principle might be an efficient method of guaranteeing mutual satisfaction. Sometimes, however, even lengthy investigation would not disclose what the buyer wants to know. With products of great complexity, the expertise needed for an adequate examination may be beyond what could reasonably be expected of most consumers. Even relatively simple products can have hidden flaws that most people would not discover until after the purchase, and to have the responsibility for closely examining every purchase would involve a considerable amount of a highly treasured modern commodity, the buyer's time. Furthermore, many exchange situations in our context involve products that cannot be examined in this way—goods that will be delivered at a later time or sent through the mail, for example. Finally, even if we assume that most buyers, by exercising enough caution, can protect their interests, the system of *caveat emptor* would take advantage of those least able to watch out for themselves. It would in effect justify mistreatment of a few for a rather questionable benefit.

In practice the buyer almost always relies on the seller for some information, and if mutually beneficial exchanges are to be expected, the information needs to meet certain standards of both quality and quantity. With regard to quality, the information provided should not be deceptive. This would include not only direct lies but also truths that are intended to mislead the buyer. Consider the following examples:

1. An aluminum siding salesperson tells customers that they will receive "bargain factory prices" for letting their homes be used as models in a new advertising campaign. Prospective customers will be brought to view the houses, and a commission of $100 will be paid for each sale that results. In fact, the price paid is well above market rates, the workmanship and materials are substandard, and no one is ever brought by to see the houses.[6]
2. A used car salesperson turns back the odometer reading on automobiles by an average of 25,000 to 30,000 miles per car. If customers ask whether the reading is correct, the salesperson replies that it is illegal to alter odometer readings.
3. A salesperson at a piano store tells an interested customer that the "special sale" will be good only through that evening. She neglects to mention that another "special sale" will begin the next day.
4. A telephone salesperson tells people who answer the phone that they have been selected to receive a free gift, a brand new freezer. All they have to do is buy a year's subscription to a food plan.
5. A salesperson for a diet system proclaims that under this revolutionary new plan the pounds

will melt right off. The system is described as a scientific advance that makes dieting easy. In fact, the system is a low-calorie diet composed of foods and liquids that are packaged under the company name but are no different from standard grocery store items.

The possibilities are endless, and whether or not a lie is involved, each case illustrates a salesperson's attempt to get a customer to believe something that is false in order to make the sale. It might be pointed out that these kinds of practices would not deceive a sophisticated consumer. Perhaps so, but whether they are always successful deceptions is not the issue. They are attempts to mislead the customer, and given that the consumer must often rely on information furnished by the salesperson, they are attempts to subvert the conditions under which mutually beneficial exchange can be expected. The salesperson attempts to use misinformation as a basis for customer judgment rather than allowing that judgment to be based on accurate beliefs. Furthermore, if these kinds of practices were not successful fairly often, they would probably not be used.

In the aluminum siding case, the customer is led to believe that there will be a discount in exchange for a kind of service, allowing the house to be viewed by prospective customers. This leaves the impression both that the job done will be of high quality and that the price paid will be offset by commissions. The car salesperson alters the product in order to suggest false information about the extent of its use. With such information, the customer is not able to judge accurately the value of the car. The misleading reply to inquiries is not substantially different from a direct lie. The piano salesperson deceives the customer about how long the product will be obtainable at a discount price. In this case the deception occurs through an omission. The telephone solicitor tries to give the impression that there has been a contest of some sort and that the freezer is a prize. In this way, the nature of the exchange is obscured.

The diet-system case raises questions about how to distinguish legitimate "puffery" from deception. Obviously, the matter will depend to some extent on how gullible we conceive the customer to be. As described, the case surely involves an attempt to get the customer to believe that dieting will be easier under this system and that what is being promoted is the result of some new scientific discovery. If there were no prospect that a customer would be likely to believe this, we would probably not think the technique deceptive. But in fact a number of individuals are deceived by claims of this type.

Some writers have defended the use of deceptive practices in business contexts on the grounds that there are specific rules applying to these contexts that differ from the standards appropriate in other contexts. It is argued, for example, that deception is standard practice, understood by all participants as something to be expected and, therefore, harmless, or that it is a means of self-defense justified by pressures of the competitive context.[7] To the extent that claims about widespread practice are true, people who know what is going on may be able to minimize personal losses, but that is hardly a justification of the practice. If I know that many people have installed devices in their cars that can come out and puncture the tires of the car next to them, that may help keep me from falling victim, but it does not make the practice harmless. Even if no one is victimized, it becomes necessary to take extra precautions, introducing a significant disutility into driving conditions. Analogously, widespread deception in business debases the currency of language, making business communication less efficient and more cumbersome.

More importantly, however, people are victimized by deceptive practices, and the fact that some may be shrewd enough to see through clouds of misinformation does not alter the deceptive intent. Whatever may be said with regard to appropriate behavior among people who "know the rules," it is clear that many buyers are not aware of having entered into some special domain where deception is allowed. Even if this is naive, it does not provide a moral justification for subverting those individuals' capacity for making a reasoned choice.

Only a few people would defend the moral justifiability of deceptive sales practices. However, there may be room for much more disagreement with regard to how much information a salesperson is obligated to provide. In rejecting the principle of *caveat emptor*, I have suggested that there are pragmatic reasons for expecting the seller to communicate some information about the product. But how much? When is it morally culpable to withhold information? Consider the following cases:

1. An automobile dealer has bought a number of cars from another state. Although they appear to be new or slightly used, these cars have been involved in a major flood and were sold by the previous dealer at a discount rate. The salesperson knows the history of the cars and does not mention it to customers.

2. A salesperson for an encyclopedia company never mentions the total price of a set unless he has to. Instead he emphasizes the low monthly payment involved.

3. A real estate agent knows that one reason the couple selling a house with her company want to move is that the neighbors often have loud parties and neighborhood children have committed minor acts of vandalism. The agent makes no mention of this to prospective customers.

4. An admissions officer for a private college speaks enthusiastically about the advantages of the school. He does not mention the fact that the school is not accredited.

5. A prospective retirement home resident is under the impression that a particular retire-

ment home is affiliated with a certain church. He makes it known that this is one of the features he finds attractive about the home. Though the belief is false, the recruiters for the home make no attempt to correct the misunderstanding.

In all these cases the prospective buyer lacks some piece of knowledge that might be relevant to the decision to buy. The conditions for ideal exchange are not met. Perhaps, however, there can be an acceptable exchange. Whether or not this is the case depends on whether the buyer has adequate information to decide if the purchase would be beneficial. In the case of the flood-damaged autos, there is information relevant to evaluating the worth of the car that the customer could not be expected to know unless informed by the seller. If this information is not revealed, the buyer will not have adequate knowledge to make a reasonable judgment. Determining exactly how much information needs to be provided is not always clear-cut. We must in general rely on our assessments of what a reasonable person would want to know. As a practical guide, a salesperson might consider, "What would I want to know, if I were considering buying this product?"

Surely a reasonable person would want to know the total price of a product. Hence the encyclopedia salesperson who omits this total is not providing adequate information. The salesperson may object that this information could be inferred from other information about the monthly payment, length of term, and interest rate. But if the intention is not to have the customer act without knowing the full price, then why shouldn't it be provided directly? The admissions officer's failure to mention that the school is unaccredited also seems unacceptable when we consider what a reasonable person would want to know. There are some people who would consider this a plus, since they are suspicious about accrediting agencies imposing some alien standards (e.g., standards that conflict with religious views). But regardless of how one evaluates the fact, most people would judge it to be important for making a decision.

The real estate case is more puzzling. Most real estate agents would not reveal the kind of information described, and would not feel they had violated any moral duties in failing to do so. Clearly, many prospective customers would want to be informed about such problems. However, in most cases failing to know these facts would not be of crucial importance. We have a case of borderline information. It would be known by all parties to an ideal exchange, but we can have an acceptable exchange even if the buyer is unaware of it. Failure to inform the customer of these facts is not like failing to inform the customer that the house is on the site of a hazardous waste dump or that a major freeway will soon be adjacent to the property.

It is possible to alter the case in such a way that the information should be revealed or at least the buyer should be directed another way. Suppose the buyer makes it clear that his primary goal is to live in a quiet neighborhood where he will be undisturbed. The "borderline" information now becomes more central to the customer's decision. Notice that thinking in these terms moves us away from the general standard of what a reasonable person would want to know to the more specific standard of what is relevant given the criteria of this individual. In most cases, however, I think that a salesperson would be justified in operating under general "reasonable person" standards until particular deviations become apparent.[8]

The case of the prospective retirement home resident is a good example of how the particular criteria of the customer might assume great importance. If the recruiters, knowing what they know about this man's religious preferences, allow him to make his decision on the basis of a false assumption, they will have failed to support the conditions of acceptable exchange. It doesn't really matter that the misunderstanding was not caused by the salespeople. Their allowing it to be part of the basis for a decision borders on deception. If the misunderstanding was not on a matter of central importance to the individual's evaluation, they might have had no obligation to correct it. But the case described is not of that sort.

Besides providing nondeceptive and relatively complete information, salespeople may be obligated to make sure that their communications are understandable. Sales presentations containing technical information that is likely to be misunderstood are morally questionable. However, it would be unrealistic to expect all presentations to be immune to misunderstanding. The salesperson is probably justified in developing presentations that would be intelligible to the average consumer of the product he or she is selling and making adjustments in the cases where it is clear that misunderstanding has occurred.

III

The condition of uncompelled exchange distinguishes business dealings from other kinds of exchanges. In the standard business arrangement, neither party is forced to enter the negotiations. A threat of harm would transform the situation to something other than a purely business arrangement. Coercion is not the only kind of compulsion, however. Suppose I have access to only one producer of food. I arrange to buy food from this producer, but given my great need for food and the absence of alternatives, the seller is able to dictate the terms. In one sense I choose to make the deal, but the voluntariness of my choice is limited by the absence of alternatives.

Ordinarily, the individual salesperson will not have the power to take away the buyer's alternatives. However, a clever salesperson can sometimes make it seem as if options are very limited and can use the customer's ignorance to produce the same effect. For example, imagine an individual who begins to look for a particular item at a local store. The salesperson extols the line carried by his store, warns of the deficiencies of alternative brands, and warns about the dishonesty of competitors, in contrast to his store's reliability. With a convincing presentation, a customer might easily perceive the options to be very limited. Whether or not the technique is questionable may depend on the accuracy of the perception. If the salesperson is attempting to take away a legitimate alternative, that is an attempt to undermine the customer's voluntary choice.

Another way the condition of uncompelled choice might be subverted is by involving a customer in a purchase without allowing her to notice what is happening. This would include opening techniques that disguise the purpose of the encounter so there can be no immediate refusal. The customer is led to believe that the interview is about a contest or a survey or an opportunity to make money. Not until the end does it become apparent that this is an attempt to sell something, and occasionally if the presentation is smooth enough, some buyers can be virtually unaware that they have bought anything. Obviously, there can be degrees of revelation, and not every approach that involves initial disguise of certain elements that might provoke an immediate rejection is morally questionable. But there are enough clear cases in which the intention is to get around, as much as possible, the voluntary choice of the customer. Consider the following examples:

1. A seller of children's books gains entrance to houses by claiming to be conducting an edu-

cational survey. He does indeed ask several "survey" questions, but he uses these to qualify potential customers for his product.

2. A salesperson alludes to recent accidents involving explosions of furnaces and, leaving the impression of having some official government status, offers to do a free safety inspection. She almost always discovers a "major problem" and offers to sell a replacement furnace.

3. A man receives a number of unsolicited books and magazines through the mail. Then he is sent a bill and later letters warning of damage to his credit rating if he does not pay.

These are examples of the many variations on attempts to involve customers in exchanges without letting them know what is happening. The first two cases involve deceptions about the purpose of the encounter. Though they resemble cases discussed earlier that involved deception about the nature or price of a product, here the salesperson uses misinformation as a means of limiting the customer's range of choice. The customer does not consciously choose to listen to a sales presentation but finds that this is what is happening. Some psychological research suggests that when people do something that appears to commit them to a course of action, even without consciously choosing to do so, they will tend to act as if such a choice had been made in order to minimize cognitive dissonance. Hence, if a salesperson successfully involves the customer in considering a purchase, the customer may feel committed to give serious thought to the matter. The third case is an attempt to get the customer to believe that an obligation has been incurred. In variations on this technique, merchandise is mailed to a deceased person to make relatives believe that some payment is owed. In each case, an effort is made to force the consumer to choose from an excessively limited range of options.

IV

How can a salesperson subvert the rationality condition? Perhaps the most common way is to appeal to emotional reactions that cloud an individual's perception of relevant considerations. Consider the following cases:

1. A man's wife has recently died in a tragic accident. The funeral director plays upon the husband's love for his wife and to some extent his guilt about her death to get him to purchase a very expensive funeral.

2. A socially insecure young woman has bought a series of dance lessons from a local studio. During the lessons, an attractive male instructor constantly compliments her on her poise and natural ability and tries to persuade her to sign up for more lessons.[9]

3. A life insurance salesperson emphasizes to a prospect the importance of providing for his family in the event of his death. The salesperson tells several stories about people who put off this kind of preparation.

4. A dress salesperson typically tells customers how fashionable they look in a certain dress. Her stock comments also include pointing out that a dress is slimming or sexy or "looks great on you."

5. A furniture salesperson regularly tells customers that a piece of furniture is the last one in stock and that another customer recently showed great interest in it. He sometimes adds that it may not be possible to get any more like it from the factory.

These cases remind us that emotions can be important motivators. It is not surprising that salespeople appeal to them in attempting to get the customer to make a purchase. In certain cases the appeal seems perfectly legitimate. When the life insurance salesperson tries to arouse the customer's fear and urges preparation, it may be a legitimate way to get the customer to consider something that is worth considering. Of course, the fact that the fear is aroused by one who sells life insurance may obscure to the customer the range of alternative possibilities in preparing financially for the future. But the fact that an emotion is aroused need not make the appeal morally objectionable.

If the appeal of the dress salesperson seems more questionable, this is probably because we are not as convinced of the objective importance of appearing fashionable, or perhaps because repeated observations of this kind are often insincere. But if we assume that the salesperson is giving an honest opinion about how the dress looks on a customer, it may provide some input for the individual who has a desire to achieve a particular effect. The fact that such remarks appeal to one's vanity or ambition does not in itself make the appeal unacceptable.

The furniture salesperson's warnings are clearly calculated to create some anxiety about the prospect of losing the chance to buy a particular item unless immediate action is taken. If the warnings are factually based, they would not be irrelevant to the decision to buy. Clearly, one might act impulsively or hastily when under the spell of such thoughts, but the salesperson cannot be faulted for pointing out relevant considerations.

The case of the funeral director is somewhat different. Here there is a real question of what benefit is to be gained by choosing a more expensive funeral package. For most people, minimizing what is spent on the funeral would be a rational choice, but at a time of emotional vulnerability it can be made to look as if this means depriving the loved one or the family of some great benefit. Even if the funeral director makes nothing but true statements, they can be put into a form designed to arouse emotions that will lessen the possibility of a rational decision being reached.

The dance studio case is similar in that a weakness is being played upon. The woman's insecurity makes her vulnerable to flattery and attention, and this creates the kind of situation in which others can take advantage of

her. Perhaps the dance lessons fulfill some need, but the appeal to her vanity easily becomes a tool to manipulate her into doing what the instructor wants.

The key to distinguishing between legitimate and illegitimate emotional appeals lies in whether the appeal clouds one's ability to make a decision based on genuine satisfaction of needs and desires. Our judgment about whether this happens in a particular case will depend in part on whether we think the purchase is likely to benefit the customer. The more questionable the benefits, the more an emotional appeal looks like manipulation rather than persuasion. When questionable benefits are combined with some special vulnerability on the part of the consumer, the use of the emotional appeal appears even more suspect.

In considering benefits, we should not forget to consider costs as well. Whether a purchase is beneficial may depend on its effects on the family budget. Ordinarily it is not the responsibility of a salesperson to inquire into such matters, but if it becomes clear that financial resources are limited, the use of emotional appeals to get the customer to buy more than she can afford becomes morally questionable. Occasionally we hear about extreme cases in which a salesperson finds out the amount of life insurance received by a widow and talks her into an unnecessary purchase for that amount, or in which the salesperson persuades some poor family to make an unwise purchase on credit requiring them to cut back on necessities. The salesperson is not responsible for making a rational calculation for the customer, but when a salesperson knowingly urges an action that is not beneficial to the consumer, that is in effect trying to get the consumer to make an irrational judgment. Any techniques used to achieve this end would be attempts to subvert the conditions of mutually beneficial exchange.

For obvious reasons, salespeople want as

many customers as possible to make purchases, and therefore they try to put the decision to purchase in the best possible light. It is not the job of a salesperson to present all the facts as objectively as possible. But if playing on a customer's emotions is calculated to obscure the customer's ability to make rational judgments about whether a purchase is in her best interest, then it is morally objectionable.

V

I have attempted to provide a framework for evaluating the morality of a number of different types of sales practices. The framework is based on conditions for mutually beneficial exchange and ultimately for an efficient satisfaction of economic needs and desires. An inevitable question is whether this kind of evaluation is of any practical importance.

If we set before ourselves the ideal of a knowledgeable, unforced, and rational decision on the part of a customer, it is not difficult to see how some types of practices would interfere with this process. We must, of course, be careful not to set the standards too high. A customer may be partially but adequately informed to judge a purchase's potential benefits. A decision may be affected by nonrational and even irrational factors and yet still be rational enough in terms of being plausibly related to the individual's desires and needs. There may be borderline cases in which it is not clear whether acting in a particular way would be morally required or simply overscrupulous, but that is not an objection to this approach, only a recognition of a feature of morality itself.[10]

NOTES

1. In a survey of the major textbooks in the field of business ethics, I discovered only one with a chapter on sales practices: David Braybrooke's *Ethics in the World of Business,* Chapter 4 (Totowa, N.J.: Rowman and Allanheld, 1983). That chapter contains only a brief discussion of the issue; most of the chapter is devoted to excerpts from court cases and the quotation of a code of ethics for a direct-mail marketing association.

2. The classic statement of the argument from economic benefits is found in Adam Smith, *The Wealth of Nations* (1776) (London: Methusen and Co. Ltd., 1930). Modern proponents of this argument include Ludwig von Mises, Friedrich von Hayek, and Milton Friedman.

3. One very clear analysis of voluntariness making use of these conditions may be found in John Hospers' *Human Conduct: Problems of Ethics,* 2nd ed. (New York: Harcourt Brace Jovanovich, 1982), pp. 385–388.

4. I will refer to the three conditions indifferently as conditions for voluntary exchange or conditions for mutually beneficial exchange. By the latter designation I do not mean to suggest that they are either necessary or sufficient conditions for the occurrence of mutual benefit, but that they are conditions for the reasonable expectation of mutual benefit.

5. There are cases, however, in which the buyer knows more about a product than the seller. For example, suppose Cornell has found out that land Fredonia owns contains minerals that make it twice as valuable as Fredonia thinks. The symmetry of my conditions would lead me to conclude that Cornell should give Fredonia the relevant information unless perhaps Fredonia's failure to know was the result of some culpable negligence.

6. This case is described in Warren Magnuson and Jean Carper, *The Dark Side of the Market-Place* (Englewood Cliffs, N.J.: Prentice Hall, 1968), pp. 3–4.

7. Albert Carr, "Is Business Bluffing Ethical?" *Harvard Business Review* 46 (January-February 1968): 143–153. See also Thomas L. Carson, Richard E. Wokutch, and Kent F. Murrmann, "Bluffing in Labor Negotiations: Legal and Ethical Issues," *Journal of Business Ethics* 1 (1982): 13–22.

8. My reference to a reasonable person standard should not be confused with the issue facing the FTC of whether to evaluate advertising by the reasonable consumer or ignorant con-

sumer standard as described in Ivan Preston, "Reasonable Consumer or Ignorant Consumer: How the FTC Decides," *Journal of Consumer Affairs* 8 (Winter 1974): 131–143. There the primary issue is with regard to whom the government should protect from claims that might be misunderstood. My concern here is with determining what amount of information is necessary for informed judgment. In general I suggest that a salesperson should begin with the assumption that information a reasonable consumer would regard as important needs to be revealed and that when special interests and concerns of the consumer come to light they may make further revelations necessary. This approach parallels the one taken by Tom Beauchamp and James Childress regarding the information that a physician needs to provide to obtain informed consent. See their *Principles of Biomedical Ethics*, 3rd ed. (New York: Oxford University Press, 1989), pp. 85–101.

9. This is adapted from a court case quoted in Braybrooke, pp. 68–70.

10. This paper was written during a sabbatical leave from Friends University at the Center for the Study of Values, University of Delaware. I wish to thank Friends University for the leave and Dr. Norman Bowie for his hospitality during my stay at the Center.

Paternalism in the Marketplace: Should A Salesman Be His Buyer's Keeper?

*James M. Ebejer
and Michael J. Morden*

The moral relationship between salespersons and their customers can range from *caveat emptor* to paternalism. We propose that between these extremes is a realistic professional ethic for sales that we will refer to as "limited paternalism."

At one extreme is *caveat emptor*—"let the buyer beware." We do not claim there is anything inherently immoral about such a position, only that it is no longer appropriate in our society. Games can be played by various rules, as long as all participants know those rules. When two old horse-traders tried to strike a bargain, it was understood that the seller could be assumed to misrepresent the condition of the animal and the buyer was warned to be on his guard. Perhaps this situation was not unfair since both participants knew the rules, entered into the agreement voluntarily, and had the opportunity to examine the merchandise. However, the contemporary consumer frequently purchases goods or services which he cannot be expected to judge for himself. The workings of an insurance policy are as mysterious to us as those of a VCR. A salesperson, with her superior understanding, is in such a position to exploit our ignorance, that few of us would want to play the game if the rule of the marketplace were understood to be strictly "let the buyer beware."

At the other extreme is the practice of paternalism. A standard definition of paternalism is "the interference with a person's liberty of action justified by reasons referring exclusively to the welfare, good, happiness, needs, interests, or values of the person being coerced" (Dworkin, 1971). In other words, pa-

Journal of Business Ethics **7** (1988) 337–339. © 1988 by Kluwer Academic Publishers. Reprinted by permission of Kluwer Academic Publishers.

ternalism occurs when an individual, presumably in a position of superior knowledge, makes a decision for another person to protect this other from some type of harm. Paternalism implies that the first person deprives the second of liberty of autonomy. This infraction on liberty is thought justified because, in the mind of the first person, it is "for his own good." Recently, a merchant refused to sell tropical fish to a patron because she felt he was not changing the water in his tank often enough. Although the merchant was infringing on the customer's liberty based on her superior knowledge, the interference was for his own good (and presumably the good of the fish). The merchant was being paternalistic.

Most of us expect paternalism in certain situations. If the service we are purchasing is an appendectomy, we typically allow the salesman (in this case the surgeon) a major role in deciding whether we need the service. We rely on the ethics of the profession to protect us from the possible exploitation. The old-fashioned physician considered such paternalism part of his role, but modern medicine emphasizes the patient's informed consent. The professionals use their superior knowledge to make the medical diagnosis, but they are expected to explain treatment options available to the patient so the latter can make the moral decision. Thus even in the most paternalistic of contexts we find that professionalism justifies only a limited paternalism.

This limited paternalism, which is typically an element in professionalism, applies when an individual in a position of superior knowledge has an active duty to explain the consequences of a decision. Here the "father-like" individual does not make the decision for the other. The only liberty that is violated is the freedom to be ignorant: the consumer is protected from an uninformed decision that could be detrimental to him.

To claim that a salesperson is professionally required to inform customers fully about a product or service, to disclose fully all relevant information without hiding crucial stipulations in small print, to ascertain that they are aware of their needs and the degree to which the product or service will satisfy them, is to impose upon the salesperson the positive duty of limited paternalism. According to this standard a salesperson is, to a limited degree, "his buyer's keeper."

Consider the following example: A woman takes her car to an auto repair shop and tells the mechanic she needs a new muffler and exhaust pipes because her car makes too much noise. While examining the car, the mechanic concludes that the excessive noise occurs because there is a hole in the tail pipe. The mechanic was told to replace the exhaust pipes and the muffler. He has three options: (1) replace the exhaust pipes and the muffler as requested by the car's owner and collect (say) $90.00; (2) talk to the owner, refuse to do as requested since all that is needed is a $20.00 tail pipe; (3) talk to the owner, explain the situation, and let her decide for herself if she really wants to spend $70.00 more than is necessary to fix the car.

When confronted with this situation, many repairmen or auto parts salespersons would choose the first option: collect as much money as possible. This is perfectly legal since the car's owner did authorize complete replacement. Some perhaps would act paternalistically by following the second option: replace the tail pipe for $20.00, but refuse to replace the longer exhaust pipe and the muffler because it is not necessary. But now he has infringed on the owner's right to decide for herself. Perhaps the owner wanted to be absolutely certain that her exhaust system was perfect and would not need work again soon. Maybe she is rich and does not mind spending the extra money. In any case, it is her car, her money, and her decision. Option number three is the best ethical choice and the standard required for professional responsibility: the mechanic has a duty to inform the owner of facts of which she might not be aware since she is not the expert. The choice should be left to the owner.

But consider a different situation: a customer in a store that specializes in stereo equipment is consulting a salesperson about the specifications, quality and prices of various amplifiers. The salesperson is considered an expert on all equipment available for sale in the show room. After some deliberation, the customer tentatively decides he would like to own a Super Max amplifier. But before making the purchase, he asks the salesperson one more question: "Is there anything else I should know about this particular model before giving you the cash?" Now, to the best of her knowledge, the salesperson has accurately communicated the advantages of the amplifier, told him the price—$400, and that this particular unit does meet his needs. However, she also knows that the same model is being sold at an appliance store across the street for only $350! Does our standard require that she tell the buyer about this possible savings? Clearly not. Although the salesperson was aware of the competitor's price, she did not withhold information that only an expert would know. Anyone could easily find out how much the amplifier sold for at the other stores. The knowledge was not part of the technical expertise that marks her as a professional and which the buyer was presumably relying upon. However, if she held back information, relevant to the decision, which a non-expert could not be expected to know, then her behavior would be unethical by our standard.

Nearly all "hard sell" techniques are unethical according to this standard. Many salespersons intentionally keep information from potential buyers. They try to sell the most expensive product a customer will buy without regard to the needs of that person. Granted, some revenue may be lost in the short term from telling customers the bad as well as the good about a product or service, but profits will increase in the long run. Once a salesperson earns a reputation for being "honest"—i.e., ethical, interested in mutual exchange to mutual advantage rather than exploitation—he will have more satisfied customers, more referrals, and, eventually, greater income from an overall increase in sales. Even where the policy might not profit the salesperson in a specific case, it is a rule which if generally followed would produce the greatest good for the greatest number. Furthermore, it treats the customer the way we ourselves would want to be treated; it is a rule we would agree to even if we didn't know whether we were going to be the salesperson or the customer; finally, it bases sales ethics on widely accepted standards of professionalism. Clearly it is consistent with our ordinary ethical assumptions.

NOTE

Gerald Dworkin: 1971, "Paternalism", in *Morality and Law*, ed. Richard Wasserstrom (Belmont, CA), p. 108.

Manipulative Advertising

Tom L. Beauchamp

Lake Jewelers closed after being in business in Detroit for 36 years. Arthur Lake, president of the local Chamber of Commerce, was not as yet financially imperilled. But he said his business was gradually being ruined by his competitors' misleading advertisements. Lake cited, in particular, "phony discounting," in which retailers present fake percentage markdowns from "suggested retail prices" that are imaginary or artificially inflated. Advertisements depict prices as bargains (50 to 78 percent off), when in fact the prices are comparatively high. Lake said that customers are "duped into thinking" they receive bargains, and "ethical" merchants find it extremely difficult to compete against such advertisements.[1]

In this paper, I assess a range of criticisms that, like this one, accuse advertisers of manipulating customers into purchases based on incorrect or inconclusive information. I am concerned exclusively with manipulations that limit free action, especially in the food and alcoholic-beverage industries and in advertising by banks, savings and loans, and brokerage houses. I begin with the rudiments of a theory of influence and manipulation, and then return to advertising.

THE CONTINUUM OF INFLUENCES

To determine whether advertising diminishes free choice, we need to examine how external influences affect free choice. The antithesis of being free is being controlled by an alien influence that deprives one of self-direction. I use terms such as *freedom* and *free to act* to refer specifically to the absence of controlling external influences or constraints.

Although coercion is a frequently analyzed form of controlling influence, coercion does not cover all relevant forms of controlling influence. It lies at one end of a continuum of influence, the end that eliminates freedom and entirely compromises free choice. At the other end of the continuum are forms of influence such as (rational) persuasion. Other points on the continuum include indoctrination, seduction, and so forth. At one end point of the continuum are completely *controlling* influences, those that fully govern or control a person's actions, rendering the person's choices and actions not meaningfully his or hers. At the other end, wholly *noncontrolling* influences in no way undermine a person's free choice.

Three broad categories or classes of influence are spread across this continuum: coercion, manipulation, and persuasion: (1) Coercive influences are controlling influences; (2) manipulative influences are sometimes controlling influences and (3) persuasive influences are not controlling influences. Many choices are not substantially free, although we commonly think of them as "free choices." These include actions under powerful family and religious influences, purchases made under partial ignorance of the quality of the merchandise, and deference to an authoritative physician's judgment. Many such actions fall far short of ideal free action because of lack of understanding or control by another person. But the vital question is whether actions are sufficiently or adequately free, not whether they are ideally or wholly free.

FROM COERCION TO PERSUASION

We need definitions of *coercion, manipulation,* and *persuasion* that express their differences.

First, *coercion* occurs if one party deliberately and successfully uses force or a credible threat of unwanted, avoidable, and serious harm in order to compel a particular response from another person. No matter how attractive or overwhelming an offer, coercion is not involved unless a threatening negative sanction is presented. Advertisements directed at a starving population that "offer" food and medical attention in return for marketable blood, as allegedly was done by Plasma International,[2] constitutes a threat and not a mere offer, and so is coercive. But such circumstances are extremely rare in advertising, and thus the problem of "coercive advertising" is contrived—not an issue that we need to address.

Second, *persuasion* is a deliberate and successful attempt by one person to encourage another to freely accept beliefs, attitudes, values, or actions through appeals to reason. The first person offers what he or she believes to be good reasons for accepting the desired perspective. In paradigmatic cases of persuasion, these good reasons are conveyed through structured verbal facts or argument. However, good reasons can also be expressed through nonverbal communication such as visual evidence. "Rational" persuasion is sometimes distinguished from "nonrational" persuasion, but I will consider only rational persuasion. ("Nonrational" persuasion is a form of manipulation, as defined below.)

The Kellogg Co., which has been attacked for its child-oriented advertisements of presweetened, ready-to-eat cereals, presents an example of self-proclaimed persuasive advertising. Executive Vice-President William E. LaMothe once testified before the Senate Select Committee on Nutrition and Human Needs that Kellogg has adopted the following approach to advertising its products: "Our company is very conscious of the fact that social responsibilities go hand-in-hand with business responsibilities. The steps that we are taking to contribute to the improvement of the understanding of the need for a complete and adequate breakfast reflect this consciousness."[3] Any company acting on the principle that advertising should "contribute to the improvement of the understanding" and using bona fide informational appeals to convince viewers to eat healthier breakfasts would be employing a policy of persuasion.

The essence of rational persuasion is inducing change by convincing a person through the merit of the reasons put forward.[4] However, "the merit of the reasons" is a tricky notion. Judgments about the credibility and expertise of a person advancing an argument affect our acceptance of a message no less than the premises and the soundness of the argument used. Does persuasion then occur? Acceding to an argument simply because one likes the person who presents the argument—as in Pepsi's television ads using famous entertainment stars—or finds the person physically attractive—as in typical magazine advertising for Virginia Slims—can be distinguished from accepting an argument because the person is an expert and therefore likely to be correct. The same arguments may be more persuasive if the reasons are presented by a professional rather than by an inexperienced amateur. Authoritative judgment often rationally persuades although fully developed persuasive arguments are not presented.

We sometimes cannot determine from the description of an attempt to influence whether the influence is a case of persuasion or a case of manipulation. The central question is not what is done, said, or suggested, but how or through what psychological processes the person responded to and was affected by the influence. Advertising can persuade and also mislead only some persons who receive the message. An FTC staff report concerning children's television noted the following about children six years and under:

> (1) They place indiscriminate trust in televised advertising messages; (2) they do not understand the persuasive bias in television advertising; and (3) the techniques, focus, and themes used in child-oriented television advertising enhance the appeal of the advertising message and the advertised product. Consequently, young children do not possess the cognitive ability to evaluate adequately child-oriented television advertising.[5]

Although children under six years of age cannot understand the intent of a commercial message, the report argues, children over six often can. Children under six are manipulated, whereas some over six are persuaded. Many questions remain unanswered about the depth and manner of television advertising's influence on both children and adults. For example, there are questions about the effect of television advertising, about the ability of persons to process cognitively the advertising information, about the ability of various persons to discriminate between the content of the program and the commercial, and about the ability of persons to resist appeals even if they understand them to be commercial in nature.

There are also questions about what counts as a good reason or even a reason at all. Suppose an advertiser believes that the reasons used in an ad are bad reasons, but knows that the persons at whom the advertisement is directed believe they are good reasons. Is this an attempt at persuasion by giving good reasons, or an attempt at manipulation by motivating purchases for bad reasons? Whether anyone except the consumer believes the reason to be a good reason sometimes seems irrelevant. For example, an advertiser may believe it is crazy to buy a soap because it smells

good when the wrapper is opened, but if people value the soap for this reason, the soap's attractive aroma seems to be a good reason to promote the product.

Cases become progressively more difficult to handle. If a person believes, based on an advertisement, that a good-tasting toothpaste enhances sex appeal, can this qualify as a good reason, or as a reason at all? If a mother believes falsely that a tasty snack food will make her baby healthier, can this be a good reason? As the ads become progressively more deceptive or harmful, one is more likely to abstain from calling them "good reasons." The criteria of "good reasons" will be governed by a broader conception of legitimate and illegitimate influence.

Consumer protection groups and sometimes government officials focus on the consumers' *response* to advertising and on its human effects, rather than on the *intention* of those who create the advertising. By contrast, those who defend controversial advertising focus more on the intentions of advertising agencies and manufacturers in marketing a product—namely, on the intent to sell a "good product." These different emphases exhibit further complications, because an advertisement created with good intentions nonetheless can be misleading or nonrationally controlling.

MANIPULATION

I move now from coercion and persuasion into the central class of influences for present purposes. Manipulation is a broad category that includes any successful attempt to elicit a desired response from another person by noncoercively modifying choices available to that person or by nonpersuasively altering another person's perceptions of available choices. A variety of concepts explains this portion of the continuum between coercion and persuasion. Current literature mentions incentives, strong offers, indoctrination, propaganda, emotional pressure, irrational persuasion, temptation, seduction, and deception. I am using the single word *manipulation* to describe various parts of this vast territory of forms of influence.

The major difference between informational manipulation and persuasion is that the former involves deception used to influence a person's choice or action, whereas persuasion is not based on deception. In being influenced by information, persuasion is an attempt to get one to believe what is correct, sound, or backed by good reasons. Manipulation is an attempt to induce one to believe what is not correct, unsound, or not backed by good reasons.

We should, however, be cautious in using words such as *misleading* and *deceptive*, which have both subjective and objective connotations. People are often misled by their own bizarre inferences or by lack of concentration. A presentation is not necessarily misleading because it is misunderstood or because it leads persons to believe what is false. The goal of eliminating all misleading subjective interpretation is a noble ideal but too demanding as a standard for public advertising.

Some writers claim that manipulation involves eliciting a desired decision through more subtle means than coercion, but, like coercion, in that the facts are packaged and presented so that the person has no real choice. To heighten an appeal to the point that a person can no longer resist the temptation to do something is, on this criterion, a manipulative way of eliminating choice.[6] This understanding of manipulation is both too broad and too narrow. It is too broad because some offers, such as competitive salary bonuses to keep an employee, can be persuasive and need not be manipulative. It is too narrow because manipulated persons may have some alternatives available, should they elect

them. They may also have capacities for resistance to an offer, should they have a reason to resist, even if the offerer knows that one option is the most attractive and the one the other person will pursue. Unlike coercion, manipulation is sometimes compatible with free choice. The manipulee may arrange and welcome the manipulative influence. A part of the difficulty in assessing the moral acceptability of advertising is that a potentially manipulative advertisement may be directed at a group of otherwise free persons, some of whom find the appeal resistible and some of whom do not. Often the influence attempt could have been persuasive but a manipulative appeal was elected instead.

MANIPULATION IN ADVERTISING

This account of manipulation and the continuum of influence applies to many forms of advertising. I shall discuss advertising in three general categories of industry.

Bank Advertising

Banks regularly advertise for new accounts, but some of these advertisements are manipulative, not persuasive. The advertisements I examined are all for fixed-term deposits that pay more than one rate over the term. They advertise a high, short-duration rate of interest in very large type, while the lower rate is noted in far smaller type, as is the fact that the lower rate is effective for a far longer term. Also relegated to the smaller print, if mentioned at all, is any statement of effective annual yield or yield over the course of the account. These advertisements are designed to convey the message to a reader that the significant rate for the thrifty-minded is the one in large type, rather than either the effective annual yield or the underlying, lower rate. A reverse priority ranking is more prudent. The ads also often present the rates as "tax-free" or "tax-exempt," when they are only tax-deferred.

A dramatic form of this kind of advertising occurred when interest rates were higher than they presently are and the competition for Individual Retirement Account (IRA) customers was more intense than it currently is. It became apparent to banks that advertising campaigns were more effective as the rates offered were adjusted to higher levels. The higher advertised rates were purely promotional for short, introductory durations and had little or no benefit on annual yields. For example, the Riggs National Bank in Washington, D.C., which advertises itself as "The Most Important Bank in the Most Important City in the World," started out advertising at 14 percent, but quickly saw the effects of the trends in advertising higher rates and rocketed up to 25 percent for a short introductory duration, after which the money is locked in at a far lower rate. Standard Federal started out with 15 percent, then quickly went to 17 percent and finally to 25 percent without otherwise changing its ads. Other banks were not about to lose customers, and they followed suit.

How successfully do these ads work to influence customers to open new accounts? An official of the Riggs Bank interviewed by the *Washington Post* confirmed that the promotional rate offered brought in a large influx of customers from the start. After Riggs raised the promotional rate from 14 to 25 percent, three times as many depositors signed up for Riggs' IRAs on the days the 25 percent rate was run than had signed up on the days the 14 percent rate had been run.[7]

More important than short duration at high rates is the inherent complication and confusion involved in interpreting the split rate in a context in which there are no uniform practices, standardized rates, or conventional expectations. This is not a mere problem of chaos in a shifting industry. It is beyond the powers of many readers to compute average effective annual yields over the life of the deposit, and yet this computation yields the only material information because withdrawals cannot be made from these accounts without loss of *all* interest—promotional as well as long-term. It is beyond the powers of many readers to make significant comparisons across the different banks. The split rate, the method of compounding, and the term of the deposit make for too many complicated calculations, even among those few customers who might figure out how to make the basic computations.

For example, Riggs' 25 percent promotional, 2-month rate was accompanied by an underlying rate of 10.87 percent for 28 months, whereas Chevy Chase Savings and Loan's 2-month 15 percent promotional rate was accompanied by an underlying rate of 11.5 percent for 28 months. The undisclosed data were that Chevy Chase had an average annual effective yield of 12.39 percent, whereas Riggs' average annual effective yield is 12.31 percent.

Food Advertising

Deceptive disclosure is likewise found in food labeling and marketing. In 1990–1991, the FDA took a stand against Ragu and Procter and Gamble for their "fresh" claims on processed, packaged foods, such as pasta sauces.[8] These two cases set a precedent for further government regulation of food labeling, which had become deceptive and often baffling. Use of terms such as *fat free, cholesterol free, fresh,* and *low sugar* traded on consumer ignorance and led to a war of subtle misrepresentation.

Several problems are involved in deceptive labeling and corresponding advertising. The first is health related. A consumer with high cholesterol typically buys products with labels stating "cholesterol free." However, these products often contain additional sugars or fats to maintain the flavor, creating further, often hidden or undisclosed health risks in the user. To cite a typical example, in 1990 the FDA forced CPC International, marketer of Mazola Corn Oil, to discontinue claims that Mazola helped reduce cholesterol levels. The FDA objected to this claim because the label failed to acknowledge that the product had a high fat content.[9] Mazola is a good product that has no cholesterol; in this respect its ads were correct. However, no margarine helps reduce cholesterol levels, although some margarines present a reduced threat to health by comparison to others. All oils are 100 percent fat, but some have a healthier fat content than others. This was hardly the message communicated by Mazola.

A similar problem occurs in percentage labeling and advertising. An Oscar Mayer turkey product that advertises itself as "98 percent fat-free" measures this claim about fat content by weight, not by caloric intake. But of the 12 calories in each super-thin slice of this turkey, approximately 9 of the calories are fat. From this perspective, a critical one for those who seek to reduce the fat content in their diet, 98 percent fat-free is equivalent to 75 percent fat-caloric content.

These forms of deception mislead consumers into believing in nonexistent health benefits, or at least in misleading claims about them. But these problems are subtle difficulties by comparison to many other advertisements for food products. Health claims in labeling had progressed in late 1991, at the time of the FDA's toughest crackdown, to the point that many manufacturers had reached the conclusion that they had to place some sort of misleading health claim on their label in order to remain competitive. More than one-third of all new food products on the market in 1991 made a claim using some health-related message, without specifying

what the message meant. The FDA effectively wrote a new set of standards for food labeling in order to stop the manipulation of consumers. The agency gave standardized meanings to terms such as *light, reduced, extra light, low-fat,* and *low in cholesterol* in a circumstance in which they were functioning more as buzzwords to attract customers than as truthful claims.[10]

It is interesting to note that this FDA decision was praised, not condemned by leading food manufacturers, such as Kraft General Foods. The reason is that nutritious products that are truthfully labeled make for good advertising and solid sales. These products do better in the market when untruthful claims for inferior products are absent. But manipulation of consumer belief is also good for sales of inferior products as long as it goes undetected or unchallenged.

Life-Style Advertising

A third genre of advertising, often used in cigarette and alcohol advertising, is known as life-style advertising. These ad campaigns do not focus on the benefits of a product, but rather on a desirable life-style that can be associated with the product. Ads aim either to create the association or psychologically reinforce associations that already exist. A typical example is making a link between alcohol consumption and having a good time at parties.

Manipulation occurs whenever life-style advertisements successfully reinforce a certain life-style, often in people who cannot legally purchase the product. For example, Brown and Williamson Tobacco Corp. attempted in 1991 to revitalize their Kool cigarette brand through creating the KOOL PENGUIN. This creature with a spiked, Vanilla Ice hairdo, attractive dark glasses, and youthful personality appeared on billboards, in magazines, and in store displays. The penguin did not directly advocate that minors smoke cigarettes, but it did reinforce youthful perceptions that smoking is cool and a bit rebellious. Company spokesperson Patrick Stone claimed that, although the KOOL PENGUIN resembles Saturday morning cartoon characters and child-hero figures, the company made no attempt to sell to minors.[11]

This interpretation is implausible. The Kool figure's appeal is strictly for the young. It invites smoking and entices a group vulnerable to such appeals. This strategy has long been used in the cigarette industry, and the controversy surrounding the KOOL PENGUIN is not new. Camel cigarettes, with noticeable success in the underage market, long used the cartoon camel figure of Joe Camel, whose coolness was expressed through a leather-jacket image. Kool's market share had fallen 4.9 percent just prior to this ad, which was created to cover lost ground. Because the adult market was at the time still declining, the only place to recover ground was with youths who either do not smoke or do not have a preferred brand.

Alcohol advertising presents a similar form of life-style advertising that critics claim reinforces underage drinking. In November 1991, Surgeon General Antonia Novella called for all beer and wine advertisers to cease television advertising immediately on grounds of its manipulative effect and health risks. To support this request she cited major breweries' advertising campaigns targeted at audiences under the legal drinking age. The Surgeon General appropriately attacked life-style advertisements associating alcohol use with beauty, sex, popularity, and good times. Beach scenes, party scenes, and romantic adventures are manipulative in that they reinforce young people's perceptions that one needs only to consume a few beers to loosen up, fit in with the crowd, and have a good time.[12] This advertising does not mention the dangers in alcohol consumption or the effects of irresponsible product use.

A similar style of advertising is found in Cisco, a "fortified dessert wine," which has a 20 percent alcohol content level, although its packaging is noticeably similar to a standard wine cooler—a clear glass container with a wraparound neck label. Most wine coolers have a 4 to 5 percent alcohol content. Purchasers, particularly underage drinkers, often do not realize Cisco's potency. Marketed under the slogan "Cisco takes you by surprise," it has been documented that Cisco consumption effects include "combativeness, hallucinations, disorientation, [and] loss of motor control and consciousness."[13] When combined with its "cooler style" packaging, Cisco's marketing success and potency led the Surgeon General appropriately to declare Cisco "a dangerous fortified wine, and the ultimate 'wine fooler'."[14]

Similarly, the G. Heileman Brewing Company's malt liquor "PowerMaster" brand created an advertising campaign that featured a black male model, with the intent of targeting young, inner-city black men, who consume roughly one-third of all malt liquors.[15] So conspicuous was this advertising that the Bureau of Alcohol, Tobacco and Firearms prohibited Heileman from further marketing of the product. Each of these advertisements used images and slogans with virtually no cognitive content. The sole objective was to entice consumers to purchase PowerMaster. The $2 billion alcohol-advertising industry often entices through images of rock and rap music, sexual suggestion, race cars, and cartoons in order to reach young audiences and manipulate them into product consumption.

HOW ADVERTISING MANIPULATES

Each example of advertising considered above is manipulative, much falling under the category earlier referred to as the manipulation of information." This informational manipulation affects freedom by deception. It renders persons at least partially ignorant, thereby limiting aspects of their decisions. Such manipulation includes withholding and exaggerating information in order to produce false beliefs or distorted perceptions. However, manipulation does not always work exclusively by rendering the manipulee ignorant of relevant information. Some advertisements initiate psychological processes of commitment that are difficult to reverse even after more information is received. People have a strong psychological tendency to continue with a decision once made, especially if an agreement has been reached, even after they become aware that the decision is going to be more costly to them than was originally thought. This phenomenon is particularly interesting for the relationship between freedom and manipulation, because it has been well documented that techniques in sales work best only if the *initial* decision is perceived by the actor to be a free choice.

AN OBJECTION IN DEFENSE OF THE ADVERTISING INDUSTRY

One objection to this analysis is that persons of normal maturity, liberty, and resistibility, do make free choices, in which case my criticism of advertising breaks down. Can we not expect persons to take care of themselves when hearing an advertisement no less than when shopping in a department store with attractive displays on every counter? Advocates often defend advertising and marketing by a rules-of-the-game model: There are more or less established, well-delineated procedures or moves for marketing a product. The consumer world is well acquainted with these rules of the game, and consumers are often in an equal bargaining position.

One can easily become upset about advertising directed at children, and other vulnerable parties, because the ordinary rules of the game are either suspended or violated. The unsuspecting child may be sacrificed to the greed of the toymaker or cookie manufacturer. But is not advertising, placed in more favorable light, analogous to activities in which all people engage—for example, purchasing a house or bargaining over the price of a rug in an overpriced store? Here bluffing, overstatement, and enticement are expected and invite similar countermoves. Although abuse and contempt are not tolerated, deception is tolerated as long as the rules of the game are known and the players are in a roughly equal bargaining position.

This defense of advertising overlooks the fact that advertisers manipulate not only the weak and unwary, but persons of normal discernment and resistibility. Advertisers know the art of subtle deception and manipulation. They use attractive rates, enticing images, and a variety of forms of suggestion to hinder reasoned choice. In my view, advertising should enable or at least not prevent an informed choice about purchase of the product or service. It should be persuasive in presentation, not manipulative. Rules of acceptable advertising should encompass more than the mere creation of a market. Advertising should be limited to the dissemination of information from which consumers are able to make an informed choice. If they are misled in the attempt to make an intelligent choice or are enticed into the choice by deception, the advertising has an enormous burden of justification—no matter the target population or the implicit rules of the game.

We need to discuss openly how false assurances and manipulative maneuvers intended to encourage persons may seriously mislead them, how to present information persuasively, and the importance of advertising directed at vulnerable populations such as underage smokers and drinkers. Disclosure "requirements" and permissible styles of presentation should be discussed, with a focus on the entire communication process and not simply on "truthtelling." When implicit rules of games are inadequate, as they are at the present time in advertising, external standards should be called upon to challenge the presuppositions that underlie the rules. When deep assumptions in the rules permit the nonunique, inessential, and less nutritious product to be advertised to children and adults alike as unique, essential, or highly nutritious, and when merchants such as Arthur Lake, with whom we began, are driven out of business by "competitive" advertising, we know that some assumptions about the rights of advertisers need to be thoroughly defended by good reasons.

We have let our rules of advertising permit too much, without restraint by a better model of adequate communication. The freedom to compete has not been adequately distinguished from the freedom to deceive in the "free-enterprise" model. My proposal, then, is that a simple moral rule should be adopted: Advertisements should be persuasive and should be judged morally inappropriate when they are manipulative. However, this is not a rule for what should be banned by federal regulation—a problem that adds another level of complexity.

NOTES

1. Walter B. Smith, "For Lake, Jewelry Has Lost Its Glitter," *Detroit News* (December 9, 1982), p. 3B.

2. T. W. Zimmerer and P. L. Preston, "Plasma International," in *Business and Society*, eds. Robert D. Hay, Edmund R. Gray, and James E. Gates (Cincinnati, Ohio: South-Western Publishing, 1976).

3. William E. LaMothe, "Testimony," in Part 5— TV Advertising of Food to Children, Hearings before the Senate Select Committee on Nutrition and Human Needs, 93rd Congress, 1st Session, 1973, p. 258.

4. See Stanley I. Benn, "Freedom and Persuasion," *Australasian Journal of Philosophy* 45 (December 1967): 265.

5. *FTC Final Staff Report and Recommendation in the Matter of Children's Advertising*, 43 Fed. Reg. 17967, TRR No. 215-60, (1981), p. 3.

6. President's Commission for the Study of Ethical Problems, *Making Health Care Decisions* (Washington, D.C.: Government Printing Office, 1982), Vol. I, p. 66–67.

7. L. Ross, "IRA Jungle Grows More Dense as Tax Time Draws Near," *Washington Post* (March 19,1984), Business Section, p. 34. See also Mary W. Walsh, "Banks' Policies on Figuring and Advertising Deposit Interest Make Picking Rates Hard," *Wall Street Journal*, October 8, 1984, Sec. 2, p. 33.

8. Laurie Freeman and Julie Liesse, "FDA Starts Getting Tough on Good Labeling," *Advertising Age* 61 (September 10, 1990), p. 87; "FDA Puts Squeeze on P&G over Citrus Hill Labeling," *Wall Street Journal*, Thursday, April 25, 1991, pp. B1, B4.

9. Steven W. Colford and Judann Dagnoli, "FDA Readies Second Strike," *Advertising Age* 62 (May 13, 1991), pp. 1, 46.

10. FDA, "Food Labeling Regulations: Information Sheet," November 6, 1991 (Washington, D.C.: DHHS, Public Health Service). The FDA Proposal was announced at a press conference, November 6, 1991. The date for compliance with the rules was set as May 8, 1993.

11. Paul Farhi, "Kool's Penguin Draws Health Officials' Heat," *Washington Post*, October 23, 1991, pp. C1, C7.

12. Paul Farhi, "Novello Urges Tough Curbs on Liquor Ads," *Washington Post*, November 5, 1991, pp. D1, D8.

13. National Council on Alcoholism and Drug Dependence, *NCADD Demands Removal of Cisco from Market*, NCADD press release, September 13, 1990.

14. Public statement of Antonia C. Novello, M.D., M.P.H., U.S. Surgeon General, Press Conference, January 9, 1991.

15. Courtland Milloy, "Race, Beer Don't Mix," *Washington Post*, July 9, 1991, p. B3.

Advertising and the Social Conditions of Autonomy

Richard L. Lippke

In *The New Industrial State,* John Kenneth Galbraith charged that advertising creates desires rather than responds to them.[1] His thesis raised in stark terms the issue of who is controlling whom in the marketplace. Yet, Galbraith did not provide a rigorous analysis of autonomy, and his remarks about the effects of advertising on individuals were often more suggestive than carefully worked out.

The claim that advertising is inimical to the autonomy of individuals has been taken up and discussed by philosophers, economists, and social theorists. Typically, these discussions provide first, an analysis of autonomy, and second, some empirical conjecture about whether or not advertising can be said to subvert it. The focus of most of these discussions has been on whether or not advertising can be justly accused of manipulating individuals into wanting and therefore purchasing specific products or services. Less attention has been paid to what I believe is another major theme in Galbraith's writings —that mass-advertising induces in individuals beliefs, wants, and attitudes conducive to the economic and political interests of corporations in advanced capitalist societies like the United States. Galbraith's concern seems to be not only that advertising is hostile to individual autonomy, but that it is an aspect of the ability of corporations to dominate the lives of other members of society.

What the effects of mass-advertising are on individuals is, it must be admitted, ultimately an empirical question. In spite of this, I will try to show how we might reasonably conclude that advertising undermines autonomy, especially under the social conditions that exist in advanced capitalist countries like the United States. . . .

My primary focus will be on persuasive as opposed to informational advertising. Though the distinction is not a sharp one, I take the latter to involve information about the features, price, and availability of a product or service. Persuasive advertising, in contrast, often contains very little direct informational content about a product or service. Whereas the former presupposes some interest on the part of individuals in the product or service, the latter seeks to cultivate an interest. This typically involves tying the product or service to the satisfaction of individuals' other, sometimes subconscious desires. It seems fair to say that current informational advertising is woefully deficient. The information that is presented is often incomplete or misleading, or both. As a result, even informational ads are deceptive or manipulative at times.[2] To that extent, they undercut the abilities of persons to make informed choices and may be destructive to the intellectual honesty that is one of the constituents of dispositional autonomy. . . .

One reason that we value autonomy is relevant to Galbraith's thesis that advertising is an aspect of the dominance of large corporations over the lives of individuals in advanced capitalist societies. Persons who are nonautonomous seem much more likely to be dominated by oth-

Richard L. Lippke, From "Advertising and the Social Conditions of Autonomy," *Business and Professional Ethics Journal* 8, No. 4 (Winter 1989). Reprinted by permission of the author.

ers. Such domination need not be consciously intended or effected by the more powerful.[3] They may simply act in ways that they perceive to be in their own interests. . . .

I

Recent discussions of advertising and autonomy are inadequate because they fail to isolate the crucial way in which the content of advertising might be subversive to autonomy. Roger Crisp, a critic of advertising, develops and tries to support the claim that ads are manipulative in an objectionable fashion. He argues that advertising "links, by suggestion, the product with my unconscious desires for [for instance] power and sex."[4] Crisp claims that persuasive advertising leaves persons unaware of their real reasons for purchasing a product, and so precludes their making rational purchasing decisions. Crisp then argues that "many of us have a strong second-order desire not to be manipulated by others without our knowledge, and for no good reason."[5] If persons become aware of how persuasive advertising affects them, by locking onto their unconscious desires, they will likely repudiate the desires induced by advertising. Such repudiated desires will not be regarded by individuals as theirs. Hence, Crisp believes he has shown how advertising is subversive to autonomy.

Crisp's approach seems to attribute both too much and too little power to advertising. Too much, because there is reason to doubt that most adults are manipulated by particular ads in the way Crisp describes. Perhaps children are so manipulated at times, and this is cause for concern. Most adults, though, seem quite able to resist what I will call the "explicit content" of ads. The explicit content of ads is the message to "buy X," along with information about where it may be purchased, its features, and how much it costs.

Most individuals learn at an early age that many ads are out to persuade them, even manipulate them. They become wary of ads and this explains why they often resist their explicit content quite easily. Even if persons do have the second-order desire Crisp attributes to them, it is not the explicit content of ads that manipulates them *without their knowledge*. The challenge is to develop an account of how advertising can have power over individuals who very often realize ads are designed to manipulate them.

This brings us to the way in which Crisp's account attributes too little power to advertising. In addition to encouraging persons to buy Brand X, many ads have what I will term an "implicit content" that consists of messages about, broadly speaking, the consumer lifestyle. This lifestyle consists of a set of beliefs, attitudes, norms, expectations, and aspirations that I will, in due course, attempt to summarize. While individuals may be aware that they are being sold particular products, the crucial issue is the extent to which they are aware of being "sold" this implicit content. . . .

II

As a first step in building my case, I offer an account of autonomy that draws on recent work on the concept. . . .

Autonomy is not a capacity that develops in isolation from the social conditions that surround individuals. It requires individuals to have certain abilities, motivations, and knowledge (or at least awareness) of alternative belief-systems and lifestyles. It also requires venues in which they can reasonably expect to display these abilities and act on these motivations. Obviously, individuals must not be subjected to coercion, deception, brainwashing, and harassment. Being shielded from these is a necessary social condition of the development and exercise of autonomy. Yet, there are other social conditions that while perhaps not, strictly speaking, necessary ones, are such that they foster and support autonomy in vital ways. Societies differ in the extent to which they provide these conditions for all individuals, and thus in the extent to which they enable autonomy.

III

. . . Much of that which is sponsored by advertising on TV, radio, and in magazines is hardly such as to encourage the development of autonomy. Program content on commercial networks is often mindless, melodramatic, simplistic in its approach to the problems of human life—or worse, violent, sexist, or subtly racist. Even commercial network news programs seem to emphasize entertainment. Dramatic visual images, "sound bites," and fifteen second summaries of events are the rule. Commercial sponsorship of the media opens the way for the exercise of subtle control over program content. But the more likely effect of that sponsorship is an emphasis on gaining and holding an audience. That which cannot do so does not get sponsored. Yet, I think we should be wary of those who claim that what the public does not choose to consume in the way of mass media reflects its autonomous choices. Other factors, such as lack of education, mindless work, and the impact of advertising may figure in such choices. In any case, what ads are wrapped around must be factored into any analysis of their likely effects. . . .

IV

. . . While advertising is sometimes deceptive and often manipulative, and in some ways akin to brainwashing . . . I am inclined to think that the way to conceptualize its character is in terms of the notion of *suppression*. Advertising suppresses autonomy by discouraging the emergence of its constitutive skills, knowledge, attitudes, and motivations.

One general feature of mass-advertising is simply its pervasiveness. Individuals are inundated with ads, no matter where they go or what activities they engage in. . . . The quantity of ads and their near inescapability are such that even the most diligent will be hard-pressed to avoid absorbing some of their implicit content. Many television shows and magazines feature or cater to the consumer lifestyle and this reinforces the implicit content.

The pervasiveness of ads is often coupled with an absence of views that challenge or reject their implicit content. In assessing the likely impact of mass-advertising, we must pay attention to societal measures to counter its effects. For instance, in the United States, there are few if any public service announcements urging individuals to be wary of ads, exposing the tactics of manipulation and seduction ads employ. . . .

If individuals lack appealing and coherent alternatives to what ads tell them about how to live, they cannot make critical, rational choices about such matters.

It is bad enough that advertising has the character of a loud, persistent bully. What is worse is that it often is not directed only at adults who might be capable of responding critically. The concern about the effects of advertising on the vulnerable, especially children, is not simply that many ads are so manipulative that they trick the vulnerable into wanting things they do not need or which are not good for them. It is also that the implicit content of ads gets absorbed by children, and habits are set up that *carry forward* into their adult lives. The ways in which they habitually perceive their lives and the social world, the alternatives they see as open to them, and the standards they use to judge themselves and others, are all shaped by advertising, perhaps without their ever being aware of it.[6]

I now turn to an analysis of the implicit content of persuasive mass-advertising. . . .

Ads subtly encourage the propensity to accept emotional appeals, oversimplification, superficiality, and shoddy standards of proof for claims. Evidence and arguments of the most ridiculous sorts are offered in support of advertising claims. Information about products is presented selectively (i.e. bad or questionable features are ignored), the virtues of products are exaggerated, and deception and misinformation are commonplace. The meanings of words are routinely twisted so that they are either deceptive or wholly lost (e.g. consider the use of words like 'sale' or 'new and improved'). Also, ads encourage the belief that important information about our lives must be entertainly purveyed and such that it can be passively absorbed.

All of these are what we might term "meta-messages." They are messages about how to deal with messages, or more precisely, about how to approach claims made by others. They are messages that tell individuals, among other things, that they cannot believe or trust what others say, that anything (or nothing!) can be proved, that evidence contrary to one's claims may be ignored, and that words can mean whatever anyone wants them to mean. They tell persons that success in communication is a matter of persuading others *no matter how it is done*. Such attitudes about thought and communication starkly oppose the habits and attitudes constituitive of critical competence: clarity, rigor, precision, patience, honesty, effort, etc. . . .

Mass production requires the existence of ready and willing consumers. Lifestyles contrary to consumption are either absent from ads (and from TV shows) or are ridiculed in them. Predominant messages in ads are "take it easy," "relax and enjoy yourself," and most especially "buy it now!" In moderation, there

may be nothing objectionable about such messages. However, where not balanced by other messages, and so not made liable to critical examination, they encourage attitudes subversive to autonomy. . . .

Numerous writers have commented on the confusion about values ads promote. Many ads tell individuals that if they will only buy X, they will acquire friendship, self-esteem, sex appeal, power, etc. Collectively, these ads tell individuals that they will be able to satisfy some of their most important desires through the purchase and use of consumer products. Where they have bought these products and still not found the relevant satisfactions, advertising has a ready answer: buy more or better products! . . .

At best ads can only *distract* individuals from clear thinking about such things as why they lack self-esteem, or why they feel powerless, or why their friendships or marriages are unsatisfactory. At worst, they can fill individuals' minds with pseudo-truths or pseudo-values bearing on issues of central significance in their lives. Numerous examples come to mind: how women are encouraged by ads to conceive of their self-worth in terms of unrealistic standards of physical beauty; how having fun is portrayed in ads for beer, wine, and alcohol; ideas about nutrition courtesy of the junk food industry; how racial disharmony, homosexuality, and poverty are missing from the social world of ads; and so on. . .

V

. . . Yet, it might be argued, why should we think societies ought to treat persuasive mass-advertising any differently? Why not, instead, think it reasonable to let individuals watch out for themselves in the face of mass-advertising? After all, some seem to.

This is a formidable objection, but it fails to

take account of the differences between individuals' encounters with advertising and their encounters with other individuals. The latter typically have three features that the former lack. First, encounters with other individuals are often either voluntarily sought out or at least voluntarily maintained. Yet, advertising is not easily avoided. It begins to work its influence on individuals when they are young and it never lets up. It is omni-present. Second, even where individual encounters with other individuals are not fully voluntary (e.g. familial or work relationships), they typically serve some important value or function in individuals' lives. This is less obviously true with respect to persuasive mass-advertising. Third, encounters with other individuals, if found unsatisfactory, can be altered by the participants. Individuals can ask, or insist, that others not deceive or manipulate them. Sometimes this works. With advertising, individuals can, at best, try to shut it out or be wary of it. It is not an agent whose "conduct" can be altered by direct appeals.

Also, the fact that some individuals manage to resist the effects of persuasive mass-advertising might be explained by their having greater access to the other social conditions of autonomy (e.g. education). Surely that does not show that a society need do nothing about an institution in its midst that arguably plays a very significant role in suppressing the autonomy of what is perhaps a very large majority of its members. As Tom Beauchamp notes, a source of influence need not be completely controlling in order to be an object of concern.[7] . . .

It is not fair to portray advertising as simply offering "truths" for consideration that compete against other beliefs in the marketplace of ideas. Whatever "truths" it offers (and I suspect they are small ones) threaten to drown out all other claims, or to render them tedious or irrelevant by comparison. Worse, as we have seen, its implicit content encour-

ages beliefs and attitudes about thought and decision-making that are hostile to those necessary to sort through claims and weed out the false or misleading ones. . . .

Finally, if advertising is inimical to autonomy in the ways I have claimed throughout this paper, it is obvious that the argument from autonomy cannot be invoked on its behalf. Those who defend persuasive mass-advertising on the basis of its contribution to individual choice would seem to have an extremely limited notion of the range of choices that individuals have about their lives. . . .

Since advanced capitalist countries like the United States are now plagued in various ways by the dominance of corporate interests, we might hope that enhancing the social conditions of autonomy for all persons will result in the cultivation, expression, and realization of more varied (and autonomous) interests.

While some will think that the only way to accomplish this result is to abandon capitalism altogether, I want to consider changes that are somewhat more modest. First, in order to modify the organization of work so as to provide a venue for the realization of worker autonomy, we might adopt the sorts of worker participation mechanisms institutionalized in countries like West Germany and Sweden.[8] These mechanisms guarantee workers participation in the economic decisions that vitally affect their lives. Second, we would need to guarantee to all individuals the level and quality of education necessary for them to develop the skills, dispositions, and knowledge constituitive of dispositional autonomy. Third, we would need to take steps to lessen if not eliminate the influence of wealth and economic power over the decisions of democratically elected political officials. This might include such things as the development of a public financing scheme for all political campaigns and the institutionalization of mechanisms to guarantee the independence of government officials from those they regulate or purchase products and services from. Fourth, steps must be taken to divorce the media from their almost exclusive reliance on commercial financial support and to provide individuals with increased access to the means of expression. . . .

What cannot be evaded is the political reality that any proposed restrictions will be steadfastly, and I suspect effectively, resisted by corporations and advertisers. On this score, the only hope may lie with the sorts of institutional changes sketched earlier. It is possible that a better educated populace with more democratic control over its corporations can take the necessary steps to curtail the suppression of autonomy effected by current mass-advertising.

NOTES

1. John Kenneth Galbraith, *The New Industrial State* (Boston, MA: Houghton Mifflin, 1967), especially pp. 198–218.

2. On the ways in which many ads deceive by presenting information in misleading ways, see, for instance, Tom L. Beauchamp, "Manipulative Advertising," *Business and Professional Ethics Journal* 3 (Spring/Summer 1984): 1–22 [and revised for this text].

3. Tom Beauchamp distinguishes between the responses of individuals to advertising and the intentions of those who create the advertising. My remarks in what follows concern the responses of individuals. I do not wish to suggest that corporations consciously intend all of the effects I delineate. See Beauchamp, "Manipulative Advertising," p. 7.

4. Roger Crisp, "Persuasive Advertising, Autonomy, and the Creation of Desire," *Journal of Business Ethics* 6 (1987): 413–418, p. 414.

5. Ibid., p. 414.

6. Cf. Lynda Sharp Paine, "Children as Consumers," *Business and Professional Ethics Journal* 3 (Spring/Summer 1984): 119–145. Paine argues persuasively that children ought not be viewed as capable of making responsible consumer choices.

7. Beauchamp, "Manipulative Advertising," p. 3.

8. On this, see G. David Garson, *Worker Self-Management in Industry: The West European Experience* (New York: Praeger Publishers, 1977).

Corporate Policy and the Ethics of Competitor Intelligence Gathering

Lynn Sharp Paine

. . . The purpose of this paper is to highlight the need for management to address the ethics of competitor intelligence gathering. Recent developments in the business environment have generated increasing interest in competitor intelligence, information that helps managers understand their competitors. Although information about rival firms has always been a valued and sought after commodity, competitor intelligence gathering has only recently begun to be systematized and legitimated as a business function. While understanding the competition is an important part of running a business, there are ethical limits on the types of competitor information that may be acquired; on the methods that may be employed to acquire it; and on the purposes for which it may be used.

Journal of Business Ethics **10**(199):423–436. © 1991 Kluwer Academic Publishers. Reprinted by permission of Kluwer Academic Publishers.

To date, however, few managers or management educators have addressed the ethics of intelligence gathering.

This paper will focus primarily on methods of acquiring competitor information. Separating legitimate from illegitimate approaches to information acquisition is, in practice, the central ethical issue for intelligence-gathering specialists. . . .

GROWTH OF COMPETITOR INTELLIGENCE GATHERING

Evidence of the growth of interest in competitor intelligence is abundant. A 1985 study which looked at the intelligence-gathering budgets of twenty-five Fortune 500 companies found that all had increased substantially over the preceding five-year period.[1] Five years earlier, one-third of the companies had not had intelligence-gathering departments at all. Respondents to a 1986 study of 50 firms anticipated a dramatic increase in their intelligence-gathering budgets and almost all foresaw rapid growth in the staff assigned to intelligence gathering over the succeeding five-year period.[2] The findings of a recent Conference Board study of more than 300 U.S. firms were similar. Nearly all respondents said that monitoring competitors' activities is important and more than two-thirds expect their monitoring efforts to increase.[3] . . .

THE DARKER SIDE

There is, however, a darker side to the growth of intelligence gathering. It is reflected in the use of ethically questionable techniques for collecting information, the increase in trade secret litigation and information crimes, and the increase in the resources devoted to corporate security. One expert on trade secret law estimates that court rulings on theft and misappropriation of information have increased four-fold over the past decade to more than 200 a year and that the actual problem of information misappropriation is at least ten times as large.[4] Another reports a surge in information crimes.[5] The American Society for Industrial Security, which includes both outside consultants and in-house security groups, was reported in 1986 to have 24,000 members and to be gaining 5000 new members a year.[6] . . .

The increase in information litigation cannot be explained solely by increasingly complex and costly technology. The increase also reflects the growing use of questionable techniques to gain access to ordinary business information generated by or about competing firms. The use of these techniques may evidence a general decline in ethical standards or a decline in resourcefulness and creativity. It may also be a by-product of increased competition and the competitor orientation of current thinking about business strategy. . . .

QUESTIONABLE METHODS OF ACQUIRING INTELLIGENCE

While surveys have examined people's willingness to engage in specific questionable practices, and at least one author has provided a list of ethical and unethical intelligence-gathering techniques, the ethical principles at issue in this area have not generally been made explicit. However, a review of studies of questionable practices, judicial opinions, news reports, popular articles, and the writings of intelligence-gathering experts, reveals that the most prevalent methods of questionable intelligence gathering fall into three broad ethical categories:

1. those involving deceit or some form of misrepresentation;
2. those involving attempts to influence the judgment of persons entrusted with confidential information, particularly the offering of inducements to reveal information; and
3. those involving covert or unconsented-to surveillance.

Norms prohibiting practices in these categories appear to be weaker than norms prohibiting theft of documents and other tangible property, a fourth category of ethically problematic intelligence gathering.

In contrast to intelligence gathering which relies on information that firms have disclosed to public authorities or to the general public or which is available through open and above-board inquiry, questionable techniques are generally employed to obtain information which the firm has not disclosed, is not obligated to disclose, and probably would not be willing to disclose publicly. But most of these techniques would be objectionable—whatever type of information they elicited—because they offend common standards of morality calling for honesty, respect for relationships of trust and confidence, and respect for privacy. While stating these principles does not resolve difficult and disputed questions concerning their interpretation and application, some of which are discussed below, understanding the principles can contribute to clearer thinking about the factors distinguishing legitimate from illegitimate practice.

Several indicators point to the use of techniques that violate or call into question these principles.

Misrepresentation

Opinion research indicates that many employees say their companies condone, and they themselves approve of, the use of various forms of misrepresentation to gather competitor intelligence.[7] For example, 45.9% of the respondents to a questionnaire administered to 451 participants in seminars on intelligence gathering approved of getting information by posing as a graduate student working on a thesis.[8] A striking 85.6% of the respondents believe their competitors would use this method of intelligence gathering. . . .

The use of misrepresentation can take many forms: conducting phony job interviews,[9] hiring students to gather intelligence under the guise of doing academic work, posing as a potential joint venturer, supplier or customer. The prevalence of phony interviews has led at least one marketing manager to remind his people that "a job interview may be a total sham, a way to get intelligence."[10] The victims of deceit may be rival firms, themselves, their suppliers and customers, or other parties with access to valuable information.

In a recently litigated case, a marketing manager and his firm were found liable for damages incurred by a competitor that had revealed confidential information to the manager and another employee when they posed as a potential customer.[11] The marketing manager, whose branch office was failing to meet his own quotas, arranged to have a new hire who had not yet joined the firm pose as a potential customer for the competitor's software. The manager attended the software presentation as a friend and consultant of the supposed customer, but without identifying himself or his employer. As a result of the misrepresentation, the pair were given a detailed demonstration of the software, in-depth answers to their questions, and access to the competitor's sales manual. They made unauthorized copies of critical information in the manual and successfully developed a competitive software program within a short period of time. In testimony reported in the court's opinion, the marketing manager referred to himself as a "scoundrel," but explained that market pressures had led him to this tactic.

Improper Influence

A second category of questionable techniques centers on attempting to influence potential informants in ways that undermine their judgment or sense of obligation to protect confidentiality or to act in their employer's best interests. Frequently, the attempt involves offering inducements or the possibility of certain advantages to those who may be able to provide valuable information. In its crudest form, this technique is bribery, the offering of something of value in exchange for the breach of a fiduciary duty. In the recent Pentagon scandals, consultants to defense contractors offered large sums of money to government officials in exchange for revealing information they were as fiduciaries legally obliged to protect. In more subtle cases not involving legal obligations of confidentiality, the inducement may work to compromise the potential informant's judgment. The source may decide to reveal information which is not, strictly speaking, confidential, but whose revelation is contrary to the employer's interests.

The inducement to disclose need not be cash; it may be a better job. The hiring of a rival's employee to gain access to confidential information appears to be a widely used and approved intelligence-gathering technique. Surveys conducted in 1974, 1976, and 1988 all found that many executives would use the practice.[12] Fifty-one percent of the smaller companies and 37% of the larger ones surveyed in 1974 said they expected employees hired from competitors to contribute all they knew to the new job, including the competitor's trade secrets.[13] And the Conference Board found that nearly half the respondents to its 1988 survey regard former employees of competitors as a very or fairly important source of information.[14] About half the executives responding to the 1976 study said they would try to hire a rival's employee to learn about an important scien-

tific discovery that could substantially reduce profits during the coming year.[15]

In 1988, *Advertising Age* asked its readers whether it was ethical to hire an account supervisor from a competitor in order to gain information about the competitor's client. Seventy-three percent of the 157 professionals responding—advertisers, agency personnel, media people, consultants, and "others"—said the practice was ethical.[16] The Center for Communications posed the same hypothetical to professors and students of marketing. Fifty-nine percent of the 626 students responding said the practice was ethical, and 70% said they would do it.[17]

The hiring of employees with access to valuable competitor information has been the subject of numerous recent lawsuits and threatened lawsuits. When Wendy's International decided to substitute Coke products for Pepsi products in its restaurants, Pepsi threatened to sue Coke for pirating executives to gain information about Pepsi's contract and programs with Wendy's and for tampering with contractual relationships.[18] Similar issues have arisen in litigation between Johns-Manville and Guardian Industries,[19] Avis and Hertz,[20] and AT&T and MCI.[21] . . .

These techniques are ethically problematic because they involve attempts to undermine relationships of trust and confidence. In many cases, the information-seeker deliberately creates a conflict of interest in the hope that self-interest will overcome the potential informant's sense of obligation to protect his employer's confidential information or to act on his behalf. One must assume that the offering of valuable inducements reflects the fact, or at least the information-seeker's belief, that the information is not publicly available and can only be acquired, or can be acquired more cheaply, by attempting to induce a breach of confidence or to otherwise influence the judgment of those acting on behalf of the rival firm.

Part of the effectiveness of these inducements is explained by employees' uncertainty about what information may and may not be disclosed. While most firms treat some information as freely available to the public and other information as strictly confidential, there is a great deal of information that could be quite valuable to a competitor and whose confidentiality status is ambiguous in the minds of many employees, suppliers, and customers. For example, a firm may regard certain information shared with a supplier as confidential while the supplier sees it as public knowledge. The annals of trade secret litigation contain many examples of this sort of discrepancy. Indeed, there may be in-house discrepancies about what information is confidential and what may be revealed. The use of disclosure incentives in these cases may be the decisive influence tipping the potential informant's judgment in the direction of disclosure.

Ethical judgments about particular intelligence-gathering practices in this category are complicated by these same uncertainties. Still, legitimate questions about the scope of employees' obligations of confidentiality do not remove the moral difficulty that attaches to offering inducements deliberately intended to undermine a person's judgment or sense of obligation.

Covert Surveillance

Covert surveillance, another category of ethically problematic intelligence gathering, includes electronic espionage as well as other unconsented-to forms of observation such as eavesdropping and aerial photography. This category, perhaps the most difficult to define, raises questions about the legitimate scope of corporate privacy. When covert surveillance involves trespass or theft of tangible property, there is a convenient legal label for condemning it. But when it involves eavesdropping in public places or observation from afar using sophisticated technology, the wrong is most readily described as a violation of corporate privacy. Although the prevailing view is that corporations have no legal right to privacy, the idea persists that businesses and their employees should be able to assume they will not be observed or listened to in certain situations.

The techniques of covert surveillance are varied. They range from planting a spy in a competitor's operation—a technique which also involves deception and perhaps inducing actual employees to violate duties of confidentiality—to strategic eavesdropping in the bar and grill favored by a competitor's employees.[22] A widely discussed case of covert surveillance which resulted in an award of damages for the target company involved aerial photography of an unfinished manufacturing plant.[23] Clever gadgets of various types are available to assist covert observation: binoculars that hear conversations up to five blocks away, a spray that exposes the content of envelopes, a gadget that can read computer screens some two blocks away by picking up radio waves emitted by the machine.[24] Inspecting the competition's trash is another type of unconsented-to surveillance that has received attention in the press and has been litigated in at least one case.[25]

Covert observation, like misrepresentation and improper influence, is yet another way to obtain information which a rival does not wish to divulge. Ethical assessments of various forms of undisclosed observation may be controversial since privacy expectations are quite variable, as are judgments about the legitimacy of those expectations.

Covert observation in or from public places is especially problematic. For example, it may be possible to ascertain the volume of product that competitors are shipping by observing from public property the number of tractor-trailers leaving the plant's loading bays and by noting the size of the product in relation to the size of the trailers.[26] Opinions vary about the legitimacy of this practice. One might say that the firm has consented to observation by not putting a fence around the property. And yet, just as it is unseemly to peer through an open window into the neighbors' living room while walking down the sidewalk, we may think observation an invasion of the firm's privacy. . . .

Unsolicited Intelligence

The questions raised by covert surveillance are closely related to those raised by the receipt of unsolicited information. Disgruntled former employees of rival firms have been known to offer highly confidential technical information as well as more general information to competitors. Two recently litigated cases involved disputes about valuable information acquired as a result of a rival's mistake. In one case, a coded customer list was inadvertently left in the memory of a computer which was purchased at an auction by a competitor. The rival gained access to the codeword from an unwitting computer operator.[27] In another case, a dealer list was accidentally left in the store of a dealer who later became a competitor.[28]

There is no question of deceit or improper influence in these cases. The ethical question centers on whether unsolicited or inadvertently revealed information should be respected as private to the competitor. If intelligence gathering is governed by respect for the competitors' voluntary disclosure decisions, then information acquired through accident or mistake, or a former employee's breach of fiduciary duty, should not be examined and utilized. Indeed, this is the view reflected in the Uniform Trade Secrets Act.[29] Some courts and commentators, however, have taken the position that privacy is for-

feited if information is accidentally revealed.[30]

The forfeiture view has some plausibility when disclosure is the result of a rival firm's carelessness. It is not unreasonable to expect a firm to suffer some loss if it acts carelessly. The view has less merit, however, when a third party, such as a supplier, inadvertently discloses a rival's valuable information. Still, in a survey discussed earlier, nearly half the marketing professionals questioned said it would be ethical to use information acquired as a result of a supplier's mistake.[31] In the survey vignette, a marketing professional is accidentally given slides prepared for a direct competitor's final presentation in a competition in which both are participating. Having examined the slides before returning them to the embarrassed employee of the slide supply house, the marketer must decide whether to use the information to alter his presentation to attack the competitor's recommended strategy. . . .

THE DEARTH OF CORPORATE GUIDANCE

Despite the growing importance of intelligence gathering and the occurrence of unethical and questionable practices, top management has not yet faced the issue squarely. Only a handful of corporations offer employees practical guidance on intelligence gathering in their codes of conduct or ethics policies. While codes of conduct are not the only, or even the most important, index of a corporations's ethical standards, they do provide some indication of ethical issues thought by the code's authors to merit attention. . . .

As a practical matter, the risks of litigation and legal liability can best be minimized by avoiding intelligence-gathering activities in the ethically problematic categories discussed above: misrepresentation, improper influence, unconsented-to surveillance, and theft.

Admittedly, the threat of legal reprisal for engaging in these practices may be minimal in certain situations. Victims of unethical practices may not know they are being targeted, or they may lack evidence to prove their case in a court of law. Moreover, the law does not provide a remedy for every violation of ethics. If the victim of misrepresentation is not individually harmed, for example, he will have no legal recourse against the intelligence gatherer. And even if substantially harmed, the victim may have no remedy if the information acquired does not qualify as a trade secret or if the target firm has not taken adequate steps to protect the information in question.

From a management perspective, however, it is quite impractical to instruct employees to fine-tune their use of questionable practices on the basis of the legal risk in particular situations. Not only is it difficult to undertake an objective assessment of legal risk when under everyday performance pressures, but the legal risk of using unethical practices depends on consequences which are difficult, if not impossible, to anticipate in advance: the kind of information that will be obtained, the use to which it will be put, the harm that the target will suffer, the adequacy of the target's security measures, the likelihood of discovery, and the evidentiary strength of the target's case. What is known in advance is that certain types of practices, namely, those involving misrepresentation, theft, improper influence, and covert surveillance, can provide the necessary foundation for legal liability. Even from the narrow perspective of legal costs, there is a good case for instructing employees to avoid questionable practices altogether rather than attempt to assess the fine points of legal risk.

INCREASING SECURITY NEEDS

More costly, perhaps, than the litigation and liability risks involved in the use of questionable practices are the increased security needs these practices generate over the long term. Every user of unethical practices must recognize his contribution to a general climate of distrust and suspicion. Insofar as individuals are more likely to engage in unethical conduct when they believe their rivals are doing so, unethical intelligence gathering contributes further to the general deterioration of ethical expectations. As the recent growth of interest in information security illustrates, declining ethical expectations translate into intensified programs for self-protection.

Firms that expect to be subjected to intelligence gathering through covert surveillance, deceit, and various forms of improper influence—especially when legal recourse is unavailable or uncertain—will take steps to protect themselves. They will tighten information security by building walls, installing security systems, purchasing sophisticated counter-intelligence technology, and instituting management techniques to reduce the risks of information leakage. Although some degree of self-protection is necessary and desirable, security can become a dominant consideration and a drain on resources.

Besides their out-of-pocket cost, security activities often introduce operational inefficiencies and stifle creativity. Avoiding the use of the telephone and restricting access to information to employees who demonstrate a "need to know" impose obvious impediments to the exchange of information vital to cooperation within the firm. When researchers, for instance, are denied information about the projects they are working on and about how their work relates to the work of others, they are cut off from stimuli to creativity and useful innovation.

Employee morale and public confidence may also be at stake. Information systems designed to insure that employees do not know enough to hurt the firm if they depart, like the dissemination of information on a "need to know" basis, proceed from a premise of distrust which can undermine employee morale. Even more clearly, information protection programs encourage an attitude of distrust toward outsiders. Employees are trained to be suspicious of public inquiries and to be wary of talking to or cooperating with outsiders who do not have security clearances. Overrestrictions on public access to information and excessive corporate secrecy generate public suspicion and hostility.

Although questionable intelligence-gathering practices may offer short-term advantages, they contribute, over the longer term, to a climate of distrust and the need for costly expenditures to tighten information security. These expenditures represent a diversion of management resources from more productive activities. Moreover, it is doubtful that firms can effectively protect their own valuable information if they encourage or tolerate loose ethical standards in acquiring competitor information. As the 1985 Hallcrest Report on private security in America concluded from studies of employee theft, "[E]ffective proprietary security programs . . . must emanate from a . . . strong sense of organizational ethics in all levels of the organization."[32] . . .

CONCLUSION

Managers who remain silent or fail to incorporate their "official" ethics policies into day-to-day management practice run the risk that they, their employees, and their firms will be involved in costly litigation over questionable intelligence-gathering tactics. More important, they jeopardize their own information security and run the risk of contributing further to the increasing demand for information protection. This demand represents a costly diversion of resources from the positive and creative aspects of doing business, a drag on innovation, and an impediment to good public relations. By supporting a competitive

system which respects the principles of common morality and the right of rivals not to divulge certain information, management supports its own vitality and the vitality of the competitive system.

NOTES

1. Information Data Search, Inc.: 1986, *Corporate Intelligence Gathering, 1985 and 1986 Surveys* (Cambridge, Massachusetts), p. 24.

2. *Id.* at p. 6.

3. Sutton, H.: 1988, *Competitive Intelligence*, Conference Board Report No. 913 (The Conference Board, Inc., New York), pp. 6–7.

4. Roger Milgrim, author of 12 *Business Organizations*, Milgrim on Trade Secrets (1988), quoted in "Information Thieves Are Now Corporate Enemy No. 1," *Business Week* (May 5, 1986), p. 120.

5. The surge in information crimes is noted by Donn B. Parker of SRI International as reported in "Information Thieves," *Ibid.*

6. Haas, A. D.: 1986, "Corporate Cloak and Dagger," *Amtrak Express* (October/November), pp. 19–20.

7. Cohen W. And Czepiec H.: 1988, "The Role of Ethics in Gathering Corporate Intelligence," *Journal of Business Ethics* **7,** pp. 199–203.

8. *Id.* at 200–201.

9. Flax, S.: 1984, "How to Snoop On Your Competitors," *Fortune* (May 14), p. 31.

10. Sutton, *Competitive Intelligence*, at p. 15.

11. *Continental Data Systems, Inc.* v. *Exxon Corporation*, 638 F. Supp. 432 (E.D. Pa. 1986).

12. Wall, "What the Competition Is Doing," at pp. 32–34; Brenner S. N. and Molander A.: 1977 "Is the Ethics of Business Changing?" *Harvard Business Review* (January-February), p. 57; "Industry Ethics Are Alive," *Advertising Age* (April 18, 1988), p. 88.

13. Wall, "What the Competition Is Doing," at p. 38.

14. Sutton, *Competitive Intelligence*, at p. 19.

15. Brenner and Molander, "Is the Ethics of Business Changing?" at p. 57.

16. "Industry Ethics Are Alive".

17. The results noted here are available from the Center for Communications, a nonprofit educational organization located in New York, New York.

18. "Pepsi to Sue Coke Over Wendy's," *Washington Post* (November 13, 1986), p. E1.

19. *Johns-Manville Corp. v. Guardian Industries Corp.*, 586 F. Supp. 1034, 1075 (E.D. Mich. 1983), aff'd, 770 F.2d 178 (Fed. Cir. 1985).

20. Lewin, "Putting a Lid on Corporate Secrets."

21. "Information Thieves", at pp. 122–123.

22. Both practices are described in Flax, "How to Snoop on Your Competitors," at pp. 28, 32.

23. *E. I. duPont deNemours v. Christopher*, 431 F. 2d. 1012 (5th Cir. 1970), *cert. denied*, 400 U.S. 1024 (1971).

24. "New Ways to Battle Corporate Spooks," *Fortune* (November 7, 1988), p. 72.

25. *Tennant Co. v. Advance Machine Co.*, 355 N.W. 2d 720.

26. Discussed in Flax, "How to Snoop on Your Competitors," at p. 33.

27. *Defiance Button Mach. Co. v. C & C Metal Products*, 759 F. 2d 1053 (2d Cir. 1985).

28. *Fisher Stoves, Inc. v. All Nighter Stove Works*, 626 F. 2d 193 (1st Cir. 1980).

29. *Uniform Trade Secrets Act With 1985 Amendments*, sec. 1 (2) (ii) (c), in *Uniform Laws Annotated*, vol. 14 (1980 with 1988 Pocket Part).

30. *Fisher Stoves; Defiance Button.* See also *Kewanee Oil Co. v. Bicron Corp.*, 416 U.S. 470, 476 (1973).

31. "Industry Ethics Are Alive."

32. Cunningham, W. C., and H. Taylor: 1985, *Private Security and Police in America*, The Hallcrest Report (Portland, Oregon: The Chancellor Press), p. 41.

Irving A. Backman v. Polaroid Corporation

United States Court of Appeals

This is a class action brought by Irving A. Backman on behalf of himself and all other persons who purchased shares of stock of defendant Polaroid Corporation on the open market between January 11 and February 22, 1979, allegedly misled by defendant's conduct that violated Section 10(b) of the Securities Exchange Act of 1934 and Rule 10b–5 of the regulations promulgated thereunder. Suit was filed in June 1979. . . . The improprieties asserted, both in the complaint and in plaintiffs' opening to the jury, as responsible for plaintiffs' purchasing shares before a substantial drop in the market, were defendant's failure to disclose unfavorable facts about its new product, Polavision, an instant movie camera. Following trial on liability, the jury found for plaintiffs. . . . On appeal, a divided panel . . . granted a new trial. On this rehearing en banc we reverse and order judgment for defendant. . . .

In their amended complaint plaintiffs alleged that defendant failed to disclose that Polavision, introduced in the spring, had been unprofitable throughout 1978, and would continue so, significantly, at least through 1979; that it had been excessively inventoried and had suffered lagging sales; that little, if any, information had been made public; that defendant knew that this undisclosed information was material to investors, and that major investment research firms had publicly projected defendant's earnings based on assumptions defendant knew were contrary to the true facts, all of which non-disclosure was in violation of the securities laws.

Secondly, plaintiffs re-alleged the above, and added that over the years defendant had advertised that it was a growth company, and that, through its successes, the investment community had come to consider it the best of the growth companies, and that its failing to make the above disclosures operated as a fraud and deceit on the investing public, was a "fraud on the market," and constituted an unlawful manipulation thereof. . . .

However, mere market interest is no basis for imposing liability. We said [in a former case]; The materiality of the information claimed not to have been disclosed . . . is not enough to make out a sustainable claim of securities fraud. Even if information is material, there is no liability under Rule 10b–5 unless there is a duty to disclose it.

A duty to disclose "does not arise from the mere possession of non-public information." . . .

In a twelve day trial [the plaintiffs] precisely followed their opening, alleging, simply, nondisclosure of material information. As summarized in their final argument,

> Polaroid . . . violated the federal securities laws which require full disclosure so that people who purchase and sell securities do so on a fair playing field; that people have the same information and people can make their investment decisions based on having all of the information and having truthful information. . . . [Y]ou have to find that Polaroid had adverse information, that information was material—i.e., that it was important—and that Polaroid knowingly and deliberately withheld it. *And that's all we're asking you to do here.* (Emphasis supplied).

The summation was not an inadvertence, but was in accord with plaintiffs' own testimony.

Q.   Now, Mr. Backman, in this action you are not claiming, are you, that the financial information put out by Polaroid was in any way false and misleading, are you?
A.   I think you'll have to refer to the complaint.

I believe the failure to disclose is just as improper as providing false information. And I believe the essence of my suit deals with the failure to disclose. . . . I do claim it was false and misleading because the failure to disclose is just as misleading a (sic) improper disclosure.

This, of course, is not so, "Silence, absent a duty to disclose, is not misleading under Rule 10b–5." . . .

We have gone into this at length, not so much to show the emptiness of plaintiff's first claim—agreed to by the full panel—but to accent our finding that there had been no falsity or misleading by defendant in any respect. In eight years of preparation and twelve days of trial, the words misrepresentation and misleading never crossed plaintiffs' lips. . . .

It appeared that Dr. Edwin H. Land, the founder and at all times president or C.E.O. of Polaroid, had added to his invention of the world-famous instant still camera another exceptional invention—an instant movie camera, Polavision. It appeared throughout the case, however, that Polavision's sales appeal did not correspond with the quality of the invention. Launched in early 1978 with great fanfare, the estimates for fall, to which production had been geared, proved to be substantially excessive. As a result, in late October, Eumig, the Austrian manufacturer, having earlier been told to increase production, was instructed to reduce by 20,000. In mid-November Eumig was told to take out another 90,000 sets, and to halt production. Plaintiffs' panel brief, quoting the fortuitous language of Eumig's cable acknowledgment, "to now finally stop production entirely," gives the impression that the halt was intended to be permanent. Conveniently, from plaintiffs' standpoint, dots in the quotation replace the subsequent sentence, "Steps have been taken to ensure a quick new start-up of production on a reduced scale." This omission aids plaintiffs in their recitation, the regrettable incorrectness of which we will come to, that "management knew that Polavision was a commercial failure." Thereafter, fourth quarter internal figures, not publicly released, confirmed that the original Polavision estimates (also not released) had been substantially excessive.

The next event was a newspaper release published on January 9, 1979, that Rowland Foundation, a charitable trust established by Dr. and Mrs. Land, was to sell 300,000 shares of Polaroid, in part for funds for a new project, and in part to diversify its portfolio. Defendant participated in the preparation of the release, but not in the action itself. It is not claimed that the release was in any way untrue. Plaintiffs' claim it misleading because additional information should then have been given the public. The sale was consummated on January 11. . . .

On February 22, 1979, immediately following the annual meeting, defendant announced further facts about Polavision's lack of success, and the market fell, shortly, by some 20%. . . .

Plaintiffs' brief now finds assisted misrepresentation because "Polaroid featured Polavision on the cover," plaintiffs point out that after President McCune "announced record worldwide sales and earnings for both the third quarter and the first nine months of 1978, . . . Mr. McCune noted that the Company's worldwide manufacturing facilities continue to operate at close to maximum capacity," whereas, in fact, Polavision's contract supplier, Eumig, was told, shortly before the report, to hold up on 20,000 units. We note, first, that the statement, taken as a whole, was true; it expressly recognized an absence of totality. Of more specific importance, it flagged, on three of its three and half pages of text, that Polavision's effect on earnings was negative. . . . With this emphasized three times, we ask did this report mislead investors to buy stock because Polavision was doing so well?

Plaintiffs quote *Roeder,* 814 F.2d at 26, that even a voluntary disclosure of information that a reasonable investor would consider material must be "complete and accurate." This, however, does not mean that by revealing one fact about a product, one must reveal all others, that, too, would be interesting, marketwise, but means only such others, if any, that are needed so that what was revealed would not be "so incomplete as to mislead." . . . Disclosing that Polavision was being sold below cost was not misleading by reason of not saying how much below. Nor was it misleading not to report the number of sales, or that they were below expectations. . . .

We come, next, to the January 9 Rowland Foundation sale release. There was nothing untrue or misleading in the release itself, but plaintiffs say, with support from the panel opinion, that it should have contained additional information in order to keep the November report from being misleading. . . .

Obviously, if a disclosure is in fact misleading when made, and the speaker thereafter learns of this, there is a duty to correct it. . . . In special circumstances, a statement, correct at the time, may have a forward intent and connotation upon which parties may be expected to rely. If this is a clear meaning, and there is a change, correction, more exactly, further disclosure, may be called for. . . . Fear that statements of historical fact might be claimed to fall within it, could inhibit disclosures altogether. And what is the limit? In the present case if the shoe were on the other foot, and defendant could have, and had, announced continued Polavision profits, for how long would it have been under a duty of disclosure if the tide turned? Plaintiffs' contention that it would be a jury question is scarcely reassuring. . . .

After indicating reluctance to accept plaintiffs' contention that the Third Quarter Report was misleading when made, the panel opinion, in holding that it could be found misleading in light of later developments, said as follows.

> [E]ven if the optimistic Third Quarter Report was not misleading at the time of its issuance, there is sufficient evidence to support a jury's determination that the report's relatively brief mention of Polavision difficulties *became* misleading in light of the subsequent information acquired by Polaroid indicating the seriousness of Polavision's problems. This subsequent information included . . . Polaroid's decision to . . . stop Polavision production by its Austrian manufacturer, Eumig, *and its instruction to its Austrian supplier to keep this production cutback secret.* We feel that a reasonable jury could conclude that this subsequent information rendered the Third Quarter Report's brief mention of Polavision expenses misleading, triggering a duty to disclose on the part of Polaroid. (Emphasis in orig.)

At the time of the Rowland sale,

> while selling the stock had absolutely nothing to do with Polaroid's financial health. . . . some might find it less than forthcoming for the press release not to have at least mentioned Polavision's difficulties so that the investing public could assess for themselves the reasons behind the sale.

That this was an improper mix was made conspicuous by plaintiffs' oral argument.

> [W]e've cited the specific passages of Mr. McCune's testimony in our brief, where Mr. McCune testified that the expression, "continued to reflect substantial expenses" was intended to convey that that condition would continue in the future. ፣ . . What we're saying is that a jury could find that this statement, even if it wasn't misleading when issued, became misleading because of the forward-looking nature.

This is a failure to recognize that what Mr. McCune said was a single, simple, statement, that substantial expenses had made Polavision's earnings negative. Though the panel opinion characterized it as "relatively brief," it was precisely correct, initially. Even if forward-looking, it remained precisely correct thereafter. . . . In arguing that the statement did not "remain true," plaintiffs' brief, unabashedly, points solely to matters outside the scope of the initial disclosure, in no way making it incorrect or misleading, originally, or later.

The shell in plaintiffs' gun at trial . . . are all percussion cap and no powder. . . . Plaintiffs have no case.

Federal Trade Commission v. Colgate-Palmolive Co. et al.

Supreme Court of the United States

The basic question before us is whether it is a deceptive trade practice, prohibited by § 5 of the Federal Trade Commission Act, to represent falsely that a televised test, experiment, or demonstration provides a viewer with visual proof of a product claim, regardless of whether the product claim is itself true. The case arises out of an attempt by respondent Colgate-Palmolive Company to prove to the television public that its shaving cream, "Rapid Shave," outshaves them all. Respondent Ted Bates & Company, Inc., an advertis-

380 U.S. 374 (1964), 85 S. Ct. 1035, 13 L. Ed. 2nd 904. Opinion by Chief Justice Earl Warren.

ing agency, prepared for Colgate three one-minute commercials designed to show that Rapid Shave could soften even the toughness of sandpaper. Each of the commercials contained the same "sandpaper test." The announcer informed the audience that, "To prove RAPID SHAVE'S supermoisturizing power, we put it right from the can onto this tough, dry sandpaper. It was apply . . . soak . . . and off in a stroke." While the announcer was speaking, Rapid Shave was applied to a substance that appeared to be sandpaper, and immediately thereafter a razor was shown shaving the substance clean.

The Federal Trade Commission issued a complaint against respondents Colgate and Bates charging that the commercials were false and deceptive. The evidence before the hearing examiner disclosed that sandpaper of the type depicted in the commercials could not be shaved immediately following the application of Rapid Shave, but required a substantial soaking period of approximately 80 minutes. The evidence also showed that the substance resembling sandpaper was in fact a simulated prop, or "mockup," made of plexiglass to which sand had been applied. However, the examiner found that Rapid Shave could shave sandpaper, even though not in the short time represented by the commercials, and that if real sandpaper had been used in the commercials the inadequacies of television transmission would have made it appear to viewers to be nothing more than plain, colored paper. The examiner dismissed the complaint because neither misrepresentation—concerning the actual moistening time or the identity of the shaved substance—was in his opinion a material one that would mislead the public.

The Commission, in an opinion dated December 29, 1961, reversed the hearing examiner. It found that since Rapid Shave could not shave sandpaper within the time depicted in the commercials, respondents had misrep-

resented the product's moisturizing power. Moreover, the Commission found that the undisclosed use of a plexiglass substitute for sandpaper was an additional material misrepresentation that was a deceptive act separate and distinct from the misrepresentation concerning Rapid Shave's underlying qualities. Even if the sandpaper could be shaved just as depicted in the commercials, the Commission found that viewers had been misled into believing they had seen it done with their own eyes. As a result of these findings the Commission entered a cease-and-desist order against the respondents.

An appeal was taken to the Court of Appeals for the First Circuit which rendered an opinion on November 20, 1962. That court sustained the Commission's conclusion that respondents had misrepresented the qualities of Rapid Shave, but it would not accept the Commission's order forbidding the future use of undisclosed simulations in television commercials. It set aside the Commission's order and directed that a new order be entered. On May 7, 1963, the Commission, over the protest of respondents, issued a new order narrowing and clarifying its original order to comply with the court's mandate. The Court of Appeals again found unsatisfactory that portion of the order dealing with simulated props and refused to enforce it. We granted certiorari, 377 U.S. 942, to consider this aspect of the case and do not have before us any question concerning the misrepresentation that Rapid Shave could shave sandpaper immediately after application, that being conceded. . . .

We are not concerned in this case with the clear misrepresentation in the commercials concerning the speed with which Rapid Shave could shave sandpaper, since the Court of Appeals upheld the Commission's finding on that matter and the respondents have not challenged the finding here. We granted certiorari to consider the Commission's conclusion that even if an advertiser has himself conducted a test, experiment or demonstration which he honestly believes will prove a certain product claim, he may not convey to television viewers the false impression that they are seeing the test, experiment or demonstration for themselves, when they are not because of the undisclosed use of mock-ups.

We accept the commission's determination that the commercials involved in this case contained three representations to the public: (1) that sandpaper could be shaved by Rapid Shave; (2) that an experiment had been conducted which verified this claim; and (3) that the viewer was seeing this experiment for himself. Respondents admit that the first two representations were made, but deny that the third was. The Commission, however, found to the contrary, and, since this is a matter of fact resting on an inference that could reasonably be drawn from the commercials themselves, the Commission's finding should be sustained. For the purposes of our review, we can assume that the first two representations were true; the focus of our consideration is on the third, which was clearly false. The parties agree that § 5 prohibits the intentional misrepresentation of any fact which would constitute a material factor in a purchaser's decision whether to buy. They differ, however, in their conception of what "facts" constitute a "material factor" in a purchaser's decision to buy. Respondents submit, in effect, that the only material facts are those which deal with the substantive qualities of a product.[1] The Commission, on the other hand, submits that the misrepresentation of *any* fact so long as it materially induces a purchaser's decision to buy is a deception prohibited by § 5.

The Commission's interpretation of what is a deceptive practice seems more in line with the decided cases than that of respondents. This Court said in *Federal Trade Comm'n v. Algoma Lumber Co.*, 291 U.S. 67, 78: "[T]he pub-

lic is entitled to get what it chooses, though the choice may be dictated by caprice or by fashion or perhaps by ignorance." It has long been considered a deceptive practice to state falsely that a product ordinarily sells for an inflated price but that it is being offered at a special reduced price, even if the offered price represents the actual value of the product and the purchaser is receiving his money's worth.[2] Applying respondents' arguments to these cases, it would appear that so long as buyers paid no more than the product was actually worth and the product contained the qualities advertised, the misstatement of an inflated original price was immaterial.

It had also been held a violation of § 5 for a seller to misrepresent to the public that he is in a certain line of business, even though the misstatement in no way affects the qualities of the product. As was said in *Federal Trade Comm'n v. Royal Milling Co.*, 288 U.S. 212, 216:

> If consumers or dealers prefer to purchase a given article because it was made by a particular manufacturer or class of manufacturers, they have a right to do so, and this right cannot be satisfied by imposing upon them an exactly similar article, or one equally as good, but having a different origin.

The courts of appeals have applied this reasoning to the merchandising of reprocessed products that are as good as new, without a disclosure that they are in fact reprocessed. And it has also been held that it is a deceptive practice to misappropriate the trade name of another.

Respondents claim that all these cases are irrelevant to our decision because they involve misrepresentations related to the product itself and not merely to the manner in which an advertising message is communicated. This distinction misses the mark for two reasons. In the first place, the present case is not concerned with a mode of communication, but with a misrepresentation that viewers have objective proof of a seller's product claim over and above the seller's word. Secondly, all of the above cases, like the present case, deal with methods designed to get a consumer to purchase a product, not with whether the product, when purchased, will perform up to expectations. We find an especially strong similarity between the present case and those cases in which a seller induces the public to purchase an arguably good product by misrepresenting his line of business, by concealing the fact that the product is reprocessed, or by misappropriating another's trademark. In each the seller has used a misrepresentation to break down what he regards to be an annoying or irrational habit of the buying public—the preference for particular manufacturers or known brands regardless of a product's actual qualities, the prejudice against reprocessed goods, and the desire for verification of a product claim. In each case the seller reasons that when the habit is broken the buyer will be satisfied with the performance of the product he receives. Yet, a misrepresentation has been used to break the habit and, as was stated in *Algoma Lumber,* a misrepresentation for such an end is not permitted.

We need not limit ourselves to the cases already mentioned because there are other situations which also illustrate the correctness of the Commission's finding in the present case. It is generally accepted that it is a deceptive practice to state falsely that a product has received a testimonial from a respected source. In addition, the Commission has consistently acted to prevent sellers from falsely stating that their product claims have been "certified." We find these situations to be indistinguishable from the present case. We can assume that in each the underlying product claim is true and in each the seller actually conducted an experiment sufficient to prove to himself the truth of the claim. But in each

the seller has told the public that it could rely on something other than his word concerning both the truth of the claim and the validity of his experiment. We find it an immaterial difference that in one case the viewer is told to rely on the word of a celebrity or authority he respects, in another on the word of a testing agency, and in the present case on his own perception of an undisclosed simulation.

Respondents again insist that the present case is not like any of the above, but is more like a case in which a celebrity or independent testing agency has in fact submitted a written verification of an experiment actually observed, but, because of the inability of the camera to transmit accurately an impression of the paper on which the testimonial is written, the seller reproduces it on another substance so that it can be seen by the viewing audience. This analogy ignores the finding of the Commission that in the present case the seller misrepresented to the public that it was being given objective proof of a product claim. In respondents' hypothetical the objective proof of the product claim that is offered, the word of the celebrity or agency that the experiment was actually conducted, does exist; while in the case before us the objective proof offered, the viewer's own perception of an actual experiment, does not exist. Thus, in respondents' hypothetical, unlike the present case, the use of the undisclosed mock-up does not conflict with the seller's claim that there is objective proof.

We agree with the Commission, therefore, that the undisclosed use of plexiglass in the present commercials was a material deceptive practice independent and separate from the other misrepresentation found. . . .

We turn our attention now to the order issued by the Commission. . . . The Court of Appeals has criticized the reference in the Commission's order to "test, experiment or demonstration" as not capable of practical interpretation. It could find no difference between the Rapid Shave commercial and a commercial which extolled the goodness of ice cream while giving viewers a picture of a scoop of mashed potatoes appearing to be ice cream. We do not understand this difficulty. In the ice cream case the mashed potato prop is not being used for additional proof of the product claim, while the purpose of the Rapid Shave commercial is to give the viewer objective proof of the claims made. If in the ice cream hypothetical the focus of the commercial becomes the undisclosed potato prop and the viewer is invited, explicitly or by implication, to see for himself the truth of the claims about the ice cream's rich texture and full color, and perhaps compare it to a "rival product," then the commercial has become similar to the one now before us. Clearly, however, a commercial which depicts happy actors delightedly eating ice cream that is in fact mashed potatoes or drinking a product appearing to be coffee but which is in fact some other substance is not covered by the present order.

The crucial terms of the present order—"test, experiment or demonstration . . . represented . . . as actual proof of a claim"—are as specific as the circumstances will permit. If respondents in their subsequent commercials attempt to come as close to the line of misrepresentation as the Commission's order permits, they may without specifically intending to do so cross into the area proscribed by this order. However, it does not seem "unfair to require that one who deliberately goes peril-ously close to an area of proscribed conduct shall take the risk that he may cross the line," *Boyce Motor Lines, Inc. v. United States*, 342 U.S. 337, 340. In commercials where the emphasis is on the seller's word, and not on the viewer's own perception, the respondents need not fear that an undisclosed use of props is prohibited by the present order. On the other hand, when the commercial not only makes a claim, but also invites the viewer to rely on his own perception for demonstrative proof of the claim, the respondents will be aware that the use of undisclosed props in strategic places might be a material deception. We believe that respondents will have no difficulty applying the Commission's order to the vast majority of their contemplated future commercials. If, however, a situation arises in which respondents are sincerely unable to determine whether a proposed course of action would violate the present order, they can, by complying with the Commission's rules, oblige the Commission to give them definitive advice as to whether their proposed action, if pursued, would constitute compliance with the order.

NOTES

1. Brief for Respondent Colgate, p. 16: "What [the buyer] is interested in is whether the actual product he buys will look and perform the way it appeared on his television set."

2. *Federal Trade Comm'n v. Standard Education Society*, 302 U.S. 112, 115–117, *Kalwajtys v. Federal Trade Comm'n*. 237 F.2d 654, 656 (C. A. 7th Cir 1956), cert. denied, 352 U.S. 1025.

CASE 1. *Food Labels and Artful Sales*

Packaged foods in supermarkets contain a list of the ingredients on the package as well as other information. Much of that information is required by law. However, research has indicated that what is said or not said on the label has an important effect on the sale of the product.

In 1983, the Kellogg Company changed

This case was written by Norman E. Bowie and Tom L. Beauchamp.

the names of two of its cereals from Sugar Frosted Flakes and Sugar Smacks to Frosted Flakes and Honey Smacks, respectively. At about the same time C. W. Post changed the name of its cereal Super Sugar Crisp to Super Golden Crisp. Market research had shown that some customers reacted negatively to the word *sugar*. However, the sugar and sweetener content of the cereal continued to be at least 50 percent of the caloric intake.

Market research has also shown that some consumers react *positively* to the word *granola*. Granola bars saw retail sales grow 290 percent from 1980 through 1985—the fastest growing segment of the candy bar market. Granola bars were first introduced into the market as health food products, and the ingredients were fashioned for consumers concerned about nutrition. However, many complained that they tasted like cardboard. Manufacturers then changed the products by adding peanut butter, chocolate chips, marshmallows, and sugar. Although the bars gradually became more like candy bars than granola in nutritional value and sugar content, they are slightly more nutritious than conventional candy bars. They have a higher fiber content, slightly less fat, and a higher percentage of complex carbohydrates. Advertising has continued to present the product through a healthful image, carrying over the public's association of the term *granola* with such concepts as "health food" and "healthy." Quaker Oats, General Mills, and Hershey Foods emphasize the "wholesomeness" and "goodness" of their granola bars in their advertising. In order to compete, conventional candy bar companies such as M&M/Mars have begun to advertise their products as healthy snacks.

The amount of sugar is not the only concern of consumers. Also important is the amount of complex carbohydrates, protein, and vitamins a food contains, as well as its fat content, sodium content, and calories. This information is found on the label, but the numbers found there are a function of serving size, and they are often presented in a way difficult for the uninitiated to interpret. The consumer's information is specified in protein content, calories, and the like *per serving*, but the larger the serving size, the higher the numbers are apt to be. Reducing the serving size lowers the number of calories and the amount of sodium. Companies have therefore begun describing as a "serving" much less than most people serve themselves as a serving.

Around 1982, the Campbell's Soup Company reduced its serving size from ten ounces to eight ounces. A can of Campbell's soup that once held two servings now held two and one-half servings. As a result, the calorie and sodium levels per serving fell. The Campbell Soup Company said that "people are eating less" and "most bowls hold eight ounces."

Questions

1. Are such marketing practices by candy, cereal, and soup companies manipulative? Deceptive?

2. Should companies be permitted to change the name, contents, or serving size without changing the product or the amount of the product?

3. The term *sugar-free* literally means free of sucrose. Since many people purchase sugar-free foods to assist them with weight loss, should a standard be required so that "sugar-free" means "free of any high-calorie sweetener"?

4. Flexi-labeling permits wording such as "contains one or more of the following." Hence, "contains sunflower oil, coconut oil, and/or palm oil" is legally permitted. Yet sunflower seed oil is a polyunsaturated fat, and the other two are saturated fats. Since polyunsaturated fats are more healthy, should flexi-labeling be prohibited?

CASE 2. *The Conventions of Lying on Wall Street*

Salomon Brothers, Inc., is one of forty firms authorized to purchase U.S. Treasury notes from the U.S. government for resale to private investors. These notes are sold periodically at Treasury auctions. Before each auction, firms receive "buy" orders from customers. The firm then tries to buy securities at a the lowest possible price.

The government places some qualifications and restrictions on the bidding. First, a firm can purchase no more than 35 percent of the notes offered at a given auction for its portfolio. Second, if a firm holds large orders from an investor, it can buy bonds directly for that customer; these bonds are *not* included in the 35 percent limit. If a firm is unable to purchase enough securities to fill its orders, the firm must then buy from competing firms at a higher rate than the auction.

In July 1991, Salomon Brothers, Inc. confessed to illegally purchasing U.S. Treasury notes on three separate occasions. They exploited the system in two ways. At the December, February, and May auctions, Salomon used customers' names to submit false bids. That is, they ordered bonds for customers who had *not* placed orders and did not know their names were being used. After the auction, Salomon added these bonds to its portfolio. On another occasion, Salomon worked with a customer to purchase a large quantity of bonds in the customers' name. Salomon then bought back a portion of the bonds, effectively making a net purchase from the auction greater than 35 percent. Using this strategy, Salomon purchased 46 percent of Treasury notes sold on one occasion and 57 percent of the securities sold on another occasion.

Treasury auctions are also affected by the prevalent practice of sharing information.

Current and former traders at several prominent Wall Street investment banks admit they regularly have shared "secrets" about the size and price of their bids at government auctions. This collusion to create a low bidding strategy results in firms paying less to the federal government. Consequently, the government makes less money to finance debt, causing an increase in taxes and interest rates.

However, the collusion is also complicated by strategies of deception. Lying has been tolerated and indeed expected for many years as part of the competition for trading. "It is part of the playing field. It's ingrained in the way the Street operates," one industry executive says. "I've stood out there on that trading floor, and they lie to each other (before the auctions). That's part of the game. It was an exception when traders actually told the truth to each other about their bidding strategy." He adds, "They lie through their teeth to each other. You want to catch the [other] guy in an awkward position and pick him off."

In a report to the U.S. Congress, the Federal Home Mortgage Company claimed that two-thirds of Wall Street firms it regularly deals with have lied to the agency to increase the chances of buying as many of the agency's securities as possible. Such deceit is so pervasive and routine on Wall Street that it has come to be regarded on the Street as the preferred and accepted way of doing business. The common practice of submitting inflated orders has come under scrutiny from securities firms and the FTC, but the practice is so pervasive that it cannot be easily remedied. A small group of dealers holds purchasing power on the market and has long operated with financial success and no serious challenges to its mode of operating.

This case was prepared by Tom L. Beauchamp.

One bond market specialists says, "I'm not condoning it or excusing it or saying it didn't go to an extreme . . . but people forget that the markets which are under the spotlight are part of that kind of distribution activity which for centuries has [been] associated with a fair amount of caveat emptor and puffery." The traditions of bluffing, deception, and puffery have created an environment in which every player in the "game" expects deception as the condition for playing.

Inflated salaries and egos fuel the temptation for collusion or deceit. Although many outsiders claim that money is the main motivator, the incentives reach to mastery and fame in competition.

Questions

1. Is Wall Street actually a "game," and can these allegations and expectations be applied equally to every participant?
2. Should the FTC ignore deceit and collusion on Wall Street since it is ingrained in the system? Why or why not?

CASE 3. *Green Advertising*

In a recent environmental study, 83 percent of respondents said they prefer buying environmentally safe products. Thirty-seven percent claimed they would pay up to 15 percent more for environmentally safe packaging. These findings present the marketer with a tangible incentive. The practice of so-called green promotion and advertising is an attempt to use corporate publicity to create a message of corporate initiative in creating a healthier, improved natural environment. To take a typical example, in 1990 Japan's Kirin Beer launched its "Earth Beer" to be marketed worldwide with a picture of the earth on a green label. Promotionally, Kirin claimed that the product was "earth friendly." However, this beer was not produced or packaged differently from Kirin's original products or the products of other beer manufacturers.

The influx of green promotion poses the question: Are companies taking action to improve the environment or is it purely publicity? Friends of the Earth President Brent Blackwelder claims that, in many cases, green advertising is not warranted by the conduct of the corporation. For example, he claims that DuPont is not a conscientious protector of the environment, although it uses green advertising. Blackwelder contends that "it's morally reprehensible to portray this type of image [in advertising] when they have this type of track record."

The background of this statement is as follows: In September 1991, the DuPont Corporation launched a television ad campaign featuring barking sea lions, jumping dolphins, and other animals enjoying fresh, unpolluted seas. The ad strongly implied that DuPont was making major changes to protect the environment. A Friends of the Earth report, by contrast, claimed that DuPont's pollution in 1989 was 14 times that of Dow Chemical Company, 20 times that of Chrysler, and 30 times that of Mobil Oil. The report claimed that DuPont has the highest ratio of pollution to profit (14 percent) and that the company paid nearly $1 million monthly from 1989 to June 1991 in fines for environmental infractions. The report also noted that after the devastating 1990 Exxon tanker accident,

---

This case was prepared by Katy Cancro, using articles in *Advertising Age* in May, June, and September 1991, and a Reuters report in *The Washington Post*, August, 28, 1991.

DuPont's oil-marketing subsidiary promoted its plans to build two new double-hulled tankers to prevent oil spills as a unique environmental strategy. However, since one out of every six crude oil tankers was already double hulled, DuPont's "change" was not a new initiative.

In response to these claims, DuPont issued a public statement that said, "It seems to be a rehash of several of DuPont's most serious environmental challenges—all of which we are working diligently to resolve." DuPont also noted that it had begun working on a few projects to benefit the environment. For example, DuPont had begun developing a chemical to reduce ozone-depleting fluorocarbons and had initiated a buy-back of fluorocarbon-producing products in an effort to preserve the ozone layer.

Questions

1. Is environmental advertising a new form of deceptive advertising?
2. Does green advertising damage the consumer, or is it a harmless method of developing the reputation of the corporation?
3. To what extent should companies be held responsible for showing a track record of environmental preservation that corresponds to its green advertising?

CASE 4. *Computer Math for Car Loans*

It is not unusual for automobile dealers to offer customers a financing plan to facilitate a new car purchase. These dealers often say that you can borrow money at a stated rate of interest, deposit it in a bank at a lower rate, and come out ahead. To sell this idea, dealers are using an Automatic Data Processing (ADP) computer software program that computes the amount of interest the customer will pay on a car loan and the amount they will earn on the same sum deposited in a certificate of deposit or savings account for the same length of time. The presentation to the customer is that the interest earned on the deposit will usually exceed the amount paid on the loan, even if the loan rate is considerably higher.

Here is a typical example used in the presentation: A customer borrows $6,469.31 for 36 months at 13 percent interest. He or she will pay $1,417.22 in interest over the three years (for a total to be paid of $7,882.52 in both principal and interest). By borrowing the money, the customer is able to leave his or her $6,469.31 in a bank account at 7.5 percent interest. In the account, the customer will earn $1,650.60 in 36 months, for a total balance of $8,119.91. From this presentation, it appears that the customer would save $233.39 by borrowing the money and leaving cash in the bank.

The Federal Trade Commission claims that this software is mathematically correct, but presents an incomplete and misleading picture to the customer. It is impossible to save money by borrowing at a higher interest rate than that which one earns from an investment. To return to the example, one cannot borrow money at 13 percent interest, earn 7.5 percent on savings, and come out ahead. The ADP software does calculate correct interest rates, but does not take into account repayment of the loan principal. As a customer repays the

---

This case was prepared by Katy Cancro and Tom L. Beauchamp from interviews with automobile dealers and by reference to "Computer Car-Loan Math Doesn't Add Up," by Albert B. Crenshaw (*Washington Post,* August 31,1991, p. C1); and "Firm, FTC Settle Charges on Claims in Auto Financing," by Gilbert Fuchsberg (*Wall Street Journal,* August 31, 1991, p. 3).

loan in monthly increments, the interest he or she earns on the savings decreases; over 36 months of withdrawals, the actual interest rate on the remaining balance in the account would be far less than $1,417.22. Therefore, interest on the savings account will be lower than the interest paid to the dealer when the car owner withdraws money to pay off the car.

Studies suggest that the average consumer does not have the ability to identify this discrepancy and recalculate the actual amount of money he or she will spend on the car, taking into account the decrease in cash in the bank. As a result consumers may make financially unsound decisions and incur a net financial loss.

For this reason the FTC sought and consummated an agreement with Automatic Data Processing that would alter the software provided to automobile dealers. ADP is prohibited by this agreement from continuing to represent the value of financing as it had; ADP agreed to delete the charts shown on screen to customers. However, the company refused to admit that the software was actually misleading or defective, and the FTC did not require such an acknowledgment. In response to FTC claims, Arthur Weinbach, senior vice-president of ADP, contended that many other software programs on the market "basically do the same thing. . . . It's been a standard industry practice."

Mr. Weinbach appears to be correct. Moreover, automobile dealers were not required by the FTC agreement to stop using their own sales approaches or charts to augment the ADP software. Many automobile dealers have continued to use the same approach even though they lack on-screen charts to show to customers. There is no regulation prohibiting automobile dealers from presenting information in this manner, and it has become standard practice to do so. As they have done even before the ADP software dealers continue to lead consumers to believe they can save money by financing a car.

Questions

1. Has the FTC in any way helped the consumer? Should the consumer be helped?
2. Is ADP merely providing dealers with a more graphic presentation of what they say anyway? Is ADP guilty of consumer deception, or is it a legitimate "buyer beware" situation?

CASE 5. *Marketing the Giant Quart*

Your company sells only in the state of New Wyoming. State law does not prohibit marketing your cola in "giant quarts." A quart is a standard measure, so a giant quart is the same size as an ordinary quart. A survey conducted by your firm indicates that 40 percent of cola buyers think that a giant quart is larger than a regular quart.

Questions

1. Would it be deceptive marketing to call your bottle a giant quart?

2. Does it make any difference in the ethics of marketing what percentage of cola buyers think that a giant quart is larger than a regular quart?
3. Suppose a firm sold a half gallon of soda for 99 cents. In ads, the half gallon size was called the giant size. The firm finds it necessary to increase the price of soda to $1.09. With the new price comes a new name—the giant economy size. Is the use of the new name deceptive?
4. Should there be a standard according to product for large, extra large, giant, and family sizes? Why?

Suggested Supplementary Readings

ALLMON, DEAN E., AND JAMES GRANT. "Real Estate Sales Agents and the Code of Ethics." *Journal of Business Ethics* 9 (October, 1990).

BEAUCHAMP, TOM L. *Case Studies in Business, Society, and Ethics.* 3rd ed. Englewood Cliffs, N.J.: Prentice Hall, 1993. Chap 2.

BELLIZZI, JOSEPH, AND ROBERT HITE. "Supervising Unethical Salesforce Behavior." *Journal of Marketing* 53 (April 1989).

BOK, SISSELA. *Lying: Moral Choices in Public and Private Life.* New York: Pantheon Books, 1978.

Business and Professional Ethics Journal 3 (Spring-Summer 1984). The entire issue is devoted to ethical issues in advertising.

CAMENISCH, PAUL. "Marketing Ethics." *Journal of Business Ethics* 10 (April 1991).

DESJARDINS, JOSEPH R., AND JOHN MCCALL. *Contemporary Issues in Business Ethics.* 2nd ed. Belmont, Calif.: Wadsworth Publishing Co., 1990.

FRIED, CHARLES. *Right and Wrong.* Cambridge, Mass.: Harvard University Press, 1978. Chap. 3.

GOODPASTER, KENNETH E. "Should Sponsors Screen for Moral Values?" *The Hastings Center Report* 13 (December 1983).

GRAY, VICTOR, AND JOHN GUTHRIE. "Ethical Issues of Environmentally Friendly Packaging." *International Journal of Physical Distribution & Logistics* 20 (1990).

HENTOFF, NAT. "Would You Run This Ad?" *Business and Society Review* 14 (Summer 1975).

HITE, ROBERT E., and others. "A Content Analysis of Ethical Policy Statements Regarding Marketing Activities." *Journal of Business Ethics* 7 (October 1988).

HUNT, SHELBY D. AND LAWRENCE CHONKO. "Ethical Problems of Advertising Agency Executives." *Journal of Advertising* 16 (1987).

KILBOURNE, WILLIAM E. "Perceptual Biases in Affirmative Disclosures in Print Ad." *Journal of Business Research* 21 (September 1990).

KING, CAROLE. "It's Time to Disclose Commissions." *National Underwriter* 94 (November 19, 1990).

LACZNICK, GENE R. AND PATRICK E. MURPHY, eds. *Marketing Ethics.* Lexington, Mass.: Lexington Books, 1985.

LEISER, B. "The Ethics of Advertising." In *Ethics, Free Enterprise, amd Public Policy,* edited by Richard DeGeorge and Joseph Pichler. New York: Oxford University Press, 1978.

PETERSON, ROBIN T. "Physical Environment Television Advertisement Themes." *Journal of Business Ethics* 10 (March 1991).

QUINN, JOHN F. "Moral Theory and Defective Tobacco Advertising and Warnings." *Journal of Business Ethics* 8 (November 1989).

SMITH, N. CRAIG, AND JOHN A. QUELCH. *Ethics in Marketing Management.* Homewood, Ill.: Irwin, 1992.

STUART, FREDERICK, ed. *Consumer Protection from Deceptive Advertising.* Hempstead, N.Y.: Hofstra University, 1974.

SULLIVAN, ROGER J. "A Response to 'Is Business Bluffing Ethical?'" *Business and Professional Ethics Journal* 3 (Winter 1984).

WALTERS, KERRY S. "Limited Paternalism and the Pontius Pilate Plight." *Journal of Business Ethics* 8 (December 1989).

Chapter Eight

Ethical Issues
in International Business

PERHAPS THE MOST important development in business in the past decade has been the recognition that markets are now international. Every U.S. firm realizes that competitors for its market share could come from any corner of the globe. Even fairly small regional firms now attempt to market their products internationally. Any firm concerned with its survival must adopt an international perspective.

Of course there is much more to the awareness of international issues than the development of international markets. International travel is becoming more prevalent, and many more people from abroad are visiting the United States. In addition, many problems that affect one country have an impact on other nations. For example, the disaster at the Soviet nuclear power plant in Chernobyl illustrated that pollution respects no national boundaries.

The subject of ethical issues in international business has no shortage of topics. Bribery is a common problem, as is the marketing of pesticides and the obligations of wealthy economies to so-called lesser developed countries. Before we can address these specific issues with much authority, an overarching problem needs to be addressed. There is a wide variety of opinion on what is acceptable conduct in international business, and a general skepticism prevails that questions whether there are any universal norms for ethical business practice. Since opinions on whether U.S. companies should bribe when conducting business in certain foreign countries depend in part on whether one believes there is a universal norm that bribery is unethical, the issue of international business norms needs to be addressed at the outset.

ARE THERE INTERNATIONAL NORMS OF BUSINESS PRACTICE?

A U.S. company involved in business abroad must face the question, "When in Rome, should it behave as the Romans do?" This question not only arises for U.S. firms doing business abroad, but for non-U.S. firms doing business in the United States. One is tempted to answer the question as follows: When operating abroad, a firm should always obey the law of the host country. But this answer is inadequate on a number of grounds. First, many differences in business practices between the home country (where the firm is headquarted) and host country are not matters governed by host country law. As noted in Chapter 5, employment at will is both legal and widely practiced in the United States. In Japan employment at will is not the customary business practice. When Japanese auto companies built auto assembly plants in the United States, the executives of these companies could not have looked to U.S. law to instruct them as to whether they should adopt the U.S. employment-at-will practice. Under U.S. law, employment at will is legally permitted but it is not legally required. Second, it is immoral for a company to obey an unjust law, for example, South Africa's Apartheid laws. The most that can be said is that corporations should obey the law of the host country as long as the law does not require the corporation to violate a universal moral norm.

How should a corporation behave when business norms of the host country differ from those of the home country and when host country law is silent concerning how business must behave? The multinational firm has at least four options: (1) Follow the norms of its home country because that is the patriotic thing to do; (2) follow the norms of the host country to show proper respect for the host country's culture; (3) follow whichever norm is most profitable; (4) follow whichever norm is morally best. (Note that these four alternatives are not all mutually exclusive; for example, following the fourth option might require following the second one as well.)

There may be no one appropriate course of action for a multinational business to take. In highly developed industrialized countries, option 3 seems to be a permissible course of action. One might think that choosing option 3 would require following option 2 as well because the most profitable way to conduct business is to follow the practices of the host country. However, Japanese companies operating in the United States have consistently not followed U.S. norms (option 2). Rather, Japanese companies have imported traditional Japanese management practices into the United States.[1] The results have been mixed, but on balance Japanese businesses operating in the United States that obey Japanese management principles are equal or superior in profitability to competing U.S. firms. One U.S. Honda plant that is operated on Japanese management principles is even more productive than comparable Honda plants in Japan. The importing of Japanese management practices with respect to employees into the United States has not created any appreciable resentment from U.S. citizens.

However, widespread acceptance of Japanese business practices has not occurred among U.S. suppliers. Japanese companies have adopted the *Keiretsu* system. Under this system, Japanese firms have stable relationships with a fixed number of suppliers. Japanese firms do not use a bidding system that is open to all potential suppliers. In practice, then, most of the parts used in Japanese auto assembly plants in the United States are made by Japanese companies. U.S. companies cannot get in the door, and not surprisingly U.S. parts manufacturers are very resentful indeed![2] If the Japanese use of the *Keiretsu* system in the United States creates sufficient resentment, Congress may rewrite U.S. trade law to Japan's detriment. However, if the resentment is kept in check, Japanese automobile companies will continue to increase their market share. Is it wrong for the Japanese to import the *Keiretsu* system into the United States? Does it show a lack of respect for U.S. culture?

The answer to these questions leads directly to this issue: Do international norms for business practice exist? Japanese firms' use of the *Keiretsu* supplier network can only be "wrong" (1) if there is an international moral norm requiring that a multinational firm respect the culture of its host country and if that moral norm is overriding in this case, or (2) if the U.S. competitive bidding procedure with respect to suppliers is morally superior to the Japanese *Keiretsu* system and if there is an international moral norm requiring that a multinational should always follow the morally superior business practice. Posing a successful argument on behalf of (2) seems unlikely since it requires establishing the moral superiority of the U.S. system.[3] However, an argument similar to (1) has been defended when the host country is an underdeveloped country.

This discussion illustrates the importance of establishing the existence and content of international moral norms for business. In his article, Norman Bowie contends that any appeals to justify home country practices over host country practices or vice versa require an appeal to international moral norms. Bowie appeals to three considerations on behalf of international moral norms. First, widespread agreement already exists among nations, as illustrated by the large number of countries that are signatories to the United Nations Declaration of Universal Human Rights and by the existence of numerous international treaties establishing norms of business practice. Second, certain moral norms must be endorsed by each society if society is to exist at all. Corporations ought to accept the moral norms that make society, and hence business practice itself, possible. Third, certain moral norms are required if business practice is to function at all. Bowie uses Kantian arguments to show that business requires a moral norm that corporations keep their contracts. However, similar arguments could be based on utilitarian considerations. If certain moral rules or traits such as truth telling or honesty give a multinational corporation a competitive advantage, then eventually these moral norms or traits will be adopted by all multinationals because those that do not will not survive.

Thomas Donaldson argues that multinationals have a moral duty to honor fundamental rights. Donaldson proposes a threefold test that any rights claim must pass if it is to be considered a fundamental right. He proposes a list of ten such fundamental rights such as the right to own property, the right to physical security, and the rights to subsistence and a minimal education. A morally responsible multinational must honor the rights of the people in host countries. Does that mean that a company has an unlimited obligation to feed the poor and provide education? Donaldson argues that honoring fundamental rights imposes no such obligation, and he distinguishes three ways that rights can be infringed: (1) A person or corporation can take action to deprive people of their rights; (2) a person or corporation can fail to protect people from having their rights violated; and (3) a person or corporation can fail to aid people in achieving their rights. Donaldson argues that the duties of multinationals are limited. Multinationals do not have a duty to aid people in achieving their rights, nor do they have an unlimited duty to provide food and education. However, multinationals do have a duty to avoid depriving people of any of their fundamental rights. In the case of six fundamental rights, multinationals have an additional duty to help people from being deprived of their fundamental rights. The reader is invited to see how persuasive Donaldson's analysis is and how many conflicts between home and host country practices Donaldson's analysis can resolve. Sometimes it might be difficult to distinguish failing to aid (which is permitted) from failing to protect (which for six of the fundamental rights is not permitted). Conflicts also exist between home and host country business practices that the rights portion of Donaldson's theory cannot resolve. For example, Donaldson is not clear how to settle the issue about Japanese companies importing *Keiretsu* supplier relationships into the United States.

EXPORTING HAZARDOUS SUBSTANCES

One of the classic differences among countries is the different rules countries have for the use of hazardous substances, especially for the use of pesticides and other chemicals. In general, the practices of the lesser developed countries are far more permissive than those of the highly developed countries. For example, many underdeveloped countries permit the use of pesticides banned by the United States. We previously discussed respect for the practices of the host country as a moral norm. However, respecting a host nation's practices in this case—allowing the use of pesticides known to be hazardous—seems morally problematic. Many have argued that the morally appropriate rules for exporting hazardous materials should be the rules of the developed countries and that applying home country rules in this case is not cultural imperialism.

Posing an argument on behalf of the developed country's rules in this matter is not difficult. Underdeveloped countries are just that. They do not have the knowledge and sophistication to evaluate the safety issues, and they do not have the money to regulate effectively. As Lynn Sharp Paine points out in her article, the producer's knowledge of its product far exceeds the user's knowledge. The producer also has the superior knowledge and resources to do the laboratory and field research necessary to acquire appropriate safety information. In light of these facts, it is argued that the morally appropriate thing for multinationals to do is to adopt the restrictive rules of the home country.

Yet another suggestion is that multinationals agree to abide by the principle of "prior informed consent" (PIC). Under a PIC rule, each exporter of a banned or restricted chemical would have to obtain through the home country government the expressed consent of the importing company to receive such a banned or restricted chemical. Although President Reagan prevented the implementation of PIC domestically, the principle has been adopted by the United Nations Environment Programme. In his article, Michael P. Walls criticizes the PIC on legal, economic, and practical grounds. One of Walls's major arguments is that PIC interferes with the sovereignty of lesser developed countries because the rules of the developed exporting countries are substituted for the rules of the lesser developed importing countries. What Walls ignores, however, are all the arguments of the sort discussed above that attempt to justify the use of the rules of the developed exporting countries in this case.

Whereas Walls criticizes the PIC as being unduly restrictive, Lynn Sharp Paine believes that the PIC is not strict enough. Paine wants a shift from what she calls demand side responsibility (importing country's responsibility) to supply side responsibility (exporting country's responsibility) on the grounds the supply side responsibility will reduce the risk to persons in the importing countries. Since the exporting countries have superior knowledge and resources, Paine argues that it is only fair that the exporters bear the cost. But wouldn't the adoption of PIC accomplish that? Paine thinks not. Some of her objectives are practical. Some hazardous pesticides would not be covered. But her interesting and controversial claim is that when government officials of the importing countries give their consent, that may not be adequate to protect the users of the product and other third parties. In nondemocratic countries, the government does not legitimately represent the people and hence cannot morally consent on their behalf. There are also problems of voluntariness, understanding, and reasonableness that often make the consent of underdeveloped importing countries morally problematic. If Paine's arguments are correct, the possibility of legal liability for the exporting multinational increases. As illustrated by the legal case at the end of this chapter—*Dow Chemical Company v. Castro Alfaro et al.*—U.S. courts are rejecting the principle of *forum non conveniens*, which entails that a U.S. company cannot be held responsible at home for harm caused abroad. If people in a foreign country can show they were harmed by the products of a U.S. company, and that the consent of their nation's government was not legitimate because it violated one of the conditions for legitimate consent, then, in the absence of *forum non conveniens*, the U.S. firm's liability for the harm would be great indeed.

The discussion of the export of potentially harmful pesticides raises some complex issues regarding how conflicts between home country business practice and host country business practice should be resolved. It is often argued that morality requires respect for the practices of the host country, especially in lesser developed countries where industrialization would radically change their way of life. Industrialization brings its share of blessings, but it also brings its share of curses. And in some countries industrialization may be supported by the majority of the inhabitants but opposed by a minority. This problem is especially evident in Brazil and other areas of South America where mining and lumbering in the Amazon rain forests threaten to eliminate indigenous tribes. Such concerns are not even limited to less developed countries. Some Italians are concerned that the widespread use of English language ads on Italian television is undermining the Italian language. The Japanese are concerned that imported products that symbolize individualism will undermine the cultural values of harmony and community so necessary in a country with little land and many people. On the other hand, as the discussion of the export of potentially harmful pesticides proves, showing respect for the culture of others sometimes requires following the rules of the home country rather than those of the host nation.

THE REGULATION OF INTERNATIONAL BUSINESS

Another instance illustrating the "home rule over host rule" practice occurred when U.S. businesspersons at least temporarily indicated that they would follow U.S. rules rather than host rules in cases of bribery. In 1977 Congress passed the Foreign Corrupt Practices Act (FCPA), which made it illegal for U.S. companies to pay bribes in order to do business abroad. Several highly publicized incidents led to the passage of the act, but the most prominent was the resignation of Japanese Premier Tanaka in 1974 after being indicted for accepting $1.7 million in bribes from the Lockheed Corporation.

Before discussing the FCPA, a distinction should be made among facilitating payments, extortion, and bribery. These distinctions are important because the FCPA permitted facilitating payments by exempting customs agents and bureaucrats whose jobs were essentially ministerial and clerical and it permitted payments in cases of genuine extortion. The chief difference between bribery and extortion is who does the initiating of the act. A corporation pays a bribe when it offers to pay or provide favors to a person or persons of trust to influence the latters' judgment or conduct. A corporation pays extortion money when it yields to a demand for money in order to have accomplished what it has a legal right to have accomplished without the payment. The difference between extortion and a facilitating payment is often one of degree.

These distinctions are important because discussion and criticism of the FCPA often confuses these activities. For example, the major criticism of the act was that the FCPA made it difficult to do business abroad and put U.S. firms at a competitive disadvantage. Stories of government officials or employees of corporations who demand payment to unload perishables or get a telephone installed are used to attack the FCPA but such payments are not bribes under the act and hence are permitted. These payments are considered to be facilitating payments.

Business leaders have argued that the FCPA has put U.S. firms at a competitive disadvantage and that U.S. export business has been hurt as a result. There is also a belief that U.S. companies are less likely to offer bribes. There is empirical evidence against these beliefs. For example, a study by Kate Gillespie, showed that U.S. export business in the Middle East had not been lost.[4] Her analysis was based on data showing the share of U.S. exports of the total exports to the countries in the region from 1970–1982. The sole exception was Iran, and the explanation for the loss there had nothing to do with the FCPA. She also showed that from 1975 to 1979, U.S. corporations were nearly twice as often involved in financial scandals in the Middle East as were the multinationals of other countries, even though the U.S. share of the exports to these countries was never more than 20 percent. Gillespie did not distinguish cases of bribery from cases of extortion so the data might show that U.S. companies were more likely to pay extortion money than other multinationals. In any case, a picture that paints the U.S. companies as moral heroes and their foreign competitors as bribers is not accurate.

Yet another criticism of the FCPA was that it was an example of moral imperialism in which the United States was forcing its moral views on the rest of the world. This argument is fallacious for at least three reasons. First, the FCPA did not force other countries or the multinationals of other countries to follow U.S. morality. It simply required U.S. companies to follow U.S. moral norms with respect to bribery when doing business abroad. Second, as we saw in the discussion of pesticides, good reasons often dictate that U.S. companies should adopt U.S. standards rather than those of host countries. Third, the belief that bribery is an unethical business practice is not unique to the United States. Nearly all countries believe that bribery is wrong. The practice of bribery may vary among countries, but the belief that bribery is wrong is universal—or nearly so. Evidence for this claim can be found in the public reaction when it is exposed. Throughout the world there is moral outrage when bribery is discovered. The bribe taker is morally disgraced and is sometimes sent to prison. Recall that Japanese Premier Tanaka resigned in disgrace when it was discovered that he was a bribe taker. This reaction is hardly to be expected in a country where bribery is morally permitted.

Despite these empirical and moral arguments, FCPA critics were sufficiently influential to have the FCPA amended in 1988. Those favoring the amendments believe that the law still outlaws bribery but is less disadvantageous to U.S. multinationals. Critics of the amendments believe that the FCPA has been gutted. Bartley A. Brennan in his article provides a detailed analysis of the 1988 amendments and refers to them as the "death" of a law.

Since there is no world government and since business practice differs throughout the world, in this age of internationalization of business some common standards for business practice are imperative. This need is particularly acute in light of the criticisms against multinationals launched by representatives of the lesser developed countries. Many informed commentators fear a growing split between the "haves" in the northern hemisphere and the "have nots" in the southern hemisphere. In addition, government officials in many countries are growing concerned about the ability of multinationals to subvert government economic activities. For example, multinationals can often use overseas operations to avoid taxes. Generally, government officials complain that multinationals use their economic power to gain favorable legislation or consideration at the expense of the public good. Although this complaint is most commonly made in lesser developed countries, it has been made in nearly every country. A few years ago, some U.S. officials contended that the Federal Reserve kept interest rates up so that the Japanese would not move their investment funds elsewhere and create a credit crunch. Some negotiated codes for the international conduct of business might lessen the number and intensity of the conflicts.

The advantages for domestic industry-wide codes discussed in Chapter 2 apply equally well for international industry-wide codes. Unfortunately the disadvantages of codes are even more acute in the international arena. Since a truly international code must apply to a number of different cultures, the drafters try to make code provisions general enough so that the codes win acceptance. As a result, however, international codes tend to be too general to implement in specific situations. Since most multinationals are from highly industrialized countries and since many of the criticisms of multinationals are from host countries that are underdeveloped countries, the latter advocate strict enforcement procedures with penalties for violation. The representatives of the developed countries resist such penalties and disputes become political, contentious, and ultimately intractable. This inability to reach agreement has already occurred at meetings of the United Nations Conference on Trade and Development.

Despite great difficulties in negotiating international codes, the benefits justify the effort. International codes can take a number of forms. Some might be truly international. Several codes regulating international business are already working their way through the United Nations, but progress is often excruciatingly slow. For example, the United Nations Code of Conduct in Transnational Corporations has been under discussion since 1972. Other codes are more regional in nature and thus agreement is often quicker. Some of the agreements of the European Economic Community provide good models. The "Guidelines for Multinational Enterprises" adopted by the Organization of Economic Cooperation and Development (OECD) is included in this chapter. Still another possibility for the development of international codes are selfregulatory codes developed by the industries in the different countries themselves. With respect to exporting hazardous products, guidelines have been adopted by the international pharmaceutical associations and the International Group of National Associations of Agrochemical Producers. As the United Nations or groups of sovereign states establish codes of conduct governing international business practice, one would predict a corresponding increase in the development of selfregulatory codes. The 1990s should be a fertile time of the development of international codes of business practice.

In his article, William Frederick examines six international codes of business practice to see if he can identify any common themes. He identifies a number of common themes such as the way multinationals should treat corporate stakeholders as well as guidelines on political payments and basic human rights. Having identified these common themes, Frederick wonders how this commonality arose. Some of it is based on shared experiences. As business becomes international, people become more knowledgeable about cultural differences in business practice and more aware of the difficulties these differences can create. Given the advantageous nature of international business, there is an incentive to resolve the difficulties those different business practices present. Common norms are then negotiated.

Interestingly, Frederick also appeals to Kantian norms, which seem to have a universal claim to validity. We are thus back at our starting point. Are there international norms of business conduct? Yes, but opinions might differ concerning how they arose. Some have argued that there are norms that are valid across cultures and that all or nearly all cultures recognize them. Others would argue that the utilitarian advantages of international business require that nations develop such norms in order to overcome the difficulties that different business practices create. On this view, the nations cannot afford not to have universal norms for business.

NOTES

1. For example, see "The Difference Japanese Management Makes," *Business Week*, July 14, 1986, pp. 47–50.
2. See Carla Rapoport, "Why Japan Keeps on Winning," *Fortune*, July 15, 1991, pp. 76–85.
3. See Alan S. Blinder, "A Japanese Buddy System That Could Benefit U.S. Business," *Business Week*, October 14, 1991, p. 32.
4. Kate Gillespie, "Middle East Response to the Foreign Corrupt Practices Act," *California Management Review* 29 (Summer 1987): 9–30.

The Moral Obligations
of Multinational Corporations

Norman Bowie

Now that business ethics is a fashionable topic, it is only natural that the behavior of multinational corporations should come under scrutiny. Indeed, in the past few decades multinationals have allegedly violated a number of fundamental moral obligations. Some of these violations have received great attention in the press.

Lockheed violated an obligation against bribery. Nestle violated an obligation not to harm consumers when it aggressively and deceptively marketed infant formula to uneducated poor women in Third World countries. Union Carbide violated either an obligation to provide a safe environment or to properly supervise its Indian employees.

Other violations have received less attention. After the Environmental Protection Agency prohibited the use of the pesticide DBCP, the American Vanguard Corporation continued to manufacture and export the product in Third World countries. U.S. cigarette companies are now aggressively market-ing their products abroad. Such actions have been criticized because they seem to treat the safety of foreigners as less important than the safety of U.S. citizens. Other charges involve the violation of the autonomy of sovereign governments. Companies such as Firestone and United Fruit have been accused of making countries dependent on one crop, while Union Miniere and ITT were accused of attempting to overthrow governments.[1]

The charges of immoral conduct constitute a startling array of cases where multinationals are alleged to have failed to live up to their moral obligations. However, the charges are of several distinct types. Some have also been brought against purely domestic U.S. firms— for example, issues involving a safe working environment or safe products. Other charges are unique to multinationals—the charge that a multinational values the safety of a foreigner less than the safety of a home country resident. Still others are charges that companies try to justify behavior in other countries

From Norman Bowie, "The Moral Obligations of Multinational Corporations," *Problems of International Justice* (edited by Steven Luper-Foy), 1988. Reprinted by permission of Westview Press, Boulder, Colorado.

that is clearly wrong in the United States, for example, the bribing of government officials.

In this essay, I will focus on the question of whether U.S. multinationals should follow the moral rules of the United States or the moral rules of the host countries (the countries where the U.S. multinationals do business). A popular way of raising this issue is to ask whether U.S. multinationals should follow the advice "When in Rome, do as the Romans do." In discussing that issue I will argue that U.S. multinationals would be morally required to follow that advice if the theory of ethical relativism were true. On the other hand, if ethical universalism is true, there will be times when the advice would be morally inappropriate. In a later section, I will argue that ethical relativism is morally suspect. Finally, I will argue that the ethics of the market provide some universal moral norms for the conduct of multinationals. Before turning to these questions, however, I will show briefly that many of the traditional topics discussed under the rubric of the obligations of multinationals fall under standard issues of business ethics.

OBLIGATIONS OF MULTINATIONALS THAT APPLY TO ANY BUSINESS

As Milton Friedman and his followers constantly remind us, the purpose of a corporation is to make money for the stockholders—some say to maximize profits for the stockholders. According to this view, multinationals have the same fundamental purpose as national corporations. However, in recent years, Friedman's theory has been severely criticized. On what moral grounds can the interests of the stockholders be given priority over all the other stakeholders?[2] For a variety of reasons, business ethicists are nearly unanimous in saying that no such moral grounds

can be given. Hence, business executives have moral obligations to all their stakeholders. Assuming that Friedman's critics are correct, what follows concerning the obligations of multinationals?

Can the multinationals pursue profit at the expense of the other corporate stakeholders? No; the multinational firm, just like the national firm, is obligated to consider all its stakeholders. In that respect there is nothing distinctive about the moral obligations of a multinational firm. However, fulfilling its obligations is much more complicated than for a national firm. A multinational usually has many more stakeholders. It has all the classes of stakeholders a U.S. company has but multiplied by the number of countries in which the company operates.[3]

It also may be more difficult for the multinational to take the morally correct action. For example, one of the appealing features of a multinational is that it can move resources from one country to another in order to maximize profits. Resources are moved in order to take advantage of more favorable labor rates, tax laws, or currency rates. Of course, the pursuit of such tactics makes it more difficult to honor the obligation to consider the interests of all stakeholders. Nonetheless, the increased difficulty does not change the nature of the obligation; multinationals, like nationals, are required to consider the interests of all corporate stakeholders.

Should a multinational close a U.S. plant and open a plant in Mexico in order to take advantage of cheap labor? That question is no different in principle from this one: Should a national firm close a plant in Michigan and open a plant in South Carolina in order to take advantage of the more favorable labor climate in South Carolina? The same moral considerations that yield a decision in the latter case yield a similar decision in the former. (Only if the interests of Mexican workers were less morally significant than were the interests of U.S. workers could any differentiation be made.)

These examples can be generalized to apply to any attempt by a multinational to take advantage of discrepancies between the home country and the host country in order to pursue a profit. Any attempt to do so without considering the interests of all the stakeholders is immoral. National firms and multinational firms share the same basic obligations. If I am right here, there is nothing distinctive about the many problems faced by multinationals, and much of the discussion of the obligations of multinationals can be carried on within the framework of traditional business ethics.

DISTINCTIVE OBLIGATIONS

Certain obligations of multinationals do become distinctive where the morality of the host country (any country where the multinational has subsidiaries) differs from or contradicts the morality of the home country (the country where the multinational was legally created). The multinational faces a modern version of the "When in Rome, should you do as the Romans do?" question. That question is the focus of this essay.

On occasion, the "when in Rome" question has an easy answer. In many situations the answer to the question is yes. When in Rome a multinational is obligated to do as the Romans do. Because the circumstances Romans face are different from the circumstances Texans face, it is often appropriate to follow Roman moral judgments because it is entirely possible that Romans and Texans use the same moral principles, but apply those principles differently.

This analysis also works the other way. Just because a certain kind of behavior is right in

the United States does not mean that it is right somewhere else. Selling infant formula in the United States is morally permissible in most circumstances, but, I would argue, it is not morally permissible in most circumstances to sell infant formula in Third World countries. U.S. water is safe to drink.

Many moral dilemmas disappear when the factual circumstances that differentiate two cultures are taken into account. It is important to note, however, that this judgment is made because we believe that the divergent practices conform to some general moral principle. The makers of infant formula can sell their product in an advanced country but not in a Third World country because the guiding principle is that we cannot impose avoidable harm on an innocent third party. Selling infant formula in underdeveloped countries would often violate that common fundamental principle; selling the formula in developed countries usually would not.

This situation should be contrasted with cases where the home and the host country have different *moral* principles. Consider different moral principles for the testing of new drugs. Both countries face the following dilemma. If there are fairly lax standards, the drug may have very bad side effects, and if it is introduced too quickly, then many persons who take the drug are likely to be harmed—perhaps fatally. On the other hand, if a country has very strict standards and a long testing period, the number of harmful side effect cases will be less, but a number of people who could have benefited from benign drugs will have perished because they did not survive the long testing period. Where is the trade-off between saving victims of a disease and protecting persons from possible harmful side effects? To bring this problem home, consider a proposed cure for cancer or for AIDS. Two different countries could set different safety standards such that plausible moral argu-

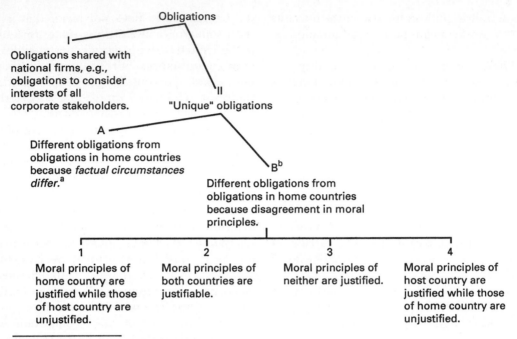

Obligations

I — Obligations shared with national firms, e.g., obligations to consider interests of all corporate stakeholders.

II "Unique" obligations

A — Different obligations from obligations in home countries because *factual circumstances differ.*[a]

B[b] Different obligations from obligations in home countries because disagreement in moral principles.

1. Moral principles of home country are justified while those of host country are unjustified.

2. Moral principles of both countries are justifiable.

3. Moral principles of neither are justified.

4. Moral principles of host country are justified while those of home country are unjustified.

[a] In my view, different obligations still conform to universal principles.
[b] It is assumed that the different moral principles referred to here and below refer to the same moral issue. It is also stipulated that "unjustified" in IIB1 and IIB4 means that the unjustified principles are in conflict with the canons of justification in ethics.

Figure 1   Obligations of multinationals

ments could be made for each. In such cases, it is morally permissible to sell a drug abroad that could not yet be sold in the United States.

If all cases were like this one, it would always be morally permissible to do as the Romans do. But alas, all cases are not like this one. Suppose a country totally ignores the problem of side effects and has no safety standards at all. That country "solves" the trade-off problem by ignoring the interests of those who might develop side effects. Wouldn't that country be wrong, and wouldn't a multinational be obligated not to market a drug in that country even if the country permitted it?

If the example seems farfetched, consider countries that are so desperately poor or corrupt that they will permit companies to manufacture and market products that are known

to be dangerous. This is precisely the charge that was made against American Vanguard when it exported the pesticide DBCP. Aren't multinationals obligated to stay out even if they are permitted?

That question leads directly to the question of whether multinationals always should do in Rome as the Romans do. To sort through that issue, Figure 1 may be useful. Thus far, I have focused on I and IIA. The remainder of the essay considers the range of ethical problems found in IIB.

In IIB4, the multinational has an obligation to follow the moral principles of the host country because on the issue at hand those of the host country are justified while those of the home country are not. Although Americans may believe that there are few such obligations because their moral principles are far more likely to be justified, it is not hard to think of a contrary case. Suppose it is a moral obligation in a host country that no corporation fire someone without due cause. In other words, in the host country employment at will is morally forbidden. Although I shall not argue for it here, I think the employment-at-will doctrine cannot stand up to moral scrutiny. Hence, in this case, multinationals are obligated to follow the moral principle of the host country. Except for economic reasons (falling demand for one's product), a multinational is morally obligated not to fire an employee without just cause.

In IIB3, if the moral principles with respect to a given issue are not justified, then the multinational is under no moral obligation to follow them (except in the weak sense where the multinational is under a legal obligation and hence under a moral obligation to obey the law). Actually, IIB3 can be further subdivided into cases where the moral principles are not justified and where the moral principles cannot be justified. Theocratic states with moral principles based on revelation but not in contradiction with rationally justified moral principles are examples of the former. When the "moral" principles based on revelation are in contradiction with rationally justified moral principles, we have an example of the latter. In this latter case, a multinational is obligated not to follow the moral principles of the host country. In these cases, when in Rome, multinationals are not to do as the Romans do.

In Case IIB2, multinationals may do in Rome as the Romans do. In this case, the moral principles of the host country are justified.

Finally, in case IIB1, the multinational is obligated not to follow the moral principles of the host country. In these cases, the principles of the host country are contrary to the canons of ethics.

In summary, then, U.S. multinationals are obligated to do as the Romans do in IIB4, are permitted to do as the Romans do in IIB2 and in IIB3 where the moral principles of the Romans are consistent with what morality would justify. U.S. multinationals are obligated *not* to do as the Romans do in IIB1 and IIB3 where the moral principles of the Romans are inconsistent with what morality would justify.

Notice, however, that the entire analysis assumes there is some means of justifying ethical principles independent of the fact that a society believes they are justified. Otherwise, for example, I could not say that the moral principles of a home country are not justified while those of the host country are. But who is to say whether the moral principles of a country are justified or when they run counter to universal morality. Besides, perhaps there is no universal morality. What then?

RELATIVISM

Cultural relativism is the doctrine that what is right or wrong, good or bad, depends on one's culture. If the Irish consider abortion to be morally wrong, abortion *is* morally wrong in Ireland. If the Swedes do not consider abortion to be morally wrong, then abortion *is not* morally wrong in Sweden. There is no universal principle to which the Swedes and the Irish can appeal that determines whether abortion really is wrong or not.

If a person is a cultural relativist, then the implications for our discussion may seem quite clear. A corporation has an obligation to follow the moral principles of the host country. When one is in Rome, one is obligated to do as the Romans do. On our chart, IIB1, IIB3, and IIB4 have no referents. There are no members of those classes just as there are no members of the class of unicorns.

The officers and managers of many multinationals often speak and act as if cultural relativism were true. Who are we, they argue, to impose our moral standards on the rest of the world? For example, the U.S. Foreign Corrupt Practices Act, which prohibits the payment of unrecorded bribes to foreign governments or officials, has come under intense attack. After all, if the payment of bribes is morally acceptable in country X, why should we impose our moral views about bribery on that country. Besides if U.S. multinationals do not bribe, German and Japanese multinationals will—or so the argument goes. Former president Jimmy Carter's attempt to include a country's record on violating or not violating fundamental human rights when making foreign policy decisions came under the same kind of criticism. Who is the United States to impose its moral values on others?

This relativistic way of thinking has always been prominent in the thinking of many social scientists. After all, discoveries by anthropologists, sociologists, and psychologists have documented the diversity of moral beliefs and punctured some of the pseudo-justifications that had been given for the superiority of white Western male ways of thinking. Philosophers, by and large, welcomed the corrections to prejudicial moral thinking, but, nonetheless, found the doctrine of cultural relativism seriously flawed.

Recently, however, the situation in philosophy has taken a surprising turn. A number of prominent philosophers have either seemed to embrace cultural relativism or have been forced by the "critics" to admit that their own philosophical positions may be consistent with it. Three examples should make the point.

In 1971, John Rawls published his monumental work *A Theory of Justice.* In that work, Rawls intended to develop a procedure (the original position) that would provide principles for a just society. Although these principles might be implemented in different ways by different societies, Rawls seemed to think that *any* just society would conform to these principles. In part, Rawls held this view be-

cause he believed the original position provided a universal justification for the principles of justice the original position produced. Early critics charged that the assumptions behind the original position were individualistic, liberal, Western, and democratic. The original position was biased in favor of individualistic Western democracies; it did not provide a universal method of justification. In a 1985 article in *Philosophy and Public Affairs,* Rawls admitted that his critics were right.

> In particular justice as fairness is framed to apply to what I call the basic structure of a modern constitutional democracy. . . . Whether justice as fairness can be extended to a general political conception for different kinds of societies existing under different historical and social conditions or whether it can be extended to a general moral conception . . . are altogether separate questions. I avoid prejudging these larger questions one way or the other.[4]

Another highly influential book in ethics, Alasdair MacIntyre's *After Virtue,* argued that the recent emphasis by ethicists on utilitarianism and deontology was seriously skewed. MacIntyre argued that a full moral theory must give a central place to the virtues. His own account was rich in description of the place of virtue in various societies. . . . However, MacIntyre's critics pointed out that what was considered a virtue in one society was frequently not considered a virtue in another— indeed one culture's virtue might be another culture's vice. MacIntyre now concedes that his earlier attempts to avoid these relativistic implications have largely failed.[5]

In theory, a cultural relativist could have two responses to CEOs of multinationals who wanted to know whether their personnel should behave, when in Rome, as the Romans do. Given that the morality of one culture cannot be shown to be superior to the morality of another, the personnel should follow the moral principles of the host country. Such an attitude of tolerance is the traditional response of most relativists.

But another response is possible. Even though the morality of one culture cannot objectively be shown to be superior to the morality of another, rather than embrace tolerance, once could simply assert the superiority of one's own culture. This is the approach taken by Richard Rorty, who has written extensively on the pretensions to objectivity in philosophy. In his 1984 article "Solidarity or Objectivity," he points out that the objectivist tries to create a dilemma for any subjectivist position. The dilemma is that

> either we attach a special privilege to our own community, or we pretend an impossible tolerance for every other group. I have been arguing that we pragmatists should grasp the ethnocentric horn of this dilemma. We should say that we must, in practice, privilege our own group, even though there can be no noncircular justification for doing so. . . . We Western liberal intellectuals should accept the fact that we have to start from where we are, and that this means that there are lots of views which we simply cannot take seriously.[6]

But how would Rorty's quotation strike the CEO of a U.S. multinational? In this case, the personnel of a multinational should *not* follow the moral principles of the host country unless they are consistent with U.S. principles. But what would this mean in terms of business practice? Given that in U.S. culture, the capitalist Friedmanite principle—maximize profits!—is the cultural norm, a U.S. multinational with a plant in South Africa would not refuse to follow the rules of apartheid or pull out. It would locate in South Africa and conform to local custom so long as it could make a profit.

Although I argued earlier that the classical view of profit maximization is seriously flawed, I did not do so from Rorty's ethnocentric position. I assumed an objective universal moral standpoint, as have those who have criticized the clas-

sical view. If Rorty's theory is correct, there is no transcultural objective perspective; because the classical view is a central principle in U.S. business and legal culture, I assume Rorty would have to accept it.

Hence, whether we are cultural relativists or ethnocentrists, some disconcerting implications seem to follow.

1. A corporation has no obligation to follow the Sullivan principles[7] in South Africa.
2. A corporation that wants to do business with the Arabs has no moral obligation to refuse participation in a boycott against Israel as a condition for doing business with the Arabs.
3. A corporation has no obligation to refrain from doing business with a state that is in systematic violation of human rights.

If these implications do follow, there seems to be something wrong with the position that entails them. Even Ronald Reagan has forbidden U.S. firms from doing business with Libya. Some set of criteria is needed for indicating when multinationals are permitted to follow the moral principles of the host country and when multinationals are forbidden to follow host-country principles. What is also needed are some principles that tell U.S. multinationals when they have an obligation to refrain from doing business either *with* a foreign (host) government or *in* a host country. However, unless cultural relativism is false, these principles will never be forthcoming.

THE ADEQUACY OF CULTURAL RELATIVISM

Although our primary concern is the obligations of multinationals, some considerations of the adequacy of cultural relativism must be made before we can speak meaningfully about the obligations of multinationals. As a starting point, I adopt a strategy used by Derek Parfit to undermine the doctrine of prudentialism.[8] Consider a continuum with three positions:

Individual Relativism	Cultural Relativism	Universalism

Individual relativism is the view that what is right or wrong, good or bad, depends on the feelings or attitudes of the individual. If an individual believes abortion is wrong, then abortion is wrong for that individual. If another individual believes abortion is not wrong, then abortion is not wrong for that individual. There is no valid cultural norm that will tell us which individual is objectively right.

The strategy is to show that any argument the cultural relativist uses against universalism can also be used by the individual relativist against cultural relativism. Similarly, any argument the cultural relativist uses against the individual relativist can be used by the universalist against the cultural relativist. As Parfit would say, the cultural relativist is constantly fighting a war on two fronts.

In this discussion, one example of this strategy will have to suffice. First, against an individual relativist, a cultural relativist would often argue that if individual relativism were the prevailing view, a stable society would be impossible. Arguments from Thomas Hobbes or decision theory would prove the point. If individual relativism were the prevailing norm, life would be "nasty, brutish, and short."

But in the present world, any arguments that appeal to social stability will have to be applied universally. In the atomic age and in an age where terrorism is an acceptable form of political activity, the stability problems that afflict individual relativism equally afflict cultural relativism. If the necessity for social stability is a good argument for a cultural relativist to use against an individual relativist, it is an equally good argument for a universalist to use against a cultural relativist.

This brief argument has not refuted relativism. It has only shown that if the stability argument works for the cultural relativist against the individual relativist, the argument also works for the universalist against the cultural relativist. Moreover, to accept the argument this far is only to show that some universal moral norms are required for stable relationships. The argument itself does not provide those universal moral norms. Multinational CEOs are likely to accept the argument thus far, however, because multinationals need a stable international environment if they are to make a profit in the long run. As any adviser for any multinational will verify, one of the chief factors affecting an investment decision in a foreign country is the political stability both of that individual country and of the region surrounding it. An unstable country or region is highly inimical to the conduct of international business.

THE MORAL MINIMUM FOR SOCIETY

Thus far we have established that multinational business requires stability and that commonly accepted moral rules are necessary for stability. But what specifically are these moral rules? To answer that question I will appeal to conceptual arguments that will assist in providing answers.

One argument that is especially effective against the charge of moral imperialism develops the point that some universal standards of conduct already have been accepted by all parties. Despite appearances to the contrary, a great deal of morality has already been internationalized either explicitly through treaty, through membership in the U.N., or implicitly through language and conduct. . . .

Note the following: The word *democracy* or *democratic* has become an honorific term. Nearly all national states claim they are democracies—people's democracies, worker democracies, but democracies nonetheless.

The August 4, 1986, *Newsweek* carried a story about repression and the denial of civil rights in Chile. The president of Chile responded to his critics by calling his dictatorship a "democratic government with authority." I have yet to come across a state that brags it is not a democracy and has no intention of being one. (Some nations do indicate they do not want to be a democracy like the United States.) Hence, there is no moral imperialism involved in saying that host countries should be democracies. The controversy involves the question, What must a government be like to be properly characterized as a democracy?

A notion of shared values can be of assistance here as well. There is a whole range of behavior, such as torture, murder of the innocent, and racism, that nearly all agree is wrong. A nation-state accused of torture does not respond by saying that a condemnation of torture is just a matter of subjective morality. The state's leaders do not respond by saying, "We think torture is right, but you do not." Rather, the standard response is to deny that any torture took place. If the evidence of torture is too strong, a finger will be pointed either at the victim or at the morally outraged country. "They do it, too." In this case the guilt is spread to all. Even the Nazis denied that genocide took place. What is important is that *no* state replies there is nothing wrong with genocide or torture. Hence, the head of a multinational need have no fear of cultural imperialism when she or he takes a stand in favor of democracy and against torture and genocide.

This conceptual argument is buttressed by another. Suppose an anthropologist discovers a large populated South Pacific island. How many tribes are on the island? Part of the answer to that question will be determined by observing if such acts as killing and murder are permitted and if they are permitted, against whom are they permitted? If they are not permitted, that counts as evidence that there is only one tribe. If people on the northern half of the island permit stealing directed against southerners but do not permit northerners to steal from one another, that provides evidence that there are at least two tribes. What often distinguishes one society from another is the fact that society A does not permit murder, lying, and stealing against members of A—society A could not permit that and still be a society—but society A does permit that kind of behavior against society B. What this strategy shows is that one of the criteria for having a society is that there be a shared morality among the individuals that make up the society.

What follows from this is that there are certain basic rules that must be followed in each society—for example, do not lie; do not commit murder. There is a moral minimum in the sense that if these specific moral rules are not generally followed, then there will not be a society at all. These moral rules are universal, but they are not practiced universally. That is, members of society A agree that they should not lie to each other, but they think it is okay to lie to the members of other societies. Such moral rules are not relative; they simply are not practiced universally.

However, multinational corporations are obligated to follow these moral rules. Because the multinational is practicing business in the society and because these moral norms are necessary for the existence of the society, the multinational has an obligation to support those norms. Otherwise, multinationals would be in the position of benefiting from doing business with the society while at the same time engaging in activity that undermines the society. Such conduct would be unjust.

THE MORALITY OF THE MARKETPLACE

Given that the norms constituting a moral minimum are likely to be few in number, it can be argued that the argument thus far has achieved something—that is, multinationals are obligated to follow the moral norms required for the existence of a society. But the argument has not achieved very much—that is, most issues surrounding multinationals do not involve alleged violations of these norms. Perhaps a stronger argument can be found by making explicit the morality of the marketplace. That there is an implicit morality of the market is a point that is often ignored by most economists and many businesspersons.

Although economists and businesspersons assume that people are basically self-interested, they must also assume that persons involved in business transactions will honor their contracts. In most economic exchanges, the transfer of product for money is not simultaneous. You deliver and I pay or vice versa. As the economist Kenneth Boulding put it: "without an integrative framework, exchange itself cannot develop, because exchange, even in its most primitive forms, involves trust and credibility."[9]

Philosophers would recognize an implicit Kantianism in Boulding's remarks. Kant tried to show that a contemplated action would be immoral if a world in which the contemplated act was universally practiced was self-defeating. For example, lying and cheating would fail Kant's tests. Kant's point is implicitly recognized by the business community when corporate officials despair of the immoral practices of corporations and denounce executives engaging in shady practices as undermining the business enterprise itself.

Consider what John Rawls says about contracts:

> Such ventures are often hard to initiate and to maintain. This is especially evident in the case of covenants, that is, in those instances where one person is to perform before the other. For this person may believe that the second party will not do his part, and therefore the scheme never gets going. . . . Now in these situations there may be no way of assuring the party who is to perform first except by giving him a promise, that is, by putting oneself under an obligation to carry through later. Only in this way can the scheme be made secure so that both can gain from the benefits of their cooperation.[10]

Rawls's remarks apply to all contracts. Hence, if the moral norms of a host country permitted practices that undermined contracts, a multinational ought not to follow them. Business practice based on such norms could not pass Kant's test.

In fact, one can push Kant's analysis and contend that business practice generally requires the adoption of a minimum standard of justice. In the United States, a person who participates in business practice and engages in the practice of giving bribes or kickbacks is behaving unjustly. Why? Because the person is receiving the benefits of the rules against such activities without supporting the rules personally. This is an example of what John Rawls calls freeloading. A freeloader is one who accepts the benefits without paying any of the costs.

> In everyday life an individual, if he is so inclined, can sometimes win even greater benefits for himself by taking advantage of the cooperative efforts of others. Sufficiently many persons may be doing their share so that when special circumstances allow him not to contribute (perhaps his omission will not be found out), he gets the best of both worlds. . . . We cannot preserve a sense of justice and all that this implies while at the same time holding ourselves ready to act unjustly should doing so promise some personal advantage.[11]

This argument does not show that if bribery really is an accepted moral practice in country X, that moral practice is wrong. What it does show is that practices in country X that permit freeloading are wrong and if bribery can be construed as freeloading, then it is wrong. In most countries I think it can be shown that bribery is freeloading, but I shall not make that argument here.

The implications of this analysis for multinationals are broad and important. If activities that are permitted in other countries violate the morality of the marketplace—for example, undermine contracts or involve freeloading on the rules of the market—they nonetheless are morally prohibited to multinationals that operate there. Such multinationals are obligated to follow the moral norms of the market. Contrary behavior is inconsistent and ultimately self-defeating.

Our analysis here has rather startling implications. If the moral norms of a host country are in violation of the moral norms of the marketplace, then the multinational is obligated to follow the norms of the marketplace. Systematic violation of marketplace norms would be self-defeating. Moreover, whenever a multinational establishes businesses in a number of different countries, the multinational provides something approaching a universal morality—the morality of the marketplace itself. If Romans are to do business with the Japanese, then whether in Rome or Tokyo, there is a morality to which members of the business community in both Rome and Tokyo must subscribe—even if the Japanese and Romans differ on other issues of morality.

THE DEFENSE OF MARKETPLACE MORALITY

Up to this point I have argued that multinationals are obligated to follow the moral minimum and the morality of the marketplace. But what justifies the morality of the marketplace? Unless the marketplace morality can be justified, I am stuck in Rorty's ethnocentrism. I can start only where I am, and there are simply a lot of views I cannot take seriously. If a CEO of a U.S. multinational should

adopt such an ethnocentric position, she or he would be accused of cultural imperialism. The claim of objectivity remains the central issue for determining the obligations of multinationals.

One possible argument is that capitalism supports democratic institutions. For example, Milton Friedman argues in *Capitalism and Freedom* that capitalism institutionally promotes political freedom.

> Economic arrangements play a dual role in the promotion of a free society. On the one hand freedom in economic arrangements . . . is an end in itself. In the second place economic freedom is also an indispensable means toward the achievement of political freedom. . . .
>
> No one who buys bread knows whether the wheat from which it is made was grown by a Communist or a Republican, by a constitutionalist or a Fascist, or for that matter by a Negro or a white. This illustrates how an impersonal market separates economic activities from political views and protects men from being discriminated against in their economic activities for reasons that are irrelevant to their productivity—whether these reasons are associated with their views or their color.[12]

Friedman also points out that freedom of speech is more meaningful so long as alternative opportunities for employment exist. However, these alternatives are impossible if the government owns and operates the means of production. In a private diversified economic community someone has a better chance to publish views that are contrary to the views of a given editor, the government, or even a majority of the public. Usually one can find some audience that is interested. Moreover, even publishers who disagree might still publish. Fear of competition often overcomes the distaste for certain ideas.

Indeed, one of the arguments for morally permitting multinationals to operate in nondemocratic countries is an extension of Friedman's point. Capitalism is allegedly a catalyst for democratic reform. If capitalism promotes democracy, then a moral argument can be made to justify capitalist investment in repressive regimes because investment will serve the moral end of making the government less repressive. This is precisely the argument that many have used to justify U.S. investment in South Africa. Indeed, the South African situation can serve as an interesting case study. The point of the Sullivan principles is to provide moral guidelines so that a company may be morally justified in having plants in South Africa without becoming part of the system of exploitation. The Sullivan principles also prevent profit-seeking corporations from morally justifying immoral behavior. No company can passively do as the South Africans do and then claim that its presence will bring about a more democratic, less racist regime. After all, if it is plausible to argue that capitalism can help create a democracy, it seems equally plausible to argue that a totalitarian regime may corrupt capitalism. The Sullivan principles help keep multinationals with South African facilities morally honest.

Moreover, the morality of the Sullivan principles depends on an empirical claim that profit-seeking corporations behaving in accordance with marketplace morality and acknowledging universally recognized human rights will in fact help transform totalitarian or repressive regimes into more democratic, more humane regimes. If that transformation does not take place within a reasonable amount of time, the moral justification for having facilities in that country disappears. Leon Sullivan recognized that point when he set May 31, 1987, as the deadline for reform of the South African government. When that reform was not forthcoming, he insisted that U.S. companies suspend operations in South Africa. . . .

What about the issue of human rights? Can multinationals ignore that question? No, they

cannot. Part of what it means to be a democracy is that respect be shown for fundamental human rights. The only justification for a multinational's doing business with a regime that violates human rights is the claim that in so doing, the country's human rights record will improve. Again, business activity under that justification will have to be judged on results.

Even if the "contribution to democracy argument" is not convincing, there is another argument on behalf of the morality of the marketplace. On the assumption that a multinational business agreement is a voluntary exchange, the morality of the marketplace is voluntarily accepted. Economic prosperity seems to be highly desired by all countries. Given that multinational business is a device for achieving prosperity, participating countries voluntarily accept the morality of the market.

CONCLUSION

I have argued that on occasion multinationals have obligations that would require them *not* to do in Rome as the Romans do—for example, in those cases where Roman practice is in violation of marketplace morality. I have also provided arguments on behalf of marketplace morality, although those arguments require that businesses have obligations to pull out of oppressive countries if there is little hope of reform.

But the appeal to the morality of the marketplace has an added benefit. What often is forgotten by business is that the market is not a morally neutral, well-oiled machine; rather, it is embedded in morality and depends upon the acceptance of morality for its success. Ultimately, the obligations of multinationals, whether in Rome, Tokyo, or Washington, are the obligations required by the market. If corporations live up to those obligations, and if capitalism really could advance the cause of democracy and human rights throughout the world, then the morally responsible multinational could be a force for social justice. However, I regret to say that I am discussing a goal and a hope rather than a reality.

NOTES

I wish to thank Steven Luper-Foy for his helpful comments on an earlier version of this essay.

1. See "There's No Love Lost Between Multinational Companies and the Third World," *Business and Society Review* (Autumn 1974).
2. For the purpose of this discussion, a stakeholder is a member of a group without whose support the organization would cease to exist. The traditional list of stakeholders includes stockholders, employees, customers, suppliers, lenders, and the local community where plants or facilities are located.
3. Of course, one large U.S. company with 10 plants in 10 different states has more classes of stakeholders than 1 U.S. company with 1 U.S. plant and 1 foreign subsidiary.
4. John Rawls, "Justice as Fairness: Political Not Metaphysical," *Philosophy and Public Affairs* 14, no. 3 (Summer 1985):224–226. Also see John Rawls, *A Theory of Justice* (Cambridge, Mass.: Harvard University Press, 1971).
5. The most explicit charge of relativism is made by Robert Wachbroit, "A Genealogy of Virtues," *Yale Law Journal* 92, no. 3 (January 1983):476–564. For Alasdair MacIntyre's discussion, see "Postscript to the Second Edition" in *After Virtue*, 2nd ed. (Notre Dame: University of Notre Dame, 1984) and his Eastern Division American Philosophical Association Presidential Address, "Relativism, Power and Philosophy" in *Proceedings and Addresses of the American Philosophical Association* 59, no. 1 (September 1985):5–22. Also see Michael Walzer, *Spheres of Justice* (New York: Basic Books, 1983).
6. Richard Rorty, "Solidarity or Objectivity," in *Post-Analytic Philosophy*, John Rajchman and Cornel West, eds. (New York: Columbia University Press, 1985), pp. 12–13.
7. The Sullivan code affirms the following principles: (1) that there be nonsegregation of the races in all eating, comfort, and work facilities; (2) that equal and fair employment practices be instituted for all employees; (3) that all employees doing equal or comparable work for the same period of time receive equal pay; (4) that training programs be developed and implemented that will prepare substantial numbers of blacks and other nonwhites for supervisory, administrative, technical, and clerical jobs; (5) that the number of blacks and other nonwhites in management and supervisory positions be increased; and (6) that the quality of employees' lives outside the work environment be improved—this includes housing, transportation, schooling, recreation, and health facilities.
8. See Derek Parfit, *Reasons and Persons* (New York: Oxford University Press, 1986), pp. 126–127.
9. Kenneth E. Boulding, "The Basis of Value Judgments in Economics," in *Human Values and Economic Policy*, Sidney Hook, ed. (New York: New York University Press, 1967), p. 68.
10. John Rawls, *A Theory of Justice* (Cambridge, Mass.: Harvard University Press, 1971), p. 569.
11. Ibid., p. 497.
12. Milton Friedman, *Capitalism and Freedom* (Chicago: University of Chicago Press, 1962), pp. 8, 21.

Fundamental Rights and Multinational Duties

Thomas Donaldson

RIGHTS

Rights establish minimum levels of morally acceptable behavior. One well-known definition of a "right" construes it as a "trump" over a collective good, which is to say that the assertion of one's right to something, such as free speech, takes precedence over all but the most compelling collective goals, and overrides, for example, the state's interest in civil harmony or moral consensus.[1]

Rights are at the rock bottom of modern moral deliberation: Maurice Cranston writes that the litmus test for whether something is a right or not is whether it protects something of "paramount importance."[2] If I have a right to physical security, then you should, at a minimum, refrain from depriving me of physical security (at least without a rights-regarding and overriding reason). It would be nice, of course, if you did more: if you treated me charitably and with love. But you must *at a minimum* respect my rights. Hence, it will help to conceive the problem of assigning minimal responsibilities to multinational corporations through the question, "What specific rights should multinationals respect?"

Notice that the flip side of a right typically is a duty.[3] This, in part, is what gives aptness to Joel Feinberg's well-known definition of a right as a "justified entitlement *to* something *from* someone."[4] It is the "from someone" part of the definition that reflects the assumption of a duty, for without a correlative obligation that attaches to some moral agent or group of agents, a right is weakened—if not beyond the status of a right entirely, then significantly. If we cannot say that a multinational corporation has a duty to keep the levels of arsenic low in the workplace, then the worker's right not to be poisoned means little.

Often, duties fall upon more than one class of moral agent. Consider, for example, the furor over the dumping of toxic waste in West Africa by multinational corporations. During 1988, virtually every country from Morocco to the Congo on Africa's west coast received offers from companies seeking cheap sites for dumping waste.[5] In preceding years, the United States and Europe had become enormously expensive for dumping, in large part because of the costly safety measures mandated by U.S. and European governments. In February of 1988, officials in Guinea-Bissau, one of the world's poorest nations, agreed to bury 15 million tons of toxic wastes from European tanneries and pharmaceutical companies. The companies agreed to pay about 120 million dollars, which is only slightly less than the country's entire gross national product. And in Nigeria in 1987, five European ships unloaded toxic waste containing dangerous poisons such as polychlorinated biphenyls, or PCBs. Workers wearing thongs and shorts unloaded the barrels for $2.50 a day, and placed them in a dirt lot in a residential area in the town of Kiko. They were not told about the contents of the barrels.[6]

Who bears responsibility for protecting the workers' and inhabitants' rights to safety in such instances? It would be wrong to place it entirely upon a single group of agents such as the governments of West African nations. As it happens, the toxic waste dumped in Nigeria entered under an import permit for "nonexplosive, nonradioactive and non-self-combusting chemicals." But the permit turned out to be a loophole; Nigeria had not meant to accept the waste and demanded its removal once word about its presence filtered into official channels. The example reveals the difficulty many developing countries have in formulating the sophisticated language and regulatory procedures necessary to control high-technology hazards. It seems reasonable in such instances, then, to place the responsibility not upon a single class of agents, but upon a broad collection of them, including governments, corporate executives, host country companies and officials, and international organizations. The responsibility for not violating the rights of people living in West Africa to be free from the dangers of toxic waste, then, potentially falls upon every agent whose actions might harm, or contribute to harming, West African inhabitants. Nor is one agent's responsibility always mitigated when another "accepts" responsibility. To take a specific instance, corporate responsibility may not be eliminated if a West African government explicitly agrees to accept toxic waste. There is always the possibility—said to be a reality by some critics—that corrupt government officials will agree to accept and handle waste that threatens safety in order to fatten their own Swiss bank accounts.

In wrestling with the problem of which rights deserve international standing, James Nickel recommends that rights that possess international scope be viewed as occupying an intermediary zone between abstract moral principles such as liberty or fairness on the one hand, and national specifications of rights on the other.[7] International rights must be more specific than abstract principles if

they are to facilitate practical application, but less specific than the entries on lists of rights whose duties fall on national governments if they are to preserve cosmopolitan relevance. . . .

As a first approximation, then, let us interpret a multinational's obligations by asking which *international rights* it should respect. We understand international rights to be the sort of moral precepts that lie in a zone between abstract moral principles and national rights specifications. Multinationals, we shall assume, should respect the international rights of those whom they affect, especially when those rights are of the most fundamental sort. . . .

[Donaldson then proposes three conditions that any purported rights claim must pass if it imposes a valid duty on a corporation. Ed.]

1. The right must protect something of very great importance.
2. The right must be subject to substantial and recurrent threats.
3. The obligations or burdens imposed by the right must satisfy a fairness-affordability test.

Let us further stipulate more precisely for our own purposes what shall be meant by the fairness—affordability test in condition number 3. The affordability part of the test implies that for a proposed right to qualify as a genuine right, all moral agents (including nation-states, individuals, and corporations) must be able under ordinary circumstances, and after receiving any share of charitable help due them, to assume the various burdens and duties that fairly fall upon them in honoring the right. "Affordable" here implies literally being *capable of paying for;* it does not imply that something is necessarily unaffordable because paying for it would constitute an inefficient use of funds, or would necessitate trading off other more valuable economic goods.

This use of the term "affordability" means

that—at least under unusual circumstances— honoring a right may be a fundamental moral duty for a given multinational even when the result is financial loss to the particular firm. For example, it would be "affordable" in the present sense for multinational corporations to employ older workers and to refuse to hire eight-year-old children as full-time, permanent laborers, and hence doing so would be mandatory even in the unusual situation where a particular firm's paying the higher salaries necessary to hire older laborers would result in financial losses. By the same logic, it would probably not be "affordable" for either multinational corporations or nation-states around the world to guarantee kidney dialysis for all citizens who need it. This sense of the term also implies that any act of forbearance (of a kind involved in not violating a right directly) is "affordable" for any moral agent.[8] To put the last point another way, I can always "afford" to let you exercise your right to vote, no matter how much money it might cost me.

Turning to the "fairness" side of the test, the extent to which it is "fair" to distribute burdens associated with a given right in a certain manner will be controversial. We assume, however, that for any right to qualify as a genuine right, some "fair" arrangement for sharing the duties and costs among the various agents who must honor the right exists, and that such an arrangement makes it possible (although not necessarily probable) for the right to be enjoyed by most people in most instances.

Next, let us stipulate that satisfying all three of the revised conditions qualifies a prospective right as what we shall call a "fundamental international right," and, in turn, as a right that must be respected by the three major types of international actors: individuals, nation-states, and corporations. This definition does not mean that individuals, na-

tion-states, and corporations must "respect" the rights in precisely the same manner. That is, it does not entail that the correlative duties flowing from the rights are the same for each type of actor. It entails only that each such actor must "respect" fundamental international rights in some manner, and that they possess some duties, however minimal, in consequence. . . .

FUNDAMENTAL INTERNATIONAL RIGHTS

We are now prepared to identify some of the items that should appear on a list of fundamental international rights, as well as to lay the groundwork for interpreting their application to multinational corporations. . . .

Though probably not complete, the following list contains items that appear to satisfy the three conditions and hence to qualify as fundamental international rights:

1. The right to freedom of physical movement
2. The right to ownership of property
3. The right to freedom from torture
4. The right to a fair trial
5. The right to nondiscriminatory treatment (freedom from discrimination on the basis of such characteristics as race or sex.)
6. The right to physical security
7. The right to freedom of speech and association
8. The right to minimal education
9. The right to political participation
10. The right to subsistence

This is a minimal list. Some will wish to add entries such as the right to employment, to social security, or to a certain standard of living. . . . Disputes also may arise about the wording or overlapping features of some rights: for example, is not the right to freedom from torture included in the right to physical security, at least when the latter is properly interpreted? We shall not attempt to resolve such controversies here. Rather, the list as presented aims to suggest, albeit incompletely, a description of a *minimal* set of rights and to serve as a beginning consensus for evaluating international conduct. If I am correct, many would wish to add entries, but few would wish to subtract them. . . .

Because by definition the list contains items that all three major classes of international actors must respect, the next task is to spell out the correlative duties that fall upon our targeted group of international actors, namely, multinational corporations.

This task requires putting the "fairness-affordability" condition to a second, and different, use. This condition was first used as one of the three criteria generating the original list of fundamental rights. There it demanded satisfaction of a fairness-affordability threshold for each potential respecter of a right. For example, if the burdens imposed by a given right are not fair (in relation to other bona fide obligations and burdens) or affordable for nation-states, individuals, and corporations, then presumably the prospective right would not qualify as a fundamental international right.

In its second use, the "fairness-affordability" condition goes beyond the judgment *that* a certain fairness-affordability threshold has been crossed to the determination of *what* the proper duties are for multinational corporations in relation to a given right. In its second use, in other words, the condition's notions of fairness and affordability are invoked to help determine *which* obligations properly fall upon corporations, in contrast to individuals and nation-states. The condition can help determine the correlative duties that attach to multinational corporations in their honoring of fundamental international rights.

As we look over the list of fundamental rights, it is noteworthy that except for a few isolated instances multinational corporations have probably succeeded in fulfilling their duty not to *actively deprive* persons of their enjoyment of the rights at issue. But correlative duties involve more than failing to actively deprive people of the enjoyment of their rights. Henry Shue, for example, notes that three types of correlative duties are possible for any right: (1) to avoid depriving; (2) to help protect from deprivation; and (3) to aid the deprived.[9]

While it is obvious that the honoring of rights clearly imposes duties of the first kind, to avoid depriving directly, it is less obvious, but frequently true, that honoring them involves acts or omissions that help prevent the deprivation of rights. If I receive a note from Murder, Incorporated, and it looks like it means business, my right to security is clearly threatened. If a third party has relevant information which if revealed to the police would help protect my right, it is not a valid excuse for the third party to say that it is Murder, Incorporated, and not the third party, who wishes to kill me. Hence, honoring rights sometimes involves not only duties to *avoid depriving*, but to *help protect from deprivation* as well. Many critics of multinationals, interestingly enough, have faulted them not for the failure to avoid depriving, but for the failure to take reasonable protective steps.

The duties associated with rights often include ones from the third category, that of *aiding the deprived,* as when a government is bound to honor the right of its citizens to adequate nutrition by distributing food in the wake of a famine or natural disaster, or when the same government in the defense of political liberty is required to demand that an employer reinstate or compensate an employee fired for voting for a particular candidate in a government election.

Nonetheless, the honoring of at least some of the ten fundamental rights by multinational corporations requires only the adoption of the first class of correlative duties, that is, only the duty to avoid depriving. The correlative duties for corporations associated with some rights do not extend to protecting from deprivation or to aiding the deprived, because of the "fairness-affordability" condition discussed earlier. . . .

It would be unfair, not to mention unreasonable, to hold corporations to the same standards of charity and love as human individuals. Nor can they be held to the same standards to which we hold civil governments for enhancing social welfare—since many governments are formally dedicated to enhancing the welfare of, and actively preserving the liberties of, their citizens. The profit-making corporation, in contrast, is designed to achieve an economic mission and as a moral actor possesses an exceedingly narrow personality. It is an undemocratic institution, furthermore, which is ill-suited to the broader task of distributing society's goods in accordance with a conception of general welfare. The corporation is an economic animal; . . . although its responsibilities extend beyond maximizing return on investment for shareholders, they are informed directly by its economic mission. . . .

[T]he application of the "fairness-affordability" criterion . . . impl[ies] that duties of the third class, to aid the deprived, do not fall upon for-profit corporations except, of course, in instances in which a corporation itself has done the depriving. Barring highly unusual circumstances, . . . whatever duties corporations may have to aid the deprived are "maximal," not "minimal," duties. They are duties whose performance is not required as a condition of honoring fundamental rights or of preserving the corporation's moral right to exist. . . .

The same, however, is not true of the second class of duties, to protect from deprivation. These duties, like those in the third class, are also usually the province of government, but it sometimes happens that the rights to which they correlate are ones whose protection is a direct outcome of ordinary corporate activities. For example, the duties associated with protecting a worker from the physical threats of other workers may fall not only upon the local police, but also to some extent upon the employer. These duties, in turn, are properly viewed as correlative duties of the right—in this instance, the workers' right—to personal security. This will become clearer in a moment when we discuss the correlative duties of specific rights.

The following table lists correlative duties that reflect the second-stage application of the "fairness-affordability" condition to the earlier list of fundamental international rights. It indicates which rights do, and which do not, impose correlative duties of the three various kinds upon multinational corporations.

A word of caution should be issued for interpreting the table: the first type of correlative obligation, not depriving directly, is broader than might be supposed at first. It includes *cooperative* as well as individual actions. Thus, if a company has personnel policies that inhibit freedom of movement, or if a multinational corporation operating in South Africa cooperates with the government's restrictions on pass laws, then those companies may be said to actively deprive persons of their right to freedom of movement, despite the fact that actions of other agents (in this example, the South African government) may be essential in effecting the deprivation.[10]

Still, the list asserts that at least six of the ten fundamental rights impose correlative duties upon corporations of the second kind, that is, to protect from deprivation. What follows is a brief set of commentaries discussing sample applica-

Correlative Corporate Duties

	Minimal Correlative Duties of Multinational Corporations		
Fundamental Rights	*To Avoid Depriving*	*To Help Protect From Deprivation*	*To Aid the Deprived*
Freedom of physical movement	X		
Ownership of property	X		
Freedom from torture	X		
Fair trial	X		
Nondiscriminatory treatment	X	X	
Physical security	X	X	
Freedom of speech and association	X	X	
Minimal education	X	X	
Political participation	X	X	
Subsistence	X	X	

tions of each of those six rights from the perspective of such correlative duties.

SAMPLE APPLICATIONS

Discrimination

The obligation to protect a person from deprivation of the right to freedom from discrimination properly falls upon corporations as well as governments insofar as everyday corporate activities directly affect compliance with that right. Because employees and prospective employees possess the moral right not to be discriminated against on the basis of race, sex, caste, class, or family affiliation, it follows that multinational corporations have an obligation not only to refrain from discrimination, but in some instances to protect the right to nondiscriminatory treatment by establishing appropriate procedures. This may require, for example, offering notice to prospective employees about the company's policy of nondiscriminatory hiring, or educating lower-level managers about the need to

reward or penalize on the basis of performance rather than irrelevant criteria.

Physical Security

The right to physical security similarly entails duties of protection. If a Japanese multinational corporation operating in Nigeria hires shop workers to run metal lathes in an assembly factory, but fails to provide them with protective goggles, then the corporation has failed to honor the workers' moral right to physical security (no matter what the local law might decree). Injuries from such a failure would be the moral responsibility of the Japanese multinational despite the fact that the company could not be said to have inflicted the injuries directly.

Free Speech and Association

In the same vein, the duty to protect from deprivation the right of free speech and association finds application in the ongoing corporate obligation not to bar the creation of labor unions. Corporations are not obliged on the basis of human rights to encourage or welcome labor unions; indeed they may oppose them using all morally acceptable means at their disposal. But neither are they morally permitted to destroy them or prevent their emergence through coercive tactics; for to do so would violate their workers' international right to association. The corporation's duty to protect from deprivation the right to association, in turn, includes refraining from lobbying host governments for restrictions that would violate the right in question, and perhaps even to protesting host government measures that do violate it. The twin phenomena of commercial concentration and the globalization of business, both associated with the rise of the multinational, have tended to weaken the bargaining power of labor. Some doubt that labor is sharing as fully as it once did from the cyclical gains of industrial productivity. This gives special significance to the right of free speech and association.

Minimal Education

The correlative duty to protect the right of education may be illustrated through the very example used to open this essay: the prevalence of child labor in developing countries. A multinational in Central America is not entitled to hire an eight-year-old for fulltime, permanent work because, among other reasons, doing so blocks the child's ability to receive a minimally sufficient education. What counts as a "minimally sufficient" education may be debated, and it seems likely, moreover, that the specification of the right to a certain level of education depends at least in part upon the level of economic resources available in a given country; nevertheless, it is reasonable to assume that any action by a corporation which has the effect of obstructing the development of a child's ability to read or write would be proscribed on the basis of rights.

Political Participation

Clearly in some instances corporations have failed to honor the correlative duty of protecting from deprivation the right to political participation. Fortunately, the most blatant examples of direct deprivation are becoming so rare as to be nonexistent. I am referring to cases in which companies directly aid in overthrowing democratic regimes, as when United Fruit Company allegedly contributed to overthrowing a democratically elected regime in Guatemala during the 1950s.

A few corporations continue indirectly to threaten this right by failing to protect it from deprivation, however. Some persist, for example, in supporting military dictatorships in countries in which democratic sentiment is growing, and others have blatantly bribed publicly elected officials with large sums of money. Perhaps the most famous example of the latter occurred in 1972 when the prime minister of Japan was bribed with 7 million dollars by the Lockheed Corporation to secure a lucrative Tri-Star Jet contract. Here, the complaint from the perspective of this right is not against bribes or "sensitive payments" in general, but to bribes in contexts where they serve to undermine a democratic system in which publicly elected officials hold a position of public trust.

Even the buying and owning of major segments of a foreign country's land and industry has been criticized in this regard. As Brian Barry has remarked, "The paranoia created in Britain and the United States by land purchases by foreigners (especially Arabs, it seems) should serve to make it understandable that the citizenry of a country might be unhappy with a state of affairs in which the most important natural resources are in foreign ownership." At what point would Americans regard their democratic control threatened by foreign ownership of U.S. industry and resources? At 20 percent ownership? At 40 percent? At 60 percent? At 80 percent? The answer is debatable, yet there seems to be some point beyond which the right to national self-determination, and national democratic control, is violated by foreign ownership of property.[11]

Subsistence

Corporations also have duties to protect from deprivation the right to subsistence. Consider the following scenario: a number of square miles of land in an underdeveloped country has been used for many years to grow beans. Further, the bulk of the land is owned, as it has been for centuries, by two wealthy landowners. Poorer members of the community work the land and receive a portion of the crop, a portion barely sufficient to satisfy nutritional needs. Next, imagine that a multinational corporation offers the two wealthy owners a handsome sum for the land, because it plans to grow coffee for export. Now *if*—and this, admittedly, is a critical "if"—the corporation has reason to *know* that a significant number of people in the community will suffer malnutrition as a result, that is, if it has convincing reasons to believe that either those people will not be hired by the company or will not be paid sufficiently if they are hired, or that if forced to migrate to the city they will receive less than subsistence wages (wages inadequate to provide food and shelter), then the multinational may be said to have failed in its correlative duty to protect individuals from the deprivation of the right to subsistence. This is true despite the fact that the corporation would never have stooped to take food from workers' mouths, and despite the fact that the malnourished will, in Samuel Coleridge's words, "die so slowly that none call it murder."

Disagreements: The Relevance of . . . Culture

The foregoing commentaries obviously are not intended to complete the project of specifying the correlative duties associated with fundamental international rights; they only begin it. Furthermore, . . . it may be that some of the fundamental rights on our list would not be embraced, at least as formulated here, by cultures different from ours. Would, for example, the Fulanis, a nomadic cattle culture in Nigeria, subscribe to this list with the same eagerness as the citizens of Brooklyn, New York? What list would they draw up if given the chance? And could we, or should we, try to convince them that our list is preferable? Would such a dialogue even make sense?[12]

I want to acknowledge that rights may vary in priority and style of expression from one cultural group to another. Yet . . . I maintain that the list itself is applicable to peoples even when those peoples would fail to compose an identical list. Clearly the Fulanis do not have to *accept* the ten rights in question for it to constitute a valid means of judging their culture. If the Fulanis treat women unfairly and unequally, then at least one fundamental international right remains unfulfilled in their culture, and their culture is so much the worse as a result. . . .

The Drug Lord Problem

One of the most difficult aspects of the proposed rights list concerns the fairness-affordability condition, a problem we can see more clearly by reflecting on what might be called the "drug lord" problem.[13] Imagine that an unfortunate country has a weak government and is run by various drug lords (not, it appears, a hypothetical case). These drug lords threaten the physical security of various citizens and torture others. The government—the country—cannot afford to mount the required police or military actions that would bring these drug lords into moral line. Or, perhaps, this could be done but only by imposing terrible burdens on certain segments of the society which would be unfair to others. Does it follow that members of that society do not have the fundamental international right not to be tortured and to physical security? Surely they do, even if the country cannot afford to guarantee them. But if that is the case, what about the fairness-affordability criterion?

Let us begin by noting the "affordability" part of the fairness-affordability condition does imply some upper limit for the use of resources in the securing of a fundamental international right (for example, at the present moment in history, kidney dialysis cannot be a fundamental international right). With this established, the crucial question becomes *how* to draw the upper limit. The argument advanced in this essay commits us to draw that limit as determined by a number of criteria, two of which have special relevance for the present issue: first, compatibility with other, already recognized, international rights; and second, the level of importance of the interest, moral or otherwise, being protected by the right, that is, the first of the three conditions. In terms of the compatibility criterion, we remember that the duties imposed by any right must be compatible with other moral duties. Hence, a *prima facie* limit may be drawn on the certification of a prospective right corresponding to the point at which other bona fide international rights are violated. As for the importance of the right, trade-offs among members of a class of prospective rights will be made by reference to the relative importance of the interest being protected by the right. The right not to be tortured protects a more fundamental inter-

est than, say, the right to an aesthetically pleasing environment.

This provides a two-tiered solution for the drug lord problem. At the first tier, we note that the right of people not to be tortured by the drug lords (despite the unaffordability of properly policing the drug lords) implies that people, and especially the drug lords, have a duty not to torture. Here the solution is simple. The argument of this essay establishes a fundamental international right not to be tortured, and it is a right that binds all parties to the duty of forbearance in torturing others. For on the first application of the fairness-affordability condition, that is, when we are considering simply the issue of which fundamental international rights exist, we are only concerned about affordability in relation to *any* of the three classes of correlative duties. Here we look to determine only whether duties of *any* of the three classes of duties are fair and affordable, where "affordable" means literally capable of paying for. And with respect to the issue of affordability, clearly the drug lords, just as every other moral agent, can "afford" to refrain from actively depriving persons of their right not to be tortured. They can afford to refrain from torturing. (Earlier in this essay, the fairness-affordability condition was interpreted to imply that any act of forbearance, of a kind involved in not violating a right directly, is "affordable" for any moral agent.) It follows that people clearly have the fundamental international right not to be tortured, which imposes at least one class of duties upon all international actors, namely the duty of forbearance.

At the second tier, on the other hand, we are concerned with whether the right not to be tortured includes a duty of the government to mount an effective prevention system against torture. Here the fairness-affordability criterion is used in a second application, which helps establish the specific kinds of correlative duties associated with the already-acknowledged-to-exist right not to be tortured. Surely all nation-states can "afford" under ordinary circumstances to shoulder duties of the second and third categories of helping prevent deprivation and of aiding the deprived, although the specific extent of those duties may be further affected by considerations of fairness and affordability. For example, in the instance described in the drug lord problem, it seems questionable that all countries could "afford" to *succeed* completely in preventing torture, and hence the duty to help prevent torture presupposed by a fundamental international right to freedom from torture probably cannot be construed to demand complete success. Nonetheless, a fairly high level of success in preventing torture is probably demanded by virtue of international rights since, as noted earlier, the ordinary protection of civil and political rights, such as the right not to be tortured, carries a negative rather than positive economic cost. We know that the economic cost of allowing the erosion of rights to physical security and fair trial—as an empirical matter of fact—exceeds the cost of maintaining them.

What the list of rights and correlative corporate duties establishes is that multinational corporations frequently do have obligations derived from rights when such obligations extend beyond simply abstaining from depriving directly to actively protecting from deprivation. It implies, in other words, that the relevant factors for analyzing a difficult issue, such as hunger or high-technology agriculture, include not only the degree of factual correlation existing between multinational policy and hunger, but also the recognition of the existence of a right to subsistence along with a specification of the corporate correlative duties entailed.

I have argued that the ten rights identified in this essay constitute minimal and bedrock moral considerations for multinational corporations operating abroad. Though the list may be incomplete, the human claims that it honors, and the interests those claims represent, are globally relevant. The existence of fundamental international rights implies that no corporation can wholly neglect considerations of racism, hunger, political oppression, or freedom through appeal to its "commercial" mission. These rights are, rather, moral considerations for every international moral agent, although, as we have seen, different moral agents possess different correlative obligations. The specification of the precise correlative duties associated with such rights for corporations is an ongoing task that this chapter has left incomplete. Yet the existence of the rights themselves, including the imposition of duties upon corporations to protect—as well as to refrain from directly violating—such rights, seems beyond reasonable doubt.

NOTES

1. Ronald Dworkin, *Taking Rights Seriously* (Cambridge, Mass.: Harvard University Press, 1977). For other standard definitions of rights see James W. Nickel, *Making Sense of Human Rights: Philosophical Reflections on the Universal Declaration of Human Rights* (Berkeley: University of California Press, 1987), especially chapter 2; Joel Feinberg, "Duties, Rights and Claims," *American Philosophical Quarterly* 3 (1966): 137–44. See also Joel Feinberg, "The Nature and Value of Rights," *Journal of Value Inquiry* 4 (1970): 243–57; Wesley N. Hohfeld, *Fundamental Legal Conceptions* (New Haven, Conn.: Yale University Press, 1964); and H. J. McCloskey, "Rights—Some Conceptual Issues," *Australasian Journal of Philosophy* 54 (1976): 99–115.

2. Maurice Cranston, *What Are Human Rights?* (New York: Tamlinger, 1973), p. 67.

3. H. J. McCloskey, for example, understands a right as a positive entitlement that need not specify who bears the responsibility for satisfying that entitlement. McCloskey, "Rights—Some Conceptual Issues," p. 99.

4. Feinberg, "Duties, Rights and Claims"; see also Feinberg, "The Nature and Value of Rights," pp. 243–57.

5. James Brooke, "Waste Dumpers Turning to West Africa," *New York Times,* July 17, 1988, p. 1, 7.

6. Ibid. Nigeria and other countries have struck back, often by imposing strict rules against the acceptance of toxic waste. For example, in Nigeria officials now warn that anyone caught importing toxic waste will face the firing squad. Ibid., p. 7.

7. James W. Nickel, *Making Sense of Human Rights,* pp. 107–8.

8. I am indebted to Lynn Sharp Paine who, in critiquing an earlier draft of this essay, made me see the need for a clearer definition of the "fairness—affordability" criterion.

9. Shue, *Basic Rights,* p. 57.

10. I am indebted to Edwin Hartman for establishing this point. Hartman has suggested that this warrants establishing a fourth significant kind of duty, i.e., "avoiding helping to deprive." For a more detailed account of this interesting suggestion, see Edwin Hartman, "Comment on Donaldson's 'Rights in the Global Market,'" in Edward Freeman, ed., *The 1988 Ruffin Lectures* (New York: Oxford University Press, forthcoming).

11. Brian Barry, "Humanity and Justice in Global Perspective," in J. Roland Pennock and John W. Chapman, eds., *Ethics, Economics, and the Law: Nomos Vol. XXIV* (New York: New York University Press, 1982), pp. 219–52. Companies are also charged with undermining local governments, and hence infringing on basic rights, through sophisticated tax evasion schemes. Especially when companies buy from their own subsidiaries, they can establish prices that have little connection to existing market values. This, in turn, means that profits can be shifted from high-tax to low-tax countries with the result that poor nations can be deprived of their rightful share.

12. Both for raising these questions, and in helping me formulate answers, I am indebted to William Frederick.

13. I am indebted to George Brenkert for suggesting and formulating the "drug lord" problem.

Chemical Exports and the Age of Consent: The High Cost of International Export Control Proposals

*Michael P. Walls**

INTRODUCTION

Throughout the 1980s, an international debate over the proper role of government in regulating exports and imports of hazardous substances, primarily pesticides and industrial chemicals, has been raging. The debate has been characterized by emotional appeals from public interest groups and steadfast opposition by the worldwide chemical industry.

Existing information exchange programs, by which regulatory information is transmitted to interested governments, have been criticized as ineffective in protecting the citizens of importing countries from harmful substances. Prior informed consent ("PIC") proposals have been promoted as the single most effective remedy for the problems of unregulated chemicals exports.

Generally, PIC would require an exporter to

*Assistant General Counsel, Chemical Manufacturers Association, Washington, D.C. This article represents the author's views. No support or endorsement by the Chemical Manufacturer's Association is intended or should be inferred. From Michael P. Walls, "Chemical Exports and the Age of Consent: The High Cost of International Export Control Proposals," *Journal of International Law and Politics* 20 (1988). Reprinted by permission.

obtain, via his own government, the express consent of importing countries to accept shipments of "banned" or "severely restricted" chemicals. Exports would be delayed until consent had been received. Although chemicals are exported to virtually every country, great emphasis has been placed on the benefits of an international PIC program, particularly for developing countries. PIC advocates contend that only PIC can help developing countries build the regulatory infrastructures necessary to ensure controlled importation and use of hazardous substances.

PIC has far-reaching consequences for international trade and international law. Export shipments could be subject to delays and trade-facilitating mechanisms, such as letters of credit, could lose their effectiveness. PIC also implicates the sovereignty of developing countries by linking regulatory decisions to the actions of exporting (and therefore probably developed) countries. At the same time, the likely result of a PIC program is that human health and the environment, particularly in developing countries, will receive no greater protection than at the present time. Finally, in this purported "age of consent," those remedies designed to alleviate the root problems of chemical misuse and underdeveloped governmental infrastructures will receive inadequate attention. . . .

PRIOR INFORMED CONSENT: ACCEPTED INTERNATIONAL STANDARD?

Background

The international impetus for PIC began with a 1981 United Nations General Assembly resolution calling for the exchange of information on "banned hazardous chemicals and unsafe pharmaceutical products." The action closely followed the Carter Administration's "Federal Policy Regarding the Export of Banned or Significantly Restricted Substances," which had established an export licensing procedure for certain hazardous substances of U.S. origin. Although the Reagan Administration quickly rescinded this policy, a move which appeared to forestall domestic efforts to implement PIC, the international push to adopt a control system for hazardous exports had already gained momentum.

In 1984, the United Nations Environment Programme (UNEP) adopted the Provisional Notification Scheme and issued a report summarizing the national experiences with export notification procedures and the existing information exchange programs for "banned" and "severely restricted" chemicals. In February of 1987, the Provisional Notification Scheme was incorporated by a UNEP Working Group into the London Guidelines for the Exchange of Information on Chemicals in International Trade (London Guidelines) and was formally adopted by the UNEP Governing Council in June of 1987. In 1984, the Organization of Economic Cooperation and Development (OECD) agreed to a Council Recommendation on information exchange for chemical exports. The United Nations Food and Agriculture Organization (FAO) followed suit in 1985 by adopting the International Code of Conduct on the Distribution and Use of Pesticides.

Notably, chemical industry efforts at self-regulation were being undertaken concurrently with the notification programs being developed by the international intergovernmental organizations: the international pharmaceutical associations adopted the Code of Pharmaceutical Marketing Practices in 1981; the International Group of National Associations of Agrochemical Producers (GIFAP) issued guidelines for the safe and effective use of pesticides; the OECD's Business and Industry Advisory Committee (BIAC) gained industry consensus on the BIAC Guides for

Manufacturers and Traders Exporting Chemicals in 1985. Numerous additional examples of the chemical industry's recognition of its responsibilities concerning international trade exist.

THE HIGH COST OF REGULATION: THE CASE AGAINST PIC

Legal Impact of PIC

Legal objections to PIC arise on several grounds, both international and domestic. PIC is inconsistent with the principle of sovereignty, under which a state has the inherent power to regulate its own affairs. By forcing an importing government to rely on the regulatory decisions contained in requests for consent, PIC, in effect, gives extraterritorial effect to the regulations of exporting countries.

Perhaps more significantly, PIC would turn the international principle of state responsibility on its head. The concept of state responsibility dictates that governments are generally responsible only for the acts of those they control. Most governments do not "control" the acts of independent business concerns, at least to the extent of control giving rise to liability on the part of the state. Nevertheless, PIC would force exporting governments to exercise a significant degree of control over the exports of those independent businesses, particularly in situations where the importing government refuses to accept the import.

PIC also has a potential effect on the assessment of liability. Shipments made in violation of a PIC regime, without the consent of the importing country, will presumably subject the exporting company to liability. Therefore, PIC effectively establishes a "multinational enterprise" principle of responsibility.

Furthermore, liability for violations of a PIC regime could presumably be assessed against exporting *countries,* for failure to exercise the requisite degree of control over shipments made without the consent of importing governments. Exporting countries might also be held liable for injuries caused by accepted imports of banned or severely restricted chemicals. The participants in the ongoing debate over PIC have given little consideration to the important issue of the responsibilities of exporting governments under such a system.

PIC is also inconsistent with U.S. law. Seven U.S. statutes, including the Toxic Substances Control Act [(hereinafter TSCA)] and the Federal Insecticide, Fungicide, and Rodenticide Act [(hereinafter FIFRA)], require some form of notification to importing countries when hazardous materials are exported. The U.S. notifications typically exceed the information exchange requirements established under the intergovernmental programs now in effect. In fact, no other country conducts as extensive a notification program as does the United States.

The United States has not adopted a definition of the terms "banned" or "severely restricted." As a result, the U.S. notifies other governments of a wide range of regulatory action taken under TSCA or FIFRA. These notices are sent despite the fact the regulatory action may not constitute a "ban" or "severe restriction" and despite the fact the recipient country may have little knowledge of the statutory, regulatory, or scientific basis for the action. For example, Section 4 of TSCA provides for toxicological testing of certain substances, but such action constitutes neither a ban nor a severe restriction on the chemical. Blanket notifications such as these may only serve to increase anxiety about chemicals in general, particularly those of U.S. origin. Rather, notifications of actions not constituting a ban or severe restriction might be better handled under a separate information exchange program to advise other governments of new health and environmental data.

Economic Impacts of PIC

The economic and trade impact of PIC is difficult to assess with certainty. The difficulty arises primarily from the lack of data on exports of banned or severely restricted chemicals, as there is no consensus on what chemicals are in fact under such regulatory restrictions. Without agreement on what body of chemicals constitute those that are banned or severely restricted, it is difficult to measure the economic impact of exports of such chemicals. It is possible, however, to identify some aspects of PIC's probable significant impact on international chemical trade. For example, depending on the particulars of a stop shipment order executed under a PIC system, and an importing government's subsequent response to similar shipments, PIC may well violate the anti-discrimination provisions of the General Agreement on Tariffs and Trade (GATT). Letters of credit and import licenses are time-limited instruments which typically expire within a given period. U.S. chemical manufacturers estimate that a three to six month delay in exports will result under PIC. These instruments could expire before the required consent to ship is received. In addition, emergency or seasonal shipments of agricultural and industrial chemicals could be compromised. Delays in export shipments will compound the warehousing and logistical problems inherent in international trade. Some facilities do not have the ability to store chemical substances for long periods of time. In turn, the possibility of increased health and environmental danger due to accidents is raised. At a minimum, PIC can be expected to drive up the cost of chemical exports to reflect the delays.

Practical Impact of PIC

The probable impact of PIC buttresses the conclusion that the proposals are ill-advised. PIC is less likely than the existing notification programs to aide the development of adequate infrastructures in developing countries. Indeed, developing countries, given the great demands on their often limited resources, will have an incentive to rely on the notifications sent under PIC to reduce the cost of an effective regulatory regime geared to the country's specific needs. PIC in no way assures that an importing government has the interest or the ability to respond to consent requests within a given time limit.

In addition, PIC may increase the incentives for illicit trade in banned and severely restricted chemicals. For example, a PIC system provides no assurance that, if the regulatory controls on exports from one country become too burdensome, importers will not seek other, less regulated sources for the chemicals. Companies forced to comply with PIC may be competitively disadvantaged if other, unregulated sources can meet the existing demand for hazardous products. Presently, shipments from the major chemical producing countries are generally accompanied by transport and use information, the companies involved have close relationships with their customers, and any information deemed necessary in the regulatory process is readily available. It is the importation of chemicals from unregulated sources, and the unregulated distribution of the chemicals at the local level, which probably account for the vast majority of problems.

Therefore, by restricting imports from more responsible suppliers, PIC may drive chemical purchasers to unrestricted sources, with a consequent increase in adverse health and environmental impacts. Hence, PIC may have the opposite effect than that intended by its proponents.

PIC ALTERNATIVES: TOWARD IMPROVED REGULATORY RESPONSE AND SAFETY IN CHEMICAL USE

PIC does not help importing countries handle banned or severely restricted chemicals better. Such a system does nothing to assist importing countries to weigh the economic, health, and environmental concerns which factor into decisions about chemical use. In view of the legal, economic, and practical impacts, several efforts to develop alternatives to PIC should result in measurable improvements in a country's ability to deal with hazardous chemicals.

A recent study conducted by the Organization for American States (OAS) indicates that PIC is not the attractive policy option its promoters suggest.[1] The OAS has recommended that the developed countries undertake a plan of action centered around improved notification and technical assistance to importing countries.[2] The key aspect of the work plan is regional seminars and workshops to discuss the decision-making process in regulatory agencies, enforcement procedures, scientific assessment of hazardous materials, institutional aspects of implementation, and communication of hazard information to users.

The Agency for International Development (AID), under a provision of the Foreign Assistance Authorization Act of 1986,[3] has convened a Committee on Health and the Environment.[4] The Committee is charged with "examining opportunities for assisting countries in the proper use of agricultural and industrial chemicals. . . . " The Committee's report should provide some guidance in the development and implementation of programs concerning hazardous materials and might be used by AID in U.S. foreign assistance programs.

The UNEP's newest *Ad Hoc* Working Group of Experts should also focus on those "modalities" of information exchange short of PIC which will further the goal of safe chemical use. One notable area for expansion of the Group's mandate is in the implementation of the London Guidelines, because not all countries have designated national representatives for the receipt of regulatory control and export notices. Furthermore, countries should be encouraged to share their experience under the London Guidelines with the International Register for Potentially Toxic Chemicals, the United Nations agency responsible for overseeing the Guidelines. In this manner, appropriate modifications to the Guidelines might be made, rather than totally abandoning a system not yet proven incapable of solving the problem it addresses.

A number of recommendations for improved notifications under the U.S. export programs have been made, which the Environmental Protection Agency has undertaken to study in an effort to make the program more effective.

Additionally, the international intergovernmental organizations, notably UNEP, should undertake to assist developing countries by identifying and anticipating their environmental problems, as well as adopting appropriate regulatory mechanisms. This type of program might be based on the developing country strategy adopted by the Environmental Protection Agency.

Private industry should also have a role in the search for viable alternatives to PIC. Exporting companies already cooperate in providing information on chemical shipments through the existing intergovernmental programs. Further development of this cooperative approach should be explored.

Even if these developments and improvements do occur, the key to success of information exchange is the establishment of infrastructures which give importing governments the ability to make their own regulatory decisions. Once such infrastructures are in place, and not before, the international community can better evaluate the need for stringent export control restrictions such as PIC.

NOTES

1. Organization of American States, *Background on the Problem of Trade in Toxic Products Banned or Severely Restricted in the Producing Countries* 1, OAS Doc. OEA/Ser. H/XIII, CIES/CECON/ 580 (1987) at 15–16.

2. Organization of American States, *Technical Meeting on Toxic Products, Final Report,* OAS Doc. OEA/ser.H/XIII, CIES/CECON/582, at 8–10, (Sept. 3, 1987).

3. Foreign Assistance Authorization Act for Fiscal Year 1987 § 539(i), Pub. L. No. 99-591, 1986 U.S. Code Cong. & Admin. News (100 Stat.) 3341–236.

4. The Committee first met on October 19, 1987, and is expected to publish its report during 1988.

Regulating the International Trade in Hazardous Pesticides: Closing the Accountability Gap

Lynn Sharp Paine

My thesis is very simple. It is that we are moving toward an international regulatory regime that will increasingly hold manufacturers and exporters of agricultural chemicals accountable for the human health and environmental consequences associated with their products.[1] As we move in that direction, pesticide producers can expect to be called to answer to various publics for the human health and environmental effects of their decisions to produce and market agricultural chemicals around the globe, particularly in developing countries. Such a regulatory system will require increased expenditures for research and field testing and may very likely reduce the availability of existing products and curtail the introduction of new ones. However, a system of what I call "supply-side" accountability is likely to emerge because it is the only kind of regulatory system capable of dealing in the near term with the existing accountability gap. I conclude by urging industry

to take the lead in defining and implementing this regime.

This may seem a bold prediction in light of the current international emphasis on a regime of "Prior Informed Consent" and the history of failed pesticide export regulation proposals in the United States and Europe. But I believe that likely defects in the implementation of the Prior Informed Consent system, [and] traditional concepts of moral responsibility . . . support this prediction. Before elaborating the argument, let me explain the problems to which various regulatory efforts have emerged as a solution.

THE ACCOUNTABILITY GAP

The problems of pesticide use and misuse persist world-wide, but they are particularly troublesome in developing countries where the human and environmental costs associated with the production, distribution, use, and disposal of hazardous agricultural chemicals are disproportionately high. Although they use about a quarter of the world's pesticide supply, developing countries suffer half the pesticide-related poisonings and about three-quarters of the deaths.

Examples of tragedy are legion. In 1988 droves of animals in the Sudan's Dinder wildlife preserve perished when farmers, intending to reduce the area's bird population, poured hazardous chemicals into lagoons and puddles. Deteriorating containers of unused pesticides donated to fight locusts in Africa have created serious problems of leakage and contamination. In 1986, the World Health Organization reported that pesticides cause an estimated 20,000 deaths and as many as one million acute poisonings each year.

The immediate causes of pesticide poisonings are varied: direct contact with hazardous chemicals, consuming food stored in discarded pesticide containers, drinking contaminated water, playing or working in freshly treated areas. The intrinsically hazardous nature of many pesticides coupled with high illiteracy rates among rural farm workers, the absence of regulatory and legal structures, lack of routine medical care, and tropical climates that make protective clothing uncomfortable, if not unbearable, are among the factors contributing to this unhappy situation. . . .

It is not surprising that pesticide-related hazards in developing countries are at issue. Pesticides manufactured for export from the major producing countries are typically exempt from domestic health and environmental regulations, and many developing countries lack an effective system of regulation and import control. Consequently, unless pesticides made for export are destined for countries with an effective regulatory system, they may entirely escape scrutiny for their human health and environmental effects. The flow of exports from the major manufacturing countries may include chemicals that have been banned or restricted at home for environmental or health reasons, those that have been voluntarily withdrawn from domestic markets because of concerns about potential environmental or health hazards, as well as those which are not subject to domestic regulations because they are manufactured for export. . . .

Of course, particular social and environmental circumstances in one part of the world may justify risks that would be unacceptable in another. And evaluation of pesticide use must proceed on a case-by-case basis. But given the absence of public standards and procedures to test and assess pesticide risks in the environments in which they are ultimately used, it is impossible for the public to feel confident that the social and environmental costs of pesticide use in developing countries are justified.

. . . There is a gigantic gap in the system of accountability for the human health and environmental consequences of pesticide use in developing countries. This gap is accompanied by highly undesirable effects on human welfare in a context which seems to suggest systematic unfairness between industrialized and developing countries. Moreover, we cannot say with confidence that these effects are necessary costs of morally sound decisions and policies. Indeed, with respect to banned and restricted pesticides exported from industrialized to developing nations, some people very much doubt that such a case can be made.

THE QUESTION OF RESPONSIBILITY

This gap in accountability has led to regulatory proposals and initiatives in a number of national and international forums, among them the United Nations Food and Agriculture Organization (FAO), the United Nations Environment Programme (UNEP), the European Economic Community (EC), the Organization for Economic Cooperation and Development (OECD), the General Agreement on Trade and Tariffs (GATT), the International Association of Chemical Manufacturers (GIFAP), and the Agricultural Chemicals Dialogue Group (ACDG). Among exporting nations, the United States and the Netherlands have enacted legislation on pesticide exports. Many recipient countries, too, have sought to regulate pesticide use and importation.

A controversial issue in all these forums has been and continues to be the allocation of responsibility for the decision to use pesticides and for the consequent human and environmental costs associated with them. In simplest terms, the question has been whether decision-making authority and responsibility rest exclusively with the demand side-users, importers, and importing nations—or with the supply side as well—producers, exporters, and exporting nations. How this question is answered has important consequences for how a regulatory system— whether a self-imposed code of conduct or a government-backed regulation—is structured and for the specific obligations it imposes.

To date, demand-side responsibility has been the dominant view. The various mechanisms that emerged in the eighties to regulate the international pesticide trade almost uniformly place responsibility for the decision to use pesticides on the demand-side of the trade relationship—on importing countries, purchasers, and users. Time and time again in the debates in Europe, the United States, and various international bodies, the view has been advanced and generally adopted that "ultimate decision making and control must rest within the sovereignty of the importing country."[2] Indeed, whenever legislation to control the export of hazardous pesticides

from the United States has been proposed, opponents have rallied behind the sovereignty of the importing country and against "paternalistic" United States legislation.[3] Export restrictions based on environmental and health standards have been rejected in principle by the governments of major pesticide exporters such as the United States, as well as by the European Community, the OECD, the UN, and the GATT. More restrictive export policies such as prohibitions on exporting banned substances, it is frequently argued, are inconsistent with free trade and with respect for the sovereignty of importing nations.

For the most part the responsibilities of producers, exporters, and their governments have been conceived in terms of providing information and, in some cases, assistance to enhance the decision making of importers, importing countries, and pesticide users. The FAO's International Code of Conduct on the Distribution and Use of Pesticides (the FAO Code) and current U.S. and EC legislation, for example, require exporters to satisfy certain labeling and packaging standards. U.S. law also requires an exporter to secure an importer's written acknowledgment whenever an unregistered pesticide is to be shipped. The EPA is then required to forward this acknowledgment through diplomatic channels to the government of the importing country. Likewise, the European Community has an export notification system covering certain designated hazardous chemicals. Although the details of these various disclosure and notification requirements vary, the underlying conception of responsibility is the same: importing countries have responsibility for protecting human health and the environment from risks associated with imported chemicals, while exporting countries are responsible for providing information to assist importers with their decisions. The 1984 OECD Council Recommendation quite explicitly rests on this allocation of responsibility.

More recently, due to continuing environmental and health problems and to shortcomings of these information provision schemes, attention has shifted to the idea of requiring suppliers of hazardous pesticides to secure the informed consent of importing country governments prior to export. While this "Prior Informed Consent" regime (described more fully below) is definitely more demanding of pesticide producers and their governments than a system of notification only, it is still conceptually rooted in the notion that decision-making authority and responsibility rest on the demand side of the trade relationship. . . .

FOUNDATIONS OF RESPONSIBILITY

Despite vigorous advocacy for demand-side accountability, a number of theoretical arguments favor a different allocation. Indeed, standard approaches to allocating responsibility—those based on risk reduction and risk distribution as well as those grounded in theories of human agency—all point in the direction of supply-side responsibility. Supply-side responsibility, it seems, would be more likely to promote risk reduction. As with many complex products based on advanced research and technology, the pesticide producer's knowledge of the product and its risks far exceeds that of the typical purchaser. Compared to the typical pesticide user, the producer can more easily and efficiently do the laboratory and field research necessary to acquire additional information about product risks. Superior knowledge and superior access to additional knowledge mean the producer is much better placed to identify product modifications and innovations that can improve safety and reduce product risk. Moreover, holding producers accountable for

the health and environmental costs of pesticide use would give them a powerful incentive to seek safer alternatives to existing products.

Disparities of knowledge and regulatory expertise at the level of nations also point to supply-side responsibility. The major exporting nations have well-developed systems for regulating pesticides to protect their citizens' health and environment. Admittedly, these systems are far from perfect: they often fail to protect citizens because of gaps in their authority, scarcity of human and financial resources, and conflicts with other objectives. Still, they are more comprehensive and more effective than the regulatory systems found in many importing countries, where resources are even scarcer and where the local agricultural extension service may consist of one person with a motorcycle and no gas. Efficient use of regulatory resources, as well as reduction of the risks of pesticide use in importing countries, suggest that exporting nations take more responsibility for evaluating the pesticides their nationals send into the world marketplace.

Fair distribution of risks and costs, another criterion for allocating responsibility, suggests the same result. It is costly, in both human and financial terms, to be the accountable party. For producers these costs are primarily financial: the costs of doing additional research, developing assessment procedures, defending and communicating assessments, and answering for failures of accountability. For demand-side players lacking financial resources and decision-making infrastructures, the costs of accountability are more likely to show up as diminished environmental and human health. Whether fairness is thought to demand distribution of costs and risks according to ability to bear them, in proportion to benefits enjoyed, or as a means of improving the lot of the least well off, fairness points toward supply-side responsibility. It is the supply-side players, in general, who can more readily bear these costs since they are, by and large, better off than the demand-side players. While it would be a difficult and challenging task to assess whether the total costs of pesticide use are distributed in proportion to the benefits enjoyed by the supply and demand sides, respectively, it seems clear that the human and environmental costs are disproportionately borne by the demand side under the current system. Supply-side responsibility would contribute to rectifying this imbalance. Moreover, as already noted, supply-side responsibility would contribute to improving the lot of the worst off.

Traditional conceptions of moral responsibility based on human agency round out the theoretical arguments for supply-side accountability. Within this framework individuals are responsible for the foreseen and foreseeable consequences of their voluntary, intentional actions. No one doubts that manufacturing and marketing a pesticide are the sorts of deliberate action for whose consequences one may be held responsible. The question is whether this responsibility, or some part of it, is transferred to or assumed by other parties—buyers, users, governments—by their own voluntary acts of purchasing, using, or permitting import of the product.

In the familiar idealized picture of market exchange, at least a partial transfer of responsibility is thought to occur as an incident of the exchange, since the buyer is presumed to be acting voluntarily and with full knowledge of the product and its attendant risks. Within the model, a voluntary act of buying is as much an act giving rise to responsibility as is the act of producing and offering for sale. An important conceptual question is whether the buyer's acceptance of responsibility for certain risks fully extinguishes the seller's responsibility for those risks. In this context, it is important to distinguish self-regarding risks to the buyer and risks to others. If voluntarism is the touchstone, it would seem that the

buyer's act can relieve the seller only of responsibility to the buyer for known, self-regarding risks assumed by the buyer. Lacking authority to act on behalf of third parties who may also be at risk from the product, the buyer cannot fully extinguish the seller's responsibility to them. At most, the exchange extends moral responsibility for these consequences to the buyer as well as the seller. And third parties may quite properly hold both buyer and seller morally accountable.

In principle, under idealized conditions of knowledge and voluntariness, economic exchange can be the vehicle for transferring to buyers responsibility for certain risks. But in the global pesticide trade these idealized conditions are frequently unsatisfied. First, and most important, it is unwarranted to assume that most pesticide buyers are knowledgeable about the risks of the products they buy. There is much evidence that pesticide purchases by Third Word importers and farmers are frequently made in ignorance of the relevant health and environmental risks. Purchasers typically do not know what risks are involved, lack access to information about those risks, and are not equipped with the resources, skills, or knowledge needed to test and assess the pesticides themselves. Even if buyers know, as they sometimes do, that the pesticide they are purchasing is not registered for sale in the exporting country, they do not know whether the pesticide poses risks to health or the environment or what those risks might be. In the absence of such knowledge, assumption of the risks of pesticide use, even purely self-regarding risks, cannot be presumed from the act of purchasing them.

Second, the magnitude and scope of third-party effects of pesticide use preclude a simple demand-side view of responsibility. From a moral perspective, as already noted, the buyer's assumption of responsibility for these effects can extend but not extinguish the seller's responsibility to those third parties. And extension of responsibility requires that these risks be knowingly and voluntarily assumed, a condition that in practice is rarely satisfied. The reality of the pesticide trade is a far cry from the idealized models that might support a regime of demand-side accountability. . . .

TOWARD SUPPLY-SIDE ACCOUNTABILITY: PRIOR INFORMED CONSENT

The Prior Informed Consent procedure currently being implemented by UNEP and the FAO may be seen as a response to some of these arguments. But a closer look will begin to explain why we are likely to move beyond "prior informed consent" to a system of supply-side accountability. Generally known as "PIC," the procedure establishes a mechanism for providing risk information and an opportunity for importing country governments to choose whether to allow the importation of certain hazardous pesticides. Precisely which pesticides will be subject to PIC is still under debate. However, the initial proposal was to include all agricultural chemicals banned or severely restricted in ten or more countries and a selected number of chemicals banned in five to nine countries.

In brief, the procedure asks governments taking action to ban or severely restrict hazardous agricultural chemicals to notify UNEP's International Register of Potentially Toxic Chemicals (IRPTC) of the control action and the reasons behind it. The Register will, in turn, inform a designated official of each participating country by means of a "Decision Guidance Document" containing information about the control action, the chemical, its toxicological characteristics, its environmental effects, and the exposure risks. Importing country authorities may then register their qualified or unqualified decision to permit or prohibit importation of the chemi-

cal. The procedure is entirely voluntary and exporting countries are expected to take steps within their authority to see that importing countries' decisions are respected.

It might be thought that implementation of this new procedure would eliminate both the need and the rationale for supply-side accountability. After all, a government official's consent to importation could be seen as proxy consent to pesticide hazards given on behalf of at-risk individuals. If those at risk have given their consent, they have no moral grounds for complaint against the producers and sellers of hazardous products. In principle, informed voluntary consent given with certain understandings by those authorized to do so could extinguish producer accountability to at-risk parties. However, in practice, given the actual conditions in many developing countries, it cannot be assumed that consent, even if ostensibly registered through the system, will satisfy the conditions necessary to do this moral work. Moreover, even if consent registered through PIC is morally effectual as an assumption of responsibility for certain risks by those on whose behalf consent is given, there will be many cases in which the consent mechanism cannot entirely relieve producers of responsibility to third parties.

Finally, it should be noticed that the proposed PIC system is built around pesticides that have been the subject of governmental control actions. That is, it presupposes a system of supply-side accountability which generates the information and product assessments upon which the consent of importing countries can be based. For pesticides produced in industrialized countries solely for export, there is no such institutionalized system of accountability. Thus, it is hard to see how there could be any morally effectual consent to the hazards of those products unless importing countries have an independent source of information and expertise or their own regulatory infrastructures.

I do not mean to suggest that PIC is undesirable. It will likely contribute to spreading information about the environmental and health risks of the chemicals included in the procedure and possibly to better informed policies and purchase behavior. However, I am suggesting that PIC is conceptually and practically inadequate to close the existing accountability gap, and that it is unlikely to eliminate the health and environmental problems that have prompted and continue to prompt calls for international regulation of hazardous pesticides. Besides the procedure's limited scope, there are serious questions about the moral effectiveness of a consent-based system given the social and economic conditions prevailing in many developing countries, the power and knowledge asymmetries between producing and importing countries, and the problem of containing the risks of agricultural chemicals.

A review of the requirements for morally effectual proxy consent suggests several potential concerns about the moral adequacy of consents registered through PIC. In practice, problems are likely to center on the voluntariness of consent, the understanding with which it is given, the authority of those giving it, and how reasonable it is.

Voluntariness

To be morally effective, consent must be given voluntarily. It must be self-directed and not the result of coercion or the over-bearing influence of others. Although it is difficult to specify what degree of external control would vitiate consent, a variety of influences short of coercion are problematic. Under PIC, voluntariness is an issue because of widespread reliance in developing countries on the pesticide industry both for information and for advice on pesticide use. Government officials designated to decide on hazardous imports, partic-

ularly those lacking expertise in the relevant areas—such as pest control methods and health and environmental risk assessment—may defer to or be overly influenced by the industry's view.

This may result from the industry's explicit and direct efforts to influence consent decisions or, more indirectly, through the selective presentation of information about their products or varying the terms and conditions of sale. The point here is not that the industry's view is necessarily correct or incorrect, but that the consenting party's decision should both be and appear to be self-chosen. The PIC procedure goes some way toward neutralizing industry influence by making available alternative sources of information. But it is doubtful that the information included in the Decision Guidance Document would, by itself, be sufficient for sound decision-making. . . .

Understanding

To the extent that industry influence takes the form of selective presentations of information through its advertising and marketing, the problem with consent may be less a matter of insufficient voluntariness and more a matter of inadequate knowledge and understanding, a second hurdle to morally effectual consent. To be morally effectual, it is not enough that consent be given by someone who is generally intelligent and mature. It must be given with adequate understanding of the risks and likely outcomes of the consented to activity, insofar as these can be known. Understanding the consequences of permitting importation of hazardous pesticides such as those on the PIC list requires a great deal of specific knowledge as well as a variety of general competencies: knowledge about the products and the social and environmental conditions under which they are likely to be used; general competencies in the areas of pest control methods and health and environmental risk assessment. As already noted, individual and institutional knowledge concerning pesticide risks and pest management techniques are in short supply in many developing countries.

Although PIC will supply certain critical pieces of information through its Decision Guidance Documents, the procedure cannot insure that this information will be assessed in light of local conditions by individuals competent and equipped with the scientific and administrative resources to do so. Information about the toxicological characteristics, environmental effects, and exposure risks of a pesticide—all to be included in the Decision Guidance Document provided through PIC—are a poor basis for understanding in the absence of background knowledge about how such characteristics are measured and how they compare with similar characteristics of other available methods of pest control. Moreover, the environmental effects and exposure risks reported in the Decision Guidance Document may be based on research conducted in quite different social and environmental circumstances. Given the scarcity of resources in many developing countries it is not unreasonable to expect that even officials with appropriate skills and competencies to assess the merits of importation will be pressed for time and resources to make the assessment.

Another defect in understanding which may be encountered in practice concerns the moral significance of consent as an assumption of responsibility. While this may be generally understood by those brought up in the tradition of liberal individualism within which the consent procedure acquires its rationale and significance, consent to importation may be understood by some as just an authorization and no more. The words of the documents proposed for PIC do not explicitly state that consent effects any acceptance of responsibility, and there remains a great deal of room for dispute about the scope of any acceptance

or transfer, assuming consent is otherwise effectual. For example, the question of responsibility for risks unknown to both producers and consenting officials remains indeterminate.

Authority

Perhaps PIC's greatest limitation springs from problems of authority. In the case of non-democratic governments, the authority of designated officials to consent to the risks of pesticide use on behalf of the country's citizens poses a formidable barrier for the moral effectualness of PIC. Even within democratic theory, notions of representation and authority must be stretched to their limit to legitimate the making of decisions that put citizens' lives and health at serious risk without their direct consent. If officials appointed to make consent decisions have no plausible basis for claiming to represent the interests of those on whose behalf they are purportedly consenting, the giving of consent is morally meaningless as an act of self-determination on the part of at-risk individuals.

Even if there is no problem of authority in the case of the official consenting on behalf of nationals of the country receiving a pesticide shipment, non-nationals inside and outside the borders of the country are also at risk. The inability to confine the effects of pesticide use within national borders virtually guarantees that sending hazardous pesticides into the global marketplace will put at risk individuals who have neither consented nor delegated authority to consent to these hazards.

Reasonableness

Finally, in practice, some consents may be morally ineffectual because they are unreasonable. The requirement that consent be reasonable in some objective sense arises because those giving consent under PIC are acting as fiduciaries obligated to exercise independent judgment on behalf of their country's citizens. Consequently, the decision to permit importation must not be corrupt—the result of a bribe or improper influence brought to bear on the official—and it must be justifiable in terms of the national well-being or public interest. The requirement of reasonableness reflects an important difference between an individual's consent to serious risks of self-regarding harm, and a government's consent on behalf of its citizens. The constraint of rationality is much stronger in the government case because of the government's obligation to its citizens. . . .

But individuals entrusted to act on behalf of others, as government officials are, have obligations of fidelity to the interests of those they represent and rationality, perhaps even prudence, in promoting and protecting those interests. The more impersonal the surrogacy relationship, the more important rationality becomes as a standard for decision-making. Imagine a government official's approving the import of a hazardous chemical expected to put thousands of people and the environment at risk while offering the sole benefit of a slight improvement in crop yield. Imagine further that a more effective, cheaper, and safer method of pest control is available. Even if this official were duly authorized and competent to register approval, and did so voluntarily with full information about the relative risks and benefits of the available alternatives, this consent would be in violation of the official's duty to act rationally on behalf of the public.

What standard should be applied in making decisions like these is far too difficult to resolve here. . . . Ultimately, whether consent is effectual under PIC depends on there being a credible case that using and importing the product is reasonable. It may, of course, be possible to make such a case for some pesticides. But the case must be made. It cannot be assumed.

These considerations explain why PIC, despite its importance and usefulness in spreading information, facilitating more informed decision-making, and enhancing self-determination, is unlikely to eliminate calls for supply-side accountability. Apart from the obvious and serious problem of PIC's limited scope, there are likely to be problems in at least some cases concerning the knowledge, understanding, authority, and justifiability with which consent to importation is given. But even in the best of cases, when it satisfies all the conditions for moral effectualness, consent by an importing country can only count as an assumption of responsibility for self-regarding risks, risks to those who have delegated decision-making authority to the consenting official. Risks to others remain unaccounted for by this scheme, except in the unusual case that the governments of all affected parties consent.

LEGAL DEVELOPMENTS

I have suggested that deficiencies in the PIC system, along with theoretical ideas about how responsibilities are properly allocated, will very likely lead to increasing support for greater supply-side accountability. Developments in [the] judicial arena in the United States lend further weight to this prediction. . . .

[One such] development pointing toward greater supply-side responsibility is a March 1990 decision of the Texas Supreme Court. The court upheld the right of some eighty Costa Rican employees to sue United States pesticide manufacturers in Texas courts for injuries allegedly suffered from exposure to hazardous pesticides the companies had exported from the United States to Costa Rica.[4] (Other courts have excluded foreign plaintiffs in this sort of case using the doctrine of forum non conveniens). The plaintiffs, workers on a Costa Rican banana plantation, allege that exposure to the United States-manufactured pesticide DBCP rendered them permanently sterile. DBCP continued to be exported even after it was banned for use in the United States by the Environmental Protection Agency in 1977. In concurring with the majority opinion permitting the plaintiffs to go forward with their suit, Judge Doggett stated that recognizing the doctrine of forum non conveniens would "immunize multinational corporations from accountability for their alleged torts causing injury abroad." Although it is impossible to predict the final outcome of this suit, it should be noted supply-side accountability is very much in line with U.S. product liability law.

IMPLEMENTING SUPPLY-SIDE RESPONSIBILITY

I have highlighted some trends, arguments, and forces pointing toward a regime of supply-side accountability. But I have said very little about how supply-side responsibility might be discharged or institutionalized. These are topics deserving full treatment in their own right, I will say just a word about them in conclusion. Supply-side responsibility means that those who decide to produce pesticides and market them in the global marketplace will be held morally accountable for those decisions and their consequences.

As a practical matter, this means that producers will need good information about the conditions under which their products will be used and an understanding of the consequences of use under those conditions. It means they will have to be careful about the markets they target and confident that the benefits of using their products in those markets exceed and can be seen to exceed whatever costs are involved. . . .

NOTES

1. I am using the word "regulation" in a very broad sense to refer to any institutionalized scheme of cooperation designed to uphold certain standards of behavior. It may, but need not, involve governments.

2. Member of the European Parliament, quoted in "Pressure Grows on Pesticide Industry to Tighten Controls on Third World Exports," 6 *Int'l Env't Rptr.* (BNA) no. 4 (April 13, 1983), p. 160.

3. In this debate about the Pesticide Export Act of 1990 (S. 2227), the EPA took the position that our responsibility as an exporter is to provide information and technical assistance to importers. The proposed bill would have had the U.S. exercise more responsibility for the health and environmental safety of pesticide exports.

4. *Dow Chemical Company and Shell Oil Company v. Domingo Castro Alfaro,* 786 S.W.2d 674 (Texas 1990).

The Foreign Corrupt Practices Act Amendments of 1988: "Death" of a Law

Barltey A. Brennan

The Members of Congress who authored this elimination of the antibribery law chose the perfect vehicle. They needed a big bill that would be handled by a myriad of committees so they could bury the few fatal lines that killed the Foreign Corrupt Practices Act deep in this forest of hundreds of thousands of words. They needed a controversial bill that would concentrate the debate on a series of economic matters that shook and divided the country and distracted the press from the death knell to antiforeign bribery law. What an opportunity to slip through a bribery repealer. The authors of the provision fully understood the gutting provision could not stand by itself. Even in a moderately complex bill the amendment would be vulnerable. But pushed by one of the many committees developing the details of this king size trade bill that was furiously contested by Congress and the President, the press and public could hardly be expected to notice the death of the Foreign Corrupt Practices Act.[1]

INTRODUCTION

An extraordinary eight year effort by some members of Congress and some business lobbyists to amend the Foreign Corrupt Practices Act of 1977 (FCPA or Act) culminated on August 23, 1988, with the enactment of the Omnibus Trade and Competitiveness Act of 1988 (Trade Act). The 1988 FCPA Amendments are only six pages in this approximately four hundred page piece of legislation

whose goals only indirectly, at best, were to amend the FCPA. Those seeking to amend the FCPA had, over an eight-year period, failed to obtain passage of such amendments when they were introduced as separate bills. Furthermore, the Trade Act itself was once vetoed by the President and was passed as a result of a series of compromises worked out in a Trade Bill Conference Committee. It is therefore not surprising that proponents of the FCPA, such as Senator Proxmire, have charged those who have been successful in amending the Act with seeking to "gut" the law.

This Article analyzes the major changes that the 1988 Amendments made to the accounting and antibribery sections of the 1977 FCPA. Throughout the discussion particular attention will be given to the way in which the 1988 Amendments address the problems created by the 1977 Act. These problems are identified in a 1981 report issued by the General Accounting Office, which conducted a survey of U.S. corporations. This Article concludes that the 1988 Amendments severely undercut the original objectives of the 1977 Act.

In reviewing the 1988 Amendments to the FCPA, it should be remembered why the 1977 Act was enacted. In the period from 1974 to 1976, approximately 435 corporations voluntarily disclosed to the Securities and Exchange Commission (SEC) that they had made improper or questionable payments to foreign officials or members of foreign political parties. Such bribery led to the

From Bartley A. Brennan, "The Foreign Corrupt Practices Act Amendments of 1988: 'Death' of a Law," *North Carolina Journal of International Law & Commerce Regulation*, volume 15 (1990), pp. 229–47. Reprinted by permission of publisher and author.

downfall of governments and officials in Japan, the Netherlands, and Korea. By weakening its statute against bribery, the United States does not present itself as a good political and economic model for other nations to follow. This message is especially inappropriate at a time when the Soviet Union and several Eastern European nations are evolving toward economies based on the U.S. model. . . .

THE ANTIBRIBERY PROVISIONS OF THE FCPA

The 1977 Antibribery Provisions

In addition to the accounting provisions of the 1977 FCPA which mandated disclosure of questionable or illegal payments, Congress also provided antibribery provisions which prohibited the bribery of any foreign official. Under this section, not all payments were prohibited. Instead, only those payments that were driven by corrupt intentions, those made to influence certain persons to commit or fail to perform certain acts, and those made for the purpose of retaining business were prohibited.

Corporate and government officials, as well as academicians and lawyers, criticized the bribery sections of the 1977 FCPA for vaguely defining what constituted compliance. Some commentators suggested that this vagueness forced U.S. corporations to forego business opportunities abroad for fear of violating the FCPA and incurring its stiff criminal sanctions. The GAO Report found that of "the 30% of our respondents who reported that the Act had caused a decrease in their overseas business, approximately 70% rated the clarity of at least one of the antibribery provisions as inadequate or very inadequate." The major ambiguities to the antibribery provisions noted by the respondents FCPA were the following:

(1) the degree of responsibility a company has for the actions of the foreign agents;

(2) the definition of the term "foreign official";

(3) whether a payment is a bribe (illegal under the FCPA) or a "facilitating payment" (legal under the FCPA); and

(4) the dual jurisdiction of the SEC and Department of Justice.

The 1988 Amendments to the Antibribery Provisions

The 1988 Amendments change the antibribery provisions of the 1977 FCPA in seven areas.

Corrupt Payments. The 1988 Amendments attempt to clarify the definition of what type of payments are prohibited. The Amendments change this definition in two respects. First, payments under the 1977 FCPA were prohibited if their purpose was to influence "*any act or decision of such foreign official in his official capacity, including a decision to fail to perform his official functions.*"[2] The 1988 Amendments alter this provision to forbid payments or offers to pay foreign officials for the purpose of "*influencing any act or decision of such foreign official in his official capacity, or inducing such foreign official to do or omit to do any act in violation of the lawful duty of such official.*"[3] Thus, it would seem at first glance that the language was changed in order to bring the FCPA into compliance with U.S. bribery laws. However, as one commentator has noted, the conferees failed because our domestic bribery statute forbids *all* corrupt payments intended to influence official functions, while the FCPA, as amended, increases the number of already existing categories of facilitating or "grease" payments.

Second, under the 1977 FCPA, payments were only illegal if made "in order to assist such issuer in obtaining or retaining business. . . . "[4] Some confusion arose as to whether lobbying fell within the definition of "retaining business." Although the Conference Committee rejected a proposed amendment that would have broadened the definition of "retaining business," the Conference Report does attempt to clarify the provision. It states that the conferees:

> wish to make clear that the reference to corrupt payments for "retaining business" in present law is not limited to the renewal of contracts or other business, but also included a prohibition against corrupt payments relating to the execution or performance of contracts or the carrying out of existing business, such as a payment to a foreign official for the purpose of obtaining more favorable tax treatment. . . . The term should not, however, be construed so broadly as to include lobbying or other normal representations to government officials.[5]

The Conference Report as noted here sought on one hand to broaden the scope of prohibited payments beyond the purpose of "retaining business" but also to liberalize its interpretation so as not to include lobbying or normal representations. These conflicting objectives may have unfortunate repercussions in light of the expansion of categories of lawfully permitted facilitating or "grease" payments discussed below.

The "Reason to Know" Standard for Third Party Payments. In addition to prohibiting payments directly to "foreign officials," the 1977 FCPA also prohibited corporate entities or officers from giving anything of value to "any person, while knowing or having reason to know that all or a portion of such money or thing of value will be offered directly or indirectly" to various persons. These payments are referred to as third party payments.

Almost fifty percent of the respondents surveyed by the GAO found the "reason to know" language either "very inadequate" or "marginally inadequate." Lawyers and legal

scholars argued that a "reason to know" standard increased the potential liability of a company and its officers for the acts of foreign agents or more closely affiliated third parties even if the company was unable to monitor or control their conduct. Several recurring questions were asked. What does "reason to know" mean? Is "reason to know" something less than full actual knowledge? If so, how much less, and should it be used in prosecution of criminal conduct? Those favoring the language as it stood under the FCPA pointed out that "reason to know" language existed in twenty-nine provisions of other federal laws. An analysis of these provisions, however, showed that thirteen of the twenty-nine provisions were civil or administrative statutes as contrasted with the FCPA, a criminal statute that provided for up to five years imprisonment. The remaining provisions fell into areas relating to federal safety standards or other types of regulatory procedures. Furthermore, similar "reason to know" language is included in eight provisions of the criminal code which has been replaced by the Federal Criminal Code Revisions.

Perhaps the most significant problem was that no precedents existed interpreting the "reason to know" language of the 1977 FCPA. In addition, because both the Department of Justice and the SEC had joint enforcement authority, a question was raised as to whether the agencies had the same interpretation of the "reason to know" language.

The 1988 Amendments delete the "reason to know" language and apply a "knowing" standard, which is defined as follows:

(A) A person's state of mind is "knowing" with respect to conduct, a circumstance, or a result if—

(i) such person is aware that such person is engaging in such conduct, that such circumstance exists, or that such result is substantially certain to occur; or

(ii) such person has a firm belief that

such circumstance exists or that such result is substantially certain to occur.

(B) When knowledge of the existence of a particular circumstance is required for an offense, such knowledge is established if a person is aware of a high probability of the existence of such circumstance, unless the person actually believes that such circumstance does not exist. . . .[6]

The "reason to know" standard has been replaced by a standard that is more difficult for prosecutors to meet. The Conference Report made it clear that "simple negligence" or "mere foolishness" was insufficient for criminal liability. However, the Committee also stated that management will be held liable for "conscious disregard," "willful blindness," or "deliberate ignorance." In other words a "head in the sand" state of mind approach by management will not be tolerated. Citing several federal cases the Conference Report noted that the knowledge requirement is not equivalent to recklessness. It requires "an awareness of a high probability of the existence of the circumstance." The Conference Report goes on to state that the FCPA covers circumstances where any "reasonable person would have realized the existence of the circumstance or result" and the defendant "consciously chose not to ask about what he had reason to believe he would discover." Courts are instructed to use a mix of subjective and objective standards to determine the level of knowledge based on this test.

It would appear that the only circumstance from which a company must now protect itself is the intentional disregarding of some mix of subjective and objective signals that illegal payments were made by an agent or employee to a third party. It is not clear at this point what the signals are. As one commentator has pointed out, the Conference Report does not cite any cases which "suggest liability where the consequences of the factual knowledge possessed by the defendant result in future conduct prohibited by the statute," yet the language of the statute imposes liability in cases where there is an awareness or belief "such result is substantially certain to occur." It would seem clear that the language substituted for the "reason to know" standard may in fact prevent serious prosecution of violators of the FCPA.

Facilitating Payments. The Amendments change the exemption for facilitating or "grease" payments. These payments are not made to obtain or retain business but merely to expedite a business activity in which the ministerial level employee is already employed. An example is the payment of thirty dollars to a customs official to move paperwork along so that a shipment of nondurable goods can be unloaded quickly. Many foreign governments permit such facilitating payments even though they are illegal in the United States and several other countries.

Under the 1977 FCPA, facilitating payments were allowed in several ways. The 1977 FCPA defined "foreign official" as any officer or employee of a foreign government or one of its departments, agencies, or instrumentalities. This definition expressly excluded any employee whose duties were "essentially ministerial or clerical." Corporate officials frequently complained that this language was unclear. Are employees of a publicly held nationalized corporation considered "foreign officials?" Is an official, or member of that official's family residing in a foreign country, who is also involved in the private sector a "foreign official?" How should the law treat individuals who simultaneously hold positions in both government and business? Can an excluded "ministerial or clerical" employee be paid a "facilitating payment" to use his influence to induce a "foreign official" to act, as long as the clerical employee does not pay the official from funds received from a U.S. corporation?

As stated above, the 1977 FCPA also proscribed only "corrupt" payments. The legislative history of the FCPA defined a corrupt payment as one made "to induce the recipient to misuse his official position in order to wrongfully direct business to the payor or his client" and requires an "evil motive or purpose." Because ministerial employees were excluded from the definition of foreign official, it is clear the FCPA was not intended to proscribe grease or facilitating payments. Moreover, social gifts or routine expenditures for marketing products were lawful. However, consistent complaints about enforcement officials' interpretation led to requests for a congressional clarification of the statute.

Despite the apparently clear legislative intent that facilitating payments to ministerial or clerical employees not be proscribed, thirty-eight percent of those responding to the GAO questionnaire rated the clarity of the provisions inadequate. The dilemma raised was that a large corrupt payment to an official with "ministerial" duties might *not* be prohibited while a small payment to expedite customs papers may be prohibited if made to a senior "official." Furthermore, middle-level employees of U.S. corporations did not fully understand what constituted a facilitating payment. The decision to make such a payment would often have to be made quickly because hesitation might cause a delay in transportation or unloading of goods.

The 1988 Amendments now allow payments to *any* foreign official if they are facilitating or expediting payments for the purposes of expediting or securing the performance of a routine governmental action. "Routine governmental action" is defined as follows:

> an action which is ordinarily and commonly performed by a foreign official in:
> (i) obtaining permit[s], licenses, or other official documents to qualify a person to do business in a foreign country;

> (ii) processing governmental papers such as visas and work order[s];
> (iii) providing police protection, mail pick up and delivery, or scheduling inspections associated with contract performance or inspections related to transit of goods across country;
> (iv) providing phone service, power and water supply, loading and unloading cargo, or protecting perishable products or commodities from deterioration; or
> (v) actions of a similar nature.

Payments can now be made to *any* foreign official, not just ministerial or clerical persons, as long as they fall within the five categories. This substantially changes the intent of the 1977 FCPA as well as the breadth of the exception. The 1977 FCPA facilitating payments language was directed at the type of foreign official (ministerial or clerical), while 1988 amendments are directed at the type of duties to be performed. The "actions of a similar nature" language greatly expands the types of activities that may be allowed as "grease" or facilitating payments.

Affirmative Defenses. In addition to expanding the "grease" payment exceptions for criminal prosecution, the 1988 Amendments also provide for two affirmative defenses for those accused of violating the FCPA. First, it is now an affirmative defense if a payment to a foreign official is lawful "under the written laws" of the foreign country. The Conference Report makes it clear "that the absence of written laws in a foreign official's country would not by itself be sufficient to satisfy this defense." Also, in interpreting what is lawful under written law, the conference committee members state that "normal rules of legal construction should apply."

This defense was added in response to complaints that U.S. companies were losing business because actions forbidden by the 1977 FCPA were permitted in foreign countries and undertaken by foreign competitors. A related problem was the lack of uniformity among nations regarding the propriety of facilitating payments. While a foreign agent might legally receive such a payment under the law of his or her country, the U.S. corporation making the payment might be violating the FCPA.

A study by Dr. John Graham of the University of Southern California, which reviewed all available empirical data, concluded that:

> (a) During the 1978–1980 period, the FCPA had no negative effect on export performance of American industry. No differences in U.S. markets shown were discovered in nations where the FCPA was reported to be a trade disincentive both in terms of total trade with each country as well as for sales in individual product categories.
> (b) During the 1977 statute, U.S. trade with bribe-prone countries has actually outpaced our trade with non-bribe-prone ones.[7]

Dr. Graham further concluded that the FCPA has not hurt the competitive position of U.S. industry. In fact, Dr. Graham's study provides support for the proposition that improper foreign payments are at least unnecessary. He suggests, therefore, that management should question payments to foreign firms on economic as well as ethical grounds.

Another complaint was that the FCPA sought to export U.S. morality. However, David D. Newsome has argued that the corrupt association of a U.S. company and a foreign official carries political implications for both actors which do not concern other foreign multinational corporations. He notes that "American businessmen often ask, 'Why us?' Why should America's multinationals be singled out for restrictions when all around them their competitors operate without such restrictions?"[8] Mr. Newsome concludes that the answer lies in the unique position which U.S. corporations have in world business ven-

tures, coupled with their role in domestic affairs of foreign nations. He states that "[o]ur companies cannot escape the fact that their activities will never be totally detached from local sensitivities relating to United States intervention of any sort in the internal affairs of another country."[9] Thus, from both an economic and a moral viewpoint, this new affirmative defense seems unnecessary and unwise.

The second affirmative defense established by the Amendments allows payments to be made for "reasonable and bona fide expenditures." Examples include travel and lodging expenses incurred by or on behalf of a foreign official, party, party official, or candidate that are "directly related to (A) the promotion, demonstration or explanation of products or services; or (B) the execution or performance of a contract with a foreign government or agency thereof." In general, this second affirmative defense codifies the procedure followed by the Justice Department under the 1977 FCPA.

Repeal of the "Eckhardt Amendment." The "Eckhardt Amendment," which was included in the 1977 Act, prevented the prosecution of employees or agents of an issuer or U.S. corporation unless the concern itself was found to have violated the FCPA. The 1988 Amendments delete the language that prevented such prosecution.

Congressman Eckhardt originally proposed such language to prevent senior management of companies from using agents or employees as "scapegoats." Also, the legislative history indicates that the sponsors of the 1977 Act were concerned that agents or employees might not have the resources to defend themselves against charges of violations of the FCPA. The 1988 Amendments now open the door for the "scapegoat" scenario. Therefore, it is now important that individual employees and agents retain their own counsel when any possibility exists of a violation of the FCPA under the "knowing" standard. The repeal of the "Eckhardt Amendment" may create a difficult working environment for employees or agents and their employers or principals.. . . .

CONCLUSION

The 1988 Amendments to the FCPA seek to redefine legally and ethically acceptable conduct for U.S. concerns doing business in foreign nations. Those who espouse an efficiency view that the "right to export" is best for the nation have succeeded in "gutting" the FCPA after an eight-year struggle. In the meantime, those who have been concerned about the legal and ethical conduct of U.S. companies doing business abroad have lost the battle to maintain the standards established by the 1977 FCPA. Scientifically sound studies (as opposed to anecdotal comments) indicated that the 1977 FCPA was at most a minor disincentive to export expansion, with other variables being far more important.[10] Moreover, the 1988 Amendments send the wrong signals to U.S. and foreign business communities at a time when new markets are opening in Eastern Europe. If we as a nation wish to encourage the adoption of an economic model based on competition for those who have experienced the poverty of a command model, bribery, under the guise of "facilitating payments," we will only give ammunition to those in Eastern Europe and elsewhere who are opposed to reform. While the proponents of the 1988 Amendments have won in the short run, a return to pre-FCPA (1977) conduct by domestic concerns doing business abroad will lead to more stringent legislation in the long term.

NOTES

1. 134 Cong. Rec. S 8528 (daily ed. June 24, 1988) (statement of Sen. Proxmire).
2. 15 U.S.C. § 78dd-2(a)(1)(A) (1982) (emphasis added).
3. *Id.* § 78dd-1(a)(1)(A)(i) (1988) (emphasis added).
4. *Id.* § 78dd-1(a) (1982).
5. H.R. Conf. Rep. No. 576, 100th Cong., 2d Sess., 134 Cong. Rec. H 1863, H 2116 (daily ed. Apr. 20, 1988), *reprinted in* 1988 U.S. Code Cong. & Admin. News 1949, at 918.
6. 15 U.S.C. § 78dd-1(f)(2)(A), (B) (1988).
7. Graham, *Foreign Corrupt Practices: A Manager's Guide,* 18 COLUM. J. WORLD BUS. 89 (1983).
8. *See* Foreign Corrupt Practices Act—Oversight: Hearings Before the Subcomm. on Telecommunications, Consumer Protection, and Finance of the Comm. on Energy and Commerce, House of Representatives, 97th Cong. 1st & 2d Sess. 176 (1981 & 1982), at 391 (statement of D. Newsome).
9. *See id.* at 391–92.
10. *Id.; see* Sternitzke, *The Great American Competitive Disadvantage: Fact or Fiction,* 10 J. INT'L BUS. STUD 25, 32–35 (1979). Sternitzke concludes that "over the last decade the lagging long run growth of American exports has been due mainly to the lose of competitiveness of American manufacturing goods in affluent markets, and has been attributable only incidentally to commodity structure or mix of American exports." *See* Graham, *Foreign Corrupt Practices: A Manager's Guide,* 18 COLUM J. WORLD BUS. 89 (1983).

The Moral Authority of Transnational Corporate Codes

William C. Frederick

Moral guidelines for corporations may be found embedded in several multilateral compacts adopted by governments since the end of the Second World War. Taken as a whole, these normative guides comprise a framework for identifying the essential moral behaviors expected of multinational corporations. Corporate actions that transgress these principles are understood to be *de facto,* and in some cases *de jure,* unethical and immoral. This set of normative prescriptions and proscriptions embodies a moral authority that transcends national boundaries and societal differences, thereby invoking or manifesting a universal or transcultural standard of corporate ethical behavior. Although this remarkable development has not run its full course and therefore is not yet all-embracing, it is well enough along for its main outlines to be evident and its central normative significance to be clear.

LANDMARK MULTILATERAL COMPACTS

The four decades between 1948 and 1988 have been remarkable for the proliferation of intergovernmental agreements, compacts, accords, and declarations that have been intended to put on the public record various sets of principles regulating the activities of governments, groups, and individuals. The core concerns of these compacts have ranged from military security to economic and social development, from the protection of national sovereignty to speci-

fying acceptable actions by multinational enterprises, from condemnations of genocide and slavery to the regulation of capital flows and the transfer of technology, from the political rights of women to the movements of refugees and stateless persons, and many others too numerous to list here. They reflect the many kinds of problems and issues that have confronted governments in the last half of the 20th century (United Nations, 1983).

This paper focuses on six of these intergovernmental compacts, which by their nature, purpose, and comprehensiveness might well be considered to be the most generic or archetypal of such agreements. Collectively they proclaim the basic outlines of a transcultural corporate ethic. This ethic effectively lays down specific guidelines for the formulation of multinational corporate policies and practices. These six compacts and their respective dates of promulgation are:

- The United Nations Universal Declaration of Human Rights (1948) [Abbreviated as UDHR]
- The European Convention on Human Rights (1950) [ECHR]
- The Helsinki Final Act (1975) [Helsinki]
- The OECD Guidelines for Multinational Enterprises (1976) [OECD]
- The International Labor Office Tripartite Declaration of Principles Concerning Multinational Enterprises and Social Policy (1977) [ILO]
- The United Nations Code of Conduct on Transnational Corporations (Not yet completed nor promulgated but originating in 1972.) [TNC Code]

The first two compacts are clearly norma-

From William C. Frederick, "The Moral Authority of Transnational Corporate Codes," *Journal of Business Ethics* 10 (1991). Reprinted by permission of Kluwer Academic Publishers.

tive in focus and intention, emphasizing human rights, but they are not addressed specifically to multinational enterprises. The principle emphasis of the Helsinki Final Act is the national and political security of the signatory governments, although this accord and its successor protocols carry strong messages concerning human rights and environmental protections, which do concern business operations. The last three compacts are aimed primarily and explicitly at the practices of multinational enterprises across a wide range of issues and problems. While three of the six accords issue primarily from European-North American governments, the other three represent the view of a much wider, even global, range of governments.

NORMATIVE CORPORATE GUIDELINES

By careful reading of these six intergovernmental compacts, one can derive a set of explicitly normative guides for the policies, decisions, and operations of multinational corporations. These guidelines refer to normal business operations, as well as more fundamental responsibilities regarding basic human rights.

Employment Practices and Policies

- MNCs should not contravene the manpower policies of host nations. [ILO]
- MNCs should respect the right of employees to join trade unions and to bargain collectively. [ILO; OECD; UDHR]
- MNCs should develop nondiscriminatory employment policies and promote equal job opportunities. [ILO; OECD; UDHR]
- MNCs should provide equal pay for equal work. [ILO; UDHR]
- MNCs should give advance notice of changes in operations, especially plant closings, and mitigate the adverse effects of these changes. [ILO; OECD]

- MNCs should provide favorable work conditions, limited working hours, holidays with pay, and protection against unemployment. [UDHR]
- MNCs should promote job stability and job security, avoiding arbitrary dismissals and providing severance pay for those unemployed. [ILO; UDHR]
- MNCs should respect local host-country job standards and upgrade the local labor force through training. [ILO; OECD]
- MNCs should adopt adequate health and safety standards for employees and grant them the right to know about job-related health hazards. [ILO]
- MNCs should, minimally, pay basic living wages to employees. [ILO; UDHR]
- MNCs' operations should benefit lower-income groups of the host nation. [ILO]
- MNCs should balance job opportunities, work conditions, job training, and living conditions among migrant workers and host-country nationals. [Helsinki]

Consumer protection

- MNCs should respect host-country laws and policies regarding the protection of consumers. [OECD; TNC Code]
- MNCs should safeguard the health and safety of consumers by various disclosures, safe packaging, proper labelling, and accurate advertising. [TNC Code]

Environmental protection

- MNCs should respect host-country laws, goals, and priorities concerning protection of the environment. [OECD; TNC Code; Helsinki]
- MNCs should preserve ecological balance, protect the environment, adopt preventive measures to avoid environmental harm, and rehabilitate environments damaged by operations. [OECD; TNC Code; Helsinki]
- MNCs should disclose likely environmental harms and minimize risks of accidents that could cause environmental damage. [OECD; TNC Code]
- MNCs should promote the development of international environmental standards. [TNC Code; Helsinki]
- MNCs should control specific operations that

contribute to pollution of air, water, and soils. [Helsinki]

- MNCs should develop and use technology that can monitor, protect, and enhance the environment. [OECD; Helsinki]

Political payments and involvement

- MNCs should not pay bribes nor make improper payments to public officials. [OECD; TNC Code]
- MNCs should avoid improper or illegal involvement or interference in the internal politics of host countries. [OECD; TNC Code]
- MNCs should not interfere in intergovernmental relations. [TNC Code]

Basic human rights and fundamental freedoms

- MNCs should respect the rights of all persons to life; liberty, security of person, and privacy. [UDHR; ECHR; Helsinki; ILO; TNC Code]
- MNCs should respect the rights of all persons to equal protection of the law, work, choice of job, just and favorable work conditions, and protection against unemployment and discrimination. [UDHR; Helsinki; ILO; TNC Code]

- MNCs should respect all persons' freedom of thought, conscience, religion, opinion and expression, communication, peaceful assembly and association, and movement and residence within each state. [UDHR; ECHR; Helsinki; ILO; TNC Code]
- MNCs should promote a standard of living to support the health and well-being of workers and their families. [UDHR; Helsinki; ILO; TNC Code]
- MNCs should promote special care and assistance to motherhood and childhood. [UDHR; Helsinki; ILO; TNC Code]

These guidelines should be viewed as a *collective* phenomenon since all of them do not appear in each of the six compacts. Table I reveals that the OECD compact and the proposed TNC CODE provide the most comprehensive coverage of the guideline categories. The relative lack of guidelines in the ECHR compact may be attributable to the considerable membership overlap with the Organization for Economic Cooperation and Development whose members subscribe to the OECD standards for multinationals. Human rights and employment conditions are clearly the leading guideline categories, while consumer protection and corporate political activity ap-

TABLE 1   Number of MNC Normative Guidelines by Category for Six Multilateral Compacts

	UDHR	ECHR	HELSINKI	OECD	ILO	TNC CODE	TOTAL
Employment Practices	6	—	—	4	10	—*	20
Consumer Protection	—	—	—	1	—	2	3
Environmental Protection	—	—	5	4	—	4	13
Political Activity	—	—	—	2	—	3	5
Human Rights (re: work)	5	2	5	—	5	5	22
TOTAL	11	2	10	11	15	14	63

*It is expected, but is not a foregone certainty, that the Transnational Corporate Code of Conduct will incorporate into its provisions regarding employment practices the bulk and central meaning of those set forth in the ILO Tripartite Declaration. Hence, their omission in this Table should not be construed to mean that they have been ignored or overlooked by the drafters of the TNC Code.

pear infrequently. Table 1 suggests that the respective compacts have "specialized" in different types of normative issues involving corporate practices, the most obvious example being the ILO's emphasis on employment issues. The argument of this paper is that the collective weight of the guidelines is more important than the absence of some of them from specific international agreements. Clearly their inclusion across the board would strengthen the case for a global normative system intended to guide corporate practices.

These normative guidelines have direct implications for a wide range of *specific* corporate programs and policies. They include policies regarding childcare, minimum wages, hours of work, employee training and education, adequate housing and health care, pollution control efforts, advertising and marketing activities, severance pay, privacy of employees and consumers, information concerning on-the-job hazards, and, especially for those companies with operations in South Africa, such additional matters as the place of residence and free movement of employees. Quite clearly, the guidelines are not intended to be, nor do they act as, mere rhetoric. Nor do they deal with peripheral matters. They have direct applicability to many of the *central* operations and policies of multinational enterprises.

THE NORMATIVE SOURCES OF THE GUIDELINES

These guides for the practices and policies of multinational companies seem to rest upon and be justified by four normative orientations. Given sets of the guidelines can be tied directly to one or more of these moral sources.

National sovereignty is one such source. All six compacts invoke the inviolability of national sovereignty. In acting on the compacts' principles, each nation is to take care not to infringe on the sovereignty of its neighbors. Hence, preservation of a nation's integrity and self-interest appears to be one of the moral foundations on which such multilateral accords rest. Multinational enterprises are urged to respect the aims, goals, and directions of a host-country's economic and social development and its cultural and historical traditions. Companies' plans and goals should not contravene these components of a nation's being and sovereignty. Nor should they interfere in the internal political affairs of host countries through improper political activities, political bribes, or questionable payments of any kind made to political candidates or public officials.

Society equity is another normative basis underlying some of the specific corporate guidelines. Pay scales are to be established in ways that will insure equity between men and women, racial and ethnic groups, professional and occupational groups, host-country nationals and parent-country expatriates, indigenous employees and migrant workers, and those well-off and those least-advantaged. The same equity principle is advocated for job opportunities, job training, treatment of the unemployed, and the provision of other work-related benefits and services.

Market integrity is yet another source of moral authority and justification for some of the guidelines identified above, as well as for a large number of other guidelines specified in other agreements that are not treated here which have to do with restrictive business practices, the transnational flow of capital investments, the repatriation of profits, the rights of ownership, and similar matters. Among the normative corporate guidelines listed earlier, those tinged with the notion of market integrity include restrictions on political payments and bribes that might inject non-market considerations into business transactions, a recognition of private collective bargaining (rather than government mandates) as a preferred technique for establishing pay scales, working conditions, and benefits for employees, and some (but not all) of the consumer protections sought in the accords.

By far the most fundamental, comprehensive, widely acknowledged, and pervasive source of moral authority for the corporate guidelines is *human rights and fundamental freedoms*. This concept is given eloquent expression in the UN Universal Declaration of Human Rights. It is then picked up and adopted by the framers of four of the other five accords analyzed in this paper. Only the OECD Guidelines for Multinational Enterprises fail to invoke the specific language or the basic meaning of human rights and fundamental freedoms as the normative principle on which these accords are erected, although the OECD Guidelines incorporate some of these rights and freedoms as specific duties and obligations of multinationals. As previously noted, a number of OECD members are signatories to the European Convention on Human Rights, thereby subscribing to the basic principles of the Universal Declaration of Human Rights.

Essentially, the Declaration of Human Rights proclaims the existence of a whole host of human rights and freedoms, saying that they are inherent in the human condition. "All human beings are born free and equal in dignity and rights." "Equal and inalienable rights" are possessed by "all members of the human family" who also manifest an "inherent dignity." Other language speaks of "fundamental human rights," "the dignity and worth of the human person," "the equal rights of men and women," and "fundamental freedoms." These rights and freedoms exist "without distinction of any kind." They are understood as a common possession of humankind, not dependent on membership in any particular group, organization, nation, or society.

This invocation of human rights, as a philosophical principle, owes much to Immanuel Kant. In effect, the Declaration of Human Rights posits the Kantian person as the fundament of moral authority. The human person is said to possess an inherent worth and dignity, as well as inalienable and equal rights and freedoms. This being true of all human beings, correlative duties and obligations are thereby imposed on everyone to respect and not to interfere with the rights of others. No one person is warranted in using another as a means to promote one's own ends and purposes, absent a freely-given informed consent. Hence, a deceptively simple algorithm based on rights and duties sets the stage for the specification of normative rules of conduct for governments, groups, individuals, and—for present purposes—multinational enterprises[1]

As powerful and compelling as the human rights principle is, it does compete with the other three normative sources—national sovereignty, social equity, and market integrity. This means that human rights are conditioned by political, social, and economic values. Rights do not stand alone or outside the normal range of human institutions, diverse as those institutions are around the globe and from society to society. The nation remains a sacred repository of group allegiance and fierce loyalty, an institution whose leaders at times are fully capable of depriving their own citizens and others of fundamental rights. Witness South Africa's apartheid system, China's brutal suppression of the student-led democracy movement, and the totalitarian excesses of Romania's communist leaders. In all three cases, the state and nation were invoked as ultimate criteria justifying the denial of human rights.

Moreover, societies everywhere erect systems of social status and class, instilling notions of "just claims" and insisting that most people should "know their place." For example, women around the globe find their rights and their life opportunities restricted by male-dominated economic and political systems. The same can be said of the widest variety of ethnic, religious, and racial groups throughout the world, whose fundamental rights and freedoms are often sacrificed on the altar of "social equity" as defined by dominant and competing groups.

Few economic institutions in modern times have appealed more powerfully than markets, whether directed by decentralized economic actors or by centralized states. Those who safeguard the integrity of markets, including officials responsible for high-level governmental or corporate policies, frequently accept the "market necessity" of closing a plant, shifting operations to lower-wage areas, or "busting" a trade union—all in the alleged interest of "allowing the market to work" or "enhancing national and corporate productivity." Doing so may deprive employees of jobs, living wages, retirement security, and other workplace rights.

Hence, in these several ways, rights everywhere are hedged in by such political, social, and economic features of human society. The behavioral guidelines for multinational corporations seem to have been woven, not from a single philosophic principle but by a blending of normative threads. At the pattern's center stand human rights and fundamental freedoms, for in the international compacts reference is found most frequently to this normative marker. But the strands of national sovereignty, social equity, and market integrity are woven into the overall pattern, coloring and giving form to the expression of human rights. Thus are human rights conditioned by societal factors.

One important trait is responsible for the normative dominance of the human rights principle. The human rights spoken of in the Universal Declaration of Human Rights are transcultural. As a principle, human rights span and disregard cultural and national boundaries, class systems, ethnic groupings, economic levels, and other human arrangements which for a variety of reasons differentiate between individuals and groups. Human rights are just that—human. They inhere in *all* humans, regardless of imposed societal classifications and exclusions. They can be defined, disregarded, or violated but they cannot be eradicated.

A transcultural character cannot be claimed for the other three normative sources. National sovereignty is by definition bound to and expressive of the nation. If "nation" is understood to embrace, not only the nation-state but also identification with and allegiance to an ethnic grouping, then it might be more accurate to speak of "socio-ethnicity" as the kind of sovereignty whose protection is sought. In any event, neither "nation-state" nor "socio-ethnic group" is or can be transcultural.

Similarly, social equity meanings rarely if ever span cultural boundaries, in spite of Marxist class theory to the contrary or even the mightiest efforts of Third World nations to see and organize themselves as the world's exploited underclass. That they *are* a global underclass, mistreated, and denied many opportunities by their more prosperous neighbors has not yet bound them together into a solid bloc that could be called transcultural.

Market integrity remains tied firmly to nation-states, even as regional interstate markets such as the European Common Market and the Andean Common Market emerge. Economic systems based on the market principle bear the marks of their national parent's political and ideological institutions. The relatively freer markets that have emerged during the 1980s in the Soviet Union, Eastern Europe, and China are heavily conditioned by the prevailing governmental philosophies of the respective countries, and their operation is not permitted to contravene the perceived needs of the state. The same may be said of markets in the United States, as one observes the ideological swings that accompany successive presidential administrations, legislative elections, and judicial decisions. United States government-imposed commercial sanctions against South Africa, the Soviet Union, Poland, Cuba, Nicaragua, Libya, and other nations reveal the nation-bound character of market operations.

Except for the human rights principle, all other normative sources that undergird the multinational corporate guidelines are thus culture bound, unable to break out of their respective societal contexts. By contrast, human rights are seen to be transcultural. They are the glue or the linchpin that holds the entire normative system together in a coherent international whole. While conditioned by desires for national (or socio-ethnic) sovereignty, social equity, and market integrity—thus finding their operational meaning within a societal context—human rights express attitudes, yearnings, and beliefs common to all humankind. In that sense, they form the core of a global system whose normative aim is to regulate the practices of multinational corporations.

This rights-based normative system finds justification in two ways. One is through deontological obligations implicit in human rights. Here, the philosopher speaks to us. The other justification is more directly operational, taking the form of lessons learned from human experience about the formation and sustenance of human values. These lessons are taught by social scientists. Each of these rationales calls for further elaboration.

RATIONALE I: DEONTOLOGICAL NORMS

The normative corporate guidelines may be seen as extensions and manifestations of broad deontological, i.e., duty-based, principles of human conduct. These principles provide a philosophic basis for defining the duties and obligations of multinational enterprises.

The concurring governments, in the several compacts mentioned here, are saying to multinational enterprises:

- Because your employees have rights to work, to security, to freedom of association, to healthful and safe work conditions, to a pay scale that sustains them and their families at a dignified level of subsistence, to privacy, and to be free from discrimination at work, the managers of multinational corporations incur duties and obligations to respect such rights, to promote them where and when possible, and to avoid taking actions that would deny these rights to the corporation's employees and other stakeholders.

- Because humans and their communities have rights to security, to health, and to the opportunity to develop themselves to their fullest potentials, corporations have an obligation to avoid harming the ecological balance on which human community life and health depend and a positive duty to promote environmental conditions conducive to the pursuit and protection of human rights.

- Because consumers have rights to safe and effective products and to know the quality and traits of the products and services they need to sustain life, companies are obligated, i.e., they have a duty, to offer such products for sale under conditions that permit a free, uncoerced choice for the consumer.

- Because human beings can lay claim to a set of human rights and fundamental freedoms enumerated in the Universal Declaration of Human Rights, multinational corporations are duty-bound to promote, protect, and preserve those rights and freedoms and to avoid trampling on them through corporate operations. The corporations' Kantian duty is implied in the Kantian rights held by all.

A moral imperative is thus imposed on corporations. The source of this deontological imperative is the rights and freedoms that inhere in all human persons. The corporation is bound, by this moral logic, to respect all persons within the purview of its decisions, policies, and actions. In some such fashion as this, the Universal Declaration of Human Rights serves as the deontological fount, the moral fundament, that defines a corporation's basic duties and obligations toward others. The Declaration's moral principles have been extended to many if not most of the multilateral compacts of the past 40 years, many of whose specific provisions take the form of normative guides for corporate actions across a large range of issues. So goes the moral logic of the accords and compacts.

This philosophic position is compelling and convincing. However, the case for a transcultural corporate ethic need not rest on philosophical arguments alone, or, more positively, the deontological position can be considerably enriched and strengthened by considering the role of human experience as a creator of human values.

RATIONALE II:
EXPERIENCE-BASED VALUES

Respect for persons, respect for community integrity, respect for ecological balance, and respect for tested human experience in many spheres of life can be understood both deontologically and as adaptive human value orientations. As value phenomena, they are compatible with the needs and experiences of the world's peoples in a technological era. The need to proclaim many of the rights that appear in the Universal Declaration of Human Rights grew directly out of the gross violations of human rights during the pre-war and war periods of the 1930s and 1940s. Those experiences inspired most of the world's governments to take collective action, in the form of a proclamation, to define an acceptable number of such rights and to urge all to nourish and safeguard them.

Since that time, societies around the globe have felt the bite and seen the promise of technology spawned and applied by multinational corporations and governments. They have experienced the benefits, and have often borne the costs, of business operations undertaken without much regard for environmental, human, and community interests. These experiences have been as compelling, if not as traumatic, as those of the pre-war and war years when human rights were trampled. They have generated widespread agreement and belief in a network of experienced-based values that sustain the lives of individuals, their communities, and their societies. It is these values that have found their way into the several multilateral compacts and accords discussed here. Corporations are urged, not just to tend to their deontological duties but also to support, and not to override, the values that have been found through experience to undergird human flourishing.

Speaking of the role played by experience in formulating value standards, sociologist Robin Williams (1979: 22, 45) reminds us that

> . . . values are learned. This means that they are developed through some kind of experience. . . . Similar repeated and pervasive experiences are often characteristic of large numbers of persons similarly situated in society; such experiences are described, discussed, and appraised by the persons involved. The communication of common appraisals eventually builds value standards, which often become widely accepted across many social and cultural boundaries. . . .
> . . . value orientations, repeatedly experienced and reformulated by large numbers of persons over extended periods, will eventually become intellectualized as components of a comprehensive world view.

The gathering together of such experience-derived values concerning the human condition has produced "a comprehensive world view" of what is thought to be morally acceptable behavior by multinational enterprises. The specific "components" of that world view are the normative corporate guidelines described earlier. Humankind is speaking here, making known the basic, minimum, socially acceptable conditions for the conduct of economic enterprise. It is a voice that speaks the language of philosophically inspired rights and duties, as well as the language of a social-scientific conception of experienced-based, adaptive human values. The outcome in both cases is movement toward a transcultural corporate ethic, which is manifested in the six multilateral compacts or codes of conduct discussed here.

Another observer (Dilloway, 1986a: 427) reveals the transcultural moral potential of such international accords:

> The final justification, therefore, for a code of rights is, first, that it defines the conditions in which human potential can develop peacefully in an interdependent milieu; and, second, that such a code, whether for the individual or for interstate relations, offers the *only* frame of common ideas that can span the diversity of cultures, religions, living standards, and political and economic systems to create a common nexus of humane practice for an emergent world community.

This view is echoed by Richard Falk (1980:67, 108):

> To think of human rights in the world as a whole . . . is itself a reflection of the emergence, however weakly, of a planetary perspective based on the notion that persons . . . warrant our normative attention.

Nor is there is any reason to restrict this "frame of common ideas"—this morality of the commons—to multinational enterprises alone. It would apply with equal force to domestic and multinational companies. Where nations have been able to identify and agree upon common ethical principles and com-

mon values that reflect the experience of even the most diverse cultures, a moral minimum has been established. It remains within the power of some governments and their citizens and businesses to exceed this minimum, while other governments' powers may be insufficiently dedicated to meet even the minimum moral standards. But this minimum—the international common morality, the "common nexus of humane practice," the planetary perspective—stands as a benchmark to be striven for. While it exists, no corporation, domestic or multinational, can legitimately claim the right to operate without referring its policies and practices to this basic moral standard, this morality of the commons that has been writ large upon the global scene.

RESERVATIONS AND QUALIFICATIONS

Four objections might be raised to the derivation of these normative corporate guidelines. . . . [The first and second objections have been omitted. Eds.]

A third difficulty arises when arguing that normative corporate guidelines form the core of a transcultural corporate ethic. The guidelines are not subscribed to by all governments, and even some of the signatory governments may override or ignore them in some circumstances. Thus, it may be charged that the guidelines fall considerably short of representing a universal world view of what multinational corporations should do. Three of the accords are clearly a product of North American-European concerns and issues, while at least one other, the ILO Tripartite Declaration, tends to express the views of employee representatives from industrial nations. Only the UN Universal Declaration of Human Rights and the UN Code of Conduct for Transnational Corporations speak with a more or less global voice, and the last of these two accords has not yet actually come into existence.

This sceptical view is compelling and must be accepted as true. The world is not yet at a point where it can claim to have formulated or projected a set of normative corporate guidelines that are universally or globally accepted and observed. Very real difficulties and genuine controversies have accompanied efforts to forge multilateral compacts that are acceptable to all parties. As noted earlier, the general absence of effective legal enforcement mechanisms weakens these intergovernmental efforts. Sharp differences between multinationals and trade unions have been prominent (Rowan and Campbell, 1983). The sometimes muted struggle between Third World nations and their richer industrial neighbors is always there as a background factor conditioning negotiations. Social ethnicity and diverse religious affiliations become stumbling blocks to consensus. Geopolitical rivalry and *real politik* frequently frustrate the best efforts to reach multilateral accord. Such obstacles are seen by many to be the essence of the international scene, putting the creation of a universal code of conduct beyond reach (Feld, 1980; Waldman, 1980; Wallace, 1982; Windsor and Preston, 1988).

However, a modicum of hope may exist in the very *process* of trying to achieve consensus, prickly as it often is. If nations can agree on procedural rules for determining a fair distribution of the benefits and costs of joining with others in multilateral compacts, more international collaboration might be forthcoming (Windsor and Preston, 1988). The outcome might then be a gradual lessening of substantive differences and a drawing together of the negotiating parties. Robin Williams (1979: 30) explains how this process works:

> . . . opposition of interests and struggles among individuals and collectiveness within a continuing polity and societal system actually can contribute to the establishment and elaboration of generalized values and symbols. . . . If successive contests and conflicts are then successfully resolved without repudiation of the values which legitimate the conflict-resolving process or mechanisms, the more highly generalized values will come more and more to be regarded as axiomatic or unchallengable. Although the specific social implications of the general value principle will be changed through successive occasions, nevertheless, all parties come to have a stake in maintaining the complex value referent as a resource for the future.

This process-based outcome is also thought to be a factor by the UN Centre on Transnational Corporations (United Nations, 1988: 361):

> . . . certain substantive principles are known and relatively undisputed in practice . . . there exists today a large body of authoritative material—agreements, declarations, statements, etc.—on the issues at hand. They are not all identical, of course, . . . but there is also considerable coincidence of views.
>
> . . . Even where binding legal obligations are not created, legitimate expectations may be established as to the application of corresponding standards within reasonable bounds.

It it worth remembering that corporations remain remarkably attuned to public perceptions of their images and reputations, displaying an often surprising sensitivity to public criticism of their policies and actions. The reasons are frequently self protective, rather than stemming from altruistic or socially responsible motives. Even so, the hovering presence and repeated expression of moral principles seemingly accepted by large public blocs and their governments may influence corporate behavior toward voluntary compliance with these normative standards.

A fourth difficulty is that the normative guidelines are obviously an incomplete set of moral instructions to enterprises. They do not cover many important matters and issues related to multinational corporate operations.

None of the five categories shown in Table I contains an exhaustive list of all possible issues and needed guidelines. One can easily identify other categories and types of issues relevant to multinational business that apparently have not found their way into this particular group of compacts. . . .

The argument of this paper does not require that all possible issues be included nor that all parties accept all of the provisions of the compacts. It is not claimed that we are witnessing more than the bare beginnings of a globally oriented system of normative principles governing corporate behavior. The only claim being made is that the general outlines of such a system are now discernible and partially operational.

LESSONS FOR POLICY MAKERS

Those who set policies, whether for public or private institutions, can find some important lessons in these multinational codes of conduct.

The most compelling lesson is that highly diverse governments and societies have been able to reach a workable consensus about some core normative directives for multinational enterprises. That should send a strong message to corporate leaders everywhere that the world's peoples, speaking through their governments, are capable of setting standards intended to guide corporate practices and policies into morally desirable channels. As noted, there continues to be much disagreement among governments about many of these issues, but failure to agree on everything should not be allowed to cloak an achieved consensus on many other issues.

Wise corporate leaders will be able to interpret this consensus as a framework of public expectations on which the policies of their own companies can be based. Global stakeholders have set out their positions on a large range of problems and issues that matter to them. In effect, corporations are being offered an opportunity to match their own operations to these public expectations. The best ones will do so. The others may wish they had if, in failing to heed the normative messages, they encounter rising hostility and increased governmental intervention in their affairs. . . .

Acting to promote this normative consensus can be encouraged if policy makers understand both the philosophic roots and the experienced-based values from which these international agreements draw their meaning and strength. The philosophic concept of the human person that one finds in these multilateral compacts, and the human and humane values that grow out of shared global experiences, are no mere passing fancy of a planetary people. Building policy on these twin foundations will bring government and business into alignment with the deep structure of human aspirations.

BEYOND MULTINATIONALS: THE CULTURE OF ETHICS

The transcultural corporate ethic described here is only one part of a much more comprehensive, universal moral order whose shadowy outlines are only partially apparent. This broader "culture of ethics" includes all of those fundamental values and moral orientations that have been proven through long experience to contribute to the sustenance and flourishing of human persons within their communities (Frederick, 1986). It will be important, and increasingly apparent, that all economic enterprises, public and private, domestic and multinational, are bound to acknowledge the moral force of this culture of ethics and to shape their policies and practices accordingly. This "moral dimension" of economic analysis and corporate decision making can no longer be set aside or treated as a peripheral matter (Etzioni, 1988). As human societies are drawn ever closer together by electronic and other technologies, and as they face the multiple threats posed by the unwise and heedless use of these devices, it will become ever more necessary to reach agreement on the core values and ethical principles that permit a humane life to be lived by all. Such planetary agreement is now visible, though yet feeble in its rudiments. This broadscale culture of ethics draws upon many societal, religious, and philosophical sources. It is a great chorus of human voices, human aspirations, and human experiences, arising out of societal and cultural and individual diversity, that expresses the collective normative needs of a global people.

NOTE

1. The algorithm is "deceptively simple" by seeming to overlook the enormous volume of argumentation, qualifications, and exceptions to Kant's views that has been produced by succeeding generations of philosophers. Extended discussion of theories of human rights may be found in Shue (1980) and Nickel (1987). Thomas Donaldson (1989) has developed a far more sophisticated view of ethical algorithms than the one offered here, and I am indebted to him for both the concept and the phrase itself.

REFERENCES

Dilloway, A. J.: 1986a. "Human Rights and Peace," in Ervin Laszlo and Jong Youl Yoo (eds.), *World Encyclopedia of Peace*, vol. 1 (Pergamon Press, Oxford), p. 427.

———: 1986b, "International Bill of Rights," in Ervin Laszlo and Jong Youl Yoo (eds.), *World Encyclopedia of Peace*, vol. 1 (Pergamon Press, Oxford), pp. 458–9.

Donaldson, Thomas: 1989, *The Ethics of International Business* (Oxford University Press, New York).

Etzioni, Amitai: 1988, *The Moral Dimension: Toward a New Economics* (Free Press, New York).

Falk, Richard: 1980, "Theoretical Foundations of Human Rights," in Paula Newberg (ed.): *The Politics of Human Rights* (New York University Press, New York).

Feld, Werner J.: 1980, *Multinational Corporations and U.N. Politics: The Quest for Codes of Conduct* (Pergamon Press, New York).

Frederick, William C.: 1986, "Toward CSR3: Why Ethical Analysis is Indispensable and Unavoidable in Corporate Affairs," *California Management Review* **28**(3), 126–41.

Nickel, James W.: 1987, *Making Sense of Human Rights: Philosophical Reflections on the Universal Declaration of Human Rights* (University of California Press, Berkeley).

Rowan, Richard L., and Duncan C. Campbell: 1983, "The Attempt to Regulate Industrial Relations through International Codes of Conduct," *Columbia Journal of World Business* **18**(2), 64–72.

Shue, Henry, 1980, *Basic Rights: Subsistence, Affluence, and U.S. Foreign Policy* (Princeton University Press, Princeton, N.J.).

United Nations: 1983, *Human Rights: A Compilation of International Instruments* (United Nations, New York).

———: 1988, *Transnational Corporations in World Development: Trends and Prospects* (United Nations, New York).

Waldman, Raymond J.: 1980, *Regulating International Business through Codes of Conduct* (American Enterprise Institute, Washington, D.C.).

Wallace, Cynthia Day: 1982, *Legal Control of the Multinational Enterprise: National Regulatory Techniques and the Prospects for International Controls* (Martinus Nijhoff, The Hague).

Williams, Robin: 1979, 'Change and Stability in Values and Value Systems', in Milton Rokeach, *Understanding Human Values* (Free Press, New York).

Windsor, Duane, and Lee E. Preston: 1988, "Corporate Governance, Social Policy and Social Performance in the Multinational Corporation", in Lee E. Preston (ed.), *Research in Corporate Social Performance and Policy*, vol. 10 (JAI Press, Greenwich, Conn.).

Dow Chemical Company and Shell Oil Company, v. Domingo Castro Alfaro et al.

Supreme Court of Texas

Because its analysis and reasoning are correct I join in the majority opinion without reservation. I write separately, however, to respond to the dissenters who mask their inability to agree among themselves with competing rhetoric. In their zeal to implement their own preferred social policy that Texas corporations not be held responsible at home for harm caused abroad, these dissenters refuse to be restrained by either express statutory language or the compelling precedent, previously approved by this very court, holding that forum non conveniens does not apply in Texas. To accomplish the desired social engineering, they must invoke yet another legal fiction with a fancy name to shield alleged wrongdoers, the so-called doctrine of *forum non conveniens*. The refusal of a Texas corporation to confront a Texas judge and jury is to be labelled "inconvenient" when what is really involved is not convenience but connivance to avoid corporate accountability.

The dissenters are insistent that a jury of Texans be denied the opportunity to evaluate the conduct of a Texas corporation concerning decisions it made in Texas because the only ones allegedly hurt are foreigners. Fortunately Texans are not so provincial and narrow-minded as these dissenters presume. Our citizenry recognizes that a wrong does not fade away because its immediate consequences are first felt far away rather than close to home. Never have we been required to forfeit our membership in the human race in order to maintain our proud heritage as citizens of Texas.

The dissenters argue that it is *inconvenient* and *unfair* for farmworkers allegedly suffering permanent physical and mental injuries, including irreversible sterility, to seek redress by suing a multinational corporation in a court three blocks away from its world headquarters and another corporation, which operates in Texas this country's largest chemical plant. Because the "doctrine" they advocate has nothing to do with fairness and convenience and everything to do with immunizing multinational corporations from accountability for their alleged torts causing injury abroad, I write separately.

THE FACTS

Respondents claim that while working on a banana plantation in Costa Rica for Standard Fruit Company, an American subsidiary of Dole Fresh Fruit Company, headquartered in Boca Raton, Florida, they were required to handle dibromochloropropane ["DBCP"], a pesticide allegedly manufactured and furnished to Standard Fruit by Shell Oil Company ["Shell"] and Dow Chemical Company ["Dow"]. The Environmental Protection Agency issued a notice of intent to cancel all food uses of DBCP on September 22, 1977. 42 Fed.Reg. 48026 (1977). It followed with an order suspending registrations of pesticides containing DBCP on November 3, 1977. 42 Fed.Reg. 57543 (1977). Before and after the E.P.A.'s ban of DBCP in the United States, Shell and

---

786 S.W. 2d 674 (Tex. 1990). Concurring opinion by Judge Doggett.

Dow apparently shipped several hundred thousand gallons of the pesticide to Costa Rica for use by Standard Fruit. The Respondents, Domingo Castro Alfaro and other plantation workers, filed suit in a state district court in Houston, Texas, alleging that their handling of DBCP caused them serious personal injuries for which Shell and Dow were liable under the theories of products liability, strict liability and breach of warranty.

Rejecting an initial contest to its authority by Shell and Dow, the trial court found that it had jurisdiction under Tex. Civ. Prac. & Rem.Code Ann. § 71.031 (Vernon 1986), but dismissed the cause on the grounds of forum non conveniens. The court of appeals reversed and remanded, holding that Section 71.031 provides a foreign plaintiff with an absolute right to maintain a death or personal injury cause of action in Texas without being subject to forum non conveniens dismissal. 751 S.W.2d 208. Shell and Dow have asked this court to reverse the judgment of the court of appeals and affirm the trial court's dismissal.

Shell Oil Company is a multinational corporation with its world headquarters in Houston, Texas. Dow Chemical Company, though headquartered in Midland, Michigan, conducts extensive operations from its Dow Chemical USA building located in Houston. Dow operates this country's largest chemical manufacturing plant within 60 miles of Houston in Freeport, Texas. The district court where this lawsuit was filed is three blocks away from Shell's world headquarters, One Shell Plaza in downtown Houston.

Shell has stipulated that all of its more than 100,000 documents relating to DBCP are located or will be produced in Houston. Shell's medical and scientific witnesses are in Houston. The majority of Dow's documents and witnesses are located in Michigan, which is far closer to Houston (both in terms of geography and communications linkages) than to Costa Rica. The respondents have agreed to be available in Houston for independent medical examinations, for depositions and for trial. Most of the respondents' treating doctors and co-workers have agreed to testify in Houston. Conversely, Shell and Dow have purportedly refused to make their witnesses available in Costa Rica.

The banana plantation workers allegedly injured by DBCP were employed by an American company on American-owned land and grew Dole bananas for export soley to American tables. The chemical allegedly rendering the workers sterile was researched, formulated, tested, manufactured, labeled and shipped by an American company in the United States to another American company. The decision to manufacture DBCP for distribution and use in the third world was made by these two American companies in their corporate offices in the United States. Yet now Shell and Dow argue that the one part of this equation that should not be American is the legal consequences of their actions.

FORUM NON CONVENIENS— "A COMMON LAW DOCTRINE OUT OF CONTROL"

As a reading of Tex.Civ.Prac. & Rem. Code Ann. § 71.031 (Vernon 1986) makes clear, the doctrine of forum non conveniens has been statutorily abolished in Texas. The decision in *Allen* v. *Bass*, . . . approved by this court, clearly holds that, upon a showing of personal jurisdiction over a defendant, article 4678, now section 71.031 of the Texas Civil Practice & Remedies Code, "opens the courts of this state to citizens of a neighboring state and gives them an absolute right to maintain a transitory action of the present nature and to try their cases in the courts of this state."

Displeased that *Allen* stands in the way of immunizing multinational corporations from suits seeking redress for their torts causing injury abroad, the dissenters doggedly attempt to circumvent this precedent. Unsuccessful with arguments based upon Texas law, they criticize the court for not justifying its result on public policy grounds.

Using the "Doctrine" to Kill the Litigation Altogether

Both as a matter of law and of public policy, the doctrine of forum non conveniens is without justification. The proffered foundations for it are "considerations of fundamental fairness and sensible and effective judicial administration." . . . In fact, the doctrine is favored by multinational defendants because a forum non conveniens dismissal is often outcome-determinative, effectively defeating the claim and denying the plaintiff recovery. . . .

Empirical data available demonstrate that less than four percent of cases dismissed under the doctrine of forum non conveniens ever reach trial in foreign court.[1] A forum non conveniens dismissal usually will end the litigation altogether, effectively excusing any liability of the defendant. The plaintiffs leave the courtroom without having had their case resolved on the merits.

The *Gulf Oil* Factors—Balanced Toward the Defendant

Courts today usually apply forum non conveniens by use of the factors set forth at length in *Gulf Oil Corp. v. Gilbert* . . . Briefly summarized, those factors are (i) the private interests of the litigants (ease and cost of access to documents and witnesses); and (ii) the public interest factors (the interest of the forum state, the burden on the courts, and notions of judicial comity). In the forty-three years in which the courts have grappled with the *Gulf Oil* fac-

tors, it has become increasingly apparent that their application fails to promote fairness and convenience. Instead, these factors have been used by defendants to achieve objectives violative of public policy. . . .

The Public Interest Factors. The three public interest factors asserted by Justice Gonzalez may be summarized as (1) whether the interests of the jurisdiction are sufficient to justify entertaining the lawsuit; (2) the potential for docket backlog; and (3) judicial comity. . . .

The next justification offered by the dissenters for invoking the legal fiction of "inconvenience" is that judges will be overworked. Not only will foreigners take our jobs, as we are told in the popular press; now they will have our courts. The xenophobic suggestion that foreigners will take over our courts "forcing our residents to wait in the corridors of our courthouses while foreign causes of action are tried," Gonzalez dissent, 786 S.W.2d at 690, is both misleading and false.

It is the height of deception to suggest that docket backlogs in our state's urban centers are caused by so-called "foreign litigation." This assertion is unsubstantiated empirically both in Texas and in other jurisdictions rejecting forum non conveniens.[2] Ten states, including Texas, have not recognized the doctrine. Within these states, there is no evidence that the docket congestion predicted by the dissenters has actually occurred. The best evidence, of course, comes from Texas itself. Although foreign citizens have enjoyed the statutory right to sue defendants living or doing business here since the 1913 enactment of the predecessor to Section 71.031 of the Texas Civil Practice and Remedies Code, reaffirmed in the 1932 decision in *Allen*, Texas has not been flooded by foreign causes of action.

Moreover, the United States Supreme

Court has indicated that docket congestion "is a wholly inappropriate consideration in virtually every other context." . . . If we begin to refuse to hear lawsuits properly filed in Texas because they are sure to require time, we set a precedent that can be employed to deny Texans access to these same courts.

Nor does forum non conveniens afford a panacea for eradicating congestion:

> Making the place of trial turn on a largely imponderable exercise of judicial discretion is extremely costly. Even the strongest proponents of the most suitable forum approach concede that it is inappropriately time-consuming and wasteful for the parties to have to "litigate in order to determine where they shall litigate." If forum non conveniens outcomes are not predictable, such litigation is bound to occur. . . . In terms of delay, expense, uncertainty, and a fundamental loss of judicial accountability, the most suitable forum version of forum non conveniens clearly costs more than it is worth.

Robertson, *supra,* 103 L.Q.Rev. at 414, 426.

Comity—deference shown to the interests of the foreign forum—is a consideration best achieved by rejecting forum non conveniens. Comity is not achieved when the United States allows its multinational corporations to adhere to a double standard when operating abroad and subsequently refuses to hold them accountable for those actions. As S. Jacob Scherr, Senior Project Attorney for the Natural Resources Defense Counsel, has noted

> There is a sense of outrage on the part of many poor countries where citizens are the most vulnerable to exports of hazardous drugs, pesticides and food products. At the 1977 meeting of the UNEP Governing Council, Dr. J.C. Kiano, the Kenyan minister for water development, warned that developing nations will no longer tolerate being used as dumping grounds for products that had not been adequately tested "and that their peoples should not be used as guinea pigs for determining the safety of chemicals."

Comment, *U.S. Exports Banned For Domestic Use, But Exported to Third World Countries,* 6 Int'l Tr.L.J. 95, 98 (1980–81) [hereinafter "*U.S. Exports Banned*"].

Comity is best achieved by "avoiding the possibility of 'incurring the wrath and distrust of the Third World as it increasingly recognizes that it is being used as the industrial world's garbage can.'" Note, *Hazardous Exports from a Human Rights Perspective,* 14 Sw.U.L. Rev. 81, 101 (1983) [hereinafter "*Hazardous Exports*"] (quoting Hon. Michael D. Barnes (Representative in Congress representing Maryland)).[3] . . .

PUBLIC POLICY & THE TORT LIABILITY OF MULTINATIONAL CORPORATIONS IN UNITED STATES COURTS

The abolition of forum non conveniens will further important public policy considerations by providing a check on the conduct of multinational corporations (MNCs). *See Economic Approach,* 22 Geo.Wash.J. Int'l L. & Econ. at 241. The misconduct of even a few multinational corporations can affect untold millions around the world.[4] For example, after the United States imposed a domestic ban on the sale of cancer-producing TRIS-treated children's sleepwear, American companies exported approximately 2.4 million pieces to Africa, Asia and South America. A similar pattern occurred when a ban was proposed for baby pacifiers that had been linked to choking deaths in infants. *Hazardous Exports, supra,* 14 Sw.U.L.Rev. at 82. These examples of indifference by some corporations towards children abroad are not unusual.[5]

The allegations against Shell and Dow, if

proven true, would not be unique, since production of many chemicals banned for domestic use has thereafter continued for foreign marketing.[6] Professor Thomas McGarity, a respected authority in the field of environmental law, explained:

> During the mid-1970s, the United States Environmental Protection Agency (EPA) began to restrict the use of some pesticides because of their environmental effects, and the Occupational Safety and Health Administration (OSHA) established workplace exposure standards for toxic and hazardous substances in the manufacture of pesticides. . . . [I]t is clear that many pesticides that have been severely restricted in the United States are used without restriction in many Third World countries, with resulting harm to fieldworkers and the global environment.

McGarity, *Bhopal and the Export of Hazardous Technologies,* 20 Tex.Int'l L.J. 333, 334 (1985) (citations omitted). By 1976, "29 percent, or 161 million pounds of all the pesticides exported by the United States were either unregistered or banned for domestic use." McWilliams, *Tom Sawyer's Apology: A Reevaluation of United States Pesticide Export Policy,* 8 Hastings Int'l & Comp.L.Rev. 61, 61 & n. 4 (1984). It is estimated that these pesticides poison 750,000 people in developing countries each year, of which 22,500 die. *Id.* at 62. Some estimates place the death toll from the "improper marketing of pesticides at 400,000 lives a year." *Id.* at 62 n. 7.

Some United States multinational corporations will undoubtedly continue to endanger human life and the environment with such activities until the economic consequences of these actions are such that it becomes unprofitable to operate in this manner. At present, the tort laws of many third world countries are not yet developed. *An Economic Approach, supra,* 22 Geo. Wash.J.Int'l L. & Econ. at 222–23. Industrialization "is occurring faster than the development of do-

mestic infrastructures necessary to deal with the problems associated with industry." *Exporting Hazardous Industries, supra,* 20 Int'l L. & Pol. at 791. When a court dismisses a case against a United States multinational corporation, it often removes the most effective restraint on corporate misconduct. *See An Economic Approach, supra,* 22 Geo.Wash.J.Int'l L. & Econ. at 241.

The doctrine of forum non conveniens is obsolete in a world in which markets are global and in which ecologists have documented the delicate balance of all life on this planet. The parochial perspective embodied in the doctrine of forum non conveniens enables corporations to evade legal control merely because they are transnational. This perspective ignores the reality that actions of our corporations affecting those abroad will also affect Texans. Although DBCP is banned from use within the United States, it and other similarly banned chemicals have been consumed by Texans eating foods imported from Costa Rica and elsewhere. *See* D. Weir & M. Schapiro, *Circle of Poison* 28–30, 77, 82–83 (1981). In the absence of meaningful tort liability in the United States for their actions, some multinational corporations will continue to operate without adequate regard for the human and environmental costs of their actions. This result cannot be allowed to repeat itself for decades to come.

As a matter of law and of public policy, the doctrine of forum non conveniens should be abolished. Accordingly, I concur. . . .

NOTES

1. Professor David Robertson of the University of Texas School of Law attempted to discover the subsequent history of each reported transnational case dismissed under forum non conveniens from *Gulf Oil v. Gilbert,* 330 U.S. 501, 67 S.Ct. 839, 91 L.Ed. 1055 (1947) to the end of 1984. Data was received on 55 personal injury cases and 30 commercial cases. Of the 55

personal injury cases, only one was actually tried in a foreign court. Only two of the 30 commercial cases reached trial. *See* Robertson, *supra,* at 419.

2. Evidence from the most recent and largest national study ever performed regarding the pace of litigation in urban trial courts suggests that there is no empirical basis for the dissenters' argument that Texas dockets will become clogged without forum non conveniens. The state of Massachusetts recognizes forum non conveniens. *See Minnis v. Peebles,* 24 Mass.App. 467, 510 N.E.2d 289 (1987). Conversely, the state of Louisiana has explicitly not recognized forum non conveniens since 1967. *See Kassapas v. Arkon Shipping Agency, Inc.,* 485 So.2d 565, 567 (La.App. 1986), *writ denied,* 488 So.2d 203 (1986), *cert. denied,* 479 U.S. 940, 107 S.Ct. 422, 93 L.Ed.2d 372 (1986); *Trahan v. Phoenix Ins. Co.,* 200 So.2d 118, 122 (La.App.1967). Nevertheless, the study revealed the median filing-to-disposition time for tort cases in Boston to be 953 days; in New Orleans, with no forum non conveniens, the median time for the disposition of tort cases was only 405 days. The study revealed the median disposition time for contract cases in Boston to be 1580 days, as opposed to a mere 271 days in New Orleans where forum non conveniens is not used. J. Goerdt, C. Lomvardias, G. Gallas & B. Mahoney, Examining Court Delay—The Pace of Litigation in 26 Urban Trial Courts, 1987 20, 22 (1989).

3. A senior vice-president of a United States multinational corporation acknowledged that "[t]he realization at corporate headquarters that liability for any [industrial] disaster would be decided in the U.S. courts, more than pressure from Third World governments, has forced companies to tighten safety procedures, upgrade plants, supervise maintenance more closely and educate workers and communities." Wall St. J., Nov. 26, 1985, at 22, col. 4 (quoting Harold Corbett, senior vice-president for environmental affairs at Monsanto Co.).

4. As one commentator observed, U.S. multinational corporations "adhere to a double standard when operating abroad. The lack of stringent environmental regulations and worker safety standards abroad and the relaxed enforcement of such laws in industries using hazardous processes provide little incentive for [multinational corporations] to protect the safety of workers, to obtain liability insurance to guard against the hazard of product defects or toxic tort exposure, or to take precautions to minimize pollution to the environment. *This double standard has caused catastrophic damages to the environment and to human lives.*"

Note, *Exporting Hazardous Industries: Should American Standards Apply?*, 20 Int'l L. & Pol. 777, 780–81 (1988) (emphasis added) (footnotes omitted) [hereinafter "*Exporting Hazardous Industries*"]. *See also* Diamond, *The Path of Progress Racks the Third World,* N.Y. Times, Dec. 12, 1984, at B1, col. 1.

5. A subsidiary of Sterling Drug Company advertised Winstrol, a synthetic male hormone severely restricted in the United States since it is associated with a number of side effects that the F.D.A. has called "virtually irreversible", in a Brazilian medical journal, picturing a healthy boy and recommending the drug to combat poor appetite, fatigue and weight loss. *U.S. Exports Banned, supra,* 6 Int'l Tr.L.J. at 96. The same company is said to have marketed Dipyrone, a painkiller causing a fatal blood disease and characterized by the American Medical Association as for use only as "a last resort," as "Novaldin" in the Dominican Republic. "Novaldin" was advertised in the Dominican Republic with pictures of a child smiling about its agreeable taste. *Id.* at 97. "In 1975, thirteen children in Brazil died after coming into contact with a toxic pesticide whose use had been severely restricted in this country." *Hazardous Exports, supra,* 14 Sw.U.L.Rev. at 82.

6. Regarding Leptophos, a powerful and hazardous pesticide that was domestically banned, S. Jacob Scherr stated that "In 1975 alone, Velsicol, a Texas-based corporation exported 3,092,842 pounds of Leptophos to thirty countries. Over half of that was shipped to Egypt, a country with no procedures for pesticide regulation or tolerance setting. In December 1976, the *Washington Post* reported that Leptophos use in Egypt resulted in the death of a number of farmers and illness in rural communities. . . . But despite the accumulation of data on Leptophos' severe neurotoxicity, Velsicol continued to market the product abroad for use on grain and vegetable crops while proclaiming the product's safety."

U.S. Exports Banned, 6 Int'l Tr.L.J. at 96.

The Guidelines for Multinational Enterprises

1. Multinational enterprises now play an important part in the economies of Member countries and in international economic relations, which is of increasing interest to governments. Through international direct investment, such enterprises can bring substantial benefits to home and host countries by contributing to the efficient utilisation of capital, technology and human resources between countries and can thus fulfil an important role in the promotion of economic and social welfare. But the advances made by multinational enterprises in organising their operations beyond the national framework may lead to abuse of concentrations of economic power and to conflicts with national policy objectives. In addition, the complexity of these multinational enterprises and the difficulty of clearly perceiving their diverse structures, operations and policies sometimes give rise to concern.

2. The common aim of the Member countries is to encourage the positive contributions which multinational enterprises can make to economic and social progress and to minimise and resolve the difficulties to which their various operations may give rise. In view of the transnational structure of such enterprises, this aim will be furthered by co-operation among the OECD countries where the headquarters of most of the multinational enterprises are established and which are the location of a substantial part of their operations. The Guidelines set out hereafter are designed to assist in the achievement of this common aim and to contribute to improving the foreign investment climate.

3. Since the operations of multinational enterprises extend throughout the world, including countries that are not Members of the Organisation, international co-operation in this field should extend to all States. Member countries will give their full support to efforts undertaken in co-operation with non-member countries, and in particular with developing countries, with a view to improving the welfare and living standards of all people both by encouraging the positive contributions which multinational enterprises can make and by minimising and resolving the problems which may arise in connection with their activities.

4. Within the Organisation, the programme of co-operation to attain these ends will be a continuing, pragmatic and balanced one. It comes within the general aims of the Convention on the Organisation for Economic Co-operation and Development (OECD) and makes full use of the various specialised bodies of the Organisation, whose terms of reference already cover many aspects of the role of multinational enterprises, notably in matters of international trade and payments, competition, taxation, manpower, industrial development, science and technology. In these bodies, work is being carried out on the identification of issues, the improvement of relevant qualitative and statistical information and the elaboration of proposals for action designed to strengthen inter-gov-

Annexed to the Declaration of 21st June 1976 by Governments of OECD Member Countries on International Investment and Multinational Enterprises, as amended in 1979 and 1984

ernmental co-operation. In some of these areas procedures already exist through which issues related to the operations of multinational enterprises can be taken up. This work could result in the conclusion of further and complementary agreements and arrangements between governments.

5. The initial phase of the co-operation programme is composed of a Declaration and three Decisions promulgated simultaneously as they are complementary and inter-connected, in respect of Guidelines for multinational enterprises, National Treatment for foreign-controlled enterprises and international investment incentives and disincentives.

6. The Guidelines set out below are recommendations jointly addressed by Member countries to multinational enterprises operating in their territories. These Guidelines, which take into account the problems which can arise because of the international structure of these enterprises, lay down standards for the activities of these enterprises in the different member countries. Observance of the Guidelines is voluntary and not legally enforceable. However, they should help to ensure that the operations of these enterprises are in harmony with national policies of the countries where they operate and to strengthen the basis of mutual confidence between enterprises and States.

7. Every State has the right to prescribe the conditions under which multinational enterprises operate within its national jurisdiction, subject to international law and to the international agreements to which it has subscribed. The entities of a multinational enterprise located in various countries are subject to the laws of these countries.

8. A precise legal definition of multinational enterprises is not required for the pur-

poses of the Guidelines. These usually comprise companies or other entities whose ownership is private, state or mixed, established in different countries and so linked that one or more of them may be able to exercise a significant influence over the activities of others and, in particular, to share knowledge and resources with the others. The degree of autonomy of each entity in relation to the others varies widely from one multinational enterprise to another, depending on the nature of the links between such entities and the fields of activity concerned. For these reasons, the Guidelines are addressed to the various entities within the multinational enterprise (parent companies and/or local entities) according to the actual distribution of responsibilities among them on the understanding that they will co-operate and provide assistance to one another as necessary to facilitate observance of the Guidelines. The word "enterprise" as used in these Guidelines refers to these various entities in accordance with their responsibilities.

9. The Guidelines are not aimed at introducing differences of treatment between multinational and domestic enterprises; wherever relevant they reflect good practice for all. Accordingly, multinational and domestic enterprises are subject to the same expectations in respect of their conduct wherever the Guidelines are relevant to both.

10. The use of appropriate international dispute settlement mechanisms, including arbitration, should be encouraged as a means of facilitating the resolution of problems arising between enterprises and Member countries.

11. Member countries have agreed to establish appropriate review and consultation procedures concerning issues arising in respect of the Guidelines. When multinational enterprises are made subject to conflicting re-

---

From T. M. Ocran, "Interregional Codes of Conduct for Transnational Corporations," *Connecticut Journal of Int'l Law* 2 (1986). Reprinted by permission.

quirements by Member countries, the governments concerned will co-operate in good faith with a view to resolving such problems either within the Committee on International Investment and Multinational Enterprises established by the OECD Council on 21st January 1975 or through other mutually acceptable arrangements.

Having regard to the foregoing considerations, the Member countries set forth the following Guidelines for multinational enterprises with the understanding that Member countries will fulfil their responsibilities to treat enterprises equitably and in accordance with international law and international agreements, as well as contractual obligations to which they have subscribed.

GENERAL POLICIES

Enterprises should:

1. Take fully into account established general policy objectives of the Member countries in which they operate;
2. In particular, give due consideration to those countries' aims and priorities with regard to economic and social progress, including industrial and regional development, the protection of the environment and consumer interests, the creation of employment opportunities, the promotion of innovation and the transfer of technology;
3. While observing their legal obligations concerning information, supply their entities with supplementary information the latter may need in order to meet requests by the authorities of the countries in which those entities are located for information relevant to the activities of those entities, taking into account legitimate requirements of business confidentiality;
4. Favour close co-operation with the local community and business interests;
5. Allow their component entities freedom to develop their activities and to exploit their competitive advantage in domestic and foreign markets, consistent with the need for specialisation and sound commercial practice;
6. When filling responsible posts in each country of operation, take due account of individual qualifications without discrimination as to nationality, subject to particular national requirements in this respect;
7. Not render—and they should not be solicited or expected to render—any bribe or other improper benefit, direct or indirect, to any public servant or holder of public office;
8. Unless legally permissible, not make contributions to candidates for public office or to political parties or other political organisations;
9. Abstain from any improper involvement in local political activities.

DISCLOSURE OF INFORMATION

Enterprises should, having due regard to their nature and relative size in the economic context of their operations and to requirements of business confidentiality and to cost, publish in a form suited to improve public understanding a sufficient body of factual information on the structure, activities and policies of the enterprise as a whole, as a supplement, in so far as necessary for this purpose, to information to be disclosed under the national law of the individual countries in which they operate. To this end, they should publish within reasonable time limits, on a regular basis, but at least annually, financial statements and other pertinent information relating to the enterprise as a whole, comprising in particular:

i) The structure of the enterprise, showing the name and location of the parent company, its main affiliates, its percentage ownership, direct and indirect, in these affiliates, including shareholdings between them;
ii) The geographical areas where operations are carried out and the principal activities carried on therein by the parent company and the main affiliates;
iii) The operating results and sales by geographi-

cal area and the sales in the major lines of business for the enterprise as a whole;

iv) Significant new capital investment by geographical area and, as far as practicable, by major lines of business for the enterprise as a whole;

v) A statement of the sources and uses of funds by the enterprise as a whole;

vi) The average number of employees in each geographical area;

vii) Research and development expenditure for the enterprise as a whole;

viii) The policies followed in respect of intragroup pricing;

ix) The accounting policies, including those on consolidation, observed in compiling the published information.

COMPETITION

Enterprises should, while conforming to official competition rules and established policies of the countries in which they operate:

1. Refrain from actions which would adversely affect competition in the relevant market by abusing a dominant position of market power, by means of, for example:
   a) Anti-competitive acquisitions;
   b) Predatory behaviour toward competitors;
   c) Unreasonable refusal to deal;
   d) Anti-competitive abuse of industrial property rights;
   e) Discriminatory (i.e., unreasonably differentiated) pricing and using such pricing transactions between affiliated enterprises as a means of affecting adversely competition outside these enterprises;
2. Allow purchasers, distributors and licensees freedom to resell, export, purchase and develop their operations consistent with law, trade conditions, the need for specialisation and sound commercial practice;
3. Refrain from participating in or otherwise purposely strengthening the restrictive effects of international or domestic cartels or restrictive agreements which adversely affect or eliminate competition and which are not generally or specifically accepted under applicable national or international legislation;

4. Be ready to consult and co-operate, including the provision of information, with competent authorities of countries whose interests are directly affected in regard to competition issues or investigations. Provision of information should be in accordance with safeguards normally applicable in this field.

FINANCING

Enterprises should, in managing the financial and commercial operations of their activities, and especially their liquid foreign assets and liabilities, take into consideration the established objectives of the countries in which they operate regarding balance of payments and credit policies.

TAXATION

Enterprises should:

1. Upon request of the taxation authorities of the countries in which they operate, provide, in accordance with the safeguards and relevant procedures of the national laws of these countries, the information necessary to determine correctly the taxes to be assessed in connection with their operations, including relevant information concerning their operations in other countries;
2. Refrain from making use of the particular facilities available to them, such as transfer pricing which does not conform to an arm's length standard, for modifying in ways contrary to national laws the tax base on which members of the group are assessed.

EMPLOYMENT AND INDUSTRIAL RELATIONS

Enterprises should, within the framework of law, regulations and prevailing labour relations and employment practices, in each of the countries in which they operate:

1. Respect the right of their employees to be represented by trade unions and other bona fide organisations of employees, and engage in constructive negotiations, either individually or through employers' associations, with such employee organisations with a view to reaching agreements on employment conditions, which should include provisions for dealing with disputes arising over the interpretation of such agreements, and for ensuring mutually respected rights and responsibilities;

2. *a)* Provide such facilities to representatives of the employees as may be necessary to assist in the development of effective collective agreements;

   b) Provide to representatives of employees information which is needed for meaningful negotiations on conditions of employment;

3. Provide to representatives of employees where this accords with local law and practice, information which enables them to obtain a true and fair view of the performance of the entity or, where appropriate, the enterprise as a whole;

4. Observe standards of employment and industrial relations not less favourable than those observed by comparable employers in the host country;

5. In their operations, to the greatest extent practicable, utilise, train and prepare for upgrading members of the local labour force in co-operation with representatives of their employees and, where appropriate, the relevant governmental authorities;

6. In considering changes in their operations which would have major effects upon the livelihood of their employees, in particular in the case of the closure of an entity involving collective lay-offs or dismissals, provide reasonable notice of such changes to representatives of their employees, and where appropriate to the relevant governmental authorities, and co-operate with the employee representatives and appropriate governmental authorities so as to mitigate to the maximum extent practicable adverse effects;

7. Implement their employment policies including hiring, discharge, pay, promotion and training without discrimination unless selectivity in respect of employee characteristics is in furtherance of established governmental policies which specifically promote greater equality of employment opportunity;

8. In the context of bona fide negotiations with representatives of employees on conditions of employment, or while employees are exercising a right to organise, not threaten to utilise a capacity to transfer the whole or part of an operating unit from the country concerned nor transfer employees from the enterprises' component entities in other countries in order to influence unfairly those negotiations or to hinder the exercise of a right to organise;

9. Enable authorised representatives of their employees to conduct negotiations on collective bargaining or labour management relations issues with representatives of management who are authorised to take decisions on the matters under negotiation.

SCIENCE AND TECHNOLOGY

Enterprises should:

1. Endeavour to ensure that their activities fit satisfactorily into the scientific and technological policies and plans of the countries in which they operate, and contribute to the development of national scientific and technological capacities, including as far as appropriate the establishment and improvement in host countries of their capacity to innovate;

2. To the fullest extent practicable, adopt in the course of their business activities practices which permit the rapid diffusion of technologies with due regard to the protection of industrial and intellectual property rights;

3. When granting licences for the use of industrial property rights or when otherwise transferring technology, do so on reasonable terms and conditions.

Case 1. *Foreign Assignment*

Sara Strong graduated with an MBA from UCLA four years ago. She immediately took a job in the correspondent bank section of the Security Bank of the American Continent. Sara was assigned to work on issues pertaining to relationships with correspondent banks in Latin America. She rose rapidly in the section and received three good promotions in three years. She consistently got high ratings from her superiors, and she received particularly high marks for her professional demeanor.

In her initial position with the bank, Sara was required to travel to Mexico on several occasions. She was always accompanied by a male colleague even though she generally handled similar business by herself on trips within the United States. During her trips to Mexico she observed that Mexican bankers seemed more aware of her being a woman and were personally solicitous to her, but she didn't discern any major problems. The final decisions on the work that she did were handled by male representatives of the bank stationed in Mexico.

A successful foreign assignment was an important step for those on the "fast track" at the bank. Sara applied for a position in Central or South America and was delighted when she was assigned to the bank's office in Mexico City. The office had about twenty bank employees and was headed by William Vitam. The Mexico City office was seen as a preferred assignment by young executives at the bank.

After a month, Sara began to encounter problems. She found it difficult to be effective in dealing with Mexican bankers—the clients. They appeared reluctant to accept her authority, and they would often bypass her in important matters. The problem was exacerbated by Vitam's compliance in her being bypassed. When she asked that the clients be referred back to her, Vitam replied, "Of course, that isn't really practical." Vitam made matters worse by patronizing her in front of clients and by referring to her as "my cute assistant" and "our lady banker." Vitam never did this when only Americans were present and in fact treated her professionally and with respect in internal situations.

Sara finally complained to Vitam that he was undermining her authority and effectiveness; she asked him in as positive a manner as possible to help her. Vitam listened carefully to Sara's complaints, then replied, "I'm glad that you brought this up, because I've been meaning to sit down and talk to you about my little game playing in front of the clients. Let me be frank with you. Our clients think you're great, but they just don't understand a woman in authority, and you and I aren't going to be able to change their attitudes overnight. As long as the clients see you as my assistant and deferring to me, they can do business with you. I'm willing to give you as much responsibility as they can handle your having. I *know* you can handle it. But we just have to tread carefully. You and I know that my remarks in front of clients don't mean anything. They're just a way of playing the game Latin style. I know it's frustrating for you, but I really need you to support me on this. It's not going to affect your promotions. You just have to act like it's my responsibility." Sara replied that she would try to cooperate, but that basically she found her role demeaning.

As time went on, Sara found that the patronizing actions in front of clients bothered her more and more. She spoke to Vitam

---

This case was prepared by Thomas Dunfee and Diana Robertson, The Wharton School.

again, but he was firm in his position and urged her to try to be a little more flexible, even a little more "feminine."

Sara also had a problem with Vitam over policy. The Mexico City office had five younger women who worked as receptionists and secretaries. They were all situated at work stations at the entrance of the office. They were required to wear standard uniforms that were colorful and slightly sexy. Sara protested the requirement that uniforms be worn because (1) they were inconsistent to the image of the banking business and (2) they were demeaning to the women who had to wear them. Vitam just curtly replied that he had received a lot of favorable comments about the uniforms from clients of the bank.

Several months later, Sara had what she thought would be a good opportunity to deal with the problem. Tom Fried, an executive vice president who had been a mentor for her since she arrived at the bank, was coming to Mexico City; she arranged a private conference with him. She described her problems and explained that she was not able to be effective in this environment and that she worried that it would have a negative effect on her chance of promotion within the bank. Fried was very careful in his response. He spoke of certain "realities" that the bank had to respect, and he urged her to "see it through" even though he could understand how she would feel that things weren't fair.

Sara found herself becoming more aggressive and defensive in her meetings with Vitam and her clients. Several clients asked that other bank personnel handle their transactions. Sara has just received an Average rating, which noted "the beginnings of a negative attitude about the bank and its policies."

Questions

1. What obligations does an international company have to ensure that its employees are not harmed, for instance, by having their chances for advancement limited by the social customs of a host country?
2. What international moral code, if any, is being violated by Security Bank of the American Continent?
3. Has the bank made the correct decision by opting to follow the norms of the host country?
4. What steps can be taken on the part of the internationals and their employees to avoid or resolve situations in which employees are offended or harmed by host country practices?
5. In this situation does morality require respect for Mexican practices, or does it require respect for Sara Strong? Are these incompatible?

CASE 2. *Transnational Oil Corporations in the Ecuadorian Amazon*

The Ecuadorian Amazon is one of the most biologically diverse forests in the world. It is home to cicadas, scarlet macaws, squirrel monkeys, freshwater pink dolphins, and thousands of other species. Many of these species have small populations, making them extremely sensitive to disturbance. Indigenous Indian populations have lived in har-

This case was prepared by D. G. Arnold and is based on Robert F. Kennedy, Jr., "Amazon Crude," *The Amicus Journal,* vol. 13, no. 2; James Brooke, "New Effort Would Test Possible Coexistence of Oil and Rain Forest," *New York Times,* February 26, 1991.

mony with these species for centuries. They have fished and hunted in and around the rivers and lakes. And they have raised crops of cacao, coffee, fruits, nuts, and tropical woods in *chakras*, models of sustainable agroforestry; each one the product of ancient tribal wisdom and backbreaking labor.

Ten thousand feet beneath the Amazon floor lies one of Ecuador's most important resources: rich deposits of heavy grade crude oil. The Ecuadorian government regards the oil as the best way to keep up with the country's payments on its $12 billion foreign debt obligations. For twenty years, American oil companies, lead by Texaco, have extracted oil from beneath the Ecuadorian Amazon. (The United States is the primary importer of Ecuadorian oil.) They have constructed 400 drill sites and hundreds of miles of roads and pipelines, including a primary pipeline which extends for 280 miles across the Andes. Large tracts of forest have been clear cut to make way for these facilities. Indian lands, including *chakras*, have been taken and bulldozed, typically without compensation. In the village of Pacayacu, the central square is occupied by a drilling platform.

The Ecuadorian government has made little effort to regulate oil company operations. However, officials estimate that the primary pipeline alone has spilled more than 16.8 million gallons of oil into the Amazon over an eighteen-year period. Spills from secondary pipelines have never been estimated or recorded; however, smaller tertiary pipelines dump 10,000 gallons of petroleum per week into the Amazon, and production pits dump approximately 4.3 million gallons of toxic production wastes and treatment chemicals into the forest's rivers, streams, and groundwater each day. (By comparison, the *Exxon Valdez* spilled 10.8 million gallons of oil into Alaska's Prince William Sound.)

Rivers and lakes have been contaminated by oil and petroleum; heavy metals such as arsenic, cadmium, cyanide, lead, and mercury; poisonous industrial solvents; lethal concentrations of chloride salt; and other highly toxic chemicals. The only treatment any of these chemicals receive occurs when the oil company burns waste pits in order to reduce petroleum content. Villagers report that the chemicals return as black rain, polluting what little fresh water remains. What is not burnt off seeps through the unlined walls of the pits into the groundwater. Cattle are found with their stomachs rotted out, crops are destroyed, and animals are gone from the forest and fish from the lakes and rivers. Health officials and community leaders report sick and deformed children, adults and children with skin rashes, abscesses, headaches, dysentery, infections, and respiratory ailments.

In 1972 Texaco signed a contract requiring it to turn over all of its operations to Ecuador's national oil company, Petroecuador by, 1992. Petroecuador has inherited antiquated equipment, rusting pipelines, and uncounted toxic waste sites. Texaco has rejected calls by environmentalists to establish a $50 million cleanup fund. Meanwhile, Conoco Ecuador Ltd., with the support of the Ecuadorian government, plans to expand drilling into the undeveloped half of Ecuador's Amazon River basin. This region includes the pristine Yasuni National Park and the Huaoroni Indigenous Reserve. The Huaorini Indians who inhabit the reserve have had little contact with the outside world. Conoco claims that modern techniques and strict regulations will ensure that both the Huaoroni, and the rain forest they inhabit, will be protected.

Questions

1. Given the stance of the Ecuadorian government, is Texaco's activity in the Amazon River basin ethically justifiable? Explain.

2. Does Texaco have a moral obligation to provide funds and technical expertise to clean up the areas of the Amazon River basin it is responsible for polluting? Does it have a moral obligation to provide medical care for the Indian tribes who are purportedly suffering from the effects of that pollution? Explain.

3. How does the conduct of Texaco influence your view of Conoco's proposal for expanding

its drilling operations? Under what conditions, if any, would you consider it morally permissible for Conoco to begin drilling in the Yasuni National Park and Huaorani Indigenous Reserve? Explain.

4. Does the example of Texaco's conduct in Ecuador suggest to you a need for enforceable regulations governing transnational corporate activity? Explain.

CASE 3. *The Nestlé Corporation*

Nestlé Corporation, a large international conglomerate, was attacked by many individuals and groups who claimed that the rising infant mortality rate in third-world nations was due to the aggressive sales promotions of the infant formula companies, which influenced women to switch from traditional breast-feeding methods to the more "modern" idea of bottle feeding. Their primary target was the Nestlé Company of Switzerland, which accounted for 50 percent of third world sales of infant formula.

The declining birthrate in industrialized countries, which began in the 1960s, caused all the infant formula companies concern. They had seen the popularity of formula feeding expand their sales tremendously during and after World War II, but in the 1960s their sales began to diminish as the market became saturated. They viewed the developing and underdeveloped countries as potential sources of new markets to restore declining sales.

As reports began to appear about women in the third world who were abandoning breast feeding, many health professionals became alarmed because of the widespread lack of basic nutritional knowledge and adequate sanitation in the third world, two conditions that were necessary for using infant formula

safely. It was estimated that only 29 percent of the rural areas and 72 percent of the urban areas in the third world had potable water for mixing formula or for sanitizing feeding equipment. The lack of sanitation facilities and the absence of clean water would only be remedied with further development. The lack of education in underdeveloped countries often meant that people did not properly mix formulas or did not follow correct sanitary procedures. Sometimes a poor family would also stretch the formula by adding extra water.

Despite these problems, the infant formula companies mounted aggressive marketing and promotional campaigns in third-world countries. These marketing and promotional practices included extensive mass media advertising, large quantities of free promotional samples to doctors and maternity wards, gifts of equipment, trips and conferences for medical personnel, and the use of company representatives called "milk nurses" whose jobs entailed promoting and explaining formula feeding to new mothers. Billboards and posters prominently displayed pictures of fat, rosy-cheeked babies, subtly suggesting that the healthiest babies were those fed formula.

By 1977, an organization called the In-

This case was written by Eugene Buchholz, Loyola University of New Orleans, and is reprinted from *Business Environment and Public Policy* with permission.

fant Formula Action Coalition (INFACT) had been formed in Minneapolis to address the problem. This organization attempted to create public awareness and economic pressure through a nationwide boycott of all Nestlé products. Nestlé was chosen because it had the largest share of the world market and also because it was based in Switzerland and could not be pressured through shareholder resolutions in the United States. The boycott, which had the support of the National Council of Churches, had little effect on Nestlé's business, but the antiformula movement did get the attention of some very powerful groups.

Despite Nestlé's initial reluctance to go along with an International Code of Breast Feeding and Infant Formula Marketing adopted by the World Health Organization in 1981, in March 1982 the company announced that it would observe the code. In a further step, Nestlé set up the Infant Formula Audit Commission, composed of doctors, scientists, and churchpeople under the direction of former Secretary of State Edmund Muskie, to monitor its own conduct.

In general, the industry, responding to recommendations from the International Council of Infant Food Industries (ICIFI) and the World Health Organization, started to demarket its products. *Demarketing* means that efforts to sell a product are reduced or stopped completely because of risks to health or safety and is usually initiated because of management decisions, public pressure, or government regulation. Demarketing is ordinarily carried out in declining markets or markets in which a company can no longer compete successfully, but in the developing countries, demarketing decisions were made for growing markets and contrary to usual business practice.

Questions

1. Should Nestlé have avoided marketing its products in lesser developed countries?
2. Is the Nestlé Corporation morally responsible for the malnutrition that resulted when the formula "was stretched" by adding extra water?
3. Did INFACT act morally in putting economic pressure on Nestlé?
4. Was the development of a voluntary code a good way to resolve the problem? Would another type of code have been a better solution?

CASE 4. *Foreign Payments*

You are in an exotic city somewhere in the Middle East, trying hard to sell military equipment to a local government. You have spent months of hard work checking out specifications, calculating costs on various kinds of configurations, and explaining the advantages of your product to the local generals. Now the deal, which will mean millions of dollars in sales for your company and an almost certain promotion for you, is about to be closed.

Before closing the deal, however, you are called to the office of the minister of war for the government. Because of a legal technicality, he says he can't award the contract to your company. You walk out of his office not knowing what has happened. An hour later, a general whom you have come to know quite well

This case was written by Eugene Buchholz, Loyola University of New Orleans, and is reprinted from *Business Environment and Public Policy* with permission.

calls and states that if you donate $500,000 to a local charity, which just happens to have a Swiss bank account, the legal problems can be resolved and you can close the deal tomorrow.

Perhaps in earlier days, a payment to the Swiss bank might have taken care of the situation and no one would have been the wiser. Now, however, the United States has a law making bribery to obtain business illegal, with stiff fines for the executives and individuals involved and up to five years in jail for the executives who carry out such actions. Several companies in your industry have been hauled to Washington recently and confronted by Securities and Exchange Commission lawyers investigating improper payments abroad. Your own company has set up a committee of outside directors who aim to crack down on such payments.

Questions

1. If you made the "donation," would you be giving a facilitating payment, paying extortion, or giving a bribe?
2. Do you think your action would be illegal under the *amended* version of the Foreign Corrupt Practices Act?
3. Ignoring the legal question, would the $500,000 "donation" to charity be wrong?
4. Since officials of companies that make the "donation" would be at a competitive advantage, how can the situation created by foreign payments be controlled?

CASE 5.   *Mitsubishi and Rockefeller Center*

On October 30, 1989, the Mitsubishi Estate Company purchased a controlling interest in Rockefeller Center, one of America's most famous landmarks. A world-renowned business address, Rockefeller Center has been home to such companies as NBC, Time-Warner, General Electric, McGraw-Hill, and Price Waterhouse. To many, this purchase appeared to be another case of Japanese investors gobbling up American jewels. Only one month earlier, SONY Corporation, the Japanese electronics giant, had purchased Columbia Productions, a major movie company.

Mitsubishi paid $846 million for a 51 percent interest in the Rockefeller Group, which also owns Radio City Music Hall and a number of other mid-Manhattan office buildings. According to Richard Voell, president and chief executive officer of the Rockefeller Group, the transaction was a way of enhancing the financial strength of the Rockefeller Group and guaranteeing the group's ability to continue its management of existing properties and diversify into some new areas of interest.

Both sides reaffirmed the commitment of the new partnership to maintaining Rockefeller Center as a modern and prestigious commercial complex that would add to the character of New York City. David Rockefeller, grandson of John D. Rockefeller, Jr., who in 1934 initiated the Rockefeller Center development, said that the arrangement with Mitsubishi "preserves the abiding commitment to Rockefeller Center and New York City" that was evident in his grandfather's action decades before.

Mitsubishi is one of Japan's largest real estate companies and one of the wealthiest in-

Reprinted with permission from *Business and Society: Concepts and Policy Issues,* by Keith Davis, William C. Frederick, and Robert L. Blomstrom (New York: McGraw-Hill, 1980).

vestment institutions in the world. Aging properties at home, combined with a need to remain competitive in the global real estate business, led Mitsubishi to look for various opportunities to acquire property outside Japan. Beyond the prestige of owning Rockefeller Center, Mitsubishi's partnership with the Rockefeller Group could lead to other developments in the United States. At a news conference, Jotaro Tagaki, president of Mitsubishi, stressed that "We are participating in the [entire] future of the Rockefeller Group."

Initially, Mitsubishi had planned to acquire 80 percent of the Rockefeller Group. In an attempt to mute public reaction, however, it bought only 51 percent. Many Americans were wary of seeing well-known United States assets purchased by wealthy Japanese interests. (In one 1989 survey by the U.S. Commerce Department, Japan had the largest direct foreign investment in the United States. Japanese investments were being courted by U.S. states, cities, and towns attracted by the potential economic benefits from increased employment, development, and taxation.) Japanese officials and business executives were surprised by the negative publicity surrounding Sony's $3.4 billion deal for Columbia Pictures; several commentators indicated American reaction was equivalent to racism toward the Japanese. Earlier in 1989, an official at one of Mitsubishi's Japanese rival real estate firms was asked not to bid on the Sears Tower in Chicago because of growing American sensitivity to Japanese holdings. The cover of an issue of *Fortune* that appeared shortly after the Mitsubishi deal was announced was entitled, "Fear and Loathing of Japan."[1]

As a result, the Japanese government has informally cautioned its business leaders against purchasing conspicuous properties in the United States. A further step by Japanese business leaders is the creation of a Committee on Public Affairs at Keidanren, the largest Japanese business association. The committee urged Japanese companies investing in the United States to take steps to become a "good corporate citizen." These should include corporate contributions to philanthropic groups and working with local governments to ease public concerns.[2]

Questions

1. Was Mitsubishi's action in any way morally inappropriate?
2. Would the issue be any different if Mitsubishi had only purchased a significant but noncontrolling interest in Rockefeller Center?
3. Several months after the Mitsubishi acquisition, a Swiss pharmaceutical firm, Roche Holding, Ltd., acquired Genetech Inc., the leading U.S. Biotechnology firm. What similarities and differences do you see in the two situations? Is either one a long-term threat to U.S. interest? Why?

NOTES

1. Lee Smith, "Fear and Loathing of Japan," *Fortune*, February 26, 1990, pp. 50–60.
2. Robert J. Cole, "Control of Rockefeller Center Is Sold to Japanese Company," *New York Times*, October 31, 1989, pp. A–1, D–6; James Sterngold, "Mitsubishi's U.S. Deal Surprises Many in Japan," *New York Times*, November 11, 1989, p. D–1; Steven R. Weisman, "Japanese Are Concerned about Rockefeller Deal," *New York Times*, November 11, 1989.

Suggested Supplementary Readings

ACQUAAH, KWAMENA. *International Regulation of Transnational Corporations*. New York: Praeger, 1986.

ADAMS, GORDON, AND SHERRI ZANN ROSENTHAL.

The Invisible Hand: Questionable Corporate Payments Overseas. New York: Council on Economic Priorities, 1976.

BASCHE, JAMES R., Jr. *Unusual Foreign Payments: A Survey of the Policies and Practices of U.S. Companies.* New York: The Conference Board, 1976.

BERLEANT, ARNOLD. "Multinationals and the Problem of Ethical Consistency." *Journal of Business Ethics* 3 (August 1982): 185–195.

CARSON, THOMAS L. "Bribery, Extortion, and 'The Foreign Corrupt Practices Act'," *Philosophy and Public Affairs* 14 (Winter 1985): 66–90.

DOLLINGER, MARC J. "Confucian Ethics and Japanese Management Practices." *Journal of Business Ethics* 7 (August 1988): 575–583.

DONALDSON, THOMAS. *The Ethics of International Business.* New York: Oxford University Press, 1989.

——— "Multinational Decision Making: Reconciling International Norms." *Journal of Business Ethics* 4 (1985): 357–366.

DUBINSKY, ALAN J., AND OTHERS. "A Cross National Investigation of Industrial Salespeople's Ethical Perceptions." *Journal of International Business Studies* 22 (1991): 651–670.

ENGLISH, PARKER. "Bribery and the U.S. Foreign Corrupt Practices Act." *Foreign Journal of Applied Philosophy* 4 (Fall 1989): 13–23.

ETUK, UDO. "Justice and Self-Interest in Transnational Operations." *Public Affairs Quarterly* 1 (October 1987): 43–58.

GETZ, KATHLEEN. "International Codes of Conduct: An Analysis of Ethical Reasoning." *Journal of Business Ethics* 9 (1990): 567–577.

GILLESPIE, KATE. "Middle East Response to the Foreign Corrupt Practices Act." *California Management Review* 29 (Summer 1987): 9–30.

GREANIAS, GEORGE C., AND DUANE WINDSOR. *The Foreign Corrupt Practices Act.* Lexington, Mass.: Lexington Books, 1982.

GUNDLING, ERNEST. "Ethics and Working with the Japanese: The Entrepreneur and the 'Elite Course'." *California Management Review* 33 (Spring 1991): 25–39.

HOFFMAN, W. MICHAEL, AND OTHERS, eds. *Ethics and the Multinational Enterprise.* Washington, D.C.: University Press of America, 1985.

JACOBY, NEIL, PETER NEHEMKIS, AND RICHARD ELLS. "Naivete: Foreign Payoffs Law." *California Management Review* 22 (Fall 1979): 84–87.

JOHNSON, HAROLD L. "Bribery in International Markets: Diagnosis, Clarification, and Remedy." *Journal of Business Ethics* 4 (December 1985): 447–455.

KAIKATI, JACK, AND WAYNE A. LABEL. "American Bribery Legislation: An Obstacle to International Marketing." *Journal of Marketing* 44 (January 1978): 38–43.

KLINE, JOHN M. *International Codes and Multinational Business: Setting Guidelines for International Business Operations.* New York: Quorum, 1985.

LANE, HENRY W., AND DONALD G. SIMPSON. "Bribery in International Business: Whose Problem Is It?" *Journal of Business Ethics* 3 (February 1984): 35–42.

LANGLOIS, CATHERINE C., AND BODO B. SCHLEGEL-MILCH. "Do Corporate Codes of Ethics Reflect National Character? Evidence from Europe and the United States." *Journal of International Business Studies* 21 (Fall 1990): 519–539.

PASTIN, MARK, AND MICHAEL HOOKER. "Ethics and the Foreign Corrupt Practices Act." *Business Horizons* 23 (December 1980): 43–47.

PRATT, CORNELIUS B. "Multinational Corporate Social Policy Process for Ethical Responsibility in Sub-Saharan Africa." *Journal of Business Ethics* 10 (July 1991): 527–541.

SINGH, JANG B., AND OTHERS. "Business Ethics and the International Trade in Hazardous Wastes." *Journal of Business Ethics* 8 (November 1989): 889–899.

SHUE, HENRY. "Exporting Hazards." *Ethics* 91 (July 1981): 579–606.

TERPSTRA, VERN, AND KENNETH DAVID. *The Cultural Environment of International Business.* 3rd ed. Cincinnati: South-Western Publishing Co., 1991.

United Nations. *Transnational Corporations in World Development: Trends and Prospects.* New York: United Nations, 1988.

VELASQUEZ, MANUEL. "International Business, Morality, and the Common Good." *Business Ethics Quarterly* 2 (January 1992): 27–43.

WINDSOR, DUANE, AND LEE E. PRESTON. "Corporate Governance, Social Policy and Social Performance in the Multinational Corporation." *Research in Corporate Social Performance and Policy* 10 (1988).

Chapter Nine

Social and Economic Justice

Economic disparities among individuals and nations have generated heated controversy over systems for distributing and taxing income and wealth. Some sustained political conflicts in the United States concern the justification of taxes, corporate profits, plant closings, international debt relief, and executive salaries and bonuses.

Several well-reasoned and systematic answers to these and related questions have been advanced, based on a theory of justice—that is, a theory of how social and economic benefits, services, and burdens should be distributed. In Chapter 1 we briefly analyzed the connection between ethical theory and problems of justice. In the present chapter, the major distinctions, principles, and methods of moral argument employed in contemporary philosophy are treated. The first four articles attempt to answer the question, "Which general system of social and economic organization is most just?" The other articles address the justice of particular policies and forms of behavior.

THEORIES OF DISTRIBUTIVE JUSTICE

What a person deserves or is entitled to is often decided by specific rules and laws, such as those governing state lotteries, food stamp allocation, health care coverage, admission procedures for universities, and the like. These rules may be evaluated, criticized, and revised by reference to moral principles such as equality of persons, nondiscriminatory treatment, property ownership, protection from harm, compensatory justice, retributive justice, and so forth. The word *justice* is used broadly to cover both these principles and the more specific rules that these principles help develop for specific situations.

Economists have sometimes complained about philosophers' approaches to justice, on grounds that a "fair price" or "fair trade" is not a matter of moral fairness: Prices may be low or high, affordable or not affordable, but not fair or unfair. It is simply unfortunate, not unfair, if one cannot afford to pay for something or if another person is paid forty times what you are paid. The reason is the market-established nature of prices and salaries. To speak of "unfair" prices, trade, or salaries is to express an opinion, but these economists reason that from a market perspective any price is fair, and no price is unfair. Salaries must be treated in the same way.

However, the economist is missing the philosopher's point. The philosopher is asking whether the market itself is a fair arrangement. What makes it fair, if so? If coercion is used in the market to set prices, is this maneuver unfair, or does it render the market not a free market? If goods such as health care and education are distributed nationally or internationally with vast inequality, can high prices on essential items such as health care goods and university tuition be fair? If a multinational company has a monopoly on an essential foodstuff, is there no such thing as a price that is too high? These kinds of questions of fairness are generally raised under the topic of justice. All are questions of distributive justice.

The term *distributive justice* refers to the proper distribution of social benefits and burdens. A theory of distributive justice attempts to establish a connection between the properties or characteristics of persons and the morally correct distribution of benefits and burdens in society. *Egalitarian* theories emphasize equal access to primary goods (see John Rawl's article); *communitarian* theories emphasize group goals and collective control as well as participation in communal life, by contrast to liberal political systems that emphasize individual welfare and rights (see Michael Walzer's article); *libertarian* theories emphasize rights to social and economic liberty and de-emphasize collective control (see Robert Nozick's essay); and *utilitarian* theories emphasize a mixed used of such criteria resulting in the maximization of both public and individual interests (see Peter Singer's article).

Systematic theories of justice attempt to elaborate how people are to be compared and what it means to give people their due. Philosophers attempt to achieve the needed precision and specificity by developing material principles of justice, so called because they put material content into a theory of justice. Each material principle of justice identifies a relevant property on the basis of which burdens and benefits should be distributed. The following list includes the major candidates for the position of justified principles of distributive justice.

1. To each person an equal share
2. To each person according to individual need
3. To each person according to that person's rights
4. To each person according to individual effort
5. To each person according to societal contribution
6. To each person according to merit

A theory might accept more than one of these principles. Some theories of justice accept all six as legitimate. Many societies use several, in the belief that different rules are appropriate to different situations.

In the utilitarian theory, problems of justice are viewed as one part of the larger problem of how to maximize value, and it is easy to see how a utilitarian might use all of these material principles to this end. The ideal distribution of benefits and burdens is simply the one having this maximizing effect. According to utilitarian Peter Singer in his essay in this chapter, a heavy element of political planning and economic redistribution is required to ensure that justice is done. Because utilitarianism was treated in Chapter 1, detailed considerations will be give in this introduction only to egalitarian, libertarian, and communitarian theories.

THE EGALITARIAN THEORY

Equality in the distribution of social benefits and burdens has a central place in many influential ethical theories. For example, in utilitarianism different people are equal in the value accorded their wants, preferences, and happiness, and in Kantian theories all persons are considered equally worthy and deserving of respect as ends in themselves. Egalitarian theory treats the question how people should be considered equal in some respects (for example, in their basic political and moral rights and obligations), yet unequal in others (for example, wealth and social burdens such as taxation).

Radical and Qualified Egalitarianism

In its radical form, egalitarian theory proposes that individual differences are always morally insignificant. Distributions of burdens and benefits in a society are considered to be just to the extent that they are equal, and deviations from absolute equality in distribution is unjust. For example, the fact that roughly 20 percent of the wealth in the United States is owned by 5 percent of the population, whereas the poorest 20 percent of the population controls only 5 percent, makes U.S. society unjust, no matter how relatively "deserving" the people at both extremes might be.

However, most egalitarian accounts are guardedly formulated, so that everyone is not entitled to equal shares of all social benefits and so that individual merit does justify some differences in distribution. Egalitarianism, so qualified, concerns itself only to some basic equalities among individuals that take priority over their differences. For example, egalitarians prefer *progressive* tax rates (higher incomes taxed more heavily than lower), rather than *proportional* rates (each unit taxed the same). This may seem odd since a proportional rate treats everyone equally. However, qualified egalitarians reason that progressive rates tax the wealthy more and distribute wealth more evenly. The goal of egalitarian schemes is to move society from inequality toward greater equality.

John Rawls's Theory

In recent years a qualified egalitarian theory in the Kantian tradition has enjoyed wide currency. John Rawls's *A Theory of Justice* has as its central contention that all economic goods and services should be distributed equally except when an unequal distribution would work to everyone's advantage or at least to the worst off in society. Rawls presents this egalitarian theory as a direct challenge to utilitarianism. His objection is that social distributions produced by maximizing utility allow for violations of basic individual liberties and rights. Being indifferent to the distribution of satisfactions among individuals, utilitarianism, in Rawls's view, permits the infringement of people's rights and liberties if it promised to produce a proportionately greater utility for all concerned.

Rawls turns to a hypothetical social contract procedure strongly indebted to what he calls the "Kantian conception of equality." Valid principles of justice are those to which all would agree if one could freely and impartially consider the social situation from the standpoint of the "original position," which is outside any actual society. Impartiality is guaranteed by a conceptual device Rawls calls the "veil of ignorance." In the original position, each person is ignorant of all his or her particular fortuitous characteristics, for example, the person's sex, race, IQ, family background, and special talents or handicaps. This veil of ignorance prevents the promotion of principles biased toward personal combinations of fortuitous talents and characteristics—for example, the various combinations of need, merit, experience, and advantage that lead different parties to promote competing principles.

Rawls argues that under these conditions people would unanimously agree on two fundamental principles of justice. The first requires that each person be permitted the maximum amount of basic liberty compatible with a similar liberty for others. The second stipulates that once this equal basic liberty is assured, inequalities in social primary goods (for example, income, rights, and opportunities) are to be allowed only if they benefit everyone. Rawls considers social institutions to be just if and only if they conform to these principles of the social contract. He rejects radical egalitarianism, arguing that inequalities that render everyone better off by comparison to being equal are desirable.

Rawls formulates what is called the *difference principle:* Inequalities are justifiable only if they maximally enhance the position of the "representative least advantaged" person, that is, a hypothetical individual particularly unfortunate in the distribution of fortuitous characteristics or social advantages. Rawls is unclear about who might qualify under this category, but a worker incapacitated from exposure to asbestos and living in poverty clearly would qualify. Formulated in this way, the difference principle could allow, for instance, extraordinary economic rewards to business entrepreneurs, venture capitalists, and corporate takeover artists if the resulting economic situation were to produce improved job opportunities and working conditions for the least advantaged members of society, or possibly greater benefits for pension funds holding stock for the working class.

The difference principle rests on the moral viewpoint that because inequalities of birth, historical circumstance, and natural endowment are undeserved, persons in a cooperative society should make more equal the unequal situation of naturally disadvantaged members. This and other Rawlsian ideas are defended in an international context by Thomas Donaldson, who espouses the view that the economically least well off in developing countries should not be harmed as a result of conditions imposed as part of international loan arrangements.

LIBERTARIAN THEORY

What makes a libertarian theory *libertarian* is the priority afforded to distinctive procedures or mechanisms for ensuring that liberty rights are recognized in social and economic practice, typically the rules and procedures governing economic acquisition and exchange in capitalist or free-market systems.

Role of Individual Freedom

Libertarian theory finds its intellectual foundations in classical writers such as John Locke and Adam Smith. Smith depicted capitalist economic systems as containing self-interested individuals who exhibit behavior patterns that collectively further the interests of the larger society. Such a system presumes a model of behavior with a substantial degree of economic freedom; individual agents can enter and withdraw from economic arrangements in accordance with their best interests.

The libertarian contends that it is a basic violation of justice to ensure equal economic returns. In particular, individuals are seen as having a fundamental right to own and dispense with the products of their labor as they choose, even if the exercise of this right leads to large inequalities of wealth in society. Equality and utility principles, from this perspective, sacrifice basic liberty rights to the larger public interest by exploiting one set of individuals for the benefit of another. The most apparent example is the coercive extraction of financial resources through taxation.

Because no moral grounds justify the sacrifice of liberty rights, the libertarian views utilitarianism and egalitarianism as perverted theories of justice. However, a libertarian is not opposed to utilitarian or egalitarian modes of distribution if they have been freely chosen by those concerned.

Robert Nozick's Theory

Libertarian theory is defended in this chapter by Robert Nozick, who refers to his social philosophy as an "entitlement theory" of justice. Nozick argues that a theory of justice should work to protect individual rights and should not propound a thesis intended to "pattern" society through arrangements such as those in socialist and (impure) capitalist countries in which governments take pronounced steps to redistribute the wealth.

The goal of state interference is presumably the redistribution of economic benefits that would otherwise concentrate in small pockets of society. A tendency has long existed to use the law and tax code to effect social goals such as the alleviation of poverty and the support of the arts. It has rarely been conceived merely as a source of revenue for essential services. Nozick resolutely resists such social engineering, and his libertarian theory invites consideration of whether such governmental intrusion is what justice demands or rather what some persons prefer.

Nozick's entitlement theory relies on three principles: *acquisition, transfer,* and *rectification.* His libertarian position rejects all distributional patterns imposed by material principles of justice and thereby is committed to a form of procedural justice. That is, for Nozick there is no pattern of just distribution independent of the procedures of acquisition, transfer, and rectification. This claim has been at the center of controversy over the libertarian account, and many competing theories of justice are reactions to such an uncompromising commitment to pure procedural justice. In several respects, Donaldson is responding to the libertarian tradition.

In the Supreme Court opinion in *Ferguson v. Skrupa,* the Court declares that legislatures, not courts, should decide on the wisdom and utility of economic and social policies such as those affecting minimum wages and poverty. However, many critics believe this conclusion to be a relatively recent position of the Court, contrasting with an older U.S. legal tradition of scrutinizing and rectifying circumstances of social and economic injustice.

COMMUNITARIAN THEORY

The moral and political theory advocating individual responsibility, free-market exchanges, and limited community control is often called *liberalism.* This approach places the individual at the center of moral and political theory and views the state as properly limited in a circumstance of conflict with individual rights such as freedom of association, expression, and religion. The state's proper role is to protect and enforce basic moral and political rights, often called *civil rights.*

Rising up against liberalism in recent years has been a tide of communitarian theories. Although a diverse lot, communitarian theories share many ideas. They see typical liberal theories such as those of Rawls and Nozick (and even Mill and Singer) as subverting communal life and the obligations and commitments that grow out of that perspective on life. These theorists see persons as intrinsically *constituted* by communal values. People are, then, best suited to achieve their good through communal life, not state protections or individual moral and political rights.

Communitarians object to the way Rawlsian liberalism has made justice the first virtue of social institutions and then has patterned those institutions to protect the individual against society. The communitarian believes that justice is a less central virtue of social life, one that is needed when communal values have broken down into conflicts of the sort litigated in court. Rather than emphasizing the state as enforcer of rights allowing individuals to pursue any course they wish, the communitarian takes a view utterly opposed to Nozick and others: The community may rightly be expected to impose on individuals certain conceptions of virtue and the good life.

The nature of the conflict between liberalism and certain communitarian values is explored in the essay in this chapter by Judith Lichtenberg, who sees industrial flight as a circumstance of historical-communal values in conflict with rights of both corporations and individuals. She argues that the question of whether plant closings are unfair to workers must be addressed, not merely whether corporations have rights to close.

The sole representative of communitarian theories in this chapter is Michael Walzer, a moderate communitarian not as opposed to liberalism as hard-line communitarians.[1] For him notions of justice are not either Kantian or utilitarian. In particular, they are not based on some "rational" or "natural" foundation external to the society. Rather, standards of justice are developed internally as the community evolves. Something has to be "given-as-basic" in every ethical theory, and the communitarian theory sees everything as deriving from communal values and historical practices. Conventions, traditions, and loyalties therefore play a vastly more prominent role in communitarian theories than they do in the other theories we encounter in this chapter.

Communitarians recognize that people have the capacity to set individual tasks and projects, as well as the capacity to challenge and reject moral rules acknowledged by the community. To this end, Walzer argues that a community ethic must be particularly vigilant to avoid "oppressing" minorities. Nonetheless, a communitarian will not accept an individual's personal values as either moral or respectable if those values depart from the moral values of the community.

VISIONS OF JUSTICE BEYOND THE FREE MARKET

Many objections to the free market typified by communitarian theory begin with assumptions that at least formally resemble the libertarian's assumptions. Nozick's unyielding commitment to individual liberty rights is a good example. The mistake in the libertarian theory, claim writers both within and without the communitarian tradition, is not the emphasis on liberty rights but rather the overriding importance ascribed to economic rights and privileges.

Many philosophers argue that a conception of fundamental individual rights more inclusive than Nozick's must be recognized in an adequate theory of justice. Even in strictly economic terms, these writers maintain, Nozick's conception of individual rights is excessively restricted. They challenge the proponents of libertarianism to answer the following questions: Why should we assume that people's economic rights extend only to the acquisition and dispensation of private property according to the free-market rules? Is it not equally plausible to posit more substantive moral rights in the economic sphere—say, rights to health care, decent levels of education, and decent standards of living?

Nozick's ideal is generally agreed to be plausible for free transactions among informed and consenting parties who start as equals in the bargaining process. But this ideal is rarely the case beyond circumstances of contractual bargaining among equals. Contracts, voting privileges, individual investing in the stock market, and family relationships may involve bluffing, differentials of power and wealth, manipulation, and the like. These factors work systematically to disadvantage vulnerable individuals. Imagine, for example, that over the course of time one group in society gains immense wealth and political influence compared with another group. Although the transactions leading to this imbalance were legitimate, the outcome is not an acceptable state of affairs. If an individual's bargaining position has been deeply eroded, does he or she have a right to protection from social inequalities that have emerged? If he or she is destined to poverty as a result, is there a legitimate claim of justice, as Rawls proposes?

If people have a right to minimal level of material means, their rights are violated whenever economic distributions leave some with less than that minimal level. A commitment to individual rights, then, may result in a theory of justice that requires a more activist role for government, even if one starts with free-market or libertarian assumptions. Many philosophers agree with Nozick that economic freedom is a value deserving of respect and protection. They disagree, however, that the principles and procedures that libertarians advocate protect that basic value.

The Principle of Need

In reaction to these problems, some reject the pure procedural commitments of the libertarian theory and replace them with a principle specifying human need as the relevant respect in which people are to be compared for purposes of determining social and economic justice. Donaldson seems to be a good example of this approach.

Much turns on how the notion of need is defined and implemented. To say that someone needs something is to say that the person will be harmed or detrimentally affected if that thing is not obtained. For purposes of justice, a principle of need would be least controversial if it were restricted to fundamental needs. If malnutrition, bodily injury, and the withholding of certain information involve fundamental harms, we have a fundamental need for nutrition, health care facilities, and education. According to theories based on this material principle, justice places the satisfaction of fundamental human needs above the protection of economic freedoms or rights.

This construal of the principle of need has provided alternatives to libertarian justice. Yet there may be some room for reconciliation between principle of need and libertarianism. Many advanced industrial countries have the capacity to produce far more than is strictly necessary to meet their citizens' fundamental needs. One might argue that *after* everyone's fundamental needs have been satisfied, *then* justice requires no particular pattern of distribution. For example, some current discussions of the right to health care and the right to a job are rooted in the idea of meeting basic medical and economic needs, but only basic needs. In this way, a single unified theory of justice might require the maintenance of certain patterns in the distribution of basic goods (for example, a decent minimum level of income, education, and health care), while allowing the market to determine distributions of goods beyond those which satisfy fundamental needs.

This approach accepts a two-tiered system of access to goods and services: (1) social coverage for basic and catastrophic needs, and (2) private purchase of other goods and services. On the first tier, distribution is based on need, and everyone's basic needs are met by the government. Better services may be made available for purchase in an economic system on the second tier. This proposal seems to present an attractive point of convergence and negotiation for libertarians, communitarians, utilitarians, and egalitarians. It provides a premise of equal access to basic goods, while allowing additional rights to economic freedom. Theories such as utilitarianism and communitarianism may also find the compromise particularly attractive because it serves to minimize public dissatisfaction and to maximize community welfare. The egalitarian finds an opportunity to use an equal access principle, and the libertarian retains free-market production and distribution. However, the system clearly does involve compromise by all parties.

Fair Opportunity

Rawls's difference principle suggests something stronger with regard to the justice of social institutions: They are to be gauged by their tendency to counteract the inequalities caused purely by luck of birth, natural endowment, or historical circumstances and events. This approach accommodates many common beliefs about justice that agree that it is unjust to distribute social burdens and benefits on the basis of purely fortuitous characteristics. But why are fortuitous characteristics such as race, religion, intelligence, national origin, sex, and social status inappropriate as principles of distributive justice?

A plausible explanation is that principles based on fortuitous characteristics treat people differently, sometimes with devastating consequences, because of circumstances beyond their control. This fairness-based reason holds that differences among persons are relevant only if those persons are responsible for them. The "fair opportunity principle," as it may be called, says that no person should be granted or denied social benefits on the basis of undeserved advantaging properties. Those inherent properties are not grounds for morally acceptable discrimination among persons, because they are not the sorts of properties that one has a fair chance to acquire or overcome.

If one accepts the fair opportunity rule in an account of distributive justice, it provides a revisionary perspective on many common forms of social distribution. A commitment to this principle suggests that whenever persons are inhibited in the advancing of their interests by "disadvantageous" properties for which they are not responsible, they should not be denied benefits because of those properties. Suppose that almost all their chief abilities and disabilities are a function of what Rawls refers to as the "natural lottery." That is, suppose that almost all their talents and deficiencies are a causal function of heredity and environment and that the individuals themselves consequently are not responsible for any of them. This could mean, for example, that one's ability to work long hours, one's competitive drive, and one's sense of dedication are undeserved—or that other disadvantageous properties such as a raspy voice, an ugly scar, or a thick accent are also undeserved. How far should we extend the range of undeserved properties in creating a right to some form of assistance?

If this theory of the causal origins of advantageous and disadvantageous properties is accepted, along with the justification based on fair opportunity previously outlined, one would be led to views about distributive justice radically different from the ones now acknowledged. It is uncertain what the full implications of this approach are, but rather than allowing radical inequalities based on effort, contribution, and merit, justice would be done if radical inequalities were diminished.

CONCLUSION

Rawls, Nozick, and their utilitarian and communitarian opponents all capture some intuitive convictions about justice, and each theory exhibits strengths as a theory of justice. Rawls's difference principle, for example, describes a widely shared belief about justified inequalities. Nozick's theory makes a strong appeal in the domains of property rights and liberties. Utilitarianism is widely used in the Western nations in the development of public policy, and communitarian theories in some form supply the prevailing model of justice in many nations.

Perhaps, then, there are several equally valid, or at least equally defensible, theories of justice. There could, on this analysis, be libertarian societies, egalitarian societies, utilitarian societies, and communitarian societies, as well as societies based on mixed theories or derivative theories of taxation and redistribution. However, this possibility raises other problems in ethical theory discussed in Chapter 1, in particular, relativism and moral disagreement, and before this conclusion is accepted, the details of the arguments in the selections in this chapter should be carefully assessed.

NOTES

1. The hard-liners include Michael Sandel, Charles Taylor, and Alasdair MacIntyre.

An Egalitarian Theory of Justice

John Rawls

THE ROLE OF JUSTICE

Justice is the first virtue of social institutions, as truth is of systems of thought. A theory however elegant and economical must be rejected or revised if it is untrue; likewise laws and institutions no matter how efficient and well-arranged must be reformed or abolished if they are unjust. Each person possesses an inviolability founded on justice that even the welfare of society as a whole cannot override. For this reason justice denies that the loss of freedom for some is made right by a greater good shared by others. It does not allow that the sacrifices imposed on a few are outweighed by the larger sum of advantages enjoyed by many. Therefore in a just society the liberties of equal citizenship are taken as settled; the rights secured by justice are not subject to political bargaining or to the calculus of social interests. The only thing that permits us to acquiesce in an erroneous theory is the lack of a better one; analogously, an injustice is tolerable only when it is necessary to avoid an even greater injustice. Being first virtues of human activities, truth and justice are uncompromising.

These propositions seem to express our intuitive conviction of the primary of justice. No doubt they are expressed too strongly. In any event I wish to inquire whether these contentions or others similar to them are sound, and if so how they can be accounted for. To this end it is necessary to work out a theory of justice in the light of which these assertions can be interpreted and assessed. I shall begin by considering the role of the principles of justice. Let us assume, to fix ideas, that a society is a more or less self-sufficient association of persons who in their relations to one another recognize certain rules of conduct as binding and who for the most part act in accordance with them. Suppose further that these rules specify a system of cooperation designed to advance the good of those taking part in it. Then, although a society is a cooperative venture for mutual advantage, it is typically marked by a conflict as well as by an identity of interests. There is an identity of interests since social cooperation makes possible a better life for all than any would have if each were to live solely by his own efforts. There is a conflict of interests since persons are not indifferent as to how the greater benefits produced by their collaboration are distributed, for in order to pursue their ends they each prefer a larger to a lesser share. A set of principles is required for choosing among the various social arrangements which determine this division of advantages and for underwriting an agreement on the proper distributive shares. These principles

are the principles of social justice: they provide a way of assigning rights and duties in the basic institutions of society and they define the appropriate distribution of the benefits and burdens of social cooperation. . . .

THE MAIN IDEA OF THE THEORY OF JUSTICE

My aim is to present a conception of justice which generalizes and carries to a higher level of abstraction the familiar theory of the social contract as found, say, in Locke, Rousseau, and Kant. In order to do this we are not to think of the original contract as one to enter a particular society or to set up a particular form of government. Rather, the guiding idea is that the principles of justice for the basic structure of society are the object of the original agreement. They are the principles that free and rational persons concerned to further their own interests would accept in an initial position of equality as defining the fundamental terms of their association. These principles are to regulate all further agreements; they specify the kinds of social cooperation that can be entered into and the forms of government that can be established. This way of regarding the principles of justice I shall call justice as fairness.

Thus we are to imagine that those who engage in social cooperation choose together, in one joint act, the principles which are to assign basic rights and duties and to determine the division of social benefits. Men are to decide in advance how they are to regulate their claims against one another and what is to be the foundation charter of their society. Just as each person must decide by rational reflection what constitutes his good, that is, the system of ends which it is rational for him to pursue, so a group of persons must decide once and for all what is to count among them as just and unjust. The choice which rational men would make in this hypothetical situation of equal liberty, assuming for the present that this choice problem has a solution, determines the principles of justice.

In justice as fairness the original position of equality corresponds to the state of nature in the traditional theory of the social contract. This original position is not, of course, thought of as an actual historical state of affairs, much less as a primitive condition of culture. It is understood as a purely hypothetical situation characterized so as to lead to a certain conception of justice. Among the essential features of this situation is that no one knows his place in society, his class position or social status, nor does any one know his fortune in the distribution of natural assets and abilities, his intelligence, strength, and the like. I shall even assume that the parties do not know their conceptions of the good or their special psychological propensities. The principles of justice are chosen behind a veil of ignorance. This ensures that no one is advantaged or disadvantaged in the choice of principles by the outcome of natural chance or the contingency of social circumstances. Since all are similarly situated and no one is able to design principles to favor his particular condition, the principles of justice are the result of a fair agreement or bargain. For given the circumstances of the original position, the symmetry of everyone's relations to each other, this initial situation is fair between individuals as moral persons, that is, as rational beings with their own ends and capable, I shall assume, of a sense of justice. The original position is, one might say, the appropriate initial status quo, and thus the fundamental agreements reached in it are fair. This explains the propriety of the name "justice as fairness": it conveys the idea that the principles of justice are agreed to in an initial situation that is fair. The name does not mean that the concepts of justice and fairness are the same, any more than the phrase "poetry as metaphor" means that the concepts of poetry and metaphor are the same.

Justice as fairness begins, as I have said, with one of the most general of all choices which persons might make together, namely, with the choice of the first principles of a conception of justice which is to regulate all subsequent criticism and reform of institutions. Then, having chosen a conception of justice, we can suppose that they are to choose a constitution and a legislature to enact laws, and so on, all in accordance with the principles of justice initially agreed upon. Our social situation is just if it is such that by this sequence of hypothetical agreements we would have contracted into the general system of rules which defines it.

. . . It may be observed, however, that once the principles of justice are thought of as arising from an original agreement in a situation of equality, it is an open question whether the principle of utility would be acknowledged. Offhand it hardly seems likely that persons who view themselves as equals, entitled to press their claims upon one another, would agree to a principle which may require lesser life prospects for some simply for the sake of a greater sum of advantages enjoyed by others. Since each desires to protect his interests, his capacity to advance his conception of the good, no one has a reason to acquiesce in an enduring loss for himself in order to bring about a greater net balance of satisfaction. In the absence of strong and lasting benevolent impulses, a rational man would not accept a basic structure merely because it maximized the algebraic sum of advantages irrespective of its permanent effects on his own basic rights and interests. Thus it seems that the principle of utility is incompatible with the conception of social cooperation among equals for mutual advantage. It appears to be inconsistent with the idea of reciprocity implicit in the notion of a well-ordered society. Or, at any rate, so I shall argue.

I shall maintain instead that the persons in the initial situation would choose two rather different principles: the first requires equality in the assignment of basic rights and duties, while the second holds that social and economic inequalities, for example inequalities of wealth and authority, are just only if they result in compensating benefits for everyone, and in particular for the least advantaged members of society. These principles rule out justifying institutions on the grounds that the hardships of some are offset by a greater good in the aggregate. It may be expedient but it is not just that some should have less in order that others may prosper. But there is no injustice in the greater benefits earned by a few provided that the situation of persons not so fortunate is thereby improved. The intuitive idea is that since everyone's well-being depends upon a scheme of cooperation without which no one could have a satisfactory life, the division of advantages should be such as to draw forth the willing cooperation of everyone taking part in it, including those less well situated. Yet this can be expected only if reasonable terms are proposed. The two principles mentioned seem to be a fair agreement on the basis of which those better endowed, or more fortunate in their social position, neither of which we can be said to deserve, could expect the willing cooperation of others when some workable scheme is a necessary condition of the welfare of all. Once we decide to look for a conception of justice that nullifies the accidents of natural endowment and the contingencies of social circumstance as counters in quest for political and economic advantage, we are led to these principles. They express the result of leaving aside those aspects of the social world that seem arbitrary from a moral point of view. . . .

THE ORIGINAL POSITION AND JUSTIFICATION

. . . The idea here is simply to make vivid to ourselves the restrictions that it seems reasonable to impose on arguments for principles of justice, and therefore on these principles themselves. Thus it seems reasonable and generally acceptable that no one should be advantaged or disadvantaged by natural fortune or social circumstances in the choice of principles. It is also seems widely agreed that it should be impossible to tailor principles to the circumstances of one's own case. We should insure further that particular inclinations and aspirations, and persons' conceptions of their good, do not affect the principles adopted. The aim is to rule out those principles that it would be rational to propose for acceptance, however little the chance of success, only if one knew certain things that are irrelevant from the standpoint of justice. For example, if a man knew that he was wealthy, he might find it rational to advance the principle that various taxes for welfare measures be counted unjust; if he knew that he was poor, he would most likely propose the contrary principle. To represent the desired restrictions one imagines a situation in which everyone is deprived of this sort of information. One excludes the knowledge of those contingencies which sets men at odds and allows them to be guided by their prejudices. In this manner the veil of ignorance is arrived at in a natural way. . . .

TWO PRINCIPLES OF JUSTICE

I shall now state in a provisional form the two principles of justice that I believe would be chosen in the original position. . . .

The first statement of the two principles reads as follows.

First: each person is to have an equal right to the most extensive basic liberty compatible with a similar liberty for others.

Second: social and economic inequalities are to be arranged so that they are both (a) reasonably expected to be to everyone's advantage, and (b) attached to positions and offices open to all. . . . [The Difference Principle]

By way of general comment, these principles primarily apply, as I have said, to the basic structure of society. They are to govern the assignment of rights and duties and to regulate the distribution of social and economic advantages. As their formulation suggests, these principles presuppose that the social structure can be divided into two more or less distinct parts, the first principle applying to the one, the second to the other. They distinguish between those aspects of the social system that define and secure the equal liberties of citizenship and those that specify and establish social and economic inequalities. The basic liberties of citizens are, roughly speaking, political liberty (the right to vote and to be eligible for public office) together with freedom of speech and assembly; liberty of conscience and freedom of thought; freedom of the person along with the right to hold (personal) property; and freedom from arbitrary arrest and seizure as defined by the concept of the rule of law. These liberties are all required to be equal by the first principle, since citizens of a just society are to have the same basic rights.

The second principle applies, in the first approximation, to the distribution of income and wealth and to the design of organizations that make use of differences in authority and responsibility, or chains of command. While the distribution of wealth and income need not be equal, it must be to everyone's advantage, and at the same time, positions of authority and offices of command must be accessible to all. One applies the second principle by holding positions open, and then, subject to this constraint, arranges social and economic inequalities so that everyone benefits.

These principles are to be arranged in a serial order with the first principle prior to the second. This ordering means that a departure from the institutions of equal liberty required by the first principle cannot be justified, or compensated for, by greater social and economic advantages. The distribution of wealth and income, and the hierarchies of authority must be consistent with both the liberties of equal citizenship and equality of opportunity.

It is clear that these principles are rather specific in their content, and their acceptance rests on certain assumptions that I must eventually try to explain and justify. A theory of justice depends upon a theory of society in ways that will become evident as we proceed. For the present, it should be observed that the two principles (and this holds for all formulations) are a special case of a more general conception of justice that can be expressed as follows.

> All social values—liberty and opportunity, income and wealth, and the bases of self-respect—are to be distributed equally unless an unequal distribution of any, or all, of these values is to everyone's advantage.

Injustice, then, is simply inequalities that are not to the benefit of all. Of course, this conception is extremely vague and requires interpretation.

As a first step, suppose that the basic structure of society distributes certain primary goods, that is, things that every rational man is presumed to want. These goods normally have a use whatever a person's rational plan of life. For simplicity, assume that the chief primary goods at the disposition of society are rights and liberties, powers and opportunities, income and wealth. These are the social primary goods. Other primary goods such as health and vigor, intelligence and imagination, are natural goods; although their possession is influenced by the basic structure, they are not so directly under its control. Imagine, then, a hypothetical initial arrangement in which all the social primary goods are equally distributed: everyone has similar rights and duties, and income and wealth are evenly shared. This state of affairs provides a benchmark for judging improvements. If certain inequalities of wealth and organizational powers would make everyone better off than in this hypothetical starting situation, then they accord with the general conception.

Now it is possible, at least theoretically, that by giving up some of their fundamental liberties men are sufficiently compensated by the resulting social and economic gains. The general conception of justice imposes no restrictions on what sort of inequalities are permissible; it only requires that everyone's position be improved. . . .

Now the second principle insists that each person benefit from permissible inequalities in the basic structure. This means that it must be reasonable for each relevant representative man defined by this structure, when he views it as a going concern, to prefer his prospects with the inequality to his prospects without it. One is not allowed to justify differences in income or organizational powers on the ground that the disadvantages of those in one position are outweighed by the greater advantages of those in another. Much less can infringements of liberty be counterbalanced in this way. Applied to the basic structure, the principle of utility would have us maximize the sum of expectations of representative men (weighted by the number of persons they represent, on the classical view); and this would permit us to compensate for the losses of some by the gains of others. Instead, the two principles require that everyone benefit from economic and social inequalities. . . .

THE TENDENCY TO EQUALITY

I wish to conclude this discussion of the two principles by explaining the sense in which

they express an egalitarian conception of justice. Also I should like to forestall the objection to the principle of fair opportunity that it leads to a callous meritocratic society. In order to prepare the way for doing this, I note several aspects of the conception of justice that I have set out.

First we may observe that the difference principle gives some weight to the considerations singled out by the principle of redress. This is the principle that undeserved inequalities call for redress; and since inequalities of birth and natural endowment are undeserved, these inequalities are to be somehow compensated for. Thus the principle holds that in order to treat all persons equally, to provide genuine equality of opportunity, society must give more attention to those with fewer native assets and to those born into the less favorable social positions. The idea is to redress the bias of contingencies in the direction of equality. In pursuit of this principle greater resources might be spent on the education of the less rather than the more intelligent, at least over a certain time of life, say the earlier years of school.

Now the principle of redress has not to my knowledge been proposed as the sole criterion of justice, as the single aim of the social order. It is plausible as most such principles are only as a prima facie principle, one that is to be weighed in the balance with others. For example, we are to weigh it against the principle to improve the average standard of life, or to advance the common good. But whatever other principles we hold, the claims of redress are to be taken into account. It is thought to represent one of the elements in our conception of justice. Now the difference principle is not of course the principle of redress. It does not require society to try to even out handicaps as if all were expected to compete on a fair basis in the same race. But the difference principle would allocate resources in education, say, so as to improve the long-term expectation of the least favored. If this end is attained by giving more attention to the better endowed, it is permissible; otherwise not. And in making this decision, the value of education should not be assessed only in terms of economic efficiency and social welfare. Equally if not more important is the role of education in enabling a person to enjoy the culture of his society and to take part in its affairs, and in this way to provide for each individual a secure sense of his own worth.

Thus although the difference principle is not the same as that of redress, it does achieve some of the intent of the latter principle. It transforms the aims of the basic structure so that the total scheme of institutions no longer emphasizes social efficiency and technocratic values. . . .

. . . The natural distribution is neither just nor unjust; nor is it unjust that men are born into society at some particular position. These are simply natural facts. What is just and unjust is the way that institutions deal with these facts. Aristocratic and caste societies are unjust because they make these contingencies the ascriptive basis for belonging to more or less enclosed and privileged social classes. The basic structure of these societies incorporates the arbitrariness found in nature. But there is no necessity for men to resign themselves to these contingencies. The social system is not an unchangeable order beyond human control but a pattern of human action. In justice as fairness men agree to share one another's fate. In designing institutions they undertake to avail themselves of the accidents of nature and social circumstance only when doing so is for the common benefit. The two principles are a fair way of meeting the arbitrariness of fortune; and while no doubt imperfect in other ways, the institutions which satisfy these principles are just. . . .

There is a natural inclination to object that those better situated deserve their greater advantages whether or not they are to the bene-fit of others. At this point it is necessary to be clear about the notion of desert. It is perfectly true that given a just system of cooperation as a scheme of public rules and the expectations set up by it, those who, with the prospect of improving their condition, have done what the system announces that it will reward are entitled to their advantages. In this sense the more fortunate have a claim to their better situation; their claims are legitimate expectations established by social institutions, and the community is obligated to meet them. But this sense of desert presupposes the existence of the cooperative scheme; it is irrelevant to the question whether in the first place the scheme is to be designed in accordance with the difference principle or some other criterion.

Perhaps some will think that the person with greater natural endowments deserves those assets and the superior character that made their development possible. Because he is more worthy in this sense, he deserves the greater advantages that he could achieve with them. This view, however, is surely incorrect. It seems to be one of the fixed points of our considered judgments that no one deserves his place in the distribution of native endowments, any more than one deserves one's initial starting place in society. The assertion that a man deserves the superior character that enables him to make the effort to cultivate his abilities is equally problematic, for his character depends in large part upon fortunate family and social circumstances for which he can claim no credit. The notion of desert seems not to apply to these cases. Thus the more advantaged representative man cannot say that he deserves and therefore has a right to a scheme of cooperation in which he is permitted to acquire benefits in ways that do not contribute to the welfare of others. There is no basis for his making this claim. From the standpoint of common sense, then, the difference principle appears to be acceptable both to the more advantaged and to the less advantaged individual. . . .

BACKGROUND INSTITUTIONS FOR DISTRIBUTIVE JUSTICE

The main problem of distributive justice is the choice of a social system. The principles of justice apply to the basic structure and regulate how its major institutions are combined into one scheme. Now, as we have seen, the idea of justice as fairness is to use the notion of pure procedural justice to handle the contingencies of particular situations. The social system is to be designed so that the resulting distribution is just however things turn out. To achieve this end it is necessary to get the social and economic process within the surroundings of suitable political and legal institutions. Without an appropriate scheme of these background institutions the outcome of the distributive process will not be just. Background fairness is lacking. I shall give a brief description of these supporting institutions as they might exist in a properly organized democratic state that allows private ownership of capital and natural resources. . . .

In establishing these background institutions the government may be thought of as divided into four branches.[1] Each branch consists of various agencies, or activities thereof, charged with preserving certain social and economic conditions. These divisions do not overlap with the usual organization of government but are to be understood as different functions. The allocation branch, for example, is to keep the price system workably competitive and to prevent the formation of unreasonable market power. Such power does not exist as long as markets cannot be made more competitive consistent with the requirements of efficiency and the facts of geography and the preferences of households. The allocation branch is also charged with identifying and correcting, say by suitable taxes and subsidies and by changes in the definition of property rights, the more obvious departures from efficiency caused by the failure of prices

to measure accurately social benefits and costs. To this end suitable taxes and subsidies may be used, or the scope and definition of property rights may be revised. The stabilization branch, on the other hand, strives to bring about reasonably full employment in the sense that those who want work can find it and the free choice of occupation and the deployment of finance are supported by strong effective demand. These two branches together are to maintain the efficiency of the market economy generally.

The social minimum is the responsibility of the transfer branch. . . . The essential idea is that the workings of this branch take needs into account and assign them an appropriate weight with respect to other claims. A competitive price system gives no consideration to needs and therefore it cannot be the sole device of distribution. There must be a division of labor between the parts of the social system in answering to the common sense precepts of justice. Different institutions meet different claims. Competitive markets properly regulated secure free choice of occupation and lead to an efficient use of resources and allocation of commodities to households. They set a weight on the conventional precepts associated with wages and earnings, whereas a transfer branch guarantees a certain level of well-being and honors the claims of need. . . .

It is clear that the justice of distributive shares depends on the background institutions and how they allocate total income, wages and other income plus transfers. There is with reason strong objection to the competitive determination of total income, since this ignores the claims of need and an appropriate standard of life. From the standpoint of the legislative stage it is rational to insure oneself and one's descendants against these contingencies of the market. Indeed, the difference principle presumably requires this. But once a suitable minimum is provided by transfers, it may be perfectly fair that the rest of total income be settled by the price system, assuming that it is moderately efficient and free from monopolistic restrictions, and unreasonable externalities have been eliminated. Moreover, this way of dealing with the claims of need would appear to be more effective than trying to regulate income by minimum wage standards, and the like. It is better to assign to each branch only such tasks as are compatible with one another. Since the market is not suited to answer the claims of need, these should be met by a separate arrangement. Whether the principles of justice are satisfied, then, turns on whether the total income of the least advantaged (wages plus transfers) is such as to maximize their long-run expectations (consistent with the constraints of equal liberty and fair equality of opportunity).

Finally, there is a distribution branch. Its task is to preserve an approximate justice in distributive shares by means of taxation and the necessary adjustments in the rights of property. Two aspects of this branch may be distinguished. First of all, it imposes a number of inheritance and gift taxes, and sets restrictions on the rights of bequest. The purpose of these levies and regulations is not to raise revenue (release resources to government) but gradually and continually to correct the distribution of wealth and to prevent concentrations of power detrimental to the fair value of political liberty and fair equality of opportunity. For example, the progressive principle might be applied at the beneficiary's end.[2] Doing this would encourage the wide dispersal of property which is a necessary condition, it seems, if the fair value of the equal liberties is to be maintained.

NOTES

1. For the idea of branches of government, see R. A. Musgrave, *The Theory of Public Finance* (New York: McGraw-Hill, 1959), Ch. 1.
2. See Meade, *Efficiency, Equality and the Ownership of Property*, pp. 56f.

The Entitlement Theory

Robert Nozick

The term "distributive justice" is not a neutral one. Hearing the term "distribution," most people presume that some thing or mechanism uses some principle or criterion to give out a supply of things. Into this process of distributing shares some error may have crept. So it is an open question, at least, whether *re*distribution should take place; whether we should do again what has already been done once, though poorly. However, we are not in the position of children who have been given portions of pie by someone who now makes last minute adjustments to rectify careless cutting. There is no *central* distribution, no person or group entitled to control all the resources, jointly deciding how they are to be doled out. What each person gets, he gets from others who give to him in exchange for something, or as a gift. In a free society, diverse persons control different resources, and new holdings arise out of the voluntary exchanges and actions of persons. . . .

The subject of justice in holdings consists of three major topics. The first is the *original acquisition of holdings,* the appropriation of unheld things. This includes the issues of how unheld things may come to be held, the process, or processes, by which unheld things may come to be held, the things that may come to be held by these processes, the extent of what comes to be held by a particular person, and so on. We shall refer to the complicated truth about this topic, which we shall not formulate here, as the principle of justice in acquisition. The second topic concerns the *transfer of holdings* from one person to another. By what processes may a person transfer holdings to another? How may a person acquire a holding from another who holds it? Under this topic come general descriptions of voluntary exchange, and gift and (on the other hand) fraud, as well as reference to particular conventional details fixed upon in a given society. The complicated truth about this subject (with placeholders for conventional details) we shall call the principle of justice in transfer. (And we shall suppose it also includes principles governing how a person may divest himself of a holding, passing it into an unheld state.)

If the world were wholly just, the following inductive definition would exhaustively cover the subject of justice in holdings.

1. A person who acquires a holding in accordance with the principle of justice in acquisition is entitled to that holding.
2. A person who acquires a holding in accordance with the principle of justice in transfer, from someone else entitled to the holding, is entitled to the holding.
3. No one is entitled to a holding except by (repeated) applications of 1 and 2.

The complete principle of distributive justice would say simply that a distribution is just if everyone is entitled to the holdings they possess under the distribution. . . .

Not all actual situations are generated in accordance with the two principles of justice in holdings: the principle of justice in acquisition and the principle of justice in transfer. Some people steal from others, or defraud them, or enslave them, seizing their product and preventing them from living as they choose, or forcibly exclude others from competing in exchanges. None of these are permissible modes of transition from one situation to another. And some persons acquire holdings by means not sanctioned by the principle of justice in acquisition. The existence of past injustice (previous violations of the first two principles of justice in holdings) raises the third major topic under justice in holdings: the rectification of injustice in holdings. If past injustice has shaped present holdings in various ways, some identifiable and some not, what now, if anything, ought to be done to rectify these injustices? . . .

HISTORICAL PRINCIPLES AND END-RESULT PRINCIPLES

The general outlines of the entitlement theory illuminate the nature and defects of other conceptions of distributive justice. The entitlement theory of justice in distribution is *historical;* whether a distribution is just depends upon how it came about. In contrast, *current time-slice principles* of justice hold that the justice of a distribution is determined by how things are distributed (who has what) as judged by some *structural* principle(s) of just distribution. A utilitarian who judges between any two distributions by seeing which has the greater sum of utility and, if the sums tie, applies some fixed equality criterion to choose the more equal distribution, would hold a current time-slice principle of justice. As would someone who had a fixed schedule of trade-offs between the sum of happiness and equality. According to a current time-slice principle, all that needs to be looked at, in judging the justice of a distribution, is who ends up with what; in comparing any two distributions one need look only at the matrix presenting the distributions. No further information need be fed into a principle of justice. It is a consequence of such principles of justice that any two structurally identical distributions are equally just. . . .

Most persons do not accept current time-slice principles as constituting the whole story about distributive shares. They think it relevant in assessing the justice of a situation to consider not only the distribution it embodies, but also how that distribution came about. If some persons are in prison for murder or war crimes, we do not say that to assess the justice of the distribution in the society we must look only at what this person has, and that person has, and that person has, . . . at the current time. We think it relevant to ask whether someone did something so that he *deserved* to be punished, deserved to have a lower share. . . .

PATTERNING

. . . Almost every suggested principle of distributive justice is patterned: to each according to his moral merit, or needs, or marginal product, or how hard he tries, or the weighted sum of the foregoing, and so on. The principle of entitlement we have sketched is *not* patterned. There is no one natural dimension or weighted sum or combination of a small number of natural dimensions that yields the distributions generated in accordance with the principle of entitlement. The set of holdings that results when some persons receive their marginal products, others win at gambling, others receive a share of their mate's income,

others receive gifts from foundations, others receive interest on loans, others receive gifts from admirers, others receive returns on investment, others make for themselves much of what they have, others find things, and so on, will not be patterned. . . .

To think that the task of a theory of distributive justice is to fill in the blank in "to each according to his _____" is to be predisposed to search for a pattern; and the separate treatment of "from each according to his _____" treats production and distribution as two separate and independent issues. On an entitlement view these are *not* two separate questions. Whoever makes something, having bought or contracted for all other held resources used in the process (transferring some of his holdings for these cooperating factors), is entitled to it. . . .

So entrenched are maxims of the usual form that perhaps we should present the entitlement conception as a competitor. Ignoring acquisition and rectification, we might say:

> From each according to what he chooses to do, to each according to what he makes for himself (perhaps with the contracted aid of others) and what others choose to do for him and choose to give him of what they've been given previously (under this maxim) and haven't yet expended or transferred.

This, the discerning reader will have noticed, has its defects as a slogan. So as a summary and great simplification (and not as a maxim with any independent meaning) we have:

> *From each as they choose, to each as they are chosen.*

HOW LIBERTY UPSETS PATTERNS

It is not clear how those holding alternative conceptions of distributive justice can reject the entitlement conception of justice in holdings. For suppose a distribution favored by one of these non-entitlement conceptions is realized. Let us suppose it is your favorite one and let us call this distribution D_1; perhaps everyone has an equal share, perhaps shares vary in accordance with some dimension you treasure. Now suppose that Wilt Chamberlain is greatly in demand by basketball teams, being a great gate attraction. (Also suppose contracts run only for a year, with players being free agents). He signs the following sort of contract with a team: In each home game, twenty-five cents from the price of each ticket of admission goes to him. (We ignore the question of whether he is "gouging" the owners, letting them look out for themselves.) The season starts, and people cheerfully attend his team's games; they buy their tickets, each time dropping a separate twenty-five cents of their admission price into a special box with Chamberlain's name on it. They are excited about seeing him play; it is worth the total admission price to them. Let us suppose that in one season one million persons attend his home games, and Wilt Chamberlain winds up with $250,000, a much larger sum than the average income and larger even than anyone else has. Is he entitled to this income? Is this new distribution D_2, unjust? If so, why? There is *no* question about whether each of the people was entitled to the control over the resources they held in D_1; because that was the distribution (your favorite) that (for the purposes of argument) we assumed was acceptable. Each of these persons *chose* to give twenty-five cents of their money to Chamberlain. They could have spent it on going to the movies, or on candy bars, or on copies of *Dissent* magazine, or of *Monthly Review*. But they all, at least one million of them, converged on giving it to Wilt Chamberlain in exchange for watching him play basketball. If D_1 was a just distribution, and people voluntarily moved from it to D^2, transferring parts of their shares they were given under D_1 (what was it for if not to do something with?), isn't D_2 also just?

If the people were entitled to dispose of the resources to which they were entitled (under D_1) didn't this include their being entitled to give it to, or exchange it with, Wilt Chamberlain? Can anyone else complain on grounds or justice? Each other person already has his legitimate share under D_1. Under D_1, there is nothing that anyone has that anyone else has a claim of justice against. After someone transfers something to Wilt Chamberlain, third parties *still* have their legitimate shares; *their* shares are not changed. By what process could such a transfer among two persons give a rise to a legitimate claim of distributive justice on a portion of what was transferred, by a third party who had no claim of justice on any holding of the others *before* the transfer? To cut off objections irrelevant here, we might imagine the exchanges occurring in a socialist society, after hours. After playing whatever basketball he does in his daily work, or doing whatever other daily work he does, Wilt Chamberlain decides to put in *overtime* to earn additional money. (First his work quota is set; he works time over that.) Or imagine it is a skilled juggler people like to see, who puts on shows after hours. . . .

The general point illustrated by the Wilt Chamberlain example is that no end-state principle or distributional patterned principle of justice can be continuously realized without continuous interference with people's lives. Any favored pattern would be transformed into one unfavored by the principle, by people choosing to act in various ways; for example, by people exchanging goods and services with other people, or giving things to other people, things the transferrers are entitled to under the favored distributional pattern. To maintain a pattern one must either continually interfere to stop people from transferring resources as they wish to, or continually (or periodically) interfere to take from some persons resources that others for some reason chose to transfer to them. . . .

Patterned principles of distributive justice necessitate *re*distributive activities. The likelihood is small that any actual freely-arrived-at set of holdings fits a given pattern; and the likelihood is nil that it will continue to fit the pattern as people exchange and give. From the point of view of an entitlement theory, redistribution is a serious matter indeed, involving, as it does, the violation of people's rights. (An exception is those takings that fall under the principle of the rectification of injustices.) . . .

LOCKE'S THEORY OF ACQUISITION

. . . [Let us] introduce an additional bit of complexity into the structure of the entitlement theory. This is best approached by considering Locke's attempt to specify a principle of justice in acquisition. Locke views property rights in an unowned object as originating through someone's mixing his labor with it. This gives rise to many questions. What are the boundaries of what labor is mixed with? If a private astronaut clears a place on Mars, has he mixed his labor with (so that he comes to own) the whole planet, the whole uninhabited universe, or just a particular plot? Which plot does an act bring under ownership?. . .

Locke's proviso that there be "enough and as good left in common for others" is meant to ensure that the situation of others is not worsened. . . .

. . . I assume that any adequate theory of justice in acquisition will contain a proviso similar to [Locke's]. . . .

I believe that the free operation of a market system will not actually run afoul of the Lockean proviso. . . . If this is correct, the proviso will not . . . provide a significant opportunity for future state action.

Rich and Poor

Peter Singer

One way of making sense of the non-consequentialist view of responsibility is by basing it on a theory of rights of the kind proposed by John Locke or, more recently, Robert Nozick. If everyone has a right to life, and this right is a right *against* others who might threaten my life, but not a right *to* assistance from others when my life is in danger, then we can understand the feeling that we are responsible for acting to kill but not for omitting to save. The former violates the rights of others, the latter does not.

Should we accept such a theory of rights? If we build up our theory of rights by imagining, as Locke and Nozick do, individuals living independently from each other in a 'state of nature', it may seem natural to adopt a conception of rights in which as long as each leaves the other alone, no rights are violated. I might, on this view, quite properly have maintained my independent existence if I had wished to do so. So if I do not make you any worse off than you would have been if I had had nothing at all to do with you, how can I have violated your rights? But why start from such an unhistorical, abstract and ultimately inexplicable idea as an independent individual? We now know that our ancestors

From Peter Singer, "Rich and Poor," in *Practical Ethics* (New York: Cambridge University Press, 1979), pp. 166, 168–179. Reprinted with permission of the publisher.

were social beings long before they were human beings, and could not have developed the abilities and capacities of human beings if they had not been social beings first. In any case we are not, now, isolated individuals. If we consider people living together in a community, it is less easy to assume that rights must be restricted to rights against interference. We might, instead, adopt the view that taking rights to life seriously is incompatible with standing by and watching people die when one could easily save them. . . .

THE OBLIGATION TO ASSIST

The Argument for an Obligation to Assist

The path from the library at my university to the Humanities lecture theatre passes a shallow ornamental pond. Suppose that on my way to give a lecture I noticed that a small child has fallen in and is in danger of drowning. Would anyone deny that I ought to wade in and pull the child out? This will mean getting my clothes muddy, and either cancelling my lecture or delaying it until I can find something dry to change into; but compared with the avoidable death of a child this is insignificant.

A plausible principle that would support the judgment that I ought to pull the child out is this: if it is in our power to prevent something very bad happening, without thereby sacrificing anything of comparable moral significance, we ought to do it. This principle seems uncontroversial. It will obviously win the assent of consequentialists; but non-consequentialists should accept it too, because the injunction to prevent what is bad applies only when nothing comparably significant is at stake. Thus the principle cannot lead to the kinds of actions of which non-consequentialists strongly disapprove—serious violations of individual rights, injustice, bro-

ken promises, and so on. If a non-consequentialist regards any of these as comparable in moral significance to the bad thing that is to be prevented, he will automatically regard the principle as not applying in those cases in which the bad thing can only be prevented by violating rights, doing injustice, breaking promises, or whatever else is at stake. Most non-consequentialists hold that we ought to prevent what is bad and promote what is good. Their dispute with consequentialists lies in their insistence that this is not the sole ultimate ethical principle: that it is *an* ethical principle is not denied by any plausible ethical theory.

Nevertheless the uncontroversial appearance of the principle that we ought to prevent what is bad when we can do so without sacrificing anything of comparable moral significance is deceptive. If it were taken seriously and acted upon, our lives and our world would be fundamentally changed. For the principle applies, not just to rare situations in which one can save a child from a pond, but to the everyday situations in which we can assist those living in absolute poverty. In saying this I assume that absolute poverty, with its hunger and malnutrition, lack of shelter, illiteracy, disease, high infant mortality and low life expectancy, is a bad thing. And I assume that it is within the power of the affluent to reduce absolute poverty, without sacrificing anything of comparable moral significance. If these two assumptions and the principle we have been discussing are correct, we have an obligation to help those in absolute poverty which is no less strong than our obligation to rescue a drowning child from a pond. Not to help would be wrong, whether or not it is intrinsically equivalent to killing. Helping is not, as conventionally thought, a charitable act which it is praiseworthy to do, but not wrong to omit; it is something that everyone ought to do.

This is the argument for an obligation to

assist. Set out more formally, it would look like this.

> First premise: If we can prevent something bad without sacrificing anything of comparable significance, we ought to do it.
>
> Second premise: Absolute poverty is bad.
>
> Third premise: There is some absolute poverty we can prevent without sacrificing anything of comparable moral significance.
>
> Conclusion: We ought to prevent some absolute poverty.

The first premise is the substantive moral premise on which the argument rests, and I have tried to show that it can be accepted by people who hold a variety of ethical positions.

The second premise is unlikely to be challenged. Absolute poverty is, as [Robert] McNamara put in, 'beneath any reasonable definition of human decency' and it would be hard to find a plausible ethical view which did not regard it as a bad thing.

The third premise is more controversial, even though it is cautiously framed. It claims only that some absolute poverty can be prevented without the sacrifice of anything of comparable moral significance. It thus avoids the objection that any aid I can give is just 'drops in the ocean' for the point is not whether my personal contribution will make any noticeable impression on world poverty as a whole (of course it won't) but whether it will prevent some poverty. This is all the argument needs to sustain its conclusion, since the second premise says that any absolute poverty is bad, and not merely the total amount of absolute poverty. If without sacrificing anything of comparable moral significance we can provide just one family with the means to raise itself out of absolute poverty, the third premise is vindicated.

I have left the notion of moral significance unexamined in order to show that the argument does not depend on any specific values

or ethical principles. I think the third premise is true for most people living in industrialized nations, on any defensible view of what is morally significant. Our affluence means that we have income we can dispose of without giving up the basic necessities of life, and we can use this income to reduce absolute poverty. Just how much we will think ourselves obliged to give up will depend on what we consider to be of comparable moral significance to the poverty we could prevent: colour television, stylish clothes, expensive dinners, a sophisticated stereo system, overseas holidays, a (second?) car, a larger house, private schools for our children. . . . For a utilitarian, none of these is likely to be of comparable significance to the reduction of absolute poverty; and those who are not utilitarians surely must, if they subscribe to the principle of universalizability, accept that at least *some* of these things are of far less moral significance than the absolute poverty that could be prevented by the money they cost. So the third premise seems to be true on any plausible ethical view—although the precise amount of absolute poverty that can be prevented before anything of moral significance is sacrificed will vary according to the ethical view one accepts.

Objections to the Argument

Taking Care of Our Own. Anyone who has worked to increase overseas aid will have come across the argument that we should look after those near us, our families and then the poor in our own country, before we think about poverty in distant places.

No doubt we do instinctively prefer to help those who are close to us. Few could stand by and watch a child drown; many can ignore a famine in Africa. But the question is not what we usually do, but what we ought to do, and it is difficult to see any sound moral justification for the view that distance, or community membership, makes a crucial difference to our obligations.

Consider, for instance, racial affinities. Should whites help poor whites before helping poor blacks? Most of us would reject such a suggestion out of hand, [by appeal to] the principle of equal consideration of interests: people's needs for food has nothing to do with their race, and if blacks need food more than whites, it would be a violation of the principle of equal consideration to give preference to whites.

The same point applies to citizenship or nationhood. Every affluent nation has some relatively poor citizens, but absolute poverty is limited largely to the poor nations. Those living on the streets of Calcutta, or in a drought-stricken region of the Sahel, are experiencing poverty unknown in the West. Under these circumstances it would be wrong to decide that only those fortunate enough to be citizens of our own community will share our abundance.

We feel obligations of kinship more strongly than those of citizenship. Which parents could give away their last bowl of rice if their own children were starving? To do so would seem unnatural, contrary to our nature as biologically evolved beings—although whether it would be wrong is another question altogether. In any case, we are not faced with that situation, but with one in which our own children are well-fed, well-clothed, well-educated, and would now like new bikes, a stereo set, or their own car. In these circumstances any special obligations we might have to our children have been fulfilled, and the needs of strangers make a stronger claim upon us.

The element of truth in the view that we should first take care of our own, lies in the advantage of a recognized system of responsibilities. When families and local communities look after their own poorer members, ties of affection and personal relationships achieve ends that would otherwise require a large, impersonal bureaucracy. Hence it would be absurd to propose that from now on we all regard ourselves as equally responsible for the welfare of everyone in the world; but the argument for an obligation to assist does not propose that. It applies only when some are in absolute poverty, and others can help without sacrificing anything of comparable moral significance. To allow one's own kin to sink into absolute poverty would be to sacrifice something of comparable significance; and before that point had been reached, the breakdown of the system of family and community responsibility would be a factor to weigh the balance in favour of a small degree of preference for family and community. This small degree of preference is, however, decisively outweighed by existing discrepancies in wealth and property.

Property Rights. Do people have a right to private property, a right which contradicts the view that they are under an obligation to give some of their wealth away to those in absolute poverty? According to some theories of rights (for instance, Robert Nozick's) provided one has acquired one's property without the use of unjust means like force and fraud, one may be entitled to enormous wealth while others starve. This individualistic conception of rights is in contrast to other views, like the early Christian doctrine to be found in the works of Thomas Aquinas, which holds that since property exists for the satisfaction of human needs, 'whatever a man has in superabundance is owed, of natural right, to the poor for their sustenance.' A socialist would also, of course, see wealth as belonging to the community rather than the individual, while utilitarians, whether socialist or not, would be prepared to override property rights to prevent great evils.

Does the argument for an obligation to assist others therefore presuppose one of these other theories of property rights, and not an individualistic theory like Nozick's? Not necessarily. A theory of property rights can insist on our *right* to retain wealth without pronouncing on whether the rich *ought* to give to the poor. Nozick, for example, rejects the use of compulsory means like taxation to redistribute income, but suggests that we can achieve the ends we deem morally desirable by voluntary means. So Nozick would reject the claim that rich people have an 'obligation' to give to the poor, in so far as this implies that the poor have a right to our aid, but might accept that giving is something we ought to do and failure to give, though within one's rights, is wrong—for rights is not all there is to ethics.

The argument for an obligation to assist can survive, with only minor modifications, even if we accept an individualistic theory of property rights. In any case, however, I do not think we should accept such a theory. It leaves too much to chance to be an acceptable ethical view. For instance, those whose forefathers happened to inhabit some sandy wastes around the Persian Gulf are now fabulously wealthy, because oil lay under those sands; while those whose forefathers settled on better land south of the Sahara live in absolute poverty, because of drought and bad harvests. Can this distribution be acceptable from an impartial point of view? If we imagine ourselves about to begin life as a citizen of either Kuwait or Chad—but we do not know which—would we accept the principle that citizens of Kuwait are under no obligation to assist people living in Chad?

Population and the Ethics of Triage. Perhaps the most serious objection to the argument that we have an obligation to assist is that since the major cause of absolute poverty is overpopulation, helping those now in poverty will only ensure that yet more people are born to live in poverty in the future.

In its most extreme form, this objection is taken to show that we should adopt a policy of 'triage'. The term comes from medical policies adopted in wartime. With too few doctors to cope with all the casualties, the wounded were divided into three categories: those who would probably survive without medical assistance, those who might survive if they received assistance, but otherwise probably would not, and those who even with medical assistance probably would not survive. Only those in the middle category were given medical assistance. The idea, of course, was to use limited medical resources as effectively as possible. For those in the first category, medical treatment was not strictly necessary; for those in the third category, it was likely to be useless. It has been suggested that we should apply the same policies to countries, according to their prospects of becoming self-sustaining. We would not aid countries which even without our help will soon be able to feed their populations. We would not aid countries which, even with our help, will not be able to limit their population to a level they can feed. We would aid those countries where our help might make the difference between success and failure in bringing food and population into balance.

Advocates of this theory are understandably reluctant to give a complete list of the countries they would place into the 'hopeless' category; but Bangladesh is often cited as an example. Adopting the policy of triage would, then, mean cutting off assistance to Bangladesh and allowing famine, disease and natural disasters to reduce the population of that country (now around 80 million) to the level at which it can provide adequately for all.

In support of this view Garrett Hardin has offered a metaphor: we in the rich nations are like the occupants of a crowded lifeboat adrift in a sea full of drowning people. If we try to save the drowning by bringing them aboard our boat will be overloaded and we shall all drown.

Since it is better that some survive than none, we should leave the others to drown. In the world today, according to Hardin, 'lifeboat ethics' apply. The rich should leave the poor to starve, for otherwise the poor will drag the rich down with them. . . .

Anyone whose initial reaction to triage was not one of repugnance would be an unpleasant sort of person. Yet initial reactions based on strong feelings are not always reliable guides. Advocates of triage are rightly concerned with the long-term consequences of our actions. They say that helping the poor and starving now merely ensures more poor and starving in the future. When our capacity to help is finally unable to cope—as one day it must be—the suffering will be greater than it would be if we stopped helping now. If this is correct, there is nothing we can do to prevent absolute starvation and poverty, in the long run, and so we have no obligation to assist. Nor does it seem reasonable to hold that under these circumstances people have a right to our assistance. If we do accept such a right, irrespective of the consequences, we are saying that, in Hardin's metaphor, we would continue to haul the drowning into our lifeboat until the boat sank and we all drowned.

If triage is to be rejected it must be tackled on its own ground, within the framework of consequentialist ethics. Here it is vulnerable. Any consequentialist ethics must take probability of outcome into account. A course of action that will certainly produce some benefit is to be preferred to an alternative course that may lead to a slightly larger benefit, but is equally likely to result in no benefit at all. Only if the greater magnitude of the uncertain benefit outweighs its uncertainty should we choose it. Better one certain unit of benefit than a 10% chance of 5 units; but better a 50% chance of 3 units than a single certain unit. The same principle applies when are we trying to avoid evils.

The policy of triage involves a certain, very great evil: population control by famine and disease. Tens of millions would die slowly. Hundreds of millions would continue to live in absolute poverty, at the very margin of existence. Against this prospect, advocates of the policy place a possible evil which is greater still: the same process of famine and disease, taking place in, say, fifty years time, when the world's population may be three times its present level, and the number who will die from famine, or struggle on in absolute poverty, will be that much greater. The question is: how probable is this forecast that continued assistance now will lead to greater disasters in the future?

Forecasts of population growth are notoriously fallible, and theories about the factors which affect it remain speculative. One theory, at least as plausible as any other, is that countries pass through a 'demographic transition' as their standard of living rises. When people are very poor and have no access to modern medicine their fertility is high, but population is kept in check by high death rates. The introduction of sanitation, modern medical techniques and other improvements reduces the death rate, but initially has little effect on the birth rate. Then population grows rapidly. Most poor countries are now in this phase. If standards of living continue to rise, however, couples begin to realize that to have the same number of children surviving to maturity as in the past, they do not need to give birth to as many children as their parents did. The need for children to provide economic support in old age diminishes. Improved education and the emancipation and employment of women also reduce the birthrate, and so population growth begins to level off. Most rich nations have reached this stage, and their populations are growing only very slowly.

If this theory is right, there is an alternative to the disasters accepted as inevitable by supports of triage. We can assist poor countries to raise the living standards of the poorest members of their population. We can encourage the governments of these countries to enact land reform measures, improve education, and liberate women from a purely child-bearing role. We can also help other countries to make contraception and sterilization widely available. There is a fair chance that these measures will hasten the onset of the demographic transition and bring population growth down to a manageable level. Success cannot be guaranteed; but the evidence that improved economic security and education reduce population growth is strong enough to make triage ethically unacceptable. We cannot allow millions to die from starvation and disease when there is a reasonable probability that population can be brought under control without such horrors.

Population growth is therefore not a reason against giving overseas aid, although it should make us think about the kind of aid to give. Instead of food handouts, it may be better to give aid that hastens the demographic transition. This may mean agricultural assistance for the rural poor, or assistance with education, or the provision of contraceptive services. Whatever kind of aid proves most effective in specific circumstances, the obligation to assist is not reduced.

One awkward question remains. What should we do about a poor and already overpopulated country which, for religious or nationalistic reasons, restricts the use of contraceptives and refuses to slow its population growth? Should we nevertheless offer development assistance? Or should we make our offer conditional on effective steps being taken to reduce the birthrate? To the latter course, some would object that putting conditions on aid is an attempt to impose our own ideas on independent sovereign nations. So it is—but is this imposition unjustifiable? If the argument for an obligation to assist is sound, we have an obligation to reduce absolute poverty; but v e have no obligation to make sacrifices that, to the best of our knowledge, have no prospect of reducing poverty in the long run. Hence we have no obligation to assist countries whose governments have policies which will make our aid ineffective. This could be very harsh on poor citizens of these countries—for they may have no say in the government's policies—but we will help more people in the long run by using our resources where they are most effective.

Spheres of Justice

Michael Walzer

COMPLEX EQUALITY AND PLURALISM

Distributive justice is a large idea. It draws the entire world of goods within the reach of philosophical reflection. Nothing can be omitted; no feature of our common life can escape scrutiny. Human society is a distributive community. That's not all it is, but it is importantly that: we come together to share, divide, and exchange. We also come together to make the things that are shared, divided, and exchanged; but that very making—work itself—is distributed among us in a division of labor. My place in the economy, my standing in the political order, my reputation among my fellows, my material holdings: all these come to me from other men and women. It can be said that I have what I have rightly or wrongly, justly or unjustly; but given the range of distributions and the number of participants, such judgments are never easy.

The idea of distributive justice has as much to do with being and doing as with having, as much to do with production as with consumption, as much to do with identity and status as with land, capital, or personal possessions. Different political arrangements enforce, and different ideologies justify, different distributions of membership, power, honor, ritual eminence, divine grace, kinship and love, knowledge, wealth, physical security, work and leisure, rewards and punishments, and a host of goods more narrowly and materially conceived—food, shelter, clothing, transportation, medical care, commodities of every sort, and all the odd things (paintings, rare books, postage stamps) that human beings collect. And this multiplicity of goods is matched by a multiplicity of distributive procedures, agents, and criteria. There are such things as simple distributive systems—slave galleys, monasteries, insane asylums, kindergartens (though each of these, looked at closely, might show unexpected complexities); but no full-fledged human society has ever avoided the multiplicity. We must study it all, the goods and the distributions, in many different times and places.

There is, however, no single point of access to this world of distributive arrangements and ideologies. There has never been a universal medium of exchange. Since the decline of the barter economy, money has been the most common medium. But the old maxim according to which there are some things that money can't buy is not only normatively but also factually true. What should and should not be up for sale is something men and women always have to decide and have de-

cided in many different ways. Throughout history, the market has been one of the most important mechanisms for the distribution of social goods; but it has never been, it nowhere is today, a complete distributive system.

Similarly, there has never been either a single decision point from which all distributions are controlled or a single set of agents making decisions. No state power has ever been so pervasive as to regulate all the patterns of sharing, dividing, and exchanging out of which a society takes shape. Things slip away from the state's grasp; new patterns are worked out—familial networks, black markets, bureaucratic alliances, clandestine political and religious organizations. State officials can tax, conscript, allocate, regulate, appoint, reward, punish, but they cannot capture the full range of goods or substitute themselves for every other agent of distribution. Nor can anyone else do that: there are market coups and cornerings, but there has never been a fully successful distributive conspiracy.

And finally, there has never been a single criterion, or a single set of interconnected criteria, for all distributions. Desert, qualification, birth and blood, friendship, need, free exchange, political loyalty, democratic decision: each has had its place, along with many others, uneasily coexisting, invoked by competing groups, confused with one another.

In the matter of distributive justice, history displays a great variety of arrangements and ideologies. But the first impulse of the philosopher is to resist the displays of history, the world of appearances, and to search for some underlying unity: a short list of basic goods, quickly abstracted to a single good; a single distributive criterion or an interconnected set; and the philosopher himself standing, symbolically at least, at a single decision point. I shall argue that to search for unity is to misunderstand the subject matter of distributive justice. Nevertheless, in some sense the philosophical impulse is unavoidable. Even if we choose pluralism, as I shall do, that choice still requires a coherent defense. There must be principles that justify the choice and set limits to it, for pluralism does not require us to endorse every proposed distributive criterion or to accept every would-be agent. Conceivably, there is a single principle and a single legitimate kind of pluralism. But this would still be a pluralism that encompassed a wide range of distributions. By contrast, the deepest assumption of most of the philosophers who have written about justice, from Plato onward, is that there is one, and only one, distributive system that philosophy can rightly encompass.

Today this system is commonly described as the one that ideally rational men and women would choose if they were forced to choose impartially, knowing nothing of their own situation, barred from making particularist claims, confronting an abstract set of goods.[1] If these constraints on knowing and claiming are suitably shaped, and if the goods are suitably defined, it is probably true that a singular conclusion can be produced. Rational men and women, constrained this way or that, will choose one, and only one, distributive system. But the force of that singular conclusion is not easy to measure. It is surely doubtful that those same men and women, if they were transformed into ordinary people, with a firm sense of their own identity, with their own goods in their hands, caught up in everyday troubles, would reiterate their hypothetical choice or even recognize it as their own. The problem is not, most importantly, with the particularism of interest, which philosophers have always assumed they could safely—that is, uncontroversially—set aside. Ordinary people can do that too, for the sake, say, of the public interest. The greater problem is with the particularism of history, culture, and membership. Even if they are com-

mitted to impartiality, the question most likely to arise in the minds of the members of a political community is not, What would rational individuals choose under universalizing conditions of such-and-such a sort? But rather, What would individuals like us choose, who are situated as we are, who share a culture and are determined to go on sharing it? And this is a question that is readily transformed into, What choices have we already made in the course of our common life? What understandings do we (really) share?

Justice is a human construction, and it is doubtful that it can be made in only one way. At any rate, I shall begin by doubting, and more than doubting, this standard philosophical assumption. The questions posed by the theory of distributive justice admit of a range of answers, and there is room within the range for cultural diversity and political choice. It's not only a matter of implementing some singular principle or set of principles in different historical settings. No one would deny that there is a range of morally permissible implementations. I want to argue for more than this: that the principles of justice are themselves pluralistic in form; that different social goods ought to be distributed for different reasons, in accordance with different procedures, by different agents; and that all these differences derive from different understandings of the social goods themselves— the inevitable product of historical and cultural particularism. . . .

MEMBERSHIP AND JUSTICE

The distribution of membership is not pervasively subject to the constraints of justice. Across a considerable range of the decisions that are made, states are simply free to take in strangers (or not)—much as they are free, leaving aside the claims of the needy, to share their wealth with foreign friends, to honor the achievements of foreign artists, scholars, and scientists, to choose their trading partners, and to enter into collective security arrangements with foreign states. But the right to choose an admissions policy is more basic than any of these, for it is not merely a matter of acting in the world, exercising sovereignty, and pursuing national interests. At stake here is the shape of the community that acts in the world, exercises sovereignty, and so on. Admission and exclusion are at the core of communal independence. They suggest the deepest meaning of self-determination. Without them, there could not be *communities of character*, historically stable, ongoing associations of men and women with some special commitment to one another and some special sense of their common life.[2]

But self-determination in the sphere of membership is not absolute. It is a right exercised, most often, by national clubs or families, but it is held in principle by territorial states. Hence it is subject both to internal decisions by the members themselves (*all* the members, including those who hold membership simply by right of place) and to the external principle of mutual aid. Immigration, then, is both a matter of political choice and moral constraint. Naturalization, by contrast, is entirely constrained: every new immigrant, every refugee taken in, every resident and worker must be offered the opportunities of citizenship. If the community is so radically divided that a single citizenship is impossible, then its territory must be divided, too, before the rights of admission and exclusion can be exercised. For these rights are to be exercised only by the community as a whole (even if, in practice, some national majority dominates the decision making) and only with regard to foreigners, not by some members with regard to others. No community can be half-metic, half-citizen and claim that its admissions policies are acts of self-determination or that its politics is democratic.

The determination of aliens and guests by an exclusive band of citizens (or of slaves by masters, or women by men, or blacks by whites, or conquered peoples by their conquerors) is not communal freedom but oppression. The citizens are free, of course, to set up a club, make membership as exclusive as they like, write a constitution, and govern one another. But they can't claim territorial jurisdiction and rule over the people with whom they share the territory. To do this is to act outside their sphere, beyond their rights. It is a form of tyranny. Indeed, the rule of citizens over non-citizens, of members over strangers, is probably the most common form of tyranny in human history. . . .

FREE EXCHANGE

Free exchange is obviously open-ended; it guarantees no particular distributive outcome. At no point in any exchange process plausibly called "free" will it be possible to predict the particular division of social goods that will obtain at some later point.[3] (It may be possible, however, to predict the general structure of the division.) In theory at least, free exchange creates a market within which all goods are convertible into all other goods through the neutral medium of money. There are no dominant goods and no monopolies. Hence the successive divisions that obtain will directly reflect the social meanings of the goods that are divided. For each bargain, trade, sale, and purchase will have been agreed to voluntarily by men and women who know what that meaning is, who are indeed its makers. Every exchange is a revelation of social meaning. By definition, then, no x will ever fall into the hands of someone who possesses y, merely because he possesses y and without regard to what x actually means to some other member of society. The market is radically pluralistic in its operations and its outcomes, infinitely sensitive to the meanings that individuals attach to goods. What possible restraints can be imposed on free exchange, then, in the name of pluralism?

But everyday life in the market, the actual experience of free exchange, is very different from what the theory suggests. Money, supposedly the neutral medium, is in practice a dominant good, and it is monopolized by people who possess a special talent for bargaining and trading—the green thumb of bourgeois society. Then other people demand a redistribution of money and the establishment of the regime of simple equality, and the search begins for some way to sustain that regime. But even if we focus on the first untroubled moment of simple equality—free exchange on the basis of equal shares—we will still need to set limits on what can be exchanged for what. For free exchange leaves distributions entirely in the hands of individuals, and social meanings are not subject, or are not always subject, to the interpretative decisions of individual men and women.

Consider an easy example, the case of political power. We can conceive of political power as a set of goods of varying value, votes, influence, offices, and so on. Any of these can be traded on the market and accumulated by individuals willing to sacrifice other goods. Even if the sacrifices are real, however, the result is a form of tyranny—petty tyranny, given the conditions of simple equality. Because I am willing to do without my hat, I shall vote twice; and you who value the vote less than you value my hat, will not vote at all. I suspect that the result is tyrannical even with regard to the two of us, who have reached a voluntary agreement. . . .

Free exchange is not a general criterion, but we will be able to specify the boundaries within which it operates only through a careful analysis of particular social goods. . . .

THE MARKETPLACE

There is a stronger argument about the sphere of money, the common argument of the defenders of capitalism: that market outcomes matter a great deal because the market, if it is free, gives to each person exactly what he deserves. The market rewards us all in accordance with the contributions we make to one another's well-being.[4] The goods and services we provide are valued by potential consumers in such-and-such a way, and these values are aggregated by the market, which determines the price we receive. And that price is our desert, for it expresses the only worth our goods and services can have, the worth they actually have for other people. But this is to misunderstand the meaning of desert. Unless there are standards of worth independent of what people want (and are willing to buy) at this or that moment in time, there can be no deservingness at all. We would never know what a person deserved until we saw what he had gotten. And that can't be right.

Imagine a novelist who writes what he hopes will be a best seller. He studies his potential audience, designs his book to meet the current fashion. Perhaps he had to violate the canons of his art in order to do that, and perhaps he is a novelist for whom the violation was painful. He has stooped to conquer. Does he now deserve the fruits of his conquest? Does he deserve a conquest that bears fruit? His novel appears, let's say, during a depression when no one has money for books, and very few copies are sold; his reward is small. Has he gotten less than he deserves? (His fellow writers smile at his disappointment; perhaps that's what he deserves.) Years later, in better times, the book is reissued and does well. Has its author become more deserving? Surely desert can't hang on the state of the economy. There is too much luck involved here; talk of desert makes little sense. We would do better to say simply that the writer is entitled to his royalties, large or small.[5] He is like any other entrepreneur; he has bet on the market. It's a chancy business, but he knew that when he made the bet. He has a right to what he gets—after he has paid the costs of communal provision (he lives not only in the market but also in the city). But he can't claim that he has gotten less than he deserves, and it doesn't matter if the rest of us think that he has gotten more. The market doesn't recognize desert. Initiative, enterprise, innovation, hard work, ruthless dealing, reckless gambling, the prostitution of talent: all these are sometimes rewarded, sometimes not.

But the rewards that the market provides, when it provides them, are appropriate to these sorts of effort. The man or woman who builds a better mousestrap, or opens a restaurant and sells delicious blintzes, or does a little teaching on the side, is looking to earn money. And why not? No one would want to feed blintzes to strangers, day after day, merely to win their gratitude. Here in the world of the petty bourgeoisie, it seems only right that an entrepreneur, able to provide timely goods and services, should reap the rewards he had in mind when he went to work.

This is, indeed, a kind of "rightness" that the community may see fit to enclose and restrain. The morality of the bazaar belongs in the bazaar. The market is a zone of the city, not the whole of the city. But it is a great mistake, I think, when people worried about the tyranny of the market seek its entire abolition. It is one thing to clear the Temple of traders, quite another to clear the streets. The latter move would require a radical shift in our understanding of what material things are for and of how we relate to them and to other people through them. But the shift is not accomplished by the abolition; commodity exchange is merely driven underground; or it takes place in state stores, as in parts of Eastern Europe today, drearily and inefficiently.

The liveliness of the open market reflects our sense of the great variety of desirable things; and so long as that is our sense, we have no reason not to relish the liveliness. . . .

THE RELATIVITY AND THE NON-RELATIVITY OF JUSTICE

Justice is relative to social meanings. Indeed, the relativity of justice follows from the classic non-relative definition, giving each person his due, as much as it does from my own proposal, distributing goods for "internal" reasons. These are formal definitions that require, as I have tried to show, historical completion. We cannot say what is due to this person or that one until we know how these people relate to one another through the things they make and distribute. There cannot be a just society until there is a society; and the adjective *just* doesn't determine, it only modifies, the substantive life of the societies it describes. There are an infinite number of possible lives, shaped by an infinite number of possible cultures, religions, political arrangements, geographical conditions, and so on. A given society is just if its substantive life is lived in a certain way—that is, in a way faithful to the shared understandings of the members. . . .

We are (all of us) culture-producing creatures; we make and inhabit meaningful worlds. Since there is no way to rank and order these worlds with regard to their understanding of social goods, we do justice to actual men and women by respecting their particular creations. And they claim justice, and resist tyranny, by insisting on the meaning of social goods among themselves. Justice is rooted in the distinct understandings of places, honors, jobs, things of all sorts, that constitute a shared way of life. To override those understandings is (always) to act unjustly.

Just as one can describe a caste system that meets (internal) standards of justice, so one can describe a capitalist system that does the same thing. But now the description will have to be a great deal more complex, for social meanings are no longer integrated in the same way. It may be the case, as Marx says in the first volume of *Capital,* that the creation and appropriation of surplus value "is peculiar good fortune for the buyer [of labor power], but no injustice at all to the seller."[6] But this is by no means the whole story of justice and injustice in capitalist society. It will also be crucially important whether this surplus value is convertible, whether it purchases special privileges, in the law courts, or in the educational system, or in the spheres of office and politics. Since capitalism develops along with and actually sponsors a considerable differentiation of social goods, no account of buying and selling, no description of free exchange, can possibly settle the question of justice. We will need to learn a great deal about other distributive processes and about their relative autonomy from or integration into the market. The dominance of capital outside the market makes capitalism unjust.

The theory of justice is alert to differences, sensitive to boundaries. It doesn't follow from the theory, however, that societies are more just if they are more differentiated. Justice simply has more scope in such societies, because there are more distinct goods, more distributive principles, more agents, more procedures. And the more scope justice has,

the more certain it is that complex equality will be the form that justice takes. Tyranny also has more scope. Viewed from the outside, from our own perspective, the Indian Brahmins look very much like tyrants—and so they will come to be if the understandings on which their high position is based cease to be shared. From the inside, however, things come to them naturally, as it were, by virtue of their ritual purity. They don't need to turn themselves into tyrants in order to enjoy the full range of social goods. Or, when they do turn themselves into tyrants, they merely exploit the advantages they already possess. But when goods are distinct and distributive spheres autonomous, that same enjoyment requires exertion, intrigue, and violence. This is the crucial sign of tyranny: a continual grabbing of things that don't come naturally, an unrelenting struggle to rule outside one's own company. . . .

JUSTICE IN THE TWENTIETH CENTURY

. . . Contemporary forms of egalitarian politics have their origin in the struggle against capitalism and the particular tyranny of money. And surely in the United States today it is the tyranny of money that most clearly invites resistance: property/power rather than power itself. But it is a common argument that without property/power, power itself is too dangerous. State officials will be tyrants, we are told, whenever their power is not balanced by the power of money. It follows, then, that capitalists will be tyrants whenever wealth is not balanced by a strong government. Or, in the alternative metaphor of American political science, political power and wealth must check one another: since armies of ambitious men and women push forward from one side of the boundary, what we require are similar armies pushing forward from the other side. John Kenneth Galbraith developed this metaphor into a theory of "countervailing powers."[7] There is also a competing argument according to which freedom is served only if the armies of capitalism are always and everywhere unopposed. But that argument can't be right, for it isn't only equality but freedom, too, that we defend when we block a large number of (the larger number of) possible exchanges. . . .

Money can buy power and influence, as it can buy office, education, honor, and so on, without radically coordinating the various distributive spheres and without eliminating alternative processes and agents. It corrupts distributions without transforming them; and then corrupt distributions coexist with legitimate ones, like prostitution alongside married love. But this is tyranny still, and it can make for harsh forms of domination. And if resistance is less heroic than in totalitarian states, it is hardly less important. . . .

The appropriate arrangements in our own society are those, I think, of a decentralized democratic socialism; a strong welfare state run, in part at least, by local and amateur officials; a constrained market; an open and demystified civil service; independent public schools; the sharing of hard work and free time; the protection of religious and familial life; a system of public honoring and dishonoring free from all considerations of rank or class; workers' control of companies and factories; a politics of parties, movements, meetings, and public debate. But institutions of this sort are of little use unless they are inhabited by men and women who feel at home within them and are prepared to defend them. It may be an argument against complex equality that it requires a strenuous defense—and a defense that begins while equality is still in the making. But this is also an argument against liberty. Eternal vigilance is the price of both.

EQUALITY AND SOCIAL CHANGE

Complex equality might look more secure if we could describe it in terms of the harmony, rather than the autonomy, of spheres. But social meanings and distributions are harmonious only in this respect: that when we see why one good has a certain form and is distributed in a certain way, we also see why another must be different. Precisely because of these differences, however, boundary conflict is endemic. The principles appropriate to the different spheres are not harmonious with one another; nor are the patterns of conduct and feeling they generate. Welfare systems and markets, offices and families, schools and states are run on different principles: so they should be. The principles must somehow fit together within a single culture; they must be comprehensible across the different companies of men and women. But this doesn't rule out deep strains and odd juxtapositions. Ancient China was ruled by a hereditary divine-right emperor and a meritocratic bureaucracy. One has to tell a complex story to explain that sort of coexistence. A community's culture is the story its members tell so as to make sense of all the different pieces of their social life—and justice is the doctrine that distinguishes the pieces. In any differentiated society, justice will make for harmony only if it first makes for separation. Good fences make just societies.

We never know exactly where to put the fences; they have no natural location. The goods they distinguish are artifacts; as they were made, so they can be remade. Boundaries, then, are vulnerable to shifts in social meaning, and we have no choice but to live with the continual probes and incursions through which these shifts are worked out. Commonly, the shifts are like sea changes, very slow. . . . But the actual boundary revision, when it comes, is likely to come suddenly, as in the creation of a national health service in Britain after the Second World War:

one year, doctors were professionals and entrepreneurs; and the next year, they were professionals and public servants. We can map a program of such revisions, based on our current understanding of social goods. We can set ourselves in opposition, as I have done, to the prevailing forms of dominance. But we can't anticipate the deeper changes in consciousness, not in our own community and certainly not in any other. The social world will one day look different from the way it does today, and distributive justice will take on a different character than it has for us. Eternal vigilance is no guarantee of eternity. . . .

NOTES

1. See John Rawls, *A Theory of Justice* (Cambridge, Mass., 1971): Jürgen Habermas, *Legitimation Crisis,* trans. Thomas McCarthy (Boston, 1975), esp. p. 113; Bruce Ackerman, *Social Justice in the Liberal State* (New Haven, 1980).

2. I have taken the term "communities of charac-

ter" from Otto Bauer (see *Austro-Marxism* [13], p. 107).

3. Cf. Nozick on "patterning," *Anarchy, State, and Utopia* pp. 155 ff [this text, Chap 9].

4. See Louis O. Kelso and Mortimer J. Adler, *The Capitalist Manifesto* (New York, 1958), pp. 67–77, for an argument that makes the distribution of wealth on the basis of contribution analogous to the distribution of office on the basis of merit. Economists like Milton Friedman are more cautious, but this is surely the popular ideology of capitalism: success is a deserved reward for "intelligence, resolution, hard work, and a willingness to take risks" (George Gilder, *Wealth and Poverty* [New York, 1981], p. 101).

5. See Robert Nozick's distinction between entitlement and desert, *Anarchy, State, and Utopia* (New York, 1974), pp. 155–60.

6. Karl Marx, *Capital,* ed. Frederick Engels (New York, 1967), p. 194; I have followed the translation and interpretation of Allen W. Wood, "The Marxian Critique of Justice," *Philosophy and Public Affairs* 1 (1972): 263ff.

7. John Kenneth Galbraith, *American Capitalism* (Boston, 1956), chap. 9.

The Ethics of Conditionality in International Debt

Thomas Donaldson

Increasingly, international financial agencies such as the International Monetary Fund (IMF) and the World Bank lend money to developing countries under conditions that aim at economic reforms, a practice dubbed "conditionality." The standard characteristics of conditionality include restrictions on credit from the domestic banking system, currency devaluation, an agreement to liberalize the

economy by removing trade restraints and internal economic controls, and the reduction of government deficits.

Let us begin by noting an oddity about such lending. If, as creditor institutions claim, the austerity typically associated with such conditionality is in the interest of the borrowing country, why then does the borrower so often object to it? One would expect a debtor

From Thomas Donaldson, "The Ethics of Conditionality in International Debt," *Millennium: Journal of International* to pay for good advice, not have to be enticed to accept it. This oddity not only draws attention to the fact that lenders and borrowers often disagree about the wisdom of given structural reform programs, but implies that global lenders who structure conditions are responsible for the shape and fairness of those conditions. The conditions imposed are, in the most important sense, *their* conditions. Being fair, in turn, requires a recognition of the distinction between the interests of those who contract for loans and those who suffer or succeed under their conditions, and while the very poor of a Third World country stand to be harmed or helped dramatically by austerity programs, their interests are seldom material factors in the loan approval process.

I will argue that:

The economically least well off in a developing country ought not be made worse off, even in the short-to-medium term, as a result of conditions imposed as a part of an international loan arrangement made by an intergovernmental loan agency.

I mean by this that the economically least well off ought not be made worse off as a result of the conditions of the loan relative to the level of welfare they would have achieved without the loan. I shall defend the proposition in two ways: first, by appealing to the moral concept of justice, including Rawlsian constructions of distributive justice and the rights-respecting obligations entailed by the concept of justice; and, second, by appealing to the criterion of consistency in moral analysis. . . .

THE HISTORY OF THE PROBLEM:

. . . The IMF has moved from a situation immediately following WW II when its mission was narrowly construed as one of encouraging liberal trade relations and making short term loans to handle balance of payments problems, as its formal charter prescribes, to one where issues of development are taken seriously. Indeed, the IMF has undergone a dramatic shift in its debtor portfolio, and is now frequently the lender of last resort for the developing world.

The reason for the shift lies primarily in the diminished sources of alternative funds. The shift to a floating currency market in the 1970s and other economic forces spawned credit and balance of payments problems precisely at a time when development funds of the World Bank were becoming scarcer.[1] Into the breach stepped the private banks, who, flush with oil money from the Arab states, accounted by 1980 accounted for 80% of all loans to developing countries, in contrast to only 40% in 1970.[2]

When in 1982 Brazil and Mexico lost their creditworthiness, they and private banks turned to the IMF. The nations did so to obtain desperately needed funds; the banks to establish conditions that would help guarantee repayment of their loans. A global train of national defaults in the 1980s were followed by the imposition of new, creditor-imposed austerity measures. Real interest rates (i.e., interest rates adjusted for inflation) for much of Latin America exceeded 30% during the 1980s, rates at which most economists agree make growth difficult or impossible.[3] Debt repayments, constrained by increasing interest rates as well as austerity, loan-related conditions and worsening terms of trade (especially the lowering commodity prices for developing country's exports), combined in the 1980s to give Latin America a dismal decade. . . .

Critics complain that because it is easier to cut the prerogatives of the politically weak, austerity programs in Latin America and elsewhere have a disproportionate and negative impact upon the poor.[4] Demand control policies are subject to the obvious objection that when demand is curtailed, the rich and middle class can give up inessentials, while the poor are left to their own resources. There is no doubt that debt puts enormous pressure on governments to cut welfare programs, and when governments fail to meet IMF specified criteria, the Fund is capable of responding quickly.

Criticism of structural adjustment occurs in a context of adjustment programs' growing adherence to free market development strategy. A Fund sponsored study of nine IMF adjustment programs in seven countries[5] revealed that most of the programs contained: "fiscal policies designed to reduce government deficits; monetary and credit policies to restrain domestic credit expansion . . . ; exchange rate policies, combined with domestic pricing policies . . . ; and labor market policies to restrain real wages in the organized sector, and increase the flexibility of wages and labor markets."[6] Structural reform is encouraged through the IMF's Extended Fund Facility. It augments the Fund's old standby arrangements, and allows repayment schedules to be extended to as long as six years (in contrast to the six months-to-a-year format of the standby arrangements) and thus accommodates medium-term, structural reform programs.

During the 1980s the tone of the IMF's response to criticism of austerity programs shifted. In the early 1980s the Fund insisted that issues of distribution were improper objects of its concern, since it dealt with sovereign countries, who were formally responsible for such matters. But recent IMF publications indicate a willingness at least to study distributive issues and to provide the results of its findings to prospective loan recipients. Nevertheless, the Fund has not backed away from its insistance that distributive concerns are ultimately the sole business of the nation state.

The Fund's literature tends to justify austerity programs' impact on the economically least well off in two ways: first, by noting that even short term negative results for the eco-

nomically least well off, in the context of reasonable economic restructuring, may well bring long-term benefits; and, second, by denying that the short term negative impacts are as severe as critics have claimed. Yet even Fund believers who insist that adjustment programs play a positive role in protecting the long-term interests of the poor, grant that in the short run the poor frequently suffer—and the short term can be devastating.[7]

Let us grant the IMF's denial that short term impact upon the economically least well off is invariably negative. In some countries, for example, small farmers dominate the agricultural scene and are helped by the expanded opportunities brought by either devaluation (in foreign markets) or the removal of price controls. . . . [But] in claiming that the economically least well off of a third world country ought not to suffer, even in the short term as a result of conditions imposed as a part of an international loan arrangement, it is important to specify that this means they ought not be made worse off as a result of the conditions of the loan *relative to the level of welfare they would have achieved without the loan.*

MORAL THEORY

One way of criticizing debt programs is by pointing to their politically destabilizing effects. But this misses the more fundamental moral issue confronting major lending organizations, namely, how do we frame such obligations regardless of political vicissitudes? Also, interestingly enough, recent analysis suggests that the political case against austerity conditions may be overstated. In recent research, Scott Sidell argues that there is no compelling evidence to assert that political instability on average increases in the face of mounting debt and debt conditionality.[8]

Instead, we can find support for the proposition under consideration by appealing to two uniquely moral concepts, namely, that of justice, including distributive justice, and moral consistency.

GENERAL JUSTICE CONSIDERATIONS:

We may presume that, at a minimum, any theory of justice will also be a theory which entails that bone fide rights be respected. . . .

Let us use [a] list of fundamental international rights for which I have recently argued, namely:[9]

1. The right to freedom of physical movement
2. The right to ownership of property
3. The right to freedom from torture
4. The right to a fair trial
5. The right to non-discriminatory treatment (i.e., freedom from discrimination on the basis of such characteristics as race or sex.)
6. The right to physical security
7. The right to freedom of speech and association
8. The right to minimal education
9. The right to political participation
10. The right to subsistence

. . . Every right entails a duty, that is, every right entails that other persons and institutions not violate the right. But correlative duties involve more than failing to actively deprive people of the enjoyment of their rights. Shue, for example, notes that three types of correlative duties are possible for any right, namely duties to 1) avoid depriving; 2) help protect from deprivation; and 3) aid the deprived.[10] While it is obvious that the honoring of rights clearly imposes duties of the first kinds, i.e., to avoid depriving directly, it is less

obvious, but frequently true, that honoring them involves acts or omissions that help prevent the deprivation of rights. As I have argued elsewhere, multinational corporations have obligations primarily of the first and second kind, while governments have obligations of all three kinds. For example, a multinational corporation has an obligation not to bribe a high government official because it has an obligation to help protect the right to political participation; and it has an obligation to refrain from hiring eight year old children for permanent, full time labor because it has an obligation to help protect the right to a minimal education. In both instances, the corporation's possible direct denial of the rights to political participation and minimal education is not at issue. What is at issue, rather, is the organization's correlative obligation to protect the rights from deprivation.

Similarly, governmental organizations have a moral obligation frequently to aid the deprived, i.e., the third category of obligation. If citizens are starving to death, most would agree that the local national government is obliged to step in and provide food, at least insofar as it is capable. And if citizens are denied even a minimal education, the government must similarly do what it can to provide one.

The very moral status of an international organization such as the World Bank or the IMF is ambiguous. One might argue that its functions resemble that of private banks to a point where its responsibilities should mirror those of private, not government, institutions. Yet surely this view neglects the obvious fact that these organizations are composed entirely of member nations states that are themselves government bodies. Hence, in at least one important sense, both bodies are governmental organizations. Space prevents us from undertaking a thoroughgoing discussion of the issue of the moral status of international lending agencies, and, instead, I propose to nuance it by noting that for purposes of assigning moral status, such agencies are partially, but perhaps not wholly, to be understood as government entities. This means that they are at least responsible for shouldering the correlative obligations attaching to rights that are appropriate for private banks (of the first and second kind), and are also responsible for shouldering *some* correlative obligations appropriate to government agencies (of the third kind), although we shall leave unspecified for present purposes what those duties are.

It follows that the IMF and the World Bank have obligations to refrain from directly depriving people of their rights, as well as, in some instances, to help protect such rights from deprivation. In turn, it follows that any loan arrangement which has the effect of depriving or of failing adequately to protect the economically least well off of a given country of their right to subsistence, or their right to a minimal education, is an arrangement that is unjust, and which ought not be undertaken. I follow Henry Shue in defining the right to subsistence as a right to "minimal economic security," entailing, in turn, a right to, e.g., "unpolluted air, unpolluted water, adequate food, adequate clothing, adequate shelter, and minimal preventative public health care."[11] While what counts as a "minimally sufficient" education may be debated, and while it seems likely, moreover, that the specification of the right to a certain level of education will depend at least in part upon the level of economic resources available in a given country, it is reasonable to assume that any action by a corporation which has the effect of, say, blocking the development of a child's ability to read or write will be morally proscribed on the basis of rights.

Hence, we can say that at a minimum the IMF should refuse to engage in an arrangement that will result in conditions in which the economically least well off are unable to possess adequate food, adequate clothing, minimal education, and minimal preventative public health care. This is a simple requirement of justice, and has obvious application to international lending polices. For in many of the poor debtor countries, the economically least well off, if made still worse off, will fall or stay below levels of adequate education and subsistence.

DISTRIBUTIVE JUSTICE CONSIDERATION

The issue of distributive justice is trickier than that of general justice. Distributive justice, a concept which refers to justice in the distribution of goods, may appear to be irrelevant in international contexts. Indeed, it is not uncommon to hear that while justice in the distribution of key goods such as wealth, food, or health care, is an appropriate topic for national contexts, it is not for international contexts. The recent and monumental analysis of distributive justice undertaken by John Rawls[12] explicitly exempts international considerations from the reach of his famous two principles, i.e., (1) that everyone is entitled to maximal liberty, and (2) that inequalities in the distribution of primary goods are unjust unless everyone, including the average person in the worst affected group, stands to benefit. Rawls's reasons for nationalizing distributive justice are tied to his belief that distributive claims can be evaluated meaningfully only against a background scheme of cooperation that yields goods subject to distribution. Since nation states are customarily the agents that provide the mechanisms necessary for facilitating cooperative arrangements and for pooling and distributing the fruits of such arrangements, and since such mechanisms are conspicuously not provided on the international scale, it seems both idealistic and implausible to speak seriously of distributive justice on an international scale.

Rawls's underlying reasons stem from the notion of the "circumstances of justice" articulated by the English philosopher, David Hume. . . . Hume argued that people usually find themselves in circumstances manifesting four general characteristics which limit the possibility of justice: dependence, moderate scarcity, restrained benevolence, and individual vulnerability. Rawls refers to the circumstances of justice as "the normal conditions under which human cooperation is both possible and necessary," and gives special attention to the condition of dependence and of moderate scarcity, the latter of which he defines as the existence of natural resources "not so abundant that schemes of cooperation become superfluous," nor "conditions so harsh that fruitful ventures must inevitably break down."[13] He explicitly denies that the former characterizes international relations in a way to make the two principles generally relevant, and he may wish to deny in the instance of some third world nations that the latter is applicable.

In the end, however, it seems clear that considerations of distributive justice do apply to international transactions such as lending to poor countries. To begin with, Rawls may be wrong about the scope of his own theory. As Brian Barry often notes, no scheme of cooperation need exist in order to demonstrate the unjustness of allowing toxic air pollution, generated in one country for the benefit of that country, to waft over into the unpolluted atmosphere of a second country.[14] . . .

Hence, one is brought to wonder whether the so-called circumstances of justice are, in truth, necessary either for the meaningful application of such terms as "just" and "unjust," or for the existence of just institutions. For example, it seems at first glance that if people have either an extravagant abundance of material goods, or an extreme scarcity, then issues of justice will not arise. But first impressions may be misleading. Suppose an extravagant abundance of material goods exists; might not questions of justice nonetheless arise over, say, the bestowing of awards in public contests, or in structuring systems of seniority and status? Or, alternatively, suppose that a dramatic scarcity of goods exists. Might not questions of justice arise in determining, say, who should be utterly deprived in order for others to survive?

Yet, even if Rawls were correct in limiting the *general* application of the two principles in the international realm on the grounds of insufficient interdependence, two considerations show that distributive justice is applicable in the specific instance of international loan arrangements. First, the important distribution issues affecting developing countries do not depend on *inter*-national distributive comparisons (distributions *among* nations), but on *intra*-national comparisons (distributions *within* a nation). Hence Rawls's principles have important application, even when inter-national distributive comparisons are excluded. In saying that the economically least well off of a third world country ought not suffer as a result of a loan arrangement, we are not making a claim about the distribution of resources among all nations of the world, but only about the distribution of a single country's resources.

Second, the mere existence of an international loan arrangement is not only testimony to a cooperative endeavor, but representative of an underlying economic association in which at least the developed and probably also the developing countries benefit. For the developed world to be left without benefit of the commodities and markets provided by the developing countries would certainly be an economic blow. While the relationship may not be one of absolute dependence, extreme dependence is not required by the concept of the conditions of justice. And certainly no representative of the IMF has ever suggested that the IMF's activities qualify as *pure* charity, that is, charity of a kind such that the developed nations expect no benefits from virtue of their association. This, in turn, implies a satisfaction of the first condition of justice and the relevance of the concept of distributive justice.

It follows that at least insofar as one accepts Rawls's claim that distributive justice entails the principle that no inequality promoting policy is just if it has the effect of failing to aid the worst off class of person, i.e., the "second principle," then no policy affecting a developing country can be labeled just that makes the economically least well off worse off. Hence, any loan arrangement entered into by the World Bank, the IMF, or any other intergovernmental lending agency which has the effect of increasing the poverty of the very poor in a third world country would fail to satisfy the Rawlsian test of distributive justice.

MORAL CONSISTENCY

The final consideration supporting the proposition under consideration invokes the notion of moral consistency. In particular, I am concerned with the tendency of the international lending agencies to insist on the absolute sovereignty of nation states, especially with respect to the issue of the distributive impact of loan arrangements, and the way such an insistence relates to other accepted policies.

Consider, for example, the widely shared conviction among representatives of global lending agencies that the absence of a European or U.S. style government, including even the absence of a truly democratic government, is insufficient to prohibit such loans and moral grounds. That is, almost every international lending agency agrees that a nation ought not be blacklisted from lending simply for reason of nondemocratic practice. The rationale, sometimes explicit, sometimes implicit, turns on the obvious prospect of benefiting those subject to non-democratic rule even through an arrangement with the rulers themselves. The ruled may benefit even though they did not voluntarily engage in the agreement. . . . The justification of lending to non-democratic regimes presumes that lending agencies can fathom the difference between the interests of the rulers and the ruled, and act accordingly. If so, then there is no reason why they cannot act accordingly also with respect to the issue of distributive justice.

This brings us again to the irony presented at the beginning of the article, namely, why if, as creditor institutions claim, the austerity typically associated with such conditionality is in the interest of the borrowing country, why then does the borrower so often object to it? Again, one would expect a debtor to pay for good advice, not to be enticed to accept it. The answer here, as above, lies in noting that the politicians who contract for loans are not the same persons as those who must suffer or succeed under the loans' conditions, and, as already noted, this distinction is inconsistent with a full reliance on the rationality of decisions made by national governments.

Indeed, the argument that concerns of justice are the exclusive territory of debtor country governments is inconsistent at a still deeper level. Even if we regard international lending arrangements as purely voluntary transactions between consenting parties and leave aside the issue of the contracting rights of governments in contrast to the people they govern, the stipulation of a condition by one party in a proposed voluntary agreement is never regarded as an invasion of the freedom or sovereignty of the other party—since, of course, the other party can voluntarily reject the condition and refuse to engage in the transaction. This is precisely why the loan conditions that are so commonly inserted in international arrangements, i.e., of reducing price controls and inducing monetary restraint, are *not* regarded as a violation of sovereignty. Ordinarily, fiscal policy is regarded as the proper and exclusive province of a sovereign government. The reason why we may not regard the fiscal policy conditions of IMF adjustment agreements to be in violation of national sovereignty is that such conditions are the features of a voluntary statement of reciprocal intent between two sovereign, free agents. But clearly it would be inconsistent to proceed to argue that restrictions on the distributive impact of a given loan arrangement, when set as a condition by an international lending agency to a loan arrangement, violates the national sovereignty of the borrowing country. One cannot have matters both ways.

CONCLUSION

It may be argued that the proposition under consideration *would* be acceptable if were it not for the phrase "even in the short to medium term." If the economically least well off must suffer today in order to benefit tomorrow, then how can justice and moral consistency condemn the requisite "medicine"? But this rhetorical question, which poses a hypothetical state of affairs, is misleading, and truth in this instance does not accommodate our hypotheses. First, there is insufficient reason to believe that the economically least well off *must* suffer now in order to achieve their own long term improvement. A social cushion for the poor in austerity programs is an acceptable, much analyzed option. Nor is there any reason to believe that preventing the very poor in the short to medium term from suffering more than they would have in the absence of a loan agreement will shipwreck the future prospects of an adjustment program.

Short term injustice would be more tempt-

ing—though even then not justified—if optimistic economic predictions were certain and incorrigible. If we knew for certain that the economically least well off could *only* benefit in the long-term by suffering in the short term, and that the policies that caused them to suffer would *without question* bring long term benefits, our welfare calculations would be different. Yet, even modern economic theory has not reached the point where it allows epistemological certainty about such propositions in individual cases. We cannot predict with absolute certainty that adjustment programs of a certain kind, whether free market or other, will in a given instance deliver the desired result.

For example, it is doubtful that pricist extremists are right when they say that if only prices could be left to market forces, everything would be fine, and that, in turn, no independent public sector action would be necessary. As Paul Streeten notes, even if prices were allowed to rise to a "natural" level in Tanzania, farmers would not benefit by producing more. In Tanzania, roads are so inadequate that even if farmers produced more in response to higher prices, the crops could not be transported.[15] The problem is one of infrastructure, not prices, and the cooperation of the public authority is essential. . . .

It is also well to remember that justice is not a concept admitting of short-term or long-term qualifications. The logic of the concept of justice does not allow one to trade off justice here for justice there, or to trade off justice now for justice later. If an act or policy is unjust, it must not be undertaken. And it must not be undertaken either now or in the future. . . .

NOTES

1. Irving S. Friedman, "The International Monetary Fund: A Founder's Evaluation," in *The*

Political Morality of the International Monetary Fund. Ethics and Foreign Policy (New York: Transaction Books) ed., Robert J. Myers, Vol. 3 (1987), pp. 21–22.

2. Henry B. Schechter, "IMF Conditionality and the International Economy: A U.S. Labor Perspective," in *The Political Morality of the International Monetary Fund. Ethics and Foreign Policy* (New York: Transaction Books) ed., Robert J. Myers, Vol. 3 (1987), p. 5.

3. John Williamson, "Reforming the IMF: Different or Better?" in *The Political Morality of the International Monetary Fund. Ethics and Foreign Policy* (New York: Transaction Books) ed., Robert J. Myers, Vol. 3 (1987).

4. Special concern for the poor is evident in the U.S. Catholic Conference Administrative Board in its "Statement on Relieving Third World Debt," *Origins* (October 12, 1989), Vol. 19, No. 19, 1, 307–314.

5. Chile, the Dominican Republic, Bhana, Kenya, the Philippines, Sri Lanka, and Thailand.

6. Peter Heller, "Fund-Supported Adjustment Programs and the Poor," *Finance & Development* (Washington, The World Bank, December 1988), pp. 2–5. See also the original study, i.e., Peter S. Heller, A. Lans Bovenberg, Thanos Catsambas, *et al,* "The Implications of Fund-Supported Adjustment Programs for Poverty. Experiences in Selected Countries" (Washington: International Monetary Fund, May 1988).

7. Heller, Bovenberg, Catsambas, *et al.,* p. 32.

8. Scott R. Sidell, *The IMF and Third-World Political Instability. Is There a Connection?* (London: The MacMillan Press Ltd., 1988).

9. See especially Thomas Donaldson, *The Ethics of International Business* (New York: Oxford University Press, 1989), chapter 5.

10. Henry Shue, *Basic Rights: Subsistence, Affluence, and U.S. Foreign Policy* (Princeton, N.J.: Princeton University Press, 1980), p. 57.

11. Shue, pp. 20–23.

12. John Rawls, *A Theory of Justice* (Cambridge, Mass.: Harvard University Press, 1971).

13. Ibid., pp. 126–28.

14. Brian Barry, "The Case for a New International Economic Order," in J. Roland Pennock and John W. Chapman, eds., *Ethics, Economics, and the Law: Nomos Vol. XXIV* (New York: New York University Press, 1982).

15. Paul Streeten, "Structural Adjustment: A Survey of the Issues and Options," *World Development,* (Boston University) Vol. 15, No. 12 (Pergamon Journals Ltd., 1987), p. 1474.

On Alternatives to Industrial Flight: The Moral Issues

Judith Lichtenberg

Staughton Lynd writes: "Workers in Youngstown and elsewhere are beginning to ask: Why is the company allowed to make a shutdown decision unilaterally? Since the decision affects my life so much, why can't I have a voice in the decision? The communities in which shutdowns occur are starting to ask the same questions."[1]

The thrust of Lynd's questions is moral, not practical. He is asking why companies *ought* to be allowed to exclude workers and communities from shutdown decisions, and he is suggesting that the latter have a *right*—a moral right, which ought perhaps to be made a legal right—to participate in these decisions.

A portion of this article appeared in Center for Philosophy and Public Policy's newsletter, QQ v. 4, No. 3 (Fall 1984). Permission for publication granted by the author.

From some perspectives, these questions seem to answer themselves. The free market defender may say: "It is the company that owns the factory, makes the investments and takes the risks; in accepting jobs, workers freely consent to certain ground rules." Thus, the firm has the right to move whenever it chooses. The committed democrat, on the other hand, may insist that in matters that crucially affect a person's life, that person ought to have some say: "What touches all must be decided by all."[2] A shutdown decision touches deeply the lives of workers, their families, and their communities; they ought to have a say in what happens to the factory on which their livelihoods depend.

These are polar views, framed in the strongest terms—in terms of rights, moral "musts." But there are positions short of the poles that, though expressing some of the same underlying concerns, do not state the issues as inescapable moral imperatives. Defenders of laissez-faire may think not that firms have a natural or God-given *right* to make shutdown decisions unilaterally, only that our kind of economic system is preferable (for which they may have a variety of reasons), and for it to work, firms must completely control investment decisions. Similarly, advocates of workers' participation in company decisions may think not that they have a *right* to participate, but simply that the possibly disastrous consequences of plant closings make a moral claim on our concern.

How can we adjudicate between these conflicting points of view? Suppose we go back to Lynd's questions and the view implicit in his essay—one that challenges the status quo, in which workers have no voice in shutdown decisions. What reasons are there for thinking that the status quo is not as it should be, that workers and communities ought to have some say in decisions about whether a plant stays or goes?

At least two basic kinds of arguments support worker participation. One focuses on the idea that, although in our legal system factories belong to stockholders, workers may acquire a kind of moral property right, a moral claim to some control over their workplaces. The other emphasizes that, through their relationships over time with workers, firms have incurred obligations to them that preclude unilateral shutdown decisions.

The first view rests on the labor theory of property, originally developed by John Locke.[3] The germ of the theory is that property rights are acquired by "mixing one's labor" with, and thereby adding value to, external objects. To make this view workable requires many qualifications, but its essential core is persuasive: Having worked on an object and transformed it into a socially valuable commodity gives one *some* claim to the fruits of one's labor. How much of a claim, and how it compares to that of the entrepreneur who has mixed a different kind of labor and has taken risks the worker has not, are questions a complete theory of property must address.

The second argument for workers' rights to a say in shutdown decisions expresses the idea that when a company has dug deep over generations into people's lives, perhaps affecting a whole community, it incurs obligations to those people and that community. Although the company may have entered freely, it is no longer at liberty simply to withdraw from relationships that have developed over years or even generations.

These are mere sketches of arguments, and I shall not flesh them out here. For some, no elaborate argument is necessary; for others, none will be convincing. Here I shall assume that, as matters of abstract moral right, these views seem persuasive; it seems plausible at least in the abstract that workers have some moral claim to the factories in which they labor and that companies have incurred obligations to these workers and communities that they are not free simply to renounce.

The sticking point is in the phrase *in the abstract.* I said earlier that the thrust of Lynd's questions is moral, not practical. But this is too simple; moral questions are not altogether separable from practical ones. Indeed, much of the controversy about employee versus management claims in plant shutdowns rests precisely on disagreement about what would in fact happen if owners were not free to make such decisions unilaterally. To decide, then, whether the abstract moral arguments for worker participation are plausible when concrete, we need to know more about the consequences of such legal and institutional changes.

What obstacles, then, do abstract moral right and obligation encounter? What arguments can be made against the rights of workers or the duties of owners?

One important argument is that plants like those in the Youngstown area are no longer sufficiently profitable; therefore, it is both natural and right (or at least not wrong) to abandon them for more profitable ventures. *Not sufficiently profitable;* that looks like an easy cover for greed. What profits are sufficient? What the traffic will bear?

But this cynical response may be misguided—or at least premature. The idea that a company can be profitable, yet not sufficiently profitable, can be explained in terms other than sheer avarice; it can be explained by the economics of investment. Unless a plant's rate of return equals the standard rate—that is, unless it is competitive with other ventures in which investment might be made—it will not endure beyond the short run.

This is not to deny that corporations may seek profits above the standard rate of return. It may be their natural tendency to seek the highest profits possible; to suppose so is not to ascribe to them base motives, only the desire for gain often found among human beings. But many economists argue that the tendency to seek higher profits, though it may be motivated only by self-interest, benefits others too. They say that the profit motive leads to the creation of more wealth, and in the long run, not only firms and corporations, but also workers and the general population benefit. The wealth spreads or trickles down. If companies are prevented from closing and seeking higher profits elsewhere, it is argued, in the long run the total pie will shrink, and everyone, workers included, will suffer.

Two claims are implicit here. First, permitting companies to move when they deem fit is *efficient,* that is, will produce more wealth overall.[4] Second, this greater overall wealth will be *distributed* in a way that benefits workers. Each of these claims needs to be considered more carefully.

DOES MANAGEMENT'S FREEDOM TO MOVE INCREASE EFFICIENCY?

The idea that if owners, rather than workers, are legally entitled to make shutdown decisions, the economy will be more efficient, is refuted by a well-known theorem of economics. According to this theorem, if the two parties (in this case, owners and workers) are free to bargain with each other, and each is guided only by economic motives, the most efficient outcome will be reached no matter who possesses the legal entitlement.[5] For whichever side stands to benefit most will simply buy out the other side's entitlement if it doesn't possess the entitlement itself.

Take a simple example. Suppose a company will realize savings in labor costs of $4 million a year if it moves a plant from Ohio to South Carolina. Suppose also that the Ohio workers will lose $3 million, the difference between their present wages and their income, from other jobs or from unemployment compensation if the plant moves. In this case, it is efficient for the factory to move, for efficiency is a matter of realizing the greatest net benefit overall. Now whoever is legally entitled to make the shutdown decision, the plant will move. Suppose the owners have the entitlement. It won't be in the workers' interests to pay more than $3 million to get the plant to stay, and it won't be in the owners' interests to accept less than $4 million. No agreement will be reached, and the plant will move. Now suppose the workers possess the entitlement. Then it will be in the owners' interests to pay up to $4 million to the workers to be allowed to move, and it will be in the workers' interests to accept something above $3 million to allow the plant to move. Owners and workers will reach an agreement under which the plant moves—the efficient outcome.

Now imagine instead that the owners will realize savings of $4 million if the plant relocates, but the workers will lose $5 million. Then it is efficient for the plant to stay. Suppose the workers possess the entitlement. It won't be in the owners' interests to pay more than $4 million to be permitted to move, and it won't be in the workers' interest to accept less than $5 million. No agreement will be reached, and the plant will stay. What if the owners possess the entitlement? Then it will be in the workers' interests to pay up to $5 million to prevent the plant from going, and it will be in the owners' interests to accept something above $4 million. Owners and workers will come to an agreement under which the plant stays—again, the efficient outcome.

There is, then, no merit to the claim that allowing workers to have some control over shutdown decisions is bad for the economy because it is inefficient. The difference between the system in which owners are entitled to make these decisions and the system in which workers are is not a difference in the *total* amount of wealth produced, but in *who* gets the better economic deal. So, for example, in the first case, where owners will save $4

million if the plant moves, but workers will lose $3 million, if the owners have the entitlement, they will move straightaway, saving $4 million while the workers lose $3 million; whereas if the workers have the entitlement, they will be able to bargain for a better deal. The question is not how much wealth, but in whose hands?

DOES MANAGEMENT'S FREEDOM TO MOVE BENEFIT WORKERS?

Now if it is a question of improving the lot of already well-off owners as against much less well-off workers, many people will see no dilemma. And yet it will be argued that the issue is not so simple. For it is often said that if the company realizes higher profits, it will invest them in ways that are good for the economy, and so in the long run for all Americans. But if it pays out what would have been those profits in the form of higher wages, the income will not be saved and invested. Since workers do not have enough income to save, they will spend it on consumer goods, groceries and the like, which do the economy no good.

This argument depends on the assumption that income spent on consumer goods is not invested. True, it is not invested by the consumer. But money spent on groceries increases the profits of the supermarket, which in turn may invest those profits. Some would argue that this sort of investment does not benefit the economy in the way investment by steel companies (and similar producers) does. But this is a disputed question among economists, and it ought not to be assumed without argument, therefore, that money spent on consumer goods has no effect on savings and investment.

There is a more important argument for the view that corporate autonomy benefits workers. When factories close down in the old industrial centers of the North and Northeast, they move to places that have traditionally been poorer: to the South, now fashionably called "the Sunbelt," or to Third World countries whose standard of living is much below that of the average American. The new factories create jobs for workers in these places and may greatly improve their standard of living. This fact seems to confront us with a discomforting dilemma. We are now forced to weight not the welfare of workers against that of owners, but rather the welfare of Youngstown workers against that of workers in South Carolina or Korea. And framed in these terms, it may seem there are good grounds for preferring South Carolinians or Koreans. For these people, especially those in the Third World, are generally much poorer than workers in Ohio, even laid-off workers. Shouldn't we give more weight to the welfare of the worse off than the better off?

So the concern with Youngstown workers might appear to rest on a partial view; when we extend our vision beyond one town or one region, a different picture seems to emerge.

Or does it? Will workers worldwide be better off on balance if plants are permitted to move when they choose, or not? We are interested in what will happen *in the long run,* and predicting what will happen far in the future is extremely difficult. The controversy is at this point in danger of degenerating to mere assertion and counterassertion, for we do not have the tools to settle this dispute empirically.

The argument must proceed at a different level. We can begin by asking why it is that Ohio workers are better off now than their counterparts in the American south or in the Third World. There seem to be several reasons. When the Northeast became industrialized in the nineteenth century, practical necessity dictated the location of factories; they were built close to the source of raw materials, or convenient to waterways or railroads.

Labor was relatively scarce, so workers were in an advantageous bargaining position compared to most modern factory workers. But the position of these earlier American workers was improved immeasurably by the facts of their coexistence under the same management, their similar interests, and the forces making it necessary for factories to be where they were. It became clear that collectively they could exert a power they didn't possess as individuals. They formed unions and were able to extract concessions from the companies. Owners and managers were no longer able to say, "take what we offer or leave it." They were forced to operate partly on workers' terms.

So the situation remained as long as there was no viable alternative to the factories staying where they were; companies could not set the terms of work unilaterally. But as technology developed the situation changed; the reasons keeping factories in the Northeast (such as convenience to waterways) were less weighty, and the attractions of moving (primarily, cheap, unorganized labor elsewhere) became increasingly compelling. There was at this point only one way the company could avoid having to come to a mutually satisfactory agreement with its employees, and that was to move, or threaten to, if workers did not accept management's terms.

Now it is obvious what the effects of shutdowns or relocations are on workers in threatened factories. But we are at the moment considering their effects on workers elsewhere; we are considering the claim that such workers, in greater need, may benefit by such actions. But the two issues are not separate. When Ohio workers have achieved a certain degree of power, companies undermine that power in the only way now available to them: by threatening not to "play the game" anymore. But this has consequences far beyond Ohio. It means undermining the hard-won strides labor has made over the years, and that affects not only the communities in which shutdowns occur, but workers elsewhere as well. For there will always be unorganized workers to act as a magnet for companies when their own employees get into a position to make unwelcomed demands.

Thus, even though the in the short-run workers in South Carolina or Korea might benefit from Ohio plant closings—and might benefit from them more, economically, than Ohio workers are harmed—over time, corporate autonomy in shutdown decisions is a setback for labor, not an advance. This is even more obvious if we think not only in the narrowest economic terms, not simply in terms of dollars, but also in terms of self-respect and the ability to determine important aspects of one's own life. What workers benefiting from plant closings would gain in the short-run are jobs and money—nothing to sneeze at, to be sure. But what they would not gain and what Ohio workers and ultimately all workers would lose is the power to affect in any way a crucial aspect of their lives, their work and livelihood. For they would be forever at the mercy of employers who can say: "take it or leave it."[6]

FREEDOM TO MOVE AND FAIR PLAY

"Take it or leave it" is not only *harmful* to workers, but also *unfair* to them.

Consider an analogy. A child with a Monopoly game offers to play with other children. They play contentedly for a while, but eventually some of the other children are putting hotels on Pennsylvania Avenue and Boardwalk, and the game's owner is broke. He's a bad sport, declares the game at an end ("It's my game"), takes his game and goes home.

Obviously, the child is acting unfairly. He was free to play or not play. But having

agreed to play, he is not free to quit simply because the terms no longer suit him. (It would be different if he began to feel sick or had to finish his homework.) Similarly, we may conclude that the company is acting unfairly if it says, "You play our way or not at all." But the analogy may appear to have its limits. For although in quitting, the child is clearly being unfair, most people would probably say that it would be wrong to force him to continue to play. Would it be similarly wrong to force the company to stay? If so, our conclusion may seem innocuous: the company is acting unfairly, but nothing can be done about it. (After all, "life is unfair.")

The question is this: What is the difference between those situations in which we think, "He's being unfair, but it would be wrong to force him not to," and those in which we conclude, "He's being unfair and should be made to act otherwise"? There are, I think, two conditions relevant to answering this question. One has to do with the costs, of various sorts—economic, moral, political—of forcing people to be fair. It may be literally too expensive to force them, or it may involve trampling on other values, like privacy or personal freedom. The other condition concerns how much is at stake for the participating players.

Obviously, it would be ludicrous to consider bringing the coercive power of the state down upon our poor, unsporting child. It would be ludicrous because not enough is at stake for anyone and because the implications of such a policy in terms of state interference in people's private lives would be monstrous.

What about prohibiting companies from making unilateral decisions to abandon factories? We have argued above that there are no clear economic costs of doing so in terms of efficiency and the like. Nor would it seem to be especially expensive or unwieldy to set into motion the necessary enforcement apparatus. Already existing government agencies, as well as the negotiation structures of management and labor unions, can perform the relevant tasks. Without a compelling argument for owners' exclusive property rights to factories, there do not seem to be any other obvious costs of enforcement. As for the other condition, it seems clear that the stakes for participating players are very high. Obviously some people (company stockholders, perhaps) may be made worse off by the decision, but workers in the affected plants will be spared grave economic and personal hardships. And, in the long run, we have argued, so will workers in general.

There is a further similarity between the Monopoly case and plant closings. Although it would be absurd to force children legally to fulfill agreements to play Monopoly, it is at least plausible that parents would be justified in forcing them. The difference between the Monopoly case and the plant closings case, then, seems to be not that it is wrong to force in one case and not the other, but rather that the morally appropriate agents of force are different.

These considerations bring us back to our earlier discussion. We began by mentioning two (not unrelated) kinds of arguments for the conclusion that workers ought to have a say in decisions about plant shutdowns and relocations. The first, rooted in the labor theory of property, supports the view that not only owners but workers may come to have property rights in their workplaces. The other argues that in view of relationships developed over years and even generations, companies come to have certain obligations to workers that are incompatible with abrupt withdrawal. We abandoned these matters of "abstract moral right and obligation," in the belief that the controversy about factory closings hangs mostly in more pragmatic considerations. Having, we hope, dispelled some of these concerns, we have returned, in these last arguments about fairness, to the more purely moral substance of the earlier arguments. For the idea that it is unfair for companies to "play the game" only as long as it suits them and that it is legitimate to force them to do otherwise, really amounts to the view that, having agreed to play the game at all, companies have incurred obligations they are not at liberty to abandon, and workers have as a result of their investments of labor acquired rights. The Monopoly example and our inquiry into the conditions under which it is legitimate to "coerce fairness" are steps toward fleshing out further the arguments for owners' obligations and workers' rights.

The connection between fairness and the earlier arguments can now be made more explicit. In the Monopoly case as in the plant closings case, the response of "It's mine" (my game, my factory) is no longer an argument stopper. We can interpret this in either of two ways: (1) It may be yours, but that doesn't mean you can do with it whatever you please; or (2) it may have been all yours once, but other people have now acquired rights to it, so it is no longer just yours to do with as you please. The first interpretation grants the original owner an exclusive property right, but asserts that it has been limited or qualified by his own actions;[7] the second interpretation denies the original owner an exclusive property right. The difference between these may be more semantic than substantive, but which interpretation we choose may determine whether we frame the argument in terms of workers' rights or just companies' obligations.

The practical conclusion is the same in either case: Companies should not be permitted to make decisions about plant closings and relocations unilaterally. This conclusion is supported by a variety of moral considerations having to do with fairness, self-respect, autonomy, and the interests of workers in general over the long run. It is, in addition, a conclusion that seems to survive the harsh scrutiny of economics. . . .

NOTES

1. Staughton Lynd, *The Fight Against Shutdowns: Youngstown's Steel Mill Closings* (San Pedro, Calif.: Singlejack Books, 1983), 3.

2. See Michael Walzer, *Radical Principles: Reflections of an Unreconstructed Democrat* (New York: Basic Books, 1980), 275.

3. *Second Treatise of Government*, chap. 5.

4. It is important to realize that the economist's notion of efficiency concerns the total amount of wealth irrespective of how it is distributed. The situation where A has $100 and B has $1 is more efficient in this sense than the situation where A and B each have $50.

5. This is Coase's theorem. R. H. Coase, "The Problem of Social Cost," *Journal of Law and Economics* 3 (1960). The theorem assumes also that transaction costs—in this case the costs of bargaining—are zero. Since the structures for collective bargaining are already in place, transaction costs will in fact be close enough to zero in this case to make the theorem practically applicable.

6. George Steinbrenner, owner of the New York Yankees and chairman of the board of American Ship Building, told shipbuilding union leaders in Lorain, Ohio, that if they did not agree to wage and other concessions, he would close down the shipyard and throw union members out of work. "I don't know about you boys, but *I'll* be eating three meals a day," Steinbrenner said. (*Washington Post,* 5 February 1984, Fl.) What is disturbing is that the same outcome can be achieved without the assumption of maliciousness; it results naturally from structural features of the situation.

7. Property rights are, of course, always limited and qualified: To say "It's mine" never means "I can do with it anything I please." I am not at liberty to burn down my house.

William M. Ferguson, Attorney General for the State of Kansas v. Frank C. Skrupa . . . Credit Advisors

Supreme Court of the United States

In this case, . . . we are asked to review the judgment of a three-judge District Court enjoining, as being in violation of the Due Process Clause of the Fourteenth Amendment, a Kansas statute making it a misdemeanor for any person to engage "in the business of debt adjusting" except as an incident to "the lawful practice of law in this state."[1] The statute defines "debt adjusting" as "the making of a contract, express, or implied with a particular debtor whereby the debtor agrees to pay a certain amount of money periodically to the person engaged in the debt adjusting business who shall for a consideration distribute the same among certain specified creditors in accordance with a plan agreed upon."

The complaint, filed by appellee Skrupa doing business as "Credit Advisors," alleged that Skrupa was engaged in the business of "debt adjusting" as defined by the statute, that his business was a "useful and desirable" one, that his business activities were not "inherently immoral or dangerous" or in any way contrary to the public welfare, and that therefore the business could not be "absolutely prohibited" by Kansas. The three-judge court

83 S.Ct. 1028 (1963).

heard evidence by Skrupa tending to show the usefulness and desirability of his business and evidence by the state officials tending to show that "debt adjusting" lends itself to grave abuses against distressed debtors, particularly in the lower income brackets, and that these abuses are of such gravity that a number of States have strictly regulated "debt adjusting" or prohibited it altogether.[2] The court found that Skrupa's business did fall within the Act's proscription and concluded, one judge dissenting, that the Act was prohibitory, not regulatory, but that even if construed in part as regulatory it was an unreasonable regulation of a "lawful business," which the court held amounted to a violation of the Due Process Clause of the Fourteenth Amendment. The court accordingly enjoined enforcement of the statute.[3]

The only case discussed by the court below as support for its invalidation of the statute was *Commonwealth v. Stone,* 191 Pa.Super. 117, 155 A.2d 453 (1959), in which the Superior Court of Pennsylvania struck down a statute almost identical to the Kansas act involved here. In Stone the Pennsylvania court held that the State could regulate, but could not prohibit, a "legitimate" business. Finding debt adjusting, called "budget planning" in the Pennsylvania statute, not to be "against the public interest" and concluding that it could "see no justification for such interference" with this business, the Pennsylvania court ruled that State's statute to be unconstitutional. In doing so, the Pennsylvania court relied heavily on *Adams v. Tanner,* 244 U.S. 590, 37 S.Ct. 662, 61 L.Ed. 1336 (1917), which held that the Due Process Clause forbids a State to prohibit a business which is "useful" and not "inherently immoral or dangerous to public welfare."

Both the District Court in the present case and the Pennsylvania court in Stone adopted the philosophy of *Adams v. Tanner* and cases like it that it is the province of courts to draw on their own views as to the morality, legitimacy, and usefulness of a particular business in order to decide whether a statute bears too heavily upon that business and by so doing violates due process. Under the system of government created by our Constitution, it is up to legislatures, not courts, to decide on the wisdom and utility of legislation. There was a time when the Due Process Clause was used by this Court to strike down laws which were thought unreasonable, that is, unwise or incompatible with some particular economic or social philosophy. In this manner the Due Process Clause was used, for example, to nullify laws prescribing maximum hours for work in bakeries, *Lochner v. New York,* 198 U.S. 45, 25 S. Ct. 539, 49 L.Ed. 937 (1905), . . . setting minimum wages for women, *Adkins v. Children's Hospital,* 261 U.S. 525, 43 S.Ct. 394, 67 L.Ed. 785 (1923), and fixing the weight of loaves of bread, *Jay Burns Baking Co. v. Bryan,* 264 U.S. 504, 44 S.Ct. 412, 68, L.Ed. 813 (1924). This intrusion by the judiciary into the realm of legislative value judgments was strongly objected to at the time, particularly by Mr. Justice Holmes and Mr. Justice Brandeis. Dissenting from the Court's invalidating a state statute which regulated the resale price of theatre and other tickets, Mr. Justice Homes said,

> "I think the proper course is to recognize that a state Legislature can do whatever it sees fit to do unless it is restrained by some express prohibition in the Constitution of the United States or of the State, and that Courts should be careful not to extend such prohibitions beyond their obvious meaning by reading into them conceptions of public policy that the particular Court may happen to entertain."[4]

And in an earlier case he had emphasized that, "The criterion of constitutionality is not whether we believe the law to be for the public good."[5]

The doctrine that prevailed in Lochner,

Coppage, Adkins, Burns, and like cases—that due process authorizes courts to hold laws unconstitutional when they believe the legislature has acted unwisely—has long since been discarded. We have returned to the original constitutional proposition that courts do not substitute their social and economic beliefs for the judgment of legislative bodies, who are elected to pass laws. As this Court stated in a unanimous opinion in 1941, "We are not concerned . . . with the wisdom, need, or appropriateness of the legislation."[6] Legislative bodies have broad scope to experiment with economic problems, and this Court does not sit to "subject the state to an intolerable supervision hostile to the basic principles of our government and wholly beyond the protection which the general clause of the Fourteenth Amendment was intended to secure."[7] It is now settled that States "have power to legislate against what are found to be injurious practices in their internal commercial and business affairs, so long as their laws do not run afoul of some specific federal constitutional prohibition, or of some valid federal law."[8] . . .

We conclude that the Kansas Legislature was free to decide for itself that legislation was needed to deal with the business of debt adjusting. Unquestionably, there are arguments showing that the business of debt adjusting has social utility, but such arguments are properly addressed to the legislature, not to us. . . .

Whether the legislature takes for its textbook Adam Smith, Herbert Spencer, Lord Keynes, or some other is no concern of ours.[9] The Kansas debt adjusting statute may be wise or unwise. But relief, if any be needed, lies not with us but with the body constituted to pass laws for the State of Kansas.

Nor is the statute's exception of lawyers a denial of equal protection of the laws to non-lawyers. Statutes create many classifications which do not deny equal protection; it is only "individuous discrimination" which offends the Constitution. The business of debt adjusting gives rise to a relationship of trust in which the debt adjuster will, in a situation of insolvency, be marshalling assets in the manner of a proceeding in bankruptcy. The debt adjuster's client may need advice as to the legality of the various claims against him, remedies existing under state laws governing debtor-creditor relationships, or provisions of the Bankruptcy Act—advice which a nonlawyer cannot lawfully give him. If the State of Kansas wants to limit debt adjusting to lawyers, the Equal Protection Clause does not forbid it. We also find no merit in the contention that the Fourteenth Amendment is violated by the failure of the Kansas statute's title to be as specific as appellee thinks it ought to be under the Kansas Constitution.

Reversed. . . .

NOTES

1. Kan.Gen.Stat.(Supp.1961) § 21-2464.
2. Twelve other States have outlawed the business of debt adjusting. Fla.Stat.Ann. (1962).
3. *Skrupa v. Sanborn*, 210 F.Supp. 200 (D.C.D.Kan.1961).
4. *Tyson & Brother, etc. v. Banton*, 273 U.S. 418, 445, 446, 47 S.Ct. 426, 433, 434, 71 L.Ed. 718 (1927) (dissenting opinion). . . .
5. *Adkins v. Children's Hospital*, 261 U.S. 525, 567, 570, 43 S.Ct. 394, 406, 67 L.Ed. 785 (1923) (dissenting opinion). . . .
6. *Olsen v. Nebraska ex rel. Western Reference & Bond Assn.*, 313 U.S. 236, 246, 61 S.Ct. 862, 865, 85 L.Ed. 1305 (1941). . . .
7. *Sproles v. Binford*, 286 U.S. 374, 388, 52 S.Ct. 581, 585, 76 L.Ed. 1167 (1932). . . .
8. *Lincoln Federal Labor Union, etc. v. Northwestern Iron & Metal Co.*, 335 U.S. 525, 536, 69 S.Ct. 251, 257, 93 L.Ed. 212 (1949). . . .
9. "The 14th Amendment does not enact Mr. Herbert Spencer's Social Statics." *Lochner v. New York*, 198 U.S. 45, 74, 75, 25 S.Ct. 539, 546, 49 L.Ed. 937 (1905) (Holmes, J., dissenting).

CASE 1   *Baseball Economics*

In December 1981, the Baltimore Orioles hall-of-fame pitcher Jim Palmer gave a newspaper interview in Portland, Oregon. He was highly critical of the system of economic incentives operative in baseball. He argued that money controlled almost all decisions by management and players alike. Many players, he said, "make a lot more money than they should." The salaries are often determined through "panic" on the part of management, he said, which plans at all cost against a situation in which star players leave and join other teams at increased salary levels. He noted that players make $300,000 to $400,000 in their second year and sign multiyear contracts. This kind of security, he said, leads players to relax and to loose their concentration on skilled performance.

On the same day Palmer gave his interview in Portland, Baseball Commissioner Bowie Kuhn was testifying before a Congressional Subcommittee on the administration of justice and issues surrounding the costs of cable television. Kuhn described the possible introduction of massive cable television broadcasts of baseball as economically intolerable for the sport. Both gate receipts and network television revenues would decline, he held, and this would be a disaster for a sport already "treading on financial quicksand." Kuhn supported this judgment with figures to show that only nine of baseball's twenty-six teams had made a profit the previous year. He argued that the aggregate loss was $25 million. He further argued that cable television would bring competing sporting events into a city without the consent or agreement of anyone in baseball management.

Ted Turner, who owns both Turner Broadcasting System (cable) and the Atlanta Braves baseball team, also testified at the same time as Kuhn. "If baseball is in trouble," he said, "it is because they are paying the [super star] baseball players a million and half dollars a year. . . . There isn't one single example of a proven economic harm from cable television."

In 1991, ten years after Palmer's interview and this testimony before Congress, player's salaries had dramatically escalated beyond what Palmer, Kuhn, or Turner could have imagined. In late 1991, the New York Yankees gave a $1.55 million signing bonus (plus a standard contract) to an unproven 19-year-old draft choice. Earlier in 1991, the figures for proven players had dramatically escalated. The Boston Red Sox signed Roger Clemens to a four-year contract worth $21.521 million, and the New York Mets signed Dwight Gooden to a three-year contract worth $15.45 million, including performance bonuses that could send the figure another million dollars. Gooden had been highly critical of the Mets front-office for only offering Daryl Strawberry a contract for four years at $15.5 million. Strawberry left and signed with the Los Angeles Dodgers for five years at $20.25 million. As for the Mets players, they said Gooden deserved everything he got. (The Mets payroll for 1992 was the largest in history: $44,464,000.) But the general manager of the Houston Astros, Bill Wood, was annoyed and distressed: "I'll be darned if I know what we're going to do next year," he said.

A survey of Mets baseball fans indicated that most thought the salary figures outrageous and that the money should be more evenly spread across the players. However, Senator Slade Gorton had a different idea

---

This case was prepared by Tom L. Beauchamp.

about how to spread the wealth. He pointed out that minor league baseball is dying in many American towns for lack of revenue. He submitted a bill to Congress that would turn over to minor league teams a significant share of television revenues contracted for by major league baseball. He also sought to distribute the revenues to major league clubs more equally. Rich Levin of the New York Yankees said that Gorton, a republican senator, had introduced a socialist approach that would have cost the Yankees $21.6 million is redistributed money. Gorton admitted his bill had little chance of passage, but said he hoped the bill would prompt legislation in Congress to address these serious equity issues.

Questions

1. If Palmer and Gorton are claiming there is an inequity in baseball salaries and revenue distributions, are they correct? Would Nozick agree with Levin's response?

2. Do Bowie Kuhn's comments reflect a libertarian or a utilitarian theory of justice?

3. If Peter Singer's proposals were followed, what would be the obligations of major league baseball players to help the poor both within and outside of their own country?

4. Would it be unjust to pass Senator Gorton's bill to redistribute baseball revenues?

CASE 2. *Selling Cyclamates Abroad*

In 1969 the Food and Drug Administration banned cyclamates, a popular sweetening agent, from the U.S. market. The evidence regarding dangers presented by cyclamates had been heavily discussed at the time. There were scientific disagreements about the evidence. What some persons regarded as telling animal studies were regarded by others as inconclusive studies. Nonetheless, by FDA criteria cyclamates presented an unacceptable level of risk to the public.

After the ban was in place, Libby, McNeil, & Libby sold approximately 300,000 cases of cyclamate-sweetened fruit to customers in Germany, Spain, and other countries where cyclamates had not been banned and were still in use. James Nadler, Libby's vice president for international relations, announced the following justification for these sales abroad: "Fortunately the older civilizations of the world are more deliberate about judging momentary fads that are

popular in the United States from time to time." (*Wall Street Journal*, February 11, 1971.)

Such sales abroad are common practice in U.S. business when products have been banned in the home country but not in other countries. In some cases involving prescription drugs, the products are not *banned* in the United States but are required to have strong warnings about negative side effects. If these warnings are not required in other countries, the drugs are shipped and sold without attached warnings.

This practice is not unilateral. In some cases, drugs and other products banned in a foreign country are imported to the United States by manufacturers in that foreign country. In effect, this is standard business practice throughout the world.

Nonetheless, this practice has been heavily criticized as unjust to consumers, especially when warnings are omitted that could easily

This case was prepared by Tom L. Beauchamp.

be included. Commenting specifically on Libby's decision to ship the cyclamates, Robert L. Heilbroner commented as follows: "The momentary fad to which [Vice President Nadler] was referring was the upshot of nineteen years of increasingly alarming laboratory findings concerning the effects of cyclamates on chick embryos—effects that produced grotesque malformations similar to those induced by thalidomide." (*In the Name of Profit.* Doubleday & Co., 1970, p. 12.)

Questions

1. Does Heilbroner seem to be accusing Libby of an injustice? If so, what principle of justice does he think the company violated?

2. Do you think Singer or Nozick would agree with Heilbroner?

3. Assuming that it is standard business practice to do what Libby did, is Libby's announced justification adequate?

4. Is it unjust to market these products abroad without warning labels?

CASE 3.   *Cocaine at the Fortune 500 Level*

Roberto U. is a pure libertarian in moral and political philosophy. He is deeply impressed by his reading of Robert Nozick's account of justice. He lives in Los Angeles and teaches philosophy at a local university. Roberto is also a frequent user of cocaine, which he enjoys immensely and often provides to friends at parties. Neither he nor any of his close friends is addicted. Over the years Robert has tired of teaching philosophy and now has an opportunity, through old friends who live in Peru, to become a middleman in the cocaine business. He is disquieted about the effects cocaine has on some persons, but he has never witnessed these effects first hand. He is giving his friends' business offer serious consideration.

Roberto's research has told him the following: Selling cocaine is a $20 billion plus industry. Although he is interested primarily in a Peruvian connection, his research has shown conclusively that the Colombian cartel alone is large enough to place it among the *Fortune* 500 corporations. Between 0.75 and 1.1 million jobs in Colombia, Bolivia, and Peru combined are in the cocaine industry—over 5 per-

cent of the entire work force in these countries. These figures are roughly comparable to the dollar and work force figures for the diamond industry throughout the world.

Peruvian President Alan Garcia once described the cocaine industry as Latin America's "only successful multinational." It can be and has been analyzed in traditional business categories; it has its own entrepreneurs, chemists, laboratories, employment agencies, small organizations, distribution systems, giants, growth phases, and so forth. Its profit margins have narrowed in some markets, while expanding in others. It often seeks new markets in order to expand its product line. For example, in the mid-1980s "crack"—a potent form of cocaine that is smoked—was moved heavily into new markets in Europe. Between the mid-1960s and the early-1990s the demand for cocaine grew dramatically because of successful supply and marketing. Middlemen first in Miami and then in Los Angeles were established to increase already abundant profits. Heavy investments were made in airplanes, efficient modes of production, training managers, and regular sched-

This case was prepared by Tom L. Beauchamp, based on accounts in The *Wall Street Journal* and *The Economist.*

ules of delivery and distribution. In the late 1980s there was a downturn in cocaine consumption after the deaths of two prominent athletes, but in the early 1990s the industry recovered.

Roberto sees the cocaine industry as not subject to taxes, tariffs, or government regulations other than those pertaining to its illegality. It is a pure form of the free market in which supply and demand control transactions. This fact about the business appeals to Roberto, as it seems perfectly suited to his libertarian views. He is well aware that there are severe problems of coercion and violence in some parts of the industry, but he is quite certain that the wealthy clientele that he would supply in Los Angeles neither abuses the drug nor redistributes it to others who might be harmed. He is confident that his Peruvian associates are honorable and that he can escape problems of violence, coercion, and abusive marketing. However, he has just read a newspaper story that Cocaine-use emergencies—especially those involving cocaine-induced

heart attacks—have tripled in the last five years. This fact and this alone gives him pause before entering the cocaine business. He sees these health emergencies as unfortunate but unfair outcomes of the business. So his humanity but not his theory of justice gives him pause.

Questions

1. Would a libertarian—as Robert thinks—say that the cocaine business is not unjust so long as no coercion is involved and the system is a pure function of supply and demand?
2. Does justice demand that cocaine be outlawed, or is this not a problem of justice at all? Are questions of justice even meaningful when the activity is beyond the boundaries of law?
3. Is the distinction Roberto draws between what is unfortunate and what is unfair relevant to a decision about whether an activity is just?

CASE 4. *Covering the Costs of Health Care*

Medicare was passed into law in the United States to provide coverage for health care costs in populations that could not afford adequate coverage, especially the elderly. Then, as now, health care technology produced by major corporations was rapidly being developed and costs were skyrocketing. Health care costs have increased from $1 billion per year in 1965 to $733 billion in 1991. Medicare payments for physicians are more than $30 billion. Between 1984 and 1990, Medicare expenditures for physicians rose an average of 12 percent per year. These payments are expected to increase 14 percent per year in the next decade. For U.S. corporations,

health care has become an extremely burdensome expense.

Health care costs have been under intense study by the U.S. Congress. In an effort to limit future increases in physician costs, the Omnibus Budget Reconciliation Act of 1989 created a Medicare Fee Schedule that affected 34.7 million U.S. citizens. This schedule attempts to redistribute payments across specialities in medicine and geographic areas of the country. The legislation called for this restructuring to be phased in over a five-year period from 1992 to 1996. In passing the legislation, members of Congress agreed that Medicare's former payment policies fueled

This case was prepared by Tom L. Beauchamp.

unacceptable increases in expenditures for
health care services. Neither the old legislation nor the new covers the kind of catastrophic illness that can wipe out a family's assets and put a family in lifetime debt.

It has been demonstrated that there is substantial variation across the United States in
payment rates for services. Urban, specialist,
and in-patient services are typically much
higher than rural, generalist, and ambulatory
services. Surgeons make more than those in
other specialties. It has been widely agreed
that these differentials are independent of
quality of services, depending more on urban
location, the high costs of specialists, and the
like. A large supply of physicians in a single
location does not seem to stimulate competition and drive prices down; instead, higher
fees for physician services tend to be the
norm. Social scientists who have studied the
changes made in the Omnibus Budget Reconciliation Act of 1989 predict that large re-
distributions of Medicare payments among
specialties will occur, thus changing long-
standing patterns in physicians' salaries.

Recent statistics indicate that the elderly,
who were targeted for the Medicare program,
have more after-tax income than do citizens
under 65; but they also have more needs for
health care. It is projected that by the year
2030 there will be more than 60 million people over age 65—roughly double the present
number. A quarter-million millionaires in the
United States are presently eligible for Medicare coverage.

Questions

1. Is a nation obligated to provide quality
   health care for the elderly who otherwise
   could afford no care? Is the obligation
   unrelated to the ability to pay?
2. Should health care be distributed purely
   on a free-market basis? Should physicians
   charge whatever the market will bear?

3. Is Medicare justifiable on either utilitarian or egalitarian premises of justice?
4. Would a communitarian approve of
   Medicare even if he or she did not think
   the system comprehensive enough? Are
   libertarians and communitarians necessarily in opposition on the question of
   state-supported systems of health care
   coverage?

Suggested Supplementary Readings

Concepts and Principles of Justice

BEAUCHAMP, TOM L., *Philosophical Ethics*. 2nd ed.
New York: McGraw-Hill, 1991. Chaps. 8–9.

BENN, STANLEY I. "Justice." In Vol. 4 of *Encyclopedia of Philosophy*, edited by Paul Edwards. New
York: Macmillan and Free Press, 1967.

CAMPBELL, TOM. *Justice*. London: Macmillan,
1988.

FEINBERG, JOEL. "Justice and Personal Desert." In
Nomos 6: Justice, edited by Carl J. Friedrich and
John W. Chapman. New York: Atherton Press,
1963.

KIPNIS, KENNETH, and DIANA T. MEYERS. *Economic
Justice*. Totowa, N.J.: Rowman and Allanheld,
1985.

Egalitarian Theories

BARRY, BRIAN. *The Liberal Theory of Justice, A Critical
Examination of the Principal Doctrines in a Theory
of Justice by John Rawls*. Oxford, England: Clarendon Press, 1973.

DANIELS, NORMAN, ed. *Reading Rawls: Critical Studies of a Theory of Justice*. New York: Basic Books,
1975.

POGGE, THOMAS W. *Realizing Rawls*. Ithaca, N.Y.:
Cornell University Press, 1991.

RAWLS, JOHN. *Justice as Fairness: A Guided Tour*.
Cambridge, Mass.: Harvard University, 1989;
unpublished monograph.

——. "Reply to Alexander and Musgrave." *Quarterly
Journal of Economics* 88(1974): 633–655.

Libertarian Theories

FRIEDMAN, MILTON. *Capitalism and Freedom.* Chicago: University of Chicago Press, 1962.

HAYEK, FRIEDRICH. *Individualism and Economic Order.* Chicago: University of Chicago Press, 1948.

———. *The Mirage of Social Justice. Vol. 2, Law, Legislation, and Liberty.* Chicago: University of Chicago Press, 1976.

MACK, ERIC. "Liberty and Justice." In *Justice and Economic Distribution,* edited by John Arthur and William Shaw. Englewood Cliffs, N.J.: Prentice Hall, 1978.

NAGEL, THOMAS. "Libertarianism Without Foundations." *Yale Law Journal* 85 (1975).

Utilitarian Theories

FREY, R. G., ed. *Utility and Rights.* Minneapolis: University of Minnesota Press, 1984.

GOLDMAN, ALAN H. "Business Ethics: Profits, Utilities, and Moral Rights." *Philosophy and Public Affairs* 9 (1980): 260–286.

GRIFFIN, JAMES. *Well-Being: Its Meaning, Measurement, and Importance.* Oxford, England: Clarendon Press, 1986.

POSNER, RICHARD A. *The Economics of Justice.* 2nd ed. Cambridge, Mass.: Harvard University Press, 1983.

SEN, AMARTYA, and BERNARD WILLIAMS, eds. *Utilitarianism and Beyond.* Cambridge, England: Cambridge University Press, 1982.

SINGER, PETER. "The Right to Be Rich or Poor." *New York Review of Books* 6 (March 1976).

Communitarian Theories

BUCHANAN, ALLEN. "Assessing the Communitarian Critique of Liberalism." *Ethics* 99 (1989).

FREEDEN, MICHAEL. "Human Rights and Welfare: A Communitarian View." *Ethics* 100 (1990).

GUTMANN, AMY. "Communitarian Critics of Liberalism." *Philosophy and Public Affairs* 14 (1985).

KYMLICKA, WILL. *Liberalism, Community, and Culture.* Oxford, England: Clarendon Press, 1989.

MACINTYRE, ALASDAIR. *Whose Justice? Which Rationality?* Notre Dame, Ind.: Notre Dame University Press, 1988.

SANDEL, MICHAEL J. "Democrats and Community". *The New Republic* (February 22, 1988).

———. *Liberalism and the Limits of Justice.* Cambridge, England: Cambridge University Press, 1982.

WALLACH, JOHN R. "Liberals, Communitarians, and the Tasks of Political Theory." *Political Theory* 15 (1987).

WALZER, MICHAEL. "The Communitarian Critique of Liberalism." *Political Theory* 18 (1990).

Issues in International Markets, Plant Closings, and Social Policy

BOWIE, NORMAN. "Fair Markets." *Journal of Business Ethics* 7 (1988).

BUCHANAN, ALLEN. *Ethics, Efficiency and the Market.* Totowa, N.J.: Rowman and Allanheld, 1985.

EHRENBERG, RONALD G., and GEORGE H. JAKUBSON. "Why Warn? Plant Closing Legislation." *Regulation* 13 (Summer 1990).

"Note: Resurrecting Economic Rights: The Doctrine of Economic Due Process Reconsidered." *Harvard Law Review* 103 (1990).

KINIKI, ANGELO, and others. "Socially Responsible Plant Closings." *Personnel Administrator* 32 (June 1987).

KOVACH, KENNETH A., and PETER E. MILLSPAUGH. "Plant Closings." *Business Horizons* 30 (March-April 1987).

LUPER-FOY, STEVEN. *Problems of International Justice.* Boulder, Colo.: Westview Press, 1988.

MILLSPAUGH, PETER E. "Plant Closing Ethics Root in American Law." *Journal of Business Ethics* 9 (August 1990).

NOWLIN, WILLIAM A., and GEORGE M. SULLIVAN. "The Plant Closing Law: Worker Protection or Government Interference?" *Industrial Management* 31 (November-December 1989).

PRATT, CORNELIUS B. "Multinational Corporate Social Policy Process for Ethical Responsibility in Sub-Saharan Africa." *Journal of Business Ethics* 10 (July 1991): 527–541.